Europe and Finland

Defining the Political Identity of Finland in Western Europe

TEIJA TIILIKAINEN

Routledge
Taylor & Francis Group

LONDON AND NEW YORK

First published 1998 by Ashgate Publishing

Reissued 2018 by Routledge
2 Park Square, Milton Park, Abingdon, Oxon OX14 4RN
711 Third Avenue, New York, NY 10017, USA

Routledge is an imprint of the Taylor & Francis Group, an informa business

Copyright © Teija Tiilikainen 1998

Publisher's Note
The publisher has gone to great lengths to ensure the quality of this reprint but points out that some imperfections in the original copies may be apparent.

Disclaimer
The publisher has made every effort to trace copyright holders and welcomes correspondence from those they have been unable to contact.

A Library of Congress record exists under LC control number : 97038532

ISBN 13: 978-1-138-31327-9 (hbk)
ISBN 13: 978-1-138-31333-0 (pbk)
ISBN 13: 978-0-429-45766-1 (ebk)

Contents

Preface

This book, originally prepared as a doctoral thesis in political science, was started in 1991. Many people supported me and influenced my thinking when I was writing the book. I would like to point out three of them explicitly without, however, intending to lessen my gratitude to others in any way.

Heikki Patomäki taught me to question things. He showed me that there are no impartial texts and meanings and that things may always be read in other ways. The approach of my book, therefore, is a result of my debates with Heikki in the beginning of this project. I felt I could only be safe by finding an approach to which I would be committed heart and soul.

Martti Koskenniemi taught me to formulate an argument. His own thesis stood as an unattainable ideal for me of how scientific works should be constructed. Awareness of the role of argument saved me, in consequence, from having to struggle with a preliminary assessment of introductory texts, an assessment that can so often serve to obscure the writer's own position.

And last but not least, *George Maude* has taught me what scientific texts are for. Commenting several times upon every single sentence of the book George has reminded me of the fact that a book will always have a public and that it should be written for a public. A literary process should transcend the writer's own 'dialogue of the soul with itself' even if this is a worthy starting–point for the journey of exploration known as research.

Several organisations have contributed to the financing of this research project. Åbo Akademi University together with the Research Centre of the Åbo Akademi Foundation have given the invaluable professional background not only through various grants, posts and facilities which I have received but also through different forms of library and administrative assistance. A major part of the research was carried out within the framework of the research project the Citizens' Europe financed by the Academy of Finland. The book has been concluded under the auspices of the National Defence College where my willingness to finish the project has met with great understanding. Ashgate's decision to publish this book gave me great pleasure and I would like to express my gratitude for the editorial assistance I have received.

This book has been developing together with our little son, *Saska*, and is dedicated to him. Without my family, and the support and understanding of my husband *Timo Sormunen*, neither this book nor any other product of my academic career would exist.

Helsinki, 8 August 1997

Teija Tiilikainen

PART I

EUROPE

1 Introduction: The Historical Study of Political Ideas

In our time, what is at issue is the very nature of man, the image we have of his limits and possibilities as man. History is not yet done with its exploration of the limits and meanings of 'human nature'.

C. Wright Mills[1]

Introduction

One of the key questions of the present integration project is the question of the *nature* of the Europe that is being constructed. The question reaches in a strange way into the core of European political culture. The very putting of the question is an expression of European unity and of the relativity connected with it. There is that much of a common political culture and identity in Europe that it makes sense to talk about, or even to plan seriously, a Europe that would be politically united under common institutions of power. The constraints on the common culture are revealed when the question is put about the nature of this united Europe. That there is no automatic answer to this question, which would at the same time be articulated as a demand for the political unity of Europe, is significative of European culture. Political diversity is itself a key characteristic of European unity.

The purpose of this book is to approach the reasons for this

---

[1]

This quotation from C. Wright Mills is borrowed from Roger Hausheer's introduction (p.xiii) to the book *Isaiah Berlin – Against the Current. Essays in the History of Ideas (ed. by Hardy 1989)*. In addition to my commitment to a particular discipline, it stands here as an expression of my loyalty and gratitude to Berlin's thinking.

diversity in unity and to make it more concrete through one example. The first argument of the study is that differences in views concerning European political unity can be explained through differences in political culture and traditions. The second argument is that these differences again are of historical origin.

In the following chapters I will thus mainly have to do with what I have called political *cultures* and *traditions*. I will try to point out the divisions in European political culture that are decisive with respect to the present integration project. The analysis is limited to Western Europe, including Northern Europe, because the roots of the project are there. My conception about the historical origin of cultural divisions and differences reflects itself in the general structure of the book as well as in its individual chapters. Western European cultures are first analysed as far as their general relationship to the idea of political community is concerned. Thereafter the idea of a united Europe is brought into focus, first in its earlier phases and then, in the fourth chapter, in its present form. In the latter part of the book, more careful attention is paid to Finnish political culture and to the way Finland has related to the idea of a united Europe.

The idea that cultures, and underlying meanings in general, are of key value as far as knowledge about societies and social life is concerned can be linked to a particular *humanist* tradition in social sciences. One of the main orientations of this tradition starts from *history* and *historical analysis* as the focal instrument in the explanation of culture and cultural differences. This approach, which constitutes also the theoretical framework of this study, is usually known as the *history–of–ideas* approach. In the first chapter, it is my intention to introduce this theoretical framework and to define the position that the present study takes within it, that is, to explicate its theoretical arguments.

The History–of–Ideas as a Scientific Discipline

The approach of this study relays the message of Romanticism in Europe. By Romanticism, I mean the tradition that brought the idea of the particular qualities and capacities of the human being into the

Enlightenment theory which is based upon the idea of permanent essences. As humanity expresses itself through the human mind and as it is not a stable phenomenon, historical knowledge is argued as being the only means to human self-knowledge. At the basis of the Romanticist view of humanity a new meaning was already being demanded for history and historical knowledge in the nineteenth century[8]. It was, however, R.G. Collingwood in this century who put the demands into a more systematic form. According to him, the understanding of history as the history of the human mind develops its meaning from the revelation of historical particularities only. Collingwood stated that:

> The body of human thought or mental activity is a corporate possession, and almost all the operations which our minds perform are operations which we learned from others who have performed them already. Since mind is what it does, and human nature, if it is a name for anything real, is only a name for human activities, this acquisition of ability to perform determinate operations is the acquisition of a determinate human nature. Thus the historical process is a process in which man creates for himself this or that kind of human nature by re-creating in his own thought the past to which he is heir[9].

Historical knowledge shall, according to Collingwood, be understood as knowledge of what mind has done in the past and as such it is seen to reveal to the historian the powers of his own mind[10]. This position has begun to be called the *individualist position* of history and has become one of the main divides of the history-of-ideas approach.

The history-of-ideas approach can be claimed to be constituted

[8]

There is good reason to argue that the conceptions of human nature which were dominant in pre-Romanticist Western cultures have contributed to the flowering of other scientific disciplines at the expense of history (Collingwood 1983, 14-81; Berlin 1969, 41-117).

[9]

Collingwood 1983, 226.

[10]

Ibid., 218.

by the humanist and the history argument and the mutual relation of these arguments has led to the drawing of one of the main dividing lines within the approach. The approach can thus be divided into a *hermeneutical* tradition and into a *history* tradition in accordance with how the emphasis falls on the two constitutive parts. The hermeneutical tradition starts from human existence as the primary mode of being. Representatives of this tradition argue that it is impossible to treat the past independently of the present because that would presuppose that the examiner could place himself outside history and time. Because people are all said to belong to history before they belong to themselves, history is argued as disappearing in the sense of an independent past and is argued as being significant only when in fusion with the present[11]. Hermeneutics has thus turned from the methodological hermeneutism of the nineteenth century into an ontological argument about meaning and understanding as a collective form of being[12].

The history tradition can be seen as a continuance of the position that was already represented by Collingwood. This position is, in contrast to the collectivism of the hermeneutical tradition, based upon an individualist interpretation of history. J.G.A. Pocock, Quentin Skinner and John Dunn are famous for their recent support of the history position. They start like Collingwood from the idea that past thought and ideas shall be understood in their own historical contexts, that is, in those historical circumstances in which they were once formulated. They thus do not accept the idea of *perennial questions, fusion of horizons* or *autonomy of texts,* but argue instead that understanding past meanings implies that the 'historian' distances

---

[11]

Femia 1988, 156–175; Keane 1988, 204–217.

[12]

Dilthey already put forth the argument about a 'life community' and the idea that people are united in a creativity that is their essence (Dilthey 1988, 92–93). Gadamer made his 'being–in–the–world' a universal principle of human thought and argued that historical interpretation implies a fusion of horizons in which the past is mediated to the present (Anderson et.al. 1986,68 ff).

himself from the meanings and understandings of his own time and passes the gap to the relevant historical period. Using the terms of Quentin Skinner:

> Historical understanding is a product of learning to follow what Hacking has called different styles of reasoning; it is not necessarily a matter of being able to translate those styles into less outlandish ones[13].

The individualist position of the history tradition finds expression in the fact that past meanings are believed to reveal themselves to the historian in instances of individual acting. Collingwood started from reflective acts as the subject–matter of history and argued for the re-enactment of these as the historical method[14]. Pocock, Dunn and Skinner all approach past meanings in terms of linguistic action and situate the real meaning in the intentions of a speaker[15].

One of the main recent debates upon the identity of the history of ideas approach has dealt with its epistemological commitments. In this debate, representatives of the hermeneutical tradition have vigorously called into question the idea of authorial intention as the ultimate source of meaning. They have emphasised the social and dynamic capacities of texts and languages and the possibilities connected with them of taking on meanings that could not possibly have been intended by the authors[16]. The commitment to authorial intention has been argued as leading to historical antiquarianism and to political and social conservatism. Ian Shapiro makes this accusation more precise by connecting the approach of the 'history tradition' with, what he calls,

---

[13]

Skinner 1988, 252.

[14]

Collingwood 1983, 308–309.

[15]

Skinner 1969, 1976; Pocock 1971; Dunn 1972.

[16]

Shapiro 1982; Femia 1988; Taylor 1988.

a *conventionalist* view of knowledge[17]. He argues that a conventionalist epistemology which defines everything exclusively in terms of what happen to be the prevailing norms cannot tackle the question of why particular ways of seeing the world become prevalent at the times they do. Therefore, in his opinion, the conventionalist view of knowledge mistakenly supports the notion that political problems can be solved merely by understanding their linguistic history and it fails to appreciate that political languages are embedded in the real world and are instrumental in its reproduction.

Quentin Skinner is the representative of the history tradition who has defended the commitments of the tradition most visibly. He builds his defence upon the idea that people may be interested in thought and ideas for different purposes. This, he argues, is totally acceptable on the condition that commitment to one approach will not make other approaches empty. According to Skinner, authorial intention is the legitimate source if one is interested in the historical identity of texts:

> I have never denied the obvious fact that we can and do turn to major works of moral and political philosophy for all sorts of reasons, some of which may carry us far beyond the works themselves and the intellectual milieu within which they were conceived. My own concern, however, has solely been with the question of how best to approch such works if our aim is, in Dunn's luminous phrase, to recover their historical identity[18].

Another great debate going on with respect to the history–of–ideas approach deals with its truth theory. The orientation towards historical identities and the denial of any ahistorical truth norms has been argued as leading to scientific relativism and moral nihilism[19]. Representatives of the history orientation have defended their position by counter–attacking the conception of reality which forms the basis for

---

[17]

Shapiro 1982, 549 ff.

[18]

Skinner 1988, 232.

[19]

Hollis 1988, 146; King 1983, 285 ff; Shapiro 1988, 537.

the idea of truth and morality motivating these accusations against them[20].

One Application of the History–of–Ideas Approach

At a general level, this study is committed to the history–of–ideas approach and to the two arguments that were said to be constitutive of the approach as a view of reality and science (the humanist argument and the history argument). The commitment to the humanist argument is of a general nature as the main intention is to emphasise the importance of ideas, or webs of meaning, in social life and in the study of it. This is done by approaching European and Finnish politics in terms of their key ideas and by using ideas as the basis of their comparison. Throughout the following chapters, I will endeavour to show how significant the role of these mental creations is by making them visible and by indicating the nature of the consequences resulting from the cultural and historical differences in them.

The respect for the history argument expresses itself in the conception that the reasons for cultural differences are found in history that is understood in terms of shifting ideas and concepts. The exact way in which these arguments are interpreted, applied and emphasised is the next subject of the present chapter.

The Humanist Argument: Shared Meanings as the Basis of Society

The humanist argument about the nature of societies and social life derives from the idea that all social forms are expressions of human creativity. In order to understand social action or social institutions, social stability or social change, one has to grasp their underlying meanings. The first argument of this study starts from the existence of these meanings and from their importance for everything that social life and human co–existence is. It is argued that in order to understand politics and political differences one has to tackle their conceptual

---

[20]

Rorty 1982, 195 and 198; Skinner 1988, 255–256.

basis, which can this far be called simply *political culture*.

The role that meanings are seen to have as the foundation of social life can be made more precise by arguing that people act towards each other, and towards society, on the basis of shared meanings. People perceive themselves and the world around them on the basis of various, even overlapping and conflictual, webs of meaning. The divergence of terms used with reference to these intellectual constructions reveal the plurality of the theoretical dimensions that are linked with the subject. Many of the following terms are currently used in a general sense without their original emphasis.

At a very general level, one could say that it is a matter of *the answers given to the key questions* of a particular time. Terms like *concept, conception* or *idea* denote easily that what is in question is something that has been formed in an individual mind and that is expressed through it. *Norm* and *principle* refer to intellectual constructions that have a firm status in a society. *Doctrine, ideology* and *theory* refer to systems of meanings that are more complex than just a single idea. The difference between these terms is that while *theory* implies that it is a question of something that has scientific legitimation, *ideology* can, in contrast, be linked with something that is biased or unreal. The general meaning of a *doctrine* lies between these two[21]. Webs, structures or systems of *meaning* put the emphasis on the characteristic that constitutes the difference between these intellectual constructions and the processes of nature. Talking about *cultures, epochs* or *eras* indicates that it is a question of large families of ideas that extend themselves to most areas of social and cultural life. A word like *traditions* puts the emphasis upon the historical continuity of a system of ideas.

Ideas are seen here as a phenomenon that is neither purely individual nor social but that has both of these dimensions. Meaning is an individual quality in the sense that it is, in the last resort, always applied through an individual mind and includes the possibility of

---

[21]

Doctrine usually refers to an intellectual construction, the scientific position of which is not as uncontroversial as that of theory, but which is politically more uncontroversial than ideology.

individual understanding and interpretation. Meaning is a social quality in the sense that it constitutes the channel or instrument for people's co-existence and, in this role, it has to be available for anybody. Individual liberty and individual meaning are thus limited by the necessity of common understanding and common meaning[22].

Individuals' relations to meanings and ideas are consequently not entirely unbounded, or, based upon the activities of a free mind. The exact argument of the study is that meaning is *historically constructed*. The idea of a historically-constructed meaning will be explicated in detail later in this chapter in connection with the history argument. The core of the question, the idea that the individual mind is somehow bound, or conditioned, will be looked at in general terms here. The alleged dependence of the individual mind means that when it is creating new conceptions, or applying existing ones, the individual mind cannot in every respect liberate itself from existing structures of meaning. These meanings may be invisible in a way that the individual is not conscious of them. They may also be more or less built into the position that the individual himself represents.

The room for manoeuvre that the individual mind has varies in every single mental action. In every historical period there are, however, webs of meaning that are less dynamic and less visible than others. These meanings are often of a more constitutive nature with respect to the systems of power of the particular epoch[23]. One could simply argue that people's ignorance of these meanings is a result of their established and uncontroversial nature. Another factor is that those in power want to ensure that the doctrinal cornerstones of their power

---

[22]

These are key questions in the debate between liberals and communitarians (see eg. Mullhall & Swift 1992). This study does not aim to take a stand on this debate and in the question of social identities. This question is seen to be subordinate to the position of historical identities.

[23]

The 'systems of power' refer here to broader systems of governance than the national ones. One could, for instance, describe the present political epoch as a gradual dissolution of the system based upon State sovereignty.

remain untouched. This argument has been developed, for instance, by Antonio Gramsci who connected to his class theory an idea of *ideological hegemony*. He meant that the ideological control of class consciousness is a decisive factor in the strategy of class domination[24]. Gramsci argued, like Michel Foucault in his structuralism, that cultures were at a comprehensive level bound to the interests of power and that it was not possible for a single human being to liberate himself from layers of meanings[25].

The humanist ambition of the present work stems from an endeavour to render visible the mental constituents of social activities. The analytical emphasis of the work falls upon the history argument which will be the following subject in the present chapter.

The History Argument: From Past to Present Meanings

The history argument that is the other key constituent of the history–of–ideas approach takes as its starting–point the idea that meaning, and the mental structures with which human beings organise the world, is not a creature independent of time and history. Meaning and ideas must therefore be understood *in the first place* as a historical phenomenon, as a product of their own historical circumstances. The importance of historical meaning does not, however, limit itself to historical knowledge only. Concepts and ideas live in history, carrying their past meanings with them. Concepts and ideas can therefore be seen to be historically constructed, which means that the form they are having at any given time is an expression of past as well as present meanings.

---

[24]

Gramsci developed his theory of ideological hegemony as a criticism of the Marxist view of the relationship between economic and other superstructures. He argued that the ideas, symbols and emblems which organise the attitudes of a society can be just as 'material' as the economic conditions of production (Kearney 1986, 174).

[25]

Foucault went still further as he argued that power is linked with the im-position of the structures that determine the formation of discursive practices (Foucault 1972, 31 ff).

Concepts are bound to their histories both in a positive and negative sense. Past meanings can thus be seen to constitute the critical limits within which concepts and ideas function. The aim of a historical analysis is therefore not to restore the past but to remember it and retrace the path to the present[26].

The second key argument of this study is thus an application of the history tradition and of its argument that meaning is historically conditioned. The core of the argument is that as an object of the individual mind meaning is not only dependent on community and common understanding, but it is also dependent on the history and different phases that have characterised the development of the understanding in question. The idea of a historical construction of meaning does not, however, necessitate a deterministic conception of history. In accordance with the view of reality that is constitutive of the approach, history is understood as the history of human thought and, more precisely, as the history of reflective thought. The possibility of other modes of being, and of other modes of history, is not denied, but the primacy of intellectual history is demanded in the study of the human being and human societies. History is treated basically as an open system that is conducted by contingency and that does not have any specific purposes or end–points[27]. This means that history, treated as a free interplay of ideas, can be seen to give way also to human creativity and imagination. The processes of history, that is the formulation of new ideas out of old ideas, are based upon contingency and the logic of context rather than upon any general and unhistorical determinant. But even if history is an open system, it is a system and

---

[26]

Ball, Farr & Hanson (1989, 4) quote O'Neill (Critique and Remembrance in O'Neill (ed) (1976), On Critical Theory. New York: Seabury Press, 1–11).

[27]

This view distances itself from the Hegelian view of history, according to which history is a world plan, a process that is fulfilling its own purpose (eg. Collingwood 1983, 113).

can thus be distinguished from other social systems[28]. History has been called 'a world of ideas' meaning that even if the historical present is not determined by the historical past, there is still a firm relationship between them[29].

History understood as a free interplay of ideas does not have any beginning or end. Conceptual histories, therefore, cannot be connected with any absolute beginnings, but all beginnings must be treated as more or less arbitrary[30]. Therefore, the origins of a concept, or the original meaning of a concept, shall be understood here in a particular way. The origins of a concept does not refer to an act, or process, through which a concept could be claimed to have been invented. Origins and original meaning are here linked with the historical context in which a new idea has entered into a more general public consciousness. Speaking about origins does not therefore imply any claims about an absolute novelty of a system of thought. The novelty is more linked with its political significance.

My first argument was that in order to grasp countries and territories politically, and the political differences between them, one has to analyse their political cultures, that is, their focal political traditions. This has now been complemented by a claim that the closer purpose of the analysis is to reveal the historical construction of these cultures and traditions.

The historical construction of a political culture or tradition must be understood here as the history of its main concepts or ideas. Conceptual histories aim at retracing the path of a concept from the past

---

28

This argument constitutes the essence of the history tradition and distinguishes historical meaning from social meaning.

29

This is Michael B. Oakeshott's definition of history (Collingwood 1983, 153). According to him 'history is not a series but a world: which means that its various parts bear upon one another, criticise one another, make one another intelligible'.

30

It is impossible to find any absolute beginnings for concepts or ideas, because they are usually developed step by step without any pure origins.

to the present. 'Concepts, like individuals', wrote Kierkegaard, 'have their histories, and are just as incapable of withstanding the ravages of time as are individuals'[31]. Writing a conceptual history thus implies an effort to understand the present meaning of a concept through its past meanings and through the ways they were created. It implies that any present meaning is seen to express a whole, or the top of a continuous process, where any previous meaning stands as the point of departure for the one following it. Conceptual histories have to be started by placing a beginning, even if an arbitrary one, somewhere. Taking this meaning as the point of departure, the focal phases of its history, the phases connecting its original form with its present state, need to be found out.

The Plan of the Study

This study can be seen as an effort to explain why different Western European countries have a differing preparedness for integration with each other and why it seems to be forever impossible to find a common conception about the governance of an integrated Europe which would be firm enough to compete with national political communities and identities. It is claimed here that differences in political culture form the very constitutive level in the explanation of the differences in political priorities between the present EU–States. The relation between political culture and political priorities will therefore be problematised.

Political culture refers here to the whole system of political traditions that is characteristic of a particular political unity at a particular time. Political traditions can be seen as political doctrines, or political systems of meaning, which are characterised by a clear historical continuity. Political culture refers to the substance of the main political traditions as well as to their structure and the relations between them[32]. In this study, political culture is more or less based upon the

---

[31]

Ball 1988, 4.

[32]

Some cultures are, for instance, more homogeneous in their polit–

political concepts of those in power, that is, upon the concepts constitutive of power. This results partly from the main point of departure adopted for the work. The key question has been to understand focal differences in views about European integration, which locate the problem in governmental policy and at the level of political elites. Therefore, it seems logical to focus on those traditions that form the basis for State governance and for the formation of political identities at the level of the Western European States.

Political culture constitutes the basis for political values and identities and, consequently, for the formulation of political goals. The terms of political culture receive expression through the conceptions of political elites and decision–makers even if they also have to achieve a broader legitimacy among citizens. The terms of political culture live in, and are transmitted by, people's political conceptions as well as institutionalised political structures such as different types of law and norms and organisations of governance. Elements of political culture live in history, which means that political conceptions and understandings are all the time being reproduced and adapted to new historical conditions.

European unity was argued as being characterised by political diversity. The origins of this state of things can be found at the level of political traditions. Even if there certainly does exist something that has customarily been defined as *the common European political heritage,* Europe is divided as far as the more detailed political conceptions are concerned. This means, inter alia, conceptions about political community, which is the main issue of this study. In an elaborated form, the argument of the work is now that *the project of European integration is impeded by a division of political traditions concerning the idea of Europe as a political community.* The significance of this historical division reaches present political thinking when concepts and meanings always carry their past with them. It is not my intention to show that every Member State of the present European Union has its own way of understanding, and evaluating, the unification project. It is

---

ical culture, characterised by the dominance of one tradition, while others are based upon a more even balance between some three–four key traditions.

just my purpose to point out the key divisions in European culture that are significant with respect to the understanding of Europe as a political community.

As far as the main structure of the book is concerned, it is divided into two parts, which focus on the problem of European community–building from two different perspectives. The perspective of the first part (chapters two–four) is a European one. Its purpose is, in general terms, to analyse differences between political traditions in Europe by revealing their historical construction. The project is begun in the *second chapter,* which introduces an argument about the Reformation as a key divide in European political culture. The argument is justified by comparing, first, the key concepts of the three political traditions that the Reformation is claimed to have brought about. The division is then followed up to modern times by showing its impact upon the terms of modern state–building in Western Europe since the seventeenth century.

The *third* chapter continues the analysis of differences between political traditions by grasping the ways in which the traditions are related to the idea of a united Europe. One purpose of the chapter is to reveal the path of the idea of a truly united, federal Europe from its early phases to the present day. This kind of analysis will point out the culture, or cultures, which are constitutive of the whole idea and which therefore may be assumed to function also as the backbone of the present integration project. It is also assumed that this will show where the limits of other, less European, cultures go as far as the acceptance of the common European governance is concerned.

The *fourth* chapter brings the analyses to the present project of European integration. Its purpose is, above all, to make visible in the present project the consequences of the cultural and political division. The chapter is thus based upon the analysis of the conceptual differences that was started in the two previous chapters. It puts forth the argument that these conceptual differences have brought the present integration project into a deadlock as far as its key structures of governance are concerned. The lack of democracy and the dominance of bureaucratic structures are introduced as examples of structural problems of this kind.

The second part (chapters five–six) of the book approaches the problem of European community–building from the point of view of one national political culture, the Finnish. Its general purpose is to bring depth to the first part by showing the impact of political culture, and the relation between political traditions and culture and the formulation of political goals, in more detail. There are also more specific purposes connected with the analysis of the *Finnish* political culture and of its European character. The analysis purports first to place Finland culturally in the project of European integration, that is, to show its cultural commitments in the project. Through this analysis, the second part aims at making understandable the present Finnish integration policy with its limitations and possibilities. The second part also approaches political cultures from a governmental level, putting the emphasis on those traditions that have been constitutive of political power.

The *fifth* chapter thus purports to grasp the core elements of Finnish political culture by analysing the historical construction of the Finnish State. It is a common assumption that the political culture of Finland is dominated by collectivist elements and by the very high value accorded to the State. It is the purpose of the fifth chapter to test the validity of this assumption and to place Finnish political culture within the tripartition of key traditions that was constructed in the first part of the book.

The fifth chapter purports to give the foundation for the *sixth* and last chapter that focuses on the prevailing ways the Finnish political culture has of relating itself to the idea of a politically united Europe. The chapter is not intended to discuss the current forms of Finnish integration policy. Its main purpose is to find out the focal points of departure for this policy and to point out the cultural limitations and abilities of Finland as one constructor of a united Europe.

2 The Three Political Cultures of Western Europe

Introduction

One of the core factors burdening the construction of a European governance is that even if the West European countries share a common political culture, they do not share a tradition of governance at this level of ambitiousness. When talking about Western political principles, we are accustomed to refer to principles that are common to Western countries irrespective of their political division into sovereign States. Freedom of the individual, democratic government and the tradition of human rights are among the key principles unifying European countries under the Western political heritage. But principles like State sovereignty, national independence or constitutional liberty are of an equal importance and function in an opposite, divisive, direction.

The purpose of this chapter is to show how the principles that constitute the common political heritage of Western Europe were developed into effective principles of governance at the national level, but not at the European one. Western culture and civilisation is based upon the heritages of the classical cultures and of Judaic–Christianity. This heritage has given birth to the principles constitutive of the Western culture and unity of which the idea of government was neither uniform nor necessarily all–embracing. The core argument of this chapter is that a certain diversity in the character of government and the difficulties in the construction of a European government, have to be understood in the light of the West European traditions of government–building since the Middle Ages.

The point of departure in this chapter is that at the same time as the Member States of the present European Union are united by a common political culture, they are also to a very decisive extent divided inside the same culture. Christianity was first divided into the Western doctrine and Eastern doctrine, but as this study focuses on Western

Europe only, it is not concerned with this division. Western Europe was crucially influenced by the subsequent division of the Western form of the Christian doctrine, that is, by the Reformation. By dividing Western Christianity into Calvinism, Lutheranism and into the doctrine known as the Counter–Reformation, the Reformation completed a historical division in Western political culture. The main purpose of this chapter is to explicate the doctrinal significance of this division and to give some proof of the importance it has had for the later phases of the three political cultures.

Defining the Three Cultures

The Reformation can be treated as one of the main divides in the political history of Europe. In spite of the difficulty of the task, the Reformation brought the medieval political system of competing political authorities to its end. The victory of the Reformation launched the system of sovereign States in Europe. Yet, in its different forms, the Reformation, in its turn, created competing State forms.

    The Reformation did not only bring about a division in political structures. It was of equal importance with respect to a division taking place in political cultures and political thinking[1]. The key purpose of the Reformation was to suppress the powers that the Church had in political affairs. The doctrines by means of which this was put into effect had a vast impact upon later political thinking and upon the creation of the modern State in various parts of Europe. The Reformation is not the only decisive division of European political culture as many other divisions could be pointed out cutting even across the cultural borders of the Reformation itself. Nor can the Reformation

---

1

    One of the few systematical studies following this argument is Max Weber's *The Protestant Ethic and the Spirit of Capitalism* (London, Unwin University Books, 1965). The argument has a significant role also in Quentin Skinner's *The Foundations of Modern Political Thought I–II* (Cambridge, Cambridge University Press, 1978), which, however, goes much deeper into the history of European political thought.

be treated as the pure fount of its own key concepts, many of which had already been developed in earlier contexts[2]. The Reformation has, however, a unique value due to the deep and comprehensive political significance that it had upon European political thinking. Its political messages effectively spread through religious doctrines to the pious people of the end of the Middle Ages.

The Reformation divided European political culture into a Calvinist tradition, into a Lutheran tradition and into a tradition of a Counter–Reformative Catholicism. Irrespective of the many political structures and tendencies that they had in common, these traditions were still divided with respect to their key political concepts. One could characterise the three traditions as an individualist tradition, a State tradition and a tradition of Christian communitarianism as far as their main political emphasis was concerned. As the rest of the study is based upon this division, there is reason to analyse how it came into being and what its significance is for the development of modern political concepts.

Before the Reformation

The birth of the three political cultures is connected with the situation in Medieval Europe where different political authorities were competing for power. The Catholic Church appeared as one powerful actor after having taken over the political structures of the West Roman Empire when this had collapsed. The long–lasting plan of the Church, which at times it tried strenuously to put into effect, was to establish a Catholic Empire in accordance with the ideas of St. Augustine[3]. The powers of the Church were opposed by different tribes, among the most important of which were the Germans and the Franks. The position of

---

[2]

The best source for the development of European political concepts from the early Renaissance is Skinner 1978, vols I–II. See also Gierke 1900 and Nussbaum 1954.

[3]

Palmer 1984, 24–27.

the Church was based upon a continuity which it represented among the ever–changing arrangements of power in core areas of the present Western Europe. In the beginning of the second millennium, there appeared at least two different bases of power that started to challenge the medieval system. The first challenge came from the rising cities which demanded privileges from feudal rule and many of which developed into independent centres of power[4]. The second challenge came from the European monarchies where the medieval political chaos was slowly being transformed into the structures of a central State[5].

The political powers of the Catholic Church had been based from the fourth century onwards upon the Augustinian doctrine of two cities, or worlds[6]. The first of them was the original world, the world of God, where men were seen to live together in peace and harmony. The second was the world that resulted from original sin, where men were said to be born innately lustful or self–regarding. The point of departure in Augustinian political theory was that in life on earth, the two worlds are mixed with each other and that it is only God who knows to which of the two worlds everybody belongs[7]. The idea of the two worlds, where the heavenly world is the good one and the primary one and where the earthly world represents sin and lust, purported to legitimate the powers of the Church with respect to both of them.

---

[4]

The most important medieval cities were in the North of Italy and along the great rivers of the Danube and the Rhine. Of the Italian cities, Venice, Genoa, Pisa, Florence and Milan had developed into real city–states (Palmer 1984, 32).

[5]

Hinsley 1986, 69 ff.

[6]

St Augustine lived in AD 354–430 and introduced his political theory in the work *De civitate Dei*. The idea of the two swords both of which belong to the Church is of Judaic origin and came to Christianity through the Apocalypse (Russell 1947, 380–381).

[7]

Nelson 1982, 72 ff; Gerholm & Magnusson 1983, 161–167.

Forming an essential part of Western political thinking, the theory of rights was adapted to a Catholic world–view characterised by two worlds. St. Augustine's theory was in many ways the opposite of Stoicism, one of the leading schools of thought in the Roman Empire. The Stoics had developed a conception about *natural law* that was seen to consist of certain universal moral laws that all men could know by the use of reason[8]. St. Augustine denied the possibility of natural law owing to his theory of original sin. His political and legal theory was based upon a hierarchical system of rights extending itself to the level of the individual. Therefore, the Augustinian theory brought a change also in the original Christian doctrine of equal right as the basis for the Christian community[9].

In the double organisation of State and Church, every individual was seen to have his own place and rights in accordance with the legal order that had been created by God as the supreme legislator. St. Augustine replaced natural law as the supreme legal order by a Divine Order that was seen to be only in part available to human reason. The rest would be announced as a Divine Right. Individuals were supposed to be satisfied with the position they were given in the social order because of its divine origins. Augustinian political theory thus drew a picture of Christianity as a political community with God as its supreme legislator and the Church as its highest political authority on earth. The theory legitimised the medieval feudal order, which has been seen to have functioned as one powerful restraint on the development of the centralised State[10].

A remarkable change took place in Catholic political theory in the thirteenth century. The change prefigured the later changes brought on within the framework of the Renaissance, one of the key eras in the

---

[8]

The idea of natural law was based upon the rationalist philosophy of the classical cultures and it constituted a natural element in the Roman idea of a world State (Stybe 1961, 54; Nelson 1982, 70–71).

[9]

Gerholm & Magnusson 1983, 163.

[10]

Hinsley 1986, 161–163.

history of Western civilisation. The change reflected the new pressures that were directed at the position of the Catholic Church from the beginning of the second millennium. It anticipated therefore the new role that Christianity came to adopt as a political community.

St. Thomas Aquinas was the main figure behind the change in Catholic political doctrine[11]. He brought the heritage of the classical cultures back to the core of Western political thinking by combining the Aristotelian world–view with the doctrine of Catholic Christianity. In addition to its scholastic spirit, Aquinas' work tried to reconcile the Catholic doctrine with the demands for political liberty, and for a division of secular and ecclesiastical power that had arisen, above all, in the independent cities of Northern Italy[12]. The form within which St. Thomas Aquinas developed the Catholic doctrine is usually known as *Thomism*, a doctrine which was to constitute also an important basis for the Catholic Counter–Reformation centuries later.

The synthesis of Aristotle's philosophy and the Catholic doctrine implied that Aquinas was endeavouring to prove the key theses of the religious doctrine by means of 'natural reason'[13]. He argued that man was at one level a part of nature and at another level transcended it. The element in which the two qualities of the human being were fused was human reason and it was this that raised man above the biological realm and above nature itself. According to St. Thomas, reason united man directly with God[14]. Through reason, the human being was seen as gaining his share of the divine goodness and was therefore not

---

[11]

St. Thomas lived between AD 1225–1274 and received his education in various European universities. He introduced his main political ideas in the *Summa theologica* (Russell 1947, 475–476).

[12]

Skinner 1978 vol I, 12–22.

[13]

Russell 1947, 476 ff.

[14]

Nelson 1982, 91.

condemned to sin and to the dependence on God's word that St. Augustine had taught.

St. Thomas modified the pessimistic conception of a human being adopted by St. Augustine and argued that reason, not sin, was the defining characteristic of human nature. As the basis of his political theory, St. Thomas brought back the Stoic concept of natural law that had been denied by St. Augustine. By natural law, one was referring to a non–codified law, a kind of moral reason that was seen to be binding all men to certain good purposes. In the syntheses embodied in Thomism, natural law appears as the link between the natural and the supernatural. It stands as the channel through which the human being participates in the eternal law of God. The concept of natural law constituted the core of Thomist political theory along with the value accorded to human or civil law. Human law was seen to be legitimate to the extent that it accorded with natural law, which attached an important spiritual element to this law. Human law started to appear as a reflection of God's eternal law with the implication that politics was raised into a new position in the Catholic doctrine, replacing consequently the Augustinian conception of politics as a necessary evil.

In the new form of the Catholic doctrine that was created mainly by St. Thomas Aquinas in the thirteenth century, politics started to be seen again in a positive light, implying also that a certain independence vis–à–vis the Church could be accepted for the management of political affairs. Thomism therefore constituted one important doctrinal framework inside which the relations between the secular and the ecclesiastical power were elaborated before the Reformation[15]. St. Thomas himself put forth the idea that even if the Church is the higher of the two authorities, its powers should be limited to ultimate questions of a moral and spiritual character[16]. While the Dominicans stood behind Aquinas, the Franciscans were more sceptical about the abilities of

---

[15]

Skinner (1978 vol I, 53 ff) goes into much detail about these variations.

[16]

Nelson 1982, 93.

human reason and emphasised the legislative role of the Church[17].

The Political Logic of The Reformation

The Reformation, which in fact consisted of a number of Protestant[18] revolutions against the existing dogma and structures of the Catholic Church in various European countries, will be treated here as the result of a multifarious opposition raised against the Church both by groups inside the institution itself and by social and political forces external to it. The leading doctrine of the first reform movement was Lutheranism, which spread mostly in Germany, Scandinavia, and at first also in the Low Countries, England, Scotland, Switzerland and France. In many of these countries, Lutheranism had only a temporary impact and it was Calvinism that became dominant as it started to spread in the second phase of the Reformation. Calvinism replaced Lutheranism in France, where the Protestants were called Huguenots, and in Holland, Scotland and Switzerland. In England, the Reformation was completed on the basis of Calvinism even if the result, the Anglican Church, is theologically a hybrid between Catholicism and Protestantism. Catholicism maintained its position in Southern Europe, in Italy, Spain and Portugal. The Catholic Church could not ignore the heavy criticism that had been directed towards it also by internal forces and it consequently put into effect a modification of its doctrine. The series of actions that ensued are known as the Counter–Reformation, in which the Jesuits had an important role.

The doctrines of Lutheranism, Calvinism and the Counter–Reformation will next be analysed in order to point out their significance and key values in terms of political culture. The core

---

17

Stybe 1961, 146.

18

The term *Protestant* is not free from problems. It came into being during the religious strife and referred first to a small group of Lutherans. Only very gradually did the various groups of anti–Roman reformers think of themselves as collectively Protestant (Palmer 1984, 75).

argument of this chapter is that as the Protestant doctrines distanced themselves from the Christian communitarianism expressed by Catholicism, Calvinism constituted an important substratum for political individualism, while Lutheranism brought about a culture centring around the State.

The Political Heritage of Lutheranism

The political significance of the Reformation can be summed up in two points. The first is the subordination of the Church to secular rulers, implying, among other things, an abolition of its worldly glory and jurisdictional powers. The second is the loss of the Christian community's value in the religious ethic at the expense of individualism or communities of a more secular type.

Lutheranism gained a permanent position in the agrarian societies of Northern Europe, strengthening there a culture that centred firmly on the State[19]. The doctrine of Martin Luther[20] constituted an important support for secular rule and ruler, both in opposition to the Catholic Church and with respect to social and political groups within the States. Luther turned against the optimism and rationalism that had characterised the Catholic doctrine from the thirteenth century and based his theory upon an Augustinian and anti–humanist conception of the human being. He argued that 'through the one transgression of one man, Adam, we are all under sin and damnation' and are left with 'no

---

[19]

It was not, of course, an accident that the areas most receptive to Lutheranism had been characterised by centralised structures of power earlier (Dickens 1975, 67–106).

[20]

Martin Luther lived between 1483–1546 and his career as a reformer originated in the protests he raised against the traffic in indulgences (Palmer 1984, 75–76). Good explanations of Lutheran thinking are Dickens 1975, Skinner 1978 vol II.

capacity to do anything but sin and be damned'[21]. The first conclusion to be drawn from the evil nature of the human being is that no one can ever hope to be granted salvation by virtue of his own works. One of the cornerstones of Lutheranism is the doctrine of *sola fide*, by faith alone. According to Luther good works cannot bring salvation, but it must be open to anybody to perceive God's saving grace.

The conclusion that Luther drew from the doctrine of *sola fide* was that as the Church cannot do anything to help a sinner the role and powers of the Church shall be understood differently from the dominant Catholic conceptions. Luther put forth his powerful thesis that the Church shall be no more than an invisible *congregatio fidelium*, a congregation of the faithful gathered together in God's name[22]. The powers of the Church must therefore be entirely spiritual, which signifies a denial of ecclesiastical authority over temporal affairs. This means that Luther envisaged a system of individual national churches, in which the ruler was given the right to appoint and dismiss the officers, as well as to control and dispose of the Church's property[23].

The other important part of Luthers' doctrine, and the core of his political theory, deals with the nature of political authority and relations between the individual and the State. The evil character of the human being and the fact that man was considered as fallen from God implies according to Luther that a human being cannot receive knowledge of God's will through his reason. The conception that God's will can be conveyed to the people only through God's word functioned as an important support of the secular power. In Luther's theory, all powers, including those of the temporal authority, are ordained by God. Luther adopted first a more liberal conception in arguing that as the prince has a duty to use the powers God has given to him in a godly way, people

---

21

Skinner 1978 vol II, 5.

22

Ibid., 10.

23

Ibid., 15.

have no obligation to follow a ruler who is doing wrong. Having realised the political dimensions of his theory, Luther changed his mind and started to emphasise the theory of non-resistance. The final message of Lutheranism thus remained very conservative as far as the role of ordinary people was concerned. People had to be loyal to the ruler because in his hands was seen to reside the will of God. Christian liberty was according to Luther only internal and spiritual liberty whereas in worldly affairs it was the duty of a good Christian to be loyal to the ruler[24].

The value of the Christian community was challenged in Protestant doctrines by an individualist moral and ethic[25]. Both Lutheranism and Calvinism opposed the Thomist idea of a Christian community based upon natural law. Their view of human being was based upon aversion and selfishness. They argued that a Christian Church or community could not help an individual to salvation but that an individual was alone in his faith. Protestant doctrines drew, however, very different conclusions from these conceptions. The Lutheran doctrine nourished passive elements of subordination and belief in authority both by means of its ethic and political theory. It introduced faith and a feeling of actual absorption in the deity as the highest religious experience[26]. According to Lutheranism, every worldly element was an indication of worldly aversion and smallness in contrast to the unlimited glory of God. The most important thing that a human being could do was to open himself to the grace of God. The same attitude characterised Lutheran political theory. Temporal power was sanctified by regarding it as a sign of God's providence. Temporal power ought not to be resisted because that would imply a resistance to

---

[24]

Palmer 1984, 77.

[25]

The idea of a Christian community was not denied, but it lost its position as the core of the political and moral theory in the doctrines of reformed Christianity.

[26]

Weber 1965, 112.

God's will. A Lutheran political culture can thus be seen as having a strong tendency towards ruler or State absolutism.

The Political Heritage of Calvinism

Calvinism is a Protestant doctrine that brought about different vicariates in different parts of the world. The Anglican Church is among these as well as the Presbyterian Churches of Scotland and of the present United States and the Congregationalist Church of the latter. A characteristic of Calvinism was that it constituted a religious minority in many European countries and had thus to fight for its position in another way than Lutheranism. The key figure behind the Calvinist doctrine was Jean Calvin who joined the Reformation in the 1530's and started to elaborate Luther's ideas[27]. Calvinism is usually called the second wave of the Reformation. It has much in common with Lutheranism but differs, however, from it in essential questions, nourishing a very different cultural heritage in the regions under its impact.

Jean Calvin shared the Augustinian and Lutheran theory of original sin as well as Luther's conviction about the doctrine of *sola fide*. He attacked the powers and glory of the Catholic Church and emphasised the almighty nature of God who appeared in his theory as a transcendental being, regulating the tiniest details of the cosmos from eternity[28]. Even if Calvin followed Luther in demanding a separation of secular and ecclesiastic rule, he did not demand the subordination of the Church to the State as Luther did. He claimed instead that the secular rule, too, should be based upon Christian principles. His ideal therefore was a theocratic State, a State that would be ruled on the basis of God's

---

[27]

Jean Calvin, who himself used the Latin name *Calvinus* lived between 1509–1564 and introduced his main ideas in the work *Christianae religionis institutio* (Palmer 1984, 79).

[28]

Weber 1965, 104.

word[29].

The idea of a State ruled on the basis of Christian principles already gives a hint of the significant differences between Lutheran and Calvinist political theory even if these were both based upon the conception that all powers are ordained by God. The Calvinist doctrine gradually developed in a direction very different from the Lutheran theory of non-resistance and loyalty to the political authorities. When Luther ended up with the conviction that even an evil ruler had been ordained by God, and had therefore to be obeyed by the people, radical Calvinists turned this very norm upside down. According to them, rulers that failed to discharge the duties of their offices ought not to be regarded as ordained by God[30]. They argued that in such a case a people that received a ruler ordained by God had committed a mistake and selected a wrong ruler. This brought the possibility, or, more correctly, the duty, of resisting a ruler who was misusing his powers.

The theory of resistance constituted the core of Calvinist political theory along with the idea of 'magistrates of the people' appointed to restrain the wilfulness of kings[31]. These theories provided Calvinism with a secular and constitutionalist spirit that did not belong to Lutheranism. According to Calvin, the right to resist a ruler belonged to the ordinary people who should also be allowed to control the ruler's use of power.

Calvin approached modern constitutionalism by perceiving his popular magistrates as appointed by the people with the purpose of moderating the power of the kings. Calvinism, however, was not the only political culture adopting constitutionalist tones in the sixteenth century, as similar ideas were powerfully put forth by the so called

---

29

Palmer 1984, 80; Gerholm & Magnusson 1983, 253.

30

The more revolutionary protagonists of the Calvinist movement were found in England, men like *John Ponet* and *Christopher Goodman* being connected with it (Skinner 1978 vol II, 221–227).

31

Ibid., 230.

'conciliarists' within the framework of the Catholic tradition[32]. Calvinist constitutionalism was, however, more radical in the sense that it dealt with the governance of secular power, while the Catholic theory constituted only a modern legitimation for this power and put forth a very ruler–centric view as far as governance was concerned[33].

There is one further cultural element in Calvinism that can be treated as a proponent of political individualism and that bears with it an even stronger impact than the political theory connected with this doctrine. We have to turn back to the debate upon the Protestant ethic that was touched on in the previous passage and has been brought into focus by Max Weber[34]. Differences between the three political cultures in Europe seem, in an important way, to be connected with the ethic, or rules of conduct, put forth by the religious doctrines constitutive of these cultures.

The ethic of Christian doctrines centres around the question of salvation. The doctrine of predestination belongs to the dogma characteristic of Protestantism[35] and forms an important element of the tenet *sola fide*. According to it, the salvation of each individual is predestined by God, the knowledge of individual fates being available for God only. Weber argued that the doctrine of predestination nourished the inner loneliness of the single individual and supported the elements of spiritual isolationism in Protestant cultures[36]. There are, however, important differences between the Protestant cultures as far as the ideas about how a good Christian should use his life on earth are

---

[32]

Ibid., 113–134.

[33]

See page 39 of this chapter.

[34]

Weber 1965.

[35]

Gerholm & Magnusson 1983, 254; Weber 1965, 98.

[36]

Weber 1965, 95 ff.

concerned. The Calvinist ethic formed an important part of its puritan spirit, while Lutheranism promoted the value of (mystical) faith.

The point of departure in the Protestant ethic was that a good Christian had to await his destiny by obeying God's law and precepts. While Luther taught that faith was the highest religious purpose of a good Christian, and loyalty towards worldly authorities its temporal manifestation, Calvin advocated a more self–centred line of conduct for the faithful. According to him, a good Christian had to acquire the self–conviction of his own salvation by arranging his whole life into a system of good works. In Calvinism, worldly activity thus gained a spiritual value even if not as a means of salvation but as an indication of it[37]. The Calvinist ethic was not in the first place devised from a detailed list of the worldly activities of every single individual. Its emphasis was placed more upon the manner of arranging and controlling these activities. Calvinism thus fostered a puritan ethic based upon a constant self–control of one's own actions and upon a careful consideration of their ethical consequences. The purpose of this puritan ascetism can be summed up as an ability to lead an alert, intelligent life by bringing under control all spontaneous, impulsive enjoyment.

The Calvinist ethic can be treated as a powerful contribution to the individualist heritage of this culture. In contrast to Lutheranism, Calvinism brought the individual and his life and deeds into focus. This was done through an ethic that made the control of one's own life one of the key values of every individual. It was also done through a political theory that gave individuals the capacity to control the use of powers ordained by God. One could therefore argue that whereas a Lutheran culture included a strong predilection for ruler or State absolutism, a Calvinist culture appeared more easily transformable into

---

[37]

This idea of worldly activity having a religious value is usually known as a *calling*, which is a firmly Lutheran concept. Weber argues, however, that the Lutheran calling is a traditionalistic concept implying that it is something which man has to accept as a divine ordinance (Weber 1965, 85). It can therefore be seen as supporting cultural elements of sub–ordination rather than those of individualism.

modern political individualism.

The Political Heritage of The Counter–Reformation

The Counter–Reformation is an ambiguous term because it refers to the resistance and reconquest that was put into effect by the Catholic Church against the reform movements as well as to the more spontaneous and long term modification of the Catholic doctrine taking place in the sixteenth century. As this work deals with political cultures, *the Counter–Reformation* refers here to the core of political thinking that remained dominant in Catholic Europe after the Reformation and can be seen as having extended its significance directly to our days. Many efforts had been made inside the Catholic Church to modify Catholic doctrine during the decades preceding the Reformation. The *conciliarist* movement had systematically advocated a limitation of Papal powers, arguing that the highest governing authority of the Church should lie with the General Council as the representative assembly of the faithful[38].

Another great critical movement, which was partly inside the Church, was the humanist movement that advocated a more independent attitude towards the role and dogmas of the Church. Humanists emphasised the role of the Bible and recommended the study of its texts in the original languages[39]. Reforms could not, however, be carried out before the Reformation was launched and the Council of Trent, assembling several times between 1545–63, had thus to defend the Catholic doctrine against all accusations, external as well as internal ones.

The reformed Catholic doctrine that was, in part, confirmed by

---

[38]

Palmer 1984, 86; Skinner 1978 vol II, 116. Skinner shows how the roots of modern constitutionalism can be found in the conciliarist tradition, which applied its theory of the Church also to secular rule.

[39]

Erasmus of Rotterdam has become the main representative of the Humanist movement. He published the New Testament in its original Greek form (Frisch 1973 vol 3, 145–147).

the Council of Trent, was mainly a creation of Dominican and Jesuit theorists and was eagerly spread throughout the Catholic world by the Jesuits[40]. The leading country of the Counter–Reformation was Spain, which remained entirely under the impact of Catholicism in the same way as Italy, Portugal and Austria. France was officially Catholic with, however, considerable Protestant minorities, which led to continuous religious struggles up to the late seventeenth century.

Doctrinally, the Counter–Reformation was based upon a revival of Thomist ideology which had been pushed aside by other doctrines and doctrinal disputes in the fifteenth century. The Dominican Francisco Vitoria and the Jesuits Luis de Molina and Francisco Suárez were the key figures behind the counter–reformative application of Thomism[41]. These theorists attacked the Humanist and Protestant criticism of Catholic theology as well as its political implications. They first repudiated the Protestant conception that Christianity is nothing more than a *congregatio fidelium*. Their arguments were confirmed in the official decree given by the Council of Trent in 1546, according to which the Scriptures revealed that the Church was founded as a visible institution by Christ himself. No one could in consequence be said to live a fully Christian life who chose to live it outside the confines of the visible Catholic Church[42]. The jurisdictional authority of the Church was defended in the same manner. Vitoria and Suárez argued that the visible Church was an independent legislative authority operating its own code of canon law parallel with, and never in subjection to, the

---

[40]

For the creation of the theory, see Skinner 1978 vol II, 136–173; for the spread of the theory, see Dickens 1969, 75–90.

[41]

Francisco Vitoria lived between 1485–1546, gained his education in Paris, and taught at the University of Salamanca in Spain. Luis de Molina and Francisco Suárez both began their studies at that university, but moved later to Portugal and Rome respectively (Skinner 1978 vol II, 137–138 ff).

[42]

Skinner 1978 vol II, 144.

civil laws of the commonwealth[43].

The political theory of the Counter–Reformation was based upon this logic, the logic of parallel political authorities with one authority serving the purposes of God and the other the purposes of the human being. This combination, deriving from the idea that the secular power was not of Divine origin, enabled a secularisation of political theory with the result that Catholicism constituted a most important historical framework for the idea of modern constitutionalism. This achievement can be linked with the Thomist concept of the human being, which gave expression to the classicist values of the Renaissance more than the Northern cultures ever did. The political heritage of Catholicism is a communitarian one. As the community it puts forth is clearly based upon Christian principles, its heritage can be crystallised as Christian communitarianism.

Reformed Catholicism had its point of departure in the idea that an individual received salvation partly through his faith and partly through his good works. Individuals were seen as partaking in the Divine goodness both through God's word, as it was interpreted by the Church, and through natural law transmitted through human reason. Individuals were therefore seen to be communitarian by nature and the communitarianism was, due to its origin, of a Christian nature. Vitoria and Suárez raised the Christian principles of individual freedom, equality and independence to be constitutive norms of natural law. In the natural condition of mankind, individuals were therefore said to form a community governed by natural law and based upon the acknowledgement of the natural freedom, equality and independence of all the peoples. The Christian community constituted the natural community in reformed Catholicism with the implication that other communities were seen to be subordinated to it[44]. This conception

---

43

Tuck 1989, 33 ff; Skinner 1978 vol II, 145.

44

Skinner 1978 vol II, 158. It should, however, be taken into account that according to Vitoria forms of secular political authority could be established even by peoples who were not Christian (Skinner 1978 vol II, 166–172).

reflected itself later in the idea of a Christian community of States, which functions as the basis for the modern system of international law.

Thomists thus rejected firmly the Protestant conception of secular powers as powers ordained by God and introduced a theory of the State according to which the State served worldly purposes only. It was within this framework that they established a primary form of the modern constitutionalist theory, by arguing that individuals established a political rule from pure self–interest, that is, in order to guarantee the maintenance of peace and justice. Individuals that were seen to be free by nature subordinated themselves in consequence to positive laws through the medium of their own consent.

The establishment of a constitutionalist theory of the State by the theorists of the Counter–Reformation ought not to be confused with the radical theory of resistance created within the Calvinist system[45]. Even if the Thomists' State was based upon the consent of the individual, the rule of the State was not seen as being controlled by individuals. The primary meaning that the constitutionalist theory of the State had in Catholic political theory and culture was that it connected secular power with more practical, everyday purposes, while still subordinating it to the higher purposes of Christianity. Yet, in the theorizing of this extension of Thomism, the secular power was accorded a certain autonomy, a fact which has been of importance for the later development of constitutionalism. Such a theory could never, for example, comprehend a divine right of kings. It is nonetheless true that as far as the use of the secular power was concerned the Thomist conception for long provided a bulwark that was as conservative and patriarchal as the papal model of the Church was to indicate. Vitoria and Suárez were thus among those Thomists who argued that secular rule was absolutist by definition. As the natural condition of mankind had not included all the powers assigned to a ruler at the inauguration of the commonwealth, the powers could not be seen to have been delegated to the ruler. According to Suárez since many powers are lacking in a natural community, it followed that, after this form of authority had been assigned to a ruler, he had to stand above the entire

---

[45]

Tuck 1989, 33–57; Skinner 1978 vol II, 174–184.

community as well as above each individual member[46].

The culture surrounding the birth of the modern State in Catholic Europe had thus a firm communitarian emphasis. The doctrine of reformed Catholicism was based upon the idea of a
Christian community both as far as its ethic and political theory were concerned. In their spiritual life, the people were supposed to lean on the Church and on the community of the faithful that it gave expression to. Although the people's worldly activities were not connected with spiritual purposes, politics appeared in a positive light as it appeared to be a realisation of a true human nature. Christianity thus constituted the real political community regulating other processes of community-building through its norms and morality.

The Modern Doctrines of State–Building in Western Europe

The significance of the Reformation, and of the birth of the three political cultures that it implied, can be illustrated through the ways in which it nourished the formation of modern States in Europe[47]. The political position of the European State was confirmed in the peace treaties of Augsburg (1555) and Westphalia (1648). The first established the principle *cuius regio eius religio* according to which every monarch could decide upon the religion of his country. The treaty of Westphalia recognised European States as the supreme political

---

[46]

Skinner 1978 vol II, 178ff. The communitarian Thomists did not thus accept the idea of an absolute individual liberty elaborated mainly by Jean Gerson. The idea was fused into the constitutionalist theory of State by Protestant Humanists (Selden, Hobbes) in the seventeenth century (Tuck 1989, 82 ff).

[47]

This is perhaps not the best way of making explicit the differences between the three cultures. There is still a certain legitimacy in the approach since the State, even if it is more directly linked with the Protestant cultures, has appeared to be one of the key concepts of Western political thought and a cornerstone for political cultures for centuries.

authorities in Europe and officially brought to an end the efforts of the Counter–Reformation[48]. The key form of the European State was elaborated conceptually between these two treaties in the midst of the religious wars of France. Jean Bodin made a significant extension to his defence of ruler absolutism by treating absolute sovereignty as an analytical implication of the concept of State[49]. He made a decisive contribution to the creation of the concept of a modern State through his argument that every political community should be characterised by an absolute and perpetual power that would stand above the laws of that community.

So far, it has been argued here that the Reformation split Western political culture into certain differentiable political traditions, that is an individualist tradition, a State–centric tradition and a tradition of a Christian community. In the process of State–building, these traditions expressed themselves as three models for the modern State. These can be called *the liberal* State, *the absolutist* State and *the republican* State. These concepts (illustrating a process of 'modernisation') are foundations for the liberation of the State from its medieval divine authority. There are hardly any pure cases of any of these models in Western Europe nor is the existence of these models limited to their 'original' culture only. Purporting to express the dominant form of the individual processes of State–building, these terms of modernisation render visible some essential differences between the processes, and, consequently, between the three political cultures. Before one goes into these processes of modernisation something has to be said about the background, that is, about the main trends of conceptualising political power in medieval Europe. It is just these trends that according to the argument of this study were questioned in different ways by the three political cultures.

There were many processes which led to a gradual reinforcement of monarchical powers in Europe during the first centuries of the second

---

[48]

Palmer 1984, 141–146.

[49]

Skinner 1978 vol II, 287; Hinsley 1986, 120–125.

millennium. One of them was the victory of regional monarchy over the universal authorities represented by the Pope and the Emperor. On the part of the Catholic Church, this was based upon the Thomist doctrine recognising the value, and the relative independence, of secular powers. The point of departure for monarchical powers was a double legitimation. From early times European kings had been elected by the community they ruled, receiving thus, at least symbolically, its consent. The other basis of legitimation was a theocratical one. The growing independence of European monarchs nourished a conception of their position as *Rex Dei Gratia*, which, in the last resort, surpassed the idea of popular consent. As a culmination of this centralisation of powers to the king, monarchical powers became hereditary in many European countries from the thirteenth century[50].

The Reformation was just one step in this all–European development towards strengthening of monarchical powers. The modernisation of political thinking it brought about had, on the contrary, quite different substrata in different cultures of the Reformation.

The Liberal State

The formation of modern States was launched in Calvinist Europe, in the British Isles and in the Spanish Low Countries, that is, the part constituted by the present Netherlands. In these countries, the growing merchant class was the first social group in Europe to break the rule of feudalism and to question the absolute powers of the monarchs. This activity gained its legitimation from radical Calvinism and from the seed of political individualism that this doctrine included. In England, the foundations of the modern State were laid in the conflict of power between King and Parliament ending up with the Glorious Revolution (1688) and the Bill of Rights (1689). Parliament became the bastion of radical Calvinists demanding a right for this organ to control the monarchical powers. Parliament was powerful, due to its construction, and was still being strengthened due to the transfer into private property

---

[50]

Hinsley 1986, 104.

that was put into effect at its direction[51]. The Glorious Revolution was a victory of the Protestants and of the supporters of Parliament (the Whigs) over the Catholic King James II. In the Bill of Rights, the new rulers, William and Mary, recognised that the power of laws was superior to that of the King. They also gave their consent to the ideas that taxes could not be collected nor an army maintained without the consent of Parliament[52].

The events surrounding the Glorious Revolution can be regarded as the core of the formation of the modern State in England because of the secularisation of Calvinist political doctrine and the modernisation of the natural law principle of *dominium* that were linked with these events. These processes completed the formation of a purely individualist political theory that had a necessary basis in Calvinism and in the humanist theory of law connected with it[53]. The birth of the modern State thus took place within the framework of a liberal State, meaning that instead of its medieval divine origin the State gained its legitimation from its position as a guarantor of individual liberties. It has been argued that this is the dominant understanding of the State in Calvinist cultures.

The first precondition for the birth of the liberal State was achieved by raising the principle of individual liberty from its medieval position as a principle of natural law into being a natural characteristic of the human being without any necessary linkage to the idea of a natural community. The key figure behind this conceptual development was the Dutchman Hugo Grotius, whose thoughts were further

---

[51]

Palmer 1984, 165–177. The strength of the English Parliament was, according to Palmer (p.168) based upon the fact that its chambers did not emphasise differences between Estates as most of the European Diets did.

[52]

Duroselle 1990, 234; Palmer 1984, 174.

[53]

For the development of the individualist political theory, see Tuck 1989.

elaborated by John Selden and Thomas Hobbes in England[54]. Grotius created the idea that the institution of private property as well as the right of punishment for wrongdoing were natural principles belonging to every human being. Selden and Hobbes, by emphasising the non-natural–law character of these principles, contributed consequently to their utilisation as points of departure for the modern political community[55].

The position of absolute individualism having thus been modernised, the State started to gain its modern legitimacy as a guarantor of individual liberties. The main theorists responsible for the creation of these ideas were Hobbes and John Locke who connected the old social contract theory of the State with their position of absolute individualism. The character and extension of the liberal State can thus be defined in Lockean words as:

> The great and chief end, therefore, of men uniting into commonwealths, and putting themselves under government, is the preservation of their property (meaning according to Locke) the mutual preservation of their lives, liberties and estates[56].

The liberal theory of the State, that has been linked with the Calvinist political tradition, could then be given different forms as far as its governance is concerned. While the theory of Hobbes was more conservative in this respect, and written as a defence of absolute monarchical powers, Locke adopted a position closer to Calvinist

---

54

Tuck 1989, 58–142.

55

The work of Hobbes has been more important, because Hobbes' individualism was based upon a new materialist, scientific theory. The absolute liberty of human beings is regarded as a consequence of the material state of things and of the psychological character of the human being as a desiring, power–seeking animal (Hobbes 1962; Nelson 1982, 136).

56

Locke 1962, 180.

radicalism. According to Locke individuals do not assign all of their liberties to the State, but keep a part of them to themselves. Lockean individuals have thus the possibility of controlling the government and of ensuring that this does not violate their liberties.

Calvinism had nourished a culture of political liberties in its other core areas, too, in the Netherlands and in Switzerland, which were the only countries in early modern Europe with a representative form of government. Both countries were religiously divided, though, with a relatively tolerant Calvinist rule. Their governance was based upon autonomous provinces connected under a common Federal Council[57]. The tradition of political liberalism did not, of course, limit itself to Calvinist Europe even if it has had its origin in this culture. Constituting one of the main political traditions in Europe, it has spread to the other cultures of the Reformation and has had an impact upon their modernisation.

The Republican State

The modern State is a product of the Reformation in Europe. This chapter has tried to explain how Catholic political theory, which did not originally allow the political division of Christianity, had to adapt itself to this state of affairs through its Counter–Reformation doctrine. As a political culture Catholicism, therefore, had a dual structure. Its secular and pre–constitutionalist idea of political communities was connected with an absolutist conception of rule according to the Papal model[58]. The dominant significance of Catholicism vis–à–vis the strengthening monarchical rule in Europe was thus conservative. The theocratic legitimation of monarchical powers functioned as an important weapon against attacks in the name of more modern structures of power[59].

---

[57]

Lagerroth 1955, 353–355 and 516–518.

[58]

See page 39.

[59]

Lagerroth 1955, 288.

The revolutionary effect of Catholicism emanated from the communitarian structures of Catholic political thinking and is based upon the significance that the Enlightenment had upon Catholic cultures. The liberation of human reason from the power of all supernatural authorities[60] and the creation of a human society based upon the developing rational capacities of the human being formed the core ideas of the Enlightenment. The Enlightenment, which had started in England, reached its culmination in France, contributing to the solution of religious conflicts in that country. The Enlightenment favoured religious toleration by releasing politics from religious considerations. Henceforward, politics was in the domain of reason only and religious commitments became a private matter[61]. The Enlightenment had a great impact upon European political thinking even if it did not put forth a political theory of its own. It called into question the divine origin of political authorities or political principles and raised citizens' rights and welfare to be the core of a political authority[62]. Its concept of the human being expressed a continuity with the Aristotelian and Thomist traditions. The human being was considered as having been originally good and rational. He was, however, seen as having been damaged by ignorance and bad conditions of living and it was therefore the great purpose of the Enlightenment to change these factors [63].

60

As the Enlightenment was essentially stimulated by the first achievements of modern natural science, its concepts ('human reason' and 'natural/supernatural') were based upon the materialist and mechanist worldview of this (see for example Scruton 1991, 81ff).

61

This was in correspondence with the ideology of Voltaire, the leading French advocate of the Enlightenment (Friedell 1974, 637–646).

62

Männikkö 1988, 554–555.

63

Gerholm & Magnusson 1983, 357 ff; Eriksson & Frängsmyr 1993, 125 ff; Männikkö 1988, 554.

The republican State will thus be seen as the dominant tradition of the modern State in Catholic Europe and as an expression of an enlightened Christian communitarianism. The French revolution of the year 1789 was the key manifestation of the formation of a modern State within the framework of republicanism. Belgium, as well as areas in Northern Italy and Southern Germany, also showed a strong commitment to this ideology. One indication of their cultural unity was the fact that they formed the area that adapted itself best to the Napoleonic rule, based upon the principles of the French revolution[64]. These States formed the core of the wave of revolutions in the name of political rights and liberties in the 1830's. The 'risorgimento' of Italy taking place in the middle of the century was also significantly affected by the republican ideology.

The republican State–building can be seen as a revolution of the third estate against *l'ancien régime*. The perspective of this revolution was broader than that of the Glorious Revolution, because republicanism purported to achieve a change in the whole system of political governance. Republican processes of State–building were not therefore revolutions in the name of liberties only, but they were also revolutions in the name of the political majority and of the political rights of individuals. The Great French revolution, for instance, was a revolution that extended itself to broad groups of society and was directed against various social and political evils and inequalities. The secularisation of political authority taking place within the framework of republicanism replaced Christian morality, as the basis for the community, by human reason and made the State a necessary condition for the communitarian life and the flowering of human nature.

As a political ideology enlightened Catholicism can be traced to the party of the *politiques* in sixteenth century France[65]. Jean Bodin was one of the chief figures of this influential group of moderate Catholics advocating religious toleration in the middle of the Huguenot wars.

---

[64]

Palmer 1984, 404.

[65]

Skinner 1978 vol II, 241–254.

Their arguments for religious liberty were based upon the idea that religious disputes arise solely from ignorance of the truth. Bodin, for instance, argued that unless a given belief happened to rest upon most plain and doubt–free demonstrations there could never be any hope of ensuring that it might not, by disputations and force of argument, be obscured and made doubtful. He then made it clear that he saw no such indubitable foundations for any religious creed. They were mainly based upon the assurance of faith and belief only[66]. The moral of the uncertainty connected with religions was complete tolerance. The maintenance of the commonwealth was thus seen to be an even more compelling duty for government than the maintenance of the established religion.

Jean–Jacques Rousseau was the person who completed the secularisation of Christian communitarianism as the basis for the modern State. In Rousseau's enlightened world–view, the human being appeared to be the creator of all those social and political rules and conventions that had formerly been regarded as expressions of God's will. Human civilisation, including its norms and language, constituted for Rousseau a necessary condition for the use of the human reason. In entering society, men, it was argued, learned to relate themselves to one another on the basis of moral rules rather than mere feeling. As such, they were seen to be truly free for the first time. According to Rousseau, the social contract created moral liberty, which alone rendered a man master of himself[67].

The republican ideology is based upon an extensive concept of politics and political life as it replaces Christian identity and Christian virtues with republican ones. Citizenship and political participation become the great virtues of the human being and a condition for the fulfilment of his humanity. States thus appear to be the necessary conditions for human liberty due to their legislative character and, in particular, due to their character as a framework for the *general will*.

---

[66]

Ibid., 248.

[67]

Nelson 1982, 193.

The *general will* is a moral will that is characterised by the participation of all members of the community. While the essence of the liberal State was individual freedom from other individuals and from society, the republican State expressed the freedom of the individual as freedom for something, that is, for the occupation of his humanity and human capacities.

The Absolutist State

The third process of modern State–building began in the Lutheran cultures of Northern Europe towards the end of the nineteenth century. In contrast to the liberal or republican processes, the third process of State–building was not a revolution in the name of people's rights or liberties. Being a prolongation of Lutheran concepts, it was conservative at the European level. As the political culture of rural Northern Europe, Lutheranism came under the attack of new centres of political power more slowly than the cultures of Southern or Central Europe. Due to its unambiguously ruler–centricism, Lutheranism was also ideologically better equipped to withstand potential attacks. The secularisation of Lutheran political theory can be perceived as a defence of the State in the face of new political identities, the liberal and republican ones[68].

The secularisation of the Lutheran States took place through German nationalism. The key product of this political force is, of course, the German State that was united under Prussian leadership in 1871. German unification and the birth of the modern German State can be perceived as the birth of the German nation and its subordination to the Prussian State. The act of unification was a reaction to external

---

[68]

The secularisation of the Lutheran doctrine was not, however, conservative in every respect. In the framework of German nationalism, important social reforms were launched such as the abolition of serfdom and the old castle system in Prussia (Palmer 1984, 412–414). The conservative character of Lutheranism refers to the key constituents of the European political system and not to the internal political structures in the States.

political developments as well as a reflection of internal social and political pressures. In addition to Germany, the influence of German Romanticism and nationalism spread into the Nordic countries. Finland is the one of these countries in which modern State–building was firmly based upon a German tradition of nationalism.

The Lutheran political tradition centred around the sanctity of the State and respect for collective forms. The original medieval conception that political powers were powers ordained directly by God had been moderated by the Enlightenment and by enlightened absolutism, a form of governance in several Lutheran countries[69]. But even if the enlightened absolute monarchs started to emphasise the prosperity and welfare of their citizens as the purpose of their rule, these goals could be easily overruled by considerations of power politics. These conservative and collectivist political concepts were turned into a modern nationalist political doctrine in the political and cultural predicament of the early nineteenth century caused by the Napoleonic rule.

The cradle of the German nationalist movement was in Jena, in Prussia, the latter being the leading German State that had suffered more than any German State from French rule. Political nationalism was preceded by a cultural nationalism which was based upon the idea of a national character, or spirit, as the core of nationality, and dividing nations from each other. Herder, for instance, started from the idea that every nation should cultivate its own national character and Fichte took the argument further by demanding that German national character, which he claimed to be more noble than the others, should be protected against external threats[70]. Hegel was the key figure behind political

---

[69]

Examples of enlightened absolutes are Fredrick II of Prussia (1740–1786) Catherine II of Russia (1762–1796), Gustavus III of Sweden (1746–1792) and Joseph II of Austria (1765–1790) (Duroselle 1990, 221). Of course, these monarchs and their States were by no means all Lutheran, but the political image they veered towards was best exemplified in the Lutheran political tradition.

[70]

Palmer 1984, 409–412; Lagerroth 1955, 380–386. The cultural basis of

nationalism and behind the secularisation of the core of the Lutheran theory. In his political theory, Hegel gave a specific place to the German nation, but it is evident that this theory reached a generality much broader than this particular case.

The secularisation of the Lutheran theory implied that the State started to appear as the source of its own legitimation. This became possible through Hegelian metaphysics. Hegel put forth the argument that the essence of reality was the self–fulfilment of an absolute spirit. Freedom was the essence of this spirit and the State was, according to Hegel, the external manifestation of freedom[71]. The State was to be perceived as a subject and right of its own provided with the authority to impose obligations on the individual. Even if Hegel's theory still included many semi–mystical elements, it purported to provide the State with a secular legitimation.

By the 1840's, nationalism had developed into an important emotional bond which absorbed the continuing loyalty of an increasing number of individual Germans[72]. Nationalism was essentially stimulated by French victories and by the mid–nineteenth century it started to take on increasingly political tones. The unification of the thirty–eight German States did not succeed without a strong military–political leadership. This position was adopted in the 1860's by Prussia led by the Iron Chancellor Otto von Bismarck. Bismarck was a political realist on the hunt for the Prussian interest rather than an idle nationalist[73]. Through several wars, Bismarck united the German States under Prussian power. The German Empire, or *Reich*, was established with a constitution that came into force in 1871.

German nationalism was, of course, a necessity in the political situation of a Germany divided in a political as well as in a religious sense (Knischewski 1996, 128).

[71]

Russell 1947, 767–769; Peters 1966, 130–142.

[72]

Greenfeld 1992, 386.

[73]

Hovi 1988, 667–670; Palmer 1984, 520–527.

The constitution of the German Empire gave expression to a nationalist understanding of the State[74]. It was based upon the primacy of the State vis-à-vis any other political unit. State powers appeared as their own legitimation. State sovereignty was seen as belonging *by definition* to the supreme German State, the Empire, instead of the autonomous parts constituting it. The State was treated as a legal subject of its own and as prior to society. In accordance with this position, the State was considered to be the sole source of any norms or law including those of the constitution. Regulations and limitations of State powers were seen to be based upon the self-binding capacities of the State. The German constitution treated State powers as indivisible. Legislative as well as executive powers belonged to the Federal Council which was led by the Prussian king, the Emperor of the *Reich*. The constitution has been defined as a monarchical one as it gave the Emperor the right to impede amendments to it. The constitution did not include a list of civil rights or liberties and the protection it gave to individuals or minorities remained, in other respects, too, very weak. The constitution could be amended by a normal legislative procedure which made it possible for the Federal Council to regulate, or even to forbid, focal civic rights or liberties through the operation of simple mechanisms[75].

Conclusions

In this chapter, I have tried to explicate the crucial significance that the Reformation has had in European political thinking. The argument has been that the Reformation brought about a division of Western European political culture, which is certainly not the only division, but which has had an overwhelming significance in the explanation of the basic difficulties in the present effort to unite Europe under one political

---

[74]

Jyränki 1989, 229.

[75]

Ibid., 229–257.

rule. The Reformation has been interpreted here as completing the division of Western Christianity into three rather distinct cultures with three different modes dominant in their political thinking.

The Protestant cultures dissociated themselves from the idea of a Christian community which was maintained by the Catholic Church and which leaned upon the State as the ultimate political community. Protestantism and the Protestant doctrine on salvation, according to which salvation is based upon faith alone, pushed forward a secularisation of politics and a separation of ecclesiastical from worldly affairs.

The Calvinist political heritage has been individualist, whereas the Lutheran political theory centres around the might of the State. A constitutive explanation for this difference was found in the Calvinist and Lutheran ethic. When the highest secular duty of a good Lutheran was to be a humble servant of the civil authorities, a good Calvinist had to arrange his own life into a system of good works as an indication of his faith. Calvinism emphasised individualist structures as far as its political doctrine was concerned, too. It functioned as a pre–phase to the liberal theory of State, which was the dominant State tradition in England and in the Netherlands. The Glorious Revolution, in a way, expressed the culmination of the Calvinist tradition.

Lutheranism and Counter–Reformative Catholicism nourished a more collectivist political culture. Lutheranism forbade resistance to a secular rule even if this were an evil rule. The high value given to the State was maintained in the core areas of Lutheranism in the form of a nationalist political theory of a very extreme type. It treated the State as a reality of its own and as the supreme form of Western civilisation. The political doctrine of the Counter–Reformation started from Christianity as a political community which meant an assertion of the powers of the Catholic Church. The communitarian culture of the Counter–Reformation was transmitted to modern State–building in Europe through the Enlightenment. The republican tradition maintained the key concepts of Catholic communitarianism even if they appear in a heavily secularised form.

The practical conclusion that can be drawn from this analysis of political cultures is that being socialised in different cultural environments, with different sets of key political values, people tend to conceive the process of European unification in very different terms. The terms can be analysed through the division of European political culture that has been the subject of this chapter. The next task is to extend the analysis to 'Europe'.

3 The Idea of a United Europe

Introduction

Political diversity is a key characteristic of European culture. Europe has been politically divided as long as the idea of *Europe* as a geographical and cultural entitity has existed. Throughout this history, the cultural unity of Europe has, however, also given rise to political demands purporting to bring the cultural unity under one political governance. We are finding a continuance of these demands in the present project of European unification.

The main purpose of this work is to render comprehensible the serious political difficulties connected with the present effort to build a common governance in Europe. This will be done from the starting point of the arguments put forth in the two previous chapters. The first chapter set out the argument that political concepts and understandings have to be understood through their histories, that is, through the chain of their past meanings. The second chapter developed an argument according to which the Reformation constituted one of the key divides as far as European political culture is concerned. Core differences in European political culture must therefore be understood in the light of the Reformation by following the core forms of political thinking that it introduced.

The two following chapters will bring together two discourses in order to explicate the relationship between the two political developments, that of the Reformation and that of European unification. The division of European political culture brought about by the Reformation has conditioned the project of European unification by imposing cultural and political limits upon it. Both of these projects are, however, products of history, which means that the understandings of political community, including the European one, have been bound to the historical context of a particular time in question. This chapter will analyse the development of the idea of European unity in order to point out the impact of these two conditions, the one of history and the other of culture[1].

Three Positions of Europe

The idea of Europe as a political community is a product of Catholic Christianity and is based upon its manner of defining Christendom in the beginning of the second millennium. The Europeanism of the Catholic political tradition extends itself into our days through Catholic social and political movements. Federalism is a characteristic of Catholic social theory which starts from the idea that the whole of Christianity shall be organised in accordance with the same model as the relations of an individual Christian to his immediate social environment. The other path from Catholic Europeanism to present–day integration goes through the Enlightenment. The Enlightenment implied a secularisation of Catholic concepts without, however, losing the connection with the idea of a federal Europe. The Enlightenment made Europe appear a civilisation, a politically and socially distinct entity the peoples of which should be united through a system of governance based upon the core principle of European politics. The principle was defined as 'liberty through community' and as an expression of this at the European level was found in a federal system. The Catholic political tradition is thus, due to its doctrine of Christian communitarianism, the original tradition of European unification, the tradition in which the idea of Europe as a federation originates.

Protestant doctrines carried a different conception of Europe that originated in the denial of Christianity as a political community. Both the Calvinist and the Lutheran doctrines were based upon the State as

---

[1]

There are many works dealing with the development of the European idea but they do not, in general, problematise the cultural unity of Europe. See, for instance, Voyenne 1953, Barraclough 1963, Duroselle 1965 and 1990, Hay 1968, Heater 1992, Johansson 1993 and Wilson & van der Dussen 1995/

the ultimate political community. The Calvinist tradition, bringing about the individualist conception of the State was, however, more internationally oriented as relations between States were conceptualised on the same model as relations between individuals provided with the same capacity of cooperation. The Calvinist tradition approached Europe through a position of liberal internationalism. Europe did not constitute the core political framework of liberal plans as it did in Catholic plans. It appeared, however, as a suitable first stage in liberal projects aiming at a universal peace, democracy or a market economy. Lutheranism which conjured up a State–centric political tradition, is of all the three traditions doctrinally the most distant from the idea of a united Europe. From its point of view, the idea of European unification appears just as one political instrument to reinforce the power of the State.

Next, it is my intention to give an account of the origins of the Catholic idea of Europe as a political community and to follow its path to the modern form of European federalism. Then the positions taken by the Protestant cultures towards the European idea will be explicated in more detail.

The Birth of Europe

The idea of Europe as a political community is not more than six hundred years old. Its first phases are essentially connected with the role of the Catholic Church, and with the Pope as its leader, in European politics. The project of European political unification can be seen to have had its beginning in the efforts of the Papacy to protect Christendom against external threats during the first centuries of the second millennium. The birth of a political Europe was a confluence of two separate developments constitutive of the present Europe.

The first is the constitution of a geographical unity called Europe. The geographical notion originated in the tripartition of the world introduced by the classic cultures[2]. A world conceived of in this fashion, the three continents being divided by the Mediterranean, the Don and the Nile, and the whole being surrounded by a circumambient Ocean, also became the Judaic–Christian cosmogony even if the first notions of Christendom did not coincide territorially with Europe[3].

The second constituent of the present Europe is the idea of a Christian community, *Christendom*, characterised by a territory and clear borders with respect to the external world. It is frequently argued that the territorial view of Christianity was above all compelled by the vigour and success of Moslem attacks during the last three centuries of the first millennium[4]. The idea of the Christian people forming a political community was established by the twelfth and thirteenth century. It was much due to the position adopted by the Catholic Church and the Papacy that *Christendom* started to be identified with the geographical area of Europe during the following centuries. The fall of Constantinople left the Catholic Church as the defender of the whole of Christianity and made its borders still more exposed.

As the political centre, as well as the borders of Christendom, had been moved towards the West and Christianity had been spread to Scandinavia, Europe and Christendom started to appear as the same thing. When this decisive step towards a European political identity was taken, Christendom was already seen as consisting of different nations[5]. In its original form, the idea of European unification thus implied a unification of the Christian nations, or the *Respublica Christiana*, with respect to an external, and, in particular, a Turkish threat. The idea was

2

First, the Greeks seem to have divided the world into Europe and Asia and only in the times of Herodotus was a tripartite division adopted and Africa brought in (Hay 1968, 2).

3

Hay 1968, 1–36.

4

Ibid., 24; Johansson 1993, 54; Delanty 1995, 26.

5

Hay 1968, 76–81.

put forth by the Church, which can therefore be treated as the first political basis for the idea of European unity. Even during the first millennium, the Church had put forth claims for a political rule of Christendom and for the creation of a real *Respublica Christiana* in accordance with the doctrine of St. Augustine[6]. These claims lacked first, as it was stated above, a territorial identity, as they were based upon a revival of the West Roman Empire and upon the universal status aspired to by Christianity[7]. As the territorial identity of Christendom started to be established, and Christendom became identified with Europe, the Popes still made claims for a Papal supremacy of Christendom. Due to the prevailing political structure of Europe, the terms in which their claims were couched already pointed more in the Thomist than in the Augustinian direction[8].

European political unification thus had its beginning in the idea of a *terra Christiana,* a Christian territorium that was threatened by a common enemy. The policy of unification was led by the Church that made claims for, at least a moral, leadership of the Christian world. The Reformation implied a breakdown of Christendom as a territorial political concept as it questioned the political powers of the Catholic Church in great parts of Europe and established the *cuius regio eius religio* principle. The great religious and civil wars shaking the social and political structures of Europe throughout the sixteenth and seventeenth centuries were another factor working concretely against

---

[6]

Palmer 1984, 18.

[7]

Charlemagne in his empire is known as the most 'European' of the Christian emperors that were allied with the Pope (Heater 1992, 2). The Holy Roman Empire continued as a potential, on occasions actual, force for unity from the mid–tenth to the mid–fourteenth century.

[8]

Duroselle 1990, 135–138. Pope Innocent III (1198–1216) has, for instance, been said to have argued that secular rulers owed the Pope the same allegiance as did the bishops. The Pope thus reminded lay sovereigns of their duties, and called them to order if they infringed the moral code.

the conception of European unity.

Europe as A Christian *Societas*

As a result of the Reformation, the Catholic Church lost its leading political position and the political point of emphasis in Europe was moved northwards. Christendom gained a new meaning in the process of a Counter–Reformation that purported to adapt Catholic doctrine to existing political conditions. This meaning was still of Thomist origin and took its stand on Christendom as a moral order and as a community with the principle of State sovereignty as one of its constitutive norms. Another crucial political principle of the Christian community was the idea that Christian rulers should not make war upon each other. These ideas formed the cornerstones of a Christian *societas* that replaced the territorial and imperial notion of Christendom.

A Christian *societas* started from the idea that even if Christendom was divided into sovereign States it still constituted a single community with particular rules and norms. The Catholic and Calvinist thinkers, most often lawyers, were very close to each other in their pre–Enlightenment conceptions of a Christian society, the Catholics being still more than the Calvinists committed to the material substance of Christianity as a political community[9]. They argued that all Christians were united through their reason in a normative code of God. This code was seen to be of divine origin both as far as its substance and authority were concerned. This constituted the key argument by which Catholics defended the jurisdictional powers of the Catholic Church.

It was not a long way from the Christian *societas* to the Catholic idea of a European federation which evolved hand in hand, and even as a counterforce, to the modern tenets of statehood. In accordance with the Thomist conception, Catholics treated the human being as a social creature and as a member of various communities. Seeing the State just

---

[9]

Wight 1991, 8; for a discussion see Koskenniemi 1989, 73–85.

as one man–made community, they denied its absolute character. Later, the idea of Christianity organised politically on the basis of the same model, from the level of the individual to the highest level, was conceptualised into aspirations to construct a full–scale federal government in Europe.

The Challenge of The Enlightenment

The Enlightenment meant a revival of Europe as a cultural and political unity. At the same time, it brought about a division of the Catholic political tradition through a secularisation of Catholic political concepts[10]. The political and cultural position of France was of key importance in the process whereby Europe was made to appear a civilisation[11]. This implied a position of social and cultural superiority adopted towards other parts of the world. For instance, the leading philosopher of the Enlightenment, Voltaire, considered the Europe of his own time to be the most civilised continent. He assumed, in accordance with Enlightenment concepts, that human nature was basically the same all over the world and that differences between people resulted from the differing extent to which reason had been 'cultivated'. Europe, he argued, would flourish still more splendidly if it were not for incessant, unnecessary wars[12].

The Enlightenment celebrated Europe as the highest level of social and political civilisation achieved in the world and as a pioneer of future progress. The three tenets of the Enlightenment, liberty, equality and reason were treated as the core of European political

---

[10]

See, 46–47.

[11]

Here the impact of the French language and culture is decisive, because it was claimed to represent the supreme form of Europeanism (Duroselle 1965, 118 ff; Duroselle 1990, 234).

[12]

den Boer 1995, 61.

civilisation and as the framework of European unity. The secularisation
of the Christian *societas*, and the birth of the first modern concept of
Europe as a political community, were based upon the Enlightenment
and upon its tradition of political republicanism. Republicanism called
forth an idea of a European federation that did not derive from the
liberal interpretation of State sovereignty, but was based upon the
political primacy of Europe. The tradition of republican federalism also
differentiated itself from the more liberally–oriented federalist plans in
its political goals, which were much broader than the peace whose
realisation constituted the supreme goal of the eighteenth–century
liberal internationalism[13].

Jean–Jacques Rousseau was the key advocate of republicanism.
The idea of citizenship and political participation treated as a
precondition of humanity formed the core of political republicanism.
Rousseau applied the same principle to the States of Europe arguing
that their relationship to each other should be seen analogously to the
relationship between the individual and the State. In both cases, security
and true liberty were seen to be enjoyed only through participation in
the greater whole[14]. Rousseau's republican federalism was based upon
the idea of European republics which would be represented by a
republican organ, a Diet, at the European level. Even if Rousseau's
federalism distanced itself clearly from most of the earlier federalist
plans, it still made one crucial concession in favour of the idea of State
sovereignty. Rousseau did not, in other words, push the analogy of State
and Federation to the ultimate stage. The power of the whole in the
State was called by Rousseau sovereign, and thus in the Federation of
States sovereignty was not abandoned by the partners[15].

The republican tradition formed the basis for modern European
federalism, which was developed into an ambitious political project in

---

13

Hinsley 1963, 33–91.

14

Heater 1992, 80.

15

Forsyth 1981, 94; Heater 1992, 81.

the nineteenth century. Its key theorist then was the Comte de Saint–Simon[16]. He devised a detailed federalist plan for Europe which already included the core ideas of the present–day federalism. As a pioneer of modern sociology, and of the positivist tradition of social science, Saint–Simon endeavoured to create a political structure in Europe based upon a scientific political analysis which, he argued, supported the need for European unification.

Saint–Simon's theory of Europe did not, in detail, apply the positivist approach as its federalism was in the first place based upon historical and cultural justifications. According to Saint–Simon:

> Europe once formed a confederal society, united by common institutions, subjected to a general government which was to the peoples what national governments are to individuals. A similar arrangement is the only one that can correct everything....We affect a supreme distrust of the centuries we call the Middle Ages..and we do not remember that it was the only time when the political system of Europe was founded on a true basis, on a general organisation.... All agree that the present political system...dates only from the sixteenth century [17].

Saint–Simon provided his federalism also with modern justifications. A federal government appeared the only political system that could restore peace and social coherence, guaranteed earlier by the Roman Catholic Church, to Europe. It was argued to be the type of European government that corresponded to the people's political sentiments and identities. According to Saint–Simon, the family sentiments of Europeanism took precedence among all Europeans over their national sentiments[18]. Saint–Simon's republican federalism had its

---

16

Comte de Saint–Simon, whose original name was Claude–Henri de Rouvroy, lived from 1760–1825 (Heater 1992, 97 ff).

17

Hinsley 1963, 102.

18

Heater 1992, 101.

point–of–departure in a parliamentary government that would bring representatives of national parliaments together at the federal level. Launched as an alliance between the two existing parliamentary governments, England and France, the European federation would at the same time imply the spread of the parliamentary government. Another strong element in Saint–Simon's plan was the idea of economic integration, which he proposed to start through a merger of English and French industries.

Catholicism Enters the Twentieth Century

The original Catholic idea of a federal Europe was thus transmitted to twentieth century political thinking by two traditions, one of which was connected with the Enlightenment, while the other expressed a Catholic reaction to it in the general spirit of Romanticism. The Enlightenment tradition of republican federalism became the core of *a Christian socialism* that has its roots in France and can be identified by such names as Charles Fourier, Philippe Buchez and Joseph Proudhon. The Catholic reaction to the Enlightenment launched a social and political movement that is generally known as *Christian Democracy*.

The tradition of Christian socialism can thus be seen to be the first modern political tradition advocating federalism in Europe. The tradition was derived from Saint–Simonian terms, according to which an all–European federation would constitute a solution to most of the prevailing political problems in Europe. Christian socialists treated the nation–States in Europe as an obstacle to the fulfilment of social and political rights and to the achievement of peace in Europe. Proudhon's political theory was the most explicit in this respect as he regarded federalism as the political form of humanity. European societies, according to Proudhon, had to be organised in a federal form from the level closest to the individual, communes, to the European level uniting the European peoples[19]. The federalist and European aspirations of

---

19

Proudhon advocated a federal France that would be composed of twelve independent governing units, each with legislative and executive

Christian socialists weakened under the Marxist tradition, but they were revived again in the interwar period and in the resistance movements of the Second World War.

One of the key Europeanists of the interwar period was the eminent French statesman Aristide Briand, who returned the aspirations of a federal Europe to the core of socialist programmes in Catholic Europe[20]. Briand made one of his key speeches in the League of Nations Assembly in 1929 stating that:

> I think that among the peoples constituting geographical groups, like the peoples of Europe, there should be some kind of federal union. It should be possible for them to get in touch at any time, to confer about their interests, to agree on joint resolutions, and to establish among themselves a bond of solidarity which will enable them, if need be, to meet any grave emergency that may arise [21].

Briand was also given the possibility of making a concrete proposal on European unification to European leaders which, however, did not gain enough acceptance. Briand's proposal and the ideology of republican federalism were eagerly advocated by the socialist parties in France and Italy. Thus during the interwar period the character of a European federation as a defence union, implying an internal disarmament, was emphasised in these programmes[22]. The ideology of republican federalism and its pacifist purposes in particular, reached its culmination in socialist resistance movements during the Second World War.

---

authorities elected by the people (Loughlin 1989, 189).

[20]

Aristide Briand (1862–1932) was a minister in different French governments twenty–five times and formed eleven ministries himself as Prime Minister. He was Foreign Minister twelve times including the whole period from 1925–32 (Heater 1992, 130).

[21]

Heater 1992, 133–134.

[22]

For the programmes of European socialist parties see Featherstone 1988.

The Birth of Christian Democracy

The Catholic reaction against the Enlightenment constitutes a bridge from the original Catholic Europeanism to the present era. The reaction that launched the formation of Catholic social and political movements all over Europe was, in the first place, a reaction against the secularising ideology of the Enlightenment. Another important element of what can be called modern political Catholicism was a resistance to any totalitarian effects and the claims of universality arising in connection with the Enlightenment State[23]. As the division between socialist and non-socialist Christian movements was not clear-cut in the nineteenth century, republican federalism and its Catholic counterpart grew intermixed in many countries.

The original form of the Christian Democrat movement was not, however, primarily that of an advocate of a federal Europe. As this role was rather taken by the movements of the Enlightenment, the goal-setting of Catholicism remained more national. Its original programme in various European countries was linked with the position of the Catholic Church and clergy[24]. The change that occurred in the doctrinal emphasis of Catholicism was conditioned by an acceptance of the main tenets of the great French revolution. The fulfilment of this condition towards the late nineteenth century was bound up with the organising of the Christian Democrat movements into modern political parties.

The federalist aspirations of modern Catholicism arise essentially in the present century. The activities of the wartime Resistance led the Catholic movements in different European countries to organise into an important political force working in favour of federalism[25]. Christian

---

23

For a comprehensive study of the Christian Democrat movement, see Fogarty 1957 (its Romanticist origins p.149 ff).

24

Fogarty 1957, 149 ff.

25

This took place through the establishment of Christian Democratic organisations at the European level. The most important of them were

Democrats, like the Christian socialists, treated the system of European States as a major cause for political destruction and war. They advocated a European federation as a solution to political problems on the basis of a view of the human being that related to the different dimensions of his personality: social as well as individual, supernatural as well as purely human. The system of political rule corresponding to this conception was a federal system organising social groupings from the level of individual and family through the State to the level of the Christian community.

One of the core statements of Resistance Catholicism was made by Pope Pius XII, who appealed for an international order based on the unshakeable, unchanging rock of the moral law: nations should live in peace and be free from coercion, with respect for one another's freedom, integrity and independence[26]. The suggestion of the Pope was interpreted in the following way in an Italian Christian Democratic programme:

For a Democratic and Christian Italy

A federation of European states governed on free principles should be set up with the framework of a renewed League of Nations expressing the solidarity of all the peoples. In both the League and the federation there should be direct representation of the people as well as of governments. General and simultaneous disarmament; armed forces (with voluntary recruitment) at the sole disposal of the international community. Right to opt for European as well as national citizenship. Citizens of all the states

---

The Christian Democratic Political International, The Union of Christian Democrats and *Nouvelles Equipes Internationales* which were all established in 1947 (Fogarty 1957, 340).
Christian Democratic parties, at the same time, gained an important position in the national context. In 1955, they held nearly two–fifths of the seats in the lower houses in the Netherlands, Belgium, Luxemburg, Switzerland, Austria, West Germany, Italy and France (Ibid., 173).

[26]

Lipgens 1985, 467.

to be legally equal. Similar principles to apply to national and international economy[27].

A Calvinist View of Europe

Protestant theories posed themselves against the Catholic idea of Christendom as a political community. Both Luther and Calvin argued that monarchical powers had been ordained by God and that the Church should be seen as a *congregatio fidelium* only. The medieval idea of Europe in which Europe was essentially based upon the unity of Christendom had been dissolved in the religious wars of the sixteenth and seventeenth centuries. One cornerstone of the Protestant view of Europe was constituted by the external meaning of State sovereignty that was developed by Protestant lawyers in the seventeenth century[28]. This can be called the liberal theory of State sovereignty as it implies that the liberal understanding of the individual is applied to the State. According to this theory, States are free and equal by nature and any norms regulating their actions have to be subordinated to these principles.This meant that an extreme individualist interpretation of the liberty of the State was set up against the more communitarian form applied in Catholic political and legal theory.

The Calvinist view of Europe reflected its general political values in the same way as the idea of a European federation was shown to reflect Catholic political values. Calvinist political theory nourished a view of international relations presenting international relations as a reconciliation of the principle of State sovereignty and world peace[29].

27

The Milan Programme of Christian Democracy 25 July 1943 in Lipgens 1985, 505–506.

28

Hinsley 1986, 179 ff; Wight 1991, 3; Nussbaum 1947, 86 ff.

29

The reconciliation of sovereignty and peace is analogous to the core of the liberal theory at the individual level, that is, the reconciliation of individual liberty and the social order (Holden 1988).

The core idea behind the Calvinist position on international relations was that relations between States did not differ from relations between individuals. This meant in the first place that State actions were seen to be subordinated to normative regulation in the same way as individuals' actions. The idea of an international society based upon positive international law regulating relations between sovereigns was created by Calvinist thinkers in the seventeenth century. Hugo Grotius was one of the leading figures contributing to the emergence of this concept through his argument that there is a system of law binding the European rulers which consists partly of positive, man–made, norms and which would be valid even if God did not exist[30]. Grotius was thus the first to insist on the need for a body of positive international law deriving from the will and practice of States. His *De Jure Belli ac Pacis* was the first systematic treatise on this law.

From Grotius began the Calvinist tradition of international peace plans in which 'Europe' appeared as the first stage[31]. The core idea was the establishment of an international organ, or committee, as a guarantor of peace to which States would assign a part of their sovereignties. The Duc de Sully's Grand Design was exceptionally European in its outlook since one of its purposes was to address the religious causes of conflict in Europe. Representatives of all the Christian European States were to form a Senate whose function was to discuss the different interests, pacify the quarrels, clear up and determine all the civil, political and religious affairs of Europe whether within itself or with its neighbours[32]. The establishment of peace was considered to be the main political problem in Europe and the existence of an international machinery of arbitration was already envisaged as being instrumental in achieving it.

---

[30]

Hinsley 1986, 188–189; Tuck 1989, 67–69.

[31]

In fact, the first liberal peace plan was put forth by Emeric Crucé two years before (1623) Grotius' *De Jure Belli* (1625), see Hinsley 1963, 20.

[32]

Heater 1992, 32.

Liberal Internationalism

The first phase of Calvinist international theory was based upon the idea that peace could be achieved by subordinating States to normative regulation in the same way as individuals in the State. The second phase was based upon the Enlightenment and upon its tenets of reason and progress. The Enlightenment and the process of industrialisation launched in the nineteenth century turned the Calvinist theory into a liberal internationalist position which has since constituted one of the main sources of opposition to the federalist theory of Europe.

Jeremy Bentham formulated the core of the liberal internationalist position through his confidence in an enlightened public opinion as a guarantor of world peace[33]. Bentham argued that there was no real conflict between national interests. According to him, the solution to unresolved problems between the States lay already at hand in the appeal to reason, to law and public opinion against the machinations of government[34]. Bentham put forth the same argument as James Mill after him, that is, no international organisations limiting State liberties were necessary, as intensive intercourse between the nations together with the existence of a critical audience would have the same effect. Both Bentham and Mill considered an international court, together with a code of international law, as a sufficient means for international governance.

The internationalist position based upon conceptions of minimal international governance and intensive intercourse between nations, was rounded off by a free–trade argument in the nineteenth century. The success of an evolving American customs union reflected itself in the ideology of the numerous Peace Societies in England and America. They started to put forth the idea that free trade and political non–intervention – respect by every sovereign State for the complete

---

33

Jeremy Bentham (lived between 1748–1832) wrote his *Plan for an Universal and Perpetual Peace* between 1786–1789.

34

Hinsley 1963, 83.

independence of every other State – were adequate means for preserving peace[35]. When this new confidence in the pacifist qualities of free trade was fused with the position of Bentham and Mill, the liberal internationalist position revealed itself in its entirety. According to it, free trade and non–intervention together would result in as little connection as possible between governments and as much connection as possible between the nations of the world[36]. The system of international law and a concomitant machinery of arbitration appeared as the only necessary form of governance at the international level.

The liberal internationalist position has constituted the dominant British approach to the question of European integration since the nineteenth century. It reached its political culmination in the establishment of the League of Nations. The latter was an organisation based essentially upon the principles of national sovereignty and non–intervention. Its functional core was a machinery of arbitration, a means of avoiding war at the point of actual crisis, not an international instrument for the continual use of governments in operating and improving the international system[37]. There was also a League Assembly in which the sinister actions of nations would be subjected to 'the overwhelming light of the universal expression of the condemnation of the world'[38].

The British policy towards the first phases of the twentieth century integration project, expressed a firm commitment to the

---

35

Ibid., 97.

36

Hinsley (1963, 97) quotes Richard Cobden who was one of the most influential 'free traders' in the British Peace Societies. His main work is *Free Trade as The Best Means for Securing Universal and Permanent Peace* (1842).

37

Hinsley 1963, 147.

38

Hinsley quotes Woodrow Wilson who was the leading politician behind the League project (Hinsley 1963, 148).

tradition of liberal internationalism[39]. The commitment expressed itself
in the vast difficulties of, above all, the Labour party to come to terms
with European integration. Labour was reluctant from the beginning to
become involved in a solely European enterprise as its hopes for
international understanding were centred on more universal forms of
cooperation[40]. Post–war Labour governments opposed all forms of
supranational governance, a fact which led, among other things, to the
original proposal behind the Council of Europe being watered down.
British governments, whether Labour or Conservative, adopted a
positive attitude towards free trade in Europe as long as it was not
connected with any forms of supranationality as was to be the case with
the EEC. As early as June 1950, the British Labour government rejected
participation in the ECSC in the following terms:

> Some people believe that the required unity of action cannot be obtained
> by co–operation between sovereign states; it must be imposed by a
> supra–national body with executive powers. They consider that the
> European countries should form a Union in both the political and
> economic spheres by surrendering the whole fields of government to a
> supra–national authority.

> The Labour Party considers that it is neither possible nor desirable under
> existing circumstances to form a complete Union, political or economic,
> in this way. Instead national policies must be progressively harmonised
> or co–ordinated by consent through co–operation between governments.
> Whether or not this process will ultimately lead to a complete Union
> cannot be foreseen. But it will be enough to solve the urgent problems of
> the immediate future.

---

[39]

The policy was formulated by a Labour government which had not been
influenced by the rhetoric of wartime federalism to the same extent as the
Conservatives (expressed, for instance, in the famous speeches of
Winston Churchill). According to Haas (1958, 159 ff), the Labour
position was accepted by the Conservatives by the end of 1940's.

[40]

Featherstone 1988, 41 ff.

The European peoples do not want a supra–national authority to impose agreements. They need an international machinery to carry out agreements which are reached without compulsion[41].

A Lutheran View of Europe

The Lutheran political theory was most firmly of all the three political theories based upon the self–sufficiency of the single State. In the pre–Enlightenment form of the Lutheran tradition, this self–sufficiency expressed itself as a supremacy of the ruler with respect to any law. As the tradition was secularised through German nationalism, the self–sufficiency took the form of the historical and cultural finality of the State. The Lutheran political heritage nourishes therefore a different, State–centric, attitude towards projects of European political unification. It also lacks an internationalist orientation corresponding to the one that has engendered the European spirit of the Calvinist cultures.

Lutheran conceptions asserting the divine origin of secular powers and the role of law as a dictum of God led to an international theory that was very Machiavellian in its terms. The Lutheran international theory was a *political* theory put up against the theological emphasis of Catholicism and the juridical approach of Calvinism. Its focal pre–Enlightenment concepts were *raison d'état* and the balance of power. The first is a Machiavellian idea that there is no ethic for the rulers or if there is, it has to serve the State. The second concept rests upon the belief that order in relations between the States is a physical state of affairs instead of a moral or legal community as recognised by both Catholicism and Calvinism.

The Lutheran international position reflected itself as a 'naturalist' position in the pre–Enlightenment internationalist discourse based upon the concepts of a Christian *societas* or the Grotian idea of positive international law between the States. The naturalist position

---

[41]

European Unity. A Statement by the National Executive Committee of the British Labour Party, 6.

implied a denial of a system of law between the States. States could not, according to the Lutheran conception, be subordinated to positive international law, as they were divine creatures and direct expressions of the divine law. This originally Hobbesian view on international relations was represented, for example, by Benedict Spinoza who denied that treaties have any binding force. He conceived them as natural reflexes of given power relations between the convenanting States[42]. Samuel Pufendorf represented a moderate Lutheran position through his argument that there was no law among nations except natural law.

The pre–Enlightenment idea of Europe as a moral community was distant from a Lutheranism that approached Europe in terms of balance of power between European rulers. Balance–of–power theories were created between the sixteenth and eighteenth centuries and they were eagerly applied by such Lutheran rulers as Frederick the Great of Prussia and Catherine II of Russia[43]. They made deliberations about how a balance of power, representing an equilibrium of pure power resources, could be achieved between European States. In these theories, which preceded European industrialisation, the territorial dimension was still the most important element of power[44]. This balance of power tradition implied according to Hinsley that 'its representatives completely abandoned the traditional belief in Christendom or Europe as a structure above or at least additional to its components States. By dealing with the interests of each State in isolation they tore Europe into its separate parts'[45].

----

[42]

Nussbaum 1954, 114.

[43]

Hinsley 1963, 177–179; Wight 1991, 19.

[44]

Fredrick the Great stated in 1743 (Hinsley 1963, 177) that 'of all the states from the smallest to the biggest one can safely say that the fundamental rule....is the principle of extending their territories'.

[45]

Hinsley 1963, 161.

The Nationalist Position

The Lutheran State–centric political tradition was secularised through German nationalism in the nineteenth century. Nationalist doctrines had their starting–point in the State as an expression of the absolute spirit, being thus a reality of its own prior to any norms or law. In nationalism, the State appeared as the ultimate moral community with the consequence that international relations were defined as its complete reverse. International relations were therefore defined as a state of anarchy lacking any binding norms or morality. The tradition of German nationalism denied the liberal idea of State sovereignty conceived of as rights in an international legal system. It perceived State sovereignty as a sociological fact and as the source of any rights whatsoever[46].

From these assumptions grew the post–Enlightenment form of the Lutheran political tradition that can be called *Machtpolitik*. This constituted the key connection between the Lutheran tradition and the present integration project in setting forth the idea of integration as a reinforcement of the nation–State and treating any element of supranationality as harmful in itself. As international relations appeared to be a state of anarchy and as the State was treated as a legitimacy of its own, the pursuit of power became the core of the international system. *Raison d'état* was turned into national interest, based ultimately upon the conditions of existence of the whole nation, and into *der Primat der Aussenpolitik*. The development of the modern tradition of *Machtpolitik* was essentially linked with the greatness of Prussia in late nineteenth–century Europe, leading first to the ending of French supremacy and then to the unification of Germany.

The Hegelian conception that as sovereignty was the true essence of the State, it was especially in the right to make war that this sovereignty expressed itself, constituted the core of Bismarckian

---

[46]

According to Hegel, State sovereignty was identical with the unity of its population. For the meaning of the sociological–fact idea in international legal science, see Koskenniemi 1989, 196 ff.

policy[47]. The famous statement of the Prussian Iron Chancellor was that 'the great questions of our time will not be settled by resolutions and majority votes – that was the mistake of the men of 1848 and 1849 – but by blood and iron'[48]. Bismarck also wrote that 'I base my conduct with other governments solely on the good or the harm that I judge them able to do to Prussia'[49]. His opinion upon the *pacta sunt servanda*–principle was revealed by the statement that 'Austria and Prussia are states too big to be bound by the text of a treaty. They can be guided only by their own interest and convenience. If a treaty stands in the way, then it must be broken'[50]. Treitschke, Lasson, Kaufmann and Jellinek were among the German scholars who shared the ruthless position of Bismarck. The period following German unification is known as the one of armed peace between European powers preparing themselves to go to war against each other[51].

From the point of view of *Machtpolitik*, Europe appeared to be just a geographical notion. The political construction of Europe was seen as representing a system of political absolutenesses where the possibility of war was as real as in any other place in the world. The German tradition of *Machtpolitik* was carried on in the twentieth century in the policy of the German National Socialists. They followed the extreme interpretation of German nationalism put forth, for instance, by Treitschke, according to which it was the historical purpose of Germany to dominate Europe. The *New Order* that the National Socialists purported to create by subordinating other European

---

[47]

Hinsley 1986, 209; Olson & Groom 1991, 45.

[48]

Wight 1991, 26.

[49]

Duroselle 1990, 333.

[50]

Ibid., 333.

[51]

den Boer 1995, 76.

States to Germany could be divided into an internal and external element, which corresponded also to the phases in which the Nazi ideology was developed[52].

In the Nazi ideology, the German right to dominate Europe was in the last resort based upon the racial supremacy of the German nation. The racial value of the *Volk* was dependent not only upon its purity but also upon the possession of an adequate *Lebensraum* and the enjoyment of a rising standard of living. If the purity of blood alone was an insufficient guarantee against economic and political depredations, it was also true that political and economic strategies could improve the inner qualities of the *Volk*[53]. The subordination of Eastern and South–Eastern Europe was legitimised by the alleged greatness of Germany. Expansion of the sovereign economy of Germany appeared incompatible with the economic sovereignty of neighbouring States. Hitler advocated the symbiosis of industrial Germany with the agrarian States and suppliers of raw materials[54].

The external element of the Nazi ideology justifying the domination of Europe was based upon the threat caused by Bolshevism. Hitler declared the German attack on the Soviet Union as a defensive war of all European peoples against Bolshevism[55]. Europe was thus defined as the sum of those peoples whom Destiny had united under German leadership to ward off the 'Asiatic–Jewish–Bolshevik' threat, on the one hand, and Anglo–American encroachments, on the other.

German nationalism is not ideologically part of the present integration project but it has functioned as one of its major external political incentives. The extreme nationalist position represented by the Nazi ideology launched an all–European federalist reaction during the

---

52

    Lipgens 1985, 37–54; Stirk 1989, 125–148.

53

    Stirk 1989, 128.

54

    Ibid., 143.

55

    Lipgens 1985, 48.

Second World War. The aspiration to bind down Germany and to prohibit another nationalist upsurge has constituted an important force behind the present integration project. There is, however, another, less extreme, doctrine growing out of the same ideological origin, which has had a direct impact upon the forms of the present project.

The other form in which the tradition of German *Machtpolitik* has been transmitted to our days is the *Realist* doctrine on international relations. Realism made its grand entry into European politics after the Second World War, when it established itself as one of the major international doctrines in many Western European countries. Realism shares the key concepts of *Machtpolitik* and purports to put forth a pure *political* understanding of international relations that would be free from economic, juridical or moral considerations. Realism distances itself from the manifestly normative doctrine of *Machtpolitik* by means of its empirical and scientific emphasis. Realism departs from State sovereignty as a fact that leads to the impossibility of perpetual peace and security at the international level. Realists consider the project of European integration as a form of international cooperation only and one that will not, and should not, change the constitutive political structure. Realists pit themselves against any supranational powers or, at least, want to keep these distant from the hard core of politics and limited to 'secondary' questions like economic or environmental cooperation.

The French President Charles de Gaulle was one of the most eminent single figures to bring the Realist tradition into the project of European integration. De Gaulle succeeded in obstructing the sort of integration about which agreement had already been reached in the Treaty of Rome establishing the EEC. De Gaulle's realism expressed itself, for instance, in the following statement:

> In the course of a press conference on 5 September [1960], after saying that to build Europe, which means that to unite Europe, is an essential aim of our policy, I declared that to this end it was necessary to proceed, not on the basis of dreams, but in accordance with realities. Now, what are the realities of Europe ? What are the pillars on which it can be built ?

The truth is that those pillars are the states of Europe....states each of which, indeed, has its own genius, history and language; but states are the only entities with the right to give orders and the power to be obeyed....[56].

Conclusions

The purpose of this chapter was to bring together the political traditions that were claimed to be constitutive of Europe. These are the Catholic political tradition that is essentially based upon European political unity and the Protestant traditions which are more inclined to emphasise other political values and which give only a secondary role to the idea of Europeanism. The chapter showed how the idea of European political unity originated in the fourteenth and fifteenth-century Catholic thinking. It was based upon the idea of an all-European federal structure, the highest level of which would take the form of a federation between the European States. The Catholic federal tradition was divided by the Enlightenment with the consequence that it has come into the twentieth-century integration project in the form of two traditions: a Catholic one and an Enlightenment one.

The chapter tried to show that as European unification has appeared as a pure political project for Catholic cultures it has had a different significance for Protestant cultures centring around State sovereignty. Of the two major Protestant cultures the Calvinist individualist doctrine nourishes a more internationalist political heritage. Its connection with the idea of a common Europe was originally formed through a tradition of peace-plans which tried to reconcile State sovereignty and international peace and order. Calvinism entered the present time in the form of a liberal internationalism. It remains loyal to its original values by assuming that peace and order between sovereignties can best be achieved by means of open and intensive intercourse between societies, which

---

56

De Gaulle 1994, 41. De Gaulle was committed to the Realist tradition through the extreme form of French nationalism which he represented.

implies minimal international governance. Free trade has constituted an essential element of liberal internationalism since the nineteenth century.

The Lutheran political tradition has the least in common with the federal orientations of Catholic Europe. When based upon the self-sufficiency of the State, the Lutheran tradition can come to terms with European unification only when this can be argued to as reinforcing the powers of the single European States. If seen through the present century's realist lens, the project of European integration appears to strengthen State sovereignty when it creates a balance of power between European States and releases their powers to be used in common in the face of an external threat or enemy.

This chapter purported simply to delineate the key forms and traditions by which the idea of a united Europe expresses itself in European political culture. The subsequent task of this study is to verify the impact that these traditions have had upon the present integration project and to point out some key conflicts called forth by the differences between the traditions.

4 The European Union: Problems in the Twentieth Century Effort of European Government–Building

Introduction

The democratic deficit is usually approached as an institutional problem of the European Union. Thus, its origin is found in the constitutive treaties conceding a majority of powers to the non–representative organs of the Union and leaving only secondary functions to the people's representation. Institutional reforms in favour of the European Parliament have proved colossally difficult to achieve because of the clearly federalist quality they have necessarily had. In this deadlocked situation, new ways of getting over the shortfall of democracy are being sought. The principles of subsidiarity and regionality confirmed by the Maastricht Treaty were once celebrated as the saving features of European democracy.

In this chapter, I will try to go behind the institutional problems by studying the democratic deficit as a problem of the legitimising of political power in Europe. Democracy here represents the least disputed rule of all the general governmental principles in the European Union. Yet it is precisely democracy that has run up a lot of organisational difficulties.

Although democracy stands as the point of departure for this analysis, it will not constitute its sole object. The European Union will be seen as an effort to build a new European government, the true character of which is of special importance here. First I will focus on the controversial nature of the European Union itself. I shall argue that the lack of agreement as to what constitutes the essential character of the Union means that democracy is being decisively contested by alternative principles of political power. The principles that interest me in this particular connection are those of national sovereignty and bureaucratic governance. In the first part of this chapter, I shall cast light on these rival conceptions and on the way they justify the threat to democracy in the European Union. Democracy is, in this part, defined in very general terms with reference to the kind of practices of power normally acknowledged as democratic.

In the second part of the chapter, I will take the present obstacles to a democratic European Union for granted and will try to work out proposals for change in this situation. This type of analysis purports to take into account the elements of historical particularity vested in the Union and to discuss its governmental structures from these premises. The idea of democracy will, for instance, be analysed in order to find out to what extent the efforts to apply it in the Union context are bound to the meaning democracy has as a principle of power in a sovereign State. The decisive issue to be aired is the governmental nature of the European Union from a broad historical perspective and its relation to the sovereign nation–State in particular. If we have reason to argue that the conditions for democracy in the European Union are not comparable to those of a sovereign State, then we should perhaps reassess the instruments of democracy in the European context. I believe that this is, indeed, the case and that I will find support and specification for this argument from the first part of my work dealing with the contested essence of the Union.

If the traditional means to democracy prove to be insufficient, the big question of the day is whether we already have alternative means available in the European Union which could meet, or could be developed to meet, the demands for its specific model of democratic government. Here, the principles of subsidiarity and regionality and the phenomenon of Union citizenship will be addressed. The final critical question is whether there are still further means of democracy in the Union repertoire, which have not yet proved their illegitimacy in the course of its history.

Democracy and the European Community

The principle of democracy has played a significant role in the plans for European unification in the twentieth century. Its meaning has, however, varied according to the specific political traditions it has been derived from. Among the resistance groups of the Second World War, the idea of a common Europe matured as a means of democracy in particular. This idea of a unification of the European people through a democratic government had its origins in nineteenth–century, mainly French and Italian, republican and socialist doctrines[1]. In our century, these reactive aspirations were pushed forward in EC politics above all by Altiero Spinelli and by various groups close to him[2].

More extensive support has, however, been won by the idea of a Europe in which democracy appears as one of the key values to be protected. This idea connects the conception of a united Europe to the broad liberal tradition which puts the emphasis in unification upon individuals' rights and liberties. As an idea of Europe, this tradition has its roots in the Calvinist tradition and in its modern international doctrine known as liberal internationalism[3].

The aims of integration have, indeed, varied considerably with respect to their economic and political emphases since the nineteenth century and the birth of modern political thinking. Since then there has, however, never been any doubt about democracy being the constitutive element of a common European government[4]. The division of opinions that has had most practical importance in Union history concerns

---

[1]

Duroselle 1958, 214.

[2]

Lipgens (ed.) 1985, 27; Pryce (ed.) 1989 and Lodge (ed.) 1986.

[3]

See 67–68 of this book.

[4]

The commitment to democracy is included in the preamble to the Maastricht Treaty: 'the contracting parties ... *confirming their attachment to the principles of liberty, democracy and respect for human rights and fundamental freedoms and of the rule of law ...* ' (emphasis added). In the new Treaty of Amsterdam the commitment is placed among the common provisions of the Treaty itself: '*The Union is founded on the principles of liberty, democracy, respect for human rights and fundamental freedoms, and the rule of law, principles which are common to the Member States*' (Art F, emphasis added).

instead the principle of State sovereignty, its legitimacy and 'natural' context in Europe.

The legitimacy of State sovereignty forms a watershed as far as the question of European government is concerned. This watershed is an expression of the general division of Western political culture which took place in the Reformation. The first dividing question is whether political power in Europe should have a centralised structure. This is thus a question of the sovereignty principle itself. The legitimacy of the principle is greatest in those parts of Europe which have a firm collectivist political heritage as in the pure Catholic cultures and in the Lutheran States in the North. The centralism is, however, more flexible and less nationalist in the first case. The Catholic cultures have traditionally tended to include in their idea of sovereignty the whole of Christian Europe, while the more nationalistically oriented Lutheran cultures have treated sovereignty as a quality of their nation–States only[5].

The other dividing question concerning the focal political conceptions in Europe does not deal with the structure of power but with its essence. This time, Europe is divided along more different lines than in the first case. Cultures with strong individualist elements tend to find the essence of political power in rules of a constitutional type. These rules are seen as constituting and limiting political power and as having as their major task a proclamation of individual rights and liberties that are treated as constitutive of the whole system. Here, it is the Catholic and Calvinist cultures that share the demand for constitutionality in the question of European government even if the structures they propose

---

5

The structure of nationalism can be regarded as an example of this decisive cultural difference. The nationalist movements of Catholic Europe treated national unification as just one necessary phase in a broader European unification, while, for example, German nationalism was based upon the idea of the nation as the highest political form. Mazzini and Hegel can be mentioned as the leading figures of these opposing traditions.

for it are quite the opposite[6]. In Lutheran Europe the essence of political power has, due to its self–legitimated character, been more connected with physical power than with rules. This does not mean that politics there entirely lacks the constitutionalist dimension, but that issues of security and defence tend to be treated as the core of political power.

The previous discussion purported to indicate that even if the main political traditions of Europe have much in common they still differ from each other in many essential questions. This has made itself apparent in the construction of the European Community. Even if democracy has been highly valued by everybody as a governmental principle, its closer application at the European level has encountered much disagreement. In the following passage, I will try to make clear how the alternative principles of political power have, in fact, benefited from this situation. Bureaucratic rule is the less deep–rooted of the two principles working against governmental democracy in the European Community. With its roots deep in EC history, bureaucracy has, however, become a typical characteristic of the organisation. The qualities of bureaucratic governmental structures which are most in conflict with democracy are its closed processes and organisation that favours narrow expertise at the expense of general citizen participation. The immediate origin of the bureaucratic nature of EC government can be found in the constitutive treaties.

If the first obstacle to democracy has its origin in the closer form of the unification plan, the second originates in the general legitimacy of this plan. The other idea that is analysed as an obstacle to democracy in Europe reflects deeper cultural differences than the idea of bureau–cracy. The age–long conflict between a Europe of sovereign States and

---

[6]

The emphasis between individualist and collectivist heritage varies in Catholic cultures. Catholicism has been able to reconcile these elements since the Counter–Reformation (Skinner 1978, vols 1 and 2). Consti–tutionality has been a key element in the integration policy of the Chris–tian Democrat parties in Europe (Cardozo and Corbett 1989, 40). The Court of Justice of the European Communities (ECJ) has made a con–siderable contribution to the development of certain parts of Commu–nity Law in a constitutional direction (Weiler 1993, 417–446; Burley and Mattli, 1993, 41–76).

a united Europe has also, in this particular case, prevented the realization of the original integration plan. National sovereignty has pulled the use of power into a State–centricist direction and hindered the development of a clear and rational system of democracy at the European level.

My intention is to open the discussion on the characteristics of Union government by analysing the conceptual origins of the constitutive treaties. The modern origins of European unification are of special importance with respect to the present forms of Union government and its heavy bureaucratic elements. These origins will be perceived in terms of two focal forces of change which were activated during the first decades of this century. The element that constitutes the conservative force will be studied subsequently. That element is the vitality of the European nation–State and its impact on the forms of European government.

Federalists, Liberals and the Unification of Europe

The present form of European integration can be seen to be a result of two different pressures for change, which strengthened during the first decades of this century. The two World Wars functioned as stimuli for these plans, the common basis of which was the achievement of a more or less permanent peace in Europe. It has to be admitted that to approach the miscellaneous field of political thinking in terms of two traditions implies a heavy simplification and appears feasible only if the grounds are clear enough. In this case, the basis for this rough categorisation is constituted by one focal quality vested in the European government that is now being constructed. The European government can be seen to be adopting either a centralising or a decentralising role with respect to the existing national governments. In the first case, it is a question of some type of federalist elements that are dominant, while in the second case, the aspirations could be described as liberal and internationalist. Any other governmental qualities are not meant to be comprehended in this division.

The first of these forces of change has been working in a federalist direction and could thus be connected with those historical traditions of unification which have been present in European politics throughout the centuries in varying shapes and intensity. A federal Europe has appeared to be the natural conception of Europe in Catholic cultures which have had grave difficulties with nationalist ideas of the northern, extreme type. The federalist forces that had been decisively nourished by the two World Wars had been looking for their moment to turn Western Europe into a federal State under a common federal government[7]. There have been at least three important federalist efforts to change European political structures since the late 1920s. They have all proceeded quite close to the objective, but have at last failed in the final straight[8]. So, the Treaty of Paris and the Treaties of Rome were nurtured in an intensely federalist spirit engendered by the Hague Congress of 1948 and by the project to establish European political union in the early 1950s. The essence of federalism then was the formation of a European federal government that would be comprised of elements like constitutional and legal supremacy vis–à–vis European States and a European representative body of some kind[9].

---

[7]

Heater 1992, 116–155. The federalist projects were numerous during the interwar period and in the 1940s and 1950s. The main area of this activity was in southern Europe, in France and Italy, but in Great Britain, too there was a measure of support for federalism in these times.

[8]

The first effort was closely associated with the French Foreign Minister Aristide Briand, who offered the representatives of other European governments a concrete proposal for the creation of a federal union in the year 1929 (Heater 1992, 130). The two other efforts were connected with the Hague Congress of the year 1948 and with the project to establish a European Political Community in the years 1952–1954 (Gerbet 1989, 35–48; and Cardozo 1989, 49–77).

[9]

The institutional emphasis tends, of course, to vary in the different federalist plans according to their origin. While the Spinellian left–wing federalists have demanded the supremacy of a European popular assembly, the Christian Democrats, for instance, have underlined the

The other force driving the European State system towards a structural change derived from typically liberal ideas. The Second World War had to some extent violated the credibility of the liberal internationalist doctrine by proving its peace plan non–durable. Its aims and concepts appeared now more pragmatical and more European if compared with the universalist spirit it manifested in the interwar period[10]. Liberal internationalism was the dominant doctrine of British foreign policy and it gained much acceptance also in Scandinavian countries. The liberals also felt that new European structures were a necessity in postwar conditions. But instead of being supranational, these structures were meant to be intergovernmental and their purpose was seen to be the regulation of freedoms between European societies rather than the constituting of a new level of centralist policy[11].
The goals of the liberal and federalist plans were different and remained so, but in the heavy longing for change that followed the antagonisms of the 1930s and 1940s the two plans became effectively intermingled in the Communities of Europe.

The Treaty of Paris and the Treaties of Rome can thus be seen to represent a combination of these historical thought–structures. Certain individuals in key positions, above all Jean Monnet and Paul–Henri Spaak, were the immediate sources of the final unification plan. The European Communities reflected their ideas as far as both the structure of the organisation and issues of substance were concerned[12].

---

[10] necessity of a European constitution which would include the protection of civil rights and liberties (Lipgens 1985).

[11] Hinsley 1963, 114 ff.

[12] Heater 1992, 150–152; Gerbet 1989, 39–45.

The fact that integration started with coal and steel is thus no coincidence. Jean Monnet had worked as a key actor in the French Commissariat Général du Plan de Modernisation et d'Équipement that had given special attention to the coal and steel industries (Diebold 1959, 17). The bringing in of atomic energy (Euratom) was also based upon Monnet's personal conceptions and connections (Küsters 1989, 78–104).

The general compromise worked out by these figures, and supported by other key political figures around them, was based upon the incorporation of federalist *goals* and liberal *means* of European unification. The European Communities that were born, including their government, also bear, of course, the trace of other more contextual political factors. These are the factors reflecting the demands and interpretations associated with the particular situations behind the birth of the treaties.

I suppose, however, that this compromise between the two historical political conceptions carries with it something essential to the problems connected with the creation of a democratic government in Europe. The federalist conception of a democratic Europe has been essentially connected with the democratic qualities of federal government. The federalist long–term democratisation project has concerned the legislative role of the European Parliament and its election by direct elections. Another project with the same purpose has been that enshrined in the concept of Union citizenship and the establishment of political rights on this basis. The liberal internationalist conception of a democratic Europe has in many ways implied a negation of the federal model. Its essence has been in the linkage of States through a variety of channels which would in most cases be of a non–governmental nature[13]. Seen from this point of view, the plurality of political processes and open political debate have thus appeared the best guarantees for democracy in Europe[14].

The problem resulting from this compromise seems to be that the present European Union has a governmental structure that is clearly federalist in its outline, but whose internal structure and division of power reflects liberal pragmatist aspirations. This combination has been apt to nourish the bureaucratic qualities of the present Union government, thus making any large–scale improvements in a democratic direction impossible. The main governmental organisation was born out

---

[13]

Holsti 1985, 27.

[14]

The whole functionalist school of integration is based upon the focal liberal premises. See, e.g., Mitrany 1975.

of the pressure of a conflict between federalist and liberal ideas. The High Authority, like its counterpart in the EEC, the Commission, represented Monnet's conception of an international institution that would contribute to the conciliation of international interests[15]. This type of organ was planned for the needs of the Franco–German coal and steel pool and it seems that its suitability for further integration was not given any significant consideration by the Founding Fathers[16].

A legislating European Parliament that would also possess some financial powers was not a part of the same plan, either. The idea of a federal type of directly elected parliament was incorporated in the unification plan only at the end of the 1950s. The Common Assembly of the EEC bears clear evidence of the ultra–federalist Union project that had failed just a few years earlier. The European Coal and Steel Community (ECSC) had already established an assembly consisting of parliamentarians from the Member States and including a weak idea of parliamentary control over the High Authority. A directly elected 'European Parliament'[17] with traditional parliamentary powers was an obviously loose part in the further organisational context and with respect to the narrow economic profile of unification.

The present Union government could be subjected to a variety of criticisms emanating from this decisive distance between the two constitutive plans. My general theme here is the problem of democracy, because it stands as one of the most fateful issues with respect to the final result of the twentieth–century effort of European unification. It is time to return to the fact that most Union powers are exercised by

---

[15]

For the 'identity crisis' of Monnet and his reasoning concerning the compromise, see Monnet 1976, 341; and Burgess 1989, 43–60. In general, Monnet was of the opinion that human nature was weak and that cooperation was achievable only by means of common rules and institutions (Burgess 1989, 46).

[16]

Diebold 1959, 47–76.

[17]

The Assembly of the Coal and Steel Community, which functioned also as the assembly of the EEC, adopted this new significant name in the year 1962 (Nugent 1989, 110).

agencies which represent narrow expertise and which are not elected by
the people. The origin of these bodies and the acceptance they have
gained during the history of the European Union can be explained
through the liberalist plan of which they constitute an immediate part.
The first element of the Union to be studied in this respect is the
emphasis put on its juridical character and the implications this
emphasis has had upon its power structure. The juridical emphasis on
unification has benefited the Court of Justice of the European Communities (ECJ) as well as the Commission – a conglomeration of activities
of the most undemocratic sort.

The Challenge of Bureaucracy

The juridical emphasis of the twentieth–century integration project is
treated here as a particular feature of the liberal plan. It bears, most of
all, evidence of the strength of the French impact in the initial phases.
Jean Monnet and his French partners did not quite share the peace–plan
outlook typical of British liberalism. According to the *laissez–faire*
spirit of the latter, the processes of international cooperation had to be
mixed with a minimum of governmental powers. The form of powers
that was most accepted was one of a conciliatory nature connected with
the settlement of disputes[18]. Due to the impact of the Catholic tradition
and the long history of monarchical powers, the value of governmental
powers has been higher in French political culture[19]. This feature
reflected itself clearly in the concept of gradual integration adopted by

---

[18]

One of the historical figures in the tradition of liberal internationalism
is Jeremy Bentham and his work *A Plan for an Universal and Perpetual
Peace* (written in 1789 as a part of his work *Principles of International
Law*). The same opposition to supranational or federal powers can be
found in Mitrany 1975, 105–132. For later liberal views on European
integration see Lipgens 1985; and for the British attitude towards the
Coal and Steel Union see Diebold 1959, 48.

[19]

See chapter 2.

the French. The essence of integration was seen as consisting of supranational juridical powers which would gradually weaken the national context. According to this conception, it was not in the first place liberties, the direction of which had to be changed or extended, but regulative rules which were the basis of political life[20].

From the beginning, and in spite of its narrow substance, the European Community was thus vested with a unique juridical machinery. The machinery was based upon the roles of the High Authority and the ECJ and upon the particular qualities of Community law[21]. This initial model of unification laid down the outlines for EURATOM and the EEC and emphasised the nature of the later EC as a juridical project in the first place. This emphasis, combined with the initial approach to integration through sectoral policies, contributed to the rise of bureaucratic structures of power in the EC. These structures were certainly not an intended element of the original plans, but their maintenance and strengthening can be seen to have resulted from the conflict between the two constitutive plans for unification.

The fact is that while the French plan was later accepted in northern Europe (meaning by this both the original and later northern members) too, as the basis for progressive integration, the idea of a gradual transfer of powers to the *federal* organisation has not been endorsed. The establishment of direct elections in the European Parliament took twenty years and the provisions for a uniform procedure have not yet been fulfilled. Parliament has not achieved real and effective legislative powers in spite of various efforts in this

---

[20]

Monnet 1976 eg., 371 and 460. For French arguments in favour of integration see Haas 1958, 114–127.

[21]

The particularity of Community law has been decisively strengthened by the policy of the ECJ (eg., Case 26/62, *N.V. Algemene Transport en Expeditie Onderneming Van Gend & Loos* v *Nederlandse Administratie der belastingen (Netherlands Inland Revenue Administration),* [1963] ECR 1; and Case 6/64, *Flaminio Costa* v *ENEL,* [1964] ECR 585). The key elements of the strong position of law, like the provision of direct applicability, were, however, already present in the constitutive treaties.

direction. The weak idea of the parliamentary control of the Commission present in the constitutive treaties has lost its relevance rather than been strengthened. The bureaucratic appearance of the European Union has been constantly reinforced due to the fact that new policy areas have been included in its powers.

Liberally–oriented internationalists have not been willing to increase democracy in Europe through supranational means, but have been loyal to their original view of a democratic Europe that could be achieved through a plurality of processes connected with the active participation of national parliaments in international affairs[22]. The northern members have traditionally been keen on developing alternative institutional structures in Europe like the Organization for European Economic Cooperation (OEEC) earlier and the Conference on Security and Cooperation in Europe (CSCE) and the European Economic Area (EEA) more recently[23]. But the long process of integration has correspondingly created more and more self–sufficient actors and institutions in the Union, which regard a development of this kind as a threat to their own position and which, therefore, push the Union in a federalist direction.

The Challenge of National Sovereignty

The problem of democracy in the European Union cannot, however, be entirely captured without touching the issue of national sovereignty.

---

[22]

This concept of a democratic Europe goes back to Bentham and its great twentieth–century proponent was Woodrow Wilson (Holsti 1985, 27). The liberal conception of European democracy has been visibly emphasised, eg. in connection with the Schuman declaration (Nicoll and Salmon 1990) and in connection with the Single European Act (Moravcsik 1991, 19–56).

[23]

In the general EC rhetoric, this phenomenon has been described as the priority given to the enlargement of the EC by the northern members and to the deepening of the Community by the southern members. For recent differences in national policies see, eg. Holland 1993, 158.

Sovereignty will be analysed here as a separate issue, while its role will be conceived as a more or less conservative force guarding the integrity of the Westphalian system and acting in opposition to European unification in its original sense. The two World Wars, which inspired a spirit of unification in the European heartland, led to a strengthened feeling of national sovereignty on the rim. It was the high value put on national sovereignty in northern Europe that watered down the all-European efforts of unification immediately following the war[24]. Sovereignty got a decisive grip on the European Community through Charles de Gaulle's policy in the 1960s. De Gaulle's concept of unification was that of a political rule which would be based upon national sovereignty and which would have its essence in external unity. Neither the idea of a federalist government nor the concept of a fragmented fusion of States' activities appeared acceptable to him. De Gaulle instead contributed to the powerful activation of a new meaning of European unity inside the European Community[25].

This new meaning of unity clearly bears with it the heritage of Protestant Europe as well as a trace of a Cold War that left Europe divided between hostile superpowers. This kind of 'unification' of European powers has its motives in global power politics more than in any peace–plan. The unification of foreign policies that has taken place since the 1970s has, due to its intergovernmental structure in particular, been an indication of the legitimacy of this 'Europe of the Sovereignties'. This tradition has brought into European integration a new

---

[24]

The best example of these hampered efforts is the Council of Europe, which ended up as a pure intergovernmental organisation (with its parliamentary organ as a debate forum) in spite of the intensity of federal aspirations connected with its birth (Gerbet 1989).

[25]

This concept was not entirely new in Europe, though. The idea of a union between European States had constituted the core of liberal peace–plans since the eighteenth century (Heater 1992 39; Voyenne 1953, 69). The immediate purpose of these unions was, however, to safeguard peace in the union in contrast to the aspirations towards external power characterising De Gaulle's union.

dimension which was not present in the original logic. This dimension has, above all, implied that the unification project has been drawn into an intergovernmental direction at the same time as new policy areas have been brought under Community powers[26]. Contrary to the original integration plans, which purported to weaken national sovereignty in favour of European peace and welfare, this intergovernmental model implied rather a reinforcement of national sovereignty for the sake of the external strength of Europe. De Gaulle saw in this form of coopera-tion between the European States a possibility of uniting the European forces under French leadership. For the smaller European States, external unity has appeared to be a valuable source of political and economic security.

With intergovernmental cooperation as the political framework, democratic processes at the European level have not appeared to be an issue of particular importance. Democracy has, on the contrary, remained a question of national governments in the first place. This means that the democratic qualities of EC politics have been approach-ed more or less in terms of the national conduct of foreign and European policies and in terms of their openness and parliamentary control. And the more that foreign and security matters have been emphasised as the substance of integration, the less democracy has appeared as a matter of importance in this connection.

This new direction of European unification has strengthened the intergovernmental qualities of the European Communities. This development culminated in the establishment of a new leading body, the European Council, in the 1970s. Again, the transfer of powers to the communitarian agencies, which was stipulated in the constitutive treaties, was decisively retarded[27]. The dispersion of Union decision-

---

[26]

My argument on the novelty of the intergovernmental dimension is based upon the fact that the original federalist and liberal plans of integration included a strategy purporting to *overcome* this dimension, which has recently taken a new grip on the whole process.

[27]

One of the most concrete acts of retardation is the Luxembourg com-promise of 1966. The planned extension of the powers of the European

making into several institutional structures has been another typical effect of intergovernmentalism[28]. It has constituted the necessary condition for the enlargement of Union powers over the areas of foreign and security policy, but at the same time it has implied a most radical departure from the original plan for unification. This intergovernmental emphasis has been apt to make worse the state of democratic decision-making in the European Union, which was already suffering from a spill–over of bureaucracy. This has led to a situation where the development of the democratic features of the Union has appeared more and more difficult to realise on the basis of the original plan and where political compromises have therefore grown amorphous[29].

The Problem of Democracy Redefined

Through a historical approach I have intended to show that the democratic deficit is a structural question of the European Union rather than a bare institutional one. It has its origins in the focal conflict of views that has prevailed about the main political characteristics of the Union. First, it seems that the federal type of government bodies were an over–estimation from the beginning, or, that their supranational powers were not sufficient to create loyalties towards a common

---

Parliament was also hampered in many ways in the 1960's (Pinder 1991, 12).

[28]

This development has been heavily opposed by federalists according to whom separate decisional structures threaten the whole existence of the European Union (this opposition can be documented from various sources, eg. Vandamme 1989; Cardozo and Corbett 1989 and concerning the debate around the Maastricht Treaty, see, eg. the Debates of the EP No. 3–417/70).

[29]

The Treaty on European Union includes various compromises whose normative clarity can be questioned (eg. the legislative processes based upon Art. 189).

European government[30]. Secondly, bringing in new sensitive policy areas and new anti–federalist Member States has made the federalist organisation a still less apparent basis for democracy in the European Union.

This background being given, I will now proceed to discuss the recent means set out for solving this problem in the European Union. The essence of the European Union being so seriously contested, it seems to me that its democratic deficit can only be extinguished through a means that is sufficiently acceptable from the point of view of all these very constitutive interests. The efforts made in the 1990's to improve the level of democracy in the European Union can be divided into two categories according to the way they relate to the two integration plans constituting the basis for this discussion. Some of these instruments of democracy can be considered as pure prolongations of the original integration plans and the democracy programmes they included. Examples of these old methods are, for instance, the reinforcements of the powers of the European Parliament in the Treaty of European Union (TEU) and the measures taken to increase the degree of openness in Union decision–making. The concept of Union citizenship will be analysed in this category due to the fact that in its very essence it comprises an integral part of the old federalist plan. Brought for the first time into the legal and political system of the Union, the concept of Union citizenship, however, includes such a new, unproved potential for democracy that it must be considered separately from the other elements in this category.

There were two elements in the Maastricht Treaty which raised great expectations of democracy and which can be treated as new instruments in the sense that their potentials have not yet been much proved in Community politics. The concepts of regionality and sub-sidiarity and their democratic potentials will, however, be discussed at the end of this chapter. Last of all, the new Treaty of Amsterdam will

---

[30]

The choice between these two statements depends on whether we are more inclined to accept the liberal plan for integration or the federalist one.

be evaluated as far as its significance for the state of democracy in the EU is concerned.

Enhancing Democracy in Accordance with the Old Plans

The original integration plans included two contradictory conceptions of the forms that a democratic government should have at the European level. Federalists strove for the establishment of a powerful European government above nation–States. The democratic nature of this planned federal government has been based upon a parliamentary body, the powers of which have been devised much in accordance with parliamentary powers at the national level. From time to time, more constitutive political powers, such as powers to stipulate the whole political and legal basis of the European Community, have been demanded for the European Parliament[31].

The federalist programme for a European parliamentary democracy has not proceeded very successfully. The European Parliament has not been able to achieve the role of legislative supremacy. Nor does it carry out any decisive control of the political executive. The development of Parliament in this direction has, on the contrary, required political compromises which have rendered the Union's political and legislative system ambiguous and complicated. The Maastricht Treaty took this original democracy programme some steps further through various channels. It established once more a new legislative process at the basis of which Parliament, for the first time, has the right of veto over legislative proposals of certain types. The

---

[31]

At least twice, a European assembly has drafted a 'constitution' for a united Europe. In the years 1952–1953 this task was given to the general assembly of the Coal and Steel Union, which drafted a further form of unification at the basis of the ECSC Treaty and the defence union that was being planned (Cardozo 1989, 54). At the beginning of the 1980s, the present European Parliament adopted a similar role and drew the outlines for the first large–scale Union treaty of the past few decades (Draft Treaty on Political Union).

right of Parliament to make legislative proposals was also slightly strengthened as well as its possibilities of exerting a democratic control over the executive. In addition to the political reasons which have hindered the effective realisation of this democracy programme, there have, however, appeared various administrative factors working in the same direction. One of them is the size of the European Parliament, which is apt to put limits on effective functioning as long as it consists of one chamber only. Another hindrance, and connected with the first one, is the ineffective organisation of party formation at the European level, which reflects itself in a lack of planning and political coherence in the parliamentary work.

European party formation stands conceptually very close to the more novel federalist element, which recent integration politics has raised as one potential solution to the democratic deficit. The concept of Union citizenship is likely to increase the level of Union democracy in various ways. Some of these ways are derived directly from the powers of the European Parliament, while others can be seen to contribute to the democratisation of the European Union at a more basic level in the citizenry. The idea of civil and human rights being laid down at the European level has constituted a vital part of the Christian Democrat plan for European unification. The decisive break–through of the idea took place in the draft Treaty of the European Parliament in 1984, after which two major modifications of the constitutive treaties have already been made in this respect[32]. The Maastricht Treaty established and recognised the concept of Union citizenship, but only subsequent legal and political practice will show its concrete significance as well as give the outlines for its further development.

The concept of Union citizenship contributes to the unification of political rights at the Union level. Even if this new federalist element will presumably have a great impact upon Union democracy in the long term, its role will first be essentially bound to the position of the

---

[32]

The Single European Act included a general reference to human and civil rights and the TEU brought in finally the whole concept of 'Union citizenship'. Art. 3 of the draft Treaty established 'Union citizenship' (eg. Lodge 1986,190) much in the same terms as the TEU (Art. 8).

European Parliament. As long as political rights laid down at the Union level are limited to parliamentary participation, the new citizenship will bring no major amendment to the situation of democracy. There is, however, a latent possibility for a more long–term change in two respects. First, I see in the concept of Union citizenship a firm instrument for the reinforcement of the European Parliament. It appears evident that as far as the concept of Union citizenship will strengthen the idea of a Union electorate it will give further legitimacy to the European Parliament and bring it closer to the European people. Another detail of equal importance in this respect is the unitary electoral system.

The other effect of 'citizenship', including and yet going beyond the first one, relates to the capacity of this concept to constitute not only an electorate, but a citizenry in a broader sense. Union citizenship is therefore of essential importance for the entire problem of building up a common European identity[33]. It is furthermore bound up with the way the formation of parties and other social and political groups proceeds at the European level. A broader justification of the concept of Union citizenship is presumable to lead to an extension of citizens' rights determined at the Union level. All in all, this could imply a pressure towards a modification of Union government in a direction which would take better account of the citizens' perspective. As I have tried to show in this chapter, the continuing legitimacy of national sovereignty and the opposition raised against a federal Europe have constituted the main obstacles to this development thus far. This growing 'citizen identity' would imply the emergence of a heavier critique of the bureaucratic and complicated character of Union decision–making.

The concept of Union citizenship has been introduced here as an intermediate form between old and new means of democracy in the European Union. It remains still to be pointed out that in addition to the federalist democracy programme to which this concept gives expression, the Maastricht Treaty launched a process of pursuing democracy through the original liberal integration plan. Here

---

33

For a debate upon this, see Tiilikainen 1997.

democracy has been linked with the openness and transparency of Union decision–making. According to the political declaration attached to the Maastricht Treaty, the European Commission should submit to the Council a report on measures designed to improve public access to information available to the institutions[34]. At the political level, the Union agencies then reached an agreement on certain measures which should be taken in order to increase Union democracy and transparency[35]. Another instrument of democracy which has been of greater importance in the liberal programme is the effective involvement of national parliaments in Union decision–making. Federalists, again, have tended to concentrate more upon the powers of the European Parliament. There was also a declaration attached to the Maastricht Treaty concerning the reinforcement of the role of national parliaments in matters of European integration[36]. Both of these liberal instruments of democracy, however, had their culmination only in the Treaty of Amsterdam.

Subsidiarity and Regionality as Means of Democracy in the European Union

The concept of Union citizenship constitutes, in theory, a significant instrument for the democratic development of the European Union. Its effective use is, however, likely to be complicated because of its

---

[34]

Declaration on the Right to Access to Information (TEU, Declaration No. 17).

[35]

Interinstitutional Declaration on Democracy, Transparency and Subsidiarity (Doc. EN\RR\239\239257).

[36]

Declaration on the Role of National Parliaments in the European Union (TEU, Declaration No. 13).

apparently federalist character[37]. It is questionable whether the journey to a democratic European Union is shorter through the principles of regionality and subsidiarity, but the character of these principles is at least more receptive of compromises. The problem of their acceptability is that the traditions of regionalism and subsidiarity belong closer to Catholic Europe, where a stronger attraction towards a united Europe already exists. The link in common between these principles is that they can both be made to work against the principle of State sovereignty and for a fragmentation of political authority without any necessary connection with federalism. Both principles have, however, grown up in a close interaction with EC government, which appears necessary in order to enable them to cope with the strength of national sovereignty. It seems to me that, at least for the time being, the fragmentation of sovereignties is decisively dependent on the centralised powers of the EU.

The expectations of democracy that have been raised by the principles of subsidiarity and regionality have in both cases been based upon their assumed capacities to work against the centralising features of the European Union. The principle of subsidiarity originates in the Catholic political tradition. Its democratic essence results from its core idea of making decisions as close as possible to the citizens. Its significance for Union democracy will therefore be connected not only with the division of powers between the Union and the Member States, but also with the division of powers between the Member States and regions, or other political unities in the Member States.

The problems in the application of the principle have already made themselves apparent at both of these levels. In general, the provisions on subsidiarity remained ambiguous in the Maastricht Treaty and have already been provided with various guidelines of interpretation[38]. As an indication of this the Treaty of Amsterdam includes a

---

37

Denmark has already been allowed to make some important reservations to the concept, while the realisation of the rights connected with it has run into great difficulties in other Member States, too.

38

Eg. Interinstitutional Agreement on Procedures for Implementing

particular protocol on the application of the principles of subsidiarity and proportionality[39]. As a result of the explicit formation of these provisions, subsidiarity has been approached in the first place as a division of power between the Union and the Member States. The ECJ will now play the key role as far as the definition and interpretation of the principle is concerned. It will thus also decide upon the role that the principle of democracy should play as a criterion for its application.

The other new dimension of Union democracy derives from the principle of regionality. This dimension reflects an aspiration to strengthen politically different kinds of historical, cultural and economic regions at the expense of the nation–State. In the context of European integration this kind of political development has been seen as a protection of the elements of plurality and heterogeneity which might otherwise risk being weakened. The importance of regions has been emphasised in various declarations and protocols since the 1980s. In 1988 a consultative board consisting of local and regional authorities was established in the Commission. In the Maastricht Treaty it was given an official status as the Committee of Regions, the powers of which are, however, quite marginal thus far.

Problems arising from the principle of regionality as a means of democracy are closely interrelated with the problems concealed behind the full use of the rule of subsidiarity. The strength and forms of regionality vary enormously between different Member States of the Union. Wessels and Engel have analysed forms of regionality in European States by dividing these into regionalised, decentralised and

---

[39] the Principle of Subsidiarity, Doc. PE 176.643, 7 58; 1992 Commission Communication to the Council and the European Parliament on subsidiarity, Bull. EC 1992/10.

The version of the new treaty available at the moment of finishing this text is just a draft version (Draft Treaty of Amsterdam CONF 4001/97). References to treaty articles as well as to protocols and declarations are therefore somewhat inexact and might not correspond to their numbering in the final version.

unitary States[40]. In addition to a federal Germany, Belgium, Italy and Spain are classified as regionalised States. In all these countries the rights of regions have been stipulated in law. In France and the Netherlands the central government is dominant in spite of the decentralisation of regions. Regions are governed by assemblies elected by the people. In unitary States like Denmark, Greece and Ireland the regions are weak, but the role of local government tends to be significant. The European Union intends to support a development of regionality which is in harmony with natural region formation in Europe. It appears evident that as a means of democracy the principle of regionality will be the most successful in those countries in which regionality and regional self–government are based upon a long tradition.

For instance, in northern Europe, where regional communities are less natural and the main emphasis is put upon local government, the democratic influence of the principle of regionality is not so self-evident. The same can be said about subsidiarity, which has certainly better chances of decentralising political power in those Member States which have more serious historical alternatives to State sovereignty.

Democracy as a Part of a Citizens' Europe – towards the Treaty of Amsterdam

The problem of democracy was raised as one of the key topics in the Intergovernmental Conference of 1996 due to the legitimacy crisis that the European Union went through in connection with the Maastricht Treaty. The way of approaching the problem of democracy has this time been a most comprehensive one as democracy has appeared as the key element in the project of 'A Citizens' Europe' which purports to reinforce the entire citizens' dimension of European integration. The core results of this project manifest themselves as Section II of the new Treaty of Amsterdam, but as the Introduction of the Treaty declares, 'making the Union more relevant and comprehensible to its citizens is

---

[40]

Kokkonen and Vartiainen 1993, 15.

a major aim which permeates the entire work of the Conference and is reflected in all chapters of the Treaty'.

The main argument of this chapter is that the lack of democracy in EU decision–making should above all be treated as a structural problem of the EU, a problem which originates in the fact that its leading concept of democracy was all too ambitious. In the Maastricht Treaty a pragmatic way of increasing democracy was adopted, meaning that small steps were taken in many separate contexts in favour of a more democratic Union. As this proved insufficient, and as even the coming enlargement will be apt to put its own demands upon the project of democracy, the new treaty is now tackling this problem more comprehensively.

As far as the question of democracy is concerned, the Treaty of Amsterdam is, in the first place, bound to the two original concepts of democracy defined here as the federalist concept and the liberal concept. The new openings, referring to possible ways out of the democracy problem, are limited mainly to a new emphasis given on the federalist strategy. When the original federalist plan of European integration was based upon the establishment of a real federal government and upon the assumption that people's political loyalties would follow this political machinery (which they never did), the new treaty gives expression to an opposite strategy adopted in this question.

The New Federalism – from Common Institutions to a Common Identity

The legitimacy crisis of the European Union, which made itself seriously known in the early 1990's, brought a new topic for the European political agenda. This was the evident gap taking place between political and social elites and ordinary people as far as their conceptions and aspirations on European integration were concerned. The crisis has, among other things, led to a new emphasis on the citizens' dimension of European integration. The various projects purporting to make integration more meaningful for citizens culminated in the attention paid to the issue in the Intergovernmental Conference preparing the Treaty of Amsterdam.

Even if the core of the new citizens' project, the entry of a comprehensive list of rights and liberties into the TEU, failed to be realised, Sections I and II of the new treaty still reinforce the role of the EU for citizens in many ways. This is done partly by bringing in new policy–areas to Union competence and partly by strengthening Union powers in existing policy–areas. The incorporation of the Schengen agreement and the Social agreement into the TEU are two of the most important changes in this respect.

The entire project of 'A Citizens' Europe' can be linked to the original federalist plan since its final purpose, based upon an assessment of the legitimacy crisis, is to bring citizens and the citizens' dimension of European integration up to the level of existing plans of integration, and not the other way around. The emphasis that the project gained in the new treaty is a socio–economic one, while a reinforcement of the political identity and unity of Union citizens might be assumed to follow indirectly or be achieved through other types of means. It is, however, a visible trait of the Treaty of Amsterdam that the key foundations of a common *political* identity, like Union citizenship or the recognition of the necessity of European party–formation in the Maastricht Treaty, gained disproportionately little attention.

The efforts to bring the EU closer to its citizens by reinforcing the role of citizens in the TEU may be connected with the problem of achieving democracy through the federalist plan. As long as the institutional structures of the EU are not decisively amended, the efforts to establish a common identity among Union citizens might simply contribute to the fulfilment of the federalist concept of democracy. It would enable a gradual amendment of Union power structures in the direction of a real federal government. One part of this process would consist of the rounding–off of Union citizenship with a complete set of rights and liberties regulated by the EU.

Long Steps along the Old Paths – The Importance of the Old Plans

In addition to the more comprehensive approach to Union democracy, the Treaty of Amsterdam succeeded in advancing both the old democracy plans. In contrast to the Maastricht Treaty, the emphasis seems to lie this time upon the liberal plan. One of the greatest achievements in this respect is the principle of openness, now raised among the key characteristics of the European Union and manifesting itself as a better access to Union documents in accordance with the details of article 191a[41]. There is also a declaration attached to the Final Act giving support to the improvement of the quality of the drafting of Community legislation. Another key amendment in the spirit of the liberal integration plan is the reinforcement of the role of national parliaments in EU decision–making. This was done by means of a new Draft Protocol to be annexed to the TEU. The protocol deals mainly with the parliaments' access to Commission documents and with the role and functions of the Conference of European Affairs Committees (COSAC).

As far as amendments in favour of a centralised, federal concept of democracy are concerned the Intergovernmental Conference seems to have been blocked by the coincidence of various grand decisions. The result was an incapacity to achieve the deepening of an integration demanded mainly in the name of the maintenance of the Union's functional capacity. Here, the significance of the Treaty of Amsterdam lies in the fact that it tries to revive the legitimacy of European integration without distancing the project once more from the citizens. The key amendments in the federalist direction deal with the role of the European Parliament. Its powers were improved by increasing the sphere of the co–decision procedure and by reinforcing its role in this procedure.

Conclusions

An effort was made in this chapter to illustrate the type and depth of political problems that the key division of European political cultures has been apt to cause in the present integration project. One of the key problems of Union governance was raised as an example of the historical conflict between the three political traditions. It was shown how the problem of democracy is in the last resort a conflict of forms where federal representative democracy, international institutional

---

[41]

This number refers to the Draft Treaty of Amsterdam (CONF 4001/97).

democracy and national democracy stand against each other. The conclusion was that there are no signs of the dissolution of this constellation, the origins of which are deep in European cultural and political history. Due to the character of the problem it can never be entirely resolved on the basis of the present institutional structure of the Union, which was shown to represent a delicate compromise between the three traditions. The argument made in this particular case was that the democratic deficit cannot be extinguished simply by increasing the powers of the European Parliament. The discussion on democracy should therefore be extended and the particular character of the European Union be taken more into account.

The new instruments that the Maastricht Treaty set up to work against the democratic deficit have appeared to be too weak to reach the core of the difficult problem. Their weakness does not lie in the concepts of Union citizenship, subsidiarity and regionality themselves, but rather in their uneven acceptability in various areas of Europe. The Treaty of Amsterdam is different in this respect as it does not so much deal with opportunities of political participation but enlarges citizens' contacts with the EU at a more general level. The key threat to this strategy is time. The paradox of the situation is that the creation of a citizenry and a common political identity, which are assumed to contribute to the democratisation of the Union in the long term, are in the short term being challenged by the yawning gap of a democratic deficit making itself painfully evident here and now. Democracy, once one of the constitutive forces of European integration, has suddenly turned into its fateful problem. This problem has to be resolved before the legitimacy of the whole of this historical idea breaks down.

PART II

FINLAND

5 The Historical Construction of Finland as a Political Community

Introduction

Political cultures consist of different sets of values. Values give rise to political doctrines and concepts that organise social life. Political cultures can be compared with each other by studying similarities and differences from the standpoint of their conceptual basis.

In the first part of this book I have made an effort to analyse the political culture of Western Europe by means of one key division in it. With the key focus of the study falling on the present project of European integration, the significance of the division was analysed from the perspective of the European political structure. It was shown how the key problem of European integration originates in Catholic, Calvinist and Lutheran political traditions that have given rise to three very different conceptions of Europe.

Finland is usually introduced as a borderland as far as political culture is concerned. Its affinity with historic Western values like liberty, democracy and the rule of law has always been axiomatic. The other tradition based, however, upon a slightly different substratum originates in geography. Having Russia for a neighbour has, for various reasons, developed into an important constituent of Finnish political thinking. Its impact does not limit itself to the domain of foreign policy only but affects political conceptions at a much more basic level. The appearance of this borderland Finland could perhaps, from a Western point of view, be described as a strange relative.

The end of the Cold War led to the revaluation of many tenable policy–lines in Finnish politics. The most comprehensive change concerned the Finnish position with respect to the European political unification that had its origin in postwar Western Europe. Finland, which had remained outside the unification project during the Cold War, emphasising its national sovereignty and its neutrality between the superpowers, started to yield to the ever–deepening unification of political structures in Europe. The Finnish decision to have a full participation in this European project implied an explicit need to harmonise Finnish politics with the politics of the European Community, that was transformed into the European Union in late 1993.

In the following two chapters it is my intention to point out the Finnish position in the present integration project by analysing the very prominent forms of Finnish political thinking. One part of this work involves the placing of Finnish political culture in relation to the political divisions brought about by the Reformation and thereafter functioning as one of the core foundations of modern political thinking in Europe. This approach is deepened through an analysis of the mutual relations and tensions between the leading political traditions in Finland. The assumption behind the analysis is that the Finnish nation–State ideology is exceptionally strong and unitary if evaluated on a European scale. It is the purpose of the following chapters to introduce the historical construction of this ideology. Another key assumption is that participation in the present European integration implies a great challenge for Finland because Finnish political culture lacks any strong connection to the tradition of a united Europe. The task of the second part of the book is divided between the two chapters so that this first one approaches Finnish political identity through the process of State-building and the latter through Finnish foreign policy.

The Birth of the Finnish Territory

Here I will try to explain how Finnish State–building rested firmly on the powers of the Lutheran and nationalist ideologies in the country. Through Finnish history, there have, however, appeared other, balancing, traditions the purpose of which has been less centralising. These traditions have constituted connecting links with the general Western community as well as with the particular Nordic community of values inside the Western connection. Collectivist elements are strong in Finnish political culture because they constitute the essential core of the Finnish State. They have, however, been strengthened also by factors of political geography. Finnish political identity–building can in this respect be returned to the early Middle Ages, when Finland was under Swedish rule.

Secular and ecclesiastic rule spread simultaneously into the medieval societies of the Nordic countries. Christian institutions came to the North from Germany as the Archbishop of Hamburg–Bremen was entitled to function as the Archbishop of all the Northern peoples[1]. The Christian Church contributed to the division of the land into legal and administrative provinces (*landskap*). Codification of the customary law into written provincial law was based upon the initiative of the Church[2]. The Church was also an important supporter of the centralisation of political power, which started to take place as a strengthening of the powers of the king during the first centuries of the second millennium[3]. As the Nordic civilisation is younger than its counterpart in southern Europe, the powers of the Catholic Church were never to the same extent in conflict with the powers of the secular rulers[4]. The Nordic kings were *Rex Dei Gratia*, which legitimated their powers but subordinated also the monarchical rule to Christian norms and principles. People were entitled to resist a king who violated divine justice. The ecclesiastical rule supported the secular rule as long as this protected its security, internal independence and privileges in society[5]. Secular rule and legislation constituted a part of the Catholic division of law, where the divine law *ius divinum* was the higher part and the

---

[1]

Vahtola 1993, 47.

[2]

Jutikkala 1965, 28.

[3]

It was the power struggle between the Emperor and the Pope in medieval Europe which made the Pope support the establishment of national Churches in Northern Europe (Pirinen 1988, 17).

[4]

Jutikkala 1965, 29.

[5]

Suvanto 1985, 140.

human law *lex humana* the lower part[6]. It is a typical characteristic of Nordic societies that monarchs did not compete for their powers with the Church but with the people.

Provinces and their self–legislation formed the historical political communities in the Nordic countries, challenging the centralising powers of a monarch and at the same time functioning as an important support for them. The provinces elected the king, who was also bound by the provincial laws. The political organ of the provinces was the 'thing' (*ting*), which cannot be treated as the direct origin of modern popular representation in spite of the fact that all peasants having a permanent abode were obliged to participate in it[7]. The king swore to uphold the sanctity of the laws. Once elected, the king visited the provinces in order to be recognised by the people (this tradition was called the '*eriksgata*'). As the monarchical powers had been strengthened, the provinces constituted a key element in the construction of the central State. Leaders of the provinces were later appointed by the king. Provinces, further, formed a basis for the 'castle provinces', as they were called, upon which the centralising tax system was based.

Other historical Nordic institutions that balanced the powers of a monarch were the councils (*riksråd*) consisting of advisers appointed by the king. Geographical perspectives were taken into account in the composition of this council, which consisted of ecclesiastic leaders, aristocrats and leaders of the provinces. Later, a larger organ called a diet (*herredag*) started to assist the king in political questions. Demands for an estate–structure in the diet increased when tasks that used to belong to the 'ting' were to a growing extent transferred to the diet. It was an important step in the centralisation of political power when the Swedish king started to call together the Estates in the sixteenth century[8]. A diet that consisted of four Estates turned out to be the most

---

[6]

Kauppinen 1992, 62.

[7]

Jutikkala 1965, 21.

[8]

Lagerroth 1955, 136.

important historical counterbalance to the ever–growing monarchical powers.

The origins of the State of Finland lie in its position as a Catholic bishopric in the very beginning of this millennium. Christianity was brought into Finland[9] by the Swedes. The Church of Rome defined the land *Findia* as belonging to the Swedish archbishopric of Lund when it was established ca. 1103[10]. A degree of independence was vested in the Finnish bishopric by the Church. In 1221, the *episcopo Finlandiae* was given the right to control trade in the Gulf of Finland and in 1229 Pope Gregory IX took the bishop, the priests and the Finnish people under his protection[11]. The Finnish territory became a part of the Catholic culture, which meant the adoption of its administrative principles, the system of Canon Law and the Latin language.

During the first centuries of the second millennium, the Finnish territories were annexed to the Swedish crown[12]. The annexation did not break the unity of the Finnish territories based upon their ecclesiastical organisation. The Swedish administration spread into Finland together with, and often slightly preceded by, the administration of the Church[13].

9

In the early Middle Ages, the Finnish tribes were called *Finns, Fenns* or *Scridefinns. Kvenland* ('the low land') was an originally Norwegian name that was used just before Christianity came to Finland. *Finland* was the name that was dominant in the beginning of the second millennium and again from the sixteenth century. The Swedish rulers used the name *Österland* from the fourteenth to the fifteenth century as the 'castle province' of Vyborg also belonged to the Swedish administration (Vahtola 1987).

10

This detail was included in the Florence document issued by the Church in 1120 (Pirinen 1988, 17; Vahtola 1993, 47).

11

Vahtola 1993, 55.

12

The first Swedish ruler active in the annexation was Birger Jarl, who died in 1266 (Vahtola 1993, 58).

13

Suvanto 1985, 112–113.

Two of the provincial Swedish laws (*Uplands–Lagen* and *Hälsinge–Lagen*) were in force in Finland[14]. Finland appeared as a jurisdictional unity, a domain of the lagman (*lagsaga*)[15], and was entitled to send its representative to the elections of the king from the fourteenth century[16]. Finland was unitary, too, as far as its economic life was concerned. Throughout the Middle Ages and even late into modern times Finland was dominated by rural sources of livelihood and urban culture remained insignificant. The impact of feudalism was even less significant in Finland than it was in other Nordic societies as the land was to a very great extent owned by the peasantry[17]. In the late Middle Ages, Finland was divided into 'castle–provinces', which strengthened the central structures of the crown and established a narrow aristocracy in the country.

Another element in Finnish political identity that can be derived from medieval times is the nature of Finland as a borderland. Throughout the Middle Ages, the Swedes were fighting over the Finnish areas against Novgorod in the east. The conflict was exacerbated by the fact that the border between the Eastern and Western Church ran along the Finnish border.

14

Brotherus 1963, 10; Kauppinen 1992, 61.

15

The Finnish domain of the lagman was, however, divided in 1435 along the river Aura (Suomen historian dokumentteja 1 1968, 128).

16

The Finnish position was expressed very well in a declaration given by the Swedish king Håkan Magnusson in 1362 : 'As the Eastland (*Österland*) forms one bishopric and one domain of the lagman and as our parents have found it faithful and dear, it is rightful that its inhabitants are given a share of the same honour and love that the other Swedish bishoprics and domains of lagman have. Therefore, each time the king has to be elected, the lagman has to come with the priests chosen and with twelve peasants to elect the king on the part of the entire people of the Eastland' (Vahtola 1993, 76).

17

Jutikkala 1965, 55.

The State Defeats the Church

The factor that broke the medieval political structure and came to have a persistent impact on the essence of social life was the Reformation. The Lutheran doctrine shaped conceptions about the character and function of secular power. Its theory of human nature turned against the original Catholic view of people as pure instruments of the Divine Good. The Lutheran doctrine divided the Christian community into the kingdom of Christ and the kingdom of the world, leaving the sinful men of the latter under the jurisdiction of a secular ruler. One of the most systematic differences with respect to previous political thinking was brought about by denying the possibilities of an inherent human justice and any impact of this kind of natural law on human behaviour. The basic Christian idea of a natural community was thus altered, and secular community–building given a more legitimate basis. The structure with which Lutheranism met natural–law thinking was in principle the same as in Calvinism. Law, as a command of God, had to be followed not because it seemed just, but precisely because it was a command from God. In the same way, the power to rule belonging to secular kings, appeared as a gift from God. Lutheranism, however, protected itself longer against the concept of people's right to resist a ruler, which was developed within Calvinism[18]. The Reformation constituted the main force behind the establishment of central and regulative State structures in Sweden–Finland.

Sweden was the first State to secede from the Roman Catholic Church during the Reformation. The possessions of the Church were transferred to the Crown, which was made hereditary. Finland was given the position of a duchy in 1556 as a reflection of the increasing power of the king[19]. A centralised system was established for the collection of taxes which gradually broke down the old administrative

---

[18]

See chapter 2.

[19]

The duke was a governor of the king in the Finnish territory, the historical provinces of which thus became united into one larger administrative unity, which was later to become the State of Finland.

structures and developed into the administrative structures of a modern regulative State. The Reformation was thus effective in the development of administrative structures of a centralised State. The situation was different as far as the political rule of the State was concerned. The centralisation of political power never led to pure ruler absolutism in Sweden–Finland. One reason for this was in the well–established institutional practices that had been in use throughout the Middle Ages.

The Reformation confirmed the role of the Estates as representatives of the people and the land and the regulation of their position through special privileges. Throughout the centuries, political rule took varying forms between ruler absolutism and Estate absolutism. The Estates demanded a part of the ruler's powers and tried to protect their position by binding the ruler to specific pacts. These pacts, where the king confirmed the conditions for his powers and the Estates swore their fidelity to the king, were regarded as *lex fundamentalis* from the seventh century[20]. The concept of fundamental law already included the core ideas of modern constitutionalism. The law was unchangeable in principle and could be amended only through an agreement between king and Estates.

The Reformation imprinted its political concepts on Finland and contributed also to developing the conceptions of the Finnish political unity. The immediate political structure of Lutheranism was one of descending power. The power in a land was seen to be given to a king by God, which made the people living in the territory his subjects. The Catholic idea of Christianity as a natural community was displaced, when the doctrine of two regimes was declared valid[21]. The people's

---

[20]

Jyränki 1989, 60 ff.

[21]

This declaration was given in Uppsala in the year 1593 and it formed the basis for the Lutheran Church in the country. Its core was formed by the statements *...una sancta ecclesia perpetua mansura sit. Est autem ecclesia congregatio sanctorum...* (one holy Church will stay forever. The Church is a congregation of the faithful)..*Non igitur commiscendae sunt potestates ecclesiastica et civilis* (Therefore the ecclesiastical and civil power shall not be mixed together, Kauppinen 1992, 140).

rights with respect to the land were given in the form of privileges, which constituted the basis for the permanent Estates. Finland was connected with the hereditary Crown through the new Finnish grand duke who gained the land from the king Gustavus Vasa:

> Therefore we are conveying the provinces mentioned belonging to us and to the Crown to our beloved son who was mentioned and to his male heirs for ever and ever...[22]

The Reformation strengthened the centralisation of power in Finland and bound it more firmly to the Swedish crown. It led to a policy of unification that was directed at the social and political life in Finland. But the Reformation contributed also to the separateness of the Finnish nation due to the conception that was put forth according to which the Christian religion should be available in the vernacular[23]. A unitary Finnish language was created by Mikael Agricola, who was the main figure of the Finnish Reformation and who also translated the New Testament and parts of the Old into Finnish. The significance of language increased as an element of national identity, but the conceptions of political unity remained basically unchanged during the Swedish era. According to these conceptions, Finland was an ancient monarchy that had been occupied by Sweden[24]. Another conception that was established during the Swedish era was the conception of Finland as a nation in the Swedish realm[25]. Respect was increasingly demanded for the Finnish language and Finnish birth, but they were not regarded as the main factors connecting people. All through the Swedish era, geographical separateness remained as the main constituent of the

---

[22]

The enfeoffment letter of Gustavus Vasa given to his son Johan. Turku 27.6.1556. (Suomen historian dokumentteja 1 1968, 189–190).

[23]

Nation referred then to the subjects of a king (Jutikkala 1965, 94).

[24]

Mäntylä 1993, 204.

[25]

Jussila 1987, 47. 'Nation' did not have its modern meaning, but referred to a people defined in historical and geographical terms.

Finnish nation[26].

Lutheranism remained in Finnish political culture as respect for the common secular power, that is for the future State, by bringing into harmony the communities of a secular and divine nature and by connecting also the first to a higher purpose. Government was furthermore given a much more comprehensive character than in cultures influenced by natural–law thinking and already manifesting the early traces of liberalism. The fact that the common power ultimately served a divine purpose implied an obligation to protect and promote the moral and religious life of the citizens[27]. Supported later by both the nationalist and socialist doctrine, the broad concept of the State has been an essential part of Finnish political identity.

Finland Becomes a Part of the Russian Empire

The main characteristics of the old political culture did not change when Finland was transferred into the empire of the Russian Tsar in the year 1809. The focal political principles of the Swedish era were handed down in the structures of the administration and legislation that Finland was entitled to maintain. The constitution that remained in force in Finland during the whole Russian era consisted of a Gustavian governmental form (1772) and of the Act of Union and Security (1789)[28]. The constitution bound Finnish political life to the ancient forms for a century and its substance was based upon an extreme ruler–

26

Jutikkala 1965, 94; Halila 1985, 11.

27

Jutikkala 1965, 22ff. In the charter establishing the first Finnish university in Turku in the year 1640 the regency (the queen was still a minor) defined the final purpose of schools and academies as 'the achievement of the right knowledge of God, honour, virtue and a Christian life' (the charter of the Academy of Turku 26.3.1640 in Suomen historian dokumentteja 1 1968, 315 ff).

28

The Law of the Diet, and an annex to it, The Order of Nobles, were promulgated in the year 1869 (Mechelin 1896, 28).

centricism. The powers of the Swedish monarch were easily transferred to the Tsar as the change of government was understood in ancient terms as a transition of the Finnish provinces from the Swedish king to the Russian Tsar[29]. The autonomous position of Finland led to certain arrangements in the central administration that constituted later the institutional basis of an independent State. The idea of particular *Finnish Estates* was established when the Tsar Alexander I called the Estates to Porvoo in 1809 and swore a ruler's oath before them[30]. A Governing Council (after 1816 called the Finnish Senate) was established in the same year to lead the administration and jurisdiction in the country.

Until modern political ideologies spread to Finland, political thinking in the country was dominated by the ancient concept of land according to which the land consisted of ruler and Estates. The role of ordinary people was to be loyal subjects and humble servants of the ruler. On the other hand, the tradition of law and the fact that Finland had had an equal right to participate in Swedish political organs can be used to explain why it was not particularly difficult for Finnish political institutions to get adjusted to the new autonomous conditions. The Finnish State did not yet constitute any basis for peoples' loyalties, while the growing State structures were understood simply as a complex that administered corporate privileges. The increasing State regulation gave birth to a bureaucratic class and it has been argued that in the political sense Finnish autonomy was an autonomy of the State bureaucracy in the first place[31].

As far as the Finnish political unity is concerned, the transfer of Finland to the Russian empire must be considered to be of primary importance. The act of transfer was given a positive value in Finnish

---

[29] Jussila 1987, 23–24.

[30] Jussila 1987, 16 ff. For the affirmation of the ruler and the Estates in Porvoo 29.3.1809, see Suomen historian dokumentteja 2 1970, 13 ff.

[31] Pulma 1993, 442.

political debate. Finland was seen to be elevated to be one of the States of the Empire[32]. Finnish political institutions were recognised and there were even some efforts to lay down a Finnish constitution, efforts which, in the end, did not succeed. It is, however, evident that these actions did not take on their full modern interpretation before liberal and nationalist ideas gained ground in Finland. The understanding of the year 1809 between the Tsar and the Finnish Estates that would later be claimed by the Finns as a treaty between two States had another tone when it came into being.

The Modern Conceptions of Finland are Born

Finnish political thinking went through decisive stages of modernisation during the latter half of the Finnish autonomy. The political conditions, that is, the position of Finland as an autonomous Grand Duchy in the Russian empire, had a significant impact upon the form and demands of modern ideologies in the country. Another thing that had an impact upon them was the fact that the Finnish political culture of that time had a great preparedness for collective forms. This collectivism was predominantly a consequence of the Lutheranism that had brought Finland under the cultural impact of Germany. This impact turned out to be decisive also as far as the modernisation of political conceptions was concerned.

The Birth of the Finnish Nation

During the latter half of the nineteenth century the view of 'the State'[33] as a duality of the monarch, with his bureaucratic–administrative machinery, and the land became contested. As Romanticism spread into the country, a conception of Finland as a cultural and historical unity

---

[32]

Jussila 1987, 22.

[33]

Neither did the term 'State' actually appear in the Finnish language in the modern sense before these times (Jussila 1987, 88).

was born. In its first phase, the new idea meant that Finland started to appear as a socio–cultural unity of its own, a unit separate from Sweden and Russia. The first wave of Romanticism in Finland is known as the Romanticism of Turku, which manifested itself as a growing interest in folklore and in the Finnish language. The awakening Finnish National Romanticism took the Swedish cultural impact on the country as its primary target. Its primary purpose was to strengthen the Finnish language and culture and suppress the corresponding Swedish elements. The creation of a Finnish national spirit was helped on by the compiling of the *Kalevala,* the Finnish national epic, and by a gradually increasing use of Finnish in journalism.

The early stage of Romanticism was already characterised by the change that was also taking place in the understanding of the political identity of Finland. As Finland became, in fact, an autonomous Grand Duchy in the Russian empire, this led to the *Finnish* political structures being given more emphasis. The evolving idea of Finland as a cultural and historical unity led first to the modification of conceptions concerning the *role* of the State and State institutions. The State, which had previously appeared as a bureaucratic machinery administering the powers of the ruler, began to be conceived of as an organism for the people and for its higher purposes[34]. The duality formed by the land, on the one hand, and the ruler with his State machinery, on the other, disappeared but the State was not yet regarded as an equivalent of the nation.

Finnish National Romanticism started to take on increasingly political tones towards the middle of the nineteenth century. It was transformed into a unitary political doctrine mainly by two academics, J.V. Snellman and Y.S. Yrjö–Koskinen. Their thinking was dominated by German Romanticism and by the ideas of G.W.F. Hegel, in particular[35]. Finnish political nationalism thus shared most of the key

---

[34]

One of the first representatives of this position was Professor J.J. Tengström (Jussila 1987, 64).

[35]

German Romanticism was the dominant source for intellectual life in Finland in the mid–nineteenth century. Juhani Paasivirta found one

ideas of nineteenth–century German nationalism. Both doctrines took as their starting–point the idea of the State as an expression of pure liberty and as the highest political form. Statehood was seen to be identical with national self–determination based upon the cultural unity and historical customs of individual nations. Individuals were seen as gaining their political maturity and full political liberty through the State and through its norm–giving capacities. In the Finnish case, the nationalist understanding of State included both conservative and subversive elements with respect to the existing political order.

Finnish political nationalism was subversive as far as the internal political structures of Finland were concerned. Its core conception of the Finnish nation as a political subject was turned in the first place against Swedish elements in society and in the State organisation and gave birth to demands for broader popular participation in political activities and decision–making. J.V. Snellman expressed the Finnish situation in the following terms: 'The national conscience of the Finnish people is mainly depressed by another power than the one binding its independence as a State' [36]. The development and ennobling of the Finnish national spirit was therefore to form a comprehensive framework for nationalist demands. The national spirit was defined by Snellman as a combination of the existing national culture and patriotism[37]. It was seen to be a process which brought individuals to act in favour of the nation on grounds of their own discretion, and a process in which a continuity of reason prevailed between different cultural states[38]. According to Snellman ' in our days it is an indication of a great ignorance if one does not know that nationality and the national spirit have always constituted, in the entire history of mankind,

reason for this in the process of nation–building that was then taking place in both countries (Paasivirta 1991, 176).

36

Paasivirta 1978, 124.

37

Snellman 1901, 11.

38

Pulkkinen 1989, 147.

the incentive to all higher human activity'[39].

The concept of the Finnish nation gave rise to heavy demands for the mental activation and political mobilisation of the Finnish people. In order to ennoble its national spirit, and to increase its national maturity, certain social and political reforms were also demanded. These included the establishment a system of popular education and a press dealing with social and political issues. The socio–economic homogeneity of the Finnish nation was to constitute the goal of the social reforms demanded.

The conservative elements in Finnish nationalism followed the Hegelian doctrine and concentrated on the position of Finland in the Russian empire and on a Statehood in these terms. According to Hegel, world history followed its own laws of necessity. As a part of this process, nations were seen as going through a process of maturation ending up in the achievement of the highest form, Statehood. Since this was a process, nationalism, for Finnish conservative nationalists, was not a political force that functioned avowedly with the aim of separating Finland from Russia[40]. Finland, as an autonomous part of the Russian Empire, was made to appear compatible with the nationalist doctrine through the idea that the Finnish nation had not yet reached its full maturity. Finland appeared instead as a nation having the preconditions for becoming a State one day. Finland, in its development as an autonomous part of Russia, was seen as entering a positive stage in a long process of maturation as Finland.

In contrast to those groups that emphasised a Finnish constitution as an indication of the Finnish Statehood, Snellman and the Finnish nationalists worked from internal and mental conditions, the state of the national spirit, as the necessary condition. For Snellman, the existence of the Finnish Estates was an important indication of the political

---

[39]

Snellman commenting on the programme of the Liberal Party on 14.12.1880 (Suomen historian dokumentteja 2 1968, 132).

[40]

The nationalist position towards Russia is known as the policy of concessions as it has implied assent to the existing political conditions between Finland and Russia more than an effort to bring about a change in them on the grounds of moral or legal considerations.

maturity of Finland. In the 1860's nationalists finally consented to the idea that Finland formed a State. Its Statehood implied, according to them, only internal independence in subordination to Russia.[41]

As an integral part of the idea of the Finnish State, the Finnish Estates were given a new meaning as a fundament of the nationalist doctrine. The Estates that in the beginning of Finnish autonomy had appeared as spokesmen for the privileges of the static Estate corporations that they represented, became perceived as a *Diet* representing the whole country and more and more apparently, the nation. Towards the end of the nineteenth century, the State started increasingly to appear as an equivalent of the nation and the Diet became the most prominent expression of Finnish Statehood.

By the end of the nineteenth century, the nationalist conception of Finland had become the leading political conception. The Finnish people no longer contented themselves with the role of humble servants of the ruler. The idea of a people *forming* a political subject, the nation, had spread itself across the broad population. The end of the nineteenth century was characterised by a revolutionary birth of civil associations among which were the first modern political parties. The elementary school system was established in 1866 and a decree for equality between the Finnish and Swedish languages was given in 1886[42]. The idea of the State as an instrument for the economic and social well-being of the people led to a reorganisation of the whole of social life. The Finnish nation was seen to have achieved modern conditions for Statehood as an autonomous part of the Russian empire, a situation that had originally been regarded as rather a privileged position. A growing Russian policy of oppression influenced popular opinion in Finland from the beginning of this century to turn from autonomy to the idea of independence.

---

[41]

Jussila 1987, 90–127.

[42]

Olkkonen 1993, 484. The decree (18.3.1886) can be found in Suomen historian dokumentteja 1 1968, 135–136.

Finland as a Constitutional Contract

From the middle of the nineteenth century, another conception of the Finnish State was systematically set up against the nationalist view of Finland as an expression of the maturing national spirit. This was a constitutionalist conception that was a reflection of the impact on Finland of the natural–rights tradition[43]. The first form in which the natural–rights tradition came into Finland emphasised individuals' economic liberties vis-à-vis the State. The economic liberalism that contributed to the change of social conditions in Finland from the eighteenth century onwards was the first individualist doctrine to challenge the old political structures. The first significant Finnish representative of the physiocratic ideas[44] was the priest Anders Chydenius, whose economic theory has been regarded as heralding the theory of Adam Smith himself[45]. The focal idea of this economic liberalism was individual liberty treated as a means of economic wealth. The changes that this new doctrine demanded of social life in Finland were the liberation of the economy from politics and allowing the economy to function on individualist conditions. Continuity with the Protestant world–view was assured by the fact that individual liberty was connected with work and that this liberty served as an instrument for wealth that could be conceived of also in collectivist terms, as

---

[43]

The German cultural impact has been important also as far as the spread of natural–rights theories are concerned. Christian Wolff and Samuel Pufendorf – both of German origin – were the representatives of this tradition through whose writings the tradition was mainly transmitted to Finland (Käkönen 1983, 38–39).

[44]

Physiocracy, a doctrine of the supremacy of nature, was originally a French economist movement that was influenced by the Enlightenment. It purported to leave the economy at the mercy of nature, because welfare was seen to grow out of the natural sources of economic life only. Land was treated as the main source of wealth (Friedell 1974, 714).

[45]

Käkönen 1983, 38 ff.

constituting a source of strength for the whole Finnish nation.

Political liberalism, by which I refer to the general European tradition of natural rights, grew out of the general reformist thinking in Finland in the nineteenth century. It became fully developed and politicised as a counterforce to the rising nationalism. Its immediate spiritual source was in Sweden, where liberals had some important achievements in the formulation of the new constitution of 1809[46]. Constitutionalism formed the main form of political liberalism in Finland in the nineteenth century, which can be treated as a reflection of its State–centric political culture.

Constitutionalism was an ideology put forth by the key groups opposing nationalist ideas in the middle of the nineteenth century. The relation between nationalism and liberalism can, by and large, be linked with the socio–cultural division of Finland during the spread of these ideologies. Nationalism was the ideology of the peasants and the rural population, to which the majority of the Finns belonged. It served to raise the Finnish population into a political class and to continue thus the development which had been started by Finnish autonomy. In this context, liberalism became an ideology of minorities that risked suppression by the mass movements caused by nationalism. The emerging liberal ideology thus had its main support among the burghers who were mostly Swedish of origin and constituted a narrow minority of the population. Another focal basis for liberalism was established among the old Swedish aristocracy and political elite, the position of which was threatened by a new Finnish–speaking political class.

The constitutionalist idea of Finland was already created in the beginning of the nineteenth century, but did not become fully politicised until the confrontation between liberals and nationalists. Constitutionalist tones were undoubtedly present in certain early nineteenth century theories of the State[47]. An interpretation of the

---

[46]

Jyränki 1989, 258–282.

[47]

The Swedish professor Israel Hwasser, for instance, argued that Finland had become a State through the peace treaty that the Finnish Estates had concluded with the Russian Emperor in 1809 (Jussila 1987, 69 ff).

Finnish position which was to take on political implications came into being in the middle of the century. According to it, Finland had been annexed to Russia in the form of a province but had become a State by means of a contract made with Tsar Alexander I in Porvoo in 1809. In the old Swedish constitution that could not be amended without the Finnish State organs, an uncontestable argument was found for Finnish Statehood. In the alleged contract between the Finnish Estates and the Russian Tsar, the latter was seen to have confirmed the validity of the Finnish constitution including the Finnish religion and the privileges of the Estates. As a consequence of the Statehood achieved in Porvoo, Finland was alleged to be in a state of real union with Russia. The Finnish position was made more precise by arguing that not having been incorporated into Russia the relationship was based upon an equality between two sovereign States[48]. The main liberal newspaper, the *Helsingfors Dagblad,* published an article upon the international position of Finland in 1863. According to it

> Obliged by existing conditions the Finnish people decided to dissociate itself from its old provincial relationship to Sweden and to enter into a new connection with Russia to which the Emperor Alexander I had invited it... Instead of having earlier been a province, Finland now became a sovereign State with definite connections to the new State to which it was united. And this is the present position of Finland in the law of nations[49].

Finnish liberalism, the emphases of which were on economic liberalism and constitutionalism, had two sets of goals, which in every case were not in harmony with each other. Liberal goals gained a more articulated form in regard to the external position of Finland, which can be explained through the fact that the old Swedish aristocracy

---

[48]

J.J. Nordström was among the first figures to introduce the idea of a Real Union. Jussila (1987) and Jyränki (1989, 408–418) show how nationalist and constitutionalist interpretations of the Finnish State grew in close interaction with each other.

[49]

Jussila 1987, 106.

functioned as the main political support of the doctrine. The constitutionalist and legalist conception of the State was most of all applied to the position of Finland as a part of Russia. This meant that Finnish independence and a separation of Finland from Russia[50] were seen to be the first conditions for all liberal objectives. Liberals emphasised the old Scandinavian connection and wanted Finland to be more oriented towards the West. They praised Swedish conditions as a contrast to the backwardness of Russia. A heavy critique was directed at the policy of the Tsar as well as at the loyalist attitude of Finnish nationalists. The policy of the Tsar as well as the whole connection with Russia was perceived more and more from a legalist position, which emphasised the need for compatibility with the Finnish constitution.

With the exception of the language question, where liberals opposed the nationalist idea of a national language, liberal and nationalist programmes for State internal social and political reforms were close to each other. The necessity of economic and social reforms was given a key emphasis in liberal programmes that started from the advantage of economic liberties for the whole society as well as for its individual members. In contrast to the strict nationalist policy concerning culture and language, general tolerance and wider liberties were demanded so as to transform this hitherto strictly regulated society. Liberty of religion was among these demands as well as freedom of the press[51].

While nationalists emphasised the Estates as the main symbol of Finnish Statehood, liberals were committed to the Finnish constitution and to constitutional regulation of State powers in general[52]. The liberal

---

[50]

In the early liberal discussion, the return of Finland to the Swedish connection was also proposed (Pulma 1993, 468).

[51]

Borg 1965, 12–20.

[52]

See eg. the first Liberal Party Programme (Borg 1965, 12–20). Liberals wanted to get confirmed the position of the constitution in norm hierarchy through the very text of the constitution. This was finally achieved in the Parliamentary Act of the year 1869 (Jyränki 1989, 416 ff).

idea of government according to which the government appeared as an arbitrator of divergent interests started to emerge in Finnish political discussion some years before Finland became independent[53]. From this conception, it was not a long way to the separation of powers doctrine that constituted the key liberal position in the process of constitution-making.

Finland as a Sovereignty of the People

The third political tradition that has had a significant impact upon the modern understanding of political community in Finland is a radicalism which in the Finnish case drew strength from the socialist and social democrat movements. Socialist ideas were introduced into Finland gradually, having their first springboard in the more practically oriented organisations aiming at the improvement of working conditions. Towards the end of the nineteenth century, the ideology started being applied to the understanding of the whole social and political system. The spread of socialist ideas was connected with social changes in Finland caused by a growing industrialism and an extensive growth in population. Structural changes in the sources of livelihood and a large migration into towns and rural municipalities constituted the basis for dissatisfaction with existing political conditions[54].

The birth of radicalism did not immediately cause a division in the political field. Demands for universal suffrage and for an equal treatment of the whole population brought the movement close to nationalism and during the period of Finnish autonomy, radicals strove for cooperation with either nationalists or liberals. The first socialist party was established in Finland in 1899 and its programme, as the ideology in Finland more generally, was influenced by the Austrian socialist movement led by Karl Kautsky[55]. The general strike

---

[53]

Lindman 1968, 256 ff.

[54]

Paasivirta 1978, 322.

[55]

Borg 1965, 29; Soikkanen 1966, 57 ff.

of 1905 and the parliamentary reform of 1906 have been treated as a decisive breakthrough for this radical thinking[56]. The civil war in 1918 ended up with a strict division of Finnish social and political life.

The radical conception of a political community was based upon the idea of popular sovereignty. Giving political power to the people was seen to involve the raising of parliament to a supreme position and the creation of a referendum system to be employed in addition to the representation. According to the radicals, political power should be regulated by the majorities directly and not through a system based upon historical or constitutional restraints. The roots of Finnish radicalism were in Marxist atheism and in Marxist economic social theory rather than in Christian humanism[57]. Therefore it was relatively easy for Finnish radicalism to adapt itself to the goals of nationalism and liberalism, which centred around the Finnish State. Before Finnish independence, the defence of the Finnish autonomy was the primary goal of Finnish socialism and socialists were prepared to work in favour of this goal together with their domestic adversaries[58]. The other main task of these Finnish radicals was seen to be to break away from the structures of the class society that was based upon relations to the

---

[56]

Ersson 1987, 120.

[57]

The core of the latter was more political, putting the emphasis on solidarity of all the people, while the Marxists worked from the class society that was of economic origin and should be dissolved by using the State as an instrument. The first programme of the Social Democratic Party (1903) was based upon a revisionist Marxism in the manner of the programmes of its German and Austrian counterparts. There was a separate Christian Workers' Association, which, however, remained short–lived (Nousiainen 1985, 45).

[58]

Soikkanen (1966, 58) points out a doctrinal reason for this and maintains that the Russian Empire was considered as an earlier stage in the historical process than the bourgeois democracy that the Finns aspired to. Therefore, support given to the latter appeared legitimate also to the socialists.

means of production [59]. In the radical doctrine, history appeared as a history of class *conflicts,* and it was the collective consciousness, based upon *material* conditions of living, that was seen to be the basis of political society.

The autumn revolution in Russia in 1917, and the radicalisation of the policy–line of the Finnish socialists, contributed to the outbreak of a civil war in Finland, which led to a split in the socialist party[60]. Cooperation between socialists and non–socialists became more difficult, which reflected itself also in the process of constitution making in Finland during the years 1917–1919.

The Forms of the Finnish State are Confirmed

The forms of the Finnish State, gaining their focal contents in the Form of Government Act of 1919, are based upon the three political traditions introduced above as well as upon the political situation of that time. When Finland gained independence, it had a government of its own consisting of a Senate and of a Parliament that represented a high level of modernity in that time. Nationalist and liberal arguments upon the forms of the new Finnish State took as their point of departure the existing structures among which the old Swedish constitution had an important role. Radicals endeavoured to change the established system with the assistance of the new Parliament which functioned as their political bastion. The civil war, which was lost by the political Left, deepened the gap between the two political camps and made the radical position more difficult to uphold in the constitutional process.

As a result of the political development of the years 1917–1918, the process of constitution–making became a conflict between the political Right and Left so that the Right was further divided into a conservative block and into a block that was more willing to change

---

[59]

The programme of the Social Democratic Party (Borg 1965, 31 ff).

[60]

As a result of the division, the Finnish Communist Party was established in the summer of 1918 (Jyränki 1978, 33).

political structures. The latter was at this stage, however, more nationalist than liberal in its orientation. The Right as a whole demanded a firm government and that certain checks be put on political life and decision–making. The idea of a firm government referred, above all, to an independent Head of State who would guarantee a firm and balanced State policy and prevent the policy from being based upon temporary impulses[61]. The emphasis put upon the role of the government in the maintenance of the social and political order was reinforced by the civil war. While the positions of nationalism and liberalism were united in the effort to prevent a monopolisation of political power by Parliament, the deeper reasons for this effort revealed two different conceptions.

One aspect of the position adopted by the political Right was based upon the nationalist idea of the State as a cultural and historical unity. These arguments derived from the idea that as a counterbalance to the will of majorities there should be an organ that stood for a national continuity and tradition and would bring in the voice of history. Even in the parliamentary reform of 1906, certain mechanisms had been established to slow down decision–making and to prevent the power of single majorities[62]. A necessary level of governmental independence was seen as being achieved through a Head of State who would counteract the risks connected with parliamentary power.

There was no unitary nationalist position as far as the constitutional character of the Head of State was concerned. One of the key conceptions connected with this position was, however, that the Finnish form of government should be a republic, in which the powers

---

[61]

Jyränki 1981, 37 ff.

[62]

A specific 'general affairs' committee was established in Parliament to moderate the transfer into a one–chamber structure and to slow down the legislative process. Another check that was written into the legislative system was the possibility for one–third of the MP's to vote a bill over to be dealt with by a new parliament after the next general election (Helander 1990, 1–5).

of the Russian Tsar would be transferred to a Finnish president[63]. The republic was seen to represent a Finnish form of government instead of a monarchy that was the form of the old Swedish constitution[64]. By 'independent Head of State' was meant a president who would have concrete political powers and who would act independently of Parliament. The president would, however, be a real republican president by getting his mandate directly from the people. At a later stage, the idea of an independent Head of State was supported also by arguments of foreign policy and the external representation of the country. According to these arguments a Head of State would bring the necessary unity and historical continuity into Finland's relations with foreign countries[65].

The other part of the position adopted by the political Right stemmed from the view of government as an arbitrator between divergent interests and from the separation–of–powers doctrine, which arose out of this view. These conceptions originated in the liberal ideology. The need for a firm government was seen to have its basis in the necessity of dividing the use of political powers between different State organs, which then effectively balanced each other. This was felt to be the best guarantee of the liberty of individuals and minorities[66]. A proper separation of powers was regarded as requiring an effective

---

[63]

Lindman 1968, 185 ff.

[64]

At one stage in the constitutional process nationalists opted for a republican form of government because it had become the new form of government in Russia from which Finland had not entirely then separated itself (Lindman 1968, 162 ff).

[65]

The alternative monarchical proposition for the Form of Government was among other things supported by the idea that it would establish a firm relationship with Germany (Lindman 1969,49; Paasivirta 1957, 262 ff).

[66]

Lindman 1968, 256 ff and 1969, 358. The role of the separation of powers doctrine is discussed in the context of the Finnish constitution, for instance, by Jyränki (1981, 24 ff).

counterforce to Parliament. This counterforce was found in an independent Head of State. In the first stages of the constitutional process, this position seemed to imply the denial of the principle of parliamentarism in the Finnish constitution, but later the combination of these doctrines was accepted as the focal basis of the constitution.

The liberal view of the Head of State was very different from the nationalist one outlined above. The conception of presidential powers that emanated from the view of government as an arbitrator was a conception of a moderating *pouvoir neutre*. It was seen to be the task of this moderating force to safeguard the balance between the different parts of the State power and to stand, by means of this role, as a guarantee of the rights of individuals and minorities. One important instrument by means of which the president was supposed to implement this position was connected with the induction and discharge of State powers. Seen from this point of view, the president's right to dissolve Parliament appeared to be in a key position[67]. The right to pick Cabinet ministers and to relieve them of their posts was demanded for the President as well. Even if this position implied that the presidential powers were firm enough, it was a question of powers standing outside the political machinery rather than being a part of it. The president was also assumed to be safeguarding the functional capacities of the political machinery itself.

The alternative conception of the Finnish State, argued against the position represented by the Right, was based upon the denial of the political structures of Finnish autonomy as the legitimate forms of the Finnish State. The Finnish Left advocated a conception of Finland

---

[67]

The other part of the powers to be used in dissolving Parliament, ie. the right to order new elections, was supported by a more nationalist argument about the president's right to 'appeal to the people'. The role of the president as a *pouvoir modérateur* has been analysed and developed in more scientific terms by Sven Lindman. In addition to the two powers connected with the role here, he also saw the power to nominate a person to certain offices to be in harmony with it (Lindman 1969, 22 and 1979, 47).

based upon popular sovereignty and thus demanded a decisive change in the political forms of autonomy. Radicals denied even the capacity of the State organs of the period of autonomy to function as temporary holders of Finnish power and demanded that Parliament should act as a constitutional conference as soon as it had declared itself as the holder of the supreme power in 1917. In terms of a political system, the radical idea of popular sovereignty implied that political powers were one and should belong undividedly to Parliament. As far as the details of the organisation were concerned, the Swiss governmental system seemed to have constituted the main ideal for the Finnish radicals in the formative years of the constitution[68]. This meant that the executive power was to be given to an organ that should be nothing more than a delegation nominated and controlled by Parliament. The chairman of the delegation could be called the President of the Republic, but he should not have any powers independent of Parliament. According to this conception judicial powers should also be controlled by the Representation.

The organs of the Finnish State were finally put together in the first Form of Government Act in 1919. Viewed against the historical backgrounds recounted in this chapter, this Act represented the first purely national declaration of Finnish political identity by bringing the various historical traditions together at a high political level. Finland was declared to be a sovereign republic, whose constitution was confirmed in the Form of Government Act and in other constitutional acts (Form of Government Act, §1). The forms of the State were firmly bound to the constitution which, as far as its status was concerned, expressed a hybrid of legal positivism and the natural–rights tradition. The constitution adopted a particular position in the legislative hierarchy as it could be amended, or exceptions be made to it, only in accordance with the forms that were given in it. On the other hand, there were no parts in the constitution that could not be amended, which emphasised the sovereignty of the legislator in this respect[69]. A list of

---

[68]

Lindman 1969, 29 ff.

[69]

Jyränki 1989, 492.

civil rights and liberties was incorporated into the constitution, but the role of these rights and liberties remained highly unclear. Being in the first place guidelines for the administration, they were not, generally speaking, meant to bind the legislative.

A dualism of the same kind made itself apparent as far as the use of State powers was concerned. The Form of Government Act (§2) began with the idea of popular sovereignty as it was stated that *in Finland all power is vested in the people*. The stipulation was then moderated, or put into constitutional forms as it was then explained, by the principle of the separation of powers. The latter part of the same paragraph divided power in Finland into a legislative, executive and judicial power and empowered the President to lead the use of the executive powers and to exercise legislative powers together with Parliament. A Council of Ministers exercised executive powers together with the President, whereas independent courts were given the use of judicial powers.

The idea of a President as an important counterforce to Parliament was confirmed by the Form of Government Act. The concrete powers given to the President expressed both nationalist and liberal reasoning. The President became a representative of national unity and continuity through the long tenures of office (six years) connected with this post and through the prohibition on any limitations in their number[70]. The core of the presidential powers was in foreign policy, the sovereign leadership of which was given to the President. Otherwise, the role of the President corresponded to the liberal conception of a *pouvoir neutre* according to which the President was responsible for the *forms* of politics and not for their contents. The President was given the right to appoint members of the Cabinet. A political practice was developed according to which the President had also, at least, a symbolical right to relieve them from their posts. The President was also entitled to

---

[70]

Jyränki 1981, 54. The length of the presidential tenure of office is six years and before 1991 the constitution did not limit the number of period of office that each president could have. In connection with the reform of presidential elections in 1991, the number of possible presidential periods of office was limited to two.

dissolve Parliament and to declare new elections[71].

The use of legislative powers was subordinated to many checks that purported to prevent the power of bare single majorities. Two of them had been established in connection with the parliamentary reform of 1906. These were the powers of the general affairs committee established in Parliament and the right of one–third of the MP's to postpone a bill to a new Parliament. The Form of Government Act still demanded the President's confirmation for every legislative proposal before coming into force. The President, however, could not defeat a proposal, the significance of his legislative veto being its postponement to a new Parliament. The right to make legislative proposals was also given to the President in the form of the right to present Government bills to Parliament.

Conclusions

Several things have worked in favour of a State centric political identity in Finland. The powers of the Catholic Church were generally not in conflict with secular rule in the Nordic countries. There were, on the contrary, many things that reinforced the political unity of Finland even before the Reformation. Finland constituting one bishopric and one jurisdictional domain in the Swedish connection were among the most important of them. In addition to its centralising effects upon political structures, the Reformation raised the idea of a Finnish language as a foundation of religious life in the country. Once Finland had been attached to the Russian empire as an autonomous Grand Duchy, with a legal and administrative system separating her from the ruling power, the necessary elements for a great nationalist awakening were there.

Collectivist forces constitute still the backbone of the Finnish

---

[71]

Jyränki (1981, 183–184) shows that while the first of these powers originated in liberal reasoning, and in Benjamin Constant's thinking in particular, the latter had a slightly different doctrinal background. It was connected with the idea of a more powerful ruler having the right to appeal to the people when the policy of Parliament was seen to be going in a 'wrong' direction.

State. The formation of a modern State in Finland cannot be seen as an uprising of the third Estate against feudal structures of power in the name of individual liberties. Nor can it be seen as a revolution of the whole society against an ancient regime in the name of political rights. The Finnish process of State–building was basically of a cultural nature giving expression to the birth of a new nation and to its self–assertion. The fervour connected with the birth of the new political identity left its imprint on other modern political ideologies that spread into Finland in the nineteenth century. Extreme individualism has been as rejected as a position in the political field of Finland as has revolutionary Communism.

brings the study of Finland into the sphere of th
European unification. It is among the last tasks o
the position from which Finland approaches the curr
project. By means of the historical analysis of Finnish
something can also be said about future Finnish priorities in the projec

The Beginning: The External Identity of Finland Takes Shape

There were two leading conceptions about the external identity of Finland even before Finnish independence. These conceptions were more or less based upon the political traditions that constituted the foundations of the modern State in Finland. The first decisive difference between these traditions was seen in connection with their relations towards Russia. Once Finland had become independent, two different lines of policy were created based on the two different views of international politics and of the Finnish place therein.

The nationalist conception of Finland was, from its early stages, directed against the Swedish influence on the country. Loyalty to and respect for the Russian power became inherent characteristics of the nationalist position from the beginning[1]. In addition to internal reasons emanating from the nationalist logic, the need for loyalty was justified by reasons drawn from international politics. Even in the beginning of Finnish autonomy, leading Finnish civil servants argued that Russian rule in Finland was a geopolitical necessity. Loyalty towards Russia would, according to this conception, bring advantages to Russia as well as to Finland as it would, by safeguarding the north–western border of Russia, reinforce the privileged and autonomous position of Finland[2]. Finnish nationalism grew into its full stature in the middle of the nineteenth century. J.V. Snellman rounded off the nationalist world-view in his campaign against the Finnish liberals, who had, in connection with the Crimean War, for the first time expressed their

---

1 Korhonen 1966, 11–12.

2 Korhonen 1966, 12; Paasivirta 1978, 72.

The Political Identity of a Borderland: An Analysis of the External Identity of Finland

Introduction

For over forty years, the 'Finnish line of foreign policy' constituted a permanent foundation for the political life of the country. 'The Line' became almost a part of the national heritage. Honoured and celebrated, it connoted Finnish independence with a special reference to the Finnish wars of the 1940's and the high toll of sacrifice the wars exacted. The integrity of this Paasikivi–Kekkonen line was under the particular protection of the two Finnish presidents, whose names it bore.

What the Finnish people learned was that where sovereignty was wanted there had to be neutrality and sympathy for the Mighty Neighbour in the East. State sovereignty as the highest value of the people was seen as something distributed in a rude game between States, where being humble was the lot of a small State. In the divided world of the superpowers the values expressed by the Finnish line of policy appeared legitimate and life with it was, in a figurative sense, safe and easy.

This chapter purports to complete the analysis of the political identity of Finland by delineating the construction of this identity through Finnish foreign policy. The main Finnish doctrines of foreign policy contribute to a firm State–centricism that has been argued as forming the key characteristic of political culture in Finland. By discussing the ways in which the relations of Finland with its political surroundings have been perceived, the chapter brings the book back to its original point of departure. By means of a simple division, or categorisation, of Western European political cultures the work purports to make the deadlocks of the current integration project comprehensible. The analysis of the external identity of Finland finally

brings the study of Finland into the sphere of the current efforts towards European unification. It is among the last tasks of this work to clarify the position from which Finland approaches the current integration project. By means of the historical analysis of Finnish identity, something can also be said about future Finnish priorities in the project.

The Beginning: The External Identity of Finland Takes Shape

There were two leading conceptions about the external identity of Finland even before Finnish independence. These conceptions were more or less based upon the political traditions that constituted the foundations of the modern State in Finland. The first decisive difference between these traditions was seen in connection with their relations towards Russia. Once Finland had become independent, two different lines of policy were created based on the two different views of international politics and of the Finnish place therein.

The nationalist conception of Finland was, from its early stages, directed against the Swedish influence on the country. Loyalty to and respect for the Russian power became inherent characteristics of the nationalist position from the beginning[1]. In addition to internal reasons emanating from the nationalist logic, the need for loyalty was justified by reasons drawn from international politics. Even in the beginning of Finnish autonomy, leading Finnish civil servants argued that Russian rule in Finland was a geopolitical necessity. Loyalty towards Russia would, according to this conception, bring advantages to Russia as well as to Finland as it would, by safeguarding the north–western border of Russia, reinforce the privileged and autonomous position of Finland[2]. Finnish nationalism grew into its full stature in the middle of the nineteenth century. J.V. Snellman rounded off the nationalist world-view in his campaign against the Finnish liberals, who had, in connection with the Crimean War, for the first time expressed their

---

[1]   Korhonen 1966, 11–12.

[2]   Korhonen 1966, 12; Paasivirta 1978, 72.

6 The Political Identity of a Borderland: An Analysis of the External Identity of Finland

Introduction

For over forty years, the 'Finnish line of foreign policy' constituted a permanent foundation for the political life of the country. 'The Line' became almost a part of the national heritage. Honoured and celebrated, it connoted Finnish independence with a special reference to the Finnish wars of the 1940's and the high toll of sacrifice the wars exacted. The integrity of this Paasikivi–Kekkonen line was under the particular protection of the two Finnish presidents, whose names it bore.

What the Finnish people learned was that where sovereignty was wanted there had to be neutrality and sympathy for the Mighty Neighbour in the East. State sovereignty as the highest value of the people was seen as something distributed in a rude game between States, where being humble was the lot of a small State. In the divided world of the superpowers the values expressed by the Finnish line of policy appeared legitimate and life with it was, in a figurative sense, safe and easy.

This chapter purports to complete the analysis of the political identity of Finland by delineating the construction of this identity through Finnish foreign policy. The main Finnish doctrines of foreign policy contribute to a firm State–centricism that has been argued as forming the key characteristic of political culture in Finland. By discussing the ways in which the relations of Finland with its political surroundings have been perceived, the chapter brings the book back to its original point of departure. By means of a simple division, or categorisation, of Western European political cultures the work purports to make the deadlocks of the current integration project comprehensible. The analysis of the external identity of Finland finally

wishes for the separation of Finland from Russia[3]. Snellman accused these people of unrealistic wishes by stating that:

> One can always dream about any alliance whatsoever but one thing that is sure is that a people that is looking for its fate in the struggle of war without being able to affect its solution in the slightest, is an imprudent people and deserves an imprudent fate, a bad sudden death......If I had the power I would like to impress indelibly on my compatriots' mind that a nation should only rely upon itself. This confidence includes a nation's neither asking for, nor trying to reach, anything other than things for the achievement and protection of which it has enough power[4].

Snellman, who was the main ideologist of the nationalist movement, and of the later Finnish party, based his thinking on international life upon German nationalism. Snellman's international thinking was derived from the idea that the State is its own purpose. Therefore, the existence and independence of the State have, according to him, to be regarded as the supreme norm and goal of every ruler. Snellman emphasised that the fate of every State was decided in war in the last resort. In questions of war and peace, the national character of any particular State was thus said to have priority over considerations of natural law or morality[5].

The Snellmanian position was brought into the twentieth century by the Old Finns, the main part of the Finnish Party from which the critics of its loyalist policy had broken away. One of its key figures, Y.S. Yrjö–Koskinen, crystallised the core position of this party in terms which can be argued to have formed one of the main norms of Finnish foreign policy since then:

---

[3]

    Korhonen 1966, 16; Paasivirta 1978, 187. These wishes did not yet constitute a broad political opinion but were limited to certain closed groups.

[4]

    Snellman's article Sota vai rauha Suomelle (War or Peace to Finland) from 1863 is published in Suomen historian dokumentteja 2 1970, 108–110.

[5]

    Snellman V 1901, 328–335.

History has placed us in such a position with respect to the great empire that we will have to live in friendship and harmony with the Russians..... But if we would above all like to protect our national standing, we are not allowed to forget that we are to a great extent dependent on the friendly sentiments of the neighbouring nation and, perhaps even more, on the favourable opinion of the common ruler[6].

The historical counterforce to the nationalist tradition arose, as far as the external identity of Finland was concerned, from the liberal tradition. Representatives of this tradition started from Sweden and Western Europe as the right political context for Finland. The liberal tradition of foreign policy can be traced to the criticism that was raised in certain emerging liberal groups against the situation arising during the Crimean War[7]. Liberals approached international relations, including relations between Finland and Russia, more in terms of legal rights and obligations than the nationalists did. Their conception of the political future of Europe was more optimistic than the one maintained by the nationalists. In accordance with the pacifist sentiments characterising liberal movements in the middle of the nineteenth century, one of the leading liberals in Finland, Leo Mechelin, introduced the idea of a diplomatic league of nations as an instrument of the European peace process[8]. A system of international law and an international society led by Western Europe formed the cornerstones of the international doctrine of Finnish liberals. Due to its special position in the Russian Empire, Finland tended to be conceived of as a subject in this system with an equal position and rights.

---

[6]

Y.S. Yrjö–Koskinen's speech in a party meeting of the Finnish Party (29.10.1901) published in Suomen historian dokumentteja 2 1970, 248–250.

[7]

These liberals demanded in their main newspaper, the *Helsingfors Dagblad*, that Finland should be declared neutral in order to keep itself outside the war between Russia and the main Western European States (Paasivirta 1978, 204–209; the article can be found in Suomen historian dokumentteja 2 1970, 107–108).

[8]

Paasivirta 1978, 226.

Liberals, in general, emphasised the particularity of the Finnish position and demanded the largest possible distance from the Russian government. Their conception of a Real Union as the governmental relationship between Finland and Russia was introduced in the middle of the nineteenth century[9]. The policy of the Russian Tsar started to be evaluated more and more from the point of view of the Finnish constitution, which brought liberals into continuing conflicts with the nationalists and with their loyalist policy. In contrast to the policy of concessions, characterising the nationalists' attitude towards the acts of Russification that began to be brought about by the Tsar towards the end of the century, the liberals launched a policy of resistance.

The liberal and nationalist traditions have constituted the historical framework for Finnish foreign policy. The international doctrine of the radical tradition, maintained by Finnish socialists, could not compete with the above–mentioned concepts that were created some decades before it came into being[10]. Historically, radicals have had to adjust themselves to a foreign policy derived from a nationalist or a liberal core. This can be seen as a part of the compromise made by the Finnish radicals in favour of the Finnish State[11]. The internationalist and pacifist orientations of radical movements in Europe have reflected themselves in the Finnish movement as a belief in international cooperation and in a permanent detente and peace process between the States. Before Finnish independence, radicals were divided between the nationalist and liberal position as far as their consent to foreign policy was concerned[12].

---

[9]

The idea of the 'Finnish' constitution was born in the middle of the nineteenth century (Jussila 1987, 84–87).

[10]

Soikkanen 1966, 57 ff; Apunen 1987, 154.

[11]

See pp. 131–133.

[12]

One part of the radical movement allied itself with liberals starting from the Finnish autonomy as the focal goal of foreign policy. The other part wanted to safeguard the existence of an independent Socialist Party which brought it closer to nationalist policy (Soikkanen 1966, 58).

During the first decades of Finnish independence the main traditions of foreign policy were blurred by the establishment of the Communist regime in Russia. For two decades, the Left–Right division influenced the thinking about the newly established Soviet State. The old loyalist position connected with the nationalist conception of foreign policy was weakened and a simplified *Machtpolitik* became its core[13]. Liberals and radicals were united by their general internationalist tendencies, which in the pre–war period expressed themselves mainly in Scandinavianism and in a confidence in the League of Nations as a solution for collective security. These traditions diverged, however, when it came to the Soviet State. Liberals, in general, perceived this State much more as a constant threat to Finland, while the radical attitude, even if incoherent, was more sympathetic towards the Eastern neighbour.

For many reasons, official policy–making was closed off to any alternative views after the Finnish involvement in the Second World War and the old nationalist position revived to form the core of Finnish foreign policy. The policy of concessions constituted a very natural ground for a more systematically structured realistic doctrine, which was legitimated by the temper of the time. The official Finnish doctrine, known as the Paasikivi–Kekkonen doctrine according to its constitutive figures, entwined itself around the principles of neutrality and a particular relationship with the Soviet Union. The goals of foreign policy as well as the identity of the State they issued from became very widely accepted in Finland. It could be argued that the late sixties and the seventies witnessed in this respect a political homogeneity, the depth of which lacks any parallel.

The purpose of this chapter being to analyse Finnish preparedness and priorities with respect to European unification it is necessary to go into the details of the external identity of Finland during the Cold War. Hence, in this chapter I am going to explicate how political realism constituted the doctrinal ground for Finnish identity and how certain

---

[13]

Kallenautio 1985, 82–86. The idea of kinship gained more ground as a part of nationalism, which was another thing that reduced the significance of the principles of the earlier loyalism (Paasivirta 1984, 227).

more specific policy–lines, like the policy of neutrality, were based upon it[14]. This political identity was internally inflexible and any change in its concepts or emphases was strictly sanctioned by the President. Therefore, the legitimacy of a realist foreign policy was not questioned nor were alternatives sought for. The world–view started to break down when the Cold War with its bipolar system of power came to an end. A normalisation of the debate on foreign policy and an open evaluation of the values and goals of the policy did not get going before Finland was pushed into making important decisions in foreign policy. The consequences that this period of transition has had for Finnish identity will be dealt with last of all in this chapter.

Sovereignty, Minority and the Self–Sufficiency of Neutrality

The Finnish postwar doctrine of foreign policy will be elucidated through the thoughts set down by the two Finnish presidents most involved in it[15]. Committed broadly to the same doctrine, they were very different with regard to their ideological backgrounds, personal characteristics and conceptions of their own role as leaders of foreign policy. President J.K. Paasikivi, an elderly statesman and banker, with his roots in the traditionalist Conservative Party, nonetheless shared strong liberalist and constitutionalist convictions[16]. The two Finnish

---

14

    Palonen approaches Finnish foreign policy from this point of view in his *The Art of the Possible on the Periphery*. J.K. Paasikivi and Urho Kekkonen in the Realpolitik Tradition (Palonen 1987).

15

    Analysing a political doctrine through the political thinking of two individuals is quite legitimate in this particular case taking into account the very specific position that the two post–war presidents had with respect to Finnish foreign policy.

16

    This position was influenced by Paasikivi's active participation in the bank sector as well as by his moderate and mediating character. The last–mentioned quality even expressed itself with regard to key value commitments: 'But isn't it after all so that the purpose of every nation,

wars had, however, manifested the urgent necessity of 'realism' in Finnish political thinking. This obliged Paasikivi, who had risen from the office of prime minister to president, to teach a doctrine that in the first place required self–discipline from himself as well as from the people. Due to the confused political situation resulting from the Finnish wars with the Soviet Union and the unquestioned authority of Paasikivi in that situation, the doctrine was widely accepted and controversies about foreign policy disappeared.

This doctrine, introducing international politics in terms of political realism, grew out of the tenets of historical necessity and the objectivity of the laws of politics[17]. The doctrine had a direct connection with the nationalist thinking that had an influence upon Paasikivi through the *National Coalition Party*[18]. While the doctrine was not set out in more detail until the period in office of his successor, President Kekkonen, nevertheless Paasikivi set forth the very bases of Finnish foreign policy in one of the first speeches he made after the war:

> One historian–thinker has said that the recognition of facts is the beginning of all wisdom...Every nation has its own facts and its own national problems and questions of life...we have to recognise the facts which have an effect on our life and future[19].

---

big and small, is *a human being*, his life and happiness?' (Paasikivi 1957, 23).

[17]

The Hegelian concept of historical determinism was transmitted to Paasikivi by one of his spiritual fathers, J.V. Snellman, and with the realist tradition he had become acquainted with through the works of Meinecke, Treitschke and Nicolson (see Patomäki 1991, 88). Paasikivi also declared that he had bought a work of Thucydides in order to develop a broader perspective on the events of his own time (Paasikivi 1966, 65).

[18]

Paasikivi was well acquainted with Snellman's ideas concerning international politics. Another representative of the historical nationalist movement who had a great impact upon Paasikivi's thinking was Y.S. Yrjö–Koskinen (Hakalehto 1970).

[19]

Paasikivi 1966, 9.

In these initial phases, the doctrine applied the realistic world–view in a narrow sense. It based itself mainly on the argument of the peculiar character of international relations and applied the consequences of this alleged state of affairs almost exclusively to the making of Soviet policy. The limits of Paasikivi's realism were well illustrated in the much–quoted statement made by him according to which the Kremlin was not a magistrates' court[20]. The doctrine was nonetheless characterised by a sense of relativism, largely as a consequence of the basically open and vacillating stand taken by Paasikivi[21]. In spite of the narrowness of its argument, the doctrine appealed to a very deep level of Finnish political understanding. Paasikivi could not have been more outspoken in the teacher's role:

> The sense of political realism has never been among the strongest characteristics of the Finnish people. Things are believed to be as they are wished to be and action is taken as though what is wished for were true....[In contrast] Peace, harmony and a neighbourly relationship of confidence with the great Soviet Union is the first precept of our civil life[22].

These constitutive assumptions were not questioned during the long period in office of President Kekkonen, but the external surroundings of Finland became, on the contrary, caught in ever more detail in terms of realism. When Kekkonen became president in the year 1956, he was still in the middle of his political career. His political personality was not as uncontroversial as the role of the old statesman Paasikivi had been in the very end of his career. By means of the

---

20

Eg. Kekkonen (1967, 72) quoting Paasikivi and referring further to Snellman.

21

Paasikivi, in spite of the firmness and absoluteness (one could also say 'anger') characteristic of his public appearances right after the wars, is known for his conciliatory and conversational way of making politics. He also often turned against the key realist concepts by criticising them and evaluating their potential risks (Paasikivi 1957, 80).

22

Paasikivi 1966, 33 and 10.

Paasikivi doctrine, Kekkonen strengthened his own leadership and established good relations with the leaders of the Soviet Union. Paasikivi's name and authority were still, long after his death, used to legitimise the continuance of the policy–line that was now in the hands of President Kekkonen[23].

The realist doctrine had its major implications for practical politics during Kekkonen's period in office, as the development of the postwar international system got off to a good start. The doctrine was adjusted to the conditions of the Cold War as well as to the personal commitments of Urho Kekkonen. In Kekkonen's thinking the basis for realism was formed by a populist nationalism leading to strong demands for national unity, particularly in foreign relations. Kekkonen did not refer systematically in his writings to any of the realist writers of his time[24], but at least Treitschke and Meinecke seem, in addition to Snellman, to have influenced his thinking on international relations[25]. Kekkonen's conception of the State reflected his ideological commitment to German nationalism[26]. This meant among other things that the independence and sovereignty of a State was, in the first place, given the meaning of external freedom[27]. This being the case, relations

---

[23]

Kekkonen 1967, 63–65; 394;. 425–426.

[24]

The speeches and writings of Urho Kekkonen, which in the most comprehensive and declaratory way manifest the tradition of political realism in international relations, place themselves in the immediate postwar years (eg. Kekkonen, 1977).

[25]

Palonen 1987, 107 ff.

[26]

Kekkonen prepared his doctoral thesis in part in Germany (1931–32). On the concept of the State, see, eg. Kekkonen 1972, 34 ff.

[27]

Kekkonen 1977, 9. The difference in this regard between the conceptions of Paasikivi and Kekkonen becomes illumined if one compares their speeches. When Kekkonen leans systematically on the freedom of the State as the primary purpose of political activity, Paasikivi problematises this thought by bringing the sovereignty of *the nation* and

between States were ultimately determined by relations of power, which elevated control of others and the promotion and protection of one's own national interests to be the first guidelines of a foreign policy.

International hostility, approached first to a great extent as a peculiarity of one epoch, took on a more and more necessitarian character as if it belonged to the structure of inter–state relations. Yet, in spite of the fact that competition and conflict were given a permanent character in international relations, the typical realist metaphor of 'anarchy' never appeared as a leading argument in the Finnish doctrine. The most persistant relic of realism was in its very purity, the argument of national interest, which demanded a very specific system of morality as the basis of foreign policy. When sufficiently drummed into the Finnish public, the hard core of realism was left in the background, though it continued to constitute a basis for the central concepts of foreign policy developed later. There were, above all, three things that were seen to be of primary importance in defining Finnish national interests. In addition to the identity that devolved on Finland in the realist world–view, a small State identity, Finnish interests had to be guided by history and geography.

If President Paasikivi left behind a demand for realism in Finnish foreign policy, the demand for neutrality was a personal creation of President Kekkonen. The policy of neutrality became the dominant element of Finnish international identity from the 1960's. Finnish neutrality should, however, be understood in the realist framework, which makes neutrality an individual security solution in the first place. Taking this doctrinal basis into account, it is easier to understand the great readiness of Finland to exchange neutrality for active participation in the European Union.

The Great Finnish Neutrality

Neutrality has constituted a part of Finnish foreign policy in several periods. Conceptually, it has not been a question of the same type of

---

the citizens' rights up to the same level as State sovereignty (Paasikivi 1966, eg.81; Kekkonen 1977, eg.7 and 13).

policy and identity, but the conception of neutrality has varied from time to time[28]. One could therefore argue that neutrality does not constitute the core of Finnish international identity in a historical sense, but that there are other elements that are still more constitutive. Variations in the content of neutrality are, among other things, indicated in the fact that neutrality has not always been as purely a security-political solution as it was during the postwar time. Considerations of security have, however, always functioned as the main arguments for the policy of neutrality, and through the discourse on State security, neutrality can be connected with two very focal identities of Finland. Geopolitical factors, the small size of Finland and its immediate proximity to a Great Power, have functioned as the historical reasons for this policy.

Neutrality therefore became one of the dominant features of postwar Finnish foreign policy. Its meaning and legitimacy grew from the realist doctrine and from the emphasis that this doctrine puts upon State security. Small State identity and geography were the closer elements which, through a realist interpretation, functioned as the immediate basis for this policy. The small State identity of Finland leans essentially on the world–view of power politics, where States are defined on the basis of their political and strategic capacities[29]. A Finnish small State identity had previously been used to legitimise a

---

[28]

In the very beginning of its independence Finland adopted a somewhat vague policy of neutrality (Kallenautio 1985, 31). This policy indicated sympathy towards Scandinavia and Great Britain and a distancing from Russia and Germany. The policy of neutrality that Finland conducted in the 1920's and 1930's had a similar content. During this period, a military alliance with another neutral State, ie. Sweden, was seen as being allowed by the concept of neutrality.

[29]

According to Hans Morgenthau, the elements of national power are geography, natural resources, industrial capacity, military preparedness, population, national character, national morale, the quality of diplomacy and the quality of government (Morgenthau 1960, 110 ff).

somewhat reserved foreign policy[30]. Urho Kekkonen created a policy of neutrality upon this identity in the 1960's. Neutrality can be seen to have worked in two directions in the divided world of the Cold War. For the Eastern bloc, it was a signal that Finland would be impartial in international crises despite its social and economic adherence to Western values. And to the Western bloc, it was a message of belonging despite the Finnish Treaty of Friendship, Co-operation and Mutual Assistance with the Soviet Union. Neutrality was reconciled with this treaty by means of an interpretation according to which the treaty both presupposed and recognised the neutral status of Finland[31].

Kekkonen's view of the international position of Finland was that because Finland was small, it had to adjust itself to the political conditions laid down by the Great Powers. A primary fact in these conditions was the proximity of Finland to the Soviet Union and the long border they shared. And in these conditions, he saw that neutrality was the necessary policy line for a small State with respect to its security. In the Finnish case, the choice of neutrality did not have any underlying altruistic purposes connected with world peace or with a change in the bipolar system of power. Neutrality was introduced as a policy-line demanded by Finnish national interests and as such, it was seen to be a solution to the immediate Finnish demands for security. Kekkonen expressed the logic of neutrality, for instance, by saying that:

---

[30] A classical statement that also both postwar presidents tended to use, was a comment that originated in the works of J.V.Snellman: 'A nation shall not ask for, nor try to reach, anything other than things for the achievement and protection of which it has enough power' (Kekkonen 1967, 103).

[31] The interpretation was made by Urho Kekkonen and it was firmly questioned by the Soviet leaders (Kekkonen 1967, 38) 'This treaty is the first document of international law, where Finnish neutrality is set forth.'(p. 121) '... the Treaty of Friendship, Co-operation and Mutual Assistance is based upon this idea. It is important for this treaty that it recognises the Finnish right to remain outside conflicts between great powers'.

A small country like Finland cannot have a great impact upon what is happening in the world. Its role in the search for its national interest is to adapt itself to actual conditions of history and economic geography rather than to strive at a change in them...[32].

Aspects of security have a decisive role in a foreign policy. Every country tries to conduct such a policy with respect to its neighbours and to other foreign countries so that its independence should be best protected....Finally it has to be stated that our people supports the policy of neutrality. It understands the national significance of the policy and gives it its full support. An imprudent and scornful attitude towards our neutrality is an exception from the rule, but very regrettable as such[33].

But neutrality is not, and must not of course be, its own purpose. Its purpose is, like the purpose of all foreign policy, to promote the interests of the country in question. And if such an accident takes place, that national interest and neutrality come into a conflict with each other, the national interest will never bend[34'].

As a product of the Cold War, Finnish neutrality had a specific meaning. The meaning was closely bound up with the purpose of neutrality as a source of security. Finnish neutrality was neutrality between the superpowers in the first place.

Finland refrained from taking part in cases in which there was a risk of a conflict between the two superpowers or their allies. During the Cold War, the risk of a superpower conflict was there in almost every issue of international politics. This meant that Finnish foreign policy became highly cautious. The attitude of reserve expressed itself in acts of foreign policy as well as in statements made and declarations

---

[32]

Kekkonen 1967, 12.

[33]

Ibid., 177–182.

[34]

Ibid., 378.

given[35]. The principle of neutrality thus constituted a fragile line in foreign policy, the success of which was seen to demand absolute loyalty from the people[36]. As years went by, the framework of relations, upon which a demand for neutrality was put, was decisively extended. Almost any question in international politics could be considered to have a bearing upon Finnish security and consequently in every issue a demand was inevitably put forth for adjustment to the principle of neutrality as it was interpreted in the Finnish case.

Later, another definition was linked with the Finnish policy of neutrality by President Kekkonen. This definition can be seen as reflecting an increase in international co-operation in the otherwise unchanged system of power in postwar Europe. This view brought a more positive and peaceful tone to the Finnish concept of neutrality in spite of the fact that it did not change its basic structure.

The new meaning that neutrality had taken on started from the idea that Finnish neutrality could also have an importance in world politics and that it could function in favour of peace and detente in the world. The geographical position of Finland, which had been treated as a difficult one between the blocs, began to be seen as facilitating the role of an arbitrator[37]. The non-egoistic goals that neutrality was now being given brought a new tone to the reserve characteristic of Finnish policy. Finland, largely because of the international role and activities

---

35

Finland had difficulties in arranging its relations with the international organisations of the West. Ideological and economic reasons functioned in support of membership, but neutrality and relations with the East worked against them. As a result, Finland engaged itself in the activities of the West through special arrangements. As far as statements about foreign policy were concerned, Finnish activity in the UN can be mentioned as an example of a careful balancing between the super-powers.

36

Good relations with the Soviet Union was the first principle, the irreplaceable value of which President Paasikivi had already tried to make clear to the public.

37

Kekkonen 1967, 145.

of President Kekkonen, found an active role in the international policy
of detente. The role culminated in Finland's hosting of the CSCE–
conference in Helsinki in the year 1975.

The Stabilisation of the Line of Neutrality

In the 1970's, the Finnish foreign policy line was stabilised in the sense
that its focal concepts were created and acceptance for them achieved.
The realistic world–view, with its nationalistic interpretations, became
less accentuated in foreign policy doctrine[38]. According to the temper
of the time, Finland paid more attention to the positive developments
that were taking place in the Cold–War system such as international
detente and the process of disarmament. The policy line adopted a more
optimistic tone if compared with preceding decades[39].

The outlook in the Finnish external policy line became more
many–sided in a world of increasing internationalisation. In spite of a
widening in outlook, the basic hierarchy of values remained as stable
and uncontroversial as before. Neutrality and good relations with the
Soviet Union constituted the uncontroversial ground of foreign policy
with which all other elements had to be in harmony. In the midst of the
increasing internationalisation of societies, President Kekkonen defined
Finnish policy in the following terms:

> As far as suspicions have been expressed about Finnish foreign policy, it
> is necessary, not to confirm them before Parliament and from this high
> position, but to state that Finland continues firmly its line of foreign
> policy that has been the official foreign policy of Finland after the
> country had got over the resistance, ignorance and fumbling that was

---

[38]

This means that systematic references to the sovereignty and inde–
pendence of the State as comprising the main values and strivings of a
foreign policy became less frequent.

[39]

See eg. the New Year speeches held by the Finnish president in the year
1974, 1975 and 1976 (Extracts from the speeches can be found in
Ulkopoliittisia lausuntoja ja asiakirjoja 1974–76).

typical of the years after the war. All Finns with a sense of responsibility give it their support nowadays....

I have often warned about speculations concerning Finnish foreign policy... In the wide area of international politics, Finnish foreign policy has been characterised by the fact that it has remained outside conflicts between the Great Powers. In acting in accordance with this precept, Finland does not forget its own national points-of-view any more than the obligations it has accepted in treaties. This is evident in the fact that Finland gives active support to those activities that promote peace in the world. Finnish foreign policy is based upon the firm basis that the Treaty of Friendship, Co-operation and Mutual Assistance with the Soviet Union has created[40].

Finnish neutrality was very firm. After a lengthy consideration, Finland concluded a free trade agreement with the EEC in the year 1972. Equivalent privileges were, however, immediately given to the CMEA-countries. In relations with the Soviet Union, great attention was paid to terms and formulations used in official declarations and communiqués. Finland demanded that its neutrality be explicitly mentioned in every official statement given in the context of bilateral State visits at a high level.

Finland and the Project of European Integration

The most apparent problem with the Finnish doctrine, based on an originally pessimistic world-view of political realism and a small State image somewhat characterised by a sense of inferiority, stemmed from the lengthy and uncontested hegemony of the doctrine. The hegemony was rendered possible by the Finnish constitution, according to which the president is the sole leader of foreign policy. The necessary factor was, however, the authoritarian model of leadership adopted by Kekkonen, which included a broad definition of what constituted the sphere of foreign policy. The specific model of thought was so deeply

---

[40] The speech of the President in the 1977 opening of parliament (Ulkopoliittisia lausuntoja ja asiakirjoja 1977 I, 14 ff).

rooted in the conceptions as well as in the routine of foreign policy that
not even the resignation of President Kekkonen liberated a political
discussion which would have relativised the doctrine.

The hegemony of political realism also determined the way of
conceiving the project of European integration. The federalist tendencies
of the immediate postwar era did not spread to Finland, which belonged
to the losers of the Second World War. European integration was thus
neither regarded as a comprehensive political and cultural effort in the
federal style nor as a peace project in the liberal manner. Being
approached from a narrow realist perspective, its meaning was above
all bound to the system of power in Europe, that is, to the division of
Europe into two blocs[41]. The project of European integration that grew
out of the numerous efforts to establish a supranational regime in
Europe was conceived as a Western European project of *economic
integration*. As such, it was of key importance for the Finnish economy,
but, being a Western project it was seen to be in conflict with Finnish
neutrality. Neutrality was also raised as the main political concern in
the extensive debate around the Finnish free–trade agreement with the
EEC–countries concluded in 1972[42].

As European integration was approached from a typical State
centric position, there was another element within it, too, that seemed
to render Finnish participation impossible. This element was constituted
by the supranational powers of the European Communities. The alleged
consequences of supranationalism revealed the strength of the realist
doctrine in Finnish politics. The opposition to supranationalism was
neither based upon an endeavour to protect the independence of the
Finnish constitution nor an endeavour to safeguard Finnish democracy.
By subordinating itself to supranational powers Finland was said to be
risking its external sovereignty and freedom of action, which were thus

---

[41]

One reason for this was, of course, the light in which the Soviet Union
saw the project of integration and its hostile attitude towards it (see, for
instance, Apunen 1977, 127 ff).

[42]

Antola & Tuusvuori 1983, 188–191.

treated as being the supreme attributes of State sovereignty[43].

Membership in the European Community did not appear as a serious political alternative for Finland before this decade. The most long–lasting official argument against membership concerned the State's external sovereignty, which, it was claimed, would become infringed as a consequence of membership. The liberation of Eastern Europe, and finally, the disappearance of the Soviet Union brought about an identity crisis in Finnish politics by breaking down the immediate visible basis of the old political doctrine. The meaning of its material tenets, neutrality and a special relationship with the neighbouring Great Power, became dubious. The political actors faced a challenge of reassessment with regard to basic concepts, in particular, the terms with which Finland would meet the European Community, and international relations in general. The debate, however, never got started before Finland, through a series of declarations made at the highest political level, arrived at the stage of applying for full membership in the EC in March 1992[44].

---

[43]

This argument was closely connected with the argument about neutrality as a reason for Finland remaining at a distance from the EC (see eg. Head of Department Erik Heinrichs', The Ministry of Foreign Affairs, speech in 1976 (Ulkopoliittisia lausuntoja ja asiakirjoja 1976, 160–172). The argument was still being utilised by the Finnish Prime Minister Harri Holkeri of the Coalition Party in numerous speeches held in Finland and abroad before the end of the year 1990 (for the last time presumably on 27.11.1990: 'Suomi hakee tietään', Ulkopoliittisia lausuntoja ja asiakirjoja 1990).

[44]

The Swedish application for EC–membership can be treated as the most immediate stimulus to the corresponding Finnish policy. The official process was started by the Finnish president Mauno Koivisto, who in his traditional New Year speech of 1992 revealed his positive attitude towards membership. His statement was followed by a government decision in February, and by a positive result in the vote of the Finnish Parliament in March 1992. The result already achieved in negotiations for membership was finally accepted in a referendum held in October 1994.

The politics of the 'historic' decision were an expression of confusion and ignorance. After having taken their stand on EC–membership much on the basis of sentiment, or on the pattern followed by others, political actors then faced the necessity of formulating their position by arguments of a more definite character. In the actor confrontation that subsequently occurred, the question that was politicised was not, however, the nature of the European Community. The actors, on the contrary, tended to take for granted the sovereignty of the State, still agreeing very broadly on the State–centric understanding of the concept. Disagreement thus took on the more unfruitful form of evaluating the compatibility of the old policy with the new context, in which case it seemed to divide the political field in an unconventional manner without leading to any proper dialogue at all[45].

The problem that had resulted from the hegemony of one doctrine was not got over before negotiations for membership were concluded and preparations for a referendum started. In the campaign preceding the Finnish referendum, debate on foreign policy was finally normalised, which meant that the official policy–line was openly criticised and alternative policies were put forth. A critical debate on foreign policy also led to the breakdown of the old realist world–view as the constitutive basis of the external identity of Finland. The European Union and a Finnish membership in it were finally evaluated from different conceptual points of view[46].

---

[45]

Although peculiar in other political contexts, this feature seems to be a general one in regard to the EC–relationship. Branner (1992, 316) makes similar findings about the beginning of Danish membership and describes, very briefly, how the situation changed in this respect.

[46]

Some examples of these perspectives are the Nordic model of the welfare state, regional development and the significance of integration upon the structure of sources of livelihood and, of course, economic considerations and the impact of integration on the condition of the Finnish economy (the structure of argument in the campaign is analysed in Tiilikainen 1996).

Adaptation to New Political Conditions

Finnish postwar foreign policy was based upon the idea that the world was bad and that the sovereignty and security of small States like Finland were constantly in danger. Therefore, the values of sovereignty and security had to stand as the primary values of all political life. In practical politics, the consideration of these supreme values was expressed by referring to *the Finnish national interest*. The concept of national interest legitimated acts of foreign policy as well as restraint from other acts. Good relations with the Soviet Union and the pursuit of a policy of neutrality were the key instruments of a Finnish foreign policy based upon the realist world–view. For decades that policy had been inviolable.

Finland first had difficulties in adapting itself and its policies to the changes taking place in Europe. Its policy was cautious. The old policy–line became less and less accentuated, but it kept its main characteristics. President Koivisto summed up Finland's international position in 1990 in the following terms:

> As for the style of our foreign policy in general, we have traditionally been cautious about taking a stand on world events. This has also been justified as an endeavour to remain uninvolved in conflicts of interests between the great powers.

> Although times have changed and superpowers are no longer diametrically opposed to each other on all issues, Finland still has to be rather reserved in her choice of words when taking an official stand. Here I refer to nothing less than the direction and style of our foreign policy.

> As we do not necessarily sing in chorus, or participate in sanctions decided upon without us, our word may sometimes bear the more weight[47].

The first elements of the postwar identity that began to be questioned were the policies it had warranted, the policy of neutrality

---

[47] New Year's Speech by the President of the Republic; 1 Jan 1990 (Ulkopoliittisia lausuntoja ja asiakirjoja 1990, 40).

and the policy of loyalty towards the Soviet Union. The meaning of Finnish neutrality had already become dubious with the breakdown of the bipolar system in Europe. Having been defined as neutrality between the superpowers in the first place this key norm of the Finnish policy had lost its immediate framework of reference. For various reasons, the leaders of the Finnish foreign policy did not, however, want to give up the principle[48]. The meaning of post–war neutrality was once again confirmed as it was finally redefined when Finnish membership in the European Union started to appear probable. The Finnish government then started to talk about *the hard core of neutrality*, which would be preserved even under the new conditions[49]. The hard core included the policy of military non–alignment and an independent defence. Neutrality was for Finland a security–policy solution only and even in the new political situation no decisive demands were introduced for a more extensive interpretation of it.

The other change taking place in Finnish foreign policy was the ending of the very heavy emphasis that had been put on relations with the Soviet Union and its replacement by a more balanced interest in the political neighbourhood. Even more than the change in of the policy of neutrality did, has the dissolution of the policy of good relations indicated how narrow the starting–point of the entire postwar policy had been. For forty years the policy of good relations made Finnish proximity to the Soviet Union look as if some natural sense of unity had united the two countries. In the emerging post–Cold War identity, proximity with Russia is perceived mainly in terms of a power politics which makes Russia appear a political threat to Finland in the first place. This conception is nonetheless balanced by a new goal, which is based upon the idea that Finland and Russia still have some security

---

[48]

President Koivisto was more positively oriented towards a change in Finnish policy from the beginning. His conception was that one should not give up the position of neutrality before one could replace it by another guarantee of security (Koivisto 1995, 548). The leading party in the Finnish government (1991–1995), the Finnish Centre, was very suspicious towards any change and put a particular value on neutrality.

[49]

See eg. Suomi ja Euroopan yhteisön jäsenyys 1992, 15.

interests in common. This new goal is the Finnish wish to avoid new political divisions in Europe[50].

Membership in the European Union as the Core of the New Finnish Identity

The old Finnish world–view faced its greatest challenge when Finland became a member of the European Union in the beginning of the year 1995. In a referendum arranged two months earlier, fifty–seven per cent of the Finnish population voted for Finnish membership. The membership was supported by the political and economic elites almost without exception. Only one of the key parties in Finland, the agrarian *Centre Party* faced the decision disunited. The deepest division brought about by the issue was of a geographical character. The question of a Finnish participation in the project of European integration divided Finland into *pro–European* cities and urban areas, the majority of which are in the South, and into a *pro–national* countryside mostly in the Central and Northern parts of the country.

A typical feature of the Finnish decision to join the European Union was that it was supported by a majority of the political elites who, just a few years earlier, had denied the membership option categorically in the name of a realist world–view. The strategy by means of which this turn–around was made possible can be called the strategy of *external change*. This strategy implied that Finland did not re–evaluate the core of its external identity, which was simply adjusted to a new political situation. The membership option was rendered positive by arguing that over a couple of years, Europe had changed dramatically and that the political and economic core of Europe now

---

[50] This idea has been particularly emphasised by the present Finnish president, Martti Ahtisaari (for instance, his inauguration speech, HS 2.3.1994). See also the Report to the Parliament by the Council of State 6.6.1995 (hereafter:'Turvallisuus muuttuvassa maailmassa'), 5.

centred around European integration[51]. Due to the breakdown of the
bipolar system in Europe, integration had lost its meaning as a project
of the West and had a new important position in a wider European
reunification. Support for Finnish membership could then easily be
built into the idea of a new Europe.

The new Finnish identity thus seems to be based upon the old
State–centric identity adapted to new conditions. An essential element
in these conditions is that there appears to be an opportunity for a
positive development of international relations even if their key
character is not assumed to have changed. Another element is the role
adopted by the European Union as the *primus motor* of this positive
development.

World politics thus appears now as a multidimensional sphere of
activity instead of the unsubtle power politics that was the basis of the
postwar policy. The State is still treated as the core unit in world
politics, but the role of other actors as citizens, ethnic groups and the
international community has also become much more visible[52]. Even if
the core character, and problems, of international relations have not
changed, the end of the Cold War is seen to have given a new chance
for a more positive conduct of international relations. The limitations
of the change have been expressed by the Finnish President Martti
Ahtisaari as follows:

> On the threshold of a new millennium, we are faced with new
> opportunities. Courage is, however, needed in seizing these opportunities.
> Relations between States are, however, always relations of power,
> exposed to constant changes and tension[53].

---

[51]

See, for instance, Notice to the Parliament by the Council of State
28.2.1992.

[52]

This is explicitly stated in Turvallisuus muuttuvassa maailmassa, 13:
'The role of the nation state is being changed, but the nation state
nevertheless preserves its role as the focal actor in international
relations'.

[53]

President Martti Ahtisaari in his speech in Helsinki 10.4.1995:

and by the Finnish government:

> The frozen system of bipolarity has been replaced by an effort towards common solutions. New possibilities have appeared for international cooperation and partnership in security policy. The post–Cold War security system is unstable and is constantly on move[54].

Finland consequently has a dual identity in the post–Cold War world. The very foundation of its political identity is still the old realist tradition with its roots in Snellmanian nationalism. The starting–point of this identity is *geopolitics* and international relations regarded as relations of power. It is often emphasised that nothing has changed in Finnish geopolitics[55]. Finland retains its long common border with a superpower. The meaning of the border is understood in firmly realist terms. As the quotations above indicate, Finnish foreign policy is based upon the assumption that no fundamental change has occurred as far as the focal character of world politics is concerned. Even if the risk of war between the European States is minimal at the moment, it has not disappeared permanently and may be more apparent again one day.

From the validity of this identity follows that State security is still very much emphasised in Finnish politics as well as among the Finnish people[56]. Security has become one of the main elements as far as

---

[54] 'Suomen tie yhdentyvässä maailmassa'.

[55] Turvallisuus muuttuvassa maailmassa, 13.

[56] See, for instance, Prime Minister Paavo Lipponen's speech held in Washington D.C. the 23rd July 1996. Geopolitics is mentioned as a key determinant in Finnish security policy even in the Report given to Parliament by the State Council (Turvallisuus muuttuvassa maailmassa, 64).

Several surveys made in the middle of 1990's have shown that the great majority of Finns have a positive attitude both to defence in general and to the Finnish system of conscription in particular (Epävarmuuden aika: Raportti Suomalaisten Asenteista 1995: Centre for Finnish Business and

Finnish participation in European integration is concerned. Considerations of security policy constituted one of the main grounds for Finnish support of membership in the European Union. Membership in the EU, it is argued, is the main framework for present Finnish security policy, which is not totally unconnected with the fact that the European Union is to a great extent accepted in Russia. The security provided by membership in the European Union is understood in traditional terms of State security in the same way as the whole project of European integration is mainly understood in terms of international cooperation[57].

The other aspect of the Finnish identity arises from the apparent contrast between the Cold War identity and the present–day identity. As the first aspect centred around the value of security as a reflection of the permanent core of international relations, the second aspect centres around *international cooperation* as a possible means for change. The second aspect has a clear connection with the historical liberal identity both as far as its concept of change and its cultural commitments are concerned. It is based upon the conception that peace and stability constitute the key goals of the change that is taking place in Europe. It is assumed that they can be achieved by creating an international system of arbitration and conflict management. It is admitted that the character of post–Cold War conflicts has changed. This change is seen to put particular demands upon the means of conflict resolution rather than upon their basic *international* structure. The framework for international change was introduced by President Ahtisaari:

Policy Studies; Puolustusvoimien sisäinen tiedote nro 12, 1996: The Defence Forces).

57

The security function of the EU was expressed by President Ahtisaari in the following way: 'As a member State of the European Union we are part of a political community of solidarity. If one member State is threatened, the threat is directed against the whole of the community' (Ahtisaari's speech in Keuruu 18.12.1996: 'Suomen turvallisuus-poliittinen tie'). As far as the Finnish understanding of the EU is concerned, see also Finland's points of departure and objectives at the 1996 Intergovernmental Conference; Report to the Parliament by the Council of State 27.2.1996, 9–11.

Cooperation is the only credible answer to our common security needs. The history of security cooperation is brief. During the Cold War we learned how to manage a peaceful relationship between two different political systems. Now our task is to manage change. After the collapse of communism, the Paris CSCE summit confirmed Western principles – human rights, the rule of law and economic liberty – as our common value basis for the whole of Europe[58].

The quotation reveals the cultural commitments in the second aspect of Finnish identity that is put against the nationalist emphasis on State security. The values upon which international peace and stability are assumed to be established are the political values common to Western Europe. The European Union is regarded as the key actor and executor of this change. In addition to the *international* ties that the EU is seen to create and maintain between its Member States, the EU is also seen as contributing to the achievement of peace and stability in Europe, by integrating European societies and by thus making the member States deeply interdependent[59]. The liberal identity of post–Cold War Finnish politics is essentially based upon Finnish membership in the European Union as a channel for Finland and the Finns for the achievement of a positive change in European politics.

The liberal doctrine puts emphasis on different qualities in the European Union than the nationalist one. When approached from the liberal point of view, the strength and efficacy of the union with respect to the implementation of its tasks is a value in itself and not only through the advantage gained from it in national contexts. In addition to the emphasis put on national values like security and welfare, Finnish EU–policy has been characterised by the unreserved support expressed towards projects promoting the process of integration itself. Finland has

---

[58]

Ahtisaari's speech at the Royal Institute of International Affairs, Chatham House, London, 18 October 1995.

[59]

Turvallisuus muuttuvassa maailmassa 1995, 9–11; President Ahtisaari's speech in Helsinki 10.4.1995. This understanding of European integration corresponds to the liberal doctrine in European politics, see chapter 2.

thus appeared as a firm advocate of the common foreign and security policy as well as of the economic and monetary union in spite of the fact that both these projects develop integration in a supranational direction at the expense of national sovereignty. The liberal identity has thus nourished a loyalist attitude towards the EU in its further development in the sense that the Union's capacity to fulfil its liberal tasks concurs with nationalist values to form the foundation of Finnish foreign policy.

Conclusions

After a long period of neutrality and an attitude of reservedness towards international conflicts, Finland has now become an active participant in international politics and a loyal member of the European Union. In many other Western European countries a rapid change like this would not have been possible. If membership could somehow have been accepted by the political elites, it would at least have been questioned by the people. In this chapter, my purpose was to evaluate the external identity of Finland from a long–term perspective in order to put these latest phases into a historical line of development.

The analysis showed that the core of the external identity of Finland has not been altered as a result of the end of the Cold War era even if its topmost commitments have changed. During this era, its identity was based upon a realist world–view originating in State centricism and in a hierarchy of values with State security as the supreme one. The move from a strict policy of neutrality to full participation in the project of European integration has, in part, been made possible by understanding the latter, in accordance with the former, as a reinforcement of Finnish security. Realism is, however, no longer the only constituent of Finnish identity, but it is again balanced by a liberal Europeanism. This identity has put Finland among the supreme advocates of European unification despite the lack of federalist elements in its political culture.

7 Conclusions: Europe and Finland; Defining the Political Identity of Finland in Western Europe

Men's beliefs in the sphere of conduct are part of their conception of themselves and others as human beings; and this conception in its turn, whether conscious or not, is intrinsic to their picture of the world. This picture can be complete and coherent, or shadowy or confused, but almost always, and especially in the case of those who have attempted to articulate what they conceive to be the structure of thought or reality, it can be shown to be dominated by one or more models or paradigms: mechanistic, organic, aesthetic, logical, mystical, shaped by the strongest influence of the day – religious, scientific, metaphysical or artistic. This model or paradigm determines the content as well as the form of beliefs and behaviour.

Isaiah Berlin
(*Concepts & Categories*, 154)

Political Identities

An interest in world–views and in differences between world–views has been the main stimulus behind this book. Paradoxically, the overwhelming number of world–views and nuances in world–views has been the main restraint. This restraint made itself evident from the very beginning of the work, when its starting–point was set forth and its analytical entities, 'Finland' on the one hand and 'Western Europe' on the other, had to be defined. The decision was made to define these political entities in terms of key world–views, that is, in terms of the world–views that have been the most serious claimants for power.

A commitment to the conception that world–views are historically constructed brought in historical continuity as a key characteristic of world–views and emphasised their character as *traditions*. A combination of different traditions could then be seen as a *culture*. As 'Finland' and 'Western Europe' appeared in this work as political projects, it was their *political* cultures that came into focus. And as these cultures were seen to be historically constructed, an analysis of their histories seemed to be the right way of approaching them.

The history–of–ideas approach, like any other approach to social and political questions, has its good sides and bad sides. The history–of–ideas approach focuses on an aspect of social and political questions that, in spite of its greater permanence, is more hidden than most of the other aspects of political life. But the object of this approach, historical understandings and identities, still forms the basis for political activities of almost any sort. Single policy lines or political interests can consequently not be understood thoroughly without being aware of their relation to those larger units of political thinking of which they form a part. Living in and being reproduced by history, these larger units of political thinking can again be fruitfully analysed only through their historical context.

An approach that focuses on the historical development of ideas may, however, easily give a picture of the world that is all too coherent and unitary. This results from the fact that the real world is characterised by such a multitude of overlapping ideas that any analysis of them necessarily becomes simplifying and tends to put into the world an order and coherence which does not belong to it. The picture of the world that the history–of–ideas approach gives may appear sterile also in the sense that it does not directly deal with those qualities that are often treated as the core of politics. As power, the lust for power or the struggle for power are only approached by means of the discursive structures to which they are bound, an analysis in terms of the history of ideas runs the risk of presenting a picture of the world that is basically a harmonious one. The weaknesses of the history–of–ideas approach do not, however, decrease the significance of this approach for the social sciences, persistently orientated as the latter are in the opposite direction, that is, towards the current verities of the natural sciences.

Western Europe

Political world–views, or traditions, centre around the question of political community. As far as Western Europe is concerned, the Reformation can be regarded as one of the key constituents of its political culture. The Reformation gave expression both to the Hellenic–Christian elements that stand for the unity of Western Europe and to the Protestant elements that stand for its division. The Reformation has been used here as the core determinant of the political culture in Western Europe. The focus of the work being on the question of political community an argument has been put forth in it according to which the Reformation brought about the three conceptions of political community that constitute the basis for Western political thinking. The individualist tradition culminated in the birth of the liberal State in seventeenth century Europe. The tradition of Counter–Reformative Catholicism has not yet reached its core goal, but is coming step by step closer to it as the project of European integration proceeds towards a European federation. The republican State that bears the immediate heritage of the Enlightenment gives expression to the tradition of Catholic communitarianism in a secularised form. The third political tradition in Western Europe is the tradition that starts from the independence and sovereignty of the State. The State tradition reached its modern culmination in a German nationalism that celebrated the State as the supreme form of world history.

If an interest in world–views was the abstract stimulus for this work, its practical hold was in the twentieth century project of European unification. The analysis of the political traditions of Western Europe was meant to contribute to a better understanding of the unification project. Therefore, the analysis of the alleged three political traditions had first to be specified as far as their positions in the political structure of Europe were concerned. From history arose, therefore, the differences in Western political culture that brought certain important explanations into the very project of European unification as well as into the insurmountable political problems connected with it.

The constitutive force of the whole unification project was found in the political movements that had their historical roots in pre–Enlightenment Catholic federalism. The political goal of these movements is a European federation which from the beginning of the present unification project has been reflected in the political organs of the project. The other historical political force in Europe working in favour of European integration is liberal internationalism which grew out of the individualist tradition. With its universalist and disregulative tendencies, liberal internationalism has, however, constituted a force against a European federation. In the present integration project, a compromise between these conceptions was first formed upon the gradualist strategy adopted for the advance of the project. Later, it has become evident that neither liberals nor representatives of the State tradition can accept the original federalist structure of government as the starting–point for their common European project.

The purpose of the first part of the book was to give a general framework for something that the second part endeavoured to put into effect. Whereas the first part could only give the broad outlines for the three core traditions in European politics, the second part has tried to clarify their significance, that is, the significance of political traditions for practical politics, through one particular case, the Finnish. The significance of the three traditions was made visible by analysing the development of the understanding of Finland as a political entity.

Finland

Finland can be treated as a typical example of a political culture that has been dominated by one political tradition. Many aspects of the history of Finland were shown to support the collectivist elements in its culture. The Lutheran Reformation planted in Finland a firm tradition of State–centricism which was finally sealed when Finland came under the impact of German nationalism in the eighteenth century. The position of Finland between its two previous ruling Powers has constituted an important support for the nationalist ideology. The Finnish experiences of the Second World War, and the two wars fought against the Soviet Union, gave a particular legitimation to this ideology as the basis for the country's external identity. The presidential leadership of foreign policy and the personalities of the post–War presidents ensured that the ideology's dominance was extended until the very end of the Cold War.

As a firm representative of the State tradition in Western Europe, Finland could be assumed to own a very weak preparedness as far as adjustment to the project of European integration is concerned. The Finnish people traditionally put a high value upon the State and models for alternative political loyalties have been few. If compared with the State tradition, the European, or international, tendencies of Finnish political culture have been narrow. Finland entirely lacks a federal tradition. As far as political conceptions are concerned, its heritage from having been a Catholic bishopric during the first half of the second millennium has been more or less overruled by the Reformation. Aspirations for the establishment of a European federation with Finland as a part of it, based upon whatsoever cultural or political grounds, have not been there.

Liberalism has constituted the main ideological link between Finland and Western Europe. Finnish liberalism has, however, been firmly affected by the dominant nationalist ideology both as far as its political and economic objectives are concerned. This has reflected itself in the internationalist tendencies of the ideology, too. The existing liberal Europeanism has thus remained very moderate in the sense that it been attached to the value of State sovereignty, yet advocating thereby cooperation and community, both economic and political, between the Western States.

If considered against this background, the Finnish decision for full participation in the integration project seemed to have been taken surprisingly easily. The explanation is that the Finnish decision to join the European Union and the necessary popular support gained for this decision did not, however, imply a revaluation of the core of Finnish external identity and a sudden uprush, for instance, of a new sense of Europeanism. The swift turn–around in official policy, and the transformation of European integration from bad to good, were made predominantly in the spirit of the old realist world–view which puts a high emphasis upon State security. Membership in the European Union was introduced with an emphasis on traditional nationalist considerations. The conception according to which membership would reinforce Finnish security and the international position of Finland seemed to have had a great value for both the people and the political elites.

This far, Finnish EU–policy has not decisively distanced itself from its initial logic. The European Union is still approached mainly as an intergovernmental organisation and its activities evaluated in nationalist terms. The limits of Finnish policy come out in regard to projects that cannot be legitimised by nationalist values. The Finnish people, consequently, do not stand behind the government's pro–EMU policy and even the matter of the Eastern enlargement of the EU remains highly controversial. The Finnish support for the key values of European unification will be weighed during the coming few years. This means the juxtaposition of national identity and European identity in significant political issues.

Europe and Finland

Different European countries have varying degrees of preparednesses for adjusting to the project of European integration. Countries with a significant Catholic political heritage carry the idea of a united Europe as a part of their political self–understanding. This does not mean that it necessarily constitutes the dominant political identity of these countries nor that it is a natural goal of their policy–making. Yet in constituting a part of these countries' historical identity, the idea is incorporated in their social and political structures and, as such, has had to be adapted to other parts of their national identity, too. Countries that are politically willing to participate in the project of European government–building, but lack a European identity have to create such an identity. This is what Finland is now faced with. And this is what makes the Finnish situation important from a broader European point-of–view, too.

The historical construction of identities was said to imply the construction of new identities out of old identities. The old identity does not determine the new but there is still a firm relationship between them. The demand for a new Finnish identity stems from the fact that since Finland is a member of the European Union Finnish politics must be more firmly based upon European considerations, the idea of a common government being one of them. As this change in politics necessitates a distance being taken from old political concepts, it gives, at the same time, room for new political thinking. This new political thinking can only be based upon the conviction that there is no necessity, not even for the small States, to adapt themselves to the dominant conceptions behind European integration. Newcomers like Finland could, on the contrary, use their virginal position for the introduction of solutions to the age-long conflicts burdening European government-building. Finnish and Swedish efforts to place openness in decision-making on the EU-agenda represents a good first step on this path. Every new initiative concerning the resolution of the structural problem of the EU, which was shown here to be working against the democratic character and the citizens' dimension of the EU in the first place, are necessary for ensuring the legitimation of the EU.

A new political identity cannot arise out of nothing, but has, as the key assumption of this work has been, to have a firm relationship to existing concepts and identities in a country. The choice of these old concepts and identities is based upon political evaluation, but in theory this demand means that a bridge must be created between the old values and the new. One could perhaps, for the sake of analysis, approach the question from the problems connected with the project of European integration and ask what Finland is able to give to the project. What are the Finnish values that could function in favour of the whole project of integration?

The Finnish position at the edge of the European Union is apt to reflect its historical identity as a borderland. This position, and the proximity to the great Eastern power, has traditionally raised security to be one of the key values of the Finnish people. The security system that is being built upon the organs of European integration should therefore constitute one of the key concerns of Finland. It should be in the Finnish interests to ensure that the European Union, at the time it is trying to respond to the unifying of the security demands of its Member States and societies, does not turn its back on anybody and thus give cause for provocation. It should also be in the Finnish interests to ensure that the significant socio-economic instrument which is the project of integration, is used in favour of a positive development in the whole of Europe and its surroundings and not only in favour of its Member States. In these efforts taken for the improvement of European security, Finland could refer back to its own situation in the Cold War system when it could only as an outsider follow the process of community-building in which it wanted to participate.

Another historical identity that could function as a positive bridge between the old identity and the new is the identity of a small power between two concurring parts. In Finnish politics, small State identity has led to a wish to avoid taking part in conflicts. This wish has emanated from the idea that small States can never afford to be on the losing side. The European Union is filled with political conflicts, some of which risk to render void the whole project of European integration. There is also the possibility that different conceptions of the forms of European integration are going to split up the whole project into parts in such a way that is in disharmony with its key purposes. Lacking a firm ideological commitment to the project of European unification, Finland could adopt a reconciling position between the historical traditions that have been shown to be so often in conflict with each other. The role of an intermediary might suit a small member that does not have these historical and political commitments, nor the same concern for its own prestige as most of the large members have.

Finland's place in a united Europe will be defined by its old political culture and traditions as well as by elements of new political thinking. The field is now open for entrepreneurs. A loyal advocate of unification or a promoter of the European idea seems nevertheless not to be what Europe is first of all asking for. How is it possible to become united and still keep a necessary level of political and cultural separateness seems to be the key question in present–day Europe. And it is not the first time we have heard that question, is it?

Bibliography

Anckar, D. (1983), *Liberalism, Democracy and Political Culture in Finland*, Åbo Akademi, Åbo.

Anckar, D. (1984), *Folket och presidenten*, Finska Vetenskaps–Societeten, Helsingfors.

Anderson, R.J., Hughes, J.A. and Sharock, W.W. (1986), *Philosophy and the Human Sciences*, Croom Helm, London.

Antola, E. and Tuusvuori, O. (1983), *Länsi–Euroopan integraatio ja Suomi*, Ulkopoliittinen instituutti, Helsinki.

Apunen, O. (1977), *Paasikiven Kekkosen linja*, Tammi, Helsinki.

Apunen, O. (1987), 'Rajamaasta tasavallaksi' in *Suomen historia 6*, Weilin + Göös, Helsinki, pp. 49–406.

Ball, T. (1988), *Transforming Political Discourse*, Oxford University Press, Oxford.

Ball, T., Farr, J. and Hanson, R.L. (eds) (1989), *Political Innovation and Con–ceptual Change*, Cambridge University Press, Cambridge.

Barraclough, G. (1963), *European Unity in Thought and Action*, Basil Black–well, Oxford.

Berlin, I. (1969), *Four Essays On Liberty*, Oxford University Press, Oxford.

Berlin, I. (1980), *Concepts and Categories*, Philosophical Essays. Edited by Henry Hardy, Oxford University Press, Oxford.

Berlin, I. (1989), *Against the Current*, Essays in the History of Ideas. Edited and with a Bibliography by Henry Hardy, Clarendon Press, Oxford.

Blichner, L. and Sangolt, L. (1993), *The Concept of Subsidiarity and the De–bate on European Cooperation*, Pitfalls and Possibilities. LOS–center Notat 9334.

den Boer, P. (1995), 'Europe to 1914: The making of an idea' in K. Wilson and J. van der Dussen (eds), *The History of the Idea of Europe*, Routledge, London, pp. 13–79.

Borg, O. (1965), *Suomen puolueet ja puolueohjelmat 1880–1964*, WSOY, Helsinki.

Branner, H. (1992), 'Danish European Policy Since 1945: The Question of Sovereignty' in M. Kelstrup (ed), *European Integration and Denmark's Participation*, Copenhagen Political Studies Press, Copenhagen, pp. 297–327.

Brotherus, K.R. (1963), *Suomen valtiollisen järjestysmuodon kehitys* WSOY, Helsinki.

Burgess, M. (1989), *Federalism and European Union*, Political Ideas, Influences and Strategies in the European Community, 1972–1987. Routledge, London.

Burley, A–M. and Mattli, W. (1993), 'Europe Before the Court' , *International Organisation* vol 47, pp. 41–76.

Cardozo, R. and Gerbet, P. (1986), 'The Crocodile Initiative' in J.Lodge (ed), *European Union: The European Community in Search of a Future*, St. Martin's Press, New York, pp.15–46.

Cardozo, R. (1989), 'The Project for a Political Community' in R.Pryce (ed) *The Dynamics of European Union*, Routledge, London, pp. 49–77.

Carr, E. H.(1939), *The Twenty Years' Crisis 1919–1939,* Harper & Row, New York.

Collingwood, R.G. (1983), *The Idea of History*, Oxford University Press, Oxford.

Delanty, G. (1995), *Inventing Europe*, Macmillan, London.

Dickens, A.G. (1969), *The Counter Reformation*, Harcourt, Brace & World, inc, London.

Dickens, A.G. (1975), *Reformation and Society in Sixteenth–Century Europe*, Harcourt Brace Jovanovich, inc, London.

Diebold, W. (1959), *The Schuman Plan*, A Study in Economic Cooperation 1950–1959, Council on Foreign Relations, New York.

Dilthey, W. (1988), *Introduction to the Human Sciences*, Harvester Wheatsheaf, London.

Dinan, D. (1994), *Ever Closer Union?* An Introduction to the European Community. Macmillan, London.

Dreyfus, H. L. (1980), 'Holism and Hermeneutics', *Review of Metaphysics* vol 34, pp. 3–23.

Dunn, J. (1972), 'The Identity of the History of Ideas' in P. Laslett, W.G. Runciman and Q. Skinner (eds), *Philosophy, Politics and Society*, Basil Blackwell, Oxford, pp. 158–173.

Duroselle, J–B. (1965), *L'idée d'Europe dans l'histoire*, Denoel, Paris.

Duroselle, J–B. (1990), *Europe, A History of Its Peoples*, Viking, London.

Eriksson, G. and Frängsmyr, T. (1993), *Idéhistoriens huvudlinjer*, Wahlström & Widstrand, Stockholm.

Ersson, S. (1987), 'Finlands kommunism' in U. Lindström and L. Karvonen (eds), *Finland, en politisk loggbok*, Almqvist & Wiksell, Stockholm, pp. 117–156.

Featherstone, K. (1988), *Socialist Parties and European Integration*, Manchester University Press, Manchester.

Femia, J.V. (1988), 'An historicist critique of "revisionist" methods for studying the history of ideas' in J.Tully (ed), *Meaning and Context*, Princeton University Press, Princeton, New Jersey, pp. 156–175.

Fogarty, M. P. (1957), *Christian Democracy in Western Europe 1820–1953*, University of Notre Dame Press, Notre Dame, Indiana.

Forsyth, M. (1981), *Unions of States*, The Theory and Practice of Confederation, Leicester University Press, New York.

Foucault, M. (1972), *The Archaeology of Knowledge*, Tavistock Publications, London.

Friedell, E. (1974), *Kulturgeschichte der Neuzeit*, Verlag C.H. Beck, München.

Frisch, H. (1973), *Europas kulturhistorie 1–4*, Politikens forlag, Kobenhavn.

Gadamer, H-G. (1979), 'The Problem of Historical Consciousness' in P. Rabinow and W. M. Sullivan (eds), *Interpretive Social Science*, University of California Press, Berkeley, pp. 82–140.

Gardiner, P. (1959), *Theories of History*, The Free Press, New York.

de Gaulle, C. (1994), 'A Concert of European States' in B.F. Nelsen and A.C-G. Stubb, *The European Union*, Lynne Rienner Publisher, London, pp. 25–41.

Gerbet, P. (1989), 'In Search of Political Union' in R. Pryce (ed), *The Dynamics of European Union*, Routledge, London, pp. 35–48.

Gerholm, T.R. and Magnusson, S. (1983), *Ajatus, aate ja yhteiskunta*, WSOY, Helsinki.

Gierke, O. (1900), *Political Theories of the Middle Age*, Cambridge University Press, Cambridge.

Greenfeld, L. (1992), *Nationalism. Five Roads to Modernity*, Harvard University Press, London.

Haas, E. (1958), *The Uniting of Europe; Political, Social and Economical Forces 1950–1957*, Stevens & Sons Lim., London.

Hakalehto, I. (1970), *J.K. Paasikivi Suomen politiikassa*, Tammi, Helsinki.

Halila, A. (1985), 'Suomi suurvalta–aikana' in *Suomen historia* 3, Weilin +Göös, Helsinki, pp. 11–218.

Hay, D. (1968), *Europe, The Emergence of an Idea*, Edinburgh University Press, Edinburgh.

Heater, D. (1992), *The Idea of European Unity*, Leicester University Press, Leicester and London.

Helander, V. (1990), *Lepäämäänjättämismekanismi*, Turun yliopisto, Valtio-opillisia tutkimuksia n:o 45, 1990, Turku.

Hindess, B. (1977), *Philosophy and Methodology in the Social Sciences*, The Harvester Press, Hassocks, Sussex.

Hinsley, F.H. (1963), *Power and the Pursuit of Peace*, Cambridge University Press, Cambridge.

Hinsley, F.H. (1986), *Sovereignty*, Cambridge University Press, Cambridge.

Hobbes, T. (1962), *Leviathan*, J.M. Dent & Sons Ltd, London.

Holden, B. (1988), *Understanding Liberal Democracy*, Philip Allan, Oxford.

Holland, M. (1993), *European Community Integration*, Pinter Publishers, London.

Hollis, M. (1988), 'Say it with flowers' in J. Tully (ed), *Meaning and Context*, Princeton University Press, Princeton, New Jersey, pp. 135–146.

Holsti, K.J. (1985), *The Dividing Discipline*, Allen & Unwin, London.

Hovi, K. (1988), 'Wienin kongressista ensimmäiseen maailmansotaan' in *Maailmanhistorian pikkujättiläinen*, WSOY, Helsinki, pp. 647–721.

Janssen, P.L. (1985), 'Political Thought as Traditionary Action: A Critical Response to Skinner and Pocock', *History and Theory*, vol 24, pp. 115–146.

Johansson, R. (1993), 'Idéer om Europa – Europa som idé' in S. Tägil (ed), *Europa – historiens återkomst*, Gidlunds bokförlag, Hedermora.

Jussila, O. (1987), *Maakunnasta valtioksi*, WSOY, Helsinki.

Jutikkala, E. (1965), *Pohjoismaisen yhteiskunnan historiallisia juuria*, WSOY, Helsinki.

Jyränki, A. (1981), *Presidentti*, WSOY, Helsinki.

Jyränki, A. (1989), *Lakien laki*, Lakimiesliiton kustannus, Helsinki.

Kallenautio, J. (1985), *Suomi katsoi eteensä, Itsenäisen Suomen ulkopolitiikka 1917–1955*, Tammi, Helsinki.

Kannisto, H. (1989), 'Ymmärtäminen, kritiikki ja hermeneutiikka' in I.Niiniluoto and E.Saarinen (eds), *Vuosisatamme filosofia*, WSOY, Helsinki, pp. 145–243.

Kauppinen, P. (1992), *Suomen valtiosääntöjen aate– ja käsitehistoriallisesta taustasta*, Tampereen yliopisto, Tampere.

Keane, J. (1988), 'More theses on the philosophy of history' in J. Tully (ed), *Meaning and Context*, Princeton University Press, Princeton, New Jersey, pp. 204–217.

Kearney, R. (1986), *Modern Movements in European Philosophy*, Manchester University Press, Manchester.

Kekkonen, U. (1967), *Puheita ja kirjoituksia 2 1956–67*, Weilin+Göös, Helsinki.

Kekkonen, U. (1972), *Demokratia ja perusoikeudet*, Weilin+Göös, Helsinki.

Kekkonen, U. (1977), *Nimellä ja nimimerkillä 1*. Otava, Keuruu.

King, P. (1983), 'The theory of context and the case of Hobbes' in P. King (ed), *The History of Ideas*, Croom Helm, London.

Knischewski, Gerd (1996), 'Post–War National Identity in Germany' in B.Jenkins and S.A. Sofos (eds), *Nation and Identity in Contemporary Europe*, Routledge, London, pp. 125–151.

Koivisto, M. (1995), *Historian tekijät*, Kirjayhtymä, Helsinki.

Kokkonen, M. and Vartiainen, P. (1993), *Alueiden Eurooppa: haasteet alueelliselle kehittämiselle*, Sisäasiainministeriö, Helsinki.

Korhonen, K. (1966), 'Kansallisvaltiollinen linja' in I. Hakalehto (ed) *Suomen ulkopolitiikan kehityslinjat 1809–1866*, WSOY, Helsinki, pp. 9–21.

Koskenniemi, M. (1989), *From Apology to Utopia*, The Structure of International Legal Argument, Lakimiesliiton kustannus, Helsinki.

Küsters, H–J. (1987), 'The Treaties of Rome' in R. Pryce (ed), *The Dynamics of European Union*, Routledge, London, pp. 78–104.

Käkönen, J. (1983), 'Anders Chydenius ja 1700–luvun suomalainen valtio-opillinen ajattelu' in J.Nousiainen and D. Anckar (eds), *Valtio ja yhteiskunta*, WSOY, Helsinki, pp. 37–58.

Laaksonen, H. (1988), 'Varhaiskeskiaika' and 'Myöhäiskeskiaika ja renessanssi' in *Maailmanhistorian pikkujättiläinen*, WSOY, Helsinki, pp. 221–365.

Lagerroth, F. (1955), *Moderna författningar mot historisk bakgrund*, Norstedt & söners förlag, Stockholm.

Lindman, S. (1968), 'Eduskunnan aseman muuttuminen 1917–1919' in *Suomen kansanedustuslaitoksen historia* VI, Eduskunnan historiakomitea, Helsinki, pp. 9–443.

Lindman, S. (1969), *Från storfurstendöme till republik*, Ekenäs Tryckeri Aktiebolag, Ekenäs.

Lindman, S. (1979), *Presidentens ställning*, Åbo Akademi, Åbo.

Lipgens, W. (ed) (1985), *Documents on the History of European Integration*, Vol 1 Continental Plans for European Union 1939–1945, de Gruyter, Berlin, New York.

Locke, J. (1962), *Two Treatises of Civil Government*, J.M. Dent & Sons Ltd, London.

Lodge, J. (ed) (1986), *European Union; The European Community in Search of A Future*, St. Martin's Press, New York.

Loughlin, J. (1989), 'Frech Personalist and Federalist Movements in the Interwar Period' in P.M.R.Stirk (ed), *European Unity in Context*, Pinter Publishers, London and New York.

Mechelin, L. (1896), *Finlands grundlagars innehåll*, Folkupplysnings-sällskapets förlag, Helsingfors.

Mitrany, D. (1975), *The Functional Theory of Politics*, London School of Economic and Political Science, London.

Monnet, J. (1976), *Memoires*, Fayard, Paris.

Moravcsik, A. (1991), 'Negotiating the Single European Act: National interests and conventional statecraft in the European Community', *International Organisation* vol 45, pp. 19–56.

Morgenthau, H. (1960), *Politics among Nations*, Knopf, New York.

Mullhall, S. and Swift, A. (1992), *Liberals and Communitarians*, Blackwell Publishers, Oxford.

Männikkö, M. (1988), 'Valistuksen aikakausi' in *Maailman historian pikkujättiläinen*, WSOY, Helsinki, pp. 509–581.

182   *Europe and Finland*

Mäntylä, I. (1993), 'Suurvaltakausi' in *Suomen historian pikkujättiläinen*, WSOY, Helsinki, pp. 181–272.

Nelson, B. (1982), *Western Political Thought, From Socrates to the Age of Ideology*, Prentice–Hall, Englewood Cliffs.

Nicoll, W. and Salmon, T. (1990), *Understanding the European Communities*, Philip Allan, London.

Nousiainen, J. (1985), *Suomen poliittinen järjestelmä*, WSOY, Helsinki.

Nugent, N. (1989), *The Government and Politics of The European Community*, Macmillan, London.

Nussbaum, A. (1954), *A Concise History of The Law of Nations*, The Macmillan Company, New York.

Olkkonen, T. (1993), 'Modernisoituva suuriruhtinaskunta' in *Suomen historian pikkujättiläinen*, WSOY, Helsinki, pp. 473–544.

Olson, W.C. and Groom, A.J.R. (1991), *International Relations Then and Now*, HarperCollins, London.

Paasikivi, J. K. (1957), *Muistelmia sortovuosilta* I, WSOY, Porvoo.

Paasikivi, J.K. (1966), *Paasikiven linja*, Puheita vuosilta 1944–1956. WSOY, Porvoo.

Paasivirta, J. (1957), *Suomi vuonna 1918*, Kirjayhtymä, Helsinki.

Paasivirta, J. (1978), *Suomi ja Eurooppa. Autonomiakausi ja kansainväliset kriisit 1808–1914*, Kirjayhtymä, Helsinki.

Paasivirta, J. (1984), *Suomi ja Eurooppa 1914–1939*, Kirjayhtymä, Helsinki.

Paasivirta, J. (1991), *Suomi ja Eurooppa 1939–1956*, Kirjayhtymä, Helsinki.

Palmer, R.R. and Colton, J. (1984), *A History of the Modern World*, Alfred A. Knopf, New York.

Palonen, K. (1987), 'The Art of the Possible in the Periphery, J.K. Paasikivi and Urho Kekkonen in the Realpolitik tradition' in J.Kanerva and K. Palonen (ed.), *Transformation of Ideas on a Periphery*, Finnish Political Science Association, Helsinki, pp. 98–115.

Patomäki, H. (1991), 'Suomen ulkopolitiikan genealogia', *Rauhantutkimus* 1991 nr 1, pp. 60–111.

Peters, R.S. (1966), 'Hegel and the Nation–State' in D.Thomson (ed), *Political Ideas*, Penguin Books, London, pp. 130–142.

Pinder, J. (1989), *European Community, The building of a union*, Oxford University Press, Oxford.

Pirinen, K. (1988), 'Keskiaika – maanosa hahmottuu' in M.Jokipii (ed), *Suomi Euroopassa*, Atena kustannus, Jyväskylä, pp. 11–37.

Pocock, J.G.A. (1971), *Politics, Language and Time, Essays on Political Thought and History*, Methuen & Co Ltd, London.

Pocock, J.G.A. (1980), 'Political Ideas as Historical Events: Political Philosophers as Historical Actors' in M. Richter (ed), *Political Theory and Political Education*, Princeton University Press, Princeton, New Jersey.

Pryce, R. (ed) (1989), *The Dynamic of European Union*, Routledge, London.

Pulkkinen, T. (1989), *Valtio ja vapaus*, Tutkijaliitto, Helsinki.

Pulkkinen, Tuija (1983), 'J.V. Snellmanin valtio–oppi' in J.Nousiainen and D.Anckar (ed), *Valtio ja yhteiskunta*, WSOY, Helsinki, pp. 61–73.

Pulma, P and Zetterberg, S. (1993), 'Autonominen suuriruhtinaskunta' in *Suomen historian pikkujättiläinen*, WSOY, Helsinki, pp. 359–472.

Rommi, P. (1974), 'Puolueet ja valtiopäivätoiminta' in *Suomen kansanedustuslaitoksen historia* IV, Eduskunnan historiakomitea, Helsinki, pp. 373–395.

Rorty, R. (1980), *Philosophy and the Mirror of Nature*, Basil Blackwell, Oxford.

Rorty, R. (1980b), 'A Reply to Dreyfus and Taylor', *Review of Metaphysics* vol 34, pp. 39–46.

Rorty, R. (1982), *Consequences of Pragmatism* (Essays: 1972–1980), The Harvester Press, Brighton.

Russell, B. (1947), *History of Western Philosophy and its Connection with Political and Social Circumstances from the Earliest Times to the Present Day*, Allen & Unwin, London.

Scruton, R. (1991), *A Short History of Modern Philosophy*, Routledge, London.

Seitkari, O. (1958), 'Edustuslaitoksen uudistus 1906' in *Suomen kansanedustuslaitoksen historia* V, Eduskunnan historiakomitea, Helsinki, pp. 9–159.

Shapiro, I. (1982), 'Realism in the Study of the History of Ideas', *History of Political Thought* vol. III, pp. 535–578.

Skinner, Q. (1969), 'Meaning and understanding in the history of ideas' republished in J. Tully (ed) (1988), *Meaning and Context*, Princeton University Press, Princeton, New Jersey, pp. 29–67.

Skinner, Q. (1976), 'Motives, intentions and the interpretation of texts' republished in J.Tully (ed) (1988), *Meaning and Context*, Princeton University Press, Princeton, New Jersey, pp. 68–78.

Skinner, Q. (1978), *The Foundations of Modern Political Thought* vols I–II, Cambridge University Press, Cambridge.

Snellman, J.V. (1901), *Valitut teokset V.* Valtio–oppi, Werner Söderström, Porvoo.

Soikkanen, H. (1966), 'Sosialistien linja' in I.Hakalehto (ed), *Suomen ulkopolitiikan kehityslinjat*, WSOY, Helsinki, pp. 57–70.

Soikkanen, H. (1975), *Kohti kansanvaltaa 1 1899–1937.* Suomen sosiaalidemokraattinen puolue 75–vuotta. Suomen sos.dem.puolue, Helsinki.

Stirk, P.M.R. (1989), 'Authoritarian and Nationalist Socialist Conceptions of Nation, State and Europe' in P.M.R.Stirk (ed), *European Unity in Context*, Pinter Publishers, London, pp. 125–148.

Stybe, S.E. (1961), *Idéhistoria, Vår kulturs ideer och tankar i historiskt perspektiv*, Rabén & Sjögren, Munksgaard.

Suomen historian dokumentteja 1–2 (1968, 1970), Otava, Helsinki.

Suvanto, S. (1985), 'Keskiaika' in *Suomen historia* 2, Weilin + Göös, Helsinki, pp. 11–212.

Taylor, C. (1980), 'Understanding in Human Science', *Review of Metaphysics* vol 34, pp. 25–38.

Taylor, C. (1988), 'The hermeneutics of conflict' in J.Tully (ed), *Meaning and Context*, Princeton University Press, Princeton, New Jersey, pp. 218–228.

Thomson, D. (ed) (1990), *Political ideas*, Penguin Books, London.

Tiilikainen, T. (1996), 'Finland and the European Union' in L. Miles (ed), *The European Union and The Nordic Countries*, Routledge, London, pp. 117–132.

Tiilikainen, T. (1997), 'Europe Needs A Common Identity?' in M. Koskenniemi (ed), *International Law Aspects of the European Union*, Kluwer, London (forthcoming)

Tuck, R. (1979), *Natural rights theories. Their origin and development*, Cambridge University Press, Cambridge.

Ulkopoliittisia lausuntoja ja asiakirjoja (vols 1958–91), Ulkoasiainministeriö, Helsinki.

Vahtola, J. (1993), 'Keskiaika' in *Suomen historian pikkujättiläinen*, WSOY, Helsinki, pp. 41–126.

Vandamme, J. (1987), 'The Tindemans Report' in R.Pryce (ed), *The Dynamics of European Union*, London: Routledge.

Voyenne, B. (1953), *Europatankens historia*, KF's bokförlag, Stockholm.

Weber, M. (1965), *The Protestant Ethic and the Spirit of Capitalism*, Unwin University Books, London.

Weber, M. (1968), *Economy and Society* vol I, Bedminster Press, New York.

Weiler, J.H.H. (1993), 'Journey to an Unknown Destination: A Retrospective and Prospective of the European Court of Justice in the Arena of Political Integration', *Journal of Common Market Studies* vol 31, pp. 417–446.

Wight, M. (1991), *International Theory – The Three Traditions*, Leicester University Press, London.

Wilson, K. and van der Dussen, J. (eds) (1995), *The History of the Idea of Europe*, Routledge, London and New York.

Other sources:

Speeches
The inauguration speech of President Martti Ahtisaari. Helsingin Sanomat 2.3.1994.

'Suomen tie yhdentyvässä maailmassa', A speech held by President Martti Ahtisaari in Helsinki 10.4.1995.

'Towards a Positive Interrelationship: The European Union, the United States and Russia in A Changing World', A speech held by President Martti Ahtisaari at the Royal Institute of International Affairs, Chatham House, London 18.10.1995.

'Suomen turvallisuuspoliittinen tie', A speech held by President Martti Ahtisaari in Keuruu 18.12.1996.

'Turvallisuus Pohjois–Euroopassa ja Itämeren alueella: Suomalainen näkemys', A speech held by Prime Minister Paavo Lipponen in Washington D.C. 23.7.1996.

Documents:

Draft Treaty of Amsterdam. CONF 4001/97.

Epävarmuuden aika: Raportti suomalaisten asenteista 1995. Helsinki: Centre for Finnish Business and Policy Studies.

Finland's points of departure and objectives at the 1996 Intergovernmental Conference. Report to the Parliament by the Council of State 27.2.1996.

Puolustusvoimien sisäinen tiedote nro 12/1996.

Suomi ja Euroopan yhteisön jäsenyys. Report to the Parliament by the Council of State. 28.2.1992.

Treaty on European Union (1992). Europe Documents 1759/60. 7.2.1992.

Turvallisuus muuttuvassa maailmassa. Report to the Parliament by the Council of State. 6.6.1995.

For Product Safety Concerns and Information please contact our EU
representative GPSR@taylorandfrancis.com
Taylor & Francis Verlag GmbH, Kaufingerstraße 24, 80331 München, Germany

du Camp devant la Rochelle le 27 Janvier 1618, pour lever 100 hommes de pied dans le pays de Baffigny, mort fans alliance ;

4. ANNE, Dame des Coutures, mariée, par contrat paffé devant *Imbault*, Notaire à Dourdan, le 12 Juin 1629, à *Philippe de Cofne*, Seigneur de Chalumelle, mort au mois de Novembre 1629, fils de *Philippe de Cofne*, Ecuyer, Seigneur de Chalumelle, Montmirault & de la Varenne, & de *Marie de Saint-Memin*, laiffant ladite ANNE D'AUSSY enceinte ;

5. Et LOUISE, Dame des Coutures & de Blancheface, qui époufa 1º le 20 Février 1637, JEAN D'AUSSY, VIº du nom, Seigneur de Paffavant, fon coufin germain ; 2º le 21 Avril 1646, par contrat paffé devant *Beaufort* & *Beauvais*, Notaires à Paris, *Jofeph de Vivant*, Chevalier, Seigneur de Caftelnau en Périgord ;

3. JEAN, qui fuit ;

4. CHARLES, Ecuyer, Seigneur des Coutures, marié, par contrat paffé devant *Trouard*, Notaire au Comté de Salm, le 19 Avril 1613, à *Efther de Hanus*, fille de *Jean de Hanus* & d'*Anne Martin*, dont il eut :

    1. JEAN, dont on ignore l'alliance ;

    2. ANNE-MARIE, mariée, le 30 Octobre 1664, à *Jean-Pierre Durant*, Seigneur de Lironcourt & de Campredon, dont il a poftérité ;

    3. Et ANNE.

5. MARIE, morte fans alliance ;

6. Et ANGÉLIQUE, femme d'*Hector d'Iquebœuf*, Seigneur de Grèves-Iquebœuf.

IX. JEAN D'AUSSY, Vº du nom, Seigneur de Paffavant & de Chamoi, Ecuyer de la Grande-Ecurie du Roi, par Brevet donné à Paris le 16 Décembre 1619, en prêta ferment le lendemain entre les mains de M. de *Bellegarde*, Grand-Ecuyer de France ; fut Aide-de-Camp des Armées du Roi, par Brevet donné à Saint-Germain-en-Laye, le 18 Août 1624 ; Lieutenant d'Artillerie dans les Evêchés de Metz, Toul & Verdun, par Lettres du 31 Octobre 1628 ; Envoyé du Roi vers les Princes de Salm, Margrave de Bade-Dourlach, Comte de Naffau-Saarbruck, & autres Princes d'Allemagne, pour les détacher du parti de l'Empereur, fuivant fes Lettres de créance, datées de Fontainebleau le 8 Octobre 1629 ; Gouverneur de Montreuil-fur-Saône, par Lettres du 28 Février 1635 ; Sergent de Bataille des Camps & Armées du Roi, par Brevet donné à Saint-Germain-en-Laye le 15 Avril 1635 ; & Colonel d'un Régiment de 1000 Chevaux-Légers étrangers, formant dix Compagnies pour le fervice du Roi, par Brevet du 1er Janvier 1637. Il époufa, par contrat paffé devant *Claude*, Tabellion au Comté de Salm, le 17 Mai 1601, *Anne Jacob*, dite de *Bruneau*, morte le 3 Août 1641, fille de *Nicolas Jacob*, Châtelain & haut Officier du Comté de Salm, & Confeiller du Duc de Lorraine pour fes affaires d'Allemagne, & d'*Alifon de Bermont*, dont font iffus cinq enfans nés en Allemagne, pour lefquels leur père obtint du Roi des Lettres de naturalité au mois d'Avril 1633 & d'autres de furannation le 28 Juin 1634, regiftrées en la Chambre des Comptes de Paris le 24 Janvier 1635, fçavoir :

1. JEAN, qui fuit ;

2. CHARLES, dont on ignore l'alliance, nommé avec JEAN fon frère & fes fœurs dans les Lettres de naturalité du mois d'Avril 1633 ;

3. MARGUERITE, mariée 1º par contrat du 1er Février 1634, à *Jean de Bey*, Seigneur de Bathily, Colonel de 1000 Chevaux-Légers étrangers pour le fervice du Roi, fans enfans ; 2º à *Guillaume de Tolofany*, Chevalier, Seigneur de la Caffaigne, Ecuyer de la Grande-Ecurie du Roi & Gouverneur des Ville & Château de Montereau. Elle eut du premier lit, pour fille unique, *Marguerite de Bey*, Dame de Bathily, morte fans alliance ;

4. MARIE, mariée 1º à *Jean Guérilbade*, Seigneur de Boifgarnier, dont, pour fille unique, *Marguerite Guérilbade*, Dame de Boifgarnier, qui fut mariée 1º à *Jean de Goffelin*, Seigneur de Martigny ; 2º par contrat du 23 Février 1636, préfens *Grandjean* & *Rouffelet*, Notaires à Metz, à *N. .. de Vivant*, Chevalier, Seigneur de Noillac, dont des enfans ;

5. Et ANNE, morte le 22 Juillet 1690, à 67 ans, inhumée le lendemain à Saint-Sulpice à Paris. Elle avoit époufé *Jacques de Guéribalde*, Seigneur de Bondaroy, près Pithiviers, dont, pour fille unique, *Anne de Guéribalde*, femme de *Jean Dufaur*, dont des enfans.

X. JEAN D'AUSSY, VIº du nom, Chevalier, Seigneur de Paffavant, & à caufe de fa femme, Seigneur des Coutures, Capitaine d'une Compagnie de 100 Chevaux-Légers étrangers, dans le Régiment du Sieur de *Bathily*, fon beau-frère, par Commiffion donnée à Compiègne le 28 Avril 1635, & enfuite Colonel du même Régiment, après la mort du Sieur *de Bathily*, par Brevet daté de Paris le 1ᵉʳ Janvier 1637, époufa, par contrat paffé devant *Boucher*, Notaire Royal à Dourdan, le 28 Février 1637, LOUISE D'AUSSY-DES-COU-TURES, fa coufine germaine, fille de JACQUES D'AUSSY, Chevalier, Seigneur des Coutures, & d'*Elifabeth de Hemery*, Dame de Blancheface, dont eft iffu un fils unique:

XI. JEAN D'AUSSY, VIIᵉ du nom, Chevalier, Seigneur des Coutures, de Paffavant, de Blancheface, & en partie de Neufville, Capitaine au Régiment de la Fère, par Commiffion, donnée à Saint-Germain-en-Laye le 20 Juillet 1671, fit hommage au Roi de fa Terre des Coutures, relevante du Château de Grez, le 20 Décembre 1668 : il fut Commandant du fecond Bataillon du Régiment, & enfuite du Château de Béfort, par Commiffion du Comte de Lefcouet, donnée à Briffac le 24 Octobre 1670, & mourut le 22 Janvier 1710, âgé de 72 ans. Il avoit époufé, par contrat paffé devant *Chaubert*, Notaire à Yèvre-le-Châtel, le 25 Octobre 1677 (la célébration le 8 Novembre fuivant) *Madeleine de Chabot*, Dame de Frefnay-Laubry, & des fiefs Chartrains de Perinet, d'Yfy & de Bains, morte à Pithiviers. Elle avoit époufé, en fecondes noces, *N... de Morainville*, dont elle n'eut pas d'enfans. Elle étoit fille de *Pierre de Chabot*, Seigneur dudit Frefnay-Laubry, & defdits fiefs, & de *Madeleine de la Taille*, Dame de Bafoche-lès-Gallerandes, fille de *Jacques*, Seigneur de Moigneville, & de *Madeleine de Loynes*, fille d'*Antoine*, Confeiller au Parlement de Paris, & de *Catherine de Charezay*, fille de *Pierre*, Baron de Thury, & de *Nicole Boilève*. De ce mariage font iffus :

1. JEAN-CHARLES, qui fuit ;
2. MADELEINE, née au mois d'Avril 1686, Religieufe à la Congrégation d'Eftampes, où elle a fait profeffion le 9 Décembre 1709, & y eft morte;
3. LOUISE, née en Septembre 1692, morte en 1693 ;
4. Et SUSANNE, née en Août 1703, Demoifelle des Coutures, non mariée en 1762.

XII. JEAN-CHARLES D'AUSSY, Iᵉʳ du nom, Chevalier, Seigneur des Coutures, de la Neufville, Frefnay-Laubry, & en partie de Bafoche-lès-Gallerandes, ancien Capitaine au Régiment de Saint-Sulpice, né le 8 Octobre 1689, époufa, dans l'Eglife de Baune en Gâtinois,

le 4 Juin 1715, en conféquence du contrat de mariage paffé devant *Langlois* & fon Confrère, Notaires à Paris, le 14 Mai précédent, *Elifabeth Blanchart*, fille de *Guillaume Blanchart*, Avocat au Parlement, & de *Marie-Anne Pezard*, dont font iffus :

1. JEAN, né le 29 Mai 1722, mort jeune;
2. JEAN-CHARLES, qui fuit;
3. JEAN *le jeune*, né en Novembre 1727, mort en bas âge;
4. MARIE, née le 25 Mars 1716;
5. ELISABETH, née le 15 Avril 1717;
6. N..., née à Paris, le 19 Mars 1719;
7. N..., née le 1ᵉʳ Septembre 1723 ;
8. Et N..., née le 30 Décembre 1724, tous morts jeunes.

XIII. JEAN-CHARLES, dit *le Baron d'*AUSSY, IIᵉ du nom, né le 30 Décembre 1725, eft entré Page de la Reine le 1ᵉʳ Janvier 1742, & premier Page de Madame la Dauphine à la création de la Maifon de cette Princeffe, le 1ᵉʳ Janvier 1745, & Cornette du Régiment d'Efcars, par Brevet du 1ᵉʳ Avril 1748; Lieutenant au même Régiment, par Lettres du 1ᵉʳ Avril 1749; a époufé, dans l'Eglife de Saint-Sulpice à Paris, le 1ᵉʳ Mars 1756, en conféquence du contrat paffé devant *Sauveige* & fon confrère, Notaires à Paris, le 28 Février précédent, *Jeanne-Louife Poiffon*, Dame de Bardy, près Pithiviers, née le 13 Février 1730, fille de *Pierre-Nicolas*, Ecuyer, Seigneur de Bardy près Pithiviers, Senive, Bonjouville en Beauce, l'Orme, Mezeret, Fougeu & Orvilliers, Confeiller, Secrétaire du Roi, Maifon, Couronne de France & de fes Finances, Greffier en Chef des Requêtes de l'Hôtel, & de *Louife-Marguerite Chalmel*, dont, jufqu'à préfent, font iffus :

1. JEAN-LOUIS, né le 11 Juillet 1757 ;
2. Et JEAN-ANTOINE, né le 3 Décembre 1759.

BRANCHE
des Seigneurs DE CONGERVILLE *& DE* MOIGNY.

VII. CLAUDE D'AUSSY, Iᵉʳ du nom, fils puîné de JEAN III, Chevalier, Seigneur des Coutures, & de *Louife de Moillart*, Dame de Congerville & de Prez en Beauce, Gouverneur de la Citadelle d'Orléans, époufa, 1° par contrat du 4 Février 1555, *Marie Lejau*, fille de *Jean*, Ecuyer, Seigneur de Vertaut, Moigny & Chambergeot, & de *Catherine de Tournebœuf*; 2° *Jeanne de Chartres*, veuve de *Charles de Blaire*, Chevalier, Seigneur de

Tome II.   E

Macheron; & 3ª *Anne de Vaufalmon*. Il n'eut point d'enfans de fes deux dernières femmes, & eut de fa première :

1. LOUIS, qui fuit ;
2. Et MARGUERITE, femme d'*Antoine de Morainville*, Chevalier, Seigneur de Guillerville.

VIII. LOUIS D'AUSSY, Chevalier, Seigneur de Congerville & de Moigny, époufa, par contrat du 8 Janvier 1589, *Louife Acarie*, fille de *Claude*, Ecuyer, Seigneur de Beaujardin, & de *Marguerite de Plumé*, dont :

IX. CLAUDE D'AUSSY, IIᵉ du nom, Chevalier, Seigneur de Moigny, Gentilhomme ordinaire de la Maifon du Roi, mort le 1ᵉʳ Septembre 1653, avoit époufé, par contrat du 18 Juillet 1628, *Geneviève Plumet*, fille de *Michel Plumet*, Bourgeois d'Eftampes, & de *Marie Lambert*. Ils furent tous deux inhumés dans l'Eglife des Cordeliers à Eftampes, laiffant de leur mariage :

1. CLAUDE, IIIᵉ du nom, Seigneur de Moigny, Avocat au Parlement & ès Confeils du Roi, qui fut maintenu dans le droit de fe qualifier *Noble*, & jouit des privilèges de la Nobleffe, par Arrêt du Confeil d'Etat du Roi, du 14 Avril 1667, & eft nommé dans un partage du 29 Octobre audit an; mort le 18 Novembre 1679, & inhumé avec fes père & mère dans l'Eglife des Cordeliers à Eftampes,
2. HENRI, qui fuit ;
3. MARGUERITE, mariée, par contrat paffé devant *le Mercier*, Notaire à Châlons-la-Reine, le 22 Juillet 1649, à *François de Féra*, Chevalier, Seigneur de Fontaine, près Eftampes;
4. Et ELISABETH, femme d'*Auguftin Dulac*, Chevalier, Seigneur de Montereau, Paroiffe de Mereville en Beauce.

X. HENRI D'AUSSY, Chevalier, Seigneur de Moigny & du Tremblay, nommé dans un acte de tutelle, du 26 Septembre 1653, & dans le partage du 29 Octobre 1667, fut maintenu dans fa nobleffe avec CLAUDE D'AUSSY, fon frère, & ELISABETH fa fœur, par ledit Arrêt du Confeil du 14 Avril 1667. Il époufa, par contrat paffé devant.... le...., *Nicole Noifel*, fille de *N*..., dont font iffus :

1. HENRI, qui fuit ;
2. Et FRANÇOIS, Chevalier, Seigneur du Tremblay, Lieutenant au Régiment de Beaujeu, en 1714; mort au Château de Moigny, fans alliance en 1750 ou 1751.

XI. HENRI D'AUSSY, IIᵉ du nom, ci-devant Capitaine au Régiment de Beaujeu, époufa, par contrat du..., *N*..., dont une fille unique, N..... D'AUSSY, dite *Demoifelle de Moigny*, née le...., 17.... non mariée en 1761.

Les armes : *d'argent, au chevron de gueules, accompagné de trois coquilles de fable, pofées 2 en chef & 1 en pointe.*

André Duchefne, Hiftoriographe de France, dans fon livre intitulé *Hiftoriæ Normanorum fcriptores antiqui*, fait mention d'un d'AUSSY, qui accompagna en 1066 GUILLAUME, Duc de Normandie, à la conquête d'Angleterre.

Dans le dénombrement des Vaffaux, dreffé fous PHILIPPE-AUGUSTE, on trouve quatre Chevaliers Bannerets du nom d'AUSSY, dans le Bailliage de Château-Landon, & deux Ecuyers du même nom dans celui de Grez en Gâtinois. (Mémoire Domeftique envoyé.)

AUSTERAY, en Provence : *de gueules, à 5 éperviers, avec leurs longes & grillets d'or.*

* AUSTRASIE. Ancien Royaume qui comprenoit toute la France au-delà du Rhin, & tout ce qui étoit entre le Rhin & la Meufe, & le cours du Rhin, depuis Bâle jufqu'à Cologne. CLOVIS, qui en fit un Royaume en faveur de THIERRY, fon fils naturel, y joignit, pour récompenfer fa valeur, une partie de l'Aquitaine, l'Albigeois, le Quercy, le Rouergue & l'Auvergne.

Metz fut la capitale de ce Royaume. THIERRY, mort en 534, régna 23 ans : THÉODEBERT, qui lui fuccéda, 14 ans; THÉODEBALD, fon fils, mort fans poftérité, âgé de 20 ans, n'en régna que 7.

CLOTAIRE, Roi de Soiffons, après la mort de ce jeune Prince, s'en empara, & laiffa en mourant l'Auftrafie, avec la Thuringe, à SIGEBERT, fon troifième fils; SIGEBERT fut maffacré dans fon camp de Vitri l'an 575. CHILDEBERT, fon fils, âgé de 6 ans, dut la Couronne à *Gombaut*, Général de l'armée Auftrafienne, qui le fit reconnoître Roi à Metz. Etant mort en 596, âgé de 25 ans, THÉODEBERT, fon fils aîné, fut Roi d'Auftrafie, & THÉODORIC ou THIERRY, fon fecond fils, Roi de Bourgogne. Celui-ci ufurpa le Royaume d'Auftrafie fur fon frère, qu'il défit à la bataille de Tolbiac. THÉODEBERT fut maffacré peu de tems après. THÉODERIC, mort en 612, n'eut que quatre fils naturels. SIGEBERT II, l'aîné, eut le Royaume d'Auſtraſie, que CLOTAIRE, légitime héritier de cette Couronne, lui fit perdre avec la vie. Ce Prince le céda, de ſon vivant, à DAGOBERT Ier, ſon fils aîné.

Le Royaume d'Auſtraſie comprenoit alors la Champagne preſque entière, juſqu'à l'Oiſe & la Marne; Laon, Cambray, les Pays-Bas, la baſſe Auſtraſie, qui étoit autrefois la première Belgique, c'eſt-à-dire la Lorraine, les Archevêchés de Trèves & de Cologne: la première & ſeconde Germanique, dont les capitales étoient Mayence & Cologne, au-delà du Rhin; la partie de la Germanie qui comprend une partie du Palatinat, la Thuringe, la Franconie, la Bavière, le Pays des Suiſſes, & leurs Alliés, & de plus l'Auvergne, l'Albigeois, le Rouergue, le Quercy, les Cévennes, & le Comté de Marſeille, étoient ſous la domination du Roi d'Auſtraſie.

SIGEBERT, fils de DAGOBERT Ier, & frère de CLOVIS II, mort en odeur de ſainteté en 656, laiſſa pour ſucceſſeur DAGOBERT II, que Grimoald fit diſparoître, pour mettre en ſa place CHILDEBERT, ſon fils; CHILDERIC II, fils de CLOVIS II, le chaſſa du trône, & DAGOBERT y remonta, en cédant une partie de l'Auſtraſie à CHILDERIC; il vécut auſſi ſaintement que ſon père. Après ſa mort, THIERRY, Roi de Neuſtrie, s'empara d'une partie du Royaume: le plus grand nombre des Auſtraſiens qui ne le voulurent pas reconnoître, ſe donnèrent des Gouverneurs. Dans la ſuite Charles Martel diſpoſa de l'Auſtraſie, comme de ſon patrimoine, en faveur de ſes fils; & le ſecond, monté ſur le trône des Mérovingiens, réunit l'Auſtraſie à la Monarchie Françoiſe, laquelle, après LOUIS le Débonnaire, perdit inſenſiblement ſon nom; la partie qui eſt entre la Meuſe & le Rhin, devint le partage de LOTHAIRE, & prit, de ſon nom, celui de LOTHARINGIA, en françois LORRAINE. Voyez ce mot.

AUTANE, en Dauphiné: d'argent, à la croix de gueules; au chef d'azur, chargé de trois étoiles d'or.

AUTEL: de gueules, à la faſce d'or, accompagnée de 6 coquilles de même, 3 en chef & 3 en pointe.

AUTEL, en Berry: de gueules, à la croix d'or, cantonnée de 18 billettes de même, 5, 5, 4 & 4.

⚜ AUTEL, illuſtre Maiſon du Duché de Luxembourg, éteinte.

HUET D'AUTEL, Chevalier, épouſa Halreſſe de la Petite-Pierre, dont vint:

JEAN D'AUTEL, Chevalier, qui épouſa Jeanne, fille de Geoffroy d'Apremont, à laquelle ſon père donna le Comté d'Apremont, au préjudice de Gobert, ſon fils. De cette alliance naquit:

HUET D'AUTEL, Comte d'Apremont, qui épouſa Agnès, fille de Wolfgang, Comte de Hohenſtein ou de la Haute-Pierre, & d'Alix, Comteſſe de Rodemach, dont il eut:

MANNE D'AUTEL, première femme de Pierre du Châtelet, Ier du nom, Seigneur dudit lieu. HUET D'AUTEL, conſtitua en dot à ſa fille, la ſomme de 3000 florins ſur la quatrième partie de la Seigneurie d'Apremont, dont il la déclara héritière, en cas qu'il mourut ſans enfans mâles;

Et ANNE D'AUTEL, mariée à Linich, Comte de Linange.

Les armes: de gueules, à la croix cantonnée de 20 billettes de même.

* AUTEUIL, dans le Mantois, Diocèſe de Chartres, Terre & Seigneurie érigée en Comté, avec union des Seigneuries de Millemont & d'Antouillet ou Autouillet, par Lettres du mois de Septembre 1660, regiſtrées le 18 Mars 1662, en faveur de François Briçonnet, Préſident de la troiſième Chambre des Enquêtes. Voyez BRIÇONNET.

AUTEVILLE, en Normandie, Election d'Avranches: d'argent, à trois faſces de ſable, au ſautoir de gueules brochant ſur le tout, à la bordure de même.

AUTIGNAL (D'), Généralité d'Alençon, Election d'Argentan, en Normandie, famille noble & ancienne qui porte: d'azur, au lion d'argent, chargé de deux cottices de gueules, l'une à la tête & à la queue, & l'autre à travers le corps, ſurmontées d'une fleurs-delys d'or au franc quartier.

AUTRÉ, en Champagne: de gueules, à 5 fuſées d'argent, poſées en faſce.

AUTREBERG, en Bourgogne: de gueules, à une aigle d'argent.

AUTREMONT, en Champagne: d'or, au lion de ſable, ſurmonté d'un lambel de 3 pendans de gueules.

AUTRET, Seigneur de Miſelieu, en Bretagne: d'or, à 5 burelles ondées d'azur. Alias: d'argent à 4 faſces ondées d'azur.

AUTREVILLE, en Dauphiné: *d'argent, à l'aigle de fable, membrée & becquée de gueules.*

*AUTREY-LE-VAY, en Franche-Comté, Terre & Baronie érigée en Comté par Lettres du mois de Février 1692, regiſtrées à Beſançon & à Dôle, en faveur de *Louis de Fabri de Moncaut.*

AUTRI, en Barrois. Voyez AULTRY.

AUTRI: *d'azur, à une faſce d'argent, accompagnée en chef de 3 merlettes d'or, & en pointe d'une mollette d'éperon de même.*

AUTRI-BRIEN: *d'argent, à trois loſanges de gueules poſés en bande.*

AUTRIC en Provence, ancienne Nobleſſe établie à Apt, où elle a toujours vécu avec diſtinction.

RAYMOND D'AUTRIC vivoit dans cette Ville en 1239. Il eſt qualifié Chevalier dans pluſieurs actes. Dans un accord qui ſe fit en 1246, entre *Bertrand-Rambaud de Simiane,* & l'*Evêque d'Apt,* RAYMOND D'AUTRIC ſervit de caution pour *Bertrand.*

ELZÉAR D'AUTRIC, un de ſes deſcendans, rendit de grands ſervices à *Raymond d'Agoult,* Seigneur de Sault. Pour l'en récompenſer, *Raymond* lui fit don, en 1392, de la Terre de Baumettes, ſituée dans la Viguerie d'Apt. Il fut ayeul de:

I. SÉBASTIEN D'AUTRIC, Seigneur de Baumettes, duquel naquit:

II. COLIN D'AUTRIC, père de:

III. GUILLAUME D'AUTRIC, marié le 28 Mai 1499, avec *Françoiſe de Saporta,* fille de *Louis,* premier Médecin de CHARLES VIII, de laquelle il eut:

IV. ELZÉAR D'AUTRIC, IIᵉ du nom, Seigneur de Baumettes, qui eut commiſſion de M. le Comte de Tende, Gouverneur de Provence, de faire une levée d'hommes pour le ſervice de Sa Majeſté, en 1548. Il épouſa, par contrat du 27 Février 1542, *Louiſe de Vintimille,* héritière de *Marc de Vintimille,* Seigneur de Bouduen, de Ramatuelle & de Sainte-Croix.

V. GASPARD D'AUTRIC, ſon fils, Seigneur de Baumettes, Bouduen, Ramatuelle & de Sainte-Croix, Chevalier de l'Ordre du Roi, & Gentilhomme de ſa Chambre, fut élu premier Conſul d'Aix, Procureur du Pays, en 1601, & Viguier Royal de Marſeille en 1606. Il é-

poufa par contrat paſſé en 1570, *Françoiſe de Simiane-la-Coſte,* de laquelle il laiſſa :

1. CLAUDE D'AUTRIC-DE-VINTIMILLE, Seigneur de Baumettes, qui fut chef d'une branche, laquelle finit en la perſonne de GUILLAUME D'AUTRIC, Conſeiller au Parlement de Provence en 1651, marié avec *Chrétienne d'Arbaud de Rognac,* de laquelle il n'eut point de poſtérité ;
2. FRANÇOIS, qui ſuit ;
3. & 4. Et deux filles mariées dans les Maiſons d'*Agoult* & de *Vincent de Lauzau.*

VI. FRANÇOIS D'AUTRIC, fils cadet de GASPARD D'AUTRIC, & de *Françoiſe de Simiane-la-Coſte,* fut marié le 6 Novembre 1630, à *Françoiſe de Caſtellane,* dont il eut :

1. JOSEPH, qui ſuit ;
2. FRANÇOIS, reçu Chevalier de Malte, & mort Commandeur ;
3. CHARLOTTE D'AUTRIC, mariée avec le Baron de Saint-Michel, du nom de *Marin.*

VII. JOSEPH D'AUTRIC-DE-VINTIMILLE, Seigneur de Baumettes & de Sainte-Croix, épouſa à Aix, l'an 1667, *Suſanne de Clapier,* fille de *Henri,* Seigneur de Vauvenargues, & de *Thérèſe de Galliffet.*

VIII. N..... D'AUTRIC, ſon fils, Seigneur de Baumettes, s'allia avec *Anne de Fougaſſe,* fille de noble *Joſeph de Fougaſſe,* & d'*Anne de Pelletier-de-Gigondas.* Il naquit de ce mariage :

IX. LOUIS D'AUTRIC, Seigneur de Baumettes, Lilleville, Haramon, & autres lieux, marié avec *Thérèſe de Crozet,* de la ville d'Avignon, de laquelle il a laiſſé :

1. LOUIS D'AUTRIC ;
2. JUSTE de Baumettes ;
3. AUGUSTIN de Lilleville ;
4. Et une fille encore jeune en 1757.

Les armes : *de gueules, à 5 éperviers d'or, poſés 2, 2 & 1, longés de fable & grilletés d'or,* depuis l'alliance avec la Maiſon de *Vintimille,* celle d'*Autric* écartèle de Vintimille-Baudouin, qui eſt *coupé d'or & de fable, à 4 épis de millet, 3 en chef & 1 en pointe de l'un en l'autre.*

(Voyez l'*Hiſtoire héroïque & univerſelle de la Nobleſſe de Provence,* tom. I, pag. 85.)

AUTRICHE. Pluſieurs Ecrivains ont pouſſé la flatterie juſqu'à chercher l'origine de cette Auguſte Maiſon dans la fable ; mais elle n'a pas plus beſoin du ſecours de l'invention, que celle de France ; elle eſt illuſtre par elle-même. CHARLES-QUINT, perſuadé de cette vérité, ne daigna pas écouter le généalogiste qui faifoit defcendre fa Maifon de la première race des .Rois de France. FERDINAND V, fon frère & fon fucceffeur à l'Empire, difoit qu'il craignoit que les fçavans, en faifant remonter fon origine fi haut, ne le fiffent defcendre d'ayeux peu recommandables.

GONTRAN *le Riche*, Comte d'*Alface* & de *Brifgau*, eft la fouche inconteftable de la Maifon d'AUTRICHE d'aujourd'hui. Il defcendoit d'ETTICHON, Comte d'*Alface*, mort à la fin du VIIᵉ fiècle. Les ténèbres qui enveloppent l'Hiftoire de ces tems, nous ayant dérobé le nom de quelques Princes de cette Maifon, qui fe trouvent entre ETTICHON & GONTRAN le Riche, nous commencerons cette Généalogie par le dernier.

I. GONTRAN *le Riche*, Comte d'*Alface* & de *Brifgau*, vivoit vers 930.

II. LENZELIN ou LANZELIN, fon fils, Comte d'Altenbourg, vivant vers 990, laiffa :

1. RADEBOTON, qui fuit ;
2. RODOLPHE ;
3. LANZELIN ;
4. Et WERNER, Evêque de Strasbourg, & fondateur de l'Abbaye de Muri en Suiffe.

III. RADEBOTON, Comte d'Altenbourg, & premier Comte d'Habsbourg en Suiffe, mort en 1027, eut :

1. OTHON ;
2. ALBERT ;
3. Et WERNER, qui fuit.

IV. WERNER ou WERNHERE, Comte d'Habsbourg, Iᵉʳ du nom, furnommé *le Pieux*, mourut en 1096, laiffant :

1. OTHON, qui fuit ;
2. Et ALBERT.

V. OTHON *le Docte*, Comte d'Habsbourg, mort en 1111, fut protecteur & bienfaiteur de l'Abbaye de Muri.

VI. WERNHERE, IIᵉ du nom, fon fils, mourut en 1143. Il fut père de :

1. WERNHERE, Comte d'Habsbourg, mort fans alliance en 1163 ;
2. Et ADELBERT ou ALBERT, qui fuit.

VII. ADELBERT ou ALBERT *le Riche*, Comte d'Habsbourg, mourut en 1199.

VIII. RODOLPHE Iᵉʳ, fon fils, Comte d'Habsbourg, mort en 1232, eut trois fils, entr'autres :

IX. ALBERT, IIᵉ du nom, dit *le Sage*, mort en 1240, qui eut pour fils :

1. RODOLPHE, qui fuit ;
2. ALBERT, Chanoine de Strasbourg ;

3. Et ERMAND.

X. RODOLPHE, IIᵉ du nom, Comte d'Habsbourg, fut élu Empereur en 1273, & paffe pour le véritable chef de la Maifon d'Autriche. Il donna l'inveftiture du Duché d'Autriche à fon fils aîné en 1282 & mourut en 1291. Depuis, les Princes de cette Maifon en ont préféré le nom à celui du Château d'Habsbourg ou de Habsburg. MAXIMILIEN Iᵉʳ fut le premier nommé Archiduc d'Autriche, c'eft-à-dire fupérieur à tous les Ducs, titre dont fon père l'honora après fon mariage. Il fut élu Empereur en 1486, & mourut en 1519.

PHILIPPE Iᵉʳ, dit *le Bel*, Archiduc d'Autriche, puis Roi d'Efpagne, né en 1478, mort en 1506, eut de fon mariage avec JEANNE d'Aragon, fille de FERDINAND V, furnommé le *Catholique*, Roi d'Aragon, CHARLES V, auteur de la Maifon d'Autriche d'Efpagne, éteinte en 1700, dans la perfonne de CHARLES II, Roi d'Efpagne, dont les Royaumes ont paffé à la Maifon de France ; & FERDINAND Iᵉʳ, Empereur, chef de la branche de la Maifon d'Autriche en Allemagne, à qui fon frère CHARLES V, abandonna en 1550, tous les biens qu'il poffédoit en Allemagne.

MATHIAS, Roi de Hongrie & de Bohême, puis Empereur, arrière-petit-fils de FERDINAND Iᵉʳ, mourut fans enfans en 1619.

FERDINAND II, fils de CHARLES d'Autriche II, dernier des fils de l'Empereur FERDINAND Iᵉʳ, & auteur des Archiducs de Grætz, puis Empereur, fut adopté par l'Empereur MATHIAS, qui le fit élire Roi de Bohême en 1617, Roi de Hongrie en 1618, & Empereur en 1619.

LÉOPOLD Iᵉʳ, quatorzième Empereur de fa famille, né le 9 Juin 1640, mort le 5 Mai 1705, fut marié trois fois. Il laiffa entr'autres enfans du 3ᵉ lit :

1. JOSEPH, qui fuit ;
2. MARIE-ELISABETH-LUCIE-THÉRÈSE, Archiducheffe d'Autriche, née le 13 Décembre 1680, déclarée le 11 Décembre 1724, Gouvernante des Pays-Bas Autrichiens, qui partit de Vienne le 4 Septembre 1725. Elle mourut le 27 Août 1741 ;
3. Et CHARLES, rapporté après fon frère aîné.

JOSEPH Iᵉʳ, né le 26 Juillet 1678, Empereur d'Autriche, mourut le 17 Avril 1711, laiffant entr'autres enfans :

1. MARIE-JOSÈPHE, née le 8 Décembre 1699, morte le 17 Novembre 1757. Elle avoit époufé, le 3 Septembre 1719, *Frédéric-Auguste* II, Roi de *Pologne* & Electeur de Saxe ;

2. MARIE-AMÉLIE, née le 21 Octobre 1701, morte le 11 Décembre 1756. Elle avoit épousé, le 5 Octobre 1722, *Charles-Albert*, Duc de *Bavière*, devenu Empereur d'Autriche, sous le nom de CHARLES VII, & mort le 20 Janvier 1745.

CHARLES VI, seizième Empereur de sa famille, né le 1er Octobre 1685, élu Empereur à Francfort le 12 Octobre 1711, après la mort de son frère aîné, mourut le 20 Octobre 1740. Il avoit épousé, le 1er Août 1708, *Elisabeth-Christine de Brunswick*, laquelle abjura le Luthéranisme & mourut le 21 Décembre 1750. Elle étoit fille de *Louis-Rodolphe*, Duc de *Brunswick-Wolfenbutel* & de *Christine-Louise*, Princesse d'*Oettingen*; de ce mariage vinrent :

1. LÉOPOLD-JEAN-JOSEPH-ANTOINE de PAUL-ERMENEGILDE-FRANÇOIS-RODOLPHE-IGNACE-BALTHASARD, Archiduc d'Autriche, né le 13 Avril 1716, mort le 4 Novembre 1716;
2. MARIE-THÉRÈSE-WALPURGE-AMÉLIE-CHRISTINE, née le 13 Mai 1717. Voyez LORRAINE.
3. MARIE-ANNE-ELÉONORE-WILHELMINE-JOSÈPHE, Archiduchesse d'Autriche, née le 14 Septembre 1718, morte sans enfans, le 16 Décembre 1744. Elle avoit épousé, le 7 Janvier 1744, le Prince *Charles de Lorraine;*
4. Et MARIE-AMÉLIE-CAROLINE-LOUISE, Archiduchesse d'Autriche, née le 5 Avril 1724, morte le 19 Avril 1730.

Les Archiducs d'*Inspruck*, qui ont commencé à LÉOPOLD d'Autriche, né en 1586, cinquième des fils de CHARLES d'Autriche, Archiduc de Grætz, & premier Archiduc d'Inspruck, étoient un rameau de la Maison d'Autriche. Ils ont fini à SIGISMOND-FRANÇOIS, Archiduc d'Inspruck, second fils du précédent, mort le 25 Juin 1662.

Les armes d'Autriche sont : *de gueules, à une fasce d'argent.*

Le Comte de Zurlauben, Maréchal des Camps & Armées du Roi, & Capitaine au Régiment des Gardes Suisses au service de France, de l'Académie des Inscriptions & Belles-Lettres de Paris, a donné, au mois de Mai 1770, *des Tables généalogiques* des Augustes Maisons d'*Autriche* & de *Lorraine*, & leurs alliances avec l'Auguste Maison de *France*, précédées d'un mémoire sur les Comtes de HABSBOURG, tige de la Maison d'AUTRICHE.

AUTRUI : *d'or, à une molette de sable au franc-quartier, au chef de gueules.*

AUTRUY : *d'argent, à 3 losanges de gueules, mis en bande.*

AUTRY, Terre & Baronie, en Champagne, Diocèse de Reims, érigée en Comté, en 1695, en faveur de la Maison de *Thuisy*.

AUTRY-LA-VILLE. Voyez AULTRY.

AUTRY ou AUTRI-DE-LA-MIVOYE. GEORGES D'AUTRY, Ecuyer, Seigneur de la Mivoye, épousa, le 4 Février 1556, *Marie David*, fille de *Jean David*, Ecuyer, Seigneur de Pertuis, & de *Jeanne de Pampelune*.

GEORGES D'AUTRUY, Ecuyer, son arrière-petit-fils, fut Lieutenant de la Compagnie des Chevaux-Légers du Duc de Savoie. Il avoit épousé, dans la ville de Turin, le 17 Septembre 1641, *Béatrix Grosso de Bauzoles*, dont il eut:

FRANÇOIS-GASTON D'AUTRY, Ecuyer, Seigneur de la Mivoye, de Varennes & de Tremblay, premier Capitaine du Régiment de son Altesse Royale Monseigneur le Duc de Savoie, marié avec *Elisabeth de Menou-Champliveau*.

JOSEPH-ADALBERT D'AUTRY, son fils, Ecuyer, Seigneur de la Mivoye, épousa, le 13 Juillet 1720, *Elisabeth de Menou*, fille de *Charles de Menou*, Chevalier, Seigneur de Cuissi, Brigadier des Armées du Roi, & Gouverneur de la Citadelle d'Arras, & de *Jacqueline de Cremeur*. De ce mariage est issue, entr'autres enfans:

ELISABETH-FRANÇOISE D'AUTRY-DE-LA-MIVOYE, née le 13 Septembre 1721, & reçue à Saint-Cyr, le 16 Janvier 1733, sur les preuves de sa noblesse.

Les armes: *d'azur, à une fasce d'argent, accompagnée en chef de trois merlettes d'or, & en pointe d'une molette d'éperon de même.*

§ AUTUN ou AUTHUM, ainsi qu'il est écrit dans les titres, famille noble & ancienne en Languedoc.

Le premier dont on ait connoissance par les différentes recherches faites à la Bibliothèque du Roi, est noble homme JEAN D'AUTUN, DE CAMPELOS, vivant en 1441 dans la Paroisse de Sainte-Cécile d'Andorge, au pays de Gévaudan.

Antoine d'Autun auſſi qualifié noble hom-me dudit lieu de Champelos, & de la même Paroiſſe, vivoit en 1471. Ils ſont tous deux mentionnés dans l'*Armorial de France* de M. d'Hozier, reg. V, part. II, pag. 3 & 10, à l'article de *Verdelan*, Seigneur de Merveil-lac & de Sarremejanne. Comme il n'a jamais exiſté qu'une famille portant le nom d'*Au-tun*, on peut conclure que Bernard ci-après deſcendoit des précédens. C'eſt par lui que nous en commencerons la filiation ſuivie, ne pouvant la remonter plus haut, à cauſe de la perte que cette famille a faite de ſes titres primordiaux, pendant les guerres des Céven-nes, qui ont agité la province de Langue-doc.

I. Bernard d'Autun, Ecuyer, Seigneur de Saint-Jean de Valeriſel au Diocèſe d'Uzès, fit ſon teſtament le 3 Juillet 1552, devant *Bru-net*, Notaire, dans lequel il nomme ſon fils Charles. Il avoit épouſé, par contrat du 28 Janvier 1525, paſſé devant *Pellet*, Notaire, *Marguerite du Ranne*, dont il eut :

II. Charles d'Autun, Ecuyer, Seigneur de Sauveplanne & de Champelos, qui fit ſon teſtament le 20 Novembre 1573, devant *Com-bière*, Notaire, où il nomme ſes fils héritiers. Il épouſa, par contrat du 17 Juin 1564, paſſé devant *Briconet*, Notaire, *Jeanne de Calmel de Gaʒel*, dont il eut :

Jean, qui ſuit ;

Et Jacques, Ecuyer, Seigneur de Champelos. Il épouſa *Eliſabeth de Pluviers*, morte en 1632, à 84 ans, qui ſe remaria avec *Char-les-Robert de la Marck*, IVᵉ du nom, Comte de Braine, Chevalier des Ordres du Roi, Maréchal de France. Elle laiſſa de ſon premier lit :

· Marguerite d'Autun, Dame de Ruival & de Champelos, morte à Avignon, le 21 Février 1616, & enterrée en l'Ab-baye de Braine, au Diocèſe de Soiſ-ſons. Elle avoit été la première femme de *Henri-Robert de la Marck*, Vᵉ du nom, Duc de Bouillon. Il mourut en ſa maiſon de Braine le 7 Novembre 1652, âgé de 77 ans, & fut enterré à côté de ſa femme. Ils eurent entr'autres enfans deux filles qui par leur mariage don-nent à la famille d'*Autun* des alliances avec les Maiſons de l'*Hôpital*, de *Beau-vau*, des Seigneurs *du Rivau*, &c.

III. Jean d'Autun, Ecuyer, Seigneur de Sauveplanne en Languedoc, Paroiſſe du Col-let de Dezes, au Diocèſe de Mende, fit ſon teſtament devant *Pinna*, Notaire, le 18 Avril 1617, en faveur de ſon fils. Il avoit épouſé, par contrat du 2 Décembre 1596, paſſé de-vant *Brajouʒe*, Notaire, *Claudine de Marin*, de laquelle il eut :

IV. Jacques d'Autun, Ecuyer, Seigneur de Sauveplanne, la Rouvière, le Theron & au-tres lieux, qui fut Lieutenant dans le Régi-ment de la Rochefoucauld, & enſuite Capi-taine au Régiment de Savines, Infanterie, dans lequel il leva une Compagnie ſous les or-dres & par commiſſion du Maréchal de Cré-quy. Il fut déclaré noble & iſſu de noble race & lignée par jugement de M. *Baʒin de Be-ʒons*, Intendant de la province de Langue-doc, le 25 Septembre 1669, ſur la production de ſes titres, faite en exécution de la déclara-tion du 8 Février 1664, & Arrêt du Conſeil du 24 Décembre 1667. Par ce jugement il fut ordonné, que tant lui que ſa poſtérité née & à naître en légitime mariage, jouiront du pri-vilège de nobleſſe ; & que ſes noms, armes & lieu de ſa demeure, ſeront inſcrits dans le catalogue des véritables nobles de la province de Languedoc. Il avoit épouſé, par contrat du 7 Mars 1641, paſſé devant *Paradis*, Notaire, *Catherine le Blanc*, Dame de la Rouvière, dont vint :

V. Pierre d'Autun, Ecuyer, Seigneur de la Rouvière, qui teſta le 19 Avril 1694, de-vant ledit *Pradel*, Notaire. Il épouſa, par con-trat du 7 Août 1683, paſſé devant *Pradel*, Notaire, *Marguerite-Cécile d'Autun*, ſa cou-ſine, fille de *Jacques d'Autun* & de *Margue-rite de Pellegrin*, native du lieu du Péage en Languedoc. Ses père & mère confirmèrent dans ce contrat la donation qu'ils avaient faite audit Pierre d'Autun de la Rouvière, leur fils, par l'acte public du 4 mai 1682. Il eut pour enfans :

1. Jacques, qui ſuit ;
2. Simon-Pierre, tige de la ſeconde branche rapportée ci-après ;
3. Joseph, mort ſans poſtérité ;
4. & 5. Marguerite-Cécile & Marie d'Au-tun.

VI. Jacques d'Autun, IIᵉ du nom, Ecuyer, Seigneur de Sauveplanne, mort le 25 Mars 1745, âgé de 58 ans, avoit épouſé *Jeanne Valentin*, décédée le 24 Janvier 1751, laiſſant :

1. Jean-Jacques d'Autun, Ecuyer, Seigneur de Sauveplanne, Lieutenant d'Infanterie,

qui a fubftitué la terre de Sauveplanne à
fon dernier frère, & eft mort fans poftérité
en 1775;

2. JEAN-MARC D'AUTUN, Ecuyer, né le 26 Octobre 1742, qui a fervi d'abord en qualité
de volontaire dans le Régiment de Touraî-
ne, puis dans celui de Befançon, Artillerie;
& a été nommé Lieutenant du corps des
Volontaires de Cornick, par Brevet du
mois de Juin 1779. Il n'eft pas marié;

3. Et JEAN-BAPTISTE-NICOLAS D'AUTUN, E-
cuyer, Seigneur de Sauveplanne, qui a fervi en qualité de volontaire dans le Régiment
de Condé, Infanterie, & s'eft retiré du fervice en 1775, après la mort de fon frère
aîné, dont il a hérité de la terre & feigneurie de Sauveplanne par fubftitution. Il n'eft
pas encore marié.

SECONDE BRANCHE.

SIMON-PIERRE D'AUTUN, Ecuyer, fecond fils
de PIERRE D'AUTUN & de *Catherine le Blanc;*
a fervi en qualité de Lieutenant dans le Régiment de Condé, Infanterie, & eft mort à
Donchery-fur-Meufe, le 15 Novembre 1775,
âgé de 88 ans. Il avoit époufé, le 5 Juillet
1721, *Marie-Anne Neveux,* de laquelle il
eut :

PIERRE D'AUTUN, Ecuyer, né le 8 Juillet
1722, qui, après avoir fervi dans le Régiment
de Touraine, en qualité de volontaire, & dans
le corps des volontaires de la Morlière, fut
reçu Manufacturier de la Draperie Royale de
Sédan, & enfuite Colonel du Milice Bourgeoife de ladite ville; il a époufé, le 18 Juillet
1748, *Jeanne-Marie Beauchamp.* De ce mariage font iffus :

1. REMY, qui fuit;

2. LOUIS-FRANÇOIS, Ecuyer, né le 26 Décem-
bre 1753, à Donchery-fur-Meufe, Major de
la jeuneffe & Milice bourgeoife de Sédan,
& Manufacturier de la Draperie Royale de
ladite ville. Il a époufé, par contrat du 12
Février 1781, *Catherine Henco,* née le 7
Juin 1762, fille de *Charles Henco,* ancien
Jufticier & Echevin de la Ville & Prévôté
d'Artout, Province de Luxembourg & de
Marie-Barbe de Haut. De ce mariage vint :

PIERRE D'AUTUN, Ecuyer, né à Sédan,
le 6 Septembre 1782.

3. MARIE-JEANNE, née le 26 Mai 1751, Religieufe à Longwuy;

4. MARIE-CHARLOTTE, née à Donchery;

5. Autre MARIE-CHARLOTTE;

6. Et MARIE-ANNE D'AUTUN.

REMY D'AUTUN, Ecuyer, Capitaine de la

Milice bourgeoife & Manufacturier de la Draperie Royale de Sédan, né à Donchery-fur-
Meufe, le 26 Mai 1752, a époufé, par contrat du 1er Décembre 1777, paffé devant *Bou-
tet* & fon confrère, Notaires au Châtelet de
Paris, & ce mariage célébré le mardi 13 Janvier 1778, à la Paroiffe de Saint-André-des-
Arts, avec *Marie-Charlotte le Sage,* née le
22 Avril 1759, fille aînée de Meffire *Jean-
Claude le Sage,* Officier Commenfal du
Roi, & de *Jeanne-Julie Duprès;* avec l'agrément & en préfence de très-haute, très-puif-
fante & très-illuftre Princeffe Louife-Julie-
Conftance de Rohan, Comteffe de Brionne,
de Charny & de Limours, veuve de très-haut,
très-puiffant & très-illuftre Prince, Monfeigneur Louis-Charles de Lorraine, Comte de
Brionne & de Charny, Pair & Grand-Ecuyer
de France, Gouverneur de la province d'Anjou; de haut & puiffant Seigneur, Monfeigneur Guy-André-Pierre, Duc de Laval-
Montmorency, Seigneur du Duché de Laval
& autres places, premier Baron de Laval,
Lieutenant-Général des Armées du Roi, Gouverneur pour Sa Majefté des villes & principautés de Sédan, Carignan, Mouzon, Rau-
court & pays indépendans, & du pays de
Tunis; de Son Excellence Alexandre, Prince
Iwan-Bariatinsky, Miniftre Plénipotentiaire
de Sa Majefté Impériale de toutes les Ruffies,
Chevalier de fes Ordres & fon grand Chambellan; & de Meffire Denis-Philbert Thiroux
de Montfauge, Receveur-Général des Finances de la Généralité de Paris, & l'un des Fermiers-Généraux de Sa Majefté. De ce mariage font fortis :

1. CLAUDE-JEAN-CHARLES, né à Sédan, le 9
Août 1779;

2. ALEXANDRE-JEAN-PIERRE, né à Paris, Paroiffe Sainte-Opportune, le 29 Septembre
1780, mort;

3. Et AUGUSTE-PIERRE-CHARLES D'AUTUN, né
le 12 Octobre 1782, à Paris, Paroiffe Saint-
Nicolas-des-Champs.

Les armes de cette famille font : *au cœur
d'argent, percé de deux flèches de même
en fautoir,* telles qu'elles font expliquées dans
le jugement de maintenue de nobleffe de
M. *de Bezons,* Intendant de la province du
Languedoc, le 25 Septembre 1669.

Les titres originaux de cette famille ont été
communiqués à l'auteur du *Dictionnaire de
la Nobleffe* par MM. D'AUTUN de Sédan, qui
en font porteurs.

Alliance de la famille d'AUTUN avec la Maifon *de la Marck*, Duc de Bouillon ; d'où dérive celle qu'elle a avec les Maifons de *Durfort*, Ducs de Duras ; de *Lorraine*, Prince de Lambefc ; du Comte d'*Egmont-Pignatelli* ; des Ducs de Luynes, & autres, &c.

AUTUN : *de gueules, à la croix dentelée d'or.*

AUVÉ, Seigneur de la Ventroufe : *d'argent, à la croix de gueules, cantonnée de douze merlettes de même, pofées 2 & 1 dans chaque canton.*

AUVELLIERS, Seigneur de Champelos, en Languedoc : *d'or, au fautoir de gueules, cantonné de quatre aiglettes de même, fur le tout d'azur, au navire d'argent, équipé de gueules, au chef coufu d'or, chargé d'une aiglette de fable.*

AUVER : *d'azur, à la fafce muraillée d'argent, de quatre traits, crénelée de même.*

*AUVERGNE. On a une Chronologie fuivie des Comtes Bénéficiaires de la Province d'Auvergne, fous les Rois de France, depuis 778 jufqu'après 928. Parmi ces Comtes, on trouve des Comtes de Touloufe, des Marquis de Gothie, des Ducs d'Aquitaine, & en dernier lieu des Comtes de Carcaffonne.

PHILIPPE-AUGUSTE confifqua le Comté d'Auvergne pour crime de félonie fur le Comte GUY, IIᵉ du nom, en 1210.

Le Roi LOUIS VIII, fon fils, au mois de Juin 1225, donna en apanage à ALPHONSE, fon cinquième fils, mort en 1271, les Comtés de Poitou & d'Auvergne. SAINT LOUIS, fon fucceffeur, rétablit en 1229, à titre d'hérédité, *Guillaume VIII*, fils de *Guy II*, dans le Comté d'Auvergne, à la réferve de la portion appelée *la Terre d'Auvergne*, qui fut depuis érigée en Duché.

Le *Comté d'Auvergne* paffa par fucceffion à l'ancienne Maifon de *la Tour*, & de celle-ci à *Catherine de Médicis*, femme du Roi HENRI II, dont la fille *Marguerite*, femme de HENRI IV, fit donation de ce Comté à *Charles d'Angoulême*, bâtard de CHARLES IX, furnommé *Comte d'Auvergne*, avec fubftitution au Dauphin, depuis LOUIS XIII. Les fils de ce CHARLES, Comte d'Auvergne, n'ayant pas laiffé de poftérité, le Comté fut réuni à la Couronne. En 1651, Louis XIV le donna au Duc de *Bouillon*, en échange de Sédan & de Ro-

Tome II.

coux, & lui céda en même tems la faculté de retirer la Baronie de la Tour, &c., engagée au feu Marquis de *Chandenier*, aux 'droits duquel étoit en dernier lieu M. le Comte de *Broglie*, mort Maréchal de France. Au *Comté d'Auvergne* Sa Majefté joignit & céda encore au Duc de *Bouillon* le Duché d'Albret, en Guyenne, le Duché de Château-Thierry, en Champagne, & le Comté d'Evreux, en Normandie.

Les armes du Comté : *d'or, au gonfanon de gueules, frangé de finople.*

Duché d'Auvergne.

ALPHONSE de France, fils du Roi LOUIS VIII, étant mort fans enfans, en 1271, la grande portion du Comté d'Auvergne fut de nouveau réunie à la Couronne, par réverfion. Le Roi JEAN, au mois de Juin 1356, donna à JEAN de France, Duc de Berry, fon troifième fils, le Gouvernement du pays d'Auvergne ; & par d'autres Lettres du mois d'Octobre 1360, il érigea pour le même, en Duché-Pairie, les Comtés de Berry & d'Auvergne.

Le Prince JEAN donna le Duché d'Auvergne pour dot, en 1400, à *Marie de Berry*, fa feconde fille, mariée à *Jean de Bourbon*, Comte de Clermont. Ce Duché refta dans la Maifon de *Bourbon*, jufqu'à la mort de *Charles*, Duc de Bourbon, Connétable de France, arrivée le 6 Mai 1527. Il fut donné, au mois de Janvier 1531, à *Louife de Savoie*, mère du Roi FRANÇOIS Iᵉʳ, morte le 22 Septembre 1531. Le Duché d'Auvergne fut alors expreffément réuni à la Couronne. Le Roi CHARLES IX le donna, le 14 Mai 1562, à fa mère CATHERINE DE MÉDICIS, pour fa dot & fon douaire avec les Duchés de Bourbonnois, de Valois, &c. HENRI III donna les Duchés d'Auvergne & de Bourbonnois, le 20 Janvier 1577, à ELISABETH d'Autriche, veuve du Roi CHARLES IX, pour fon douaire au lieu du Duché de Berry. Il fut enfuite réuni à la Couronne.

Les armes : *femé de France, à la bordure engrelée de gueules.*

AUVERGNE, Sieur de Frondval, la Motterie, en Normandie, Généralité de Rouen, famille maintenue dans fa nobleffe, le 18 Mars 1669, dont étoit MARGUERITE D'AUVERGNE, alliée, vers 1550, à *Hugues d'Ailly*, Seigneur d'Annery.

Les armes : *d'argent, à une fafce de gueu-*

les, *chargée de trois coquilles du champ, & accompagnée de fix merlettes, trois rangées en chef & trois en pointe.*

AUVERGNE (D'), en Bretagne: *de fable, à la croix d'argent, cantonnée de 4 têtes de loup arrachées de même, & lampaffées de gueules.*

✠ AUVERGNE DE GAGNY, famille noble de l'Isle de France.

JEAN D'AUVERGNE, Seigneur de Gagny, époufa, au mois de Février 1520, *Marie de Sailly*, & en eut:

JEAN D'AUVERGNE, II⁰ du nom, qui fut Lieutenant-Général au Bailliage de Senlis, marié à *Anne Baudry*, dont:

ROBERT D'AUVERGNE, Ecuyer, le premier qui fe tranfporta en Berry dans la Grofrinière, près Saint-Aignan. Il époufa *Anne de Bonnafau*, & en eut:

ANTOINE D'AUVERGNE, Ecuyer, Seigneur de la Grofrinière, marié à *Claude de Boifvilliers*, dont plufieurs enfans, entr'autres:

1. HIPPOLYTE, qui fuit;
2. & 3. Deux fils, tués au fervice étant Capitaines dans le Régiment de la Vieille-Marine;
4. 5. 6. & 7. URSULE, née en 1661; AGNÈS, née en 1663; MADELEINE, née en 1664; & MARIE-THÉRÈSE D'AUVERGNE, née en 1670, toutes les quatre reçues à Saint-Gyr au mois de Mars 1686, après avoir prouvé que JEAN D'AUVERGNE, Seigneur de Gagny, & *Marie de Sailly*, étaient leurs trifayeuls.

HIPPOLYTE D'AUVERGNE, Ecuyer, Seigneur de la Grofrinière, époufa *Elifabeth de Launay*, de laquelle vinrent 12 garçons & une fille. Plufieurs fervirent dans la guerre de la fucceffion d'Efpagne & deux furent tués à la bataille de Malplaquet le 11 Septembre 1709. De ces 12 garçons, il y en eut 3 de mariés, favoir:

1. ANTOINE D'AUVERGNE, l'aîné, Ecuyer, Seigneur de la Grofrinière, qui n'eut qu'un fils, mort fans poftérité;
2. HIPPOLYTE, qui fuit;
3. Et JACQUES, tige de la feconde branche, rapportée ci-après.

HIPPOLYTE D'AUVERGNE, II⁰ du nom, Ecuyer, Seigneur de Meune, a laiffé de fon mariage:

1. HIPPOLYTE, qui fuit;
2. N... D'AUVERGNE, qui a fervi Capitaine au Régiment de Limoufin & eft mort Chevalier de Saint-Louis;
3. Et un autre fils, qui a fervi Capitaine-Aide-Major au Bataillon de Châteauroux, eft vivant & n'a de fon mariage que deux filles.

HIPPOLYTE D'AUVERGNE, III⁰ du nom, Ecuyer, eft mort laiffant de fon mariage:

1. HIPPOLYTE, qui fuit;
2. Et N... D'AUVERGNE DES COIGNÉES, qui a fervi dans le Régiment de Bourbon, Cavalerie, eft marié, & a quatre garçons; l'aîné, HIPPOLYTE D'AUVERGNE, a été reçu élève des Ecoles Royales Militaires en 1775, & eft au Collège de Pont-le-Roi.

HIPPOLYTE D'AUVERGNE, IV⁰ du nom, Ecuyer, Seigneur de Meune, Capitaine au Régiment Provincial de Châteauroux, & Chevalier de Saint-Louis, a époufé, en 1770, *Marie Dupleffis*, dont un garçon & une fille.

SECONDE BRANCHE.

JACQUES D'AUVERGNE DE CHAMPDALOÏTTE, Ecuyer, fils puîné d'HIPPOLYTE, I⁰ʳ du nom, & d'*Elifabeth de Launay*, époufa, en 1728, *Marie de Turmeau*, dont:

1. JACQUES-AMABLE, qui fuit;
2. HIPPOLYTE, appelé *le Chevalier d'Auvergne*, qui a fervi aux Grandes-Indes, a été Capitaine d'une Compagnie d'Elèves à l'Ecole Royale Militaire, eft Chevalier de Saint-Louis, retiré du fervice, non marié;
3. JEAN, premier Capitaine de Grenadiers, au Régiment de Port-au-Prince, à Saint-Domingue, vivant fans alliance;
4. Et quatre filles.

JACQUES-AMABLE D'AUVERGNE, Chevalier de Saint-Louis, Lieutenant-Colonel réformé de Cavalerie, &, en cette qualité, Commandant de l'Equitation de l'Ecole Royale Militaire, a époufé, le 17 Mai 1764, *Ifidore-Vincent de Bongars*, fille de *Guillaume*, & nièce de Jacques de Bongars, Commandeur de l'Ordre de Saint-Lazare, Brigadier des armées du Roi, & fon Lieutenant à l'Ecole Royale Militaire. De ce mariage font iffus:

1. GUILLAUME-AMABLE, né le 27 Novembre 1764, nommé par le Roi, Elève de l'Ecole Royale Militaire, en Août 1774;
2. JACQUES, né le 9 Avril 1775;
3. HIPPOLYTE, né le 17 Mars 1776;
4. THOMAS-ALEXANDRE, né le 7 Mars 1778;
5. MARGUERITE-VINCENT, née le 28 Novembre 1767;
6. ISABELLE-APOLLINE, née le 9 Avril 1769;
7. MADELEINE, née le 6 Avril 1770, nommée par le Roi à une place de Saint-Cyr, le 18 Juin 1778;

8. Et THÉRÈSE, née le 15 Avril 1774.

Les armes : *d'argent, à la fasce de gueules, chargée de trois coquilles d'argent, & accompagnée de six merlettes de sable, trois en chef & trois en pointe.*

AUVERGNY. Voyez ESPINAY-SAINT-LUC.

AUVERY : *d'or, au dauphin pâmé d'azur.*

AUVERY : *chevronné d'argent & de sable, de 6 pièces.*

AUVEU : *enté en pointe de gueules & d'argent.*

* AUVILLARS, Vicomté au pays de Lomagne, en Gascogne, qui a été unie au Comté d'*Armagnac.* Voyez ce mot.

AUVILLIERS, Seigneur du Bouchoir : *d'argent, à 2 chevrons de gueules, accompagnés de 3 têtes de loup de sable arrachées, 2 en chef & 1 en pointe.*

AUVRAY. Il y a cinq familles de ce nom en Normandie, trois dans la Généralité d'Alençon, & deux dans celle de Caen.

La première est AUVRAY, Sieur de la Gondonnière, maintenue dans sa noblesse, le 20 Mai 1666, dont étoit CHARLES AUVRAY, Seigneur de la Gondonnière, marié, vers 1620, à *Anne de Morchêne.* Leur fille, MARGUERITE AUVRAY, épousa, le 15 Janvier 1647, *François de Droullin-de-Mesnilglaise.*

Les armes : *de gueules, à la fasce d'or, accompagnée en chef de deux roses d'or, & en pointe de deux lions passans & affrontés d'or.*

La seconde, dont La Roque parle dans son *Traité de la Noblesse,* pag. 267, est AUVRAY, Sieur des Monts, de Mainteville, maintenue dans sa Noblesse, le 31 Décembre 1666. NICOLAS AUVRAY, Ecuyer, Sieur d'Imanville, des Monts, de Martainville, Généralité d'Alençon, Election d'Argentan, fut annobli par Lettres données au Camp de Pas, en Artois, au mois de Septembre 1597. N... AUVRAY, veuve de *N... Eynard,* Grand-Maître des Eaux & Forêts de Touraine, étoit mère de Madame de *l'Hôpital-Sainte-Mesme,* & de N..., femme de *N... de Selle,* Trésorier-Général de la Marine.

Les armes : *d'argent, au chevron d'azur, chargé de trois fleurs-de-lys d'or, & accompagné de trois feuilles de sinople, deux en chef & une en pointe.*

La troisième famille, de la Généralité d'Alençon, Election de Lisieux en Normandie, est AUVRAY, Ecuyer, Sieur d'Imanville & de Meurville, maintenue dans sa noblesse, le 3 Décembre 1666. Elle porte pour armes : *de gueules, au chevron d'or, accompagné de trois croix de même, deux en chef & une en pointe.*

De la première famille d'AUVRAY, de la Généralité de Caen, dont parle La Roque, dans son *Traité de la Noblesse,* étoit CYPRIEN AUVRAY, Sieur de Lescarde, Echevin à Caen, qui fut *annobli* par Lettres du mois d'Octobre 1599, vérifiées en la Chambre des Comptes en 1599, & en la Cour des Aides, le 13 Décembre 1610.

Les armes : *d'azur, à trois coquilles d'argent, 2 & 1.*

La dernière famille du nom d'AUVRAY, est AUVRAY, Sieur de la Rocque, dont les armes sont : *palé d'azur & d'or, de six pièces, au chef de gueules, chargé d'un léopard d'or.*

AUVRECHER. La Terre d'Auvrecher, que ceux du Pays nomment, par corruption *Orchèr,* est située dans le Bailliage de Caux, sur le bord de la rivière de Seine, à une lieue de la Ville de Harfleur.

Cette Maison est connue indifféremment sous les noms d'*Avrecher,* & d'*Angerville,* ce dernier ayant été pris par les puînés, qui quelquefois ont porté tous les deux ensemble.

Les Registres de la Chambre des Comptes font mention de Monsieur GUILLAUME, Seigneur d'Auvrecher & d'Angerville, Maréchal & Sénéchal de Normandie, sous le Roi PHILIPPE-AUGUSTE, l'an 1205.

Et en effet, la Charge de Maréchal héréditaire de la Province a été d'ancienneté attachée à cette Maison : mais il y a si long-tems qu'elle est éteinte, qu'on n'en peut donner qu'une notice.

Il y a des Lettres du Roi PHILIPPE DE VALOIS, expédiées à Poissy, au mois de Mars 1345, par lesquelles il octroye une charretée de bois sec, chaque semaine, en sa forêt de Brotanne, aux Religieux du Prieuré de Notre-Dame-du-Bois-d'Auvrecher, fondé sur la Terre de GUILLAUME, Sire d'AUVRECHER, près de Harfleur, dans la Paroisse de Gonfreville-l'Auvrecher, par Frère *Pierre le Marchand,* du Tiers-Ordre de Saint-François, en récompenfe des bons fervices que ce Frère *Pierre* avoit fait à Sa Majefté en fes guerres de la mer, en la Compagnie de *Nicolas Beuchet*, fon Chevalier, Confeiller & Amiral.

Ce GUILLAUME, Sire d'Auvrecher, eut pour fils & fucceffeur:

ROBERT, Chevalier, Sire d'AUVRECHER, Maréchal de Normandie en 1363, qui époufa *Jeanne de Préaux* (a), dont il eut:

1. JEAN, qui fuit;
2. JEANNE, Dame de Turgoville, femme de *Colard d'Eftouteville*, Seigneur d'Ausbofe;
3. Et JACQUELINE, femme de *Guillaume Crefpin*, qui, à caufe d'elle s'intitula Maréchal de Normandie.

JEAN, Sire d'AUVRECHHR, Maréchal de Normandie, époufa, l'an 1390, *Marie de Bréauté*, fille de *Roger*, IVe du nom, Seigneur de Bréauté, & de *Marguerite d'Eftouteville*, dont il eut:

1. JACQUES, qui fuit;
2. Et JEANNE, morte fans enfans.

Meffire JACQUES, Sire d'AUVRECHER & de Planes, Maréchal de Normandie, décéda, fans poftérité, le 21 Octobre 1428, & avec lui gît *Noble Homme* Meffire JEAN, Seigneur d'AUVRECHER & de Planes, Maréchal héréditaire de Normandie.

Les Echiquiers des années 1390 & 1397 parlent de Meffire JEAN D'AUVRECHER, Chevalier, Maréchal de Normandie, héritier de *Jeanne de Préaux*, fa mère, plaidant contre Meffire GUILLAUME D'AUVRECHER, Vicomte de Bloffeville; ce qui montre qu'il y avoit encore d'autres branches de cette Maifon.

En d'autres Arrêts de la même Cour, ès années 1448, 1463, & 1497, il eft parlé de Madame *Jeanne d'Aunou*, veuve de Meffire JACQUES D'AUVRECHER, Chevalier; d'*Aubry Doullé*, Ecuyer, chargé du fait de *Jean d'Angerville*, de *Robert d'Angerville*, Ecuyer, de là Demoifelle fa femme, de Meffire JEAN D'AUVRECHER, Chevalier, tous héritiers de la Dame *Jeanne d'Auvrecher*.

Il y a un accord fait entre JEAN, Sire d'Au-

(a) ROBERT D'AUVRECHER, Chevalier, eft mentionné dans un contrat du 28 Février 1374, avec *Jeanne de Planes*, fon époufe, & JEAN, Seigneur d'AUVRECHER, leur fils; ce qui fait croire ou qu'il avoit eu deux femmes, ou que *Jeanne de Préaux* étoit Dame de Planes, ce qui eft plus vraifemblable.

vrecher & de Planes, Maréchal de Normandie, & *Marguerite d'Harcourt*, Dame de Ferrières, l'an 1402.

Raoul Morel de Brione, puîné de la Maifon d'*Harcourt*, en 1416, époufa PERRETTE D'AUVRECHER.

Cette Terre d'Auvrecher eft maintenant poffédée par la branche de *Potier-de-Novion*, dont le Préfident au Parlement de Paris eft mort en 1769.

Monfeigneur JEAN D'AUVRECHER eft compris dans le Rôle des grands Seigneurs de Normandie, fous le règne de CHARLES VI.

Quant à la branche D'ANGERVILLE, puînée de la Maifon d'AUVRECHER, JEAN D'ANGERVILLE fervoit l'Etat l'an 1338.

PIERRE D'ANGERVILLE rendit aveu d'un Fief dans la Paroiffe de Douville l'an 1391.

ROBERT D'ANGERVILLE, Seigneur de Grainville, rendit auffi aveu l'an 1392. Il époufa *Marguerite de Tourneville*, dont il eut: ROBERT, RICHARD, COLIN & GAUTHIER, vivant en 1396. (Voyez ANGERVILLE).

Il y a des partages faits entre FRANÇOIS D'ANGERVILLE, fils de JEAN, ROBERT & LOUIS D'ANGERVILLE, fes oncles, fils de CHARLES, & JEAN D'ANGERVILLE, Vicomte de Coutances, fils de CHARLES.

LOUIS D'ANGERVILLE, Curé de Petiville en 1508, préfenté par JEAN D'ANGERVILLE, Seigneur de Petiville.

JEAN D'ANGERVILLE, préfenté à la même Cure, l'an 1535, & JACQUES D'ANGERVILLE, auffi préfenté l'an 1550, par LOUIS D'ANGERVILLE, Seigneur de Petiville.

Traité de mariage de l'an 1608, entre ROBERT D'ANGERVILLE, frère de RENÉ, Seigneur de Gonneville, & *Ifabeau de Boifrenom*.

Accord, l'an 1640, entre FRANÇOIS & ANTOINE D'ANGERVILLE, leurs enfans.

Charte pour le Prieuré de Saint-Gilles de Pont-Audemer, de 1272, où figne ROBERT D'ANGERVILLE.

Dans les Mémoires de M. *Bigot de Longmefnil*, font mentionnés GUILLAUME D'ANGERVILLE, Seigneur de Cléville, & GUILLAUME D'ANGERVILLE, Seigneur d'Auvrecher.

Gilles d'Argouges, Seigneur de Grâtot, époufa, l'an 1443, LOUISE D'ANGERVILLE.

GUILLAUME D'ANGERVILLE époufa en 1041 *Simonne d'Ainfy*, fille de *Raoul d'Ainfy*.

Jacques de Poiffy, Seigneur de Gouy, fils de *Jean de Poiffy*, Seigneur de Gouy, & de

Catherine, Dame de Grainville-fur-Fleury, époufa JEANNE D'AUVRECHER.

Guillaume de Rupierre, Seigneur de Sarcelles, époufa, l'an 1440, JEANNE D'ANGERVILLE, fille de ROBERT, Seigneur de Grainville.

Il y a un Arrêt des francs-fiefs, de l'an 1563, qui contient que CATHERINE D'ANGERVILLE, fille de JEAN, Seigneur de Grainville, avoit époufé *Guillaume le Bouquetot*, Seigneur de Rabu, fils de *Jean Bouquetot*, Seigneur du Breuil, & de *Louife l'Éfcot*, Dame de Rabu.

Remontant plus haut, il y a un rôle de la Chambre des Comptes, de l'an 1351, où font nommés PIERRE D'ANGERVILLE, Chevalier, ROBERT, RAOUL & ROGER D'ANGERVILLE.

Les armes: *d'or, à deux quinte-feuilles de fable, pofées une au canton feneftre, & l'autre en pointe de l'écu, à un lionceau de même au premier canton.*

AUX, ou d'AUX, au Diocèfe de Condom, Province de Guyenne. Ce nom fe trouve, avec la qualité de *Noble*, dans plufieurs actes des Archives du Chapitre de Saint-Pierre de Larromieu, au Diocèfe de Condom, datés du XIe fiècle. Cette ancienne Nobleffe a eu, dans le lieu de Larromieu, différens corps de bâtimens, qui tous annoncent fon antiquité; le plus ancien exiftoit avant la conftruction de la Ville de Larromieu. Il étoit fitué à 200 pas au-deffus: on l'appeloit *Montpellier (Mons Peffulanus)*; il en refte encore quelques veftiges; & la Chapelle, qui fait partie de la maifon du Fermier.

Lorfqu'on bâtit l'Eglife Paroiffiale de Larromieu, la Maifon d'AUX fit conftruire une Maifon y attenante, où l'on voit fes armes; & cette maifon eft aujourd'hui la demeure du Doyen du Chapitre de Larromieu.

Dans le XIIe fiècle, la Ville fut entourée de murailles, & la Maifon d'AUX fit conftruire un édifice fuperbe pour ces tems-là: il eft défigné dans l'acte de fondation du Chapitre fous le nom de *Palatium*; ce n'eft plus aujourd'hui qu'une maifon honnête: il y en a une troifième, dont la porte-cochère ne marque pas moins fon antiquité que le rang diftingué de ceux qui l'habitoient. Vers le milieu du XIIIe fiècle, Meffire PIERRE D'AUX, Chevalier, defcendant de cette Maifon, eut deux enfans, ARNAUD & GUILLAUME, dont nous rapporterons ci-après la filiation:

ARNAUD embraffa l'Etat Eccléfiaftique, & après avoir été Vicaire-Général de l'Archevêque de Bordeaux, nommé du *Gout* ou *Got*, fon parent, depuis Pape, fous le nom de CLÉMENT V, fut fait Evêque de Poitiers par ce Pontife, qui lui donna enfuite l'Evêché d'Albane, le fit Cardinal, & l'envoya fon Légat en Angleterre, pour réconcilier les efprits, dit Thomas Walfingamus.

En 1318, ce Cardinal fonda le Chapitre de Saint-Pierre de Larromieu, auquel il donna le Prieuré dudit lieu, avec fes dépendances, qu'il acquit des Bénédictins de Saint-Victor de Marfeille. Et comme le revenu de ce Prieuré n'étoit pas fuffifant pour doter ce Chapitre, il y ajouta non-feulement fes biens patrimoniaux, mais il fit auffi contribuer fes parens: (*Tam in bonis noftris, quam proximorum noftrorum concefforum.*) Ce font les termes de la fondation, qui marquent qu'ils confiftent en terres, rentes, fiefs, dixmes, moulins, Seigneuries, le tout fitué en diverfes Paroiffes du Diocèfe de Condom.

Le Cardinal ARNAUD D'AUX ne laiffa à fa famille qu'un petit Domaine, fon Palais, & le droit de Patronage, fucceffivement attaché, & à perpétuité, à fes plus proches. Cette fondation prohibe le droit de Patronage aux filles, & affure la fucceffion graduelle aux mâles, &, à leur défaut, la nomination des bénéfices eft réverfible au Chapitre. Cette claufe garantit la Maifon d'AUX de toute idée d'extinction, & elle nomme à ces bénéfices depuis 450 ans.

La fondation de ce Chapitre, les guerres civiles, & peut-être la mauvaife adminiftration, ont beaucoup diminué la fortune de la Maifon d'AUX; ce qui a fans doute empêché que ceux de ce nom ne foient parvenus aux premières Charges de l'Etat; mais du moins ont-ils fait de très-belles alliances.

Suivant le Jugement de M. *Pellot*, Commiffaire député par Arrêt du Confeil, du 22 Mars 1666, pour la recherche de la Nobleffe, GUILLAUME D'AUX, frère du Cardinal, eut pour enfans:

1. GÉRAUD, qui fuit;
2. FORT, ou FORTIUS, Evêque de Poitiers;
3. PIERRE-RAYMOND, Abbé de Sainte-Marie-Majeure de Poitiers;
4. Et GUILLAUME, Chantre-Dignitaire de la même Eglife de Poitiers, Employé à la Cour de Rome.

GÉRAUD, le premier Patron du Chapitre de

enfant de *Jacques Barrin*, Chevalier, Seigneur & Marquis de la Galiffonnière, & d'*Eléonore Bidé*, Dame de la Grandville. Etant veuve, au nom, & comme tutrice & gardienne-noble de fes enfans mineurs, ci-après nommés, elle obtint un Arrêt en la Chambre des Comptes de Paris, le 11 Juillet 1717, portant délai pour faire l'hommage que lefdits mineurs devoient au Roi, à caufe du Marquifat du Bailleul, & de la Baronie de Goron, mouvant du Comté du Maine, & mourut au Château des Moutys, Paroiffe de la Valette près Nantes en Bretagne. Ses enfans furent :

1. PIERRE GILBERT-ANNE, qui fuit ;
2. LOUIS-EMÉRITE, né au Château de fon nom, le 20 Janvier 1709, qui embraffa l'Etat Eccléfiaftique ; fut ordonné Prêtre à Paris le 10 Avril 1734, nommé Vicaire-Général de l'Evêché de Limoges en 1736 ; Préfident & Député de la Chambre Eccléfiaftique de ce Diocèfe en 1737, nommé à l'Abbaye Royale du Beuil, au même Diocèfe, le 14 Septembre 1738 ; Grand-Vicaire de l'Archevêché de Tours le 5 Septembre 1739, d'où il paffa, en la même qualité, à Embrun en 1740, où il fut fait l'année fuivante Archidiacre & Chanoine de cette Eglife, & fut nommé à l'Abbaye-Royale de Bois-Groland le 2 Mars 1742. Il fe rendit utile au Roi & à l'Etat, dans cette dernière Place, par le fervice qu'il rendit à l'Armée combinée de France & d'Efpagne, par l'établiffement qu'il fit à Embrun d'un Hôpital Militaire, dont cette Place de Guerre étoit alors dépourvue, & dans lequel, par fes foins, dès le mois de Septembre 1743, jufqu'au départ de cette Armée, arrivé au mois de Février 1745, plus de 500 Soldats, tant malades que bleffés, furent journellement traités avec fuccès. Il procura également les mêmes fecours aux Officiers, tant dans fa maifon, que dans celles où il les fit placer. Il tint au commencement de 1745, en l'abfence de l'Archevêque, l'Affemblée Provinciale d'Embrun, où il fut élu l'un des Députés du fecond ordre pour l'Affemblée Générale du Clergé qui fe tint à Paris fur la fin de 1745. Il quitta ce Diocèfe en 1748, & s'attacha, en la même qualité de Grand-Vicaire, à celui de Rodez, à la Théologale Métropolitaine duquel il fut nommé le 6 Mai 1754 ; fut pourvu le 18 Décembre fuivant du Canonicat & de l'Archidiaconé de Milhau en la même Eglife, & Député du Chapitre de ce Diocèfe pendant 3 à 4 ans ; fut nommé à l'Abbaye-Royale de Notre-Dame de Barzelles-en-Berry, Diocèfe de Bourges, le 20 Janvier 1748 ; & mourut à Paris le lundi 18 Septembre 1769, regretté de toutes fes connoiffances, dont il étoit l'ami déclaré. Il fut inhumé le lendemain en la cave de la nef de l'Eglife Royale & Paroiffiale de Saint-Paul. Il étoit le *dernier mâle* de toute fa famille ;
3. N...... mort jeune ;
4. Et MARIE-CATHERINE-EUGÉNIE, dite *Mademoifelle du Bailleul*, née au Château de fon nom, le 18 Janvier 1710, morte, fans alliance, à Rennes en Bretagne, au mois de Novembre 1769, & inhumée en l'Eglife Paroiffiale de Saint-Aubin.

PIERRE-GILBERT-ANNE DU BAILLEUL, Chevalier, Seigneur & Marquis du Bailleul, Baron de Goron, Seigneur de Couefme, Lucé, Vaudemuffon, le Rocher, la Pierre, Hercé, Belleplante, &c., né au Château de fon nom le 26 Décembre 1707, reçu Page du Roi dans fa Grande-Ecurie, le 5 Janvier 1724, d'après fes preuves faites devant le Juge d'Armes de France (feu M. *Charles d'Hozier*) qui établiffent fucceffivement la poffeffion de fa nobleffe, depuis ALAIN DU BAILLEUL, fon huitième ayeul, qualifié *Chevalier, Seigneur du Bailleul*, &c., dont nous avons parlé au commencement de cet article ; Lieutenant au Régiment du Roi en 1728 ; eft mort à Mayenne au mois de Janvier 1737, d'où fon corps fut tranfporté en l'Eglife Paroiffiale de Saint-Martin de fa Baronie de Goron. Il avoit époufé, par contrat paffé devant *Julien Gobbé*, Notaire à Goron, en Février 1729, *Françoife-Thérèfe de Montecler*, qui vit aujourd'hui à Mayenne, avec fes deux filles. Elle étoit fille de *Georges-François*, Marquis de Montecler & de Defcajeuls, & d'*Etiennette-Diane de la Malrais*. Leurs enfans furent :

1. 2. & 3. N...... N...... & N...... Chevaliers, morts en bas âge ;
4. FRANÇOISE-MARIE, dite *Mademoifelle du Bailleul*, née au Château de fon nom le 8 Décembre 1729, non mariée en 1770 ;
5. LOUISE-HYACINTHE-PULCHÉRIE, dite *Mademoifelle de Goron*, née au Château du Bailleul, le 27 Janvier 1731, Religieufe Auguftine à l'Hôpital de Sainte-Julie de la ville de Château-Gontier ;
6. ANNE-VICTOIRE-FÉLICITÉ, dite *Mademoifelle de Lucé*, née au Château du Bailleul le 25 Janvier 1732, non mariée en 1770 ;
7. Et N....... dite *Mademoifelle de Couefme*, morte âgée de 4 ans.

Les armes : *d'argent, à 3 têtes de loup de*

fable, arrachées & lampaſſées de gueules, poſées 2 *&* 1.

BAILLI: *d'argent, à la quinte-feuille de fable.*

BAILLI: *d'azur, à la faſce d'argent, accompagnée en chef de trois étoiles d'or, & en pointe d'un croiſſant de même.*

BAILLIF (LE), en Bretagne: *d'argent, à un palmier arraché de ſinople, fruité de gueules.*

BAILLIF (LE), en Bretagne: *écartelé d'or & de gueules.*

BAILLIF (LE), en Bretagne: *d'azur, au chevron d'or, accompagné de quatre beſans de même, trois en chef & un en pointe.*

BAILLIF (LE): *d'azur* ou *de fable, au lévrier courant d'argent, accompagné en chef d'une étoile à huit raies de même.*

BAILLIF, Seigneur de Mainvilliers, famille éteinte, que l'auteur des *Antiquités d'Eſtampes* nomme mal-à-propos BAILLY.

JACOB BAILLIF, Maître des Requêtes de la Reine & Bailli de Pithiviers, épouſa *Louiſe Rouſſet,* veuve de *Jacques Ravault,* Seigneur de Changy. De ce mariage ſont iſſus:

1. JOSEPH, qui ſuit;
2. Et FRANÇOISE-VICTOIRE, née en 1678, morte en 1709. Elle avoit épouſé, le 13 Janvier 1699, *Charles de Tarragon,* Ecuyer, Seigneur de la Carrée.

JOSEPH BAILLIF, Chevalier de Saint-Louis, & ancien Capitaine au Régiment de Picardie, mourut ſans alliance dans ſon château de Mainvilliers, le 13 Janvier 1742.

Les armes: *d'azur, au chevron d'or accompagné de trois étoiles de même, le chevron chargé d'un pampre de vigne, garni de fruits au naturel.*

⚜ BAILLIVY, Maiſon ancienne & originaire de Toul, établie en Lorraine au commencement du dernier ſiècle, qui portoit autrefois le nom de BAILLY, ſous lequel elle a poſſédé depuis long-tems la dignité de Maître-Echevin dans la Ville de Toul, lorſque cette Ville, comme celles de Metz & de Verdun, étoit Impériale, & ſe gouvernoit, ſous l'autorité des Empereurs, par ſes propres loix. Elle a fondé ſur la fin du XVIe ſiècle les Religieuſes Prêchereſſes de cette Ville, & les Frères Prêcheurs, chez leſquels cette Maiſon a ſa ſépulture; ils lui doivent une partie de

Tome II.

leur dotation. Le premier par où commence la filiation ſuivie eſt:

JEAN BAILLY, Ecuyer, qui fut Maître-d'Hôtel de Robert de Bar, Evêque & Comte de Verdun, duquel il obtint, en 1258, pour lui & JEAN BAILLY, ſon fils, demeurant à Toul, 80 liv. monnoie de Verdun, à prendre ſur ſes rentes du ban de Tilly, en conſidération des bons ſervices qu'il lui avoit rendus, ainſi qu'au Pape, à l'Empereur & à Yolande de Flandres, Comteſſe de Bar; il promit à cet Evêque de l'accompagner au voyage de la Terre-Sainte, & il étoit un des vieux Gentilshommes de ſa maiſon. Du fils de ce JEAN BAILLY, étoit iſſu par pluſieurs degrés, JEAN BAILLY, ſurnommé BAILLIVY, Lieutenant-Général de la Cité de Toul, ainſi qu'il fut prouvé en 1620, & qu'il eſt rapporté dans des Lettres-Patentes du Roi LOUIS XIII. Il mourut le 5 Juillet 1578, & avoit épouſé *Catherine de Remy,* morte le 30 Novembre 1589, fille de *Colin de Remy,* Ecuyer, Seigneur de Bouck, mort en 1524, inhumé dans l'Egliſe des Cordeliers de Toul, dont il eut:

1. CLAUDE, qui ſuit;
2. NICOLAS, père d'un autre NICOLAS, mort ſans enfans;
3. JEAN, Seigneur de Bouveron, Lieutenant-Général de la Cité de Toul, qui, de *Catherine de Bailliart,* eut:
   1. ESTHER DE BAILLIVY, femme 1° de *Jean de Villers,* Seigneur de Saulny; & 2° de *Nicolas de la Tour,* Seigneur de Savonnières, Gouverneur de Liverdun;
   2. MARIE, morte ſans enfans de ſon mariage avec *Nicolas,* Seigneur de *Larry;*
   3. LUCIE-FRANÇOISE, mariée 1° à *Charles de Feriet,* Conſeiller d'Etat en la Chambre des Comptes de Lorraine; & 2° à *René du Meſnil-de-Vaux,* Seigneur de Mondeval, Saint-Germain & Mauvaye, Lieutenant au Gouvernement de Toul, duquel elle eut entr'autres enfans:
      ANNE DU MESNIL-DE-VAUX, femme d'*Évrard des Salles,* Baron de Gouhecourt, Lieutenant-Colonel au ſervice de France;
      Et MATHILDE-CATHERINE DU MESNIL-DE-VAUX, femme d'*Antoine des Armoiſes,* Baron d'Autreu & de Bazvilles;
4. Et CHARLES DE BAILLIVY, Seigneur de Bouveron, mort en 1644. Il avoit épouſé *Marguerite,* fille d'*Euſtache de Rho-*

N

der, Seigneur de Jubainville, & d'*Anne de Morlaincourt*, dont:

JEAN DE BAILLIVY, Seigneur de Bouveron;

Et ANNE, femme de *Jean-François*, Seigneur de *Dompmartin*, Conseiller d'Etat, Maître des Requêtes de l'Hôtel du Duc de Lorraine;

4. Et LOUIS DE BAILLIVY, Conseiller d'Etat du Duc de Lorraine, & marié à *Elisabeth de Fercet*, fille de *Nicolas*, Seigneur de Pulligny, & de *Barbe le Galland*, de laquelle il eut:

1. CLAUDE, Chanoine de Saint-Gengoux;
2. BARBE, mariée à *Gilles de Jabal*, Seigneur de Pagny-lès-Loins, de Dompmartin & Vocet-de-Blénard. Elle fut ayeule du Marquis *du Barail*, Colonel du Régiment du Roi, Infanterie, & de la Marquise de *la Tournelle;*
3. ANTOINETTE, mariée 1º à *N... des Fois;* & 2º en 1630, à *Pierre du May*, Seigneur de Vezerny;
4. CATHERINE, femme de *François de Riguet*, Seigneur de Barisey, Capitaine des Gardes de la Duchesse de Lorraine;
5. Et LOUISE DE BAILLIVY, mariée à *Henri de Belliard de Salins*, Colonel-Commandant les Mousquetaires de la Garde du Duc Charles IV.

CLAUDE DE BAILLIVY, Ier du nom, Seigneur de Mèreville, Velaine, Sancy-entre-les-Bois, Olchey, Sélincourt, Brabois, Houdemont & de la Cour-de-la-neuve-Ville, fut Conseiller d'Etat, Maître des Requêtes de l'Hôtel du Duc Henri; il obtint, avec ses frères, du Roi LOUIS XIII, le 11 Avril 1620, des Lettres-Patentes portant déclaration & reconnoissance de noblesse, & qu'ils ont prouvé être issus des plus anciennes familles nobles de Toul, & notamment de Noble Ecuyer JEAN BAILLY, qui vivoit en 1250, depuis lequel ils ont toujours vécu noblement sans mésalliance, & portent le titre de Gentilshommes. Il épousa *Anne de Vaillot*, veuve de *Balthasard*, Seigneur de *Toupet*, sœur de *Jean de Voillot*, Seigneur de *Valleroy*, Madecourt, Agécourt, Marancourt, Ministre & premier Secrétaire d'Etat du Duc Charles III, & tous deux enfans de *Jean de Voillot*, & de *Françoise de Raufain*, dont le père Nicolas de *Raufain*, Capitaine du Château de Condé-sur-Moselle, fut marié à *Nicole de Nogent*. CLAUDE DE BAILLIVY eut pour enfans:

1. CLAUDE, qui suit;
2. NICOLAS, Chanoine de la Primatiale de Nancy;
3. PHILIPPE, Religieux Capucin;
4. JEAN, rapporté après son frère aîné;
5. ANNE, femme de *Jean de Noirel*, Capitaine du Château de Gondreville;
6. Et MARIE DE BAILLIVY, femme de *Claude de Ceuillet*, Seigneur du Sauvois, Gruyer de Nancy.

JEAN DE BAILLIVY, Seigneur de Houdemont & de la Cour-de-la-neuve-Ville, Conseiller d'Etat, Maître des Requêtes de l'Hôtel du Duc Henri, épousa en 1607 *Catherine de Rennel*, fille de *Balthasard*, Seigneur de Brin, Jarville, Saint-Germain, Ministre d'Etat & Président de Lorraine, & de *Barbe de Lescut*, dont il eut:

1. CLAUDE-CHRÉTIENNE, mariée en 1639 à *Nicolas le Fèvre d'Ancy*, Seigneur dudit lieu, Pullenoy et Passoncourty;
2. Et MARIE DE BAILLIVY, femme de *César de Hoffelize*, Seigneur d'Oberfing & de Valfroicourt, Conseiller d'Etat, Maître des Requêtes de l'Hôtel du Duc Charles IV.

CLAUDE DE BAILLIVY, IIe du nom, Seigneur d'Olchey-Brabois & Sélincourt, Conseiller d'Etat, Maître des Requêtes de l'Hôtel du Duc Henri, obtint de ce prince, le 8 Mars 1522, des Lettres-Patentes de déclaration de gentillesse, confirmatives de celles accordées, en 1620, par le Roi Louis XIII, à son père & à ses oncles, & mourut en 1641. Il avoit épousé, en 1605, *Nicole d'Einville*, Dame de Gueblanges, fille de *Nicolas*, Chevalier, Seigneur de Gueblanges, Blainville, Craiencourt, Jalocourt, Horbey, Dombale & Momel-sur-Seine, & de *Marie de Vigneulles-du-Sart*. Leurs enfans furent:

1. NICOLAS, qui suit;
2. FRANÇOIS, auteur de la branche des Comtes de *Merigny*, rapporté ci-après;
3. HENRI-PHILIPPE, tige des Seigneurs de *Valleroy, Madecourt*, dont nous parlerons ensuite;
4. FRANÇOISE, mariée en 1629 à *Charles de Lampugnan*, Seigneur de Frémonville, Gentilhomme de la Chambre du Duc Charles IV, & fils d'*Octave de Lampugnan*, Gentilhomme Milanois, Conseiller d'Etat du Duc de Lorraine, & de *Jeanne Forvye*, dont elle n'eut qu'*Antoinette de Lampugnan*, Dame de Fremonville, femme de *Luc le Roy de Monluc*, Lieutenant-Colonel d'un Régiment de Cavalerie au service de France;

5. ANNE, mariée en 1631 à *Charles de Sennevois*, Chevalier, Seigneur de Balot, en Bourgogne, dont *Claude de Sennevois*, marié, en 1680, à *Georges-Anne-Louis*, Comte *de Pernès*, Marquis d'Efpinac, Brigadier des Armées du Roi, Lieutenant des Gendarmes-Dauphins, premier Gentilhomme de la Chambre du Duc de Bourbon, & élu de la Nobleffe de Bourgogne en 1709;

6. CLAUDE, mariée en 1643 à *Jean-Philippe de Malvoifin*, Seigneur de Hameville, Aboncourt &˙Boulancourt, Colonel au fervice du Duc Charles IV;

7. Et NICOLE DE BAILLIVY, femme de *Jean-Philippe du Pleffis*, commandant une Compagnie de Chevaux-Légers de la Garde de Charles IV, & Gouverneur de Dieufe, dont elle eut une fille, mariée à *N.... de Lorins*, Baron d'Eftrepy.

NICOLAS DE BAILLIVY, Chevalier, Seigneur de Gueblanges, Lieutenant d'une Compagnie des Gardes-du-Corps du Duc Charles IV & Gouverneur de Longny, époufa 1° *Yolande de Forvye*, morte fans enfans; & 2° en 1676, *Marie-Charlotte de Lardenois-de-Ville*, veuve de *Gabriel-Abraham de Myon*, Baron de Gombervaux, & fille de *Philippe de Lardenois*, Seigneur de Porchereffe, & d'*Anne de Gourcy*. Il en eut:

1. FRANÇOIS, qui fuit;
2. Et MARIE-FRANÇOISE DE BAILLIVY, morte en 1736, fans poftérité.

FRANÇOIS, Comte de BAILLIVY, Seigneur de Gueblanges, Chambellan du Duc Léopold, Lieutenant-Colonel du Régiment de Duhan, & Commandant des Ville & Château de Bar, mourut en 1728. Il avoit époufé *Anne-Marie de Chauvirey*, Dame de Gouffaincourt, veuve d'*Antoine de la Fitte*, Marquis de Pellaport, Chambellan du Duc Léopold, & fille de *Nicolas-François*, Comte de *Chauvirey*, Maréchal de Lorraine & Barrois, & de *Caroline-Marie-Gertrude de Dongeberg*. Il a eu de cette alliance:

. ANNE-MARIE DE BAILLIVY, Dame de Gueblanges, femme de *Charles-Louis*, Marquis de *Nettancourt* & de *Bellancourt*.

BRANCHE
des Comtes DE MÉRIGNY.

FRANÇOIS DE BAILLIVY, fecond fils de CLAUDE, II° du nom, & de *Nicole d'Einville*, fut Seigneur de Mérigny, Sauxures, Olchey, Sélincourt, Houffelefmont. Il époufa, en 1659, *Françoife de Rofières*, fille de *François*,

Seigneur de Chaudenay, Braux, Longeville & Nefves, en Blois, Capitaine de Saint-Mihiel, & de *Sufanne Dalaumont*, celle-ci fille de *Robert Dalaumont*, Baron de Cernay, & de *Françoife de Joyeufe*. Il eut de ce mariage:

NICOLAS-FRANÇOIS DE BAILLIVY, Chevalier, Seigneur de Mérigny, Sauxures, Houffelefmont, Olchey, Salincourt, Tourteron, Fiequelmont & Xonville, qui mourut le 27 Août 1750. Il avoit époufé, en 1687, *Louife-Dorothée de Gournay*, morte dans fon Château de Mérigny, en Décembre 1749, fœur & héritière d'*Ignace*, Comte de *Gournay*, Seigneur d'Eftreval & de Rambercourt, Bailli de Vezelize, & fille de *Renaud de Gournay*, Seigneur defdits lieux, & de *Louife de Revet*. Il laiffa:

1. IGNACE, qui fuit;
2. Et NICOLAS DE BAILLIVY, rapporté après fon frère.

IGNACE DE BAILLIVY, Chevalier, Comte de Mérigny, Seigneur dudit lieu, de Sauxures, Houffelefmont, Olchey, Sélincourt & Rambecour, Chevalier de Saint-Louis, Lieutenant-Colonel du Régiment de Rofen, Allemand, mourut en 1771. Il avoit époufé, le 2 Mai 1741, *Henriette-Armande de Saint-Blaife*, morte en 1772, fille de *Gabriel-Henri*, Comte de Changy, & de *Nicole de Montarby-de-Dampierre*. De ce mariage font iffus:

1. FRANÇOIS-XAVIER DE BAILLIVY, Chevalier, Comte de Mérigny, Capitaine au Régiment de Cavalerie Royal Lorraine;
2. CHARLES-MARIE-DIEUDONNÉ DE BAILLIVY, Capitaine au Régiment de Vermandois, Infanterie, reçu Chevalier de Malte au Grand-Prieuré de Champagne, en 1752; &˙
3. Et JEANNE-DOROTHÉE DE BAILLIVY-DE-MÉRIGNY, mariée à Nancy, le 5 Septembre 1768, à *Jean-Vincent-Anne de Malartic*, Lieutenant-Colonel au Régiment de Baffigny, Chevalier de l'Ordre Royal & Militaire de Saint-Louis.

NICOLAS DE BAILLIVY, Chevalier, Seigneur de Xonville, Tourteron & Fiequelmont, fils puîné de NICOLAS-FRANÇOIS, & de *Louife-Dorothée de Gournay*, d'abord Page du Duc Léopold, puis Capitaine de Cavalerie au Régiment de Rofen, Allemand, a époufé, le 7 Janvier 1744, *Barbe de Hault-de-Sancy*, fille unique de *Nicolas-François*, Seigneur de Rodange, & de *Barbe-Catherine de Bonet-d'Aunoux*, de laquelle il a eu:

1. IGNACE;
2. ALEXANDRE-FRANÇOIS, qui a été Moufquetaire du Roi;
3. Et LOUISE DE BAILLIVY, mariée, en 1773, à *Nicolas-François de Curel*, Chevalier, voué de Royaumeix, Seigneur de Chonville & de Lonoux, des anciens Seigneurs de *Curel*, Capitaine en premier au Corps Royal du Génie.

BRANCHE
des Seigneurs DE VALLEROY, MADECOURT, &c.

HENRI-PHILIPPE DE BAILLIVY, Chevalier, troifième fils de CLAUDE, IIᵉ du nom & de *Nicole d'Einville*, fut Commandant des Gendarmes de la Garde de Charles IV, Duc de Lorraine, & époufa, le 13 Janvier 1666, *Marie-Louife-Françoife*, fille de *Claude*, Seigneur de *Villeroy*, Madecourt, Agécourt, Maroncourt, Ath-fur-Meurtre & Brin, Miniftre, Premier Secrétaire d'Etat du Duc Charles, & Préfident unique de la Chambre des Comptes, Cour des Aides & des Monnoies de Lorraine, & de *Marie de Rennel*, dont:
1. CHARLES, qui fuit;
2. Et MARIE-NICOLE DE BAILLIVY, mariée, en 1692, à *Jean-Baptifte-Henri*, Comte de *Rennel* & du Saint-Empire, Seigneur de Jarville, alors Capitaine au Régiment de Dauphiné, puis Colonel d'Infanterie en Lorraine.

CHARLES DE BAILLIVY, Chevalier, Seigneur de Valleroy, Madecourt, Agécourt & Maroncourt, Lieutenant de la compagnie des Cadets-Gentilshommes, au fervice du Duc Léopold, époufa, 1° en 1693, *Anne-Thérèfe de Seurcot*; 2° en 1706, *Marguerite de Légéville*, fille de *Charles*, Chevalier, Seigneur de *Légéville*, Frenoufe & la Chapelle, & de *Marthe de Houx-de-Belrupt*; & 3° *Marie-Anne Vincey*. Du premier lit il a eu:
1. FRANÇOIS-LÉOPOLD;
2. CLAUDE-HYACINTHE, dite *Mademoifelle de Baillivy*;
3. MARIE-ANNE, morte en 1758, femme d'*Eudes de Bocavillier*, Seigneur de Voué, de la ville de Toul;
4. CHARLOTTE-CHRISTINE DE BAILLIVY, morte Religieufe en 1755.
Et du troifième lit:
5. 6. & 7. Trois garçons;
8. Et une fille, mariée à *N... de Finance*.
Les armes: *de gueules, au chevron d'or,*

accompagné en chef de deux étoiles de même, & en pointe, d'un triangle taillé à fafcette, aussi d'or.

BAILLON. Il y a trois familles de ce nom en France, mais on ne fçait fi elles ont la même origine, ou fi elles font différentes, parce que leurs armes ne font pas les mêmes. Paillot parle de deux, & la troifième eft DE BAILLON fimplement, & porte: *d'or, à trois têtes de fanglier de fable.*

De la famille de BAILLON de Paris, qui porte: *de gueules, à une tête de léopard d'or, bouclée de trois annelets de même*, étoient MARIE-ANNE DE BAILLON, née le 28 Juillet 1672, & JEANNE-ELISABETH DE BAILLON-DE-FORGES, née le 11 Septembre 1674, l'une & l'autre reçues à Saint-Cyr au mois de Juin 1687, après avoir prouvé qu'elles defcendoient d'ODET DE BAILLON, Seigneur de Forges, qui étoit marié, en 1557, avec *Jeanne le Crec*, & étoit trifayeul de ces deux Demoifelles.

BAILLON, en Bourgogne: *d'argent, à cinq bandes de gueules.*

BAILLON, Seigneur de Forges: *de gueules, au mufle de léopard d'or, bouclé d'un anneau de même.*

BAILLON, Seigneur de Blampignon: *d'azur, à deux épées d'argent, garnies d'or, pofées en fautoir, accompagnées en chef d'un croiffant de gueules.*

BAILLON, Seigneur de Saillant: *d'azur, au lion paffant d'or, une patte pofée fur une fouche, furmontée de trois fleurs-de-lys, le tout de même.*

BAILLON, Seigneur de la Sablonnière, de Ganne, d'Ocqueville, de Beauffaut: *d'azur, à la croix d'or, cantonnée de quatre croifettes de même.*

BAILLOT, Seigneur de Villechavant: *d'azur, à trois colonnes tofcanes, furmontées chacune d'un V, en chef, un croiffant accotté de deux étoiles, le tout d'argent.*

BAILLOU, en Touraine: *d'or, à trois hures de fanglier de gueules, 2 & 1*; d'autres les portent *de fable.*

BAILLY, ou BALLI, famille originaire du Dauphiné.

FRANÇOIS-JOSEPH DE BAILLY, Chevalier, Marquis de Valbonnais, reçu Premier Préfident de la Chambre des Comptes de Grenoble, le 4 Juillet 1729, a épousé, en 1718, *Françoise Pourroy-de-Lauberivière*, fille de *Claude-Joseph Pourroy-de-Lauberivière*, second Préfident en la Chambre des Comptes, & sœur de *Marc-Joseph Pourroy-de-Quinsonnas*, Premier Préfident du Parlement de Befançon. Il a de ce mariage:

1. Jean-Pierre, Conseiller au Parlement de Grenoble;
2. Flodoard-Eléonor, Chevalier de Malte, Gouverneur de la Ville de Romans, & Capitaine de Cavalerie dans le Régiment d'Henrichemont;
3. Marie-Sébastien, Conseiller au Parlement de Grenoble;
4. Marc-Joseph, Eccléfiaftique;
5. N..., mariée à *Claude-François de Gratet*, Comte *du Bouchage*, Conseiller au Parlement de Dauphiné;
6. N..., épouse de *Jean-Baptiste de Rigaud-de-Laigue-de-Serezin*;
7. & 8. Et deux autres filles, non mariées.

(*Tabl. de Thémis*, part. III, pag. 57).

Les armes: *d'azur, à trois fasces d'or, & une plante de lys de finople à fix fleurs d'argent renverfées fur le champ, 1, 2 & 3, feuillée de finople, à la bulbe d'argent, aufi fur le champ.*

BAILLY, en Dauphiné: *d'azur, au chevron d'hermines, accompagné de trois étoiles d'or en chef, & en pointe d'un croiffant dè même.*

BAILLY, ancienne famille de Robe. Plufieurs de ce nom ont poffédé les charges les plus confidérables.

Guillaume Bailly, Chevalier de l'Ordre du Roi, Chancelier du Duc d'Alençon & Surintendant des Armées d'Italie, fut trifayeul de:

N... Bailly, Préfident au Grand-Conseil, qui époufa *N... le Tellier*, fille de *N... le Tellier*, Seigneur de Richebourg, dont:

N... Bailly, Comte de Frefnay, Capitaine au Régiment du Roi, qui a épousé, à Tours, le 1er Avril 1764, *Edmée-Anne-Charlotte*, fille de *Gafpard-Céfar-Charles l'Efcalopier*, Intendant de Tours.

Un autre Guillaume Bailly fut Avocat-Général, Conseiller d'Honneur au Grand-Conseil, & Abbé de Saint-Thierry.

BAILLY, Seigneurs de Lardenoy: *de gueules, à une plante de trois lys d'argent,* fur une terrasse de finople, au chef coufu d'azur, chargé d'une croifette pommetée d'or, accoftée de deux coquilles de même.

BAILLY, en Normandie, Généralité de Rouen: *d'azur, à trois annelets d'or, 2 & 1.*

BAILLY, Seigneur de Petit-Val, même Province & Généralité, famille maintenue dans fa nobleffe le 10 Août 1667, qui porte: *d'azur, à la fasce d'or, accompagnée en chef de deux croiffans d'argent, & en pointe de deux molettes d'éperon de même.*

BAILLY, Seigneur de Saint-Mars, de la Croix, du Séjour, de la Bruyère: *d'or, à la fasce d'azur, chargée d'une croix ancrée du champ, & accompagnée en chef de deux glands de finople en bande & en barre appointés, & en pointe d'un arbre fur une terraffe, le tout de même.*

BAILLY, Seigneur de Beyre: *écartelé, aux 1 & 4 d'azur, à la fasce d'or, aux 2 & 3 d'argent, au chevron de gueules accompagné de trois coquilles de même, deux en chef & une en pointe.*

BAILLY-DE-GAUGÉ, famille noble, dont étoit Françoise de Bailly, fille de Philibert de Bailly, Seigneur de Gaugé & de la Gibardière, & de *Françoise Quefti*; qui époufa 1°. *Adam Godme*, Seigneur de Grange, & 2° par contrat du 8 Mars 1571, *Michel de Melun*, Seigneur d'Annemois, & en partie du Buignon, troifième fils de *Loup de Melun*, & de *Marguerite Buffetan*.

Les armes: *d'argent, à une fasce de fable & une bordure engrêlée de gueules.*

BAINAST, en Tiérache. Robert de Bainast, Seigneur d'Herleville, qui vivoit en 1471, fut le cinquième ayeul de:

Albert de Bainast, Chevalier, Seigneur de Dommart, qui époufa *Marie Lignier*, dont il eut:

Marie-Anne de Bainast-de-Pommeras, née le 16 Juillet 1675, qui fut reçue à Saint-Cyr, au mois de Juillet 1687, après avoir prouvé fa nobleffe depuis 1471.

Léon de Bainast, Ecuyer, Sieur des Mazures, fit fon teftament dans la Ville d'Amiens, le 16 Juillet 1558, & nomma fon légataire Jean de Bainast, fon fils aîné, qualifié du titre de *Chevalier de l'Ordre du Roi*, dans un titre poftérieur de 1570. Celui-ci étoit troisième ayeul de CLAUDE-CHARLES DE BAINAST, Ecuyer, Seigneur de Sept-Fontaines en Tiérache, & de la Motte-Buleux, de Vergie & de Calaminois, Maître des Eaux & Forêts dans le Comté de Ponthieu, marié avec *Anne-Charlotte de Béthify*, dont il a eu :

CHARLES-FRANÇOIS DE BAINAST, Seigneur de Sept-Fontaine, Lieutenant des Carabiniers du Roi, puis Capitaine dans le même Régiment, par Commiffion du 24 Mai 1723, & Chevalier de Saint-Louis, qui époufa, le 16 Février 1712, *Benoîte-Thérèfe Acari*, fille de *Louis Acari*, Ecuyer, Seigneur de Manenghen, & de *Marie Auftreberthe-de-le-Warde*. De ce mariage vint :

MARIE-JOSÈPHE-AUSTREBERTHE-DE-BAINAST DE-SEPT-FONTAINES, née le 6 Janvier 1714, reçue à Saint-Cyr, le 4 Juillet 1725, fur les preuves de fa nobleffe. (*Armorial de France*, reg. I, part. I, pag. 47.)

Les armes : *d'or, à un chevron abaiffé de gueules, furmonté de trois fafces de même.*

* BAINVILLE, Terre & Seigneurie près de Mirecourt, dans le Duché de Lorraine, Diocèfe de Toul, qui fut unie à celle de Valfroicourt, & érigée en Comté, fous le nom de *Hoffélize*, par Lettres du 7 Juin 1726, en faveur de *Marc-Céfar de Hoffélize*, Chambellan du Duc LÉOPOLD, en confidération de fa naiffance, de fes fervices, & de ceux de fes ancêtres. Voyez HOFFELIZE.

BAINVILLE : *d'argent, à trois jumelles de fable.*

BAISLE (DE) : *d'argent, au chevron accompagné de trois étoiles, le tout de gueules.*

BAISNE, en Provence : *de gueules, à la colonne d'or, couronnée de même, & entourée d'une vigne de finople.*

BAISSEUL : *parti de gueules & d'hermines.*

BAISSEY, en Bourgogne. Guy, Seigneur de BAISSEY, d'Yzeure & de Saint-Thibaut, mort l'an 1449, avoit époufé *Ifabeau de Saint-Seigne*, dont il eut :

1. JEAN, qui fuit ;
2. Et GILLES, Seigneur de Saint-Thibaut.

JEAN DE BAISSEY, Seigneur d'Yzeure & de Longecourt, époufa *Jeanne de Saulx*, fille du Seigneur d'Orrain & de Prangey, de laquelle il eut :

1. ANTOINE, qui fuit ;

2. Et JEAN, Baron de Beaumont, Grand-Gruyer de Bourgogne, qui époufa *Antoinette du Saix*, fille d'*Antoine du Saix*, Seigneur de Rivoire, & de *Françoife de la Baulme.*

ANTOINE DE BAISSEY, Seigneur de Longecourt, Baron de Tilchaftel, Ecuyer de CHARLES, Duc de Bourgogne, puis Chambellan des Rois LOUIS XI, CHARLES VIII, & LOUIS XII, & Bailli de Dijon, Capitaine de 100 hommes d'armes, Colonel des Suiffes & Lanfquenets, époufa *Jeanne de Lénoncourt*, fille de *Philippe de Lénoncourt*, Seigneur de Gondrecourt, Grand-Ecuyer de RENÉ, Roi de Sicile, & de *Catherine de Beauvau*, dont il eut :

1. CLAUDE, qui fuit ;
2. Autre CLAUDE, Abbé de Mézières, de la Prée & du Jar, en Poitou ;
3. JEAN, Abbé du Jar, après fon frère ;
4. ENGELBERT, Baron de *Tilchaftel*, auteur d'une branche rapportée ci-après ;
5. PHILIPPE, qui époufa 1o *Jean du Puy*, Seigneur du Coudray ; & 2o *Antoine Raffin*, Seigneur de Pecalvary ;
6. EVE, femme du Seigneur de *Chamblay* ;
7. Et CLAUDINE, femme d'*Antoine de Malin*, Seigneur de Digoine & de Château-Renaud.

CLAUDE DE BAISSEY, Seigneur de Longecourt, Colonel des Lanfquenets, & Penfionnaire des Rois LOUIS XII, & FRANÇOIS Ier, époufa *Jeanne de Crux*, dont il eut :

1. CLAUDE, Abbé de Mézières, puis de Cîteaux.
2. Et CLAUDE, femme d'*Antoine*, Seigneur de Saillant.

BRANCHE
des Seigneurs DE TILCHASTEL.

ENGELBERT DE BAISSEY, Baron de Tilchaftel, quatrième fils d'ANTOINE, Seigneur de Longecourt, & de *Jeanne de Lénoncourt*, époufa *Jeanne du Châtelet*, dont il eut :

1. JEAN, du Buron de Tilchaftel ;
2. JEANNE, femme du Seigneur de la *Rouffière* ;
3. Et CLAUDINE, femme du Seigneur *de la Roche*, en Poitou.

Les armes : *d'azur, à trois quinte-feuilles d'argent, pofées deux & une.*

BAJOLET-MARTET : *d'argent, au chevron d'azur, accompagné de 3 cannettes de fable, deux en chef & une en pointe.*

BAJORAND : *d'azur, à la croix ancrée d'or, à la bordure de même.*

BALAGNY-MOLUC : *d'or, à trois ai-*

gles d'azur, membrées & becquées de gueules, 2 & 1.

BALAI. Voyez BALAY.

BALAINVILLIERS, Seigneurie érigée en Baronie par Lettres du 21 Février 1661, enregistrées le 4 Mars suivant. Elle est actuellement possédée par N... Bernard, Maître des Requêtes. Voyez BERNARD DE BALAINVILLIERS.

BALAION-POLONA: d'hermines, à la bande de gueules.

BALAISON: d'hermines, à la bande de gueules.

BALAN: d'azur, au balancier d'or, accompagné en chef d'une étrille, accostée de deux étoiles, le tout de même, & en pointe d'un croissant d'argent.

BALANDONE, en Normandie, Généralité de Rouen, famille maintenue dans sa noblesse le 16 Juillet 1666. L'Histoire de Rouen fait mention de Nicolas Balandone, Syndic de la ville de Rouen, qui obtint des Lettres de Noblesse en 1660, & d'autres Lettres de confirmation en 1666.

Les armes: d'argent, au lion de sable, lampassé de gueules; au chef d'azur, chargé de trois molettes d'éperon d'or.

BALARIN: d'azur, au chevron d'or, au chef cousu d'argent.

BALARIN, en Provence: de gueules, à un rocher d'argent, mouvant de la pointe de l'écu, sur lequel est perchée une aigle essorante de sable, membrée d'or.

BALARIUS, en Provence: d'or, à l'aigle de sable.

BALARIUS-POLENAY, en Provence: d'azur, au chevron d'or, au chef de même.

BALATHIER, en Champagne: de sable, à la fasce d'or.

BALATHIER-DE-LANTAGE, famille établie en Dauphiné, en Champagne & en Bourgogne. Les qualités de Chevalier & de Baron ont été prises par ceux de ce nom, ainsi que celles de Noble & puissant Seigneur, il y a plus de 300 ans; qualifications fort rares alors, qui annonçoient un Noble d'extraction.

Raoul de Balathier, le premier de cette famille que l'on connoisse, vivoit le 15 Novembre 1372.

François de Balathier, Ier du nom, fut Ecuyer, Seigneur & Baron de Vaux, en Dauphiné.

Un de ses descendans fut père de cinq enfans, entr'autres de:

I. Termet de Balathier, Ecuyer, qualifié du titre de Noble Seigneur, qui épousa N.... de Montdragon, dont il eut:

II. François de Balathier, Ecuyer, Seigneur en partie de Villemorien, de Lantage, des Bordes & d'Avirey-le-Bois, marié, en 1527, à Françoise Fornir, ou de Fourny, fille de Pierre Fornir, ou de Fourny, Ecuyer, Seigneur en partie de Villemorien. De ce mariage naquirent sept enfans, entr'autres:

III. Pierre de Balathier, Ecuyer, Seigneur en partie de Lantage, des Bordes, de Vougrey & d'Avirey-le-Bois, qualifié de Noble Seigneur, & Maréchal des Logis de la Compagnie d'hommes d'armes du Seigneur de Dinteville. Il avoit épousé, le 3 Août 1556, Peronne d'Amoncourt, de laquelle il eut:

IV. Jean de Balathier, Seigneur de Lantage, des Bordes, de Vougrey, de Maleroy, de Bragelogne, de Mathaux, & du Fief de Fligny, ou Féligny, appelé depuis de Balathier, qualifié de Noble Seigneur, marié en 1591, avec Françoise de Faulcq, ou de Faoucq, veuve de Jacques de Vougrey, Chevalier de l'Ordre du Roi, Seigneur de Vougrey & de Mathaux, & fille de Louis de Faulcq, Ecuyer, Seigneur de Pouilly & de Bragelogne, eut de cette alliance cinq enfans, entr'autres:

V. Edme de Balathier, Seigneur de Lantage, des Bordes, de Bragelogne, de Vougrey, de Mathaux, de Maleroy, de Villargois & de Conclais, maintenu dans sa noblesse par les Elus de Bar-sur-Aube, le 19 Juin 1634. Il acheta, le 9 Juin 1646, d'Antoinette de la Plume, mère de sa femme, la Terre & Seigneurie de Conclais, en Bourgogne, & mourut avant le 6 Décembre 1663. Il est qualifié de Noble Seigneur, dans son contrat de mariage, passé le 11 Mai 1624, avec Antoinette de Sivry, fille de Guy de Sivry, Seigneur de Villargois, & d'Antoinette de la Plume. Il laissa sept enfans, entr'autres:

1. Roger, qui suit;
2. Jacques, qui fit ses preuves de noblesse en 1649, pour être reçu Chevalier de Malte; il quitta cet Ordre pour se marier. Il fut élu, le 8 Septembre 1674, Lieutenant de la noblesse dans l'Assemblée du ban & arrière-

ban du Bailliage de Troyes, & fut fait, le 15 Janvier 1675, Gentilhomme ordinaire du Prince de Condé;

3. Et ANTOINE, qui a formé une branche rapportée ci-après.

VI. ROGER DE BALATHIER, qualifié *Baron* de Villargois, & *Seigneur* de Lantage, de Bragelogne, de Maleroy, de Cormaillon & de Chaffelembert, affista aux Etats de Bourgogne en 1668, 1674, 1679, 1682 & 1685, & obtint, en 1682, des Commiffaires nommés par la Chambre de la Nobleffe aux Etats de cette Province, un certificat portant qu'il étoit *bon Gentilhomme, non noble fimplement.* Il acquit, le 7 Décembre 1663, de *Charles Damas,* frère de *Bénigne Damas,* les Terres & Seigneuries de Cormaillon, & de Chaffelembert, mouvantes du Comté de Marigny. Il époufa, le 6 Décembre 1663, *Bénigne de Torcy-de-Lantilly,* fille de *Michel de Torcy,* Seigneur de Lantilly, & de *Bénigne Damas.* Il eut de fon mariage:

VII. HENRI-DENIS DE BALATHIER, Seigneur de Lantage, de Villargois, de Cormaillon & de Chaffelembert, appelé *le Comte de Lantage,* qui naquit en 1670; fut reçu Chevalier de Malte en 1687; quitta depuis l'Ordre, & mourut le 31 Janvier 1727. Il avoit époufé, en 1707, *Julie-Sufanne de Launoy,* fille de *François de Launoy,* Meftre-de-Camp de Cavalerie, Seigneur de Vuagnon, de Launoy, de la Lobbe, &c., dont il laiffa:

1. ELIE-ANTOINE, qui fuit;
2. ARMAND-JOSEPH, né en 1711, reçu Chevalier de Malte en 1718, premier Capitaine des Grenadiers dans le Régiment de Rouergue;
3. LOUIS-MARIE, reçu Chevalier de Malte en 1718, mort en bas âge;
4. GUY-CLAUDE, Capitaine dans le Régiment de Rouergue;
5. BÉNIGNE-FRANÇOISE, mariée, par difpenfe de Rome, le 4 Février 1722, à CHARLES DE BALATHIER, Seigneur de Bragelogne, fon coufin;
6. LOUISE-CHARLOTTE, mariée, en 1735, avec *Hugues de Riollet,* Lieutenant au Régiment de Navarre;
7. Et BERNARDE-VICTOIRE, Religieufe Urfuline à Saulieu.

VIII. ELIE-ANTOINE DE BALATHIER, appelé *le Comte de Balathier,* Seigneur de Lantage, de Villargois, de Cormaillon, de Chaffelembert, des Efcures, de Demoux, de Mirebeau de Plaifance, & en partie de Vougrey & des Bordes, Capitaine d'Infanterie au Ré-

giment d'Artois, né en 1710, obtint, en 1745, un certificat de la Chambre de la Nobleffe des Etats de Bourgogne, portant qu'il avoit les qualités requifes pour y prendre féance, & y avoir voix délibérative. Il acheta, le 29 Avril 1746, de *Charles de Bar,* Seigneur de Lantage, la Terre & Seigneurie de Lantage. Il époufa, par contrat du 26 Janvier 1741, *Catherine de Feydeau,* fille unique de *Pierre de Feydeau,* Seigneur de Demoux & de Mirebeau, ancien Capitaine au Régiment d'Auvergne, Chevalier de Saint-Louis, & de *Marie-Anne de Brou;* ils ont pour enfans:

1. LOUIS-JULES, né le 26 Août 1742;
2. ANTOINE-MARIE, né le 7 Juillet 1743, & reçu, en 1744, Chevalier de minorité dans l'Ordre de Malte;
3. Et BÉNIGNE-PERRETTE, née le 18 Avril 1745.

BRANCHE
des Seigneurs DE BRAGELOGNE.

VI. ANTOINE DE BALATHIER, Seigneur de Bragelogne, de Maleroy, &c., troifième fils d'EDME DE BALATHIER, & d'*Antoinette de Sivry,* naquit en 1646. Il fut marié, par contrat du 24 Juillet 1668, étant alors Gendarme du Dauphin, avec *Anne-Françoife d'Abonde,* fille de *Louis d'Abonde,* Ecuyer, Seigneur de Fillebordes. Il eut de fon mariage:

VII. CHARLES DE BALATHIER, Seigneur de Bragelogne, baptifé le 19 Mars 1674; marié 1° avec *Claire-Gabrielle de la Malrais;* & 2° le 4 Février 1722, fur une difpenfe de Rome, avec BÉNIGNE-FRANÇOISE DE BALATHIER, fille de HENRI-DENIS DE BALATHIER-DE-LANTAGE, fon coufin germain. De ce fecond mariage font nés:

1. ELIE, Lieutenant dans le Régiment de Rouergue;
2. Un autre fils;
3. SUSANNE;
4. Et GUILLEMETTE, Religieufe Urfuline à Saulieu (Voyez l'*Armorial de France*).

Les armes: *de fable, à la fafce d'or.*

BALAVENNE, en Bretagne: *d'argent, à trois fermaillets ou boucles rondes, ardillonnées de fable, pofées 2 & 1, & un annelet de même en abîme.*

* BALAY, en Franche-Comté, Diocèfe de Befançon. Par Lettres du mois de Juin 1712, regiftrées à Befançon & à Dôle, les Terres de *Marigna,* de la *Boiffière* & de la *Comée,*

furent unies & érigées en *Marquifat* fous le nom de *Balay*, en faveur & pour récompenfe des fervices d'EDME-FRANÇOIS DE BALAY, ancien Lieutenant-Colonel du Régiment de Villequier, iffu d'une ancienne nobleffe du Réthelois, en Champagne : il fut admis, le 24 Avril 1712, dans la *Confrérie de Saint-Georges*, & deux de fes fœurs, dans les Chapitres nobles de *Lons-le-Saulnier* & de *Migette*.

La Maifon de BALAY eft une des plus anciennes du Comté de Bourgogne, & defcend des anciens Seigneurs de cetteVille & du Château de Balay. Les armes de cette Maifon fe voient encore en plufieurs endroits de ce Château, & quelques Seigneurs de ce nom font enterrés en l'Eglife Paroiffiale du lieu. Le plus ancien qui foit aujourd'hui connu par titres eft :

JEAN DE BALAY, Seigneur de Balay, vivant en 1274, qui vint dans le Duché de Bourgogne à la fuite de *Louis de Flandres*, y acquit des Terres, & y mourut vers 1297, ainfi que cela eft relaté dans des titres paffés dans le Duché de Bourgogne en 1297, pour les partages de fes trois fils: JEAN, JACQUES, qui fuit, & VINCENT DE BALAY. JEAN eut la Terre de Balay en Réthelois; JACQUES, celle de Saint-Martin fur la Rivière de Guye en Charolois, à la charge de payer ce qui étoit dû à VINCENT, leur frère.

JACQUES DE BALAY, Chevalier, Seigneur de Saint-Martin, fut père de:

I. THIEBAUD DE BALAY, Chevalier, Seigneur duditlieu & de Saint-Martin, vivant en 1345, qui fut au fervice des Comtes de Flandres & de Réthel. Il époufa *Ifabelle de Feillens*, fille de *Jean*, Seigneur dudit lieu, près de Mâcon, & de *Lionnette de la Baulme-fur-Cerdon*, à préfent *Saint-Amour*, dont la mère, *Marguerite de Coligny*, étoit alliée aux Comtes de Vienne & de Forcalquier; il en eut:

    1. AYMÉ, Chevalier, Seigneur de Balay, en 1367 & 1383;
    2. ETIENNE, qui fuit;
    3. Et HUGUENIN.

II. ETIENNE DE BALAY, Seigneur de Saint-Martin-fur-Guye, prenoit, en 1383, la qualité de *Damoifeau*, & depuis il eut celle de *Chevalier*. Il époufa *Marguerite de Fay*, dont la Maifon eft fondue dans celle de *Chamilly*, & en eut:

    1. PHILIBERT, qui fuit;
    Tome II.

2. Et JEAN, Chevalier, qui époufa *Jacquette de Dommarien*, fœur de *Thiébaud de Dommarien*, Gentilhomme du Diocèfe de Langres.

III. PHILIBERT DE BALAY, Chevalier, Seigneur de Saint-Martin, mort en 1421, époufa *Catherine de Rochebaron*, fœur d'*Antoine de Rochebaron*, Seigneur de Berfé & de Joncy-fur-Guye, iffu des anciens Comtes de Foreft, qui lui apporta en dot la Terre de Rains. Leurs enfans furent:

    1. JACQUES, qui fuit;
    2. Et HUGUES, Chevalier, qui fut Capitaine de 100 hommes d'armes, pour le Duc *Philippe le Bon*. Il époufa *Marie de la Foreft*, dont vingt-deux fils, entr'autres:

        JEAN DE BALAY, fi connu par fon zèle pour la Maifon de Bourgogne. Etant prifonnier de guerre, on ne lui rendit fa liberté qu'à condition qu'il ne monteroit jamais à cheval, & ne porteroit point d'armes de fer. Il monta donc une mule, s'habilla de buffle, &, armé d'une lourde maffe, il continua de donner des marques de fon courage & de fon attachement à fervir fon Prince avant & après la mort de CHARLES *le Hardi*, dernier Duc de Bourgogne.

IV. JACQUES DE BALAY, Seigneur de Saint-Martin & de Rains, époufa *Marguerite de la Faye*, fœur de *Jean* & *Gérard de la Faye*, Damoifeaux. De ce mariage vinrent:

    1. ETIENNE, dont il n'eft plus fait mention dès 1460;
    2. PIERRE, qui fuit;
    3. GÉRARD, qui, s'étant diftingué au fervice de CHARLES *le Hardi*, fut nommé Gouverneur de la Fortereffe de Sanvines en Charolois, par *Marie*, fille unique du Duc *Charles*, & femme de MAXIMILIEN D'AUTRICHE, Archiduc, & depuis Empereur. Dans les Lettres qui lui furent accordées le 24 Janvier 1476, il eft qualifié d'*Ecuyer-Tranchant* du feu Duc CHARLES, & on y loue fes fervices, furtout à la bataille de Nancy. Il fut Seigneur de Valefcot, & vivoit encore en 1511;
    4. Et JEANNE, qui époufa CLAUDE DE BALAY, Seigneur de Feillens & de Châtenay, fon parent.

V. PIERRE DE BALAY, Seigneur de Saint-Martin & de Rains, vivoit encore en 1495, qu'il fit, par acte du 16 Décembre, le partage de fes fils. Il avoit époufé *Anne de Chintrey*, fœur de *Philibert*, Seigneur dudit lieu, en Mâconnois, dont il eut:

O

1. JEAN, qui eut la Terre de Saint-Martin, & mourut fans être marié;
2. ETIENNE, qui eut celle de Rains, & vivoit encore en 1511;
3. AYMÉ, qui fuit;
4. Et CLAUDE, qui fe maria, en 1496, à Triftan Damas, fils de Jean, Seigneur de Digoine, Chevalier de la Toifon d'Or.

VI. AYMÉ DE BALAY, Ier du nom, Seigneur de Terans & de Cordillon, Ecuyer-Tranchant du Roi d'Espagne, qui fut, depuis l'Empereur CHARLES V, Capitaine, Gouverneur & Grand-Bailli de Dôle, Capitale du Comté de Bourgogne, en 1482, Chevalier de Saint-Georges, a été le premier de la Maifon de Balay qui s'eft établi en Franche-Comté. Il fut enterré avec fa femme en l'Eglife des Cordeliers de Dôle, en 1511, fous un Maufolée qui fubfifte encore. Il avoit épousé, Jeanne de Bafan, fille & héritière de Jacques, Seigneur de Terans & de Cordillon, & de Jeanne de Coutier, Dame de Longwy. De leur mariage vinrent:
1. AYMÉ, qui fuit;
2. CLAUDE, tué aux guerres d'Italie;
3. ANNE, morte fille;
4. Et ELISABETH, mariée à Henri de Boifelle, Seigneur de Largilla.

VII. AYMÉ DE BALAY, IIe du nom, Chevalier, Baron de Longwy, Seigneur de Marigna & autres lieux, bâtit un Village proche les Bois de Longwy, qu'il nomma Balay-Saulx, de fon nom, & de celui de fa feconde femme. Il fut Chevalier de Saint-Georges, & mourut en 1570. Il épousa 1º Véronique de Courcelles, morte en 1540, fille de Jean, Baron de Pourlans & d'Auvillars, & de Philiberte de Tenare; & 2º Anne de Saulx, de la même Maifon que le Maréchal de Tavannes. Il eut du premier lit:
1. ETIENNE, mort fans alliance;
2. CLAUDE, qui fuit;
3. JEANNE, alliée à Philibert de Salins, Seigneur de Vincelles;
4. ANNE, mariée à Philibert de Joly, Seigneur de Marcilly & de Dracy;
5. BÉATRIX, Abbeffe de Courcelles;
6. CATHERINE, Religieufe à Molaife.
Les enfans du fecond lit furent:
7. AYMÉ, IIIe du nom, Lieutenant de la Compagnie des Chevaux-Légers de la Garde du Roi, commandée par le Baron de Balançon: il mourut en Flandres fans alliance;
8. ETIENNE, Enfeigne de Vaiffeaux, tué à la bataille de Lépante en 1571;
9. JEANNE, qui époufa Léon Dandelot, Seigneur de Tromarey;

10. Et MARIE, qui époufa Philibert de Pra, Seigneur de Clivria, de Péfeul & de Balay-Saulx, par fa femme.

VIII. CLAUDE DE BALAY, Seigneur de Marigna & de la Boiffière, Capitaine de 50 hommes d'armes, Gouverneur & Grand-Bailli de la Province de Charolois, par Lettres du Roi PHILIPPE II, du 19 Novembre 1566, tefta le 18 Juin 1572, à Marigna, dans un Pré au bord de la rivière de Valoufe, & y mourut deux heures après, ayant une épaule emportée d'un coup de fauconneau, que lui fit tirer Geoffroy de Faulquier, d'une des Tours de fon Château de Marigna, dont il étoit Seigneur en partie. Sa veuve, Marguerite de Mouchet, fille de Guyon, Seigneur de Château-Roulliaud, &c., & d'Etiennette de Pernot, fœur du Cardinal de Grandvelle, ayant porté fes plaintes au Roi de cet affaffinat, Geoffroy & fa famille furent bannis à perpétuité des Etats du Roi d'Espagne, & fon Château & fa moitié de la Terre de Marigna furent confifqués au profit des enfans de CLAUDE DE BALAY, qui étoient:
1. ANTOINE, qui fuit;
2. Et PIERRE, mort en 1589, fans avoir pris alliance.

IX. ANTOINE DE BALAY, dit de Mouchet, Chevalier de Saint-Georges, Seigneur de Marigna, la Boiffière & de Château-Roulliaud, fut chargé par le teftament de fa mère (du 14 Décembre 1612), qui fe trouva la dernière de fa famille, de porter fon nom & fes armes. Il fut au fervice du Roi d'Espagne pendant plufieurs années, & fe maria, 1º en 1591, avec Marguerite de Favernier, fille de Richard, Seigneur d'Ogéa & de Thomaffe de Vieux; 2º & avec Guillemette de Chiffey, dont il n'eut point d'enfans. Du premier lit naquirent:
1. LOUIS-NICOLAS, tué en duel;
2. PIERRE, qui fuit;
3. PHILIBERT-EMMANUEL, auteur de la branche des Seigneurs de Château-Roulliaud, rapportée ci-après;
4. Et LAURENCE, alliée à Léonard de Pardeffus, Seigneur de Marcilly.

X. PIERRE DE BALAY, Seigneur de Marigna, la Boiffière, &c., Capitaine d'Infanterie, eut de fon mariage avec Jacqueline de Franchet, fille de Claude de Franchet-Deftaray & de Claire de Bélot-Villette:
1. HUGUES, marié à Chriftine de Bélot-Chevigney;

2. Gérard, Capitaine des Gardes du Prince d'Orange, tué à la bataille de Caſſel, en 1677;
3. Jean, qui ſuit;
4. Léonard, mort ſans poſtérité;
5. Benoît, Capucin;
6. Hugues, Religieux à Gigny;
7. Marie, alliée à *Charles de Mouſtier*, Baron d'Igny;
8. Marguerite, Religieuſe;
9. Et Marie, morte Abbeſſe de Sainte-Claire, de Poligny, en odeur de ſainteté.

XI. Jean de Balay, Seigneur de Marigna & de la Boiſſière, ſervit, l'eſpace de 32 ans, le Roi d'Eſpagne dans les guerres de Flandres, & ſe ſignala aux batailles de Senef, de Caſſel & de Saint-Denis. Il étoit Lieutenant-Colonel du Terce de Cavalerie de Bourgogne, lorſqu'ayant tué, dans un combat ſingulier, le Vicomte de Looz, Seigneur Flamand, il ſe retira, lors de la Paix, en Franche-Comté, dans ſes Terres, où il prêta ſerment de fidélité au Roi Louis XIV, entre les mains du Maréchal de Duras. Il épouſa, en 1685, *Claude-Françoiſe de Grachault*, dernière de ſon nom & de ſes armes, fille de *Melchior*, Seigneur de Raucour, & de *Marie-Thérèſe de Grivel-Perrigny*, dont :

1. Aymé-François, qui ſuit;
2. Henri, Lieutenant-Colonel au Régiment de Cavalerie de Bourbon, au ſervice de Sa Majeſté Catholique;
3. Nicolas, Religieux au noble Chapitre de Beaume, mort en 1729;
4. Hugues, Religieux de Gigny;
5 Léonard, Religieux de Nantua;
6. Aymé, Capitaine d'Infanterie au Régiment de Foreſt;
7. François-Xavier, Lieutenant aux Gardes du Roi d'Eſpagne;
8. & 9. Et Deux filles, Chanoineſſes.

XII. Aymé François, Marquis de Balay, Chevalier de Saint-Georges & de Saint-Louis, Seigneur de Marigna, &c., épouſa, en 1718, *Louiſe-Renée de Reims*, originaire de Lorraine, née Baronne du Saint-Empire, fille de *Chriſtophe*, Baron du Saint-Empire, Capitaine de Cavalerie en France, Seigneur de Lory, &c., & de *Marguerite de Richebois*. Il en a :

1. Emmanuel-Aymé-François, Marquis de Balay, né en Juillet 1724;
2. Emmanuel-Gaspard-Ferdinand, né en Juin 1736;
3. Gabrielle-Françoiſe, née en Février 1720;

4. Et Henriette-Gabrielle, née le 12 Août 1721, reçues toutes les deux Chanoineſſes à Lons-le-Saulnier en 1729.

BRANCHE
des Seigneurs de Chateau-Roulliaud.

X. Philibert-Emmanuel de Balay, Seigneur de Château-Roulliaud, &c., troiſième fils d'*Antoine* & de *Marguerite de Favernier*, épouſa, en 1645, *Catherine de Marnix*, fille de *Claude*, Seigneur de Nanieuſe & de Crille, & de *Gaſparine de Léçay*. Il en eut :

1. Claude-César, qui ſuit;
2. Henri, Grand-Prieur de l'Abbaye de Gigny;
3. & 4. Claude-Marie & Antoine;
5. Marie-Louiſe, Religieuſe Bernardine;
6. Gasparine, mariée à *Antoine-Ferdinand de Bélot-Chevigney*;
7. & 8. Anne-Louiſe & Marguerite, Chanoineſſes à Lons-le-Saulnier;
9. Et Christine-Henriette, femme de *Guillaume de Crécy*, Seigneur de Montigny, &c.

XI. Claude-César de Balay, Seigneur de Château-Roulliaud, épouſa, en 1679, *Anne-Marie du Pin*, dernière de ſon nom & de ſes armes, fille de *Pierre*, Seigneur & Baron de Jouſſeau, & de *Jeanne-Philiberte de Montrichard*. Ses enfans ſont :

1. Philibert-Marie-Joseph, qui ſuit;
2. N.... Religieux à Gigny;
3. N... mort Lieutenant de Cavalerie;
Et autres enfans, dont pluſieurs filles, Chanoineſſes.

XII. Philibert-Marie-Joseph de Balay, Baron de Jouſſeau, a épouſé, en 1724, *Nicole d'Aigrefeuille*, dont pluſieurs enfans.

L'Abbé de Longeville, Prieur de Voiſey, a dreſſé la généalogie de cette Maiſon, qui eſt probablement la même que celle-ci que nous donnons d'après Moréri, édition de 1759.

Les armes : *de ſable, au lion rampant d'or*.

BALAYNE (de), Seigneur du Champaudos & de Beauregard, en Champagne : *d'argent, à la faſce crénelée de gueules, d'un créneau & demi*.

✠ BALB ou BALBE, grande & illuſtre famille originaire de Quiers en Piémont. Comme tous les titres honorifiques de cette Maiſon ſont à Madrid, & qu'il n'eſt pas aiſé de les faire paſſer à Paris, on doit penſer que M. l'*Abbé de Crillon*, & MM. ſes neveux, doivent regretter de ne pas les avoir fous les yeux, pour que nous en puiffions donner ici la généalogie.

En effet, la généalogie d'une telle Maifon ne peut & ne doit guère paraître qu'étayée des pièces authentiques qui la canonife, d'autant plus que ces titres font pour la plupart confignés dans des Archives les plus refpectables, telles que celles du Roi de Sardaigne, celles des villes d'Afti & de Quiers, ce qui donne plus de poids aux cinq grandes branches de cette famille, ces mêmes titres fe trouvent en forme bien probante, quand ils fe trouvent ainfi confignés dans des Archives publiques & étrangères à celles de la Maifon même.

Ajoutons à ce raifonnement qu'une Maifon comme celle de *Balbe - Berton-Crillon*, étrangère en France, ou du moins qui s'y eft établie en 1745, doit être plus attentive qu'une Maifon nationale, à ne rien préfenter à la critique, & cela, en faifant paraître tous fes titres, de quelque nature qu'ils puiffent être, fans extraits, fans lacunes, & dans leur entier.

C'eft par des circonftances heureufes & particulières, que cette Maifon en doit la confervation à fes *Majorats* & fes *fidei-Commis*, à fa fubftitution, & furtout à un efprit de famille, dont les teftamens de tous les âges appellent, au défaut des mâles des teftateurs, les enfans mâles de leur Maifon, à l'exclufion de leurs propres filles, qui doivent profiter de cet avantage peu commun.

Pour ne rien précipiter, cette Maifon s'eft occupée à raffembler tous fes titres honorifiques, afin de donner une généalogie de fes différentes branches, avec l'époque de leur extinction, & la filiation directe des trois branches, qui feules, exiftent encore actuellement, deux en Piémont, & l'autre en France.

On connaîtra encore mieux l'importance de ces titres honorifiques, qui font à Madrid, par le détail rapide que nous en allons faire, & obferver qu'indépendamment de leur importance, pour conftater l'honorifique de cette Maifon, ils deviennent bien plus effentiels pour elle encore, afin de prouver que leurs auteurs, contenus dans la généalogie du Sénat, font intervenus dans les mêmes actes honorifiques, & y jouent même les plus grands rôles.

On peut juger de l'importance de ces actes, dont le premier eft la deftruction de la Ville de Teftône, que l'on croit aujourd'hui connue fous le nom de Montcallier, où l'on voit que les habitans fe rendirent à la clémence des Balbe: *Se tradiderunt clementiæ illorum de Balbis* 1179, *duodecim, Non. Kel. Auguft. Oyerio Boverio Notor. Palatino en Caftro Nigro Carii.*

Le fecond eft un acte paffé entre la Nobleffe de la Ville de Quiers, d'une part, & les *Balbe*, d'une autre, en préfence du Comte d'Acaye, choifi pour arbitre par les parties. On prétendait ôter à la Maifon des *Balbe* un des fceaux de la République, fans lèquel rien ne pouvait avoir force de loi; parce que l'on foutenait que la Maifon des *Balbe* en avoit abufé: mais on reconnut que ce fceau devait toujours être dans la Maifon des *Balbe*, & tenu par un *Balbe*, foit *Berton*, foit *Simeoni*; *qui funt eâdem famigliâ & agnatione Balborum*; on lit, dans cet acte, que ce privilège étoit fi ancien dans la Maifon des *Balbe*, que la mémoire des hommes n'en pouvoit rappeler l'origine: *à tanto tempore citrâ cujus initio, in contrarium hominum memoria, non exiftit* 1374 *die* 1 *Martii.*

Le troifième acte intitulé: *Treguæ Balborum en* 1271, *D. Ult. Menfis Maii Henrico Scutino Notor. in Cario.* On compte, dans cet acte, 108 contractans, tous de la Maifon des *Balbe*. On y diftingue trente branches différentes des *Balbe*. Cet acte eft effentiel dans tous fes détails.

Un autre acte de 1542 n'eft pas moins intéreffant pour la Maifon des *Balbe*; il eft fait au nom de tous les *Balbe* & au nom d'Egidius Secondus Bertonus de Balbis, alors établi à Avignon.

Le détail en ferait trop long; mais il eft trop important pour être omis dans aucune de fes parties; & il fuffit de dire ici que l'on voit dans l'acte de 1179 & dans ce dernier de 1542, que les *Balbe* avoient le droit de prééminence & de préfider toujours au Confeil de la République, c'eft-à-dire un *Balbe* choifi dans la Maifon des *Balbe*, ou dans fes branches. *Sicuti per fæcula præterita uti confueverunt illi de Balbis.*

Ce ne font que par ces titres ci-deffus qu'on peut appuyer l'antiquité de la race des *Balbe*, ainfi que la tradition conftante du pays, qui eft, que cette Maifon defcend de

BALBUS, iſſu de cette illuſtre Maiſon *Balbe*, originaire d'Eſpagne, ſi connue dans l'*Hiſtoire Romaine*, par les Conſuls & les Empereurs qu'elle a donnés à cet Empire. Selon cette même tradition, il vint, à la tête d'une colonie romaine, s'établir, dans le VIᵉ ſiècle, dans les Gaules Ciſalpines, entre le Pô & le Tanaro, qui eſt préciſément la véritable poſition de la Ville de Quiers.

Au reſte, ſi cette tradition peut être aſſimilée à ces fables célèbres, auxquelles pluſieurs grandes Maiſons rapportent leur origine, au moins faut-il convenir que la ſuite des actes, la nature des privilèges & la prééminence des *Balbe*, rendraient la fable de leur Maiſon plus vraiſemblable que celle des autres, leſquelles, pour la plupart, ſont ſouvent ridicules.

Il ne faut pas oublier que le Marquis de *Rivère-Simeoni des Balbe* a produit, dans ſon fameux procès, contre le marquis *d'Orméa*, premier Miniſtre du Roi de Sardaigne, au ſujet des terres de Pavarole & du Comté de Montac, en Piémont, un acte de l'an 1000, où l'on voit un SIMEONUS DE BALBIS, qualifié du titre de *Dominus*, & dans lequel acte eſt rapporté un *Henricus Bertonus de Balbis, de Querio*, d'où il réſulte que, ſi les branches de cette Maiſon étoient déjà ſéparées de leur tige dès l'an 1000, cette ſéparation ſe porte au moins vers le IXᵉ ſiècle, & ramène, avec bien de la vraiſemblance, la Maiſon des *Balbe* à l'origine que la tradition lui donne.

Telle eſt une notice hiſtorique & curieuſe ſur l'antiquité de la Maiſon des *Balbe*, que nous devons aux attentions de M. l'Abbé de CRILLON. Nous ajouterons encore que cette Maiſon des *Balbe-Balbe* & ſes branches, ſont une des ſept familles d'*Albergue*, fondatrice de la Ville & République de Quiers. Les *Balbe* des différentes branches ont toujours rempli les premières charges de la République, comme celles de Conſul, Podeſtat, Sages de la guerre, Recteur du peuple, &c., conjointement avec les ſix autres familles d'*Albergue*. Parmi les Sages de la guerre, il y avoit toujours un *Balbe*; & des cinq ſceaux de la République, il y en avoit toujours un aux mains d'un des *Balbe*.

Toutes les branches de la Maiſon de BALBE-BERTON ont conſervé, dans tous les temps, une grande union entr'elles. Ce fut pour la perpétuer, que, dans le commencement du XIIIᵉ ſiècle, JEAN-BALBIS-BERTON, qualifié

alors de *nobilis & potens vir*, fonda le majorat, dont les fonds, diminués par les guerres d'Italie, furent réparés par BENVENUTO BERTONE, Comte DI MONBELLO, en 1443; ce Majorat doit être poſſédé par le plus âgé de la Maiſon, & paſſe indifféremment de l'une à l'autre branche. L'acte de créations ſe trouve à Gênes dans la banque de Saint-Georges, ſur laquelle les fonds ſont établis.

« FRANÇOIS BALBE-BERTON DE CRILLON, Archevêque de Vienne, a poſſédé le Majorat; enſuite le Comte de BALBE-BERTON-DE-CRILLON, ſon frère; après lui le Commandeur BALBO-BERTONE DI MONBELLO, qui ſort d'une branche de Piémont. FRANÇOIS-FÉLIX BALBE-BERTON, de la Maiſon des Seigneurs de Rovigliaſco, Duc de Crillon, poſſède aujourd'hui le Majorat.

HUMBERT BALBE-BERTON, Iᵉʳ du nom, paſſa dans la Terre-Sainte à la première Croiſade, & fut tué à la priſe d'Antioche en 1099.

GEOFFROY, âgé de 23 ans, ſuivit AMÉ III, Comte de Savoie, en 1147, à la ſeconde Croiſade, en qualité de *Porte-Etendard*, qui étoit la première dignité militaire.

HUMBERT, IIᵉ du nom, & OUDAIN, accompagnèrent LOUIS *le Jeune* à la même expédition, l'an 1148.

Cette Maiſon s'eſt alliée avec les Maiſons de *Savoie*, de *Saluces*, de *Colonna*, de *Doria*, d'*Impériali*, de *Valpergues*, de *Montafia*, & autres des plus anciennes & des plus diſtinguées.

Elle a produit juſqu'à dix-ſept branches, répandues en différentes parties de l'Europe. Elle ſubſiſte encore dans celles de Quiers, de Turin & d'Avignon.

La première n'eſt jamais ſortie de Quiers, & a pour chef, ſous le nom de *Balbo*, le Comte de BALBO, ſans enfans, lequel a un frère qui n'eſt point marié.

La ſeconde branche, qui eſt celle de *Crillon*, ſous le nom de *Balbe-Berton-de-Crillon*.

La troiſième établie à Turin, ſous le nom de *Balbo-Bértone-Sambuis*, a pour chef le Comte de BERTONE, marié, fils du Comte de BALBO-BERTONE, Généraliſſime des Armées du Roi de Sardaigne, Chevalier de l'Ordre de l'Annonciade.

La quatrième eſt celle de *Balbo-Bertone-Simeoni*.

ALEXANDRE BALBO-BERTONE-SIMEONI, de

l'Ordre de Saint-Jean de Jérufalem, contribua beaucoup à l'obéiffance que l'Eglife de Paleftine rendit à ALEXANDRE III l'an 1161.

Cette Branche a fini depuis peu d'années dans les perfonnes du Comte de *Rivère*, Miniftre plénipotentiaire du Roi de Sardaigne à Rome, & de la Marquife d'*Orméa*.

La branche de *Balbo-Bértone di Monbello*, réfidente à Turin, s'eft éteinte dans ces derniers tems, par la mort du dernier Comte de *Balbo di Monbello*.

Les fubftitutions & les anciens titres de cette branche ont donné fujet à un grand procès entre les BALBE-BERTON d'Avignon & ceux de Turin. On a vu, dans ce Procès, cette Maifon prouver, par les Actes les plus authentiques, devant le Sénat de Turin, une filiation fuivie depuis l'an 1000, qui fe lit à la fin de la vie du brave *Crillon*, tom. II. Il eft intervenu plufieurs Arrêts à ce fujet; ce qui met le dernier fceau à l'antiquité de cette Maifon.

BRANCHE
DE BALBE-BERTON-CRILLON.

Le brave LOUIS DE CRILLON, qui vivoit fous le règne de HENRI III, étoit de cette branche. Il fut Chevalier de Malte en 1560, Chevalier des Ordres du Roi en 1585, enfuite Meftre-de-Camp du Régiment des Gardes Françoifes, Lieutenant-Colonel de l'Infanterie-Françoife (charge créée en fa faveur, pour contrebalancer la trop grande autorité du Duc d'Epernon, & fupprimée à fa mort), Gouverneur de Boulogne & du Boulonnois, de Toulon & des Tours, mort le 11 Décembre 1615. Voyez fon éloge dans le *Nobiliaire d'Avignon*, par l'Abbé de Pithoncurt, pag. 145 & 146.

PIERRE DE CRILLON fut tué en parant de fon corps un coup de pertuifanne, porté au Roi HENRI III.

FRANÇOIS-PHILIPPE DE CRILLON, Bailli de Malte à l'âge de 30 ans, commandoit l'armée d'URBAIN VIII. Il mourut à Fréjus, empoifonné avec fes domeftiques, en retournant à la Cour de France, où il étoit appelé pour être Capitaine des Gardes-du-Corps.

PHILIPPE-MARIE DE BALBE-BERTON-CRILLON avoit époufé, en 1651, *Françoife de Saporta*, dont il eut :

1. FRANÇOIS-FÉLIX, qui fuit;
2. DOMINIQUE-LAURENT, mort Evêque de Glandèves en 1747;

3. JEAN-LOUIS, Archevêque & Primat de Narbonne, Commandeur de l'Ordre du Saint-Efprit, Abbé Commendataire de l'Abbaye de Chaulieu, &c., mort à Avignon, le 15 Mars 1751, âgé de 67 ans;
4. SUSANNE, mariée au Marquis de *Monteil-Corfac;*
5. FRANÇOISE, Religieufe à Avignon;
6. Et CATHERINE, Abbeffe de Villiers, morte en 1763.

FRANÇOIS FÉLIX, Duc de Crillon, mort depuis quelques années, avoit époufé en 1715, *Marie-Thérèfe Fabry-de-Moncault*, fille de *Louis*, Comte de *Moncault*, Lieutenant-Général & Gouverneur de la Citadelle de Befançon. Ses enfans font:

1. LOUIS, qui fuit;
2. PONS, Eccléfiaftique, mort il y a quelques années;
3. LOUIS-SÉBASTIEN, Chevalier de Malte, Abbé de Saint-Thierry, Colonel d'un Régiment de Dragons;
4. LOUIS-ATHANASE, Agent général du Clergé de France;
5. VIRGINIE, mariée 1° à N..... *Thomas*, Seigneur de Millau; & 2° en 1742, à *Henri-Céfar-Raymond-Hyacinthe*, Comte de *Brancas*, de la branche de *Villeneuve*, dit le *Baron de Lafcours;*
6. Et EMILIE, Carmélite à Avignon. »

LOUIS BALBE-BERTON, Marquis de Crillon, puis Duc de Crillon-Mahon, Lieutenant-Général des Armées du Roi, aujourd'hui (1781) au fervice du Roi d'Efpagne, a obtenu des Lettres de naturalifation, & a été reçu, fur fes preuves faites, Chevalier de l'Ordre du Roi d'Efpagne & Capitaine-Général de fes Armées, il commandoit les troupes qui font entrées dans l'Isle Minorque, dont il s'eft emparé; & a été créé Duc de Crillon à Avignon, titre accordé par le Pape. Il a époufé, 1° le 1er Janvier 1742, *Françoife-Marie-Elifabeth Couvay*, morte le 8 Mars 1755; 2° en 1762, *Florence-Radegonde-Louife-Eléonore-Julie Bruneau de la Rabatelière*, morte au mois d'Août 1764, fans poftérité. Elle étoit d'une famille noble du Poitou, dont les titres ont été dépofés chez *Garry*, Notaire à Paris, & qui fubfifte dans *René Bruneau*, Chanoine de Saint-Hilaire de Poitiers; & 3° *Jofèphe-Athanafe-Roman-Garmon Spinofa de Los-Monteras*. Du premier lit vinrent:

1. LOUIS-ALEXANDRE-NOLASQUE-FÉLIX, qui fuit;
2. Et FRANÇOIS-FÉLIX-DOROTHÉE, né en 1748,

Chevalier de Crillon, puis dit *le Comte de Crillon*, marié en 1774, à *Marie-Charlotte Carbon*, de laquelle il a un garçon & une fille, exiftant en 1782.

Du troifième mariage font nés :

1. Louis-Antoine-François-de-Paule, né en 1775;
2. Et Marie-Thérèse-Virginie-Françoise-de-Paule, née en 1771.

Louis-Alexandre-Nolasque-Félix, Marquis de Crillon, né le 11 Décembre 1742, ancien Colonel dans les Grenadiers de France en 1767, Capitaine de Dragons en 1768, aujourd'hui Brigadier & Capitaine du Régiment d'Aquitaine, a époufé 1° par contrat du 27 Octobre 1768, *Marie-Sophie-Joféphine de la Briffe*, née le 4 Décembre 1750, morte fans poftérité en 1770, fille de *Louis-Arnaud de la Briffe*; & 2° par contrat du 23 Juin 1771, *Angélique-Madeleine de Valois de Murfay*, décédée en 1774, dont il a eu une fille, qui vivoit en 1782.

La branche de Balbe-Berton-Crillon s'eft alliée, depuis qu'elle eft à Avignon, avec les Maifons de *Seytres-Caumont*, de *Ris-d'Aragon*, de *Joyeufe*, de *Galéan*, de *Cavaillon*, de *Baronelly*, de *Grillet-Briffac*, de *Villeneuve*, & de *Simiane*.

Cette branche a donné quatre Chevaliers de l'Ordre du Roi, avant la création de l'Ordre du Saint-Efprit; un Chevalier à la création de cet Ordre, un Commandeur, des Ambaffadeurs, des Gouverneurs, des Commandans de Provinces, plufieurs Baillis de Malte, & plufieurs Prélats.

Les armes: *d'or, à cinq cottices d'azur*.

Les *Balbis* de Gênes, quoique très-noble famille, ne font pas *Balbe* de Piémont.

Il n'en eft pas de même de ceux de Venife, que l'on croit être iffus de ceux de Piémont.

Pour l'Hiftoire & l'origine de la Maifon de *Balbe-Berton-Crillon*, on peut confulter l'excellente *Hiftoire du Brave Crillon*, par Mademoifelle de Luffan, & le *Dictionnaire des Gaules*, tom. II, au mot Crillon, où l'on trouve une Généalogie de cette Maifon, telle qu'elle a été prouvée devant le Sénat de Turin en 1753.

BALBE ou BAULS, famille de Provence, éteinte.

Guillaume Balbe de S. Alban eut en 1279, du Comte de Provence, la Terre de Mui en échange de celle de Puget de Theoniers, dont

fon fils Pierre obtint la confirmation en 1297. Sa poftérité ne conferva qu'une moitié de cette Seigneurie; l'autre fut poffédée dès 1410, par *Jean de Pontevès*, Seigneur de Bazene, trifayeul de *Louis de Pontevès*, qui acquit l'autre partie de Mui par fon alliance, en 1499, avec *Matheline*, fille & héritière de Philippe Balbe. Leur poftérité a poffédé cette Terre jufqu'après le milieu du dernier fiècle, qu'elle a paffé à *Jean-Baptifte Félix*. Voyez FELIX.

Les armes : *un bélier de fable, accollé d'argent, en champ d'or*.

BALDONI, en Provence. Par les certificats que cette famille préfente, il eft conftant, dit l'Auteur de l'*Hiftoire héroïque & univerfelle de la nobleffe de Provence*, tom. I. pag. 89, qu'elle eft noble & ancienne, & alliée avec les meilleures Maifons de *Céféna*, dans la Romanie, d'où elle eft originaire. Elle vint s'établir à Avignon, vers la fin du XVe fiècle, tems auquel Cyprien de Baldoni fut nommé, par Sa Sainteté, pour réformer la Juftice dans le Comtat Venaiffin.

Joseph de Baldoni fervit avec diftinction dans les Armées des Rois Henri III & Henri IV.

Cette famille fubfifte dans Claude de Baldoni, marié, le 22 Février 1717, avec *Urfule d'Aimar*, dont il a un fils & deux filles, mariées dans les Maifons de *Beaujeu-Quiqueran*, & de *Paul-Lamanon*.

Les armes: *d'azur, à une mer d'argent, de laquelle fort une bombe d'or enflammée de gueules, à trois endroits, furmontée de trois étoiles d'or*.

BALE, *de la Religion Catholique*.

Georges-Joseph-Guillaume-Aloysius Barrinck de Baldenstein, né le 9 Février 1705, élu le 12 Janvier 1744, Evêque de Bâle.

Simon-Nicolas-Eusèbe-Ignace, Comte de Froberg, né le 23 Septembre 1694, élu le 25 Octobre 1762, Evêque de Bâle.

BALEINE (de), Seigneur de Suzemont & de Maifon, en Champagne: *d'argent, au lion de fable, armé, lampaffé, & couronné de gueules*.

BALIDART, en Champagne : *d'argent, à la fafce de finople, accompagnée de fept merlettes de même, 4 & 3*.

BALIENCOURT, famille du Brabant

éteinte, de laquelle étoit JEANNE DE BALIEN-COURT, fille & unique héritière de JEAN DE BA-LIENCOUT, & d'*Anne d'Itre*, mariée en 1581, à *Guillaume Riffart*, auquel elle porta en dot la Seigneurie d'Itre. Voyez RIFFART.

* BALINCOURT, dans le Vexin François, Diocèse de Rouen, Terre & Châtellenie unies aux Seigneuries d'Hereville, d'Arrouville & de Margicourt, & érigée en Marquifat, par Lettres du mois de Juillet 1719, en faveur de CLAUDE-GUILLAUME TESTU-DE-BALINCOURT. La Terre & Seigneurie de Mérouville, qui avoit été long-tems féparée de celle de Balincourt, par un partage des frères cadets, y a été réunie depuis, avec celle de la Chapelle Saint-Lubin. Voyez BOULOIRE & TESTU.

BALLEROY. Voyez COUR DE BAL-LEROY.

BALLEUR, Seigneur du Mefnil, en Normandie, Généralité de Rouen, famille maintenue dans fa nobleffe le 4 Octobre 1669, dont les armes font: *d'azur, à trois befans d'argent, 2 & 1*.

BALLINEUC, en Tréguier, *d'argent, à une fleur-de-lys de gueules, en abîme, accompagnée de quatre merlettes de fable, 2 en chef & 2 en pointe*.

BALLIVIÈRE. Voy. CORNU DE BAL-LIVIÈRE.

BALLUE (LA), en Tréguier: *d'argent, à trois channes de fable, 2 & 1*. C'eft un poiffon de mer qui reffemble à la perche, & a toujours le mufeau ouvert.

BALME (LA), en Bugey. PIERRE DE LA BALME, Chevalier, Seigneur du Tiret, vivant ès années 1300 & 1320, eut pour femme *Béatrix d'Oucieux*, fille de *Jean d'Oucieux*, Seigneur de Douvres, & d'*Alix de Septin*, dont il eut:

1. ANSELME, qui fuit;
2. Et N..., femme de N..., Seigneur de Donnivard.

ANSELME DE LA BALME, Chevalier, Seigneur du Tiret, époufa en 1363 *Agnès de St.-Sulpix*, fille de *Pierre*, Seigneur de *St.-Sulpix*, & de *Guillemette de Lugny*. Il en eut:

1. AMÉ, qui fuit;
2. JACQUES, Chevalier, Seigneur de Montfalcon, en Savoie;
3. Et MARGUERITE, qui tefta le 4 Août 1411. Elle avoit époufé *Guyonnet de Loras*, Damoifeau, fils de *Jean de Loras*, Seigneur de Montplaifant.

AMÉ DE LA BALME, Chevalier, Seigneur du Tiret, fut allié, vers 1402, avec *Alix de la Baume*, fille de *Pierre de la Baume*, Seigneur de Pomiers, & de *Catherine d'Eftrées*. Il en eut:

1. AYMON, ou AMÉ, qui fuit;
2. Et FRANÇOISE, femme d'*Amé de Feillens*, Seigneur de Châtenay, fils puîné de *Sibuet*, Seigneur de *Feillens* & de Châtenay, & de *Marguerite de Monfpey*, fa première femme.

AYMON, ou AMÉ DE LA BALME, Chevalier, Seigneur du Tiret, époufa le 8 Janvier 1448, *Jeannette de Verfey*, fille de *Perceval*, Seigneur de Verfey, & de *Guillemette de Châteauvieux*. Il en eut:

1. HUGUES, qui fuit;
2. Et BERTRAND, Religieux & Chambellan de Saint-Oyen-de-Joux, Prieur de Villette & de Ceffia, en 1511 & 1516.

HUGUES DE LA BALME, Seigneur du Tiret, de Nercia, de Verfey, & premier Maître-d'Hôtel du Duc de Savoie, en 1519, tefta le 12 Avril 1532. Il avoit époufé *Louife de Chandieu*, fille de *Louis*, Baron *de Chandieu*, & d'*Antoinette de Grolée*. Il laiffa:

1. PIERRE, qui fuit;
2. JEAN-LOUIS, Seigneur de *Verfey*, auteur d'une branche rapportée ci-après;
3. BERTRAND, Protonotaire Apoftolique, Prieur de Bourges, de Villette, de Clairfont & de Sainte-Hélène-du-Lac, qui tefta le 13 Décembre 1558;
4. LOUISE, Religieufe à Neufville, en Breffe;
5. FRANÇOISE, mariée 1° à *Jean-Baptifte Grimaldi-de-Bueuil*, Seigneur d'Efcros, Chambellan du Roi FRANÇOIS Ier; & 2° à *Jean de Grimaldi*, Seigneur de Levans & de Reveft;
6. Et CHARLOTTE, femme de *Louis de Moyria*, Seigneur de Mirigna, fils puîné d'*Antoine de Moyria*, Seigneur de Châtillon, de Corneille, & d'*Etiennette de Tency*.

PIERRE DE LA BALME, Seigneur du Tiret, fe maria avec *Jeanne de Montfalcon*, fille de *Marin de Montfalcon*, Baron de Flaccieu, & d'*Antoinette de Clermont*, dont il n'eut point d'enfans.

BRANCHE
des Seigneurs DE VERFEY.

JEAN-LOUIS DE LA BALME, Seigneur de Verfey, deuxième fils de HUGUES DE LA BALME, Seigneur du Tiret, & de *Louife de Chandieu*, fut Capitaine des Gens de Pied pour le fervice de fon Alteffe de Savoie, fous la Charge de Baron d'Aix, l'an 1561, & mourut en 1588. Il fut marié, 1° le 8 Juin 1544, avec *Philiberte de Saint-Point*, Dame de la Salle, fille de *Philibert*, Seigneur de *Saint-Point*, & d'*Ancelis de Chandieu*; & 2° avec *Madeleine de Ronchevol*, veuve de *Charles de Chamberan*, Seigneur de la Bernardière, & fille de *Simon de Ronchevol*, Seigneur de Pramenon, en Beaujolois, dont il n'eut point d'enfans. Il laiffa de fon premier mariage:

1. Jean-Aymé, mort fans lignée;
2. Louis-Jean, mort auffi fans hoirs;
3. Claude, mort jeune;
4. Bertrande, femme d'*Aynard de Fétans*, Seigneur dudit lieu & de Montferrand, fils d'*Etienne*, Seigneur de Fétans, & d'*Eléonore de Varey*;
5. Et Pernette, femme de *Théodore* ou *Théod de Ronchevol*, Seigneur de Pramenon, frère de *Madeleine de Ronchevol*, fa belle-mère, dont fortirent *Sébaftien, Yves*, & *Philiberte de Ronchevol*.

Jean-Louis de la Balme eut un fils naturel:

Pompée de la Balme, Seigneur de la Forêt, en Lyonnois, qui époufa, le 16 Mai 1592, *Philiberte de Ronchevol*, remariée à *Profper de Barhod*, Ecuyer. Elle étoit fille de *Théodore de Ronchevol*, Seigneur de Pramenon, dont il eut:

1. Antoine, Curé de Saint-Paul-de-Varax;
2. Jeanne-Antoinette;
3. Et Claudine-Louise.

Les armes: *de gueules, à une bande d'argent bordée d'or, accompagnée de fix befans d'argent, pofés en orle.*

Il y a encore plufieurs autres familles du nom de Balme.

Balme, Seigneur du Gouft, en Provence: *d'azur, au chevron d'or, au chef de même, chargé de trois fautoirs du champ.*

Balme, Seigneur de Saint-Julien: *coupé de gueules, au lion d'or paffant fur un coupé d'azur & de fable, l'azur chargé d'une gerbe de bled d'or, & le fable d'un rocher d'argent.*

Balme, Seigneur de Monchalin & d'Optevoz, en Dauphiné: *de gueules, à trois pals d'or, à la bande de fable, brochant fur le tout.*

Balme (la), Seigneur de Mares, en Dauphiné: *d'or, à la bande d'azur.*

Tome II.

Balmey, en Bugey. Il y a un titre à la Chartreufe de Meyria portant une conceffion faite par Garnier du Balmey, par laquelle il donne aux Chartreux de ce lieu tout ce qu'il avoit en la ville de Meyria, l'an 1116, & où il fe qualifie: *GARNERIUS DE BALMETO miles, filius NORTBOLDI, filii ROSBOLDI, filii PONCII, filii GIMOLDI DE BALMETO militis.* Ainfi l'on peut commencer cette généalogie par ce dernier nommé dans ce titre.

Gimold, Seigneur du Balmey, Chevalier, qui, felon la fupputation, devoit vivre vers 980, fut père de:

Ponce, Seigneur du Balmey, vivant l'an 1023, lequel eut pour fils:

Rithbold, Seigneur du Balmey, vivant en 1041, qui laiffa pour fils & fucceffeur:

Nortbold, Seigneur du Balmey en 1083. Celui-ci eut:

1. Garnier, qui fuit;
2. Ponce, Evêque du Belley, vivant ès années 1113 & 1120;
3. Et Guillaume, Seigneur de *Dorches*, auteur d'une branche dont nous parlerons ci-après.

Garnier, Seigneur du Balmey, Ier du nom, Chevalier, fut, comme on a vu par le titre ci-deffus, fondateur de la Chartreufe de Meyria, avec Guillaume, fon frère, l'an 1116. Il eut:

1. Aymé, qui fuit;
2. Et Garnier, rapporté plus loin.

Aymé, Seigneur du Balmey, Ier du nom, Chevalier, vivoit l'an 1160, & eut pour fils & fucceffeur:

Aymé, Seigneur du Balmey, IIe du nom, Chevalier vivant en 1213, qui fut père de:

Humbert, Seigneur du Balmey, Chevalier vivant en 1240, fon fils fut:

Guillaume, Seigneur du Balmey & de Condamine de la Doys, qui eut pour femme une nommée *Mariette*, qui lui donna plufieurs enfans:

1. Aymé, qui fuit;
2. 3. & 4. Jean, Pierre & André, Damoifeaux.

Aymé, Seigneur du Balmey, IIIe du nom, vivoit ès années 1320 & 1340. Il eut pour fils:

Girin, Seigneur du Balmey, Chevalier, qui étoit Ecuyer du Sire de Thoire & de Villars, l'an 1370, depuis lequel on a rien trouvé des Seigneurs du Balmey.

P

GARNIER DU BALMEY, IIe du nom, avant que de fe faire Religieux Convers à la Chartreufe de Meyria, eut :

1. GARNIER, qui fuit ;
2. Et HUGUES, qui fut d'Eglife.

GARNIER DU BALMEY, IIIe du nom, Chevalier, ratifia les donations faites par fon père à la Chartreufe de Meyria, en s'y faifant Religieux Convers, & laiſſa :

ROBERT DU BALMEY, Chevalier, lequel donna, à la même Chartreufe de Meyria, ce qu'il avoit à Condamine de la Doys l'an 1226.

BRANCHE
des Seigneurs DE DORCHES.

GUILLAUME DU BALMEY, Ier du nom, troifième fils de NORTBOLD, Seigneur du Balmey, fe retira en Michaille, où il fut Seigneur de Dorches, dont il prit le nom, ainſi que ſes ſucceſſeurs. Il vivoit en 1130. Il eut :

1. GUILLAUME, qui fuit ;
2. Et HUBERT, Chevalier, qui fit branche, rapportée ci-après.

GUILLAUME DU BALMEY, IIe du nom, Seigneur de DORCHES, eut de ſa femme nommée Bernarde :

1. GUICHARD, qui fuit ;
2. PIERRE, Chevalier, marié à Guyette de Moria, fille de Guy de Moria, Chevalier. Elle étoit veuve de lui en 1280, & mère de Guillaume, Guy, Jean, Béatrix & Eléonore de Dorches ;
3. ARTHOLD, qui fut père d'un autre ARTHOLD DE DORCHES, dont il eſt parlé dans des titres au Prieuré de Nantua, l'an 1270 ;
4. Et GUILLEMETTE, dont on ne fçait pas l'alliance.

GUICHARD DU BALMEY, Seigneur de DORCHES, Chevalier, qui vivoit l'an 1236, eut :

1. HUGUES, qui n'eut qu'une fille, MARGUERITE, femme de Raymond de Livron, Chevalier, Gentilhomme du pays de Gex, avec lequel elle vivoit l'an 1285 ;
2. Et HUMBERT, Seigneur de DORCHES, qui vivoit l'an 1281 ; il eut pour fils & ſucceſſeur :

AYMON DU BALMEY, Seigneur de DORCHES, dont la femme ſe nommoit Guillemette ; elle étoit veuve de lui l'an 1343, & en eut :

JEAN DU BALMEY, Seigneur de DORCHES, qui teſta le 16 Avril 1361, & dans ſon teſtament fait mention de ſa femme, nommée Aneſtonne, & de ſes enfans :

PIERRE, AMÉDÉE, PHILIPPE, HENRI, & ALIX DE DORCHES, deſquels on n'a point ſçu la poſtérité.

BRANCHE
des Seigneurs DU BALMEY.

HUBERT DU BALMEY, Chevalier, deuxième fils de GUILLAUME DU BALMEY, Ier du nom, Seigneur de Dorches, vivoit l'an 1203, & eut pour fils & ſucceſſeur :

ANDRÉ DU BALMEY, Ecuyer, vivant en 1248, père de :

1. AMÉ, qui fuit ;
2. Et GUILLAUME, Ecuyer, vivant en 1283.

AMÉ DU BALMEY vendit, avec GUILLAUME, ſon frère, au Prieur de Meyria, tout ce qu'ils prétendoient en la montagne de Châtillonnet, l'an 1288, & fut père de :

JEAN DU BALMEY, dit Allemand, Damoiſeau, qui vivoit l'an 1313, & eut :

1. GUILLAUME, dit Allemand, Damoiſeau ;
2. JEAN, Religieux à Saint-Rambert ;
3. & 4. AMÉ & PIERRE, dit Allemand, qui gît dans l'Eglife de Meyria, avec Guillemette, ſa femme.

Les armes : d'hermines, au franc canton d'argent, chargé d'une aigle à deux têtes de ſable.

BALNOT : d'azur, au lion d'argent, couronné d'or.

BALON. Il y a une famille de ce nom en Provence, originaire de Savoie. ANDRÉ DE BALON, Ier du nom, fut reçu Viſiteur alternatif des Gabelles, le 17 Octobre 1611 (charge autrefois remplie par les meilleures Maiſons de la Province). Il eut :

1. JEAN, qui ſuccéda à l'office de ſon père, & mourut ſans poſtérité ;
2. ANDRÉ, qui fuit ;
3. Et ANNE, mariée à Jean de Boniface, Seigneur de la Môle, Conſeiller au Parlement d'Aix.

ANDRÉ DE BALON, IIe du nom, fut pourvu d'une Charge de Conſeiller au Parlement de Provence en 1615, vint s'établir à Aix & épouſa en 1617, Jeanne de Raſcas-du-Canet. Il eut de ce mariage :

1. GASPARD, qui fuit ;
2. Et MADELEINE, mariée avec Alexandre de Galliffet, Seigneur du Tholonet, Préſident aux Enquêtes.

GASPARD DE BALON, Seigneur de Saint-Julien, fut reçu dans l'office de son père l'an 1662; & s'étoit allié, en 1641, avec *Anne de Vintimille,* Dame de Saint-Julien, fille de *Madelon de Vintimille,* des Comtes de Marseille, Baron d'Ollioule, & de *Louise de Coriolis.* Il eut de mariage:

1. Joseph, qui suit;
2. Et plusieurs autres enfans morts au service.

Joseph de Balon, Ier du nom, Seigneur de Saint-Julien, fut pourvu d'un Office de Conseiller au Parlement, en 1682, & marié avec *Françoise d'André,* dont il eut:

1. Pierre, qui suit;
2. Et une fille, mariée avec *César de Marc-de-Panisse,* Conseiller au Parlement de Provence.

Pierre de Balon, Seigneur de Saint-Julien, succéda à la charge de son père en 1712, & épousa *Jeanne d'Arnaud-de-Nibles,* dont:

1. Joseph, IIe du nom, reçu dans la Charge de son père & de ses ayeux en 1735;
2. & 3. Louis & Jacques, Officiers au service de France. (Voy. l'*Hist. hér. & univ. de la Noblesse de Provence,* tom. I, page 90).

Les armes: *d'azur, au lion d'or, armé & lampassé de gueules, au chef de même, chargé d'un cœur d'argent, côtoyé de deux roses de même.*

BALONE, en Bresse: *de gueules, à la bande d'argent, bordée d'un filet d'or, & accompagnée de six besans de même en orle.*

BALORRE, ancienne Maison du Duché de Bourgogne, éteinte dans Philippe, Seigneur de Balorre, dont les biens ont passé dans celle de *Rabutin,* par le mariage, en 1360, de sa fille unique & héritière Marie de Balorre, avec *Jean de Rabutin,* Seigneur d'Epiri. Depuis cette alliance les Seigneurs de *Rabutin* ont écartelé leurs armes de celles de Balorre. Voyez RABUTIN.

Les armes: *d'azur, à la croix engrêlée d'or.*

* BALSAC ou BALZAC, petite ville en Auvergne, à deux lieues de Brioude, qui a donné son nom à l'ancienne Maison dont nous allons parler. Le premier connu est:

Odo, Seigneur de Balsac, qui donna aux Comtes & Chanoines de Saint-Julien de Brioude, pour une fondation, les cens & rentes qui lui appartenoient au lieu de Balsac; la fondation est du mois de Mars 814, sous le règne de Louis le Débonnaire.

Armand de Balsac fit une fondation pareille le 15 Décembre 920, sous le règne de Raoul.

Roger de Balsac donna aux mêmes Chanoines 30 liv., l'an 941, sous le règne de Louis d'Outremer.

Gildebert de Balsac donna à la même Eglise certaine maison & champs, qui lui appartenoient, le 31 Mars 944, sous le règne de Lothaire.

Rodolphe de Balsac fut Chanoine de Brioude en 948.

Etienne de Balsac donna à la même Eglise, pour une fondation, douze cartées d'avoine, & une geline, à lui dues sur le lieu de Balsac, le 25 Juin 1060, sous le règne de Philippe.

Hector de Balsac donna aux Comtes & Chanoines de Saint-Julien de Brioude 10 livres de rente, l'an 1102, sous le règne de Louis-le-Gros.

Ferdinand de Balsac fut Chanoine de Brioude en 1150.

Raymond de Balsac, Comte & Chanoine de Brioude, laissa aux Chanoines de cette Eglise 15 livres de rente en 1150.

En 1200, on trouve Raymond de Balsac: on lui donne pour fils, Beraut de Balsac, qui, au mois de Juillet 1230, reconnut avoir vendu au Chapitre de Brioude le lieu de *Balsac,* pour 20 livres, avec faculté de rachapt, pour le tenir en fief. En 1237 il transigea avec le même Chapitre, & reconnut, en 1268, tenir en fief de cette Eglise les cens & rentes qu'il avoit ès villes de Brioude, de Coylde, & à Chaimac.

En 1278, il convint que le Mas de Lavau, avec les cens & rentes, demeureroient communs entre lui & le Chapitre.

Raymond de Balsac, Comte & Chanoine de Brioude, mourut le 29 Août 1270.

Drogon de Balsac, Chanoine de Brioude, mourut en 1283.

Autre Drogon de Balsac, Chevalier, mourut le 17 Mai 1285.

En 1363, Raoul de Balsac reconnut tenir en fief du noble Chapitre de Brioude les cens & rentes à lui appartenant en cette ville; &, en 1373, il donna à l'Eglise de Saint-Julien 2000 écus d'or, 1000 pour y être enterré, & les autres 1000 pour la fondation d'une Chapelle, où sont ses armes: *d'azur, à trois sautoirs d'argent, au chef d'or, chargé de trois sautoirs du champ.* Il mourut en 1373.

P ij

F. Raymond de Balsac, Comte & Chanoine de Brioude, donna, le 14 Décembre 1378, 15 livres à fon Chapitre, pour les Obits de Raoul de Balsac, fon frère, Damoifeau, & de *Bérengaria*, fa mère.

Les extraits cités ci-deffus & plufieurs autres de la Généalogie fuivante, font tirés des Archives de Saint-Julien de Brioude, le 12 Septembre 1609, & certifiés par les Comtes & Chanoines de cette Eglife, fignés des Gardes-Titres & de leur Secrétaire.

La Filiation fuivie de la Maifon de Balsac commence à

I. Roffec de Balsac, Ier du nom, Chevalier, qui reconnut, en 1336, tenir du Chapitre de Saint-Julien de Brioude tout ce qu'il avoit à Balfac; promit, en 1348, de payer au même Chapitre 30 livres, & inftitua une Vicairie de quatre feptiers de bled de feigle. Il tranfigea la même année avec Guillaume de Balsac, pour la donation à lui faite par feu Guillaume, fon oncle, & fe chargea de payer au Chapitre de Brioude 30 livres. En 1363, il reconnut tenir en fief du même Chapitre les cens & rentes à lui appartenant dans la ville de Brioude, les maifons y déclarées, ce qu'il avoit à la rivière d'Allier, à Coylde, & à la moitié du lieu de Balfac, avec haute, moyenne & baffe Juftice, qui fut à Meffire Guillaume de Balsac; fit hommage en 1366 à Beraud, Dauphin, à caufe de fon Château de l'Eftoing, de Broffac, de Vernuffal, &c. Il époufa *Sibylle*, & de leur mariage naquit:

II. Guillaume de Balsac, Chevalier, qui tranfigea avec le Chapitre de Brioude en 1373; dans l'acte il fe dit fils de Roffec de Balsac, *Chevalier*, & reconnoît être obligé de payer à cette Eglife dix pots de vin de fon *cuvage*, & douze quartauts de froment de rente annuelle. Il époufa *Marguerite d'Alzon*, dont il eut:

III. Jean de Balsac, Seigneur d'Entragues, d'Antoing, Rioumartin & Benfac, qui aida le Roi Charles VII de tous fes biens contre les Anglois. Il époufa *Agnès de Chabannes*, fille de *Jacques de Chabannes*, dont il eut:

1. Roffec, qui fuit;
2. Raoul ou Rodolphe, Sénéchal d'Agénois, mort fans alliance;
3. Robert, qui continua la poftérité;
4. Antoine, Evêque de Die en 1474, puis de Valence en 1475; il étoit auparavant Prieur de Saint-Caffien, dans le Diocèfe de

Béziers. Il mourut le 3 Novembre 1491, dans fon Prieuré d'Ambert;
5. Pierre, Abbé de Vézelay, en 1485, jufqu'en 1490; il affifta aux Etats de Tours;
6. Louis, ou Raymond, Chevalier de Saint-Jean de Jérufalem, Commandeur de Chazel, en Forez;

    Mondon de Balfac, cru bâtard de Louis de Balsac, eft chef des Seigneurs de *Saint-Paul*, en Armagnac:
7. Guillaume, Prieur de Clerieu;
8. N... Dame de Fougerolles;
9. Et Marguerite, mariée à *N... de Lavedan*.

IV. Roffec de Balsac, IIe du nom, Seigneur de Glifenove, Benfac, Saint-Amand, Prelat, Paulhac, Rioumartin, Seveirac, Rofières, Cuffet, Montmorillon, Saint-Clément, Châtillon-d'Azergues, Baigneul & la Rigaudière, fut Sénéchal de Nîmes & de Beaucaire, Capitaine de 100 hommes d'armes, & de 4000 Francs-Archers, Gouverneur de Pont Saint-Efprit, Chevalier de l'Ordre de Saint-Michel; il eft qualifié Confeiller, Chambellan du Roi, dans le don que Louis XI lui fit, & à fes hoirs & fucceffeurs, en 1471, des Seigneuries de Marfillac & de Caffaignes, confifquées fur *Jean*, Comte d'*Armagnac*. Il mourut le 25 Octobre 1473, & fut enterré dans l'Eglife de Saint-Julien de Brioude, à laquelle il avoit laiffé 2000 écus pour la fondation de quatre Vicaires, d'une Chapelle, d'une Cloche & d'une Meffe tous les ans. Il avoit époufé, par contrat du 16 Février 1453, *Jeanne d'Albon*, fille d'*Antoine*, Seigneur de Baigneul, il en eut:

1. Roffec, IIIe du nom, Confeiller & Chambellan du Roi, Sénéchal de Beaucaire, Seigneur de Châtillon-d'Azergues, qui donna quittance, le 23 Août 1489, à *Jean le Gendre*, de 90 livres, pour un quartier de fes gages, en qualité de Capitaine de trente Lances; elle eft fcellée de fon fceau. Il mourut, en 1489, fans poftérité;
2. Geoffroy, Seigneur de Montmorillon & de Saint-Clément, en Bourbonnois, qui fut élevé Enfant-d'Honneur du Roi Charles VIII, qui, par Lettres de l'an 1484, établit en fa faveur une Foire au Bourg de Saint-Clément; & en 1488, le qualifiant fon *Confeiller & Chambellan*, il lui fit don de tous les biens de *Jean Boudet*. En 1496 un cheval fougueux l'ayant emporté dans le Rhône, il fit un vœu à Notre-Dame de l'Eglife des Céleftins de Lyon; &, en mémoire du péril dont il avoit été préfervé, il fit

faire un tableau qui y eſt encore aujour-
d'hui, au bas duquel cet évènement eſt décrit; il teſta le 9 Juin 1509, & mourut la
même année, ſans enfans, laiſſant ſa femme ſon héritière; il avoit épouſé *Claude le
Viſte*, qui ſe remaria à *Jean de Chabannes*,
Seigneur de Vandeneſſe. Elle étoit fille de
Jean le Viſte, Préſident en la Cour des Aides, & de *Geneviève de Nanterre;*

3. ANNE, qui épouſa *Guillaume de Joyeuſe*,
fils de *Tanneguy de Joyeuſe.* & de *Blanche de Tournon;*

4. MARIE, femme de *Louis Mallet*, Seigneur
de Graville, de Marcouſſis, Milly, Montagu, Fontenai & Bois-Malherbes, Amiral
de France;

5. PHILIPPE, mariée à *Louis*, Seigneur de
Montlaur & de Maubec; que quelques-uns
diſent fille de *Robert;*

6. MARGUERITE, femme de *Philippe de l'Eſ-
pinaſſe*, Seigneur de Maulévrier;

7. Et ANTOINETTE, Religieuſe de l'Ordre de
Fontevrault, à Varinville.

IV. ROBERT DE BALSAC, troiſième fils de
JEAN, Chevalier, & d'*Agnès de Chabannes*,
fut Seigneur d'Entragues, petite Ville de
la Limagne, mouvante du Comté de Clermont, en Auvergne; puis Sénéchal de Gaſcogne & d'Agénois, après ſon frère; Capitaine
des Châteaux de Tournon, port de Penne, &
Châtelculhier, au Diocèſe d'Agen: il étoit,
en 1471 & 1472, Capitaine de 200 Lances,
pour leſquelles CHARLES de France, Duc de
Guyenne, lui faiſoit payer par quartier 1860
liv. Il ſervit le Roi Louis XI dans ſes guerres
contre le Comte d'*Armagnac*, & eut, de la
conſiſcation de ſes biens, Malauſe, Clermont-
Soꝰs-Biran, & la quatrième partie de la Seigneurie d'Aſtafort. Dans ſon contrat de mariage, du 3 Octobre 1474, il eſt qualifié RO-
BERT DE BALSAC, *Conſeiller & Chambellan
du Roi, Sénéchal d'Agénois, Baron d'Entragues & de Saint-Amand.* LOUIS XI, dont
il étoit favori, établit en ſa faveur une Foire
en ce dernier lieu. CHARLES VIII le nomma
Gouverneur de la Citadelle de Piſe, pendant
ſon voyage de Naples. Il fonda, dans ſa Seigneurie de Saint-Amand, l'an 1484, une
Egliſe Collégiale de ſix Chanoines, ſix Pré-
bendiers, & de pluſieurs Chapelains; teſta le
3 Mai 1503, & y fut inhumé. Il avoit épouſé,
le 3 Octobre 1474, *Antoinette de Caſtelnau*,
fille d'*Antoine*, Seigneur de *Caſtelnau*, & de
Bretenoux, Baron de Saint-Côme, & de *Catherine de Chauvigny*, dont il eut:

1. PIERRE, qui ſuit;

2. ROBERT, Protonotaire Apoſtolique;

3. JEANNE, qui épouſa *Amaury*, Seigneur de
Montal;

4. LOUISE, femme de *Charles de Brillac*, Seigneur d'Argy, en Touraine;

5. Et ANTOINETTE, qui épouſa *Gabriel*, Seigneur de *Noꝫières*, Bailli des Montagnes
d'Auvergne.

Jeanne, bâtarde de ROBERT DE BALSAC, épouſa *François Rigaud*, Seigneur de la Vay-
fière, fils de *Pierre Rigaud;*
N.... & *N....* autres filles bâtardes.

V. PIERRE DE BALSAC, Baron d'Entragues
& de Saint-Amand, Seigneur de Prélat,
Paulhac, Juis, Dunes, & Clermont-Sous-Biran, n'avoit que 15 ans en 1494, lorſqu'il fut
pourvu, en ſurvivance de ſon père, de la Capitainerie des Châteaux de Tournon, Fort
de Penne, & Châtelculhier. Il fut depuis Capitaine de Corbeil & de Fontainebleau, commanda l'arrière-Ban de Melun, Montargis,
Eſtampes, Chartres & Montfort, qu'il condui-
ſit en Hainaut; il prêta ſerment en 1523, entre les mains du Maréchal de Chabannes,
Gouverneur d'Auvergne, pour la Lieutenance de Roi en cette Province. Il enleva *Anne
Mallet-de-Graville*, ſa couſine, & l'épouſa
malgré l'Amiral, qui penſoit à déſhériter ſa
fille, lorſque le Prieur des Céleſtins de Marcouſſis la lui préſenta, avec ſon gendre, le
Vendredi-Saint, comme il étoit ſur le point
d'adorer la Croix, & obtint leur pardon, en
mémoire du Myſtère du Jour. PIERRE DE BAL-
SAC, par ſon teſtament, pria MARGUERITE DE
VALOIS, Reine de France, ſœur de FRANÇOIS
Iᵉʳ, de prendre ſes enfans en ſa protection, à
cauſe des grands procès qu'on lui avoit ſuſci-
tés, tant de la part de ſon beau-père, que pour
la ſucceſſion de GEOFFROY DE BALSAC, ſon couſin. Cette Princeſſe s'en fit décharger par
Lettres du Roi, données à Compiègne, au
mois de Novembre 1531. PIERRE DE BALSAC
épouſa donc *Anne Mallet*, Dame de Montagu, fille de *Louis Mallet*, Seigneur de Graville, Amiral de France, & de *Marie de Bal-
ſac*. Elle portoit pour devife un inſtrument
hydraulique, qu'on nomme *chantepleure*,
avec ces mots: *Muſas natura, lacrymas for-
tuna*. Il eut pour enfans:

1. GUILLAUME, qui ſuit;

2. THOMAS, tige des Seigneurs de *Montagu;*

3. LOUISE, mariée en 1523 à *Charles Martel*,
Seigneur de Bacqueville. Il eut, après la

Reine de Navarre, la tutelle de ses beaux-frères & belles-sœurs, qui lui intentèrent procès pour lui faire rendre compte;

4. JEANNE, qui épousa *Claude d'Urfé*, Chevalier de l'Ordre du Roi, Gouverneur de M. le Dauphin, & Bailli de *Forez*;

5. ANTOINETTE, Abbesse de Malnoue;

6. Et GEORGETTE, mariée, par contrat du 10 Mai 1538, en présence de la Reine de Navarre, & du Connétable, à *Jean Pot*, Seigneur de Chemaut;

Et d'autres enfans, morts jeunes.

VI. GUILLAUME DE BALSAC, né à Marcoussis le 14 Décembre 1517, eut pour parrain N... *de Montmorency*, & pour marraine *Madeleine de la Roche-Guyon*, & fut Seigneur d'Entragues, de Marcoussis, Malherbes, & Baron de Clermont; se fit émanciper, & partagea les biens de son père & de sa mère avec son frère THOMAS, en 1540. Il étoit Capitaine de 200 Chevaux, & Lieutenant de la Compagnie des Gendarmes de FRANÇOIS de Lorraine, Duc de Guise, sous lequel il servit au siège de Metz, en 1552, & à la bataille de Renty, en 1554, où il fut dangereusement blessé, & mourut quelques jours après, à Montreuil. Il avoit épousé à Compiègne, en présence de la Cour, le 18 Octobre 1538, *Louise de Crévant-d'Humières*, fille de *Jean*, Seigneur d'Humières, & de *Françoise de Contay*, dont il eut:

1. HENRI, né à Malherbes le 30 Mars 1540, mort jeune;

2. FRANÇOIS, qui suit;

3. CHARLES, qui a fait la branche des Comtes de *Clermont*;

4. JEAN, né le .... Février 1543, mort au Collège de Navarre, à Paris, & enterré à Marcoussis;

5. GALÉAS, Seigneur de Tournanfuye, aujourd'hui Graville, mort, sans alliance, en 1573, d'une blessure qu'il avoit reçue au siège de la Rochelle;

6. CHARLES, Seigneur de Dunes, Comte de Graville, Chevalier des Ordres du Roi, en 1595, dit *le Bel-Entraguet*, Lieutenant-Général au Gouvernement d'Orléans, Gouverneur de Saint-Dizier, & Capitaine de 50 hommes d'armes. Ce fut contre lui que le Comte de *Quélus* prit querelle en 1576, &, à cinq heures du matin, le Dimanche, 27 Avril de la même année, se fit dans le Marché-aux-Chevaux, près la Porte Sainte-Antoine, le fameux duel de Quélus, Maugiron & Livarot, contre Entragues, Riberac & Schomberg. Maugiron & Schomberg restèrent

morts sur la place, Ribérac mourut le lendemain, Livarot reçut un coup sur la tête dont il fut malade six semaines. Quélus fut blessé de 19 coups, dont il mourut le 29 Mars suivant: Entragues en fut quitte pour une égratignure. HENRI III lui accorda sa grâce quelque tems après. Il mourut à Toulouse, l'an 1599, ayant été fiancé à une fille du Maréchal de *Montluc*;

7. ROBERT, mort le 18 Mars 1548, à l'âge de quatre mois;

8. LOUISE, alliée, le 9 Juin 1571, à *Jacques*, Baron de *Clere*, en Normandie, fils de *Jean de Clere*, & d'*Anne de Fouquesolles*;

9. Et CATHERINE, mariée en 1572, à *Edme Stuart*, Comte de Lennox, Seigneur d'Aubigny, d'où sont issus les Ducs de Lennox, & les Seigneurs d'*Aubigny*. Après la mort de son mari, elle envoya ses enfans à JACQUES, Roi de la Grande-Bretagne, qui les avoit demandés, pour les établir à sa Cour.

VII. FRANÇOIS DE BALSAC, Seigneur d'Entragues, de Marcoussis, & du Bois-Malherbes, Conseiller du Roi en ses Conseils, Capitaine de 50 hommes d'armes, Gouverneur d'Orléans, & Lieutenant-Général de l'Orléanois, & Pays adjacens, fut fait Chevalier des Ordres du Roi, par HENRI III, en 1578, lors de la première promotion. Il épousa 1° *Jacqueline de Rohan*, fille & héritière de *François de Rohan*, Seigneur de Gié & du Verger, & de *Catherine de Silly*; 2° *Marie Touchet*, Dame de Belleville, fille de *Jean Touchet*, Seigneur de Beauvais & du Quillart, Conseiller du Roi, Lieutenant-Particulier au Bailliage, & Présidial d'Orléans, & de *Marie Mathi*. Elle avoit été maîtresse du Roi CHARLES IX: elle en avoit eu *Charles*, bâtard de VALOIS, Duc d'Angoulême, qui a fait la branche des derniers Ducs d'*Angoulême*.

Du premier mariage vinrent:

1. CHARLES, qui suit;

2. CÉSAR, Seigneur de Gié, premier Colonel-Général des Carabiniers, Conseiller du Roi, en ses Conseils, Lieutenant-Général en ses Armées, & au Gouvernement d'Orléans; se voyant sans enfans, il substitua son nom & ses armes à *Léon d'Illiers*, fils de sa sœur; il avoit été nommé Chevalier des Ordres du Roi, le 15 Janvier 1629, & mourut avant d'avoir été reçu. Il épousa, en 1612, *Catherine Hennequin d'Assi*, veuve du Baron *de Dunes*, son cousin. Elle eut pour troisième mari *Nicolas de Brichanteau*, Marquis de Nangis, Chevalier des Ordres du Roi. Elle étoit fille d'*Antoine*, Seigneur d'*Assy*;

3. CHARLOTTE-CATHERINE, née en 1568, qui fut nommée par le Roi CHARLES IX, & par la Reine CATHERINE DE MÉDICIS, & mariée le 23 Novembre 1588, à *Jacques d'Illiers,* Seigneur de Chantemerle, qui mourut la nuit de Noël 1611; elle en eut, entr'autres enfans, *Léon d'Illiers,* Seigneur d'Entragues & de Chantemerle, qui fut fubftitué, par fon oncle maternel, au nom & aux armes d'*Entragues.* C'eft de lui que defcendent les Seigneurs d'*Illiers d'Entragues;*

4. & 5. N.... & N.... autres enfans, morts jeunes.

Du fecond mariage fortirent:

6. HENRIETTE, Marquife de Verneuil, morte le Mercredi des Cendres, 9 Février 1633, en fa 64e année, mère de *Henri de Bourbon,* Duc de Verneuil, Chevalier des Ordres du Roi, fils naturel du Roi HENRI IV;

7. Et MARIE, mère de *Louis de Baffompierre,* Abbé de Cléry, Evêque de Saintes, en 1649, fils naturel de *François de Baffompierre,* Maréchal de France.

VIII. CHARLES DE BALSAC, Seigneur d'Entragues, s'appeloit auparavant *Guillaume:* fon nom lui fut changé en la Confirmation. Il fut Seigneur de Marcouffis, du vivant de fon père, puis Capitaine de 50 hommes d'armes, & Gouverneur des Duchés d'Orléans & d'Eftampes. Il époufa 1° *Marie de la Chaftre,* fille de *Claude de la Chaftre,* Seigneur de la Maifon-Forte, Maréchal de France, & de *Jeanne Chabot;* 2° *Jeanne Gaignon,* fille de *Jean,* Seigneur de Saint-Bohaire, & de *Jeanne d'Angennes:*

Du premier lit fortirent:

1. & 2. *N.....& N.....* morts en bas âge.

Et du fecond lit:

3. CHARLES, tué en duel, l'an 1616, à l'âge de 20 ans;

4. CLAUDE, Seigneur de Marcouffis, mort fans alliance, le 26 Janvier 1618, inhumé près fon père, aux Céleftins de Marcouffis;

5. ANNE, morte jeune, du verfement d'un carroffe;

6. Et FRANÇOISE, Religieufe à Faremoutier, puis transférée à Bonlieu, près Châteaudu-Loir, où elle eft morte en 1650, âgé de 55 ans.

BRANCHE
des Seigneurs DE CLERMONT-SOUS-BIRAN.

VII. CHARLES DE BALSAC, dit *le Jeune,* troifième fils de GUILLAUME & de *Louife de Crévant-d'Humières,* fut Seigneur de Clermont-Sous-Biran, Gentilhomme de la Cham-

bre, & Capitaine de 100 Archers de la Garde du Corps du Roi HENRI III; il fuivit ce Prince en Pologne, qui, après fon retour, le fit Chevalier de fes Ordres, le 31 Décembre 1583: il fut tué à la bataille d'Ivry, le 14 Mars 1590. Il avoit époufé *Hélène Bon,* veuve de *Charles de Gondi,* Seigneur de la Tour, Maître de la Garderobe du Roi, & fille de *Pierre Bon,* Seigneur de Meuillon, Gouverneur de Marfeille, & de *Marguerite de Robins-de-Gravefon,* dont il eut:

1.° HENRI, qui fuit;

2. CHARLES, qui fit la branche des Seigneurs de *Dunes;*

3. JEAN, Abbé d'Evron & de Saint-Quentinlez-Beauvais, nommé à l'Evêché de Grenoble, mort le 15 Mai 1608;

4. LOUIS, Chevalier de Malte, mort à l'âge de 21 ans, en 1618, faifant fes caravanes;

5. NICOLAS, Abbé de Saint-Martin-aux-Bois, puis d'Evron & de Saint-Quentin, après fon frère, Coadjuteur d'Autun, mort le 16 Janvier 1610;

6. Et HÉLÈNE, morte jeune, ou LOUISE, felon Moréri.

VIII. HENRI DE BALSAC, Marquis de Clermont-d'Entragues, Comte de Graville, Baron de Dunes, Seigneur de Mezières, obtint l'érection de fa terre de Clermont-Sous-Biran, en Agénois, en *Marquifat,* par Lettres données à Paris, au mois de Janvier 1617, & vérifiées au Parlement de Bordeaux, le 2 Décembre fuivant. Il époufa *Louife l'Huillier,* fille unique de *Nicolas l'Huillier,* Seigneur de Boulancourt, Préfident en la Chambre des Comptes de Paris, & de *Louife Boudet,* dont il eut:

1. LOUISE, morte au mois de Mars 1682. Elle avoit époufé, le 3 Septembre 1647, *Louis de Bretagne-Avaugour,* Marquis d'Avaugour, Comte de Vertus & de Goello, dont elle fut la feconde femme;

2. Et MARIE, morte le 9 Novembre 1691, âgée de 74 ans. Elle avoit époufé, le 28 Mai 1651, *Jean-Gafpard-Ferdinand,* Comte de *Marchin* & du Saint-Empire.

BRANCHE
des Barons DE DUNES.

VIII. CHARLES DE BALSAC, Seigneur de Dunes, fecond fils de CHARLES, Seigneur de Clermont d'Entragues, Chevalier des Ordres du Roi, & d'*Hélène Bon,* Dame de Meuillon, fut inftitué héritier par le teftament, du 4 Avril 1598, de fon oncle CHARLES DE BALSAC, dit *le*

Bel-Entraguet, Baron de Dunes. Il époufa, le 28 Juin 1606, *Catherine Hennequin*, qui fe remaria à César de Balsac, Seigneur de Gié, coufin germain de fon premier mari ; & en troifièmes noces, elle époufa *Nicolas de Brichanteau*, Marquis de Nangis, Chevalier des Ordres du Roi. Elle étoit fille d'*Antoine Hennequin*, Seigneur d'Affi. Leurs enfans furent :

1. Jeanne, mariée à *Louis Hurault*, Seigneur du Marais, Enfeigne des Gendarmes du Roi, dont un fils *Charles Hurault*, Comte du Marais ;
2. Alphonsine, mariée, le 10 Octobre 1628, à *Charles Martel*, Seigneur de Monpinçon, & de Fontaine-Martel, dont deux filles ;
3. Et Elisabeth, mariée le 21 Février 1634, avec *Gafton de Renty*, Seigneur de Landelles, renommé pour fa piété, & dont la vie a été écrite par Jean-Baptifte de Saint-Jure.

BRANCHE
des Seigneurs de Montagu.

VI. Thomas de Balsac, fils puîné de Pierre, Seigneur d'Entragues, & d'*Anne Mallet-de-Graville*, Dame de Montagu, fut Seigneur de Montagu la Brifette, Chevalier de l'Ordre du Roi, & Gentilhomme de fa Chambre. Il fit au Roi, le 12 Avril 1575, pour les Seigneuries de Gouverts, Châtres & la Roue, qui lui étoient échues par le partage fait avec Guillaume, fon frère. Il eft enterré, avec fa femme, dans le Sanctuaire de l'Eglife des Céleftins de Marcouffis, du côté de l'Évangile, fous un tombeau de marbre que Charles, leur fils, Evêque & Comte de Noyon, leur fit faire, & où il eft auffi inhumé. Il époufa *Anne Gaillard*, fille de *Michel*, Seigneur de Longjumeau, & de *Souveraine d'Angoulême*, fœur naturelle du Roi François Ier. Il eut pour enfans :

1. Jean, qui fuit ;
2. Robert, Seigneur d'Ambonville, la Brifette, & Châtres fous-Montlhéry. Il époufa *Marie le Maître*, morte fans enfans, fille de *Gilles le Maître*, Seigneur de Ferrières, Capitaine d'une Compagnie de Chevaux-Légers, & de *Marie de Hennequin* ;
3. Charles, Evêque & Comte de Noyon, Pair de France. Voyez fon article, dans le P. Anfelme ;
4. Louise, mariée à *Jean de Créquy*, Seigneur de Raimboval, dont elle eut *Claudine de Créquy*, femme de *François de Monchy*, Seigneur de Longueval ;
5. Anne, mariée à *Antoine de Monchy*, Chevalier, Seigneur de Mont-Cavrel, dont des enfans ;
6. Claudine, Dame de Boifroger ;
7. Et autre Louise, Abbeffe de Saulvoir, Ordre de Cîteaux, près Laon, morte en 1628.

Selon Moréri il eut encore une fille nommée Souveraine de Balsac, mariée à N...., Seigneur de *Saint-Sulpix*, en Normandie.

VII. Jean de Balsac, ou Pierre, felon Moréri, Seigneur de Montagu, Chevalier de l'Ordre du Roi, Chambellan du Duc d'Alençon, Lieutenant de la Compagnie du Prince de Condé, & Surintendant de fa Maifon, eut les Seigneuries de Châtres, de Viviers, & de la Roue ; il fuivit en Hongrie le Duc de Guife, lorfqu'il alla au fecours de l'Empereur contre le Turc ; fut Gouverneur de Saint-Jean-d'Angély, puis de Brouage, & mourut, le 8 Décembre 1581, âgé de 36 ans. On voit fon épitaphe fur un marbre noir, contre un pilier, entre deux tombeaux, dans le Sanctuaire des Céleftins de Marcouffis. Il époufa *Madeleine Olivier*, veuve de *Louis de Sainte-Maure*, Comte de Neelle, fille de *François Olivier*, Seigneur de Leuville, Chancelier de France, & de *Jeanne de Cérifay*, dont il eut :

Anne, mariée 1° à *François de Lisle*, Seigneur de Treigny, Gouverneur de Corbeil & de la Baftille en 1594, de la Chapelle en 1598, & d'Amiens en 1607, mort l'an 1611, avec foupçon d'avoir été empoifonné, dont poftérité ; & 2° à *Louis Séguier*, Baron de Saint-Briffon, Prévôt de Paris, dont elle n'eut point d'enfans.

Les armes : comme ci-devant, colonne 246.

BALTHAZAR, famille illuftre & Patricienne de la République de Lucerne en Suiffe, originaire du *Val-Maygia*, aujourd'hui Bailliage dépendant des douze premiers Cantons.

I. Thierry Balthazar, Ier du nom, vint s'établir à Lucerne, où il obtint, en 1531, le droit de Bourgeoifie, habile au gouvernement ; il étoit Capitaine au fervice de la République de Lucerne. Il eut de fon mariage avec N...*Hug*, fille de *Jean Hug*, Avoyer ou Chef du Canton de Soleure :

II. Georges Balthazar, qui renouvela fon droit de Bourgeoifie à Lucerne, & laiffa de fon mariage avec *Anne-Marie Somazzi* :

III. Guillaume Balthazar, Ier du nom, Capitaine, qui fut nommé du Grand-Confeil de la République de Lucerne en 1580, Bailli

de Habsbourg en 1589, Sénateur du Petit-
Conseil en la même année, & Bailli du Val-
Entlibuch en 1599. Il mourut en 1621, ayant
eu de son mariage avec *Afre*, fille de *Jodoc
Krebsinger*, Avoyer de la Ville & Canton de
Lucerne :

1. JEAN, qui suit ;
2. THÉODORIC ou THIERRY, dont on parlera ci-
après ;
3. Et MADELEINE, mariée à *Antoine Haas*,
d'une ancienne famille Patricienne de Lucerne.

IV. JEAN BALTHAZAR, du Grand-Conseil de
Lucerne en 1599, du Petit-Conseil en 1621,
Bailli du Val-Entlibuch en 1625, mourut en
1630. Il eut de son mariage avec *Madeleine
Ekart* :

1. MELCHIOR, qui suit ;
2. LOUISE, mariée à *Corneil Bachmann* ;
3. Et ANNE, mariée à *Guillaume Meyer*.

V. MELCHIOR BALTHAZAR, du Grand-Conseil en 1632, du Petit-Conseil la même année, & Trésorier de la République de Lucerne en 1651, mourut en 1661. Il avoit épousé
1° *Anne-Marie Castanéa* ; & 2° *Jacobée-Se-
gesset-de-Brunegg*.

Il eut du premier lit :

1. JEAN-MELCHIOR, qui suit ;
2. NICOLAS, dont on rapportera la postérité
ci-après ;
3. Et. MADELEINE, mariée à *Jost-Renouard
Hartmann*, de Lucerne.

VI. JEAN MELCHIOR BALTHAZAR, du Grand-
Conseil de Lucerne en 1639, mourut en 1657.
Il eut de son mariage avec *Dorothée Mittler* :

1. JODOC-MELCHIOR, Gardien du Couvent des
Cordeliers de Lucerne, sous le nom de *P.
Otton* ;
2. JEAN-CHARLES, qui suit ;
3. DENIS, Capucin ;
4. ANNE-MARIE, qui épousa *Jean-Melchior
Fleischlin*, de Lucerne ;
5. LOUISE, mariée à *Jean-Jost Fleischlin* ;
6. CATHERINE, mariée à *Guillaume Thuring*,
de Lucerne ;
7. DOROTHÉE, Religieuse au Couvent d'Im-
bruch, à Lucerne ;
8. Et ROSE, Religieuse de l'Abbaye de Gna-
denthal, Ordre de Cîteaux.

VII. JEAN-CHARLES BALTHAZAR, du Grand-
Conseil de Lucerne en 1669, Chancelier du
Canton de ce nom en 16.... Sénateur du Petit-Conseil en 1699, élu Bailli du Landgraviat de Turgovie en 1701, fut élevé d'une
voix unanime, cette même année, à la pre-

mière dignité de l'Etat de Lucerne, qui est
celle d'*Avoyer*, fut en même tems Banneret
de la Ville, & un des plus illustres Magistrats que la Suisse ait eus. Il étoit en grande
estime auprès des Ambassadeurs des deux
Puissances Rivales, la France & l'Autriche,
& il eut la sagacité de cultiver & de ménager
ces deux Ministres, pour le bien de sa patrie.
Il mourut en 1703, & eut de son mariage
avec *Marguerite Schuomacher*, d'une famille Patricienne de Lucerne :

1. JACQUES-CHARLES, qui suit ;
2. FRANÇOIS-OURS, auteur de la seconde branche, rapportée ci-après ;
3. & 4. CHARLES & JOSEPH, Jésuites ;
5. Et JEAN-ANTOINE, aussi Jésuite, qui fut, pendant de longues années, Missionnaire dans
les Royaumes du Mexique & du Pérou. Il
pénétra le premier dans l'intérieur de la
Californie ; fut élu Visiteur-Général des
Missions, & Préfet Provincial de son Ordre
dans la Province du Mexique, & mourut à
Mexico, le 23 Avril 1763, étant Recteur du
Collège de cette Ville.

VIII. JACQUES-CHARLES BALTHAZAR, du Petit-Conseil d'Etat de Lucerne, en 1712, mourut en 1727. Il avoit épousé, 1° sans enfans,
Catherine-Elisabeth Dulcicker ; & 2° *Anne-
Marie Cysat*.

Du second lit vinrent :

1. JOSEPH-LOUIS-XAVIER, qui suit ;
2. Et MARIE-ROSE, mariée à *Antoine-Léonce-
Irénée Schuomacher*, Conseiller d'Etat de
Lucerne.

IX. JOSEPH-LOUIS-XAVIER BALTHAZAR, Gouverneur du Château de Wycken en 1746,
Conseiller d'Etat de la République de Lucerne, a épousé, en 1747, *Marie-Thérèse Schuomacher*.

SECONDE BRANCHE.

VIII. FRANÇOIS-OURS BALTHAZAR, second
fils de l'Avoyer JEAN-CHARLES, & de *Marguerite Schuomacher*, fut Chancelier de la République de Lucerne, puis Sénateur du Petit-
Conseil en 1727, Directeur-Général des Bâtimens de la République, Représentant du
Corps Helvétique à Bâle, en 1733 & 1742,
durant la guerre allumée entre les Maisons de
Bourbon & d'*Autriche*, & Intendant-Général de la ville de Lucerne en 1748. Il fut un
des plus vertueux, des plus zélés & des plus
respectables Magistrats du Corps Helvétique.
Il est mort le 30 Mai 1763, âgé de 73 ans, 6

mois & 23 jours. On voit son épitaphe en Allemand à Lucerne, dans l'Eglise Paroissiale
du Chapitre de Saint-Léger. Il a laissé plusieurs ouvrages de sa composition en Allemand, & a eu de son mariage avec *Anne-
Marie Schuomacher* :

1. JOSEPH-ANTOINE-FÉLIX, qui suit;
2. MARIE-ANNE, mariée à *François-Dominique Peyer-im-Hoff*, Sénateur de Lucerne;
3. Et MARIE-JACOBÉE, mariée à *Joseph-Igna-
   ce-François-Xavier Pfyffer-de-Heidegg*,
   Sénateur du Petit-Conseil de Lucerne, &
   Bailli du Landgraviat de Turgovie.

IX. JOSEPH-ANTOINE-FÉLIX BALTHAZAR, né
à Lucerne, Conseiller d'Etat, du Petit-Conseil en 1763, Intendant-Général de l'Hôpital de la ville de Lucerne en 1765. C'est à ce
magistrat, digne fils de son père, que la Suisse,
ennemie du Pyrrhonisme, doit l'Apologie du
fondateur de sa liberté *(Guillaume Tell)*. Il
a eu plusieurs enfans de l'un & de l'autre sexe
de son mariage avec *Marie-Elisabeth Pfyffer d'Alhshoffen.*

TROISIÈME BRANCHE.

VI. NICOLAS BALTHAZAR, second fils de MEL-
CHIOR, & d'*Anne-Marie Castanéa*, mort en
1701, Stathouder & Banneret de la ville de
Lucerne, avoit épousé 1º *Catherine de Sonnenberg*; & 2º sans enfans, *Marie-Elisabeth Schuomacher*. Il a eu du premier lit:

VII. BÉAT-FRANÇOIS BALTHAZAR, du Grand-
Conseil de Lucerne en 1693, Bailli de Krientz
en 1699, du Petit-Conseil en 1702, Banneret de la ville de Lucerne, qui renouvela, en
1715, comme Ambassadeur de son Canton,
l'alliance à Soleure avec la France. Il mourut
en 1730, & avoit épousé *Marie-Elisabeth
Dulcicker*, dont :

1. FRANÇOIS-NICOLAS-LÉONCE, qui suit;
2. JEAN-ULRIC-MAURICE, auteur de la quatrième branche, rapportée ci-après;
3. BASILE, Religieux & Archiviste de l'Abbaye de
   Saint-Gall, Ordre de Saint-Benoît, qui
   a composé en Latin la continuation de
   l'Histoire de ce célèbre Monastère. Elle est
   en manuscrit dans les Archives de cette
   Abbaye;
4. MARIE-CATHERINE, mariée à *Jean-Martin
   Schnider-de-Wartensée*, Sénateur de Lucerne;
5. MARIE-ELISABETH, mariée à *Jacques-Joseph-
   Rodolphe Mohr*, Sénateur de Lucerne;
6. MARIE-FRANÇOISE, mariée à *Henri Goel-
   delin-de-Tieffenau*, Capitaine.

VIII. FRANÇOIS-NICOLAS-LÉONCE BALTHA-
ZAR, Sénateur du Petit-Conseil en 1730,
Bailli de Munster en 1733, Directeur-Général des Bâtimens de l'Etat; Avoyer ou Chef
du Canton de Lucerne, depuis le mois de Décembre 1766, & Banneret de cette même ville en 1769, a eu de son mariage avec *Jean-
ne-Baptiste de Sonnenberg* :

IX. JOSEPH-JEAN-BAPTISTE BALTHAZAR, du
Grand-Conseil de Lucerne, qui a épousé *Marie-Josèphe de Fleckenstein.*

QUATRIÈME BRANCHE.

VIII. JEAN-ULRIC-MAURICE BALTHAZAR,
second fils de BÉAT-FRANÇOIS, & de *Marie-
Elisabeth Dulcicker*, du Grand-Conseil, &
Sous-Secrétaire de la République de Lucerne, a épousé *Marie-Bernardine Pfyffer*,
dont :

1. XAVIER, qui suit;
2. VINCENT, Religieux de l'Abbaye de Notre-
   Dame de la Pierre, Diocèse de Bâle;
3. Et MARIE-ANNE-CATHERINE, mariée à *Ale-
   xis-Christophe-Jean-Baptiste Goeldelin-
   de-Tieffenau*, Chevalier de l'Ordre Royal
   & Militaire de Saint-Louis, Lieutenant-
   Colonel au service de France, & Sénateur
   du Conseil intérieur de la République de
   Lucerne.

IX. XAVIER BALTHAZAR.

CINQUIÈME BRANCHE.

IV. THÉODORIC ou THIERRY BALTHAZAR, IIe
du nom, second fils du Capitaine GUILLAUME
Ier, & d'*Afre-Krebsinger*, épousa *Jacobée
de Krus*, d'une famille Patricienne de Lucerne, dont il eut :

V. GEORGES BALTHAZAR, du Grand-Conseil de Lucerne en 1628, Bailli de Krientz
& de Horb en 1629, & du Comté de Habsbourg en 1633 & 1643, qui fut nommé Sénateur
du Petit-Conseil en 1648, & mourut en 1658.
Il eut de son mariage avec *Pétronille Wis-
sing*, de Lucerne :

1. JEAN-FRANÇOIS, qui suit;
2. JODOC-THÉODORIC, rapporté après son frère
   aîné;
3. Et CATHERINE, mariée à *Louis Durler*, du
   Grand-Conseil de Lucerne.

VI. JEAN-FRANÇOIS BALTHAZAR, du Grand-
Conseil de Lucerne en 1649, du Petit-Conseil en 1658, mourut en 1669. Il eut de son
mariage avec *Marie-Jacobée de Sonnenberg* :

1. HENRI, Chanoine du Chapitre de Lucerne;

2. Pétronille, mariée 1° à *Jean-Joft Bir-cher;* & 2° à *Joft-Melchior Zelger;*

3. Et Marie-Jacobée, mariée à *Louis Mah-ler,* de Lucerne.

SIXIÈME BRANCHE.

VI. Jodoc-Théodoric Balthazar, fecond fils de Georges, & de *Pétronille Wiffing,* du Grand-Confeil de Lucerne en 1659, Bailli du Comté de Baden en 1667, fut nommé du Petit-Confeil de la République de Lucerne en 1669, Bailli du Comté de Sargans en 1675, Intendant-Général de l'Hôpital de Lucerne en 1681, Bailli du Landgraviat de Turgovie en 1688, Major-Général du Canton de Lu-cerne en 1693, & Bailli du Comté de Rot-tenbourg en 1695. Il mourut en 1704, & eut de fon mariage avec *Anne-Barbe Pfyffer-d'Alhshoffen*:

1. Jacques, qui fuit;

2. Jean-François, Chanoine du Chapitre de Munfter;

3. Charles-André, dont on rapportera la poftérité ci-après;

4. Robert, né en 1674, élu Abbé de Saint-Urbain, ordre de Cîteaux, Diocèfe de Conftance, le 11 Mai 1726, mort le 9 Novembre 1751, âgé de 77 ans. Il fut le reftaurateur de fon Abbaye, & l'enrichit d'une Biblio-thèque & d'une collection de Médailles;

5. Marie-Catherine, mariée à *Jodoc-Jofeph Mohr,* Vice-Avoyer;

6. Barbe-Claire, mariée 1° avec *François-Louis Hartmann,* Sénateur de Lucerne; & 2° avec *François-Melchior Hartmann,* auffi Sénateur de Lucerne;

7. Et Marie-Barbe-Françoise, élue Abbeffe d'Efchenbach, ordre de Cîteaux, en 1713, & morte en 1737.

VII. Jacques Balthazar, du Grand-Con-feil de Lucerne en 1678, Bailli de Weggis en 1681, & du Comté de Baden en 1699, fut nommé du Petit-Confeil de Lucerne en 1704, Avoyer & Banneret de cette République en 1713, réfigna la même année la dignité d'A-voyer, à caufe de fon grand âge & de fes in-firmités, & mourut le 29 Janvier 1723, âgé de 75 ans. On voit à Lucerne fon épitaphe dans l'Eglife des Cordeliers. Il avoit été, en 1712, Major-Général des troupes de Lucerne durant la guerre civile, qui s'étoit élevée en-tre les cinq premiers Cantons Catholiques, & les Cantons Réformés de Zurich & de Ber-ne. Il eut de fon mariage avec *Anne-Ma-rie-Catherine Meyer*:

1. François-Jean, Sénateur de Lucerne, qui, de fon mariage avec *Marie-Elifabeth Bir-cher,* a eu Marie-Anne Balthazar, femme du Sénateur *Joft-Jofeph-Xavier Meyer*;

2. Jodoc-Théodoric, Lieutenant au fervice d'Efpagne;

3. Jacques-Rodolphe, Capitaine, qui, de fon mariage avec *Anne-Elifabeth de Flecken-ftein,* eut:

     Jacques-Charles-Martin Balthazar, Chanoine & Cuftode du Chapitre de Munfter;

     Et Joseph-Leger Balthazar, Chanoine du Chapitre de Lucerne;

4. Jean-Martin, qui fuit;

5. Jean-Leger, Seigneur de Tannenfels, Cha-noine & Cuftode du Chapitre de Munfter;

6. Catherine, mariée à *François-Théodore Dorer,* de Bade;

7. Et Marie-Anne, mariée 1° à *François-Louis Bur,* du Grand-Confeil de Lucerne; & 2° à *Henri-Maurice Pfyffer-de-Heid-degg.*

VIII. Jean-Martin Balthazar, Capitai-ne, époufa *Catherine Felber,* laquelle, de-venue veuve, fe remaria à *Jean-Charles-Chriftophe Pfyffer,* Seigneur d'Alhshoffen, Statthalter, ou Stathouder de la République de Lucerne. Elle a eu de fon premier mari:

1. Joseph-Antoine, Chanoine de Munfter;

2. Martin, Religieux de l'Abbaye de Saint-Urbain;

3. Jean, qui fuit;

4. Marie-Anne, mariée 1° avec le Baron *de Reding,* Colonel d'un Régiment Suiffe de fon nom, au fervice d'Efpagne; & 2° avec *Jodoc-François Hartmann,* du Grand-Con-feil de Lucerne;

5. Et Aloysie, mariée à *Jodoc Pfyffer-d'Alhf-hoffen,* Capitaine des Cent-Suiffes de la Garde du Pape.

IX. Jean Balthazar, du Grand-Confeil de Lucerne, Major de la garnifon de la ville de ce nom, a plufieurs enfans de fon mariage avec *Elifabeth Mohr.*

SEPTIÈME BRANCHE.

VII. Charles-André Balthazar, fils puî-né de Jodoc-Théodoric, & d'*Anne-Barbe Pfyffer-d'Alhshoffen,* Capitaine, Secrétaire du Sénat en 1703, fut nommé du Grand-Confeil de Lucerne en 1705; & tué en 1712, à la bataille de Vilmergen, contre les Ber-nois; il avoit époufé 1° *Elifabeth de Krus;* & 2° *Elifabeth Schwytzer.*

Il eut du premier lit:

1. Jean-Martin, qui fuit;
2. Et Marie-Anne, mariée à *Alphonfe-Igna-ce Dulliker*.

VIII. Jean-Martin Balthazar, Sénateur de Lucerne, époufa 1° *Marie-Marguerite de Cyfat;* & 2° N.....*Meyer*.

Il eut du premier lit:

1. Deodat, Capucin;
2. Et Marie-Anne, mariée à *Charles-Rodol-phe Corragione-d'Orello*.

Les armes: *d'azur, à trois étoiles d'or, 1 & 2,pofées dans un triangle de même,char-gé d'un triangle renverfé auffi d'or*. Ci-mier: *un cafque grillé & couronné d'or,re-hauffé d'un demi-homme habillé d'azur, le vifage barbu, la tête couverte d'un bonnet de fable, tenant à la main droite une fleur-de-lys d'azur, & avec la gauche un marteau de fable*.

BALTHAZARD, famille illuftre & an-cienne, originaire de Tranfylvanie, d'où elle fortit en 1320, dit le *Mercure* du mois de No-vembre 1742. Le Colonel Balthazard , tué en 1590, étoit Maréchal-de-Camp fous le Roi Henri IV. Gacho de Balthazard, tué à la bataille de Prague en 1620, fuivit la for-tune de Frédéric V, Roi de Bohême, dont il étoit Capitaine des Gardes-du-Corps. Il laiffa de *Marguerite de Rahire:*

Jean de Balthazard de Simeren, qui vint en France au fervice du Roi Louis XIII,après la première bataille de Nortlingue, fous le Duc de Saxe-Weimar, en 1634. Y ayant été attiré par la réputation que s'y étoit acquife le Colonel de Balthazard, fon oncle, Jean fe diftingua beaucoup dans la guerre de Guyen-ne fous le Prince de Condé. Il fut envoyé en Catalogne, pour y fervir en qualité de Lieute-nant-Général fous le Prince de Conty, & en chef en fon abfence pendant la campagne en 1654. Il fut auffi Colonel d'un Régiment d'Infanterie, & Meftre-de-Camp d'un Régi-ment de Cavalerie,aujourd'hui nommé Royal-Cravates. Il fut envoyé, avec le caractère d'Ambaffadeur extraordinaire dans les Cours de Brunfwick & Lunebourg pour y négocier la paix, laquelle étant faite, Charles-Louis, Electeur, Comte Palatin du Rhin, l'engagea, avec la permiffion du Roi, d'entrer à fon fer-vice, & le fit Généraliffime de fes troupes & fon Miniftre d'Etat en 1657. Depuis il fe re-tira en Suiffe dans le Canton de Berne, où il

acheta des Terres. Il époufa *Marguerite de Brignac de Montamont*, dont il eut:

Genève de Balthazard , Vicomte d'Altezy, qui fut Colonel d'un Régiment de Dragons au fervice du Roi d'Angleterre. Il eut deux fils:

L'aîné fut tué à l'affaire de Claufen en Allemagne, en 1735;
Et le cadet à la bataille de Malplaquet le 11 Septembre 1709.

Et Armand de Balthazard, qui ne put conti-nuer le fervice, à caufe de fa mauvaife fan-té. Il eut quatre fils, qui ont donné en toute occafion des marques de leur valeur, à l'exemple de leurs ancêtres:

1. Etienne-Gacho de Balthazard, Capi-taine commandant les Grenadiers du Régiment de Hoffy, Suiffe, tué à l'âge de 24 ans, en 1712, au fiège du Quef-noy;
2. Marc-Louis-Isaac de Balthazard, Seigneur de la Vincelay, Colonel com-mandant le Régiment Suiffe de Dies-bach, mort à Dunkerque en 1742, âgé de 53 ans;
3. Jean-Alexandre de Balthazard, Ma-réchal des Camps & Armées du Roi, Colonel d'un Régiment Suiffe de fon nom, mort à Paris le 25 Novembre 1753, âgé de 64 ans;
4. Armand-Louis de Balthazard de Lor-ny, premier Capitaine & commandant les Carabiniers du Régiment Royal Allemand Cavalerie, tué le 20 Sep-tembre 1742, âgé de 36 ans, étant for-ti de Prague pour donner la chaffe aux Huffards. Il a laiffé, de *Marie-Thérèfe le Vayer*, deux fils & une fille.

BALUE, famille éteinte dans le XVIe fiè-cle, qui a donné dans Jean de Balue, un E-vêque d'Angers, enfuite Cardinal, du titre de *Sainte-Sufanne*, Evêque d'Albe & de Pré-nefte, Abbé Commendataire de Fécamp, du Bec, & de St.-Ouen de Rouen. Son efprit & fa bonne mine le firent parvenir & goûter du Roi Louis XI; il éprouva pendant fa vie la bonne & la mauvaife fortune, & mourut E-vêque de Prenefte,en 1481.Voyez les *Grands Officiers de la Couronne*, & Moréri.

Les armes : *d'argent, au chevron de fable, accompagné de trois têtes de lion de gueu-les, 2 & 1*.

BALUE, en Bretagne: *d'argent, à trois pots de fable, 2 & 1*.

BALUZE, Maifon originaire de Tulle,

qui a donné un faint Prêtre dans JEAN BA-
LUZE, mort fous le règne de FRANÇOIS Ier, &
dans ANTOINE BALUZE, qui s'eft rendu célèbre
fous LOUIS XIII, dans les importantes négociations dont il fut chargé. Il mourut à Paris le 12 Septembre 1681, & laiffa un fils,
JEAN-CASIMIR BALUZE, né à Varfovie en 1648,
qui ne s'eft pas moins fait honneur que fon
père. Voyez Moréri.

BAMBERG, FRÉDÉRIC - JOSEPH - MARIE,
Comte de *Sansheim*, né le 16 Février 1708,
élu Evêque de Bamberg le 21 Avril 1757.

BAN-DE-LA-FEUILLÉE (DU), en Bourgogne. JEAN DU BAN-DE-LA-FEUILLÉE eft compris dans la Montre de l'arrière-ban de Châtillon-fur-Seine, convoqué le 15 Octobre 1542,
à caufe de ce qu'il tenoit à la Vannerie & à la
Folie. Ce même JEAN DU BAN, Ecuyer, avec
fa femme, rendit aveu au Roi le 30 Juillet 1540, du Fief de la Feuillée, mouvant du
Château de Châtillon-fur-Seine, & de la
moitié par *indivis* de la Seigneurie de la
Vannaire, mouvante de la Seigneurie de
Chaumont-le-Bois. Il avoit époufé Colette
de *Mazilles*, dont il eut:

    JACQUES, qui fuit;
    Et LOUISE DU BAN, veuve de *Louis Duval*,
      Ecuyer.

JACQUES DU BAN, Ecuyer, en partie Seigneur de la Feuillée, qui donna, le 22 Juin
1549, une procuration générale, fignée de
Louvencourt, Notaire au Châtelet de Paris,
à *Pierre d'Efchères*, fon beau-frère, Ecuyer
en partie de la Vannaire. Il époufa, le 26 Novembre 1554, *Evandeline de Nogent*, fille
de *François de Nogent*, Ecuyer, Seigneur
d'Aubetrée, & de *Claudine de Caftres*, lefquels, par un acte du 5 Avril 1559, figné de
Frettes, Notaire à Châtillon, confentent que
leur fille renonce aux conventions accordées
par fon contrat de mariage, & revienne à leur
fucceffion après leur décès. De ce mariage vint:

BAPTISTE DU BAN, Ecuyer, Seigneur de la
Feuillée & de la Vannaire, qui fut compris
dans le Rôle des Gentilshommes du Bailliage
de la Montagne, fait en 1568, à caufe de la
convocation de l'arrière-ban de Bourgogne.
Il obtint à fon profit une Sentence le 19 Avril
1583, figné *Jaulpy*, rendue au Bailliage de
la Montagne, contre LOUISE DU BAN, fa tante,
veuve de *Louis Duval*, Ecuyer. Il époufa,
par contrat du 23 Février 1579, reçu par le

Clerc & *Raoul*, Notaires à Saint-Florentin,
Denife de Beaujeu, fille de Noble *François
de Beaujeu*, Seigneur de Chafeul & de Jauge, & de *Claude de Méry*, laquelle, après la
mort de fon mari, fit une vente d'héritages le
18 Novembre 1589, fignée *Petit*, Notaire à
Châtillon-fur-Seine; elle eut la Garde-Noble de fes enfans. Par une procuration du 29
Septembre 1607, fignée *Petit*, Notaire à Châtillon-fur-Seine, donnée par *Denife de Beaujeu*, Dame de la Feuillée, par laquelle elle
confent au mariage de fon fils JEAN, on voit
qu'elle étoit veuve de *Jean de Drouet*, fon
fecond mari. Du premier mariage font iffus:

    GIRARD, JACQUES & JEAN, qui fuit.

JEAN DU BAN, Ecuyer, Sieur de la Feuillée
& de la Vannaire, qui, devenu veuf, fit l'inventaire des biens laiffés par fon époufe au
Bailliage de la Montagne, le 24 Octobre 1630,
à fes enfans. Il avoit époufé, par contrat du
12 Octobre 1607, reçu par *Piot*, Notaire à
Montigny-le-Roi, *Edmée de la Rochette*,
fille de Meffire *Jean de la Rochette*, Chevalier, Seigneur d'Efpinan, & de *Sufanne de
Pradine*. Ses enfans font:

    1. & 2. BAPTISTE-JÉRÔME & ALEXANDRE-BLAISE;
    3. Et PIERRE, qui fuit.

PIERRE DU BAN, Ecuyer, Seigneur de la
Vannaire, fit une reprife du Roi, en la Chambre des Comptes de Bourgogne, à caufe de la
Seigneurie de la Feuillée, qui lui étoit échue
de la fucceffion de feu fon père. Il obtint des
brevets, commiffions, pouvoirs & provifions
de Cornette, Capitaine, Meftre-de-Camp, &
Brigadier de Cavalerie; de Maréchal-de-
Camp, Lieutenant-Général de Gray, de Dôle
& de Châtillon-fur-Seine. Elles lui furent
données fucceffivement par le Roi depuis le
mois de Juin 1643 jufqu'au mois de Décembre 1674, & fut nommé Élu de la Nobleffe
des Etats de Bourgogne au mois de Janvier
1677. Il étoit Meftre-de-Camp d'un Régiment de Cavalerie, & Brigadier des Camps
& Armées du Roi, lorfqu'il époufa, par contrat du 26 Juillet 1666 (reçu par *Calignon*,
Notaire au Bailliage de Rofnay), *Françoife
de Bretel*, fille de Meffire *Antoine de Bretel*,
Chevalier, Seigneur de Valentigni & d'Aunay, Capitaine du Duché de Beaufort, &
d'*Edmée Goyet-de-Becherade*. De ce mariage font nés:

    1. PIERRE-JEAN-BAPTISTE, Chevalier, Seigneur
      de la Feuillée, de Chaumont-le-Bois & de

la Vannaire, baptiſé le 5 Octobre 1668, en l'Egliſe de Saint-Martin de Chaumont-le-Bois, Diocèſe de Langres, dont nous ignorons la poſtérité;

2. ANTOINE, qui ſuit;

3. PIERRE-JEAN-BAPTISTE, dit *de la Feuillée*, reçu Page du Roi dans ſa Grande-Ecurie, le 31 Mars 1686, tué à la bataille de la Marſaille en Piémont, en 1693, étant alors Capitaine de Cavalerie;

4. FRANÇOIS, dit *le Comte de Frolois*, reçu Page du Roi dans ſa Grande-Ecurie en 1688, puis Gouverneur de Châtillon-ſur-Seine en 1713;

5. CHARLES-FRANÇOIS, reçu auſſi Page du Roi dans ſa Grande-Ecurie au mois de Mai 1698, puis Major d'un Régiment de Cavalerie;

6. Et EDME, Seigneur de Morvillier, Lieutenant-Colonel du Régiment de Marcillac, Cavalerie.

ANTOINE DU BAN, Comte de Frolois, Seigneur de la Feuillée, de Mézières & de Valentigni, Meſtre-de-Camp d'un Régiment de Cavalerie, marié le 6 Février 1712, à *Hélène-Thérèſe de Sercey-de-Saint-Prix*. Leurs enfans furent:

1. FRANÇOIS-HENRI DU BAN-DE-LA-FEUILLÉE, né le 28 Janvier 1713;

2. Et EDME-CLAUDE DU BAN-DE-MEZIÈRES, né le 25 Février 1714. Tous deux reçus Pages du Roi dans ſa Grande-Ecurie, le 12 Mai 1728, ſur les preuves de leur nobleſſe, juſtifiée par titres depuis JEAN DU BAN, leur cinquième ayeul, Ecuyer, Seigneur de la Feuillée & de la Vannaire, lequel fit hommage au Roi en ſa Chambre des Comptes de Dijon, le 17 Mars 1518, à cauſe de la moitié de la Maiſon-Forte de la Feuillée, mouvante en Fief du Duché de Bourgogne, qui lui appartenoit du chef de *Colette de Maʒilles*, ſa femme.

Les armes : *écartelé , aux* 1 & 4 *contrécartelé , d'aʒur à trois feuilles de chêne d'or, poſés* 2 & 1; & *d'aʒur à la bande de gueules, dentée d'argent;* & *aux* 2 & 3 *de Goyet, qui eſt d'aʒur au chevron d'or, accompagné de trois pélicans de même, deux en chef* & *un en pointe.*

Et ſelon l'*Armorial de France*, reg. I, part. I, pag. 47 & 48, cette famille porte: *d'aʒur, à trois feuilles de chêne d'or,* 2 & 1.

* BANAINS, Terre qui fut acquiſe de la famille d'*Andrevet*, avec celle de Beneins, par *Pierre de Corſant*, Maréchal-de-Camp des Armées du Roi, qui en obtint l'érection

en Vicomté par Lettres du mois de Mars 1644, puis en Comté par Lettres de 1649. (*Tablettes Généalog.*, part. IV, p. 309).

BANASTRE, Sieur de Routtes, du Meſnil, d'Arcauville, en Normandie, Généralité de Roüen, famille maintenue dans ſa Nobleſſe, le 23 Novembre 1668. La Roque, dans ſon *Traité du Ban & Arrière-Ban*, dit qu'en la Montre de 1470, Vicomté de Caudebec, pour JEHAN BANASTRE, perſonnage ancien, ſe préſenta *Jehan Picot*, armé de brigandine, ſallade & vouge. ISABEAU BANASTRE, & *Richard d'Herbouville*, vivoient vers la fin du XVᵉ ſiècle.

Les armes: *de gueules, à la bande d'argent, accompagnée de trois molettes d'éperon de même,* 2 *en chef* & 1 *en pointe.*

BANCE: *d'aʒur, au chevron d'or, accompagné en chef de deux molettes d'éperon de même,* & *en pointe d'une foi d'argent.*

BANCENEL, famille noble de Salins en Franche-Comté, qui a pour tige ETIENNE BANCENEL, qualifié *Noble* dans un contrat de mariage avec *Marguerite d'Orchamps*, & qui ſubſiſte dans ANTOINE-FRANÇOIS BANCENEL, Ecuyer, Seigneur de Champagne, marié le 29 Août 1754, avec *Marie-Claire-Iſabelle Marchand*, fille de *Joſeph-Emmanuel Marchand-de-la-Châtelaine*, Seigneur de Badennance, Chevalier d'Honneur en la Chambre des Comptes de Dôle, & de *Marie-Jeanne de Reinac*. Ses enfans ſont:

1. HENRI-FRANÇOIS-JOSEPH BANCENEL;

2. Et CHARLOTTE-JOSÉPHINE BANCENEL.

Les armes: *d'aʒur, à trois quinte-feuilles d'or,* 2 *en chef* & 1 *en pointe, une tête de léopard d'or, miſe en cœur.* Cimier: *un lion naiſſant d'or.*

BANCHAREAU, ou BANCHEREAU, Seigneur de la Serre: *échiqueté d'or* & *de gueules; au chef du premier, chargé de trois roſes du ſecond.*

BANCQUELOT: *d'argent, à la croix de gueules.*

BAND (LA), en Bretagne: *d'or, à la faſce de gueules, chargée de trois molettes d'éperon d'argent.* Deviſe : *Ped Bebret*, qui veut dire: *Prie ſans ceſſe.*

BANDES : *d'or, au mouton de ſable.*

* BANDEVILLE, Seigneurie érigée en

Marquifat par Lettres du mois d'Avril 1682, enregiftrées au Parlement le 15 Décembre fuivant, & en la Chambre des Comptes le 30 Janvier 1683, en faveur de *Nicolas Doublet*, mort le 23 Mars 1695. Voyez DOUBLET.

BANDINI, famille noble & ancienne de Florence. Pierre-Antoine Bandini fut Sénateur de cette République. Il eut de *Caffandre Cavalcante Bartolomei;*

> Octave Bandini, né en 1558, qui vint en France étudier la Philofophie & la Langue Françoife. Il fut Protonotaire Apoftolique, en 1579, fous Grégoire XIII, Gouverneur de Fermo fous Sixte V, Vice-Légat à Bologne fous Clément VIII, Archevêque de Fermo, en 1596, & Cardinal-Prêtre, du titre de *Sainte-Sabine* fous le même Pape. Il mourut en 1629, âgé de 72 ans;
>
> Et Mario Bandini, qui fervit en France fous Henri IV. Voyez Moréri.

BANDOCHES: *d'argent, à trois chevrons de gueules, chargés de trois tours d'or.*

BANES, Seigneur de la Baftie, en Dauphiné: *d'azur, à trois croiffans adoffés & mal ordonnés.*

BANES, Seigneur de Cabiac, en Normandie: *d'azur, au demi-bois de cerf arraché d'or, chevillé de dix cornichons dreffés en pals, parti de gueules à la tour donjonnée d'argent.*

¶ BANNE D'AVÉJAN, & fuivant les titres latins, de *Banâ* ou de *Bannâ.* Cette Maifon tire fon nom de la terre de Banne, au Diocèfe de Viviers, en Bas-Languedoc, & eft diftinguée dans l'ordre de la Nobleffe, tant par fes alliances que par fon ancienneté. L'*Armorial de France*, reg. II, part Ire, en commence la généalogie à

I. Guigon de Banne, Damoifeau, regardé comme la tige de cette Maifon, & qui peut être forti d'Arnaud de Banne, nommé dans une Charte de 1181, ou de Hugues, mentionné dans celle de 1203. Il fit une donation en 1222 à la Maifon du Temple des Jalez, au Diocèfe du Puy-en-Velay, de tous les biens qu'il avoit dans l'Eglife de Saint-Pierre de Banne. Ces actes fe confervent dans les archives du Prieuré de Saint-Gilles, de l'Ordre de Malte. Il eut pour fils:

II. Pons de Banne, Damoifeau, Seigneur d'Avéjan, qualifié *Pontius de Banâ, Domicellus, filius quondàm Guigonis de Banâ,*

Domicelli, dans plufieurs actes de reconnoiffances en latin, ou d'hommages; les uns du 5 des Ides d'Avril 1275, les autres du jour des Nones de Janvier 1286. Il vivoit encore en 1290, & fut père de:

III. Pierre de Banne, Ier du nom, Seigneur d'Avéjan, qualifié Noble & Damoifeau, Co-Seigneur de Banne, qui obtint une fentence du Viguier Royal de Marvéjols, le 9 Octobre 1320, contre les Officiers Royaux de cette ville, qui le troubloient dans la poffeffion de fes droits, en empêchant les habitans de lui prêter le ferment qu'ils lui devoient. Il vivoit encore le 11 Mars 1345 & avoit alors pour enfans:

> 1. Arnaud, qui fuit;
> 2. Vierne, Religieufe Auguftine;
> 3. Et Aigline, mariée à *Gaucelin-Gilles*, du lieu de Saint-Ambroife, qui n'eut que trois filles, mortes *ab inteftat.*

IV. Arnaud de Banne, Damoifeau, Seigneur d'Avéjan, Co-Seigneur du Château de Banne, ainfi qualifié dans une reconnoiffance qui lui fut rendue, le 17 Août 1365, demeuroit en la Paroiffe d'Avéjan, dont il poffédoit auffi la Seigneurie, comme il confte par un acte latin du 12 Décembre 1366. Il avoit époufé 1° N...; & 2° *Ferrande de Caftillon*, fille de noble *Raymond*, Seigneur de Caftillon, laquelle vivoit encore veuve le 5 Juillet 1384. Du premier lit il eut:

> 1. Bermond, qui fuit;
>
> Et du fecond:
>
> 2. Louis, feulement nommé dans un acte de 1378;
> 3. Pierre, rappelé dans le même acte, & mort fans alliance;
> 4. Et Héraclée de Banne, mariée, par contrat du 20 Janvier 1378, à noble *Guillaume d'Aygaliers*, du lieu de Bagnols, au Diocèfe d'Uzès. Elle eut en dot la fomme de 600 florins d'or de France, que fa mère, ainfi que Louis & Pierre, fes deux frères, lui conftituèrent.

V. Bermond de Banne, Damoifeau, Seigneur d'Avéjan, Co-Seigneur du Château de Banne, fuccéda à fon père & à fon frère Pierre, & eft qualifié Noble & Damoifeau, comme fes prédéceffeurs, dans les titres de famille & dans des titres étrangers, notamment dans une reconnoiffance faite le 11 Janvier 1400 à noble *Guillaume de Pradel.* Il vivoit encore le 28 Janvier 1414, & mourut peu de tems après, laiffant de *Smaragde de Roux:*

1. RAYMOND, inftitué héritier par le teftament
de fa mère, du 7 Décembre 1418, & dont
on a un extrait dans une ordonnance de
M. de Bezons du 29 Octobre 1668;
2. PIERRE, qui fuit;
3. JEAN, Prieur d'Avéjan, connu par deux titres des 19 Octobre 1451 & 15 Février
1464;
4. Et DEGANNE DE BANNE.

VI. PIERRE DE BANNE, IIe du nom, Damoifeau, Seigneur d'Avéjan, Co-Seigneur de Caftillon & de Banne, mentionné dans plufieurs
reconnoiffances & autres actes des 4 Novembre 1428, 10 Août 1433, 8 Mai 1434, 6 Juillet 1437, 13 Février 1442, 23 Août 1458, &
du 16 Mars 1460, qui fourniffent la preuve
de fa filiation & fa nobleffe; fit fon teftament le 19 Octobre 1451, choifit fa fépulture
dans le Cimetière de l'Eglife Saint-Pierre
d'Avéjan, au tombeau de fes pères, & y rappelle fes enfans. Il vivoit encore le 17 Juillet
1475, & avoit époufé, par contrat du 7 Février 1429, Mirande de Montjoc, fille de noble Pierre de Montjoc, qui lui conftitua en
dot une fomme de 620 florins, & 30 florins
de bagues & joyaux, à condition qu'elle renonceroit à tout droit de légitime en faveur
de noble Joffelin de Montjoc, fon frère. De
leur mariage vinrent:
1. JEAN, qui fuit;
2. 3. 4. & 5. CLAUDINE, ISABELLE, AGNETTE &
VÉRANE, toutes quatre léguées par leur
père;
6. Et BLANCHE DE BANNE, née depuis le teftament de fes père & mère, & légataire de
JEAN, fon frère, en 1516.

VII. JEAN DE BANNE, Damoifeau, Seigneur
d'Avéjan, Co-Seigneur de Banne & de Caftillon, fit fon teftament le 4 Mai 1516, par lequel il élit, comme fon père, fa fépulture au
tombeau de fes parens & prédéceffeurs, Seigneurs d'Avéjan, & il y rappelle fes trois fils
ci-après nommés. Il avoit époufé, par contrat
du 15 Février 1464, Hélips ou Alix de Luffan, fille de noble Olivon de Luffan, Seigneur de Sénéchas, au Diocèfe d'Uzès, & de
la Paufe, en la Paroiffe de Malbofc, au Diocèfe
de Viviers, & de noble Françoife de Folhar-
quier, dont vinrent:
1. PIERRE, qui fuit;
2. LOUIS, Prêtre, Prieur de Saint-Raphaël de
Château-Gelais, en Gafcogne, qualifié de
plus, dans un titre du 21 Février 1523,
Protonotaire du Saint-Siège; à cette dernière qualité, il joint celle de Prieur du

Prieuré d'Avéjan, qu'on lui trouve dans
deux actes des 5 Mars 1530 & 12 Août
1538;
3. Et JACQUES DE BANNE, mort fans avoir été
marié, comme on l'apprend d'une enquête
faite les 27 & 28 Novembre 1597, devant
un Commiffaire de la Cour du Sénéchal de
Beaucaire & de Nîmes.

VIII. PIERRE DE BANNE, IIIe du nom, Seigneur d'Avéjan, Co-Seigneur de Caftillon, fit
un teftament le 11 Mars 1514. Il avoit époufé, 1° par contrat du 5 Février 1488, Jeanne
de Barjac, fille de noble Bertrand de Barjac, Seigneur du Boufquet & de Vacquières;
& 2° noble Catherine de Montaigu, veuve
de N... de Salagnac, laquelle eft rappelée,
ainfi que Jeanne de Salagnac, fa fille, dans le
teftament de PIERRE DE BANNE, qui eut de fa
première femme:
1. ANTOINE, qui fuit;
2. JEAN, auffi mentionné dans le teftament de
JEAN DE BANNE, fon ayeul;
3. SÉBASTIEN, que fon ayeul fubftitua à fes
deux fils aînés;
4. MARGUERITE, Religieufe à Avignon, lors du
teftament de fon ayeul, en 1516;
5. JACQUETTE, mariée à N... de Ponfard ou
Poinfard, Ecuyer, du lieu de Saint-Lau-
rent-des-Arbres;
6. Et AGNETTE ou AGNÈS DE BANNE, mariée,
le 5 Mars 1530, à Guillaume de Cuculon,
qualifié noble de la ville de Mornas au
Diocèfe d'Orange. Ces filles font non-feulement rappelées, comme leurs frères, dans
le teftament de leur ayeul, mais de plus,
entre JACQUETTE & AGNETTE, celui-ci en
met une, à laquelle il donne le nom de
JEANNE.

IX. ANTOINE DE BANNE, Baron de Ferreyrolles, Seigneur d'Avéjan, & Co-Seigneur des
Seigneuries & Mandemens de Caftillon, Cor-
ry, Malbofc, &c., également inftitué héritier
de fon père & de fon ayeul, en 1514 & 1516.
Il tefta le 19 Août 1548, & étoit mort le 10
Novembre 1555. Il avoit époufé le 21 Février 1523 (vieux ftyle) Gabrielle Aubert ou
d'Albert, fille & héritière univerfelle de noble Thomas Aubert, Seigneur de Bouffar-
gues & de Marthe des Porcellets, dont il eut:
1. CLAUDE, qui fuit;
2. JEAN, Prieur d'Avéjan;
3. ANTOINE, qualifié Seigneur de Saint-Pri-
vat, en 1593 & 1597;
4. LOUIS, mort à la guerre, où, fuivant l'enquête de 1597, il étoit allé avec le Seigneur
de Ventabren, du furnom de Quiqueran;

5. FLORETTE, mariée à *Antoine Maurin*, de la Ville de Saint-Efprit ;

6. JEANNE, époufe de noble *Jean de Calvet*, Ecuyer, Seigneur de Fontanilles & du Solier, au Diocèfe de Mende, qui donna, le 10 Novembre 1555, à CLAUDE DE BANNE, fon beau-frère, une quittance de la dot conftituée à fa femme par feu ANTOINE, fon père ;

7. CATHERINE, mariée en 1556 à *Simon Bonhomme*, Ecuyer de la Ville de Bagnols, dont elle étoit veuve en 1597 ;

8. MARGUERITE ;

9. AGNETTE, morte fans alliance ;

10. Et LOUISE DE BANNE, mariée à *Claude Santel* ou *Sautel*, Ecuyer, Seigneur de la Baftide, Virac, &c., du lieu de Barjac, Diocèfe & Viguerie d'Uzès. Elle eut en dot 500 écus d'or fol, comme on le voit par une quittance que Claude Sautel donna à fon beaufrère le 8 Juin 1580.

X. CLAUDE DE BANNE, Seigneur d'Avéjan, Baron de Ferreyrolles, &c., embraffa le calvinifme le 7 Août 1567 ; mais par un teftament qu'il fit le 2 Août 1588, il déclara qu'il vouloit être enterré dans le Cimetière de l'Eglife d'Avéjan, au tombeau de fes prédéceffeurs. Il mourut au mois de Mars 1604, & avoit époufé, par contrat paffé à Nîmes, le 7 Août 1567, & infinué le 23 Novembre fuivant, en la Cour du Sénéchal de Beaucaire & de Nîmes, *Dauphine de Montcalm*, fille de *François*, Ecuyer, Seigneur de Saint-Véran, & de *Louife des Porcellets*. Ce contrat porte expreffément que le mariage devoit être célébré dans l'Eglife de la Religion Réformée. Elle tefta le 15 Juin 1632, & vivoit encore le 4 Juin 1635. Ils eurent de leur mariage cinq garçons & trois filles, que le teftament de leur père rappelle dans l'ordre que voici :

1. PIERRE, qui fuit ;

2. JACQUES, tige de la branche des Seigneurs de *Terris* & de *Montgros*, rapportée en fon rang ;

3. 4. & 5. LOUIS, CLAUDE & CHARLES, mentionnés après leur frère aîné ;

6. MARGUERITE, femme, en 1612, de noble *Jean de Ribeirols*, Seigneur du Pont ;

7. FRANÇOISE, légataire de fa mère en 1632, & mariée du vivant de fon père (fuivant une tranfaction de 1610) à noble *Jacques de Gout*, Seigneur de la Charrière, dont une fille, que *Dauphine de Montcalm* appelle dans fon teftament Damoifelle *Dauphine de Gout*, femme de M. *Gueydan*, peut-être *Honoré Gueydan*, nommé dans un titre du 25 Janvier 1629 ;

8. Et ISABEAU DE BANNE, mariée, par contrat paffé au Château d'Avéjan le 20 Juillet 1605, à noble *Jean de Gas*, dit *de Baignols*, Seigneur de Saint-Gervais, au Diocèfe d'Uzès, & Co-Seigneur de Saint-Marcel-d'Ardèche.

XI. PIERRE DE BANNE, IVe du nom, Seigneur d'Avéjan, Baron de Ferreyrolles, fut donataire & héritier univerfel de fon père en 1588. Devenu par fon mariage poffeffeur de la juftice haute, moyenne & baffe, fur une partie du village de la Nuéjol, & d'autres que le Roi HENRI IV avoit donnés en inféodation à François de Coladon, fon beau-père, il rendit, le 20 Septembre 1612, l'hommage dû à Sa Majefté, & en donna fon aveu le 19 Octobre 1612. Il fit trois teftamens, en date des 28 Mai 1605, 30 Janvier 1612, & 1er Novembre 1622, qui ont tous à peu près les mêmes difpofitions, & déclara qu'il vouloit être enterré à la manière de ceux de la Religion prétendue Réformée, dans le Cimetière d'Avéjan, au tombeau de fes prédéceffeurs. Il avoit époufé, par contrat du 2 Mai 1593, paffé en la Ville du Vigan, en préfence du Miniftre de la Religion prétendue Réformée, *Anne de Caladon*, fille de noble *François*, Sieur de la Valette, & de *Gabrielle d'Eftaing de Pomérols*. *Anne de Caladon* tefta, le 30 Janvier 1612, & voulut être inhumée ou à la Nuéjol, ou à Avéjan ; fit plufieurs legs, laiffa fa fucceffion à fon mari, à condition de porter les armes de fa Maifon, & à la charge de la remettre à un de leurs enfans mâles, ou, par fubftitution graduelle aux filles forties de leur mariage, pourvu cependant qu'elles ne fuffent pas mariées. Leurs enfans furent :

1. FRANÇOIS, inftitué héritier univerfel par le premier teftament de fon père, & mort avant le fecond ;

2. JACQUES, rapporté ci-après ;

3. JEAN, fait légataire de fon père en 1622 ;

4. GABRIELLE, qui étoit alors mariée à *Charles de Rochemore*, Seigneur de la Devéze ;

5. MARIE, mariée par contrat paffé au Château d'Avéjan, le 25 Janvier 1629, à *Charles d'Agulhac*, Seigneur de Lézeau & de Rouffon, fils de noble Jacques, & de *Madeleine d'Audibert-de-Luffan* ;

6. Et FRANÇOISE DE BANNE, femme de *Joachim de Gabriac*, Seigneur de Saint-Paulet.

XI. LOUIS DE BANNE, Seigneur de Méjannes, troifième fils de CLAUDE & de *Dauphine de*

Montcalm, marié 1º à *N...,* & 2º à *Anne de Leuze,* qui fit un teftament le 31 Juillet 1646. Du premier lit il eut:

1. DAUPHINE DE BANNE, mariée à *Charles de Rofel,* Seigneur de Saint-Sébaftien.

Et du fecond lit:

2. JACQUES, Sieur de Méjannes, connu par une donation de fon ayeule du 4 Juin 1635, & par l'Ordonnance de M. de *Bezons,* devant qui il produifit les titres juftificatifs de fa nobleffe en 1668;

3. Et une autre DAUPHINE.

XI. CLAUDE DE BANNE, Seigneur de Cabiac, quatrième fils de CLAUDE, & de *Dauphine de Montcalm,* tefta le 20 Octobre 1656, & mourut le 2 Juin 1658, âgé de 82 ans. Il avoit époufé, par contrat du 28 Avril 1610, *Gabrielle de Rouverie de Chabrières,* de laquelle il laiffa:

1. PIERRE DE BANNE, qui produifit fes titres avec fon coufin, en 1668, devant M. de *Bezons.* Il avoit époufé, par contrat du 18 Octobre 1646, *Jacquette de Carcenac,* dont vint:

JEANNE DE BANNE DE CABIAC, mariée, par contrat du 16 Novembre 1667, à *François de Georges - d'Aramon,* Baron de Lédenon, fils de noble *Louis de Georges,* Seigneur de Taraut, Baron de Lédenon, frère puîné de *Henri de Georges,* tué en 1621, à l'attaque du baftion de Montpellier, étant Gouverneur de la Ville de Blaye, Grand-Sénéchal de Guyenne, & commandant en cette occafion le Régiment de Normandie.

2. Et HONORÉ, qualifié Prieur de Cieuré, & Chanoine de Nîmes, dans le contrat de mariage de fa nièce.

XI. CHARLES DE BANNE, Seigneur de Révégueys, cinquième fils de CLAUDE, & de *Dauphine de Montcalm,* & nommé dans la tranfaction du 23 Avril 1610, avec fon frère aîné, fut accordé le 21 Décembre 1611, avec *Jeanne de Tuffain,* & fit fon teftament le 13 Juin 1628, dans lequel font compris fes enfans, favoir:

1. ANTOINE DE BANNE, qui époufa (felon un mémoire de famille) le 2 Avril 1633, *Marie des Ours,* fille d'*Abraham,* Seigneur de la Genette, & de *Jeanne d'Airagues,* & n'en eut qu'une fille;

2. JACQUES, qui produifit devant M. de *Bezons,* en 1668, les titres juftificatifs de la jonction de fa branche avec celle de fes coufins;

3. JEAN, qui étoit mort dès le 23 Novembre 1648;

4. & 5. FRANÇOIS & PIERRE;

6. Et MARGUERITE DE BANNE, rappelée avec ANTOINE, fon aîné, dans le teftament de leur ayeule du 15 Juin 1632.

XII. JACQUES DE BANNE (fils de PIERRE IV), qualifié haut & puiffant Seigneur, Baron de Ferreyrolles, Seigneur d'Avéjan, de la Nuéjol, & du Mandement de Montjarderin, pour lequel il rendit hommage à Sa Majefté, à Rodès, le 29 Avril 1634, entre les mains de Jean-Baptifte de Verthamon, un des Commiffaires généraux députés pour la réformation & liquidation de l'ancien Domaine de Navarre, & la réception des foi & hommage, étoit, dès l'an 1631, Guidon de la Compagnie des Gendarmes du Comte de Tournon, fervit en Italie fous le Maréchal de Créquy, qui, en qualité de Lieutenant-Général de l'Armée, lui donna, du Camp de Wezin, le 29 Juin 1636, un paffe-port ou congé, pour repaffer en France & donner ordre à fes affaires. En 1635, il avoit fait un femblable voyage, pendant lequel il fe maria. Suivant deux Lettres que lui écrivit le Maréchal de Schomberg, en 1637, il rejoignit fa troupe, & fe rendit à fes invitations; mais pendant fon abfence fa maifon Seigneuriale de la Nuéjol fut pillée & rafée par les rebelles & les déferteurs du parti royal. En conféquence il obtint de LOUIS XIII des Lettres de fauvegarde, datées de Saint-Germain-en-Laye, le 4 Novembre 1637, pour fa perfonne & fes biens, eu égard aux bons & grands fervices qu'il avoit rendus dans l'Armée d'Italie; & le 1er Mai 1647, il obtint encore du Roi, en confidération de fes fervices, l'exemption de tout logement de gens de guerre dans fes Terres d'Avéjan, de Ferreyrolles, &c. Enfin, affigné le 13 Août 1668, avec JACQUES DE BANNE, Seigneur de Méjannes, fon coufin, & plufieurs autres de fa famille, pour faire devant M. de *Bezons,* Intendant en Languedoc, la production de fes titres, il fut maintenu dans fa nobleffe par Ordonnance du 29 Octobre 1668, qui déclara qu'ils feroient infcrits dans le catalogue des véritables nobles, comme tous les Gentilshommes du Royaume. Il vivoit encore le 31 Mars 1694, âgé de 81 ans, & avoit fi conftamment profeffé la Religion proteftante comme fes deux derniers prédéceffeurs, & étoit fi attaché aux fentimens qu'il tenoit de l'éducation, que fon fils aîné ayant fait abjuration, en 1655, à la Fère en Picardie, où il étoit à la fuite de Louis XIV, durant le fiège de Landrecie, il conçut de cette converfion un reffentiment que rien ne put calmer malgré une lettre dont l'honora ce Monarque, à ce fujet, le 14 Octobre 1655. En effet, par fon teftament du 17 Avril 1658, il légua feulèment à fon aîné une fomme de 8000 livres, & inftitua héritier univerfel de tous fes biens fon fecond fils en lui fubftituant fon troifième. Il avoit époufé, par contrat paffé au Château de Saint-Chaiftol, le 16 Septembre 1635, *Marguerite de la Fare,* fille de *Jacques*, Seigneur, Baron de la Fare, &c., & de *Gabrielle d'Audibert de Luffan.* Ses enfans furent:

1. Denis, qui fuit;
2. Jacques, Capitaine au Régiment Dauphin, le 1er Avril 1674, mort en Irlande, où il étoit allé fervir, à caufe de la Religion prétendue Réformée qu'il profeffoit;
3. Christophe, tué en Flandres en 1678, étant Capitaine dans le même Régiment;
4. Marie, Religieufe au Couvent des Dames des plans, proche Montdragon;
5. Françoise, Religieufe en l'Abbaye de Bagnols;
6. Gabrielle, mariée, par contrat du 1er Avril 1674, avec *Jacques-Jofeph de Rocquart*, Seigneur de Vinfobres, &c., fils de *Jacques*, & de *Lucrèce de Salvix*;
7. Et Marguerite ou Marguerite-Louise de Banne, nommée par le Roi, le 11 Mars 1704, Abbeffe d'Hières, au Diocèfe de Toulon.

XIII. Denis de Banne d'Avéjan, Baron de Ferreyrolles, Seigneur d'Avéjan, de la Nuéjol, du Mandement de Montjarderin, &c., né le 7 Août 1639, Page du Roi dans fa Petite-Ecurie en 1655, réduit par fon père, en 1658, à un fimple legs de 8000 livres, pour avoir abjuré les fentimens dans lefquels il avoit été élevé (entre les mains de l'Archevêque de Lyon, fuivant fon certificat du 31 Janvier 1669), eut, dès le 13 Juin 1647, commiffion de Capitaine d'une Compagnie d'Infanterie de nouvelle levée, fous la charge du Marquis de la Fare, fon oncle, n'étant pas encore âgé de huit ans; fut Enfeigne de la Compagnie du Fay, au Régiment des Gardes-Françoifes en 1661; fait Sous-Lieutenant le 29 Janvier 1665, Lieutenant en 1668, & Capitaine le 21 Avril 1672, à caufe de fes bons fervices; fit avec le Roi la campagne de Hollande, fut bleffé au fiège d'Unna en 1673; fe trouva en 1674 aux fièges de Maeftricht, de Befançon, de Dôle, à la bataille de Senef, aux

fièges de Condé, de Valenciennes, de Cambray, de Gand & d'Ypres, au combat de Saint-Denis, où il avoit fous fes ordres un bataillon du Régiment des Gardes, & à la prife de Courtray; fut fait Chevalier de l'Ordre de Notre-Dame du Mont-Carmel & de Saint-Lazare, par Lettres du 3 Mars 1680; eut, le 31 Décembre 1680, la Commanderie de Beaugency, dépendant du Grand-Prieuré de Bretagne, où il fut reçu le 8 Mars 1681; nommé Brigadier d'Infanterie le 26 Avril 1689; fe diftingua à la bataille de Fleurus, aux fièges de Mons & de Namur, & furtout au combat de Steinkerque, où, l'épée à la main, il chargea les ennemis avec tant de bonheur, qu'ils ne purent fe rallier; fut fait Gouverneur de Furnes, au mois de Janvier 1693; Maréchal-de-Camp le 30 Mars 1693, Commandeur de l'Ordre Militaire de Saint-Louis le 8 Mai fuivant, eut la Lieutenance-Colonelle du Régiment des Gardes le 28 Décembre 1696, fut nommé Grand'Croix de l'Ordre de Saint-Louis le 20 Mars 1699, & Lieutenant-Général des Armées du Roi le 29 Janvier 1702. Enfin, Louis XIV lui donna, le 13 Décembre 1702, le commandement des Troupes Françaifes dans les Ville & Citadelle de Nancy pour la fûreté de la frontière du Royaume. Il s'y conduifit avec tant de fageffe, qu'il mérita la confiance du Duc de Lorraine & l'eftime générale. Il y tefta le 14 Septembre 1707, & y mourut le 17, âgé de 69 ans. Il avoit obtenu, le 4 Août précédent, un Arrêt qui le déchargeait de toute affignation, en conféquence de l'Ordonnance rendue en faveur de fon père par M. de Bezons. Il avoit époufé, par contrat paffé à Paris le 24 Avril 1672, *Louife-Elifabeth de Vallot*, fille d'*Antoine*, Seigneur de Maignan, &c., mort Confeiller d'Etat ordinaire, & de *Catherine Gayant*, dont:

1. Edouard-Denis, né le 10 Septembre 1676, élevé Page de la Petite-Ecurie du Roi, nommé Capitaine aux Gardes fur la démiffion de fon père, le 1er Juin 1705, & mort peu de jours après des bleffures qu'il avoit reçues au fiège de Huy en Flandres;
2. Jean-Baptiste-Bonaventure, né le 1er Octobre 1679, mort le 18 Septembre 1699, Prieur de Saint-Sauveur-de-Gaillac;
3. Louis, qui fuit;
4. Charles, nommé Evêque d'Alais le 8 Janvier 1721, & Abbé Commendataire de l'Abbaye de Montebourg, Diocèfe de Coutances en 1723;

R ij

5. MARIE, née le 16 Août 1677, femme de *Jacques-Joseph*, Marquis de *Perrufis*, Seigneur de Barles ;

6. ANNE-ELISABETH, Abbeffe d'Hières en 1717, & en 1742 Abbeffe des Fons-Sainte-Claire, à Alais, morte le 11 Novembre 1774, dans la 95e année de fon âge;

7. MARIE, Religieufe Profeffe en l'Abbaye de Bagnols, morte à l'Abbaye d'Alais, où elle avoit été transférée ;

8. Et autre MARIE DE BANNE, morte Supérieure de la Vifitation-Sainte-Marie, rue du Bac, à Paris.

XIV. LOUIS DE BANNE D'AVÉJAN, Marquis d'Avéjan, Baron de Ferreyrolles, Seigneur de la Nuéjol, Montjarderin, Baron des Etats de Languedoc, né le 29 Octobre 1683, d'abord Moufquetaire, dès l'âge de 15 ans, fucceffivement Maréchal-de-Camp le 20 Février 1734, fervit en cette qualité le 15 Juin 1734 & le 1er Mai 1735, fous les Maréchaux d'Asfeld, de Noailles & de Coigny ; & fut enfin nommé Lieutenant-Général des Armées le 1er Mars 1738. Par l'érection de fa terre d'Avéjan en Baronie, au mois d'Octobre 1732, il eut entrée & féance aux Etats de Languedoc, & le Roi lui accorda encore une nouvelle grâce au mois d'Avril 1736, qui fut de créer, par d'autres Lettres-Patentes, la même Terre d'Avéjan en Marquifat, telle qu'elle avoit été compofée & réunie par les Lettres de 1732. Il eft mort à Paris le 23 Mai 1738, & avoit époufé, par contrat du 29 Avril 1709, *Marie-Angélique Dufour-de-Nogent*, fille de *Jean*, Seigneur de Nogent-les-Vierges, & de Villers-Saint-Paul, & d'*Angélique-Catherine Guinet*. De ce mariage font iffus :

1. PHILIPPE-ANNE, qui fuit;

2. Et CATHERINE-AUGUSTE DE BANNE D'AVÉJAN, Dame de Sandricourt, morte fans avoir été mariée.

XV. PHILIPPE-ANNE DE BANNE (a), Marquis d'Avéjan, Baron des Etats de Languedoc, Baron de Ferreyrolles, Seigneur de la Nuéjol, &c., né le 14 Mars 1719, a été reçu le 6 Janvier 1729, dans la première Compagnie des Moufquetaires, fait Cornette le 12 Novembre 1734, Enfeigne le 24 Mai 1738, & eft mort fans alliance en 1741.

_____

(a) La Chenaye-Desbois l'appelle JACQUES.
(Note des Editeurs).

BRANCHE
des Seigneurs DE TERRIS & DE MONTGROS.

XI. JACQUES DE BANNE, Seigneur de Terris, fecond fils de CLAUDE, & de *Dauphine de Montcalm*, nommé dans le teftament de fon père du 2 Août 1588, & dans la tranfaction faite le 23 Avril 1610, entre fes frères & lui, eut, le 30 Juin 1621, commiffion de Gafpard, Comte de Coligny, Seigneur de Châtillon, Gouverneur de Montpellier & d'Aigues-Mortes, pour lever un Régiment de guerre à pied françois pour le fervice du Roi, & de le commander dans la Province du Bas-Languedoc, & partout ailleurs où il lui feroit ordonné. Il tefta au mois de Mai 1636. Il avoit époufé, 1° par contrat du 5 Mars 1603, *Louife de Brignon*, fille unique de *Claude de Brignon*, & de *Marguerite de Carlat* ; & 2° le 18 Août 1613, *Louife de Grimoard-de-Beauvoir-du-Roure*, morte en Février 1637, fille de *Jacques*, Seigneur de Braye, & de *Sufanne d'Yzarn*. Du premier lit vinrent :

1. PIERRE DE BANNE, Seigneur de Cavennes, mort fans poftérité. Il produifit fes titres en 1668, devant M. de Bezons, & avoit époufé, le 15 Octobre 1660, *Louife de Rocher ;*

2. MARGUERITE, mariée le 18 Août 1613, par fon père, avec *Charles d'Ilaire.*

Et du fecond lit :

3. JEAN, qui fuit ;

4. HERCULE, nommé feulement dans le teftament de fa mère ;

5. CHARLES, Seigneur de Terris, Capitaine au Régiment de Montpezat, Infanterie, par Commiffion du 24 Juin 1649, mort fans enfans, depuis fa production de titres, faite devant M. de Bezons. Il avoit époufé, le 2 Novembre 1653, Demoifelle *Pierre Imbert ;*

6. Et HENRI DE BANNE, Seigneur de Châteauvieux, compris dans la même production.

XII. JEAN DE BANNE, Seigneur de Montgros, héritier univerfel de fa mère, en 1632, & de fon père, en 1636. Il tefta le 18 Février 1654, voulut être enterré dans le cimetière de la Religion Réformée, & mourut à Blauzac le 24 Février 1654. Il époufa 1° *Sufanne de Rofel*, morte fans poftérité ; & 2° le 14 Août 1649, *Gabrielle de Chabas*, fille de noble *Daniel*, & de *Diane de Brueis*. Du fecond mariage vint :

XIII. PIERRE DE BANNE, Ve du nom, né le

21 Juin 1650, Seigneur de Montgros & du fief de Lignemaille, dont il fit hommage au Roi en fa Chambre des Comptes, Aides & Finances de Montpellier, le 9 Août 1679. Ayant été affigné devant M. de *Bezons*, en même tems que JACQUES DE BANNE D'AVÉJAN, fon coufin, PIERRE DE BANNE, Seigneur de Cavennes, fon oncle, & les autres ci-deffus nommés, il fut reconnu avec eux, fur production de titres, par cet Intendant, le 29 Octobre 1668, pour noble & iffu de noble race. Il mourut en 1709, & avoit époufé, par contrat du 9 Décembre 1676, *Françoife de Barre*, fille de *Pierre*, & de *Françoife de Rouftaing-du-Vieux*. Il eut de fon mariage :

1. CHARLES, qui fuit ;
2. HENRI, tué à Crémone en 1702 ;
3. & 4. Deux filles, mortes en bas âge ;
5. Et DIANE-JEANNE DE BANNE, mariée, par contrat du 15 Septembre 1702, à *Louis Fraiffines*, Co-Seigneur de Blauzac, fils de *Jérémie*, Seigneur de Ménudière, & de *Marguerite Martin*.

XIV. CHARLES DE BANNE, Seigneur de Montgros & de Lignemaille, né le 13 Septembre 1679, a fait deux campagnes en Catalogne, en qualité de volontaire dans le Régiment de Leisler, où étoit Capitaine le Sieur de *Chalas d'Agueillonne*, fon grand-oncle paternel, tué au fiège de Barcelone; & la troifième campagne dans le Régiment de Villevieille. Il avoit époufé, 1º le 15 Janvier 1705, *Marie Lefils*, fille d'*Etienne*, & de *Jeanne l'Evefque* ; & 2º le 23 Février 1707, *Marie-Anne Fraiffines*, fille de *Louis*, & de *Marie d'Olivet*. Il a eu du premier lit :

1. PIERRE, qui fuit ;

Et du fecond :

2. JEAN, mentionné après fon frère ;
3. LOUIS, mort Chanoine de la Cathédrale d'Alais, Prieur Commendataire des Abbayes de Viarge & de Chavanon, Ordre de Grandmont ;
4. GABRIELLE, morte Religieufe à l'Abbaye de Saint-Bernard d'Alais ;
5. CATHERINE, appelée *Mademoifelle de Montgros* ;
6. MARIE-PIERRE DE BANNE DE MONTGROS, femme de N... de *Saint-Vincent*, morte ayant laiffé un fils ;
7. MARGUERITE, reçue à Saint-Cyr le 13 Décembre 1730, puis mariée à N... d'*Anglas*, dont elle eft veuve, & a trois garçons & une fille ;

8. Et MARIE-ANNE DE BANNE, qui a été reçue à Saint-Cyr, le 4 Décembre 1733.

XV. PIERRE DE BANNE, VIᵉ du nom, Marquis d'Avéjan, Baron des Etats de Languedoc, Seigneur de Montgros & de Lignemaille, ancien Moufquetaire du Roi dans fa première Compagnie, où il a été reçu le 1ᵉʳ Octobre 1731, a eu rang & commiffion de Capitaine de Cavalerie le 1ᵉʳ Juin 1739, & a époufé, le 27 Octobre 1745, *Marie-Françoife d'Arbaud de Blauzac*, dont il a :

1. JEAN DE BANNE, Comte d'Avéjan, Capitaine au Régiment Meftre-de-Camp-Général, Cavalerie, en 1775, paffé Capitaine au premier Régiment des Chevaux-Légers.
2. Et MARIE DE BANNE D'AVÉJAN.

XV. JEAN, dit *le Comte de Banne*, Seigneur du Marquifat de Sandricourt, d'Amblainville & autres lieux, fils de CHARLES DE BANNE, & de *Marie-Anne Fraiffines*, fa feconde femme, « Aide-Major de la première Compagnie des Moufquetaires, où il entra le 1ᵉʳ Août 1722. Il y fut fait Maréchal-de-Logis, & Aide-Major, avec Brevet de Meftre-de-Camp de Cavalerie, le 27 Février 1735 ; Chevalier de Saint-Louis le 3 Juin 1740, Brigadier de Cavalerie le 1ᵉʳ Mai 1745, & Maréchal-de-Camp le 10 Mai 1748. Il a quitté les Moufquetaires en Janvier 1750, avec 30000 liv. d'argent comptant, & 7000 liv. de penfion. Il a été nommé Gouverneur de la ville d'Ardres en Picardie, & a époufé, le 11 Juin 1759, au château de Chaumontel près Luzarches, » *Marie-Geneviève de Thouron d'Arcilly*, fille de *Jules-Charles*, Seigneur de Bertinval, & de *Geneviève Befnier*, dont :

GENEVIÈVE-LOUISE ;
Et SUSANNE DE BANNE D'AVÉJAN.

Les armes : *écartelé, aux 1 & 4 d'azur, à trois fleurs-de-lys d'or, au chef retrait de même, qui eft* D'ESTAING ; *aux 2 & 3 d'azur, à trois flambeaux d'or, allumés, de gueules, rangés en trois pals*, qui eft de LA FARE, & *fur le tout d'azur, à une demi-bane ou ramure de cerf d'or, pofée en bande*, qui eft de BANNE. L'écu fommé d'une *couronne de Marquis*. Supports : *deux cerfs au naturel contournés & en repos*.

BANNOIS (LE), Seigneur de Pontfout, en Normandie, Généralité de Caen : *fafcé, ondé d'or & d'azur de fix pièces, la première fafce d'or chargée de trois merlettes de gueules*.

BANNOIS (le), ancienne Nobleffe de Normandie, Election d'Avranches : *d'azur, à la fafce d'argent, au chef d'or, chargé de trois merlettes de gueules.*

BANQUEVILLE, en Normandie : *d'or, à trois marteaux de gueules, 2 & 1.*

BANS (des), en Touraine : *d'argent, à l'aigle éployée de fable.*

BANVILLE : *de gueules, au pal d'argent, accompagné de fix molettes d'éperon de même.*

BANVILLE, Seigneur de Truttemne, de la Pierre & du Moutin, en Normandie, Généralité de Caen, Elections de Vire & de Caen : *vairé de fix tires, ou menu-vair.*

BAOUEC, en Bretagne : *de gueules, à une croix annillée d'argent.*

BAPTENDIER, famille originaire de la Province de Maurienne en Savoie, annoblie en 1521. JEAN-BAPTISTE DE BAPTENDIER, réfidant à Marfeille, où il vit fans alliance, voulant jouir de la nobleffe que les fervices militaires avoient acquis à fa famille en Savoie, préfenta requête en la Cour des Comptes, Aides & Finances de Prove. pour demander l'enregiftrement des pièces qui prouvoient fon origine, & fon état de Noble. Après avoir examiné les pièces par lefquelles il confte, *que les BAPTENDIER n'ont fait aucun acte de dérogeance, & ont fervi toujours avec diftinction dans l'Epée & dans la Robe,* la Cour ordonna, par Arrêt du 2 Avril 1740, qu'elles feroient enregiftrées. On les trouve au Regiftre *Corfica,* fol. 49.

Les armes : *de gueules, au pal d'or, chargé d'un lion de fable.* Devife : *Durat cum fanguine virtus avorum.*

BAPTISTE, Seigneur de Kermabian, en Bretagne, iffu d'un Juveigneur de la Maifon noble de *la Châtaignaye,* porte pour armes : *d'or, à trois tours couvertes & crênelées d'azur, jointes enfemble, & d'une même hauteur.*

BAR. Les Ducs & Comtes de Bar ont commencé à BRUNON, Archevêque de Cologne, frère de l'Empereur OTHON II, furnommé *le Grand.* Il partagea, en 958, le Gouvernement de la Lorraine avec FRÉDÉRIC Ier, Comte de Bar, fon neveu, qui fit bâtir, en 951, la Ville de Bar-le-Duc.

SOPHIE, Comteffe de Bar, fille de FRÉDÉRIC II, Duc de Lorraine, époufa, en 1027, *Louis,* Comte de *Montbeliard* & *de Mouffon,* auquel elle porta le Comté de Bar. On préfume que l'Erection du Comté de Bar en Duché fut faite par le Roi JEAN. Ce Duché eft un des Fiefs de la Couronne.

ROBERT DE BAR, Comte de Soiffons, Vicomte de Meaux, Grand-Bouteillier de France, mourut à la bataille d'Azincourt le 25 Octobre 1415. Ce fut en fa faveur que les Châtellenies de la Fère, Marle & Montcornet furent érigées en Comté, fous le nom de Comté de Marle. Sa fille unique JEANNE DE BAR porta les Comtés de Marle & de Soiffons à fon mari *Louis de Luxembourg,* Comte de St.-Pol ; & de cette Maifon ils font entrés par alliance dans celle de *Bourbon.*

LOUIS, Cardinal, Duc de Bar, fuccéda à fon neveu ROBERT dans le Duché en 1415, & le donna en 1419, avec le Marquifat de Pont-à-Mouffon, à RENÉ d'ANJOU, Roi de Naples & de Sicile, fon petit-neveu, qu'il adopta, à la charge de porter fon nom & fes armes après fa mort, arrivée en 1430.

Ce RENÉ D'ANJOU avoit époufé, en 1418, ISABELLE DE LORRAINE, fille du DUC CHARLES. Le Duché de Bar fut ainfi uni à celui de Lorraine.

YOLANDE D'ANJOU, Ducheffe de Lorraine & de Bar, fille de RENÉ D'ANJOU, Roi de Naples, époufa, en 1444, FERRY DE LORRAINE, IIe du nom, Comte de Vaudemont & de Guife, Sire de Joinville, & fuccéda au Duché de Lorraine & de Bar en 1473, par la mort de NICOLAS D'ANJOU, Duc de Calabre, de Lorraine & de Bar.

LÉOPOLD, Duc de Lorraine, fit hommage en perfonne au Roi LOUIS XIV, du Duché de Bar, le 25 Novembre 1699, & FRANÇOIS-ETIENNE, Duc de Lorraine & de Bar, fon fils aîné, depuis Empereur, l'a cédé à la France par un traité de paix, avec le Duché de Lorraine, & a eu en échange le Grand-Duché de Tofcane.

Le Roi STANISLAS, de Pologne, avoit été mis en poffeffion des Duchés de Lorraine & de Bar, conformément aux traités de Vienne des 3 Octobre 1735, 28 Août 1736 & 18 Novembre 1738, à fa mort le 23 Février 1766, ils ont été réunis à la Couronne.

Les armes : *d'azur, femé de croix recroifettées au pied fiché d'or, & deux bars ou barbeaux adoſſés de même, brochant ſur le tout.*

* BAR (LE), Terre & Seigneurie qui fut donnée en 1236, en échange par le Comte de Provence à *Rambault de Graſſe,* IIIᵉ du nom, iſſu des anciens Comtes d'Antibes, ſeptième ayeul de *Claude de Graſſe,* Chevalier de l'Ordre du Roi, qui obtint de FRANÇOIS Iᵉʳ l'érection du Bar en Comté, titre qui fut confirmé à ſon fils *Claude II de Graſſe,* par Lettres de HENRI III, de 1580. Voy. GRASSE.

BAR, en Berry. Cette famille étoit anciennement diviſée en pluſieurs branches, que l'on diſtinguoit, dit M. *d'Hozier,* par les noms de *Baugy, Villemenard* & *Buranlure.* Elle ne ſubſiſte plus qu'en deux, dont l'une établie en Nivernois, qui eſt l'aînée, & l'autre en Berry, qui eſt la cadette. La première poſſède actuellement les Terres de Limanton, Soſay, la Boutière & Neufvy-le-Barrois-ſur-Allier. La ſeconde poſſède les Terres de Bonnebuche, de Savigny, &c.

La branche qui a le plus fleuri eſt celle de *Baugy,* laquelle a donné un Chambellan du Roi CHARLES VII, Maître des Comptes, Général des Finances, & Bailli de Touraine; deux Evêques de Saint-Papoul, & un Evêque Comte de Beauvais, diſent Louvat, *Hiſtoire des Antiquités de la Ville de Beauvais,* & le P. Anſelme, *Hiſtoire des Grands-Officiers de la Couronne,* tom. II.

La branche de *Buranlure* a donné des Comtes de Lyon, une Dame de Remiremont, des Chevaliers de l'Ordre du Roi, & de celui de Saint-Jean de Jéruſalem.

Les alliances de ces branches ſont avec les Maiſons de *Châteauneuf-ſur-Cher,* de *Montberon, Thiſard-Vinon,* du *Chenay, Chabannes, Maumigny,* du *Meſnil-Simon, Montolieu, Crèvecœur, Gaucourt, Courtenay, Damas, Langeac,* de *Jaucourt,* de *Villaines,* &c.

JEAN DE BAR, IVᵉ du nom, Chevalier, Seigneur de Baugy, la Guierche, Eſtrechy, Vicomte de Savigny, fut Chambellan des Rois CHARLES VII & LOUIS XI, Maître des Comptes à Paris, Bailli de Touraine, Capitaine des Châteaux de Tour & d'Amboiſe, Général des Finances. Chartier, dans ſes *Chroniques,* ainſi que Monſtrelet, & Chaumeau, le mettent au nombre de ceux qui ſervirent à la rédaction de la Coutume de Normandie. Il fut

fait *Chevalier* après la priſe de Verneuil, lorſque les François étoient ſur le point de combattre les Anglois. Il donna à l'Egliſe de Saint-Urſin à Bourges pluſieurs beaux Livres d'Egliſe en vélin, enrichis de quelques figures en mignature, & un Crucifix, devant lequel il eſt à genoux avec ſes enfans & leurs femmes, & les hommes ſont en armures & cottes d'armes, chargées de leurs armoiries. Il mourut en 1469, & fut inhumé aux Jacobins de Bourges, où l'on voit ſon tombeau & ſon effigie en pierre. Ses enfans furent:

1. DENIS, d'abord Evêque de Tulle en 1472, & enſuite de Saint-Papoul en 1496, mort le 31 Mars 1517;
2. CHARLES, Religieux de l'Ordre de Saint-Bernard, Abbé de Lory, qui ſuccéda à ſon frère dans l'Evêché de Saint-Papoul, & mourut en 1558;
3. ROBERT, qui ſuit;
4. JACQUES, Auteur de la branche de *Palanon,* éteinte dans ſon petit-fils MATHIEU DE BAR, mort ſans poſtérité;
5. Une fille, morte en 1471, mariée à *Charles de Gaucourt,* Capitaine de la Maiſon du Roi LOUIS XI;
6. Et une autre fille, morte femme en ſecondes noces de *Pierre d'Oriolle,* Chancelier de France.

ROBERT DE BAR, Seigneur de Baugy, la Guierche & Chantelou, Vicomte de Savigny, Echanſon du Roi, fut Député de la Nobleſſe aux Etats de Tours en 1484. Il teſta le 4 Mai 1478, & mourut le 13 Décembre 1498. Il eut de *Madeleine de Châteauneuf:*

1. FRANÇOIS, qui ſuit;
2. Et MADELEINE, morte le 20 Août 1516. Elle avoit épouſé, par contrat du 2 Février 1494, *Jean de Courtenay,* IVᵉ du nom, Seigneur de Bléneau, de Champignelles & de Villard, dont elle fut la ſeconde femme. Etant veuve, elle fut tutrice & eut la garde-noble de ſes enfans. En cette qualité, elle donna pouvoir à FRANÇOIS DE BAR, ſon frère, Seigneur de Baugy, de faire hommage au Roi de la Seigneurie de la Grange en Brie le 12 Octobre 1512. Elle fit auſſi hommage de la Seigneurie de Bléneau à *René d'Anjou,* Baron de Mezières, & Seigneur de Puiſaye, le 16 Octobre 1514.

FRANÇOIS DE BAR, Chevalier, Seigneur de Baugy & autres lieux, fonda l'Hôpital de Baugy le 24 Janvier 1505, & mourut environ l'an 1530. Il eut de *Renée de Montberon,* fille de *René de Montberon,* & de *Louiſe de Sainte-Maure:*

1. FRANÇOIS, qui fuit;
2. N..., Religieufe à Orſan;
3. JACQUETTE, mariée à *François de Chery*;
4. MARGUERITE, mariée à *Gilbert de Bonnay*;
5. JEANNE, mariée à *Jean de Damas*;
6. Et FRANÇOISE, mariée à *Jean de Jaucourt*.

FRANÇOIS DE BAR, IIe du nom, Chevalier, Seigneur de Baugy, Chantelou, Eſtrechy, Pouligny, Chaumoux, Paracy, Fontbary & des Eſſarts, Baron de la Guierche, Vicomte de Savigny & du Preau, eut un grand procès avec les Sieurs de *Jaucourt*, ſes neveux, pour les partages des Terres de Baugy & Eſtrechy, &, par un Arrêt qui intervint en 1572, les trois quarts de la Terre de Baugy, & moitié de celles d'Eſtrechy & Salerieux, lui furent adjugées, tant de ſon chef, que par ſucceſſion, & l'autre quart de Baugy & moitié d'Eſtrechy & Salerieux, auxdits Sieurs de *Jaucourt*. En lui finit la branche aînée, étant mort ſans poſtérité de *Catherine de Chabannes*, fille de *Joachim*, Marquis de Curton, Comte de Rochefort & de Seigne, Vicomte de la Roche & de Savigny, & de *Louiſe de Pompadour*, ſa ſeconde femme.

BRANCHE des *Seigneurs* DE VILLEMENARD & DE BURANLURE.

PIERRE DE BAR, Ier du nom, Ecuyer, Seigneur de Villemenard & de Saint-Germain-Dupuy, ſecond fils de JEAN, IIIe du nom, obtint le 3 Décembre 1436, la permiſſion du Roi CHARLES VII, de fortifier la maiſon de Villemenard, parce qu'elle étoit une Place frontière des ennemis de la France, qui occupoient Montargis. Il eut entr'autres enfans:

DÉSIRÉ DE BAR, Ecuyer, Seigneur de Villemenard, &c., qui teſta le 17 Mai 1519, en faveur de ſon fils:

JEAN DE BAR, Chevalier, Seigneur de Villemenard, Buranlure, Eſtivaux, &c., qui ſe trouva à la rédaction de la Coutume de Lorris en 1531, & fit partage, entre ſes enfans, de tous ſes biens & de ceux de ſa femme, le 30 Avril 1553. Il épouſa, le 11 Mars 1515, *Françoiſe de Vinon*, fille de *Jean*, Ecuyer, Seigneur de Perrière, Buranlure & Eſtivaux, & de *Marguerite Segault*, dont il eut:

1. FRANÇOIS, qui fuit;
2. Et JEAN, né le 24 Novembre 1532, Seigneur de Villemenard & de Saint-Germain-Dupuy, auteur de la branche des Seigneurs de *Villemenard* & de *Silly*, qui eſt éteinte.

FRANÇOIS DE BAR, Chevalier de l'Ordre du Roi, Gouverneur & Maître des Eaux & Forêts de Berry, Seigneur de Buranlure, né le 31 Janvier 1517, eut pour parrain DÉSIRÉ DE BAR, ſon ayeul, & pour marraine Madame la Ducheſſe de *Brabant*. Il ſe maria à *Paule Ducheſnay*, fille d'*Edme*, Chevalier, Seigneur de Neuvy-le-Barrois, de Langeron & des Barres, & de *Geoffredine le Roux*, de laquelle ſont ſortis:

1. ANTOINE, qui fuit;
2. Et EDME, auteur de la branche des Seigneurs de *Billeron* & de *Bonnebuche*, rapportée ci-après.

ANTOINE DE BAR, Chevalier, Seigneur de Buranlure, Vicomte de Villemenard, Thibau & Signy, Chevalier de l'Ordre du Roi, l'un des 100 Gentilshommes de ſa Maiſon, Gouverneur du Comté de Sancerre, fut exempt du Ban & Arrière-Ban ordonné par le Roi CHARLES IX. Le Marquis de Nesle fut commis pour lui donner le Collier de l'Ordre de Saint-Michel, le 5 Mars 1571. Le Roi lui écrivit d'aſſembler ſes vaſſaux, amis & Gentilshommes de ſon voiſinage, pour joindre le Baron de la Châtre, chargé de faire le ſiège de Sancerre. Il s'en acquitta ſi dignement, qu'après la réduction de la Ville, le Baron de la Châtre l'en établit Gouverneur, par ordre du Roi, le 20 Octobre 1573. Il ſe maria, 1° le 9 Novembre 1560, à *Françoiſe le Roi*, fille de *Guillaume* & de *Claude de Pontville*; & 2° le 13 Décembre 1584, à *Madeleine de Babute*, veuve d'*Etienne de Maumigny*. Il eut de ſa première femme:

1. GUILLAUME, qui fuit;
2. JEAN, auteur de la branche des Seigneurs de *Grimonville*, éteinte en mâles, & qui ſubſiſte encore en deux filles, dont une eſt mariée à *N..... de Saint-Jérôme*, en Berry;
3. Et PIERRE, Chevalier de l'Ordre de Saint-Jean de Jéruſalem, Commandeur de Celle, en Berry.

GUILLAUME DE BAR, Seigneur de Buranlure, ſe maria, le 25 Juillet 1584, à *Henriette de Maumigny*, fille d'*Etienne* & de *Madeleine Babute*, dont il eut:

1. SYLVAIN, qui fuit;
2. Et LOUIS, Chevalier de l'Ordre de Saint-Jean de Jéruſalem.

SYLVAIN DE BAR, Chevalier, Seigneur de Buranlure, la Broſſe & Vieilmanay, épouſa, le 19 Janvier 1620, *Gabrielle du Meſnil-Simon*, fille de *Charles*, & de *Marie d'Avantigny*. Il a eu:

1. PIERRE, qui fuit;
2. & 3. JEAN, & autre JEAN ; tous les deux Chevaliers de l'Ordre de Saint-Jean de Jérusalem.

PIERRE DE BAR, Chevalier, Seigneur de Buranlure, la Broffe, les Aries, le Jarrier, &c., commanda la Compagnie d'Ordonnance de M. le Duc d'Enghien, fe trouva aux batailles de Fourchen en Catalogne, proche la Tour de Segre, de Fribourg & de Nortlingen, où il fut dangereufement bleffé. Il époufa, 1º par contrat du 24 Avril 1643, *Marie de Lorron*, fille de *Charles*, Baron de Limanton, &c., & de *Claude de Courtenay* ; & 2º LOUISE DE BAR, fille de JEAN-JACQUES, Chevalier, Seigneur de Bonnebuche, &c., & d'*Hélène de Crèvecœur*. Il eut du premier lit :

HENRI-LOUIS, qui fuit.

Et du fecond lit :

N..... DE BAR, dit *le Marquis de Buranlure*, Chancelier de l'Ordre de Saint-Lazare, fous M. le Duc d'Orléans, Régent, Colonel du Régiment de l'Isle-de-France, mort fans poftérité;

Deux autres garçons;

Et trois filles, dont l'une fut Fille d'honneur de Madame la Princeffe.

HENRI-LOUIS DE BAR, Chevalier, Seigneur, Baron de Limanton & de Saufay, fut dans fa jeuneffe Aide-de-Camp de M. le Duc d'Orléans, frère unique du Roi ; & fe maria, vers 1659, à *Jeanne de Las*, fille de *Charles de Las*, & de *Jeanne de Changy*, Dame de Montigny-fur-Canne en Nivernois, d'où font fortis :

1. CHARLES-GABRIEL, qui fuit;
2. PIERRE, Lieutenant-Colonel du Régiment de Bourbon, Cavalerie, Brigadier des Armées du Roi, mort le 9 Janvier 1657;
3. HUGUES-NICOLAS, Prieur de Saint-Etienne en l'Isle de Ré, premier Aumônier de Madame la Ducheffe d'Orléans, femme de M. le Duc d'Orléans, Régent;
4. & 5. Et deux filles, dont une Religieufe, & l'autre mariée.

CHARLES-GABRIEL DE BAR, Chevalier, Seigneur, Baron de Limanton, Saufay, &c., Lieutenant-Colonel du Régiment de Bourbon, Cavalerie, a époufé, le 4 Avril 1714, *Anne-Gabrielle d'Arlay*, fille de *Barthélemy*, & de *Marie Cartier*, Dame de la Boutière, de laquelle il a eu :

1. BARTHÉLEMY, qui fuit;
2. CHARLES-MICHEL, Prieur de Saint-Etienne dans l'Isle de Ré, avant fon oncle HUGUES.

Tome II.

NICOLAS, Vicaire-Général du Diocèfe de Nevers, mort l'an 1748;
3. Et autre BARTHÉLEMY, Chevalier de l'Ordre de Saint-Jean de Jérufalem, Capitaine au Régiment de Fleury, Cavalerie. Il a hérité de la Seigneurie du Bouchet, poffédée par fon oncle PIERRE, par teftament de 1755.

BARTHÉLEMY DE BAR, Seigneur de Limanton, Saufay en Nivernois, la Boutière près d'Autun & Neufvy-le-Barrois-fur-Allier, ci-devant Capitaine au Régiment de Bourbon, Cavalerie, eft marié, & a des enfans.

BRANCHE
des Seigneurs DE BILLERON, DE BONNE-BUCHE, &c.

EDME DE BAR, fecond fils de FRANÇOIS, & de *Paule Duchefnay*, fe maria à *Marguerite le Roi*, fille de *Guillaume*, & de *Claude de Pontville*, dont il a eu :

1. JEAN-CLAUDE, qui fuit;
2. CHARLES;
3. Et JEANNE, qui partagea avec fes frères le 27 Juillet 1582, mariée à *Hardouin de l'Efbahy*.

JEAN-CLAUDE DE BAR, Chevalier, Seigneur de Billeron, Lugny, Eftivaux, &c., époufa, par contrat du 20 Juillet 1589, *Gilberte de Montolieu*, fille de *François*, Chevalier, Seigneur de Brion, & de *Jacquette de Courtois*, dont :

1. JEAN-JACQUES, qui fuit;
2. Et MARIE.

JEAN-JACQUES DE BAR, Chevalier, Seigneur de Billeron, Lugny, Eftivaux & Bonnebuche, époufa *Hélène de Crèvecœur*, de laquelle font fortis :

1. CHARLES, qui fuit;
2. Et LOUISE, mariée à PIERRE DE BAR-DE-BURANLURE, qui l'époufa en fecondes noces.

CHARLES DE BAR, Chevalier, Seigneur de Billeron, de Bonnebuche, la Vauvrille & du Brion, Lieutenant-Colonel d'un Régiment de Cavalerie, fe maria à *Jeanne Broffier*, fille de *Guillaume*, Tréforier-Général de l'Extraordinaire des Guerres & de la Cavalerie-Légère, dont il a eu :

1. JEAN-CHARLES, qui fuit;
2. Et LOUISE, Religieufe.

JEAN-CHARLES DE BAR, Chevalier, Seigneur de Villeron, Bonnebuche, Flavigny & la Vauvrille, Lieutenant de Roi en Berry, fe maria, le 1er Août 1715, à *Anne-Françoife Heufe-*

S

de-Vauloger, Dame de Bonnay, en Bourbonnois, dont il a eu :

JEAN-CHARLES DE BAR, Chevalier, Seigneur de Bonnebuche, &c., Lieutenant de Roi en Berry, & Lieutenant au Régiment des Gardes-Françoifes, né le 25 Décembre 1723, marié, le 2 Avril 1751, à *Scholaſtique-Marthe-Henriette de Gois* ou *Goiet*, fille de *Jacques*, Seigneur du Vivier, &c.

Les armes: *faſcé d'or & d'azur de neuf pièces*, ou *d'or.*

BAR, en Champagne: *d'or, à la bande de gueules.*

BAR, en Provence: *d'or, au lion de ſable, couronné d'argent.*

BAR (DE), en Languedoc: *écartelé, aux 1 & 4 d'azur, à deux bandes d'or; aux 2 & 3 de gueules, au lion d'or.*

BAR (DE), en Limouſin: *d'argent, à trois faſces de gueules.*

BAR-SUR-SEINE : *d'azur, à trois bars ou barbeaux d'or, poſés l'un ſur l'autre en demi cercle, à la bordure componée de neuf pièces d'or, & de ſable.*

BAR-PRESSAIE: *de gueules, ſemé de croix recroiſetées, au pied fiché d'or, à deux barbeaux adoſſés de même, brochant ſur le tout, ſurmontés d'un loſange d'argent.*

BARACH, à Louance, en Bretagne: *écartelé d'or & d'azur.*

BARACH, à Louance, en Bretagne: *de gueules, à une faſce d'argent, accompagnée de ſix annelets d'or, 3 en chef rangés, & 3 en pointe, poſés 2 & 1.*

BARADAD, ou BARADAT, en Champagne & en Guyenne. On trouve, JEAN DE BARADAT, originaire du Condomois & d'Armagnac, qui vivoit en 1495. Il eut pour deſcendans, entr'autres, trois frères:

FRANÇOIS, qui ſuit;

HENRI, Evêque & Comte de Noyon, Pair de France en 1627, mort en 1659;

Et PIERRE, Lieutenant-Général des Armées du Roi, qui commanda à Caſal dans le Montferrat, fit le ſiège de Valence-ſur-le Pô, & mourut en 1682, laiſſant:

HENRI-FRANÇOIS DE BARADAT, le dernier mâle de cette branche, qui, ayant quitté le ſervice en 1714, après la paix d'Utrecht, embraſſa l'état eccléſiaſtique, &

fut nommé par le Roi à une Prébende de Reims en 1720.

FRANÇOIS DE BARADAT, Seigneur de Damery, chef de la Maiſon, eut beaucoup de part à la faveur de LOUIS XIII. Il ſervit avec diſtinction ſous le Maréchal de Thoiras, & mourut en 1683. Il eut pour fils:

MARC DE BARADAT, enfant-d'honneur auprès de LOUIS XIV, qui mourut d'une bleſſure qu'il reçut à la bataille de Saint-Gothard en Hongrie , en 1664, ne laiſſant qu'un fils mort en bas âge;

JEAN-MARC DE BARADAT, qui mourut à Veniſe ſans avoir été marié;

HENRI DE BARADAT, Abbé de Signy;

Et LOUIS DE BARADAT, Evêque de Vabres en 1672.

LISANDER DE BARADAT, quatrième fils de JEAN DE BARADAT, IIe du nom, & de *Marguerite de Copin*, eſt auteur des Vicomtes de *Verneuil*, qui n'ont formé que deux degrés.

On trouve encore JOACHIM DE BARADAT, Seigneur de *Maujuſſon*, ſecond fils de CARBONEAU DE BARADAT. Cette branche a fini à ſon petit-fils JEAN DE BARADAT, Seigneur de *Maujuſſon*, Capitaine au Régiment de Piémont.

Voyez le *Nobiliaire de Champagne*, imprimé grand in-fol.

Les armes : *d'azur, à la faſce d'or, accompagnée de trois roſes de même, deux en chef & une en pointe.*

BARAILH ou BARRAILH. De cette famille étoient JEAN DE BARRAILH, Grand-Croix de l'Ordre Royal & Militaire de Saint-Louis depuis 1754, Vice-Amiral le 25 Août 1753, mort le 25 Août 1762, âgé de 91 ans.

Et le Marquis de BARAILH, Lieutenant-Général & Commandant en Flandre.

Les armes: *d'argent, au chevron d'azur, ſurmonté d'une faſce de gueules, chargée de trois beſans du champ.*

BARAL, en Picardie: *de gueules, à trois barillets d'or, 2 & 1.*

BARALY: *d'or, au lion de gueules, au chef d'azur, chargé de trois étoiles du champ.*

BARANDIÈRE (LA). ANTOINE-LOUIS DE LA BARANDIÈRE, Comte de là Gorge, épouſa *Marie-Anne-Joſéphine de la Chauſſée d'Eu*, dont il eut:

FRANÇOIS-BRUNO DE LA BARANDIÈRE, Comte de la Chauſſée d'Eu, marié le 1er Mars 1751, à *Marie-Anne-Auguſtine de la Vieuville*, veuve le 9 Mars 1750, de *Jacques-Augufte-Laurent-Ferdinand-Philippe-Marie d'Alpozzo*, Marquis de la Trouffe.

BARANGUE: *d'azur, au chevron d'argent, accompagné de trois coqs d'or, deux en chef & un en pointe*

BARANTIN: *d'azur, à la fafce d'or, accompagnée en chef de trois étoiles de même, & en pointe de fix ondes.*

BARAS, en Provence: *d'or, à trois fafces d'azur.*

BARASTRE, Seigneur du Mefnil, en Normandie, Généralité de Rouen, famille maintenue en fa nobleffe le 28 Juillet 1668, dont les armes font: *de gueules, à une épée d'argent en pal, accompagnée de trois étoiles de même, une en chef & deux en flancs.*

BARAT, Seigneur de Beauvais, en Normandie, Généralité d'Alençon, famille maintenue dans fa nobleffe le 4 Avril 1667, qui porte pour armes: *d'argent, à la croix ancrée de fable, vidée en cœur d'argent.*

BARAT-MONTRAVERSIER: *d'argent à une anille de fable.*

BARATES: *de fable, à trois mains dextres d'or, 2 & 1.*

BARATIER, en Dauphiné, famille noble, de laquelle eft ANTOINE BARATIER, né le 4 Juillet 1713, Officier-Pointeur d'Artillerie le 1ᵉʳ Novembre 1729, Commiffaire extraordinaire le 6 Mars 1734, ordinaire le 11 Décembre 1741, Chevalier de Saint-Louis en 1744, Lieutenant-Général de l'Artillerie, & Commiffaire-Provincial les 30 & 31 Décembre 1746; Major en chef de l'Artillerie en 1747 & 1748, Lieutenant le 29 Octobre 1750, il eut rang de Lieutenant-Colonel le 8 Décembre 1755, & de Colonel le 1ᵉʳ Mai 1756, Colonel d'une Brigade, & Brigadier d'Infanterie les 1ᵉʳ Janvier & 10 Février 1759, Maréchal-de-Camp le 20 Février 1761, & enfin Chef de la Brigade de fon nom le 7 Mars 1761.

Les armes: *d'argent, au lévrier de fable, accollé de gueules.*

BARATON, Maifon originaire de Touraine, qui a donné un Grand-Echanfon de France dans FRANÇOIS DE BARATON, Chevalier, Confeiller-Chambellan du Roi en 1516. Elle a fini à LOUIS DE BARATON, qui n'eut, de *Jacqueline Paumart*, qu'une fille, ANNE DE BARATON, Dame de Rivareine, mariée en 1572.

Les armes: *d'or, à la fafce fufelée de gueules, accompagnée de fept croix ancrées de fable, 4 en chef & 3 en pointe;* d'autres portent: *trois croix recroifetées de fable, 2 en chef & 1 en pointe.*

BARATON, Seigneur de la Romagère, en Berry: *de gueules, à deux fafces d'or, accompagnées en chef de deux étoiles d'argent, & en pointe d'un croiffant de même.*

BARAUDIN, Capitaine de Frégate. Il a été nommé, en Août 1767, Capitaine des Vaiffeaux du Roi.

BARAULT. *d'azur, à la croix d'or, cantonnée de quatre foleils de même.*

* BARBANÇOIS (DE), en Berry. Cette noble & ancienne Maifon tire fon nom d'une Terre fituée dans la Marche. On trouve à la fin du XIᵉ fiècle un GUILLAUME DE BARBANÇOIS, qui fit donation à l'Abbaye de Notre-Dame du Pré-Benoît, conjointement avec Meffieurs de *Chauvigny*, de *Broffe* & autres, de tout ce qui leur appartenoit aux environs de ladite Abbaye; tous les Donataires y font qualifiés collectivement de *Chevaliers* ou *Damoifeaux*.

Cette Maifon s'eft tranfplantée, vers la fin du XIIIᵉ fiècle en Berry, où elle a toujours pris des alliances dans des Maifons nobles & illuftres, telles que celles d'*Amblard*, de *Boifé*, de *Chamborant*, de *la Châtre*, de *Douzan*, de *le Féron*, *Lavaud*, *Bridiers*, *Bertrand*, *Lezai-Lufignan*, du *Puy-Vatan*, du *Pleffis-Richelieu*, de *Rieux*, de *Villaines*, & autres très-nobles, fans s'être jamais méfalliée.

Elle n'a jamais difcontinué de fervir l'Etat: ce qui eft conftaté, tant par les preuves faites chez les différens Généalogiftes de la Cour, & autres, que par l'*Hiftoire du Berry* de la Thaumaffière, p. 600 & fuiv.; l'*Hiftoire du tems*, par Guillaume Paradin, liv. IV, chap. II & fuiv., & les différentes Chartes des diverfes Abbayes.

Ceux de cette Maifon ont toujours porté les qualités de *Damoifeaux, Ecuyers* & *Chevaliers*, titres affectés aux Gentilshommes de nom & d'armes, avant qu'ils parvinffent à l'Ordre de Chevalerie. Plufieurs ont été faits Chevaliers de l'Ordre du Roi, & Officiers de Compagnies d'Ordonnances. Cette Maifon a donné un Gouverneur d'Iffoudun & Lieutenant-Général des Troupes du Roi en Berry, un Capitaine du Ban & Arrière-Ban, un Tréforier-Général & Commiffaire du même Ban, des Maréchaux-de-Camp, un Capitaine des Gardes du Grand Condé, un Capitaine-Colonel d'Infanterie, & de généreux Chevaliers, toujours prêts à combattre pour le fervice de leur Prince & la défenfe de leur honneur, témoin le fameux HÉLION DE BARBANÇOIS, IIᵉ du nom, qui, à l'âge de 70 ans, combattit en préfence & par Ordonnance du Roi FRANÇOIS Iᵉʳ, l'an 1538, & tua Meffire François de Saint-Julien, Seigneur de Veniers, brave & généreux Chevalier & en la fleur de fon âge; & PIERRE DE BARBANÇOIS, fon petit-fils, qui eut quatre duels mémorables.

La Terre de Barbançois refta dans cette Maifon depuis le XIᵉ fiècle jufqu'au XVᵉ, qu'elle fut vendue.

Cette Maifon poffédoit encore vers la fin du XIIIᵉ fiècle la Châtellenie de Sarzai en Berry, mouvante, & à deux petites lieues de la Baronie de la Châtre. Cette Terre, qui confiftoit en un ancien & fort Château flanqué de plufieurs groffes tours, en haute, moyenne & baffe-juftice, &c., fut vendue, en 1720, à M. de la Porte; &, ce qui eft affez remarquable, elle n'eft jamais tombée en partage, & avoit, depuis plus de 500 ans, toujours appartenu aux aînés de préciput & avantage, par la difpofition de leurs pères, foigneux du luftre de leur ancienne maifon. Elle a auffi poffédé en divers tems les Terres de Réville, Charon, Auzans, Coudière, Corbilly, les Chezaux, Barbette, Fonteny, la Coullardière, Limanges, Fougères, les Gerbaux, Chouday, Angibaut, Roche, la Bize, Villegongis, & autres. Cette dernière eft encore aujourd'hui poffédée par LÉON-FRANÇOIS DE BARBANÇOIS, chef de toute fa Maifon, en faveur duquel elle a été érigée en Marquifat fous le nom de Barbançois-Villegongis, par Lettres-Patentes du Roi données à Marly au mois de Mars 1767, & regiftrées au Parlement le 18 Mai 1768. Le premier de cette Maifon eft:

I. MATHIEU DE BARBANÇOIS, lequel eft dit Seigneur de Sarzai dans un titre latin de 1300, & dans un autre de 1338, où il eft qualifié Damoifeau. Il vendit, en 1348, à Jean Gendrault, & autres, le bois de la Lande, & par le contrat qui eft auffi en latin, il eft qualifié Nobilis vir MATTHÆUS DE BARBANÇOIS, Domicellus, Dominus de Sarzai, &c., qui étoient, comme nous l'avons dit, les plus hautes qualités que priffent pour lors

les Gentilshommes de nom & d'armes, avant qu'ils fuffent faits Chevaliers.

II. GUILLAUME DE BARBANÇOIS, fon fils, Damoifeau, Seigneur de Sarzai, fervit le Roi JEAN contre les Anglois, affembla jufqu'à 40 lances, avec lefquelles il s'oppofa aux courfes qu'il faifoient dans le Berry, & reprit fur eux la ville de la Châtre & les forterefles de Briantes, du Chaffin & du Lys, dont ils s'étoient rendus maîtres. Il avoit acheté en 1378, de Louis Gofon, la feizième partie des Dîmes de la Paroiffe de Sarzai, & échangea, par contrat du jour & fête de Saint-Martin de l'an 1383, différens héritages qu'il avoit en la Paroiffe de Cluys, contre une autre portion des Dîmes de Sarzai, avec Louis de Crévant; dans l'un & l'autre de ces deux contrats il eft qualifié Damoifeau. Il obtint des Lettres d'abolition du Roi CHARLES VI, le 7 Février 1385, au fujet du dégât que fes troupes avoient fait dans la ville de la Châtre. Il avoit époufé, par contrat de 1362, Jeanne d'Amblard, fille de N..... d'Amblard, d'une famille illuftre du Berry, & de N... de la Châtre, dont il eut:

1. JEAN, Damoifeau, Seigneur de Sarzai, marié 1º à N...; & 2º à Marguerite Graffeville, veuve de Perrin de Bourges, Ecuyer, Seigneur de Villepaple, de laquelle il eut:

MACÉ DE BARBANÇOIS, Damoifeau, Seigneur de Sarzai, qui mourut fans poftérité de Perrette de Bourges, fille de Perrin, dont il partagea la fucceffion avec Louis, Mérigot & Jeanne de Bourges, femme de Jean de Pons, fes beaux-frères & belle-fœur, par acte de l'an 1418;

JEAN DE BARBANÇOIS, qui inftitua fes oncles, fes héritiers;

Et JEANNE DE BARBANÇOIS, à laquelle fa mère & fon frère donnèrent en dot 400 écus vieux, ou réaux de 64 au marc, lors de fon mariage, en 1438, avec Jean Ducher, Ecuyer, Seigneur de Signat, & qui tranfigea avec HÉLION & ARCHAMBAUT DE BARBANÇOIS, fes oncles, par acte du 15 Novembre 1442, moyennant 90 réaux d'or.

2. ARCHAMBAUT, Chevalier, qui ne laiffa qu'un fils nommé JEAN, lequel vendit, par contrat de 1470, à JEAN, fon coufin germain, fils d'HÉLION, fon oncle, tous fes droits, & mourut fans poftérité;

3. Et HÉLION, qui fuit.

III. HÉLION DE BARBANÇOIS, Iᵉʳ du nom,

Damoiſeau, Seigneur de Sarzai & de Charon, lequel arrenta certains héritages à Jean Chaumeau, par aĉte du 15 Mai 1449, dans lequel il eſt qualifié, *Nobilis vir HELYAS DE BARBANÇOIS Domicellus, Dominus de Sarʒaïo, &c.* Il fit, ainſi que ſa femme, donation à JEAN DE BARBANÇOIS, leur fils aîné, par aĉte du 1er Août 1440, de tous leurs meubles, acquêts & conquêts, & ſpécialement des Terres de Charon & de Heurtebize, & étoit mort en 1462. Il avoit épouſé *Catherine de Villaines*, fille de *Guillaume*, & de *N...de l'Age.* Leurs enfans furent:

1. JEAN, qui ſuit;
2. Et JACQUETTE, qui fut mariée par contrat du 21 Novembre 1448, avec *Georges de la Châtre*, Chevalier, Seigneur de Breuillebault, Grand-Fauconnier de France.

IV. JEAN DE BARBANÇOIS, Damoiſeau, Seigneur de Sarzai, de Charon, de Coudière, Corbilly, les Chezaux, Auzans, Barbette, Fonteny, la Coullardière, Limanges, Réville, des Fougères & des Gerbaux, donna à bail, en 1475, la Terre de Barbançois, & fit ſon teſtament le 12 Septembre 1476, par lequel il choiſit ſa ſépulture en l'Egliſe Paroiſſiale de Sarzai, laiſſa le ſoin de ſes funérailles à ſa femme & à FRANÇOIS DE BARBANÇOIS, ſon fils aîné du premier lit, & aumôna 100 écus d'or aux pauvres. Tous ſes enfans, tant du premier que du ſecond lit, ſont dénommés dans ce teſtament, par lequel il partage entre les mâles tous ſes biens, & fait différens legs, tant à ſes filles, qu'à ſa femme. Il avoit épouſé, 1º par contrat du 27 Décembre 1453, du vivant de ſon père & de ſa mère, *Françoiſe de Boiſé*, fille de *Jacques de Boiſé*, Ecuyer, Seigneur de Courtenay, &c., & de *Souveraine de Blanchefort*; & 2º, par contrat de l'an 1467, *Iſabeau du Puy-de-Vatan*, qui s'étoit remariée, en 1476, avec *Gilbert-Bertrand*, Chevalier, Seigneur *du Lys-Saint-Georges.* Elle vivoit encore ès années 1477 & 1480, ſuivant différens aveux & dénombremens.

Les enfans du premier lit furent:

1. FRANÇOIS, qui ſuit;
2. JACQUES, Religieux de l'Abbaye de Déols;
3. JACQUELINE, mariée, par contrat de l'an 1470, avec *Guyot Ajaſſon*, IIe du nom, Seigneur de Vot & de Grandſaigné, fils de *Henri*, Seigneur des mêmes lieux.

Ceux du ſecond lit ſont:

4. ANTOINE, auteur de la branche des Seigneurs *de Charon*, rapportée ci-après;

5. GUYOT, Chevalier de Saint-Jean de Jéruſalem & de Rhodez, lequel fit vente, en 1494, à ANTOINE, ſon frère, de tous ſes biens patrimoniaux;
6. MARGUERITE, mariée à *N... de Saint-Martin*, lequel donna quittance en 1490, d'une ſomme de 700 livres, à FRANÇOIS & ANTOINE DE BARBANÇOIS, ſes beaux-frères;
7. & 8. CATHERINE & ISABEAU.

V. FRANÇOIS DE BARBANÇOIS, Ier du nom, Damoiſeau, Seigneur de Sarzai, de Coudière, Corbilly, Chézaux, Auzans, Barbette, Fonteny, la Coullardière, Limanges, Réville, des Fougères & des Gerbaux, eut de ſi grands avantages par le teſtament de ſon père, qu'ils lui furent conteſtés par *Iſabeau du Puy*, ſa belle-mère, comme tutrice & gardienne-noble de ſes enfans, & par JACQUES DE BARBANÇOIS, ſon frère germain, en 1477, qui ſe ſoumirent à l'arbitrage de Meſſire *Antoine de Blanchefort*, Chevalier, Seigneur du Bois-à-l'Amy; de *Jacques de Bridiers*, Ecuyer, Seigneur du Gué; de Meſſire *Jean de Roches*, Chevalier, Seigneur de Chabannes; & de *Pierre de Saint-Julien*, Ecuyer, Seigneur de Véniers, d'après l'avis deſquels ils tranſigèrent le 16 Février 1477. Il étoit Préſident des Comptes à Moulins, ſuivant les Lettres de Proviſions expédiées le 15 Août 1524, en faveur de René d'Orme, qui lui ſuccéda en cette charge. Il avoit épouſé *Marguerite d'Auʒans*, laquelle, comme tutrice & gardienne noble de leurs enfans mineurs qui ſuivent, rendit aveu de la Terre de Sarzai en 1496.

1. HÉLION, qui ſuit;
2. & 3. JEAN & FRANÇOIS.

VI. HÉLION DE BARBANÇOIS, IIe du nom, Chevalier, Seigneur de Sarzai, d'Auzans, & de 14 autres Terres conſidérables, fut pourvu, par Lettres du 26 Avril 1538, de la charge de Gentilhomme ordinaire de la Chambre du Roi FRANÇOIS Ier, en récompenſe des ſervices importans qu'il avoit rendus en pluſieurs occaſions à ce Prince, & *en conſidération de ſon ancienne Nobleſſe*, & Chevalier de l'Ordre du Roi. Sa valeur & ſon mérite étoient ſi connus, que nous ne pouvons oublier ici ce dont l'Hiſtoire conſerve aujourd'hui la mémoire à la poſtérité & à l'honneur de ce Gentilhomme, & de la Maiſon de BARBANÇOIS, qui eſt le combat qu'il eut au mois de Juillet 1538 contre *François de Saint-Julien*, Chevalier, Seigneur de Veniers, par ordre du Roi FRANçois Ier, Messire *Charles de Gaucourt* avoit rapporté au Sieur de *Sarzai*, que le Sieur de *Veniers* lui avoit dit que *Jean de la Tour*, Chevalier, Seigneur de Châteauroux, *avoit lâché le pied, & pris la fuite en la bataille de Pavie*; ce qu'ayant appris ce dernier, il fit citer devant le Roi FRANÇOIS Ier ledit Sieur de Sarzai, pour soutenir les paroles qu'il avoit dites. Le Sieur de Sarzai se présenta devant S. M. à Chenonceaux, à Amboife & à Blois, & fut ouï par MONSIEUR, en préfence du Grand-Maître de France, du Chancelier, du Cardinal de Langres, de l'Evêque de Soiffons, du Préfident *Poyet*, & autres du Confeil du Roi, lequel ordonna que ledit Sieur de Sarzai *ameneroit fon Difeur*, qui étoit le Sieur de *Gaucourt*; &, pour ce faire, lui octroya commiffion pour le faire ajourner à Paris le 7 Janvier 1537. Ce dernier, ayant paru au Confeil, avoua avoir dit les paroles proférées par le Sieur de Sarzai, & qu'il les tenoit du Sieur *de Veniers*; fur quoi le Confeil ordonna, le 22 du même mois, que le Sieur de Sarzay feroit comparoître ledit Sieur de *Veniers*, lequel, interrogé fur ce que les Sieurs de *Gaucourt* & de Sarzai avoient affuré de lui, dénia leur avoir dit ces paroles; &, quoique le Sieur de Sarzai lui eût maintenu le contraire, le Roi leur permit, par Arrêt du Confeil, pour vuider & décider le débat & différend entre le Sieur de Sarzai, *Demandeur en cas d'honneur*, & le Sieur de *Veniers*, *Défendeur*, de fe trouver en perfonnes le 1er Octobre 1537, là où feroit S. M. *pour*, en fa préfence, ou de ceux par Elle commis, *combattre l'un & l'autre en champ clos, & faire preuves de leurs perfonnes, pour la juftification de l'honneur de celui auquel la victoire en demeurera*, fur peine, à celui qui feroit de fe faire refufant, d'être réputé non Noble, lui & fa poftérité, à jamais, & d'être privé des droits, privilèges & autres peines en tels cas accoutumées. *Dauphin*, Héraut-d'armes de France, préfenta le 1er Juillet 1538, au Sieur de Sarzai, par ordre du Roi, en préfence de *Pierre de Saint-Eftève*, fon Echanfon, & Gentilhomme ordinaire de fa Maifon, & de *François de Marçonnay*, Gentilhomme de fa Vènerie, l'écrit figné de la main du Sieur de *Veniers*, contenant trois fortes d'armes, qu'il étoit tenu déclarer; à quoi le Sieur de Sarzai fit réponfe, qu'il avoit envoyé à Paris *Bourgogne*, Hérault d'armes de Fran-

ce, par lequel il les lui enverroit par écrit dans 24 heures. Le combat fut remis en la ville de Moulins, pour être fait en préfence du Roi. Ce combat en occafionna un autre, qui n'étoit pas moins illuftre, entre le Sieur de Sarzai & CHARLES DE BARBANÇOIS, fon fils aîné, où l'on vit éclater la piété filiale, & la générofité d'un père vigoureux au-delà de fon âge. Le fils pria fon père de lui permettre de combattre pour fa querelle, difant *que ce feroit chofe honteufe à un Gentilhomme, en la fleur de fon âge, de fouffrir que fon père, âgé de 70 ans, combattît avec un jeune & vigoureux Chevalier, adroit, difpos, & expérimenté au fait d'armes.* Le père ne voulut pas expofer fon fils pour fa querelle, & lui répondit fièrement qu'*il les frotteroit bien tous deux, & avoit affez de force, de courage & de vigueur pour mettre fon adverfarge à raifon.* Ainfi, non-obftant la réfiftance du fils, ces deux champions entrèrent en champ clos, avec les cérémonies en tel cas requifes & accoutumées; & ce vieillard fit bien voir qu'il avoit autant de force que de courage, car il bleffa le Sieur *de Veniers*, qui mourut 15 jours après le combat. L'Hiftoire remarque encore que, pendant l'action, CHARLES DE BARBANÇOIS prioit à deux genoux, & les larmes aux yeux, le Dieu des combats, pour qu'il lui plût accorder la victoire à fon père, & que ce bon vieillard, ayant remporté l'avantage, alla trouver fon fils, pour en rendre grâces à Dieu dans la même Eglife. Ce combat eft l'un des derniers qui ont été faits par Ordonnance du Souverain. Voyez l'*Hiftoire du Tems*, par Guill. Paradin, liv. IV, chap. II; & celle du *Berry*, pag. 603 & fuiv. Il époufa, par contrat du 25 Octobre 1507, *Aimée du Pleffis-Richelieu*, fille aînée de *François*, IIe du nom, Seigneur de Richelieu, & de *Guyonne de Laval*, grand'tante du Cardinal de *Richelieu*, & de *Nicole du Pleffis-Richelieu*, laquelle eut d'*Urbain de Maillé*, Maréchal de France, *Claire-Clémence de Maillé*, époufe du Grand Condé, & fœur de *Jeanne du Pleffis-Richelieu*, femme de *Mathurin du Theil*, Ecuyer, Seigneur du Frefne; partagea avec ce dernier, par acte du 15 Octobre 1518, les biens provenans de la fucceffion de *Guyonne de Laval*, leur belle-mère, lefquels confiftoient dans les Terres de Cerbouan, Touffe, Tranaille, Rimbault, la Roche-Saint-Mas, Pélifton, Petit-Gué-de-la-Forêts, & de la Barrière, qu'il vendit par contrat du 29 du même mois.

Ses enfans furent :

1. CHARLES, qui suit ;
2. GABRIEL, Chevalier, Seigneur de Saint-Auzans, qui fut père d'ANDRÉ DE BARBANÇOIS, homme d'armes de la Compagnie d'Ordonnance de M. de la Bourdaisière ;
3. GEORGES, qui testa en faveur de ses frères en 1547, & servoit encore en 1548, dans l'armée que le Roi envoya en Ecosse ;
4. JEAN, qui rendit foi & hommage pour ses biens, en 1550, & étoit Gentilhomme de la Chambre du Duc DE MONTPENSIER, suivant ses Lettres de retenue de l'an 1559 ;
5. ANTOINE, Religieux à Déols ;
6. ANNE, mariée avec *Louis de Constant*, Chevalier, Seigneur de Font-Pertuis ;
7. CHARLOTTE, femme de *Louis le Chat*, Chevalier, Seigneur de Traffy ;
8. Et MARIE.

VII. CHARLES DE BARBANÇOIS, Chevalier de l'Ordre du Roi, Seigneur & Baron de Sarzai, de Grand-Maison, & de douze autres Terres, fut élu en 1545, pour commander, en qualité de Capitaine, le ban & arrière-ban de la Province de Berry ; fit un marché en conséquence pour l'habillement de sa Compagnie, avec des Marchands de drap de la ville de Bourges, le 1ᵉʳ Juillet 1545 ; signala son courage à la défense de la ville d'Issoudun, que les Religionnaires tenoient assiégée en 1562, sur lesquels il fit trois sorties si furieuses, qu'il les obligea de lever le siège, sans avoir été secouru que de PIERRE DE BARBANÇOIS, son fils, qui s'étoit jeté dans cette Place avec quelque Noblesse ; les habitans, en reconnoissance, firent réédifier une tour abattue par le canon des ennemis, à laquelle ils donnèrent le nom de *Sarzai*, & firent fondre des canons à son nom & à ses armes, pour éternelle mémoire de la valeur de celui qui les avoit si généreusement défendus. Il fut Député de la Noblesse de cette Province aux Etats-Généraux en 1565. Le Roi CHARLES IX, pour reconnoître ses services, le fit Lieutenant-Général & Commandant de ses Troupes en Berry, par Lettres du 29 Janvier 1567 ; l'honora, le 24 Mai 1568, du Collier de son Ordre, qui lui fut donné par M. le Duc DE MONTPENSIER, le 6 Juin suivant ; & le fit Gouverneur des ville & château d'Issoudun, par Lettres du 2 Septembre 1568 ; dans laquelle Place il rendit pendant plusieurs années, & dans des

tems difficiles & de guerres civiles, de très-grands services au Roi. CHARLES DE BARBANÇOIS transigea, par acte du 26 Août 1544, qui fut homologué au Siège Royal d'Issoudun, le 15 Juillet 1545, avec ses frères & sœurs, & sa mère, au nom & comme leur gardienne-noble & tutrice, qui lui contestoient la donation qui lui avoit été faite par son père lors de son mariage ; & rendit foi & hommage de la Terre de Sarzai en 1556. Ayant eu procès au Conseil-Privé du Roi HENRI II, cette même année, avec Messire *Olivier Guérin*, Chevalier, Seigneur de la Beauce, pour paroles d'honneur proférées l'un contre l'autre, ce Prince, en considération *de ce qu'ils étoient de bonne, noble & ancienne race, & des grands & signalés services qu'eux & leurs prédécesseurs lui avoient rendus & à la Couronne*, leur accorda des Lettres de pardon le 1ᵉʳ Juillet 1556. Il avoit été marié, 1° par contrat du 17 Juin 1534, avec *Anne de Louan*, fille de *Joachim*, Ecuyer, Seigneur de Grand-Maison, & de *Louise d'Aymer* ; & 2° en 1545, avec *Anne Bertrand*, de la Maison du *Lys-Saint-Georges*, de laquelle il n'eut point d'enfans.

Ceux du premier lit furent :

1. PIERRE, qui suit ;
2. Et LOUISE, mariée, par contrat du 8 Mai 1556, à *Gilbert Bertrand*, IIᵉ du nom, Sieur de Saint-Julien.

VIII. PIERRE DE BARBANÇOIS, Chevalier, Seigneur de Sarzai de Réville, & de douze autres Terres, fit ses premières armes dès l'âge de 15 ans. Il étoit en 1568 Guidon de la Compagnie d'Ordonnance du Marquis de Boisé, puis Enseigne de celle du Comte du Bouchage, & en 1577 de celle du Maréchal de Cossé ; il succéda à son père dans le Gouvernement de la ville d'Issoudun, & passoit pour l'une des meilleures épées de son temps. Il fut reçu, en 1568, Chevalier de l'Ordre du Roi ; en 1573 Gentilhomme de la Chambre de FRANÇOIS, Duc d'Alençon ; en 1578 de celle du Duc d'Anjou ; & peu après l'un des Gentilshommes de la Maison du Roi de la première bande. Il eut quatre duels mémorables : le *premier* au siège de Brouage, contre un Capitaine du Régiment de Picardie, qu'il tua ; le *second*, au siège de Poitiers, où il s'étoit jeté pour la défense de cette Place & le service du Roi, contre un Capitaine nommé *Cerifié* ; le *troisième*, contre un nommé *Baudin* ; & le *quatrième*, contre le grand Capitaine *Aragon*, qui fe fit derrière les Chartreux à Paris, en préfence de 4,000 perfonnes. Il lui donna deux grands coups d'épée, & le laiffa mort fur la place. HENRI III, ayant été informé comment l'action s'étoit paffée, lui envoya fa grâce par M. le Comte du Bouchage, par Lettres du mois de Juin 1584, & lui donna pour récompenfe fa Compagnie de Gens-d'armes. Il mourut en 1590, & avoit époufé, par contrat du 7 Novembre 1560 (extrait de célébration du 25 Décembre fuivant), *Françoife de Leẓai-des-Marais*, qui tefta le 7 Août 1597, elle étoit de l'illuftre & ancienne Maifon de *Leẓai-Lufignem*, première fille & fecond enfant de noble & puiffant Seigneur Meffire *René de Leẓai*, Chevalier de l'Ordre du Roi, Seigneur Châtelain des Marais-de-Lezai, &c., & de *Françoife d'Alleri*, dont il eut :

1. CHARLES, Chevalier, Seigneur de Sarzai, qui fut Maréchal des Camps & Armées du Roi, & Chevalier de fon Ordre, dont le Collier lui fut donné par le Maréchal de Souvré, le 29 Janvier 1620; il avoit rendu aveu des Terres de Sarzai, de Bellefonds & autres, ès années 1607, 1612 & 1617, & avoit fait un teftament en 1591, par lequel il inftitua LÉON DE BARBANÇOIS, fon frère, fon héritier univerfel, n'ayant point d'enfans d'*Anne l'Allier*, laquelle l'inftitua également fon unique héritier, par fon teftament de 1630;

2. LÉON, qui fuit;

3. CLAUDINE, qui fut mariée, par contrat, du 8 Avril 1589, à *François d'Huiffel*, Ier du nom, ou d'*Wiffel*, Ecuyer, Seigneur de Beauregard, Touzel, Chaillou, Arteuil, & de la Charité-en-Brie, Lieutenant des toiles des chaffes du Roi, Capitaine & Maître des Eaux-&-Forêts des Baronies de Meilland, Charenton, Chaudeuil, Poudix, &c., fils de *Jean*, Ecuyer, & de *Chriftine de Patoufleau*, dont poftérité;

4. Et LOUISE, femme de *Jean du Rieux*, Ecuyer, Seigneur de Villepréau, Fontbuffeau, Saint-Martin, Sainte-Catherine, Villaudrin, &c., & Sénéchal de la Baffe-Marche.

IX. LÉON DE BARBANÇOIS, Ier du nom, Chevalier, Seigneur de Sarzai, de Réville, Chouday, Angibault, & de huit autres Terres, fut Gentilhomme ordinaire de la Chambre du Roi en 1616; Maréchal-de-Camp en 1630, Chevalier de l'Ordre de Saint-Michel en 1631, dont le Collier lui fut donné par le Maréchal de Souvré; Confeiller & Grand-Maître-d'Hô-

tel de la Maifon du Roi en 1636, & Maréchal-des-Logis de Sa Compagnie de Gens-d'armes en 1640. Il fe fignala en plufieurs occafions, notamment à l'attaque de Saint-Antonin, où il força le corps-de-garde avec quelques Gens-d'armes du Roi, qui y avoient été commandés pour faire un premier effort; & à l'attaque de l'Isle-de-Ré, où le Roi LOUIS XIII lui fit l'honneur de lui donner, *à caufe de fa bravoure & de fa valeur*, la Cornette blanche dans le champ de bataille. Ce Prince, peu avant fa mort, rendit un témoignage éclatant de fa fidélité, & des fervices qu'il lui avoit rendus, ainfi qu'au Roi HENRI-LE-GRAND, pendant plus de 40 années. LÉON DE BARBANÇOIS, Ier du nom, avoit époufé, par contrat du 22 Février 1610, *Françoife du Rieux*, fille de *Jean*, Ecuyer, Seigneur de Villepréau, Fontbuffeau, Villaudrin, Saint-Martin, Sainte-Catherine, &c., Sénéchal de la Baffe-Marche, & de *Barbe de Réchigne-voifin*, & petite-fille d'*Antoine du Rieux*, & d'*Antoinette Boueri*, fes ayeuls. Il rèndit hommage pour fes Terres de Sarzai & autres, en 1627, & eut de ce mariage :

1. LÉON, qui fuit;

2. Et ANNE, femme de *Maximilien Lignaud*, Chevalier, Seigneur de Lage-Bernard, Coulonges, Luffac-les-Eglifes, Tilly, Saint-Martin, &c.

X. LÉON DE BARBANÇOIS, IIe du nom, Chevalier, Seigneur & Marquis de Sarzai, Seigneur de Réville, Lineux, Mouville, Villegongis, Angibault, Chouday, &c., Meftre-de-Camp du Régiment de Conty, Çavalerie, par commiffion du 11 Novembre 1651, & Gouverneur des ville & citadelle de Bourg-fur-Mer en 1662, avoit époufé, par contrat du 4 Juillet 1645, *Jacqueline de Neuchèẓe*, qui tefta en 1671, fille de *Jacques*, Chevalier, Seigneur de Baudiment, Beaumont, Mayet, Beriulle, la Rivière, Villegongis, & autres Terres, & de *Jeanne de Launay* qui lui firent, par le même contrat, donation entre vifs de tous leurs biens, à la réferve de l'ufufruit leur vie durant. Leurs enfans furent :

1. FRANÇOIS, qui fuit;

2. LOUIS, Comte de Sarzai, Capitaine de Çavalerie, mort fans alliance;

3. Autre FRANÇOIS, dit *le jeune*, auteur du rameau établi en Bourbonnois fous le nom des Seigneurs de *Dorne*, &c., rapporté ci-après;

4. CHARLES, Chevalier de l'Ordre de Malte,

d'abord Capitaine de Dragrons au Régiment de Liſtenois, puis de Cavalerie dans celui d'Eſclainvilliers, qui eut une jambe emportée, à l'affaire de Donawert, en 1703;

5. MARIE-ANNE, mariée à *N*..., Marquis de *Fougières*, Seigneur de Creux en Bourbonnois, dont des enfans;

6. & 7. CLAUDE-FRANÇOISE, & JACQUELINE, Religieuſe à Gerzai;

8. Et MARIE, Religieuſe à la Châtre.

XI. FRANÇOIS DE BARBANÇOIS, IIᵉ du nom, Chevalier, Seigneur & Marquis de Sarzai, de Villegongis, &c., connu ſous le nom de *Marquis de Sarzai*, fut Capitaine de Dragons au Régiment d'Eſtiſſac, & ſervoit dans la guerre terminée par le Traité de Ryſwick. Il avoit épouſé, par contrat du 30 Janvier 1690, *Jacqueline-Eugénie Marin*, dont il eut:

1. CLAUDE, Chevalier, Lieutenant au Régiment de Dauphiné, Infanterie, qui mourut en Novembre 1707, en la vallée de Quéros;

2. Et PIERRE-JACQUES-FRANÇOIS-HONORÉ, qui ſuit;

XII. PIERRE-JACQUES-FRANÇOIS-HONORÉ DE BARBANÇOIS, Chevalier, Seigneur de Villegongis, Chezelles, Vimeuil, & autres Terres en Berry, de Montmarin, Courcelles-le-Roi en Gâtinois, &c., ancien Capitaine d'Infanterie au Régiment de Dauphiné, & Chevalier de Saint-Louis, avait épouſé, par contrat du 27 Mai 1716, *Marie-Jeanne de Marçai*, fille de *Louis*, Chevalier, Seigneur de Blaire, dont il eut entr'autres enfans:

XIII. LÉON-FRANÇOIS DE BARBANÇOIS, Chevalier, Seigneur de Villegongis, Chezelles, Vimeuil & autres Terres en Berry, Montmarin, Courcelles-le-Roi, &c., en Gâtinois, né le 17 Avril 1717, qui a été d'abord Page du Roi dans ſa Petite-Ecurie en 1732, d'où il a paſſé, en 1735, au Régiment des Gardes-Françoiſes, où il eſt depuis 1767 Capitaine avec Brevet & rang de Colonel d'Infanterie, grade auquel il eſt parvenu par ſon ſeul ſervice; il s'eſt trouvé en ladite qualité, le 27 Juin 1743, à la bataille de Dettingen, aux ſièges de Menin & d'Ypres en 1744, à celui de Tournay au commencement de 1745, & à la bataille de Fontenoy, le 11 Mai de cette année; a fait, avec ſon Corps, toutes les Campagnes de Flandres; a été reçu Chevalier de Saint-Louis en 1747, s'eſt trouvé au ſiège de Maeſtricht en 1748, a fait la Campagne de Weſtphalie en 1762, & s'eſt trouvé, le 25

Tome II.

Août de cette année, à la Bataille de Gruningen.

Ce fut en conſidération de ſes ſervices, & de ceux de ſes ancêtres, que le Roi érigea, en ſa faveur, la Terre de Villegongis en Berry, & lieux en dépendans, en Marquiſat, ſous le nom de *Barbançois-Villegongis*, par Lettres-Patentes données à Marly au mois de Mars 1767, qui furent enregiſtrées au Parlement de Paris le 18 Mai 1768. Il avoit épouſé, par contrat du 6 Août 1754, *Louiſe-Hélène le Féron*, dite *Mademoiſelle de Savigny*, qui fut préſentée le 28 Avril 1765, & mourut à Villegongis le 23 Mars 1767. Elle étoit fille & ſeptième enfant de *Nicolas le Féron*, Chevalier, Seigneur d'Orville & de Louvres en Pariſis, Conſeiller du Roi en ſes Conſeils, & Préſident en la première Chambre des Enquêtes du Parlement de Paris, & de *Jeanne-Louiſe-Mélanie Berger*. Les enfans iſſus de ce mariage ſont:

1. CHARLES-HÉLION, Chevalier, né le 28 Août 1760, dit *le Comte de Barbançois-Villegongis*;

2. HECTOR-LOUIS, Chevalier, né le 18 Septembre 1763, reçu Chevalier de Malte de minorité en la Langue d'Auvergne, par bref du 1ᵉʳ Avril 1764, prorogé par autre du 11 Janvier 1766, & réintégré par autre du 21 Août 1769, appelé *le Chevalier de Barbançois-Villegongis*;

3. MARGUERITE-LOUISE, née le 5 Décembre 1755, dite *Mademoiſelle de Barbançois*;

4. MÉLANIE-HÉLÈNE, née le 29 Septembre 1756, dite *Mademoiſelle de Villegongis*;

5. GABRIELLE-CLAIRE-CHARLOTTE, née le lundi 31 Juillet 1758, dite *Mademoiſelle de Chezelles*, & morte le 13 Avril 1760;

6. Et GABRIELLE-MARIE, née le 27 Janvier 1763, dite *Mademoiſelle de Courcelles*.

BRANCHE
des Seigneurs DE DORNE, *iſſue de celle des Seigneurs* DE SARZAI.

XI. FRANÇOIS DE BARBANÇOIS, dit *le jeune*, Chevalier, né le 4 Décembre 1665, fut reçu Chevalier de Malte & Page du Grand-Maître le 15 Avril 1680; eut en partage les Terres & Seigneuries de Dorne, Arrivolle, Barodrais, &c., & s'établit en Bourbonnois; fut Capitaine de Dragons, & Lieutenant des Gardes de Son Alteſſe Royale Monſeigneur le Duc d'ORLÉANS, Régent du Royaume; & s'allia, 1° par contrat du 17 Juillet 1703, avec *Marie-Anne de Réfuge*, fille de *Pompone*

T

Seigneur de Villevault, & de *Françoife d'El-bene*, de laquelle il n'eut point d'enfans; & 2° par contrat du 7 Juillet 1706, avec *Catherine de Chafpoux-de-Verneuil*, fille de *Jacques*, Ecuyer, Seigneur de Verneuil, Confeiller du Roi, Tréforier de France, Honoraire au Bureau des Finances à Tours, & de *Claire Renaudot*. De ce dernier mariage font nés :

1. FRANÇOIS-HÉLION, Chevalier, baptifé le 28 Août 1710, & reçu Page du Roi dans fa Grande-Ecurie le 23 Avril 1725, d'après fes preuves de nobleffe remontées par titres à HÉLION DE BARBANÇOIS, fon cinquième ayeul, & citées dans l'*Armorial de France*, reg. I, part. I, p. 48. Il fut tué le 27 Juin 1743, à la bataille de Dettingen, Capitaine au Régiment de Dauphiné, Infanterie ;
2. EUSÈBE, qui fuit ;
3. Et CLAIRE-CHARLOTTE, laquelle vivoit encore fans alliance en 1758.

XII. EUSÈBE DE BARBANÇOIS, Ier du nom, connu fous le nom de *Comte de Sarzai*, Chevalier, Seigneur de Dorne, Arrivollé, Barodrais, &c., eft aujourd'hui Chevalier de Saint-Louis, & ancien Capitaine d'Infanterie. Il a de *N.... le Bouché :*

XIII. EUSÈBE DE BARBANÇOIS, IIe du nom, Chevalier, qui a d'abord été élevé Page du Roi dans fa Grande-Ecurie, & eft Lieutenant de Cavalerie au Régiment de Royal-Pologne.

BRANCHE
des Seigneurs DE CHARON, *iffue de celle*
des Seigneurs DE SARZAI.

V. ANTOINE DE BARBANÇOIS, quatrième fils de JEAN, Damoifeau, Seigneur de Sarzai, de Charon, & de douze autres Terres, & d'*Ifabeau du Puy-de-Vatan*, fa feconde femme, eut en partage la Seigneurie de Charon & autres Terres, par le teftament de fon père, du 12 Septembre 1476. Il avoit, par fon teftament du 7 Juillet 1494, inftitué pour fon héritier, LÉON DE BARBANÇOIS, fon neveu, à la charge qu'il renonceroit aux fucceffions de fes père & mère, au profit de JEAN & de FRANÇOIS DE BARBANÇOIS, fes frères; & fondé en l'Eglife Paroiffiale de Maleret, une Chapelle en l'honneur de *Saint-Antoine*, fon Patron, laquelle il dota de 30 liv. de rentes; mais ce teftament n'eut point lieu; car, ayant époufé, le 29 Janvier 1499, *Marie de Bridiers*, il fut annulé par la naiffance de :

VI. JEAN DE BARBANÇOIS, Chevalier, Seigneur de Charon, lequel affifta au Procès-verbal de rédaction de la Coutume de Berry en 1539 & fut un des dix Gentilshommes élus pour faire Remontrances pour le fecond Etat. Il avoit époufé *Bertrande de Cluys*, qui le rendit père de :

1. CLAUDE, qui fuit ;
2. Et MARGUERITE, mariée, par contrat du 15 Octobre 1554, avec *Claude de Mauffabré*, Ecuyer, Seigneur de la Sobardière.

VII. CLAUDE DE BARBANÇOIS, Chevalier, Seigneur de Charon, &c., fut d'abord Enfeigne de la Compagnie de M. le Duc DE MONTPENSIER, puis Gentilhomme ordinaire de la Chambre du Roi, & Chevalier de fon Ordre. Il époufa, par contrat du 11 Mai 1569, *Marguerite de Bridiers*, dont il eut :

VIII. LOUIS DE BARBANÇOIS, Chevalier, Seigneur de Charon, &c., qui fut Gentilhomme ordinaire de la Chambre du Roi, & Capitaine d'une Compagnie de Chevaux-Légers. Il avoit époufé, par contrat du 17 Juillet 1607, *Edmée de Bourges*, dont il laiffa entr'autres enfans :

IX. SYLVAIN DE BARBANÇOIS, Chevalier, Seigneur de Charon, lequel fut Guidon de la Compagnie des Gens-d'armes de M. le Prince. Il époufa, le 13 Juin 1634, *Marguerite Bertrand*, dont il laiffa :

1. FRANÇOIS, Chevalier, Seigneur de Charon, qui mourut fans poftérité. Il avoit époufé, par contrat du 18 Octobre 1660, *Marie de Chamborant* ;
2. & 3. JEAN & LOUIS, tous deux Chevaliers de Malte ;
4. Et GUY, Chevalier, Comte des Roches, Capitaine des Gardes du Grand CONDÉ, mort le 9 Janvier 1682, fans poftérité de *Marie-Françoife de Bigny*, remariée avec *Henri*, Palatin de *Dio de Montperroux*, Comte de Breffe. Elle vivoit encore en 1692, & étoit fille de *Louis-Armand de Bigny*, Comte d'Aifnay, employé, le 1er Octobre 1667, au rang des Nobles d'extraction de la Généralité de Bourges, & d'*Ifabelle de Château-Bodeau*.

Les armes : *de fable, à trois têtes de léopard d'or, arrachées & lampaffées de gueules, & pofées 2 & 1*. Supports : *deux licornes d'argent*. Cimier : *une licorne de même naiffante du cafque*, & *couronne de Marquis*.

La branche aînée a pour armes : *écartelé, au 1 d'argent, à trois chevrons de gueules*, qui eft du Pleffis-Richelieu ; *au 2 burelé d'ar-*

gent & d'azur de 10 *pièces*, qui eſt de Lezai-Luſignem; au 3 *plein d'hermines*, qui eſt du Rieux; & au 4 *de gueules, à neuf molettes d'éperons d'argent poſées en bannière*, qui eſt de Neuchèze; & fur le tout, de la Maiſon de BARBANÇOIS.

BARBANÇON, famille dont la branche aînée a été fondue dans la Maiſon de *Ligne*. Une autre branche, par un mariage avec l'héritière de *Werchin*, prit le nom & les armes: *d'azur, ſemé de billettes d'argent, au lion de même, brochant ſur le tout*, & ſe fondit dans *Melun-Epinoy*; & la dernière branche de BARBANÇON s'éteignit dans la Maiſon *du Prat*, dont le gendre du Maréchal de *Maubourg* porta le titre de *Comte de Barbançon*. La branche des Princes de BARBANÇON a été formée par

ROBERT DE LIGNE, ſecond fils de JEAN DE LIGNE, Baron de Barbançon, premier Prince d'Arenberg. Voyez LIGNE.

La ſubſtitution du nom & des armes de BARBANÇON a été faite à FRANÇOIS DU PRAT, d'abord appelé *Chevalier de Nantouillet*, puis Comte de BARBANÇON, par LOUIS DE BARBANÇON, Seigneur, Marquis de Cany & autres Terres en Picardie, qui étoit frère de ſa biſayeule paternelle, & le dernier mâle de cette illuſtre Maiſon.

Il y a en Berry une autre famille du nom de BARBANÇON.

Les armes de BARBANÇON: *d'argent, à trois lions de gueules, couronnés & armés d'or.*

* BARBANTANE, Terre & Seigneurie ſituée en Provence, Dioceſe d'Avignon, qui eſt aujourd'hui poſſédée par *Paul-François de Puget-Deſcapaſſolle-de-Réal*. Voyez PUGET.

BARBARIGO, famille originaire de Veniſe, qui a donné pluſieurs Cardinaux, ſçavoir: MARC-ANTOINE; GRÉGOIRE, Cardinal, Evêque de Padoue, mort en odeur de ſainteté, le 19 Juin 1697; & JEAN-FRANÇOIS, Cardinal & auſſi Evêque de Padoue, né le 25 Avril 1658, mort à Padoue le 26 Janvier 1730.

BARBARO. Cette ancienne & illuſtre Maiſon, l'une des plus diſtinguées de Veniſe, portoit anciennement pour armes: *d'azur, à trois roſes d'or, poſées* 2 & 1. De cette famille étoit MARC BARBARO, Provéditeur de l'Armée Vénitienne envoyée par le Sénat contre les Infidèles, qui occupoient la Terre Sainte l'an 1123; lequel fut attaqué par un grand nombre de Vaiſſeaux de l'armée du Calife d'Egypte, où il perdit, dans le combat, le pavillon ou l'étendard de ſon vaiſſeau, & tua le Capitaine d'une galère des ennemis, dont il ſe rendit maître. Il déploya la toile du turban de ce Capitaine, &, s'étant ſervi d'un des bras qu'il lui avoit coupé, pour faire un cercle de ſang ſur cette toile, il en fit le pavillon de ſon vaiſſeau, marqué de ce *cyclamor*, & le retint pour armes, que ſes deſcendans ont conſervées & continuent de porter, qui ſont: *d'argent à un cercle* ou *cyclamor de gueules*. Cette action eſt peinte dans la ſalle du *Scrutin*, à Veniſe, de la main de Santo-Peranda. (Extrait tiré du P. Meneſtrier, Jéſuite, édition de 1679, in-12, pag. 536 & 537.)

BARBAZAN. Voici une Maiſon ſi ancienne qu'on n'en peut parler que confuſément, ſans même en pouvoir donner la généalogie; elle tire ſon origine du pays de Bigorre.

AYMERY DE BARBAZAN, Chevalier, fleuriſſoit ſous le règne de PHILIPPE *le Bel*, & fut employé par GASTON, Ier du nom, Comte de Foix, & MARGUERITE, Vicomteſſe de Béarn, ſa mère, l'an 1311, pour recevoir en leurs noms les Villes & Châteaux de la Baronie de Cachalon, & pays adjacens.

MENAUD DE BARBAZAN, Chevalier, ſe trouve peu de tems après, auquel le Roi PHILIPPE *le Long* donna, l'an 1317, 120 livres de rente, en hommage ſur Beaumarchez, & au même tems ARNAUD DE BARBAZAN étoit Evêque de Pampelune, au Royaume de Navarre.

GUILLEM DE BARBAZAN épouſa, en 1326 *Mabile de Montlezun,* fille d'*Arnaud-Guillem de Montlezun*, Comte de Pardiac, & de *Giraude de Biran*.

ARNAUD-GUILLEM, Seigneur de BARBAZAN, fut marié 1º à *Simonne de Lavedan*; & 2º à *Marguerite d'Andouins*. Il eut du premier lit:

NAVARRE DE BARBAZAN, morte avant ſon père. Elle avoit épouſé, *Guillaume-Raymond de l'Eſcur*, Chevalier.

Du ſecond lit vint:

JEANNE DE BARBAZAN, qui ſurvécut peu de tems à ſon père. Elle mourut ſans lignée.

THIBAUD DE BARBAZAN, frère puîné d'ARNAUD-GUILLEM, Chevalier, Seigneur de MAR-

ceillan, au Comté de Fezenſac, ſe rendit célèbre ſous les Rois PHILIPPE DE VALOIS, JEAN &
CHARLES V, & fut, l'an 1340, nommé Capitaine & Gouverneur de la Ville de Bazas, puis
Sénéchal de Carcaſſonne l'an 1378. Il eut:

MENAUD DE BARBAZAN, qui, après la mort de
ſa couſine JEANNE, plaida pour la Terre de
BARBAZAN, contre les enfans de *Guillaume-
Raymond de l'Eſcur*, & par Arrêt de l'an
1406, la moitié lui en fut adjugée. Il eut:

1. ARNAUD-GUILLEM, qui ſuit;
2. Et JEAN, mort avant ſon père, laiſſant pour
   enfans: LÉONNET, & OUDINE, femme du
   Seigneur de *Faudoas*.

ARNAUD-GUILLEM, Seigneur de BARBAZAN,
rendit de ſi bons & utiles ſervices au Roi CHAR-
LES VII, qu'il le fit ſon premier Chambellan,
Lieutenant-Général au pays & Comté de
Champagne. Il mourut en combattant vaillamment à la bataille de Belleville, près Nancy, l'an 1432. Il eut pour femme *Sybille de
Montaut*, qui lui donna une fille, JEANNE DE
BARBAZAN, mariée à *Jean*, Comte d'*Eſtrac*.
Après la mort d'icelui, *Beraud*, Seigneur
de *Faudoas*, fils d'OUDINE DE BARBAZAN, ſa
ſœur, fondé ſur les ſubſtitutions faites par
MENAUD DE BARBAZAN, ſon ayeul, intenta procès pour la ſucceſſion du défunt; & par Arrêt du Parlement obtint, entr'autres Seigneuries, celle de BARBAZAN, dont il prit le nom;
l'an 1442 il fut pourvu de l'Office de Sénéchal d'Agénois, & eut pour femme *Annette
de Billy*, dont:

1. JEAN, qui ſuit;
2. Et ISABEAU DE FAUDOAS, dite de *Barbazan*,
   femme, l'an 1459, *de Pierre de Montmorin*, Seigneur de Saint-Herem.

JEAN, Seigneur de BARBAZAN, eut pour fils
BERAUD, Seigneur & Baron des Baronies de
Faudoas, de Barbazan & de Montagut; lequel épouſa *Jeanne de Cardeillac*, dont naquit une fille unique :

CATHERINE DE BARBAZAN, Dame de tous ces
lieux. En elle prit fin cette grande & ancienne Maiſon de BARBAZAN. Elle épouſa, au Château de Faudoas, en 1517, *Antoine de Rochechouart*, Baron de Saint-Amand, Sénéchal de Toulouſe.

Les armes : *d'azur, à la croix d'or.*

BARBEAU, en Provence : *coupé d'argent
& de gueules, le premier chargé de 3 roſes
de gueules, 1 & 2, & le deuxième de deux
barbaux affrontés d'or, & mis en chevron.*

* BARBÉE, Terre & Seigneurie ſur le
Loir, en Anjou, à deux lieues de la Flèche,
relevant en partie du Comté de Duretal, qui
a appartenu à ISABEAU DE BOURBON, Comteſſe
de Vendôme, & qui paſſa, à titre de ſucceſſion à ſon frère JEAN DE BOURBON, Comte de
la Marche & de Caſtres, qui la vendit, en
1379, à *N... de la Roche-Abillon*. Elle a été
depuis poſſédée long-tems par la Maiſon de
Montalais, d'où elle paſſa, dans le XVIe ſiècle, à *Geoffroy de Dureil*, & dans le XVIIe
à *Guillaume Gilles-de-la-Bérardière*, Capitaine de Cavalerie. Voyez GILLES-DE-
LA-BÉRARDIÈRE.

BARBEIRAC. Cette famille, originaire de
Saint-Martin de Caſtillon, en Provence, étoit
compriſe parmi la nobleſſe de cette Province
au commencement du XVIe ſiècle.

JEAN DE BARBEIRAC, Capitaine des Gardes
de M. le Maréchal de Damville, & Gouverneur du lieu & Château de Viens, fut tué au
ſervice du Roi, dans un combat livré contre
les ennemis de Sa Majeſté. Il avoit épouſé,
par contrat paſſé devant *Claude Lautier*,
Notaire à Saint-Martin de Caſtillon, le 12
Septembre 1573, *Marguerite Blain*, dont il
laiſſa:

HENRI, qui ſuit; HERCULE, JACQUES & PIERRE.

HENRI DE BARBEIRAC tranſigea avec ſes frères, le 24 Novembre 1621, par-devant *Raymond*, Notaire de Céreſte, par laquelle tranſaction HENRI fut mis en poſſeſſion des biens
de ſon père, moyennant une certaine ſomme
qu'il donna à ſes trois frères. Il teſta le 26
Mai 1662 par-devant *Vaſpaud*, Notaire à Céreſte. Il avoit épouſé, le 2 Juin 1624, par
contrat paſſé à Seine, *Julie de Buille*, fille du
Capitaine *Charles de Buille*, de la Ville de
Seine, & eut de ſon mariage:

1. JEAN, qui ſuit;
2. ANTOINE;
3. Et CHARLES, Docteur en Médecine à Montpellier, que ſon père inſtitua héritier. Il avoit
   épouſé, le 2 Mars 1656, par contrat paſſé
   devant *Pellerin*, Notaire à Montpellier,
   Catherine de Bracis.

JEAN DE BARBEIRAC, Avocat en la Cour, Juge de la Baronie de Céreſte, teſta le 22 Septembre 1674, à Céreſte, en faveur de ſes deux
fils, HENRI, qui ſuit, & ANTOINE, auxquels,
en cas de décès ſans enfans, il ſubſtitua ſes
deux frères, l'un établi à Béziers & l'autre à
Montpellier.

Henri de Barbéirac, Juge de Cérefte, fut maintenu dans fa nobleffe par les Commiffaires du Roi députés pour la vérification des titres de Nobleffe, le 26 Août 1716. Il époufa, par contrat paffé le 23 Février 1696, par-devant *Chartrons*, Notaire à Locmaria, *Anne d'Ailhaud*, & laiffa de fon mariage :

Henri de Barbeirac, qui refte feul de cette branche, établie à Cérefte.

Les armes : *d'argent, au cheval-barbe de fable courant ; au chef d'azur, chargé d'un croiffant d'argent, accofté de deux étoiles d'or.* (Mémoire envoyé).

* BARBEN, Terre & Seigneurie en Provence, Diocèfe d'Aix, qui fut acquife, en 1472, du Roi René, Comte de Provence, par *Jean de Forbin*, IIe du nom, arrière-petit-fils de *Pierre de Forbin*, & de *Françoife d'Agoult*. Voyez FORBIN.

BARBERE, en Bretagne : *de fable, à une fafce de gueules, chargée d'une étoile d'or, & accompagnée de trois trèfles de même,* 2 *en chef & 1 en pointe.*

BARBERIE-DE-SAINT-CONTEST, famille de Normandie, Généralité de Rouen.

Dominique-Claude Barberie, Seigneur de Saint-Conteft, mort Confeiller d'Etat ordinaire, après avoir été Maître des Requêtes, & Miniftre Plénipotentiaire au Traité de Bade, conclu le 7 Septembre 1714, a eu pour fils :

1. François-Dominique, Seigneur de la Chateigneraye, en Poitou, & autres Terres, né en Janvier 1701 ; D'abord reçu Confeiller au Parlement de Paris le 29 Décembre 1724, Maître des Requêtes le 24 Décembre 1728, nommé Intendant de Pau en 1737, & de Bourgogne en 1740 ; Ambaffadeur auprès des Etats-Généraux des Provinces-unies, le 16 Octobre 1749, Miniftre & Secrétaire-d'Etat des Affaires Etrangères le 11 Septembre 1751, mort à Verfailles le 24 Juillet 1754. Il avoit époufé, le 27 Septembre 1735, *Jeanne-Monique des Vieux*, morte le 1er Janvier 1746, fille de *Louis-Philippe des Vieux*, Fermier-Général, & fœur de *Philippe-Etienne des Vieux*, aujourd'hui Préfident en la première Chambre des Requêtes du Parlement de Paris. De ce mariage eft iffue :

   Marguerite-Marie-Louise-Victoire, née le 13 Mars 1738, devenue fille unique, par la mort, fans alliance, de fon frère. Elle a époufé, 1° le 6 Juin 1753, *Louis-*

Henri-Félix du Pleffis-Châtillon, Comte de Château-Meillant, Sous-Lieutenant des Chevaux-Légers d'Orléans, mort fans enfans le 25 Août 1754, âgé de 28 ans ; & 2° le 18 Mai 1756, *Charles-Louis-Jofeph-Alexandre de Canonville*, Marquis de Raffetot, Sous-Lieutenant des Chevaux-Légers Dauphin, & depuis Capitaine-Lieutenant des Chevaux-Légers de Berry ;

2. Et Henri-Louis, qui a été reçu Confeiller au Parlement de Paris le 16 Juillet 1731, Maître des Requêtes le 23 Décembre 1735, nommé Intendant de Limoges en 1743, & de Champagne en 1750, & appelé *Sieur de la Chateigneraye.*

Jacques de Barberie, frère de Dominique-Claude, Marquis de Courteilles, Confeiller-Honoraire au Parlement de Paris, Maître des Requêtes-Ordinaire-Honoraire de l'Hôtel du Roi, ci-devant Intendant des Généralités d'Alençon & de Berry, mourut le 17 Avril 1731. Il avoit époufé *Elifabeth Doumengin*, fille de *Jacques Doumengin*, Seigneur d'Elize, dont il eut :

Jacques-Dominique Barberie de Courteille, Confeiller d'État, ci-devant Ambaffadeur de France auprès du corps Helvétique, aujourd'hui l'un des fix Intendans des Finances, qui époufa 1° *N... de Savalette de Magnanville ;* & 2° le 20 Mars 1746, *Marie-Madeleine-Mélanie Fyot*, fille de *Jean-Philippe Fyot de la Marche*, premier Préfident du Parlement de Bourgogne, & de *Jeanne-Marguerite Baillet*. Du premier lit eft iffue :

   Madeleine-Mélanie-Henriette, mariée, par contrat figné le 3 Octobre 1764 (mariage célébré le 10), à *Aimeri-Louis Roger*, Comte de *Rochechouart-Faudoas.*

Et Michel-Antoine de Barberie-de-Courteille, Abbé Commendataire de l'Abbaye de Beaulieu, Ordre de Saint-Auguftin, Diocèfe de Boulogne, depuis le mois de Novembre 1730.

Il y a un Marquis *de Saint-Conteft* qui, étant Capitaine dans Royal-Dragons, a acheté la feconde Cornette des Moufquetaires-Noirs en Avril 1766.

Les armes : *d'azur, à trois têtes d'aigle d'or, arrachées,* 2 & 1.

BARBERIN, Maifon originaire de Saintonge, de laquelle étoit Julie-Célefte Barberin-de-Reignac, morte à Verfailles, le 20 Avril 1754, âgée de 58 ans, époufe de *Char-*

les-Yves-Thibaut, Comte *de la Rivière.*

LOUIS DE BARBERIN, Seigneur, Comte de Reignac, Maréchal-de-Camp, Commandant au Neuf-Brifack, en Alface, eft mort en 17..., & MARIE-LOUISE DE BARBERIN, fa fille & unique héritière, veuve le 1er Mars 1740, de *Charles-François du Campet*, Seigneur, Comte de Saujon, en Aunis, Brigadier de Cavalerie, & Enfeigne des Gardes-du-Corps, s'eft remariée, en Novembre 1747, à *Jofeph-Augufte*, Comte de *Laval-Montmorency.*

Les armes: *d'azur, à trois abeilles d'or*, 2 & 1.

BARBERINI, Maifon originaire d'Italie, qui a donné un Pape & plufieurs Cardinaux. Le premier qui fe retira en France fut THA-DÉE BARBERINI, Prince de Paleftrine & Préfet de Rome. Il mourut à Paris en 1647. Il étoit frère aîné d'ANTOINE BARBERINI, Cardinal du Saint-Siège, Archevêque & Duc de Reims, Evêque de Paleftrine, Pair & Grand-Aumônier de France, né le 5 Août 1608. Quelques démêlés que lui & fa famille eurent avec le Pape Innocent X, avant fa promotion à la Papauté, le fit réfoudre de fe retirer d'Italie & de paffer en France, où il fut comblé d'honneurs & d'avantages: il mourut à fon Château de Némy, à fix lieues de Rome, le 3 Août 1671.

URBAIN DE BARBERINI, Prince de Paleftrine, &c., Grand d'Efpagne, né en 1666, Chevalier de la Toifon d'Or, en 1687, mourut le 28 Septembre 1722, fans poftérité de trois femmes qu'il eut. Voyez Moréri.

Les armes: *d'azur, à trois abeilles d'or*, 2 & 1.

BARBESI, en Bourgogne: *d'argent, à la croix de fable chargée de 5 befans d'or.*

BARBETS: *d'argent, au bœuf paffant de gueules, au chef de même, chargé d'une clef du champ, mife en fafce.*

BARBEY, en Normandie, Généralité de Rouen. Suivant l'*Armorial de France*, PIERRE BARBEY, Ecuyer, Vicomte de Fécamp, Lieutenant-Général en l'Election de Montivilliers, époufa, vers 1620, *Sufanne de Morant*, dont:

CHARLES BARBEY, Sieur de Bofc-Roger, Sénéchal de Fécamp, marié, le 4 Avril 1655, avec *Adrienne de Rouffel-de-Goderville.*

Les armes: *coupé, au 1 d'azur & d'or, de fix pièces; au 2 de gueules, au lion d'or.*

BARBEY, en Baffe-Normandie: *d'azur, au chevron d'argent, accompagné de trois dards de même, la pointe en bas*, 2 & 1.

BARBEY, Seigneur de Fontenailles, en Normandie, Généralité de Caen, famille annoblie en 1594, qui porte pour armes: *d'azur, au chevron d'or; accompagné de trois fers de lance de même, ceux du chef renverfés.*

BARBEZIÈRES (DE), Seigneur de Chemerault, de la Roche: *d'argent, à une fafce de cinq lofanges & deux demi-lofanges de gueules*, aliàs *cinq fufées de gueules.*

BARBEZIÈRES, même famille que la précédente: *écartelé, au 1 d'argent; au 2 d'azur, à une croix denchée d'argent; au 3 d'hermines, au chef de gueules, & au 4 d'or, à l'aigle éployée de gueules*, aliàs *de fable.*

BARBEZIEUX, Seigneurie en Saintonge, que poffédoit *Antoine de la Rochefoucauld*, mort en 1557, Général des Galères. Il fit la branche des Seigneurs de BARBEZIEUX. Voyez ROCHEFOUCAULD.

BARBEZIEUX, en Aquitaine: *burelé d'argent & d'azur, à trois chevrons de gueules, brochant fur le tout.*

BARBEZIEUX, en Comté: *d'or, à l'écuffon d'azur en cœur.*

BARBIER, Seigneur de Vannerelle, en Normandie, Généralité d'Alençon, famille maintenue dans fa nobleffe le 31 Août 1667, qui porte: *d'azur, au chevron d'or, accompagné de trois trèfles de même, 2 en chef & 1 en pointe.*

BARBIER: *d'azur, au chevron d'or, accompagné de trois rofes de même, 2 en chef & 1 en pointe; au chef d'argent, chargé d'un lion de fable paffant.*

BARBIER, Seigneur de la Rivière, famille dont il y a eu un Evêque de Langres: *d'azur, au chevron d'or, accompagné de trois croix au pied fiché de même, 2 en chef & 1 en pointe.*

BARBIER (LE), Seigneur de Kerjan, Tamelin, Kercoent, &c., à Léon, en Bretagne: *d'argent, à deux fafces de fable.* Devife: *fur ma vie.*

BARBIER (LE), famille de Beauce, dont une fille a été reçue à Saint-Cyr en 1734. Voy. l'*Armorial de France*, reg. I, p. 49.

Les armes : *d'argent, à trois mains dextres de fable appaumées & pofées 2 & 1.*

BARBIER: *d'azur, au cygne d'argent.*

BARBIN, en Champagne, famille qui vient d'un BARBIN, Maître des Requêtes fous le Roi JEAN en 1360, dont le fils fut Procureur-Général du Parlement. Le petit-fils du Procureur-Général, CHRISTOPHE-BARBIN, a été Gouverneur de Melun vers 1530. Il a laiffé de fon mariage :

> DREUX BARBIN, Commandant d'un bataillon de la Marine, père de MATHIAS, qui fuit;
> Et CLAUDE, Surintendant de la Maifon de la Reine.

MATHIAS, Baron de Broyes, a été Gentilhomme de la Chambre, Confeiller d'Etat d'Epée, & Gouverneur de Corbie. Il a eu pour fils :

HENRI, Baron de Broyes, Commandant d'un bataillon de Picardie, qui a laiffé :

> Le Comte de Broyes, qui n'a eu que deux filles;
> Le Chevalier de Broyes, mort fans poftérité;
> Une fille, mariée au Marquis *d'Anglure-Savigny;*
> Et CLAUDE-ANTOINE de Broyes, Seigneur de Dampierre & d'Autry, marié avec *Françoife Boileau,* dont:
>
>> JEAN-ARMAND BARBIN, Comte de Broyes, Baron d'Autry, marié à Paris, en la Paroiffe de Saint-Nicolas-des-Champs, le 10 Avril 1747, avec *Louife de Mafcrany,* fille de *Louis de Mafcrany,* Seigneur, Comte de Château-Chignon, d'Hermé, de Villiers, de Servolle & autres lieux, Maître des Requêtes Honoraire, & de *Marie Picot-de-Clorivière.* (*Mercure de France* du mois de Juillet 1747, page 202.)

Les armes : *d'azur, au chevron d'or, accompagné de deux rofes d'argent en chef, & d'un lion d'or en pointe.*

BARBOYERS: *écartelé, au 1 d'argent; au 2 d'azur, à une croix denchée d'argent; au 3 d'hermines, au chef de gueules; & au 4 d'or, à l'aigle éployée de gueules,* aliàs *de fable.*

BARBU (LE), au Quiliou, en Cornouaille: *d'or, à un fautoir d'azur péri en trèfle.*

BARBY: *écartelé, aux 1 & 4 de gueules, à la rofe d'argent; aux 2 & 3 d'argent, à l'aigle de gueules.*

BARBY: *d'argent, à..... à la bande d'or, brochant fur le tout.*

* BARCELONE, Ville de Catalogne, au Royaume d'Efpagne, avec titre de Comté : fes Gouverneurs, nommés *Comtes,* fe rendirent Souverains fous CHARLES-*le-Chauve* en 873 ou en 884, fous CHARLES-*le-Gros.* Ils ont commencé à WIFRED, I.er du nom, & ont fini à RAYMOND BERENGER V, mort fans poftérité en 1166.

D'eux font fortis les anciens Comtes d'*Utgel,* les Comtes de *Béfalu,* les Comtes de *Cerdagne,* & Rois d'Aragon. Voyez Moréri.

BARCILON, en Provence. I. Noble THOMAS DE BARCILON, qui vivoit à Barcelone en 1330, eft la tige de cette famille. Il avoit époufé *Marie de Marquet,* de laquelle il eut:

> 1. JACQUES, qui fuit ;
> 2. Et ARNAUD, qui embraffa l'Etat Eccléfiaftique; il gagna les bonnes grâces de ROBERT D'ANJOU, qu'il fuivit en Provence, lorfqu'il en fut fait Comte, & devint Evêque de Vence en 1337.

II. JACQUES DE BARCILON, qui fuivit fon frère, tefta le 18 Juillet 1359 (*Valentin,* Notaire). Il avoit époufé, dans la Ville de Vence, le 8 Octobre 1328, *Jacquette Robion,* héritière des Co-Seigneurs de Saint-Paul-lez-Vence, & laiffa:

III. FRANÇOIS DE BARCILON, qui, de *Jeanne de Lafcaris-de-Caftelar,* eut:

> 1. PIERRE, I.er du nom, auteur des branches éteintes des Seigneurs de *Mauvans,* de *Mazaugues* & de *Verrayon;*
> 2. Et autre PIERRE, qui fuit.

IV. PIERRE DE BARCILON, II.e du nom, auteur de la branche des Seigneurs de *Roquefort* & de *Québris,* époufa, en 1425, *Philippe de Cairace,* de la Ville de Nice, dont :

V. GEORGES DE BARCILON, qui laiffa de *Marguerite Adorne:*

VI. GEORGES DE BARCILON, II.e du nom, père de:

VII. PIERRE DE BARCILON, III.e du nom, marié, en 1353, avec *Honorée de Mauvans.* Il eut pour fils:

VIII. PAUL DE BARCILON, marié à *Maguelone de Barcilon-Mauvans,* fa coufine, de laquelle il eut:

IX. CLAUDE DE BARCILON, marié, le 5 Mars 1628, avec *Lucrèce de Grimaldi-Levins,* des Comtes de *Beuil,* dont:

1. Scipion-Joseph, qui fuit;
2. Et Marie, alliée, en 1653, avec noble *Pierre de Flotte*, Seigneur de Québris.

X. Scipion-Joseph de Barcilon, Seigneur de Roquefort, époufa, en 1651, *Marguerite de Reymond d'Eoux*, dont:
1. Claude, qui fuit;
2. & 3. Et deux filles, mariées dans les Maifons de *Villeneuve-Tourettes*, & de *Clary-d'Ubraye*.

XI. Claude de Barcilon, IIe du nom, Seigneur de Québris & de Roquefort, marié avec Mademoifelle de *Sabran-Baudinard*, a eu entr'autres enfans:
1. Elzeard, qui fuit;
2. Et Jean-Gaspard, reçu Chevalier de Malte en 1732.

XII. Elzeard de Barcilon, Seigneur de Québris, a des enfans de fon mariage avec *Anne-Urfule d'Aftier*, fille de *Nicolas*, Tréforier-Général de France, & d'*Anne-Urfule de Maifredy*.

La Branche de *Mauvans* a donné deux Confeillers à la Cour des Comptes de Provence, & un Chevalier de l'Ordre de Malte en 1643. On trouve dans les Archives du Roi, que Bertrand Barcilon fit hommage de la Terre d'Aubéran en 1511.

Les armes: *d'azur, à deux fautoirs alaifés ou raccourcis d'or, rangés en fafce, & furmontés d'une étoile de même, pofée au milieu du chef,*

BARCOS (de), Seigneur du Planty: *parti d'or & de gueules, au fautoir breteffé de l'un en l'autre.*

BARDE (la). Jean de la Barde, Confeiller d'Etat, Ambaffadeur de France en Suiffe, obtint que la Seigneurie de Marolles, en Gâtinóis, fut érigée en Marquifat, par Lettres du mois de Juin 1661, enregiftrées au Parlement le 10 Décembre fuivant, & en la Chambre des Comptes le 23 Avril 1663. Il mourut en Juillet 1692, âgé de 90 ans, ayant eu de *Marie Regnouard*, morte en 1674, entr'autres enfans: Claude de la Barde, Marquis de Marolles, Confeiller au Parlement, décédé le 1er Août 1671, fans poftérité; & Anne-Marie de la Barde, femme de *Jean de Brion*, Marquis de Combroude, Baron de Salvert, Confeiller au Parlement; leurs enfans, fubftitués au nom & armes de la Barde furent: Jean-Antoine, mort fans poftérité le 15 Décembre 1708; & Noel-François, qui, deftiné à l'état

eccléfiaftique, le quitta, & devint Marquis de Combroude & de Marolles; il a époufé, le 22 Août 1714, *Marie-Agnès de Pommereu*, dont:
N... de Brion de la Barde, Marquis de Marolles, qui a époufé la veuve du Préfident *le Couturier;*
Et N.... de Brion de la Barde, qui eft au fervice.

Les armes: *coupé d'azur fur or, l'azur chargé d'une molette d'éperon d'or, & l'or de trois coquilles de fable, 2 & 1.*

BARDEL, en Provence: *d'azur, au ferpent tortillé en rond ou en colimaçon d'argent, au chef de gueules, chargé de trois étoiles d'or.*

BARDEL, en Dauphiné: *de gueules, au ferpent ondoyant & tortillé d'argent, mis en pal, couronné d'or à cinq rayes.*

BARDET: *de gueules, à la croix ancrée d'argent.*

BARDIN, en Dauphiné: *d'azur, à la bande d'or, chargée de trois rofes de gueules.*

BARDIN: *de finople, à trois dauphins d'argent, 2 & 1.*

BARDON, en Périgord, famille qui a été maintenue dans fa nobleffe par Jugement rendu à Périgueux, le 26 Janvier 1667, par M. de Montozon, Commiffaire fubdélégué de M. Pellot, Intendant de cette Généralité, par lequel il donna acte à François-Louis Bardon, Seigneur de Ségonzac, de la repréfentation qu'il avoit faite des mêmes titres que ceux qui font énoncés dans cette preuve pour la juftification de fa nobleffe.

Aymar de Bardon, fils de noble Jean de Bardon, & de noble *Marguerite Marqueiffat*, époufa, par contrat du 8 Mars 1518 (reçu par *Duval*, Notaire à Migno-le-Folquier), noble *Bernine de Fenet*. Dece mariage vint:

Geoffroy de Bardon, marié, par contrat du 16 Janvier 1537 (reçu par *Salnauds*, Notaire à Migno-le-Folquier, dans la Paroiffe de Luffac, en Sarladois), avec *Marguerite de Charbonnière*, fille de noble *Jean de Charbonnière*, & de N... *Comteffe Maffaige*. De ce mariage vint:

Raymond de Bardon, qui époufa, par contrat du 4 Juillet 1572 (reçu par *Rodignac*, Notaire à Plas, en Périgord), *Madeleine Vigier;* elle tefta le 12 Février 1583, fit fes légataires Charles & Alix, fes enfans, & infti-

tua fon héritier univerfel MARC, fon fils aîné (acte reçu par *la Rarafe*, Notaire à Ségonzac). Elle étoit fille d'*Hélie Vigier*, Ecuyer,
Seigneur de Ségonzac, & d'*Ifabeau de Cha-
bans*. De ce mariage font iffus:

1. MARC, qui fuit;
2. CHARLES, Ecuyer;
3. Et ALIX BARDON.

MARC, Comte de BARDON, Chevalier, Seigneur de Caftel, de Bonnefons & de Ségonzac, eut une commiffion de Capitaine d'Infanterie dans le Régiment de Riberac, fignée
par le Roi le 18 Octobre 1615. Il fut taxé
pour fa part de la contribution au ban & à
l'arrière-ban de la Province de Périgord, à
la fomme de 100 livres, dont quittance lui fut
donnée, le 28 Juillet 1639, par le Commiffai-
re-Receveur de cette taxe, & fignée *de la
Contaudie*. Il obtint, au mois de Février
1623, des Lettres-Patentes, en forme de
Charte, par lefquelles le Roi érigea, en fa faveur, en titre de Baronie, la Terre & Seigneurie de *Ségonzac*, mouvante du Comté
de Périgord, tant en confidération des bons &
recommandables fervices qu'il avoit rendus au
voyage de Béarn, aux fièges de Saint-Jean
d'Angély, de Clairac, de Montravel & de
Tonneins, & pendant la rébellion de ceux
de la *Religion prétendue Réformée*, qu'en
reconnoiffance des fervices que fes ancêtres avoient rendus en plufieurs occafions
aux Rois prédéceffeurs de Sa Majefté. Ces
Lettres font fignées Louis, & fur le repli, par
le Roi, *Brulard*, fcellées en cire verte, & enregiftrées au Parlement de Bordeaux, le 27
Mai 1623. Dans des Lettres de *Committi-
mus*, obtenues le 9 Mai 1624, il eft qualifié
l'un des *Ecuyers* de la Grande-Ecurie de Sa
Majefté. Il tefta le 23 Juin 1646, fit fes légataires Dame *Finette de Belcier*, fa femme,
LOUIS-JACQUES, LOUIS-MADELEINE & MARGUE-
RITE BARDON, fes enfans, & inftitua fon héritier univerfel FRANÇOIS-LOUIS BARDON, fon
fils aîné. Cet acte eft figné *Ségonzac*. Il fe
maria, par contrat du 18 Septembre 1602,
reçu par *Combret*, Notaire à Caftillon-fur-
Dordogne, avec *Finette de Belcier*, Dame
de la Maifon noble de Labatut. Leurs enfans
furent:

1. FRANÇOIS-LOUIS, qui fuit;
2. LOUIS-JACQUES;
3. LOUIS-MADELEINE;
4. Et MARGUERITE BARDON.

Tome II.

FRANÇOIS-LOUIS BARDON, Chevalier, Seigneur & Baron de Ségonzac, eut une Commiffion de Capitaine d'Infanterie dans le Régiment de Cugnac, le 14 Mars 1635. Il tefta le 30 Janvier 1667; fit fes légataires,
LOUIS BARDON, FRANÇOIS-LOUIS-ARMAND, &
FRANÇOIS BARDON, fes enfans, & inftitua fon
héritier univerfel MARC, fon fils aîné (Acte
reçu par *Rey*, Notaire à Ségonzac). Il fe maria, par contrat du 22 Mai 1640 (reçu par
Rey, Notaire à Menfignac, en Périgord), à
Marguerite de Fayard, fille de Meffire
Antoine de Fayard, Seigneur de Menfignac & de Beaulieu, & de *Nicole de Montferrand*.

Leurs enfans furent:

1. MARC, qui fuit;
2. LOUIS, Seigneur de la Vergne;
3. FRANÇOIS-LOUIS-ARMAND;
4. Et FRANÇOIS BARDON.

MARC, Comte de BARDON, Chevalier, Seigneur & Baron de Ségonzac, fervit dans l'arrière-ban de la Nobleffe de Guyenne, fuivant
un certificat du 3 Juillet 1674, qui lui fut
donné par le *Maréchal d'Albret*, Gouverneur de cette Province. Il s'allia, par contrat du 11 Novembre 1671 (reçu par *de Pau-
ly*, Notaire à Plaffac, en Périgord), avec
Jeanne de la Cauffe, fille de Meffire *Louis
de la Cauffe*, Chevalier, Seigneur de Plaffac,
& de *Gabrielle de Mellet*. De ce mariage eft
forti:

FRANÇOIS-LOUIS BARDON-DE-SÉGONZAC, né le
11 Septembre 1672, duquel nous n'avons
pas la poftérité.

Il y a du nom de BARDON un Capitaine au
Régiment d'Aquitaine, Infanterie, Chevalier
de Saint-Louis.

Les armes: *d'or, à l'aigle de fable becquée & membrée de gueules, becquetant
la tête d'un barbeau de fable pofé en fafce,
& le tenant fous fes ferres; à une croifette
de gueules, pofée au canton dextre du chef;
cafque couronné d'un cercle de Baron.*

BARDON, en Bretagne: *de gueules, à 3
coquilles d'or, 2 & 1.*

BARDON, Seigneur de Parteville, de Belmont: *de fable, au bourdon d'or, pofé en
pal, chargé au milieu d'une coquille de même, & accofté en chef de deux molettes d'é-
peron, auffi de même.*

* BARDONENCHE, Maifon de Dauphi-

U

né, d'ancienne nobleffe & Chevalerie. La Vallée de *Bardonenche*, voifine de celle d'Oulx, vers les frontières de Piémont, a donné fon nom à cette Maifon, qui la poffédoit dès le XIe fiècle, fous la feule mouvance de l'Empire, dans le tems d'Anarchie, où, après la réunion du Royaume de Bourgogne à l'Empire, chaque Seigneur fe rendit indépendant dans fon canton; ce qui dura jufqu'à ce que les Dauphins, augmentant leur puiffance, foumirent peu à peu tous ces différens Seigneurs & les obligèrent à leur faire hommage. Les différentes branches de cette Maifon s'étant extrêmement multipliées, divifèrent la Vallée de *Bardonenche* en autant de Co-Seigneuries appelées *Pareries*: & on comptoit, en 1330, jufqu'à 30 Nobles de cette Maifon, demeurant dans la *Vallée*, & y poffédant fief & jurifdiction, dont ils firent hommage au Dauphin, qu'ils ne reconnurent Souverain que dans le XIVe fiècle. Le nom qui fe lit dans les anciens titres latins eft de *Bardonnenchia*: quand on écrivit les actes en françois, les mêmes fe nommèrent indifféremment *Bardonefche* ou *Bardonenche*. Le premier dont on ait connoiffance eft Pons de Bardonenche, témoin à une donation faite en 1078, au Monaftère d'Oulx. Pierre de Bardonenche eft préfent à la donation faite en 1119, par Amédée III, Comte de Savoie, au même Monaftère: ces actes font au Cartulaire d'Oulx. La filiation eft fuivie depuis:

I. Rodolphe de Bardonenche, qui fut témoin avec Hugues, fon fils, à une donation faite, en 1186, au Monaftère d'Oulx, par *Hugues*, Duc de Bourgogne, & Comte d'Albon, & par fa femme *Béatrix*, fille & héritière du Dauphin Guigues IV.

II. Hugues de Bardonenche eft dit fils de Rodolphe, dans l'acte ci-deffus. Il paroît comme caution avec Boniface, Pierre & Aynard de Bardonenche, dans un accord fait, en 1197, entre quelques particuliers & les Chanoines Réguliers d'Oulx. Il fut encore caution avec Aynard, fon fils, dans une vente que fit, en 1200, au Prévôt d'Oulx, l'Abbé de Saint-Juft-le-Suye & fon Chapitre. Cet Hugues, & Aynard, fon fils, vendirent, en 1202, au même Prévôt, la Vallée-Froide au prix de 1000 fols.

III. Aynard de Bardonenche, fils d'Hugues, felon les deux actes mentionnés, eft qua-

lifié *Chevalier*, dans l'hommage que lui rendit, le 9 des calendes de Novembre 1214, *Hugues Guers*, fils de *Raymond*, habitant à *Bardonenche*; il eft auffi qualifié *Chevalier* dans la tranfaction paffée le 2 des nones de Mars 1225, entre *Soffrey*, Evêque de Grenoble, *Guigues d'Albon*, & *Guiffrey de Salvain-de-Boiffieu*, & qui eft dans le Cartulaire de l'Eglife de Grenoble; & dans l'hommage que le Dauphin Guigues-André de Bourgogne fit à l'Evêque de Gap, en 1232. On connoît fon alliance par une donation qu'il fit en 1228, au Chapitre d'Oulx, de tout ce qu'il avoit dans la Vallée-Froide, ne s'y réfervant que les droits de juftice, les mines d'argent, & le quart des bêtes fauves qui s'y prendroient. Aynard de Bardonenche, Chevalier, & la Dame *de la Chambre*, fa femme, inveftiffent de cette donation *Gérente*, Prévôt d'Oulx. Aynard eut pour fils:

IV. Pierre de Bardonenche, Damoifeau, qualité que prenoient les fils de *Chevaliers*, qui fut témoin à l'hommage du Dauphin Guigues à l'Evêque de Gap en 1251. Il fit hommage, en 1252, au même Dauphin, fans reconnoître fa Terre, ainfi que s'exprime l'acte qui eft à la Chambre des Comptes de Grenoble, au regiftre *Probus*. Il eut pour fils:

1. Perceval, qui fuit;
2. Burnon, vivant en 1289, qui fut père d'Aynar & de Burnon II. Celui-ci eut Aynard, qui fut père de Burnon III, mort fans enfans; c'eft ce qu'on apprend de leurs reconnoiffances féodales jufqu'en 1413;
3. Mathieu, qui fut père de Jean, qui rendit hommage de la Co-Seigneurie de *Bardonenche* en 1318; & de François, Chevalier, qui eut de grands démêlés avec le Dauphin Humbert II, & fut dépouillé de tous fes biens. Il eut un fils nommé Hugues;
4. François, dont la poftérité finit en 1420, dans Jeanne, mariée à noble *Albert de Nefache* ou *Nafaiffe*;
5. Et Jean, qui eut auffi poftérité. Il fit plufieurs branches des Co-Seigneurs de *Bardonenche*. Plufieurs paffèrent en Piémont, qui touche cette *Vallée*, & prirent des alliances dans les Maifons les plus confidérables de Piémont & de Savoie, comme on peut le voir dans le *Pourpris Hiftorique* de Charles-Augufte de Sales, Evêque de Genève.

V. Perceval de Bardonenche, Bailli ou Gouverneur du Gapençois, vivoit en 1290, felon plufieurs actes de la même Chambre des

Comptes, aux regiſtres *Copiarum* dans le regiſtre *Probus*, Il vivoit en 1303, & eut pour fils:

VI. Pons de Bardonenche, qui vivoit en 1320, ſuivant les mêmes regiſtres où il eſt appelé quelquefois *Poncet*. Il eut pour fils:

1. Constant, qui ſuit;
2. Pierre, qui eſt qualifié *Damoiſeau* avec ſon frère Constant, & fils de Poncet dans l'acte d'échange qu'ils firent avec le Dauphin, le 13 Novembre 1333. Ils lui donnèrent les portions qu'ils avoient dans la *Vallée de Bardonenche*, qui étoient franches & indépendantes de toute ſujétion envers le Dauphin; & ce Prince leur donna la Seigneurie du *Percy* & du *Monétier* en Trièves, & des rentes au même lieu, & à Saint-Jean d'Hérant. Cet échange occaſionna le changement de domicile de la branche aînée, qui paſſa du Briançonnois au pays de Trièves, qu'elle a toujours habité depuis, & où elle a acquis de nouvelles Terres. Pierre fut tué à la bataille de Poitiers en 1356, & eut pour fils Léon, dont la fille Galliane, vendit, avec Borsac, ſon couſin, le quart du *Monétier du Percy*, en 1359; elle épouſa noble *François-du-Thau*;
3. Et Guillaume, auſſi appelé *Guillermet*, qui paſſa une reconnoiſſance au Dauphin en 1330, avec ſes frères, pour la Parerie de *Bardonenche*. Il la vendit en 1352 à Humbert, ancien Dauphin, alors Patriarche d'Alexandrie; c'eſt ce qui réſulte d'un hommage rendu le 13 Août 1352, au Dauphin Charles, par *Jeannon de Navaiſſe*, Damoiſeau, fils de *Lantelme*, qui rappelle auſſi l'hommage fait en 1214 à Aynard de Bardonenche, l'un des ancêtres de Guillaume. La poſtérité de celui-ci finit en 1416, dans Jean, ſon petit-fils, qui ne laiſſa que des filles.

VII. Constant de Bardonenche fut tué avec Pierre, ſon frère, à la bataille de Poitiers en 1356. On voit à Poitiers leurs tombeaux & leurs armoiries. Il eut pour fils:

1. Frelin ou François;
2. Lantelme, Damoiſeau;
3. Et Borsac, qui ſuit.

VIII. Borsac de Bardonenche fit hommage, en 1359, de la Terre du Percy & du Moétier. Il teſta le 30 Juillet 1361, & inſtitua Ant , e, ſon fils, & le poſthume dont ſa femme étoit ence te; ce fut Pierre, qui ſuit.

Antoine eut un fils, nommé Louis, qui fut père de Justet.

IX. Pierre de Bardonench vivoit encore en 1385; il eut pour enfans:

Frelin ou François;
Et Lantelme, qui ſuit.

X. Lantelme de Bardonenche, Co-Seigneur du Percy, Seigneur du Monétier, &c., fut compris parmi les Nobles dans la réviſion des feux de 1428. Il teſta le 10 Février 1433, & fit héritiers les deux fils qu'il avoit eus de *Jeanne du Puy-Boſon*, François, & Durand, qui ſuit.

XI. Durand de Bardonenche partagea avec ſon frère François, le 2 Avril 1443, les biens de Lantelme, leur père. Il teſta le 5 Juin 1457, & eut de *Marguerite d'Hellis*, ſœur de noble *Barthélemy d'Hellis*:

1. Jean, qui ſuit;
2. Pierre, co-héritier de ſon père. Il teſta le 24 Juin 1482, laiſſant de *Cécile Ricon*, ſœur de la femme de ſon frère, deux filles, *Jeanne* & *Françoiſe*;
3. Jean, Religieux;
4. Et Catherine, mariée à noble *Hugues de Ponet-de-Sinard*,

XII. Jean de Bardonenche, Ier du nom, eſt compris dans les rôles de l'arrière-ban de Trièves aux années 1472 & 1482. Il teſta avec ſon frère Pierre, le 24 Juin 1482. Les enfans nommés dans ſon teſtament ſont:

1. Jean, qui ſuit;
2. & 3. Imbert & Marie.

XIII. Jean de Bardonenche, IIe du nom, teſta le 26 Juillet 1548. Il avoit épouſé *Jeanne de Chambrier*, fille d'*André*. Il en eut Jean, qui ſuit, & Raymond.

XIV. Jean de Bardonenche, IIIe du nom, donna des marques de ſa valeur à la journée de Cériſolles en 1543; & fut compris parmi les Nobles dans la réviſion des feux de 1549. Il épouſa 1º *Claudine de Forbin-de-Souliers*, morte en 1552; & 2º *Anne de Beaumont-Combourfier*, fille de *Jean*.

Il eut du premier lit:

1. Raymond;
2. Jean, qui ſuit;
3. Antoinette, mariée à *Antoine de Vaujani*;
4. Et Marguerite.

Du ſecond lit vinrent:

5. Humbert, dont la poſtérité eſt éteinte;
6. Pierre, allié à *Ennemonde du Thau*, fille d'*Etienne*;
7. Et Renée, mariée à noble *Gabriel Paſchal*.

XV. Jean de Bardonenche, IVe du nom, mort en 1632, âgé de 92 ans, avoit épouſé, le 27 Avril 1574, *Jeanne de Revilianf*, qui teſta le 23 Janvier 1606. Elle étoit d'une très-ancienne Maiſon originaire de Piémont, établie depuis le XIII° ſiècle dans le Gapençois, & fille de *Michel de Reviliat*, Seigneur de Chabertan, & de *Marguerite de Pierre*. Il eut de ſon mariage:

1. ALEXANDRE, qui ſuit;
2. ANDRÉ, auteur de la branche des *Tenaux*, qui eſt éteinte. Il avoit épouſé, en 1624, *Ennemonde de Reynard*;
3. JEAN;
4. CÉSAR, mort en 1671, qui a fait la branche de *Souvile;* ſes fils paſſèrent en Pruſſe pour fait de Religion, leur poſtérité y ſubſiſte;
5. PIERRE, Prieur de Saint-Laurent de Grenoble, Conſeiller-Clerc au Parlement de Dauphiné.
6. 7. 8. 9. & 10. JUDITH, MARGUERITE, JEAN-NE, RENÉE, & SARA.

XVI. ALEXANDRE DE BARDONENCHE, Ier du nom, Seigneur de Toranne, Treſannes, Saint-Martin de Clelles, &c., ſe diſtingua au ſervice de HENRI IV, ſous M. de Leſdiguières, & commandoit les gens de pied à la bataille de Pontcharra en 1591. Il fut fait priſonnier avec le Duc de Créquy, lors de l'entrepriſe ſur la place d'Aiguebelle. Il mourut fort vieux en 1666, & teſta la même année. Il avoit épouſé 1° *Chriſtophe Bloſſet*, fille de *Guillaume*, dont il n'eut que des filles, & 2° *Lucrèce de Montchenu*, fille de *Jean*, & de *Louiſe de Brenieu*, dont:

1. ALEXANDRE, qui ſuit;
2. Et CÉSAR, rapporté après ſon frère.

XVII. ALEXANDRE DE BARDONENCHE, II° du nom, Vicomte de Clermont en Trièves, Seigneur de Monétier, Toranne, Treſannes, Saint-Martin de Clelles, &c., Conſeiller d'Etat, teſta en 1711, & fit ſon héritier le fils de JEANNE, ſa fille, rapporté ci-après. Il avoit épouſé 1° le 27 Septembre 1646, *Marie Darmand*, fille de *Pierre*, dont il n'eut point d'enfans mâles; & 2° *Melchionne d'Engilboud*, fille de *René*, dont:

1. RENÉ, Vicomte de Bardonenche, Chevalier-d'honneur au Parlement de Grenoble, mort avant ſon père, ſans enfans, de *Marguerite Eyraud-de-Saint-Marſolle*;
2. Et JEANNE, mariée à CÉSAR DE BARDONEN-CHE, II° du nom.

XVII. CÉSAR DE BARDONENCHE, Ier du nom, ſecond fils d'ALEXANDRE Ier, & de *Lucrèce de Montchenu*, Seigneur de Champigney, ſe maria, le 20 Mars 1653, avec *Anne de Peccat*, fille de *Jacques*, & d'*Anne-de-Clermont-de-Chatte*. Il en eut:

1. CÉSAR, qui ſuit;
2. Et LUCRÈCE, alliée avec N... *de Lyobard*, Comte de Romans.

XVIII. CÉSAR DE BARDONENCHE, II° du nom, Seigneur de Champigney, épouſa 1° le 18 Juin 1684, JEANNE DE BARDONENCHE, ſa couſine germaine, fille d'ALEXANDRE DE BARDONENCHE, II° du nom, & de *Melchionne d'Engilboud;* & 2° *Eliſabeth Odos-de-Bonniot*, veuve de N..... *Darmand-de-Brion*. Du premier lit il a eu:

1. RENÉ-ALEXANDRE, qui ſuit;
2. Et ANDRÉ, qui a commandé un bataillon du Régiment de la Couronne, mort en 1755.

Du ſecond lit naquirent:

3. RENÉ, mort Capitaine au Régiment de Limouſin, tué au ſiège de Berg-op-Zoom en 1746;
4. ANDRÉ, Sieur de Clainville;
5. Et MARGUERITE, mariée à *Laurent de Chaléon*, Conſeiller au Parlement de Grenoble.

XIX. RENÉ-ALEXANDRE DE BARDONENCHE, Chevalier, Vicomte de Trièves, Seigneur du Monétier, Toranne, Treſannes, Saint-Martin, &c., mort en 1741, avoit épouſé, le 3 Mai 1714, *Marie de Leſtang-de-Murat*, fille d'*Antoine*, Préſident à Mortier au Parlement de Grenoble, & de *Virginie Davity*, dont:

1. ANTOINE-CÉSAR, qui ſuit;
2. DAVID-ANSELME;
3. ABEL-ANDRÉ, Chanoine de l'Egliſe Noble de Saint-Chef;
4. ANTOINE-RENÉ, Chanoine de la Cathédrale de Grenoble, Vicaire-Général à Vienne;
5. CHARLES-GABRIEL, Capitaine au Régiment d'Infanterie du Roi;
Et trois filles, Religieuſes.

XX. ANTOINE-CÉSAR DE BARDONENCHE, Vicomte de Trièves, Seigneur du Monétier, de Toranne, Tréſanne, Saint-Martin, &c., a épouſé, le 25 Août 1743, *Marie-Madeleine de Vachon-de-Belmont*, fille de *Nicolas*, & de *Juſtine-Angélique de la Porte-de-Lartaudière*. Il en a:

1. RENÉ-CÉSAR-ANTOINE, né en 1746, Lieutenant au Régiment de la Marine;
2. JOSEPH-ANTOINE, né en 1747;
Et pluſieurs filles.

Tous ceux du nom de Bardonenche portoient pour armes: *d'argent au treillis de gueules, cloué d'or;* des branches y ajoutèrent des briſures différentes; mais elles n'ont jamais abandonné *le treillis,* & celle qui ſub-

sifte porte *en chef une aigle naissante de sa-*
ble. Mor ri, édition de 1759, tom. II, pag.
116.

BARDOT : *d'azur, à trois têtes de léo-*
pards d'or, au chef d'argent, chargé d'une
croix de sable pattée, au pied fiché.

BARDOUF, Seigneur de Beaulieu, en Normandie, Généralité d'Alençon. Il est parlé dans
l'*Histoire de la Maison d'Harcourt,* pag.
600, de Messire ROBERT BARDOUF, Chevalier,
Seigneur de Putot-en-Auge, qui plaidoit en
1398, pour le fief d'Aon, dont l'acquisition
avoit été faite par feu Monseigneur *Guillau-*
me de Thieuville, Evêque de Coutances, le
1er Février 1392.

Les armes : *d'argent, à la croix de sable*
au pied fiché, ou terminée par le bas en pieu,
chargée en cœur d'une molette d'éperon du
champ.

BARDOUIL, Seigneur de la Bardouillière
& de Saint-Lambert, même Province & Généralité, famille maintenue dans sa noblesse, le
22 Juin 1667. ROBERT DE BARDOUIL, Seigneur
de la Bardouillière, eut une fille, MARGUERITE
DE BARDOUIL, mariée le 20 Septembre 1503,
à *Jean de Fontaines*, Ecuyer, Seigneur de
Boiscard. L'abbé de Vertot, en son *Histoire*
de Malte, parle d'ANTOINE BARDOUIL-DE-LA-
BARDOUILLIÈRE, du Diocèse d'Evreux, qui fut
reçu Chevalier de Malte le 17 Mars 1638.

Les armes : *de sable, à la fasce d'or, ac-*
compagnée de 3 branches de fer d'argent,
terminées de 3 fers de lance, & posées 2 en
chef & une en pointe ; à la bordure d'or.

BARDOUIL, ou BARDOVIL, Seigneur
de Surville, de la Bichardière, en Normandie,
Généralités de Rouen & d'Alençon, familles
maintenues dans leur noblesse le 26 Août
1668, dont les armes sont : *d'azur, à la croix*
d'argent, ancrée & flamboyée d'un rayon de
même à chaque angle.

BARDOUL, en Bretagne : *d'argent, au*
limier de sable, accompagné de trois molet-
tes d'éperon de gueules, 2 & 1.

BARDOUL, Seigneur de Neufville, de
Vaux, de Charleval, de Magny & de Bardoul,
en Normandie, Généralité d'Alençon, famille
maintenue dans sa noblesse le 30 Avril 1666,
dont les armes sont : *parti d'argent & de*
gueules, au lion léopardé de l'un en l'autre.

BARDOUL, Seigneur de la Lande, de

Pevensé, en Normandie, Généralité d'Alençon : *d'or, à trois écrevisses de sable.*

BARE-PIERRE-FORT : *d'or à un gui-*
don d'azur ; au chef de gueules chargé d'un
léopard d'argent.

BAREAU, ou BARREAU : *d'azur, à trois*
sceptres Royaux d'or, mis en trois bar-
res, à la bande de gueules brochant sur le
tout.

BAREITH, branche cadette de la Maison
Electorale de *Brandebourg.* Voyez BRAN-
DEBOURG.

BARELLIER, en Picardie : *d'argent, à la*
bande crénelée d'azur, chargée de trois ba-
rils d'argent.

BARELLIÈRE, en Bretagne : *d'or, à une*
croix de gueules, cantonnée de quatre lion-
ceaux de même.

BARENTIN, en Picardie, famille dont
l'antiquité se prouve par la possession immé-
moriale de la Terre des Belles - Ruries, en
Touraine, dont elle a joui & jouit encore,
ainsi que de celles de la Malmaison, à trois
lieues de Paris, qui a été possédée par dix Conseillers au Parlement, de père en fils, dont
l'un a été Prévôt des Marchands de Paris.

JACQUES-HONORÉ BARENTIN, premier & an-
cien Président du Grand - Conseil, père de
CHARLES-HONORÉ, qui suit, avoit pour sœur
MARGUERITE BARENTIN, mariée 1º au Mar-
quis de *Souvré*, premier Gentilhomme de la
Chambre, & 2º au Marquis de *Laval Bois-*
Dauphin; du premier lit elle eut *Anne de*
Souvré, mariée à M. *de Louvois.*

CHARLES-HONORÉ BARENTIN fut Maître des
Requêtes & Intendant de Dunkerque ; il a eu
de *Marie-Reine de Montcharle* :

CHARLES-AMABLE-HONORÉ BARENTIN, successivement Conseiller au Parlement, Maître
des Requêtes, Intendant d'Orléans, & Conseiller d'Etat, mort le 9 Juin 1762, âgé de 66
ans. Il avoit épousé, le 17 Juillet 1724, *Ma-*
rie- Catherine le Fèvre, née le 15 Décembre 1706, fille d'*Henri-François-de-Paule*
le Fèvre d'Ormesson, Conseiller d'Etat &
Intendant des Finances, dont il eut :

N.... BARENTIN, reçu en Juillet 1764, Avocat-Général du Parlement de Paris, après M.
le Pelletier-de-Saint-Fargeau, devenu Président à Mortier au même Parlement.

al'Abbé de Barentin, que nous croyons frère ou coufin de l'Avocat-Général.

D'une autre branche étoit Joseph Barentin, Seigneur de Minières, d'Hardivilliers & de Mons, Lieutenant des Vaiffeaux du Roi, né dans le Vendômois, arrière-petit-fils de Pierre, Ecuyer, Sieur des Gats, & Commiffaire des Guerres, qui avoit époufé, le 26 Décembre 17....., *Elifabeth Laugier*, dont:

François-Joseph Barentin, né le 25 Décembre 1713;

Et Elisabeth-Susanne Barentin-des-Minières, née le 5 Avril 1715, reçue à Saint-Cyr, le 23 Novembre 1723, fur fes preuves de nobleffe.

De la branche de Barentin-Montchal, étoit Charles-Jean-Pierre Barentin, Comte de Montchal, Brigadier de Cavalerie, ci-devant Capitaine-Lieutenant des Gendarmes de Flandres, mort en Auvergne, le 16 Avril 1763, âgé de 59 ans. Il avoit époufé, le 10 Mars 1735, *Louife-Madeleine Bertin-de-Vaugien*, fille de *Bruno-Maximilien Bertin*, Seigneur de *Vaugien*, Confeiller au Parlement de Paris, & de *N...* *Pagot-du-Plouy*, dont, entr'autres enfans, un Capitaine de Cavalerie.

C'eft tout ce que nous favons de cette famille, dont nous n'avons reçu aucun *Mémoire*, & fur laquelle cependant l'on peut confulter l'*Armorial de France*, reg. I, part. I, pag. 50. Les armes: *d'azur, à trois fafces, la première d'or, furmontée de trois étoiles d'or, & les deux autres ondées d'argent.*

BARENTON, en Picardie: *d'azur, à trois bandes d'or.* [*Lieux.*]

BARET (du), Seigneur de Luné: *d'azur, à trois fafces d'or, accompagnées d'une étoile de même en chef.*

BARFUSE: *de gueules, à la fafce d'argent, chargée de trois bars ou barbeaux de finople.*

BARFUSÉE: *de pourpre, à la fafce de finople.*

BARGE (la), en Champagne: *d'argent, à la bande de fable, accompagnée en chef d'une couronne de même.*

BARGE (la), en Dauphiné: *d'argent, à la bande de fable.*

BARGETON, Seigneur de Cabrières, en Languedoc. Pierre de Bargeton époufa *Marguerite Bocorut*. Denis-Mathieu de Bargeton, leur troifième fils, né le 12 Juin 1682, Sous-Lieutenant dans le Régiment de Santerre en 1707, Capitaine dans le même Régiment en 1712, Major de la Ville de Maubeuge le 6 Avril 1738, Chevalier de Saint-Louis le 18 Mars fuivant, a époufé, en 1731, *Claudine-Antoinette Dufaux*, dont il eut:

1. Jacques-Charles-Denis de Bargeton, né le 4 Novembre 1736;
2. Daniel, né le 14 Octobre 1739;
3. Marie-Margüerite, née le 16 Décembre 1732, reçue à Saint-Cyr le 7 Janvier 1741;
4. Louise-Antoinette, née le 26 Décembre 1733, & reçue auffi à Saint-Cyr;
5. Et Marguerite-Madeleine, née le 11 Novembre 1740. Voyez l'*Armorial de France*, reg. II, part. II, pag. 2.

Les armes: *d'azur, à un chevron d'or, accompagné d'une rofe d'argent pofée à la pointe de l'écu, & un chef auffi d'argent, chargé de trois croifettes de gueules.*

BARIER, ou BARIOLET: *d'azur, au griffon d'or, tenant une étoile de même en fon bec.*

BARIÈRES: *d'azur, à deux bâtons noeteux d'or, mis en bonnet, accompagné de cinq étoiles de même, pofées en orle.*

BARIL, Seigneur de Chantelou, Election d'Avranche, en Normandie, annobli aux francs-fiefs en 1632, famille qui porte: *d'argent, à l'épervier de gueules, coupé d'azur, au lion léopardé d'argent.*

BARILLER (le), en Bretagne: *d'argent, au chevron d'azur, accompagné de trois trèfles de finople, 2 en chef & 1 en pointe.*

BARILLON, ou BARRILLON, originaire d'Auvergne, dès le tems de Louis XI. Cette famille vint s'établir à Paris fous le règne de François Ier. Le Chancelier *du Prat* fit époufer fa nièce, *Claude du Prat*, à Jean de Barillon, Seigneur de la Ville de Murat, dans la Haute-Auvergne.

Jean-Jacques de Barillon, Préfident au Parlement de Paris, époufa *Bonne Fayet*, fille du Préfident *Fayet*; ils furent l'un & l'autre plus diftingués par une piété folide, que par les grands biens qu'ils poffédoient.

Henri de Barillon, leur fils, né le 4 Mars 1639, nommé Evêque de Luçon, mourut en 1699, décoré de toutes les vertus qui font les Saints Evêques.

BRANCHE
des Seigneurs D'AMONCOURT.

PAUL BARILLON D'AMONCOURT, Marquis de Branges, Seigneur de Mancy, de Morangis & de Châtillon-fur-Marne., Confeiller d'Etat Ordinaire, fut Ambaffadeur Extraordinaire en Angleterre. Il mourut le 23 Juillet 1691, laiffant de *Marie-Madeleine Mangot*, décédée le 17 Octobre 1694 :

ANTOINE DE BARILLON D'AMONCOURT, Marquis de Branges, Seigneur de Mancy, de Châtillon-fur-Marne, &c., Maître des Requêtes honoraire de l'Hôtel du Roi, mort à Paris le 29 Juin 1741, âgé de 70 ans. Il avoit été d'abord Confeiller au Parlement de Paris, le 12 Janvier 1692, puis Maître des Requêtes en 1700. Il fut nommé, au mois de Janvier 1710, à l'Intendance de Rouffillon, & de Cerdaigne, & de l'Armée du Roi en Catalogne, d'où il fut transféré en Mars 1711, à celle de Pau, en Béarn, qu'il n'exerça que jufqu'en 1713. Il avoit époufé *Anne Doublet*, décédée le 21 Mai 1727, dont il a laiffé :

ANTOINE-PIERRE DE BARILLON D'AMONCOURT, Confeiller au Parlement de Paris, où il a été reçu le 9 Juin 1719 : marié le 3 Février 1727, avec *Françoife-Nicole de Landes*, Dame d'Houville, dans le Pays Chartrain, dont il eut :

ANTOINE-MARIE DE BARILLON D'AMONCOURT, né le 11 Mars 1736 ;

BONNE DE BARILLON, morte le 13 Août 1755, veuve de *François le Camus*, Marquis de Bligny, Maréchal des Camps & Armées du Roi ;

Et ANNE-PHILIBERTE DE BARILLON, époufe de *Charles-Gabriel de Tardieu*, Marquis de Maleyffie, Lieutenant de Roi à Compiègne. Voyez *le Mercure de France* du mois de Juillet 1741, pag. 1691.

BRANCHE
des Seigneurs DE MORANGIS.

ANTOINE DE BARILLON DE MORANGIS, Seigneur de Louans & de Montigny, Maître des Requêtes ordinaire de l'Hôtel du Roi, fucceffivement Intendant à Metz & au pays Meffin, & dans les Généralités d'Alençon, de Caen & d'Orléans, mourut le 18 Mai 1686, laiffant de *Catherine-Marie Boucherat*, fille du Chancelier de France de ce nom, mort le 15 Mars 1733 :

JEAN-JACQUES BARILLON DE MORANGIS, Maî-

tre des Requêtes ordinaire de l'Hôtel du Roi, l'un des quarante Doyens du quartier, mort à Paris, fans avoir été marié, le 29 Mai 1741, âgé de 63 ans. Il avoit été d'abord Avocat du Roi au Châtelet de Paris le 13 Août 1695, enfuite Confeiller au Parlement de Paris le 8 Avril 1699, & en dernier lieu Maître des Requêtes le 17 Juin 1706. Il a laiffé pour héritières :

ANNE-FRANÇOISE DE BARILLON DE MORANGIS, fa fœur, morte en 1745. Elle avoit époufé, le 29 Juin 1695, *Antoine-Cleriadus de Choifeul*, Marquis de Beaupré d'Aillecourt, mère du feu Evêque de Châlons & du Cardinal-Archevêque de Befançon, & de leurs frères mariés ; & *Louife-Marie-Gabrielle de Gourgues*, fa nièce, époufe de *Louis-François de Saint-Simon*, Marquis de Sandricourt, Lieutenant-Général des Armées du Roi, fille de *Jean-François de Gourgues*, Marquis d'Aulnay, &c., & de GABRIELLE DE BARILLON DE MORANGIS, fa première femme, morte le 15 Avril 1700, âgée d'environ 21 ans. *Mercure* du mois de Juin 1741, pag. 1470.

Les armes : *écartelé, aux 1 & 4 d'azur, au chevron accompagné de deux coquilles en chef, & d'une rofe en pointe, le tout d'or ; aux 2 & 3 de gueules, au fautoir d'or, qui eft* D'AMONCOURT.

La branche de *Morangis* porte : *écartelé de Boucherat.*

BARILLON, en Bretagne : *de gueules, à trois barillets d'or, cerclés de fable, 2 & 1.*

BARILLON-LA-COSTE : *d'argent, au lion de gueules, à la bande d'or, brochant fur le tout.*

*BARINGUE, Terre qui fut démembrée de la Baronie de Navailles, & cédée à *Bertronnet de Navailles*, tige des Seigneurs de la Batut-Figuères. N... de Navailles, fa petite-fille, la porta en dot à *Ramonet de Caftaing*. De cette Maifon elle a paffé dans celle de *Lomagne-Terride*. Voyez ce mot.

BARJAC, Baron de Rochegude, Diocèfe d'Uzès : *d'azur, au bélier effaré d'or.*

BARJAC, même Province : *d'argent, à trois pals de fable, au chef de gueules, chargé de trois étoiles d'or.*

BARJOT. Ceux de ce nom fe prétendent originaires du Comté de Bourgogne, & venir d'un puîné des Comtes de Varrax, ainſi que l'a remarqué Guichenon, dans ſon *Hiſtoire de Breſſe*. Pierre de Saint-Julien, Livre III de ſes *Antiquités de Mâcon*, dit que les Comtes de Varrax, ou Varrace, s'appeloient *de la Pallu*, & que cette Seigneurie de la Pallu étoit poſſédée depuis long-tems par les BARJOT; que GUILLAUME BARJOT, Secrétaire du Roi, fut père de:

CLAUDE, Maître des Comptes du Roi en la Chambre de Dijon, & père de deux Préſidens au Grand-Conſeil;

Et GUILLAUME, Seigneur de la Pallu & de la Salle qui eut entr'autres enfans:

GUILLAUME, Seigneur de la Pallu, Maître-d'Hôtel de CHARLES IX;

Et PHILIBERT, Seigneur de la Salle, Lieutenant-Général au Bailliage du Mâconnois. Pierre de Saint-Julien dit que PHILIBERT BARJOT ſervit le Duc de Bourgogne en pluſieurs importantes occaſions.

Dans des *Mémoires Domeſtiques*, qui nous ont été communiqués, nous trouvons un PHILIBERT BARJOT, Seigneur d'Auneuil, Conſeiller d'Etat, né en 1410, marié à *Marie de Tournebulle*, de la Maiſon de *Magis*. Il en eut pluſieurs enfans. Ses aînés ſont auteurs des branches qui ſe ſont perpétuées, tant dans le Beaujolois & la Bourgogne, où elles étoient déjà établies, que dans le Lyonnois, le Bourbonnois & l'Auvergne.

Leur principal ſurnom paroît avoir été *de la Pallu*, & *de la Combe*. La branche des BARJOT-DE-LA-PALLU s'eſt éteinte dans N.... DE BARJOT-DE-BRION, Dame de la Pallu, dernière héritière de cette branche; celle des BARJOT-DE-LA-COMBE ſubſiſte encore, à ce qu'on croit, à Meaux, dans le Mâconnois.

Il y a eu encore la branche des BARJOT-MONTFAVIER, dont étoit BENOÎT-BARJOT, né à Beaujeu en 1575, qui laiſſa de *Conſtance du Cran*:

JEAN BARJOT, Chanoine de Beaujeu en 1643;

Et PHILIBERT BARJOT, auſſi Chanoine.

Il eſt à croire qu'après la mort de ces deux Chanoines, ſeuls & uniques héritiers de leur branche, leurs biens ont paſſé à des héritiers maternels.

Ces branches aînées, avec celle de JEAN BARJOT, dernier fils de PHILIBERT; dont nous allons donner la filiation, ſe ſont tellement perdues de vue, qu'on n'en a eu aucune connoiſſance. Les titres ſont reſtés entre les mains

des aînés, & les deſcendans de JEAN BARJOT, dernier fils de PHILIBERT, n'ont les preuves de leur filiation, par partages & contrats de Mariage, que depuis la ſéparation de ces branches aînées, & il ne leur reſte, ſur leurs aînés, que les indications que nous venons de donner.

BRANCHE
des Seigneurs DE MOUSSY & DE RONCÉE.

I. JEAN D'ORVAL, dernier fils de PHILIBERT, fut Seigneur d'Orval & de la Pallu. Il s'attacha au Comte de Beaujeu. La Terre d'Orval lui tomba en partage, & lui & ſes enfans continuèrent d'en prendre le nom. Il eut d'*Henriette de Bourbon*, fille naturelle de PIERRE DE BOURBON, Comte de Beaujeu, & mari d'ANNE DE FRANCE, fille de LOUIS XI:

II. CLAUDE DE BARJOT, Iᵉʳ du nom, Seigneur d'Orval, né en 1440, qui paroît avoir été marié 1º avec *Antoinette de Luxembourg-Montmorency*, & 2º avec *Claudine de Balzac*. Il eut de cette dernière:

III. GUILLAUME DE BARJOT, Seigneur d'Orval, né en 1474, qui fut Gouverneur du Bourbonnois, & marié à *Thomaſſe du Gellay*, dont il eut:

IV. CLAUDE DE BARJOT, IIᵉ du nom, Seigneur de Roches, Capitaine des Chevaux-Légers de la Reine, qui fut chargé de quelques négociations à Rome, & auprès de pluſieurs Princes étrangers. Il ſe maria, en 1514, avec *Antoinette le Viſte-de-Saint-Bonnet*, dont il eut CLAUDE, qui ſuit, & PHILIBERT BARJOT. JEAN BARJOT, Conſeiller au Parlement, Seigneur de Mouſſy, probablement fils cadet de GUILLAUME, ſe voyant ſans enfans d'*Olive de Tétigny*, fille de *François de Tétigny*, & de *Marie*, fille de l'Amiral de *Coligny*, tué à la Saint-Barthélemy, fit embraſſer à CLAUDE & PHILIBERT BARJOT, de même nom que lui, & ſes couſins, le parti de la Robe; en faveur du don & ſubſtitution qu'il leur fit de tous ſes biens. CLAUDE eut la Terre de Mouſſy, & PHILIBERT celles d'Auneuil & de Marchefroy. Il eſt auteur de la branche des BARJOT-D'AUNEUIL, & fut, comme ſon frère, Conſeiller d'Etat, & premier Préſident au Grand-Conſeil.

V. CLAUDE DE BARJOT, IIIᵉ du nom, Seigneur de Mouſſy, épouſa, 1º en 1561, *Anne d'Avayolles*; & 2º *Philippe de Naillac*, proche parente du Grand-Maître de Malte, veuve d'*André de Beauvau-de-Paimpéan*. Elle étoit

fille de *René de Naillac,* premier Ecuyer du
Roi Charles IX.

Du premier lit vint:

1. Léonor, qui fuit.

Et du fecond lit:

2. Et Claude, reçu Chevalier de Malte, de minorité.

VI. Léonor de Barjot, Seigneur de Mouf-
fy, Ier du nom, époufa, en 1588, *Renée de
Beauvau-de-Paimpéan,* fille d'*André,* & de
Philippe de Naillac, fa belle-mère. Il en eut:

1. Claude, marié à *Charlotte des Barres,* remariée à *Henri de la Ferté-Senneterre,*
ou *Senecaire,* Maréchal de France;

2. Et Léonor, qui fuit.

VII. Léonor de Barjot, IIe du nom, dit le
Marquis de Mouffy, époufa, en 1629, *Léonore de Voyer d'Argenfon.* Il en eut:

1. René, qui fuit;

2. Claude, reçu Chevalier de Malte le 3 Juillet 1648;

3. Eléonore, mariée à *René Robin,* Marquis
de la Tremblaye;

4. Et N.... mariée à *Louis le Teftu,* Marquis
de Balincourt.

VIII. René de Barjot, dit le *Marquis de
Mouffy,* mort en 1677, époufa en 1654
Charlotte de Maillé-Kerman, & a eu:

1. René, qui fuit;

2. Et Charles, dit le *Comte de Roncée,* marié avec *Marie-Anne d'Appelvoifin-de-la-
Roche-du-Maine.* Elle eft morte, & a laiffé
deux filles non mariées, l'une *Mademoifelle
de Roncée,* morte en 1761; l'autre *Mademoifelle de Lillette,* morte en 1762, qui
poffédoient les terres de la Jumellière & de
Champdefonds; Alexis de Barjot, leur
coufin germain, rapporté ci-après, a été
leur principal héritier.

IX. René de Barjot, Seigneur de Mouffy,
IIe du nom, né le 16 Janvier 1658, mort le 17
Mai 1729, s'allia, en 1691, avec *Louife de
Johanne-de-la-Carre-de-Saumery,* fille de
Jacques, Marquis de Saumery, Gouverneur
de Chambord, & de *Catherine Charron de
Menars,* morte le 30 Novembre 1743. De la
famille de *la Carre-de-Saumery,* originaire
d'Efpagne, font l'Evêque de Rieux, le Comte
de Saumery, & l'Abbeffe de Réconfort. René
Barjot a laiffé:

X. Alexis de Barjot, Marquis de Roncée, né à Paris le 16 Décembre 1695, mort le
8 Mars 1763. Il avoit époufé, en Janvier
1726, *Geneviève-Alphonfine Borderie-de-*
Tome II.

Vernejoux, née à Paris le 11 Juin 1700, &
a laiffé:

1. Paul-Jean-Baptiste-Alexis, qui fuit;

2. Geneviève-Alphonsine, mariée, le 16 Août
1747, à *Armand-François,* Comte de *Dur-
fort-Boiffières;*

3. Louise-Renée, morte le 16 Mai 1765. Elle
avoit époufé, en Septembre 1749, *Jean-Baptifte Savary,* Marquis de Lancofme, de la
Maifon de *Savary-de-Brèves* & de *Gerfay;*

4. Et Marguerite-Charlotte, mariée, le 3
Juin 1750, à *Jean-Nicolas de Johanne-de-
la-Carre-de-Saumery,* Marquis de Sau-
mery-de-Johanne, mort fans poftérité, le 11
Juin 1757.

XI. Paul-Jean-Baptiste-Alexis de Barjot, Comte de Roncée, né le 11 Juin 1731,
ancien Sous-Lieutenant de la Gendarmerie
en Mars 1749, fut grièvement bleffé à la bataille de Minden. Il s'eft marié en 1751 à
*Adélaïde-Julie-Sophie Hurault-de-Vi-
braye,* Dame de Compagnie de feu Madame
la Princeffe de Condé, dont:

Marie-Joséphine-Caroline de Barjot-de-
Roncée, née le 22 Décembre 1759.

Les defcendans de Jean de Barjot, fils cadet de Philibert, ont formé deux branches
principales.

Celle des Barjot, Seigneurs de *Mouffy* &
de *Roncée,* dont nous venons de donner la
filiation, & laquelle a produit: un Evêque
de Rennes, trois Confeillers-d'Etat, nombre
de Chevaliers de l'Ordre du Roi, avant la
création de l'Ordre du Saint-Efprit, des Capitaines de 100 hommes d'armes, des Commandans de l'Arrière-Ban, des Lieutenans
des Gardes-du-Corps, des Guidons de Gendarmerie, des Officiers aux Gardes-Françoifes, &c.

L'autre branche eft celle des Seigneurs
d'*Auneuil* & de *Marchefroy,* éteinte dans la
perfonne de N... de Barjot, dit le *Comte de
Mafy,* premier Ecuyer de Mademoifelle de
Montpensier, fille de Gaston, Duc d'Orléans.

Ses alliances font avec la Maifon de *Beauvau,* deux fois; celles de *Maillé, la Fayette,
Senneterre, la Paliffe, Chabannes, Ar-
naud-de-Pomponne, Voyer d'Argenfon,
Maillé-Kerman,* &c.

Lorfque le Connétable de Bourbon fortit
du Royaume, il fut accompagné, dans fa fuite, par un Barjot, & par fon gendre *Henri-
Arnaud de Pomponne,* qui firent ferrer les
chevaux de ce Prince à rebours, pour cacher

leur marche. Moréri & des Mémoires ne parlent que de *Henri Arnaud;* mais BARJOT y étoit auſſi ; & *Arnaud* n'étoit attaché au Connétable qu'à cauſe de ſon mariage avec CATHERINE DE BARJOT.

Outre la Terre de Mouſſy, qui étoit depuis long-tems dans la branche de ce nom, & qui fut ſubſtituée en 1559 à CLAUDE DE BARJOT, *Anne d'Avayolles ,* ſa première femme , lui apporta en 1560 celle de *Roncée ,* en Touraine.

Les branches des Maiſons de *Naillac,* de *Beauvau* & de *Paimpéan ,* qui ſe ſont fondues dans celle de BARJOT-DE-MOUSSY, par les héritiers de ces deux branches, ont auſſi apporté un nombre de terres conſidérables, entr'autres la Baronie de la Jumellière & de Champdefons , la terre de *Paimpéan ,* qui a deux Baronies, celle de Roches, celle de Cholette, terre & petite Ville que RENÉ DE BARJOT, Baron de Cholette, fit ériger en Marquiſat, pour lui & ſes deſcendans. Ce Marquiſat a paſſé à M. *de Broon,* Marquis de Tourmeaux, fils d'un BARJOT ; & elle eſt actuellement dans la branche de *Maulevrier-Colbert.* La terre de Mouſſy eſt auſſi ſortie de la Maiſon de BARJOT ; & c'eſt le père du Marquis de *Roncée* d'aujourd'hui, ſur la tête duquel elle étoit libre de ſubſtitution, & qui l'a vendue. Il n'y a aujourd'hui que la terre de *Roncée* qui ſoit ancienne dans cette famille; les autres terres qu'elle poſſédoit encore étoient celles de *la Pallu,* de *Montfavier* & d'*Orval,* dont deux branches ont porté les noms.

Les armes : *d'azur, au griffon d'or, le franc-canton rempli d'une étoile de même ;* ſupports : *deux lions d'or ;* cimier : *une tête de licorne d'argent..... ;* deviſe : *l'haurœ non l'haure.*

BARLATIER, en Provence. Cette famille noble eſt diviſée en deux branches, qui ont leur demeure à Aix.

BERNARDIN BARLATIER eſt la tige des Seigneurs de *Saint-Julien.* Il fut reçu Secrétaire du Roi en la Chancellerie de Provence en 1720 , & épouſa *Honorée de Pin,* de laquelle il a laiſſé :

1. PAUL, qui ſuit ;
2. ANTOINE, vivant ſans alliance;
Et ſept filles, dont l'aînée a été mariée avec *Michel de Reynaud,* Tréſorier de France, & les ſix autres ſont Religieuſes.

PAUL DE BARLATIER, Seigneur de Saint-Julien, a eu de *Françoiſe d'Eyſſautier :*

1. BERNARDIN, qui ſuit ;
2. JACQUES-LOUIS-ANTOINE, Chevalier de l'Ordre Militaire de Saint-Louis, Capitaine dans le Régiment Royal-Comtois;
3. FRANÇOIS-MICHEL, mort Lieutenant au Régiment de Breſſe ;
4. LOUIS-PAUL , Capitaine au même Régiment;
5. JEAN-AUGUSTIN, Eccléſiaſtique ;
Et ſix filles, dont cinq Religieuſes, & la ſixième, MADELEINE - GABRIELLE , mariée avec *Auguſtin-Sauveur Ribe,* Tréſorier de France.

BERNARDIN DE BARLATIER , Seigneur de Saint-Julien, reçu Conſeiller au Parlement, le 10 Octobre 1736, a épouſé *Marie-Lucrèce de Raouſſet-la-Croix,* de la ville de Taraſcon.

LOUIS-MATHIEU DE BARLATIER, Seigneur de Mas, fait la ſeconde branche de cette famille. Il eſt Conſeiller au Parlement de Provence, depuis 1740, & marié avec *Anne-Cécile d'Eſtienne,* fille de noble *Honoré d'Eſtienne,* de laquelle il a deux fils : l'aîné eſt deſtiné à remplir l'Office de ſon père; & le cadet ſert ſur les Vaiſſeaux du Roi, en qualité d'Enſeigne.

On trouve, dans le regiſtre des Déclarations du Parlement, qu'en 1592 cette Cour choiſit le Capitaine BARLATIER pour commander dans le Château de Rognes, & le conſerver ſous l'obéiſſance du Roi ; & au *primum ſumptum* de *Teyſſeire,* Notaire, conſervé aux écritures de *Claude Minuty,* à Aix, on voit que, par acte du 9 Décembre 1512, nobles Louis & GUILLAUME BARLATIER, fils de noble ANTOINE BARLATIER & de *Marguerite Marin,* contractent enſemble. (Voy. l'*Hiſt. héroïq. & univ. de la Nobleſſe de Provence,* tom. I, p. 94.)

Les armes : *d'azur, à la croix alaiſée d'or, cantonnée de quatre étoiles de même.*

* BARLES, en Provence, Evêché de Digne, Terre & Seigneurie qui ne relève que du Roi. Cette Terre fut donnée, le 7 Août 1355, par JEANNE Ire, Comteſſe de Provence, & LOUIS DE FRANCE, Duc d'Anjou, que cette Princeſſe avoit adopté pour ſon héritier, à *Jean de Laudun,* & à ſa poſtérité.

Louiſe d'Oraiſon, iſſue de *Jean de Laudun,* héritière de ſa Maiſon, porta, le 31 Mars 1478, cette terre à ſon mari *Philippe d'Aqua,* ou de l'*Aigue.*

Antoine-Honoré d'Aqua, fils aîné de *Philibert*, prit le nom d'*Oraifon*; & *Alphonfe d'Aqua d'Oraifon*, un des defcendans d'*Antoine-Honoré*, vendit, le 4 Octobre 1641, la Terre & Seigneurie de *Barles*, à *Jeanne de Peruzzi*, Dame de Montdevergues, veuve de *Jérôme de Lopis*, dont le fils,

François de Lopis, mort Lieutenant-Général des Armées du Roi, après avoir été employé dans plufieurs négociations, par le Cardinal *Mazarin*, laiffa, par fon teftament, la Terre & Seigneurie de *Barles*, à *François de Peruzzi*, fon coufin iffu de germain. Voyez PERUZZI.

BARLET, en Bourgogne: *d'or, au lion de fable, armé & couronné de gueules.*

BARME: *d'azur, au chevron d'or, chargé de trois rofes de gueules.* Une autre famille porte, au lieu des trois rofes, *trois pots de gueules.*

BARNIER, en Languedoc: *d'azur, au chevron d'or, accompagné de trois grives d'argent, 2 en chef & 1 en pointe; au chef coufu d'or, chargé de trois étoiles de gueules.*

BARNIOLLES, Seigneur du Mefnil, en Normandie, Généralité de Rouen, famille maintenue en fa nobleffe le 20 Janvier 1668, qui porte: *de gueules, à une épée d'argent en pal, accompagnée de 3 étoiles de même, 2 en chef & 1 en flanc.*

BARNOIN, en Provence. Louis XIV accorda des Lettres d'annobliffement à PIERRE BARNOIN, de la Ville de Digne, Préfident à Marfeille, enregistrées aux Archives de Sa Majefté en Provence, le 27 Juin 1659, l'Arrêt du Confeil d'Etat du 22 Août 1750, & Lettres-Patentes expédiées en conféquence, le 29 dudit mois & même année, par lefquelles le Roi, en exceptant des révocations d'annobliffement portées par les Édits des mois de Septembre 1664, & Août 1715, des Lettres de confirmation de nobleffe & d'annobliffement, en tant que de befoin, accordées au mois de Juin 1659 à PIERRE BARNOIN, bifayeul de JOSEPH-HYACINTHE BARNOIN, le maintient, ainfi que fes enfans, poftérité & defcendans, nés & à naître en légitime mariage, dans tous les droits & privilèges de la Nobleffe, tant qu'ils ne feront aucun acte de dérogeance; & ce, nonobftant & fans s'arrêter à celle de CYPRIEN BARNOIN, fon père, dont

Sa Majefté le relève. Lefdits Arrêts & Lettres-Patentes furent vérifiés le 4 Février 1751, & enregiftrés au Regiftre *Fontenoy*, fol. 265.

Autres Lettres d'annobliffement, accordées par le Roi Louis XV, à LOUIS-CHARLES BARNOIN, Tréforier de France, en la Généralité d'Aix, le 12 Août 1748. Il eft marié avec une fille de la famille de *Crofe-de-Perthuis*, dont il a poftérité. (Voy. Artefeuil, tome I, pag. 95.)

Les armes: *fafcé d'or & d'azur de 6 pièces; au chef d'argent, chargé de 3 étoiles de gueules.*

BAROIS, Seigneur de Beaubuiffon, en Normandie, Généralité de Rouen, famille maintenue dans fa nobleffe le 12 Janvier 1668, qui porte: *d'argent, au lion de fable, lampaffé de gueules, au chef d'azur, chargé de trois fautoirs, de deux branches d'olivier, chacun d'argent.*

BARON, Seigneur de Thibouville, de Vallevit, en Normandie, Généralité de Rouen, famille maintenue dans fa nobleffe, le 7 Janvier 1668. JACQUES BARON, Seigneur de Thibouville, étoit Lieutenant-Particulier-Civil au Bailliage de Rouen en 1668, & portoit pour armes: *de gueules, à 5 befans d'or, 3 & 2.*

BARON: *d'azur, à une bande d'or, accoftée de 2 befans de même.*

BARON, en Dauphiné: *d'or, à un ours contourné, naiffant de fable, tenant de fa patte dextre une épée haute d'argent, accompagné de deux rofes de gueules en chef, & d'une étoile d'azur en pointe.*

BARONAT: *d'or, à un guidon d'azur, au chef de gueules chargé d'un léopard d'argent.*

BARONNAT, en Languedoc: *d'or, à trois guidons d'azur, chargés d'un écuffon d'argent; au chef de gueules, chargé d'un lion paffant d'argent.*

BARONNIE (DE LA), Seigneur de Cely: *de gueules, au chevron d'argent, chargé de cinq mouchetures d'hermines de fable, accompagné de trois molettes d'éperon d'argent, 2 en chef & 1 en pointe; au franc-quartier d'azur, chargé d'un chevron d'or, accompagné en chef de 2 gerbes de blé de même.*

BARQUES, ou BARQUET (du), Seigneur du Bourg, en Normandie, Généralité d'Alençon, famille maintenue dans fa nobleffe le 17 Février 1667, qui porte : *de fable à 3 croiffans d'argent*, 2 & 1. D'autres lui donnent : *d'azur, à 3 trèfles d'or, pofés 2 & 1.*

§ BARQUIER, en Provence, ancienne nobleffe, illuftre dans fon origine, laquelle a produit des perfonnages diftingués dans l'Eglife, l'Épée & la Robe, & a été alliée aux meilleures Maifons d'Italie ; mais victime des malheurs des tems & des troubles qui agitèrent la Provence, elle fe trouva vers le milieu du fiècle dernier déchue de fa première fplendeur. Privée des avantages de la fortune & de la plupart de fes titres qui ont été brûlés ou difperfés, elle étoit tombée dans une forte d'oubli, qui, fans donner atteinte à fa nobleffe, lui fit perdre fon éclat. Elle a néanmoins toujours tenu un rang diftingué dans la ville d'Antibes où elle eft établie, & n'a pas ceffé depuis plus de trois fiècles d'y occuper les premières charges ; c'eft pour parvenir à réparer lefdites pertes, qu'en 1778, Meffire ALEXANDRE DE BARQUIER, rapporté ci-deffous, obtint de Sa Majefté un ordre à M. le Procureur-Général de lui donner un libre accès au tréfor des Chartes de la Couronne, où les titres appartenant à la ville d'Antibes, avoient été transférés, lors de la vente de cette Seigneurie, au Roi HENRI IV, par les Maifons de *Grimaldi* & de *Lorraine*, & de lui délivrer des copies authentiques des pièces qui lui manquaient pour juftifier pleinement de fa nobleffe. De ces titres & de ceux qui s'étoient confervés dans la famille, if réfulte que le nom de BARQUIER a éprouvé des variations confidérables dans fon orthographe, felon le tems, la différence des idiomes, & le plus ou le moins d'exactitude des Notaires, favoir : BARQUIER, BARGUIER, BALGUIER, BARQUE, BARQUEROT, &c. Voulant nous conformer à la délicateffe de cette famille, qui ne veut rien avancer qui ne foit prouvé par les actes les plus authentiques, nous nous contenterons ici de donner un extrait de fes différens titres depuis le XVe fiècle.

VICTOR DE BARQUIER, neveu de JEAN, Evêque de Nice, Docteur ès loix, vivoit en 1420, & occupoit dans cette ville un rang confidérable. Il avoit porté les armes dans fa jeuneffe, & s'étoit diftingué dans plufieurs occafions.

JEAN DE BARQUIER, Damoifeau, Seigneur de Malvans, homme d'armes des Ordonnances du Roi, fut un des Seigneurs qui vinrent avec Georges de Grimaldi, au fecours de Marfeille, menacée d'une feconde furprife de la part des Catalans. Il eft cité des premiers avec Pierre d'Arbaud, dans un acte d'aveu rendu par les Confuls & les Habitans de la ville d'Antibes au Seigneur de ladite ville, du 18 Avril 1441, reçu par *Pierre Froment*, Notaire d'Antibes. Il fervit avec Pierre de Courtenay, du fang Royal de France, dans la compagnie du Maréchal de Loheac, ce qui eft prouvé par un rôle en parchemin, original de ladite compagnie, daté de 1460.

GUILLAUME DE BARQUIER (*nobilis Guillelmus Barquerii*), rendit hommage, le 23 Juillet 1464, à Gafpard de Grimaldi, des Princes de Monaco & d'Antibes.

HONORÉ DE BARQUIER, Capitaine de Vaiffeau, mentionné dans l'acte ci-deffus, fe diftingua contre les infidèles des côtes d'Afrique.

JACQUES DE BARQUIER, Chevalier, Seigneur en partie de Rochefort & de la Salle, Grand-Bailli & Préfident de la Cour temporelle de la ville d'Antibes (*curiæ temporalis*), vivant en 1490, paroît comme médiateur dans une tranfaction entre les Seigneurs de Grimaldi d'une part, & les Confuls d'Antibes de l'autre.

BERTRAND DE BARQUIER, Gouverneur & premier Conful de la ville d'Antibes (*Dux & Conful*), Capitaine de 200 hommes de pied avec lefquels il repouffa les Sarrafins ou Maures d'Afrique qui avoient fait une defcente fur les côtes d'Antibes, & en dévaftoient le territoire. Il avoit pour fecond Conful en ordre inférieur un d'Hugolen ; ce qui mérite d'autant plus d'être obfervé, que ce dernier étant d'une Maifon très-ancienne de Provence, qui dès 1400 avoit donné des Commandeurs à l'ordre de Saint-Jean de Jérufalem, & d'une branche affez riche, pour avoir fondé en 1516 le Couvent des Cordeliers d'Antibes, rien ne prouve mieux le rang diftingué dont ce premier jouiffoit parmi la nobleffe du pays. Une autre obfervation non moins importante, c'eft que la Maifon que le même BERTRAND poffédoit dans Antibes, a paffé de père en fils à BALTHASARD DE BARQUIER. (Voyez ci-deffous.) On voit encore fur la porte les armes de la famille.

LOUIS DE BARQUIER, Chevalier (*dit* BARQUE-

ROT), fe diftingua dans les guerres d'Italie fous le règne de CHARLES VIII. Il eft compris en qualité d'Officier avec Pierre de Mouftier, Jean de Caftellane, & plufieurs autres Gentilshommes Provençaux, dans un rôle d'hommes d'armes de 1501 fervant pour le Roi de France à Cayau, au Royaume de Naples.

BARTHÉLEMY DE BARQUIER, vivant en 1509, eft cité au nombre des plus nobles citoyens de la ville d'Antibes (a) & de fon diftrict (*proceres & magni viri*), favoir: avec Antoine de Caronne, Pierre de Bompar, Pierre de Solis, Gafpard de Robion (des Seigneurs de Saint-Paul), Barthélemy de Bergundi, Alphonfe de Teneris, Antoine de Valence (des Seigneurs de Touton), Barthélemy d'Albert, Bernard de Sabran, Jean de Langui, Balthafard d'Hugolen, André de Galeau, Jean de Lance, André d'Ancone, & Mathieu Calvi.

PIERRE DE BARQUIER, Chevalier, fut Capitoul de Touloufe en 1579 (tems où cette charge n'étoit conférée qu'à la nobleffe).

HONORÉ DE BARQUIER, IIᵉ du nom, Capitaine d'Antibes, fe fignala dans cette ville, en 1536, lorfqu'elle fut affiégée par l'Empereur CHARLES-QUINT, & fut caufe en partie de fa réfiftance opiniâtre. Il eut :

1. JEAN, qui fuit;
2. Et ANTOINE DE BARQUIER, Ecuyer, vivant en 1564.

JEAN DE BARQUIER, IIᵉ du nom, premier Conful d'Antibes en 1587, ainfi que fes ancêtres, époufa *Bartholomée d'Albert*, des Comtes Alberti, Maifon illuftre de Florence, & tige des Ducs de Luynes & de Chaulnes, dont il eut :

1. FRANÇOIS (*dit* LA BARQUE), Chevalier de Malte, qui, l'an 1626, fe diftingua dans un combat contre un vaiffeau Turc;
2. Et BARTHÉLEMY DE BARQUIER, auteur de la première branche.

BALTHASARD DE BARQUIER, Ecuyer, né à Antibes le 6 Octobre 1659, premier Conful de la ville d'Antibes, «Confeiller Secrétaire du Roi en la Chancellerie, près la fouveraine Cour des Comptes de Provence, par Lettres données à Verfailles le 31 Décembre 1712, exerçoit encore cette charge le 22 Avril 1734,

qu'il mourut *ab-inteftat*. Il eft inhumé en l'Eglife paroiffiale de la ville d'Antibes, » & avoit époufé, le 17 Janvier 1689, *Hippolyte de Raynaud*, fille d'*Efprit de Raynaud*, & de *Blanche de Roftan*, dont:

1. PIERRE; qui fuit;
2. ESPRIT, mort, fans alliance, le 12 Mars 1733;
3. ANNE, née le 4 Octobre 1689, morte au berceau;
4. Et une autre fille, mariée, le 8 Octobre 1713, à *Henri Currault*, Juge Royal de la ville d'Antibes.

PIERRE DE BARQUIER, Ecuyer, né le 30 Novembre 1691, mort le 27 Février 1738, avoit époufé, le 4 Février 1722, *Elifabeth de Calvi*, décédée le 4 Décembre 1770, fille d'*Honoré de Calvi* & de *Gabrielle de Calvi*, fa coufine germaine, fille unique d'une famille noble originaire de Gênes, établie à Graffe. De ce mariage font iffus:

1. BALTHASARD, qui fuit
2. PIERRE-JOSEPH, né le 20 Mars 1728, « Lieutenant au Régiment de Picardie en 1743, Capitaine en 1748, & Chevalier de Saint-Louis en 1762. Il a obtenu, au Camp de Compiègne, en 1769, un *Bon du Roi*, pour une Majorité de Régiment, avec une gratification annuelle de 300 livres, en attendant qu'il en fût pourvu; & le 28 Janvier 1773, il a obtenu fa retraite avec 400 livres d'appointement, & la confervation des 300 livres de gratification annuelle qui lui avoient été accordées en 1769, en confidération de fes fervices; »
3. ANTOINE, *Abbé de Barquier*, né le 1ᵉʳ Mai 1733, Curé d'Antibes;
4. JEAN, né le 3 Septembre 1734, Lieutenant au Régiment de Piémont le 1ᵉʳ Septembre 1755, tué le 5 Novembre 1757, d'un coup de canon, à la bataille de Rosbach, en Saxe;

Deux autres garçons & deux filles, morts au berceau.

BALTHASARD DE BARQUIER, IIᵉ du nom, Chevalier, né le 23 Avril 1723, Seigneur de Claufonne, Député de la Nobleffe de Provence aux comptes dudit Pays, Chevalier de Saint-Louis, Capitaine au Régiment de Piémont, & Maire d'Antibes, lequel, après 22 ans de fervice dans le même Régiment, & avoir fait toutes les campagnes depuis 1741 jufqu'à la dernière paix, & s'être diftingué principalement à la bataille de Rosbach, où l'un de fes frères fut tué à fon côté, s'eft retiré en 1763 avec une penfion de 400 liv. fur le Tréfor

---

(a) La ville d'Antibes, alors plus peuplée qu'elle n'eft aujourd'hui, renfermait dans fon fein beaucoup de nobleffe, iffue la plupart des plus illuftres Maifons d'Italie, qui avoit cherché en 1300 un afile contre la tyrannie.

Royal à Antibes, où il eſt mort en 1778. Il avoit épouſé, le 21 Novembre 1768, *Radegonde Lombard-Tarradeau*, d'une ancienne famille de la ville de Draguignan, & fille de *François de Lombard*, Seigneur de Tarradeau, & de *Marguerite de Broulhony de Fabregues* (famille noble, originaire d'Angleterre), dont:

1. JEAN-ANTOINE-BALTHASARD-MAURICE DE BARQUIER, Chevalier, né le 2 Septembre 1769, admis aux Pages de S. A. S. Monſeigneur le Duc d'Orléans;
2. Et MARGUERITE-FRANÇOISE-ADÉLAÏDE DE BARQUIER, née le 1er Août 1774;

SECONDE BRANCHE.

Elle a pour auteur:

JEAN DE BARQUIER, Écuyer, qui laiſſa:

1. JEAN-BAPTISTE, qui ſuit;
2. ANTOINE, Docteur en Théologie, Prêtre de la Congrégation de l'Oratoire, qui s'eſt rendu célèbre dans ſon ordre, & qui y eſt mort, après avoir compoſé quelques ouvrages qui ne ſont pas imprimés;
3. ANDRÉ, Officier de Marine, Capitaine d'un Brigantin, tué au combat de la Hogue, le 29 Mai 1692;
4. Et JEAN DE BARQUIER, mort ſans alliance.

JEAN-BAPTISTE DE BARQUIER fut premier Conſul de la ville d'Antibes. Il épouſa, en 1709, *Marie d'Auſſel*, fille d'*Honoré d'Auſſel*, noble commerçant de la ville de Nice, & d'*Honorée de Bayon*, de l'illuſtre Maiſon de *Libertat*. La famille d'*Auſſel*, éteinte aujourd'hui, étoit ancienne, & a pour tige, *Bertrand d'Auſſel*, Gentilhomme du Comté de Nice, qui en 1164 fut témoin à une Chartre de vente de Guillaume de Saint-Alban, à l'Evêque de Nice. Elle s'étoit adonnée au commerce, comme le pratique encore la nobleſſe d'Italie. De ce mariage vinrent:

1. ALEXANDRE, qui ſuit;
2. JACQUES, mort à Montpellier, ſans alliance;
3. FRANÇOIS, Chevalier de BARQUIER, mort Capitaine d'Infanterie au Port-au-Prince en 1774, après avoir ſervi avec honneur en Amérique, dans la dernière guerre, comme en font foi les certificats des différens Gouverneurs de Saint-Domingue;
4. JEAN-BAPTISTE, appelé Dom *Vincent*, Prieur de la Chartreuſe de Rouen, « Religieux d'une grande piété & d'un mérite diſtingué; »
5. CÉCILE, morte fiancée du Marquis de *Lenſſanade*, Miniſtre à la Cour d'Eſpagne;
6. THÉRÈSE, mariée à *François Borrelly*, ancien Capitaine de vaiſſeau au ſervice d'Eſpagne;
7. Et ANNE DE BARQUIER, mariée à *François d'Iſnard*, Seigneur de Malvans, Juge de la ville de Vence.

ALEXANDRE DE BARQUIER, Chevalier, Seigneur titulaire de Malvans & de Clauſonne, ancien Capitaine d'Infanterie au Régiment de Bourbon, Conſeiller, Penſionnaire du Roi; a commencé de ſervir en 1744, s'eſt diſtingué à l'attaque des lignes de Weiſſembourg & au village des Picards, où il fut bleſſé, & reſta ſeul d'Officier à la tête de 14 Grenadiers, débris de deux Compagnies entières. Il s'eſt trouvé au ſiège de Fribourg, & a rendu des ſervices importans dans Antibes, en 1746, lors du bombardement de cette place, ſuivant le certificat du Comte de Sade, Maréchal de Camp & Armées du Roi, mort Commandant de ladite Ville. Il a épouſé, par contrat du 9 Juillet 1749, à Marſeille, *Geneviève de Poivre*, des Barons de Poivre, morte au Port-au-Prince, Isle Saint-Domingue, habitation *Barquier*, en 1777. (Elle étoit iſſue au XVe degré de *Thibaut*, Sire, Baron de *Poivre* & de Bayouville en Champagne, Chevalier Banneret, filleul de Thibaut, Comte de Champagne, ainſi qu'il a été prouvé), & fille d'*Antoine de Poivre*, de Bayouville, & de *Catherine Donadieu*. De ce mariage vinrent:

1. & 2. Deux garçons, morts jeunes;
3. JOSEPH-DAVID, dit *le Comte de Barquier*, né le 7 Juin 1757, Officier au Régiment du Colonel-Général Cavalerie, depuis 1779;
4. ANNE-MARIE, mariée en 1772 à *Michel Arnoux*, de Marſeille;
5. ANNE-CATHERINE-SOPHIE, morte en 1779. Elle avoit épouſé, en 1773, *Jean-Pierre Duprat*, Baron de Precy, Capitaine d'Infanterie, & Ingénieur ordinaire du Roi au Département de la ville d'Antibes;
6. ALEXANDRINE, morte à 17 ans;
7. Et FÉLICITÉ DE BARQUIER, qui vit ſans alliance.

TROISIÈME BRANCHE

Elle a pour chef:

PIERRE DE BARQUIER, Maire d'Antibes, lequel a:

1. Un fils, qui n'eſt pas encore marié;
2. Et ADELAÏDE DE BARQUIER, mariée au Chevalier de *Leſrat*, ancien Lieutenant-Colonel du Régiment de Foix, Lieutenant de Roi, commandant la ville d'Antibes, & Chevalier de Saint-Louis.

ANNE-CHARLOTTE DE BARQUIER, fœur de PIERRE, eſt veuve d'*Honoré de Serra*, Seigneur en partie de Clauſonne, ancien Officier de Dragons, Juge & Préſident en la Maîtriſe des Ports de la ville d'Antibes.

Les alliances directes ou indirectes de cette famille ſont avec les Maiſons de *Grimaldi*, *Laſcaris*, *Doria*, *Pignatelli*, *Léon*, *Hugolen*, *Galean*, *Tondutti*, *Rouverio*, *Ruffi*, *Alberti*, *Graſſi*, *Solis*, *Ancone*, *Calvi*, *Villeneuve*, *Libertat*, *Duprat*, *Broulhony - Fabregues*, &c.

Les armes : *d'azur, au bras vêtu mouvant du flanc, dextre de l'écu, tenant une branche de laurier d'argent, ſurmonté en chef de trois étoiles auſſi d'argent* ; ſupports : *deux lions tenant une bannière fuſelé d'argent & de gueules ; couronne de Marquis* ; devife : *Dulce & decorum eſt pro patriâ mori.*

BARRAL, Marquis d'Arvillard, Comte de Barral, Baron de la Roche-Commier, ancienne Nobleſſe du Dauphiné.

Elle remonte à JEAN DE BARRAL, qui eut pour frère GUIGUES.

Le Dauphin, au mois d'Octobre 1323, inféoda le droit de *Picot*, ou *Vingtain*, à ces deux frères, qui, le 5 Juin 1328, tranſigèrent avec d'autres Nobles qui demeuroient dans la Vallée d'Allevard. (Le *Picot* ou *Vingtain*, eſt un droit de Fief qui ſe perçoit ſur les vins qui ſe vendent dans les Mandemens d'Allevard.)

Les mêmes frères firent, le 4 Septembre 1328, à *Guigues de la Roche*, un albergement ; & le Dauphin HUMBERT leur accorda, le 10 Décembre 1337, & à d'autres Nobles, des franchiſes dans le Mandement d'Allevard.

Cette famille conſerve une reconnoiſſance du 19 Mai 1364, par laquelle GUIGUES DE BARRAL eſt reconnu fils de JEAN DE BARRAL, qui paſſa, le 1er Mars 1392, des inveſtitures à Noble homme *Guillaume Morard*. Ce GUIGUES DE BARRAL, qui ſe reconnoît Vaſſal du Dauphin, eut pour fils: FRANÇOIS, qui ſuit.

C'eſt ce qui eſt prouvé par une reconnoiſſance de CLAUDE & URBAIN DE BARRAL, faite au Dauphin, où ils ſont dits arrière-petits-fils de GUIGUES.

FRANÇOIS eut pour fils:

AYMARD DE BARRAL, qui rendit, en 1413,

hommage au Roi, & le 3 Décembre 1415, il paſſa un accenſement à Noble homme *François de Montfort*. Dans une Sentence rendue le 21 Mars 1435, entre lui & les héritiers de *Rodolphe de Commiers*, il eſt dit fils de FRANÇOIS DE BARRAL. Il épouſa *Léonnelle de Commiers*, fille de Noble & Puiſſant homme Meſſire *Raoul de Commiers*, Chevalier, Co-Seigneur de Saint-Jean-le-Vieil, qui eut pour dot mille florins d'or. Il laiſſa :

HUVET, ou HUMBERT DE BARRAL, qui eut pour femme *Marie Genton*, dont on lui connoît :

1. CLAUDE, qui ſuit ;
2. AYMARD, qui mourut peu de tems avant le 6 Mars 1484. Il eut de ſon mariage avec *Anne-Antoinette de Cezerain* :

    CATHERINE, mariée au Sieur *de Crel*, dit *Poillet* ;
    Et PHILIBERTE, qui fut femme de noble *Jean Monnet* ;

3. Autre AYMARD, Ecuyer, Seigneur de Magny ;
4. URBAIN, qui teſta le 8 Juin 1517, en faveur de PIERRE & de CLAUDE, IIe du nom, ſes neveux, fils de CLAUDE Ier ;
5. GUILLAUME, Grand-Prieur de l'Abbaye d'Ainay, à Lyon, qui teſta le 14 Décembre 1520, & inſtitua auſſi pour ſes héritiers PIERRE, & CLAUDE, IIe du nom, ſes neveux, fils de CLAUDE DE BARRAL, ſon frère ;
6. AYMARDE, mariée, par contrat du 9 Janvier 1481, à noble homme *Claude Truchet* ;
7. JEANNE, femme de Noble *Pierre Charrat* ;
8. Et GABRIELLE, dont le nom paroît dans deux actes des 6 Mars 1484 & 7 Septembre 1490.

CLAUDE DE BARRAL, Ier du nom, ſuivant une expédition du 6 Mars 1484, & un original en parchemin du 8 Mars de la même année, eſt dit fils d'HUVET ou d'HUMBERT DE BARRAL. Il rendit hommage au Roi, avec URBAIN, ſon frère, le 7 Octobre 1507. Dans cet acte ils ſe reconnoiſſent tous deux Hommes-Liges, Nobles & Vaſſaux du Roi, & rendent hommage du droit de *Picot*, ou *Vingtain*, dans le Mandement d'Allevard. Un autre acte, du 12 Janvier 1508, fait voir que l'un & l'autre avoient chacun un droit de *Picot*, ou *Vingtain*. On ignore le nom de la femme de CLAUDE, dont les enfans furent :

1. PIERRE, mort ſans poſtérité ;

2. CLAUDE, qui fuit;
3. GUIGUES, Religieux de l'Abbaye d'Ainay, à Lyon;
4. Et GUILLAUME, mort auffi fans poftérité.

CLAUDE DE BARRAL, IIe du nom, époufa *Michelette Vachon,* dont il eut:

1. LOUIS, qui fuit;
2. Et CLAUDE, Seigneur de Saint-Germain, Capitaine & Major de la Ville de Metz, qui tefta en faveur de GASPARD, fon neveu. Il époufa *Angèle de Bellehouffe,* qui étoit du Pays de Luxembourg. Il n'eut que:

    ANNE, Religieufe au Couvent de Bonpère, à Marienbourg, fur le·Rhin;
    Et CATHERINE, Religieufe au Couvent de Sainte-Claire, à Metz.

LOUIS DE BARRAL, Capitaine-Châtelain de Voiron le 14 Janvier 1570, fut nommé, par Lettres-Patentes du 3 Avril 1570, Commandant dans les même Ville & Château. Il eut auffi, le 6 Juillet fuivant, Commiffion de Capitaine de gens de pied, qu'il eut ordre d'affembler en plus grand nombre qu'il lui feroit poffible, & dont il eut le Commandement en confidération de fon expérience & intelligence au fait de la guerre, & de fon zèle pour le fervice du Roi. Enfin il fut créé Lieutenant-Provincial des Mines & Minières du Lyonnois, Forez, Beaujolois & Bourbonnois, par Lettres du 30 Novembre 1597. Il époufa, par contrat du 25 Février 1565, *Anne de Chambaran,* d'une noble & ancienne race, fœur de *François de Chambaran,* Ecuyer, homme d'armes de la Compagnie du Seigneur de Boiffac, & fille de *Claude de Chambaran,* & de *Claude de Ponchon.* Ses enfans furent:

1. ENNEMOND, mort dans la Ville de Carmagnolle au-delà des Monts, où il commandoit la Compagnie du Sieur de Preffeing;
2. CLAUDE, Ecuyer, Capitaine-Châtelain du Mandement de Voiron, Gouverneur, pour le Roi, du Château d'Entremont, & de la Garnifon qui étoit entretenue dans le Comté;
3. Et GASPARD, qui fuit;

GASPARD DE BARRAL, par le teftament de fon oncle CLAUDE, en 1623, devint, avec fon frère aîné CLAUDE, héritier de fes biens, & il y eut, le 18 Novembre 1623, un accord fait entre lui & la veuve de fon oncle. Il fut pourvu, le 31 Mai 1649, d'un Office de Maître des Requêtes ordinaire de la Reine-Mère, & d'un autre Office de Maître des Requêtes de la

même Reine, le 27 Mars 1665, & tefta le 22 Mai 1667. Il époufa, par contrat du 13 Novembre 1621, *Hélène de Chafte-de-Geffande-Clermont,* qui, par fon teftament du 10 Septembre 1665, chargea fes enfans héritiers de porter fon nom & fes armes écartelées avec les leurs. Elle étoit coufine germaine d'*Annet de Chafte-de-Geffan,* Grand-Maître de l'Ordre de Malte, & fille de noble *Jean de Chafte-de-Geffan,* & de *Pernette de Sallignon.* Leurs enfans furent:

1. FRANÇOIS, qui fuit;
2. CLAUDE, tué les armes à la main au fiège de Turin en 1640, au fervice de Sa Majefté;
3. Et LOUIS-BENOÎT, Capitaine d'Infanterie, puis Gouverneur du Château de Culan, tué à la tête de fa Compagnie, au fiège de Montrond.

FRANÇOIS DE BARRAL-DE-CLERMONT, Ecuyer, Seigneur d'Allevard, de Saint-Pierre d'Allevard, de la Ferrière, de Pinfot, de la Baftie-d'Arvillard, &c., fut nommé le 14 Juin 1644 Subftitut-Général des trois Ordres du Dauphiné, & pourvu, le 28 Février 1661, d'un Office de Confeiller au Parlement de Grenoble. Il acquit la Terre d'Allevard de *Charles de Chabot,* Marquis de Saint-Maurice, le 15 Septembre 1668; & le 4 Avril 1669, Meffire *Michel Pomine,* Docteur ès droits, fubrogea FRANÇOIS DE BARRAL, par acte paffé chez *Caftain,* Notaire à Allevard, à l'enchère & délivrance faite au profit du Sieur *Pomine,* du droit de *Picot* & *Vingtain* du Mandement d'Allevard, comme étant provenu de l'ancienne & noble famille de BARRAL, de laquelle eft iffu ledit FRANÇOIS, lequel acheta la Terre d'Allevard & celle de la Baftie-d'Arvillard, de *Jofeph d'Arvillard,* Seigneur & Baron de la Roche, le 16 Février 1692; il tefta le 25 Décembre 1695, & mourut Doyen du Parlement de Grenoble. Il avoit époufé, par contrat du 3 Février 1663, *Louife de Guerin,* fille de *François de Guerin,* Confeiller au Parlement, & de *Juftine du Faure.* Leurs enfans font:

1. JOSEPH, qui fuit;
2. JOSEPH-ANTOINE, Seigneur du Bellier, mort jeune;
3. JUSTINE, femme de *Sébaftien de Rachais,* Seigneur de Montferrat, Chevalier de Saint-Louis, & Colonel d'un Régiment d'Infanterie de fon nom;
4. ANNE, femme de *Gabriel du Mottet,* Confeiller au Parlement de Grenoble;

5. Emérantine, Prieure du Monaſtère des Religieuſes Chartreuſes de Prémol;

6. Et Louise, Religieuſe Jacobine au Monaſtère Royal de Montfleury.

Joseph de Barral, Marquis de la Baſtie d'Arvillard, Seigneur d'Allevard, de la Ferrière, de Pinſot, de la Chapelle du Bard, de Saint-Pierre d'Allevard, de Rochechinard, de Montferrat & du Bellier, né en 1677, fut pourvu d'un Office de Conſeiller au Parlement de Grenoble en 1698, & de celui de Préſident au même Parlement le 15 Juillet 1708. Il acheta la Maiſon-Forte d'Allevard, le 4 Décembre 1719, de Joſeph de Morard; le 14 Août 1733, il fut inveſti, à la Chambre des Comptes de Dauphiné, des Terres d'Allevard & de la Baſtie d'Arvillard, & le 11 Août 1739 il obtint l'érection de la Terre d'Arvillard en Marquiſat. Les Lettres de cette érection furent vérifiées au Parlement de Grenoble le 5 Septembre 1739; il fut Commandant en chef en Dauphiné pour Sa Majeſté, & eut du Roi une penſion de 3000 livres, pour récompenſe de ſes ſervices. Il teſta le 30 Août 1747. Il avoit épouſé, par contrat du 4 Janvier 1709, *Marie-Françoiſe de Blondel*, fille de *François*, Comte de Siſſonne. Il en a eu:

1. Jean-Baptiste-François, qui ſuit;
2. Jean-Sébastien, né le 15 Octobre 1710, Docteur en Théologie de la Maiſon de Navarre, ci-devant Abbé & Comte d'Aurillac, nommé en 1752 à l'Evêché de Caſtres, en Languedoc, & ſacré le 12 Décembre 1752;
3. Charles-Gabriel-Justin de Barral-de-Rochechinard, né le 4 Mars 1712, Conſeiller au Parlement de Grenoble. Il a obtenu, au mois d'Août 1750, l'érection de ſa Terre de Montferrat en Marquiſat;
4. Joseph-Claude-Mathias, né le 6 Septembre 1714, Aumônier du Roi, Abbé & Comte d'Aurillac, Evêque de Troyes en 1761;
5. François-Antoine, né le 20 Février 1716, Chevalier de Saint-Louis, Lieutenant-Colonel, & Commandant d'un bataillon du Régiment de Belfunce;
6. Charles-Louis, né le 10 Juin 1717, Seigneur du Bellier & de Montagneux, Chevalier de Saint-Louis, & ci-devant Capitaine au Régiment de Belfunce;
7. N..., Cornette du Régiment de Cavalerie de Clermont-Prince, tué, le 27 Juin 1743, à la bataille de Dettingen, ſur le Mein, étant Aide-de-Camp du Comte de Clermont, Prince du Sang;

8. Pierre-Alexandre, né le 26 Août 1724, Docteur de Sorbonne, Prieur d'Ambial, & Vicaire-Général du Dioceſe de Montpellier;
9. Louise-Jacqueline, née le 28 Juin 1713, mariée à *Jean-Emmanuel de Guignard*, Vicomte de Saint-Prieſt, Maître des Requêtes, & Intendant du Languedoc;
10. Justine-Augustine, née le 4 Août 1718, Religieuſe à Montfleury;
11. Louise-Françoise, née le 15 Mai 1720;
12. Marie-Françoise-Sophie, née le 13 Avril 1727, auſſi Religieuſe à Montfleury;
13. Marie-Félicité, née le 19 Juillet 1728;
14. Et N..., morte jeune.

Jean-Baptiste-François de Barral-de-Montferrat, Chevalier, Comte de Barral, Marquis de la Baſtie d'Arvillard, Baron de la Roche-Commier, Seigneur d'Allevard, de Saint-Pierre, de la Ferrière, de Pinſot, de la Chapelle du Bard, &c., né le 2 Novembre 1709, fut pourvu, le 31 Mai 1731, d'un Office de Conſeiller au Parlement de Grenoble, & le 6 Juin 1741 de celui de Préſident à Mortier au même Parlement. Il a obtenu, le 11 Juillet 1751, des Lettres d'Erection en Comté de la Terre d'Allevard, & il y a eu à ce ſujet deux Arrêts d'enregiſtrement au Parlement & à la Chambre des Comptes de Grenoble. Le 4 Août 1751, il a fait hommage en la même Chambre des Comptes du Comté d'Allevard & du Marquiſat d'Arvillard; mais par Lettres-Patentes du mois de Mars 1753, enregiſtrées au Parlement de Grenoble, & en la Chambre des Comptes de cette même Ville, Sa Majeſté a changé le nom de la Terre, Seigneurie & Comté d'Allevard en celui de Barral, en conſidération des grands ſervices que la famille de Barral a anciennement rendus en défendant la Terre d'Allevard contre les inſultes des ennemis qui en ſont voiſins, & en même tems pour reconnoître par-là les importans ſervices de cette famille dans les dignités qu'elle a remplies, tant dans l'Egliſe que dans les principales Charges de la Magiſtrature, & dans différens Emplois Militaires dont elle a été honorée.

Le même Jean-Baptiste-François de Barral a encore obtenu l'érection de la Terre de la Roche-Commier en Baronie, par Lettres-Patentes du mois de Mars 1755, vérifiées au Parlement & à la Chambre des Comptes de Grenoble au mois d'Avril ſuivant. Il s'eſt marié, 1° le 14 Septembre 1735, à *Jeanne-Marie-Dominique de Peyrenc-de-Saint-Cyr*, fille de *Louis de Peyrenc-de-Saint-Cyr*, Gentilhomme ordinaire du Roi, & de *N*.... *Barberie-de-Courteille*, fœur de *Jacques-Dominique de Courteille*, Confeiller-d'Etat, Intendant des Finances, ci-devant Ambaffadeur du Roi en Suiffe, dont il n'a eu qu'un enfant mort au berceau; & 2° le 1er Avril 1741, à *Marie-Charlotte-Françoife-Antoinette de Chaumont-Quitry*. Il laiffa:

1. ARMAND-FRANÇOIS-JOSEPH, né au mois de Mai 1744, mort le 8 Juillet 1753;
2. PIERRE-FRANÇOIS, Comte de Barral, né le 30 Décembre 1745, ci-devant Chevalier de Malte, reçu de minorité le 17 Décembre 1747, qui a payé fon paffage à Malte le 11 Décembre 1749; marié, par contrat figné le 15 Février 1764 (célébration le 16), à *Marie-Séraphine de la Motte;*
3. Un fils, né le 18 Juillet 1763;
4. LOUISE-JOSÈPHE-CLAUDE-SOPHIE, née le 12 Novembre 1753;
5. MARIE - FRANÇOISE - HENRIETTE-ADÉLAÏDE, née le 31 Janvier 1757;
6. Et BARBE-SOPHIE-JEANNE, appelée *Mademoifelle de la Roche-Commier*, née le 2 Décembre 1759, ~~morte.~~

Les armes: *de gueules, à trois bandes d'argent, & un chef auffi d'argent, chargé de trois cloches d'azur, bataillées d'or.*

Cette Généalogie, dreffée fur les titres, fe trouve conforme à ce qu'on lit fur cette famille dans la nouvelle édition du *Dictionnaire* de Moréri.

BARRAS. Cette famille eft une des plus anciennes de Provence, qui a pris fon nom de la Terre de Barras, dans la Viguerie de Digne. Elle eft connue dès le XIe fiècle, fuivant les Chartes des Croifades d'Embrun, où l'on trouve un BARRAS fe croifer avec diftinction pour la conquête de la Terre-Sainte.

Un autre BARRAS de BARRAS, Seigneur de Saint-Eftève, vivoit vers l'an 1230. Il eut de *Louife du Puget:*

1. RAYMOND, qui fuit;
2. & 3. FERRAND & GUILLAUME, Ier du nom, qui furent tous deux Chevaliers de l'Ordre de Saint-Jean de Jérufalem, dont ils devinrent Grands-Commandeurs;
4. Et DAUPHINE DE BARRAS, mariée à *Guillaume de Signe*, Seigneur de Puymichel, dont naquit SAINTE-DELPHINE, époufe de *Saint-Elzéar-de-Sabran.*

RAYMOND eut deux fils:

GUILLAUME, IIe du nom, qualifié *Miles*, dans un acte paffé le 24 Février 1291;

Et BERTRAND, tige des Seigneurs de *Mirabeau*, dont un cadet fe retira à Arles, & duquel les Seigneurs de *Lençac*, établis dans cette Ville, fe difent iffus.

JEAN DE BARRAS fut Sénéchal de Provence en 1280.

RAYBAUD DE BARRAS fut un des ôtages envoyés au Roi d'Aragon, pour la délivrance de CHARLES II, Duc d'Anjou, détenu prifonnier à Barcelone.

JACQUES DE BARRAS, Ier du nom, iffu par divers degrés de GUILLAUME, Ier du nom, tranfigea le 15 Février 1398 avec les Frères Prêcheurs de Sifteron, au fujet d'un legs fait par fes prédéceffeurs. Il eut pour defcendant au XIIe degré:

JOSEPH DE BARRAS, chef du nom, qui a époufé, par contrat du 9 Juin 1754, *Jeanne-Elifabeth Boniface de Fombeton*, dont eft iffu:

JEAN-JOSEPH-HIPPOLYTE DE BARRAS, né & baptifé le 12 Juillet 1756.

LOUIS DE BARRAS eft tige des Seigneurs de *Saint-Laurent*, branche cadette, qui fubfifte dans fes defcendans.

Voyez Artefeuil, tom. I, pag. 96 & fuiv.; & Gaufridy, Bouche, Notradamus, le Moine des Isles d'or, les Chartes des Croifades d'Embrun du XIe fiècle, rapportées par le père Hardouin, &c.

Les armes: *fafcé d'or & d'azur de fix pièces*; devife: VAILLANCE DE BARRAS.

BARRE (DE LA). M. DE LA BARRE D'ARBOUVILLE, chef de la branche aînée, nous a envoyé un mémoire qui dit que cette ancienne famille noble eft originaire de Flandres, qu'elle a donné de Grands-Baillis de Gand, & un fouverain Bailli de Flandres. C'eft ce qu'a fans doute ignoré feu M. le Marquis de *Prunelé*, Seigneur de Tignonville, qui, dans fon Mémoire la difoit originaire de Beauce; mais c'eft une branche qui s'y eft établie en 1330, & dont voici la filiation:

I. GUILLAUME DE LA BARRE, Ier du nom (*a*),

(*a*) Le Marquis de *Prunelé*, dans fon Mémoire, inféré dans la deuxième édition du *Dictionnaire de la Nobleffe*, par de la Chenaye-Desbois, pag. 744 & fuiv., le dit pourvu de l'office de Châtelain en la Sénéchauffée de Ponthieu, par Lettres-Patentes données à Paris, le 18 Juillet 1426, par le Duc de Bedford, Régent en France pour HENRI VI, Roi d'Angleterre, foi-difant

Chevalier, Seigneur de Chauvincourt & d'E-
rainville, Paroisse d'Alainville-aux-Bois,
près Dourdan, épousa, vers 1430, *Robine
d'Orval*, fille de *Jean d'Orval*, Écuyer, Seigneur d'Ozouer-le-Marché, dont il eut:

II. JEAN DE LA BARRE, Chevalier, marié à
Clémence de Saint-Quentin. Il fut père de:

III. JEAN DE LA BARRE, IIe du nom, Ecuyer,
qui s'allia avec *Marguerite*, dont il eut:

   JEAN, qui suit;

   Et GUILLAUME, mort Commandeur des Commanderies de Châlons, Metz & Nancy,
   ainsi qu'il paroît par un ancien *Mémoire* de
   famille.

IV. JEAN DE LA BARRE, IIIe du nom, E-
cuyer, Seigneur de Rinville, ainsi qu'il est
prouvé par des aveux, & dénombremens,
épousa *Jeanne de Souplainville*, fille de *Guillaume de Souplainville*, Chevalier, Bailli &
Gouverneur de Montargis. De ce mariage
vint:

V. GUILLAUME DE LA BARRE, IIe du nom,
Ecuyer, Seigneur de Rinville, Châtelain en
titre d'office de la Sénéchaussée de Ponthieu,
ce qui est justifié par la commission à lui donnée par HENRI VI, Roi d'Angleterre, en date
du 18 Juillet 1426. Le *Mémoire*, sans nommer sa femme (a), lui donne pour fils:

VI. JEAN DE LA BARRE, IVe du nom, Ecuyer,
Seigneur de Rinville, dont il fit hommage le
20 Juin 1483, au Chapitre de l'Eglise de Paris & de Bandeville; & par sa femme, Seigneur de Groslieu, Arbouville & Vaubenard,
mort le 8 Mars 1489, & inhumé dans l'E-
glise de Saint-Germain de Dourdan. Il avoit
épousé, par contrat passé devant *Rolère*, Tabellion à Estampes, le 18 Novembre 1455,
Marie Desmazis, née le 28 Mars 1440, remariée à *Jean II*, Seigneur *de Montmorency*,
Grand-Chambellan de France, dont descend
la branche des Ducs de ce nom. Elle étoit
fille de *Jean Desmazis*, Ecuyer, Seigneur de
Brières, Marchais, &c., Capitaine & Bailli
des Ville & Château d'Estampes & de Dourdan, & de *Jeanne de Brouillard*, fille de

---

Roi de France, lors mineur. Il lui donne pour
père & mère, JEAN DE LA BARRE, Ecuyer, &
Jeanne de Souplainville, sa seconde femme.
                      (Note des Editeurs).

(a) M. le Marquis *de Prunelé* donne à ce GUIL-
LAUME, pour femme, *Robine d'Orval*, que M. *de
la Barre d'Arbouville* donne à GUILLAUME, Ier
du nom, qui est venu s'établir en Beauce.

   Tome II.

Guillaume de Brouillard, Chambellan du
Roi, & de *Marguerite d'Orgemont*. Du
mariage de JEAN DE LA BARRE, IVe du nom,
vinrent:

  1. JACQUES, qui suit;

  2. JEAN, auteur de la branche des Seigneurs de
    Laage en Poitou, rapportée ci-après;

  3. MARGUERITE, femme, le 12 Août 1495, de
    Nicolas du Bouchet, Ecuyer, Seigneur d'E-
    trechy en Brie;

  4. Et CLAUDINE (elle est nommée CATHERINE
    dans le *Mémoire* de feu M. le Marquis *de
    Prunelé*), femme de *Claude de Saintoyré*,
    Ecuyer, Seigneur de Sous.

VII. JACQUES DE LA BARRE, Ier du nom, &
deuxième Seigneur d'Arbouville, Groslieu &
Vaubenard, mort le 11 Juillet 1528, avoit
épousé *Jeanne du Bouchet*. Ils furent inhumés l'un & l'autre dans la Chapelle de Groslieu, & eurent pour enfans:

  1. FRANÇOIS, qui suit;

  2. LOUIS, auteur de la branche des Seigneurs
    de *la Chauffée*, établie en Nivernois, rap-
    portée ci-après;

  3. MARGUERITE, femme, le 2 Septembre 1514,
    de *Louis d'Estouteville*, Chevalier, Seigneur
    de Villeconin;

  4. Et ANNE, femme, le 1er Décembre 1515,
    de *Jean de Réviers*, Ecuyer, Seigneur de
    Soufy. Voyez RÉVIERS.

VIII. FRANÇOIS DE LA BARRE, Chevalier de
l'Ordre du Roi, l'un des 100 Gentilshommes
de son Hôtel, Seigneur d'Arbouville, Groslieu, Vaubenard, d'Harocourt, des grand &
petit Jouanais & de Bandeville, épousa, par
contrat passé devant *Guy*, Tabellion à Estampes, le 6 Juillet 1532, *Pernelle de Fleury*,
fille de *François de Fleury*, Chevalier, Seigneur de Ruperfond, & de *Jeanne de Re-
quiers*, Dame d'Harocourt, dont:

  1. JACQUES, qui suit;

  2. Et ANNE, femme de *Louis de Duisson*, Che-
    valier, Seigneur de Rougemont. Elle par-
    tagea devant *Chantosme*, Notaire à Bre-
    taucourt, le 25 Mars 1569, avec son frère,
    la succession de ses père & mère. Le second
    Mémoire dit qu'elle épousa *Jean de Sinxe*,
    Chevalier, Seigneur de Quatrevaux &
    d'Ormeville. C'est sans doute en secondes
    noces.

IX. JACQUES DE LA BARRE, IIe du nom, Chevalier, Seigneur d'Arbouville, Groslieu, Harocourt, des grand & petit Jouanais, Gentilhomme ordinaire de la Maison du Roi, mort

en 1587, avoit épousé 1° *Louise d'Argenson*, fille de *François d'Argenson*, Chevalier, Seigneur d'Aveснes & de Montchery, & de *Jeanne de Cochefilet*; & 2° le 25 Avril 1577, *Claude de Duyson*, fille d'*Etienne*, Chevalier, Seigneur de Boisminard, & de *Marthe de Percy*, Dame de Guigneville *(a)*. Il eut du premier lit:

1. ANTOINE, qui suit;

Et du second:

2. N..., mariée à *Jacques de Neucard*, Chevalier, Seigneur de Boissy;
3. Et N..., mariée à *François de Poilloue*, Chevalier, Seigneur de Saelas.

X. ANTOINE DE LA BARRE *(b)*, Ecuyer, Seigneur d'Arbouville, Groslieu, d'Harocourt, le grand & petit Jouanais, d'Hattonville & de Boisminard, mort le 1er Septembre 1641, avoit épousé *Marie le Roux*, dont:

1. JACQUES, qui suit;
2. ANDRÉ, Capitaine au Régiment du Plessis-Praslin, tué au siège de Crémone en 1702;
3. Et MARGUERITE, mariée à *César de Galmet*, Ecuyer, Seigneur de Lintrie & de la Croix.

XI. JACQUES DE LA BARRE, IIIe du nom, Chevalier de l'Ordre du Roi, Seigneur d'Arbouville, Groslieu, Hattonville, Boisminard, épousa, le 16 Novembre 1631, *Marie Desmazis*, fille de *Gédéon-Sanguin Desmazis*, Chevalier, Seigneur du Tronchet, Chalo-Saint-Mars, Brégy, Vicomte de Beaumont en partie, homme de la Chambre du Roi, Enseigne de ses Gardes-du-Corps, & d'*Anne de*

Rochechouart, fille de *Louis de Rochechouart*, & de *Marie de Castelnau-Mauvisière*, dont:

1. LOUIS-ALEXANDRE, qui suit;
2. LOUIS, dit *le Chevalier de Groslieu*, Chevalier des Ordres de Saint-Lazare & du Mont-Carmel, mort le 11 Août 1666, Commandant le Vaisseau des dix Ordres pour le service du Roi, après avoir pris quatre Vaisseaux Anglois, & en avoir fait échouer deux. Voyez Moréri au mot GROSLIEU;
3. PAUL, Chevalier, Seigneur de Boisminard, Capitaine au Régiment de Rambures, mort sans alliance;
4. Et MARIE, alliée à *Paul de la Mouchetière*, Chevalier, Seigneur de Guignonville.

XII. LOUIS-ALEXANDRE DE LA BARRE, Chevalier, Seigneur d'Arbouville, Groslieu & Hattonville, épousa, sous l'autorité de LOUIS XIV, *Elisabeth Doufrère*, dont:

1. LOUIS-ALEXANDRE, qui suit;
2. PAUL-GÉDÉON, marié à *Héloïse de Bouseube*, veuve de *N...... de Dillon*, Capitaine dans le Régiment du Milord *Dillon*, son frère, laquelle fut élevée à Saint-Cyr;
3. Et MARGUERITE, morte fille.

XIII. LOUIS-ALEXANDRE DE LA BARRE, Chevalier, Seigneur d'Arbouville, Groslieu & Hattonville, mort le 3 Mars 1740, avoit épousé, *Henriette de Languedoue de la Villeneuve*, morte à Groslieu en 1740, fille de *Chrétien de Languedoue de la Villeneuve*, Chevalier, Seigneur d'Ouarville, Reclinville, Montguignard, & de *Marie d'Alègre*. Leurs enfans sont :

1. LOUIS-HENRI-RENÉ, qui suit;
2. PAUL-ARMAND-ALEXANDRE, dit *le Chevalier* DE LA BARRE, marié à *Madeleine Pichonel*;
3. MARIE-MARGUERITE-JULIE, dite *Mademoiselle d'Arbouville*, née le 28 Septembre 1724, morte le 13 Mai 1762. Elle avoit été mariée, le 29 Janvier 1753, dans l'Eglise de Saint-Gilles à Estampes, à *Hector de Tarragon*, Chevalier, Seigneur de Mainvilliers, ancien Capitaine au Régiment de Bassigny, dont un fils;
4. Et ADÉLAÏDE, morte fille le 12 Mai 1762.

XIV. LOUIS-HENRI-RENÉ DE LA BARRE, Chevalier, Seigneur d'Arbouville, Groslieu, Hattonville & Reclinville, a épousé, en 1750, *Denise-Jeanne-Baptiste de Mosset*, fille de *Pierre de Mosset*, Chevalier, Seigneur de Chillois & des Roches, Brigadier des Armées du Roi, dont il n'y a point d'enfans en 1772.

(a) Le *Mémoire* de M. de Prunelé dit que ce JACQUES épousa, 1° le 12 Octobre 1563, *Marthe Acarie*, morte sans enfans, fille de *Girard*, Ecuyer, Seigneur de Liffermeau, & de *Marie Chantault*, Dame d'Hattonville ou Hottonville; 2° par contrat passé devant *Monteneil*, Notaire à Houdan, le 28 Août 1567, *Louise d'Argenson*, fille de *François*, Ecuyer, Seigneur d'Avenne, & de *Jeanne de Cochefilet*; & 3° *Claude de Duyson*. Ce mémoire donne à cette troisième pour fils, CLAUDE, dont la postérité masculine est éteinte, & non deux filles, comme le marque le second *Mémoire*, d'après lequel nous écrivons.

(b) Cet ANTOINE, suivant le Marquis de Prunelé, eut trois femmes : la première, *Marie de la Motte*, fille d'*Antoine*, Ecuyer, Seigneur de Saint-Firmin, morte sans enfans. La seconde, *Marie de Hilaire*, aussi morte sans enfans; & la troisième, cette *Marie le Roux*. Pourquoi le Chevalier d'*Arbouville*, qui est si au fait de sa Généalogie, a-t-il oublié ces deux mariages?

BRANCHE
des Seigneurs de LA CHAUSSÉE.

VIII. LOUIS DE LA BARRE *(a)*, Seigneur de la Chauſſée & de Villemue en Nivernois, ſecond fils de JACQUES, Ier du nom, Seigneur d'Arbouville, &c., & de *Jeanne du Bouchet*, vivoit encore en 1550, avec *Jacquette de Fontenay*, ſa femme, dont il eut :

1. FRANÇOIS, marié à *Marguerite de Clèves*, fille naturelle de *Charles*, Duc de Nevers, dont il n'eut qu'une fille, nommée ANNE DE LA BARRE, mariée à *Jean de Meung*, Chevalier, Seigneur de Doys, laquelle n'eut point d'enfans ;
2. PHILIBERT, qui ſuit ;
3. Et MARGUERITE.

IX. PHILIBERT DE LA BARRE, Ecuyer, Seigneur de la Chauſſée & de Villemue, eut d'*Anne de Béron*, quinze enfans, entr'autres :

1. ALAIN, l'aîné, tué au ſiège de la Mure en Dauphiné ;
2. CLAUDE, marié à *Eliſabeth de Murat*, de laquelle vinrent :
   FRANÇOIS & ETIENNE, tous deux tués au ſervice ; le dernier d'une mouſquetade au côté, au-deſſus de la hanche, étant Capitaine au Régiment de Langeron ;
   Et MARGUERITE, Dame de Villemue, mariée ;
3. Et SIMON, qui ſuit.

X. SIMON DE LA BARRE, Ecuyer, Seigneur de la Chauſſée & de Chevroux près Clamecy en Nivernois, épouſa 1° *Aimée de Sillerieu* ; & 2° *Anne de Brou*. Il eut du premier lit :

1. THOMAS, qui ſuit ;
Et du ſecond :
2. ALEXANDRE, qui étoit encore bien jeune lors du ſiège de Corbie en 1636, & dont on ignore l'alliance.

XI. THOMAS DE LA BARRE, Chevalier, Seigneur de Lorgues, juſtifia de ſa nobleſſe devant l'Intendant de Moulins, le 7 Juin 1667, & eſt le biſayeul de N... DE LA BARRE, Capitaine de Cavalerie.

BRANCHE
des Seigneurs DE LAAGE en Poitou.

VII. JEAN DE LA BARRE, ſecond fils de JEAN, IVe du nom, & de *Marie Deſmaʒis*, fut Ar-

cher de la Garde du Roi, & vint s'établir près de Saint-Maixent en Poitou, où il épouſa, le 12 Octobre 1492, *Jeanne de Poiſpaillie*, dont :

1. JEAN, qui ſuit ;
2. Et JACQUES, auteur de la branche de la Gueslonnière, ſur laquelle nous n'avons point reçu de *Mémoire*.

VIII. JEAN DE LA BARRE, IIe du nom de cette branche, auſſi Archer de la Garde du Roi, s'établit près de Chatelleraut en Poitou, & y épouſa *Tiennette de Maiʒe*, Dame de la Salle, dont :

IX. MAURICE DE LA BARRE, titré *Lieutenant de Robe-Courte*, dans une donation à lui faite par le Roi, en date du 11 Septembre 1572. Le 8 Décembre 1573, Sa Majeſté le fit Capitaine du Château de Châteauneuf-ſur-Charente ; puis le 1er Juin 1574, il fut fait un de ſes 100 Gentilshommes. Il épouſa, le 3 Février 1577, *Claude de Laage*, qui lui porta la Terre de ſon nom, & en eut :

X. HENRI DE LA BARRE, auſſi l'un des 100 Gentilshommes du Roi, & Capitaine de 100 hommes dans le Régiment de Laval, qui épouſa, le 25 Mars 1641, *Renée le Merre*. De ce mariage vint :

XI. HENRI-JOSEPH DE LA BARRE, Seigneur de Laage, Mouſquetaire du Roi, puis Subdélégué des Maréchaux de France. Il épouſa, le 21 Août 1670, *Françoiſe de Préʒeau*, dont :

XII. JOSEPH DE LA BARRE, Seigneur de Laage, Mouſquetaire du Roi, marié, le 21 Août 1701, avec *Marie-Madeleine Mangot*, de laquelle ſont ſortis :

1. JOSEPH-FRANÇOIS, qui ſuit ;
2. & 3. PIERRE & JACQUES ;
4. & 5. HENRIETTE & MARIE DE LA BARRE.

XIII. JOSEPH-FRANÇOIS DE LA BARRE, Seigneur de Laage, Chevalier de Saint-Louis, Capitaine au Régiment de Richelieu le 17 Juillet 1731, a épouſé, le 16 Janvier 1738, *Marie-Jeanne de Blom,* fille de Meſſire *Sylvain de Blom*, Chevalier, Seigneur de Beaupuy en Poitou, dont :

1. ALEXIS-THIBAUT-GASPARD, qui ſuit ;
2. HENRI-THIBAUT DE LA BARRE-DE-LAAGE, d'abord élève de l'Ecole Royale-Militaire, puis Cornette au Régiment de Lanant, Dragons ;
3. MARIE-DOROTHÉE, femme de N... *de Véty de Villeneuve*, Marquis de Vittée ;
4. Et VICTOIRE DE LA BARRE, morte élève à l'Abbaye Royale de Saint-Cyr.

(a) Le Marquis de *Prunelé* le dit ſecond fils de JEAN DE LA BARRE, & de *Marie Deſmaʒis*.
(Note des Editeurs.)

XIV. Alexis-Thibaut-Gaspard de la Barre, Seigneur de Laage, d'abord Page du Roi, puis Capitaine-Commandant de la Colonelle du Régiment des Huffards de Chamborant, a époufé *Geneviève Lévêque*, Américaine, de laquelle on ignore s'il a des enfans.

Les armes: *d'argent, à la bande d'azur, chargée de 3 coquilles d'or & accompagnée de 2 merlettes de fable, l'une en chef & l'autre en pointe.* Supports: *deux lions.*

BARRE (la), en Berry, famille noble dont il eft parlé dans l'*Armorial de France*, reg. I, part. I, pag. 51.

Jean de la Barre, Ecuyer, fut marié, le 13 Mai 1464, avec *Bonne de Maroles*, Dame de Gérigny.

François de la Barre, un de fes defcendans, frère de Gabriel de la Barre, reçu Chevalier de Malte au Grand-Prieuré de France, le 3 Novembre 1608, étoit bifayeul de Michel de la Barre, Ecuyer, Seigneur des Troches & de Cloux; marié, le 18 Mars 1719, avec *Marie de Reugni*, fille de *François de Reugni*, Ecuyer ordinaire du Roi, & Aide-de-Camp dans les Armées de Sa Majefté, & d'*Anne de Champfeu*. De ce mariage font iffus:

1. Pierre-Marie de la Barre-de-Chassenay, Chevalier, baptifé le 18 Février 1722;
2. Et Eustache-Catherine de la Barre-des-Troches, Chevalier, baptifé le 12 Décembre 1723, & reçu Page de la Chambre du Roi, le 2 Janvier 1736, fur les preuves de fa noblefle.

Michel de la Barre, rapporté ci-deffus, étoit neveu de Pierre de la Barre, Seigneur des Nouettes, Chevalier de Saint-Louis, & Major du Régiment d'Anjou, Cavalerie.

Les armes: *d'azur, à 3 feuilles de chêne d'or, tigées de même, pofées 2 & 1, & garnies chacune d'un gland d'or.*

BARRE (la), Seigneur du Pleffis, de Bonnières, de Bermenil, en Normandie, Généralité de Rouen, famille maintenue en fa nobleffe, le 23 Janvier 1667, dont les armes font: *d'azur, à trois croiffans d'or, 2 & 1.*

BARRE (la), Seigneur de Nanteuil, en Normandie, Généralité de Rouen, famille maintenue en fa nobleffe, le 13 Décembre 1668, qui porte: *de gueules, à trois merlettes d'argent, 2 & 1.*

BARRE (la), Seigneur de Gouverville, en Normandie, Généralité de Rouen, famille maintenue dans fa Nobleffe, le 14 Février 1670, dont les armes font: *d'azur, au chevron d'or, accompagné en chef de deux oifeaux de même, & en pointe d'une étoile d'argent.*

BARRE (la), Seigneur de Mouféron: *de gueules, à la bande de vair.*

BARRE (la), en Touraine: *d'or, à 6 croiffans de fable, 3, 2 & 1.*

BARRE (la), en Touraine: *d'azur, à la bande d'or, accofté de 2 croiffans montans de même.*

BARRE (la), en Touraine: *d'argent, à trois lions de fable, armés, lampaffés & couronnés d'or, pofés 2 & 1.*

BARRE (la): *d'or, au gros mâtin d'azur, aboyant, accompagné de trois étoiles de gueules, deux en chef & une en pointe.*

BARRE (la): *d'azur, à la bande d'or.*

BARRE (la), Seigneur de Cerçay: *d'azur, à la bande d'argent.*

BARRE (la): *d'argent, au chevron de gueules, accompagné de trois molettes d'éperon de fable, deux en chef & une en pointe.*

BARRE (la), en Bretagne: *de gueules, au chevron d'argent, accompagné de trois étoiles de même, 2 & 1.*

* BARRE (la Grande Barre), Fief & Terre, fubdélégation d'Alençon en Normandie, érigée en Marquifat depuis peu d'années en faveur de M. le Marquis *de la Cervelle.*

BARRE (la), Seigneur de Gaudreville. De cette famille étoit Jean de la Barre, Seigneur de Gaudreville, qui époufa, vers l'an 1400, *Agnès Valleton*, qui le rendit père de Colinette de la Barre, Dame de Gaudreville, femme, le 10 Octobre 1423, de *Guy Prunelé*, Seigneur de la Porte, en partie de Rieux & d'Alzonne, en Languedoc, dont la poftérité fubfifte. Voyez PRUNELÉ.

Les armes: *d'argent, freté de gueules.*

* BARRE-DE-BIERNÉ (la). Les Terres compofant le Marquifat de la Barre au Maine, ayant été acquifes par le Marquis de Torcy, il en obtint l'érection en Comté fous la dénomination de *la Barre-de-Bierné*, par Lettres du mois d'Octobre 1735, enregiftrées au Parlement de Paris, le 10 Décembre 1735.

Ce Comté eft échu à *Jeanne-Marie-Con-*

ſtance de *Mailly*, épouſe du Marquis de *Voyer*, par le partage fait en date du... Décembre 1758, depuis lequel partage le ſecond fils du Marquis de *Croiſſy* a quitté le nom de *Comte de Bierné*, & ſon pere l'a nommé *Marquis de Torcy*: il eſt Sous-Lieutenant dans la Gendarmerie. Voyez COLBERT.

BARRE-DE-MARTIGNY (LA), en Brie, famille repréſentée par trois freres:

ANTOINE DE LA BARRE, qui a laiſſé:

LOUIS-FRANÇOIS-PAUL DE LA BARRE, dit *le Chevalier de la Tillaye*, Seigneur de la Tillaye-lez-Coutrevou, en Brie, & dè la Gueriniere, en Beauce, Chevalier de Saint-Louis, Capitaine retiré d'Infanterie, veuf de N... dont il a une fille, née en 1756.

LÉANDRE DE LA BARRE, pere de N.... DE LA BARRE, appelé le *Marquis de Martigny*, né le 4 Décembre 1705, marié à *Nicole-Suſanne Roẓer*.

Et JEAN-BAPTISTE DE LA BARRE, d'abord appelé le *Chevalier de Martigny*, aujourd'hui le *Marquis de Martigny*, Chevalier de Saint-Louis, Meſtre-de-Camp de Cavalerie, retiré du ſervice avec penſion & appointemens, à la fin de 1767, étant Maréchal-des-Logis de la premiere Compagnie des Mouſquetaires, Seigneur de Martigny, Miline-l'Apoſtole, du fief de Cornillon, &c., né le 11 Juillet 1690, marié, le 1ᵉʳ Mars 1732, à *Catherine-Hélène de Lauzieres-de-Cardaillac*, Comteſſe de Thérines, morte le 17 Juin 1766. Il a pour enſ... ſ:

1. ELISABETH, née le 2 Décembre 1740, à St-Germain-lez-Couilly, admiſe ſur ſes preuves de nobleſſe, & élevée à la Maiſon Royale de Saint-Louis à Saint-Cyr; mariée, le 6 Juin 1763, à *Auguſte-Jean-François-Antoine de Labroue*, Baron de Vareilles-Summieres. Voyez LABROUE;
2. Et JEAN-BAPTISTE-FRANÇOIS, né le 2 Août 1742, qui a été Mouſquetaire dans la premiere Compagnie, & ſert actuellement dans le Corps des Dragons de la Légion-Royale.

Les armes: *écartelé, au 1 d'or, à 3 fuſées de ſable, rangées en faſce; aux 2 & 3 d'argent, à 3 faſces de ſable; & au 4 d'or, à 5 cotices de gueules.*

BARRE-PUFFÉ: *d'azur, à la faſce d'or, chargée d'une étoile de gueules.*

BARRÉ, Seigneur de Montfort, des Coutures, en Normandie, Généralité d'Alençon, famille annoblie en 1547.

ANTOINE BARRÉ, Sieur de Couſtau ou Coutures, épouſa, vers 1580, *Jeanne Tardif*, Dame de Douſſey. Leur fille, MARIE BARRÉ, fut mariée à *Nicolas Potier*, Seigneur d'Ocquiere, Secrétaire d'Etat, ſur la démiſſion de *Louis Potier*, Seigneur de Gèvres, ſon oncle.

PIERRE-ALEXANDRE BARRÉ, Seigneur de Bordigny & des Autieux, épouſa, vers 1710, *Marie-Anne du Vaucel-de-Berville*.

Les armes: *de gueules, à 3 bandes d'or; au chef d'argent, chargé de 3 hures de ſangliers de ſable.*

Une autre branche, qui a été maintenue dans ſa Nobleſſe, le 31 Janvier 1767, Seigneur des Autieux, Généralité d'Alençon, porte pour armes: *d'azur, à 3 faſces d'or ſurmontées de trois têtes d'oiſeaux d'argent.*

BARRÉ: *coupé d'argent & de gueules, l'argent chargé d'un lion léopardé de gueules, & le gueules de trois bandes d'or.*

⚜ BARREL, DES BARRES OU DE BARREL, ancienne Nobleſſe originaire de Champagne, nommée dans leurs titres latins *Barrezus* ou *Barrelli*, dont le premier connu eſt:

JEAN DES BARRES, qui vivoit en 1097, & fut noyé à la rupture du Pont de Lepte. Toutes les hiſtoires d'alors font la mention la plus honorable de GUILLAUME DES BARRES, Comte de Rochefort, iſſu de JEAN, l'un des plus grands guerriers de ſon ſiecle, ſurnommé l'Achille de ſon tems, qui exiſtoit avec éclat ſous le regne de PHILIPPE-AUGUSTE. « Il fut ayeul de JEAN DE CHAMPRONT, marié à *Clémence de Dreux*. » On voit par un état des Chevaliers François qui ſuivirent le Roi Saint-Louis à la Terre-Sainte en 1247, que JEAN DES BARRES, IIᵉ du nom, étoit du nombre des plus illuſtres croiſés. « Un autre JEAN fut Maréchal de France en 1318. » Depuis ces tems reculés, les Seigneurs des BARRES ont vécu dans la Province de Champagne, d'une maniere diſtinguée, ayant donné pluſieurs Officiers Généraux aux Armées de nos Rois.

I. CLAUDE DES BARRES (a), Chevalier, qui

_____

(a) La Chenaye-Desbois le dit fils de CLAUDE DES BARRES, Seigneur de Bréchainville, & de *Michelle Hédelin*, & lui donne pour enfans:
1. EVRARD, qui étoit Grand-Maître de l'Ordre du Temple, & commandoit l'Armée de LOUIS VII, quand il arriva en Afrique;
2. HUBERT, qui fut Prieur des Bouconvilliers;

descendoit des Seigneurs des Barres, ci-deſſus mentionnés, eſt connu en Provence, par le contrat de mariage d'un de ſes fils. Il épouſa, ainſi que le porte cet acte, *Marie-Marguerite Gouffier*, ſœur d'*Artus Gouffier*, Comte d'Eſtampes, Gouverneur du Dauphiné. Il eut entr'autres enfans:

Pluſieurs fils, qui formèrent diverſes branches;
Et Augustin, qui ſuit.

II. Augustin des Barres (*a*), le plus jeune de ſes frères, ayant quitté la Maiſon paternelle pour quelques mécontentemens domeſtiques, s'établit en Provence ſous le nom de Barrel. Il conſte qu'il fut bienfaiteur de l'Ordre de Saint-Jean de Jéruſalem, ſuivant un acte du 24 Mars 1521, s'étant enſuite attaché à la Cour d'Henri, Roi de Navarre, il devint Gentilhomme de ſa Chambre, comme il eſt juſtifié par un paſſe-port donné à Paris le 3 Septembre 1582, ſigné de ce Prince & contreſigné par Deloppes, ſon Secrétaire, duement ſcellé. Ce paſſe-port eſt conçu dans des termes qui font connoître l'état que tenoit le Seigneur de Barrel à la Cour du Roi de Navarre. Il épouſa, à Avignon, par contrat du 30 Octobre 1535 (*b*), reçu par *Dalmas* & *Maugoni*, Notaires d'Avignon, *Etiennette de Renaud*, de la Maiſon d'*Alenc*, dont il eut:

III. Jean-Pierre de Barrel, qui paſſa pluſieurs actes à Avignon, ès années 1611 & 1643, reçus par *Fort* & *Bellou*, Notaires. Il avoit épouſé, par contrat du 19 Mars 1588, paſſé devant *Laville*, Notaire, *Jeanne de Marrel*, d'une famille diſtinguée du Dauphiné, fille de *Pierre de Marrel*, & de Dame *des Iſnards*. Leurs enfans furent:

Guillaume, qui ſuit;

---

3. Et Claude, qui fut Gentilhomme ordinaire de la Chambre du Roi.

Les armes: *d'azur, au chevron d'or, accompagné de 3 coquilles de même.*

(*a*) La Chenaye-Desbois le dit fils de noble Honoré Barrel, Syndic de la ville d'Aix en 1492, ainſi qu'il conſte par les regiſtres de cette communauté, & de *Jeannette de Vachères*.

(*b*) La Chenaye-Desbois dit qu'Augustin de Barrel ſe maria en 1525, & eut pour fils:

Michel de Barrel, qui épouſa, en 1569, *Peyronne d'Almeran*, dont naquit:

Jean-Pierre de Barrel, ſubſtitué après ſon père, aux biens de *Jacques de Renaud*, des Seigneurs d'*Alenc*, par teſtament du 27 Août 1582, & marié, en 1607, à *Jeanne de Martel*, dont il eut Guillaume de Barrel. (*Note des Editeurs*).

Et Anne de Barrel, mariée à *Jean de Boulſicaud*, Gentilhomme de la ville d'Arles.

IV. Guillaume de Barrel, Seigneur en partie du Reveſt, le Gubran & Vachères, Terres qu'il acquit par acte paſſé en 1679, devant *Arnaud*, Notaire de Forcalquier, s'adonna à l'étude des Loix & devint un des plus grands Juriſconſultes de ſon tems, fut fait Docteur ès droit de l'Univerſité d'Avignon en 1632, fut nommé premier Profeſſeur Royal en celle d'Aix, choiſi en 1671 pour aſſeſſeur & Procureur de la Province, fit ſon teſtament le 14 Novembre 1684, devant *Beauzin*, Notaire d'Aix, par lequel il voulut être inhumé dans l'Egliſe de Saint-Jean de Jéruſalem & en la Chapelle de Notre-Dame d'Eſpérance, appartenant à l'Ordre de Malte, laquelle lui fut donnée en reconnoiſſance de ſervices rendus à l'Ordre par ſa famille. L'acte en fut paſſé en 1676 devant *Alpheran*, Notaire. Il y eſt dit que Guillaume de Barrel & ſes deſcendans jouiront de ladite Chapelle à perpétuité, qu'ils auront le droit d'y faire placer leurs armes, d'y faire bâtir un caveau pour leur ſépulture, & d'y avoir un banc diſtingué. Il avoit épouſé, par contrat du 19 Décembre 1638, paſſé devant *Vaugier*, Notaire d'Aix, *Madeleine de Ruffi*, veuve de N.... *Arbaud*, Seigneur de *Porchères*, & fille de noble François de *Ruffi*, & de *Sibylle de Ravel*, des Barons d'*Eſclapon*, dont:

1. Joseph, qui ſuit;
2. Jacques, Officier dans les Armées du Roi;
3. Et Jean-François de Barrel, Chanoine, Docteur en Théologie à l'Univerſité d'Aix.

V. Joseph de Barrel, Co-Seigneur du Reveſt, le Gubran, Vachères & autres lieux, fut convoqué, en 1675, à la levée du ban & arrière-ban ordonnée par le Roi, & lorſque Sa Majeſté eut conſenti de convertir en argent les ſervices perſonnels qu'elle étoit prête de lui faire, Joseph de Barrel ſatisfit ſur-le-champ à ce qui lui fut impoſé. Il fut nommé Aſſeſſeur d'Aix & Procureur des gens des trois Etats de Provence en 1685, prêta hommage au Roi pour ſes Terres en 1704, & fut maintenu en 1704 dans ſa nobleſſe par les Commiſſaires-Généraux députés pour le Roi en exécution de ſes déclarations des 4 Septembre 1696, 30 Mai 1702 & 30 Janvier 1703. Il avoit épouſé, par contrat du 8 Février 1670, paſſé devant *Beauzin*, Notaire d'Aix, ſigné des principaux Gentilshommes de la Provence, parens refpectifs des parties, *Anne de Pontevès*, des Comtes de Carles, fille de Meffire *Jean-Baptifte de Pontevès*, Chevalier, Seigneur de la Foreft & autres lieux, & de *Catherine de Richery*, dont vint:

VI. FRANÇOIS-XAVIER DE BARREL, Chevalier, Seigneur en partie des lieux du Reveft, le Gubran & Vachères, qui fut envoyé au ban & arrière-ban en 1707, donna l'aveu & dénombrement de fes Terres, à l'exemple de fes père & aïeul, prêta hommage au Roi & ferment de fidélité en 1723, en la Chambre des Comptes de Provence, tranfigea le 13 Novembre 1750, avec la Dame de *Monery* fa belle-fille, & tefta le lendemain, devant *Gollier*, Notaire d'Avignon. Il avoit époufé, par contrat du 27 Mai 1696, paffé devant *Beauxin*, Notaire d'Aix, *Elifabeth de Chanut*, fille unique de *Louis de Chanut Valhères*, Co-Seigneur du Reveft & de Pierrefer, & de *Gabrielle de Montolieu*. Elle porta à fon mari un tiers de la Terre du Reveft, outre ce qu'il poffédoit de fon chef, depuis plufieurs générations. De ce mariage vinrent:

   1. HONORÉ-GUILLAUME (a), qui fuit;
   2. JEAN-CLAUDE, Prêtre, Doyen des Chanoines de Saint-Martin, mort en 1774;
   3. Et JOSEPH-FRANÇOIS-GABRIEL, appelé l'*Abbé du Reveft*, Chanoine de l'Églife Métropolitaine de la ville d'Avignon.

VII. HONORÉ-GUILLAUME DU BARREL, Chevalier, Seigneur en partie du Reveft, de Gubran & Vachères, ajouta à fon nom celui de Pontevès, en exécution du teftament d'*Anne de Pontevès*, fon aïeule. Il tranfigea, au nom de fon époufe fur la fucceffion d'*Anne-Thérèfe de Monery*, fa tante, avec les autres cohéritiers de ladite Demoifelle, le 14 Janvier 1738, devant *Carteau*, Notaire d'Avignon. Il eft mort à Paris le 16 Octobre 1750, & a été inhumé dans l'Eglife de Saint-Sulpice. Il avoit époufé, par contrat du 20 Juin 1726, paffé devant *Gaudin*, Notaire d'Avignon, *Marie-Thérèfe de Monery*, d'ancienne Maifon, originaire de Nice, fille de Meffire *Jean-François de Monery*, & de *Jeanne de la Vigière*. De ce mariage font iffus:

   1. JEAN-FRANÇOIS-XAVIER, qui fuit;
   2. Et JEAN-ALBERT DE BARREL, dit *le Chevalier du Reveft*, mort jeune.

VIII. JEAN-FRANÇOIS-XAVIER DU BARREL-PONTEVÈS, Chevalier, Co-Seigneur de Gubran & Vachères, Seigneur du Reveft & du Villars, ayant réuni les différentes portions de fes Terres, dont il a prêté hommage au Roi les 13 Août 1760 & 24 Juillet 1767, a époufé, par contrat du 23 Octobre 1753, paffé devant *Brunet* & fon confrère, Notaires à Arles, *Julie-Thérèfe de Barras*, des anciens Barons de Mirabeau, fille de Meffire *Jean-François de Barras*, Chevalier, ancien Capitaine au Régiment de Chartres, Seigneur de Lanfac, Fos-les-Martigues, &c., & de *Marthe du Begou*, de la ville d'Arles, dont pour fils unique:

IX. HONORÉ-GABRIEL-ELZÉAR, Baron de BARREL-PONTEVÈS, Seigneur des fufdits lieux, né & baptifé à Avignon, le 3 Octobre 1761, a été admis, après avoir fait fes preuves, en date du 12 Août 1774, au nombre des Pages de MONSIEUR, frère du Roi. Il eft aujourd'hui Capitaine de Cavalerie au Régiment des Cuiraffiers du Roi, par Commiffion du 12 Juillet 1781, quelques mois après fa fortie des Pages. Il a époufé, le 7 Janvier 1782, devant *Bayle*, Notaire d'Aix, *Marguerite-Emilie d'Efmivy de Moiffac*, fille de Meffire *Jean-Louis-Honoré d'Efmivy*, Chevalier, Seigneur, Baron de Moiffac, Confeiller du Roi en la Cour du Parlement de Provence, & de *Marguerite-Rofe de Villeneuve*. De ce mariage font nés:

   1. FRANÇOIS-XAVIER-EMILIEN, né le 10 Octobre 1782;
   2. Et JULES-JOSEPH-VICTOR-AURÈLE DE BARREL-PONTEVÈS, Chevalier du Reveft, né le 10 Mars 1784.

On trouve dans les hommages, aveux, dénombremens, tranfactions & autres actes originaux qui nous ont été préfentés, & qui fervent à prouver la Généalogie de cette famille, déchargée du droit de franc-fief en 1704, les qualifications de Nobles, d'Ecuyers, d'illuftres Seigneurs & de Chevaliers, données à ceux qui les ont paffés. Nombre de certificats & de titres très-authentiques conftatent fon ancienne extraction. Outre les alliances ci-deffus mentionnées, elle eft encore alliée aux Maifons de *Caftellane*, de *Valbelle*, de *Benaud-Lubières*, de *Clapiers-Saint-Tropès*, de *Quiqueran de Beaujeu*, d'*Arlatan*, de *Lauris*, de *Gras*, de *Viguier*, de *Brun-de-Boades*; & en Italie, aux Comtes de *Blan-*

(a) La Chenaye-Desbois le dit fecond fils de JOSEPH, qui précède. (*Note des Editeurs*).

chety, aux Marquis de *Monti,* & aux Comtes de *Vanuzzi,* &c., &c.

Les armes: *écartelé, aux* 1 *& 4 de gueules, à un pont d'or de 3 arches,* qui eft de Pontevès; *aux 2 & 3 d'or, au loup raviffant d'azur,* qui eft d'Agoult; & fur le tout: *fafcé d'azur & d'or de fix pièces & une bande de gueules brochant fur le tout, chargée de 3 quinte-feuilles d'argent,* qui eft de BARREL.

On peut confulter fur cette famille, les Archives de Malte, à Arles, années 1521 & 1676; les Archives du Roi, reg. des hommages, aux années 1684, 1704, 1723, 1760, 1767; celles de l'Hôtel de Ville d'Arles, aux années 1671, 1685; celles de la Chambre Apoftolique du Comtat, année 1692; celles de l'Univerfité d'Avignon, année 1632; celles de l'Univerfité d'Aix aux années 1660, 1665; celles des Affemblées du corps de la Nobleffe de Provence, l'*Hiftoire héroïque & univerfelle de la Nobleffe de Provence; les Tablettes Généalogiques,* &c., &c.

BARRÊME, famille originaire de Marfeille. Artefeuil (*Hiftoire héroïque & univerfelle de la nobleffe de Provence*) dit qu'on trouve plufieurs actes paffés en 1404, 1405 & 1406, & commence la Généalogie de cette famille par

I. ANTOINE DE BARRÊME, qui a paffé lefdits actes, dans lefquels il eft qualifié *Nobilis & circonfpectus vir*. Il étoit Juge des premières appellations, & avoit époufé *Eléonore de Puget,* dont il eut:

II. GUILLAUME BARRÊME, qui tefta le 3 Décembre 1443, en faveur de fon fils. Il avoit époufé, le 5 Décembre 1432, *Marthe de Ftalco,* de Tarafcon, dont il eut:

III. ANTOINE BARRÊME, IIe du nom, qui fit fon teftament le 15 Septembre 1508. Il avoit époufé *Madeleine de Saint-André,* dont il laiffa:

IV. JEAN BARRÊME, qui eut d'*Hélène l'Artilles :*
1. GUILLAUME, qui fuit;
2. Et JEAN, mort au fervice du Roi.

V. GUILLAUME BARRÊME, IIe du nom, époufa, par contrat du 12 Juin 1520, *Catherine de Procionce,* dont il eut:

VI. RENÉ BARRÊME, Ier du nom, qui fe retira à Avignon, où il fut Juge en 1565, & enfuite Procureur du Roi en la Sénéchauffée d'Arles. Il tefta le 12 Novembre 1602. Il avoit époufé, le 23 Février 1558, *Claire de Cadenet,* & en eut:

1. JEAN, qui fuit;
2. PONS, qui s'établit à Tarafcon, & dont le fils JACQUES BARRÊME, marié avec *Anne de Privat-de-Molière,* n'eut qu'une fille, époufe, en 1657, de noble *André de Meyran,* Seigneur d'Ubaye;
3. RENÉ, dont la poftérité eft rapportée après celle de fon frère aîné;
4. MADELEINE, mariée avec *Honoré de Laugier de Monblanc;*
5. Et CATHERINE, mariée avec noble *Jacques d'Afme.*

BRANCHE des Seigneurs DE MONTRAVAIL.

VII. JEAN BARRÊME, IIe du nom, furnommé le *petit-guerrier,* fut Seigneur de la Terre de Montravail, pour laquelle il préta hommage au Roi en 1634; & fut pourvu à Tarafcon des Offices de Juge, Capitaine & Viguier pour le Roi en 1598 & 1606. Il devint enfuite Confeiller & Maître-des-Requêtes ordinaire de la Reine MARGUERITE DE VALOIS; & en récompenfe de fes fervices, HENRI IV lui donna une penfion annuelle par Brevet du 13 Janvier 1610. Il époufa, le 15 Octobre 1596, *Honorade de Laurens,* fœur de *Gafpard de Laurens,* Archevêque d'Arles, & laiffa de ce mariage:

1. FRANÇOIS, qui fuit;
2. Et RENÉ, dont la branche s'eft éteinte dans la famille de *Robin.*

VIII. FRANÇOIS BARRÊME fut marié, 1° par contrat du 16 Janvier 1628, avec *Alexandrine de Rolland;* & 2° avec *Alexandre de Lazari,* fille de noble *François,* Milanois, allié au Pape INNOCENT XI. Il eut de fon premier mariage:

1. PIERRE, qui fervit dans le Régiment d'Anjou, & fut pourvu de la Charge de Juge & Viguier de Tarafcon après la mort de fon père;
2. Et LUDOVINE, mariée, le 29 Décembre 1652, avec *Antoine de Servan.*

Et du fecond:
3. Et JEAN, qui fuit.

IX. JEAN BARRÊME, IIIe du nom, fut Seigneur de Montravail, fuccéda aux Charges de fon père & de fon frère; & époufa, par contrat paffé le 19 Juin 1651, *Madeleine de Grégoire,* de laquelle il eut:

1. MATHIAS, qui fuit;
2. Et MARIE, mariée avec *Pierre de Joffaud,* dont le frère mourut à Landau, Maréchal des Camps & Armées du Roi.

X. Mathias Barrême épouſa, le 7 Août 1679, *Marguerite de Geoffroy*, & eut :

XI. Jean-Baptiste Barrême, pourvu des Charges de ſes ayeux, & marié avec *Delphine de Servan*, dont :

1. Joseph, qui ſuit ;
2. Joseph-Antoine, Capitaine dans le Régiment de Saint-Chaumont, Infanterie ;
3. Et Marie, qui épouſa *Antoine-Germain de Conygham*, Seigneur d'Ovirat en Champagne, mort Capitaine au Régiment de Quercy, dont la famille a donné des Gouverneurs de Provinces.

XII. Joseph Barrême, Juge & Viguier de Taraſcon le 16 Juillet 1745, exerce ces Charges, & eſt marié avec *Marguerite Boutard*.

BRANCHE
des Seigneurs DE MANVILLE.

VII. René Barrême, II⁰ du nom, Seigneur de Manville, fut pourvu, le 12 Février 1602, de l'Office de Procureur du Roi qu'avoit exercé René, Iᵉʳ du nom, ſon père, & enſuite de celui de Juge d'Arles. Il fut député par délibération du Conſeil de cette Communauté, conjointement avec l'Archevêque de la même Ville, pour aller demander au Roi certaines grâces & certains privilèges. Saxi, dans ſon livre intitulé : *Pontificium Arelatenſe, &c.* cap. 117, fait mention de cette députation, & parle avec éloge de René Barrême, qui épouſa 1° *Catherine de Petil*, & 2° par contrat du 23 Décembre 1611, *Diane de Barras*.

Du premier lit vinrent :

1. Pierre, Chanoine de l'Egliſe d'Aix, Conſeiller-Clerc au Parlement de Provence ;
2. René, III⁰ du nom, mort Prêtre à l'Oratoire ;
3. Et Honorade, mariée, en 1619, avec *Simon de Raoux*, Ecuyer. .

Du ſecond lit ſont nés :

4. Charles, qui ſuit ;
5. Louis, Docteur en Théologie, Prédicateur du Roi, Abbé de Chamoſin ;
Et deux filles, Carmélites.

VIII. Charles Barrême, Seigneur de Manville, Juge-Royal d'Arles, obtint du Roi des Lettres-Patentes qui le confirment dans ſa Nobleſſe ; elles furent enregiſtrées aux Archives de Sa Majeſté en Provence, le 27 Novembre 1663, reg. *Opreſſa*, fol. 328. Il épouſa, par contrat du 1ᵉʳ Juillet 1636, *Marguerite d'Aguillinqui-de-Châteaufort*, fille de Gaſ-

pard, & d'*Honorade de Forbin*, des Seigneurs de *la Barben*, dont il eut :

1. Jean-Baptiste, qui ſuit ;
2. René, IVᵉ du nom, Chanoine de l'Egliſe d'Aix, Conſeiller-Clerc au Parlement de cette Ville, après le décès de Pierre, ſon oncle ;
3. Joseph, qui, après avoir commandé le ſecond Bataillon du Régiment Lyonnois, eſt mort Commandant du Château de Pierre-Ancife, Chevalier de Saint-Louis & de Saint-Lazare de Jéruſalem ;
4. Louis, décédé ſans alliance ;
5. Et Thérèse, mariée, en 1675, dans la Maiſon de *Montfort-Faraman*.

IX. Jean-Baptiste Barrême, Seigneur de Manville, Lieutenant-Général au Siège d'Arles, & après la mort de ſon père, Juge de cette Ville, épouſa, par contrat du 12 Octobre 1683, *Gabrielle de Gras-de-Preigne*, dont il eut :

1. Charles, qui ſervit quelque tems dans le Régiment de Lyonnois en qualité d'Officier. Il ſuccéda aux biens de ſon oncle d'Aguillinqui, & devint par-là Seigneur de Châteaufort & de Saint-Veran, dont il prêta hommage au Roi le 4 Mai 1730. Il épouſa, le 7 Septembre 1723, *Marie-Renée de Damian-Vinſargues* ;
2. René, Chanoine de l'Egliſe d'Arles ;
3. Et Joseph, qui ſuit.

X. Joseph Barrême, Seigneur de Manville & autres lieux, Juge d'Arles, marié, le 11 Novembre 1717, avec *Pierrette de Piquet*, fille de noble *Jean-Baptiſte*, & de *Pierrette d'Aſguières*, dont il eut :

XI. Guillaume Barrême, Seigneur de Manville & autres lieux, marié, le 24 Juin 1750, avec *Eliſabeth de Campan*, fille de *Jacques*, Conſeiller en la Cour des Comptes, Aides & Finances de Montpellier.

Les armes : *de ſable, à deux triangles entrelaſſés d'argent, enfermant une molette d'éperon d'or chargée d'un tourteau de gueules.*

BARRES (DES), Seigneur de Cuſſigny : *d'azur, à la faſce d'or, chargée d'une étoile de gueules, & accompagnée de trois croiſſans d'argent, 2 en chef & 1 en pointe.*

BARRES (DES). Antoine-Henri-Claude, Marquis DES Barres, Enſeigne des Gardes-du-Corps a épouſé *Henriette-Agnès-Félicité*, ſeconde fille de *François Teſtu*, Marquis de *Balincourt*, dont :

François-Henri;
Et Guillaume-Félicité-Geneviève.

Les armes : *d'or, à la croix ancrée de sinople.*

BARRES (des), Seigneur de Chaumont : *losangé d'or & de gueules.*

BARRES (des), à Langres : *d'azur, au chevron d'or, accompagné de trois coquilles de même.*

BARRETO, famille noble du Portugal, qui a donné un Gouverneur Général des Indes Orientales dans François Barreto, qui fervit avec diftinction; dans Melchior Nunez Barreto, Jéfuite, le premier miffionnaire qui ait prêché l'Evangile dans l'Empire de la Chine en 1555; un patriarche d'Ethiopie dans Jean Nunez Barreto, auffi Jéfuite; dans François Barreto de Meneses, un Officier qui fervit avec diftinction dans la guerre contre l'Efpagne; & dans Nuno Barreto Fuseiro, le fondateur du Couvent des Religieufes de la Conception à la Luz, à une lieue de Lifbonne. Voyez Moréri, nouveau fupplément.

BARRIER, Seigneur de Pierrepont en Normandie, Généralité d'Alençon, famille maintenue dans fa Nobleffe le 1ᵉʳ Août 1667. La Roque, dans fon *Traité de la Nobleffe,* p. 261, parle d'Hippolyte Barrier, demeurant à Falaife, qui fut annobli par Lettres expédiées à Paris en Avril 1594, regiftrées à la Chambre des Comptes en 1596, & à la Cour des Aides l'an 1615.

Les armes : *d'azur, à la fafce d'or, chargée d'un lion iffant de gueules, accompagnée de quatre croix aléfées d'argent, trois en chef, & une en pointe, cette dernière furmontée d'une tour de même, accoftée de deux trèfles d'or.*

BARRIGUE, famille noble originaire de Portugal, dit l'Auteur de l'*Hiftoire héroïque & universelle de la nobleffe de Provence,* pag. 105 & fuiv.

Un Pierre de Barrigue, Commandant de Cavalerie, fit en diverfes occafions des prodiges de valeur contre les Maures d'Afrique. Un Lopez Barriga, Commandant l'avantgarde de l'armée du Général *Aluide,* affiégea & prit le Château d'Amangor au Royaume de Maroc, dont la fituation, fur un rocher au bord d'une rivière, engagea le Roi Jean III à lui donner des armes parlantes.

Il eft fouvent parlé, dans l'*Hiftoire de Mal-*

te, par M. l'Abbé de Vertot, de Pierre de Barrigue, qui en étoit Vice-Roi.

Ceux de cette Maifon qui fuivirent la fortune du Roi Antoine, perdirent tous leurs biens, & fe réfugièrent avec lui en France.

I. Gérard de Barrigue, l'un d'eux, eut :
1. Amiel, qui fuit;
2. Et Mathieu, qui vint s'établir à Marfeille, ainfi que fon frère, pour y réparer leurs pertes par le commerce. Ils y ont formé deux branches : l'une des Seigneurs de *Fontanieu,* & l'autre des Seigneurs de *Montvalon.*

II. Amiel de Barrigue eut pour fils :
1. Gérard-Hilaire, qui fuit;
2. Et Marc-Antoine, dont le fils Ignace-Amiel de Barrigue-de-Fontanieu, Confeiller, Secrétaire du Roi, a poftérité de fon mariage avec *Thérèfe de Gautier,* des Seigneurs d'*Eyguières.*

III. Gérard-Hilaire de Barrigue, Confeiller, Secrétaire du Roi, eut :
1. François-Amiel, qui fut reçu Confeiller au Parlement de Provence le 24 Avril 1714. Il avoit époufé *Marie-Marthe de Gauthier,* des Seigneurs de *Valabres,* & mourut fans enfans;
2. Et Joseph-Marc, qui eft chef de la feconde branche des Seigneurs de *Fontanieu,* établie à Marfeille.

BRANCHE
des Seigneurs de Montvalon.

II. Mathieu de Barrigue, fecond fils de Gérard, fut Echevin de Marfeille en 1678. Il eut pour fils :

III. Honoré de Barrigue, Seigneur de Montvalon, qui alla s'établir à Aix, où il acheta une Charge de Secrétaire du Roi, Contrôleur en Chancellerie en 1702. Il avoit époufé, en 1677, *Claire la Garde,* fille de *Gabriel la Garde,* d'une noble & ancienne Maifon, & de *Marguerite de Feris,* dont le frère étoit Commandeur de Malte & Colonel du Régiment de Guyenne. Honoré de Barrigue eut de fon mariage :

IV. André de Barrigue, Seigneur de Montvalon, reçu Confeiller au Parlement de Provence en 1702, qui eft encore Confeiller vétéran au même Parlement, & eft le premier qui, en faifant paffer fa Charge à fon fils, ait été diftingué par une furvivance indéfinie. Il fut député du Parlement en 1726, pour la pourfuite d'un procès au Confeil de Sa Majefté, contre la Cour des Comptes de Provence. Il a fait imprimer quelques ouvrages, qui, joints à ſes longs ſervices, lui ont attiré du Roi une penſion de 1000 livres en 1752. Il avoit épouſé *Julie-Darie de Boyer*, des Seigneurs d'*Eguilles* & d'Argens, fille d'une Dame de *Forbin*, dont il a eu :

1. Honoré, qui ſuit;
2. François-Félicité, Capitaine dans le Régiment de Penthièvre, mort en Bohême, où il commandoit un poſte avec quatre Compagnies, en 1743;
3. Marc-Antoine, reçu Conſeiller-Clerc au r~arlement de Provence, le 23 Janvier 1742, & pourvu en 1746 de l'Abbaye de Saint-Rambert, de nomination Royale, l'un des Vicaires-Généraux de l'Archevêque d'Aix;
4. Et Angélique-Marguerite, mariée avec *Céſar de Cadenet*, des Seigneurs de *Charleval*.

V. Honoré de Barrigue, Seigneur de Montvalon, reçu dans la Charge de ſon père le 14 Octobre 1729, a épouſé, en 1734, *Louiſe-Polixène d'Iſnard*, fille de Joseph, Seigneur d'*E¸clapon*, & de *Polixène de Gantès*, de laquelle il a :

Joseph-André;
Polixène, qui a épouſé, au mois de Juin 1757, *Georges ʋe Rollands*, Marquis de Cabanne & de Reauʋ.ʟe, ci-devant Chevalier de .ʜalte;
Et quelques filles.

Les armes : *de gueules, à la tour donjonnée d'or, ſur un roc de même, iſſant d'une mer de ſinople. Il ſort deux étendards de la tour à droite du haut, & à gauche d'un créneau plus bas.*

BARRILLIÈRE, Seigneur du Bot, en Bretagne : *d'argent, à trois merlettes de ſable, 2 & 1.*

BARRIN DE LA GALISSONNIÈRE. La Seigneurie de la grande Querche en Bretagne a été érigée, en Marquiſat, par Lettres du mois d'Août 1701, enregiſtrées le 4 Septembre 1702, en faveur de Jacques-François Barrin de la Galissonnière, dont le fils N… Barrin de la Galissonnière, Seigneur de Peſcheſeul au Maine, Conſeiller au Parlement de Rennes, s'eſt marié à N… *de la Borde*, fille du Lieutenant de Roi du Maine. Leurs enfans ſont :

1. N….. Barrin de la Galissonnière, reçu Page du Roi;
2. Et Madeleine-Félicité, mariée en Novembre 1728, à *François de Vaucouleurs*, Seigneur de l'Anjamet.

Le Marquis de la Galissonnière, Commandant à la Nouvelle-France, Vice-Amiral, eſt de cette famille. Peu de tems après avoir battu la Flotte Angloiſe qui venoit ſecourir le Port-Mahon, il mourut le 27 Octobre 1756, à Nemours, venant à Fontainebleau rendre compte de ſa conduite.

Les armes : *d'azur, à trois papillons d'or, poſés 2 & 1.*

BARROSA ou BARROSO, nom d'une illuſtre Maiſon d'Eſpagne, connue ſous le nom de Barroso. Elle a donné un Cardinal dès 1327, dans Pierre Gomez de Barroso, Evêque de Carthagène; un Archevêque de Séville, & un Archevêque de Braga en Portugal. Voyez Moréri.

BARSCAOU, à Boteguiry, en Léon : *écartelé, aux 1 & 4 de ſable, à 3 quintefeuilles d'argent, 2 & 1; aux 2 & 3 de ſable, à un cerf paſſant d'argent.* Deviſe : *Amſery*, qui veut dire *temporiſer.*

BART, famille originaire de Dunkerque, qui doit ſon luſtre à Jean Bart, Chevalier de l'Ordre Militaire de Saint-Louis, Capitaine de Marine, &c., dont les belles & éclatantes actions lui firent mériter, de Louis XIV, des Lettres de Nobleſſe pour lui & ſes enfans, poſtérité & lignée, tant mâles que femelles, nés & à naître en légitime mariage. Ce Prince le décora du titre & qualité de *Gentilhomme*, voulant que lui & ſa poſtérité ſe puſſent dire & qualifier d'*Ecuyer*, & puſſent parvenir à tous degrés de *Chevalerie*, jouir de tous honneurs & de tous privilèges accordés à la Nobleſſe. Il lui a été permis, & à ſa poſtérité, de porter les écuſſons & armoiries timbrées, telles qu'elles furent empreintes, avec faculté de charger ſes armes d'*une fleur-dè-lys d'or à fond d'azur*, &c. Les Lettres de Nobleſſe inférées dans le *Mercure* du mois d'Octobre 1694, font mention de toutes les belles actions du Chevalier Jean Bart. Il a laiſſé :

Jean, qui a hérité de toute ſa bravoure, & eſt mort à Dunkerque le 30 Avril 1755, Vice-Amiral & Grand-Croix de l'Ordre Royal & Militaire de Saint-Louis;
Et N… Bart, Capitaine au ſervice de la Compagnie des Indes, & depuis Capitaine de Port au Cap-François.

BARTAIGE, à Léon : *d'argent, au fretté*

d'azur de fix pièces, brifé en chef d'un croif-fant de gueules.

BARTAUT: *d'or, à la croix de fable, chargée de cinq coquilles d'argent.*

BARTELEMI, en Provence : *d'azur, à la montagne ou rocher d'or, accompagnée de deux étoiles de même, une en chef & une en pointe.*

BARTELLE-LA-MOIGNON, en Bourgogne: *d'argent, à trois hermines de fable, 2 & 1.*

BARTET, Seigneur de Bonneval : *d'azur, à trois petits poiffons, barbeaux d'argent, rangés en barre.*

BARTHALASSE: *de gueules, au chef d'argent, chargé de trois rofes du champ.*

* BARTHE (DE LA). C'eft une Seigneurie anciennement compofée des quatre Vallées d'Aure, de Neftez, de Magnoac & de Barrouf-fe, dont la *Barthe* eft le chef-lieu. Ce petit Pays fait les limites de l'ancien Comté de Cominges, qui s'étend fur la frontière d'Ef-pagne, & eft enclavé, pour la plus grande partie, dans les Monts-Pyrénées. Ses anciens Seigneurs l'ont poffédé fous le titre de Vi-comté. Il fut réuni à la Couronne, après la mort du dernier Comte d'*Armagnac*, fous le règne de Louis XI, en 1481.

Ce Pays a donné fon nom à l'ancienne & illuftre Maifon de LA BARTHE, qui defcend des anciens Comtes d'Aragon, dont elle a retenu les armes, qui font: *d'or, à 4 pals de gueules, & une tête de bouc* pour cimier. Voyez l'*Hif-toire de Béarn*, par M. de Marca; Oihenart, *Notice de Gafcogne*, pag. 525; l'*Hiftoire des Grands Officiers de la Couronne*, tom. VII, pag. 208 & fuiv. ; celle *du Languedoc*, &c.

Cette Maifon, qui a donné un Maréchal de France, un Gouverneur de Paris & de l'Ifle de France, deux Archevêques d'Auch, un Evêque d'Albi, un de Lectoure, & un de Touloufe, des Abbés Commendataires, &c., & a toujours fervi avec honneur & diftinction, fubfifte aujourd'hui dans les branches des Sei-gneurs de *Gifcaro*, de *Valentine*, de *Ca-feaux*, de *Laffégan* & de *Thermes*.

C'eft à AURIOL-MANSE, premier Vicomte de LA BARTHE, par lequel nous commencerons, avec le P. Anfelmè, & les différens *Mémoi-res domeftiques* qui nous ont été communi-

qués par Meffieurs les Vicomte de LA BARTHE, & Comte de *Thermes*, la Généalogie de cette Maifon.

Voici la filiation chronologique des Ducs d'Aquitaine, Rois & Comtes de Touloufe, & Comtes d'Aragon, dont on fait defcendre AURIOL-MANSE.

SÉVENUS fut Duc de toute l'Aquitaine, & vivoit en 600. Il laiffa cinq enfans:

AMANT, fon fils aîné, Duc de la Novempo-pulanie, Capitaine de Gafcogne, qui vivoit en 620 & 627, fonda le Monaftère de Saint-Sever, & ne laiffa que :

GISÈLE, qui fut mariée, du vivant de fon Père, à CHARIBERT, Roi de Touloufe, à qui elle porta le Duché de la Novempopulanie. Il étoit fils de CLOTAIRE, Roi de Touloufe, & neveu de DAGOBERT, Roi de France. Suivant la nouvelle *Hiftoire du Languedoc*, il laiffa deux fils, BOGGIS & BERTRAND.

BOGGIS, qui vivoit depuis 631 jufqu'en 685, fut Duc d'Aquitaine, & eut d'*Aude* ou *Ode:*

EUDES, furnommé *le Grand*, Duc d'Aqui-taine, puis Duc de Gafcogne, par *Valtrude*, fa femme, fille & unique héritière de *Valachie*, Duc de Gafcogne.

AZNAIR, Ier du nom, fon troifième fils, après les guerres qu'il eut à foutenir, avec fes frères & fes neveux, contre CHARLES MARTEL, PÉPIN & CHARLEMAGNE, fe retira en Efpagne, & fut Comte d'Aragon. Il vivoit en 735.

GARSIMIO, fon fils, Comte d'Aragon, & Duc de Gafcogne, après la mort de fes oncles & de fes coufins germains, jura une haine irrécon-ciliable à CHARLEMAGNE, fe mit à la tête des Gafcons, & fut tué dans une bataille qu'il li-vra en 818 à ce Prince; il étoit alors fort âgé. Il ne laiffa qu'un fils unique nommé

AZNAIR, IIe du nom, qui vivoit en 785, & fut Comte d'Aragon. Il laiffa deux fils : GA-LINDE, Comte d'Aragon, vivant en 840, qui n'eut qu'une fille, mariée à SANCHE, Roi de Navarre, & SÉMENON, qui fuit.

SÉMENON, qui fuccéda à GALINDE, fon frère aîné, dans le Comté d'Aragon, ne régna pas long-tems. Il fut père de :

FORTUNIUS, Comte d'Aragon, qui vivoit en 880. Celui-ci laiffa:

1. AZNAIR, IIIe du nom, dont on ignore le fort;
2. Et ARNAUD, qui fuit.

ARNAUD, Ier du nom, & premier Comte d'Aure, des quatre Vallées, d'Arné, d'Arago-net, de Barrouffe, de l'Arbouft, Campan, &

pays adjoints, qui faifoient partie de l'Aragon, vivoit en 900.

GARCIE, fon fils, fecond Comte d'Aure, &c., allié à *Fachilène*, fille de *Renaud Garcie*, premier Comte d'Aftarac, eut pour la dot de fa femme, le Comté de Magnoac. Ses enfans furent:

1. GUILLAUME-AURIOL, mort fans poftérité;
2. Et ARNAUD, qui fuit.

ARNAUD, IIe du nom, troifième Comte d'Aure & de Magnoac, vivoit, ainfi que fon frère, ès années 952 & 975. On trouve dans les cartulaires d'Auch, qu'ils prenoient quelquefois les titres de *Princes & Comtes d'Aftarac*, fans doute parce que le Comté de Magnoac fait partie de la Principauté d'Aftarac. Il eut de fon époufe, dont on ignore le nom:

1. GARCIE-ARNAUD, quatrième Comte d'Aure, dont on ignore la poftérité;
2. AURIOL-MANSE, connu fous le nom du premier Vicomte de LA BARTHE, & par lequel nous allons commencer la Généalogie de cette Maifon;
3. Et FORTAN-SANCHE, Religieux à Simorre.

I. AURIOL-MANSE DE LA BARTHE, premier Vicomte de la Barthe, Seigneur des quatre Vallées, de Neftez & de Barroufe, vivoit en 1020, fuivant les *cartulaires d'Auch, de Simorre* & l'*Hiftoire du Languedoc*. Il eut de fon époufe, dont on ignore le nom:

1. SANCHE, qui fuit;
2. AIMERIC, auteur, à ce qu'on préfume, d'une branche, mais inconnue, & peut-être éteinte;
3. Et GARCIE, Archevêque d'Auch.

II. SANCHE, Ier du nom, fecond Vicomte de LA BARTHE, rendit hommage, le 12 Mars 1078, à *Centulle*, Ier du nom, & à *Béatrix*, fon époufe, Comte & Comteffe de Bigorre, pour les Terres & Seigneuries qu'il poffédoit dans ce Comté. Il vivoit encore en 1083 & 1086, difent l'*Hiftoire du Languedoc*, le *cartulaire de Simorre*, & *un manufcrit de Saint-Oran*. Il laiffa pour fils unique:

III. AUGER, troifième Vicomte de LA BARTHE, Comte d'Aure, des quatre Vallées, de Magnoac, d'Arné, & Seigneur de Barroufe, l'Arbouft, Campan, & Pays adjoints, en Périgord, qui vivoit en 1100, fuivant Oihenart, & le *cartulaire de Simorre*. Ses enfans furent:

1. ARNAUD-GUILHEM, qui fuit;

2. ARNAUD-ESPARRE, auteur de la branche des Seigneurs d'*Arné* & de *Montcorneil*, rapportée ci-après;
3. BERNARD, premier Abbé de l'Echelle-Dieu;
4. Et ODON-GUILHEM, Moine de Simorre.

IV. ARNAUD-GUILHEM, Ier du nom, Vicomte de LA BARTHE, & autres lieux, eut:

1. SANCHE, qui fuit;
2. Et CONTOURS DE LA BARTHE, née avant 1180, mariée à *Bernard*, Comte de *Cominges*, dont le mariage fut déclaré nul au mois de Novembre 1197.

V. SANCHE, IIe du nom, Vicomte de LA BARTHE, &c., fonda l'an 1235, dans l'Abbaye de Bonnefons, un anniverfaire pour lui & pour fes parens, & donna pour cette fondation, fix feptiers de froment, trois charges de vin, & 20 fols *Morlas*, à prendre fur les Terres d'*Antichan*, d'*Illeu* & de *Poft*, qu'il avoit acquifes des Seigneurs de Cardaillac. Il eut de *Mathilde de Cominges*, fille de *Bernard*, Comte de Cominges, & de *Marie*, Dame de *Montpellier*, fa troifième femme:

VI. ARNAUD-GUILHEM, IIe du nom, Vicomte de LA BARTHE, & autres Terres, qui vivoit en 1259, & ne laiffa que:

1. VÉRONIQUE DE LA BARTHE, mariée en 1263, avec *Arnaud-Bernard d'Armagnac*, tué dans un combat particulier, en 1272, par *Géraud de Cafomont*, Seigneur de Hautpuy, pour raifon de la mouvance de ce Château. Cet *Arnaud-Bernard d'Armagnac*, troifième fils de *Roger*, Comte d'Armagnac & Vicomte de Féfenzac, & de *Pincette d'Albret*, ne laiffa point d'enfans de fon mariage. Voyez l'*Hiftoire de Béarn*, pag. 779;
2. Et BRUNISSENDE, qui fuit.

VII. BRUNISSENDE DE LA BARTHE, après la mort de fa fœur aînée, fans enfans, hérita de tous les biens de fes père & mère, dont elle jouiffoit en 1283, & qu'elle porta à fon mari, *Bertrand de Fumel*, Ier du nom, fils puîné du Baron de *Fumel*, en Quercy. Il devint, par fon mariage, Vicomte de LA BARTHE, Comte d'Aure & de Magnoac, Seigneur de Barroufe, &c., & écartela fes armes qui étoient, *d'azur, à 3 fumées d'or, fortant du bas de l'écu*, de celles de la Barthe, qui font *d'or, à 4 pals de gueules*, dont fa poftérité retint le nom. De ce mariage vinrent:

1. ARNAUD-GUILHEM, qui fuit;
2. BERTRAND;
3. GAUSSENTE, mariée, en 1291, à RAYMOND

de la Barthe-Montcorneil, Comte & Seigneur d'Arné & de Montcorneil, son cousin à la mode de Bretagne, au IV° degré, dont il sera parlé ci-après;

4. Et Sibylle, mariée à *Bertrand de Durfort*, Seigneur de Clermont.

VIII. Arnaud-Guilhem de la Barthe-Fumel, III° du nom, Vicomte de la Barthe, d'Aure & de Magnoac, Seigneur de Barrousse, s'allia avec *Mascarose d'Armagnac*, fille de *Géraud V*, Comte d'Armagnac & de Fésenzac, & de *Marthe de Béarn*, & nièce d'*Arnaud-Bernard d'Armagnac*, époux de Véronique de la Barthe, sa tante, dont :

1. Géraud, qui suit;
2. Arnaud-Guilhem, Evêque de Lectoure, puis d'Albi;
3. Roger, qualifié *Ecuyer, Sire de Montesquieu*, dans une quittance donnée à Touloufe, le 13 Octobre 1350, à *Jean Chauvel*, Tréforier des Guerres. Il brifoit ses armes *d'une bande chargée de 3 lions.*
4. N.... de la Barthe, mariée au Seigneur de Pujols.

Il eut aussi deux fils naturels :

Guillaume, dit *Guillaume-Bourc de la Barthe*, & Guillaume-Bourc de la Barthe, dit *le Jeune*, tous les deux mentionnés & qualifiés dans deux quittances de *Jean de Chauvel*, Tréforier des Guerres du 1er Avril 1340 & 1347; l'un de *Vieil Capitaine de Villeneuve d'Agénois*, & l'autre de *Capitaine de Sainte-Foy*.

On trouve un Guillaume de la Barthe, Chevalier, Capitaine du Mont-Semproing & de Saint-Paftour, lequel fit montre de lui & de neuf Ecuyers de sa Compagnie, dont l'un étoit Bernard de la Barthe, le 30 Septembre 1352.

Et Pierre de la Barthe, Chevalier, Capitaine de Moncuc-de-Vaux, lequel y fit montre avec 14 Ecuyers, le 29 Novembre 1352.

IX. Géraud, Vicomte de la Barthe, d'Aure & de Magnoac, *aliàs* dénommé Girard, Capitaine de Sainte-Livrade, donna quittance à *Jean Chauvel* de 500 liv. *Tournois*, sur ses gages & sur ceux de 100 Ecuyers de sa Compagnie, le 3 Avril 1345. Il en donna une autre à ce même Tréforier, le 10 Octobre 1350, de la somme de 9774 liv., 9 sols *Tournois*, sur ses gages de Chevalier Banneret, & une autre pour ses gages de Chevalier, & ceux de 296 Sergens de pied. Il fut marié 1° avec *Trenca Lienhana*, 2° avec *Eléonore de Saluces*, 3° avec *Miramonde de Bonneville*, & 4° avec *Brunissende de Lautrec*, Vicomtesse

de Lautrec. Il n'eut d'enfans que de cette quatrième femme, qui sont :

1. Jean, qui suit;
2. Saure, mariée à *Guigues de Lévis*, Seigneur de la Roche, à qui elle porta la Vicomté de Lautrec;
3. Et Mascarose, seconde femme de *Jean*, Comte d'*Aftarac*, I° du nom.

X. Jean, Vicomte de la Barthe, Seigneur de Neftez, Cieutad, de Barrousse, &c., Comte d'Aure & de Magnoac, est qualifié *Jean de la Barre, Ecuyer, Sire d'Aure & de Magnoac, Capitaine de Villeneuve d'Agénois*, dans une quittance qu'il donna en 1363, de la somme de 256 écus, & de deux tiers d'écu, sur ses gages & ceux des Gens-d'armes de sa Compagnie, pour la garde de cette place, depuis le 8 Décembre 1358 jusqu'au 1er Mai 1359. Il s'engagea, par acte passé à Touloufe, le 21 Octobre 1370, au Duc d'Anjou, Lieutenant de Roi ès parties du Languedoc, de défendre & garder le Pays d'Agénois, & y faire la guerre aux ennemis avec 100 hommes d'armes de sa Compagnie, pour la somme de 1500 francs d'or, à compte de laquelle il donna, par le même acte, quittance de celle de 200 francs d'or. Il en donna une autre de pareille somme, le 1er Février 1377, au Duc d'Anjou, qui lui en avoit fait don, par Lettres datées de Gaillac en Albigeois, le 11 Avril 1376, pour le récompenser de ce qu'après avoir pris le Châtel de Châteaufort en Bigorre, il l'avoit gardé & le gardoit encore à ses dépens. Il avoit été marié 1° avec *Marguerite de Madaillan*, Baronne de Cançor, en Agénois; & 2° avec *Jeanne d'Albret*, veuve de *Guillaume Raymond*, Seigneur de Caumont. Elle étoit fille d'*Amanieu*, Seigneur de Verteuil, & de *Mabille de l'Efcouffan*, Dame de Langoiran. Il n'eut point d'enfans de ces deux alliances; & par son teftament de 1398, il ratifia la donation qu'il avoit faite à noble Arnaud Guilhem de la Barthe, fils de Raymond, II° du nom, Comte & Seigneur d'Arné & de Montcorneil, des Terres de Bourifp, Saint-Lari & Ilhan, en Aure, en contre-échange desquelles ledit Arnaud-Guilhem de la Barthe avoit cédé tous les droits qu'il avoit sur la Terre de Magnoac. Il inftitua son héritier universel, *Bernard*, VII° du nom, Comte d'*Armagnac*, son cousin au III° degré, en faveur duquel il difposa de la Vicomté de la Barthe. Il mourut le 5 Octobre 1398; & le Comte d'Armagnac prit poffeffion de fon hérédité les 17 & 18 du même mois. Ses fucceffeurs l'ont poffédée jufqu'à la réunion qu'en fit à la Couronne le Roi Louis XI en 1481.

BRANCHE

des Seigneurs d'Arné & de Montcor-neil, *iffue des premiers Vicomtes* de la Barthe.

IV. Arnaud-Esparre de la Barthe, Comte & Seigneur d'Arné & autres Terres, fecond fils d'Auger, troifième Vicomte de la Barthe, Comte d'Aure, d'Arné, &c., mourut fort âgé le 10 Octobre 1210, & eut de fon mariage avec *Condarine*, entr'autres enfans :

1. Sanche, qui fuit;
2. Et Géraud, Evêque de Touloufe, enfuite Archevêque d'Auch en 1170, qui fit le voyage de la Terre-Sainte, & mourut en 1190. *Le cartulaire de Simorre* & le *martyrologe* ou *le nécrologe de Saint-Orens d'Auch*, font mention de ce Prélat & de fon père.

V. Sanche de la Barthe, Ier du nom de fa branche, fut préfent en 1227 avec *Grimoaud*, Evêque de Cominges, & *Bernard*, Comte de Cominges, à la donation que Centulle, Comte d'Aftarac, fit à l'Archèvêque d'Auch des Dîmes qu'il poffédoit dans fon Comté; l'acte original de cette donation eft dans les archives d'Auch. Sanche de la Barthe eut pour fils :

VI. Géraud de la Barthe, qui fit, l'an 1242, une donation au Monaftère de Bouleau, ce qui eft prouvé par un cartulaire de cette Abbaye. De fa femme, dont on ignore le nom, il eut :

1. Bernard, qui, voyant que la branche aînée de fa Maifon alloit s'éteindre par deux filles, Véronique & Brunissende, dont nous avons parlé, crut que l'hérédité des quatre Val-lées lui appartenoit. Il s'en qualifia *Comte;* & fous ce titre, & en qualité de *Souverain*, il donna des privilèges aux habitans; mais dans la fuite il tranfigea, & fe fit Abbé. *Voyez le Cartulaire de Farrancolin;*
2. Et Raymond, qui fuit.

VII. Raymond de la Barthe, Ier du nom, Comte & Seigneur d'Arné & de Montcorneil, époufa, l'an 1270, la fille aînée & héritière de la branche de *Montcorneil*, dont il eut :

VIII. Arnaud-Guilhem de la Barthe, Ier du nom, Comte & Seigneur d'Arné & de Montcorneil, au Comté d'Aftarac, qui épou-

Tome II.

fa, en 1291, *Gauffente de la Barthe-Fumel,* fa coufine au IVe degré, fille de *Bertrand de Fumel*, Baron de Fumel en Quercy, & de *Bruniffende de la Barthe.* Cette *Gauffente de la Barthe-Fumel* fit rentrer dans la Maifon de la Barthe les Terres que fa mère avoit portées dans celles de *Fumel.* Ce fut à caufe de cette alliance, que lui & fes defcendans ont écartelé leurs armes de celles de *Fumel.* Il eut pour fils unique :

IX. Jean de la Barthe, Ier du nom, Comte & Seigneur d'Arné & de Montcorneil, Seigneur de Bourifp, Saint-Lari & Ilhan en Aure, qui ratifia, au nom de fa femme, le bail qui avoit été fait, du bois de *Las-Méades*, dans la Paroiffe de Guifery, en faveur des habitans de ce lieu. Il époufa *Endelade de Lafferan*, fœur & unique héritière d'*Hugues de Lafferan*, Co-Seigneur de Saintrailles & Guifery, dans le Magnoac, & de *Blanchefleur de Lafferan*, tous enfans de N..... *de Lafferan*, & de *Giraude de Saint-Loup.* De ce mariage vint :

X. Raymond de la Barthe, IIe du nom, Comte d'Arné, Seigneur de Bourifp, Saint-Lari, Ilhan en Aure, & de Montcorneil en Aftarac, qui rendit hommage pour cette dernière Terre au Comte d'Aftarac en 1379. On lui donne pour femme une fille du Seigneur *de Montcorneil*, & pour fils & héritier :

XI. Arnaud-Guilhem de la Barthe, IIe du nom, Comte d'Arné & de Montcorneil, & de Guifery dans le Magnoac, qui céda à Jean, dernier Vicomte de la Barthe, fon coufin au VIe degré, tous les droits qu'il avoit fur la Terre de Magnoac, en échange des Terres de Bourifp, Saint-Lari, Ilhan en Aure, dont ce dernier lui fit donation, laquelle il ratifia par fon teftament du 5 Septembre 1398, où *Bernard*, VIIe du nom, Comte d'*Armagnac*, eft inftitué fon héritier univerfel, & ce fut en fa faveur que ce *Jean*, dernier Vicomte de la Barthe, difpofa de la Vicomté de la Barthe, que, comme nous l'avons dit ci-deffus, Louis XI réunit à la Couronne en 1481. Arnaud-Guilhem de la Barthe, IIe du nom, eut de fa femme, dont on ignore le nom :

1. Jean, qui fuit;
2. Et Bertrand, Prieur de Saint-Mont, élu Abbé de Simorre, Diocèse d'Auch, en 1434, dit le *Gallia Chriftiana*, édition nouvelle, tom. I, col. 1016.

XII. Jean de la Barthe, IIe du nom, Com-

Y

te d'Arné & de Montcorneil, Seigneur de Guifery, dans le Magnoac, Bourifp, Saint-Lari, & Ilhan en Aure, Chevalier, Sénéchal d'Aure en 1453, afferma, le 6 Octobre 1463, le port de Montarcy dans les montagnes d'Aure, à noble *Sentoret de Béon*, Seigneur d'Augean en Aftarac, & tefta le 17 Janvier 1494. Il avoit époufé, par contrat du 9 Avril 1422, *Efclarmonde de Rivière*, fille de *Bernard*, Chevalier, Vicomte de Labatut. Il eut :

1. ARNAUD-GUILHEM, qui fuit ;
2. BERNARD, auteur de la branche des Seigneurs de *Gifcaro*, rapportée ci-après ;
3. N... DE LA BARTHE, Seigneur de Sépuze, & de Hauffon, père de :
   GUILLAUME DE LA BARTHE ;
   Et DOMENGE DE LA BARTHE, mariée, le 18 Avril 1492, à *Lancelot de Cardaillac ;*
4. ROGER, Abbé de Simorre en 1455 ;
5. OTHON, auteur d'une branche (fuivant les *Mémoires domeftiques*), laquelle eft inconnue ;
6. Et AGNÈS, mariée, par contrat du 7 Octobre 1450, à *Aimery de Cominges*, Chevalier, Seigneur de Puy-Guilhem.

XIII. ARNAUD-GUILHEM DE LA BARTHE, IIIᵉ du nom, Comte & Seigneur d'Arné, de Montcorneil & de Guifery, premier Baron d'Aftarac, & Sénéchal d'Aure, eut un procès contre *Ifabelle d'Armagnac*, Dame des Quatre Vallées, qui lui difputoit la Seigneurie de Retpoy'en Magnoac. A ce fujet il fit faire une enquête, le 20 Mars 1474, où les témoins déclarèrent qu'il en étoit *Seigneur-Haut-Jufticier*, ainfi que JEAN DE LA BARTHE, *fon père*, & ARNAUD-GUILHEM DE LA BARTHE, *fon ayeul*. Il avoit époufé *Mondine de Léaumont*, fille de *Raymond*, Seigneur du Puy-Gaillard. Elle étoit Demoifelle d'ISABELLE D'ARMAGNAC, fœur de JEAN, Comte d'ARMAGNAC, qui lui donnèrent en faveur de ce mariage, par acte du 12 Août 1443, 600 écus d'or, fur les revenus de la Terre d'Aure, dix livres, deux robes, l'une de drap, & l'autre de damas. De ce mariage vinrent :

1. JEAN, qui fuit ;
2. ROGER, Abbé de Simorre en 1492 ;
3. PIERRE, auteur de la branche des Seigneurs de l'*Artigolle*, rapportée ci-après ;
4. PEX, Abbé de Faget ;
5. CATHERINE, qui fut Demoifelle d'ISABELLE D'ARMAGNAC, laquelle lui légua 150 écus, avec un habillement de camelot & un d'écarlate ;

6. ANTOINETTE, mariée, par contrat du 11 Décembre 1480, à *Pierre de Lagorfan*, Seigneur de Bellegarde. JEAN DE LA BARTHE, Abbé de Simorre, fon oncle, & PEX DE LA BARTHE, Abbé de Faget, fon frère, affiftèrent à la cérémonie de fon mariage ;
7. Et JEANNE, mariée à *Arnaud-Guillaume de Cominges*, Seigneur de Puy-Guilhem, dont des enfans.

XIV. JEAN DE LA BARTHE, IIIᵉ du nom, Comte & Seigneur d'Arné, de Montcorneil & de Guifery, Chevalier, Sénéchal d'Aure, &c., reçut le 16 Novembre 1498, en préfence d'ARNAUD-GUILHEM DE LA BARTHE, fon père, le ferment de fidélité des habitans de Guifery. BERTRAND DE LA BARTHE, fon coufin germain, rapporté ci-après, jouiffoit encore en 1504 de certains droits fur la Vallée d'Aure, puifque cette même année il lui céda & tranfporta tous les droits qu'il avoit fur les montagnes appelées *Montabrin*, *Prédicil*, *Bufeau*, *Buiffannet*, *Forduranfa*, *Périper*, *Jurat* & *Eftinocière*, qui avoient été données à fes auteurs pour leurs légitimes. Il reçut quittance, le 4 Octobre 1526, dè PIERRE DE LA BARTHE, fon frère, qui lui avoit vendu fa légitime, pour en employer la fomme à l'achat de la Terre de l'Artigolle. Il époufa *Brunette d'Ifalguier*, fille de *Jacques*, & d'*Anne de Foix-Rabat*, dont :

1. MATHIEU, qui fuit ;
2. ROGER, Religieux-Profès de l'Ordre de St.-Benoît, & Prieur de St.-Déodé en 1530 ;
3. & 4. BERNARD & FÉLIX, qui vivoient en 1530 ;
5. GABRIELLE, mariée, par contrat du 28 Janvier 1525, à *Odet de Soréac*, Seigneur de Meun en Bigorre ;
6. BARBE, qui vivoit encore en 1544, femme de *N.... d'Eaux* ou *d'Aux*, dit *de la Forgue ;*
7. Et N.... DE LA BARTHE, mariée à JEAN DE LA BARTHE, fils de PAUL, Seigneur de Gifcaro, à qui elle porta la Terre d'Arné.

XV. MATHIEU DE LA BARTHE, Chevalier, Seigneur de Montcorneil & de Guifery, Sénéchal d'Aure, tranfigea, le 20 Février 1544, avec BARBE DE LA BARTHE, fa fœur, en préfence de *Pierre de Saint-Lari*, Seigneur de Bigorre, de *Jean d'Arcifac* & de *Jean de Soréac*. Il obtint, le 11 Janvier 1553, confirmation du droit qu'il avoit de prendre le bois mort dans la forêt de Pampafan. Il avoit époufé, par contrat du 20 Avril 1530, *Catherine de Lomagne*, fille de *François*, Baron de

Montagnac & de Correnſan, & de *Jeanne de la Roche-Fontenilles*, dont :

1. JEAN, qui ſuit ;
2. ARNAUD, Maréchal-des-Logis de la Compagnie de 5o Lances de M. de Bellegarde, lequel donna quittances en ladite qualité, 1° de 37 livres 12 ſols, le 19 Décembre 1568, ſignée *de Montcorneil*, dit *de la Barthe ;* & 2° de 137 livres 10 ſols, le 1er Octobre 1569 ;
3. FRANÇOISE, qui teſta le 13 Mai 1605. Elle avoit épouſé, par contrat du 12 Novembre 1554, *Jean de Guiſcard,* Seigneur de la Coſte ;
4. GABRIELLE, femme de *Balthaſard d'Alard,* Seigneur de Régolières ;
5. HÉLÈNE, mariée à *Triſtan de Caſtelnau,* Baron de Servies ;
6. MARGUERITE, femme de *François du Lac,* Seigneur de Cairech & de Boiſſe ;
7. Et PAULE, qui tranſigea avec ſes ſœurs pour la ſucceſſion de leur frère aîné, le 4 Mars 1589. Elle donna à ſon mari, par ſon teſtament du 30 Mai 1595, & par ſon codicille, tous ſes biens, n'ayant point d'enfans. Elle étoit la ſeconde femme de *Michel d'Aſtarac,* Seigneur de Fontrailles, Sénéchal d'Armagnac, & Gouverneur de Lectoure, fils de *Jean-Jacques* & *d'Anne de Narbonne*

XVI. JEAN DE LA BARTHE, IVe du nom, Chevalier, Seigneur de Montcorneil & de Guiſery, avoit acheté, le 21 Juillet 1576, le Moulin de *Couran* en Guiſery, que ſa veuve vendit, avec *Aimeric de Narbonne & de Loumagne,* ſon père, le 12 Août 1602, à *Jean,* Seigneur de *Meun,* & mourut ſans enfans en 1580. Il avoit épouſé *Marguerite de Narbonne,* fille *d'Aimeric de Narbonne* & *de Loumagne*.

BRANCHE

des Seigneurs DE L'ARTIGOLLE, *iſſue de celle des Seigneurs* D'ARNÉ & DE MONTCORNEIL.

XIV. PIERRE DE LA BARTHE, troiſième fils d'ARNAUD-GUILHEM, IIIe du nom, Chevalier, Seigneur d'Arné & de Montcorneil, & de *Mondine de Léaumont,* paſſa quittance pour ſa légitime, à JEAN, IIIe du nom, ſon frère, le 4 Octobre 1526, ſomme qu'il employa comme nous l'avons dit, à l'achat de la Terre de l'Artigolle. Il épouſa *Béatrix de Roux,* fille de *Guillaume,* Seigneur de Gréville, qui s'obligea de lui payer, pour reſtant de la dot de ſa femme, par acte du 5 Février

1547, la ſomme de 300 livres. Lorſqu'elle fit hommage & donna dénombrement au Sénéchal de Touloufe, elle étoit veuve & tutrice, le 9 Avril 1540, de ſes enfans :

1. BERNARD, qui ſuit ;
2. Et MARGUERITE, mariée, par contrat du 25 Août 1564, à *Jean de Ville*.

XV. BERNARD DE LA BARTHE, Chevalier, Seigneur de l'Artigolle, épouſa, par contrat du 9 Mars 1553, *Françoiſe de Cardaillac,* avec laquelle il fit, le 13 Avril 1563, l'acquiſition d'une pièce de Terre. Etant veuve, elle conſtitua au nom de ſes enfans, le 25 Août 1564, la dot de MARGUERITE DE LA BARTHE, ſa belle-ſœur. On ne connoît de ſa poſtérité que :

XVI. ODET DE LA BARTHE, Chevalier, Seigneur de l'Artigolle, qui épouſa, par contrat du 2 Octobre 1576, *Catherine de Soubiette de Singla,* dont vint :

XVII. PHILIPPE DE LA BARTHE, Chevalier, Seigneur de l'Artigolle, Maréchal-des-Logis de la Compagnie des Gendarmes du Duc d'Epernon, qui s'allia, par contrat du 4 Juin 1624, avec *Catherine de Goutz,* dont il eut :

XVIII. JEAN DE LA BARTHE, Chevalier, Seigneur de l'Artigolle, Sénéchauſſée de Magnoac, & Election d'Aſtarac, Maréchal-des-Logis des Gendarmes du Duc d'Epernon, ſuivant une lettre de ce Duc du 14 Mars 1650, qui fut depuis Lieutenant d'une Compagnie au Régiment d'Epernon, ſuivant un paſſeport du 16 Novembre 1658. Il eut acte de la repréſentation de ſes titres de Nobleſſe devant M. *Pellot,* Intendant en Guyenne, le 1er Juin 1667. Il ne laiſſa de ſon mariage, du 29 Mai 1663, avec *Gérarde de Caſaux,* que :

XIX. CALIXTE DE LA BARTHE, Dame de l'Artigolle, née en 1667, dont on ignore l'alliance.

BRANCHE

des Seigneurs DE GISCARO, *iſſue de celle des Seigneurs* D'ARNÉ & DE MONTCORNEIL.

XIII. BERNARD DE LA BARTHE, ſecond fils de JEAN, IIe du nom, Comte d'Arné & de Montcorneil, & *d'Eſclarmonde-de-Rivière,* fut Seigneur de Giſcaro, Diocéſe de Lombès. Il reçut le ſerment de fidélité des habitans du lieu de Giſcaro, le 30 Avril 1450, & rendit lui-même foi & hommage au Roi, de cette Terre, au nom de ſa femme, en 1469 ;

avoit acheté, en 1466, la Terre de Péléfixe, tefta devant *Martial Tillorès*, Notaire de Simorre, le 5 Novembre 1485, & fit un codicille le 6 Décembre 1491. Il avoit épousé, avant 1450, *Jeanne de Béon*, fille & unique héritière de N.... *de Béon*, Chevalier, Seigneur de Gifcaro & de Lafségan. De ce mariage vinrent:

1. BERTRAND, qui fuit;
2. JEAN, auteur des Seigneurs de *Thermes*, rapportés ci-après;
3. ARNAULD-GUILHEM, auteur de la branche des Seigneurs de *Lafségan*, rapportée après celle des Seigneurs de *Thermes*;
4. Et BERNARD, Prieur de Sarrancolin, & Abbé de Simorre.

XIV. BERTRAND DE LA BARTHE, Chevalier, Seigneur de Gifcaro, jouiffoit encore de certains droits fur la Vallée d'Aure en 1504, puifque cette même année il céda & tranfporta à JEAN DE LA BARTHE, IIIᵉ du nom, Seigneur de Montcorneil, Sénéchal d'Aure, fon coufin, tous les droits qu'il avoit fur les montagnes appelées *Montabrin*, *Prédicil*, *Bufeau*, *Buiffannet*, *Forduranfa*, *Périper*, *Jurat* & *Eftinocière*; droits qu'ils n'avoit confervés que parce qu'ils avoient été donnés à fes auteurs pour leurs légitimes. L'original de cet aête, paffé devant Notaire, eft dans les regiftres de l'Abbaye de Gimont. Il tefta le 6 Décembre 1517, & eut de *Sibylle du Mona*, fille d'*Arnaud*, Seigneur de Savignac:

XV. JEAN DE LA BARTHE, Chevalier, Seigneur de Gifcaro & de Boucaignères par fa mère, qualifié *Maréchal-des-Logis* de la Compagnie de 50 hommes d'armes de M. de Martigues, dans deux quittances des 3 Juin 1566, & 4 Janvier 1567, vivoit encore en 1580. Il avoit époufé *Catherine de Péguilhem*, belle-fœur de JEAN DE LA BARTHE, Seigneur de Thermes, fon oncle, & eut pour fils unique:

XVI. PAUL DE LA BARTHE, Chevalier, Seigneur de Gifcaro & de Boucaignères, qui rendit hommage & donna dénombrement defdites Terres devant le Sénéchal *de Touloufe*, le 24 Novembre 1540, & tefta le 30 Décembre 1570. Il avoit époufé, par contrat du 31 Janvier 1529, *Marie d'Armantieu-de-la-Palu*, fille de noble *Bertrand d'Armantieu*, Seigneur de la Palu, & mère de 32 enfans mâles & de 4 filles. Le plus jeune des garçons étoit âgé de 14 ans, lorfque le Maréchal *de Bellegarde* & *René de Rochechouart*-

Mortemart, leurs parens, les préfentèrent au Roi, leur père étant à leur tête. *Marie d'Armantieu*, leur mère, eut deux fœurs, toutes les deux mariées, l'une qui eut 28 enfans, & l'autre 24; de forte que ces trois fœurs enfemble eurent 88 enfans, *chofe remarquable & rare*. Des 36 enfans de PAUL DE LA BARTHE, ceux dont on a connoiffance font:

1. MATHIEU, qui fuit;
2. JEAN, marié à N..... DE LA BARTHE, fille & unique héritière du Seigneur d'Arné, qui lui porta en dot cette Terre qui s'étoit confervée dans une des branches depuis 1291;
3. PHILIPPE, marié à *Jeanne de Paris* en Dauphiné, dont il eut un fils nommé JACQUES DE LA BARTHE, qui prit le nom & les armes de *Françoife de Châteaudouble*, & dont la poftérité (fi elle fubfifte en Dauphiné) nous eft inconnue;
4. Un autre JEAN, qui vivoit en 1570 & 1578;
5. ADRIEN, Chevalier, Gouverneur de Nîmes, enfuite de Toulon, marié à *Françoife de Seilles-de-Roquefec*, dont nous ignorons auffi s'il y a eu poftérité;
6. GABRIEL, auteur de la branche des Seigneurs de *Montignac*, rapportée ci-après;
7. JACQUES, auteur de la branche des Seigneurs de *Valentine*, rapportée après celle des Seigneurs de *Montignac*;
8. & 9. JEANNOT & CHARLES, qui vivoient en 1570 & 1578;
10. Un autre CHARLES, Religieux Bénédiêtin à Mas-Grafnier, lors du teftament de fon père;
11. CATHERINE, mariée au Seigneur de *Gaillarville*;
12. MARGUERITE, mariée au Seigneur de *la Lignée*;
13. ANNE, mariée à noble *Simon Dumont*, Chevalier, Seigneur de Malas;
14. Et ANNE-PÉLÉGRIE.

XVII. MATHIEU DE LA BARTHE, Chevalier, Seigneur de Gifcaro & de Boucaignères, tefta le 11 Juin 1603 au profit de fon fils. Il avoit époufé, par contrat du 10 Juin 1571, *Antoinette de Goth*, fille de *Jean*, Seigneur de Rouillac, & de *Catherine de Montlezun*, Dame d'Anfan. Elle étoit morte lors du teftament de fon père fait au Château de Roquefort le 29 Juin 1590, par lequel il laiffe des legs aux enfans d'elle & du Seigneur de Gifcaro fon mari. Ils eurent:

XVIII. ARNAUD-GUILHEM DE LA BARTHE, Chevalier, Seigneur de Gifcaro, qui mourut le 20 Avril 1622. Il avoit époufé, le 11 Janvier

1599, *Catherine de Murviel*, fille de *François*, Chevalier, Seigneur de Murviel, & de *Catherine de Rouges-de-la-Haye*, & laissa :

1. JEAN-JACQUES, qui suit ;
2. GUILLAUME, Chanoine de Montauban ;
3. & 4. ARNAUD & CHARLES, Chevaliers de Malte ;
5. JEAN-LOUIS, dont nous n'avons point de connoissance ;
6. CATHERINE, Religieuse à Toulouse ;
7. & 8. MARGUERITE & FRANÇOISE.

XIX. JEAN-JACQUES DE LA BARTHE, Chevalier, Seigneur de Giscaro, Capitaine au Régiment des Gardes-Françoises, épousa, par contrat du 8 Janvier 1623, *Agnès de Brion*, fille de *Scipion*, Seigneur de Casteljaloux, & de *Louise de Montagut*, dont :

XX. JEAN-LOUIS DE LA BARTHE, Chevalier, Seigneur de Giscaro, qui fut Colonel d'un Régiment d'Infanterie, & ensuite Capitaine des Chevaux-Légers. Il eut acte de la représentation de ses titres devant le Sieur *Lartigue*, Subdélégué de M. *Pellot*, Intendant en Guyenne, le 15 Juin 1667. Il avoit épousé, par contrat du 6 Août 1655, *Catherine de Polastron*, remariée à *Jean-Louis*, Seigneur de *Saint-Pastour*. Elle étoit fille de *Denis*, Seigneur de la Hillière, & de *Marguerite du Bouzet*. Il eut pour fille & unique héritière :

N... DE LA BARTHE, mariée 1° à *N... de Sérignac*, Seigneur de Belmont ; & 2° à *N... de Barboutan-de-Rivière*, Vicomte de Labatut.

BRANCHE
des Seigneurs DE MONTIGNAC, *issue de celle des Seigneurs* DE GISCARO.

XVII. GABRIEL DE LA BARTHE, Ier du nom, sixième fils de PAUL, Seigneur de Giscaro, & de *Marie d'Armantieu-de-la-Palu*, vivoit encore en 1597. Il épousa, par contrat du 31 Mars 1566, *Marie de Villepinte*, fille & unique héritière du Seigneur de *Montignac*, dont il eut :

1. PAUL, qui vivoit encore le 8 Mars 1614 ;
2. GABRIEL, qui suit ;
3. Et FRANÇOIS, qui fit, le 8 Mars, conjointement avec GABRIEL, son frère, une renonciation en faveur de PAUL, leur frère aîné. Il avoit épousé, par contrat du 13 Août 1610, *N... de Fosseries*, dont il eut :

SÉBASTIEN DE LA BARTHE, Chevalier, Seigneur en partie de Giscaro, qui eut acte de la représentation de ses titres de noblesse devant le Sieur *Lartigue*,

Subdélégué de M. *Pellot*, Intendant en Guyenne, le 1er Juin 1667. Il avoit épousé, par contrat du 17 Février 1657, *Anne d'Abadie*. Nous ignorons s'il a eu postérité.

XVIII. GABRIEL DE LA BARTHE, IIe du nom, Chevalier, Seigneur de Montignac, fut marié, 1° par contrat du 7 Décembre 1597, avec *Astruge de Caussade*, de laquelle il n'eut point d'enfans ; & 2° par contrat du 21 Novembre 1615, avec *Bernarde de Claverie*, dont il eut entr'autres enfans :

XIX. JACQUES DE LA BARTHE, Chevalier, Seigneur de Montignac, qui fut baptisé le 21 Mai 1623, & eut acte de la représentation de ses titres de noblesse devant le Sieur *Lartigue*, Subdélégué de M. *Pellot*, Intendant en Guyenne, en 1667. Nous ignorons s'il a contracté alliance.

BRANCHE
des Seigneurs DE VALENTINE, *issue de celle des Seigneurs* DE GISCARO.

XVII. JACQUES DE LA BARTHE, Chevalier, septième fils de PAUL, Chevalier, Seigneur de Giscaro, & de *Marie d'Armantieu-de-la-Palu*, fut institué héritier par *Jacques de Bazordan*, Abbé du Mas-Grasnier, frère de *Simon de Bazordan*, Chevalier des Ordres du Roi, & petit-fils de PAULE DE LA BARTHE, sœur du Maréchal de Thermes. Il testa le 12 Novembre 1609, & fut marié, 1° par contrat passé à Valentine le 30 Avril 1570, avec *Gratiane-Marie de Gabarret*, lors veuve, avec une fille nommée *Marthe-Marie*, de *N......* *d'Ustou* : elle étoit héritière & Dame du Sol & des Domaines dépendans de la Maison de *Tarasté*, situés à Valentine, & c'est de-là que les Seigneurs de la Barthe sont quelquefois qualifiés *Seigneurs de Tarasté* ; & 2° avec *Marguerite d'Ustou*, qui l'institua son héritier universel, & de laquelle il n'eut point de postérité. De plusieurs enfans qu'il eut de sa première femme, dont quelques-uns furent tués au service, ceux dont nous avons connoissance sont :

1. ANTOINE, qui suit ;
2. Et CATHERINE, mariée à noble *Jean de Croso*, Seigneur de Monti.

XVIII. ANTOINE DE LA BARTHE, Ier du nom, Chevalier, Seigneur de Valentine, testa au profit de son fils aîné le 14 Août 1631. Il avoit épousé, 1° par contrat passé devant *Jean*

Sailles, Notaire d'Eftadens en Cominges, le 12 Octobre 1596, *Marguerite d'Ustou*, nièce de *Marguerite*, dont nous venons de parler, & fille de *Frise*, Chevalier, Seigneur de Montgaillard; & 2° *N... de Binot-de-Gourdan*. Il n'eut point d'enfans de fon fecond mariage; ceux du premier font :

1. Louis, qui fuit;
2. Jacques, Chanoine d'Auch;
3. Jean, auteur de la branche des Seigneurs de *Caseaux* & de *Gimont*, rapportée ci-après;
4. Guillaume, Curé de Valentine;

Et trois filles, qui furent mariées.

XIX. Louis de la Barthe, Ier du nom, Chevalier, Seigneur de Valentine, acheta, par contrat paffé à Tarbes le 23 Avril 1656, la Terre de Montignac en Bigorre. Il demeuroit à Gifcaro, Pays de Bigorre, le 1er Juin 1667, lorfqu'il eut acte de la repréfentation de fes titres de nobles devant le Sieur *Lartigue*, Subdélégué de M. *Pellot*, Intendant en Guyenne. Il fut marié, 1° par contrat du 18 Avril 1623, avec *Agnès de Benque*, lors veuve fans enfans, du Seigneur de *Laux*, & fille de *Philippe de Benque*, Chevalier, Seigneur de Maran, de la Grange, & de *Françoise de Bajourdan*; & 2° à *N.....*

Les enfans du premier lit furent :

1. Antoine, qui fuit;
2. Blaise, mort jeune;
3. N..., mariée à *N... de Lort*, Seigneur de Montramée en Conferans;
4. N..., mariée à *N... de Potton*, Chevalier, Seigneur de Cornac en Pardiac.

Du fecond lit il n'eut que :

5. N..., mariée à *N... de Cardaillac*, Seigneur de Mauvéfin.

XX. Antoine de la Barthe, IIe du nom, Chevalier, Seigneur de Valentine, de Bordes, de Montignac & de Tarafté, s'allia, par contrat du 1er Mai 1656, avec *Georgette de la Mothe*, fille d'*Augier*, Chevalier, Seigneur d'Iffaut, & de *Marguerite*, dénommée dans l'Hiftoire de Faudoas, *Ifabeau de Rochechouart*, dont il eut :

1. Louis, qui fuit;
2. Jean, Capitaine au Régiment de Médoc;
3. Et Alexandre.

XXI. Louis de la Barthe, IIe du nom, Chevalier, Seigneur de Valentine, de Bordes, de Montignac & de Tarafté, eut acte de la repréfentation de fes titres de nobleffe, & y fut maintenu par jugement de M. de *Lamoignon*, Intendant en Languedoc. Il avoit époufé, par contrat paffé à Rofès en Conferans, le 29 Juillet 1680, *Françoise de Méritens-de-Rofès*, fille de *Louis de Méritens*, Chevalier, Seigneur de Rofès, & de *Marguerite de Vafon*, dont il eut :

1. Louis, qui fuit;
2. Jean-Valentin, qui a embraffé l'Etat Eccléfiaftique;
3. Roger, qui s'eft auffi fait d'Eglife;
4. Et N...... mariée au Seigneur de *Cafter*.

XXII. Louis de la Barthe, IIIe du nom, Chevalier, Seigneur de Valentine, de Gifcaro en partie, de Bordes, de Montignac, &c., s'allia, par contrat du 25 Juillet 1713, avec *Catherine de la Forgue-de-Saincłot*, fille de *Jean de la Forgue*, Chevalier, Seigneur de Saincłot, & de *Marie-Anne de Saincolren*, dont il a eu :

1. Louis, qui eft Chanoine;
2. Joseph, qui fuit;
3. Jean-Maurice, Chevalier, Capitaine d'Infanterie;
4. François, Chanoine de Gaudens, & Bachelier de Sorbonne;

Trois garçons, morts en bas âge;
Quatre demoifelles, vivantes fans alliances;
Et N....... Religieufe.

XXIII. Joseph de la Barthe, Ier du nom, Chevalier, Seigneur de Valentine, de Gifcaro en partie, &c., a époufé, par contrat du mois de Février 1745, *Marie-Marguerite de la Hitte*, dont il a :

1. Joseph, qui fuit;
2. Calixte, Chevalier, Sous-Lieutenant au Régiment d'Aquitaine, Infanterie;
3. 4. & 5. Marie, Elisabeth & Marie-Louise.

XXIV. Joseph de la Barthe, IIe du nom, Chevalier, eft aujourd'hui Lieutenant au Régiment d'Aquitaine, Infanterie.

BRANCHE
des Seigneurs de Caseaux, de Gimont, & iffue de celle des Seigneurs de Valentine.

XIX. Jean de la Barthe, Chevalier, troifième fils d'Antoine, Ier du nom, Chevalier, Seigneur de Valentine, &c., & de *Marguerite d'Ustou*, fa première femme, étoit Maréchal-des-Logis des Moufquetaires de la Garde ordinaire du Roi avant 1637; fut Capitaine au Régiment de Picardie, Infanterie, en 1639, & depuis Gouverneur d'Auch. Il avoit été préfent au fiège de Montauban, & avoit époufé, par contrat paffé devant *de Cuffon*, Notaire de Caftelnau & de Barberens, le 6 Juillet 1642, *Catherine d'Orbeffan*, fille de noble *François*, Chevalier, Seigneur de Monladet, & de *Jeanne de Goût*, Dame de Cafeaux. De ce mariage vinrent :

1. PHILIPPE, Chevalier, qui fut Capitaine au Régiment de la Marine, Infanterie ;
2. Et ANTOINE, qui fuit.

XX. ANTOINE DE LA BARTHE, Chevalier, Seigneur de Cafeaux, fervit d'abord en Catalogne en qualité de Lieutenant au Régiment de la Marine, Infanterie, puis en 1673 en celle de Capitaine dans le même Corps; & en 1674, fous le Maréchal d'Albret, dans la convocation du Ban de la Nobleffe; fut bleffé au col & au bras en 1675, en montant la tranchée au fiège de Bellegarde ; eft qualifié *Marquis de Cafeaux* dans un Brevet qu'il obtint du Roi cette même année à caufe de fes bleffures, pour aller prendre les eaux de Barrège. La guerre s'étant allumée plus que jamais en 1690, il fut détaché avec 100 hommes pour patrouiller autour de Bergues. Cette commiffion, dont il s'acquitta avec honneur, lui valut, au mois de Mars 1690, le commandement & l'infpection des ports & redoutes du retranchement d'Honfcotte, depuis la Môcre jufqu'à la Sinhl. En 1691 il eut la même infpection fur les lignes d'Enfcotte & poftes en dépendans, jufqu'à l'Abbaye d'Yvertam. Il paffa enfuite en Sicile avec fon Régiment, où il s'acquit une fi grande réputation, qu'il fut nommé, en 1692, Commandant de la Brongue, par M. de Mornas, obligé d'évacuer cette Place; fit toutes les autres Campagnes avec le même Régiment; fut Commandant de la ligne fur le Canal de Loo, en 1694, où il fervit 18 mois; fut fait, en 1695, Sergent-Major du Régiment de la Mothe; réformé avec ce Régiment en 1698, & rétabli la même année en qualité de Capitaine dans celui de Limoufin, où il a fervi jufqu'à fa mort. Il avoit fervi en tout 50 ans, & avoit époufé, par contrat paffé devant *Paffalaigne*, Notaire à Agen, le 9 Juin 1668, *Françoife d'Hugues*, Demoifelle de Compagnie de la Reine, veuve fans enfans de M. *de Vernet*, & fille de noble *Jean d'Hugues*, Chevalier, Gentilhomme ordinaire de la Chambre du Roi, Capitaine & Major du Régiment d'Eftiffac, Commandant de Bergerac, & Gouverneur de Caftelviel, & de *Marguerite de Vergouffane*, Dame du Paradon, & Dame d'Honneur de la Reine ANNE D'AUTRICHE. De ce mariage vint entr'autres enfans :

XXI. PHILIPPE-FRANÇOIS DE LA BARTHE, Chevalier, Seigneur de Cafeaux, & Co-Seigneur d'Arné, qui fut Lieutenant, en 1670, au Régiment Dauphin, & tefta, le 22 Février 1713, en faveur de PHILIPPE DE LA BARTHE, fon fils aîné. Il avoit époufé, par contrat paffé devant *Maumus*, Notaire à l'Isle-Jourdain, le 26 Juillet 1693, par lequel il y eut donation mutuelle & réciproque, *Jeanne de Belleforêt*, fille de noble *Jean-Jacques*, Chevalier, Seigneur d'Engaye, & d'ANNE-LOUISE DE LA BARTHE, Dame de Champaigne & de la Maguère, de la branche de *Laffégan*. De ce mariage vinrent :

1. LOUIS, mort jeune ;
2. PHILIPPE, lequel, n'ayant point eu d'enfans de fa femme, dont on ignore le nom, difpofa en faveur de JEAN-BERNARD DE LA BARTHE, fon frère, des biens que fon père lui avoit laiffé par fon teftament du 22 Février 1713 ;
3. JEAN-BERNARD, qui fuit ;
4. Et BERNARD, qui n'a laiffé que trois filles.

XXII. JEAN-BERNARD DE LA BARTHE, Chevalier, Seigneur de Cafeaux, Co-Seigneur d'Arné, &c., Lieutenant au Régiment de Médoc, a époufé, par contrat paffé devant *Jean Ducaffe*, Notaire de Tournai en Bigorre, le 17 Juin 1733, *Marie-Anne d'Angos-de-Boncarrés*, fille de noble *Jean-François*, Chevalier, Seigneur de Boncarrés, de Luc, de Bourg-Efpielh, &c., & de *Marie de Gironde*, Dame de Caftel-Sacrat. De ce mariage font nés :

1. JEAN-FRANÇOIS, qui fuit ;
2. JEAN-ANNE, rapporté après fon frère aîné ;
3. MARIE, mariée à *Jean de Marmiesle*, Chevalier d'honneur au Parlement de Touloufe ;

Et trois filles, Demoifelles.

XXIII. JEAN-FRANÇOIS DE LA BARTHE, Chevalier, Seigneur de Cafeaux, & Co-Seigneur d'Arné, appelé *le Comte de la Barthe*, eft aujourd'hui Capitaine au Régiment de Médoc.

XXIII. JEAN-ANNE DE LA BARTHE, Chevalier, appelé *le Vicomte de la Barthe*, fecond fils de JEAN BERNARD, Chevalier, Seigneur de Cafeaux & Co-Seigneur d'Arné, & de *Marie-Anne d'Angos-de-Boncarrés*, d'abord Offi-

cier, & fucceffivement Sous-Lieutenant, Lieutenant & Capitaine au Régiment de Médoc;
depuis Capitaine au Régiment des Grenadiers
de France, par commiffion du Roi du 19
Mars 1770, a époufé, par contrat du 21 Mars
1770, & de célébration du 24, *Marie-Anne-
Louife Varnier*, fille d'*Antoine*, Ecuyer, ancien Confeiller du Roi, Auditeur des Comptes
de Dauphiné, & de *Marie-Madeleine de Roman.*

BRANCHE
des Seigneurs DE THERMES, *iffue de celle
des Seigneurs* DE GISCARO.

XIV. JEAN DE LA BARTHE, Chevalier, fecond fils de BERNARD, Chevalier, Seigneur de
Gifcaro, & de *Jeanne de Béon*, époufa *Jeanne de Péguilhem*, fille & héritière de *N... de
Péguilhem*, Chevalier, Seigneur de Thermes
en Aftarac, & de *Marie de Vilambis*, dont il
eut :

1. PAUL, qui fuit;
2. JEANNE-MATHILDE, qui eut de *Pierre*, Chevalier, Seigneur d'*Orbeffan*, *Marguerite
   d'Orbeffan*, laquelle fut mariée, par contrat
   du 11 Mars 1522, avec *Pierre de Saint-Lari*, Baron de Bellegarde, dont elle eut *Roger de Saint-Lari*, Maréchal de France,
   qui fut inftitué héritier de PAUL DE LA BAR-
   THE, Maréchal de France, & Seigneur de
   Thermes, fon grand-oncle, dont il époufa
   la veuve par difpenfe ;
3. Et PAULE, qui eut du Seigneur de *Bazordan*, fon mari, le Capitaine de *Bazordan*,
   qui fut tué Meftre-de-Camp au fiège de
   Montauban le 22 Octobre 1562.

XV. PAUL DE LA BARTHE, Chevalier, Seigneur de Thermes, par fa mère, Chevalier de
l'Ordre du Roi, Capitaine de 50 hommes de
fes Ordonnances, Gouverneur de Paris & de
l'Isle-de-France, dit *le Maréchal de Thermes*,
étoit né à Conferans en 1482. Peu avantagé
des biens de la fortune, il fit fes premières armes dans la guerre d'Italie, où il fe fignala au
fiège de Naples en 1528, au retour duquel il
fut pris par les Corfaires, & racheté ; fervit à
la conquête du Piémont en 1536, au ravitaille-
ment de Thérouanne en 1537, & au fiège de
Perpignan en 1541 ; fut Gouverneur de Savillan en 1542, Colonel-Général de la Cavalerie-Légère à la bataille de Cérifolles en
1544, où il mit en déroute la Cavalerie Florentine ; donna jufqu'au milieu du bataillon
du Prince de Salerne, où il demeura prifonnier, fon cheval ayant été tué fous lui; paffa

enfuite en Ecoffe, comme Lieutenant de Roi,
où il fe comporta généreufement pendant la
guerre de 1549 ; fut envoyé l'année fuivante
en Ambaffade vers le Pape PAUL III, foutint
avec valeur le fiège de Parme contre les Im-
périaux, au mois de Novembre de cette année. Il pratiqua la ligue avec les Siennois, les
fit foulever le 5 Août 1552, & commanda
l'armée que le Roi envoya à leur fecours. Il
paffa enfuite en l'Isle de Corfe, où il fit des
progrès; commanda en Piémont durant l'abfence du Maréchal Duc de Briffac en 1550; le
Roi lui fit don du Comté de Cominges, Sénéchauffée de Touloufe, le 10 Février 1555;
après la prife de Calais, il en fut Gouverneur;
le Roi le créa en 1558 Maréchal de France.
il fe rendit maître de Dunkerque & de Berghes-Saint-Winock, & perdit auffitôt après
la bataille de Gravelines, où il fut bleffé &
fait prifonnier le 14 Juillet 1558. Malgré fa
défaite, qui lui donna le furnom de *Malheu-
reux Capitaine*, il fut en grande confidération jufqu'à fa mort, arrivée à Paris le 6
Mai 1562; il fut inhumé aux Céleftins dans
la Chapelle des dix Martyrs. Il avoit acquis
peu de richeffes, dont il difpofa en faveur de
Roger de Saint-Lari, Seigneur de Bellegarde, & Maréchal de France, fon petit-neveu, n'ayant point eu d'enfans de *Marguerite de Saluces-Cardé*, remariée par difpenfe, le 20 Août 1565, à *Roger de Saint-Lari*,
fille de *François*, Chevalier, Seigneur de
Cardé, laquelle donna, le 8 Mai 1562, quittance à *Raoul Moreau*, Tréforier des Guerres, de 750 liv. pour fubvenir aux frais de
fa fépulture. M. de Thou, en fon Hift., liv.
XXXVI, dit que *le Maréchal de Thermes
étoit un homme de bien, & un fage Capitaine, auffi illuftre dans la paix que dans
la guerre.* Sa vie a été écrite par M. Brantôme. Voyez les *Mémoires* de M. de Langey,
& les *Commentaires* de Fr. Rabutin.

BRANCHE
des Seigneurs DE LASSÉGAN, *iffue de celle
des Seigneurs* DE GISCARO.

XIV. ARNAUD-GUILHEM DE LA BARTHE, Chevalier, troifième fils de BERNARD, Chevalier,
Seigneur de Gifcaro, & de *Jeanne de Béon*,
reçut en apanage de fes père & mère la Terre
de Laffégan, dont il donna le dénombrement
devant le Sénéchal de Touloufe en 1503. BER-

NARD, fon frère, Prieur de Sarrancolin, du confentement de ROGER DE LA BARTHE, Abbé de Simorre, fon oncle, lui donna une vigne dans la ville de Simorre, en 1500, & JEAN DE LA BARTHE, Seigneur de Thermes, fon autre frère, le fit fon Exécuteur teftamentaire le 8 Février 1510. Il mourut en 1518, & avoit été marié deux fois. On ignore le nom de fa première femme; la feconde fut *Anne de Biran*, d'une ancienne Nobleffe de Gafcogne.

Il eut du premier lit:

1. PHILIPPE, qui fuit.

Et du fecond lit:

2. PIERRE, Chevalier, Capitaine d'Infanterie, Gouverneur de Toulon en Provence, qui partagea avec fon frère, par acte du 6 Mars 1546, les biens provenant de la fucceffion de leur père;

3. MADELEINE, mariée à *Jean de Maffent*, Seigneur de l'Hâs;

4. CATHERINE, femme de *François de Polaftron*, Seigneur du Bofc;

5. & 6. JEANNE & autre CATHERINE.

XV. PHILIPPE DE LA BARTHE, Ier du nom, Chevalier, Seigneur de Laffégan, Chevalier de l'Ordre du Roi, rendit hommage & dénombrement de fa Terre au Sénéchal de Touloufe le 18 Mars 1539 & en 1556; donna quittance le 13 Novembre 1520 d'une partie de la dot de *Catherine de Marquefave*, fa femme, fille d'*Odinet de Marquefave*, Seigneur de la Trape, d'une très-ancienne Maifon. Il eut:

1. FRANÇOIS, Chevalier, qui s'allia avec *Ifabelle de Vize*, fille de *Jean de Vize*, Seigneur de Sajas, & de *Jeanne de Saint-Lari*, laquelle étant veuve de lui fans enfans, tranfigea avec CARBON DE LA BARTHE, fon beau-frère, au fujet de fa dot, par acte du 16 Février 1561;

2. CARBON, qui fuit;

3. Et ARNAUD.

XVI. CARBON DE LA BARTHE, Chevalier, Seigneur de Laffégan & de la Maguère, Chevalier de l'Ordre du Roi en 1566, Enfeigne de la Compagnie de M. de Maffez, fuivant une quittance de la fomme de 100 liv. qu'il donna le 26 Janvier 1569, laquelle eft fignée *Carbon de Laffégan*, fut Capitaine de 50 hommes d'armes des Ordonnances du Roi en 1572; Maréchal-de-Camp, Commandant & Gouverneur des Comtés d'Aftarac, Cominges & Bigorre; fut chargé de plufieurs commiffions importantes par les Rois CHARLES IX & HENRI III, qui lui témoignèrent,

par plufieurs lettres, la fatisfaction de fes fervices; eft qualifié *Maréchal-de-Camp des Troupes du Roi en Guyenne* dans des lettres que ce Prince lui adreffa les 6 & 12 Janvier 1576, 21 Mars & 8 Mai fuivant; tranfigea avec ARNAUD DE LA BARTHE, fon frère, le 8 Octobre 1551; tefta en faveur de JEAN-FRANÇOIS DE LA BARTHE, fon fecond fils, le 25 Avril 1575, & fut marié, 1° par contrat du 24 Novembre 15..., avec *Suprême de Roquelaure*, fille de *Jean*, Chevalier, Seigneur de Saint-Aubin, & de *Bertrande de Bézolles*; & 2° par contrat du 19 Avril 1574, avec *Marguerite de Groffolles*, veuve de *Jean-François d'Aulin*, Seigneur d'Aulin, dont on ignore la poftérité. Elle étoit fille de *Raymond*, Seigneur & Baron de Flamarens, Chevalier de l'Ordre du Roi.

Il eut du premier lit:

1. PHILIPPE, qui fuit;

2. JEAN, Chevalier, qui eut différend avec fon frère, qui lui difputoit un legs que fon père lui avoit fait par fon teftament ci-deffus daté, lequel fe termina par Sentence arbitrale du 8 Février 1594, d'après laquelle il tranfigea avec lui le 17 Novembre 1596;

3. Et FRANÇOIS.

XVII. PHILIPPE DE LA BARTHE, IIe du nom, Chevalier, Seigneur de Laffégan, de la Hage-Forgues, de Garravet, Campaigne, la Maguère, &c., partagea avec JEAN, fon frère, le 18 Octobre 1596. Il rendit aveu & dénombrement de fa Terre, le 10 Janvier 1610, fuivant & conformément à ceux rendus par PHILIPPE DE LA BARTHE, fon ayeul, & par ARNAUD-GUILHEM, IIe du nom, fon bifayeul, auquel elle fut donnée en apanage, comme nous l'avons dit ci-devant; fut fait Chevalier de l'Ordre du Roi, par Lettres données à Saint-Germain-en-Laye, le 28 Juillet 1570, & commis pour en donner le Collier au Baron de *Pontejac*, par autres Lettres datées de Poitiers le 8 Juillet 1577; fut Commandant au Comté d'Aftarac par Lettres du 15 Mars 1573, & vivoit encore en 1629. Il avoit été marié, 1° par contrat du 8 Juin 1592, avec *Marthe de Murviel*, fille de *François*, Chevalier, Seigneur de Beauvais, & de *Catherine de Touges-Noaillan*, Dame de la Hage-Forgues, &c., & 2° par contrat du 21 Mai 1602, avec *Julienne Carbonneau*, de laquelle il n'eut point d'enfans.

Du premier lit vinrent:

1. Gabriel, qui fuit, auteur de la branche des Seigneurs de la *Maguère;*
2. Jean - François, Chevalier , Seigneur de Campaigne, & de la Maguère, qui fut maintenu en fa noblefle, par Jugement rendu le 18 Mai 1635, par MM. de *Verthamon* & de *Gourgues,* Commiffaires députés par S. M. pour le régalement des Tailles de l'Election de Périgueux. Il vivoit encore en 1660, Il avoit époufé, par contrat du 8 Avril 1629, *Jeanne de Saubolle,* dont il eut :

  Philippe de la Barthe, Chevalier, Seigneur de Campaigne, Aide-Major du Régiment de Piémont, qui fut maintenu dans fa noblefle par Jugement rendu le 15 Mars 1668, par M. *Pellot,* Intendant en Guyenne, & mourut fans poftérité. Il avoit époufé, par contrat du 6 Septembre 1660, *Gabrielle de la Pleynie;*

  N... de la Barthe, Chevalier, Seigneur de Rochebonne, qui fut Major au Régiment d'Auvergne, par commiffion du 20 Septembre 1658;

  Et Anne-Louise de la Barthe, qui eut de *Jean - Jacques de Belleforêt,* fon mari, Chevalier, Seigneur d'Engaye, une fille , nommée *Jeanne de Belleforêt,* qui fut mariée, par contrat du 26 Juillet 1693, avec Philippe - François de la Barthe, Chevalier, Seigneur de Cafeaux, dont nous avons ci-devant parlé, à qui elle porta les Seigneuries de Campaigne & de la Maguère, & les autres biens de fes oncles & ayeuls.

3. Et Odet, dont la poftérité fera rapportée ci-après fous le nom des *Seigneurs de Laffégan.*

BRANCHE
des Seigneurs DE LA Maguère.

XVIII. Gabriel de la Barthe, Chevalier, Seigneur de la Maguère, de la Hage-Forgues, de Gavarret, de Tancouet & de Larrocan, s'allia, par contrat du 27 Octobre 1620, à *Françoise d'Efparbès-de-Luffan,* fille de *François,* Chevalier, Seigneur de Luffan, & d'*Anne Dantin,* & fœur de *Philippe d'Efparbès.* Il eut de ce mariage, entr'autres enfans :

XIX. Philippe de la Barthe, IIIe du nom, Chevalier, Seigneur de la Maguère, de la Hage-Forgues, de Marignac & de Gavarret, qui époufa, par contrat du 18 Octobre 1651, *Jeanne de Guerrier,* fille de *Pierre,* Chevalier, Seigneur de Beaufort & de Carpette, &

de *Marie de Sainctes,* qui le fit père de :

XX. François de la Barthe, Chevalier, Seigneur de la Maguère, Baron de la Hage-Forgues, de Marignac, de Gavarret, &c., qui tefta le 28 Mars 1710, & avoit époufé, par contrat du 10 Février 1695, *Anne d'Efcodéca-de-Boiffé,* fille de *Jean-Henri,* Marquis de Boiffé, & de *Marthe de Cominges-Péguilhem.* Ses enfans furent :

  1. Joseph-François-Clément, qui fuit;
  2. Jean-Henri, Chevalier, né le 25 Décembre 1701, qui fut reçu Chevalier de Malte au Grand-Prieuré de Touloufe en 1723, & depuis Commandeur;
  3. Et Jeanne-Marie, mariée, par contrat du 4 Janvier 1725, avec *Jean-Pierre de Siregand,* Comte d'Erce. Voyez SIREGAND.

XXI. Joseph-François-Clément de la Barthe, Chevalier, Seigneur & Baron de la Hage-Forgues, de la Maguère, Gavarret & de Marignac, a été Moufquetaire du Roi de la première Compagnie, & eft mort fans poftérité de *Louife de Sers-de-Manzac.*

BRANCHE
des Seigneurs DE Lasségan & DE Thermes.

XVIII. Odet de la Barthe, Chevalier, Seigneur de Laffégan, troifième fils de Philippe, IIe du nom, & de *Marthe de Murviel,* fa première femme, partagea avec Gabriel & Jean-François, fes frères, le 19 Avril 1637, & tefta le 20 Juillet 1665. Il avoit époufé, le 2 Avril 1636, *Marguerite-Renée de Biran,* fille de *Barthélemy-Scipion de Biran,* Chevalier, Seigneur de Caftelgeloux, & de *Louife de Magnaut-de-Montégut,* fille de *Louis de Magnaut-de-Montégut,* & de *Marguerite de Roquelaure,* tante d'*Antoine,* Maréchal de France, de laquelle il eut :

  1. Pierre, qui continua la poftérité des Seigneurs de *Laffégan,* éteinte;
  2. Et Guillaume, qui fuit.

Le P. Anfelme donne un troifième fils, nommé Jean, qui fut maintenu en fa noblefle avec fes frères en 1667.

XIX. Guillaume de la Barthe, Chevalier, eut pour fon apanage le Domaine de Mondeau, par donation qui lui en fut faite par la Dame *de Biran,* fa mère, le 21 Février 1677. Il eut acte de la repréfentation de fes titres de noblefle, conjointement avec les Seigneurs de la Hage-Forgues, & de Laffégan, devant M. *Pellot,* Intendant en Guyenne, le 31 Juillet

1667, & devant M. *le Gendre*, le 18 Février 1700. Il testa le 13 Août 1702, & avoit épousé, le 13 Septembre 1689, *Louise Duffour*, fille d'*Arnaud Duffour*, Seigneur de Loran, & de *Jeanne de la Mazère*, dont pour fils unique :

XX. François de la Barthe, Chevalier, Comte de Mondeau, d'Arrogues, Baron de Thermes en Armagnac, & de la Mazère, qui épousa, le 7 Février 1717, *Marie-Anne Saint-Lari-de-Bellegarde*, fille d'*Antoine*, de la même Maison que *Roger de Saint-Lari-de-Bellegarde*, Maréchal de France, & de *Christine de Lasséran*, dont :

1. Antoine, qui suit ;
2. Jean-Baptiste, mort Lieutenant de Dragons, au service d'Espagne ;
3. Henri, Cornette au Régiment Dauphin, Cavalerie ;
4. François-Louis, Chanoine, Chantre, & Grand-Vicaire du Diocèse de Sarlat ;
5. Et Françoise, mariée, le 14 Février 1750, à *Paul-François*, Comte de *Vendômois*, Capitaine au Régiment de Fleury, Cavalerie, & Chevalier de Saint-Louis.

XXI. Antoine de la Barthe, Baron de la Mazère, Comte de Thermes en Armagnac, Seigneur d'Izotges, Arparens, Laubade & Viel-Capet, Chevalier de l'Ordre Militaire de Saint-Louis, a épousé, le 12 Janvier 1750, *Claude de Bréthous*, fille de *Léon de Bréthous*, Seigneur, Baron de Cap-Breton & Labenne, & de *Jeanne Picot*, dont :

1. François-Louis, né le 13 Septembre 1756 ;
2. Et Marie-Anne-Jeanne-Louise, née le 7 Septembre 1760.

Les armes : *écartelé, aux 1 & 4 d'or à quatre pals de gueules*, qui est de la Barthe ; *aux 2 & 3 d'azur à trois fumées d'or sortantes du bas de l'écu, & se terminant en pointes arrondies*, qui est de Fumel. *Une aigle éployée à deux têtes d'or derrière l'écu, & le soutenant sur l'estomac.* Supports: *deux lions d'or, armés & lampassés de gueules.* Cimier: *une tête de bouc au naturel, & Couronne de Marquis.*

BARTHÉLEMY-DE-GRAMONT, famille originaire de Rouergue, établie à Toulouse, il y a environ 200 ans.

Pierre Barthélemy, Seigneur de Puymaurin en Auvergne, & de Gramont en Rouergue, &c., vivoit sous le règne du Roi Charles VIII. Cette famille a donné beaucoup de Conseillers & de Présidens au Parlement de Toulouse. François Barthélemy, Seigneur de *Gramont*, & ses descendans, Gabriel, Pierre qui suit, & Gabriel II, l'ont été successivement.

Pierre Barthélemy-de-Gramont, IIe du nom, Président aux Enquêtes du Parlement de Toulouse, mort en 1630, a laissé de *Jacquette Sabathery* :

François Barthélemy-de-Gramont, Evêque de Saint-Papoul en 1675, mort en 1716.

Jacques Barthélemy-de-Gramont, Baron de Lanta, épousa, par contrat du 25 Avril 1678, *Catherine de Riquet*, fille de *Pierre-Paul de Riquet*, Seigneur de Bonrepos, & de *Catherine de Milhau*, dont il eut :

Pierre, qui suit ;
Et Jean-Mathias Barthélemy-de-Gramont, successivement Chanoine de Saint-Sernin de Toulouse, Abbé de Calers en 1717, nommé Evêque de Perpignan le 17 Octobre 1723, & sacré le 26 Mai 1726, mort en Juillet 1743, âgé de 55 ans.

Pierre Barthélemy-de-Gramont, IVe du nom, Baron de Lanta, a été Capitaine d'Infanterie au Régiment du Roi.

(Voyez *le Mercure de France* du mois de Juillet 1743, pag. 1656).

Les armes : *d'azur, à trois bandes d'or.*

BARTHÉLEMY, en Picardie: *d'argent, au levrier couronné de sable, accollé d'or ; coupé d'azur, au massacre du cerf d'or.*

BARTHÉLEMY, en Provence, famille éteinte, qui s'étoit illustrée par les Chevaliers qu'elle avoit donnés à l'Ordre de Malte & par ses alliances dans les Maisons de *Villeneuve*, de *Forbin d'Oppède*, d'*Arlatan*, de *Clapier-Vauvenargues* & autres. Elle portoit : *d'azur, au rocher de six coupeaux d'or en cœur, accompagné de trois étoiles de même, 2 & 1.*

BARTHÉLEMY-D'ORVILLE: *de sinople, à trois têtes de lion d'or, arrachées & lampassées de gueules, 2 & 1.*

BARTHELIER, famille qui habite la Ville de Lisle, au Comtat Venaissin, depuis environ 400 ans.

Hermand Barthelier s'allia à *Catherine de Burgondion*, & vint s'établir à l'Isle, au Comtat Venaissin, où il acquit des biens. Il eut de son mariage trois enfans, qu'il nomme dans son testament, fait le 3 Février 1363, par-devant *Bertrand Gautier*, Notaire ; il y prend la qualité de *Chevalier du Saint-Empire-Romain*, & de *Chambellan* du feu Empereur Louis; il fait un legs à son fils Raymond; & à sa fille Catherine, & nomme héritier de ses biens de Bavière, & de ceux qu'il a acquis à l'Isle, son autre fils Pierre.

Cette famille s'est distinguée, non-seulement dans les Croisades d'Orient, mais encore dans celles que la Noblesse Allemande fit aux Prussiens Idolâtres, invitée par Conrad, Duc de Massovie, qui ne savoit comment résister à ce Peuple barbare & cruel. Jean Barthelier, qui conduisoit plusieurs Gentilshommes Allemands dans cette Croisade, ayant vaincu une partie de ce Peuple, fit construire un Château fortifié, qu'il nomma *Barthelier*, mot qui, en langue du Pays, signifie *barrière terrassée*.

Comme les noms propres des familles n'étoient pas fixes en ces tems-là, on ignore s'il donna son nom à ce Château, où si c'est de ce Château que cette famille a pris le sien.

Elle subsiste dans ladite Ville de l'Isle, & a pour chef Claude-Pompée-François de Barthelier, Co-Seigneur de Venasque, ancienne Capitale du Comtat Venaissin, marié, le 6 Octobre 1742, avec *Madeleine de Silvang*; dont il a:

1. François-Pompée-Libéral de Barthelier-Venasque, né le 26 Juillet 1743, Lieutenant au Régiment de Vermandois, depuis le 1er Novembre 1755;
2. Louis-Alexandre-Urbain, né le 25 Mai 1744;
3. Joseph-Ferdinand, né le 26 Août 1745;
4. Lucrèce-Marguerite-Elisabeth, née le 20 Octobre 1746;
5. Et Françoise-Laure-Madeleine, née le 15 Février 1754.

Les armes: *d'azur, à trois étoiles d'or; au chef cousu de gueules, chargé d'une colombe d'argent, portant au bec un épi d'or.* Supports & cimier: *deux sauvages armés de massues.* Devise & cri de guerre: *Cœli enarrant gloriam.*

BARTHELOT: *d'azur, au chevron d'or, accompagné de trois trèfles de même, 2 en chef & 1 en pointe.*

BARTHOLY: *taillé & crénelé d'or & de gueules, à deux étoiles de l'un en l'autre.*

BARTOLLE: *d'or, au lion de gueules, la queue fourchée.*

BARTOMIER, famille de l'Isle-de-France,

qui portoit: *d'azur au chevron d'or, accompagné en chef de deux roses d'argent, & en pointe d'un trèfle d'or*, & de laquelle étoit Susanne-Louise-Marguerite Bartomier, née le 3 Mars 1676, & reçue à Saint-Cyr, au mois d'Avril 1687, après avoir prouvé sa Noblesse depuis Jean Bartomier Ier, Seigneur d'Olivet, qui épousa, en 1564, *Geneviève Brachet*.

BARTON-DE-MONTBAS, ancienne Noblesse de la Marche.

Bernard Barton, Vicomte de Montbas, avait épousé, avant 1500, *Marie de Sully*, fille de *Guyon*, Seigneur de Voullion, & de *Jeanne de Prie*, dont il eut:

. Perrette Barton-de-Montbas, qui épousa, par contrat du 7 Septembre 1506, *Hélion de la Châtre*, Seigneur de Bruillebault.

Pierre, Vicomte de Montbas, qui pouvoit être fils de Bernard, naquit en 1489, & épousa, en 1509, *Isabelle*, fille de *Jacques de Lévis*, Seigneur de Châteaumorand, & de *Louise de Tournon*.

François, Vicomte de Montbas, Lieutenant-Général des Armées du Roi, & Meftre-de-Camp du Régiment de Cavalerie du Cardinal Mazarin, épousa *Denise de Maillé*, fille de *Remi*, Seigneur de Bénehart, & de *Dorothée Clausse-de-Fleury*.

N.... Vicomte de-Montbas, dans la Marche, épousa la sœur du Maréchal de *Fabert*, veuve du Sieur *Déjardin*, Secrétaire-Général de l'Infanterie sous le Duc d'Epernon.

Anne Barton-de-Montbas épousa *Pierre le Long*, Seigneur de Chevillot, & en eut *Anne le Long*, veuve en 1573 de *François de Talaru*, Seigneur de Chalmazel, laquelle épousa en secondes noces *Pierre de Châteauneuf*, dont un fils unique, auteur des Seigneurs de *Rochebonne*.

Jeanne Barton-de-Montbas épousa *François de la Berrodière*, Seigneur de l'Isle-Rouet, dont *Françoise*, femme de *Robert de Combaut*, Vicomte d'Arcy-sur-Aube, dont *Claudine de Combaut*, qui épousa, en 1596, *Charles*, Baron *de Clerc* & de Panilleuse, dont *Marie de Clerc*, qui épousa *François Martel*, & en eut *Charles-Martel*, Comte de Clerc, &c.

La famille de Barton-de-Montbas subsiste dans le Vicomte de Montbas, qui fait sa résidence au Château de Montbas, ou à Bellac, en Basse-Marche, & il a pour frère cadet:

Pierre Barton-de-Montbas, Chevalier de

Saint-Louis, ancien Capitaine au Régiment de la Marche-Prince, Lieutenant de Meſſieurs les Maréchaux de France, né à Bellac, marié à Toulon avec *Claire-Françoiſe Chantelot-de-la-Chaiſe*, d'une famille originaire de Bourbonnois, éteinte, & fille d'*Antoine Chantelot-de-la-Chaiſe*, Chevalier de Saint-Louis, Capitaine des Vaiſſeaux du Roi, & d'*Anne de Gombaud*, d'une famille noble établie à Bordeaux, dont :

  1. Louis, né le 6 Septembre 1761 ;
  2. Et Anne-Marie-Claire, née au Château de Montbas, & morte à Toulon.

\- Les armes : *d'azur, au cerf giſant ou à la repoſée d'or, onglé & ramé de même ; au chef échiqueté d'or & de gueules.* Supports : *deux ſauvages portant une ceinture de ſinople.*

BARVAU, à Tréguier : *de ſable, à deux branches de palmes d'argent, adoſſées & poſées en pal.*

* BARVILLE, en Gâtinois. C'est un Bourg près Boine & Gaubertin, qui a donné ſon nom à une famille ancienne.

1. Pierre, Sire de Barville, nommé Ecuyer, Seigneur de Gaubertin, reçut un aveu le Dimanche avant la Saint-Lucas 1371, & étoit mort avant le 17 Novembre 1409. Il laiſſa de *Marion* :

  1 Guillaume, qui ſuit ;
  2. Et Pierre, dont on ignore l'alliance.

II. Guillaume de Barville, Ier du nom, Ecuyer, Seigneur de Gaubertin, Maiſoncelles, Tillay-le-Godin & Maſcheron, partagea avec ſon frère, ſous le ſcel d'Yerre, le 6 Décembre 1430, & ſuivant un acte du 10 Juillet 1410, il eut pour femme *Jacqueline de Boulainvilliers*, dont :

III. Jean de Barville, Ecuyer, Seigneur deſdits lieux, qui vendit, avec ſa femme, la Terre de Manchecourt à l'Amiral de Graville, *Louis de Malet*, Seigneur de Maleſherbes. Il épouſa *Perette de Courtenay-Blénau*, dite de *Manchecourt*, fille de *Guillaume*, Chevalier, Seigneur dudit Manchecourt & de Trazant. Ses enfans furént :

  1. Guillaume, qui ſuit ;
  2. Et Marie, femme, par contrat du 15 Mai 1481, de *Charles de Bosbec*, Chevalier, Baron dudit Bosbec, dont poſtérité.

IV. Guillaume de Barville, IIe du nom, Ecuyer, Seigneur de Maiſoncelles & de Trazant, épouſa *Jacqueline de Garlande*, Dame de Coudray, fille d'*Amanjou* ou *Amonis*, Chevalier, Seigneur d'Argeville, Chambellan du Roi, Gouverneur de Montlhéry, & de *Bertrande d'Allonville*, dont :

V. Guillaume de Barville, IIIe du nom, Chevalier, Seigneur de Maiſoncelles & du Coudray, où l'on voit ſon épitaphe à côté d'*Iſabeau de Duis*, ſa ſeconde femme, qu'il avoit nommée ſon exécutrice, par ſon teſtament du 30 Avril 1483. Il avoit épouſé 1° *Guillemette du Tartre* ; & 2° *Iſabeau de Duis*, qui étoit veuve le 1er Juin 1488, qu'elle donna procuration devant *Geoffroy*, Notaire à Yerre-le-Chatel, à Charles de Villers. Elle mourut en 1500.

Il eut de ſon premier mariage :

  1. Philippe, Seigneur de Maiſoncelles, mort ſans alliance.

Et du ſecond :

  2. Gilles, Chanoine de Sens, Archidiacre de Melun, Prieur de Saint-Sauveur, mort en 1555 ;
  3. Louis, qui ſuit ;
  4. Un autre Philippe, Chevalier de Saint-Jean de Jéruſalem ;
  5. Marguerite, femme 1° de *N.... Hérouan*, Seigneur de Courtainville ; en Chartrain, dont poſtérité ; 2° d'*Aubert le Fèvre*, Seigneur de Caumartin, dont la poſtérité ſubſiſte ;
  6. Marie, femme de *Jean Coëtin* ;
  7. Julienne, femme, par contrat devant *Péret*, Notaire, le 3 Janvier 1496, de *Jean Tapperant*, Ecuyer ;
  8. Jeanne, femme de *Guillaume Langlois*, Ecuyer ;
  9. & 10. Julienne, la jeune, & Barbe, Religieuſes à Saint-Dominique de Montargis ;
  11. Et Artuze, femme, par contrat devant *Jourdain de Bèze*, Notaire au Coudray, en Beauce, le 3 Avril 1502, de *Perrot de Caſebonne*, Ecuyer, Seigneur de Romainville, dont trois filles mariées.

VI. Louis de Barville, Chevalier, Seigneur de Coudray, Maiſoncelles, du Buiſſon, & Ligerville, vendit, devant *Bouchet*, Notaire à Beaune, le 19 Mai 1515, portion d'un bien de ſa femme. Il avoit épouſé, *Jacquette de Longueau*, fille de *Bertrand*, Chevalier de l'Ordre du Roi, Seigneur de Parville, Saint-Michel, & de *Marie de la Taille-de-Bondaroy*. Il eût :

  1. Gilles, qui ſuit ;
  2. Jean, Chanoine de Sens, Docteur en Théologie, & Prieur de Saint-Sauveur, après la

mort de Gilles, fon oncle, en 1555, qui mourut en 1571;

3. Philippe, Chevalier de Malte en 1552, & Commandeur de Loifon, en Artois, en 1576;

4. Artuze, femme, par contrat paffé devant *Olivier*, Notaire au Caudray, le 11 Novembre 1523, de *Jean de Goulard*, Ecuyer, Seigneur en partie d'Invillier;

5. Julienne, femme de *N......* Jupereau, Ecuyer;

6. Marie, femme de *Valentin de la Roque*, Seigneur de Montfezin;

7. Et Jeanne, femme, par contrat du 10 Août 1538, d'*André de Bufferant*, Ecuyer, Seigneur de Chaumont.

VII. Gilles de Barville, Ier du nom, Chevalier, Seigneur du Coudray en 1545, Maifoncelles en 1553, du Buiffon & Ligerville en 1559; l'un des 100 Gentilshommes de la Maifon du Roi; tefta le 24 Février 1573, & avoit époufé par contrat, préfent *Pierre le Roi*, Notaire au Châtelet de Paris, le 3 Janvier 1539, *Marie de la Vernade*, fille de *Pierre*, Baron de Broue, Maître des Requêtes, & d'*Anne Briçonnet*, dont:

1. Gilles, qui fuit;

2. Et Jean, Seigneur de Ligerville, dont la poftérité fera rapportée ci-après.

VIII. Gilles de Barville, IIe du nom, Chevalier, Seigneur du Coudray & Maifoncelles, premièrement Confeiller au Parlement, puis Capitaine de Chevaux-Légers, fous M. le Duc d'Anjou, mort en 1610, avoit époufé, par contrat du 14 Décembre 1605, *Jeanne de Piédefer*, fille de *Robert*, Seigneur de Guyencourt, & de *Lucrèce de Prunelé*, fille de *Gilles*, Seigneur de la Porte, dont:

1. Robert, qui fuit;

2. Et Anne, femme de *N.... Vion*, Chevalier, Seigneur de Treffancourt, près Meulan.

IX. Robert de Barville, Chevalier, Seigneur du Coudray & Maifoncelles, Capitaine de Chevaux-Légers, époufa, par contrat du 29 Septembre 1645, *Marie Fiot*, veuve de *Pierre Baillet*, Préfident en la Chambre des Comptes de Dijon, dont il n'eut point d'enfans, & donna à *Robert Vion*, fon neveu, la Terre du Coudray & Maifoncelles, à la charge de joindre le nom de Barville à celui de *Vion*, ce qui n'a pas duré long-tems; il n'en refte aujourd'hui que trois filles, dont les deux cadettes font mariées, l'aînée à M. *Graffin*, ci-devant Colonel d'un Corps de Troupes-Légères de fon nom, & aujourd'hui Brigadier

des Armés du Roi, Chevalier de Saint-Louis.

VIII. Jean de Barville, Seigneur de Ligerville, Page, & enfuite Maître-d'Hôtel de Charles IX, mort en 1601, avoit époufé 1o *Jacqueline de Saint-Mefmin*, fille d'*Agnan*, Ecuyer, Seigneur de Breuil, morte fans enfans; & 2o en 1578, *Jacqueline*, Dame de Boüe & d'Echilleufe, dont:

1. Louis, qui fuit;

2. Bertrand, Seigneur de Barville, qui accompagna le Duc d'Alençon, depuis Henri III, en Pologne, & époufa *Marie de Saint-Martin*, fille de *François*, Chevalier, Seigneur de Garuenne, & de *Louife du Pleffis*, dont:

> Jacqueline de Barville, femme de *Jean de Roffart*, Ecuyer, Seigneur de la Gatine, au Perche, Moncheroille;
>
> Et N.... femme de *N.... de Roffart*, Seigneur de la Boulaye, au Perche;

3. N... dite *Mademoifelle de Ligerville*, femme de *Charles de Montaçant*, aliàs *Monteclard*, Ecuyer, Seigneur de la Planchette & Mignerel;

4. Louife, femme, par contrat du 7 Février 1609, de *Charles de Cambray*, Seigneur de Gironville;

5. Anne, femme, en 1564, d'*Hubert le Chat*, Seigneur de Ruys, près Nevers;

6. Et Charlotte, femme, en 1572, d'*Honoré de la Vallette*, Ecuyer, Seigneur de la Broffe, au Perche.

IX. Louis de Barville, troifième fils de Gilles, Ier du nom, Seigneur de Maifoncelles & du Buiffon, & de *Marie de la Vernade*, fut Seigneur du Buiffon, du Chefne & de Romainville. Il époufa, à Yerre, *Louife de la Taille*, fille de *Guillaume*, Ecuyer, Seigneur de Doffainville, & d'*Antoinette de Frefnay*, dont:

1. Gilles, qui fuit;

2. Louis, Seigneur du Chefne, mort au fiège de Montpellier, fans enfans;

3. Bertrand, qui fera rapporté ci-après;

4. Charles, mort Capucin;

5. Lancelot, rapporté après la poftérité de Bertrand;

6. Marc, Ecuyer, Seigneur de Boiffy-le-Girard, Paroiffe d'Autruy, qui époufa, en 1632, *Ifabelle de Chambon*, morte en 1643, fille de *Guillaume*, Seigneur de Godinville, & de *Marguerite du Roux*, dont:

> Charles, Ecuyer, dont on ignore l'alliance;
>
> Et Louis, Ecuyer, Seigneur de Boiffy, marié à *Anne Fougeroux*, fille de *Pierre*, & d'*Elifabeth de Chevillart*;

7. JEANNE, femme de *Chriſtophe Garcout-de-Longueau*, Ecuyer, Seigneur de Parville, dont des enfans ;

8. Et JUDITH, morte ſans alliance.

X. GILLES DE BARVILLE, IIIe du nom, Ecuyer, Seigneur de Doſſainville, Folleville, Montville & Popinville, mort en 1632, avoit épouſé, par contrat du 8 Juin 1614, *Marie de Blaire*, veuve de *Louis du Faur*, Seigneur de Mareau & Fittes, dont :

1. FRANÇOIS, Seigneur de Doſſainville, Enſeigne d'une Compagnie d'Infanterie, mort en Allemagne, à 20 ans, en 1636, des bleſſures qu'il avoit reçues ;

2. CHARLES, Seigneur de Monvilliers, mort en 1635 à l'Armée, commandée par le Cardinal de la Valette ;

3. MARIE, femme, en 1650, d'*André Galteau*, Ecuyer, Seigneur de Puiſſelet ;

4. Et BERNARDE, femme de *Charles le Clerc-de-Fleurigny*, Baron de la Forêt-le-Roi.

IX. BERTRAND DE BARVILLE, Ecuyer, Seigneur des Epars, troiſième fils de Louis, & de *Louiſe de la Taille*, épouſa *Madeleine de Champs*, fille de *Céſar*, Ecuyer, Seigneur du Portail, dont :

1. ACHILLE, qui ſuit ;

2. MADELEINE, fille ;

3. Et N…. Religieuſe.

X. ACHILLE DE BARVILLE, Ecuyer, Seigneur des Epars, & à cauſe de ſa femme, Seigneur de Puiſſelet-le-Marais, épouſa, en 1690, par diſpenſes, *Marie Galteau*, ſa couſine germaine, fille unique d'*André*, Ecuyer, Seigneur de Puiſſelet-le-Marais, & de MARIE DE BARVILLE, dont :

1. ANDRÉ-JULES, qui ſuit ;

2. BERTRAND, dit *le Chevalier de Barville*, Capitaine dans le Régiment de Soiſſonnois, Commandant du Château vieux de Perpignan, où il eſt mort ſans alliance ;

3. MARIE-ANTOINETTE, non mariée ;

4. Et MARIE-ELISABETH-JULIE, née le 3 Mai 169….., mariée le 12 Juin 1716, & veuve, ſans enfans, le 7 Mai 1740, de *Louis Pierre*, Sénéchal de Bournaes, Chevalier de Saint-Louis, ancien Exempt des Gardes-du-Corps, Gouverneur de Bitche, en Lorraine-Allemande, Maréchal des Camps & Armées du Roi.

XI. ANDRÉ-JULES, Comte DE BARVILLE, Chevalier, Seigneur de Puiſſelet-le-Marais, Capitaine de Fuſiliers, Colonel du Régiment de Soiſſonnois, Maréchal des Camps & Armées du Roi, Gouverneur de Villefranche, Chevalier de Saint-Louis, mort en Janvier

1731, avoit épouſé, en 1716, *Charlotte le Goux*, morte à Puiſſelet en 174…., dont pluſieurs enfans. Les vivans ſont :

1. LOUIS-ACHILLE, né le 24 Mars 1724, Capitaine au Régiment de Soiſſonnois, Chevalier de Saint-Louis, Seigneur de Puiſſelet-le-Marais, Terre qu'il a vendue à M. *de Mainon*, Seigneur de Farcheville, le 24 Avril 1758, non marié en 1765 ;

2. & 3. JULIE, & CHARLOTTE, Religieuſes à la Préſentation, à Paris ;

4. N….. Religieuſe à la Maiſon Royale de Saint-Louis, à Saint-Cyr ;

5. Et JEANNE-MADELEINE, née en 1728, élevée à Saint-Cyr, fille en 1765.

BRANCHE

des Seigneurs DE ROMAINVILLE.

X. LANCELOT DE BARVILLE, cinquième fils de LOUIS, & de *Louiſe de la Taille*, Chevalier, Seigneur de Romainville & de Boiſſy-le-Girard, Capitaine au Régiment d'Orléans, épouſa, en 1642, *Iſabelle de Compigny*, fille de *Nicolas*, Ecuyer, Seigneur de Compigny, qui obtint des Lettres-Patentes au mois de Mai 1625, qui lui permirent de changer ſon nom de le *Fèvre*, en celui de *Compigny*, & de *Françoiſe de Melun*, morte le 18 Janvier 1641, dont :

1. FRANÇOIS, Chevalier, Seigneur de Romainville, marié, 1° en 1671, à *Suſanne de Villereau*, veuve de *Céſar de la Taille*, Seigneur de Tertinville ; & 2° avec *N…. Oꝛon*, qui lui ſurvécut ;

2. ROBERT, qui ſuit ;

3. & 4. HENRI & CHARLES, morts ſans alliances.

XI. ROBERT DE BARVILLE, Chevalier, Seigneur de Romainville, Page & enſuite Ecuyer de Madame la Princeſſe de Carignan, épouſa, en 1672, *Marie Gentil*, fille de *Guillaume*, Lieutenant au Bailliage de Pithiviers, & de *Marie Laureau*, dont entr'autres enfans :

1. LOUIS-ROBERT, qui ſuit ;

2. Et N…. morte ſans enfans, en Février 1714, de *René-François de Vion*, Chevalier, Seigneur de Teſſancourt, près Meulan, du Coudray & Maiſoncelles, en Beauce.

XII. LOUIS-ROBERT DE BARVILLE, Chevalier, Seigneur de Romainville & Moigneville, né en 1694, épouſa, le 23 Janvier 1714, *Marie-Claude Hémard*, Demoiſelle de Boiſſy, morte à Pithiviers, fille de *Claude*, Seigneur du Freſne, Contrôleur des grandes & petites

Chancelleries,& de *Marie-Madeleine le Tellier*, dont font iffus :

1. Louis-François, qui fuit ;
2. Alexandre-Joseph ;
3. Marie, née le 8 Juillet 1717, morte en Janvier 1754, laiffant deux garçons & quatre filles, de fon mariage avec *François Touffaint Berteau*, Ecuyer, Seigneur d'Invillier ;
4. Et Louise, Demoiselle de Barville, née le 30 Décembre 1732, non mariée en 1765.

XIII. Louis-François de Barville, Chevalier, Seigneur de Frefne, ancien Capitaine au Régiment de la Marine, né le 17 Juillet 1716, époufa 1° *Marie-Geneviève de la Cour-d'Invillier*, morte le 2 Avril 1760; & 2° le.... Novembre 1763, *Marie-Marguerite de Meauffé*, Demoifelle de Souplainville, fille de *Louis*, Chevalier, Seigneur de Ville-Breton-le-Pontier, en Dunois, Capitaine de Cavalerie, & Chevalier de Saint-Louis, & de *Marie-Marguerite-Agathe le Noir-de-Jouy*, Dame de Souplainville.

Il a du premier lit :

N.... de Barville-de-Romainville.

Les armes : *d'azur, au lion d'or, accompagné de fept fleurs-de-lys de même mifes en orles*, 3, 2, 2.

Il y a d'autres branches ou familles de ce nom, fur lefquelles on n'a pas fourni de *Mémoires*.

✣ BARVILLE, au Perche. Cette Maifon répandue dans le Maine, la Normandie & autres lieux, porte : *d'argent, à deux bandes de gueules*.

EXTRAITS DES DIFFÉRENS ACTES ET TITRES
qui nous ont été communiqués.

1260. *Univerfis præfentes litteras infpecturis Officialis fagienfis, falutem in Domino : Noveritis quod cùm ventere- tur inter viros religiofos Capitulum Sancti Gervafii Sagienfis, ex unâ parte, & Guillelmum de Barvill, militem, ex alterâ fuper,.... quod dicti Religiofi dicebant quod dictus miles, in præjudicium ipforum Religioforum, quoddam foffatum propè molendinum de Barvill ad eofdem Religiofos fpectans, confiruxerat, per quod rota dicti molendini impediebatur currere, &c. Datum de concenfu partium, anno Domini millefimo ducen-*

tefimo fexagefimo, die Sabbati poft feftum S. Albini (1).

Du Samedi devant la Purification de la Vierge 1311, acte entre Robin de Barville, Ecuyer, & *Guillo de Blavette*.

Mercredi avant la fête de la Pentecôte 1336, acte qui joute les hoirs de feu Huet ou Hue de Barville, Ecuyer.

Le 5 Juin 1350, Jean de Barville paffe un acte à fon profit.

Le 20 Avril 1361, donation entre *Jean de Blavette*, Ecuyer, & Jeanne de Barville, fon époufe.

Le 1ᵉʳ Juin 1380, échange entre Guillaume-Colin de Barville, Ecuyer, & *Jean de Blavette*, Ecuyer, des héritages tenans aux héritiers de feu Jean de Barville, Ecuyer, & à Jean de Barville.

Le 2 Octobre 1382, aveu rendu à Guillaume-Colin de Barville, Seigneur de Barville, dans lequel eft citée *Jeanne de Marcouville de Montgoubert*, fa femme.

Le 11 Juin 1391, contrat d'acquêts faits par Jean de Barville, Ecuyer, & par *Robine*, fa femme, de *Jean Blavette*, Ecuyer, de 28 fols de rente.

1394. Aveu rendu à noble Jean de Barville.

Le 6 Juillet 1401, vente faite à Jean de Barville l'aîné, Ecuyer.

Les 13 & 28 Avril 1402, différens aveux rendus à Jean de Barville l'aîné, Ecuyer.

Le 28 Avril 1403, tranfaction paffée entre Jean de Barville, Ecuyer, & Demoifelle *Robine*, fille de défunt *Colin Carel*, & fœur aînée de *Jean Carel*, Ecuyer. Ledit *Jean Carel* accorde audit Jean de Barville préfent, & à ladite *Robine*, fa femme, abfente, à caufe d'elle, & à leurs hoirs, pour toutes, telles parts & portions qui peuvent appartenir à ladite *Robine*, fa fœur, dans tous les héritages quelconques, demeurés du décès dudit défunt *Colin Carel* & feue fa femme, *douze livres* de rente à prendre fur la Paroiffe de Burre & fur celle de Saint-Julien-fur-Sarthe, & *cent livres* tournois, payables en quatre paiemens.

Le 12 Mars 1420, *Julien Blavette*, Ecuyer,

---

(1) Cette charte eft en original au Chartrier de Blavette, appartenant à MM. *Clément de Boiffy*, qui font Seigneurs de Barville au Perche, d'où les branches des Seigneurs de Barville font étendues dans la Normandie, le Poitou & le Berry.

pour demeurer quitte de 44 fols de rente foncière envers Guillaume de Barville, Ecuyer, fils, héritier de Jean de Barville, Ecuyer, & de *Robine Carel*, fa femme, vend audit Guillaume de Barville des héritages affectés à ladite rente, fitués Paroiffe de Barville, amplement fignés & confrontés audit acte. Lefquels héritages avoient été originairement acquis par ladite *Robine*, femme de Jean de Barville, de *Julien de Blavettè*; qu'audit acte étoit préfent, à la minute de *Robert de la Lande*, Notaire, Jean de Barville, Prêtre, Ecuyer, le 24 Septembre 1428.

Le 23 Janvier 1451, Guillaume de Barville, Ecuyer, reçoit quittance d'un rachat, à caufe de la mort de Jacques de Barville, fon frère aîné.

Le 2 Août 1453, partage entre noble Guillaume de Barville, Ecuyer, d'une part, & *André de Valandry*, auffi Ecuyer, & Dame Marie de Barville, fa femme, des biens à eux venus & échus de la fucceffion de feu Jean de Barville, Ecuyer & Seigneur dudit lieu de Barville, & de ladite Marie de Barville, enfemble des héritages qui leur pourront échoir après le décès de la Dame *Robine Carel*, leur mère, préfente; & du confentement de Meffire Jean de Barville, Prêtre, frère dudit défunt Jean de Barville, & de ladite *Robine Carel*, mère defdits Guillaume & Marie de Barville.

AUTRE EXTRAIT.

Noble homme Guillaume de Barville, s'eft fait rendre, le 13 Octobre 1461, aveu, comme ayant le droit de feu Jean de Barville, l'aîné en fon vivant, Ecuyer, Seigneur de Barville. Il époufa, *Marie de Feugerêts*, dont il eut:

1. Jean de Barville, Seigneur de Barville au Perche & de la Gaftine, Paroiffe de Louze, Baronie de Sonnois, au pays du Maine, qui époufa *Jeanne Belard*, qui lui apporta en dot la Seigneurie de Boitron, celle du Jardin & la métairie de la Mauguinière, Paroiffe de Chalange, qu'il donna par échange, en 1496, à Bertrand de Barville, fon frère, qui fuit;
2. Bertrand de Barville, qui eut en partage la Terre & Seigneurie de la Ligeardière, fituée dans la Paroiffe de Pervenchères, qu'il donna par échange à Jean de Barville ci-deffus, fon frère aîné, pour la métairie de la Mauguinière, en 1496;

Tome II.

3. Nicolas de Barville, Seigneur de la Lande, qui ratifia, le 5 Juillet 1506, une tranfaction du 30 Juin audit an, entre Jean de Barville, fon frère aîné, fils de Guillaume de Barville, & de *Marie des Feugerêts*, fe faifant fort de fes frères & fœurs, & de *Florent-Sébaftien* & Bertrand des Feugerêts, des biens de la fucceffion de *Bertrand des Feugerêts*, & de *Marie Duhamel*, fa femme;
4. Alexandre de Barville, Ecuyer, Seigneur de la Terrière, Archer de la Garde du Roi, en 1497, & en 1503, fous Myolant, qui avoit époufé *Florine de Thouars*. Sa poftérité exiftoit en 1580, fuivant un acte de tutelle, par lequel *Jean de Marcouville*, Seigneur de Mongoubert, & Alexandre de Barville, Sieur de la Terrière, furent établis tuteurs & curateurs des enfans mineurs de défunt Christophe de Barville & de *Marie Duhamel*, fa femme; ledit Christophe de Barville, fils de Jean, Seigneur de Barville & de la Gaftine;
5. Jehannot, qui fit décréter la Terre de Boislandry fur Thomas de Barville, fon frère, Archer de la Garde du Roi, en 1515, & époufa *Sufanne de Thouars*;
6. Thomas de Barville, Seigneur de *Rofais* & *du Boislandry*, auteur d'une branche rapportée plus loin;
7. Et Marguerite de Barville, laquelle acheta des biens le 2 Novembre 1557, de *Jeanne Belard*, fa belle-fœur & de Christophe de Barville, fon neveu. Elle époufa *Philippe de Blavette*.

PREMIÈRE BRANCHE.

Le 15 Novembre 1496, échange entre noble homme Meffire Jean de Barville, fils aîné de Guillaume, & de Marie des Feugerêts, & petit-fils de Jean, & de *Robine de Carel*, Chevalier dudit lieu de Barville & Bertrand de Barville, Ecuyer, fon frère, Archer de la Garde du Roi, paffé devant les Notaires Royaux de la ville de Breft. Ledit Chevalier quitte, délaiffe, par ladite voie d'échange, audit Bertrand de Barville, Ecuyer, fon frère, le lieu, manoir, & métairie de la Mauguinière, appartenant audit Chevalier de Barville à caufe de la Dame *Belard*, fon époufe, Paroiffe de Chalange, & ledit Bertrand de Barville auroit, par retour, en récompenfe de ce, quitté & délaiffé audit Jean de Barville, Chevalier, le lieu, Terre & Seigneurie de la Ligeardière, fife en la Paroiffe de Pervenchères, & le 7 Mars 1497, ladite Dame *Belard*, ratifie ledit acte

A a

devant les Tabellions en la Châtellenie de Perrière.

Le 12 Mai 1495, compte que *Marie des Feugerêts*, tutrice & garde-noble de fes enfans, leur rend. Ils partagent la fucceſſion de ladite *Marie*, de leurs père & mère, le 24 Mai 1495.

Le 6 Juin 1506, NICOLAS DE BARVILLE, Ecuyer, Seigneur de la Lande, ratifie une tranfaction dont copie eſt en tête, tenant lieu de partage le 30 Juin 1506, entre Meſſire JEAN DE BARVILLE, Ecuyer, fils de *Guillaume de Barville*, & de *Marie des Feugerêts*, fe faiſant fort de fes frères & fœurs, d'une part, & *Florent-Sébaſtien* & *Bertrand des Feugerêts*, des biens provenus de fucceſſions de *Bertrand des Feugerêts*, Ecuyer, & de *Marie Duhamel*, fa femme.

CHRISTOPHE DE BARVILLE, Seigneur dudit lieu, y demeurant, à préfent fils aîné de Meſſire JEAN DE BARVILLE, & auſſi aîné héritier principal de FRANÇOIS DE BARVILLE, fon frère, tant en fon nom, que comme Procureur de *Jeanne Belard*, fa mère, veuve de Meſſire JEAN DE BARVILLE, Chevalier, & encore de GUILLAUME DE BARVILLE, Ecuyer, fon frère puîné, Sieur de la Barre, & fe faiſant fort de *Jeanne Belard*, fa mère, & dudit GUILLAUME DE BARVILLE, fon frère, demeurant auſſi en ladite Paroiſſe de Barville, d'une part, *Claudine Mauny*, veuve de noble homme FRANÇOIS DE BARVILLE, Sieur de la Gaſtine, fils aîné & principal héritier de défunt MeſſireJEAN DE BARVILLE, Chevalier dudit lieu de Barville, d'autre part. Appert ledit CHRISTOPHE DE BARVILLE, tant pour lui que pour fes frères & fœur, & encore comme fe faiſant fort de ladite Dame *Belard*, fa mère, avoir tranfigé fur le procès mu par-devant le Bailli du Perche, avec ladite *Claudine Mauny*, veuve dudit FRANÇOIS DE BARVILLE, frère de lui CHRISTOPHE, au fujet du douaire à elle dû, & qui auroit été fixé d'abord par le contrat de mariage de ladite *Claudine Mauny* & dudit FRANÇOIS DE BARVILLE, à la fomme de 240liv. par an, à prendre, après fon décès, fur la Terre, Fief & Seigneurie de la Gaſtine, & encore fur le domaine & métairie de Barville, & autres Fiefs & Seigneurie à lui appartenant de proches en proches, qu'il avoit affectés audit douaire préfix, lequel a été enfuite réduit à la fomme de 120 liv. affectée feulement fur la Terre de la Gaſtine, fuivant & au défir de

ladite tranfaction, enfuite de laquelle eſt l'acte de ratification de ladite *Jeanne Belard*, atteſté dudit *Auvray* de *Jean Gueſtre*, Tabellion, le 26 Juillet 1541. CHRISTOPHE DE BARVILLE n'eut que deux filles dont la feconde, nommée MARIE DE BARVILLE, époufa, par contrat du 7 Janvier 1573, *Léon Malard*, & lui porta la Terre de Barville, poſſédée aujourd'hui par M. *Clément*, qui fert à la Chambre des Comptes, dont le frère, Avocat-Général à la Cour des Aides, porte le nom.

Noble homme GUILLAUME DE BARVILLE, Seigneur de la Gaſtine, eut commiſſion de la Cour le 17 Novembre 1562, pour faire la revue des Gentilshommes de l'arrière-ban pour la province du Maine. Il époufa, par contrat paſſé devant *Guilovau*, Notaire à Mamers, le 20 Février 1556, *Marie de Gueroult*.

Noble homme FRANÇOIS DE BARVILLE, Ecuyer, Seigneur de la Gaſtine, fils aîné & principal héritier de GUILLAUME, époufa, par contrat paſſé devant *Guillaume Touſte*, Tabellion à la Perrière, le 6 Septembre 1580, *Marthe Dufay*, fille de noble homme *Gallerand Dufay*, & de *Catherine Boiſſel*.

GALLOIS DE BARVILLE, fils aîné & principal héritier de FRANÇOIS, fera rapporté plus loin.

ORDONNANCE DE MAINTENUE DE NOBLESSE.

Par une Ordonnance rendue par *Claude de Paris*, Intendant de la province de Normandie, & *Etienne Paſcal*, Préfident en la Cour des Aides de Clermont-Ferrand, Commiſſaires-Généraux pour Sa Majeſté, en exécution de la déclaration & arrêt du Conſeil, pour l'exécution du droit de franc-fief, & décharge de toute indemnité des 28 Février & 31 Mars 1640; ladite ordonnance en date du 3 Juillet 1640, & fignée en fin d'icelle de Paris & Paſcal. Et plus bas, par mefdits Sieurs *Corneillan*.

Appert que, vu la requête préfentée à Noſſeigneurs les Commiſſaires par *François de Barville*, Sieur de Lanbonnière, attendu fa qualité & ancienne extraction de noble race, vu auſſi les pièces par lui produites, favoir deux actes & deux contrats des années 1493, 1506 & 1541, par lefquels fe voit que JEAN DE BARVILLE, qualifié Chevalier, Seigneur de Barville, eſt fils de GUILLAUME, auſſi qualifié Ecuyer. Plus deux contrats des années 1546, 1557, par lefquels appert que dudit JEAN DE

BARVILLE eſt iſſu GUILLAUME DE BARVILLE, auſſi qualifié Ecuyer, Seigneur dudit lieu; plus d'une commiſſion émanée de Meſſire *Louis de Couaſmes*, Ecuyer, Seigneur de Lucé & Gouverneur du Maine, de l'année 1562, par laquelle le dit GUILLAUME DE BARVILLE avoit été commis pour faire les montres & prendre le ferment des nobles & compagnie de l'arrière-ban pour Sa Majeſté audit Comté du Maine; plus autres actes & contrats des années 1575, 1578 & 1580, par leſquels il eſt juſtifié que dudit GUILLAUME eſt iſſu FRANÇOIS DE BARVILLE, qualifié Ecuyer, Seigneur de la Gaſtine, plus un acte de 1587, par lequel la veuve dudit FRANÇOIS, ayant la garde-noble de ſes enfans, eſt reçue à faire foi & hommage dudit fief de la Gaſtine; plus autres contrats & actes des années 1587 & 1602, par leſquels il appert que dudit FRANÇOIS Ier eſt iſſu autre FRANÇOIS, IIe du nom, qui étoit le ſuppliant, auſſi qualifié Ecuyer, Seigneur de la Gaſtine; plus un autre contrat de mariage d'entre ledit FRANÇOIS II & *Marie de Belard*. Le tout conſidéré, ledit DE BARVILLE, ſuppliant, comme noble de race, a eu main-levée de la ſaiſie faite de ſes fiefs de Barville & de Lanbonnière.

GALOIS DE BARVILLE, Ecuyer, Seigneur de la Gaſtine & de Chanceux, épouſa par contrat du 8 Décembre 1611 (en préſence de puiſſante Dame *Marie le Voyer*, ayeule de *Renée de Carion*, & veuve de Meſſire *Jean des Vallées*, Chevalier des Ordres du Roi, *Renée de Carion*, fille d'*Antoine de Carion*, Ecuyer, & de *Renée des Vallées*. De ce mariage ſont iſſus:

1. GALLOIS DE BARVILLE, Chevalier, Seigneur de la Gaſtine, Paroiſſe de Louze, province du Maine, Baronie de Sonnoy, Chevalier de l'Ordre du Roi, Lieutenant - Colonel au Régiment de l'Iſle de France, marié, en 1630, à *Marie le Paumier*, dont un fils ſans poſtérité, & pluſieurs filles, dont l'aînée lui porta la Terre de la Gaſtine;

2. ANTOINE DE BARVILLE, marié, en 1645, avec *Renée de More*, dont:

 ANTOINE DE BARVILLE-BEAUREPERE, qui ſe maria avec MARGUERITE DE BARVILLE, ſœur de PIERRE DE BARVILLE, Sieur de la Bonneville, & fille de RENÉ DE BARVILLE, Sieur de Saint-Germain, & d'*Anne de Puiſaye*, couſine au VIIe degré; ladite MARGUERITE étant deſcendue de BERTRAND DE BARVILLE, ci-après;

3. JEAN DE BARVILLE, Sieur du Châtellier, vi-

voit en 1667. Il avoit épouſé *Marthe de Vaſcouſeil*, dont:

 LOUIS DE BARVILLE, Sieur des *Aulnais*. Cette branche ſubſiſtoit encore il y a quelques années.

4. & 5. GUILLAUME DE BARVILLE & FRANÇOIS DE BARVILLE, morts ſans poſtérité;

6. RENÉ DE BARVILLE, qui avoit épouſé *Marie de Broſſet*, dont eſt iſſu:

 PIERRE-ANTOINE DE BARVILLE, mort à Dreux, âgé de 84 ans, laiſſant un fils:

 HENRI, qui a été Lieutenant de Milice. Il s'eſt marié en Lorraine, & a eu trois fils:

 L'Aîné a embraſſé l'état Eccléſiaſtique;

 Le Second, eſt Sous-Lieutenant réformé dans la Légion de Lorraine;

 Et le Troiſième, Lieutenant en ſecond au Régiment de Rouergue, dont a été Colonel le Comte de Cuſtine;

7. Et PIERRE DE BARVILLE, Major de Bouillon, qui a eu:

 Deux garçons, dont le dernier, élevé à l'Ecole Royale Militaire, eſt mort Lieutenant dans le Régiment de Normandie;

 Et ſix filles, dont trois ſont encore vivantes, ſavoir: Deux Religieuſes, l'une à l'Abbaye de Poiſſy, & élevée à Saint-Cyr; & la troiſième, penſionnaire aux Dames Miramiones.

DEUXIÈME BRANCHE.

BERTRAND DE BARVILLE, ſecond fils de GUILLAUME, & de *Marie des Feugerêts*, fut Archer de la Garde du Roi, en 1495, partagea avec JEAN DE BARVILLE, ſon frère aîné, le 24 Mai 1495, dans les biens de *Marie des Feugerêts*, leur mère, laquelle avoit rendu compte à ſes enfans, en qualité de tutrice, le 12 mai 1495, devant *Pierre le Bel*, Tabellion de la Châtellenie de la Perrière. Le 7 Mars 1496, Dame *Jeanne Belard*, femme autoriſée de Meſſire noble homme *Jean de Barville*, ſon mari, Chevalier, Seigneur dudit lieu de Barville, ratifie un contrat d'échange dont copie eſt tranſcrite en tête de ladite ratification faite entre ledit JEAN DE BARVILLE ſon mari, BERTRAND DE BARVILLE, Ecuyer, ſon frère, atteſté des Notaires Royaux le 15 Novembre 1596, par lequel contrat ledit Chevalier DE BARVILLE auroit quitté & délaiſſé, par ladite voie d'échange, audit BERTRAND DE BAR-

VILLE, Ecuyer, fon frère, le lieu, manoir & métairie de la Mauguinière, appartenant audit Chevalier de BARVILLE, à caufe de ladite Dame *Belard*, fon époufe, Paroiffe de Chalange; & ledit BERTRAND DE BARVILLE auroit, pour retour & récompenfe de ce, quitté & délaiffé audit JEAN DE BARVILLE & à fes co-héritiers, le lieu, Terre & Seigneurie de la Ligeardière, avec toutes fes dépendances, fituées en la Paroiffe de Pervenchères. BERTRAND DE BARVILLE époufa 1° *N... de Callonne; &* 2° *Renée de la Noue.*

Le 5 Août 1533, fentence exercée devant *Gervais Gaucher*, Lieutenant de la Sergenterie de Seez, fous M. le Bailli de Caen; appert avoir été mandé par Lettres royaux obtenues par FRANÇOIS DE BARVILLE, Ecuyer, fils de BERTRAND, auffi Ecuyer, prenant fon fait & caufe d'envoyer à la Cour certaines informations faites contre *Noël Malet*, détenu prifonnier en la conciergerie de Rouen, & décrété de prife de corps avec fes complices.

Appert le 10 Novembre 1539, devant *Huvé* & fon confrère, Notaires, noble homme FRANÇOIS DE BARVILLE, Seigneur de Vaudon, après avoir pris poffeffion de la métairie de Lavardin, fituée Paroiffe de Saint-Aubin-de-Locquenay, près la Chapelle Soive, à lui appartenant, à caufe de la fucceffion de feue *Sainte-Renée de la Noue*, femme de noble homme BERTRAND DE BARVILLE, fes père & mère.

Le 22 Avril 1540, tranfaction entre noble homme FRANÇOIS DE BARVILLE, Archer de la Garde du Roi, qui fe trouva aux obfèques de FRANÇOIS Ier. Le Sieur FRANÇOIS DE BARVILLE, Sieur de *Vaudon*, d'une part, & *Guillaume-François-Marin Belard*, au fujet du procès mu entr'eux, par rapport aux droits que lefdits *Belard* prétendoient alors en la métairie de la Mauguinière, qui avoit été cédée par JEAN DE BARVILLE, Chevalier, à *Jeanne de Belard*, fon époufe, qui étoit héritière de *Guillaume de Belard*, fon fils, vivant Ecuyer.

Le 28 Février 1555, devant le Notaire du Mesle-fur-Sarthe, appert que noble homme CYPRIEN DE BARVILLE, Archer de la Garde du Roi en 1555 & 1565, fils & préfomptif héritier de FRANÇOIS DE BARVILLE, Ecuyer, Sieur de la Mauguinière, Paroiffe de Chalange, d'une part, & *Mathurine de Sormont*, fille de noble *Jean*, d'autre part, avoir contracté mariage entr'eux.

Le 6 Février 1562, devant le Notaire de Sainte-Efcolaffe, partage entre noble homme CYPRIEN DE BARVILLE, Sieur de la Mauguinière, & JEAN DE BARVILLE, Archer de la Garde du Roi, Ecuyer, Sieur du Buiffon fils, & héritier de défunt FRANÇOIS DE BARVILLE, Ecuyer, Sieur du lieu de la Mauguinière, des biens à eux venus & échus par la mort dudit FRANÇOIS DE BARVILLE leur père, tous deux Archers de la Garde du Roi, le 5 Juillet 1577.

Marie Thonin, veuve de noble FRANÇOIS DE BARVILLE, donne, devant le Notaire du Mans, quittance à CYPRIEN DE BARVILLE, Ecuyer, de la fomme de 200 livres, pour refte de fes deniers dotaux.

Le 5 Janvier 1579, tutelle devant le Juge de la Châtellenie d'Effey. Les enfans mineurs iffus de défunt noble JEAN DE BARVILLE, Sieur du Buiffon, & de *Gratiane Mallard*, fa veuve, où font dénommés noble homme François MALLARD, Sieur de Fontaines, Chevalier de l'Ordre du Roi, aïeul maternel defdits mineurs & CYPRIEN DE BARVILLE, oncle maternel.

Le 28 Novembre 1585, devant les Tabellions de Sainte-Efcolaffe, appert noble homme PHILIBERT DE BARVILLE, Archer de la Garde du Roi, & JEAN DE BARVILLE, fils & héritiers de défunt noble CYPRIEN DE BARVILLE, Sieur de la Mauguinière, en la Paroiffe de Chalange; ledit JEAN DE BARVILLE, affifté de noble homme *Charles de Sormont*, fon curateur, ordonné par juftice, avoir procédé entr'eux au partage en deux lots de biens à eux échus par le décès dudit CYPRIEN DE BARVILLE. leur père, & ledit PHILIBERT eft qualifié d'aîné, Archer de la Garde du Roi.

Noble homme JEAN DE BARVILLE, Ecuyer, Sieur de Saint-Germain, Archer de la Garde du Roi, affifté de CHARLES DE BARVILLE, Ecuyer, Sieur de Boislandry, & de JEAN DE BARVILLE, Ecuyer, Sieur de la Fiance, coufin dudit Sieur de *Saint-Germain*, & de *Charles de Sormont*, Ecuyer, Sieur dudit lieu, oncle dudit DE BARVILLE, époufa, par contrat paffé devant *Froger*, Notaire à Saint-Hilaire-le-Lierre, le 26 Janvier 1587, *Jeanne de Brehanon*, fille de noble *Jacques de Brehanon*, & d'*Antoinette de Soucelle*, veuve en fecondes noces, de *Marin de la Goupillière.*

Le 4 Avril 1595, fentence rendue par *Jacques de Barbier*, Sieur de Bonelles, Commiffaire départi fur le fait & convocation du ban du Bailliage d'Alençon, appert *Marie de Faurie*, veuve de PHILIBERT DE BARVILLE, avoir été déchargée de la taxe à laquelle elle avoit été impofée en fadite qualité de tutrice des enfans mineurs dudit défunt & d'elle, pour raifon de la métairie de la Mauguinière, Paroiffe de Chalange, venue & échue à fefdits enfans, de la fucceffion de CYPRIEN, père dudit PHILIBERT, aïeul defdits enfans, laquelle métairie avoit été en partie acquife par FRANÇOIS DE BARVILLE, père dudit CYPRIEN, & par BERTRAND DE BARVILLE, Ecuyer, père dudit FRANÇOIS.

Le 31 Décembre 1616, devant les Tabellions d'Argentan, le contrat de mariage entre JEAN DE BARVILLE, Ecuyer, Sieur de Saint-Germain, fils & feul héritier de défunt JEAN DE BARVILLE, Chevalier, Sieur dudit lieu, & de *Jeanne de Brehanon*, fes père & mère d'une part, & *Marie Gautier*, fille de noble homme *Jacques Gautier*, Sieur de Launay & de Montreau, Vicomte d'Argentan d'Exmes, & de *Barbe de Vauquelin*, fes père & mère, d'autre part.

Le 28 Janvier 1643, devant le Notaire de Courtomer, partage entre RENÉ DE BARVILLE, Ecuyer, Sieur de Saint-Germain, & GUILLAUME DE BARVILLE, Ecuyer, Sieur dudit lieu, frères & héritiers de défunt JEAN DE BARVILLE, Ecuyer, Sieur de Saint-Germain, & de *Marie Gautier*, leur père & mère, des biens à eux échus de la fucceffion dudit défunt Sieur de Saint-Germain leur père; lefdits lots faits par GUILLAUME, le puîné des deux, & les choix faits par RENÉ DE BARVILLE, comme aîné.

GUILLAUME eut un fils nommé JACQUES, qui fut Lieutenant-Colonel au Régiment de Grancey.

RENÉ DE BARVILLE, affifté de fon frère GUILLAUME, époufa, par contrat du 28 Janvier 1649, *Anne de Puifaye*, fille de *Pierre*, Ecuyer, Sieur de Beaufoffé, & de *Marguerite Dubois*.

PIERRE DE BARVILLE, Ecuyer, Sieur de Bonneville, fils aîné & principal héritier de RENÉ DE BARVILLE, époufa, affifté de GUILLAUME DE BARVILLE, fon oncle paternel, par contrat du 1668, HÉLÈNE DE BROSSARD, fille unique & héritière de *Gabriel de Broffard*, Ecuyer, Sieur Devaux, & de *Jacqueline Gallan*.

RENÉ-GASPARD DE BARVILLE, Ecuyer, Sieur de Bonneville, fils aîné de PIERRE DE BAR-

VILLE, né en 1678, Capitaine d'Infanterie & Chevau-Léger de la Garde du Roi, Chevalier de Saint-Louis, mort en 1761, avoit époufé, par contrat du 23 Août 1717, *Madeleine Charbonnier*, fille de *Nicolas Charbonnier*, Ecuyer, Sieur de Champré, & d'*Anne Duclos*, dont il eut:

1. RENÉ-GASPARD-THOMAS, né le 12 Septembre 1718, mort en bas âge;
2. NICOLAS DE BARVILLE, né le 11 Septembre 1721, Chevau-Léger en 1734, Cornette des Carabiniers en 1746, dont il s'eft retiré Lieutenant de Meftre-de-Camp, avec commiffion de Capitaine en 1761, à caufe de fes infirmités, fuite de fes bleffures, mort Chevalier de Saint-Louis en 1777. Il avoit époufé, en 1752, *Catherine de Carel*, dont il a laiffé:

    1. ANTOINE, né en 1754, forti de l'Ecole Royale Militaire en 1771, pour entrer Sous-Lieutenant au Régiment des Carabiniers de MONSIEUR, & Chevalier de Saint-Lazare;
    2. ETIENNE, né le 10 Septembre 1762, entré, en Juillet 1772, à l'Ecole Royale Militaire, & Lieutenant au Régiment de la Sarre;
    3. NICOLAS, né le 9 Septembre 1764, entré à l'Ecole Royale Militaire en 1776;
    4. Et une fille, appelée *Mademoifelle de Barville*, née en 1759, non mariée.

3. GASPARD-ANTOINE, né le 3 Mai 1723, Capitaine de Cavalerie, Sous-Brigadier des Chevaux-Légers de la Garde du Roi, ancien Lieutenant & Infpecteur-Général de la Capitainerie Royale des Chaffes de Fontainebleau, & ancien Ecuyer de MONSIEUR, frère du Roi, Chevalier de Saint-Louis;
4. JEAN-RENÉ-FRANÇOIS, né le 23 Octobre 1726, mort volontaire au Régiment de Bourbon, Infanterie, au fiège de Fribourg, en 1744;
5. ANNE-MARIE-MADELEINE DE BARVILLE, née le 19 Août 1720, mariée à *Adrien-Pierre Defmoutis*, Ecuyer, Seigneur du Bois Hébert & de la Morandière, dont font iffus:

    Un garçon, Page de fon Alteffe feu Monfieur le Comte de *Clermont*, & enfuite Chevau-Léger de la Garde du Roi;
    Une fille, morte à Saint-Cyr;
    Et ANNE-RENÉE-FRANÇOISE DE BARVILLE, dite *Demoifelle des Moutis*, née le 7 Juillet 1750, mariée à *N... de la Haye*, Seigneur de la Barre, Capitaine-Commandant au Régiment de Beaujolois, dont font iffus un fils & deux filles.

« 6. Et MADELEINE-RENÉE, née le 3 Novembre 1724, & reçue à Saint-Cyr, le 3 Mars

1734, fuivant l'*Armorial de France*, reg. Ier, part. Ire, pag. 51. »

Le 6 Février 1562, ont été les partages entre CYPRIEN DE BARVILLE, Ecuyer, Sieur de la Mauguinière, & JEAN DE BARVILLE, Ecuyer, Sieur du Buiffon, fon frère, lefquels étoient fils de FRANÇOIS DE BARVILLE, Ecuyer, Sieur de Vaudon & de la Mauguinière, & petits-fils de BERTRAND DE BARVILLE, frère de JEAN, Seigneur de Barville, qui avoit époufé la Dame *Belard*, lefquels JEAN, Seigneur de Barville & BERTRAND DE BARVILLE frères, étoient fils de GUILLAUME DE BARVILLE, & de *Marie des Feugerêts*. Les BARVILLE DE LA MAUGUINIÈRE font aînés des BARVILLE DU BUISSON; CYPRIEN DE BARVILLE DE LA MAUGUINIÈRE & JEAN DE BARVILLE DU BUISSON étoient tous deux Archers de la Garde du Roi.

FRANÇOIS DE BARVILLE, fils & héritier de défunt JEAN DE BARVILLE, Ecuyer, Sieur du Buiffon; Lieutenant d'une Compagnie de Chevaux-Légers pour le fervice de fon Alteffe le Duc de Savoie, Chevalier de l'Ordre du Roi, Gentilhomme ordinaire de la maifon de Sa Majefté, époufa, par traité du 20 Juillet 1609, *Marie de Gefne*, fille d'*Henri*.

Le 3 Décembre 1652, partage entre ETIENNE DE BARVILLE, Ecuyer, Sieur du Buiffon, & HENRI DE BARVILLE, fon frère, de la fucceffion de feu FRANÇOIS DE BARVILLE, en préfence de *Marie de Gefne*, leur mère.

Le 4 Décembre 1659, reconnoiffance du traité de mariage d'HENRI, Ecuyer, Sieur du Buiffon, fils de défunt noble homme FRANÇOIS DE BARVILLE DU BUISSON, avec *Françoife des Vallées*.

CADETS DES BARVILLE DU BUISSON.

Noble JEAN DE BARVILLE, Ecuyer, Seigneur de Vauhulin, fils de défunt noble homme JEAN DE BARVILLE, Sieur du Buiffon, & de *Gratienne Mallard*, époufa, par contrat du 9 Mai 1592, *Catherine d'Ambray*, fille du Baron de l'Aigle, fœur de *Nicolas d'Ambray*, Baron de l'Aigle.

1598, aveu rendu à noble Dame *Catherine d'Ambray*, Dame & Baronne de Belzaize, époufe de noble JEAN DE BARVILLE, Capitaine d'une Compagnie de 100 Chevaux-Légers.

CHARLES DE BARVILLE, fils de feu JEAN DE BARVILLE, Ecuyer, Seigneur de Belzaize, nommé Chevalier de Saint-Michel, en 1619, & Capitaine d'une Compagnie de Moufquetai-

res à cheval de 100 hommes en 1635, marié par contrat paffé au Châtelet, le 20 Avril 1618, avec HIPPOLYTE-ANGÉLIQUE *de Morainvilliers*.

CHARLES DE BARVILLE, fils de Meffire CHARLES DE BARVILLE, Chevalier, Seigneur de Belzaize, époufa, par contrat du 14 Juillet 1644, *Louife d'Hellainvilliers*, fille de N... *d'Hellainvilliers*, Chevalier, Seigneur de Sommaire, & de noble Dame *Catinat*.

Le 26 Novembre 1657, tranfaction devant les Notaires de l'Aigle, entre Meffire *Jacques des Acres*, Chevalier, Seigneur & Marquis de l'Aigle, & Meffire CHARLES DE BARVILLE, Chevalier, Seigneur & Baron de Belzaize & de Vimoutiers.

AUTRE BRANCHE.

THOMAS DE BARVILLE, fils de GUILLAUME DE BARVILLE, & de *Marie des Feugerêts*, fut partagé par JEAN DE BARVILLE, fon frère aîné, le 24 Mai 1495, avec BERTRAND DE BARVILLE & fes autres frères, dans les biens de *Marie des Feugerêts*, leur mère, laquelle avoit rendu compte à fes enfans, comme tutrice, le 12 Mai 1495; il partagea avec fes co-héritiers les biens de *Marie le Guerou*, fa belle-mère, & JEANNOT DE BARVILLE, fon frère, fit décréter fa terre de Boislandry. Ce THOMAS DE BARVILLE étoit Archer de la Garde du Roi, à la montre faite à Reims, le 1er Décembre 1507, du nombre de 100 lances fous Robert de la Mark. Il époufa *Périne le Couturier*, fille de *Macé*, & de *Marie le Guerou*, dont il eut:

JEAN DE BARVILLE, Seigneur de Boislandry, qui fut émancipé par fon père, le 19 Juillet 1529. Il eft qualifié Archer de la Garde du Roi, dans une fentence du 17 Novembre 1544, par laquelle il fut envoyé en poffeffion de la Terre de Boislandry, qui avoit été décrétée par JEANNOT DE BARVILLE, fon oncle, & il affifta en cette qualité aux obféques de FRANçois Ier, en 1547. Il ne vivoit plus le 10 Mars 1560. Il avoit époufé, par contrat du 1er Décembre 1542, *Catherine de Lance*, qui eut, le 10 Mars 1560, la garde-noble de fes enfans, & obtint une fentence contre *François Rochenis*, fon gendre, & MARIE DE BARVILLE, fa fille, le 15 Mars 1574, par laquelle elle fut maintenue dans fa nobleffe, tant de fon chef que de celui de fon mari. Elle étoit fille de noble homme *Jean de Lance*, & de *Catherine de Floc*.

CHARLES DE BARVILLE, fils de JEAN, Ecuyer, Seigneur de Boislandry, de la Fiance & de la Matraſſière, Archer de la Compagnie de M. de Matignon, en 1575, homme d'armes de la Compagnie de Monſeigneur le Prince de Conty, partagea en 1585 avec JEAN DE BARVILLE & ſes ſœurs, la ſucceſſion d'OLIVIER DE BARVILLE, ſon frère aîné, & celle de ſes père & mère le 15 Mars 1590. Il demeuroit dans la Paroiſſe de Gaſtine en 1611, & ne vivoit plus le 26 Novembre 1615, que ſa veuve *Barbe d'Amilly*, afferma la Terre de Boislandry.

JEAN DE BARVILLE, Chevalier, Seigneur de Boislandry, Naumoraſſin en Touraine, comparut avec les autres nobles de la Province de Touraine, avec un Gentilhomme à ſa ſuite, quatre chevaux & armes complètes, à la montre qui en fut faite à Amboiſe, le 30 Août 1635, tranſigea le 20 Décembre 1637; maintenu dans la poſſeſſion de la Terre de Fontaine, comme héritier de *Guillaume de Damas*, par arrêt du Parlement du 12 Janvier 1677. Il épouſa, par contrat du 24 Février 1626, *Helène de Rochefort*, fille d'*Imbert de Rochefort*, Seigneur de Villedieu en Berry, Chevalier de l'Ordre du Roi, Gentilhomme de ſa Chambre, & de *Françoiſe Crevant*.

JEAN-FRANÇOIS DE BARVILLE, Chevalier, Seigneur de Naumoraſſin, Boislandry, Fontaine, du Buiſſon, produiſit les titres juſtificatifs de ſa nobleſſe, depuis 1524, devant *Tubeuf*, en 1666, tranſigea avec FRANÇOIS DE BARVILLE, ſon frère, ſur le partage de la ſucceſſion de ſes père & mère, & épouſa, par contrat du 12 Décembre 1664, *Charlotte Duham*, Dame de Montdetour, fille de *Charles*, Chevalier, Seigneur de Tanay en Thimeraye, de Morteville, de Montdetour & de Neuville.

CHARLES DE BARVILLE, Seigneur de Boislandry, Naumoraſſin, Chanteloup, Capitaine d'Infanterie dans le Régiment d'Hunière, Gentilhomme de Monſeigneur le Prince de Conty, Capitaine de Cavalerie au Régiment de Furſtenberg en 1693, Chevalier de Saint-Lazare en Janvier 1696; fut maintenu dans ſa nobleſſe par M. *Phélypeaux*, Intendant de la Généralité de Paris, le 11 Mars 1701, fut Colonel d'un Régiment de ſon nom. Il eſt mort ſans poſtérité. Il avoit épouſé, par contrat du 4 Mai 1699, devant *Carnot*, Notaire au Châtelet de Paris, *Marie-Anne Jacquinot*, fille de *Daniel Jacquinot*, Sieur des Preſſoirs,

dans la Forêt de Fontainebleau, & de *Nicole Miron*.

N..., ſœur de CHARLES DE BARVILLE, a épouſé N... *de Boiſmarmin*,

BRANCHE
des Seigneurs de NOCEY, au Perche.

« Suivant le *Traité de la Nobleſſe*, par La Roque, édit. de 1678, pag. 415, ANTOINE DE BARVILLE réclama en 1518, la ſucceſſion de *Louiſe de Martel*, ſa mère, comme ſeul fils & héritier d'elle & de CONSTANTIN DE BARVILLE, ſon père, contre *Léonard & Charles Martel*, réputés bâtards d'*Antoine Martel*, Seigneur de Bacqueville. »

Suivant un Mémoire qui nous a été fourni par cette famille, nous trouvons:

Noble homme BIN ou BERTRAND DE BARVILLE, Chevalier, qui épouſa, *Peronelle de Beaumont*, fille de *Thibaut de Beaumont*, & d'*Iſabelle de Logny*, dont:

GUILLAUME DE BARVILLE, Ecuyer, Seigneur de Nocey, marié le 22 Juillet 1413, avec *Marie Royer*, fille de *Guitte Royer*. Il eut:

1. JEAN, qui ſuit;
2. PIERRE;
3. Et PÉTRONILLE DE BARVILLE.

JEAN DE BARVILLE, Ecuyer, Seigneur de Nocey, marié avec *Flavette* ou *Fraxette le Bouteiller*, dont il eut:

1. JEAN, qui ſuit;
2. ROBERT, dont on ignore la deſtinée;
3. Et ANNE DE BARVILLE, mariée à *Jean de Villeneuve*.

JEAN DE BARVILLE, IIe du nom, marié à N..., dont eſt iſſu:

ROBERT DE BARVILLE, Seigneur de la Mauſonnière, qui épouſa *Marguerite le Baleur*, fille de *N... le Baleur*, dont vinrent:

1. RENÉ, qui ſuit;
2. JEANNE, mariée à *François de la Motte*;
3. Et ANNE DE BARVILLE, mariée à *Guillaume Roquer*.

RENÉ DE BARVILLE, marié le 19 Janvier 1499, à *Jeanne de Courboyer*, fille de *James de Courboyer*. De ce mariage vint:

JEAN DE BARVILLE, IIIe du nom, Ecuyer, Seigneur de Nocey, qui tranſigea, le 15 Novembre 1525, avec ANNE DE BARVILLE, ſa tante, ſur le partage des biens de ROBERT DE BARVILLE, & de *Marguerite le Baleur*, ſes aïeul & aïeule. Il épouſa *Jeanne de Cochefilet*, dont entr'autres enfans:

RENÉ DE BARVILLE, II° du nom, Ecuyer, Seigneur de Nocey, fut fait Capitaine à l'arrière-ban, par commiffion du 18 Août 1569. Il mourut à Nantes, en revenant de l'arrière-ban, & y fut enterré aux Jacobins, le 17 Mars 1540. Il avoit époufé, 1° le 9 Septembre 1551, *Anne des Feugerêts-Deftouches*; & 2° *Philippe de Vauviffan*. Il eut du premier lit:

1. JEAN, qui fuit;
2. Et FRANÇOISE.

Et du fecond lit:

3. Autre JEAN;
4. LOUIS;
5. Et RENÉE DE BARVILLE.

JEAN DE BARVILLE, IV° du nom, Chevalier, Seigneur de Nocey, marié à *Françoife*, laquelle devenue veuve, eut la tutelle de fes enfans, le 24 Juin 1587, & la garde-noble, le 14 Octobre 1598, & rendit aveu aux Chanoines de Chartres au nom de fes enfans qui furent:

1. FLORIMOND, qui fuit;
2. Et FRANÇOISE, mariée à N... *Dumouchel*.

FLORIMOND DE BARVILLE, Ecuyer, Seigneur de Nocey, Capitaine au Régiment du Perche le 14 Mars 1624, obtint un jugement, par lequel il fut confervé au rang des nobles de fa Province. Il avoit époufé, le 17 Septembre 1609, *Anne de Fontenay*, dont il eut entr'autres enfans:

ANDRÉ DE BARVILLE, Chevalier, Seigneur de Nocey, qui leva une Compagnie de 100 hommes de pied, le 21 Juillet 1644, dans le Régiment du Cardinal Mazarin, fut enfuite Capitaine d'une Compagnie de Chevaux-Légers de 50 hommes, par commiffion du 17 Mars 1652. Il avoit époufé, le 15 Octobre 1634, *Barbe Girard*, fille de noble homme *Jacques Girard*, & de *Barbe Rignard*, dont pour enfans:

1. FLORIMOND, tué à Saint-Gothard en Hongrie;
2. ANDRÉ, qui fuit;
3. PIERRE, qui époufa *Marie-Catherine de Beauvau*, veuve de *Claude-Louis de Bullion*, Marquis d'Attilly;
4. CHARLES, mort fans enfans, Lieutenant-Colonel du Régiment Dauphin;
5. JEAN-ETIENNE, mort garçon, Lieutenant de Roi au Fort-Bareau;

Et plufieurs filles.

ANDRÉ DE BARVILLE, II° du nom, Chevalier, Seigneur de Nocey, Major au Régiment de la Salle, marié, 1° en 1677, avec *Renée Sevin*,

morte fans enfans; 2° en 1687, avec *Efther-Louife Turpin*, & 3° en 1699, avec *Marie-Madeleine de Cleuche*. Il eut du fecond lit:

1. ANDRÉ-MADELEINE, qui fuit;
2. PIERRE, marié;
3. ANDRÉ-LOUIS, tué Capitaine de Grenadiers, au fiège de Berg-Op-Zoom, en 1747;
4. Et une fille.

Et du troifième lit:

5. Un fils, mort fans poftérité;
6. Et une fille.

ANDRÉ-MADELEINE DE BARVILLE, Chevalier, Seigneur de Nocey, Capitaine au Régiment Dauphin, tué en 1734, à la bataille de Parme, avoit époufé en 1715, *Marie-Marguerite de Rofnivineau*, dont font iffus:

1. ANDRÉ, mort fans poftérité, Capitaine de Carabiniers;
2. LOUIS-MADELEINE, tué Enfeigne aux Gardes-Françoifes, au fiège de Maeftricht en 1748;
3. LOUIS-AUGUSTE, qui fuit;
4. Et une fille, morte en bas âge.

LOUIS-AUGUSTE DE BARVILLE, Chevalier, Seigneur de Nocey, Capitaine de Carabiniers, a époufé, en 1758, *Marie-Marguerite de Rofnivineau*, fa coufine germaine.

Les armes: *d'or, au fautoir de gueules, engrelé & cantonné de quatre lions de fable*.

BRANCHE

des Seigneurs DE BARVILLE, *établie dans l'élection de Lifieux, Intendance d'Alençon, que nous croyons fortie de la précédente.*

JEAN DE BARVILLE, Ecuyer, Seigneur de Barville, eft mentionné dans un acte du 8 Mars 1492, il époufa *Jeanne le Gris*, qui vivoit en 1483, lors du mariage de fa fille GUILLEMETTE, fille du Baron de *Montreuil*. Ils eurent pour enfans:

1. CONSTANTIN DE BARVILLE, dont la fucceffion fut partagée, en 1654, entre fes fœurs. Il avoit époufé *Jacqueline Martel*, morte fans poftérité, fille de *Jean Martel*, & de *Renée de Malet de Graville*;
2. GILETTE DE BARVILLE, qui eut en partage les Terres, Fiefs & Seigneuries de Barville, la Vavaffaurie d'Efperaudes, comme aînée dans la fucceffion de fon frère. Elle époufa *Richard de Livet*. La Terre de Barville eft toujours dans la famille de *Livet*, dont les poffeffeurs portent le nom, joint à celui de *Livet*;

3. Guillemette de Barville, qui eut 1000 liv. tournois de dot comme deuxième héritière de fon frère. Elle époufa, en 1483, *Etienne Vipart*, Baron de *Bethomas*, dont le fils, nommé *Hector de Bethomas*, eut, à caufe de fa mère, les Terres & Seigneuries d'Yvetot;

4. Jacqueline de Barville, laquelle eut en partage les Terres & Seigneuries de Bourg-Nainville, la Concinnière, la Tillaye, le fief de Vaucou & une partie de la Seigneurie d'Yvetot. Elle époufa *Gabriel de Pommereuil*;

5. Et Charlotte de Barville, mariée à *Guillaume le Breton*, Seigneur de la Couture, dont les enfans eurent le Fief, Terre & Seigneurie d'Anières & partie du Fief de Clipin dans la Paroiffe de..... avec des rentes fur le petit Cormilly.

Armes.

Les anciens Chevaliers de Barville portoient pour armes, & leurs fucceffeurs les ont confervées: *d'argent à deux bandes de gueules, avec un cafque mi-tourné d'acier aux 5 grilles dorées*. Le hachement & le bourlet aux *fermaux du cafque*; fupports: *2 lions d'or, armés & lampaffés de gueules*; devife: *foldat & brave*; fymbole: *un coq éployé d'argent, becqué, membré, crêté de gueules, couronné d'or*; *placé fur le dos d'un lion, léopardé d'or, armé & lampaffé de gueules*, avec les mêmes mots: *foldat & brave*; cri de guerre: *Dieu à nous*, ce que les anciens Seigneurs de Barville figuroient par une foi de carnation *couronnée d'azur*, avec ces mêmes mots: *Dieu à nous*, comme voulant fignifier que *Dieu nous donne fa protection quand nous fommes fidèles à garder fa foi*.

Ces mêmes armes font élevées en boffe au pignon de l'Eglife de Barville, Diocèfe de Seez, Election de Mortagne au Perche, fous la Généralité d'Alençon.

La branche des Seigneurs de Saint-Germain porte: *d'argent, à la bande de gueules*.

BARWICK ou BERWICK. Voyez FITZ-JAMES.

BAS (le), famille divifée en plufieurs branches, établies à Paris & à Befançon.

François le Bas, Ecuyer, Seigneur de Lefcheneau, originaire du Berry, fut Secrétaire de la Chambre du Roi le 7 Janvier 1639, Tréforier des Ponts & Chauffées, en Champagne, le 1er Octobre 1645; Maître-d'Hôtel

Tome II.

ordinaire de Sa Majefté le 6 Juillet 1653, & Confeiller d'Etat le 10 Mars 1657. Il mourut, revêtu de cette Charge, au mois de Mars 1666. De fon mariage, accordé le 22 Février 1653, avec *Catherine Roger*, fille de *Pierre Roger*, Confeiller, Secrétaire du Roi, Greffier en Chef du Grand-Confeil, font nés entr'autres enfans:

1. Claude le Bas-de-Montargis, Marquis du Bouchet-Valgrand, Seigneur de Vanvres, Maintenu dans fa nobleffe par Arrêt des Commiffaires-Généraux du Confeil, rendu en 1701; fait la même année Tréforier-Général de l'Extraordinaire des Guerres & Garde du Tréfor-Royal en 1708; Commandeur-Secrétaire des Ordres du Roi en 1716, & Confeiller d'Etat en 1722; marié en 1693 avec *Henriette-Catherine Hardouin-Manfard*, dont il n'a eu que:

N..., mariée à M. *Hénault*, Préfident en la première Chambre des Enquêtes du Parlement de Paris;

Et Charlotte, mariée à *Louis*, IIe du nom, *Marquis d'Arpajon*;

2. Louis, auteur d'une feconde branche, dite *de Girangy*, qui fuit;

3. Et Michel-François, chef d'une troifième branche, dite *du Pleffis*, rapportée ci-après.

Louis le Bas-de-Girangy, Ecuyer, Seigneur de Claye, &c., Tréforier-Général des Gardes-du-Corps des Grenadiers à Cheval de Sa Majefté, mort à Paris en 1722, fut marié, 1° en 1698 avec *Marie-Anne de Sauvion*, dont il n'a point eu d'enfans; 2° le 16 Octobre 1706, avec *Marie-Catherine Quentin*, fille de *Jean Quentin*, Ecuyer, Seigneur de Villiers-fur-Orge. Il eut de fon fecond mariage:

1. Louis-Michel, mort en 1711;

2. Charles-Louis, mort en 1713;

3. Pierre-René, qui fuit;

4. Louis-César, né le 23 Décembre 1717, fait Capitaine dans le Régiment des Dragons de la Reine, en 1742, & Chevalier de Saint-Louis en 1746;

5. Marie-Catherine, morte en 1737, femme de Charles le Bas, Seigneur du Pleffis-Saint-Jean, fon coufin;

6. Angélique, morte en 1712;

7. Marie-Thérèse, née en 1713, mariée en 1731 à *Jean-Baptifte le Clerc*, Seigneur de Boifguiche, de Riberpré & du Hamel;

8. Henriette-Catherine, morte en 1715;

9. Et Anne-Madeleine, née en 1721, mariée, en 1740, à *Claude-François Boquet-de-Courbouzon*, Confeiller au Parlement de Befançon.

PIERRE-RENÉ LE BAS-DE-GIRANGY, Ecuyer, né en 1715, fut fait Gentilhomme ordinaire de la Maifon du Roi en 1736, Capitaine de Cavalerie dans le Régiment de Chépy, depuis Bellefonds, en 1737, & Chevalier de Saint-Louis en 1745. De fon mariage, accordé le 1er Février 1747, avec *Marie-Anne-Sufanne Roualle*, fille de *Louis Roualle*, Ecuyer, Confeiller du Roi, Payeur des rentes de l'Hôtel-de-Ville de Paris, font iffus :

1. LOUIS-RENÉ, né le 3 Septembre 1748;
2. Et ALEXANDRE-PAUL-NARCISSE, né le 24 Mai 1750.

BRANCHE
des Seigneurs DU PLESSIS.

MICHEL-FRANÇOIS LE BAS-DU-PLESSIS, Ecuyer, Seigneur du Pleffis-Saint-Jean, dit *Praslin*, de Pailly, de Clévant & de Lefcheneau, cinquième fils de FRANÇOIS LE BAS, & de *Catherine Roger*, naquit en 1663. Il fut, Confeiller du Roi, Tréforier-Général de l'extraordinaire des Guerres, fur la démiffion de fon frère, & en obtint des provifions le 6 Décembre 1709. Il mourut en 1725, laiffant plufieurs enfans de fon mariage avec *Charlotte de Serre*, entr'autres :

1º CHARLES LE BAS, Ecuyer, Seigneur du Pleffis-Saint-Jean, dit *Praslin*, de Pailly & autres lieux, Confeiller au Parlement de Paris, marié fur une difpenfe de Rome, par contrat du 9 Février 1726, avec MARIE-CATHERINE LE BAS-DE-GIRANGY, fa coufine germaine dont il a eu :

1. CÉSAR-CHARLES, né en 1727, Confeiller au Parlement en 1748, & mort en 1749;
2. CHARLES-NICOLAS, né le 26 Janvier 1737;
3. & 4. CHARLOTTE-CLAUDE, & N... mortes, l'une en 1729, & l'autre en 1730, une heure après leur naiffance.

2. NICOLAS LE BAS-DU-PLESSIS, Ecuyer, baptifé en 1695, Capitaine d'une Compagnie dans le Régiment Dauphin, étranger, en 1716, mourut en 1744. Il avoit époufé, 1º le 23 Juillet 1726, *Louife-Françoife le Griffe*, morte le 22 Janvier 1728, fans enfans; & 2º le 28 Février 1729, *Charlotte-Françoife Roffignol*. Il laiffa de ce fecond mariage :

1. CLAUDE, Ecuyer, né le 3 Février 1734;
2. FRANÇOIS-NICOLAS, né le 23 Mai 1740;
3. CHARLOTTE, née le 19 Décembre 1729, mariée le 18 Mai 1750, à *François-Marie-Bruno Daguay*, Avocat-Général du Parlement de Franche-Comté;

4. Et ANTOINETTE-FRANÇOISE, née le 16 Juillet 1732.

3. JOSEPH LE BAS-DE-CLÉVANT, Ecuyer, Seigneur de Pugey, Marquis de Bouclan & de Varignolle, né à Nancy le 26 Décembre 1697, fut Confeiller au Parlement de Befançon en 1729, puis Confeiller-Honoraire du même Parlement. Le Roi érigea en fa faveur en titre de Marquifat, par Lettres du mois de Novembre 1749, la Terre de Bouclan, au Comté de Bourgogne. Cette Terre lui eft venue & à fa femme, par fucceffion, de *Marie-Rofe Maréchale*, Baronne de Bouclan, veuve de *Jean Lampinet*, Confeiller au Parlement de Befançon. De fon mariage, accordé le 15 Septembre 1725, avec *Marie-Thérèfe Hermand-de-Varignolle*, veuve de *Jean-Ferdinand Lampinet*, Seigneur de Bouclan & de Pugey, font iffus :

1. CHARLES-ALEXIS LE BAS-DE-BOUCLAN, Ecuyer, né le 21 Mai 1728;
2. LOUIS-MARIE LE BAS-DE-PUGEY, né le 13 Mai 1729;
3. LAURENT-MARIE LE BAS-D'AIGREMONT, né le 25 Mai 1730;
4. FERDINANDE-ANTOINETTE LE BAS-DE-CLÉVANT, née le 2 Octobre 1731;
5. Et MARGUERITE-THÉRÈSE LE BAS-PUGEY, née le 21 Décembre 1732.

4. ANNE-CLAUDE LE BAS DU PLESSIS-DE-CLOUANGE, Ecuyer, né à Metz le 6 Février 1704, étoit Sous-Diacre lorfqu'il obtint, le 24 Février 1730, des provifions de l'Office de Confeiller-Clerc au Parlement de Paris, & s'étant fait relever du Sous-Diaconat, par Sentence de l'Officialité de Metz, du 10 Juillet 1743, il fe maria, le 1er Août 1743, avec *Catherine Fadot-de-Grandmaifon*, dont il a eu :

ARMAND-HENRI LE BAS-DE-CLOUANGE, Ecuyer, né le 22 Janvier 1746.

5. Et LOUIS-DOMINIQUE LE BAS-DE-COURMONT, Ecuyer, né à Metz le 25 Août 1706, fut Fermier-Général. Il fe maria, 1º par contrat du 31 Mai 1729, à *Marie-Anne Saget*, morte fans enfans le 28 Mars 1738; & 2º le 27 Mars 1740, à *Louife-Elifabeth le Noir*, fille unique de *Séraphin le Noir*, Confeiller du Roi, Tréforier-Général, Receveur & Payeur des rentes de l'Hôtel de Ville de Paris, & d'*Elifabeth Jourdan-de-la-Salle*. De ce fecond mariage font iffus :

1. LOUIS-MARIE, né le 29 Septembre 1741;
2. CHARLES-CLAUDE, né le 17 Juin 1747;
3. LOUIS-DOMINIQUE, né le 15 Juillet 1749;

4. ELISABETH-LOUISE, née le 20 Octobre 1742;

5. LOUISE-NICOLE, née en 1743, morte en 1748;

6. ANGÉLIQUE-CHARLOTTE, née le 4 Décembre 1744;

7. Et CHARLOTTE, née le 29 Mai 1746.

(Voyez l'*Armorial de France*, reg. IV).

Les armes: *d'or, à un lion de gueules, accompagné de trois arbres de sinople, arrachés, posés, deux en chef & un en pointe.*

BAS (LE), à Pont-Audemer, en Normandie, Généralité de Rouen, famille maintenue en sa noblesse le 21 Novembre 1667. N... LE BAS, Vicomte de Pont-Audemer, la même année, eut pour fils ALPHONSE LE BAS, Conseiller au Parlement de Rouen.

Les armes: *d'argent, au chevron d'azur, accompagné de trois roses de gueules, feuillées & tigées de sinople, deux en chef & une en pointe, cette dernière surmontée d'un croissant d'azur.*

BAS (LE), Seigneur du Hamel, en Normandie, Généralité de Caen, famille annoblie en 1576: *de gueules, à la croix ancrée d'argent, cantonnée de quatre croissans de même.*

BAS-VEXIN (LE), près Rennes: *d'argent, à une aigle de sable, membrée de gueules.*

BASCHI, Maison originaire d'Italie.

I. UGOLINO DE BASCHI, Seigneur de Baschi, près du Tibre, en Ombrie, de Vitozzo, dans le Diocèse de Soana & de Montemarano, vivoit en 1080. Il laissa:

II. NÉRI DE BASCHI, qui fut père de:

III. UGOLINO DE BASCHI, dont le fils:

IV. UGOLINO DE BASCHI, Seigneur de Baschi, de Vitozzo, de Montemarano, &c., qui vivoit en 1220, eut pour enfans:

UGOLINO, qui suit;

Et FRANÇOISE DE BASCHI, mariée à *Aldobrandino Aldobrandeschi*, Comte de Soana & de Pitigliano, mort en 1285, laissant *Marguerite Aldobrandeschi*, Dame de Grosseto, Soana & Pitigliano, femme de *Guy de Montfort*, Comte de Nole, mort en 1288.

V. UGOLINO DE BASCHI, Seigneur de Baschi, de Vitozzo, de Montemarano, &c., vivant l'an 1260, épousa 1° *Gemma Aldobrandeschi-de-Pitigliano*; & 2° *Necca Farnèse*, fille d'*Antoine Farnèse*, & de CATHERINE DE BASCHI. Du premier lit vinrent:

1. NÉRI, qui suit;

2. Et BINDO DE BASCHI, Général des Troupes de la ville de Todi, à la bataille de Monte-

molino, le 5 Septembre 1310; Capitaine des Gibelins, qui voulurent s'emparer d'Orviéto, le 20 Août 1313, tué dans cette occasion. Il fut le trisayeul de NICOLAS DE BASCHI, Seigneur de Castel-Agara, arbitre des différends qu'il y avoit entre REINIER DE BASCHI, Seigneur de Vitozzo, & BERTHOLE DE BASCHI, Seigneur de Castellar, le 10 Avril 1426.

Il eut du second lit:

Un fils, qui mourut sans postérité.

VI. NÉRI DE BASCHI, Seigneur de Baschi, de Montemarano, de Vitozzo, &c., Capitaine des Troupes du St.-Siège, fut Vicaire de l'Empereur à Pise en 1310. Ceux d'Orviéto l'ayant fait prisonnier à Castel-Franco en 1317, le firent mourir. Il fut père de BENDOCCIO, qui suit, & d'UGOLINO DE BASCHI, Seigneur de Vitozzo, qui a fait la branche des Marquis d'AUBAIS, rapportée ci-après.

VII. BENDOCCIO DE BASCHI, Seigneur de Baschi, Ténaglie, Mezzanello, mort avant 1355, eut de *Maccalila de Gli-Atti*, sœur du Cardinal *François de Gli-Atti*, lequel mourut le 4 Septembre 1361:

VIII. RANUCE DE BASCHI, Seigneur de Baschi & de Carnano, marié avec URSINA DE BASCHI, fille de CELLO DE BASCHI, qui fut père de:

IX. UGOCCIONE DE BASCHI, Seigneur de Baschi, Carnano, Salviano, &c., qui laissa de *Violande d'Alviano*:

1. BERNARDIN DE BASCHI, Chevalier de Rhodes, Commandeur de Saint-Justin de Pérouse, qui servit en 1480, à la défense de Rhodes, assiégée par MAHOMET II;

2. Et RANUCE, qui suit.

X. RANUCE DE BASCHI, Seigneur de Baschi, Carnano, &c., Lieutenant de *Frédéric de Montefeltro*, Duc d'Urbin, Général de l'Armée du Pape SIXTE IV, avoit épousé *Sixte Baglioni*, fille de *Pallucio Baglioni*, Comte de Castel-di-Piro & de Grafignano, & de *Catherine Savelli*, qui étoit sœur du Cardinal *Jean-Baptiste Savelli*, mort le 1er Février 1495. Il en eut:

1. ANTOINE, qui suit;

2. Et UGOCCIONE DE BASCHI, Seigneur de Carnano, Lieutenant de *Barthélemy*, Seigneur d'Alviano, Général de l'Armée des Vénitiens, qui reçut LOUIS DE BASCHI-SAINT-ESTÈVE au Château de Baschi, en 1530. Il épousa 1° *Léonore della Cervara*; & 2° *Sigismonde Orsini-de-Mugnano*, dont les enfans moururent sans postérité.

XI. Antoine de Baschi, Seigneur de Baschi, qui épousa Lucrèce de Baschi, de laquelle il eut:

XII. Jean-Raymond de Baschi, Seigneur de Baschi, qui épousa Bernardine de Baschi, assassinée au Château de Baschi en 1553, fille d'Hercule de Baschi, Seigneur de Sarmognano & de Camille de Baschi. De cette alliance vint:

XIII. Ranuce de Baschi, Seigneur de Baschi, vivant l'an 1584, qui épousa *Cornélie Santinelli*, des Comtes *della Metola*, dans le Duché d'Urbin. Il en eut:

XIV. François de Baschi, &c., qui épousa *Adrienne de Simoncelli*, sœur du Cardinal *Hierôme Simoncelli*, qui étoit petit-neveu du Pape Jules III. Il en eut:

1. Ranuce de Baschi, qui s'attacha aux intérêts de la France. Le Pape Innocent XI lui ayant donné l'Evêché de Sinigaglia, dans la Marche d'Ancône, il fut sacré par le Cardinal d'Estrées, à Rome, le 14 Juin 1682, & il y mourut le 25 Septembre 1684;
2. Le Comte Martio de Baschi, nommé Commandant de l'Infanterie que le Pape envoyoit au secours des Vénitiens, en Mai 1659;
3. Et Joseph-Gilles, qui suit.

XV. Joseph-Gilles de Baschi, Comte de Baschi, épousa *Honesta Fiumi*, des Comtes de *Sterpeto*, en Ombrie, & fut père de:

XVI. François de Baschi, Comte de Baschi-Saint-Estève, né le 9 Juillet 1710, Chevalier des Ordres du Roi, Conseiller d'Etat d'Epée, Ambassadeur de Sa Majesté, en 1755, en Portugal, ensuite à Venise en 1762, qui a épousé, le 6 Avril 1740, *Charlotte-Victoire le Normand*, née le 5 Novembre 1712, fille de *Guillot le Normand* & d'*Elisabeth Francine*, dont:

1. François de Baschi, né le 3 Août 1745, marié en 1770 à *Susanne-Caroline* de Baschi, sa cousine, fille d'Henri-Louis, Marquis du Cayla;
2. Jeanne-Charlotte-Victoire-Elisabeth, née en 1741, mariée, le 1er Juillet 1754, à *Charles-Antoine de Guérin*, Marquis de Lugeac;
3. Elisabeth-Guillelmine-Françoise, née le 21 Décembre 1742, mariée, le 1er Juillet 1754, à *Charles-Théophile de Béfiade*, Marquis d'Avaray, mort le 17 Avril 1757;
4. Henriette-Louise-Madeleine, née le 20 Mai 1744, mariée le 21 Juin 1765, à *François*, Comte *de Monteynard*, Colonel dans les Grenadiers de France;

5. Et Jeanne-Marie-Louise, née le 22 Septembre 1750.

BRANCHE des Marquis d'Aubais.

VII. Ugolino de Baschi, Seigneur de Vitozzo, de Montemarano, second fils de Néri, Seigneur de Baschi & de Vitozzo, fut surnommé *Buffa*. Il fut exclu, le 8 Février 1322, avec les autres Seigneurs de sa Maison, du Gouvernement d'Orviéto, par ceux de cette Ville, qui avoient fait mourir son père, & qui craignoient son ressentiment & sa puissance. Il étoit mort en 1355; & avoit épousé une sœur de *Gisello de Gli-Ubaldini*, Général des Troupes de la ville de Pise, de laquelle il eut:

VIII. Reinier de Baschi, Seigneur de Vitozzo & de Montemarano, qui fut un des principaux Capitaines de l'Armée, avec laquelle le Cardinal *Gilles Albornos* recouvra Viterbe & beaucoup d'autres places de l'Etat de l'Eglise, en 1354. Il fit une Guerre fort vive aux *Ursins* & aux *Farnèse*; & ce ne fut qu'après plusieurs prières réitérées de *Nicolas*, Patriarche d'Aquilée, frère naturel de l'Empereur Charles IV, & son Vicaire-Général en Toscane, qu'il consentit à faire une trève avec eux, le 5 Mai 1355. Il fut Général des Pisans contre les Florentins, à la bataille de Bagno à Véna, donnée le 7 Mai 1363. Il testa en 1367, & fit un legs à Boccace. Il avoit épousé *Etiennette Gateschi*, des Seigneurs de *Viterbe*, de laquelle il eut:

1. François de Baschi, Seigneur de Vitozzo & de Silvena, bisaïeul d'Hercule de Baschi, Seigneur de Sermogano, vivant en 1530;
2. Et Etienne, qui suit.

IX. Etienne de Baschi, Seigneur en partie de Vitozzo, signa la Trève faite avec les Ursins, le 5 Mai 1355. Il étoit mort en 1375, & eut pour fils:

X. Guichard de Baschi, Seigneur en partie de Vitozzo, de Marano, de Latera, qui se ligua avec les Gouverneurs de Rome & de Vico & les *Farnèse*, pour faire la guerre aux Siennois, en 1384. Il s'attacha ensuite à Louis II d'Anjou, Roi de Naples, Comte de Provence, qui lui donna la charge de son Ecuyer, & passa avec lui en Provence. Il fit son testament au Château de Thoard le 7 Septembre 1425, & mourut bientôt après. Il avoit épousé *Jacquette Farnèse*, fille de *Ranuce Farnèse*, sa cousine du troisième au quatrième degré; ce qui l'ayant obligé de demander une difpenfe, le Pape la lui accorda. Il en eut:

XI. Berthold de Baschi, Seigneur en partie de Vitozzo, Ecuyer de Louis, Roi de Naples, qui fit plufieurs voyages en Italie après la mort de fon père, & tranfigea avec fes coufins, Reinier & Angelo de Baschi, fur les droits qu'il avoit à la Terre de Vitozzo, en 1426, 1428 & 1429. Il acheta, le 19 Avril 1422, de *Jean de Barras*, le Château de Saint-Eftève, & la plus grande partie de ceux de Thoard, de Barras & de Tournefort, dans le Diocèfe de Digne en Provence, & fit fon teftament le 19 Octobre 1461. Il avoit épousé, 1° par contrat paffé à Avignon, dans le Palais du Cardinal Amédée de Saluces, *Philippe de Pontevès*, Dame de Caftellar, laquelle tefta le 11 Juillet 1429; elle étoit fille de *Bérenger*, & de *Catherine de Barras*, Dame de Caftellar; 2° le 22 Avril 1434, *Marguerite Adhémar*, qui tefta le 25 Juillet 1452, fille de *Louis Adhémar*, Seigneur de Monteil & de la Garde, & de *Dauphine de Glandevès*; & 3° le 7 Mars 1453, *Catherine d'Allamanon*, morte avant le 1er Décembre 1470, fille d'*Hugonin d'Allamanon*. Il eut de fa première femme:

1. Siffred de Baschi, Seigneur de Caftellar, qui tefta le 1er Septembre 1476, & mourut fans enfans;
2. Honorade de Baschi, mariée le 14 Décembre 1440, à *Arnaud de Villeneuve*, Seigneur des Arcs & de Trans, dont les filles furent mariées dans les Maifons de *Foix* & de *Brancas*.

De fa feconde femme vinrent:

3. Thadée, qui fuit;
4. Perron de Baschi, qui fuivit Jean d'Anjou, Duc de Calabre, dans fes expéditions en Italie. Il fut enfuite pourvu d'une charge de Maître-d'Hôtel du Roi Charles VIII, qui l'envoya, en 1493, en ambaffade vers le Pape, & les Républiques de Venife & de Florence. L'année fuivante, il fut envoyé au Pape Alexandre VI, pour lui demander l'inveftiture du Royaume de Naples. Charles VIII l'envoya encore en plufieurs autres négociations.

Du troifième lit vint:

5. Et Honoré de Baschi, né en 1454, qui étoit Abbé du Thoronet en 1487, & de Saint-Thiers de Saône, au Diocèfe de Die, en 1498.

XII. Thadée de Baschi, Seigneur de Saint-Eftève, de Barras, de Tournefort, & de la plus grande partie des Thouars, tefta le 27 Avril

1509, & étoit mort le 4 Août 1509. Il épousa 1° *Honorade Monge*, qui tefta le 3 Mars 1505; & 2° le 7 Juin 1506, *Jeanne de Barras*, morte en 1531, fille d'*Antoine*, Seigneur de la Robine & de Mirabeau, & de *Baudette de Brignolles*. Il eut de fa première femme:

1. Mathieu de Baschi, Seigneur de Saint-Eftève, mort en 1542, fans enfans. Il avoit épousé, le 4 Novembre 1502, *Catherine de Frégofe*, fille d'*Auguftin de Frégofe*, & de *Gentille*, fille de *Frédéric de Montefeltro*, Duc d'Urbin, & fœur du Cardinal *Frédéric de Frégofe*, & d'*Octavien de Frégofe*, Doge de Gênes.

Et du fecond lit vint:

2. Et Louis, qui fuit.

XIII. Louis de Baschi, né peu après le teftament de fon père, refta long-tems en Italie avec le Cardinal de *Frégofe*. Ayant fuccédé à fon frère, il rendit hommage au Roi, le 15 Mars 1542, pour les Terres de Saint-Eftève, Barras, Tournefort & Thoard, & mourut le 3 Janvier 1588. Il avoit épousé, le 27 Avril 1537, *Melchionne de Matheron*, Dame de Levens, d'Auzet de Trévans, & en partie de Barras, de Tournefort, d'Eftoblon & d'Aiglun, qui tefta le 4 Février 1557. Elle étoit fille & héritière d'*Antoine de Matheron*, Seigneur d'Auzet, & d'*Andrivette de Forbin*. Il eut pour enfans:

1. Frédéric, Seigneur de Levens, qui fervit avec fes frères en Piémont, & au fiège du Havre-de-Grâce. Il fut fait Gouverneur de Sifteron le 30 Décembre 1567, & étoit mòrt en 1569;
2. Louis, qui fuit;
3. Octavien, baptifé le 3 Février 1546, Chevalier de Malte, Commandeur de Douzens, lequel fe noya en paffant la rivière d'Aude, le 22 Octobre 1579;
4. Thadée, Seigneur de Stoblon, Général des Razats en Provence, qui battit *Crillon* le 14 Juin 1574, s'empara de Riès le 6 Juillet fuivant, & fut fait Gouverneur de Seine, le 4 Octobre 1577. Il mourut le 30 Mai 1579, d'une bleffure qu'il avoit reçue fept jours auparavant, en fe rendant maître du Château de Trans;
5. Alexandre, Seigneur de Saint-Pierre & d'Auzet, Commandant à Thoard, en Octobre 1586. Il tefta le 1er Janvier 1626, & fit la branche des Seigneurs de *Saint-Pierre*, qui s'éteignit dans la perfonne de Catherine de Baschi, fon arrière-petite-fille, morte en 1714, femme de *Louis le Camus*;
6. Et Honorade, mariée le 17 Septembre

1573, à *Barthélemy*, Seigneur de Pontis. Elle fut mère de *Louis de Pontis*, connu par les Mémoires publiés fous fon nom.

XIV. Louis de Baschi, Seigneur d'Auzet, fut Capitaine d'une bande de 200 hommes de pied. Henri III, étant à Ferrare, au mois d'Août 1574, lui ordonna de fe rendre auprès du Comte de Carces, à Aix; il obéit, mais il fut affaffiné dans cette ville d'un coup de piftolet, le 18 Septembre 1574. Il avoit époufé, le 4 Octobre 1569, *Louife de Varei*, Dame de Manteyer & de Saint-André, qui fe remaria à *Charles du Faur*, Seigneur de la Serre, & tefta le 6 Août 1615. Elle étoit fille de *Balthafard*, Seigneur de Manteyer, & d'*Authoronne de Guigonis*, & laiffa:

XV. Balthasard de Baschi Seigneur de Saint-Eftève, de Barras, de Tournefort, & de la plus grande partie de Thoard, né le 27 Juillet 1571, qui fervit dans l'armée du Roi en Provence en 1589; il fut fait Gentilhomme ordinaire de la Chambre de Henri IV, le 18 Septembre 1595; & fe noya à la fin de Janvier 1598, dans la rivière du Viftre audeffous du Cayla. Il avoit époufé, le 28 Juin 1591, *Marguerite du Faur*, Dame d'Aubais, du Cayla, Zunas, Gavernes, Montleau, morte à Nérac, le 9 Septembre 1609, après s'être remariée, le 29 Septembre 1607, à *Jean de Peyre*, qui fut tué au mois de Juillet 1608. Elle étoit fille de *Charles du Faur*, Seigneur de la Serre, & de *Jacqueline de Boxène*, Dame d'Aubais & du Cayla, fa première femme. Leurs enfans furent:

> Charles, qui continua la branche des Seigneurs de *Saint-Eftève*, laquelle fubfifte aujourd'hui dans la perfonne de François de Baschi, Comte de Bafchi-Saint-Eftève, fon arrière-petit-fils;
> Et Louis, qui fuit.

XVI. Louis de Baschi, né à Aubais le 22 Octobre 1595, héritier de fa mère, fut, par le Baron d'Aubais & du Cayla, Seigneur de Junas, de Gavernes, de Sauffines & de Saint-Félix. Louis XIII lui donna, le 14 Octobre 1629, une Compagnie de 50 Chevaux-Légers, & il empêcha, en 1632, que la ville de Nîmes ne prit le parti du Duc de Montmorency. Il fe diftingua à la bataille d'Ayefnes en 1635; & le 24 Janvier 1638, le Roi lui donna un des premiers Régimens de Cavalerie qui avoient été levés en France. Le 11 Juin 1642, ce Prince lui donna une commiffion pour commander la Cavalerie de l'Armée de Catalogne, en qualité de Meftre-de-Camp-Général; il fe diftingua fort à la bataille de Lérida, le 7 Octobre 1642; fut fait Maréchal-de-Camp le 31 Décembre 1642, & mourut au Château d'Aubais le 13 Novembre 1646. Il avoit époufé, le 17 Juin 1614, *Anne de Rochemore*, morte le 17 Novembre 1667, fille de *Louis de Rochemore*, Maître des Requêtes, & Préfident du Sénéchal de Nîmes, & d'*Anne de Barrière*, Dame de Nages & de Solorgues, dont il eut:

XVII. Charles de Baschi, Baron d'Aubais & du Cayla, Seigneur de Junas, Gavernes, Saint-Félix, né à Aubais le 26 Juillet 1623, qui fut Capitaine de Chevaux-Légers dans le Régiment de fon père, & fe diftingua à la bataille de Thionville en 1639; il fut bleffé à celle de Lérida, en 1642, & mourut le 31 Janvier 1668. Il avoit époufé, le 24 Avril 1640, *Marguerite Cauffe*, Dame de Rigoles & de Magdas, morte le 10 Septembre 1676, fille de *Jean*, Seigneur des mêmes Terres, & de *Violande dè Béedos*, dont il eut:

> 1. Louis, qui fuit;
> 2. Et Henri, Seigneur de Rigoles, qui a fait la branche des Marquis de *Pignan*, rapportée ci-après.

XVIII. Louis de Baschi, Marquis d'Aubais, Baron du Cayla, Seigneur de Junas, Gavernes, Saint-Félix, &c., né le 21 Mars 1646, mourut le 7 Juin 1703. Il avoit époufé, le 4 Novembre 1673, *Anne Boiffon*, née le 8 Décembre 1655, morte le 21 Mars 1686, fille d'*Ifaac Boiffon*, & de *Marguerite Richard*, dont il eut:

> 1. Charles, qui fuit;
> 2. Et Madeleine de Baschi, née le 3 Août 1683, mariée, le 12 Mai 1705, à *Jacques de Caffagnet*, Marquis de Firmarcon.

XIX. Charles de Baschi, Marquis d'Aubais, Baron du Cayla, Seigneur de Junas, Gavernes, Saint-Chriftin, &c., né au Château de Beauvoifin, le 20 Mars 1686, a époufé, en Juin 1708, *Diane de Rozel*, Dame de Cors & de Beaumont, née le 14 Novembre 1683, morte au Château d'Aubais, le 16 Décembre 1765, fille unique de *Louis de Rozel* & de *Jacquette Jauffaud*, dont:

> 1. Jean-François, qui fuit;
> 2. Diane-Henriette, morte le 28 Mars 1755. Elle avoit époufé, le 5 Juin 1732, *Jofeph de Monteynard*, Marquis de Monfrein;
> 3. Jacqueline-Marie, née le 19 Août 1719,

mariée le 26 Novembre 1741, à *Alexan-dre-François-Joseph*, Comte *d'Urre*, dont trois garçons & une fille ;

4. Et EUPHROSINE, née le 25 Septembre 1724, morte au Château de Galargues, le 5 Mars 1749. Elle avoit épousé, le 20 Février 1743, *Anne-Joachim-Annibal*, Marquis *de Roche-more.*

XX. JEAN-FRANÇOIS DE BASCHI, Marquis du Cayla, né à Aubais, le 23 Décembre 1717, & mort le 28 Février 1758, a laissé de son mariage, contracté le 11 Août 1745, avec SUSANNE-FRANÇOISE DE BASCHI-DE-PIGNAN, sa cousine, morte le 20 Octobre 1773 :

HENRI-LOUIS, Comte du Cayla, né le 17 Juin 1746, & mort le 16 Février 1749 ;

SUSANNE-CAROLINE, mariée en 1770 à FRAN-ÇOIS DE BASCHI, son cousin ;

DIANE-HENRIETTE-LOUISE-GODEPHLINE ;

GABRIELLE-PAULINE ;

Et GABRIELLE-ALEXANDRINE, morte à Mont-pellier le 23 Novembre 1759.

BRANCHE
des Marquis DE PIGNAN.

XVIII. HENRI DE BASCHI, second fils de CHARLES DE BASCHI, Baron d'Aubais, & de *Marguerite Cauffe*, Dame de Rigoles & de Magdas, né à Aubais, le 31 Octobre 1647, fut héritier de sa mère, & par-là Seigneur de Ri-goles & de Magdas, & en partie de Saint-Ro-mans, & servit en Flandres en qualité de Ca-pitaine de Cavalerie au Régiment de Tilla-det. Il mourut au Château de Pignan, le 16 Février 1727. Il avoit épousé, le 1er Septem-bre 1678, *Elisabeth de Richard*, Dame de Pignan, Sauffan, las-Ribes, la Vacaresse, &c., morte à Pignan, le 20 Septembre 1719, fille de *François de Richard*, Seigneur de Sauf-fan, & de *Louise d'Hebles*, Dame de las-Ri-bes ; il en eut :

1. JEAN-LOUIS DE BASCHI DE PIGNAN, connu sous le nom *de Cayla*, né le 20 Octobre 1685, Colonel du Régiment de la Reine, Cavalerie, à la tête duquel il fut tué au com-bat de Castiglione, dans le Mantouan, le 9 Septembre 1706 ;

2. HENRI, qui suit ;

3. FRANÇOIS DE BASCHI DE SAUSSAN, connu pareillement sous le nom *de Cayla*, né le 14 Décembre 1688, Colonel du Régiment de la Reine, Cavalerie, en Septembre 1706, Brigadier des Armées du Roi, le 1er Fé-vrier 1719, Lieutenant-Général des Armées du Roi, Inspecteur de Cavalerie, & Gou-verneur de Saint-Omer, mort à Montpel-

lier, le 27 Février 1766, qui a épousé, le 3 Février 1722, *Marie Guillot*, née le 15 Août 1700, morte à Montpellier, le 17 Août 1724, fille de *Jean Guillot*, Seigneur de Fesc, de Sardan & de Salinelles, & de *Fran-çoise de Gondin*. Il a laissé JEANNE-MARIE-MADELEINE-SUSANNE DE BASCHI-PIGNAN, née le 17 Juillet 1724, morte à Montpel-lier le 14 Décembre 1764. Elle avoit épou-sé, le 8 Mars 1746, *François*, Marquis *de Roquefeuille ;*

4. PHILIPPE DE BASCHI-DE-LA-VACARESSE, né le 8 Septembre 1690, Major du Régiment de son frère, mort en.....;

5. MARC-ANTOINE DE BASCHI, né le 22 Juin 1699, Capitaine de Cavalerie dans le Régi-ment de la Reine, mort en.....;

6. Et SUSANNE DE BASCHI, née le 1er Octobre 1681, mariée 1° en Avril 1700, à *Marc-Antoine de Pierre*, Sieur d'Arennes, Lieu-tenant-Colonel des Dragons de Fontboif-fard, mort le 24 Juin 1708 ; & 2° le 27 Juin 1714, à *Jean de Bocaud*, Seigneur de Ja-cou & de Teirand, Président à la Cour des Aides de Montpellier.

XIX. HENRI DE BASCHI, Marquis de Pi-gnan, par Lettres-Patentes du mois d'Avril 1721, Baron de las-Ribes, né à Montpellier le 13 Mai 1687, épousa, le 11 Août 1720, *Anne-Renée d'Estrade*, née le 16 Avril 1700, morte à Montpellier le 4 Novembre 1725, fille de *Geoffroy*, Comte *d'Estrade*, Lieute-nant-Général des Armées du Roi, & de *Char-lotte le Normand*, de laquelle il a eu :

1. CHARLOTTE-SUSANNE-ELISABETH DE BASCHI, Demoiselle de Pignan, née le 10 Février 1722 ;

2. Et SUSANNE-FRANÇOISE, née le 20 Avril 1724, morte le 20 Octobre 1773, qui avoit épousé, le 11 Août 1745, JEAN-FRANÇOIS DE BASCHI, Marquis du Cayla, son cousin, mort le 28 Février 1758.

La Maison de Baschi porte pour armes : *d'argent, à la fasce de sable.* Les Comtes de Baschi, en Italie, écartèlent *aux 1 & 4 de gueules, au lion d'or.* Les branches établies en France, ont mis pour brisures leur écu *d'argent, chargé d'une fasce de sable, dans un écu de gueules,* & ont surmonté cet écu *d'une couronne de Comte, cousue d'or.* Le Marquis d'Aubais porte aujourd'hui : *écar-telé, au 1 d'or, à six fleurs-de-lys d'azur, 3, 2, 1,* qui est de Farnèse ; *au 2 d'or, à l'ours en pied de sable, armé & lampassé de gueu-les, & éclairé d'argent,* qui est de Bermond-d'Anduze ; *au 3, parti au 1 d'argent, au chef de fable*, *l'écu bordé de gueules*, qui eſt de Pelet; *au 2 faſcé d'or & de gueules de fix pièces*, qui eſt de Languſſel; *au 4 d'a-zur à deux jumelles d'or, accompagnées de fix befans d'argent, trois en chef, & trois en pointe*, qui eſt de du Faur; & ſur le tout *d'argent, à la faſce de fable,* qui eſt de Baſchi.

Supports: *un bacchus & une bacchante,* tenant une bannière à droite aux armes de Baſchi, & à gauche à celles de Bermond-d'Anduze. Le Marquis de Pignan : *écartèle aux 1 & 4* de Baſchi; *de gueules, en écuſſon en hermines d'argent chargé d'une faſce de fable, & couronné d'une couronne de comte, couſue d'or; aux 2 & 3 d'azur au lévrier paſſant d'argent, furmonté de trois roches d'échiquier, de même 2 & 1, & 1 chef d'azur, parti, & chargé au 1 d'une fleur-de-lys d'or, & au 2 d'un mouchoir, fanglant, accoſté à dextre d'un piſtolet en pal, & à feneſtre d'une flèche auſſi en pal, le tout d'argent,* qui eſt d'Hèbles, ſuivant la conceſſion accor-dée par Henri IV, en Janvier 1608, à *Jean d'Hebles*, Baron de las-Ribes.

(Moréri, Edit. de 1759).

BASCLE-D'ARGENTEUIL (le), origi-naire de Touraine.

Guillaume le Bascle, Grand-Sénéchal de Guyenne en 1240, fut père de :

I. Meſſire Henri le Bascle, Chevalier de l'Hôtel du Roi. On lit dans l'*Hiſtoire de Saint Louis*, par Joinville, pag. 348, & dans celle de Ducange, pag. 398, qu'il fut un de ceux qui accompagnèrent Saint Louis au deuxième voyage de la Terre-Sainte en 1270. Il tenoit un ſi haut rang parmi les Chevaliers, qu'il eſt nommé le ſixième après *Philippe de Nemours*. De lui vint :

II. Pierre le Bascle, Chevalier, Sire de Baſcle, nommé dans le chapitre des Robes diſtribuées aux Officiers de Philippe le Har-di, en 1274, épouſa, en 1287, *Iſabeau de Meudon*, Dame de Barbé, près Sens, de la-quelle il laiſſa :

III. Jean le Bascle, Ier du nom, Seigneur du Puy-Baſcle, le Pin & Saint-Louant, qui ſe trouva à la bataille de Crécy, en 1346, pour le ſervice du Roi Philippe de Valois, & s'en-gagea par la ſuite au ſervice du Roi de Na-varre, & fut tué à la bataille de Cocherel, en 1364, où, au rapport de Froiſſard, il com-mandoit un des trois corps d'Armée de ce

Prince. Il avoit épouſé *Jeanne de Cottereau*, grand'tante de *Jean de Cottereau*, Baron de Maintenon, Secrétaire d'Etat, dont il eut:

IV. Jean le Bascle, IIe du nom, Seigneur du Puy-Baſcle, le Pin & Saint-Louant, qui fut marié à *Charlotte-Angélique d'Argen-teuil.* De ce mariage fortirent:

1. Guillaume, mort ſans alliance;
2. Jean, qui ſuit ;
3. Un autre Jean, tige des Seigneurs du *Pin* & de *Saint-Louant*, dont la filiation eſt rap-portée par le Chevalier l'Hermite-Soulier, dans ſon Inventaire de la Nobleſſe de Tou-raine, & par M. de la Rivière, dans une Généalogie particulière qu'il a faite de cette Maiſon en 1659 ;
4. Et Gillette, femme de *Jean Galbrun.*

V. Jean le Bascle, IIIe du nom, Seigneur du Puy-Baſcle, de la Martinière, de Varen-ne, en Loudunois, épouſa en 1440 *Yolande le Maire*, fille de *Jean*, Seigneur de la Ro-chejacquelin, & de *Jeanne Quatrebarbes,* grand'tante d'*Hyacinthe Quatrebarbes,* Mar-quis de la Rongère, Chevalier des Ordres. Il a eu de ce mariage :

1. Guy, Doyen de Gergeau ;
2. Hugues, qui ſuit ;
3. Pierre, Seigneur de la Martinière, homme d'armes de la Compagnie de Jean d'Am-boiſe, Seigneur de Buſſi;
4. François, Seigneur de Varenne, en Loudu-nois, Conſeiller, Maître-d'Hôtel ordinaire du Roi Charles VIII, en 1492, Gouver-neur de l'Iſle-Bouchard, & premier Maî-tre-d'Hôtel de Monſeigneur le Dauphin, mort ſans enfans de *Marguerite d'Argy ;*
5. Et Charlotte le Bascle, femme de *Jean de Grailly*.

VI. Hugues le Bascle, Seigneur de Puy-Baſcle, élevé, en 1467, enfant d'honneur de la Reine Marie d'Anjou, femme du Roi Char-les VII, Maître-d'Hôtel du Roi en 1483, puis Echanſon du Duc de Normandie, frère de Louis XI, épouſa, en 1478, *Marguerite de Mandelot*, Baronne d'Argenteuil, Arcy & Moulin, fille unique de *Claude*, Seigneur des mêmes lieux, & grand'tante de *François de Mandelot*, Seigneur de Paſſy, Chevalier du Saint-Eſprit, le 31 Décembre 1582. De ce mariage vinrent :

1. Guillaume, Doyen de Gergeau;
2. Antoine, qui ſuit ;
3. Huguette , Dame de Moulin, mariée 1o à *Thomas d'Hériot*, Lieutenant des Gardes-du-Corps du Roi; & 2o à *Thomas d'Eſtra-*

ton, Guidon fous la charge de M. d'*Aubigny*;

4. Et JEANNE, mariée à *Guillaume de Béthoulat*, Seigneur du Défert.

VII. ANTOINE LE BASCLE, Ier du nom, Seigneur de Puy-Bafcle & de Moulin, Baron d'Argenteuil, s'allia, par contrat du 17 Octobre 1519, à *Marguerite de la Touche-Limoufinière*, petite-fille de *Jean de la Touche*, & de *Jeanne de Rohan*, & fille de *Renaud de la Touche*, & de *Françoife de Rochechouart*, de laquelle il eut:

1. ANTOINE, qui fuit;
2. Et Louis, dont eft fortie la branche des Seigneurs de *Puy-Bafcle*, & de la *Cour-d'Avon*.

VIII. ANTOINE LE BASCLE, IIe du nom, Seigneur du Puy-Bafcle, Baron d'Argenteuil, & Seigneur de Varenne, Capitaine de 50 Chevaux, s'allia, par contrat du 22 Janvier 1545, à *Françoife de Bouffeval*, Dame de Villiers-les-Eaux, fille de *Jean*, Seigneur de Bouffeval, Capitaine & Gouverneur du Château de Dijon, & d'*Hélène le Courtois* Il eut:

IX. FRANÇOIS LE BASCLE, Baron d'Argenteuil, d'Arcy & de Moulin, Seigneur de Santenay, Chevalier de l'Ordre du Roi, Gentilhomme ordinaire de fa Chambre, Meftre-de-Camp d'un Régiment d'Infanterie, fous les Rois HENRI III & HENRI IV, premier Chambellan de Monfeigneur le Comte de Soiffons, fecond Prince du Sang, qui époufa, 1° par contrat du 24 Décembre 1577, *Denife d'Hériot*, fa coufine, Baronne de Moulin, fille de *Patrice d'Hériot*, Lieutenant des Gardes-du-Corps Ecoffois, & de *Barbe de Chaftenay*; & 2° en 1591, ou par contrat du 5 Juin 1592, *Marie de Lenoncourt*, d'une des plus illuftres Maifons de Lorraine, veuve de *Robert des Réaux*, & fille de *Claude de Lenoncourt*, Seigneur des Marolles, & d'*Anne de Maumont*, Dame de Château-Chinon en Berry.

Du premier lit vint:

PATRICE, qui fuit;

Et du fecond lit:

FRANÇOIS LE BASCLE, IIe du nom, Seigneur d'Arcy, Château-Chinon & Beauregard, premier Gentilhomme de la Chambre de Monfeigneur le Comte de Soiffons. Il eut la réputation d'un des hommes les plus braves de fon fiècle, & il eft l'auteur de la branche des Comtes d'*Argenteuil*, Barons de *Chapelaine*, en Bourgogne, & qui fubfifte dans

Tome II.

la perfonne du Marquis d'Argenteuil, Aide-Major des Gardes-du-Corps du Roi en 1770.

X. PATRICE LE BASCLE, Baron d'Argenteuil, d'Arcy & de Moulin, Meftre-de-Camp d'Infanterie, fuivant un titre du 25 Avril 1613, fut tué au fiège de Noyers en Bourgogne, en 1631. Il avoit époufé, par contrat du 25 Juillet 1608, *Colombe de Boucher*, Comteffe d'Epineuil, Dame de Pouy, veuve de *Louis de Saint-Blaife*, Seigneur dudit Pouy, de laquelle il eut:

1. LOUIS, qui fuit;
2. CHARLES, tige de la branche des Comtes de *Moulin*;
3. MATHIEU, Prieur d'Ancilcerveux;
4. Et CATHERINE, femme de *Paul-François de Beaujeu*, Gentilhomme ordinaire de la Chambre de Monfeigneur le Duc d'Orléans, Capitaine des Gardes-du-Corps du Duc de Mantoue, Chevalier de fon Ordre, & fon Envoyé en Hongrie.

XI. LOUIS LE BASCLE, Comte d'Epineuil, Baron d'Argenteuil, Seigneur de Pouy, élevé Page, fut Gentilhomme ordinaire de la Chambre du Roi LOUIS XIII; Capitaine d'une Compagnie de 100 hommes de pied François, par Brevet du 16 Octobre 1646, & retenu par LOUIS XIV à 2000 livres de penfion annuelle. Il fe maria, 1° par contrat du 31 Janvier 1640, à *Catherine de Torcy*, des Marquis de Torcy, Barons de Greuille, fille de *Claude de Torcy*, Seigneur de Lantilly, & de *Françoife de Chaugy*; & 2° par contrat du 11 Février 1652, avec *Françoife de Ponville*, Dame de Mailly, petite-fille d'*Edme de Ponville*, Seigneur de Mailly, Maître-d'Hôtel ordinaire du Roi, Maréchal de fes Camps & Armées, & de *Diane de Poitiers*, proche parente de *Diane de Poitiers*, Ducheffe de Valentinois, & fille d'*Edme de Ponville*, Seigneur de Mailly, & de *Louife de Combault*, & petite nièce de *Robert de Ponville*, Chevalier des Ordres, le 31 Décembre 1583. De fon premier mariage il a eu:

1. FRANÇOIS, qui fuit;
2. FRANÇOISE, Chanoineffe & Comteffe de Remiremont, depuis femme de *Pomponne de Vienne*, Seigneur de Soligny.

Et du fecond lit il eut:

3. LOUIS, Seigneur de Mailly, Capitaine de Cavalerie, mort fans alliance;
4. CLAUDE-JEAN-BAPTISTE, reçu Chevalier de Malte, le 16 Juillet 1674, Capitaine de Cavalerie au Régiment de Bourgogne, tué à la bataille de Spire, en 1703;

C c

5. CHARLES-BLAISE, auffi Chevalier de Malte, reçu le 1er Avril 1676, & mort au fervice de fon Ordre, dans les guerres de la Morée ;

6. JEAN-PIERRE, auffi reçu Chevalier de Malte le 8 Novembre 1678;

7. NICOLAS, auffi reçu Chevalier de Malte le 16 Octobre 1683 ;

8. CATHERINE-ELÉONORE, Chanoineffe & Comteffe d'Efpinal, le 3 Novembre 1679, élue Doyenne du Chapitre au mois de Septembre 1708, & Adminiftratrice de ladite Abbaye en 1728;

9. Et LOUISE-FRANÇOISE, qui fit fes preuves pour Remiremont, & fut enfuite Comteffe & Chanoineffe d'Efpinal.

XII. FRANÇOIS LE BASCLE D'ARGENTEUIL, IIe du nom, Comte d'Epineuil, Seigneur de Pouy, Lieutenant-Colonel de Cavalerie du Régiment d'Efclainvilliers, par Brevet du 16 Décembre 1688, Chevalier de l'Ordre de Saint-Louis, s'allia, par contrat du 24 Mai 1689, avec *Anne-Elifabeth le Tenneur*, de laquelle eft venu pour fils unique :

XIII. JEAN-LOUIS LE BASCLE, Marquis d'Argenteuil, Comte d'Epineuil, Seigneur de Pouy, Lieutenant-Général des Provinces de Champagne & de Brie, par Brevet du 4 Septembre 1716, Gouverneur de la ville de Troyes, par le même Brevet, mort le 18 Décembre 1753, dans fa 61e année, en fon Château de Pouy en Champagne. Il avoit époufé, par contrat du 14 Novembre 1712, *Louife-Anne-Victoire de Rogres-de-Champignelles*, Dame de Villemaréchal, Saint-Ange, Chevrinvilliers, morte le 14 Février 1764, à Troyes, âgée de 69 ans, fille unique de *Louis-Charles, Comte de Rogres*, & de *Marie-Anne le Charron*. De cette alliance font venus :

1. JEAN-LOUIS-NICOLAS, qui fuit ;

2. JACQUES-FRANÇOIS, né le 21 Mars 1723, Chevalier de Malte, Capitaine de Cavalerie au Régiment de Fiennes en 1744, enfuite Exempt des Gardes-du-Corps du Roi, Compagnie de Villeroy, en 1755, & Meftre-de-Camp de Cavalerie en 1760 ;

3. Et LOUISE-ANNE-ELISABETH, née le 26 Octobre 1713, reçue Chanoineffe, & Comteffe de Remiremont, par acte du 28 Novembre 1726, enfuite mariée, le 29 Juillet 1738, à *Jofeph-Augufte de Chaftenay*, Comte de Lanty.

XIV. JEAN-LOUIS-NICOLAS LE BASCLE, Marquis d'Argenteuil, Comte d'Epineuil, Seigneur de Pouy, Villemaréchal, né le 19 Octobre 1714, Capitaine de Cavalerie au Régiment du Roi, par Brevet du 25 Mars 1734,

Lieutenant-Général des Provinces de Champagne & de Brie, Gouverneur de la ville de Troyes, par provifions de 1745; Chevalier de Saint-Louis en 1746, nommé à un Guidon de Gendarmerie le 14 Mars 1748, a époufé, le 12 Avril fuivant, *Marie-Angélique-Philippe le Veneur*, morte le 27 Janvier 1773, fille d'*Henri-Charles le Veneur*, & de *Marie-Catherine de Pardieu*, coufine iffue de germaine, d'*Anne-Gabrielle le Veneur*, Ducheffe de Châtillon. De ce mariage font venus :

1. JEAN-LOUIS-MARIE, né le 30 Novembre 1749, Officier dans le Corps des Carabiniers;

2. EUSTACHE-LOUIS-TANNEGUY, né le 10 Mars 1752, Chevalier de Malte de minorité;

3. HENRI-LOUIS-FRANÇOIS-PHILIPPE, né le 2 Décembre 1756, Chevalier de Malte de minorité;

4. MARIE-LOUISE-VICTOIRE, née le 7 Janvier 1751;

5. FLORENCE-HENRIETTE-MARIE-PHILIPPINE-VICTOIRE, née le 19 Novembre 1754;

6. Et ANNE-GABRIELLE, née le 5 Novembre 1759, brévetée Chanoineffe & Comteffe de Neuville-les-Dames.

Généalogie dreffée fur un *Mémoire* envoyé.

Les armes : *écartelé, au 1 de gueules, à trois fafces entées en ondes d'argent*, qui eft Rochechouart; *aux 2 & 3 d'azur, femé de fleurs-de-lys d'or*, qui eft Anjou-Méziers; *au 4 de gueules, à neuf macles d'or, accoftés en fafces, 3, 3 & 3*, qui eft Rohan; & fur le tout *de gueules, à trois macles d'argent, pofés 2 & 1*, qui eft Bafcle.

BASEMONT, en Dauphiné : *d'azur, à deux ferpens adoffés, tortillés & entrelaffés en triple fautoir d'or; au chef coufu de gueules, chargé d'une colombe d'argent, membrée d'or*.

BASIAN. Les Barons de BASIAN ont pour tige GASTON DE BOURBON, Seigneur de Bafian, quatrième fils de CHARLES, Bâtard de Bourbon, Baron de Caudes-Aigues, & de *Louife du Lyon*, qui époufa, le 25 Février 1534, *Sufanne Dupuis*.

N... DE BOURBON, Baron de Bafian, iffu de lui au VIe degré, s'eft marié au Diocèfe d'Auch, à la fin du mois d'Août 1725.

Les armes : *d'azur, à trois fleurs-de-lys d'or, à la bande de gueules & une barre d'or*.

BASIRE, Sieur de Boifguillaume, en Normandie, Généralité de Rouen, famille maintenue dans fa nobleffe, le 6 Juillet 1666. On trouve, dans le *Traité de la Nobleffe*, par la

Roque, pag. 459, Jean Basire, Maître Monnoyeur de Saint-Lo, qui n'avoit point dérogé par fa charge.

Les armes: *d'azur, à la bande ondée d'argent.*

BASIRE, Seigneur de Villodon, en Normandie, Généralité de Caen, famille annoblie en 1473: *d'azur, au pied de griffon d'or, onglé de même, & accompagné en flanc, au-deffus des griffes, de deux feuilles de même.*

BASLEVRIER: *de fable, au chef d'or, chargé de trois cornets de gueules, enguichés d'argent.*

BASNY: *d'or, à l'aigle de gueules, furmontée d'un lambel de trois pendans d'azur.*

* BASOCHES, Subdélégation de Falaife. La Baronie de Bafoches étoit, il y a plufieurs fiècles, poffédée par les Rois de France, qui en firent donation à la famille de Meffieurs de *Faucon,* Gentilshommes Ecoffois, après leur paffage & leur établiffement en France. Ils l'ont poffédée très-long-tems; & ayant fait perte de biens, elle fut vendue & paffa dans la Maifon de M. de *Vaffy,* qui la poffède encore aujourd'hui.

BASOUGES, à Tréguier: *d'azur, à trois écuffons d'argent, pofés 2 & 1.*

BASSAY-LONGECOURT: *d'argent, à trois quinte-feuilles de gueules, 2 & 1.*

BASSET, Seigneur de Normanville: *d'or, au chef emmanché de trois pièces de gueules, au franc-canton d'hermines.*

BASSOMPIERRE, dans le Barrois, Maifon qui a donné un Chevalier des Ordres du Roi, Colonel des Suiffes & Maréchal de France dans François de Bassompierre, né le 22 Avril 1579; l'homme qui avoit le plus de brillant & de vivacité d'efprit, duquel on a des Mémoires qui contiennent l'Hiftoire de fa vie & de ce qui s'eft paffé de plus remarquable à la Cour de France depuis 1598 jufqu'à fon entrée à la Baftille le 25 Février 1631, d'où il ne fortit qu'après la mort du Cardinal de *Richelieu,* le 19 Janvier 1643. Il mourut d'apoplexie le 12 Octobre 1646.

L'*Hiftoire des Grands-Officiers de la Couronne* commence la Généalogie de cette Maifon par

I. Olery de Dompierre, Sire de Bassompierre, qui reconnut du confentement d'*Agnès,* fa femme, le lundi d'avant l'Afcenfion 1292, être homme-lige, & avoir repris d'*Henri,*

Comte de Bar, après le Duc de Lorraine, fa forte maifon de Baffompierre, voulant que s'il avoit deux enfans mâles, celui qui tiendroit Baffompierre, fut homme-lige du Comte. Il eut:

1. Simon, qui fuit;
2. Et Jean.

II. Simon, Sire de Bassompierre, reprit auffi d'*Henri,* Comte de Bar, au mois d'Avril 1293, fa forte maifon de Baffompierre. Il étoit mort en 1333. Il laiffa de *Jeanne:*

1. Olery, qui fuit;
2. Et Jean.

III. Olery, IIe du nom, Sire de Bassompierre, émancipé lorfque fa mère fit hommage au Comte de Bar en 1333, ne vivoit plus en 1352. Il laiffa de fa femme, dont on ignore le nom:

IV. Simon, IIe du nom, Sire de Bassompierre, qui étoit fous la tutelle de fon oncle en 1352. Il fit hommage au Duc de Bar, le 16 Juillet 1393, de fa fortereffe de Baffompierre. Il fut père de:

V. Geoffroy, Ier du nom, Sire de Bassompierre & de Longchamp, qui vendit le 20 Novembre 1403, avec fa femme, au Duc de Bar, tout ce qu'il avoit au ban & finage de Longchamp, qu'il tenoit en Fief de l'Evêque de Verdun. Il fut, en 1416, un des Chevaliers de l'Ordre de Chevalerie ou Confrérie, formée par plufieurs Gentilshommes Lorrains. Il eut de fon mariage avec *Jeanne Rincxette :*

1. Jean, qui fuit;
2. Et Simon, marié à *Alix de Baudricourt,* fœur du Maréchal de France de ce nom, & fille de *Robert de Baudricourt* & d'*Alix de Chambley,* dont il ne paroît pas qu'il ait eu des enfans, tous les biens de la Maifon de *Baudricourt* étant paffés dans celle d'*Amboife,* par le mariage de la nièce du Maréchal & de ladite *Alix,* fa fœur. Voyez BAUDRICOURT.

VI. Jean, Sire de Bassompierre, fit hommage de fa Terre au Duc de Bar le 16 Février 1423. Il eut part à la Confédération faite le 19 Septembre 1435, entre plufieurs Seigneurs Lorrains pour le rétabliffement de la Paix publique. Il époufa 1° *Jeanne d'Orne,* fille de *Jean* & de *Gillette de Levaveline,* dont il n'eut point d'enfans; & 2° *Jeanne de Puligny,* fille de *Perrin* & de *Catherine d'Harouel,* laquelle, étant veuve, fit le 2 Mai 1456, foi & hommage au nom de fes enfans à RENÉ, Roi de Jérufalem, Duc de Lorraine & de Bar, de fa maifon forte de Baffompierre. Les enfans fortis de ce mariage furent :

1. GEOFFROY, qui fuit ;
2. HERMENGARDE, femme de *Louis de Saucy ;*
3. N..., Religieufe, puis Abbeffe à Trèves ;
4. Et MARGUERITE.

VII. GEOFFROY, IIe du nom, Sire DE BAS-SOMPIERRE & d'Harouel, Chevalier, Confeiller & Chambellan de RENÉ II, Duc de Lorraine & de Bar, accompagna, en 1477, ce Prince à la bataille qui fe donna la veille des Rois devant Nancy, contre le Duc de BOURGOGNE. En 1489, il conduifit fous fa bannière une Compagnie de Gafcons aventuriers, & fit pour le fervice du Duc, des courfes jufqu'aux portes de Metz ; il fut du nombre des Seigneurs Lorrains, auxquels le Duc ANTOINE adreffa fon Ordonnance du 15 Mai 1511, pour gouverner le Pays en fon abfence. Il mourut en 1524, & eut de *Philippe Wiffe,* fille de *Vautrain,* Seigneur de Gerbeviller, & de *Claude de Vautrouville* ou *Watronville,* felon le Père Anfelme :

1. CHRISTOPHE, qui fuit ;
2. Et YOLANDE, mariée à *Antoine de Ville.*

VIII. CHRISTOPHE, Sire DE BASSOMPIERRE & d'Harouel, Ier du nom, fe diftingua d'abord par fon adreffe dans les joûtes que fit la Nobleffe des environs chez le Comte DE SARBRUCH, lorfqu'il fut vifité par le Duc NICOLAS, au commencement de l'année 1472. *Dufay* & lui furent les deux vainqueurs. Il époufa, en 1494, *Jeanne de Ville-fur-Illon,* fille de *Colignon,* Sire de Ville, Bailli de Vofges, & de *Mahaut de Ville,* dont il eut :

1. MAXIMILIEN, marié à une Comteffe de *Leiningen* ou *Linange,* dont il eut un fils nommé THÉODORIC, mort fans poftérité ;
2. THIERRY, Grand-Prévôt de Mayence, & Chanoine de Wurtzbourg ;
3. FRANÇOIS, qui fuit ;
4. YOLANDE, mariée à *Louis des Armoifes,* Seigneur d'Autcey ;
5. N..., mariée 1° au Comte de *Vefterbourg ;* 2° au Seigneur de *Vautru-de-Bourgogne ;* & 3° au Seigneur de *Port-fur-Seille ;*
6. Et N..., Dame & Chanoineffe de Remiremont.

IX. FRANÇOIS, Sire DE BASSOMPIERRE, d'Harouel & de Remonville, dit *le Baron d'Harouel, Bailli de Vofges, & Chef du Confeil du Cardinal de Lorraine,* fut l'un des Exécuteurs du teftament d'ANTOINE, Duc de Lor-

raine. Le Roi de France HENRI III s'étant emparé de la Lorraine pendant la minorité du Duc CHARLES III, qu'il emmena en France pour l'y faire élever, FRANÇOIS DE BASSOMPIERRE fe retira vers l'Empereur CHARLES-QUINT, dont il avoit été Page. Il fut Colonel des Lanfquenets en plufieurs guerres, puis Gentilhomme de la Chambre & Capitaine de la Garde Allemande. Après que l'Empereur CHARLES-QUINT eut remis fes Etats entre les mains du Roi fon fils, FRANÇOIS DE BASSOMPIERRE fe retira auprès du Duc d'*Arfchot.* Il fit fon teftament le 16 Avril 1543. Il avoit époufé, par contrat du 6 Septembre 1529, *Marguerite de Dompmartin* ou *Dammartin,* dit Moréri, fille de *Guillaume,* Baron de Fontenay, & d'*Anne de Neufchâtel-Montagu.* Il laiffa de fon mariage :

1. CLAUDE-ANTOINE, Gouverneur & Bailli de Vofges & de l'Evêché de Metz, marié à *Anne du Châtelet,* que le Père Anfelme nomme *Barbe,* fille de *Perrin,* Seigneur de Dueilly, & de *Bonne Baudoche,* dont il n'eut qu'une fille nommée GABRIELLE, mariée à *Erard de Livron,* Seigneur de Bourbonne, Grand-Maître de Lorraine, dont plufieurs enfans.
2. BERNARD, Colonel d'un Régiment de Lanfquenets, mort à Vienne au retour du fiège de Ziguel en Hongrie, fans laiffer d'enfans de fon époufe, héritière de la Maifon de *Maugiron* & d'*Imonblery ;*
3. CHRISTOPHE, qui fuit ;
4. YOLANDE, Abbeffe d'Epinal ;
5. MARGUERITE, mariée à *Jacob de Raville,* Comte d'Afperg, Seigneur d'Ausbourg, Maréchal héréditaire de Luxembourg ;
6. Et ANNE, nommée par le Père Anfelme, ANNE-MARGUERITE, mariée 1° à *Gafpard de Nettancourt,* fils de *Georges,* Seigneur de Vaubecourt, & d'*Anne d'Hauffonville ;* & 2° par contrat du 27 Avril 1566, à *Jean de Cuffigny,* Seigneur de Viage, Baron de Lézines, duquel elle eut une fille Abbeffe d'Epinal, & un fils marié à la fœur du Marquis de *Marcouffay,* qui a laiffé trois fils.

X. CHRISTOPHE, IIe du nom, Baron DE BASSOMPIERRE, Seigneur d'Harouel & de Baudricourt, Grand-Maître-d'Hôtel & Chef des Finances de Lorraine, Colonel de 1500 Reiftres, entretenus pour le fervice du Roi en 1570, remit en 1585 fes Etats & fes penfions au Roi HENRI III, pour entrer dans le parti de la Ligue, qu'il fervit avec zèle. Il fe joignit en 1589, avec quatre Cornettes de Reiftres, au Duc de Mayenne, &, après la conver-

fion d'HENRI IV, il procura les Traités de
Paix faits, le premier, à Saint-Germain-en-
Laye le 16 Novembre 1594, l'autre à Folem-
bray au mois de Décembre 1595, entre le
Roi & le Duc de Lorraine CHARLES III. Il
fonda en cette même année les Minimes de
Nancy. Il épousa, en 1572, *Louise le Picart*,
fille de *Georges*, Seigneur de Radeval, & de
Louise de la Motte-Bléquin, dont :

1. FRANÇOIS, IIe du nom, Chevalier des Ordres du Roi, Maréchal de France, né le 22
Avril 1579, qui mourut le 12 Octobre
1646, laissant deux fils naturels : N......
DE BASSOMPIERRE, Seigneur de la Tour, né
d'une Princesse, mort peu de tems après
fon père, & LOUIS DE BASSOMPIERRE, né de
Marie-Charlotte de Balʒac-d'Entragues,
qui fut Evêque de Saintes & premier Aumônier de PHILIPPE de France, Duc
d'Orléans, mort le 1er Juillet 1676;
2. JEAN, mort sans postérité, d'une blessure
qu'il reçut devant Oftende ;
3. GEORGES-AFRICAIN, qui suit ;
4. DIANE, morte à Rouen en 1584, âgée de 10
ans ;
5. HENRIETTE, première femme, en 1603, de
Timoléon d'Espinay, Seigneur de Saint-
Luc, Maréchal de France ;
6. Et CATHERINE, mariée à *Tanneguy le Veneur*, Comte de Tillières & de Carouges,
Chambellan de la Reine de la Grande-Bretagne, & Ambassadeur en Angleterre, dont
plusieurs fils & filles.

XI. GEORGES-AFRICAIN DE BASSOMPIERRE,
Marquis de Remonville, Seigneur du Châtelet, Baudricourt, Gouverneur & Bailli de
Vosges, Grand-Ecuyer de Lorraine, mort en
1632, avoit épousé, le 21 Juin 1610, *Henriette de Tornielle*, fille de *Charles-Emmanuel*, Comte de Tornielle, Grand-Maître &
Chef des Finances de Lorraine, & d'*Anne du
Châtelet*, Dame d'honneur de la Duchesse
de LORRAINE, dont :

1. ANNE-FRANÇOIS, Marquis de BASSOMPIERRE
& de Remonville, Grand-Ecuyer de Lorraine, Bailli de Vosges, & Général de l'Artillerie de l'Empereur, mort sans alliance;
2. CHARLES, qui suit ;
3. GASTON-JEAN-BAPTISTE, auteur de la branche de BAUDRICOURT, rapportée ci-après ;
4. MARIE-YOLANDE-BARBE, mariée par contrat
du 7 Avril 1633, à *Alexandre-Timoléon
d'Halwin*, Seigneur de Vailly, Capitaine
des Gardes de GASTON DE FRANCE, Duc
d'Orléans ; leur fille *Josephe-Barbe d'Halwin* fut mariée, le 29 Octobre 1688, avec

Ferdinand-François-Joseph de Croy, Duc
d'Havré ;
5. MARGUERITE-ANNE, Abbesse d'Epinal, &
depuis mariée, en 1639, à *Charles*, Marquis
d'*Haraucourt* & de Faulquemont, Comte
de Dalem, Maréchal de Lorraine, Général
de la Cavalerie de l'Electeur de Bavière,
& Gouverneur de Marsal ;
6. Et HENRIETTE, ou NICOLE-HENRIETTE,
Dame & Secrète de Remiremont.

XII. CHARLES, Marquis de BASSOMPIERRE,
Baron de Dammartin, Colonel d'un Régiment
dans les Troupes de Lorraine, & Maréchal-
de-Camp, fut fait prisonnier à la défaite du
Duc CHARLES DE LORRAINE, par le Duc de
Saxe-Weimar, le 15 Octobre 1638. Il étoit
mort avant 1665, & avoit épousé, en 1644,
Henriette d'Haraucourt-Chambley, fille de
Ferry, Seigneur de Chambley & de Dom-
bale, dont il laissa :

1. ANNE-FRANÇOIS-JOSEPH, qui suit ;
2. CHARLES, Marquis DE BASSOMPIERRE, Général de Cavalerie pour le service de l'Empereur LÉOPOLD, son Chambellan, & depuis
Maréchal de Lorraine & Barrois, Gouverneur & Bailli de Vosges, qui, de *Marie-
Louise de Beauvau*, fille de *Louis*, Marquis de Beauvau, Capitaine des Gardes de
S. A. R. LÉOPOLD Ier, Duc de Lorraine &
de Bar, n'a laissé qu'un fils mort sans postérité ;
Et trois filles, mortes à Nancy, Religieuses à
la Visitation.

XIII. ANNE-FRANÇOIS-JOSEPH, Marquis DE
BASSOMPIERRE & de Remonville, Baron du
Châtelet, épousa *Diane de Beauvau*, fille de
Louis, Marquis de Beauvau, Capitaine des
Gardes du Duc LÉOPOLD, & d'*Anne de Li-
gny*, sa seconde femme, dont :

1. ANNE-FRANÇOIS-JOSEPH, IIe du nom, qui a
servi quelque tems en qualité de Capitaine
au Régiment du Roi, Infanterie, & est mort
le 20 Mai 1734, à Paris, âgé d'environ 48
ans, retiré dans une maison du Faubourg
Saint-Antoine, vivant dans une très-grande
dévotion, & pratiquant de grandes auste-
rités, sans laisser d'enfans. Il avoit épousé,
le 3 Juin 1733, *Louise d'Oglettorp*, Demoiselle Angloise, sœur de la Marquise de *Me-
ʒières*, & fille de *Théophile*, Chevalier, Ba-
ronet, Seigneur de Weftbrook, Drauhold
& Godalming dans le Comté de Surry, Grand-
Ecuyer des Rois d'Angleterre CHARLES II
& JACQUES II, Major-Général de leurs Armées, & d'*Eléonore Wal-de-Rathkenny*.
Il a laissé pour héritières ses deux sœurs;
2. LOUISE-LUCIE, mariée à *François-Emma-*

nuel, Marquis de *Ligny*, Seigneur du Pleſ-
ſis-Billy, Meſtre-de-Camp de Cavalerie,
Sous-Lieutenant des Gendarmes d'Anjou;
3. Et FRANÇOISE-LOUISE, morte le 25 Novembre 1758. Elle avoit épouſé, en 1717, *François-Joſeph de Choiſeul*, Marquis de Stainville. Voyez CHOISEUL.

BRANCHE
des Seigneurs DE BAUDRICOURT.

XII. GASTON-JEAN-BAPTISTE, Marquis de
BASSOMPIERRE & de Baudricourt, Gouverneur
& Bailli de Voſges, Lieutenant-Général des
Armées du Duc de Lorraine, CHARLES IV,
troiſième fils de GEORGES-AFRICAIN & d'*Henriette de Tornielle*, ſe diſtingua particulièrement à la bataille de Binghen au Palatinat,
où il commandoit le corps de réſerve avec lequel, ayant arrêté les efforts des ennemis &
donné lieu au reſte de l'armée de ſe rallier, il
procura le gain de la bataille. Il épouſa *Henriette de Rollin*, fille d'*Henri*, Conſeiller
d'Etat du Duc CHARLES IV, & Surintendant
de ſes troupes, & de *Jeanne Oris-de-Jubain-
ville*, dont il eut:

1. FRANÇOIS-CHARLES, Meſtre-de-Camp de Cavalerie pour le ſervice du Roi, Chambellan
de S. A. R. LÉOPOLD Ier, qui, de ſon mariage
avec*Marie-Madeleine*,Comteſſe du*Hamal*,
Chanoineſſe de Maubeuge, n'a laiſſé qu'une
fille, HENRIETTE-CHARLOTTE de BASSOM-
PIERRE, mariée, le 25 Février 1728, à *Charles-Marie*, Marquis de *Choiſeul;*
2. HENRI-DOMINIQUE, Chambellan du Duc
LÉOPOLD, & Guidon des Chevaux-Légers
de ſa Garde, mort à Nancy en 1721, ſans
poſtérité;
3. JEAN-CLAUDE, qui ſuit;
4. CHARLES-LÉOPOLD, Enſeigne de Vaiſſeau,
mort à Toulon ſans poſtérité le 6 Juillet
1709;
5. N........ morte Religieuſe au Couvent de
Charmes;
6. CATHERINE, morte à Nancy le 25 Août
1734, ſans avoir été mariée;
7. FRANÇOISE-THÉRÈSE, morte au Château
d'Andrezel en Brie, le 1er Mars 1749,
âgée de 73 ans. Elle avoit épouſé, à Paris
le 15 Juin 1712, *Jean-Baptiſte-Louis Picon*, Seigneur & Marquis d'Andrezel &
de Mayanne, Secrétaire du Cabinet du
Roi & des Commandemens de M. le Dauphin, Commiſſaire-Ordonnateur dans les
Armées d'Italie, mort à Conſtantinople
le 26 Mars 1727, Ambaſſadeur du Roi
à la Porte, âgé de 64 ans. Ils ont laiſſé de

leur mariage, deux fils & une fille. *Jean-
Baptiſte-Louis Picon* eut un fils naturel,
N....... *Ponci-de-Nenville*, Prêtre & Prédicateur, qui mourut le 26 Avril 1727, de
la petite vérole à Paris, à l'âge de 30 ans
ou environ. *Ponci* étoit l'anagrame de *Picon*, nom de la famille du Marquis d'Andrezel;
8. Et ELISABETH-THÉRÈSE, mariée à *Jean-
François-Louis Picon-de-Granchamp*, Capitaine au Régiment de Cambréſis, dont
deux fils & une fille.

XIII. JEAN-CLAUDE, Marquis de BASSOM-
PIERRE, Baudricourt, Remonville, &c., Ca-
pitaine-Lieutenantcommandant les Chevaux-
Légers de la Garde des Ducs de Lorraine
LÉOPOLD Ier & FRANÇOIS III, depuis Empe-
reur ſous le nom de FRANÇOIS Ier, & leur
Chambellan, épouſa, le 15 Janvier 1711,
Jeanne-Eliſabeth de Nettancourt, fille d'*Ed-
mond*, Comte de Nettancourt, Baron de Fré-
nel, & de *Marie le Joli*, Fille d'honneur de
S. A. R. MADAME, Ducheſſe de Lorraine,
dont:

1. LÉOPOLD-CLÉMENT, qui ſuit;
2. & 3. Deux garçons morts en bas âge;
4. & 5. MARIE-LOUISE & HENRIETTE-CHAR-
LOTTE, Chanoineſſes à Pouſſey.

XIV. LÉOPOLD-CLÉMENT, Marquis de BAS-
SOMPIERRE, né en 1715, Meſtre-de-Camp de
Cavalerie, & Enſeigne de Gendarmerie, Brigadier des Armées du Roi à la promotion du
31 Décembre 1747, Chambellan du Roi de
Pologne feu STANISLAS Ier, Duc de Lorraine
& de Bar, épouſa, le 21 Décembre 1734, *Charlotte de Beauvau*, Abbeſſe de Pouſſey, fille
de *Marc de Beauvau-Craon*, Marquis d'Harouel & autres lieux, Prince du Saint-Empire, Grand d'Eſpagne de la première claſſe,
& Chevalier de la Toiſon-d'Or, & d'*Anne-
Marguerite de Ligniville*, dont:

1. MARC-LOUIS FRANÇOIS, né à Nancy le 5 Novembre 1735;
2. CHRISTOPHE-FRANÇOIS, né à Nancy le 1er
Avril 1739;
3. STANISLAS-CATHERINE, né à Lunéville le 16
Septembre 1741, mort le 1er Octobre 1741;
4. Et ANNE-MARGUERITE, née à Nancy le 25
Octobre 1736, morte le 17 Avril 1762, à
Lunéville. Elle avoit épouſé, par contrat du
4 Juillet 1761, *Jacques-Joſeph*, Marquis de
Boiſſe. (Voy. *Grands Officiers de la Couronne*, tome VII, & Moréri, édition de 1759.)

Les armes: *d'argent, à trois chevrons de
gueules, & une couronne murale.*

BASSOMPIERRE, Seigneur de Nuife-mont: *écartelé, aux 1 & 4 d'argent, au lion de fable, couronné d'or; aux 2 & 3 d'a-zur, au lion d'argent, lampaffé de gueules.*

◊ BASTARD. On lit dans le *Tréfor généa-logique* de Dom Caffiaux, Religieux Bénédic-tin de la Congrégation de Saint-Maur, que cette famille noble eft originaire de Bretagne. On préfume qu'une branche, depuis la fin du XIVᵉ fiècle, alla s'établir à Fleurance, capi-tale du Comté de Gaure. Elle étoit repréfen-tée alors par THOMAS DE BASTARD, qui fuit, & GUY DE BASTARD, qu'on préfume frère de THO-MAS. Il fut un de ceux qui furent envoyés pour figner le traité de paix entre le Roi d'Angleterre & le Comte de Flandres en 1371. Voyez Rymer, tom. V & VI, pag. 676 & 716.

THOMAS DE BASTARD, Chevalier, demanda, le 24 Juin 1350, la permiffion au Roi d'An-gleterre de paffer dans fes Etats pour termi-ner un duel. Il eut pour fils:

PIERRE, qui fuit;

Et ROBINET.

PIERRE DE BASTARD, Damoifeau, vivoit en 1378, fuivant un extrait des Chartes du Roi. Il confentit, le 11 Juin 1457, un acte, comme procureur fondé de noble ROBINET DE BAS-TARD, fon frère, en faveur d'Antoine de Cha-bannes, Comte de Dammartin, Seigneur de Blanquefort, Confeiller du Roi, Chambellan, Grand-Pannetier & Sénéchal de Carcaffonne & de Béziers. L'Extrait original eft au cabi-net des Religieux Bénédictins de St.-Martin-des-Champs à Paris.

On lui donne pour enfans:

CHARLES, qui fuit;

Et LOUISE DE BASTARD, mariée à *Payen le Taut*, Ecuyer, Seigneur de Semenges, dont:

    JEANNE LE TAUT, mariée à *Jean de Vi-gnerot*, Seigneur de Pont-Courlay, d'où fortent les Maifons des Ducs de *Richelieu* & d'*Aiguillon*.

CHARLES DE BASTARD, Ecuyer, Seigneur de Terland en Berry, Maître-d'Hôtel du Roi, fut nommé Commiffaire pour paffer les mon-tres & revues des gens de guerre, par Lettres de Pierre, Duc de Bourbonnois & d'Auver-gne, en date du 13 Juillet 1495; & en confé-quence il paffa, le 21 Juillet 1495, près la ville de Sufe en Piémont, la revue de la com-pagnie de M. de Graville, Amiral de France & Chambellan du Roi. Ceci eft extrait du re-giftre des rôles des montres, dépofé au cabi-net des Religieux Bénédictins de Saint-Mar-tin-des-Champs. Il eut pour fils:

PIERRE DE BASTARD, auteur de la première branche.

Cette famille noble de BASTARD s'eft divi-fée en plufieurs branches, dont nous allons donner la filiation, d'après l'inventaire des titres produits devant les Commiffaires-Gé-néraux députés fur ce fait de la Nobleffe, dont l'original eft au Tréfor des Archives du Lou-vre, fur lequel eft intervenu arrêt contradic-toire du Confeil d'Etat du Roi rendu à Saint-Germain-en-Laye, le 25 Novembre 1671, qui maintient JEAN DE BASTARD, Capitaine d'In-fanterie, & fon neveu JEAN DE BASTARD, Con-feiller du Roi & Commiffaire député pour la réformation des domaines de Sa Majefté, leur poftérité née & à naître en légitime mariage dans la qualité de Noble & d'Ecuyer, & or-donne qu'ils jouiront de tous les privilèges, honneurs & exemptions dont jouiffent les Gentilshommes du Royaume.

PREMIÈRE BRANCHE.

I. PIERRE DE BASTARD, fils de CHARLES, men-tionné ci-deffus, étoit Archer de la Compa-gnie de Gamaches, à la revue paffée en 1494 & de celle de M. d'Efpiry, en la revue paffée en la ville d'Aft en Italie, le 8 Juin 1496, fuivant un extrait tiré des montres dépofées à la Bi-bliothèque du Roi, & délivrées par M. la Cour, alors Garde de ce cabinet. Il fut nommé Gou-verneur du Comté de Gaure vers la fin du XIVᵉ, ou au commencement du XVᵉ fiècle, puifqu'il en prend le titre dans un acte de vente, en date du 12 Août 1501, d'une mai-fon en faveur des Confuls de Fleurance. On ignore le tems de fa mort, mais on préfume qu'il mourut à Fleurance vers 1531, époque où il fonda un *obit* dans l'Eglife paroiffiale de ladite ville. Dans fon contrat de mariage du 8 Septembre 1505, retenu par *Montibus*, avec *Geralde de Foiffin*, fille de *Jean de Foiffin*, Ecuyer, Seigneur du Bofq, Lieute-nant-Général du fiège de Lectoure, il fe dit fils de CHARLES DE BASTARD, Seigneur de Ter-land. Il eut de fon mariage:

    1. CLAUDE, qui fuit;

    2. JEAN, auteur d'une branche rapportée en fon rang;

    3. PIERRE, dont on ne connoît que le nom;

    4. ODIETTE, qui, affiftée de fon mari, renonça

à tous droits, voies & actions qu'elle pouvoit prétendre à l'hérédité de son père & de sa mère, en faveur de CLAUDE & JEAN DE BASTARD, ses frères, moyennant les prix & somme de 500 liv. tournois, non compris les habits nuptiaux, par transaction passée le 20 Juin 1541, devant *Margoet*, Notaire Royal de Fleurance;

5. Et DOUCE DE BASTARD, mariée à noble *Jacques de Sarta*, Sieur de Las Laques.

II. CLAUDE DE BASTARD, Seigneur du Bosq, homme d'armes dans la compagnie du Duc de Guise, suivant la revue passée à Vauclufe en 1532, donna devant Pierre Carnu, Commissaire député par le Sénéchal d'Armagnac, le 8 Mars 1544, déclaration des biens nobles ou fiefs qu'il possédoit: en conséquence, il fut taxé pour la onzième partie d'un Chevau-Léger pour l'arrière-ban, comme il conste de l'extrait de ladite déclaration, ou dénombrement, dont l'original est aux Archives du bureau des Finances de la Généralité de Montauban. Il prend la qualité de Capitaine dans différens actes, & notamment dans un achat qu'il fit le 22 Mars 1553. Le Roi FRANÇOIS Ier l'avoit gratifié, en 1540, pour ses services rendus dans les guerres de Piémont, d'une chaîne de 100 liv. d'or. Le Brevet est au cabinet des Religieux de Saint-Martin-des-Champs. On présume qu'il mourut au service vers 1557 ou 1558. Il avoit épousé, par articles sous seing-privé, le 10 Janvier 1535, *Marie de Campan*, fille de *Pierre de Campan*, Ecuyer, Seigneur de Sarros en Artarac, & donna quittance, le 15 Mai 1536, à son beau-père, de la somme de 400 liv. tournois, pour partie de la constitution de la dot. *Marie de Campan*, devenue veuve, constitua pour son procureur, fondé par acte du 3 Septembre 1590, Me Tartanac, Procureur en la Cour du Sénéchal d'Armagnac, siège de la Vicomté de Lectoure, à l'effet de défendre son fils aîné PIERRE, absent, étant à la guerre, sur certaine augmentation donnée à sondit fils par Me Fabri, Conseiller audit siège. Elle testa le 2 Juillet 1592, & ordonna par une clause de son testament olographe, que son corps seroit enterré dans la chapelle nommée de BASTARD. Elle eut pour enfans:

1. PIERRE, qui suit;
2. DOMINIQUE, qui épousa *Anne de Mons*, fille de noble *Jean de Mons*, Sieur d'Ardennes, dont il eut:

MARIE;

FRANÇOISE & ANNE DE BASTARD.

3. Et AMANIEU DE BASTARD, qui mourut au service sans postérité.

III. PIERRE DE BASTARD, IIe du nom, Seigneur du Bosq, partagea avec JEAN DE BASTARD, Ecuyer, son oncle, une métairie, nommée les Oliviers, située dans la juridiction de Fleurance. Il fut homme d'armes de la compagnie de M. de Monluc, suivant un certificat de ce Seigneur du 30 Mai 1568. Ses talens pour le service militaire, & son attachement pour le parti que le Roi de Navarre soutenoit, lui mérita, de la part de ce Prince, d'être traité d'*ami* dans la lettre qu'il lui écrivit le 24 Mars 1576; titre flatteur pour un sujet, surtout lorsqu'il est donné par un Souverain en état de l'apprécier. Cette lettre finit par ces mots écrits de la main du Roi: *Votre bon ami*, HENRI. Il est à présumer que PIERRE DE BASTARD, IIe du nom, mourut jeune au service dans les guerres qui troublèrent ce siècle, vers 1590. Il avoit épousé *Bernalde Delpuech*, qui, étant veuve, fut contrainte en 1610, par Me Larrieux, Curé & Recteur de la ville de Fleurance, à payer 8 liv. de rente pour un *obit* que noble CLAUDE DE BASTARD, Capitaine, père de son mari, avoit fondé par son testament le 14 Septembre 1557. Elle étoit fille de noble *Bernard Delpuech* ou *Dupuy*, Seigneur de la Barthe. Ils eurent pour enfans:

1. NICOLAS, qui suit;
2. DOMINIQUE, qui épousa *Charlotte de Perès*, dont il eut:

MARIE, mariée à noble *Arnaud Merlin*, Ecuyer, Capitaine;
Et JEANNE, femme de noble *Jean de Maras*.

3. JEAN, Ecclésiastique, nommé Prieur de la chapelle St.-Jean-Donase, *aliàs* d'Abbasse, dite Pitampoy, sur la nomination faite par NICOLAS DE BASTARD, son frère;
4. Autre JEAN, auteur du troisième rameau de la première branche, rapporté ci-après;
5. ANNE, mariée à Me *Antoine de Lucas*, Procureur du Roi au Sénéchal de Lectoure;
6. Et JEANNE DE BASTARD, femme de noble *Antoine de Pons*.

IV. NICOLAS DE BASTARD, Seigneur du Bosq, fut homme d'armes, servit à cheval dans la Compagnie de M. le Dauphin, & se trouva à la revue faite près Conches en Normandie le 20 Octobre 1606; quitta le parti des armes pour embrasser celui de la robe. Il vivoit encore en 1652, puisqu'il obtint conjointement avec Jean de Bastard, fon frère, Capitaine du Prince de Conty, une fauve-garde & exemption de logement de gens de guerre, en date du 19 Février 1652, après avoir juftifié leur qualité de Gentilhomme. On ignore l'époque de fa mort. Il réfulte, de la procuration confentie par *Bernarde del Puech*, fa mère, à l'effet de l'infinuation de la donation qu'elle lui fit lors de fon contrat de mariage paffé par *Lormand*, Notaire de Fleurance, le 1er Octobre 1618, qu'il époufa *Jeanne de Rébéfies*, fille de noble *Sébaftien de Rébéfies*, Seigneur de la Rouquette. Ses enfans furent :

1. Jean, qui fuit ;
2. Dominique, Seigneur de St.-Denis-fur-Garonne, auteur de la feconde branche rapportée plus loin ;
3. Antoine, qui embraffa l'état Eccléfiaftique, & fut Chanoine-Infirmier du Chapitre de Saint-Orens d'Auch, enfuite Abbé & Prieur d'Eauze ;
4. Et Joseph de Bastard, Gendarme, mort jeune.

V. Jean de Bastard, Ier du nom, fut nommé Commiffaire du Roi à la réformation des domaines de Sa Majefté, par commiffion datée des 10 Octobre 1667, 21 Avril 1668, & 3 Mars 1673. Il obtint fon relax par Arrêt du Confeil d'Etat du Roi, contradictoire avec le traitant, le 25 Novembre 1671, tefta le 1er Avril 1676 & mourut quelques mois après. Il avoit époufé, par contrat du 10 Juillet 1644, retenu par *Lormand*, Notaire de Fleurance, Marie de Bastard, fa parente, du confentement de fon père & de fa mère. Il eut :

1. Antoine, qui fuit ;
2. Jean, Abbé & Prieur d'Eauze, qui tefta le 6 Juillet 1688 ;
3. Gaspard, Gendarme, enfuite Cornette au Régiment de la Valette, mort jeune au fervice ;
4. Autre Antoine, Prêtre, Chanoine-Infirmier du chapitre de St.-Orens d'Auch ;
5. Et Françoise de Bastard, mariée à Mre *Jean de Larrieu*, Lieutenant principal.

VI. Antoine de Bastard, né le 19 Novembre 1654, tefta le 23 Novembre 1722, inftitua pour héritier fon fils aîné, réduifit fes autres enfans à une légitime de 3000 liv. chacun, & mourut le 19 Septembre 1735. Ses enfans procédèrent à l'ouverture de fon teftament le 22 Septembre 1735. Il avoit époufé Demoifelle *Anne de la Caze*, fille de noble *Bernard de la Caze*, dont il eut :

1. Jean, qui fuit ;

2. Dominique, Chanoine & Archi-Prêtre de l'Eglife de Sos, Métropolitain de l'Archevêque d'Auch ;
3. Louis, Sous-Lieutenant au Régiment de Foix le 1er Juillet 1703, Lieutenant le 18 Octobre 1705, Capitaine au même Régiment le 14 Novembre 1706, bleffé à la défenfe de Lille en 1708, à celle de Bouchain en 1711, créé Chevalier de Saint-Louis en 1731, retiré du fervice, à caufe de fes bleffures, en 1735 ; mort en 1773 ;
4. Jacques, mort jeune au fervice ;
5. Jean-Gaspard, Chanoine & Archidiacre de Lectoure, Vicaire-Général du Diocèfe pendant 50 ans, obtint une penfion de 1200 liv. fur l'Evêché de Couzerans, & mourut le 8 Février 1773 ;
6. Dominique, Chanoine le Saint-Orens d'Auch ;
7. Et Thérèse de Bastard, mariée à Meffire *Jean d'Efpons*.

VII. Jean de Bastard, IIe du nom, baptifé le 7 Août 1680, dans l'Eglife Paroiffiale de Fleurance, Comté de Gaure, fut émancipé le 9 Juillet 1700, tefta le 14 Juillet 1751, & mourut le 16 Août 1751. Il a oit époufé, le 23 Février 1710, acte retenu par *Limoufin*, Notaire Royal à Fleurance, Demoifelle *Louife de Goudin*, fille de Meffire *Jean-Pierre de Goudin*, Confeiller du Roi en l'Election de Lomagne, affifté de fes père & mère, parens & amis. Il a eu de fon mariage :

1. Antoine, qui fuit ;
2. Jean-Pierre, Comte d'Eftang, Seigneur de Cantiran, rapporté après la poftérité de fon frère aîné ;
3. Autre Antoine, Capitaine au Régiment de Foix, Chevalier de Saint-Louis, qui a fervi près de 25 ans, a été bleffé plufieurs fois, a perdu un bras à la journée du 10 Août 1746, d'un boulet de canon, dans l'action où le Général Gotta perdit 6000 hommes, & fut obligé de repaffer en défordre le Tidon. Cette bleffure l'obligea de quitter le fervice 3 ans après ; il obtint 700 liv. de penfion, & mourut le 16 Janvier 1780 ;
4. Et Jean-Gaspard de Bastard, rapporté après fes frères.

VIII. Antoine de Bastard, IIIe du nom, Ecuyer, Seigneur de Bartère, baptifé le 7 Octobre 1710, a tefté le 20 Août 1771, & inftitué fon fils unique, héritier général univerfel ; il fubftitua fes biens à fes quatre filles, eft mort le 8 Juillet 1773. Il avoit époufé, acte paffé par maître *Moncaffin*, Notaire de Touloufe, le 18 Novembre 1732, noble *Hé-*

lène de Nogeroles dè la Mothe, fille de noble *Jean de Nogeroles*, & de *Marie de Larroquau*, affifté de fes père, frères, parens & amis. Il a laiffé :

1. JEAN-JOSEPH DE BASTARD, né le 2 Décembre 1743, qui n'étoit pas marié en 1780;
2. MARIE-LOUISE, mariée à noble *Hilaire de Coquet de Saint-Lary*, Seigneur dudit lieu ;
3. GUILLEMETTE, mariée à noble *Jean-Marie de Lort*, ancien Confeiller au Parlement de Touloufe, & profeffeur de Droit François dans ladite ville ;
4. JEANNE-MARIE ;
5. Et JOSÈPHE-HÉLÈNE DE BASTARD.

Premier Rameau de la première Branche.

VIII. JEAN-PIERRE DE BASTARD, Chevalier, Comte & Baron d'Eftang, Seigneur de Caupène, de Cantiran, & autres lieux, né le 25 Octobre 1711, fecond fils de JEAN DE BASTARD, IIᵉ du nom, & de *Louife de Goudin*, a été Volontaire au Régiment de Foix, & bleffé très-dangereufement à la bataille de Parme; ce qui l'obligea de quitter le fervice. Les nobles de la ville de Nogaro, en conformité des Edits de 1764 & 1765, préalablement avertis par le Maire du lieu, s'affemblèrent le 19 Septembre 1765, dans la maifon dudit JEAN-PIERRE DE BASTARD, & l'élùrent d'un commun accord & voix unanime Député de leur corps, par acte retenu par *Dupouy*, Notaire de ladite ville. Par fon teftament olographe, il a fait JEAN, fon fils, héritier général & univerfel, & eft mort le 4 Septembre 1778. Il avoit époufé, le 24 Septembre 1743, comme il réfulte de la célébration du mariage fignée *du Rey*, Curé dè Caumont, *Marie-Louife de Cattelan*, fille de Meffire *Jean-Louis de Cattelan*, Chevalier, Confeiller au Parlement de Touloufe, Seigneur, Comte de Caumont, de Saint-Arromès & Gaichanès, & de noble *Marguerite de Rouffel*, affifté de fes père frères, parens & amis. Il laiffa :

IX. JEAN DE BASTARD, Chevalier, Comte & Baron d'Eftang, né le 17 Août 1744, Seigneur de Cantiran & de Caupène, Confeiller du Roi, Chevalier d'honneur de la Cour des Aides & Finances de Montauban, marié, le 2 Décembre 1782, à *Marie-Elifabeth de Brunet de Villeneuve-Lévis*, fille de haut & puiffant Seigneur Meffire *Marc-Antoine de Brunet-Lévis* de Pujols & Caftelpels, Marquis de Villeneuve, Vicomte de Lautrec, Seigneur de Portirague, Baron de Montredon & des Etats

de la Province du Languedoc, & de haute & puiffante Dame *Marie-Anne-Urfule de Fargeon*, nièce de M. le Marquis *de Caftries*, Miniftre de la Marine & Maréchal de France, &c.

Second Rameau de la première Branche.

VIII. JEAN-GASPARD DE BASTARD, Ecuyer, quatrième fils de JEAN, IIᵉ du nom, né le 8 Août 1717, a époufé, le 16 Août 1758, *Françoife-Bonaventure du Barry*, fille de noble *Urbain du Barry du Colomé*, Préfident en l'Election de Lomagne, & de Dame *le Fieret de Baudribofc*, affiftée de fon frère aîné, parens & amis. Il a plufieurs enfans encore jeunes.

Troifième Rameau de la première Branche.

IV. JEAN DE BASTARD, IIIᵉ du nom de fa branche, dernier fils de PIERRE DE BASTARD, IIᵉ du nom, fut Capitaine d'Infanterie, & obtint, conjointement avec fon neveu, JEAN DE BASTARD, Iᵉʳ du nom de la branche aînée, fon relax, portant maintenue de nobleffe, par Arrêt du Confeil d'Etat du Roi, contradictoire avec les traitans, le 25 Novembre 1671. On ignore l'époque de fa mort. Il avoit époufé *Marie de Margouet*, fille de Mᵉ *Jacques de Margouet*, ancien Procureur du Roi, dont il eut :

1. BLAISE, qui fuit ;
2. JEANNE, mariée à noble *Philippe d'Arquier* ;
3. Et MARIE, époufe de noble *Charles de Cornet*.

V. BLAISE DE BASTARD fut Capitaine d'Infanterie, fit ceffion d'une fomme de 800 liv. à prendre fur Philippe d'Arquier, en faveur de Mᵉ Guillaume Puimiffon, Confeiller au Parlement de Touloufe, & mourut jeune au fervice. Il époufa noble *Judith d'Afpis de Saint-Cricq*, qui, devenue veuve, fut en arbitrage fur certains différens élevés entre JEAN DE BASTARD, père de fon époux, relativement aux biens donnés à fon mari par fon contrat de mariage, & qui devoient revenir à fa fille. Leurs différens finirent par une transaction paffée entr'eux le 23 Avril 1663, & l'acte fut retenu par *Lagaffon*, Notaire Royal de Fleurance. De ce mariage vint :

MARGUERITE DE BASTARD, mariée à noble *Frix de Mons*.

SECONDE BRANCHE.

V. DOMINIQUE DE BASTARD, Chevalier, Seigneur de Saint-Denis fur Garonne & des Iſles Chrétiennes, Tréſorier de France de la Généralité de Touloufe, ſecond fils de NICO-LAS DE BASTARD, & de *Jeanne de Rébéſies*, teſta le 24 Janvier 1692, & mourut le 27 Mai 1696. Il réſulte d'une procuration donnée par ſon père, pour conſentir aux accords des articles de ſon mariage, en date du 29 Juin 1658, qu'il épouſa *Civile Louſteau*, qui laiſſa, par ſon codicille du 22 Octobre 1707, à Meſſire ANTOINE DE BASTARD, Ier du nom, ſon neveu, deux flambeaux d'argent pour preuve de ſon amitié. Elle mourut le 1er Juin 1709. Ses enfans furent:

1. NICOLAS, qui ſuit;
2. JEAN, Eccléſiaſtique, Chanoine & Doyen du Chapitre de Montauban;
3. ANTOINE, auſſi Eccléſiaſtique, Prieur & Abbé royal d'Eauze;
4. DOMINIQUE, Sieur de Lisle, qui ſuivit d'abord le parti des armes, enſuite fut Lieutenant-Général de la Sénéchauſſée de Lectoure, & épouſa demoiſelle *de Lucas*, ſa parente, fille de noble *Louis de Lucas*, dont il n'eut pas d'enfans;
5. CATHERINE, mariée à Jean DE BASTARD, appartenant à la quatrième branche, rapportée en ſon rang;
6. MARIE, mariée à noble *Bernard d'André*, Ecuyer, Seigneur d'Eſcalquens;
7. Et autre MARIE, femme de Meſſire *Dominique de Louſteau*, Conſeiller du Roi en ſa Cour des Aides & Finances de Bordeaux.

VI. NICOLAS DE BASTARD, Chevalier, Seigneur de Saint-Denis ſur Garonne & des Isles Chrétiennes, & Grand-Maître des Eaux & Forêts de Guyenne, paſſa acte d'accord avec JEAN DE BASTARD, ſon frère, Doyen du Chapitre de Montauban, au ſujet de leurs droits paternels & maternels, & mourut le 22 Février 1722. Il avoit épouſé, 1° le 22 Septembre 1692, *Françoiſe-Marguerite de Jean;* & 2° par contrat paſſé le 17 Juillet 1704, devant *Meunier & Donat*, Notaires à Paris, *Deniſe Moreau*. Du premier lit vinrent:

1. DOMINIQUE, qui ſuit;
2. ANTOINE, dont la poſtérité ſera rapportée après celle de ſon aîné;
3. JEAN, Capitaine-Commandant au Régiment de Mailly, auſſi Chevalier de Saint-Louis;
4. DOMINIQUE-NICOLAS, Sieur de Lisle, auſſi Capitaine & Chevalier de Saint-Louis, qui s'eſt retiré à Lectoure, & eſt mort en 1765;
5. MARIE, femme de noble *Antoine de Galard*, Marquis de Lisle;

6. MARGUERITE-LOUISE, Religieuſe au Couvent de Longages, Ordre de Fontevrault.

Du ſecond lit ſont nés:

7. NICOLAS DE BASTARD, Capitaine de Dragons, mort ſans alliance;
8. Et CIVILE DE BASTARD, mariée, le 29 Janvier 1722, à Meſſire *Jean-Florimond de Raymond*, Chevalier, Seigneur de la Garde & de Huguet.

VII. DOMINIQUE DE BASTARD, Chevalier, Seigneur de Saint-Denis ſur Garonne & des Isles Chrétiennes, Grand-Maître des Eaux & Forêts de Guyenne & de Béarn, teſta le 2 Mars 1729; & étant mort, Meſſire Jean-Florimond de Raymond, comme tuteur des enfans mineurs de DOMINIQUE, fit procéder à l'ouverture du teſtament, le 27 Avril 1736. Il avoit épouſé, le 5 Décembre 1721, *Marie-Catherine de Bequey*, ce qui réſulte de la procuration donnée à cet effet, par NICOLAS, ſon père, en faveur de Claude Barbier, Seigneur de Lafferre, Conſeiller du Roi en ſa Cour des Aides & Finances de Bordeaux, pour ratifier en ſon nom, les articles du mariage de ſon fils. Ses enfans furent:

1. FRANÇOIS-DOMINIQUE, qui ſuit;
2. JEAN-DOMINIQUE, appelé le *Baron de Saint-Denis*, Capitaine au Régiment de Guyenne, & Chevalier de Saint-Louis, mort au ſervice, ſans alliance;
3. MARIE-MARGUERITE, morte auſſi ſans alliance;
4. Et MARIE-CATHERINE DE BASTARD, femme de *Jean de Caſtaing*, fils de noble *Octavien de Caſtaing*, Colonel d'Infanterie.

VIII. FRANÇOIS-DOMINIQUE DE BASTARD, Chevalier, Seigneur de Saint-Denis ſur Garonne & des Isles Chrétiennes, Grand-Maître des Eaux & Forêts de Guyenne & de Béarn, après ſes père, & ayeul; ſe maria, 1° du conſentement de ſa mère, qui étoit abſente, mais repréſentée par Meſſire JEAN DE BASTARD, Chevalier de Saint-Denis, ſon oncle, fondé de procuration, avec noble *Jeanne-Françoiſe-Catherine de la Mazelière*, Dame de Reaux, morte ſans enfans; & 2° par acte retenu par *Audebert*, Notaire d'Agen, en date du 19 Août 1768, avec noble *Anne de Redon*, fille de Meſſire *Jean de Redon*, Seigneur de Maiſon-Noble-de-la-Chapelle & de Soufferies, & de *Jeanne du Goût*, aſſiſté de ſes parens & amis. De ce mariage il y a trois enfans vivans, dont les noms nous ſont inconnus.

TROISIÈME BRANCHE

VII. ANTOINE DE BASTARD, Capitaine au Régiment de Pons, appelé *le Chevalier de Bastard*, Chevalier de Saint-Louis, fecond fils de NICOLAS DE BASTARD, & de *Françoife-Marguerite de Jean*, tefta en 1744, & mourut à Paris en 1745. Il avoit époufé, en 1721, à Trèves, *Barbe-Marguerite de Rifaucourt*, morte à Béziers, en 1769, fille de Meffire *Humbert d'Igny de Rifaucourt*, Chevalier, Seigneur de Guerpont & de Silmon, Baron du Saint-Empire, Lieutenant des Maréchaux de France. Ils ont laiffé pour enfans :

1. FRANÇOIS-ANTOINE, qui fuit ;
2. Et ETIENNE-CHARLES DE BASTARD, Vicaire-Général, Sacriftin & Chanoine de Béziers.

VIII. FRANÇOIS-ANTOINE DE BASTARD, né en 1725, Chevalier de Saint-Louis ; n'eft pas encore marié.

QUATRIÈME BRANCHE.

II. JEAN DE BASTARD, Ier du nom de fa branche, fils de PIERRE, Ier du nom, & de *Geralde de Foiffin*, tranfigea avec fon frère aîné, CLAUDE, le 14 Mars 1538, avec Antoine & François de la Fitte, frères, Sieurs de la Barthe, & avec ODIETTE, fa fœur, le 20 Juin 1541. Il tefta le 13 Mars 1583 ; inftitua fes enfans mâles héritiers égaux, & laiffa à fes filles une légitime telle que de droit. On ignore l'époque de fa mort. Il avoit époufé *Dominge de Vaquier*, dont il eut :

1. JACQUES, qui fuit ;
2. GASPARD ;
3. BERTRAND ;
4. ANDRÉ ;
5. Et CATHERINE DE BASTARD.

III. JACQUES DE BASTARD, homme d'armes de la Compagnie de M. d'Anjou, enfuite Capitaine, fit un codicille le 18 Septembre 1618. Il avoit époufé *Violente de Mérat*, dont le teftament clos, le 7 Novembre 1600, ordonne par une claufe particulière, qu'elle veut être enterrée dans l'Eglife Paroiffiale de Fleurance, & dans la Chapelle de la famille des BASTARD. JACQUES DE BASTARD, fon mari, requit l'ouverture dudit teftament, le 13 Avril 1601. Elle étoit fille de noble *Blaife de Mérat*, Seigneur de Luc. Leurs enfans furent :

1. BLAISE, qui fuit ;
2. PIERRE ;

3. GASPARD ;
4. Autre PIERRE ;
5. JEAN ;
6. Et DOMINGE DE BASTARD, mariée à Meffire *Léonard de Piney*.

JACQUES DE BASTARD eut auffi pour fils naturels :

GASPARD & BLAISE. Leur père, par fon codicille du 18 Septembre 1618, leur laiffa une penfion alimentaire.

IV. BLAISE DE BASTARD tefta le 17 Octobre 1626, inftitua pour héritier fon fils, rappela fon père dans fon teftament, & mourut jeune ; mais on ignore à quelle époque. Il avoit époufé *Paule de Laufit*, Damoifelle. Il eut de ce mariage :

1. LÉONARD, qui fuit ;
2. Et SUSANNE DE BASTARD, mariée à *Jean de Pommarede*.

V. LÉONARD DE BASTARD, né à Fleurance en 1600, fut Député de la ville de Touloufe pour affifter aux Etats-Généraux de la Province qui fe tinrent à Béziers, par délibération du 8 Novembre 1642, tranfigea le 14 Novembre 1645, d'accord avec fes oncles, JEAN, GASPARD & PIERRE DE BASTARD, fur les différens furvenus relativement à la légitime qui lui devoit revenir de *Violente de Mérat*, fon ayeule. Il obtint, le 8 Janvier 1669, de M. *Bazin de Bezons*, Intendant de la province du Languedoc, fon arrêt de relax, en maintenue de nobleffe, & mourut le 25 Novembre 1693. Il avoit époufé, le 29 Juillet 1634, *Perrette d'André*, fille de noble *François d'André*, & de *Jeanne du May*, petite-fille du Préfident *du May*. Dont il a eu :

1. JEAN, qui fuit ;
2. JEANNE-THÉRÈSE, mariée à noble *Louis du Confeil* ;
3. Et CATHERINE DE BASTARD, Religieufe au Couvent de Longages, Ordre de Fontevrault.

VI. JEAN DE BASTARD, IIe du nom de fa branche, Seigneur de la Fitte, fut Député à Paris, par acte de l'Affemblée du corps de ville de Touloufe le 11 Février 1672, & de nouveau le 3 Janvier 1676, & aux Etats de la province tenus à Nîmes, & tefta le 22 Octobre 1729. Il avoit époufé, par contrat du 2 Avril 1682, retenu par *Saux*, Notaire Royal de Touloufe, CATHERINE DE BASTARD, fa parente, fille de Meffire DOMINIQUE DE BASTARD, & de *Civile de Loufteau*. De ce mariage vinrent

1. Dominique, qui fuit;
2. Antoine, Chanoine de Saint-Gaudens;
3. Dominique-Simon, Profeffeur de Droit françois;
4. Bernard, Officier d'Infanterie;
5. Jean-Baptiste, auffi Chanoine de Saint-Gaudens;
6. Cibile-Thérèse-Marie, Religieufe au Couvent de Longages;
7. Autre Marie, Religieufe de Sainte-Claire-du-Salins;
8. Françoise, Religieufe au Couvent de Sainte-Catherine;
9. Jeanne-Cibile, Religieufe de Notre-Dame du Coin-du-Sac;
10. Et Catherine de Bastard.

VII. Dominique de Bastard, Seigneur de la Fitte & de Pominet, &c., né le 18 Janvier 1683, reçu Confeiller au Parlement de Touloufe en 1704, Doyen en 1753, premier Préfident nommé en 1762, Confeiller d'Etat en 1774, mourut au mois de Novembre 1777. Il avoit époufé, le 14 Octobre 1719 (acte retenu par *Bande*), *Marie-Anne Eimar*, qui tefta le 7 Octobre 1768, inftituant fon mari pour héritier univerfel. Elle étoit fille de Meffire *Samuel Eimar*, Receveur des Tailles du Diocèfe de Mende, & de *Louife de Guyot*. De ce mariage font nés:

1. François, qui fuit;
2. Jean-François, Lieutenant-Colonel du Régiment des Grenadiers Royaux qui fut reçu, & prit fa place le 1ᵉʳ Décembre 1759, aux Etats-Généraux de la province du Languedoc, en qualité d'Envoyé du Baron d'Ambres, après avoir juftifié & fait preuve de nobleffe requife. Il a été reçu en 1773, Chevalier de l'Ordre de Saint-Lazare & du Mont-Carmel, fur fes preuves de nobleffe faites par M. *Chérin*, Généalogifte, & fignées du Chancelier de l'Ordre;
3. Paul-Dominique, rapporté après fon frère aîné;
4. Marie, Abbeffe du Monaftère Royal de Fabas;
5. Louise-Civile-Dominique, Religieufe;
6. Et Catherine de Bastard, mariée à noble *Baillet de Berdolle*, Baron de Goudourville, Comte de Cufor, Seigneur de Saint-Vincens, &c.

VIII. François de Bastard, Seigneur de la Fitte & Pominet, né le 16 Décembre 1722, fucceffivement Confeiller au Parlement de Touloufe, Maître des Requêtes, premier Préfident en 1762, Confeiller d'Etat en 1768, Chancelier & Surintendant des Finances de Monfeigneur le Comte d'Artois en 1773, eft mort en Janvier 1780. Il avoit époufé, par contrat retenu par Mᵉ *Chaumel*, Notaire à Paris, le 15 Août 1759, *Elifabeth-Françoife de Parfeval*, dont il eut:

1. Anne-Philibert-François, qui fuit;
2. Et Elisabeth-Adélaïde-Françoise de Bastard, mariée, en Juillet 1778, à *Charles*, Marquis de *Vergennes*, Chevalier, Confeiller du Roi en tous fes Confeils, Maître des Requêtes ordinaire de fon Hôtel, fils du Marquis de *Vergennes*, Ambaffadeur de Sa Majefté très-chrétienne auprès de la République de Venife, & neveu du Comte de *Vergennes*, actuellement Miniftre & Secrétaire d'Etat des Affaires Etrangères.

IX. Anne-Philibert-François de Bastard, Seigneur de la Fitte, né le 30 Juin 1761, n'eft pas encore marié.

VIII. Paul-Dominique de Bastard, troifième fils de Dominique, & de *Marie-Anne Eimar*, né le 2 Juillet 1741, reçu Garde-Marine en 1754, Capitaine de Cavalerie dans Royal Picardie en 1757, réformé en 1762, Confeiller au Parlement de Touloufe en 1771, s'eft marié, en Juillet 1780. Il n'a pas encore de poftérité.

Les armes de la famille de Bastard, telles qu'on les voit encore empreintes dans plufieurs Eglifes, font: *au 1 d'or à l'aigle d'empire éployée, & au 2 d'azur à une fleur-de-lys d'or*. On les voit auffi fur la porte de leur chapelle: *au 1 d'azur à 2 aigles d'or au naturel, perchées fur un tonneau, accompagné d'un croiffant d'argent, & au 2 d'azur à la fleur-de-lys d'or*, & fur le tout: *d'azur à la bande d'argent, de droite à gauche chargé de 6 coquilles d'or 2, 1, & 1, 2*.

BASTEROT, en Guyenne, particulièrement à Bordeaux, & dans le Pays de Médoc, famille originaire de Suiffe. Le premier de ce nom, connu en France, étoit fous Louis XII, environ l'an 1500, Capitaine de 100 hommes d'armes, & Gouverneur de la Ville de Saint-Macaire, en Guyenne, & dans le même tems, à peu-près, il y avoit un Basterot, Evêque de Siquença, en Efpagne, dans le Royaume de Caftille, qui étoit oncle du Gouverneur de Saint-Macaire, fous les règnes de Ferdinand & d'Isabelle. Ses defcendans s'établirent dans la Ville de Bazas; un d'eux quitta le Bazadois, & vint s'établir, en 1570, à Lefparre,

Capitale du Bas-Médoc. Il eut un fils nommé Louis, qui étoit père d'Arnaud, dont vinrent:

Gabriel, chef de la branche aînée, qui fuit;
Et François, auteur de la seconde branche.

PREMIÈRE BRANCHE.

Gabriel de Basterot eut pour enfans :
1. Barthélemy, qui fuit;
2. François, ancien Capitaine de Grenadiers au Régiment de Bourbonnois;
3. Gabriel, Prêtre, Doyen de l'Eglife Cathédrale de Saint-André de Bordeaux, & Abbé Commendataire des Abbayes de Notre-Dame de Madion, Diocèfe de Saintes, & de Saint-Pierre de l'Isle de Médoc, Diocèfe de Bordeaux, & Vicaire-Général du même Diocèfe, mort en 1759;
4. François de Basterot-de-la-Barrière, mort Enfeigne de Vaiffeaux du Roi en 1719;
5. Un autre François de Basterot-de-Saint-Vincent, rapporté après fon frère aîné;
6. Et N...., morte en 1730, épouse de N.... Lavaiffière-de-Verdufan, Tréforier de France au Bureau de Bordeaux.

Barthélemy de Basterot, Confeiller au Parlement de Bordeaux, mort en 1751, a laiffé de N.... de Poitiers:
1. Gabriel-Barthélemy, qui fuit;
2. N..... mort Lieutenant au Régiment de Bourbonnois;
3. N.... Cornette au Régiment de Saluces, tué à la bataille de Rocoux, le 11 Octobre 1746;
4. N.... mort au Collège, en bas âge;
5. Et Marguerite-Madeleine, épouse de François-Xavier de Filhot, Confeiller au Parlement de Bordeaux.

Gabriel-Barthélemy de Basterot, Confeiller au Parlement de Bordeaux, Seigneur de Dignac-le-Godet, Blayat & Valerac, s'eft marié à Marie d'Augeard; de quatre enfans qu'il a eus, il lui refte N.... de Basterot, née en Décembre 1747.

François de Basterot-de-Saint-Vincent, fixième des enfans de Gabriel, Subdélégué de l'Intendance de Bordeaux, a épousé, en 1716, Marie Basterot, fa coufine germaine, dont:
1. Guillaume de Basterot-de-la-Barrière, Chevalier de Saint-Louis, Lieutenant de Vaiffeaux du Roi, ancien Capitaine de l'une des Compagnies Franches de la Marine, Seigneur de la Barrière, de la Verdaffe, de Geiran & de Touffas, qui s'eft marié en 1760, à Honorée-Efther Chadeau-de-la-Clocheterie, dont François, né en 1762;

2. N.... Religieufe à Sainte-Urfule de Libourne;
3. Et Marguerite, mariée en 1741 à Pierre de Sainerie, Ecuyer.

SECONDE BRANCHE.

François de Basterot, fils puîné d'Arnaud, a fervi dans fa jeuneffe, fur les galères, en qualité de Garde-Etendart. Il étoit en Sicile à l'expédition de Meffieurs du Quefne & de Vivonne. Il a été marié deux fois.

De fon premier mariage il a eu:
1. N.... qui fuit;
2. Paul, rapporté après fon frère;
3. Marie, qui a épousé François de Basterot-de-Saint-Vincent, son coufin germain;
4. Françoise, morte en 1763, veuve de Jean de Cazenave, Ecuyer;
5. Une autre Françoise, Religieufe à Sainte-Urfule de Libourne;
Et plufieurs autres enfans morts en bas âge.

N... de Basterot, Préfident à la Cour des Aides de Guyenne, a épousé 1° N... de Gromen; & 2° N... Février.
De fon premier mariage eft née:
1. N.... Religieufe à Sainte-Urfule de Libourne.
Et du fecond lit il a eu:
2. N.... âgée de 22 ans;
Et trois filles, dont l'aînée eft âgée de 27 ans, la feconde de 25, & Religieufe à Sainte-Urfule de Libourne, & la dernière étoit âgée de 12 ans en 1766.

Paul de Basterot, ancien Lieutenant au Régiment de Bourbonnois, a épousé Marie Ancre, dont quatre garçons & trois filles. L'aîné des garçons eft Chanoine de l'Eglife Collégiale de Saint-Surin de Bordeaux; en 1764 il étudioit pour être reçu Docteur de Sorbonne, étoit au Séminaire de Saint-Sulpice à Paris, & Chapelain de Laudiras. (Mémoire envoyé par la famille.)

Les armes: d'argent, à l'arbre de finople, au lion d'azur s'appuyant fur le tronc de l'arbre. Supports: deux lions d'azur.

BASTIDE, en Provence. François de Bastide, iffu d'une famille qui a toujours été revêtue des premières Charges du fiège & Sénéchal d'Hières, obtint du Roi Louis XV des Lettres de Nobleffe, dans le mois d'Août 1751. Elles furent vérifiées & enregiftrées à la Cour des Comptes, Aides & Finances de

Provence, le 4 Novembre de la même année, aux Tréforiers de France, deux jours après, & au Parlement, le 26 Juin 1752.

On trouve, dans les Archives d'Hières, une tranfaction paffée, le 10 Avril 1477, entre *Palamède de Forbin*, premier Préfident en la Cour des Comptes de Provence, & la Communauté de cette Ville, dans laquelle un Bastide eft qualifié *Nobilis Amedeus de Baftida*. Cette tranfaction fut reçue par *Jacques Giraud*, Notaire & Tabellion d'Hières.

Les armes: *d'argent, à une baftide ou maifon de gueules, ouverte de fable, & garnie de cinq fenêtres de même, trois en chef & une à chaque côté de la porte, ladite maifon fur une terraffe de finople; au chef coufu d'azur, chargé de trois étoiles d'or.*

BASTIDE: *d'azur, à deux chevrons d'or, pofés l'un fur l'autre, & accompagnés en pointe d'une rofe d'argent.*

BASTIDE (la), en Languedoc: *d'azur, à la tour d'argent, maçonnée de fable.*

BASTIE, Terre à laquelle furent unies celles de Chenavel, l'Isle de Barrioz, Chavagna & Langé, en Bugey, qui furent érigées en Baronies par Lettres d'Emmanuel-Philibert, Duc de Savoie, du 20 Décembre 1570, en faveur d'*Antoine du Breul*, Ecuyer. Voyez BREUL.

BASTIE (de la), Seigneur de Vercel: *écartelé, aux 1 & 4, coupé d'or & de fable, l'or chargé d'une hure de fanglier du fecond, & le fable chargé d'un chevron du premier; aux 2 & 3 d'argent, à l'aigle d'azur, membrée & languée de gueules.*

BASTIE (de la): *de gueules, au chef d'argent, chargé de trois rofes du champ.*

*BASTIE D'ARVILLARD (la), en Dauphiné, Diocèfe, Parlement & Intendance de Grenoble; Terre et Seigneurie qui fut érigée en Marquifat, par Lettres du mois d'Août 1739, enregistrées au Parlement de Grenoble, & en la Chambre des Comptes de la même ville le 21 Novembre 1750, en faveur de *Jofeph de Barral-de-Clermont*. Voyez BARRAL.

BASTIER (le), Seigneur du Quefnois, en Normandie, Généralité de Rouen, famille maintenue dans fa nobleffe le 17 Décembre 1668.

N.... le Bastier, Ecuyer, Seigneur de Rinvilliers, Capitaine dans le Régiment du Roi, eut une fille, Barbe-Françoise le Bastier, mariée, vers 1730, à *Jean-Jacques Goffelin*, Sieur de Bois Montel, Brigadier des Gardes-du-Corps.

Les armes: *d'argent, au chevron d'azur, accompagné de trois rofes de gueules, deux en chef & une en pointe.*

BASTIN, famille établie en Provence, depuis plus de deux fiècles. Pierre de Bastin époufa *Catherine d'Arnaud*, dont il eut:

Jean de Bastin, Ier du nom, Ecuyer, Capitaine dans le Régiment du Comte de Tende, qui eft qualifié de *Noble* dans fon contrat de mariage, du 3 Février 1559, avec *Catherine Martine*, fille de *Pierre Martine*, auffi Ecuyer, & de *Catherine de Gombert*, laquelle eut de fon père 500 écus d'or pour dot. Il eut entr'autres enfans:

1. Jean, qui fuit;
2. Un autre Jean, marié le 1er Septembre 1612, à *Louife d'Ifnard*, fille de *Pierre d'Ifnard*, Ecuyer, de la Ville de Salon, & de *Madeleine de Marc*;
3. Jean, Ecuyer, marié à *Marguerite de la Mothe-d'Ariez*;
4. Et Susanne, mariée à noble *Gafpard Benoît*, Ecuyer.

Jean de Bastin, IIe du nom, Ecuyer, eft auffi qualifié de *Noble & d'Ecuyer*, dans les titres qui le concernent. Il époufa, le 15 Mai 1616, *Anne de Boiffon*, fille de *Jean de Boiffon*, Seigneur de Champ-Jacob, citoyen de Marfeille, Gentilhomme ordinaire de la Maifon de M. le Duc de Guife, & de *Catherine de Garnier*. Leurs enfäns furent:

1. Jean, qui fuit;
2. Un autre Jean, Lieutenant d'une des Galères du Roi. Il périt fur la Galère du Marquis de Caftellane, au fameux naufrage des Galères, fous M. de la Ferrière. Il avoit époufé, le 31 Octobre 1671, *Anne de Serre*, fille de *Cornélio de Serre*, Ecuyer, & d'*Urfule de Sauffon*, de Marfeille.
3. Barthélemy, un des 100 Gentilshommes de la Garde de fon Alteffe Monfeigneur le Duc de Beaufort, Grand-Amiral;
4. Et Jean-Baptiste, qui fit 12 campagnes fur les Galères du Roi, avec fon frère aîné.

Jean de Bastin, IIIe du nom, Ecuyer, avoit fervi depuis 1636 jufqu'en 1662. Il tomba malade au retour de la campagne qu'il fit au détroit de Gibraltar, avec l'efcadre de fix Galères, commandée par le Baron de Thermes,

Lieutenant-Général. Il fut bleffé de deux coups de moufquet au grand combat de 15 galères de France, contre un pareil nombre de celles d'Efpagne, fous le Commandement de M. de Pontcourlay, en 1638. Il fe trouva auffi en 1641 au fiège de Tarragone, & au combat donné contre 41 galères d'Efpagne, venues au fecours de cette place, & dont il y en eut 11 coulées à fond. Enfin il fervit pendant plufieurs années, en qualité de Lieutenant-Commandant en chef fur diverfes galères du Roi, en tems de pefte, tant pour garder les côtes que pour amener des bleds à la Ville de Marfeille, fa patrie. Il avoit été marié 1° à *Françoife de Patéou* ; & 2° par contrat du 3 Mars 1662, à *Anne de l'Efcaçe*, fille de *Thomas de l'Efcaçe*, & d'*Anne de Mouftier*. Il eut, entr'autres enfans, de fon fecond mariage :

JEAN-BAPTISTE DE BASTIN-DE-COLOMBI, Ecuyer, qui, ayant prouvé, par pièces & titres fuffifans, la qualité de noble & d'Ecuyer, fut maintenu dans fa nobleffe par jugement de *Pierre Cardin-le-Bret*, premier Préfident du Parlement d'Aix, & Intendant de la Provence, rendu à Aix le 25 Octobre 1701. Il époufa, par contrat du 28 Juin 1693, *Gabrielle de Bionneau*, fille de *Jean-Baptifte de Bionneau-d'Eyragues*, & d'*Anne-Marie d'Efcanavel*, dont il eut :

1. JEAN-BAPTISTE, ancien Capitaine en fecond des galères, Chevalier de Saint-Louis en 1738, marié au mois de Juin 1746. Il a eu deux filles ;
2. ANDRÉ, qui fuit ;
3. & 4. PIERRE-ANTOINE, & BARTHÉLEMY, morts jeunes ;
5. & 6. Deux fils, morts en bas âge ;
7. JEAN-BAPTISTE-MARTIN, né le 11 Novembre 1707, Prêtre en 1730, Bachelier en Théologie, & nommé par le Roi, en 1733, à un Canonicat de l'Eglife-Royale de Saint-Quentin, dont il eft Chanoine-Honoraire depuis 1755 ;
8. JOSEPH, mort en 1720 ;
9. N..., morte en bas âge ;
10. CLAIRE, Religieufe Carmélite à Marfeille, fous le nom de *Sœur Claire de l'Incarnation*, morte en odeur de Sainteté, le 13 Avril 1733, à l'âge de 32 ans, dont elle en avoit paffé 13 dans la Religion ;
11. Et GABRIELLE, mariée à *Scipion d'Armand-de-la-Garcinière*, dont il a eu trois fils & deux filles. Les trois garçons ont fervi

dans la Marine, & il ne refte que JEAN-BAPTISTE, nommé le Chevalier d'*Armand*, qui eft Capitaine-Aide-Major des Troupes de la Marine, à St.-Domingue, depuis 1751.

ANDRÉ DE BASTIN-DE-COLOMBI, Ecuyer, ancien Lieutenant de Dragons, a été tué en 1747 au fiège de Berg-op-Zoom, étant pour lors Lieutenant dans les Volontaires Bretons. Il fut marié en 1728 à *Madeleine Venture-de-Paradis*, & a laiffé :

1. JEAN-BAPTISTE, qui fuit ;
2. LOUISE-GABRIELLE, mariée avec *Jean-Baptifte Baillot-de-Montpellier* ;
3. Et CHARLOTTE.

JEAN-BAPTISTE DE BASTIN-DE-COLOMBI, Ecuyer, a été reçu Lieutenant d'Infanterie en 1745, & Garde-du-Corps du Roi en 1751, &c.

Il eft fait mention dans l'*Hiftoire de Provence*, par Gaufridy, de l'accident arrivé en 1590 au Capitaine de BASTIN, qui fut malheureufement tué à Aix.

La famille de BASTIN eft alliée aux meilleures Maifons de la Provence, comme avec celles de *Caftellane*, de *Vintimille*, de *Forbin-de-Janfon*, de *Flotte*, &c.

Les armes : *de gueules, fretté d'or*.

BASTOIN, en Provence : *de fable, fretté d'or, femé d'écuffons d'argent & de mûres de gueules*.

BASTONEAU, Seigneur d'Azay : *d'azur, au chevron d'or, accompagné en chef de deux quint-feuilles, & en pointe d'un bâton écotté, pof à pal, le tout de même*.

BASUEL, famille originaire de Bâle en Suiffe.

GEORGES-GUILLAUME DE BASUEL, Lieutenant-Colonel au Régiment de Mauny, Suiffe, Chevalier de Saint-Louis & de l'Ordre de l'Eperon, époufa, à Langres, N... *de Girard*, d'une famille noble de la province de Champagne, dont il eut entr'autres enfans :

ETIENNE-GUILLAUME, qui fuit ;
Et une fille, mariée à *N... de Rofe*, Marquis de *Dammartin* dont eft forti le Marquis de *Rofe Dammartin*, d'aujourd'hui, & Mademoifelle de *Dammartin*, qui vit fans alliance.

ETIENNE-GUILLAUME DE BASUEL, Ecuyer, Officier au Régiment d'Affry, mort en 1729, avoit époufé, à Lille en Flandres, *Marie-*

Louise-Thérèse de Flaction, dont il eut entr'autres enfans :

Un fils, mort jeune au service ;

Et JEANNE DE BASUEL, née au mois de Septembre 1737, mariée à Paris, le 4 Septembre 1759, à *Pierre-Edme de Baubard-de-la-Grurie*, qui a servi dans les Volontaires de Flandres.

Les armes : *d'azur, au bafilic d'or, aîlé & couronné de même.* Supports : *deux lions.*

* BASVILLE, ou BAVILLE, Terre & Seigneurie dans le Pays Chartrain, poffédée dans le XVIe fiècle par *Charles de Lamoignon*, reçu Confeiller au Parlement de Paris. *Guillaume*, premier Préfident du même Parlement, en faveur duquel les Terres & Seigneuries de Bafville & de Boiffy furent érigées en Marquifat par Lettres de Décembre 1670, regiftrées au Parlement & à la Chambre des Comptes de Paris, les 8 & 20 Janvier 1671, mourut le 10 Décembre 1677. Il eft le bifayeul de *Chrétien-Guillaume de Lamoignon*, Marquis de BASVILLE, le fixième de fa famille, Préfident du Parlement de Paris. Voyez LAMOIGNON.

BATAILHE, Seigneur de Frances : *d'or, à l'arbre de finople, fur une terraffe de même.*

BATAILLE DE MANDELOT, en Bourgogne. GUILLAUME BATAILLE, Seigneur du Tillot, fut pourvu par le Roi LOUIS XI, le 25 Mai 1478, d'un Office de Confeiller au Parlement de Bourgogne. Il mourut le 15 Février 1499.

PHILIPPE BATAILLE, un de fes defcendans au VIe degré, Ecuyer, Seigneur de Mandelot, de Mavilli & de l'Auxey, commença à fervir le Roi en 1690. Il fut Aide-Major d'un Régiment d'Infanterie, le 16 Avril 1704, puis Capitaine dans le même Régiment, par Commiffion du 16 Avril 1706. Il époufa, le 21 Février 1709, *Louife de Vellerot*, dont :

1. HENRI-CHARLES, qui fuit ;
2. CHARLES-CLAUDE, né le 5 Octobre 1720 ;
3. NICOLAS, né le 4 Novembre 1721 ;
4. MARIE-LOUISE-CHARLOTTE, née le 3 Octobre 1711 ;
5. LOUISE-MARIE-ANDRÉE-BÉATRIX, née le 24 Octobre 1712 ;
6. JEANNE-MARGUERITE-BERNARDE, née le 18 Octobre 1718, & reçue à Saint-Cyr, le 11 Août 1730 ;
7. Et MARIE-ANNE, née le 16 Mars 1723.

HENRI-CHARLES BATAILLE DE MANDELOT, né le 12 Novembre 1713, Capitaine des Vaif-

Tome II.

feaux du Roi & Chevalier de Saint-Louis, mort le 11 Avril 1762, avoit époufé, le 19 Décembre 1751, *Françoife de Damas*, remariée, le 7 Avril 1772, à *Louis-Claude de Clermont*, Marquis de *Montoifon*. Elle étoit fille de *Louis de Damas*, Comte de Vellerot, & de *Catherine de Chaugy*. Elle eut :

HENRI-CAMILLE BATAILLE DE MANDELOT, né le 2 Mars 1763 (53)

(Voyez l'*Armorial de France*, reg. Ier, part. Ire, pag. 52).

Les armes : *d'argent, à trois flammes de gueules, mouvantes de la pointe de l'écu.*

BATAILLE, en Champagne : *d'azur, à trois fafces crénelées d'or.*

BATAREL, en Bretagne : *d'argent, à deux léopards de fable, couronnés de même.*

BATARNAY ou BASTERNAI. La Maifon de BATARNAY tire fon origine de la Province de Dauphiné, où la Terre du Bouchage eft fituée.

JOACHIM, Seigneur de BATARNAY, eft le premier de cette famille dont nous ayons connoiffance ; fon fils fut :

ANTOINE, Seigneur de BATARNAY & de Charnes, lequel époufa *Catherine Gaftonne*, dont il eut :

1. ANTOINE, qui fuit ;
2. IMBERT, Seigneur *du Bouchage*, auteur d'une branche ;
3. Et JACQUES, Evêque de Valence en 1480.

ANTOINE DE BATARNAY, IIe du nom, Seigneur de Vaugris & de la Vicomté d'Evrecy, Bailli de Caen en 1481, époufa *Renée de Houllefort*, Dame de Hamars, Vienne, Saint-Martin, de Sallon, Planes, Aunay & Eftrehan, en Beffin, fille & héritière *de May de Houllefort*, Confeiller du Roi, Bailli de Caen, Seigneur de Marneaux, & de *Louife de Hamars*, fa première femme. De ce mariage fortirent :

1. MARGUERITE, Dame de Hamars, femme de *Jean d'Harcourt*, Sire & Châtelain d'Auvilliers, fils de *Jean d'Harcourt*, Buron de Bonneftable, & de *Catherine d'Arpajon* ;
2. Et MARGUERITE, femme de *François de Laval*, Seigneur de Marfilly, mort fans enfans, l'an 1575, fils de *Guy de Laval*, Seigneur de Loué, & de *Charlotte de Sainte-Maure.*

BRANCHE
des Seigneurs DU BOUCHAGE.

IMBERT DE BATARNAY, fecond fils d'ANTOINE,

E e

Seigneur de Batarnay & de Charnes, & de *Catherine Gaſtonne*, fut Seigneur du Bouchage, Comte de Feſenzac, par don du Roi Louis XI, & épouſa *Georgette de Montchenu*, fille de *Falcon de Montchenu*, Seigneur de Châteauneuf, & de *Galaure*, Dame *du Bouchage*, dont il eut :

  1. François, qui fuit ;

  2. Et Jeanne, femme de *Jean de Poitiers*, Seigneur de Saint-Vallier, fils d'*Edouard de Poitiers*, Seigneur de Saint-Vallier, & de *Jeanne de Boulogne*.

François de Batarnay, Baron du Bouchage & d'Authon, s'allia avec *Françoiſe de Mᵉillé*, fille de *François*, Seigneur de *Maillé*, & de *Marie de Rohan*. De ce mariage fortirent :

  1. René, qui fuit ;

  2. Et Anne, mariée l'an 1536 à *Jean de Daillon*, Comte du Lude, Sénéchal d'Anjou.

René de Batarnay, Comte du Bouchage, Baron d'Authon, Seigneur de Montréſor, mort en 1587, avoit épouſé, l'an 1527, *Iſabeau de Savoie*, fille de *René*, bâtard légitimé *de Savoie*, Comte de Villars & de Tende, Grand-Maître de France, & d'*Anne de Laſcaris*. Il laiſſa :

  1. Claude, qui fuit ;

  2. Françoiſe, femme de *François d'Ailly*, Vidame d'Amiens ;

  3. Marie, morte en 1592, femme de *Guillaume*, Vicomte de *Joyeuſe*, Maréchal de France ;

  4. Jeanne, femme de *Bernard de Nogaret*, Seigneur de la Valette, Amiral de France ;

  5. Et Gabrielle, femme de *Gaſpard de la Châtre*, Seigneur de Mançay, Capitaine des Gardes-du-Corps du Roi.

Claude de Batarnay, Comte du Bouchage, n'eut point d'enfans, & fut tué à la bataille de Saint-Denis, laiſſant ſes ſœurs héritières de ſes biens. Il avoit épouſé, l'an 1561, *Jacqueline*, Comteſſe *de Montbel* & d'Entremonts, remariée à *Gaſpard de Coligny*, Seigneur de Châtillon. Elle étoit fille & héritière de *Sébaſtien de Montbel*, Chevalier de l'Ordre de Savoie, & de *Béatrix Pacheco*.

Les armes de cette famille éteinte : *Ecartelé d'or & d'azur*.

BATELLE-DE-TRESME : *d'azur, à la bande d'or*.

BATESTE. Le nom de Bateste ne vient point d'une Terre, ainſi on n'en peut donner une véritable origine que par la conjecture de la Terre d'*Outrelaiſe*, qui eſt ſituée dans le Bailliage de Caen, & qui a toujours été poſſédée par ceux de cette famille.

Les armes : *d'azur, à deux faſces d'argent*.

Pierre Louvet, dans ſon *Hiſtoire Beauvoiſine*, fait mention de Philippe Bateste, Chevalier en 1196.

Prossin & Guillaume Bateste ſont repréſentés dans les Rôles de la Chambre des Comptes de 1313, comme *Ecuyers* de l'Hôtel du Roi Philippe-le-Long, & dans le même tems Etienne Bateste étoit un des Officiers du même Roi.

Les Chartes de la Couronne de France remarquent Guillaume Bateste.

Dans une Charte de 1324 il eſt parlé de Jean Bateste, Chevalier.

Monſeigneur Philippe Bateste, Chevalier, eſt auſſi employé entre les Grands du Royaume, ſous le Roi Philippe-le-Long, l'an 1339. Il épouſa *Péronnelle de Brionne*, fille de *Raoul-Morel de Brionne*, Seigneur de Heuditot, & de *Péronnelle d'Auvrecher*, dont il eut quatre fils & deux filles.

  1. Philippe, Seigneur d'Outrelaiſe ;

  2. Jean-Robert ;

  3. Alain-Philippot ;

  4. Et Jeanne.

Il y a un Arrêt du Parlement de Paris, de 1346, prononcé en faveur de Guyot Bateste, Chevalier, & *Béatrix de Poitiers*, ſa mère.

Thomas Bateste comparut pour un fief fis à Franconville, qui avoit appartenu à Jacques Bateste, ſon père.

Henri V, Roi d'Angleterre, ayant confiſqué les biens de *Jeanne de Brionne*, & de Philippe Bateste, ſon mari, les rétablit, par Lettres données au Château de Rouen, la huitième année de ſon règne, au mois d'Avril, ſignées *Sturgeon*, ſe retenant la haute & ſouveraine Juſtice & les terres qui ſeroient près de la Ville de Falaiſe & celle de Caen, dont il prétendit faire tirer des pierres pour bâtir un Palais dans ſa Ville de Rouen.

Philippe Bateste, leur fils, rendit enfuite aveu de ſes biens au mois de Janvier 1392.

Dans les Armoriaux, dreſſés ſous le Roi Charles VI, *Monſeigneur* Philippe Bateste, & *Monſeigneur* Jean Bateste, Chevaliers, y ſont enrôlés.

Dans les Regiſtres du Tabellionage de Caen, de 1457, il eſt parlé de Bertrand Bateste.

Le même BERTRAND BATESTE, Seigneur de Quilly, demeuroit dans la Sergenterie de Breteuille, fur l'Aife, Election de Falaife, & fit fa preuve l'an 1463.

Les Echiquiers de Normandie, de 1463, difent que *Drouet de Pont-Audemer*, Chevalier, & Damoifelle ROBINE BATESTE, fon époufe, auparavant femme de *Jean Boislichauffe*, avoient des différends contre plufieurs autres.

Aux montres du Bailliage d'Alençon, faites l'an 1477, JEAN BATESTE, Seigneur d'Outre-laife, y comparut des premiers.

Les Échiquiers de l'an 1497 contiennent un Arrêt donné au profit de THOMAS BATESTE & la Demoifelle fa femme; & en une autre inftance eft nommé Meffire LOUIS BATESTE, Prieur de Noyers.

En l'an 1517, RENÉ BATESTE, Seigneur de Rocquereuil, eft nommé dans les Regiftres du Tabellionnage de Thury.

Il y a un Arrêt, donné au Parlement de Rouen entre GASPARD BATESTE & *Charles de Piedeleu*, Baron d'Aunay.

CHRISTINE BATESTE, Dame de Quilly, époufa *Guillaume Girard*, dont fortit *Jeanne Girard*, Dame de Quilly, en 1520, femme de *François de Sainte-Marie*, Seigneur du Mefnil-Gondouin.

Il y eut une autre preuve de nobleffe de cette famille, faite l'an 1598.

On a encore connoiffance d'une autre branche de cette Maifon, qui prit alliance avec une des filles de *François de Vaulx*, Seigneur de Merville, & de *Fontaine Eftoupefour*, vivant en 1490.

Les armes: *d'azur, à deux fafces d'argent*.

BATHORI, famille noble de Tranfylvanie, qui a donné plufieurs Princes à cet Etat, & un Cardinal en 1584, fous le Pontificat de GRÉGOIRE XIII. Voyez Moréri.

BATS, ou BATZ (DE), Maifon originaire de Béarn, connue & diftinguée dès le XIe fiècle, dont étoient ARNAUD-RAYMOND DE BATZ, Seigneur de Batz & de Séroneac; BERNARD DE BATZ, Evêque de Lefcar; & RAYMOND-ARNAUD DE BATZ, Vicomte de Coarafe, près de Pau, une des douze anciennes Baronies de Béarn; les defcendans des Comtes & Sires de *Coarafe*, & des Barons de *Batz*, près d'Orteits, s'établirent au XVe fiècle dans l'Albret, Diocèfe de Condom; ils ont poffédé les Sei-

gneuries de Gontaut, de Lille & de Trenqueleon, & occupé, jufqu'à ce jour, des emplois diftingués dans le Militaire, tant au fervice des Rois de Navarre que de ceux de France.

CHARLES DE BATZ, Baron de Trenqueleon, a époufé, en Juillet 1750, *Anne-Louife de Malide*, fille de *Louis de Malide*, mort Brigadier des Armées du Roi, Capitaine au Régiment des Gardes-Françoifes, tante des Ducheffes de *Lauraguais*, & de la *Rochefoucauld*, dont deux garçons & deux filles. L'aîné des garçons fut reçu Page aux Ecuries du Roi en 1769.

ALEXANDRE DE BATZ, Baron de Mirepoix, & Seigneur de Sainte-Criftie, en Armagnac, Lieutenant des Maréchaux de France, dans le Condomois, ancien Capitaine au Régiment de Conty, Chevalier de Saint-Louis, s'eft marié, en Juin 1759, à *Marie de la Claverie-de-Soupets*, arrière-petite-fille de *Jean-François de la Claverie*, Baron de Soupets, Meftre-de-Camp de Cavalerie, Confeiller d'Etat d'épée, dont un garçon & une fille.

GASPARD DE BATZ, ci-devant Abbé de Châtres, aujourd'hui de l'Abbaye-Royale de Saint-Ferme, Baron du Puy & de Dieulivol, eft Grand-Vicaire d'Auch, & a été préfenté au Roi en 1745.

CHARLES DE BATZ, ancien Capitaine des Grenadiers au Régiment d'Auvergne, eft Chevalier de Saint-Louis.

Et UTÉRIN-GASPARD DE BATZ, Baron de Lapeyre, Seigneur de Lalane & Dars, en Albret, Brigadier des Armées du Roi, Capitaine des Grenadiers au Régiment des Gardes-Françoifes, & Chevalier de l'Ordre de Saint-Louis, eft mort de fes bleffures, reçues à la bataille de Fontenoy.

Les armes: *de gueules, parti d'azur au lion d'or, dreffé fur cinq pointes de rocher d'argent, pofées trois & deux*. Support: *un Saint-Michel de couleur de chair, aîlé & vêtu à la Romaine, d'argent, armé d'une pique d'or, plongée dans la gueule d'un dragon terraffé, de couleur naturelle*.

Les Marquis de *Caftelmore* portent le nom de BATZ. LOUIS-GABRIEL DE BATZ, Marquis de Caftelmore, avoit époufé *Conftance-Gabrielle-Madeleine du Moncel-de-Lourailles*, morte le 9 Juillet 1764, âgée de 44 ans. Elle avoit époufé, 1° le 16 Août 1740, *Jofeph Bonnier de la Moffon*, & étoit fille de *Jacques-Alexandre*, Préfident à Mortier à Rouen, et de *Marie-Françoife*, aliàs *Marie-Madeleine-Cécile Maignant de Bernières*.

BATTEFORT, Marquis de l'Aubepin, qui porte : *de gueules, à une épée d'argent mise en pal, au chef coufu d'azur, chargé de deux rofes d'argent*. Voyez AUBEPIN.

BATTENDIER : *d'or, au lion de fable entre deux pals de gueules*.

BATUT-DE-LA-PEYROUSE, famille de la Vicomté de Turenne dans le Bas-Limoufin.

JEAN DU BATUT, Ier du nom, Seigneur de la Peyroufe, Confeiller du Roi HENRI IV, & Maître des Requêtes de fon Hôtel en l'Etat de Navarre fut le bifayeul de JEAN DU BATUT, IIIe du nom, qui fut nommé à la charge de Syndic-Général de la Vicomté de Turenne en 1706. Il eut, de *Marie-Françoife de la Gorce*, un fils unique :

JOSEPH-JACQUES DU BATUT, Ecuyer, Seigneur de la Peyroufe, en Touraine, du Roch, &c., qui époufa, le 18 Avril 1728, *Marie de Lefcot*, dont il eut :

1. JEAN, IVe du nom, né à Turenne en 1729;
2. MARIE-FRANÇOISE, née le 1er Août 1730 ;
3. MARIE-ANNE-THÉRÈSE, née le 24 Mars 1732 ;
4. Et MARIE, née le 20 Août 1735.

Voyez l'*Armorial de France*, reg. II, part. II.

Les armes : *d'azur, à un lion d'or, au chef d'argent, chargé d'une étoile de gueules*.

◊ BATZ (DE), en Gafcogne, famille maintenue dans fa nobleffe le 2 Août 1668.

I. MATHIEU DE BATZ, Capitaine dans le Régiment de Vignolles, époufa *Marthe de Vignolles*, dont :

II. ETIENNE DE BATZ, Ecuyer, Docteur ès droits, Confeiller du Roi au fiège de Saint-Sever, qui fe maria, par contrat du 1er Février 1552, avec *Jeanne de Tauzin*, fille de *Bernard*, Avocat au Parlement de Bordeaux, & de *Marguerite d'Eftoupignan*. Il eut :

III. PIERRE DE BATZ, Ecuyer, Seigneur de la Mothe, du Levy & d'Artiguebarde, Confeiller du Roi, Lieutenant-Particulier au fiège de Saint-Sever, & Avocat au Parlement de Bordeaux, qui tefta le 19 Juin 1640. Il avoit époufé, par contrat du 4 Novembre 1595, *Catherine de la Borde*, fille de *Chriftophe*, Confeiller du Roi au fiège de Saint-Sever, & de *Jeanne de Paret*. De ce mariage font iffus :

1. PIERRE, qui fuit;
2. Autre PIERRE, lequel étoit fur le point d'embraffer l'état Eccléfiaftique lors du teftament de fon père ;
3. JEAN, auteur de la troifième branche, rapportée ci-après ;
4. N.... DE BATZ, mariée à *Jean du Junea*, dont elle étoit veuve lors du teftament de fon père ;
5. N..., femme pour lors de *Pierre de Cloche*, Avocat ;
6. CATHERINE, mariée à *Jean du Vacquier*, Sieur d'Aubaignan, de Lartigue, &c. ;
7. Et JEANNE DE BATZ, morte lors du teftament de fon père, ainfi que la précédente. Elle avoit époufé *Michel Vincens*, bourgeois de Grenade.

IV. PIERRE DE BATZ, Vicomte d'Aurice, Baron de la Mothe, Seigneur d'Efcoubès, de Saint-Araille & du Levy, Confeiller du Roi, Lieutenant-Particulier au fiège de Saint-Sever, époufa, par contrat du 3 Juin 1636, *Catherine le Blanc*, morte le 18 Mai 1676, fille d'*Alcibiade le Blanc*, Seigneur & Baron de la Batut, & de *Louife de Caftet*. Leurs enfans furent :

1. BERNARD, baptifé le 13 Décembre 1637;
2. JOSEPH, qui fuit;
3. Et N... DE BATZ, Religieufe Bénédictine.

V. JOSEPH DE BATZ, Vicomte d'Aurice, Baron de la Mothe, Seigneur d'Efcoubès, de Saint-Araille & du Levy, Confeiller du Roi, Lieutenant-Particulier au fiège de Saint-Sever, maintenu dans fa nobleffe le 2 Août 1668, tefta le 15 Décembre 1691, & mourut avant le 7 Janvier 1696. Il avoit époufé, le 20 Avril 1667, *Jeanne de Captan* (nommée *Marie* dans le contrat de mariage d'ANTOINE DE BATZ, fon fils), morte le 7 Mars 1674, fille de *Jean de Captan*, Confeiller du Roi, Receveur & Contrôleur alternatif des décimes du Diocèfe d'Aire, & de *Madeleine de Tauzin*. Il laiffa :

1. ANTOINE, qui fuit;
2. DANIEL, Eccléfiaftique ;
3. Et LOUIS, auteur de la feconde branche rapportée ci-après.

VI. ANTOINE DE BATZ, baptifé le 28 Janvier 1671, Vicomte d'Aurice, Baron de la Mothe, Seigneur d'Efcoubès, de Saint-Araille & du Levy, Confeiller du Roi, Lieutenant-Particulier au fiège de Saint-Sever, puis Confeiller au Parlement de Bordeaux, obtint, le 2 Janvier 1697, un jugement des Commiffaires-Généraux, députés par le Roi pour les francs-fiefs, qui le décharge de la taxe faite sur lui comme propriétaire des maisons nobles de la Mothe & d'Aurice, & fut maintenu dans sa nobleffe, par ordonnance de M. *Bazin de Bezons*, Intendant de Bordeaux, rendue le 3 Janvier 1698. Il vivoit encore le 11 Avril 1715, date de son teftament, & avoit époufé, 1º par contrat du 7 Janvier 1696, *Catherine Dalon*, fille de *Raymond*, Chevalier, Confeiller du Roi en fes Confeils, premier Préfident du Parlement de Navarre, & de *Catherine du Ribaud*; & 2º *Sufanne-Elifabeth du Vigier*, morte fans enfans. Il eut du premier lit une fille, &

VII. JEAN-BAPTISTE DE BATZ, Vicomte d'Aurice, Baron de la Mothe, Seigneur d'Efcoubès, de Saint-Araille & du Levy, &c., né le 26 Février 1708, marié par contrat du 18 Février 1730, avec *Rofe de Caupène*, fille de *Jean*, qualifié dans cet acte Marquis d'Amon & de Saint-Pé, Baron de Pommarès, de Caftelfarazin, &c., & de *Jeanne-Bédorrède Galyraffe*. De ce mariage font iffus:

1. JEAN-PIERRE, Ecuyer, né le 5 Janvier 1737, qui a fervi dans le régiment de Navarre;
2. RAYMOND, Ecuyer, baptifé le 7 Novembre 1740, Vicomte d'Aurice, Baron de la Mothe, Seigneur d'Efcoubès, &c., Officier au Régiment de Navarre, marié, le 22 Août 1764, à *N... de Fillol*, dont JEAN-BAPTISTE DE BATZ, Ecuyer, Vicomte d'Aurice, Lieutenant au Régiment de Berry, Infanterie;
3. Et JEANNE-MARIE-THÉRÈSE DE BATZ, née le 13 Octobre 1731.

SECONDE BRANCHE.

VI. LOUIS DE BATZ, Ecuyer, Seigneur de Saint-Araille, troifième fils de JOSEPH, & de *Jeanne de Captan*, né le 19 Février 1674, Capitaine d'Infanterie dans le Régiment Royal, fit fon teftament le 19 Avril 1724, par lequel il déclara avoir eu un fils & une fille, de fon mariage par acte fous feings privés du 28 Février 1696, avec *Jeanne Dartigues*, fille de *Guillaume*, bourgeois de la ville de Saint-Sever, & de *Marguerite Darmandieu*. Son fils fut:

VII. JEAN-PIERRE DE BATZ, Ecuyer, né le 9 Janvier 1710, ci-devant Officier dans le Régiment de Lorraine, qui a époufé, par articles fous feings privés du 13 Mars 1731, *Catherine-Gérarde de Captan*, fille d'*Antoine*, Ecuyer, Chevalier de Saint-Louis, ancien Capitaine de Cavalerie dans le Régiment

de Condé, & de *Jeanne de Monbeton-de-Bourrouillon*. Leurs enfans font:

1. ANTOINE, Ecuyer, né le 27 Septembre 1732, Lieutenant au Régiment de Navarre, puis Capitaine au même Régiment, Chevalier de Saint-Louis, Lieutenant-Colonel d'Infanterie, marié, le 15 Novembre 1769, à *Marie-Louife de Hilon*, dont font iffus:
   1. JEAN-PIERRE, Ecuyer, né le 12 Juillet 1772;
   2. CATHERINE, née le 10 Septembre 1770;
   3. Et HENRIETTE DE BATZ, née le 20 Septembre 1774.
2. JOSEPH, né le 12 Février 1749;
3. Autre JOSEPH, né le 9 Juin 1752;
4. N......, Religieufe de Saint-Dominique à Prouillan, près Condom;
5. ROSE-JOSÈPHE, née le 16 Février 1735;
6. CATHERINE, née le 27 Janvier 1736;
7. ROSE, née le 22 Août 1740, reçue à Saint-Cyr le 21 Juin 1751 fur fes preuves de nobleffe;
8. Et MARIE DE BATZ, née le 1er Août 1744.

TROISIÈME BRANCHE.

IV. JEAN DE BATZ, Ecuyer, troifième fils de PIERRE, & de *Catherine de la Borde*, époufa, par contrat du 11 Juin 1647, *Marguerite de la Lanne*, fille de *Pierre*, Sieur de Diuffe, Abbé de Mafcaras, & de *Jeanne de Lurbe*. Il en eut:

V. JEAN-PIERRE DE BATZ, Baron de Diuffe, Seigneur de Buannes, de Montaut & de Mafcaras, déchargé du droit de francs-fiefs, par ordonnance de M. *Bazin de Bezons*, Intendant de Bordeaux, rendue le 5 Octobre 1693 fur la production qu'il lui avoit fait de fes titres de nobleffe depuis 1552. Il époufa, par contrat du 2 Juillet 1676, *Françoife de Nogues*, fille de *Jean*, Baron d'Affat, Confeiller d'Etat, Commiffaire en la Chambre de Juftice, & de *Françoife d'Orthe*, dont:

VI. ANTOINE DE BATZ, Ecuyer (nommé JACQUES dans l'extrait baptiftère de fon fils), Seigneur de Bannes & en partie de Montaut, qui a époufé, par contrat du 24 Avril 1722, en préfence de CLÉMENT DE BATZ, fon parent, Docteur en théologie, & Chanoine de l'Eglife de Saint-Martin d'Oléron, *Françoife de la Goyte*, fille de *Jean*, Lieutenant-Général d'épée au Sénéchal de Tartas, & de *Françoife de Larrey*. De ce mariage eft iffu:

JEAN-PIERRE DE BATZ, Ecuyer, né le 9 Janvier 1723.

(Armorial de France, reg. V, part. I.)

Les armes : *d'azur, à un chevron d'or, accompagné de trois chicots de même posés en pal, 2 en chef & 1 en pointe ; au chef d'argent, chargé d'un lion de gueules naissant.*

BAUBARD DE LA GRURIE, en Champagne. Voici la filiation suivie de cette famille, dreffée fur les titres communiqués.

Le premier dont il foit fait mention, eft JEAN DE BAUBARD, Ecuyer, qualifié dans plufieurs actes du titre de Chevalier, Seigneur de Chambour, & mari de *Claude de Matignon*, fille de *Pierre de Matignon*, Ecuyer, Chevalier, Seigneur d'Enon & autres lieux. De ce mariage vinrent :

1. JEAN, qui fuit ;
2. Et PIERRE, Capitaine d'une compagnie de 100 hommes de pied, tué dans un combat fingulier.

JEAN DE BAUBARD, II° du nom, Ecuyer, Seigneur de Chambour, époufa, au mois de Septembre 1488, *Marie de Picotte*, de laquelle il eut :

JEAN, qui fuit ;
Et CHARLES, Lieutenant au Régiment de la Ferté.

JEAN DE BAUBARD, III° du nom, Ecuyer, Seigneur de Chambour, & autres lieux, homme d'armes de la compagnie du Seigneur de Bellon, fut marié, le 13 Novembre 1540, par contrat paffé devant *l'Epine*, Notaire Royal en la Prévôté de Ceriziers, à *Claude de Salazar*, fille de *Galeas de Salazar*, Ecuyer, Seigneur de Ferrière, Vaudeurs, les Sièges, &c. De ce mariage vint :

JEAN DE BAUBARD, IV° du nom, Ecuyer, Seigneur de Chambour, Planfy, &c., qui époufa, 1° par contrat paffé le 17 Octobre 1600, devant *Renaud*, Notaire Royal à Sens, *Marguerite de Thévenin* ; & 2° le 15 Décembre 1623, *Gabrielle de Sillière*, fille de *Jacques de Sillière*, ou *Sillier*, Ecuyer, Seigneur du Fey, & de *N... de Léonne*, dite *de Foiffy* ; Les enfans du premier lit furent :

1. MARGUERITE DE BAUBARD, dite *demoifelle de Chambour*, née au mois d'Avril 1602, mariée à *Louis de Bérulle*, Chevalier, Seigneur de Montaguillon ;
2. EDMÉE DE BAUBARD, née le 15 Novembre 1609, mariée à *Pierre de Liége*, Ecuyer, Seigneur de Saint-Mars ;
3. ALEXANDRE, qui fuit.
Et du fecond lit :
4. ELISABETH, morte à Saint Cyr.

ALEXANDRE DE BAUBARD, Ecuyer, Seigneur de Chambour, né le 15 Avril 1621, Lieutenant au Régiment de Gramont, Cavalerie, marié, en 1646, par contrat paffé devant *Marquaire*, Notaire Royal à Foiffy, à *Anne de Chicault*, dite *de Milly*, fille de *Charles de Chicault*, Ecuyer, Seigneur de Mont-Audhoard & du Milly, & d'une femme dont on ignore le nom. De ce mariage eft né :

FRANÇOIS-HENRI DE BAUBARD, Ecuyer, Seigneur de Chambour & de la Grurie, ancien Capitaine & Aide-Major au Régiment de la Ferté, né le 11 Janvier 1654, qui fut marié à *Agathe de Bigot*, fille de *Jean de Bigot*, Ecuyer, Seigneur du Domat, & d'*Anne de Fréville*, dite *de Rapficourt*, dont il n'a point eu d'enfans ; & 2° le 6 Avril 1681, par contrat paffé devant *Augé*, Notaire Royal à Saint-Liébault, *Gabrielle le Paule*, dite *Demoifelle de Villemoiron*, fille de *Pierre le Paule*, Ecuyer, Seigneur en partie de Bercenay en Othe, & de *N... Journée du Montois*, dont eft iffu :

PIERRE DE BAUBARD, Ecuyer, Seigneur de la Grurie, né le 7 Mars 1684, Capitaine au Régiment de Beaujolois, & Chevalier de Saint-Louis, qui fe maria, le 10 Avril 1707, à *Luce Janneau de Jardelay*, fille de *N... Janneau*, Seigneur de Jardelay, Capitaine de Dragons, & de fa femme, dont on ignore le nom. Il eut :

1. PIERRE-NICOLAS, qui fuit ;
2. PHILIPPE-ALEXANDRE, né le 17 Avril 1715 ;
3. N... DE BAUBARD, né au mois d'Avril 1717, Lieutenant au Régiment de Picardie, tué aux guerres d'Italie ;
4. FRANÇOIS, dit *le Chevalier de la Grurie*, né le 14 Mars 1718, auffi Lieutenant au Régiment de Picardie, tué en Bohême.

PIERRE-NICOLAS DE BAUBARD, Ecuyer, Seigneur de la Grurie, né le 11 Août 1709, fut maintenu dans fa noblesse, avec fon frère PHILIPPE-ALEXANDRE DE BAUBARD, le 21 Décembre 1717. Il a époufé, en 1733, *Cécile de Lobin*, Dame des Ouches, de laquelle font iffus :

1. PIERRE-EDME, qui fuit ;
2. Et CHARLES-FRANÇOIS, dit *le Chevalier de Baubard*, né en 1740, lequel fit preuve de nobleffe en 1752, pour entrer à l'École Royale Militaire ; mais il mourut peu de temps après.

PIERRE-EDME DE BAUBARD, né le 31 Juillet 1737, après avoir fervi pendant quelques années dans les Volontaires de Flandres, s'eft marié à Paris le 4 Septembre 1759, à *Jeanne de Basuel*, née au mois de Septembre 1737, fille d'*Etienne-Guillaume*, Ecuyer, Officier au Régiment d'Affry, & de *Marie-Louise-Thérèse de Flaction*, dont un enfant au berceau.

Les armes: *d'or, u sautoir d'azur, accompagné de quatre aigles de sable.*

BAUBIGNY, *d'azur, à trois mains dextres d'or, posées 2 & 1.*

BAUCEY, en Bourgogne : *de gueules, à la croix ancrée a'or.*

BAUCHES, Seigneur de His, en Normandie, Généralité de Caen, famille annoblie pour services en 1597 : *d'azur, à un poignet dextre d'argent, tenant une épée en pal, accompagnée à chaque flanc d'une étoile, & surmontée en pointe d'une nuée, le tout de même se terminant en demi-cercle au haut de l'écu, & renfermant un soleil d'or.*

BAUCHET, en Bourgogne : *d'argent à une merlette de sable, au chef d'azur, chargé de trois besans d'or.*

BAU...LERC-D'ACHERE : *de gueules, au chevron d'or, accompagné en chef de trois têtes de loup, & en pointe d'un loup entier, le tout de même; au chef cousu d'azur, chargé d'un croissant d'or.*

BAUD (LE), en Bretagne : *d'argent à une quinte-feuille de gueules.*

BAUD, en Provence : *d'or, au mouton rampant de sable, brisé d'une cotice d'argent.*

BAUDA, en Champagne : *d'or, à trois bandes de gueules.*

BAUDAIN : *d'azur, au chevron d'argent, accompagné de trois quinte-feuilles d'or, 2 en chef, & une en pointe; au chef de même, chargé de trois merlettes de sable.*

BAUDAR, Seigneur de Vaudesin : *d'azur, au dard d'or, posé en pal, la pointe en haut.*

BAUDART, Seigneur de Colombi, Généralité de Caen en Normandie. GERVAIS BAUDART, Ecuyer, rendit, suivant la Roque, aveu pour un quart de fief de Chevalier, nommé Garsailles, situé à Espanai, Vicomté de Falaise, le 19 Mars 1371.

PIERRE BAUDART, Sieur de la Baudardière, épousa en 1440, *Jeanne de Graveron*, Dame de Reviers en Bessin.

ELISABETH BAUDART, née le 8 Août 1674, fut reçue à Saint-Cyr au mois de Mars 1686, après avoir prouvé qu'elle descendoit de PIERRE BAUDART.

GUILLAUME BAUDART, Ecuyer, Seigneur de Colombi, est cité dans un contrat daté du 6 Juin 1457; il eut pour fils :

THOMAS BAUDART, Seigneur de Colombi, qui fut père de :

JACQUELINE BAUDART, mariée, 1° le 7 Juillet 1501, à *Roger de Baillehache*, Seigneur de Descajeux, & 2° à *Michel d'Harcourt*, Seigneur de Mont-Louis.

Par une Ordonnance des Commissaires députés par le Roi HENRI IV, sur le fait de la Noblesse, datée du 8 Juin 1599, la famille de *Baudart* fut déclarée noble d'ancienneté.

Les armes : *d'azur, à trois fasces ondées d'argent.*

BAUDE DE LA VIEUVILLE. ETIENNE-AUGUSTE DE BAUDE DE LA VIEUVILLE est Officier au Régiment des Gardes-Françoises : c'est en sa faveur, & en considération de ses services, que le Marquisat de Châteauneuf acquis par son père N.... de BAUDE DE LA VIEUVILLE, a été de nouveau érigé en Marquisat, par lettres du mois de Juin 1746, enregistrées à Nantes le 23 Novembre suivant. Voyez VIEUVILLE.

* BAUDEAN. La Terre & Vallée de Baudean dans les Monts Pyrénées en Bigorre a donné le nom à la Maison de Baudean, que l'on tient être issue de la race des anciens Rois de Navarre. Elle est d'ancienne Chevalerie & une des premières & des plus distinguées des Provinces de Béarn & de Bigorre. Il faut remarquer que le nom de BAUDEAN s'écrivoit & se prononçoit autrefois BEUDEA, tel qu'il se voit dans les titres gascons.

La famille de BAUDEAN tomba en quenouille vers 1400, & fut relevée par *Pierre de Momas*, cité plus loin. La filiation de la Maison de *Momas*, commence à RABIDAT DE MOMAS, qualifié *puissant Chevalier*, qui du consentement de GUILLAUME, son fils, fit donation à l'Abbaye de la Réole en Béarn de certains biens au lieu de Momas vers 980. Dans le même tems, *Sanche*, Duc *de Gascogne*, donna le lieu de Pardiès, qui étoit une dépendance de sa Cour, & Seigneurie de Momas. *Centule-Gaston*, Vicomte *de Béarn*, *Guillaume Rabi*, Vicomte de Marenne, & le Vi-

comte *de Louvigner* firent auffi des libérali-
tés au même Monaftère. Voyez Marca, *Hiftoire de Béarn,* liv. IV, chapit. 4, pag. 267.

On trouve enfuite RAYMOND-FUERT, Seigneur DE MOMAS, Chevalier, qui fit foi &
hommage au Vicomte *de Béarn* en 1345. Il
fervit dans les guerres de Gafcogne contre les
Anglois en 1346, &c. Il eut entr'autres enfans :

ARNAUD, qui fuit ;

ASSIVAT ;

Et MARIE DE MOMAS, mariée à *Gaillard de
Luc,* Seigneur de Luc en Béarn.

ARNAUD DE MOMAS, Seigneur de Momas,
fut du nombre des Chevaliers & Ecuyers qui
paffèrent en revue au Château d'Orthès en
1376, pour fervir contre les Anglois. Il rendit
hommage de fes Terres à *Gafton,* Vicomte *de
Béarn,* en 1391. Il époufa *Berneȝe de Béarn,*
& donna quittance de fa dot à *Gafton de
Foix,* Vicomte de Béarn, le 24 Mars 1400.
Ses enfans furent entr'autres :

JEAN, qui fuit ;

Et DOUCINE, mariée, en 1519, avec *Auger
d'Andouins,* Seigneur de Doazon.

JEAN DE MOMAS, Seigneur dudit lieu, eut
pour fils :

PIERRE, Seigneur DE MOMAS, qui époufa
Jeanne de Loubie, & en eut :

LOUIS, Seigneur DE MOMAS, père de :

LOUISE, Dame héritière de la Terre de Momas, qu'elle porta en mariage, en 1442, à
Jean, Seigneur de *Caubios,* en Béarn.

La filiation des Seigneurs de BAUDEAN &
de PARABÈRE commence à :

I. PIERRE DE MOMAS, Damoifeau, cadet des
Seigneurs DE MOMAS en Béarn, né vers 1376.
Il fut préfent à la reconnoiffance de la dot de
Jeanne de Baudean, fille de *Navarrot,* Seigneur d'Aux, au Comté de Pardiac, confentie par *Aȝemar,* Seigneur de Marambat le 8
Septembre 1398. Il affifta auffi à la reconnoiffance de la dot de *Catherine de Villepinte,*
époufe de *Pierre,* Seigneur de *Saint-Aunis*
près de Parabère, le 11 Février 1411, & fervit avec *Jean,* Comte *de Foix* contre les Anglois en 1430 & 1431. Il avoit époufé, vers
1412, *Simonne de Baudean,* Dame de Parabère en Bigorre, Terre qui appartenoit, en
1266, à *Efpain de Baudean,* Seigneur de
Baudean. Ils eurent différend vers 1414, fur
les limites de leur Terre, avec les habitans
des lieux de Monfegur, de Labatut-Higueres

& de Cafteyde. *Jean,* Comte *de Foix* & de
Bigorre, en confidération des Seigneurs &
Dame *de Parabère,* nomma pour Arbitres
Bertrand de Navailles & le Seigneur *de Caf-
tetber,* qui terminèrent l'affaire par Sentence
de l'an 1427. *Simonne de Baudean* étoit
veuve en 1452, & difpofa de fes biens, le 30
Août 1454, en faveur de fes deux fils :

JEAN, qui eut pour fon partage la Terre de
Baudean, & a continué la poftérité des Seigneurs de BAUDEAN de mâles en mâles, jufqu'à HENRI, Baron de BAUDEAN, qui repré-
fente aujourd'hui cette branche ;

Et ARNAUD, tige des Comtes de *Parabère,* dont
nous allons parler, qui eut pour fon partage la Terre de Parabère.

Seigneurs Comtes de PARABÈRE.

II. ARNAUD DE MOMAS, fils puîné de PIERRE,
fut apanagé par *Simonne de Baudean,* fa
mère, de la Terre de Parabère en Bigorre, par
acte de 1454. Il étoit mort en 1490, & laiffa
pour fucceffeur :

III. ARNAUD-GUILLAUMÈ DE BAUDEAN, Seigneur de Parabère, qui en cette qualité confentit un bail à fief audit lieu en 1498. Il reçut la même année le ferment de fidélité des
habitans de fa Terre, & paffa un accord avec
eux & avec l'Abbé & les Religieux de la Réole près de Parabère, au fujet du Terroir des
Barthes, lequel il promit de faire ratifier &
approuver par fa femme, & par fon fils qui
étoit encore adulte. Il avoit époufé, vers 1479,
Chriftine d'Andouins, fille d'*Arnaud,* Seigneur de Doazon & de Caftera en Béarn,
dont :

IV. LOUIS DE BAUDEAN, Chevalier, Seigneur de Parabère, qui n'avoit que 14 à 15
ans en 1498, lorfqu'il confentit avec fa mère
à l'accord paffé avec les habitans de Parabère,
l'Abbé & les Religieux de la Réole. Il fit
vente de plufieurs fiefs dépendans de la Seigneurie de Parabère, par acte de 1514. Les
Seigneurs *de Parabère* furent toujours atta-
chés aux Rois de Navarre qui leur faifoient
l'honneur de les traiter de *Coufins* en leur
écrivant. LOUIS DE BAUDEAN DE PARABÈRE, tué
au fiège de Pampelune, avoit époufé, en 1512,
Catherine du Fourc, fille de *Carbonel,* Chevalier, Seigneur de Montaftruc au Comté d'Armagnac, de laquelle il eut entr'autres enfans :

V. BERNARD DE BAUDEAN, Seigneur de Parabère, qui fut toujours attaché au Roi de
Navarre. Il tefta au Château de Parabère le

Avril 1554, & avoit épousé, le 27 Avril 1562, *Jeanne de Caubios*. Cette Dame racheta, le 8 Janvier 1577, les Fiefs qui avoient été aliénés, en 1514, par Louis de Baudean, Seigneur de Parabère, père de son mari. Elle étoit fille de *Guillaume*, Seigneur de *Caubios* & d'Uzain, & de *Catherine de la Fargue*; & sœur des Seigneurs *de Caubios*, tués au siège de Metz en 1552. Ses enfans furent:

1. Pierre, Seigneur de Parabère, Capitaine-Gouverneur de Beaucaire, qui fut un homme d'un mérite singulier. Ses amours avec la Dame *de la Tourette*, de la Maison de *Villeneuve*, de Provence, & leur mort tragique arrivée dans l'Eglise des Cordeliers de cette ville, où ils furent ensemble assassinés d'une manière barbare, sont connus;
2. Jean, qui suit;
3. Et Jeanne, mariée, le 24 Décembre 1577, avec *Jean de Marrenx*, Seigneur de Montgaillard en Armagnac.

VI. Jean de Baudean, Chevalier, Comte de Parabère, & de Nouillan, Marquis de la Mothe-Sainte-Heraye, Seigneur de Saint-Sauran & de Roche, Châtelain de la Roche-Ruffin, de Salle & de Fougeray, Gentilhomme ordinaire de la Chambre du Roi de Navarre, Capitaine d'un Régiment de son nom, connu par les Historiens sous le nom *de vieux Régiment de Parabère*, Gouverneur de la Ville & Château de l'Isle-Jourdain en 1585, puis de Niort qu'il emporta par escalade sous Henri III, fit prisonnier le Baron de Malicorne, Gouverneur du Poitou, & fut fait Lieutenant-Général des Armées du Roi. Fidèlement attaché au Roi Henri IV, qu'il servit dans toutes ses expéditions, il fut honoré de la bienveillance de ce Prince, qui lui donna les deux Lieutenances Générales de la Province de Poitou, lesquelles furent réunies en sa personne ayant toujours été séparées jusqu'à lui comme elles l'ont encore été depuis; fut fait Maréchal de France le 14 Septembre 1622, & nommé Chevalier des Ordres, mais non reçu par sa mort arrivée le 14 Décembre 1622, causée par les grandes blessures qu'il avoit reçues. Il avoit épousé, le 23 Décembre 1591, *Louise de Gilier*, veuve de *François de Sainte-Maure*, Comte de Montausier. De ce mariage naquirent.

1. Henri, qui suit;
2. Et Charles, Comte de Nouillan, dont la postérité sera rapportée après celle de son aîné.

VII. Henri de Baudean, Chevalier, Comte de Parabère, Marquis de la Mothe-Sainte-Heraye, Baron de Pardaillan, Capitaine de 100 hommes d'armes des Ordonnances du Roi, Gouverneur de Niort, Lieutenant-Général & Gouverneur du haut & bas Poitou, pays d'Angoumois, d'Aunis & de la Rochelle, nommé Chevalier de l'Ordre du Saint-Esprit à la promotion du 14 Mai 1633, mort le 11 Janvier 1653, dans la 60e année de son âge, avoit épousé, le 13 Novembre 1611, *Catherine de Pardaillan-d'Armagnac*, fille & héritière de *François-Jean-Charles de Pardaillan-d'Armagnac*, Seigneur Comte de Panjas, Baron de Pardaillan, &c., & de *Jeanne du Monceau de Tignonville*.

De ce mariage naquirent:

1. Jean de Baudean, Comte de Parabère, Marquis de la Mothe-Saint-Heraye, premier Baron d'Armagnac, Baron de Montaut, de Pardaillan & de Grammont, Lieutenant-Général du haut Poitou, mort le 12 Mars 1695, âgé de 80 ans, sans enfans. Il avoit épousé 1º *Henriette de Voisin-de-Montaut*, morte à Paris en 1680; & 2º *Françoise de Sancerre;*
2. Alexandre, qui suit;
3. Philippe, reçu Chevalier de l'Ordre de St.-Jean de Jérusalem, en 1637, tué au combat de Retimo, en Candie, dans le Bataillon de Malte, au secours des Vénitiens, en 1647;
4. César, Abbé de Saint-Vincent de Metz, de la Réole en Bigorre, de Notre-Dame de Noyers, mort en 1678;
5. Charles-Louis, Mestre-de-Camp de Cavalerie, mort sans alliance;
6. Achille, Chevalier de Malte, tué en duel;
7. Henri, appelé *le Chevalier de Parabère*, Capitaine de Cavalerie dans le Régiment de Mestre-de-Camp-Général, mort en 1678, sans alliance;
8. Louise, mariée, en 1633, à *David*, Comte de *Souillac*, Marquis d'Azerac, & de Castelnau d'Eauzan, Seigneur de Rouffignac;
9. Catherine-Berenice de Baudean, mariée, le 1er Août 1649, à *Louis Bouchard-d'Aubeterre*, Marquis de Saint-Martin, Seigneur de Folles;
10. Charlotte, Abbesse de la Mothe-Sainte-Heraye, où elle est morte;
11. Et Catherine de Baudean, nommée Dorothée dans les *Grands Officiers de la Couronne*, première Abbesse de la Mothe-Sainte-Heraye, fondée & dotée par Henri de Baudean, son père, à la nomination des Seigneurs Comtes de *Parabère*.

VIII. Alexandre de Baudean, Comte de Pardaillan & de Parabère, Chanoine d'honneur de l'Eglise Cathédrale d'Auch, Baron du petit Château de Beauran, Seigneur de la Rouffelière-Rouhault, d'Antigny, de Bazoches & de la Fosse, Lieutenant-Général des Armées du Roi & au Gouvernement du haut & bas Poitou, mort e 28 Juin 1702, âgé de 83 ans, avoit épousé *Jeanne-Thérèse de Mayaud*, dont:

1. Jean-Henri de Baudean, Marquis de Parabère, Capitaine de Cavalerie dans le Régiment du Roi, mort à Namur en Décembre 1692;
2. César-Alexandre, qui suit;
3. Alexandre, Comte de Neuillan, appelé *le Comte de Pardaillan*, Mestre-de-Camp de Cavalerie du Régiment de Parabère;
4. Henri, Marquis de Parabère, fait Brigadier des Armées du Roi, à la promotion du 20 Février 1734, chef d'une Brigade du Régiment Royal des Carabiniers, qui a quitté le service en 1735, & est mort le 28 Juillet 1741, dans la 52e année de son âge. Il avoit épousé, le 8 Février 1720, *Marie-Andrée Fargès*, décédée en couches le 7 Décembre 1720, de deux enfans qui sont morts;
5. & 6. Esclarmonde & Jeanne-Thérèse, Religieuses à Cerisiers, Ordre de Fontevrault;
7. & 8. Henriette-Dorothée & Marie ou Marguerite, selon le P. Anselme, toutes deux Religieuses à Sainte-Croix de Poitiers.

IX. César-Alexandre de Baudean, Comte de Parabère & de Pardaillan, Chanoine d'honneur né de la Cathédrale d'Auch, Mestre-de-Camp d'un Régiment de Cavalerie, Brigadier des Armées du Roi, mort le 13 Février 1716, de la petite-vérole, & inhumé aux Minimes de la Place Royale, avoit épousé, le 8 Juin 1711, *Marie-Madeleine de la Vieuville*, fille de *René-François*, Marquis *de la Vieuville*, Chevalier d'honneur de la Reine, & Gouverneur du haut & bas Poitou, & de *Marie-Louise de la Chauffée d'Eu*, Dame d'Atours de la Duchesse de Berry, dont:

1. Louis-Barnabé, qui suit;
2. Louis-Henri, né le 15 Mars 1715, d'abord ecclésiastique, ensuite nommé *le Chevalier de Parabère*, Lieutenant des Vaisseaux du Roi, puis Major-Général de l'Escadre du Du d'Anville, mort le 28 Septembre 1746;
3. Et Gabrielle-Anne de Baudean, née au mois d'Octobre 1716, mariée, le 18 ou 19 Juillet 1735, à *Frédéric-Rodolphe*, Comte de *Rottenbourg*, Mestre-de-Camp de Cavalerie en France, mort en 1752.

X. Louis-Barnabé de Baudean, Comte de Parabère & de Pardaillan, Seigneur de Beauran, Chanoine d'honneur-né de la Cathédrale d'Auch, né le 14 Mars 1714, ci-devant Capitaine au Régiment Royal des Carabiniers, & Chevalier de Saint-Louis, a épousé 1º *Françoise-Claire de Gourgues*, morte sans enfans le 13 Décembre 1757; & 2º le 18 Mars 1760, *Jeanne-Claude-Bernardine Gagne de Perigny*, fille de *Philibert-Bernard*, Président à Mortier au Parlement de Bourgogne, & de *Jeanne-Marie Thesut de Ragy*, De ce second mariage il a:

Alexandre-César, qui suit;
Et Adelaide-Julie-Amelie de Baudean-Parabère, née en 1770.

XI. Alexandre-César de Baudean, Comte de Parabère, est né en 1766.

Branche sortie de la précédente.

VII. Charles de Baudean, Comte de Neuillan, Seigneur de Saint-Sauran, la Roche-Ruffin, Sainte-Souline, & des Moulières, fils puîné de Jean, Comte de Parabère, & de *Louise de Gilier*, Conseiller du Roi en ses Conseils d'Etat & Privé, Capitaine de 50 hommes d'armes des Ordonnances, Gouverneur de la Ville & Château de Niort, épousa *Françoise* ou *Louise* (selon le P. Anselme), *Tiraqueau*, veuve d'*Eusèbe du Puy du Fou*, Seigneur de la Sevrie, & fille d'*Adam Tiraqueau*, Seigneur de Laubier, Gouverneur de Vouvent. Elle eut de son premier mari — *Françoise du Puy du Fou*, mariée à *Hilaire de Laval de Lezay*, aîné de la Maison de *Laval*, dont elle n'eut point d'enfans, & de son second mariage avec Charles de Baudean, vinrent:

1. Charles, Gouverneur de Niort, Capitaine de Cavalerie, tué à la bataille de Lens, en 1648, sans avoir été marié;
2. Susanne, l'une des Dames d'honneur de la Reine Anne d'Autriche, morte le 15 Février 1700, âgée de 74 ans. Elle avoit épousé, par contrat du 19 Février 1651, *Philippe de Montaut de Benac*, IIe du nom, Duc de Navailles, Maréchal de France. Voyez MONTAUT;
3. Et Angelique de Baudean, mariée à *Charles*, Comte de *Froulay*. Voyez FROULAY.

Cette Généalogie des Comtes *de Parabère* est extraite en partie du *Mercure de France* du mois de Décembre 1746, des tom. V & IX de l'*Histoire des Grands Officiers de la Couronne*; du Cabinet des Ordres du Roi, & enfin des titres originaux qui nous ont été préfentés.

Outre les alliances, dont il eft fait mention dans cette Généalogie, la branche de BAUDEAN-PARABÈRE en a aufli contracté avec les Maifons de *Rohan*, de *Montmorency*, la *Trémoille*, *Vienne*, en Bourgogne, *Noailles*, *Crequy*, *Caumont la Force*, *Gramont*, & plufieurs autres grandes Maifons du Royaume.

Les armes: *écartelé, aux 1 & 4 d'or, à un pin fruité & arraché de finople*, qui eft de BAUDEAN; *aux 2 & 3 d'argent, à deux ours levés de fable*, qui eft de MOMAS.

La branche des Comtes *de Parabère* porte : *écartelé, contrecartelé aux 1 & 4 DE NAVARRE; aux 2 & 3 D'ARMAGNAC- RODÈS, & un écuffon en cœur aux armes de Pardaillan ; & fur le tout celles de* BAUDEAN & de MOMAS comme ci-devant.

BAUDENIS ou BAUDENYS, Sieur de Monteterre, Election de Carentan, en Normandie, ancienne nobleffe qui porte: *d'argent, au fautoir engrelé de gueules, cantonné de quatre têtes de lion de fable, arrachées, lampaffées de gueules.*

BAUDEQUIN-DE-PEUTHY. On nous a envoyé un Mémoire fur cette Famille noble originaire du Duché de Bourgogne, établie depuis plufieurs fiècles en Flandres & dans le Brabant.

On y trouve que PAUL DE BAUDEQUIN étoit natif de la ville de Dijon, & d'extraction noble & ancienne, c'eft ce qu'apprennent vifiblement plufieurs anciens documens & mémoires de la même Ville. Il fut dès fa jeuneffe attaché au fervice de PHILIPPE-LE-BON, Duc de Bourgogne, & fervit en qualité d'homme d'armes. Il mourut en 1426, & avoit époufé *Charlotte Amandre*, dont il eut:

PAUL DE BAUDEQUIN, Echanfon de CHARLES-LE-HARDI, Duc de Bourgogne, qui fe maria avec *Jeanne de Cuiry*, dont:

DENIS DE BAUDEQUIN, aufli Echanfon de la Panneterie de l'Empereur MAXIMILIEN, marié à l'héritière de Bourgogne, fille de CHARLES-LE-HARDI. DENIS DE BAUDEQUIN s'allia avec *Jeanne de Machéco*, d'une illuftre Maifon qui fubfifte encore en Bourgogne. De ce mariage vint:

PHILIPPE DE BAUDEQUIN, Sommelier de la

Panneterie & Greffier en chef des Bureaux de l'Empereur CHARLES-QUINT. Il mourut en 1571, & fut enterré dans l'Eglife Paroifliale de Saint-Jacques de Caudenbergh à Bruxelles. Il avoit époufé *Marie de Zombergh*, fille d'*Aimond de Zombergh*, Capitaine-Châtelain de la ville de Rupelmonde, & en eut, entr'autres enfans :

1. CHARLES, mort fans hoir, en 1650, enterré dans l'Eglife Paroifliale de Peuthy, qui avoit été créé Chevalier par Philippe III, Roi d'Efpagne en 1603, Gentilhomme ordinaire de fa Chambre, & fon Introducteur des Ambaffadeurs à la Cour de Madrid;
2. CLAUDE, qui fuit;
3. Et CATHERINE, Dame d'Honneur de la Princeffe d'Orange, & veuve du Seigneur de *Moens de Zelem*. Elle fut enterrée comme fon frère dans l'Eglife de Peuthy.

CLAUDE DE BAUDEQUIN fut membre de l'Etat Noble de la Châtellenie & Ville de Lille, Douai, Orchies, &c. Il eut, entr'autres enfans de fa première femme, *Marie de la Rivière*, fille de *Philippe*, Ecuyer & Seigneur d'Allencour & de Warmes, & d'*Ifabelle de Launoy-d'Ablains* :

PHILIPPE DE BAUDEQUIN, créé Chevalier par Lettres-Patentes de 16.., de PHILIPPE IV, Roi d'Efpagne, Seigneur d'Allencour, la Haye, Peuthy & Battenbourg; Commiffaire au renouvelement de la Loi de la ville de Lille en Flandres ; Membre & Député de la même Province, & Fondateur en partie du Couvent des Carmélites Déchauffées de la même Ville, où il eft inhumé fous une tombe de marbre avec fes huit quartiers. Il avoit époufé *Claudine d'Ennetières*, fille de *Jean*, Chevalier, Seigneur d'Harlebois, Confeiller des Domaines & Finances de S. M. le Roi d'Efpagne aux Pays-Bas, & de *Françoife Van den Berghe de la Croix-au-Mont*. De ce mariage vinrent:

1. FERDINAND, Capitaine de Cuiraffiers au fervice du Roi d'Efpagne, qui fut marié, & laiffa deux garçons, morts Chanoines, & quatre filles; l'une mariée en Artois, & deux autres Religieufes;
2. CLAUDE-EUGÈNE, qui fuit;
3. Et CHARLES-EUGÈNE, rapporté après la poftérité de fon aîné.

CLAUDE-EUGÈNE DE BAUDEQUIN, Seigneur de Peuthy, Battenbourg, de Huldenbergh, Smyesbergh, &c., Grand-Bailli de la Ville & du Territoire de Vilvorde, fut aufli Capitai-

ne d'une Compagnie de Cuiraffiers au fervice du Roi d'Efpagne. Il avoit époufé *Marie-Madeleine de Croix de Dadizcele*, fille
de *Jean*, Chevalier & Seigneur de Dadizcele;
& d'*Ifabelle Van-Schoore de Roftuyne*,
dont il a eu:

CHARLES-PHILIPPE-MARTIN DE BAUDEQUIN,
Chevalier, Seigneur de Peuthy, Battenbourg,
Huldenberg, Smeysberg, Autem, Kalverkee-
te, la Plaigne, Sains & Launoy, Grand-Bailli
de la Ville & Territoire de Vilvorde. Il a été
élevé à la dignité de Baron, titre applicable
fur telle Terre acquife ou à acquérir qu'il
voudra nommer fous la dénomination de
S. M. Impériale & Royale, par Lettres-Patentes datées de Vienne du 20 Mars 1766. Il
a époufé, par contrat du 25 Mars 1735, *Marie-Anne d'Eynatten-de-Schoonhoven*, fille
de *Nicolas*, Baron d'Eynatten, Seigneur de
Terheyden, de Terhaegen, Gerardmont, Confeiller penfionnaire de la ville de Louvain, &
Député ordinaire aux Etats du Duché de
Brabant, & d'*Anne-Véronique de Joncis-
de-Duffel*, petite-fille de *Théodore d'Eynatten*, Ecuyer, Seigneur de Terheyden & Terhaegen, Echevin de la ville de Louvain, &
d'*Anne-Mathilde Van-Ophem de Wayems*,
& arrière-petite-fille d'*Arnoul d'Eynatten-
de-Schoonhoven*, Ecuyer & Seigneur de Terheyden & Terhaegen, Echevin·de la ville
de Louvain, & de *Françoife de Borgraef*.
De cette alliance font nés:

1. IDESBALD-ALBERT-JOSEPH, Baron de Baudequin, reçu à l'Etat Noble du Duché de
   Brabant, en qualité de Baron de Huldenbergh;
2. Et MARIE-MADELEINE-THÉODORE, Chanoineffe au noble Chapitre de Mouftiers-fur-
   Sambre.

SECONDE BRANCHE.

CHARLES-EUGÈNE DE BAUDEQUIN, Chevalier,
Seigneur du Metz & de Sainghin, Capitaine
d'une Compagnie de Cuiraffiers au fervice de
S. M. C., fecond fils de PHILIPPE, & de *Claudine d'Ennetières*, époufa, par contrat paffé
à Lille le 4 Février 1673, *Ifabelle-Jeanne
de Waziers*, fille de *Jean-André*, Chevalier,
Seigneur du Verbois-la-Volandre, & de *Madeleine de Heffel*, dont entr'autres enfans:

PHILIPPE-ANDRÉ DE BAUDEQUIN, Chevalier,
Seigneur du Metz, de Sainghin & de Flers,

qui fe maria, par contrat paffé à Lille le 5
Novembre 1707, avec *Marie-Antoinette de
Grofpré*, fille de *Guislain-Robert de Gros-
pré*, Chevalier, Seigneur de Gorguehel & de
Bruyelle, & de *Marie-Jeanne de Blondel*,
dont entr'autres enfans:

ANDRÉ-FRANÇOIS-JOSEPH DE BAUDEQUIN,
Chevalier, Seigneur de Biez, mort avant fon
père. Il avoit époufé, par contrat paffé à Lille
le 25 Mai 1743, *Marie-Françoife-Corneille
Dumont*, fille de *François-Louis-Jofeph Dumont*, Baron de Weftoutre, Grand-Bailli de
Bailleul, & de *Marie-Catherine de Pollinc-
hoven*, Dame de Weftoutre, dont:

1. PHILIPPE-JOSEPH, Seigneur de Sainghin, du
   Metz, Flers & Bruyelle, Exempt des Gardes-du-Corps du Roi, né le 5 Avril 1744,
   mort à Paris, non marié, en Février 1765,
   & inhumé dans l'Eglife de Saint-André-
   des-Arts;
2. Et MARIE-CLAIRE-JOSÈPHE DE BAUDEQUIN,
   née le 3 Mars 1745, héritière univerfelle
   de fon frère. Elle a époufé, le 4 Juin 1770,
   François-Philippe-Nicolas-Ladislas, Comte de *Diesbach*, Baron du Saint-Empire
   Romain, Officier-Major au Régiment des·
   Gardes-Suiffes en France, fille de *Fran-
   çois-Jofeph-Romain*, Comte de *Diesbach*,
   Baron du Saint-Empire, Seigneur de la
   Cour, Commandeur de l'Ordre Royal &
   Militaire de Saint-Louis, Maréchal de
   Camp, Colonel d'un Régiment-Suiffe de
   fon nom, & de *Marie-Dominique-Théré-
   fe de Mullet*, Dame de Deux, Achiets,
   Wacquetin & d'Erviliers, &c.

Les armes: *d'argent, à la hure de fanglier de fable, défendue du champ;* l'écu
fommé d'une *couronne de Comte*. Supports:
*deux fauvages de carnation couronnés &
ceintrés de feuille de lière de finople*. Cimier: *un cafque de Baron, chargé de 5
grilles, furmonté d'une couronne de Marquis, fommée d'un vol banneret, parti mi-
fable & mi-argent & ornée de lambrequins
de même*.

BAUDET: *d'or, au mouton de fable*.

BAUDET: *de gueules, à trois hameçons
d'argent, 2 & 1*.

BAUDIER, en Champagne. CLAUDE BAU-
DIER, Gouverneur de Rhétel, époufa *Sufanne
d'Afpremont*, fille d'*Abfalon*, Baron de Nanteuil, & de *Claude d'Y*, Dame de Novien-le-
Comte, dont:

Catherine de Baudier, mariée, le 15 Mars 1660, à *Georges de Reignard*, père de *Charles-Joseph de Reignard*, dont la fille, *Marguerite-Catherine de Reignard-des-Bordes*, décédée le 17 Novembre 1757, avoit été mariée.

Les armes : *d'argent, à trois têtes de maures de fable, pofées 2 & 1, & tortillées du champ.*

BAUDIERE, en Languedoc : *d'azur, à cinq épées d'argent pofées en pal.*

BAUDIÈRE ou BAUDIEZ, en Bretagne : *d'or, à trois fafces ondées d'azur, furmontées au côté droit d'un trèfle de même.*

BAUDIMANT, en Poitou : *d'argent, à trois merlettes de fable, 2 & 1.*

BAUDIMENT : *d'or, à trois aigles éployées de finople ou de fable, pofées 2 & 1.*

BAUDIN : *bandé d'argent & de gueules de fix pièces.*

BAUDINCOURT : *d'argent, à l'aigle éployée de fable, chargé d'un écuffon d'argent, furchargé d'un chapeau de Cardinal, de gueules.*

BAUDINEL, en Bourgogne : *d'or, à la croifette de finople, au chef d'azur, chargé de trois croiffans d'argent.*

BAUDINET, en Bourgogne : *d'azur, à trois fafces d'or, furmontées de trois croiffans d'argent, divifés de gueules.*

BAUDOCHE : *d'argent, à trois chevrons de gueules ; au chef d'azur, chargé de trois tours d'or.*

BAUDON : *d'azur, au pélican dans fon aire, furmonté un peu à dextre d'un foleil, le tout d'or.*

BAUDON, en Provence : *de gueules, à une épée garnie d'argent dans fon fourreau de fable, pofée en pal, la pointe en bas, & tortillée de fon baudrier ou ceinturon, auffi de fable.*

BAUDOT. Cette famille a été long-tems établie à Ambène, Election de Conches, Généralité d'Alençon, en Normandie. Son premier domicile étoit au Hameau de la Fleurière, où elle fit conftruire une Chapelle Domeftique qui fubfifte encore aujourd'hui, quoique délaiffée. Depuis elle en fit con-

ftruire une autre contre le chœur de l'Eglife, qui lui à fervi de féance & de fépulture.

Edmond de Baudot, Ier du nom, Ecuyer, Seigneur d'Ambène & du Boyon, auteur commun des deux branches des Sieurs d'Ambène & du Boyon, eft celui qui, après la réunion du Comté d'Evreux à la Couronne, fit confirmer les droits & privilèges des Riverains de la forêt de Breteuil, par Arrêt du Parlement de Rouen, où il eft dénommé. Ce droit eft inféré dans les franchifes de ladite forêt, le 11 Juin 1578. Il fut inhumé dans le chœur de l'Eglife d'Ambène, le 9 Avril 1614; il laiffa :

1. & 2. N... & Edmond, qui fuivent ;
3. Et N... père de François de Baudot, Ecuyer, Sieur d'Ambène, Gouverneur en 1669, de la Ville & Tour-Grife de Verneuil.

N....... Baudot, Seigneur de Néquèfe, Euneval, près Conches, époufa, vers 1620, *Catherine de Croifmare*, fille de *Charles de Croifmare*, Seigneur de Portmot.

La branche aînée des Seigneurs d'*Ambène* eft tombée en quenouille.

Edmond Baudot, IIe du nom, fils puîné d'Edmond Ier Seigneur d'Ambène & du Boyon, époufa, en 1628, *Catherine Giraud*, dont il eut :

Edmond Baudot, IIIe du nom, qui a fervi long-tems dans les Chevaux-Légers, & y eft mort en 1677. Il avoit époufé, en 1653, *Anne Agis*, fille de Meffire *Louis Agis*, Chevalier, Seigneur du Longpré, & de *Marie de Bardouil*, & nièce d'*Antoine de Bardouil*, Commandeur de l'Ordre de Saint-Jean de Jérufalem, dont vinrent :

1. Jean, qui fuit ;
2. Louis, tué au choc de Leuze le 18 Octobre 1691, après onze ans de fervice dans les Gardes du Roi ;
3. Et Alexandre, rapporté après fon frère aîné.

Jean de Baudot, Brigadier des Gardes du Roi, après avoir reçu plufieurs bleffures à Leuze & à Steenkerque, eut le bras droit emporté d'un coup de canon à la bataille de Malplaquet. Il avoit époufé, en 1695, *Marie de Lorme*, veuve de *René de Moucheron*, Ecuyer, Seigneur de Freulmon, tué à Leuze le 18 Octobre 1691. Il en eut :

1. Jean-René, qui fuit ;
2. Et Alexandre-Charles, qui s'eft retiré

Port-Etendard des Gardes du Roi, & Chevalier de Saint-Louis.

JEAN-RENÉ DE BAUDOT, après avoir servi plusieurs années dans les Gardes du Roi, s'est retiré pour cause de maladie, & a épousé, le 13 Septembre 1736, *Elisabeth de Mays*. De ce mariage naquirent :

- 1. JEAN-RENÉ-ALEXANDRE, qui suit ;
- 2. Et JEAN-RENÉ, né le 23 Octobre 1739, qui sert dans les Gardes du Roi, Compagnie de Villeroy.

JEAN-RENÉ-ALEXANDRE DE BAUDOT, né le 4 Juillet 1737, qui a fait deux Campagnes en Westphalie, sous les ordres du Maréchal Duc de Richelieu, a épousé, le 22 Août 1759, *Marguerite-Françoise Descorches*, sa cousine germaine, fille de *Maurice-François Descorches*, Ecuyer, Sieur de Sainte-Croix, & de *Renée-Marguerite de Moucheron*.

ALEXANDRE DE BAUDOT, fils puîné d'EDMOND III, s'est retiré Commandant de Bataillon dans le Régiment d'Albigeois. Il a épousé *Marie-Simonne Leroy*, fille de *Gabriel Leroy-d'Aquest*, Ecuyer, Sieur de Noue, & d'*Anne-Madeleine Godot*. De ce mariage il eut :

- 1. JÉRÔME-LOUIS DE BAUDOT, né le 8 Octobre 1728 ;
- 2. Et ALEXANDRE DE BAUDOT, Ecuyer, Sieur du Breuil, né le 13 Décembre 1729. Ils servent tous les deux depuis 15 ans dans les Gardes du Corps, Compagnie de Luxembourg.

Cette famille, qui a plusieurs Arrêts de décharge & de maintenue de noblesse, & des épitaphes & des armes peintes dans l'Eglise d'Ambène, est connue depuis plusieurs siècles, suivant qu'il est justifié par un Procès-verbal dûment en forme, fait le 21 Décembre 1761.

Les armes : *de sable, au chevron d'or, accompagné de trois molettes d'éperon de même, 2 en chef & 1 en pointe.*

BAUDOT, Seigneur de Frementel, en Normandie, Généralité d'Alençon : *d'azur, à l'aigle abaissée d'or, accompagné en chef, à dextre d'un soleil, & à senestre d'une épée ou poignard, la pointe en bas, en pal, le tout de même.*

BAUDOUIN, Seigneur du Baffet ou Boisset, de la Guenssue, du Prey, en Normandie, Généralité de Rouen, famille maintenue en sa

noblesse, le 1er Septembre 1667 ou 1669. On lit dans l'*Histoire de Rouen*, que NOEL BAUROUIN fut annobli en 1598. JÉRÉMIE BAUDOUIN, Sieur de Beuville, Auditeur de la Chambre des Comptes de Normandie, mort en 1630, avoit épousé *Barbe Nagerel*, morte le 3 Avril 1631. PIERRE BAUDOUIN, Seigneur du Baffet, Conseiller au Parlement de Rouen, en 1671, étoit Doyen du Parlement en 1717.

Les armes : *d'argent, à la croix de sable, cantonnée aux 1 & 4 d'une croix de Malte d'azur, aux 2 & 3 d'une tente de gueules.*

BAUDOUIN, Sieur de Grandouit, du Fresné, aussi en Normandie, Généralité d'Alençon, famille maintenue dans sa noblesse, le 16 Mai 1667. BERNARD-BAPTISTE BAUDOUIN, Ecuyer, seigneur des Pins, Cornette dans le Régiment du Colonel-Général de Cavalerie, épousa *Marie-Anne Bellette*, fille d'*Olivier Bellette*, seigneur de Gourmai, Vicomte de Vreidey, & *Marie de Beauvais*, dont il eut, entr'autres enfans, MADELEINE-ELISABETH BAUDOUIN-DES-PINS, reçue à Saint-Cyr le 26 Mars 1708, sur les preuves de sa noblesse, établie par titres depuis PIERRE BAUDOUIN, son quatrième ayeul, Seigneur d'Aizy, qualifié de *Noble & d'Ecuyer*, au mois d'Avril 1521.

Les armes : *d'azur, au chevron d'argent, accompagné en chef de deux roses d'or, & en pointe de trois trèfles d'argent, 2 & 1, surmontées d'une fleur-de-lys d'or, à la pointe du chevron.*

BAUDOUIN, en Picardie. PIERRE BAUDOUIN, Ecuyer, Seigneur de Soupire, fut Conseiller-Notaire & Secrétaire du Roi, Maison & Couronne de France, en 1589, Grand-Maître Enquêteur & Général Réformateur des Eaux & Forêts en Bourgogne, pourvu en 1595, de la Charge de Secrétaire des Finances, & du Conseil d'Etat & Privé, par Brevet du 18 Juillet 1617, & Intendant des Finances par commission du 2 Mai 1618, jusqu'en 1627. De son mariage avec *Catherine Cordier*, il a eu :

DANIEL BAUDOUIN, Ecuyer, Seigneur de Soupire, Conseiller-Maître-d'Hôtel ordinaire du Roi, par Lettres de retenue du 1er Novembre 1646, marié, le 3 Août 1637, avec *Marie de Flécelles*, dont :

- 1. SÉRAPHIN, qui suit ;

2. Et PIERRE, Capitaine aux Gardes en 168.

SÉRAPHIN BAUDOUIN, Seigneur de Verneuil, de Baune, de Courtonne & le Soupire, Chevalier d'Honneur au Bailliage & Siège Présidial de Vermandois, fut maintenu dans sa noblesse, par ordonnance de M. *Machault*, Maître des Requêtes & Commissaire départi dans la Généralité de Soissons, du 0 Février 1669. Il épousa, le 12 Mai 1625, *eneviève-Simonne de la Mouche*, dont il eut:

1. FIDEL-SÉRAPHIN ou FÉLIX-SÉRAPHIN, selon le *Mercure de France* du mois d'Avril 1738, Seigneur de Soupire, de Verneuil, de Courtonne, de Baune & de Chéry, né le 23 Mars 1696, Lieutenant dans le Régiment des Gardes-Françoises, Chevalier de Saint-Louis, pourvu le 12 Mai 1716, de l'Office de Conseiller du Roi & de Chevalier d'Honneur au Présidial de Laon. Il est marié;
2. Et ANTOINE-SÉRAPHIN, né le 5 Mai 1697, Chevalier de Saint-Louis, & Capitaine dans le Régiment d'Heudicourt.

Les armes: *d'azur, au lion d'or, au chef de même, chargé de trois roses de gueules; le lion lampassé de gueules.*

BAUDOUIN, Seigneur de Keraudrun, en Ruis: *de gueules, à dix-neuf billettes d'argent, au canton de même, chargé d'une billette de gueules.*

BAUDOUIN, en Bretagne: *de gueules, à la croix pattée d'or, ou d'or, à la croix pattée de gueules.*

BAUDOUIN, Seigneur d'Estavigny: *azur, au chevron d'argent, accompagné en chef de deux étoiles d'or, & en pointe d'un épi de bled de même.*

BAUDOUIN, Seigneur de Chamoult: *d'argent, à l'arbre de sinople, au pied nourri; au chef de gueules, chargé d'un croissant d'argent, accosté de deux étoiles d'or.*

BAUDOUIN ou BAULDIN, en Franche-Comté, de la ville de Salins, famille éteinte dans le XVᵉ siècle. VAULCHIER BAUDOUIN eut de *Guye de Beaufort*:

GUILLAUME BAUDOUIN, Ecuyer, Seigneur de Beaufort, mort le dernier de son nom, qui disposa de ses biens le 8 Décembre 1419 en faveur de l'Eglise Collégiale de Saint-Anatoile de Salins. Il choisit sa sépulture au cloître de cette Eglise, où ses père & mère avoient

été inhumés. Voyez le *Nobiliaire de la ville de Salins*, p. 18.

*BAUDOUR, Terre & Pairie située en Hainaut, sur laquelle les Seigneurs de *Haynin* avoient une rente de 100 livres, très-ancienne monnoye, laquelle a été depuis remise à 300 livres. Cette Terre étoit tenue en fief du Comté de Hainaut, à cause du Château de Mons. *Claude de Haynin*, Seigneur d'Amfroipret, vendit ou aliéna ladite rente. Les Seigneurs de *Haynin* avoient dans la Terre de Baudour quatre journaux de pré, gissant en l'étendue de la Justice de ladite Terre, consistant en trois différentes pièces, & un autre journal gissant au Pont-Tourine, qui servit à fonder une Chapelle.

BAUDOYER ou BODOYER (LE), en Bretagne: *fascé d'argent & de gueules de six pièces.*

BAUDRA ou BEAUDRAP, Seigneur du Mesnil, de la Prumerie, en Normandie, Généralité de Caen, annobli en 1597: *d'azur, au chevron d'argent, accompagné en chef de deux étoiles d'or, & en pointe d'un croissant de même.*

BAUDRAN-DE-PRADEL ET DES GRAVES, dans le Lyonnois. BENOÎT BAUDRAN, Ecuyer, Seigneur de Pradel, des Graves, de Laroue, de Ronzuel, dans la Principauté de Dombes, fut institué héritier universel de *Jean-François de Pradel*, Ecuyer, Seigneur de Laroue, son oncle maternel, par son testament du 9 Juin 1719, à la charge de porter le nom & les armes de *Pradel-Fautrain*, auxquelles il pouvoit joindre celles de BAUDRAN. Il fut maintenu dans sa noblesse, le 1ᵉʳ Septembre 1736, sur les preuves qu'il fournit, & qui remontoient à son sixième ayeul, GONNET DE BAUDRAN, Damoiseau, qui fit son testament le 7 Mai 1445. De son mariage célébré à Pampelune, le 11 Février 1718, avec *Marie-Ignace de Laudaverre*, sont nés deux fils jumeaux, le 27 Mars 1725. Voyez l'*Armorial de France*, reg. II, part. II.

Les armes: *d'azur, à une bande d'or, accompagnée de trois molettes d'éperon de même, 1 en chef & 1 à chaque flanc, & d'un croissant d'argent, à la pointe de l'écu.*

BAUDRE (DE), en Normandie, ancienne noblesse, qui a donné son nom à la Paroisse de St.-Ouen-de-Baudre, Election de Saint-Lô;

dont l'origine fe perd dans l'antiquité des tems. Nous ne pouvons en remonter la filiation fuivie & certaine qu'à

I. GEOFFROY DE BAUDRE, Chevalier, Seigneur de la Paroiffe de Saint-Ouen-de-Baudre, qui fut père de

II. GUILLAUME DE BAUDRE, qualifié *Miles*, dans la charte latine des dons qu'il fit aux Religieux de l'Abbaye de Saint-Lô en 1278, de Monfeigneur GUILLAUME DE BAUDRE, Chevalier, dans l'Ordonnance de l'Echiquer de Normandie de 1291, & d'autres dont nous parlerons. Ledit GUILLAUME DE BAUDRE fit donation, fuivant une charte latine, en 1236, à cette Abbaye de Saint-Lô, Diocèfe de Coutances, de demi-acre de terre, jouxte l'aumône qu'il avoit faite à l'Hôpital de la même ville, pour le falut de fon âme, & de celle de tous fes ancêtres, fuivant une charte en latin, où il avoit mis fon fceau, dans laquelle charte il eft dit fils de GEFFROY DE BAUDRE. Par une autre charte également en latin, datée du 8 Décembre 1278, il confirme toutes les donations que lui & fes prédéceffeurs avoient faites aux Religieux de cette Abbaye, & leur cède le droit qu'il avoit & pouvoit avoir au patronage de l'Eglife de Saint-Ouen-de-Baudre, &c. Par autres titres, en date du mois d'Avril 1278, où il eft également qualifié *Miles*, Seigneur dudit lieu de Baudre, cède & remet à Nicolas-Barthélemy & Olivier le Noir, les redevances des fervices que lui, & fes tenans, lui devoient pour l'héritage qu'ils tenoient de lui; GUILLAUME DE BAUDRE eut pour enfans:

1. GEFFROY, qui fuit;
2. Et JEAN DE BAUDRE.

III. GEFFROY DE BAUDRE, IIe du nom, Ecuyer, & Seigneur du lieu, fiefe à cens, & délaiffe à Hélie le Beau, fon homme, & à fes parchainiers, tous les fervices de charrues, de bêtes, de pêche, corvées, &c., qu'ils lui devoient par Lettres fcellées & confirmées du fceau dudit Seigneur, en date du mois de Mai 1299. Par autres Lettres du Lundi après Noël, l'an 1346, Pierre Huc de Sainte-Croix de Saint-Lô, vend audit GEFFROY DE BAUDRE, cinq boiffeaux de froment de rente, &c. Ce titre a été référé & confirmé par devant le Vicomte de *Carentan*, le 10 Décembre 1412; ledit GEFFROY DE BAUDRE eut:

1. JEAN;
2. COLIN, qui fuit;

3. Et GUILLAUME DE BAUDRE.

IV. COLIN DE BAUDRE, Ecuyer, prit par échange de Richard Hubert, quatre pièces de terre, fifes à Saint-Ouen-de-Baudre, par contrat paffé devant *Richard Duquefney*, Tabellion-Juré à Saint-Lô, l'an 1370; on ignore le nom de fa femme, ainfi que des précédentes. Il eut pour enfans:

V. JEAN DE BAUDRE, Ecuyer, qui clame de Denis le Maître, dit *Papin*, deux tennements d'héritage fis en la Paroiffe de Saint-Ouen-de-Baudre, par contrat paffé devant *Pierre de la Lande*, Lieutenant-Général, de Jean le Chien, Vicomte de Coutance, le 17 Novembre 1402. Dans ce titre, & les fuivans, ledit JEAN DE BAUDRE y eft dit fils de COLIN, cedit JEAN retira ce droit de fang & de lignage, de Jean Pigny, 10 livres de rente par contrat paffé devant le Tabellion de Saint-Lô, le 2 Février 1408. Autre acte paffé devant le même, le 7 Septembre 1409; d'anciens extraits généalogiques de la famille lui donnent pour femme *Guillemette Maubeuc*, de laquelle il eut:

1. JEAN;
2. Et GUILLAUME DE BAUDRE, qui fuit.

VI. GUILLAUME DE BAUDRE, IIe du nom, Ecuyer, fit fes preuves de nobleffe, lors de la recherche de Monfaut en 1463, Sergenterie de Saint-Lô, Paroiffe de Saint-Ouen-de-Baudre; il réclama ès plaids du Roi notre Sire à Bayeux, tenus par les gens & Officiers du Roi, la Sergenterie, fief au Buiffon de la grande Forêt, comme appartenant à *Jeannette Potier*, fa femme, par lettres du 13 Mai 1432. Il eut:

1. GUILLAUME, qui fuit;
2. Et NICOLAS DE BAUDRE.

VII. GUILLAUME DE BAUDRE, Ecuyer, IIIe du nom, partagea avec fon frère NICOLAS la fucceffion de GUILLAUME, fon père, & celle de leur mère, par lots fous feing du 5 Juillet 1504, reconnus par JEAN, RICHARD ET GILLES, fes enfans, procureur pour eux, par-devant *Claude Dufrefne*, Confeiller du Roi au Parlement de Rouen, Commiffaire en cette partie, le 29 Avril 1528. Ce GUILLAUME eut en partage les terres & rentes fituées dans la Paroiffe de Litheau, Monfiquet, la Bazoque, & Saint-Ebremont de Seuilly, avec la Seigneurie, &c. Et NICOLAS, les terres & rentes fituées Paroiffe de Saint-Ouen-de-Baudre, Sainte-Croix, Saint-Thomas de Saint-Lô,

Gourfaleur, la Mancellière, & Condé-fur-Vire. Suivant une ancienne partie de généalogie, qui doit avoir été juftifiée à MM. les élus de Bayeux, par ordre du Roi, en 1523, ledit GUILLAUME DE BAUDRE avoit époufé *Catherine de Parfourru*, fille du Sieur de Pierrefitte, de laquelle il eut:

    1. JEAN, qui fuit;
    2. RICHARD;
    3. Et GILLES DE BAUDRE.

VIII. JEAN DE BAUDRE, IIᵉ du nom, Ecuyer, fervit pour lui & NICOLAS, fon oncle, au ban & arrière-ban, fous Jean d'Harcourt, commandant la nobleffe, dont la famille a l'atteftation en parchemin, pour avoir main-levée de leurs fiefs nobles, du 14 Septembre 1523. La filiation depuis cedit JEAN, qui forme ce degré, à remonter jufqu'à GUILLAUME, Iᵉʳ du nom, qui fait le IIᵉ degré, eft prouvée inconteftablement par l'Arrêt du Parlement de Rouen du 13 Juin 1576, dans lequel elle eft rapportée en entier, & fuivant la Sentence du Bailliage de Saint-Lô, du 14 Juillet 1713, confirmée par Arrêt du Parlement, le 11 Décembre 1714, obtenu par GUILLAUME DE BAUDRE, iffu au Vᵉ degré, de RICHARD DE BAUDRE, frère de ce dit JEAN DE BAUDRE, chef de ce degré. Il époufa, par contrat fous feing, du 15 Août 1505, *Anne Guerault*, lequel fut reconnu ès affifes de Carentan, devant *Jacques Dary*, Lieutenant de ladite Vicomté, le 9 Mars 1528, inftance dudit JEAN. Il eut:

    1. JACQUES;
    2. THOMAS;
    3. Et GUILLAUME DE BAUDRE, qui fuit;

IX. GUILLAUME DE BAUDRE, IIIᵉ du nom, Ecuyer, Seigneur du Roucheray, partagea avec fon frère JACQUES, & les enfans mineurs de THOMAS, les biens de JEAN, leur père, par lots fous feing, du 5 Mai 1561, reconnus devant les Tabellions de Bréquenard, le 27 Novembre 1586. Il s'allia, par contrat fous-feing, du 31 Juillet 1583, reconnu devant *Pierre le Moigne*, Tabellion en la Seigneurie de Saint-Vez, & *Guillaume Piquot*, pris pour adjoint le 3 Juin 1609, à *Jeanne de Pierre*. Il eut:

    1. LOUIS;
    2. PIERRE;
    3. MICHEL, qui fuit;
    4. Et GUILLAUME DE BAUDRE.

X. MICHEL DE BAUDRE, Ecuyer, partagea avec PIERRE & GUILLAUME, fes frères, les biens

Tome II.

de feu GUILLAUME leur père, & ceux de *Jeanne de Pierre*, leur mère, vivant alors, & de fon confentement, par lots fous feing, du 2 Avril 1617, reconnus devant les Tabellions de la haute Juftice de Cerify, le 5 Avril 1617. Il époufa, par contrat fous feing, du 16 Janvier 1622, reconnu devant les Tabellions du Comté & haute Juftice de Torigny, le 13 Mai 1624, *Anne le Vaillant*. Il eut pour enfant:

XI. OLIVIER DE BAUDRE, Ecuyer, qui fit les preuves de fon ancienne nobleffe, lors de la recherche de M. de *Chamillart*, qui lui donna fon certificat fur parchemin, avec l'empreinte de fes armes, comme il lui avoit prouvé être noble, dès le tems de Monfaut, & fait mention des trois degrés paternels ci-deffus, dont la famille conferve l'original en date du 17 Janvier 1668. Il époufa, du vivant de fon père, par contrat fous feing du 7 Mars 1651, reconnu devant les Tabellions de la Sergenterie de Bréquenard, pour le fiège de Catillon, le 18 Janvier 1656, *Marguerite de Balleroy*. Il eut pour fils:

XII. JEAN DE BAUDRE, Ecuyer, IIIᵉ du nom, qui époufa, par contrat du..., mariage célébré à Caen, Paroiffe Saint-Julien, le 1ᵉʳ Août 1698, *Louife le Chanoine*. Il eut:

    1. OLIVIER-LOUIS-HERVÉ, marié à *Marguerite de Cabaçac*, mort fans poftérité;
    2. EMILE-VICTOR, Capitaine au Régiment de Cambréfis, mort au fervice du Roi, auffi fans poftérité;
    3. Et AUGUSTIN DE BAUDRE, qui fuit.

XIII. AUGUSTIN DE BAUDRE, Ecuyer, Chevalier de l'Ordre Militaire de Saint-Louis, Capitaine de Grenadier au Régiment de Rohan, partagea les biens de JEAN, fon père, & de *Louife le Chanoine*, fa mère, avec fes deux frères, par lots fous feing, le 10 Mars 1743. Il acquit, pendant fon vivant, la terre, feigneurie & patronage d'Afnières, & les fiefs des grand & petit Fournet. Il s'allia, par contrat paffé le...., mariage célébré dans l'Eglife paroiffiale de Sainte-Marie-Madeleine de Cerify-l'Abbaye le 11 Juillet 1746, à *Louife-Marguerite le Patout*, Dame des fiefs de Saint-Remy & de Baven. Il eut:

    1. PAUL-HENRI-AUGUSTIN, né le 28 Août 1748, Capitaine de Cavalerie, mort fans poftérité;
    2. N..., mort jeune;
    3. CHARLES-FRANÇOIS-LOUIS, Chanoine en l'Eglife Cathédrale de Bayeux;
    4. JACQUES-EMILE-VICTOR DE BAUDRE, qui fuit;

5. N......., mariée à Meffire *Jean-Nicolas de Berruyer*, Ecuyer, Chevalier de Saint-Louis;

6. N...., mariée à *N... de Grainville*, Ecuyer, fils du Seigneur de Saint-Quentin;

7. Et N...., mariée à *N... de Baupte*, Ecuyer.

XIV. Jacques-Emile-Victor de Baudre, Chevalier, Seigneur & Patron d'Afnières, des grand & petit Fournet, élevé à l'Ecole militaire, Chevalier de l'Ordre de Saint-Lazare, & Sous-Lieutenant au Régiment Royal-Rouffillon, Cavalerie, a époufé, par contrat fous feing du 9 Novembre 1782, *Jeanne-Louife-Félicité du Fayel*, fille de *Claude-Félix du Fayel*, Chevalier, Seigneur de Berné, &c., Chevalier de Saint-Louis, & de *Jeanne-Elifabeth du Chatel*, Dame de Lizon & autres fiefs.

Voilà tout ce que nous pouvons dire maintenant de la Maifon *de Baudre;* il y a plufieurs autres branches aujourd'hui exiftantes, qui ont fourni, dans tous les tems, de braves Officiers dans les troupes du Roi; mais nous en ignorons la filiation, faute de mémoire.

Les armes: *d'argent, au croiffant de gueules, accompagné de fix merlettes, de même*, 3 *en chef*, 2 *en fafce*, & 1 *en pointe.*

BAUDRE, en Bretagne: *d'argent, à cinq billettes de fable, pofées en fautoir.*

*BAUDRICOURT ou BAUDRECOURT en Lorraine, Diocèfe de Toul. La Baronie de Saint-Menge fut érigée en Marquifat fous la dénomination de *Marquifat de Baudricourt,* par Lettres du Duc *Léopold*, du 8 Novembre 1719, en faveur de *Jean Claude*, Marquis de *Baffompierre* & de Remauville. Voyez BASSOMPIERRE.

Liebault de Baudricourt, Chevalier, Confeiller & Chambellan de *Robert*, Comte de Bar, qui le fit Gouverneur de la ville & Marquifat de Pont-à-Mouffon en 1384, eft le premier de cette Maifon que l'on connoiffe: il vivoit en 1387. Elle a fini à Jean, Seigneur de Baudricourt, de Choifeul, &c., Confeiller, Chambellan du Roi, Chevalier de fon Ordre, Bailli de Chaumont & Gouverneur ès pays, Duché & Comté de Bourgogne, Mâconnois, Charolois, Auxerrois & Marche de par-deçà, dit le *Maréchal de Baudricourt.* Il s'engagea dans le parti du Duc de Bourgogne: il affifta le Comte de Charolois dans la guerre du bien public en 1465. Le Roi Louis XI, connoiffant fon mérite, l'attira à lui, le combla de bienfaits, le fit Chevalier de fon Ordre, lui donna le revenu de la Terre de Vaucouleurs le 23 Juin 1472, le fit Bailli de Chaumont en 1479, Capitaine de 4000 Francs-Archers, & fon Lieutenant-Général en la ville d'Arras, Gouverneur de Bourgogne le 18 Mars 1480. Il ne rendit pas de moindres fervices au Roi Charles VIII, particulièrement à la journée de Saint-Aubin du Cormier en Bretagne, en 1488, ayant beaucoup contribué au gain de la bataille. Il fut pourvû quelque tems après, par ce Prince, de la charge de Maréchal de France: il le fuivit en fon expédition de Naples, & mourut à Blois le 11 Mai 1499.

Les armes: *d'or, au lion de fable, couronné & lampaffé de gueules.* Voyez le P. Anfelme, tom. VII, pag. 113.

BAUDRICOURT: *d'argent, à la croix de gueules.*

BAUDRIER-LA-MARCHE: *d'argent, au chef d'or, chargé d'une fleur-de-lys d'azur.* Une autre famille de ce nom porte: *d'argent, au chef de gueules.*

BAUDRY, Seigneur de Semilly, Neufvillette, en Normandie, Généralité de Rouen, dont Girard Baudry-de-Semilly, Echevin de Rouen, qui obtint des Lettres de Nobleffe en 1645, & fut maintenu le 12 Mars 1667. Les armes: *d'azur, au chevron d'or, accompagné en chef de deux croix de Malte de même, & en pointe d'un trèfle d'argent.*

BAUDRY, Seigneur de Bretteville, en Normandie, Généralité de Rouen, famille maintenue dans fa nobleffe, le 28 Décembre 1666. Nicolas Baudry, Seigneur de Bretteville & de Rafaut, Avocat au Parlement de Normandie, dit l'*Hiftoire de Rouen*, obtint des Lettres de nobleffe en 1593; & Charles Baudry, Confeiller au même Parlement, vivoit en 1607, & eut pour fils, Nicolas Baudry. Les armes: *d'argent, au chevron d'azur, accompagné en chef de deux rofes & en pointe d'un cœur, le tout de gueules.*

BAUDRY, Seigneur de Thonfy, Piencourt, en Normandie, Généralité de Rouen, famille maintenue dans fa nobleffe, le 27 Janvier 1668. Dans l'*Hiftoire Généalogique des Maîtres des Requêtes*, pag. 16, on trouve Simon Baudry, Maître des Requêtes en 1344, qui portoit: *d'or, à 3 mains de gueules.* L'Abbé de Vertot parle de Louis BAUDRY-DE-PIENCOURT, du Diocèse de Lisieux, reçu Chevalier de Malte le 30 Mai 1612 ; & Masseville, dans son *Histoire de Rouen*, dit que PLACIDE BAUDRY-DE-PIENCOURT, fut nommé à l'Evêché de Mende, vers 1680. Il avoit été auparavant Religieux de l'Ordre de St.-Benoît, & Abbé Commandataire de l'Abbaye Royale de St.-Leufroy, au Diocèse d'Evreux, où il succéda à un oncle. Messieurs de *Piencourt* ont été les deux derniers Abbés Réguliers de cette ancienne Maison, dont la destruction s'est consommée sous le second Abbé.

Les armes: *de sable, à 3 mains senestres appaumées d'or.*

BAUDRY, en Bourgogne: *d'or, à trois mains senestres de gueules, posées 2 & 1.*

BAUDRY, Seigneur de Canroft, en Normandie, Généralité de Rouen, famille maintenue dans sa noblesse le 30 Janvier 1668 : *d'azur, au chevron d'argent, accompagné en chef de deux lapins affrontés d'or, & en pointe d'une tête d'argent contournée, tortillée de même.*

BAUDRY-TACHEREAU, voyez TACHEREAU-DE-BAUDRY.

BAUFFREMEZ, noble & ancienne famille qui rapporte son origine aux anciens Seigneurs de *Wavrin*, desquels un cadet prit le nom de la Terre de *Bauffremez*, située dans la Châtellenie de Lille, qu'il eut en partage. La Maison de BAUFFREMEZ est reçue dans les Chapitres nobles des Pays-Bas, & est alliée aux meilleures Maisons de ce Pays.

FRANÇOIS DE BAUFFREMEZ, Baron d'Esnes, Seigneur de Cauroir, de Brimeu, &c., eut pour fils:

JEAN DE BAUFFREMEZ, Chevalier, Seigneur d'Esnes & d'Hailly, qui épousa *Catherine de Heuchin*, dont il eut:

ADRIEN DE BAUFFREMEZ, en faveur duquel la Terre, Seigneurie & Pairie d'Esnes, dans le Cambrésis, fut érigée en Baronie par Lettres-Patentes du Roi d'Espagne, du 13 Septembre 1650. Il épousa *Jeanne-Marie de la Potte-des-Pierres*, dont vinrent:

Deux fils, morts sans alliance au service de Louis XIV, ayant été successivement Colo-

nels d'un Régiment d'Infanterie de leur nom;

Et CHARLES-ALEXANDRE, qui suit.

CHARLES-ALEXANDRE, dit *le Marquis de Bauffremez*, fut marié, en 1716, à *Françoise-Louise de Croix*, remariée, par contrat du 21 Novembre 1724, à *François-Eugène de Bethune*, Comte de Saint-Venant. Elle étoit fille de *Charles-Adrien*, Comte de *Croix*, Seigneur de Wayembourg, & de *Marie-Philippine de Croix*, héritière de *Wasquehal*. Il eut:

FRANÇOISE-CAROLINE-JOSÈPHE DE BAUFFREMEZ, héritière de la Maison, née le 28 Octobre 1722. Voyez les *Tablettes Généalogiques*, part. VIII, pag. 424.

* BAUFFREMONT, ancienne Baronie située dans le Bailliage de Saint-Mihel, en Barrois, qui a donné son nom à une ancienne & illustre Maison, qui a eu deux Chevaliers du Saint-Esprit, & quatre de la Toison d'Or.

En 1314 *Etienne de Montaigu*, Ier du nom, Seigneur de Sombernon, sorti d'un puîné de la Maison de Bourgogne, épousa MARIE DE BAUFFREMONT, Dame des Couches, dont il eut ETIENNE, II° du nom, & PHILIBERT, tige des Seigneurs des *Couches*.

PIERRE DE BAUFFREMONT, Chevalier de la Toison d'Or, Seigneur de Charni, &c., fit publier, en 1443, à l'exemple des anciens Preux, que douze Chevaliers garderoient à une lieue de la Ville de Dijon, un *Pas près d'un arbre*, que Paradin nomme l'*arbre des Hermites*, & d'autres l'*arbre de Charlemagne*. Il épousa, le 30 Septembre 1448, *Marie*, légitimée de Bourgogne, fille de PHILIPPE, dit *le Bon*, Duc de Bourgogne, dont il eut trois filles.

GUILLAUME DE BAUFFREMONT, frère de PIERRE, eut un fils nommé PIERRE, Baron de Senecey, de Scey, &c., lequel laissa:

NICOLAS DE BAUFFREMONT, qui fut Baïlli de Châlons, Gouverneur d'Auxonne, &c. Il fut appelé pour être présent à la réformation de la Coutûme de Bourgogne, en 1570. Il se trouva, en 1576, aux Etats de Blois, où il harangua le Roi HENRI III. Sa harangue fut imprimée l'année suivante à Paris, chez Mathurin Breville, & depuis on l'a mise dans le *Recueil des Etats de France*, imprimé à Paris l'an 1651. Outre cette pièce, il en composa d'autres, & mourut, en son Château de Senecey, le 10 Février 1582. De Thou, Davila, Belleforêt, Daudrins, Dupleix, Louis-

Jacob de Rubis, &c., en parlent avec éloge. Nicolas de Bauffremont eut de *Denife Palatin*, fille de *Claude*, Vice-Chancelier de Milan, & premier Préfident au Parlement de Bourgogne:

    1. Claude, qui fuit;

    2. Et Georges, qui a fait la branche des Seigneurs de *Crufilles*, Marquis de *Scey*, &c.

Claude de Bauffremont, Bailli de Châlons, Gouverneur d'Auxonne, Baron de Senecey, &c., mourut en 1596, & laiffa de *Marie de Brichanteau*, morte en 1580, fille de *Nicolas*, Seigneur de Beauvais-Nangis, & de *Jeanne d'Aguerre*:

Henri de Bauffremont, Baron de Senecey, Lieutenant de Roi au Comté Mâconnois, mort en 1622, qui avoit époufé *Marie-Catherine de la Rochefoucauld*, Comteffe, puis Ducheffe de Randan, première Dame d'Honneur de la Reine Anne d'Autriche, & Gouvernante de la perfonne du Roi Louis XIV, durant fon bas âge, morte le 10 Mai 1677, âgée de 89 ans. De cette alliance il eut:

    1. Henri, Gouverneur d'Auxonne & de Mâcon, Meftre-de-Camp du Régiment de Piémont, tué par un Allemand, à la bataille de Sédan, le 6 Juillet 1641, fans avoir été marié;

    2. Louis, Comte de Randan, mort à la même bataille;

    3. Et Marie-Claire, Marquife de Senecey, première Dame d'Honneur de la Reine Anne d'Autriche, morte le 29 Juillet 1680. Elle avoit époufé, en 1637, *Jean-Baptifte-Gafton de Foix*, Comte de Fleix, tué au fiège du Fort de Mardick, le 13 Août 1646.

Les autres branches des cadets de la Maifon de Bauffremont ont produit des Hommes illuftres, entr'autres:

E. Claude de Bauffremont, Seigneur de Scey, &c., Gouverneur de Franche-Comté, lequel eut, d'*Antoinette de Vienne*, Dame de Liftenois & d'Argues, fille de *François de Vienne*, & de *Bénigne de Granfon*.

    1. Antoine, qui fuit;

    2. Jean, Seigneur de Clervaux;

    3. Charles-Louis, rapporté après fon frère aîné;

    4. Et Claude, Tréforier de Saint-Martin de Tours, nommé Evêque de Troyes en 1561, mort le 24 Septembre 1592, âgé de 64 ans.

Antoine de Bauffremont, Seigneur de Liftenois, Marquis d'Arc, en Barrois, &c., fut

Confeiller d'Etat, Capitaine de 50 hommes d'Ordonnances, Gentilhomme de la Chambre du Roi Henri III, en 1585, & Chevalier d'Honneur du Parlement de Bourgogne, où il fut reçu le 11 Février 1561. Il n'eut qu'un fils, mort fans être marié.

Charles-Louis de Bauffremont, Marquis de Meffimieu, Grand d'Efpagne, Chevalier de la Toifon d'Or, & Général de Bataille, époufa une de fes coufines du même nom, dont il laiffa:

    1. Ferdinand, Marquis de Liftenois, mort en 1657;

    2. Claude-Paul, Marquis de Liftenois, Colonel d'Infanterie & de Dragons au fervice de France, tué à la bataille de Saint-François, à Etheim, le 4 Octobre 1674;

    3. Jean-Baptiste-Joseph-Hyacinthe, Abbé de Luxeul, mort;

    4. Pierre, qui fuit;

    5. Charles-Emmanuel, Baron de Scey, puis Abbé de Luxeul, après fon frère;

    6. Et Desle, Demoifelle de Bauffremont, morte en 1705.

Pierre de Bauffremont, Marquis de Liftenois, fut élevé Enfant d'Honneur auprès du Roi d'Efpagne. Après la conquête de la Franche-Comté il vint en France, & fon frère ayant été tué, le Roi le gratifia de deux Régimens qu'il avoit. Il mourut le 28 Août 1685. Il avoit époufé, le... Avril 1681, *Marie des Barres*, fille de *Bernard*, Préfident au Parlement de Dijon, dont il eut:

    1. Jacques-Antoine, Marquis de Liftenois, Grand-Bailli d'Aval, en Franche-Comté, Colonel de Dragons, bleffé dangereufement à Munderkingen, fur le Danube, en 1703. Il le fut encore en 1704 à la défenfe des lignes de Schellenberg, près Donavert; fut fait Chevalier de la Toifon d'Or en 1709; Maréchal-de-Camp en 1710, & fut tué dans une fortie de la Ville d'Aire, le 24 Septembre 1710. Il avoit époufé, le 10 Janvier 1706, *Françoife-Louife*, morte en 1769, fille de *Louis*, Comte de *Mailly*, & de *Marie-Anne de Sainte-Hermine*, dont il eut:

        Louise-Françoise, morte au mois de Mai 1716.

    2. Louis-Bénigne, Marquis de Bauffremont, puis de Liftenois, Sous-Lieutenant des Gendarmes Bourguignons, qui fut bleffé avec fon frère, à Schellenberg en 1703, & à la bataille donnée à Malplaquet, près de Mons, le 11 Septembre 1709; & eut le Régiment de Dragons de fon frère, après fa mort. Il fut nommé Chevalier de la Toifon

d'Or en 1711, fe fignala à la rencontre près d'Arleux, le 12 Juillet de la même année, & fut fait Brigadier d'Armée en Août 1719. Il eft mort le 18 Juillet 1755. Il époufa, le 5 Mars 1712, *Héléne de Courtenay*, née le 7 Janvier 1689, morte le 14 Juin 1768, fille du Prince *Louis-Charles*, dont:

1. Louis, Prince d'Empire, par Diplôme du mois d'Octobre 1757, Seigneur du Duché de Pont-de-Vaux, Lieutenant-Général des Armées du Roi, Colonel du Régiment de Dragons de fon nom, né le 21 Novembre 1712, mort le 13 Mai 1769, qui avoit époufé, en 1735, *Marie-Sufanne-Simonne-Ferdinande de Tenarre de Montmain*, Dame de la Croix Etoilée de l'Impératrice Reine, fille d'*Henri-François de Tenarre*, Marquis de Montmain, dont:

> Louise-Bénigne-Marie-Octavie-Françoise-Jacqueline-Laurence, née en 1750, mariée, le 22 Novembre 1762, à *Jofeph* de Bauffremont.

2. Charles-Roger, né le 4 Octobre 1713, Colonel de Dragons & Brigadier le 20 Mars 1747;

3. Joseph, né le 24 Septembre 1714, d'abord Chevalier de Malte, Capitaine des Vaiffeaux en 1742, Chef d'Efcadre en 1755, & Lieutenant-Général des Armées navales, qui prit, avec permiffion du Roi, le titre de *Prince de Liftenois*, en époufant, par contrat du 22 Novembre 1762, *Louife-Bénigne-Marie-Octavie-Françoife-Jacqueline-Laurence de* Bauffremont, fa nièce;

4. Et Pierre, né le 14 Octobre 1717, dit *le Chevalier de Bauffremont*, nommé, en 1734, Guidon des Gendarmes Bourguignons, mort peu de tems après.

Le Grand-Maître & le Confeil de l'Ordre de Malte ont accordé au Marquis & à la Marquife de Bauffremont la permiffion de porter la Croix de Malte, à caufe du droit que cette Dame a de nommer un Commandeur dans la Tofcane, en qualité de fondatrice aux droits de fes ayeux. Ce droit s'étend à la poftérité de l'un & de l'autre fexe.

Les armes: *vairé d'or & de gueules.*

Baugé, en Breffe, dont les armes étoient: *d'azur, au lion d'hermines.*

Wigues ou Hugues, Seigneur de Baugé, eft celui qui a donné commencement à cette ancienne & illuftre Maifon. Il vivoit du tems de *Warin*, premier Comte de Mâcon, fous le règne de l'Empereur Louis-*le-Débonnaire*, l'an 839. Il mourut l'an 867, laiffant:

Fromond, Seigneur de Baugé en 889, lequel laiffa entr'autres:

Hugues, IIe du nom, Seigneur de Baugé en 940, qui eut une grande guerre contre *Gérard*, Evêque de Mâcon, fur lequel il s'empara de l'Abbaye de Saint-Clément, & mourut l'an 958, laiffant:

Hugues, IIIe du nom, Seigneur de Baugé, qui renouvela la vieille querelle avec *Théotelme*, Evêque de Mâcon, pour l'Abbaye de Saint-Clément, l'an 967. Il décéda vers 970, & eut pour fils & fucceffeur:

Lambert, Seigneur de Baugé, vivant l'an 971, qui mourut peu de tems après fon père, en 980, laiffant:

Hugues, IVe du nom, Seigneur de Baugé, qui fuccéda à fon père en 980, & fut père de:

Rodolphe, Seigneur de Baugé & de Breffe en 1015. Ce fut à lui que *Gaulenus*, Evêque de Mâcon, concéda l'Abbaye de Saint-Laurent de Mâcon, l'an 1023. Son fils fut:

Raynald, ou Renaud, Seigneur de Baugé, & de Breffe, mort l'an 1072, ayant eu pour fils & fucceffeur:

Gaulseran, Seigneur de Baugé & de Breffe, en 1098. Il eut un différend avec *Landry*, Evêque de Mâcon, & mourut l'an 1110, laiffant:

1. Ulric, qui fuit;
2. Hugues, Chanoine en l'Eglife de Mâcon, l'an 1120;
3. Gaulseran, duquel parle Severt, dans fes *Annales* fous l'an 1150, fous *Jofferand*, Evêque de Mâcon;
4. Et Etienne, Evêque d'Autun, mort l'an 1140. Il eut pour fucceffeur *Robert de Bourgogne.*

Ulric, Ier du nom, Seigneur de Baugé & de Breffe, fe croifa pour le voyage de la Terre-Sainte l'an 1120, au retour duquel, ayant perdu fa femme, il fe retira dans un hermitage de la forêt de Brox, près Bourg, où il vécut le refte de fes jours Religieux, fous la Règle de Saint-Benoît. Ceci arriva l'an 1125. Il avoit époufé *N.... de Savoie*, fille d'*Amé*, Ier du nom, Comte de Savoie, & d'*Alix de Suze*. Il laiffa:

1. Ulric, mort jeune;
2. Raynald, qui fuit;
3. Blandin, Chevalier, nommé dans une Charte pour l'Eglife de Mâcon, l'an 1152;
4. Humbert, Archidiacre, puis Evêque d'Au-

tun par le décès de *Robert de Bourgogne*, puis Archevêque de Lyon l'an 1148;

5. Et ETIENNE, Evêque de Mâcon en 1167.

RAYNALD, IIe du nom, Seigneur de BAUGÉ & de Breffe, mourut l'an 1153, laiffant :

1. ULRIC, mort avant fon père ;
2. Et RAYNALD, qui fuit.

RAYNALD, IIIe du nom, Seigneur de BAUGÉ & de Breffe, mort l'an 1180, laiffa :

1. ULRIC, qui fuit;
2. GUY, Chevalier ;
3. Et RAYNALD, Seigneur de Saint-Trivier, en Breffe.

ULRIC, IIe du nom, Seigneur de BAUGÉ & de Breffe, mourut en 1220; il fut marié 1° avec *N... de Châlon*, veuve de *Jofferand*, Ier du nom, Seigneur de *Brancion*, & fille de *Guillaume*, Ier du nom, Comte de Châlon, avec laquelle il vivoit l'an 1185; & 2° avec *Alexandrine de Vienne*, fille de *Gérard*, Comte de Vienne & de Mâcon.

Il eut du premier lit :

GUY DE BAUGÉ, Seigneur de Mirebel, mort avant fon père au voyage de la Terre-Sainte, l'an 1215. Il eut une fille, MARGUERITE DE BAUGÉ, Dame de Mirebel, femme d'*Humbert*, V^e du nom, Seigneur de Beaujeu, fils de *Guichard*, V^e du nom, Seigneur de Beaujeu, & de *Sibylle de Hainaut*.

Et du fecond lit :

1. RAYNALD, qui fuit ;
2. HUGUES, Seigneur de Saint-Trivier & de Cufery, en 1250, dont il fit hommage au Duc de Bourgogne ;
3. Et BÉATRIX, vivante l'an 1227, femme d'*Amé de Genève*, Seigneur de Gex.

RAYNALD, IVe du nom, Seigneur de BAUGÉ & de Breffe en 1230, fit plufieurs dons à la Chartreufe de Montmerle, en Breffe, & tefta le 18 Août 1249, laiffant de fa femme, dont le nom ne nous eft pas connu, mais qui, après fa mort, fe remaria à *Pierre le Gros*, Seigneur de Brancion :

1. GUY, qui fuit ;
2. RAYNALD, Seigneur de Saint-Trivier, de Bourg & de Sagy, mort fans être marié, ayant fait hommage au Duc de Bourgogne l'an 1255;
3. ALEXANDRE, Seigneur de Saint-Trivier, de Bourg, de Sagy & de Cufery, après fon frère, mort auffi fans être marié, en 1266;
4. SIBYLLE, Religieufe à Notre-Dame-du-Lys ;

5. BÉATRIX, femme de *Guichard*, Seigneur de Châtillon-de-Michaïlle;
6. Et JEANNE, morte fille.

GUY, Seigneur de BAUGÉ & de Breffe, vivoit l'an 1252, & tefta le 5 Avril 1255. Il avoit époufé *Béatrix de Montferrat*, veuve d'*André de Bourgogne*, Dauphin de Viennois & Comte d'Albon, & fille de *Boniface*, dit *le Géant*, Marquis de *Montferrat*, & de MARGUERITE DE SAVOIE, & laiffa une fille unique :

SIBYLLE, Dame de BAUGÉ & de Breffe, femme, en 1272, d'AMÉ, IVe du nom, furnommé *le Grand*, Comte de Savoie, fils de THOMAS, IIe du nom, Comte de Maurienne, & de *Béatrix de Fiefque*. D'eux font fortis les Ducs de *Savoie*, Seigneurs de *Baugé* & de *Breffe*.

Quant aux Comtés de Baugé & de Breffe, ils font maintenant du Domaine de la France, depuis que HENRI-*le-Grand* les conquit fur le Duc de Savoie, qui les avoit ufurpés pendant la Ligue.

La Ville de Baugé fut démembrée de la Breffe par *Emmanuel-Philibert*, Duc de Savoie, qui l'érigea en Marquifat, & la donna en propriété, avec la Seigneurie de Récoles, à *Renée de Savoie-Tende*, veuve de *Jacques*, Seigneur d'*Urfé*, en échange du Comté de Tende & de la Souveraineté de Maroc, par accord du 16 Novembre 1575.

Jofeph-Marie de Lafcaris, Marquis d'*Urfé*, arrière-petit-fils de *Renée de Savoie*, étant mort fans enfans, le 13 Octobre 1724, le Marquifat de Baugé, & les autres biens de la Maifon d'*Urfé*, ont paffé, avec le furnom de *Lafcaris*, à *Louis-Chriftophe de la Rochefoucauld*, Marquis de Langheac, du chef de fon ayeule *Marie-Françoife d'Urfé-Lafcaris*, fœur de *Jofeph-Marie*. Voy. LASCARIS & ROCHEFOUCAULD.

Il y a une Ville du nom de *Baugé*, fituée fur la rivière de Coueïnon, en Anjou, nommée en latin *Balgium*.

BAUGENCI : *échiqueté d'or & d'azur, à la fafce de gueules.*

BAUGY-LEDVILLE : *d'azur, à trois trônes d'or, pofés en pal 2 & 1, furmontés en chef d'une molette de même.*

BAUHIN, ou BAUHYN, famille illuftre en France, dont étoit THOMAS BAUHIN, Confeiller en la Grande Chambre à Paris, qui vivoit en 1344, & fut préfent, lorfque le Roi

PHILIPPE DE VALOIS fit enregiftrer au Parlement la confirmation de l'Univerfité de Paris, le 21 Mai 1345. Cette famille a toujours été florissante, furtout dans la Robe; elle est maintenant divifée en trois branches, dont l'une est à Paris, la feconde à Dijon, & la troisième à Bâle, en Suisse. Cette dernière a fourni cinq ou fix Médecins de réputation. Voyez Moréri.

BAULAC, en Bourgogne : *d'argent, à la croix pattée de fable*.

BAULAND, en Bresse: *d'or, à la bande alaifée d'azur*.

BAULD (DE), à la Vigne-le-Houlle, en Vennes: *d'azur, à dix billettes d'or*, 4, 3, 2 & 1.

❧ BAULNY-DE-LA-GRANGE, famille noble établie à Saint-Juvin en Champagne, depuis 300 ans & plus. Les guerres civiles & étrangères qui ont défolé la France, & fait éprouver à plufieurs Provinces des ravages de toute efpèce, ayant été particulièrement funeftes à celle de Champagne, fous les règnes de Charles VI, Charles VII, & du tems de la Ligue & de la Fronde, elles ont non-feulement ruiné quantité de familles nobles, mais encore leur ont ôté jufqu'aux moyens de prouver leur extraction, en détruifant, par le pillage & l'incendie, jufqu'aux traces de leur origine. Dans ce tems fâcheux le village de Saint-Juvin, au Comté de Grandpré, où la famille de BAULNY fe trouve établie depuis plus de 300 ans fans interruption, a fingulièrement fouffert de tous ces défaftres, furtout pendant la guerre de la Fronde, fous la minorité de LOUIS XIV. Il fut prefqu'entièrement détruit & réduit à 70 feux environ, de plus de 400. La famille de BAULNY perdit confidérablement par ces deftructions; récemment encore un incendie, le 12 Mars 1752, qui confuma prefque toute l'habitation du Sieur DE BAULNY-DE-CIERGES, père du Sieur DE BAULNY-DE-LA-GRANGE, l'a privée d'une partie des titres nécessaires, pour prouver une filiation fuivie de fa Nobleffe de race. Ces faits ont été conftatés par un acte en forme, figné d'un grand nombre de Gentilshommes des plus qualifiés de la Province de Champagne, & confirmés par des Lettres-Patentes. Ainfi nous nous contenterons de donner la notice fuivante, d'après les titres originaux qui nous ont été communiqués.

SIMON DE BAULNY, Ecuyer, rendit aveu & dénombrement, le 20 Janvier 1501, à Ifabeau Halwin, Comtesse de Grandpré, pour quelques portions aux Seigneuries de Marq & de la Grande-Befogne. Il fut quart-aïeul de JEHAN DE BAULNY, Ecuyer, qui, né fur la fin du XVIe fiècle, n'eft mort qu'entre 1660 & 1670. De plufieurs enfans qu'il eut, il ne refta que deux fils, dont la poftérité foit connue, HENRI, qui fuit, & JEAN, dit *le Jeune*, auteur de la feconde branche, dont on parlera ci-après.

HENRI DE BAULNY, l'aîné de tous, fut père de GUILLAUME DE BAULNY, qui eut pour fils : PIERRE DE BAULNY, Seigneur de Cierges & de la Grange-aux-Bois, Capitaine d'Infanterie, mort le 3 Décembre 1765. Il avoit époufé *Victoire-Madeleine de Schrœder de Peck*, fille de *Georges de Schrœder*, Baron de Peck, & de *Claire Rouffel*, alliée, du côté de fon père & de fa mère, à un grand nombre des meilleures Maifons d'Allemagne & de Lorraine. De ce mariage font iffus :

1. LUC-GEORGES-GUILLAUME, qui fuit;
2. Et MARIE-SIMONNE DE BAULNY, née en 1727.

LUC-GEORGES-GUILLAUME DE BAULNY-DE-LA-GRANGE, Ecuyer, Baron du Peck, du chef de fa mère, Seigneur en partie de Cierges, de la Grange-aux-Bois, Marcq & la Grande-Befogne, né à Saint-Juvin le 19 Novembre 1725, Lieutenant d'Infanterie le 26 Mars 1746, reçu Garde-du-Corps du Roi le 22 Mai 1752, dans la Compagnie de Noailles, avec rang de Capitaine de Cavalerie, dès 1761, fait Chevalier de Saint-Louis le 30 Avril 1771, Penfionnaire du Roi, Garde de fa Manche le 31 Décembre 1780, & Brigadier des Gardes-du-Corps depuis le commencement de l'année 1783, n'eft pas encore marié.

JEHAN DE BAULNY, dit *le Jeune*, Ecuyer, auteur de la feconde branche, fut bifaïeul de PIERRE-CÉSAR, qui fuit, & de CHARLES, Chanoine à Reims, Prieur de... & Penfionnaire du Roi.

PIERRE-CÉSAR DE BAULNY, mort en 1772, a laiffé :

1. THIBAUT, Chanoine de l'Eglife métropolitaine de Reims, & Archidiacre de Champagne;
2. Et CÉSAR-LOUIS DE BAULNY, Ecuyer, Tréforier de la guerre de l'Isle de Corfe, ci-devant Tréforier de l'armée de Rochambeau dans l'Amérique feptentrionale, & ancien

Tréforier-Général adjoint de l'ordinaire des guerres, & de la Maifon Militaire du Roi.

Les armes : *un écu de gueules à trois befans d'or, pofés deux en chef, & l'autre en pointe ; & pour brifure à la branche cadette, un lambel à trois pendans d'argent.*

BAULON, en Bretagne: *de vair, au fautoir de gueules.*

BAULT (le), en Bretagne : *d'argent, à une quinte-feuille de gueules.*

BAULT-DE-LANGY, en Nivernois: *de gueules, au chevron d'or, accompagné de trois merlettes de fable, 2 en chef & 1 en pointe.*

'BAULT - DE - ROMAINVILLE. Romainville eft une Terre qui fut érigée en Baronie, par Lettres du mois de Février 1646, enregiftrées le 29 Janvier 1666, en faveur de PIERRE DE BAULT, Baron de Saint-Frique; il obtint, par d'autres Lettres du mois de Mai fuivant, la permiffion d'établir des Foires & Marchés en fa Baronie de Romainville. La Seigneurie de Candé fut auffi érigée en Vicomté, par Lettres du 20 Avril 1656, enregiftrées au Parlement le 22 Janvier 1657, en faveur d'HENRI DE BAULT, Seigneur de Saint-Frique.

BAUME. Il y a plufieurs Maifons illuftres de ce nom, dont nous allons donner des extraits généalogiques, d'après les Auteurs qui en ont parlé.

BAUME (DE LA), en Languedoc : *de gueules, à la fafce d'or, accompagnée de trois gantelets d'argent, deux en chef & un en pointe.*

BAUME (DELA), Seigneur de Forfac : *écartelé, au 1 d'azur, au loup paffant d'or; au 2 de fable, au lion d'or; au 3 de Bourbon-Condé, qui eft d'azur, à trois fleurs-de-lys, 2 & 1, au bâton péri en bande de gueules ; & au 4 d'argent, à l'aigle de fable, membrée & becquée de gueules; & fur le tout, d'or, à la fleur-de-lys de gueules.*

BAUME-LE-BLANC DE LA VALLIÈRE. Voyez BLANC (LE) DE LA VALLIÈRE.

BAUME-CORNILLON : *de gueules, à la bande d'or, chargée de trois corneilles de fable, pofées dans le fens de la bande.*

BAUME D'HOSTUN (LA), en Dauphiné,

Diocèfe de Valence, Parlement & Intendance de Grenoble. C'eft un Marquifat qui fut érigé en Duché, fous le nom feul d'*Hoftun*, par Lettres-Patentes du mois de Mars 1612, en faveur de *Camille d'Hoftun*, Comte de Tallart. Voyez HOSTUN & TALLART.

BAUME-MONTREVEL (DE LA), Maifon des plus anciennes de la Breffe, fuivant Guichenon, en fon *Hiftoire de Breffe & de Bugey*, part. III, pag. 12 & fuiv., & Chafot-de-Nantigny. Elle a des prérogatives d'honneur peu communes, & des marques de grandeur qui fe rencontrent rarement ailleurs. Elle a donné deux Cardinaux, Archevêques de Befançon, deux Grands-Maîtres des Arbalêtriers, deux Maréchaux de France, un Maréchal & Amiral de Savoie, un Régent de Savoie, & Tuteur du Comte AMÉ VI, un Vice-Roi de Naples, 17 Gouverneurs & Lieutenans de Province, deux Chevaliers de Saint-Michel fous Louis XII & FRANÇOIS Ier, deux du Saint-Efprit, quatre de la Toifon-d'Or, & quatre de l'Annonciade. Les Auteurs modernes parlent diverfement de l'origine de cette maifon. Le plus ancien Seigneur DE LA BAUME dont on puiffe parler fûrement, eft

I. SIGEBALDE OU SIGEBAULD DE LA BAUME, Chevalier, qui vivoit ès années 1140 & 1160, & fit quelques donations à l'Abbaye d'Ambronay. Il fut père de :
1. & 2. REYNALD & GUILLAUME, Eccléfiaftiques;
3. Et BERNARD, qui fuit.

II. BERNARD DE LA BAUME, Chevalier qui vivoit en 1190, donna quelques héritages à la Chartreufe de Seillons. Ses enfans furent :
1. ISMIO, qui fûit;
2. Et AMÉ-GUY, qui époufa *Guillemette*, dont THIBAUT & ALIX DE LA BAUME, vivant en 1254.

III. ISMIO DE LA BAUME, Chevalier, fit quelque bien, en 1215, à la Chartreufe de Meyria. Il eut pour enfans :
1. GÉRARD, mort fans poftérité;
2. PHILIPPE, Chevalier;
3. ETIENNE, qui fuit;
4. & 5. THIERRY & EUDES;
6. Et ACHARD, qui fit quelqu'échange en 1252, avec les Chartreux de Seillons. Il époufa *Elifabeth de Beyniers*, & en eut HUMBERT & GEOFFROY DE LA BAUME.

IV. ETIENNE DE LA BAUME, Chevalier, vivant en 1272, époufa *Martine de la Baulme*, dont:

1. Pierre, qui fuit ;
2. Josserand, Seigneur de Ciriez ;
3. Et Guichard, Chanoine de Lyon & de Saint-Juft, vivant en 1309.

V. Pierre de la Baume, Seigneur de Valufin, Bailli de Breffe, de Bugey & de Novaleyfe, fut l'un des Seigneurs de Savoie, qui promirent au Comte Amé, de reconnoître pour fon fucceffeur le fils aîné qui naîtroit du mariage d'Edouard de Savoie, & de Blanche de Bourgogne ; il vivoit en 1308, & époufa *Marguerite de Vaffalieu*, morte en 1348, & enterrée dans la Chartreufe de Meyria, veuve de *Joffelin*, Seigneur *de Grolée*, & fille *d'Etienne*, Seigneur *de Vaffalieu*, dont il eut :

1. Etienne, qui fuit ;
2. Verruquier, Seigneur de Broces, rapporté après fon frère ;
3. Guichard, Doyen de l'Abbaye de Tournus, vivant en 1330 ;
4. Etienne, Chanoine, enfuite Doyen de l'Eglife de Lyon en 1323.
5. Et Sibylle, alliée à *Etienne*, Seigneur de *Belregard* en Comté.

VI. Etienne de la Baume, IIe du nom, dit *le Galois*, Seigneur de Valufin, rendit de grands fervices à Amé IV, Comte de Savoie, & au Roi Philippe *de Valois*, qui le fit Grand-Maître des Arbalétriers de France en 1338, lui donna le Gouvernement de Penne-d'Agénois, puis celui de Cambray, qu'il défendit vaillamment contre Edouard III, Roi d'Angleterre, l'an 1339. Le Roi le fit Lieutenant-Général de fes Armées, & Amé, V^e du nom, Comte de Savoie, lui donna la même charge vers l'an 1350 ; mais deux ans après le Roi Jean le rappela en France pour le fervir contre les Anglois : il mourut en 1362. Il époufa *Alix de Châtillon*, Dame de Montrevel, fille & héritière de *Renaud*, Seigneur de Montrevel, dont il eut :

1. Guillaume, qui fuit ;
2. Lucie, Dame de Curtafray, mariée, en 1363, à *Amé*, Seigneur de Viri en Génevois.

Il eut auffi pour fils naturels :

Guillaume, vivant en 1402 ;

Et Etienne, Seigneur de Saint-Denis-de-Chauffon en Bugey, & de Chavannes en Comté, Amiral & Maréchal de Savoie, Chevalier de l'Ordre de l'Annonciade, qui fe diftingua à la prife de Gallipolis, & affifta au Traité de Paix fait en 1383, entre Amé VI, Comte de Savoie, & *Edouard*, Seigneur *de Beaujeu*. Il vivoit en 1402. Il eut de fon mariage avec *Françoife de Bacin* :

Tome II.

Antoinette de la Baume, mariée à *N...* Seigneur de Salleneuve ;

Et Isabelle de la Baume, femme de *Louis de Rivoire*, Seigneur de Gerbais, de Domeffin & de Belmont en Savoie.

VII. Verruquier de la Baume, Seigneur de Broces, fecond fils de Pierre, & de *Marguerite de Vaffalieu*, fut Confeiller ordinaire d'Amé V, Comte de Savoie, furnommé le *Comte-Verd*, & fe trouva en cette qualité au mariage de ce Prince avec Jeanne de Bourgogne en 1347, & au Traité d'alliance qui fe fit la même année entre les Maifons de Bourgogne & de Savoie. Il fut père de :

1. Pierre, qui fuit ;
2. Etienne, mort fans alliance ;
3. Et Agnès, femme de *Guillaume de Molon*, Chevalier, Seigneur de Villereverfure.

VIII. Pierre de la Baume vivoit en 1400, & n'eut qu'un fils :

Pierre, IIIe du nom, Chevalier, Seigneur de Chaftenay, qui époufa *Henriette de Marchand*, fille de *Guillaume*, Seigneur de Chavaux, dont il n'eut qu'une fille, Antoinette de la Baume, Dame de Chavaux, mariée à *Jean de Colomb*, Ecuyer, Seigneur de la Salte-de-Manzia.

VII. Guillaume de la Baume, fils aîné d'Etienne, IIe du nom, & d'*Alix de Châtillon*, Seigneur de l'Abbergement, &c., fut élevé en France & nommé Confeiller & Chambellan du Roi Philippe *de Valois*, par Lettres du 14 Décembre 1345. Il fut fucceffivement Tuteur d'Amé VI, Comte de Savoie, furnommé le *Comte-Verd* ; & l'Hiftoire de Savoie lui donne l'éloge d'avoir été un des plus fages Chevaliers de toute la Gaule. Il eut beaucoup de part aux grandes entreprifes de fon temps, fut aimé des Rois de France, & mourut en 1360, avant fon père, d'une bleffure qu'il reçut au fiège de Carignan. Il avoit époufé, en 1348, *Clémence de la Palu*, fille de *Pierre*, Seigneur de Varembon, Gouverneur & Bailli d'Amiens, & de *Marie ae Luyrieux* ; & 2° le 1er Juin 1357, *Conftantine Alleman*, Dame d'Aubonne, qui tefta le 6 Août 1376. Elle fe remaria à *François*, Seigneur de *Saffenage*, & étoit fille de *Hugues*, Seigneur de Valbonnais, & de *Sibylle de Châteauneuf*.

Du premier lit fortirent :

1. Philibert, qui fuit ;
2. Béatrix, qui tefta le 23 Juillet 1675. Elle avoit époufé, 1° en 1350, *Simon*, Seigneur de *Saint-Amour*, en Comté ; & 2° *Triftan*

H h

de Châlon, Seigneur de Châteaubelin, d'Orgelet & de Chavannes;

3. Et ALIX, qui époufa, 1º en 1360, *Jean de Corgenon*, Seigneur de Meillonas & de Chaumont; & 2º le 8 Mai 1362, *Guy de Montluel*, Seigneur de Châtillon & de Choutagne.

Du fecond lit vint:

4. JEAN, rapporté après fon frère.

VIII. PHILIBERT DE LA BAUME, Baron de Montrevel, de l'Abbergement, &c., fuivit le Comte de Savoie en la guerre qu'il fit aux Valefans, affifta au Traité de Paix fait en 1383, entre le Comte de Savoie & le Seigneur de Beaujeu, & mourut fans alliance, laiffant pour enfans naturels:

1. GUILLAUME, Seigneur de la Charme, qui mourut en 1430, n'ayant pas eu d'enfans de *Gillette de Dortans;*

2. Et AIMÉE, femme d'*Antoine de Monfpey*, Seigneur de la Tour-de-Replonge, Grand-Châtelain de Bugey.

VIII. JEAN DE LA BAUME, Iᵉʳ du nom, quatrième fils de GUILLAUME & de *Conftantine Alleman*, fa feconde femme, Comte de Montrevel, Seigneur de Valufin, de l'Abbergement, de Montfort & de Montagni, fe fit connoître à la prife du Château d'Ornacieu en Dauphiné en 1379. LOUIS DE FRANCE, Duc d'Anjou, adopté par la Reine JEANNE de Naples, ayant levé, en 1383, une armée pour la conquête des Etats de cette Princeffe, lui en donna la conduite, & le fit depuis Comte de Cinople en Calabre. Il fervit enfuite AMÉ VIII, premier Duc de Savoie, qui le fit Chevalier de l'Ordre de l'Annonciade en 1409, & Lieutenant-Général en Breffe. Dès 1404, LOUIS DE FRANCE, Duc d'Orléans, lui avoit donné le Collier de fon Ordre du Porc-Epic, & l'avoit employé pour fes affaires. Le Duc de Bourgogne & les autres Princes de fon tems s'efforcèrent fouvent de l'attirer dans leur parti. Le Roi CHARLES VI lui donna des marques de bienveillance, le créa fon Confeiller & Chambellan, & à la prière de HENRI V, Roi d'Angleterre, le fit enfin Maréchal de France, le 22 Janvier 1421. On dit qu'il délivra le même Roi affiégé dans Meaux, & qu'il le fervit utilement contre les Anglois, lefquels voulant tâcher de fe l'acquérir, lui firent donner le Gouvernement de Paris. Il fervit long tems, & vivoit encore en 1435; car fon teftament eft du 25 Janvier de la même année. Il époufa, par contrat du 5 Novembre 1384,

Jeanne de la Tour, fille unique d'*Antoine*, Seigneur de la Tour d'Illeins & d'Arconciel en Suiffe, & de *Jeanne de Villars*, dont:

1. JEAN, qui fuit;

2. JACQUES, Seigneur de l'Abbergement, &c., qui s'attacha au fervice de JEAN, Duc de Bourgogne, à la recommandation duquel le Roi le pourvut le 26 Janvier 1418, de la Charge de Maître des Arbalétriers de France. Le Duc de Savoie le fit fon Lieutenant-Général & Bailli de Breffe; & il vivoit encore l'an 1466. Il fut marié 1º à *Catherine de Thurey*, fille. & héritière de *Gérard*, Seigneur de Noyers, Morillon & Jarcieu, & de *Gillette de Coligny;* & 2º à *Jacqueline de Seiffel*, Dame de Soudrans & de Monts, veuve de *Guillaume*, Seigneur de Saint-Trivier & de Branges, & eut pour fille unique du premier lit FRANÇOISE DE LA BAUME, Dame de Noyers, &c., morte fans enfans en Novembre 1459. Elle avoit époufé, par contrat du 10 Juin 1439, *Jean de Seyffel*, Seigneur de Barjat & de la Rochette, Maréchal de Savoie;

3. PIERRE, auteur de la branche des Seigneurs du *Mont-Saint-Sorlin*, puis Comtes de *Montrevel*, rapportée ci-après;

4. ANTOINETTE, Dame d'Attalens & de Sermoyé, mariée, le 24 Octobre 1403, à *Antoine*, Seigneur de Saint-Trivier & de Sandrans;

5. Et JEANNE, femme de *Claude*, Seigneur de *Saint-Amour* & de *Châteauneuf*. ●

IX. JEAN DE LA BAUME, IIᵉ du nom, Seigneur de Bonrepos, Valufin & de Pefmes, fut Echanfon du Duc de Bourgogne, par Lettres du 22 Décembre 1404, Prévôt de Paris en 1420, Confeiller & Chambellan du Roi, & mourut avant fon père. Il n'eut de fon mariage avec *Jeanne de Châlons*, Comteffe de Tonnerre & d'Auxerre en partie, morte le 16 Mai 1451, fille de *Louis*, Comte d'Auxerre, & de *Marie de Parthenay*, que:

X. CLAUDE DE LA BAUME, Comte de Montrevel, Seigneur de Valufin, &c., qui fut Confeiller & Chambellan du Roi LOUIS XI, & des Ducs de Bourgogne & de Savoie, & vivoit en 1481. Il époufa, le 9 Septembre 1427, *Gafparde de Lévis*, fille de *Philippe*, Comte de Villars, &c., & d'*Antoinette d'Andufe*, Dame de la Voûte, dont:

1. JEAN, qui fuit;

2. CLAUDE, Seigneur de l'Abbergement, Vicomte de Ligny-le-Châtel, Chambellan du Duc de Bourgogne en 1473, & des Rois CHARLES VIII & LOUIS XII, en 1483 &

1501, mort fans enfans de *Marie d'Oifelet*. Il laiffa une fille naturelle, *Claudine*, alliée, le 14 Janvier 1501, à *Pierre d'Eftrées*, Seigneur de l'Efpinay ;

3. Louise, mariée, le 11 Mars 1454, à *Ferri*, Seigneur de Cufance, Belvoir & Darcey en Auxois ;

4. Et Claudine, femme, le 14 Juillet 1455, de *Claude de la Guiche*, Seigneur de Chaffaut & de Martigny-le-Comte.

XI. Jean de la Baume, IIIᵉ du nom, Comte de Montrevel, fut Confeiller & Chambellan du Duc de Bourgogne le 2 Mai 1460, & le Roi Louis XI le, fit Capitaine de la ville de Paris en 1467, & fon Confeiller & Chambellan le 29 Juin 1481, ainfi que le Roi Charles VIII, le 13 Novembre 1483. Il époufa, le 5 Mai 1467, *Bonne de Neufchaftel*, morte en 1491, veuve d'*Antoine de Vergy*, Seigneur de Montferrand, & fille de *Thibaut*, Seigneur de Neufchaftel, ayant eu pour fille unique, Bonne de la Baume, qui porta de grands biens à Marc de la Baume, Seigneur de Buffy, fon coufin.

BRANCHE.

des Seigneurs du Mont-Saint-Sorlin, Comtes de Montrevel.

IX. Pierre de la Baume, troifième fils de Jean, Iᵉʳ du nom, & de *Jeanne de la Tour-d'Illeins*, Comte de Montrevel, fut Seigneur du Mont-Saint-Sorlin, de la Roche-du-Vanel, d'Illeins, &c., & Ecuyer tranchant, en 1418, du Duc de Bourgogne. Il époufa, le 2 Mars 1424, *Alix de Luyrieux*, fille de *Humbert*, Seigneur de la Cueille & de Savigny-en-Revermont, & de *Jeanne de Saffenage*, dont il eut :

1. Jean, Religieux de Cluny, Prieur & Seigneur de Couzien, Diocèfe de Belley ;

2. Quentin, Seigneur du Mont-Saint-Sorlin, Co-Seigneur de Marbos, Chambellan du Duc de Bourgogne, mort à la bataille de Granfon le 2 Mars 1476 fans poftérité de *Claude de Toraife*, fille de *Jean*, Seigneur de Torpes, & d'*Agnès de Varax ;*

3. Guillaume, Seigneur d'Illeins, &c., Chevalier de la Toifon-d'Or, Chambellan du Duc de Bourgogne, puis du Roi Charles VIII, Gouverneur de Breffe pour le Duc de Savoie, qui fuivit le parti de Charles, Duc de Bourgogne, de Marie, fa fille, & de l'Empereur Maximilien, & mourut en Août 1490, fans enfans d'*Henriette de Longvy*, Dame de Choix, fille de *Jean*, Seigneur de

Raon, & de *Jeanne de Vienne*, Dame de Paigny ;

4. Guy, qui fuit ;

5. Alix, mariée, 1º le 12 Avril 1442, à *Guillaume de Saint-Trivier*, Seigneur de Branges ; & 2º à *Claude de Lagny*, Seigneur de Ruffey ;

6. Jeanne, morte en 1510, âgée de 97 ans. Elle avoit époufé *Claude de Dinterville*, Seigneur des Chenets & de Commarin, fils de *Jean*, Seigneur des Pins, & d'*Agnès de Courtiamble*, fa première femme ;

7. Et Françoife, qui époufa *Antoine du Saix*, Seigneur de Refleins en Beaujolois.

X. Guy de la Baume, Seigneur de la Roche-du-Vanel, d'Attalens, puis Comte de Montrevel, après la mort de Jean, IIIᵉ du nom, fon coufin, Chevalier de la Toifon-d'Or en 1516, & Chevalier d'honneur de Marguerite d'Autriche, Douairière de Savoie, mort en 1516, époufa *Jeanne de Longvy*, fille de *Jean*, Seigneur de Raon & de Givry, & de *Jeanne de Vienne*, Dame de Paigny, dont :

1. Marc, qui fuit ;

2. Pierre, Chanoine de Saint-Jean & Comte de Lyon, Abbé de Saint-Claude de Notre-Dame de Pignerol, de Saint-Juft, de Suze, & de Mouftier-Saint-Jean, puis Prince du Saint-Empire, Evêque de Tarfe, enfuite de Genève. Le Duc de Savoie l'envoya au Concile de Latran, où il parut avec éclat. Il prit poffeffion de l'Evêché de Genève en 1523, & s'y oppofa avec zèle à la fureur des Hérétiques, qui le chafferent deux fois de la Ville. Le Pape Paul III le créa Cardinal au mois de Janvier 1539, & il fut Archevêque de Befançon en 1542. Il mourut le 4 Mai 1544, & fut enterré dans l'Eglife de Saint-Juft ;

3. Claude, auteur de la dernière branche des Seigneurs du Mont-Saint-Sorlin, Comtes de Montrevel, rapportée ci-après ;

4. Louise, mariée, le 2 Octobre 1472, à *Claude de Savoify*, Seigneur de Seigneley, fils de *Philippe*, & de *Marguerite de Lugny* ;

5. Et Jeanne, morte le 6 Mai 1517. Elle avoit époufé *Simon de Rye*, Seigneur de Rye, de Balançon & de Dicey.

XI. Marc de la Baume, Seigneur de Buffy, puis Comte de Montrevel, après la mort de fon père, fe trouva à la journée de Novarre en 1513. Le Roi Louis XII lui accorda 1000 liv. de penfion, & il fut fait Lieutenant-Général au Gouvernement de Champagne & de Brie, fous M. de Guife, par le Roi François Iᵉʳ. Il tefta le 19 Novembre 1526, & fut marié, 1º le 10 Juillet 1488, avec BONNE DE LA BAUME, fille unique de JEAN, IIIᵉ du nom, Comte de Montrevel, & de *Bonne de Neufchaſtel;* & 2º en 1508, avec *Anne*, Dame de *Châteauvillain,* de Grancey, &c., veuve de *Jacques de Dinteville,* Grand-Veneur de France.

Du premier lit ſortirent:

1. FRANÇOIS, Seigneur du Mont-Saint-Sorlin, mort ſans poſtérité avant ſon père. Il avoit épouſé, le 23 Août 1517, *Claude de Prie,* laquelle ſe remaria à *Claude de Sainte-Maure;*
2. JEAN, qui ſuit;
3. ETIENNETTE, morte ſans lignée. Elle avoit épouſé, l'an 1514, *Ferdinand de Neufchaſtel,* Seigneur de Montagu, Fontenay & d'Amance, dernier mâle de cette illuſtre & ancienne Maiſon.
4. GÉRARDE, morte jeune;
5. Et CLAUDINE, alliée à *Aymar de Prie,* Seigneur de Montpoupon, Grand-Maître des Arbalétriers de France.

Du ſecond lit naquirent:

6. JOACHIM, Comte de Châteauvillain, Baron de Grancey, &c., qui prit par permiſſion du Roi, & au déſir de ſa mère, le nom de *Châteauvillain* ſans quitter celui DE LA BAUME. Le Roi HENRI II érigea en ſa faveur la Seigneurie de Châteauvillain en Comté, & le fit Gouverneur & ſon Lieutenant-Général au Duché de Bourgogne. Sa mère lui donna, le 2 Janvier 1534, tous ſes biens en le mariant à *Jeanne de Moy,* fille de *Nicolas,* Seigneur de Moy, & de *Françoiſe de Tardes,* Dame de Nehon & d'Anfreville. Il eut pour fille unique, ANTOINETTE DE LA BAUME, Comteſſe de Châteauvillain, qui s'allia avec *Jean d'Annebaut,* Baron de la Hunaudaye, Bailli d'Evreux, fils de *Claude,* Seigneur d'Annebaut, & de *Françoiſe de Tournemine;*
7. ANNE, mariée, 1º en 1526, à *Pierre d'Aumont* l'aîné, Seigneur d'Eſtrabonne, de Lons, de Couches & de Nolai; & 2º à *Jean de Hautemer,* Chevalier, Seigneur de Fervaques & du Fournet;
8. Et CATHERINE, mariée à *Jacques d'Avaugour,* Seigneur de Courtalin, Boiſrufin, &c., fils de *Pierre,* Seigneur des mêmes Terres, & de *Marguerite de Saint-Paër.*

MARC DE LA BAUME eut auſſi un fils naturel:

ETIENNE, dont la poſtérité s'eſt éteinte dans ANNE DE CASTRES-DE-LA-BAUME, mariée, le 10 Janvier 1652, à *Charles le Baſcle,* Seigneur de Moulin. La Maiſon de *Baſcle* eſt une des plus conſidérables du Royaume,

& a produit un Prévôt de Paris en 1348. Voyez BASCLE.

XII. JEAN DE LA BAUME, IVᵉ du nom, ſecond fils de MARC & de BONNE DE LA BAUME, ſa couſine, Comte de Montrevel, Chevalier de l'Ordre du Roi, Capitaine de 50 hommes d'armes de ſes Ordonnances, portoit la qualité de Seigneur de Pesmes du vivant de ſon père, fut pourvu de la Charge de Conſeiller & Chambellan de PHILIPPE, Archiduc d'Autriche, Duc de Bourgogne, fut enſuite établi Gouverneur de Breſſe, & Lieutenant-Général pour le Roi au Duché de Savoie, par Lettres du 1ᵉʳ Décembre 1540, & mourut en 1552. Il avoit épouſé, 1º le 4 Août 1527, *Françoiſe de Vienne,* Dame de Buſſy, veuve de *Jacques d'Amboiſe,* Seigneur de Buſſy, & fille de *François,* Seigneur de Liſtenois, & de *Bénigne de Grandſon;* 2º le 8 Août 1531, *Avoye d'Alègre,* morte ſans enfans en 1534, fille de *François,* Seigneur de Précy, & de *Charlotte de Chalons,* Comteſſe de Joigny; & 3º le 28 Juillet 1536, *Hélène de Tournon,* Dame de Vaffalieu, qui vivoit encore en 1570, fille de *Juſt,* Seigneur de Tournon, & de *Jeanne de Viſſat,* Dame d'Arlenc:

Du premier lit vinrent:

1. AIMÉE, Dame de la Ferté-Chaudron, mariée, le 16 Décembre 1546, à *Jean,* IVᵉ du nom, premier Marquis *de la Chambre,* Comte de Luille, Vicomte de Maurienne, fils de *Jean,* Comte de la Chambre & de Luille, & de *Barbe d'Amboiſe;*
2. Et FRANÇOISE, alliée, le 16 Décembre 1546, à *Gaſpard de Saulx,* Seigneur de Tavannes, Maréchal de France, fils de *Jean,* Seigneur d'Aurains, & de *Marguerite de Tavannes.*

Du troiſième lit ſortit:

3. Et FRANÇOISE, mariée, 1º par diſpenſe le 17 Septembre 1548, à FRANÇOIS DE LA BAUME, Baron du Mont-Saint-Sorlin, ſon parent; & 2º le 20 Novembre 1566, à *François de Kernevenoy,* Seigneur de Carnavalet & de Noyon, Chevalier de l'Ordre du Roi, Grand-Ecuyer, & Gouverneur de la perſonne, Chef du Conſeil & Surintendant de la Maiſon de HENRI, Duc d'Anjou, depuis Roi de France.

BRANCHE
des derniers Seigneurs DU MONT-SAINT-SORLIN, *Comtes de Montrevel.*

XI. CLAUDE DE LA BAUME, troiſième fils de GUY, Comte de Montrevel, & de *Jeanne de*

Longvy, fut Baron du Mont-Saint-Sorlin, &c., Chevalier de la Toifon d'Or, Maréchal & Gouverneur du Comté de Bourgogne, & Chambellan du Roi d'Efpagne, & mourut l'an 1541. Il avoit époufé, 1º le 30 Août 1502, *Claudine de Toulongeon,* dont il n'eut point d'enfans; & 2º le 28 Décembre 1532, *Guillemette d'Igni,* remariée l'an 1548, à *Jean d'Andelot,* Seigneur de Myons. Elle étoit fille & héritière de *Clériadus,* Seigneur d'Igni, Rizacourt, &c., & de *Claire de Clermont,* & eut de fon premier mariage :

1. FRANÇOIS, qui fuit ;
2. CLAUDE, Abbé de Charlieu, de Saint-Claude, &c., qui fut nommé, à l'âge de 16 ans, Coadjuteur de PIERRE, fon oncle, Archevêque de Befançon, par le Pape PAUL III, en 1543. Les Chanoines qui ignoroient ce que le Pape avoit fait en faveur de CLAUDE, qui étoit fort jeune, élurent dans le même tems *François Bonnalot,* Abbé de Luxeu. Ce Prélat s'oppofa avec beaucoup de zèle aux erreurs de Calvin, & les étouffa entièrement dans le Comté de Bourgogne. Il fit recevoir le Concile de Trente à Befançon, & fut ami des gens de Lettres. Le Pape GRÉGOIRE XIII le fit Cardinal en 1578. Il mourut le 14 Juin 1584, à Arbois, lorfqu'il alloit prendre poffeffion de la charge de Vice-Roi de Naples ;
3. PÉRONNE, mariée, l'an 1560, à *Laurent de Gorrevod,* IIᵉ du nom, Comte de Pontdevaux, Gouverneur de Breffe ;
4. Et CLAUDINE, Abbeffe de Saint-Andoche.

Il eut auffi un fils naturel :

PROSPER DE LA BAUME, Abbé de Bégard, Evêque de Saint-Flour, en Auvergne.

XII. FRANÇOIS DE LA BAUME, Baron du Mont-Saint-Sorlin, puis Comte de Montrevel, après la mort de JEAN, IVᵉ du nom, fon beau-père & fon coufin, accompagna, en 1552, l'Empereur CHARLES-QUINT au fiège de Metz, fut fait Lieutenant-Général de la Compagnie d'Ordonnance du Duc de Savoie, le 1ᵉʳ Juillet 1560, & Gouverneur de Savoie & de Breffe, le 20 Janvier 1561, & mourut en 1565. Il avoit époufé, le 17 Septembre 1548, FRANÇOISE DE LA BAUME, fa coufine, qui fe remaria, en 1566, avec *François de Kernevenoy,* Seigneur de Carnavalet, & il eut de fon premier mariage :

1. ANTOINE, qui fuit;
2. EMMANUEL-PHILIBERT, né le 30 Décembre 1561, Page du Duc de Savoie, puis Gentilhomme ordinaire de la Chambre du Roi,

tué en Flandres d'un coup de moufquet au talon, fans avoir été marié ;
3. PROSPER, né le 20 Mars 1562, Doyen de Befançon, Abbé de Saint-Paul de la même Ville, de Charlieu & du Miroir, mort le 7 Janvier 1599;
4. MARGUERITE, Dame du Mont-Saint-Sorlin, née le 1ᵉʳ Novembre 1559, mariée, 1º le 11 Décembre 1572, à AIMÉ DE LA BAUME, Seigneur de Crèvecœur; & 2º le 14 Novembre 1578, à *Africain d'Anglure,* Prince d'Amblife, Baron de Bourlemont;
5. Et ANNE, née le 13 Janvier 1564, mariée à *Charles-Maximilien de Grillet,* Comte de Saint-Trivier, premier Chambellan du Duc de Savoie.

XIII. ANTOINE DE LA BAUME, Comte de Montrevel, Marquis de Saint-Martin-le-Châtel, né le 28 Juin 1557, fut fait Gentilhomme ordinaire de la Chambre du Roi CHARLES IX, & Capitaine de 30 lances des Ordonnances par HENRI III, en 1579. Il fut depuis premier Gentilhomme de la Chambre du Duc de Savoie, & étoit Lieutenant du Vicomte de Château-Clou, à la bataille d'Iffoire en Auvergne, où il fut fait prifonnier. Il fut tué au fiège de Vefoul en Comté, en 1595. Il avoit époufé, le 20 Février 1583, *Nicole de Montmartin,* fille & héritière de *Philibert,* Grand-Gruyer & Colonel-Général de l'Infanterie au Comté de Bourgogne, & de *Claudine de Pontallier.* Leurs enfans furent :

1. CLAUDE-FRANÇOIS, qui fuit;
2. PHILIBERT, Marquis de Saint-Martin, né le 26 Mars 1586, fait Chevalier au fiège d'Oftende en 1602, mort d'une chûte en courant le cerf, & qui, de *Lambertine,* Princeffe de Ligne, fille de *Lamoral,* Prince de Ligne, Gouverneur de l'Artois, & de *Marie de Melun,* eut pour fille unique LAMBERTINE-MARIE DE LA BAUME, mariée 1º à *Ernefl-Chriflophe,* Comte de *Rietberg* & d'Oft-Frife, Maréchal-de-Camp des Armées Impériales; & 2º le 29 Novembre 1642, à CHARLES DE LA BAUME, Baron de Pefines, fon coufin;
3. JEAN-BAPTISTE, Seigneur de Saint-Romain, Baron de Montmartin, Marquis de Saint-Martin-le-Châtel, né en 1593, deftiné à l'Eglife, mais qui embraffa la profeffion des armes, & fe fignala, fous le nom de *Baron de la Baume* & de *Marquis de Saint-Martin,* dans les plus grandes affaires qui fe pafsèrent de fon tems, tant en Allemagne qu'aux Pays-Bas, au fervice de l'Empereur & du Roi d'Efpagne, où il acquit beaucoup de réputation. Il mourut à Grei, chargé de

bleffures, fans laiffer de poftérité. Il avoit époufé, par difpenfe, l'an 1540, *Lambertine*, Princeffe *de Ligne*, fa belle-fœur;

4. CLAUDINE-PROSPÈRE, née le 31 Mars 1588, mariée, le 20 Août 1608 , à *Claude de Rye*, Baron de Balençon, Gouverneur de Bréda, Chevalier de l'Ordre de Saint - Jacques, Gouverneur de Namur;

5. Et MARGUERITE, née le 20 Août 1590, Abbeffe de Saint-Andoche d'Autun.

XIV. CLAUDE-FRANÇOIS DE LA BAUME, Comte de Montrevel, &c., né le 18 Mars 1586, fut fait Chevalier par l'Archiduc ALBERT, au Camp devant Oftende, le 3 Février 1602, Meftre-de-Camp du Régiment de Champagne, & Confeiller d'Etat par LOUIS XIII, le 11 Avril 1619. Il fe fignala au combat du Pont-de-Cé, en 1620. Le Roi lui donna le Gouvernement des Isles de Sauveterre & d'Oléron, & le fit Maréchal-de-Camp, le 25 Avril 1621. Il fe trouva enfuite au fiège de Saint-Jean d'Angely, & mourut le 31 Mai 1621, d'une moufquetade qu'il reçut en forçant les barricades du Faubourg de Taillebourg, ayant été nommé Chevalier des Ordres du Roi, dont il avoit le brevet. Il avoit époufé, le 5 Juin 1602, *Jeanne d'Agoult-de-Montauban-de-Vefc-de-Montlaur*, fille de *François-Louis*, Comte de Saul𝔵 &c., Chevalier des Ordres du Roi, & de *Chrétienne d'Aguerre*, Dame de Vienne. Il eut de cette alliance :

1. FERDINAND, qui fuit ;

2. CHARLES, auteur de la branche des Marquis de *Saint-Martin*, rapportée ci-après;

3. MARIE, Dame de Grimault, alliée à *Efprit Alart*, Seigneur d'Efplan, Gouverneur de Meulan, Grand-Maréchal-des-Logis de la Maifon du Roi;

4. MARGUERITE, mariée à *François de Galles*, Baron de Mirebel en Dauphiné, &c., Colonel-Général de l'Infanterie Italienne en France;

5. JEANNE, Religieufe en l'Abbaye de Jouarre;

6. Et FRANÇOISE.

XV. FERDINAND DE LA BAUME, Comte de Montrevel, Chevalier des Ordres du Roi, fut Meftre-de-Camp du Régiment de Champagne, qu'il commanda, n'ayant que 17 ans, aux fièges de Saint-Jean d'Angely & de Royans, où il fut dangereufement bleffé; & s'en étant démis, il fervit le Roi dans les plus importantes occafions de la Guerre, & fe trouva au fiège de la Rochelle, &c. Le Roi le fit Confeiller d'Etat, Capitaine de 100 hommes d'armes, Maréchal de fes Camps & Armées, Lieutenant-Général en Breffe & Comté de Charolois, & enfin l'honora du Collier de fes Ordres en 1661. Il mourut le 20 Novembre 1678, âgé de 75 ans. Il avoit époufé, par contrat du 1er Octobre 1623, *Marie Ollier de Nointel*, dont il eut :

1. CHARLES-FRANÇOIS, qui fuit;

2. LOUIS, Prieur de Marbos;

3. FRANÇOIS, Chevalier de Malte ;

4. NICOLAS-AUGUSTE, Comte de Montrevel, Chevalier des Ordres du Roi, qui fut élevé à la Cour avec les enfans d'Henri de Lorraine, Comte d'Harcourt, Grand-Ecuyer de France. Lorfque le Roi arma pour la Guerre d'Italie, après l'affaire des Corfes, il fut gratifié d'une Compagnie de Cavalerie. Une affaire d'honneur qui lui arriva à Lyon, dont il fortit deux fois avec avantage, l'obligea de quitter le Royaume. Il y revint en 1667, & fe diftingua fi bien au fiège de Lille, que le Roi, à la prière de M. de Turenne, augmenta, fa confidération, le Régiment-Colonel d'une Compagnie, à la tête de laquelle il fut dangereufement bleffé, l'année fuivante, d'un coup de moufquet à la cuiffe, en dégageant un convoi que les ennemis avoient enveloppé au Pont-d'Efpières. Il fut un des premiers qui fe jeta dans le Rhin, lorfque l'Armée Françoife le paffa en 1672. Il y reçut plufieurs bleffures, entr'autres un coup de fabre au vifage. Ses fervices lui méritèrent le Régiment d'Orléans, Cavalerie, qu'il commanda avec diftinction, furtout à Senef, au fecours d'Oudenarde & de Maeftricht, & à Turquentin. Il fut fait enfuite Colonel du Régiment Royal Cavalerie; & le Roi le gratifia en même tems de la Lieutenance-Générale de Breffe. Il fe diftingua à Caffel, & fut Commiffaire-Général de la Cavalerie, ayant fervi en cette qualité avec grande réputation dans les plus vives actions qui fe pafsèrent en Allemagne. En 1688, il fut fait Maréchal-de-Camp; il avoit fervi au fiège de Luxembourg, & fervit encore à la bataille de Fleurus & à la prife de Namur; fut Lieutenant-Général en 1693, commanda, en cette qualité, des corps féparés, & fut chargé de garder la frontière tous les hivers pendant cinq années; eut auffi le Gouvernement de Mont-Royal, & fut créé Maréchal de France le 14 Janvier 1703. Il eut le Commandement-Général du Languedoc contre les Fanatiques, qu'il défit en diverfes occafions; celui de Guyenne en 1704, & enfin le Commandement-Général dans les Provinces d'Alface & de Franche-

Comté. Il mourut à Paris le 11 Octobre 1716, âgé de 70 ans, fans enfans. Il avoit épousé, en 1665, *Isabelle de Veyrat-de-Paulian*, Dame de Cuisieux, fille de *Jean*, Seigneur de Paulian, & *d'Isabelle de Saint-Gilles*, & veuve 1° d'*Augustin de Forbin*, Seigneur de Souliers; & 2° d'*Armand de Cruffol*, dit *le Comte d'Uzès*;

5. MARIE, Abbesse de Saint-Andoche d'Autun;
6. Et ISABELLE-ESPRIT, mariée le 17 Février 1648, à *Louis-Armand*, Vicomte *de Polignac*, Marquis de Chalançon.

XVI. CHARLES-FRANÇOIS DE LA BAUME, Marquis de Saint-Martin, servit au voyage d'Artois, l'an 1645, où il fut blessé & fait prisonnier; servit en qualité de volontaire sous le Prince de Condé en Catalogne, en Flandres, & pendant les mouvemens de Paris, & mourut avant son père, en 1666. Il avoit épousé, le 2 Janvier 1647, *Claire-Françoise de Saulx*, Marquise de Lugny, Comtesse de Brancion, &c., fille & héritière de *Charles*, Baron de Tavannes, Bailli de Mâconnois, & de *Philiberte de la Tour-Occors*, dont:

1. FERDINAND-FRANÇOIS, Marquis de Savigni, mort le 24 Juin 1662;
2. JACQUES-MARIE, qui suit;
3. ESPRIT, Abbé de St.-Cernin & de St.-Germain, au Diocèse d'Autun, mort au mois de Septembre 1721;
4. EUGÈNE, Chevalier de Malte, Mestre-de-Camp de Cavalerie, qui, ayant été réformé à la Paix de Ryswick, fut gratifié d'un autre régiment de Cavalerie, vacant, en 1700, par la mort du Marquis de Molac;
5. MARIE-JOSÉPHINE, dite *Mademoiselle de la Baume*, morte sans avoir été mariée, le 6 Décembre 1749, âgée de 84 ans;
6. Et MARGUERITE, dite *Mademoiselle de Montrevel*, Dame de Crusilles & de Brancion, morte le 29 Octobre 1714, âgée de 59 ans, en odeur de sainteté.

XVII. JACQUES-MARIE DE LA BAUME, dit *le Comte de Brancion*, Marquis de Saint-Martin, après son père, & Comte de Montrevel par la mort de son ayeul, fut Mestre-de-Camp de Cavalerie, en 1675, & Brigadier des Armées du Roi, le 30 Mars 1693, fut tué à la bataille de Nerwinde le 29 Juillet suivant. Il épousa *Adrienne-Philippine-Thérèse de Lannoy*, Comtesse du Saint-Empire, morte à Paris le 29 Mars 1710, fille de *François*, Comte de Lannoy, & de l'Empire, & de *Mechthild de Berghes*, fille d'Honneur de la Reine. Il eut:

1. MELCHIOR-ESPRIT, Comte de Montrevel, né

en 1680, tué en Italie, le 27 Octobre 1701, étant Capitaine de Cavalerie;
2. NICOLAS-AUGUSTE, qui suit;
3. Et JEAN-BAPTISTE, dit *le Chevalier de la Baume*, Capitaine de Cavalerie, après son frère, mort le 24 Juin 1707

XVIII. NICOLAS-AUGUSTE DE LA BAUME, Comte de Montrevel, &c., Capitaine de Cavalerie, puis Mestre-de-Camp en 1704, reçut à la bataille de Calcinato en Italie, le 19 Avril 1706, 14 blessures de fer & de feu, à la tête & aux mains qu'il eut toutes hachées, & un coup qui lui perça le corps d'outre en outre; sa Compagnie fut taillée en pièce. Le Roi le fit Brigadier de ses Armées, le 1er Février 1719, & Maréchal-de-Camp, le 7 Mars 1734. Il mourut le 13 Janvier 1740. Il avoit épousé, le 23 Juillet 1731, *Florence du Châtelet*, fille puînée de *Florent*, Comte de Lomont, Lieutenant-Général des Armées du Roi, Grand-Croix de l'Ordre de Saint-Louis, &c., & de *Marie-Gabrielle-Charlotte du Châtelet*, héritière de la branche de *Pierrefite*. De ce mariage est sorti:

XIX. FLORENT-ALEXANDRE-MELCHIOR DE LA BAUME, Comte de Montrevel, né le 18 Avril 1736, Colonel d'un Régiment d'Infanterie de son nom, en 1759, aujourd'hui Berry, depuis 1762, marié, le 10 Avril 1752, à *Elisabeth-Céleste-Adélaïde de Choiseul*, née le 27 Janvier 1737, morte le 18 Octobre 1768, fille de *César-Gabriel de Choiseul*, Duc de Praslin.

BRANCHE des Marquis DE SAINT-MARTIN.

XV. CHARLES DE LA BAUME, second fils de CLAUDE-FRANÇOIS, Comte de Montrevel, & de *Jeanne d'Agoult-de-Montauban*, né le 20 Mars 1611, fut Marquis de Saint-Martin, Baron de Pesmes & de Caromb, &c., & Lieutenant de la Mestre-de-Camp du Régiment des Gardes; il se retira depuis aux Pays-Bas, au service du Roi d'Espagne, qui lui donna le Régiment de Bourgogne, & fut Gouverneur de Dol en 1658. Il épousa 1° par dispense, le 29 Novembre 1642, ALBERTINE-MARIE DE LA BAUME, sa cousine, veuve d'*Ernest-Christophe*, Comte de Rietberg, & d'Ost-Frife, & fille unique de PHILIBERT DE LA BAUME, Marquis de Saint-Martin, & de *Lambertine*, Princesse *de Ligne*; & 2° en 1663, *Thérèse-Anne-Françoise de Trazegnies*, fille d'*Othon*, Marquis de Trazegnies, & de *Jacqueline de Lalain-Hoochſtraten*. Du premier lit vint:

1. FRANÇOIS-ANDRÉ, mort en bas âge.

Du ſecond lit ſont iſſus:

2. CHARLES-ANTOINE, qui ſuit;
3. MARIE-FRANÇOISE, *aliàs* JACQUELINE, alliée, le 9 Avril 1684, à *François-Joſeph Damas-du-Breuil*, Marquis d'Antigny;
4. Et ALBERTINE-ÉRIGITE, mariée le 4 Juin 1687, à *Charles de Gaucourt-de-Cluys*, Lieutenant-Général au Gouvernement de Berry, veuf de *Marguerite Tiercelin de Rancé*, mort le 20 Mai 1713. Il étoit fils de *Charles*, Seigneur de Cluys, & de *Gilberte d'Aſſy*.

XVI. CHARLES-ANTOINE DE LA BAUME, Marquis de Saint-Martin, Baron de Peſmes & de Caromb, eſt mort à Paris le 23 Juillet 1745, âgé de 75 ans. Il avoit épouſé *Marie-Françoiſe de Poitiers-Vadans*, fille de *Ferdinand-François*, Baron de Vadans, dit *le Comte de Poitiers*, & de *Marguerite-Françoiſe d'Achey*, ſa première femme. De ce mariage ſont nés:

1. CHARLES-FERDINAND-FRANÇOIS, qui ſuit;
2. Et FRÉDÉRIC-EUGÈNE, dit *le Comte de la Baume*, Colonel du Régiment de Rouergue, & Brigadier des Armées du Roi, le 1er Août 1734, mort ſans alliance le 5 Avril 1735.

XVII. CHARLES-FRANÇOIS-FERDINAND DE LA BAUME, Marquis de Saint-Martin, né au mois de Mars 1695, fait Colonel du Régiment de Rouergue le 1er Février 1719, puis Meſtre-de-Camp de Cavalerie, mort le 19 Novembre 1736, épouſa, le 29 Juillet 1723, *Eliſabeth-Charlotte de Beauvau-Craon*, né le 26 Novembre 1705, ſeconde fille de *Marc de Beauvau*, appelé *le Prince de Craon*, & de *Marguerite de Ligneville*. Il en eut:

1. ESPRIT-MELCHIOR, qui ſuit;
2. DIANE-GABRIELLE, Dame de Peſmes, Chanoineſſe de Remiremont, puis mariée, le 1er Septembre 1755, à *Claude-Antoine-Cleriadus de Choiſeul*, appelé *le Marquis de Choiſeul-Beaupré;*
3. Et N.... Chanoineſſe de Remiremont.

XVIII. ESPRIT-MELCHIOR DE LA BAUME, Marquis de Saint-Martin, Baron de Peſmes & de Caromb, appelé *le Marquis de Montrevel*, né au mois d'Août 1733, & mort à Paris le 4 Juillet 1754.

Les armes: *d'or, à une bande d'azur vivrée.* Guichenon, *Hiſtoire de Breſſe;* le Père Anſelme, *Hiſtoire des Grands-Officiers de la Couronne*, & Moréri, tom. II, pag. 210 & ſuiv., parlent de cette Famille.

BAUME-DE-PLUVINEL (LA), en Dauphiné.

I. GABRIEL DE LA BAUME, Seigneur de la Rochelle, fils puîné de PIERRE DE LA BAUME, & de *Jeanne de la Croix*, forma la branche de la BAUME-PLUVINEL. Il épouſa, le 30 Avril 1604, *Catherine de Pluvinel*, fille unique & héritière de noble *Jean de Pluvinel*, Maître-d'Hôtel de HENRI IV, & nièce d'*Antoine de Pluvinel*, premier Ecuyer du même Prince, Chevalier de ſes Ordres, Sous-Gouverneur de LOUIS XIII, Ambaſſadeur en Hollande, Gouverneur de la Groſſe-Tour de Bourges. De ce mariage naquirent:

1. ANTOINE, qui ſuit;
2. LOUIS, Conſeiller-Clerc au Parlement de Grenoble, Prévôt de la Collégiale de Creſt, & Doyen de la Cathédrale de Die;
3. Et JEANNE, mariée à noble *Pierre de Gallien-de-Chabon*, Seigneur de Chabon, Saint-Auban, &c.

II. ANTOINE DE LA BAUME fut chargé par le teſtament de *Jean de Pluvinel*, ſon grand-père maternel, de porter ſon nom & ſes armes écartelées avec les ſiennes. Il fut élevé Page de LOUIS XIII, & à ſa ſortie gratifié de la Charge d'Ecuyer de la Grande-Ecurie, par proviſions du 11 Novembre 1628, enſuite Gouverneur des Ville, Tour & Château de Creſt, par Brevet du 13 Juin 1641, & poſtérieurement pourvu de la Charge d'Ecuyer de la Petite-Ecurie, par Brevet du 13 Octobre 1648. Il fut député de la Nobleſſe à l'Aſſemblée tenue à Saint-Marcellin le 4 Août 1651. Il étoit Seigneur des Terres de Quint, Pontaix, Eygluy, la Rochette, Soû, la Maiſon-Forte, de Clavel, &c. Il s'allia, le 13 Février 1650, avec *Lucrèce-Alexandrine de Raphaélis*, fille de *Jean de Raphaélis*, Marquis de la Roque, & de *Lucrèce du Puy-Montbrun*. Il eut de ſon mariage:

1. JOSEPH, qui ſuit;
2. MARIE, qui s'allia avec Meſſire *Pierre de l'Eſcot*, Préſident au Parlement de Grenoble, Seigneur de Chaſſelay, &c.;
3. GABRIELLE, mariée à Meſſire *Juſt de Beaumont*, Marquis d'Autichamp, Seigneur de la Roche-ſur-Gione, Saint-Lambert, &c.;
4. & 5. Et deux autres filles Religieuſes à l'Abbaye de Sainte-Colombe-lès-Vienne.

III. Joseph de la Baume, Marquis de Pluvinel, Seigneur des Terres de la Vallée, de Quint, Pontaix, Eygluy, Barsac, la Vacherie, Chatte, la Rochette, la Roque, l'Auriol, &c., fut reçu en survivance au Gouvernement des Ville, Tour & Château de Creft, par Brevet du 12 Mai 1679. Il fit ériger les Terres d'Eygluy, Omblefes, la Rochette, la Vacherie, en Marquifat, le 10 Janvier 1693. Il recueillit les biens par fubftitution, de Meffire *Jean-Jofeph François de Raphaelis*, Marquis de la Roque, avec Meffire *François des Rolands*, Marquis de Roville, ledit Seigneur Marquis de la Roque leur oncle, Gouverneur de Villeneuve, n'ayant point laiffé d'enfans de *Marie de Béthune*, ci-devant Chanoineffe de Remiremont. Joseph de la Baume époufa, par contrat du 11 Février 1687, *Marie-Diane Alleman*, fille d'*Aimar Alleman*, Seigneur de Chatte-Puvelin, Saint-Juft, la Maifon-Forte, de la Bérodière, &c., & de *Françoise de Ponat*, dont:

1. Jean-François, Marquis de la Roque, Elu de la Nobleffe du Comtat, marié à *Chriftine de Théʒan*, fille de *Paul de Théʒan*, tous les deux morts fans enfans;
2. Joseph-Séraphin, qui fuit;
3. Jeanne, mariée à *Ignace de Blain-de-Marcel*, Marquis du Poët, Seigneur de Mornans, Saint-André, la Batie, &c.;
4. Gasparde, mariée à *Pierre de Boutin*, Comte de Valouze, Brigadier des Armées du Roi;
5. Louise-Antoinette, mariée à *Auguftin de Vefc*, Marquis de Béconne, Seigneur d'Eurre, Upie, Barcelone', &c.;

Et quatre filles, Religieufes.

VI. Joseph-Séraphin de la Baume, Marquis de Pluvinel & de la Roque, Seigneur des Terres ci-deffus, fubftitué aux biens de fes père & mère, fut Page du Roi Louis XIV, & enfuite Capitaine de Cavalerie au Régiment de Germinon. Il époufa, le 24 Mars 1737, *Laurence-Antoinette de Lattier*, fille de *Jérôme*, Seigneur de Salettes, Saint-Jean, &c., & d'*Agathe du Puy-Montbrun*, dont:

1. Joseph-Antoine-Augustin, qui fuit;
2. Pierre-Antoine-Joseph, Chevalier de Malte, appelé le *Chevalier de Pluvinel*, Officier dans l'Etat-Major du Régiment de Royal-des-Vaiffeaux;
3. Et Antoine-Joseph-Bernard, auffi Chevalier de Malte.

V. Joseph-Antoine-Augustin de la Baume, Marquis de la Roque, Cornette au Régiment de Clermont-Prince, a époufé, par contrat du

28 Avril 1768, *Louife-Victoire de Valernod*, fille de *Jofeph*, Seigneur du Fay-Chavanieu, la Batie en Lyonnois, Baron de la Batie-fur-Cerdon, Château-Gaillard, Maifon-Forte, des Rioû, &c., & de *Louife de Montferrand*. De ce mariage eft née:

Louise-Josèphe.

Leurs alliances font avec les Maifons d'*Alleman, du Puy-Montbrun, des Rolands, des Penne, d'Agoult, Chattelard-Marcieu, la Tour, Chaponay, Verfeil, Brifon, Beaumont, Sibud, Blain-du-Poët, Boutin-de-Valouze, de Vefc, Valernod, Murat, Viennois, Lattier, d'Urre-Tholon, de Lers-de-Jony, la Devèʒe, Roftaing-Champferrier, Montferrand, Pina, Gallien-de-Chabon, la Garde, Gigondas-Sobirat, Laftic, Bruyère-Saint-Michel*, &c.

Des différentes branches de cette Maifon, il y a eu deux Confeillers d'Etat: Pierre Ier fut Confeiller d'Etat par Brevet du 1er Avril 1607, & Maître des Requêtes de la Reine Marie de Médicis; & Pierre II a été Confeiller d'Etat par Brevet du 24 Avril 1624.

Les armes: *d'or, à la bande vivrée d'aʒur, chargée d'une moucheture d'hermines de fable, & furmontée d'une encolure de cheval*, comme on le voit dans les anciennes tapifferies de la Maifon & ailleurs. Devife: L'Honneur guide mes pas. Cette généalogie a été vue & vérifiée fur les titres originaux à Creft le 18 Juin 1769, par M. *de Bruyère-Saint-Michel*, Syndic de la nobleffe du Bas-Dauphiné.

BAUME, ou BAULME-SAINT-AMOUR (la). Il y en a qui croient que cette Maifon eft la même que celle des Comtes de *Montrevel*, dont nous avons parlé, col. 526, les armes étant prefque pareilles: celles-ci font *d'or, à la bande d'aʒur*. Mais il faut remarquer, dit Piganiol de la Force, que le nom de cette Maifon, qui eft de la Province de Bugey, s'écrit par un *l*, qui fait *la Baulme*, à la différence de celle de Montrevel, qui s'écrit fimplement *la Baume*.

I. Hugues de la Baulme, Chevalier, Ier du nom, vivoit l'an 1080, & fut préfent à une donation faite par Guillaume, Comte de Bourgogne, au Prieuré de Saint-Pierre de Mâcon, l'an 1096. Il laiffa:

1. Hugues, qui fuit;
2. Gontier, Chevalier, en 1120, qui époufa la Dame de *Micigua*, dont il eut:

1. Humbert;
2. Guichart;
3. & 4. Pierre & Bernard, Chevaliers;
3. Et Soffrey, Chevalier, lequel eut pour fils:
    1. Guillaume;
    2. Hismir, Prieur de Brenod en 1146;
    3. & 4. Guy & Miles, Chevaliers.

II. Hugues de la Baulme, IIe du nom, Chevalier, fut un des principaux bienfaiteurs de la Chartreufe de Megria, en l'an 1120. On ne fçait dans qu'elle Maifon il prit alliance, mais il eut fept enfans mâles, lefquels, après fon décès, firent bâtir chacun un Château près de Cerdon, aux lieux dont ils poffédoient les Seigneuries, fçavoir:

1. Hugues, qui fuit;
2. Etienne, Seigneur de Saint-Julin;
3. Aimé, Seigneur de la Balme-fur-Cerdon;
4. Guillaume, Seigneur de *la Picarderie*, qui a fait branche;
5. Isar, Seigneur de *Langes*, qui a auffi fait branche;
6. Hismir, Seigneur de la Verruquerre;
7. Et Guy, Seigneur de Salencune.

III. Hugues de la Baulme, IIIe du nom, Seigneur de la Balme-fur-Cerdon en 1147, époufa *Alix de Binan*, fille de *Roland de Binan*, Chevalier, & fe fit Chartreux après le décès de fa femme, laiffant:

1. Humbert, qui fuit;
2. Guillaume, Chevalier, auteur de la branche de *la Balme* & des *Ferreaux*;
3. Etienne, Chevalier;
4. Et Alix, femme de *Garnier*, Seigneur *du Balmey*, Chevalier.

IV. Humbert de la Baulme, Seigneur de la Balme-fur-Cerdon, & de Fromentes, en 1200, prit pour femme *Huguette de Beauregard*, Dame de Fromentes, dont il eut:

1. Etienne, Chevalier, mort fans lignée;
2. Humbert, qui fuit;
3. Faucon, Chevalier, qui donna tous fes biens à la Chartreufe de Megria, en 1230;
4. Anselme, qui fit la branche des Seigneurs des *Boches*;
5. Régnier, qui fut d'Eglife;
6. Et Mabile.

V. Humbert de la Baulme, IIe du nom, Seigneur de la Balme, de Fromentes, mort l'an 1289, eut de fon époufe, nommée *Marguerite*:

1. Jean, qui fuit;
2. Guillaume, Abbé de Saint-Oyen-de-Loux en 1283, puis d'Ambronay en 1298;

3. Pierre, Evêque de Bellay en 1265;
4. Jean, Abbé d'Ambronay en 1328, puis Evêque de Bellay en 1330;
5. Et Guigonne.

VI. Jean de la Baulme, Seigneur de la Balme-fur-Cerdon, & de Fromentes en 1337, époufa *Marguerite de Coligny*, fille d'*Etienne de Coligny*, Ier du nom, Seigneur d'Andelot, & d'*Ifabelle de Forcalquier*. De ce mariage fortirent:

1. Etienne, qui fuit;
2. Geoffroy, Chanoine & Comte de Lyon, mort l'an 1341;
3. Humbert, Chanoine à Saint-Paul de Lyon, puis Chanoine & Comte de Lyon, en 1360;
4. Aimé, Abbé d'Ambronay en 1338, puis de Saint-Vincent de Befançon en 1351;
5. Amblard, Seigneur de *la Balme-fur-Cerdon*, qui a fait branche;
6. André, Chanoine à Saint-Nifier de Lyon;
7. Lionnette, femme de *Jean*, Seigneur de *Ferllens*;
8. Et Marguerite, femme de *Jean*, Seigneur de *Corgenon*.

VII. Etienne de la Baulme, Seigneur de la Balme-fur-Cerdon, & de Fromentes, Confeiller & Chambellan du Duc de Savoie en 1346, mourut vers 1360. Il avoit époufé *Huguette de Beauregard*, fille de *Vauchier*, Seigneur de Beauregard, en Comté, & de *Jeanne du Corveiffia*. Il laiffa:

1. Humbert, qui fuit;
2. Aimée, femme de *Perronin d'Eftrez*, Seigneur d'Efpey, en Breffe;
3. Huguette, femme d'*Etienne de Doncieux*, Chevalier;
4. Et Jeanne, femme de *Hugonin*, Seigneur de *Dorlans*, Chevalier.

VIII. Humbert de la Baulme, IIIe du nom, Seigneur de Fromentes, Cormoran & Monthous en 1383, mourut en 1391. Il avoit époufé *Catherine de Luyneux*, fille d'*Humbert de Luyneux*, Seigneur de la Cucille, & d'*Aynarde de Rivoire*. Il laiffa:

1. Bon, Seigneur de Fromentes, mort fans être marié;
2. Seguirard, Seigneur de Monthous, décédé jeune;
3. Jean, Religieux, puis Chambrier d'Ambronay en 1415;
4. Pierre, mort jeune;
5. Huguette, Dame de Fromentes, héritière de fes frères, femme de *Jacmart*, Seigneur de *Coligny* & d'Andelot;
6. Aynarde, Dame de Monthous, en Géne-

vois, femme de *Guy de la Pallie*, Seigneur de Varembon ;

7. Et MARIE, femme d'*Amé de Gorlée*, Seigneur de Paſſin.

PREMIÈRE BRANCHE
des Seigneurs de la BALME-SUR-CERDON *& du* MORTEREY.

VII. AMBLARD DE LA BAULME, Seigneur de la Balme-ſur-Cerdon, cinquième fils de JEAN DE LA BAULME, Seigneur de Fromentes, & de *Marguerite de Coligny*, épouſa, en 1346, *Marguerite de Sales*, fille de *Pierre*, II° du nom, Seigneur de *Sales*, & de *Clémence de Bronne*, dont il eut :

1. PIERRE, qui ſuit ;
2. PERCEVAL, rapporté après ſon frère ;
3. JEAN, Religieux à Ambronay, Prieur de Villette ;
4. GUILLAUME, Abbé de Saint-Oyen-de-Rous, vulgairement dit *Saint-Claude* en 1397 ;
5. LOUIS, Chevalier en 1417 ;
6. Et MARIE, femme de *Joſſerand*, Seigneur du *Saix*, Chevalier.

VIII. PIERRE DE LA BAULME, Seigneur de Sales & de Pommiers, épouſa, l'an 1573, *Catherine d'Eſtrés*, fille de *Girard d'Eſtrés*, Seigneur de Banains, Chancelier de Savoie, & de *Guigonne*, dont il eut :

1. CLAUDINE, femme de *Jean de Chambut*, II° du nom, Seigneur de Conflens, fils de *Louis-Claude de Chambut*, Seigneur de Conflens, & de *Béatrix de Saint-Amour* ;
2. JEANNE, femme de *Claude de Chambut*, frère dudit *Jean* ;
3. ALIX, femme d'*Amé de la Balme*, Seigneur du Tiret, fils d'*Anſelme de la Balme*, Seigneur du Tiret, & d'*Agnès de St.-Sulpis* ;.
4. Et MARGUERITE, morte fille.

VIII. PERCEVAL DE LA BAULME, deuxième fils d'AMBLARD, Seigneur de la Balme-ſur-Cerdon, & de Perès en 1375, eut pour femme *Iſabelle des Roches*, Dame de Perès, fille de *Barthélemy des Roches*, Seigneur deſdits lieux, & de *Lucie de Sachems*, dont ſortirent :

1. AMBLARD, qui ſuit ;
2. CLAUDE, Seigneur d'Aſnières, qui épouſa *Claudine de Grolié* ;
3. GUILLAUME, ſurnommé *Mortelet*, qui fit branche ;
4. Et ODET, Prieur des Déferts en 1399, & de Saint-Eutrope, Ordre de Cluny en 1439.

IX. AMBLARD DE LA BAULME, II° du nom, Seigneur de Perès & de la Balme-ſur-Cerdon,

mort l'an 1479, épouſa 1° *Louiſe de Mathéfélon*, fille d'*Henri de Mathéfélon*, Seigneur de Martigna ; & 2° *Jeanne de Gormolles*, veuve de *Guy de Marmont*, Seigneur de Broft, & fille de *Jean*, Seigneur de Germoles, en Mâconnois, & de *Marguerite de Jays*. De cette dernière il eut :

1. GUILLAUME, qui ſuit ;
2. PERCEVAL, Seigneur de Morterey, Evêque de Bellay, & Patriarche de Gradiſque ;
3. JEAN, Chanoine à Saint-Paul de Lyon en 1461 ;
4. JEANNE, femme d'*Antoine du Saix*, Seigneur d'Arnens ;
5. Et AYNARDE, Religieuſe à Neufville.

X. GUILLAUME DE LA BAULME, Seigneur de la Balme-ſur-Cerdon, mort l'an 1500, épouſa *Françoiſe de la Balme*, Dame de Morterey & de la Tour de Cerdon, fille & héritière d'*Antoine de la Balme*, Seigneur deſdits lieux, & de *Lionnette de Pierre-Gourde*, dont il eut :

1. BERTRAND, qui ſuit ;
2. CLAUDE-LOUISE, femme de *Gabriel de Laure*, Seigneur de Broſtel, en Dauphiné ;
3. FRANÇOISE, femme de *Claude de Seyturier*, Seigneur de Cornod ;
4. Et MARIE, mariée 1° à *Antoine de Chevriers*, Seigneur de Douvres ; & 2° à *Philippe de Ville*, Ecuyer.

XI. BERTRAND DE LA BAULME, Seigneur de la Balme-ſur-Cerdon en 1532, épouſa *Marguerite de Poyſieux*, fille de *Jean de Poyſieux*, Seigneur du Paſſage, dont il eut :

1. CLAUDE, qui ſuit ;
2. Et JACQUELINE, femme de *Pierre de Portans*, Seigneur de Berchier, au pays de Vaux.

XII. CLAUDE DE LA BAULME, Seigneur de la Balme-ſur-Cerdon, Conſeiller & Maître-d'Hôtel de la Reine de Navarre en 1561, épouſa *Charlotte de la Fontaine*, fille de *Simon de la Fontaine*, Seigneur du Boys, en Bugey, & de *Charlotte du Bois-Gaigneuf*. De ce mariage ſortirent :

1. MARIE, Dame de la Balme-ſur-Cerdon, mariée, l'an 1581, à *Claude de Mareſte*, Seigneur de Chavanne, en Breſſe, dont il eut une fille unique ;
2. Et JEANNE, morte ſans avoir été mariée.

BRANCHE
des Seigneurs DE PERÈS, *Comtes de Saint-Amour.*

IX. GUILLAUME DE LA BAULME, dit *Morte-*

let, Seigneur de Perès, troifième fils de Perceval de la Baulme, Seigneur de la Balme-
fur-Cerdon, & *d'Ifabelle des Roches,* fut
Echanfon de Philippe, Duc de Bourgogne,
& fon Grand-Maître des Eaux & Forêts de-
çà les Monts, en 1461, & mourut en 1470. Il
avoit époufé *Louife de Genoft,* fille de *Jean
de Genoft,* Seigneur de la Ferle. Il laiffa :

1. Philibert, qui fuit ;
2. Louis, Seigneur de *Montfalconnet,* auteur
   d'une branche rapportée ci-après ;
3. Anne, femme de *Philibert du Breuil,* Seigneur de Perès ;
4. Marguerite, Prieure de Neufville, en
   Breffe ;
5. Jeanne, Religieufe audit Prieuré de Neufville ;
6. Et Louise, femme de *Georges de la Gellière,* Seigneur de Cornaton & de Serre.

X. Philibert de la Baulme, Seigneur de
Perès & de Morterey, Chevalier de l'Ordre,
& Echanfon du Roi Louis XI en 1461, &
Grand-Ecuyer de Savoie, époufa 1° *Phili-
berte de Saint-Trivier,* fille d'*Antoine de
Saint-Trivier,* & d'Efteauge, dont il n'eut
point d'enfans ; 2° *Françoife Bouchard-de-
Montflory,* veuve du Seigneur de *Liffaire ;*
3° *Péronne de Poupet,* fille de *Charles de
Poupet,* Seigneur de la Chaux, premier Som-
melier du Corps de l'Empereur Charles-
Quint, dont il n'eut point de lignée ; & 4°
Eléonore de la Rate, veuve d'*Humbert de
Varaix,* Seigneur de Belmont. Il eut du fe-
cond lit :

Jeanne-Philiberte de la Baulme, mariée à
Charles de Poupet, Seigneur de la Chaux.

Du quatrième lit font nés :

1. Philibert, qui fuit ;
2. Claude, Seigneur du Morterey ;
3. Anatole, Seigneur de *Romans,* qui fit
   branche ;
4. Benoîte, femme de *Claude de la Poype,*
   Seigneur de Saint-Julien ;
5. Péronne, Religieufe à Neufville ;
6. Et Gabrielle, Religieufe en la Chartreufe
   de Saletter, en Dauphiné.

XI. Philibert de la Baulme, II° du nom,
Seigneur de Perès & de Corgenon en 1531,
mort en 1568, avoit époufé *Françoife Damas,* fille de *François Damas,* Baron de Digoine, & de *Jeanne de Saint-Balais.* Il laiffa :

1. Louis, qui fuit ;
2. Antoine, Abbé de Baume, en Comté en
   1545 ;
3. Aimé, Seigneur de Crevecœur, qui époufa

Marguerite de la Baume, fille de *François
de la Baume,* Comte de Montrevel, & de
Françoife de la Baume, dont il eut Guillaume, mort jeune ;
4. Alexandre, Seigneur de la Falconnière,
   mort fans hoirs ;
5. Jean, Seigneur du Morterey, marié, en
   1561, à *Philiberte de Feurs,* fille de *Claude
   de Feurs,* Seigneur des Zones, & de *Claudine de la Baume,* dont il n'eut point d'enfans ;
6. Et Péronne, femme de *Claude de Binan,*
   Seigneur de Chamberie.

XII. Louis de la Baulme, dit *Corgenon-
de-Poupet-d'Efthintufe,* Comte de Saint-
Amour & de Vinceftre, Chevalier de l'Ordre
de Savoie, époufa, 1° l'an 1560, *Claudine de
la Teffonnière,* Dame de Chancins, fille &
héritière de *Philibert de la Teffonnière,* Seigneur de Chancins, & de *Claudine de la
Baulme ;* & 2° en 1574, *Catherine de Bruges,* fille de *René de Bruges,* Seigneur de la
Gruthufe, Prince d'Efthintufe, & de *Béatrix
de la Chambre.*

Du premier lit vinrent :

1. Françoise, mariée 1° à *Pierre de Nanton,*
   Seigneur d'Afnières, fils de *François de
   Nanton,* Seigneur de Pifay, & de *Philiberte
   de Feurs,* & 2° à *Gabriel de Treffondant,*
   Seigneur de Suancourt ;
2. Et Catherine, femme de *Pierre-Antide de
   Dorlans,* Seigneur de Dorlans, Usfelle &
   Efmondaux.

Du fecond mariage fortirent :

3. Emmanuel-Philibert, qui fuit ;
4. Guillaume, mort jeune, en 1579 ;
5. Charles-Emmanuel, Seigneur de la Chaux,
   mort fans hoirs en 1584 ;
6. Philippe, Prieur de Vaux, puis Abbé de
   Luxeul ;
7. Antoine, Baron de la *Chaux,* qui a fait
   branche ;
8. Et Françoise-Catherine.

XIII. Emmanuel-Philibert de la Baulme,
dit de *Poupet,* de *Bruges,* & de *Corgenon,*
Comte de Saint-Amour, Marquis de Saint-
Genis & d'Yenne, époufa, l'an 1599, *Hélène
Pèrenot-de-Gravelle,* fille de *Frédéric Pere-
not,* Seigneur de Champagné, Baron de Re-
nais, Gouverneur d'Anvers, Chef des Finances aux Pays-Bas, & de *Marie de Bercan.*
De ce mariage fortirent :

1. Jacques-Nicolas, qui fuit ;
2. Philibert, Seigneur de Perès, Baron de
   Beaujeu, Bailli d'Aval, au Comté de Bourgogne, marié à *Dorothée de Rye,* fille de

Claude de Rye, Baron de Balaucon, & de
*Claudine-Prospère de la Baume-de-Mont-
revel;*
3. JEAN, mort jeune;
4. CATHERINE, femme de *Jean-Claude de Lévis*, Baron de Maumont, Marquis de Châteaumorand;
5. CAROLINE, femme d'*Emenfroy-François*,
IIe du nom, Baron d'*Oysselet;*
6. Et GENEVIÈVE, morte jeune.

XIV. JACQUES-NICOLAS DE LA BAULME,
Comte de Saint-Amour, Marquis de Saint-
Genis, Chevalier d'honneur au Parlement de
Bourgogne, Gouverneur de Dôle, & Gentilhomme de la Chambre du Roi Catholique,
vivant en 1661, épousa *Marie des Porcel-
lets-de-Malliane*, fille d'*André des Porcellets*, Seigneur de Malliane, Maréchal de Barrois, & d'*Elisabeth de Cernay*, dont il eut:
1. PHILIPPE, Marquis de Saint-Genis;
2. CHARLES-ANTOINE, Baron de Montmirail;
3. Et MARIE.

BRANCHE
des Seigneurs DE LA CHAUX.

XIII. ANTOINE DE LA BAULME, Seigneur &
Baron de la Chaux, troisième fils de LOUIS DE
LA BAULME, Comte de Saint-Amour, & de
Catherine de Bruges, sa seconde femme,
épousa *Jeanne de Richardot*, fille de *Jean de
Richardot*, Seigneur d'Ottigny, & de *Jeanne
de Couriol*, dont il eut:
CATHERINE, femme d'*Albert-Eugène de
Genève*, Marquis de Lullins, Chevalier de
l'Ordre de Savoie, Grand-Ecuyer de Madame
Royale, fils de *Clériadus de Genève*, Marquis
de Lullins, Chevalier de l'Ordre de Savoie,
& de *Sabine de Hornes*.

BRANCHE
des Seigneurs DE MONTFALCONNET.

X. LOUIS DE LA BAULME, Seigneur de Mont-
Falconnet, second fils de GUILLAUME DE LA BAUL-
ME, dit *Mortelet*, Seigneur de Perès, & de
Louise de Genost, épousa *Philiberte de Teney*, fille de *Jean de Teney*, Seigneur de la
Falconnière, & d'*Anne de Buenc*, dont il eut:
1. PHILIBERT, dit *de Montfalconnet*, Chevalier de l'Ordre de Saint-Jacques, Grand-E-
cuyer, & premier Maître-d'Hôtel de l'Empereur CHARLES-QUINT, mort sans être
marié;
2. ANTOINE, Seigneur de la Griffonnière, Commandeur de l'Ordre de Saint-Jacques, en
Espagne;
3. Et CLAUDINE, qui épousa 1º *Philibert de la*

Tessonnière, Seigneur de Chancins; & 2º
Claude de Fleurs, Seigneur d'Estours.

BRANCHE
des Seigneurs DE ROMANS.

XI. ANATOLE DE LA BAULME, Seigneur de
Romans, dit *Moricaut*, troisième fils de PHI-
LIBERT DE LA BAULME, Seigneur de Perès, &
d'*Eléonore de la Rate*, sa quatrième femme,
épousa, l'an 1549, *Isabeau de Varax*, fille de
Pierre de Varax, Seigneur de Romans, & de
Jeanne de Clermont, dont il eut:
1. PIERRE, Seigneur de Romans, mort sans
enfans;
2. AIMÉ, qui suit;
3. CLAUDE, Seigneur de Villette, mort sans
hoirs en 1565;
4. Et PÉRONNE, femme d'*Aimé de Belontes*,
Seigneur de Grand-Champ.

XII. AIMÉ DE LA BAUME-VARAX, Seigneur
de Romans, épousa, l'an 1577, *Claudine de
Ponceton*, fille d'*Alexandre de Ponceton*,
Seigneur de Franchelins, & de *Jeanne de
Grandis*, dont sortirent:
1. PIERRE-MARC, Seigneur de Romans, mort
sans avoir été marié;
2. Et AIMÉ-HECTOR, mort aussi sans hoirs.

BRANCHE
des Seigneurs DE BOSCHES.

V. ANSELME DE LA BAULME, Chevalier, quatrième fils d'HUMBERT DE LA BAULME, Seigneur
de la Balme-sur-Cerdon en 1212, & d'*Huguette de Beauregard*, eut:
1. ANSELME, qui suit;
2. Et PIERRE, Abbé d'Ambronay en 1229.

VI. ANSELME DE LA BAULME, Chevalier, IIe
du nom, mort en 1279, laissa:
1. PIERRE, qui suit;
2. AMÉ, Chevalier, mort sans hoirs, en 1234;
3. MARGUERITE, femme de *Jean de Coussy*,
Seigneur de Genissia;
4. ELÉONORE, femme de *Guillaume de Bussy*,
Seigneur d'Eria;
5. & 6. HUGUETTE & GILLETTE, mortes filles.

VII. PIERRE DE LA BAULME, Chevalier, Seigneur de Bosches en 1297, épousa *Sucelis de
Frans*, dont il eut:
1. PIERRE, qui suit;
2. Et AMÉ, Chevalier, mort en 1373.

VIII. PIERRE DE LA BAULME, IIe du nom,
Seigneur de Bosches & de Termeut en 1339,
épousa *Marguerite de la Balme*, fille de
Perrault de la Balme, Chevalier, dont sortirent:

1. Amé, qui fuit;
2. Guillaume, Prieur de Meximieux en 1332;
3. Antoinette, morte fille;
4. Florence, femme de *Guillaume*, Seigneur de *Marmont;*
5. Et Marguerite, femme d'*André de Megria*, Chevalier.

IX. Amé de la Baulme, Seigneur de Bofches en 1347, fonda la Chartreufe de Megria en 1361. Il eut pour fils :

X. Pierre de la Baulme, IIIe du nom, Seigneur de Bofches, mort en 1397, qui eut de *Philippine* :

1. Jean, qui fuit;
2. André, Damoifeau, qui époufa, en 1430, *Ancelife de Charno*, fille de *Guerry*, Seigneur de Charno, mort fans hoirs;
3. Perceval, Prieur de Saint-Robert;
4. Pierre, Religieux à Ambronay;
5. & 6. Jeanne & Antoinette.

XI. Jean de la Baulme, Seigneur de Bofches, époufa *Antoinette de Varcy*, fille de *Guichard de Varcy*, Chevalier, après la mort de laquelle il fe rendit Chartreux, & mourut Procureur de la Chartreufe de Poléfins, l'an 1447, laiffant :

Marguerite de la Baulme, Dame de Bofches, femme de *Pierre*, bâtard de *Grolée*.

BRANCHE

des Seigneurs de la Balme, en Valromey.

IV. Guillaume de la Baulme, Seigneur de la Balme, en Valromey, fecond fils de Hugues de la Baulme, IIIe du nom, Seigneur de la Balme-fur-Cerdon, & d'*Alix de Binan*, en 1200, eut :

1. Pierre, qui fuit;
2. 3. & 4. Girard, Etienne & Guillaume, Chevaliers ;
5. Et Marguerite.

V. Pierre de la Baulme, Seigneur de la Balme & de Prangin, en Valromey, en 1237, prit pour femme *Ancelife*, dont il eut :

1. Humbert, qui fuit;
2. Pierre, Seigneur de Prangin, en 1250, père de Guillaume de la Baulme, Seigneur de Prangin, qui eut une fille, Pétronille, Dame de Prangin, femme de *Pierre*, Seigneur de *Luycieux;*
3. Et Thomas, mort fans hoirs.

VI. Humbert de la Baulme, Seigneur de la Balme, dit l'*Efcornas*, en 1260, laiffa :

1. Jean, qui fuit;
2. Et Hugues, Seigneur *du Bouchet*, qui fit branche, rapportée ci-après.

VII. Jean de la Baulme, Seigneur de la Balme, en Valromey en 1300, eut pour enfans :

1. Etienne, qui fuit;
2. Pierre, Chevalier en 1309;
3. Et Guillaume, Chevalier, dit *Maucler*, qui époufa, en 1311, *Marguerite de Portebeuf*, fille d'*Etienne de Portebeuf*, Seigneur de la Poype, & de *Lugues de la Paliffe*.

VIII. Etienne de la Baulme, Seigneur de la Balme, en Valromey, vivant en 1310, eut:

1. Guillaume, qui fuit;
2. Et Humbert, dit *des Rios*, Chevalier, père de Pierre, né en 1343, Chevalier; de François, Damoifeau, né en 1358; & d'Agnès, vivante l'an 1366.

IX. Guillaume de la Baulme, Seigneur de la Balme & des Terraux en 1352, eut pour fils:

X. Jean de la Baulme, Seigneur des Terraux & des Grez en 1398, qui époufa *Ifabelle de Clermont*, dont il eut:

1. Claude, qui fuit;
2. Guillaume, dit *Udrifet*, Seigneur des Grez;
3. Jacques, Religieux d'Ambronay;
4. Claudine, mariée 1° à *Lancelot de Châtillon-de-Michaille*, Seigneur du Château de Cult; & 2° à *Jean de la Baulme*, fon parent, Seigneur du Bouchet, en Dauphiné;
5. Et Catherine, femme de *Guillaume de Chalard*.

XI. Claude de la Baulme, Seigneur des Terraux & de Molières en 1438, fut marié avec *Béatrix de Gerbais*, dont il eut:

1. Guillaume, qui fuit;
2. Pierre, Seigneur de Molières, qui eût pour enfans :
   1. Antoine;
   2. Georges;
   3. Henri;
   4. Claude, qui fut père de :
      André & Guillaume, Seigneurs de Montaigre, vivant ès années 1512 & 1530;
   5. & 6. Aubert & Pierre, Seigneurs de Molières, vivant en 1491.
3. Et Hugues, dit *Sarrazin*, Damoifeau, qui époufa *Guye de Châtillon*, fille de *Guillaume de Châtillon*, Seigneur de Chapelles, & de *Guillemette de Montburon*, dont il eut Antoine, Seigneur de Grez.

XII. Guillaume de la Baulme, Seigneur des Terraux, mort l'an 1461, époufa *Jeanne de Montfalcon*, fille de *François de Montfalcon*, Chevalier, Seigneur de Flaccieu, & d'*Alix de Verbos*, dont il eut:

Louise de la Baulme.

BRANCHE
des Seigneurs DU BOUCHET.

VII. HUGUES DE LA BAULME, Seigneur du Bouchet, en Dauphiné, vivant en 1330, deuxième fils d'HUMBERT, Seigneur de la Balme, dit *l'Efcornas*, eut pour fils:

VIII. HUMBERT DE LA BAULME, Seigneur pu Bouchet, mort l'an 1372, qui époufa *Béatrix de l'Avés*, dont il eut:

1. JEAN, qui fuit;
2. & 3. ANCELISE & GABRIELLE;
4. 5. & 6. ANNEMONDE, AGNÈS & MARIE.

IX. JEAN DE LA BAULME, Seigneur du Bouchet, époufa, l'an 1386, CLAUDINE DE LA BAULME, fa parente, veuve de *Lancelot de Châtillon-de-Michaille*, Seigneur de Château-de-Cult. Elle étoit fille de JEAN DE LA BAULME, Seigneur des Terraux, & d'*Ifabelle de Clermont*. Il en eut:

1. ETIENNE, qui fuit;
2. Et HUGONET, qui tefta l'an 1455, faifant fes neveux héritiers, n'ayant pas de lignée de *Florette*.

X. ETIENNE DE LA BAULME, Seigneur du Bouchet en 1422, eut:

1. JEAN, qui fuit;
2. Et HENRI.

XI. JEAN DE LA BAULME, IIᵉ du nom, Seigneur du Bouchet en 1470, eut:

1. FRANÇOIS, qui fuit;
2. Et GILLES, Ecuyer, qui fut père de CLAUDE DE LA BAULME, Baron de la Hagria, marié, en 1495, à *Charlotte de Boulainviller*, fille de *Pierre de Boulainviller*, Seigneur de Serpois, & de *Pérette de Boiffet*.

XII. FRANÇOIS DE LA BAULME, Seigneur du Bouchet, époufa *Marie d'Hallencourt*, Dame de Boyrieu, dont il eut pour fille unique:

GUIGONNE DE LA BAULME, Dame du Bouchet, femme de *Louis*, Seigneur de *Longecombes*, en Bugey.

BRANCHE
des Seigneurs DE LA PICARDERIE & DE GENESËY.

III. GUILLAUME DE LA BAULME, OU DE LA BALME, Seigneur de la Picarderie, quatrième fils de HUGUES DE LA BAULME, IIᵉ du nom, Seigneur de la Balme-fur-Cerdon, laiffa:

1. JOSSERAND, qui fuit;
2. Et BÉRAUD, Chevalier.

IV. JOSSERAND DE LA BAULME, Seigneur de la Picarderie en 1248, laiffa un fils:

V. JEAN DE LA BAULME, dit *Picard*, Seigneur de Genefey en 1271, dont le fils fut:

VI. JEAN DE LA BAULME, dit *Picard*, IIᵉ du nom, Seigneur de Genefey, de la Balme & de Seure en 1334. Il eut:

VII. JEAN DE LA BAULME, IIIᵉ du nom, Chevalier, Seigneur de la Balme & de Genefey, en 1378, qui eut d'*Alix*:

1. LOUIS, qui fuit;
2. Et ANTOINE, Seigneur de *Corleyfon*, qui a fait branche.

VIII LOUIS DE LA BAULME, Seigneur de Genefey en 1442, mourut fans enfans.

BRANCHE
des Seigneurs DE CORLEYSON.

VIII. ANTOINE DE LA BAULME, Damoifeau, Seigneur de Corleyfon en 1441, fecond fils de JEAN DE LA BAULME, IIIᵉ du nom, Seigneur de Genefey, eut:

1. JEAN, qui fuit;
2. ODET, Seigneur de Corleyfon en 1486;
3. JEANNE, mariée 1º à *Didier*, de la Charme, Seigneur de Pitafoux; & 2º à *Jacques de Ferlay*, Seigneur de la Vernonfe;
4. CLAUDINE, femme de *Louis Bochard*, Ecuyer;
5. Et CATHERINE, Dame de Corleyfon.

IX. JEAN DE LA BAULME, Seigneur de Genefey, après fon oncle, en 1484, époufa *Catherine de Saint-Julien*, fille de *Pierre de Saint-Julien*, Chevalier, dont il eut:

1. LOUIS, mort fans hoirs, du vivant de fon père;
2. Et CLAUDINE, femme de *Pierre de Charno*, Seigneur de Faucoges, en Comté.

BRANCHE.
des Seigneurs DE LANGES.

III. ISARD DE LA BAULME, ou de la Balme, Seigneur de Langes, cinquième fils de HUGUES DE LA BAULME, IIᵉ du nom, Seigneur de la Balme-fur-Cerdon, laiffa de fon époufe, dont le nom nous eft inconnu:

1. GUILLAUME, qui fuit;
2. ACHARD, Chanoine de Mâcon en 1220, mort en 1242;
3. AMÉ, Chevalier;
4. Et PONCE, Chevalier en 1210.

IV. GUILLAUME DE LA BAULME, Seigneur de Langes, vivant en 1220, fut père de:

V. ISARD DE LA BAULME, IIᵉ du nom, Seigneur de Langes & de Mailla, vivant en 1245, qui eut:

1. HUMBERT, qui fuit;

2. Et YOLANDE, Dame de Mailla, femme de *Hugues*, Seigneur de *Moyeia*.

VI. HUMBERT DE LA BAULME, Seigneur de Langes en 1284 & 1320, eut de *Marceline:*

1. HUMBERT, qui fuit;
2. JEAN, dit *de Langes*, Seigneur de Morterey;
3. Et GUILLAUME, dit *de Langes*, Chevalier en 1340.

VII. HUMBERT DE LA BAULME, dit *de Langes*, II° du nom, Seigneur de Morterey, de l'Ane & de Langes en 1347, époufa 1° *Huguette Jullien*; & 2° *Alix de Beaufort*, Dame de Nublans. Il eut du premier lit:

1. JEAN, Religieux à Ambronay;
2. HUMBERT, Religieux à Saint-Ouyn de Roux;
3. & 4. PERCEVAL & CLAUDE;
5. JEANNETTE, Religieufe à Neuville;
6. & 7. FRANÇOISE & LOUISE.

Et du fecond lit :

FRANÇOIS, qui fuit.

VIII. FRANÇOIS DE LA BAULME, dit *de l'Ane*, Seigneur de Morterey & de Langes, mourut en 1435. Il avoit époufé, l'an 1398, *Pernette de Gafpard*, fille de *Guillaume de Gafpard*, Damoifeau. Il laiffa :

1. ANTOINE, qui fuit;
2. GUILLAUME, mort fans hoirs;
3. CLAUDE, Seigneur de *Langes*, qui a fait branche ;
4. PIERRE, Prieur de Vobles, en Comté ;
5. & 6. AMÉ & FRANÇOISE.

IX. ANTOINE DE LA BAULME, Seigneur de Morterey, Confeiller & Chambellan du Duc de Savoie en 1463, époufa *Lionnette de Pierre-Gourde*, fille de *Hugues*, Seigneur de Pierre-Gourde & de Cornon, & d'*Alix de Grolée*, dont il eut:

FRANÇOISE DE LA BAULME, Dame de Morterey, femme de GUILLAUME DE LA BAULME, Seigneur de la Balme-fur-Cerdon.

BRANCHE
des Seigneurs DE RAMASSE & DE CHARANTONNAY.

IX. CLAUDE DE LA BAULME, Seigneur de Langes & de Ramaffe, troifième fils de FRANÇOIS DE LA BAULME, dit l'*Ane*, Seigneur de Morterey, & de *Pernette de Gafpard*, époufa, en 1470, *Jeanne de Benier*, fille de *Claude de Benier*, Seigneur de Corbertod, & de *Sibylle de Briod*, dont il eut:

1. SIBUET, qui fuit;
2. HENRIETTE, Religieufe à Villers-fur-Saône;

3. Et CATHERINE, femme de *Claude de Châtillon*, Seigneur de Ralamandes.

X. SIBUET DE LA BAULME, Seigneur de Ramaffe, de l'Ane & de Charantonnay en 1530, époufa *Claudine*, Dame *de Charantonnay*, dont il eut:

1. JEAN, Seigneur de Ramaffe en 1572, mort fans hoirs;
2. PIERRE-MARC, Seigneur de Ramaffe, après fon frère, mort auffi fans être marié;
3. CLAUDE, Prieur de Vion, en Savoie;
4. ANGÉLIQUE, femme de PIERRE, Seigneur de *Montaigne;*
5. NICOLARDE, femme du Seigneur de *Châteauneuf;*
6. Et JACQUELINE.

BRANCHE
des Seigneurs DE VERTRIEU.

Il y a grande apparence que les Seigneurs de VERTRIEU, en Dauphiné, font iffus de la famille de la BAULME, Seigneurs de la Balme-fur-Cerdon, tant par la commune tradition, qu'à caufe de la conformité des armes, qui font d'or, *à la bande de gueules*, qui pourroit être prife pour *brifure*, nous les mettons en ce lieu pour ne rien omettre de cette Maifon.

AMBLARD DE LA BAULME, Seigneur de Vertrieu, vivant l'an 1340, époufa *Béatrix de Léras*, dont il eut:

JEAN DE LA BAULME, Seigneur de Vertrieu en 1400, qui époufa *Claudine d'Armefin*, fille d'*Amé d'Armefin*, Chevalier, Seigneur de Connelieu, & de *Philippine d'Afpremont*, dont fortit:

JEAN DE LA BAULME, II° du nom, Seigneur de Vertrieu, qui époufa *Béatrix de Grolée*, fille d'*Aymard de Grolée*, Seigneur de Nuys & de Mefpreu, & d'*Ifabelle de Grolée*, dont il eut :

1. AMBLARD, qui fuit;
2. ROBERT, Chanoine-fcrutain & Comte de Lyon en 1471;
3. ANSELME, Religieux d'Ambronay, Doyen de la Tiamehère en 1504;
4. EUSTACHE, Religieux d'Ambronay, Doyen de Villeverfure en 1504;
5. LOUIS;
6. Et HECTOR, Doyen de Villeverfure, & Religieux d'Ambronay, mort l'an 1523.

AMBLARD DE LA BAULME, II° du nom, Seigneur de Vertrieu en 1515, époufa *Gabrielle de Poifieux*, dont il eut pour fille unique :

FRANÇOISE DE LA BAULME, Dame de Vertrieu,

mariée, en 1491, avec *Allaude de la Poype*, Seigneur de Cernens & de Foffieu, en Dauphiné.

BRANCHE
des Seigneurs DE MARES.

Les Seigneurs de Mares fe difent auffi if-fus de la Maifon de la BAULME-fur-Cerdon; ils portent les même nom & mêmes armes.

AMÉ DE LA BAULME, Seigneur de Mares, fe retira en Dauphiné, où il époufa, en 1439, *Perrette de Mares*, Dame du lieu, en la Pa-roiffe de Joannage. Il en eut:

1. PERCEVAL, qui époufa, en 1480, *Jeanne de Roucée*, fille de *Jean de Roucée*, Seigneur de Cofpet, au pays de Vaud, & de *Jean-nette de Montburon*, dont il n'eut point d'enfans;
2. Et ETIENNE, qui fuit.

ETIENNE DE LA BAULME, Seigneur des Ma-res en 1490, fut père de:

BARTHÉLEMY DE LA BAULME, Seigneur de Mares, mort l'an 1534, qui eut:

1. PIERRE, qui fuit;
2. & 3. FLORENCE & ANNE.

PIERRE DE LA BAULME, Seigneur de Mares en 1543, mourut en 1587. Il avoit époufé *Jacquette de Vauchier*, & laiffa:

1. FRANÇOIS, qui fuit;
2. CATHERINE, femme, en 1576, de *Laurent Dupuy*, Seigneur de Marcel;
3. Et CLAUDINE.

FRANÇOIS DE LA BAULME, Seigneur de Mares & de Cherna, mourut l'an 1600. Il avoit époufé, 1° l'an 1587, *Anne de Paleguin*, fille de *Gafpard de Paleguin*, Seigneur de Befemon, & de *Sufanne de Ferou*; & 2° *Péronne de Dorlans*, fille d'*Antoine*, Seigneur *de Dor-lans*, & de *Ferne de Ciucia*. Il eut du pre-mier mariage:

1. GUILLAUME, qui fuit;
2. LAURENCE;
3. Et SUSANNE, mariée, le 14 Avril 1602, avec *Annibal de Torchefelon*, Seigneur de Mai-gné, fils de *Claude de Torchefelon*, Seigneur de Maigné.

GUILLAUME DE LA BAULME, Seigneur de Ma-res en 1615, époufa *Gafparde de Chaillot*, fille de *Gafpard de Chaillot*, Vice-Bailli du Briançonnois, & de *Gafparde de Faure*. Il eut:

1. LOUIS, Seigneur de Mares;
2. Et FRANÇOISE, femme de *Chriftophe de Ri-verie*, Seigneur de Clerimberg.

De la même Maifon étoient GUILLAUME DE LA BAULME, Ecuyer, & AGNÈS, fa femme, en 1297.

Tome II.

Et GUY DE LA BAULME, ou DE LA BALME, & *Ifabelle de Frangié*, fa femme en 1314.

De la Maifon DE LA BAULME-SAINT-AMOUR, étoit JACQUES-PHILIPPE DE LA BAULME, Comte de Saint-Amour, ancien Meftre-de-Camp de Dragons, mort au Château de Chantonnay, en Franche-Comté, le 26 Novembre 1761.

Les armes: *d'or, à la bande d'azur*, que quelques-uns difent *engrêlée*. On trouve dans l'*Hiftoire Généalogique des Sires de Salins*, pag. 19, une famille du nom DE LA BAULME, en latin *Balma*, que l'Abbé Guil-laume, Auteur de cet Ouvrage, dit paroître avoir été originaire de la Ville de Salins. *On voit*, dit-il, *dans les Chartres des anciens Sires de Salins, les noms de plufieurs Gen-tilshommes de cette Maifon, qui s'établit en-fuite dans la Baronie d'Arlay, & y fut con-nue fous le nom de la* BAULME, *ou de la* BAL-ME. De cette Maifon étoient:

GUY DE LA BAULME, Chevalier, qui fit hom-mage, en 1245, à JEAN, Comte de Bourgogne, d'une vigne fituée fur le territoire de Salins.

Et JEAN DE LA BAULME, Chanoine de Befan-con & Archidiacre de Favernay, qui difpofa de fes biens, en 1349, & chargea fes héritiers de faire conftruire un Hôpital dans la Terre d'Orgelet, fuivant les intentions de GUILLAU-ME DE LA BAULME, fon frère, qui avoit deftiné à cet ufage 250 florins.

BAUME-SUZE (LA). Voici encore une Maifon du nom de la BAUME, qui n'a rien de commun avec les autres, & qui tire fon ori-gine de la Province de Dauphiné.

I. LOUIS DE LA BAUME, Chevalier, eft le pre-mier de cette Maifon dont on ait connoiffan-ce: il eft nommé, dans les Comptes de *Jean le Flament*, Tréforier des Guerres, en 1380, & eut pour fils:

II. LOUIS DE LA BAUME, II° du nom, qui, par fon mariage contracté, en 1426, avec *An-toinette de Saluces*, Dame de Suze, devint Seigneur de cette Terre. Leur fils fut:

III. BERTRAND DE LA BAUME, Seigneur de Suze, qui époufa, l'an 1459, *Françoife de Fayn*, dont il eut:

1. PIERRE, qui fuit;
2. CHARLES, Chevalier;
3. LOUIS, Chevalier;
4. JEANNE, mariée 1° à *Gabriel de Gruiel*, Sei-gneur de la Borde, & 2° à *Jean de Plana*;
5. Et PHILIPPE, femme de *Jacques de Monta-gu*, Seigneur de Candis & de Vic.

J j

IV. Pierre de la Baume, Seigneur de Suze, épousa, l'an 1490, *Françoise Allois*, fille
de *Louis Allois*, Seigneur de Vaſſieu, & en
eut :

1. Guillaume, qui ſuit ;
2. Rostang, Religieux de l'Ordre de Cîteaux,
   Abbé de Maz, puis Evêque d'Orange, mort
   l'an 1551 ;
3. Jean, Seigneur de Pleſian ;
4. Philippe, femme de *Henri de Grace ;*
5. Et Claire, femme de *Guillaume*, Seigneur
   de *Grimon.*

V. Guillaume de la Baume, Seigneur de
Suze, épouſa *Catherine d'Albaron*, fille de
Jacques d'Albaron-de-Lers & de Montfrin,
& de *Marguerite de Clermont,* dont il eut :

1. François, qui ſuit ;
2. Antoinette, femme de *Louis d'Euvre*,
   Seigneur du Puy-Saint-Martin ;
3. Et Marguerite, femme d'*Aymar*, Seigneur de *Vinay.*

VI. François de la Baume, Comte de Suze,
Chevalier des Ordres du Roi, Lieutenant-Général pour Sa Majeſté en Provence, & Général de l'Egliſe au Comté Venaiſſin, mort l'an
1587, eut pour femme, *Françoiſe de Lévis*,
fille de *Gilbert de Lévis*, Comte de Venta-
dour, & de *Jeanne de Laire.* De ce mariage
ſortirent :

1. Rostang, qui ſuit ;
2. Georges, Seigneur *de Pleſian*, qui a fait
   une branche ;
3. Ferdinand, Baron de Lers & de Rochefort, mort au ſiège d'Iſſoire l'an 1577 ;
4. Antoine, Baron *de Beaumez*, qui a fait
   branche ;
5. Louise, femme d'*Antoine de Saſſenage*,
   Seigneur du Pont-de-Royan ;
6. Catherine, femme de *Jean-Claude Alleman*, Baron d'Uriage ;
7. Marguerite, femme de *Pompée de Pontevès*, Seigneur de Buons ;
8. Et Charlotte, femme du Comte de *Saint-
   Renièze* en Vivarais.

VII. Rostang de la Baume, Comte de Suze
& de Rochefort, épouſa 1° *Madeleine Deſprez*, fille de *Melchior Deſprez*, Seigneur de
Montpézat, & d'*Henriette de Savoie ;* &
2° *Catherine de Meuillon*, fille de *François de Meuillon*, Baron de Breſſieu, & de
Marguerite de Guaſſe-de-Lupe. Il eut du
premier lit :

1. Jacques, qui ſuit ;
2. Et Marguerite, femme de *Henri de Beaumanoir*, Marquis de Lavardin.

Du ſecond lit vinrent :

3. Anne, Comte *de Rochefort*, qui a fait une
   branche ;
4. Louis-François, Evêque de Viviers ;
5. François, Chevalier de Malte ;
6. Charles, auſſi Chevalier de Malte ;
7. Marguerite, femme de *Juſt-François de
   Fay*, Baron de Garlande ;
8. Madeleine, Religieuſe ;
9. Marie, femme de *Joachim de Montagu*,
   Marquis de Bouzols ;
10. Charlotte, femme du Marquis de *Cham-
    bonnes ;*
11. Anne, morte fille ;
12. Jeanne, femme de *N… de Fougaſſes*, Sei-
    gneur de Taillades ;
13. Et Henriette.

VIII. Jacques-Honorat de la Baume, Comte de Suze, Marquis de Villars, prit pour
femme, *Françoiſe des Porcellets-de-Mail-
lane*, dont il eut pour fils unique :

IX. Bernard de la Baume, Comte de Suze,
Marquis de Villars, mort ſans être marié.

BRANCHE
des Seigneurs de Rochefort.

VIII. Anne de la Baume, Comte de Rochefort, fils de Rostang de la Baume, Comte
de Suze, & de *Catherine de Meuillon*, ſa ſeconde femme, épouſa *Catherine de la Croix-
Caſtries*, dont :

1. Gaspard-Joachim, qui ſuit ;
2. Anne-Tristan ;
3. Et Catherine, Religieuſe.

IX. Gaspard-Joachim de la Baume, Comte
de Suze, Marquis de Breſſieu, épouſa, en
1682, *Marthe d'Albon.* Il fut père de :

X. Louis-François de la Baume, Comte de
Suze & de Rochefort, Marquis de Breſſieu,
mort en 1746, qui avoit épouſé, en 1709, *Marie de Roſtaing-du-Vauches*, dont :

1. Louis-Charles, Comte de Suze & de Ro-
   chefort, Marquis de Breſſieu ;
2. Antoine-Françoise-Hugone, mariée, le 2
   Mars 1741, à *Paul-Alphonse-François-
   Antoine de Theſan-Venaſque*, Vicomte de
   Nebouſan ;

Et deux filles, Religieuſes.

Les armes : *d'or, à trois chevrons de ſable, au chef d'azur, chargé d'un lion naiſſant d'argent, couronné d'or, armé & langué de gueules.*

BRANCHE
des Seigneurs de Plésian.

VII. Georges de la Baume, Seigneur de

Plefian, fecond fils de François de la Baume, Comte de Suze, & de *Françoife de Lévis*, prit pour femme *Jeanne de Maugiron*, de laquelle il eut plufieurs enfans dont nous ne pouvons parler, faute de Mémoires.

BRANCHE
des Seigneurs de Baumez.

VII. Antoine de la Baume, Seigneur de Baumez, quatrième fils de François de la Baume, Comte de Suze, & de *Françoife de Lévis*, époufa *Marie de Laire*, Dame de Glaudage, dont il eut:

1. Charles, Baron de Baumez, Abbé de Mazan;
2. Catherine, femme de *N... de Châteauneuf*, Comte de Rochebonne;
3. Et Françoise, femme de *Louis-Efcalin Adhémar*, Marquis de la Garde.

Les armes comme ci-deffus.

* BAUMES, Terre & Seigneurie qui eft la feconde Baronie du Comtat Venaiffin. Elle paffa, vers le milieu du XIVᵉ fiècle, dans la Maifon de *Peyre*, avec les Terres & Seigneuries de Bedouin, d'Auriol & de Carousbe, par le mariage de *Marguerite de Bedoffir*, fille & héritière de *Bertrand*, Prince d'Orange, & *ab-inteftat* de *Catherine de Baucio*, fa mère, avec *Aftorg de Peyre*. En 1574, cette Baronie fut confifquée, pour caufe de Religion, fur *Antoine-Aftorg de Peyre*, & donnée par le Pape à *Henri de Montmorency*, Pair & Connétable de France. Cependant *Antoine-Aftorg* y eft rentré en 1599; fon fils *Geoffroy-Aftorg-Aldebert* la vendit en 1604 à la Maifon de *Fortia-de-Piles*, qui en a joui depuis, & l'a confervée jufqu'à préfent.

BAUMETTE: *de gueules, à cinq éperviers, avec leurs longes & fonnettes d'or, pofées 3 & 2, ou en fautoir.*

BAUNE (de la), en Normandie: *d'argent, au chevron d'azur, accompagné en chef de deux croiffans de même, & en pointe de trois tours de fable rangées en face, celle du milieu plus élevée.*

BAUNE (de la): *d'or, à un arbre arraché de finople, accofté de deux croiffans de gueules.*

◊ BAUPTE (de), famille des plus anciennes de la province de Normandie, où elle poffédoit, dans les premiers tems, de très-grands biens. Elle impofa fon nom de Baupte à une

Paroiffe, enfuite à une contrée entière, appelée encore aujourd'hui le *Pays Bauptois*. La Paroiffe de Baupte appartenoit encore à cette famille en 1100, ainfi qu'on le remarque par quelques aveux rendus à Joseph de Baupte, Chevalier, Seigneur dudit lieu & de Bauptois.

Les guerres que la province a effuyées dans prefque tous les tems, & même encore depuis peu, près Cherbourg & autres endroits, ont difperfé les branches de cette famille & fes anciens titres; mais celles qui fe font perpétuées ont toujours confervé la pureté des fentimens de ceux qui les leur ont tranfmis, ainfi que le nom.

Quoique cette famille foit *noble de race*, & que l'annobliffement s'en perde dans les tems les plus reculés, Louis XIV jugea à propos de le renouveler dans la perfonne d'Anténor de Baupte, Sieur de Jugauville, rapporté ci-après.

Jean de Baupte, tige d'une branche cadette, aujourd'hui repréfentée par les Seigneurs de *Moon*, fe trouvant dans le cas d'acquérir des fiefs mouvans de Sa Majefté, fe pourvut d'un office de Secrétaire du Roi, pour avoir l'exemption des droits de lods, & ventes des biens qu'il projetoit d'acquérir. Les Lettres de Louis XIV, du mois de Juin 1653, pour Anténor de Baupte, l'office de Secrétaire du Roi, obtenu par ledit Jean, donneroient, au befoin, un double titre d'annobliffement; mais cette vertu n'enlève pas à cette famille l'ancienneté de la nobleffe dans laquelle fes ancêtres étoient nés & ont vécu; au contraire, elle la fortifie & la corrobore. Les defcendans confervent encore, pour cet effet, une partie de leur fortune dans la contrée de leur nom, qui eft le pays de Baupte, chef-lieu du Bauptois. Elle a, dans tous les tems fervi les Souverains, comme il eft prouvé par les Lettres que Louis XIV jugea à propos d'accorder à Anténor en 1653, & par la confirmation de celles qu'il donna à Pierre, un de fes fils, au mois d'Octobre 1664. Ceux qui exiftent aujourd'hui, à l'exemple de leurs ayeux, continuent de fervir.

Anténor de Baupte, Ecuyer, Sieur de Jugauville, fervit fous Louis XIII, & fut ennobli fans finance, lui & fes enfans, nés & à naître en loyal mariage, par Lettres-Patentes de Louis XIV, en forme de charte, données à Paris au mois de Juin 1653; lefquelles Lettres, acceptées par ledit Anténor, furent préfentées à la Cour des Aides, le 13 Mai 1654, aux fins de leur enregiftrement. Cette Cour ordonna, comme en pareil cas, par Arrêt du 21 Février 1657, les informations de droit, qui furent faites & finies au mois d'Oĉtobre 1657. ANTÉNOR DE BAUPTE mourut le 15 Octobre 1660 & fut inhumé le lendemain, en la Paroiffe de Vuide-Fontaine en Normandie. Ses Lettres de Nobleffe furent enregiftrées par Arrêt du 8 Août 1661, à la requête de fon fils PIERRE. Il avoit époufé N.... *de Poupet*, dont il eut:

1. ROBERT, Ecuyer, Sieur de Jugauville, marié à *Françoife de Mauconvenant;*
2. Et PIERRE, qui fuit;

PIERRE DE BAUPTE, Ecuyer, Sieur de Contrepont, fervit Sa Majefté dans fes armées de Flandres & d'Italie, particulièrement au fiège de Tortone & autres, en qualité de Lieutenant au Régiment d'Infanterie du Comte du Pleffis-Praslin, ès années 1639, 40, 41, 42 & 1643, s'acquitta dignement de la commiffion qu'il avoit reçue du Roi, fous les ordres du Maréchal du Pleffis-Praslin, pour faire mettre bas les armes aux mutins de la ville de Bordeaux, & faire ceffer l'attaque du Château Trompette; pour l'exécution de laquelle commiffion il expofa plufieurs fois fa vie; fervit auffi quatre années confécutives, en qualité de Garde-du-Corps du Roi, notamment au fiège du Caftelet, où il reçut plufieurs bleffures en montant des premiers à la brèche avec les Enfans-Perdus. C'eft en confidération de fes fervices rendus pendant plus de 20 ans, que Louis XIV, qui, par déclaration du mois d'Août 1664, enregiftrée à la Cour des Aides, le 8, avoit révoqué toutes les Lettres d'annobliffement expédiées depuis le 1er Janvier 1639, confirma PIERRE DE BAUPTE, fans finance, par Lettres données à Paris au mois de Décembre 1664, lui, fes enfans & defcendans nés & à naître en loyal mariage, dans la *nobleffe* accordée à feu ANTÉNOR DE BAUPTE, fon père. Elles furent enregiftrées à la Cour des Aides, le 12 Janvier 1665. Il produifit les titres de fa nobleffe devant M. *Chamillart*, Intendant de la Généralité de Caen, qui lui en délivra un certificat, le 22 Mars 1668. Il avoit époufé, *Anne Jourdan du Mefnil*, dont:

1. ROBERT, qui fuit;
2. BONAVENTURE, Ecuyer, Prêtre;
3. JEAN, tige de la branche de *Moon*, rapportée ci-après;

4. Et autre ROBERT DE BAUPTE, Ecuyer, marié à N... *de Cuves.*

ROBERT DE BAUPTE, Ecuyer, Seigneur de Champcey, époufa 1º *Françoife-Elifabeth le Verrier de Thoville;* & 2º par contrat du 3 Février 1702, *Madeleine du Halley*, veuve de *Pierre le Sauvage*, Ecuyer. Du premier lit il a eu:

1. ROBERT, qui fuit;
2. CHRISTOPHE-BONAVENTURE, Ecuyer, Seigneur de Champcey, mariée à *Jeanne de la Bellière de Vains;*
3. Et ANGE-FÉLIX DE BAUPTE, rapporté après fon aîné.

ROBERT DE BAUPTE, Ecuyer, Sieur de la Monguerrière, baptifé le 1er Novembre 1698, époufa *Marie-Perrine du Prey de Pierreville*, dont:

1. JACQUES-MARIE-ROBERT, Ecuyer, baptifé le 15 Mars 1755;
2. Et MARIE-CAROLINE-ANNE-FRANÇOISE DE BAUPTE, baptifée le 17 Avril 1752.

ANGE-FÉLIX DE BAUPTE, Ecuyer, Sieur de Contrepont, obtint des Lettres de relèvement en la Chancellerie du Palais à Rouen, le 17 Février 1720, contre CHRISTOPHE-BONAVENTURE DE BAUPTE, Ecuyer, fon frère aîné, au fujet des fucceffions de leurs père & mère, & mourut le 20 Avril 1723. Il avoit époufé, *Marie le Vavaffeur*, de laquelle il a laiffé:

ANGE-FÉLIX DE BAUPTE, IIe du nom, Ecuyer, Seigneur de Saint-Manvieu, du Hamel, &c., appelé *le Chevalier de Contrepont*, ancien Lieutenant de frégate du Roi, retiré du fervice à caufe de fes bleffures. Il a époufé le 10 Février 1739, en la Paroiffe Notre-Dame de Grandville, *Marie le Pelletier*, dont:

1. ANGE-FÉLIX-FRANÇOIS-MARIE, Ecuyer, baptifé le 23 Avril 1748, Officier de Marine;
2. LOUIS-MARIE, Ecuyer, baptifé le 20 Avril 1750, auffi Officier de Marine;
3. ANTÉNOR-MARIE, Ecuyer, baptifé le 7 Février 1756, Officier de Marine;
4. ANGÉLIQUE-ANDRÉE-CHARLOTTE DE BAUPTE, baptifée le 29 Novembre 1746.

BRANCHE
des Seigneurs DE MOON.

JEAN DE BAUPTE, Ecuyer, troifième fils de PIERRE, Sieur de Contrepont, & d'*Anne Jourdan du Mefnil*, pourvu d'un office de Secrétaire du Roi, mort le 25 Février 1771, avoit époufé *Renée Hébert de Beaumer*, fille & héritière de *Gilles Hébert*, Ecuyer,

Sieur de Beaumer, mort le 12 Août 1676, & de N.... *de Marguerie de Vierville*, dont il a eu :

FRANÇOIS DE BAUPTE, Ecuyer, Seigneur de Moon, mort le 10 Juin 1749, qui avoit épouſé *Marie - Gillette de Bauquet*, Dame de Moon, morte le 30 Juin 1749, fille d'*Henri de Bauquet*, Ecuyer, Sieur de la Buiſſonnière, & de *Marie de Groſourdy*. De ce mariage ſont iſſus :

1. JEAN-FRANÇOIS-HENRI, Chevalier, Seigneur de Moon ;
2. LOUIS - CHARLES, appelé *le Chevalier de Baupte ;*
3. Et MARIE-GENEVIÈVE DE BAUPTE, dite *Mademoiſelle de Beaumer*.

Les tems reculés ayant fait perdre de vue à quelques branches de cette famille leurs vraies armoiries, il s'y étoit gliſſé quelque changement; mais les ayant recouvrées, toutes les branches les reprennent telles qu'elles ſont en effet, & connues de tout tems, ſavoir : *de ſable, au pal d'or, chargé d'une flèche de gueules.*C'eſt ainſi qu'elles ſont blaſonnées en tête du certificat de M. Chamillart.

BAUQUEL, Seigneur de la Roque, de Mauny, Creuilly, Grandval & d'Huberville, en Normandie, Généralité de Rouen, famille maintenue dans ſa Nobleſſe le 28 Novembre 1667, qui porte pour armes: *de gueules, au chevron d'or, accompagné de trois pommes de même, feuillées & tigées de ſinople, deux en chef & une en pointe.*

BAUQUEMARE, Sieur du Victot en Normandie, Généralité d'Alençon, famille maintenue dans ſa nobleſſe le 3 Janvier 1668. L'*Hiſtoire des Maîtres des Requêtes* dit que JEAN DE BAUQUEMARE, fameux Avocat du Parlement de Rouen, fut père de JACQUES DE BAUQUEMARE, Premier Préſident de la même Cour en 1565. Il mourut en 1584. La Roque, dans ſon *Traité de la Nobleſſe*, p. 367, dit que ce Premier Préſident du Parlement de Normandie fut fait *Chevalier* par le Roi CHARLES IX, par Lettres données à Gaillon le 25 Septembre 1566. Suivant l'*Hiſtoire de Rouen*, ſon fils fut Gouverneur du Vieux Palais en 1590.

JOSEPH DE BAUQUEMARE, Maître des Requêtes, GUILLAUME DE BAUQUEMARE, Conſeiller au Parlement de Rouen, & NICOLAS DE BAUQUEMARE, Seigneur de Francville, ſuivant l'*Hiſtoire de Rouen*, obtinrent des Lettres de Nobleſſe en 1572.

JEAN DE BAUQUEMARE, Chevalier, Seigneur de Bourdeni, Maître des Requêtes, mort en 1619, avoit épouſé *Anne de Hacqueville*, Dame d'Oms-en-Bray, morte en 1638.

Les armes: *d'azur, au chevron d'or, accompagné de trois têtes de léopards de même, deux en chef & une en pointe.*

BAUQUET, Seigneur de Turqueville & de Sureville, en Normandie, Généralité de Caen, famille annoblie en 1543 : *d'argent, au chevron de gueules, accompagné de trois loſanges de même, deux en chef & une en pointe.*

BAUQUET, en Normandie, Election de Carentan, famille qui peut bien être une branche de la précédente: *de gueules, au chevron d'or, accompagné de trois loſanges d'argent, deux en chef & une en pointe.*

BAURE : *écartelé, aux 1 & 4 d'argent, à trois mouchetures d'hermines de ſable, 2 & 1; aux 2 & 3 d'argent, à trois faſces de gueules.*

BAUSSAN. FRANÇOIS DE BAUSSAN, Seigneur de Richegrou, ancien Capitaine au régiment de Piémont, mort le 7 Avril 1719; laiſſa de *Marguerite de Mareſcot*, décédée le 27 Avril 1710, pour fils aîné:

FRANÇOIS DE BAUSSAN, Seigneur de Pichegrou, d'Arpentigny, &c., né le 27 Octobre 1675, Maître des Requêtes ordinaires de l'Hôtel du Roi, depuis 1711, & Intendant de la Généralité d'Orléans depuis le mois d'Août 1731 ; & auparavant de celle de Poitiers depuis le mois de Juillet 1728, ci-devant Conſeiller au Parlement de Paris, où il avoit été reçu le 18 Février 1699, eſt mort ſubitement à Paris le 26 Février 1740. Il avoit épouſé, 1° en Janvier 1708, *Marie-Anne Rellier*, morte le 26 Février 1722, fille unique de *Louis Rellier*, Intendant & Secrétaire du feu Duc de Vendôme, & d'*Anne-Eliſabeth Heiſs;* & 2° le 25 Avril 1725, N...... *le Fer-de-Bauvais*, de la ville de Saint-Malo, veuve de *Charles-François-Claude de Marbeuf*, Préſident au Parlement de Bretagne.

Il a eu du premier lit pour fille unique:

MARIE - MARGUERITE - ELISABETH DE BAUSSAN, née le 23 Janvier 1709, mariée, le 1er Mars 1728, avec *Geoffroy - Macé Camus*, Seigneur de Pontcarré, mort à Paris le 28 Janvier 1767. Voyez CAMUS - PONT-CARRÉ.

Et du fecond lit il a eu :

CLAUDE-ADRIEN DE BAUSSAN, qui fuit.

CLAUDE-ADRIEN DE BAUSSAN, Chevalier, Seigneur de Torry, ancien Ecuyer du Roi, mort le 7 Novembre 1731, âgé d'environ 50 ans, fut nommé par le Roi pour commander l'équipage que Sa Majefté envoya pour conduire la Reine en France. Il avoit époufé *Angélique de Marefcot*, remariée 2° à *François Renouard*, Comte de Villayer & d'Auteuil, mort le 5 Juin 1738; & 3° le 2 Mai 1751, à *Jean-François-Louis Aubery-de-Vâtan*, Capitaine au Régiment des Gardes-Françoifes. De ce mariage vint :

ALEXANDRE DE BAUSSAN, qui fut reçu, en 1751, Maître des Requêtes, & mourut le 19 Janvier 1755, âgé de 28 ans. Il avoit époufé MARIE-FRANÇOISE DE BAUSSAN, fa coufine germaine, remariée, le 23 Février 1756, à *Jofeph-Charles-Roch-Palamède de Forbin de Maynier*, Baron d'Oppede. Elle étoit fœur de N.... DE BAUSSAN, Capitaine de Cavalerie.

Les armes : *d'azur, à un chevron d'or, accompagné de trois glands de même, deux en chef & un en pointe.*

BAUSSANCOURT, en Champagne.

Première Branche.

LOUIS-MARCEL DE BAUSSANCOURT, Seigneur du Petit-Mefnil, Chaumefnil, Mefnil-Fouchard, a époufé *Jeanne-Françoife le Perry*. Il a eu :

EDME-FRANÇOIS-MARCEL DE BAUSSANCOURT, Seigneur du Mefnil-Fouchard, la Maifon des Champs, le Chanel, Vauchonvilliers, Valfutenay, né le 10 Octobre 1723, Chevalier de Saint-Louis, Moufquetaire du Roi, dans la feconde Compagnie, retiré avec Commiffion de Capitaine de Cavalerie & penfion en 1755, marié, en 1756, à *Madeleine-Jacobée de Vienne*, dont il a eu quatre garçons & une fille.

Seconde Branche.

Elle eft repréfentée par LOUIS-FÉLIX DE BAUSSANCOURT, Docteur de Sorbonne ;

Et FRANÇOIS DE BAUSSANCOURT, Provincial des Minimes.

Les armes : *d'argent, au lion de fable, la queue fourchée paffée en fautoir, chargé fur l'épaule féneftre d'une étoile d'or.*

BAUSSEN, Sieur du Defert, de Haudi-

court, ancienne Nobleffe, Election de Caen, en Normandie; famille alliée à celle de *Foucault* par le mariage de JEAN DE BAUSSEN avec *Catherine de Foucault*.

Les armes : *d'azur, à l'agneau pafcal d'argent.*

BAUSSET, ancienne nobleffe, originaire de Provence. On voit, dans l'*Hiftoire des Evêques de Marfeille*, GEOFFROY DE BAUSSET avec la qualification de *Miles* fignée au bas d'une tranfaction paffée entre trois frères & l'Evêque de Marfeille fous la médiation de l'Archevêque d'Arles pour la poffeffion du port de Portgatte, en 1150.

Dans la même Hiftoire, GUILLAUME DE BAUSSET figne avec plufieurs Gentilshommes au bas d'un acte de Jugement paffé entre les Evêques de Marfeille & de Toulon, & les Chartreux de Montrieux, en 1174.

Dans la même Hiftoire il confte par une tranfaction, paffée en 1255 entre l'Evêque de Marfeille, BENOIT & GUILLAUME DE BAUSSET, que ce GUILLAUME poffédoit des droits Seigneuriaux dans la Châtellenie du Bauffet, comme ceux des bains, clef des portes, &c., qu'il cède au fufdit Evêque.

En 1310, noble GEOFFROY DE BAUSSET, fils de BERTRAND, qualifié de *Miles*, paffe un acte d'*infolutoudation* en faveur d'*Adalafie*, fa femme. Cette *Adalafie* avoit fondé, dans la ville d'Aubagne, une Chapelle fous le nom de *Sainte-Croix*, à la condition que le *Jus-patronat* en refteroit à la famille de fon mari.

En 1350, GUILLAUME DE BAUSSET, Damoifeau, en conféquence du pacte de fondation d'*Adalafie*, nomme *Icard*, Prêtre, pour defservir la Chapelle de *Sainte-Croix*. Cette Chapelle, qui exifte encore, a toujours appartenu depuis ce tems-là, à la branche aînée, qui en eft encore en poffeffion. Ce GUILLAUME eut un fils :

JEAN DE BAUSSET, Ier du nom, Capitaine de la Galère Royale à Marfeille, qui époufa, en 1390, *Elipfe de Cepeta*.

En 1395 il nomma à la Chapelle de Sainte-Croix, fondée par fon ayeule *Adalafie*. En 1437, le Roi RENÉ lui fit don par Lettres-Patentes, & en confidération de fes fervices, du Greffe de la Sénéchauffée de Toulon. En 1436, la Reine ELISABETH lui avoit auffi accordé d'autres grâces par brevet. Ces deux pièces font enregiftrées, la première à la Cour des Comptes de Provence, & la feconde aux

Archives du Greffe de Marfeille. Il eut un fils:

Jean de Bausset, IIᵉ du nom, Capitaine de la Galère Royale; qui avoit partagé avec fon père le don que le Roi René lui avoit fait. Ayant accompagné ce Prince à la guerre de Naples à la tête d'une Compagnie de 45 Arbalêtriers, il en obtint en 1442 un paffeport pour revenir en France; ce paffeport eft enregiftré à la Cour des Comptes de Provence. Il époufa, en 1429, *Dulcèle de Boniface,* dont il eut plufieurs enfans, entr'autres:

Antoine de Bausset, Iᵉʳ du nom, héritier de fon père par teftament en 1454, Capitaine de la Galère Royale, qui avoit époufé *Laurence de Hamelle,* ce qui eft prouvé par plufieurs actes paffés par eux en 1477 & 1498, & d'autres paffés par leurs enfans en 1526. Il fit fon héritier fon fils:

François de Bausset, Iᵉʳ du nom, Capitaine de la Galère Royale. En 1506, partant avec fa Galère pour le fervice du Roi, il fit une procuration en faveur d'un Notaire de Marfeille, pour nommer en fon nom, pendant fon abfence, à la Chapelle de Sainte-Croix d'Aubagne, fi le cas y advenoit. Il époufa *Elifabeth de Guiran,* qui mourut avant fon mari; elle tefta en 1499, lui laiffant la jouiffance de fes biens. Elle conftitua héritier fon fils:

Pierre de Bausset, Iᵉʳ du nom, qui fit en 1569, l'achat de la Seigneurie de Roquefort. Il époufa, en 1526, *Antoinette de Gilles,* & eut:

1. Nicolas, qui fuit;
2. François, qui fit branche;
3. Barthélemy, qui fut Aumônier de la Reine Catherine de Médicis, & Prévôt de l'Eglife Cathédrale de Marfeille;
4. Laurent, qui fut Chanoine de Barjols & Fréjus, enfuite Prévôt de l'Eglife Cathédrale de Marfeille après la mort de fon frère;
5. Et Jean, qui mourut garçon.

BRANCHE
aînée de la Maifon de Bausset, *Seigneurs de Roquefort.*

Nicolas de Bausset, Iᵉʳ du nom, fils aîné de Pierre, Seigneur de Roquefort, fut pourvu par le Roi Henri II, du Gouvernement de Lille, & Château d'If près Marfeille; Charles IX le confirma dans cette place, & Henri III, en récompenfe de fes fervices, en accorda la furvivance à fon fils aîné Jean. Celui-ci

étant mort, ainfi que François fon fecond fils, Henri IV accorda la furvivance de ce Gouvernement à fon troifième fils, Claude-Antoine, & un droit de 6 pour cent fur tous les navires qui aborderoient à Marfeille; les Lettres-Patentes font de 1597. Lorfque Charles IX fit fon entrée à Marfeille, il eut l'honneur de le recevoir chez lui avec la Reine fa mère, fes frères & Henri de Bourbon, Roi de Navarre. A fa mort, M. *du Vair,* premier Préfident du Parlement de Provence, enfuite Garde des Sceaux, vint à Marfeille mener fon deuil, & prononcer fon Oraifon funèbre, telle qu'on la voit dans les Œuvres de ce Magiftrat. Il époufa 1° *Françoife de Verdhillon;* & 2° *Jeanne Dasbaud,* dont il n'eut point d'enfans. De la première il eut:

1. 2. Jean & François, morts fans poftérité;
3. Et Claude-Antoine, qui fuit.

Claude-Antoine de Bausset, Seigneur de Roquefort, fe maria, en 1583, avec *Louife de Pifcatoris,* dont il eut:

1. Pierre, qui fuit;
2. & 3. Michel & François, qui embrafsèrent l'Etat Eccléfiaftique;
4. N...., mariée à *Louis Duchaine,* Préfident à Mortier du Parlement de Provence;
5. N...., mariée à *Nicolas d'Albert,* Confeiller à la Cour des Aides de la même Province;
Et plufieurs autres filles.

Pierre de Bausset, IIᵉ du nom, Seigneur de Roquefort, époufa, en 1616, *Lazarine de Salveti.* Il eut de ce mariage:

1. Jean-Baptiste, qui fuit;
2. Joseph, Chanoine de Barjols;
3. Et Michel, mort fans poftérité.

Jean-Baptiste de Bausset époufa, en 1653, *Chrétienne de Cypierre,* dont font iffus:
Joseph-Charles, qui fuit;
Et deux autres enfans, morts fans poftérité.

Joseph-Charles de Bausset, Seigneur de Roquefort & de Saint-Martin, époufa, en 1678, *Marguerite de Cabrède-Thomaffin,* dont il eut:

1. Michel-Jean-Baptiste, qui fuit;
2. Joseph-Bruno, Evêque de Béziers;
3. Pierre, qui a formé une feconde branche;
4. François, Chevalier de l'Ordre de Saint-Louis, Officier des Galères du Roi, mort fans poftérité;
Et plufieurs filles, Religieufes, dont les deux aînées font mortes Abbeffes de l'Abbaye du Saint-Efprit de Béziers.

Michel-Jean-Baptiste de Bausset, Seigneur de Roquefort, fut premier Conful d'Aix,

& premier Procureur du Pays aux années 1736 & 1737; Syndic de la Nobleffe de Provence aux années 1749, 1750 & 1751. Il époufa, en 1722, *Marie-Thérèfe de Gantel-Guittou*, dont font iffus:

1. Joachim, qui fuit;
2. Emmanuel-François, Vicaire-Général & Chanoine-Camérier de Béziers, Abbé Commandataire de l'Abbaye de Saint-Florent, Ordre de Cîteaux, Agent Général du Clergé, & nommé en 1766 à l'Evêché de Fréjus;
3. Anne, mariée à noble *Guillaume de Guillermy*, de Marfeille;
4. Et Dauphine, mariée 1º à *François-Louis d'Allard*, Seigneur de Néoulles, Confeiller au Parlement de Provence, & 2º à M. le Marquis *de Lombard*, Seigneur de Caftelet.

Joachim, Marquis de Bausset, Seigneur de Roquefort, ayant fervi fur les Galères du Roi, époufa, en 1751, *Françoife de Thomaffin-de-Raillane*, dont il eut:

1. Nicolas-Jean-Baptiste-Gabriel, qui fert dans le Régiment de Commiffaire-Général, Cavalerie;
2. Marie-Joseph;
3. Emmanuel-François-Paul-Hilarion, Eccléfiaftique;
4. François-Pierre-Gabriel-Raymond-Ignace-Ferdinand, nommé à un Canonicat par le noble & infigne Chapitre de Saint-Pierre de Vienne;
Et quatre filles brevetées dans le Chapitre des Dames Chanoineffes, Comteffes de Neuville.

C'eft à cette branche, comme l'aînée, qu'appartient & s'eft perpétuée la nomination du Recteur de la Chapelle de Sainte-Croix-d'Aubagne, fondée par Geoffroy de Bausset, en 1310.

BRANCHE
des Seigneurs DE SAUVIAN.

Pierre de Bausset, IIIº du nom, fils de Joseph-Charles, Seigneur de Roquefort & de Saint-Martin, époufa aux Indes, Demoifelle *de Léridé*, ce qui a formé la feconde branche; de façon que la feconde, qui exiftoit déjà, eft devenue la troifième. Il s'eft établi en Languedoc, où il a acquis le Comté de Sauvian. De fon mariage font iffus quatre garçons & deux filles, l'aînée eft mariée à M. *de Gros*, Préfident à la Cour des Aides de Languedoc.

Le Comte de Bausset, l'aîné des garçons, eft Officier dans le Régiment du Roi, & a époufé, au mois de Juin 1765, *N... de Jarente-Dorgeval*, dont il a un fils, né à Béziers en 1768.

TROISIÈME BRANCHE.

François de Bausset, IIº du nom, fils de Pierre, Seigneur de Roquefort, eft la tige de la troifième branche, & époufa, en 1561, *Claire Bertrand*, dont font iffus:

Nicolas, qui fuit;
Et une fille, mariée à noble *Alexandre de Gafpari*.

François de Bausset, commandoit le Régiment de Provence, à la bataille de Jarnac contre les Huguenots, où il reçut un coup de fufil.

Nicolas de Bausset, IIº du nom, contribua, en 1596, à réduire la ville de Marfeille fous l'obéiffance du Roi, en y introduifant le Duc de Guife au péril de fa vie & de fes biens, dans le tems que Cazaux vouloit la livrer aux Efpagnols. Henri IV, en confidération de cet important fervice, le pourvut de l'Office de Lieutenant-Général à Marfeille, & il fut députe par cette Ville pour aller prêter ferment de fidélité au Roi. Il époufa, le 26 Décembre 1593, *Ifabeau de Félix*, dont il eut:

1. Antoine, qui fuit;
2. & 3. Pierre & Philippe; le premier Prévôt, le fecond Chanoine de l'Eglife Cathédrale de Marfeille;
4. N... mariée à *Henri d'Armand*, Marquis de Mifon;
Et N... mariée à noble *François d'Auguftine*, Seigneur de Septème.

Antoine de Bausset, Lieutenant-Général en la Sénéchauffée de Marfeille, fut fait Confeiller d'Etat & Privé des Confeils du Roi en 1651. Il époufa, en 1617, *Gabrielle de Fornier*, dont font iffus:

1. Nicolas, qui fuit;
2. & 3. François & Alexandre, Chevaliers de Malte;
4. Philippe, Eccléfiaftique;
5. N... mariée à *Jean-Baptifte d'Arcuffia*, Seigneur d'Efparron & du Reveft;
6. Et N..., morte Religieufe.

Nicolas de Bausset, IIIº du nom, Confeiller d'Etat & Lieutenant-Général en la Sénéchauffée de Marfeille, époufa, en 1648, *Diane d'Eftuard-de-Velleron*, dont il eut:

1. Pierre, qui fuit;
2. Antoine-Marseille, Chevalier de Malte, mort Grand-Croix & Bailli du Manoque;

3. & 4. François & Joseph, Chanoines de l'Eglise Cathédrale de Marseille;

Et Geneviève, mariée à Messire *Henri de Jarente*.

Pierre de Bausset, II° du nom, Conseiller d'Etat, Lieutenant-Général en la Sénéchaussée de Marseille, épousa, en 1680, *Théodore d'Audiffret*, dont il eut:

1. Louis-François, mort Religieux;
2. François, Chevalier de Malte, qui quitta la Croix pour se marier, & qui suit;
3. Pierre, Chanoine à Marseille;
4. Et Anne, mariée à *Louis Sauveur-Renau*, Marquis de Villeneuve, Baron de Forcalquier, Ambassadeur Extraordinaire & Plénipotentiaire à la Porte Ottomane, Conseiller d'Etat, & nommé au Ministère des Affaires Etrangères.

François, Marquis de Bausset, Page, Mousquetaire, & Chevalier de Malte, épousa, en 1724, *Marie de Mayossau-Fortune*, dont sont issus:

1. Mathieu-Nicolas, qui suit;
2. Antoine-Hilarion, Capitaine de Vaisseau du Roi;
3. Lopis-Sauveur-Hippolyte, Lieutenant-Colonel des Grenadiers-Royaux;
4. Et Sophie, mariée à noble *Claude-François de Causse*, Seigneur de Serviés, Vallongue, &c.

Mathieu-Nicolas, Marquis de Bausset, Chevalier de Saint-Louis, a servi sur les Galères du Roi. Il a été Ministre Plénipotentiaire du Roi auprès de l'Electeur de Cologne, & ensuite auprès de l'Impératrice de Russie, & est mort à Pétersbourg en 1768. Il avoit épousé, par contrat du 13, célébration 19 Mars 1763, *Adélaïde-Constance de Selle*, née en 1743, dont il a eu deux garçons: l'aîné né à Paris en 1764, & le second né en Russie en 1767.

Les armes: *d'azur, à une montagne à trois pointes d'argent, surmontée d'un chevron d'or, & de deux étoiles à six rayes en chef;* Couronne de Marquis. Supports: *deux génies aîlés.* Cimier: *une aigle naissante.* Devise, sur un ruban *d'azur, lizeré d'or, & écrit en lettres d'or:* Sola salus servire Deo.

Baussy, en Normandie, Généralité de Caen, annobli aux Francs-Fiefs: *d'argent, à trois peignes ou démêloirs ou rateaux, à cinq dents de gueules, 2 & 1.*

Baut (le), en Bretagne: *d'azur, à dix billettes d'or, posées 4, 3, 2 & 1.*

     Tome II.

* Bautange, Terre & Seigneurie en Bourgogne, Diocèse de Lyon, Parlement & Intendance de Dijon, érigée en Marquisat en faveur de *N..... Potet*, Maître des Requêtes, par Lettres enregistrées en la Chambre des Comptes de Dijon, le 26 Novembre 1676. Par d'autres Lettres de 1696, registrées le 14 Décembre 1697, le titre de Marquisat de Bautange fut confirmé en faveur de *François Guyet*, Comte de Louhans, Baron de Saint-Germain-de-Plan, Chaumire, Auroux, Seigneur de la Faye, Maître des Requêtes en 1689, Intendant à Pau en 1699, de Lyon en 1701, Intendant des Finances depuis 1704, jusqu'en Septembre 1715. Il a laissé de *Claude Quarré*, morte le 10 Novembre 1749:

Philiberte Guyet, morte en Mai 1728, sans enfans. Elle avoit épousé, en Mars 1702, *Jérôme Chamillart*, Gouverneur de Dol, Maréchal-de-Camp, dit *le Comte de Chamillart*.

Bautot: *d'argent, à trois coqs de sable, barbés & crêtés de gueules, 2 & 1.*

* Bautru, famille originaire d'Anjou, qui a produit des personnages recommandables, tant par leur esprit que par leurs services rendus à l'Etat.

Nicolas Bautru, Capitaine des Gardes-de-la-Porte, obtint que Nogent-le-Roi fut érigé en Comté, par Lettres du mois d'Août 1636, enregistrées au Parlement & en la Chambre des Comptes, les 3, 7 & 23 Décembre 1636. Il obtint aussi que la Seigneurie de Tremblai fut érigée en Marquisat par Lettres du mois de Juin 1655, enregistrées le 14 Avril 1657. Il fut père de:

Armand de Bautru, Comte de Nogent, tué, en 1672, au passage du Rhin, laissant de *Diane-Charlotte de Caumont-Lauzun*:

Louis-Armand, qui suit;

Et Marie-Antoinette de Bautru, morte le 4 Août 1742. Elle avoit épousé, le 12 Août 1686, *Charles-Armand Gontaut-de-Biron*, mort Doyen des Maréchaux de France.

Louis-Armand de Bautru, Comte de Nogent, Seigneur d'Ormoy, Vacheresse, Russin, &c., Lieutenant-Général des Armées du Roi. Il avoit été fait successivement Mestre-de-Camp du Régiment de Dragons du Roi, en 1693, Brigadier le 8 Octobre 1696, Lieutenant-Général de la Basse-Auvergne au mois d'Août 1700, Maréchal-de-Camp le 23 Décembre 1702. Il avoit servi, en 1703, au siège de Brizac, sous les Ordres du Duc de Bour-

                            K k

gogne,& s'étoit trouvé, le 15 Novembre 1703, à la bataille de Spire, où il s'étoit diftingué à la tête du Régiment-Dragons du Roi. Il fe trouva le 11 Août 1705 à la bataille d'Hoch-ftett, & fut Lieutenant-Général le 26 Octobre 1706. Il mourut le 7 Juin 1736, âgé de 68 ans, laiffant:

HENRIETTE-EMILIE, morte le 27 Octobre 1757. Elle avoit époufé, par contrat du 14 Avril 1743, *Louis*, Marquis de *Melun*, avec lequel elle a vendu le Comté de Nogent au Duc d'Ayen, aujourd'hui Duc de Noailles, pour joindre à la Terre de Maintenon.

De la même famille étoit GUILLAUME DE BAUTRU, Comte de Serrant, Confeiller d'Etat ordinaire, Introducteur des Ambaffadeurs, Ambaffadeur vers l'Archiducheffe en Flandres, & Envoyé du Roi en Efpagne, en Angleterre & en Savoie. C'étoit un des beaux efprits de fon fiècle. Il eut de *Marthe Bigot*:

GUILLAUME DE BAUTRU, IIIᵉ du nom, Comte de Serrant, Chancelier de PHILIPPE, fils de France, Duc d'Orléans, mort en 1711, âgé de 93 ans, qui n'a laiffé que des filles. Voyez Moréri.

Les armes: *d'azur, au chevron, accompagné en chef de deux rofes, & en pointe d'une tête de loup arrachée, le tout d'argent.*

BAUVIÈRE, famille de Champagne, qui porte: *d'argent, à quatre fafces de gueules,* & de laquelle étoit EDMÉE DE BAUVIÈRE, née le 12 Octobre 1676. Elle prouva fa Nobleffe depuis l'an 1548, que vivoient DIDIER DE BAUVIÈRE, Ecuyer, & *Henriette de Sainte-Livière*, fes trifayeul & trifayeule.

BAUVOY, en Normandie, Election de Vire: *écartelé, aux 1 & 4 de gueules, à la rofe d'argent; aux 2 & 3 auffi de gueules, au lion d'argent.*

BAUX, ancienne Maifon de Provence. Les Barons de ce nom étoient Seigneurs en partie de la Vicomté de Marfeille, Princes d'Orange, & ont porté le titre de Rois d'Arles. On ne fçait fi la Maifon de BAUX, illuftre par fa grandeur, a donné fon nom au Château de Baux, où fi c'eft ce Château qui le lui a donné.

Le plus ancien de cette Maifon, dont on ait connoiffance, eft GUILLAUME, dit *Hugues*, qui vivoit en 1040 & 1050. ALIX, Baronne de Baux, fe voyant fans poftérité, inftitua, en 1425 & 1426, pour fes héritiers, ceux de fa Maifon qui étoient dans le Royaume de Na-

ples, & à leur défaut, les defcendans de MARIE, fa fœur.

La Maifon de BAUX a été puiffante & illuftre dans le Royaume de Naples. Elle y a poffédé des Terres confidérables, & les premières charges de l'Etat.

BERNARDIN DE BAUX, Chevalier de Saint-Jean de Jérufalem, fut Général des Galères de France en 1518; il donna des preuves de fa valeur au fiège de Marfeille en 1524. Il mourut de la pierre à Marfeille, le 12 Décembre 1527, ayant fait, par fon teftament, le Roi fon héritier. Il eft enterré dans l'Eglife des Jacobins de Marfeille.

Pour la Baronie de Baux, elle fut unie au domaine Comtat de Provence, & y eft reftée jufqu'en 1641, que LOUIS XIII l'érigeant en Marquifat, la donna, avec la Ville de Saint-Remi, à *Honoré de Grimaldi*, IIᵉ du nom, Prince de Monaco, qui, ayant fecoué le joug des Efpagnols, fe mit fous la protection de la France. Voyez GRIMALDI.

On peut, fur l'ancienne Maifon de BAUX, confulter l'*Hiftoire d'Orange*; Noftradamus; Bouche, *Hiftoire de Provence*; Chorrier, *Hiftoire de Dauphiné*; Moréri, &c.

Il y a en Provence une Famille noble de BAUX, qui porte pour armes: *de gueules, à la comète à raies d'argent.*

BAUYN-D'ANGERVILLIERS. LOUIS BAUYN-D'ANGERVILLIERS eut pour fils:

PROSPER BAUYN, Confeiller à la Cour des Aides, reçu le 25 Novembre 1553, puis Confeiller au Parlement le 14 Janvier 1568, qui époufa, le 4 Septembre 1563, *Etiennette Goret*. Il laiffa:

PROSPER BAUYN, Confeiller en la Cour des Aides, puis au Parlement, reçu le 31 Janvier 1612, dont vinrent:

PROSPER, qui fuit;

Et N... BAUYN, père de:

ANDRÉ-PROSPER, Seigneur de Jalais, Intendant du Rouffillon & de Perpignan;

Et PIERRE BAUYN-DE-BERSAN, ci-devant Sous-Lieutenant au Régiment des Gardes-Françoifes.

PROSPER BAUYN, Seigneur d'Angervilliers, Maître de la Chambre aux deniers du Roi, mort le 18 Juin 1700, avoit époufé *Gabrielle-Choart-de-Buzanval*, dont il eut:

PROSPER-NICOLAS BAUYN, Seigneur d'Angervilliers, né le 15 Janvier 1675, Miniftre & Confeiller d'Etat ordinaire, Secrétaire d'Etat

& des Commandemens du Roi, ayant le département de la Guerre, mort au Château de Marly, le 15 Février 1740. Il avoit épousé, le 14 Juin 1694, *Marie-Anne de Maupeou*, fille de *Guillaume*, Conseiller au Châtelet de Paris, & de *Marie de la Forêt*. Il n'en a laissé que·

MARIE - LOUISE BAUYN - D'ANGERVILLIERS, morte le 7 Septembre 1761. Elle avoit épousé, 1° le 11 Août 1728, *Jean-René de Longueil*, Marquis de Maisons & de Poissy, Président au Parlement de Paris, mort le 13 Septembre 1731; & 2° le 21 Janvier 1733, *Armand-Jean de Saint-Simon*, Marquis de Ruffec, Grand d'Espagne, mort le 20 Mai 1754.

Il y a la branche de BAUYN-DE-CORMERY, qui a donné un Officier-Général des Armées du Roi, & celle de BAUYN-DE-PÉREUSE, issue de LOUIS-PROSPER, & de *Françoise Courtin*, fille de *Charles*, Seigneur de Péreuse.

Voyez sur cette famille le *Mercure* du mois de Février 1740, pag. 396, & l'*Armorial de France*, reg. I, part. I, pag. 53.

Les armes: *d'azur, à un chevron d'or, accompagné de trois mains droites & d'argent, posées en fasce, deux en chef & l'autre à la pointe de l'écu.*

BAVALLAN, en Vennes: *d'argent, à deux fasces de sable.*

BAVELINGHEN, dans le Boulonnois. HEREMAR, Seigneur de BAVELINGHEN, Chevalier, vivoit en 1093, & eut pour fils:

EUSTACHE, Seigneur de BAVELINGHEN, qui donna à l'Abbaye d'Ardres, la Terre qu'*Everard de Pithem* tenoit de lui, par une chartre passée en 1136. Il épousa *Adecis de Guines*, fille naturelle de *Manassès*, Comte de *Guines*, dont il eut:

1. EUSTACHE DE BAVELINGHEN, mort jeune, après avoir été créé Chevalier;
2. BAUDOUIN, mort jeune;
3. HUGUES, qui suit;
4. GRÉGOIRE, Abbé du Monastère d'Ardres, mais volontairement déposé avant sa bénédiction;
5. SIMON, Chevalier;
6. FRUMOL, Chevalier;
7. Et AVOISE DE BAVELINGHEN, mariée à *Baudouin*, Seigneur d'*Ermelinghen*, Connétable de Bourbonnois.

HUGUES, Seigneur de BAVELINGHEN, succéda à son père, & épousa *Mahaut*, autrement dite *Marthe*, fille de *Laurette de Hamrs*, dont vint:

ADELIS, Dame de BAVELINGHEN, mariée, 1° en 1196, à *Arnould*, Seigneur de *Cayeu*; & 2° à *Daniel de Gand*, frère de *Liger*, deuxième Châtelain de Gand. Voilà tout ce que nous sçavons de cette ancienne Maison.

BAVET, en Bresse: *d'azur, au chevron d'or, accompagné de trois roses d'argent, 2 en chef & 1 en pointe.*

BAVEUX: *de gueules, au chevron d'argent.*

BAVIÈRE. Il y a peu de Maisons plus anciennes que celle de Bavière, tant dans l'Empire que dans l'Europe. On croit qu'ALDIGER ou ALDEGER s'établit vers 456 en Bavière. Les Rois & Ducs de Bavière ses successeurs, finirent à TASSILLON, subjugué par CHARLEMAGNE. Des descendans de cet Empereur furent aussi Rois de Bavière.

Nous ne dirons pas, comme a fait M. du Mai, dans son *Etat de l'Empire*, que plusieurs écrivains tirent ces Princes *de la cuisse de Charlemagne*, peut-être remonte-t-elle plus haut que ce grand Empereur. Leur Généalogie ne craint pas de commencer au VII° siècle.

OTHON, Duc de WITTELSBACH, surnommé l'*Illustre*, Comte de Schiren, auteur certain de la Maison de Bavière, descendoit de l'ancienne Maison de Franconie, qui a donné dans CONRAD I°°, un Roi de Germanie, au commencement du X° siècle, aussitôt après l'extinction de la postérité de CHARLEMAGNE. Aussi le héros de l'illustre famille de Bavière, MAXIMILIEN-MARIE, ne fait pas difficulté de marquer dans son manifeste contre l'Empereur LÉOPOLD, qu'il y avoit des Empereurs dans sa Maison, lorsqu'on ne trouvoit encore que des Gentilshommes dans les auteurs des Maisons d'Autriche & de Habsbourg. OTHON DE WITTELSBACH fut investi de la Bavière & du Palatinat en 1180, soit que ce fut en épousant l'héritière de ces deux Principautés, soit que ce fut par la faveur de l'Empereur FRÉDÉRIC I°°, qui en priva HENRI *le Lion*, l'un des chefs de la Maison de Brunswick. Peut-être les deux causes y ont-elles concouru. OTHON épousa, en 1180, *Gertrude de Saxe*, dont il eut:

LOUIS I°° DE BAVIÈRE, qui fut déclaré Electeur par l'Empereur FRÉDÉRIC I°°, en 1215. On sait que les grands Fiefs ne s'accordoient dans ces anciens tems qu'à des Seigneurs de haute naiffance. Il époufa *Ludmille*, & laiffa :

LOUIS II DE BAVIÈRE, Duc de WITTELS-BACH, qui époufa, vers 1225, *Agnès*, héritière du Palatinat & des droits d'HENRI-le-Lion, Duc de *Saxe*, fur la Bavière, elle étoit fille d'*Henri*, Comte Palatin. Ils eurent :

LOUIS II DE BAVIÈRE, dit *le Sévère*, mort en 1294, qui époufa 1° *Marie de Brabant*, fille d'*Henri*, dit *le Magnanime*, Duc de *Brabant*; 2° *Anne*, fille de *Conrad*, Duc de Mazovie; & 3° *Mathilde*, fille de l'Empereur RODOLPHE Ier. Du fecond lit vint :

LOUIS DE BAVIÈRE, tué dans un tournoi en 1288. Il eut de *Mathilde* :

RODOLPHE, auteur de la branche *Palatine du Rhin*, ou *Rodolphine*;

Et LOUIS, qui fonda la branche de *Bavière* ou *Wilhelmine*, rapportée plus loin.

Ces deux branches alternèrent pendant quelque tems pour l'Electorat.

BRANCHE
PALATINE DU RHIN ou RODOLPHINE.

RODOLPHE, Duc DE BAVIÈRE, Electeur de l'Empire & Comte Palatin du Rhin, eut pour petit-fils :

ROBERT III DE BAVIÈRE, élu Empereur le 16 Mai 1400, & mort le 18 Mai 1410.

De la branche Palatine font iffues les branches fuivantes :

1. Branche des Ducs de *Simmeren*, devenue Electorale en 1559. La reftitution du Bas-Palatinat lui a été faite & la création d'un nouvel Electorat en fa faveur, avec huitième rang feulement; le droit de vocation à l'Electorat de Bavière à défaut d'enfans mâles, dans la branche *Wilhelmine*, & à charge d'extinction du nouveau droit au mois d'Octobre 1648. Après la mort du dernier mâle de cette branche, CHARLES II, Duc DE BAVIÈRE, Comte Palatin du Rhin, arrivée le 26 Mai 1685, cet Electorat paffa dans la branche de *Neubourg*.

2. Branche des Ducs de *Deux-Ponts*, iffue de celle de *Simmeren*, éteinte le 9 Juillet 1661.

3. Branche des Ducs de *Neubourg*, iffue de celle de *Deux-Ponts*, devenue Electorale, & éteinte le 31 Décembre 1742.

4. Branche des Princes de *Sulzbach*, iffue de celle de *Neubourg*, rapportée ci-après.

5. Branche des Ducs de *Landsberg*, iffue de celle de *Deux-Ponts*, éteinte en 1681.

6. Branche des Ducs de *Klebourg*, dont font iffus les Rois de Suède, éteinte le 12 Décembre 1718.

7. Un rameau forti de la branche de *Klebourg*, qui hérita du Duché de *Deux-Ponts* à la mort de CHARLES XII, Roi de Suède, éteint en 1731.

8. Branche des Princes de *Birkenfeld*, éteinte le 28 Mars 1671.

9. Branche de *Bifchweiler*, puis de *Birkenfeld*, aujourd'hui de *Deux-Ponts*, rapportée plus loin.

10. Branche de *Gelnhaufen*, qui viendra en fon rang.

11. Branche des Comtes de *Lutzelftein* ou de *la Petite-Pierre*, de *Veldents* & de *Lautered*, éteinte le 29 Septembre 1694.

12. Et les Comtes de *Lœwenftein-Wertheim*, dont les aînés font Princes de l'Empire, mentionnés plus loin.

BRANCHE
des Princes de SULZBACH.

THÉODORE DE BAVIÈRE, Comte Palatin du Rhin, né le 14 Février 1659, mort le 11 Juillet 1732, avoit époufé, le 9 Juin 1692, *Marie-Éléonore-Amélie de Heffe-Rothenbourg*, morte le 27 Janvier 1720, dont il eut entr'autres enfans :

JOSEPH-CHARLES-EMMANUEL, né le 2 Novembre 1694, Prince héréditaire, mort le 18 Juillet 1729, laiffant :

1. MARIE-ELISABETH-ALOYSE-AUGUSTE-INNOCENTE-GABRIELLE-EULALIE, née le 17 Janvier 1721, mariée, le 17 Janvier 1742, à CHARLES-THÉODORE DE BAVIÈRE, fon coufin germain;

2. AMÉLIE-MARIE-ANNE, née le 22 Juin 1722, mariée, le 17 Janvier 1742, à CLÉMENT-FRANÇOIS DE PAULE, Duc de BAVIÈRE;

3. Et FRANÇOISE-DOROTHÉE, née le 15 Juin 1724, mariée, le 5 Février 1746, à FRÉDÉRIC DE BAVIÈRE-BIRKENFELD, Prince de Deux-Ponts.

FRANÇOISE-CHRISTINE, née le 26 Mai 1696, Abbeffe des Abbayes Impériales de Thorn & d'Effen, en Weftphalie, & Prieure du Couvent des Carmélites de Duffeldorf;

ERNESTINE-ELISABETH-JEANNETTE, née le 15 Mai 1697, mariée, le 19 Septembre 1719, à GUILLAUME, Landgrave de *Heffe-Wanfried*, mort le 1er Avril 1731. Depuis fon veuvage, elle eft Prieure Carmélite à Neubourg;

JEAN-CHRÉTIEN-THÉODORE, qui fuit;

Et ANNE-CHRISTINE-LOUISE DE BAVIÈRE, née le 3 Février 1704, morte le 12 Mars 1723. Elle avoit époufé, le 13 Mars 1722, *Charles-Emmanuel de Savoie*, Prince de Piémont, devenu roi de Sardaigne, fous le nom de *Charles-Emmanuel III*.

JEAN-CHRÉTIEN-THÉODORE DE BAVIÈRE, Comte Palatin du Rhin & Prince de Sulzbach, né le 23 Janvier 1700, mourut le 20 Juillet 1733. Il avoit époufé, 1° le 15 Février 1722, *Henriette de la Tour*, héritière du Marquifat de Berg-op-Zoom, née le 11 Octobre 1708, morte le 28 Juillet 1728, fille de *François-Egon*, dit *le Prince d'Auvergne*; & 2° par procuration le 20 Décembre 1730, & en perfonne, le 25 Janvier 1731, *Eléonore-Philippine-Chrétienne-Sophie de Heffe-Rhinfels*, née le 18 Octobre 1712, fille d'*Erneft-Léopold*, Landgrave de *Heffe-Rhinfels*. Il laiffa du fecond lit:

CHARLES-THÉODORE DE BAVIÈRE, Comte Palatin du Rhin, Archi-Tréforier de l'Empire, Duc de Bavière, Juliers, Clèves & Berg, Prince de Mœurs, Marquis de Berg-op-Zoom, Comte de Veldents-Sponheim, de la Marck & de Varenfperg, Seigneur de Ravenftein, &c., Souverain-Chef & Grand-Maître de Saint-Hubert, Vicaire né de l'Empire dans le cercle du Rhin, conjointement avec l'Electeur de Bavière, pendant la vacance du Trône Impérial, Directeur des Cercles du Haut-Rhin & de Weftphalie, &c., né Prince de Sulzbach, le 10 Décembre 1724, Electeur le 31 Décembre 1742. Il a époufé, le 17 Janvier 1742, MARIE-ELISABETH-ALOYSE-AUGUSTE-INNOCENTE-GABRIELLE-EULALIE DE BAVIÈRE-SULZBACH, fa coufine, née le 17 Janvier 1721, Dame de l'Ordre de la Croix-Etoilée, fille de JOSEPH-CHARLES-EMMANUEL, Comte Palatin du Rhin, Prince héréditaire de Sulzbach, dont:

Un fils, mort en naiffant, le 28 Juin 1761.

BRANCHE
de BISCHWEILER, *puis de* BIRKENFELD, *aujourd'hui de* DEUX-PONTS.

CHRISTIAN Ier DE BAVIÈRE, Duc de Birkenfeld, mort le 27 Avril 1654, laiffa entr'autres enfans:

CHRISTIAN, qui fuit;

Et JEAN-CHARLES, auteur de la branche de *Gelnhaufen*, rapportée ci-après.

CHRISTIAN II DE BAVIÈRE, Duc de Birkenfeld, mort le 7 Avril 1717, eut entr'autres enfans:

CHRISTIAN III DE BAVIÈRE, Comte Palatin du Rhin, Colonel du Régiment d'Alface, Infanterie en 1696, Duc de Birkenfeld, puis Duc de Deux-Ponts, par droit d'agnation, le 17 Septembre 1731, & mis en poffeffion feulement par décret du Confeil aulique, le 1er Avril 1734, qui mourut le 3 Février 1735. Il avoit époufé, le 21 Septembre 1719, *Caroline de Naffau-Saarbruck*, née le 12 Août 1704, morte à Darmftadt, le 25 Mars 1774, fille de *Louis-Craton*, Comte de *Naffau-Saarbruck*. Leurs enfans furent:

CHRISTIAN, qui fuit;

FRÉDÉRIC, appelé *Prince Palatin de Deux-Ponts*, né le 27 Février 1724, Chevalier de l'Ordre de Saint-Hubert, Colonel du Régiment d'Alface en Février 1735, puis fucceffivement Brigadier, Maréchal-de-Camp, & Lieutenant-Général des Armées de France, par promotion particulière le 16 Février 1746, Chevalier de la Toifon-d'Or, Grand-Croix de l'Ordre Militaire de MARIE-THÉRÈSE, Gouverneur du Duché de Juliers, & Feld-Maréchal du Cercle du Haut-Rhin. Il profeffoit la Religion Catholique & mourut le 15 Août 1767. Il avoit époufé, le 5 Février 1746, FRANÇOISE-DOROTHÉE DE BAVIÈRE-SULZBACH, née le 15 Juin 1724, fille de JOSEPH-CHARLES-EMMANUEL, Comte Palatin du Rhin, Prince héréditaire de Sulzbach. De ce mariage font iffus:

1. Prince CHARLES-AUGUSTE, né le 29 Octobre 1746, Colonel au Palatinat;
2. Prince MAXIMILIEN-JOSEPH, né le 27 Mai 1756;
3. Princeffe MARIE-AMÉLIE-AUGUSTE, née le 10 Mai 1752, mariée par procuration le 17, & en perfonne le 29 Janvier 1769, à *Frédéric-Augufte*, Electeur Duc de *Saxe*;
4. Et Princeffe MARIE-ANNE, née le 18 Juillet 1753.

Princeffe HENRIETTE-CHRISTINE-CHARLOTTE-PHILIPPINE-LOUISE, née le 9 Mars 1721, morte en Avril 1774. Elle avoit époufé, le 11 Août 1741, *Louis IX*, Landgrave de *Heffe-Darmftadt*;

Et Princeffe CHRISTINE, née le 16 Novembre 1725, mariée le 19 Avril 1741, à *Charles-Augufte-Frédéric*, Prince de *Waldeck*, mort le 29 Août 1763.

CHRISTIAN IV, Duc de Bavière, Comte Palatin du Rhin, Duc de Deux-Ponts, né le 6

Septembre 1722, héritier préfomptif de l'E-lectorat, Chevalier de l'Ordre de Saint-Hubert, n'eft pas encore marié.

BRANCHE
de GELNHAUSEN.

JEAN-CHARLES, Duc de Bavière, Comte Palatin du Rhin, fecond fils de CHRISTIAN Ier, Duc de Birkenfeld, époufa, 1º en 1685, SOPHIE-AMÉLIE DE BAVIÈRE-DEUX-PONTS, veuve de *Sigefroy*, Comte de *Hohenlohe*; & 2º le 26 Juillet 1696, *Marie-Efther de Witzleben*. Il eut du fecond lit:

1. Prince FRÉDÉRIC-BERNARD, né le 6 Mars 1697, Général des Troupes de l'Electeur Palatin, mort le 5 Août 1739. Il avoit époufé, le 3 Mars 1737, *Erneftine-Louife de Waldeck*, née le 6 Novembre 1705, fille d'*Antoine-Ulric*, Prince de *Waldeck*, dont: La Princeffe LOUISE-CAROLINE, née le 22 Janvier 1738.
2. Prince JEAN, qui fuit;
3. Princeffe CHARLOTTE-CATHERINE, née le 19 Novembre 1699, mariée, en Décembre 1745, à *Frédéric-Guillaume*, Prince de *Solms-Braunfels;*
4. Prince GUILLAUME, Duc de Bavière, appelé *Prince Palatin de Birkenfeld*, né le 4 Janvier 1701, ancien Capitaine de Cuiraffiers au fervice de l'Empereur CHARLES VI, a été fait Chevalier de l'Ordre de Saint-Hubert le 2 Février 1731;
5. Et Princeffe SOPHIE-MARIE, née le 5 Avril 1702, mariée, le 24 Août 1722, à *Henri XXV*, Comte de *Reufs-Géra*, mort en 1748.

Prince JEAN, Duc de Bavière, né le 24 Mai 1698, Duc de Birkenfeld, ancien Colonel d'Infanterie au fervice de l'Empereur CHARLES VI, a été fait Chevalier de l'Ordre de Saint-Hubert le 2 Février 1731, puis Gouverneur de Juliers. Il époufa, le 29 Août 1743, *Sophie de Daun*, née le 29 Août 1719, fille de *Charles*, Rhingrave *de Daun*. Leurs enfans furent:

1. Prince JEAN-CHARLES-LOUIS, né le 18 Septembre 1745;
2. Prince GUILLAUME, né le 10 Novembre 1752;
3. Et Princeffe LOUISE-CHRISTINE, née le 17 Août 1748, mariée, le 28 Octobre 1773, à *Henri XXX*, Comte de *Reufs-Géra*.

BRANCHE
des Princes DE LŒWENSTEIN-WERTHEIM-RO-CHEFORT, *de la Religion Catholique*.

Elle eft repréfentée par trois frères, favoir:

1. Prince CHARLES-THOMAS DE LŒWEN-STEIN-WERTHEIM, né le 7 Mars 1714, marié, le 25 Juillet 1736, à *Marie-Charlotte-Antoinette de Holftein-Wie-fenbourg*, née le 18 Février 1718, fille de *Léopold*, Duc de *Holftein-Wiefenbourg*, dont:
    Princeffe LÉOPOLDINE-CAROLINE, née le 28 Décembre 1739, morte le 8 janvier 1765. Elle avoit époufé, le 19 Mai 1761, *Charles-Albert-Chrétien*, Prince de *Hohenlohe-Schillingsfurft*.
2. Prince LÉOPOLD DE LŒWENSTEIN-WERT-HEIM, né le 16 Février 1716;
3. Et Prince THÉODORE-ALEXANDRE DE LŒ-WENSTEIN-WERTHEIM, né le 14 Septembre 1722, marié, le 28 Avril 1752, à *Catherine-Louife-Eléonore*, Comteffe de *Linange-Dachsbourg-Bockenheim*, née le 1er Février 1735, fille de *Charles-Louis*, Comte de *Linange-Dachf-bourg-Bockenheim*. De ce mariage font nés:
    1. Princeffe MARIE-GABRIELLE, née le 20 Juillet 1759;
    2. Et Prince DOMINIQUE-CONSTANTIN, né le 16 Mai 1762.

BRANCHE
de BAVIÈRE *ou* WILHELMINE.

LOUIS DE BAVIÈRE, fecond fils de LOUIS *le Sévère*, fut un Prince rempli de courage, qui foutint avec beaucoup de grandeur la dignité Impériale, à laquelle il fut appelé en 1314. Il la pofféda pendant 33 ans, malgré les oppofitions qu'il trouva dans fon règne, & mourut le 11 Octobre 1347. Il eft la tige des branches fuivantes:

1º Branche des Ducs de *Bavière* à Landf-hut, éteinte.
2º Branche des Ducs de *Bavière*, à Munich, qui fuit.
3º Branche de *Leuchtenberg*, éteinte en 1688.
4º Et Branche de *Wartenberg*, éteinte, dont étoit FRANÇOIS-MARQUARD, Comte de Wartenberg, né en 1673.

BRANCHE
DE BAVIÈRE à Munich.

MAXIMILIEN Ier, Duc de Bavière, invefti de la dignité Electorale du Palatinat le 25 Février 1623, mourut le 27 Septembre 1651. Il laiffa entr'autres enfans:

FERDINAND-MARIE, Duc de Bavière, né le 21 Octobre 1636, qui mourut le 27 Mai 1679. Il avoit épousé, le 22 Juin 1652, *Henriette-Adélaïde de Savoie*, morte le 18 Mars 1676. Ils eurent entr'autres enfans :

1. MAXIMILIEN-MARIE, qui suit ;
2. Et JOSEPH-CLÉMENT DE BAVIÈRE, né le 5 Décembre 1671, Electeur de Cologne, mort le 12 Novembre 1723. Il eut, avant d'être promû aux Ordres Sacrés, deux fils naturels :

   1. JEAN-BAPTISTE-VICTOR ;
   2. Et ANTOINE-LIVIN, Comte de Grofberg. Voyez GROSBERG-BAVIÈRE.

MAXIMILIEN-MARIE, Duc de Bavière, né le 10 Juillet 1662, fut dépouillé de l'Electorat, par décret Impérial du 29 Avril 1706, puis rétabli avec même rang & prérogatives qu'avant la suppression en Mars 1714, & mourut le 26 Février 1726. Il avoit épousé, 1o le 15 Juillet 1685, *Marie-Anne*, Archiduchesse d'*Autriche*, morte le 24 Décembre 1692 ; & 2o le 15 Août 1694, *Thérèse-Cunégonde Sobieski*, morte le 11 Mars 1730. Du second lit vinrent entr'autres enfans :

1. MARIE-ANNE-CAROLINE, née le 4 Août 1696, qui fit profession au Couvent des Religieuses de Sainte-Claire de Munich le 29 Octobre 1719, & mourut en 1750 ;
2. CHARLES-ALBERT, qui suit ;
3. FERDINAND-MARIE, né le 5 Août 1699, mort le 9 Décembre 1738. Il avoit épousé, le 9 Février 1719, LÉOPOLDINE-ELÉONORE DE BAVIÈRE, née le 22 Octobre 1691, fille de PHILIPPE-GUILLAUME, Comte Palatin de Neubourg. Il laissa entr'autres enfans :

   CLÉMENT-FRANÇOIS-DE-PAULE, titré *Duc Clément*, né le 19 Avril 1722, mort le 6 Août 1770. Il avoit épousé, le 17 Janvier 1742, AMÉLIE-MARIE-ANNE DE BAVIÈRE, née le 22 Juin 1722, fille de JOSEPH-CHARLES-EMMANUEL, Prince héréditaire de Sulzbach, dont une fille, morte en naissant en 1748 ;
   Et une autre fille, morte en naissant, à Munich, le 1er Juin 1754.

4. CLÉMENT-AUGUSTE, né le 16 Août 1700, Archevêque & Electeur de Cologne ;
5. Et JEAN-THÉODORE DE BAVIÈRE, né le 3 Septembre 1703, Evêque, Prince de Liège & Cardinal.

Il eut aussi d'*Agnès-Françoise Louchier*, de la ville de Tournay, veuve de *Ferdinand*,

Comte d'*Arco* & du Saint-Empire, un fils naturel :

EMMANUEL-FRANÇOIS-JOSEPH. Voyez BAVIÈRE-VILLACERF.

CHARLES-ALBERT, Duc de Bavière, né le 6 Août 1697, élu Empereur le 4 Janvier 1742, sous le nom de CHARLES VII, mourut le 20 Janvier 1745. Il avoit épousé, le 5 Octobre 1722, *Marie-Amélie d'Autriche*, née le 21 Octobre 1701, morte le 11 Décembre 1756, fille de *Joseph* Ier, Empereur d'*Autriche*. Leurs enfans furent :

1. MARIE-ANTOINETTE-WALPURGE-SYMPHOROSE, née le 19 Juillet 1724, mariée, le 20 Juin 1747, au Prince *Frédéric-Christian*, Electeur de *Saxe*, & Prince Royal de Pologne, mort le 5 Décembre 1763 ;
2. THÉRÈSE-BÉNÉDICTINE, née le 6 Décembre 1725, morte le 29 Mars 1743 ;
3. MAXIMILIEN-JOSEPH, qui suit ;
4. MARIE-JOSÈPHE, née le 7 Août 1734, mariée le 10 Juillet 1755, à *Guillaume-Georges-Bernard-Sibert-Philippe*, Prince de *Bade* ;
5. Et JOSÈPHE-MARIE-WALPURGE DE BAVIÈRE, née le 30 Mars 1739, morte le 28 Mai 1767. Elle avoit épousé, le 23 Janvier 1765, JOSEPH II, Empereur d'*Autriche*.

Il eut aussi, d'une Demoiselle de qualité, une fille naturelle :

MARIE-JOSÈPHE-CAROLINE, née en 1720, légitimée, Comtesse de Hochenfels-Bavière, mariée à EMMANUEL-FRANÇOIS-JOSEPH, dit *le Comte de Bavière*, Marquis de Villacerf.

MAXIMILIEN-JOSEPH DE BAVIÈRE, né le 28 Mars 1727, titré d'abord *Prince Electoral de Bavière*, puis Electeur le 20 Janvier 1745, Grand-Maître de l'Ordre de Saint-Georges, a épousé, le 8 Juillet 1747, *Marie-Anne-Sophie de Saxe*, née le 29 Août 1728, fille d'AUGUSTE II (*Frédéric*), Roi de *Pologne*.

Cette Maison a donné deux Empereurs à l'Allemagne, des Rois à la Suède, au Danemark & à la Norwège ; divers Electeurs à l'Empire, des Comtes à la Hollande, &c.

BRANCHE de GROSBERG-BAVIÈRE.

JOSEPH-CLÉMENT-CAJÉTAN-FRANÇOIS-ANTOINE-GASPARD-MELCHIOR-JEAN-BAPTISTE-NICOLAS, Duc des deux Bavières & du haut Palatinat, né en 1671, Archevêque de Cologne, Prince Electeur du Saint-Empire, Evêque & Prince de Liège, de Hildesheim, premier Grand-Maître de l'illustre Ordre de l'Archange Saint-Michel en Bavière, institué en 1699, mort à Bonn, à 8 heures du ſoir, le 12 Novembre 1723, a eu (n'étant pas promû pour lors aux Ordres ſacrés) de Dame *Conſtance de Grouſſelier,* Dame de Ruysbeck, de Gravenſteyn, &c., morte vers 1724, deux fils, reconnus de leur père, par acte ſigné à Bonn le 3 Avril 1717, lequel y déclare avoir interpoſé ſes bons offices pour leur obtenir de S. M. Impériales, des Lettres de légitimation, octroi & grâces, plus amplement ſpécifiées dans leſdites Lettres de légitimation impériales. Ces deux fils auſſi légitimés par Patentes de Sa Majeſté Louis XV, données à Paris en Octobre 1719, ſont:

1. Jean-Baptiste-Victor-François-Marie-Joseph-Antoine-Cajétan-Laudelin-Paul-Michel, qui ſuit;
2. Et Antoine-Livin-Joseph-François-Cajétan-Marie-Michel-Jean-Baptiste-Ignace-Isaac-Emmanuel, Comte de Grosberg-Bavière, né à Lille, Commandeur & Grand-Croix de l'illuſtre Ordre de Saint-Michel en Bavière, Chambellan de Clément-Auguste, Duc de Bavière, Electeur de Cologne, Capitaine des Gardes Wallones, & Lieutenant-Général des Armées de S. M. C. en Eſpagne, mort à Barcelone le 22 Mai 1757, dans ſa 47° année, ſans avoir été marié.

Jean-Baptiste-Victor-François-Marie-Joseph-Antoine-Cajétan-Laudelin-Paul-Michel, Comte de Grosberg-Bavière, né à Lille en 1706, Seigneur de Ruisberg, de Gravenſteyn, &c., Grand-Croix & Commandeur de l'Ordre de Saint-Michel en Bavière le 23 Décembre 1738, & depuis, ayant ſatisfait de rechef à la preuve d'extraction, requiſe par la réformation générale, nommé par S. A. le Grand-Maître de l'Ordre, par décret du 7 Mai 1765, Chambellan de Clément-Auguste, Duc de Bavière, Electeur de Cologne, Grand-Maître de l'Ordre Teutonique, accepté Chambellan par l'Empereur Charles VII; mais n'ayant pu recevoir la clef d'or à cauſe de la mort de cet Empereur, il a été Chambellan de Jean-Théodore, Duc de Bavière, Prince & Evêque de Liège, Grand-Maître de l'illuſtre Ordre de Saint-Michel en Bavière; ſon Conſeiller intime d'Etat, & ſon Miniſtre Plénipotentiaire à la Cour de Bruxelles; ci-devant Miniſtre des Cours de Bonn & de Liège près de Sa Majeſté Louis XV; Miniſtre actuel du Prince de Liège à ladite Cour de Bruxelles, & Chambellan de S. A. le Duc de

Bavière, par décret du 20 Décembre 1768. Il a épouſé, en 1729, *Marie-Joſéphine-Ferdinandine-Roſe,* Baronne *de Colins* & de Sainte-Gertrude-Machelen, née à Bruxelles le 20 Mars 1708, Dame de Waeyneſſe, de Plettenbroeck, de Wavere, de Sautbergen, &c., fille unique de *Pierre-Antoine,* Baron *de Colins,* Seigneur & Baron de Sainte-Gertrude-Machelen, & d'*Anne-Eléonore Edwards,* dite *Trévor,* iſſue d'une Maiſon Royale d'Angleterre. De ce mariage il a eu:

1. François-Joseph-Léonard - Maximilien-Emmanuel, Comte de Grosberg-Bavière, dit *le Baron de Sainte-Gertrude Machelen,* Seigneur de Waeyneſſe & de Plettenbroeck, &c., Page de Jean-Théodore, Duc de Bavière, Evêque & Prince de Liège, mort au Château de Seray, âgé d'environ 14 ans, & enterré dans la Chapelle de la Cour de Liège;
2. Albert-Léonard-François-Hubert-Dominique, qui ſuit;
3. Anne-Marie-Gertrude, Comteſſe de Grosberg-Bavière, morte enfant;
4. Marie-Henriette-Joséphine - Guislaine, Comteſſe de Grosberg-Bavière, Dame de Waeyneſſe, de Plettenbroeck, &c., mariée, à Bruxelles, le 5 Octobre 1768, à *Joſeph-Ferdinand-Guislain,* Comte *de Cuypers,* Banneret, Seigneur d'Alſingen, S'hertoghen, &c., troiſième fils de *Jean-François-Daniel-Joſeph,* Comte *de Cuypers,* Seigneur de Rymenam, d'Opſtalle, de Muyſelwick, de Zoetingen, &c., & de *Claire-Jeanne Gielis-Hujoel,* ſa première femme. Voyez CUYPERS;
5. Marie-Charlotte-Auguste, Comteſſe de Grosberg-Bavière;
6. Et Marie-Antoinette-Ursule-Guislaine, Comteſſe de Grosberg-Bavière, Dame de Cour de S. A. Madame l'Electrice de Bavière.

Albert-Léonard-François-Hubert-Dominique, Comte de Grosberg-Bavière, Baron de Sainte-Gertrude-Machelen, baptiſé le 7 Avril 1740, entré au ſervice de France, a été Capitaine d'Infanterie au Régiment d'Horion; puis, en 1760, Capitaine de Cavalerie au Régiment de Rougrave, réformé à la paix; & par Patentes, ſignées à Maſſeyck le 3 Septembre 1761, a été fait Lieutenant-Colonel d'Infanterie du Prince de Liège, au Régiment du Comte de Bairlamont; Cornette de la Garde-du-Corps des Archers du Prince; Meſtre-de-Camp de Cavalerie en 1765, au ervice de France, Grand-Croix & Commandeur de l'Ordre de Saint-Michel en Bavière. Il fatisfit depuis au décret de réforme fous le Grand-Maître actuel dudit Ordre; a été Chambellan, par décret figné à Munich le 22 Août 1759, de Jean-Théodore, Duc de Bavière; & eft Chambellan par autre décret figné à Munich le 20 Décembre 1768, de S. A. Electorale le Duc de Bavière, & a été préfenté le 18 Mars 1772. (Mémoire envoyé par M. le Comte de Cuypers).

BRANCHE
des Marquis de VILLACERF.

Emmanuel-François-Joseph, dit le Comte de Bavière, fils naturel de Maximilien-Marie, Duc de Bavière, & d'Agnès-Françoise Louchier, de la ville de Tournay, veuve de Ferdinand, Comte d'Arco & du Saint-Empire, fut Marquis de Villacerf, par l'acquifition qu'il a faite de ce Marquifat, Grand d'Efpagne de la première Claffe, Lieutenant-Général des Armées du Roi, & tué à la bataille de Lawfeld, le 2 Juillet 1747. Il avoit épousé Marie-Josèphe-Caroline, Comteffe de Hochenfels-Bavière, née en 1720, fille légitimée de Charles VII, Empereur d'Autriche & Duc de Bavière, & d'une Demoifelle de qualité. Il n'eft refté de ce mariage que:

Marie-Amélie-Caroline-Josèphe-Françoise-Xavière de Bavière, née à Francfort-fur-le-Mein, le 2 Décembre 1744, tenue fur les Fonds-Baptifmaux le 3, par l'Impératrice Marie-Amélie, femme de Charles VII, Comteffe de Hochenfels, Dame de Villacerf, dans le Comté de Troyes en Champagne, Grande d'Efpagne par fucceffion paternelle. Elle a époufé, le 3 Février 1761, Armand-Charles-Emmanuel, Marquis d'Hautefort.

Les armes actuelles de la Maifon de Bavière font: écartelé, aux 1 & 4 fufelé d'argent & d'azur; aux 2 & 3 de fable, à un lion d'or, couronné de même.

BAVIGNAN, en Champagne: d'azur, à deux épées d'argent, paffées en fautoir, les pointes en bas, les gardes & poignées d'or.

BAY. Le Roi d'Efpagne Philippe V, pour récompenfer les fervices d'Alexandre Maitre-de-Bay, Chevalier, Seigneur de Laëre, Lieutenant-Général de fes Armes, premier Lieutenant de fes Gardes-du-Corps, l'éleva à la dignité de Marquis de Bay, par Lettres du 23 Juillet 1704. Voyez MAITRE-DE-BAY.

* BAYARD, Terre dans le Dauphiné, dont le célèbre Chevalier Bayard portoit le nom.

Il fe nommoit Pierre du Terrail-de-Bayard, & fut un des plus fages & vaillans Capitaines de fon tems. Il commença de fervir à la bataille de Fornoue avec honneur, fous Charles VIII, & fut employé à la conquête de Milan, en 1499, par Louis XII. Il combattit à la bataille de Marignan contre les Suiffes, à côté de François Ier, qui voulut être fait Chevalier de fa main. Il fut mortellement bleffé à la retraite de Rebec, en 1524, & mourut univerfellement regretté.

Pierre du Terrail, fon ayeul, fut tué à la bataille de Montlhéry, en 1465; fon bifayeul, à celle d'Azincourt en 1415; fon trifayeul, à celle de Poitiers, aux pieds du Roi Jean, en 1356; & fon père fut bleffé dangereufement à celle des Eperons. Le dernier de cette Maifon fut tué au fiège de Gravelines, en 1644; & le nom & la Terre du Terrail paffèrent, par la fœur de celui-ci, dans la Maifon d'Eftaing; car elle époufa Jacques, Baron de Planfat, tige des Comtes de Saillent, l'un des fils de Jean, IIIe du nom, Vicomte d'Eftaing. Voyez l'Hiftoire du Chevalier Bayard; & Chorrier, Hiftoire de Dauphiné.

BAYARD, famille originaire de Picardie. Georges Bayard, Seigneur des Catelais, Capitaine des Vaiffeaux du Roi, & Chevalier de Saint-Louis, avoit époufé Laurence Cadot-de-Sebeville, dont un fils & une fille nommée Madeleine-Laurence-Christine Bayard, mariée, le 15 Mai 1741, avec Jean-François-Nicodéme le Roux-de-Gilbertprey, Gouverneur de Valogne.

BAYC, au Meryonec, près Guerrande, en Bretagne: de gueules, à trois huchets d'argent, liés de même en fautoir, 2 & 1.

* BAYE, Terre, Seigneurie, & l'une des quatre anciennes Baronies de Champagne, fituée dans le Diocèfe de Sens, & au-dedans du Bailliage, dont elle relève. Elle appartenoit, lors du Procès-verbal de rédaction des Coutumes de cette Ville, du 4 Novembre 1555, au Duc de Nivernois, Pair de France, Gouverneur de Brie, Champagne & Luxembourg; elle appartient aujourd'hui à François Berthelot, Baron de Baye, Lieutenant-Général des Armées du Roi, & Commandeur de Saint-Louis, &c. Voyez BERTHELOT.

BAYER, Seigneur de Boport: écartelé,

aux 1 *& 4 d'argent, au lion de fable, couronné d'or, armé & lampaffé de gueules ; aux* 2 *& 3 de gueules, au dextrochère d'argent, tenant une bague d'or, accompagnée de trois croix fleuronnées au pied fiché de même, une en chef & deux en pointe.*

BAYER, Maifon originaire de Bavière, établie depuis long-tems en Hongrie. JEAN BAYER fut d'abord Recteur du Collège d'Eperies, enfuite Miniftre à Neuhfel en 1667, annobli en 1669 par l'Empereur LÉOPOLD. C'étoit un homme habile dans les mathématiques & dans plufieurs autres sciences. Son zèle ardent pour les Proteftans lui occafionna des affaires férieufes, que fa famille reffentit même après fa mort. Son petit-fils THÉOPHILE-LE-GEOFFROY BAYER, né en 1694, & mort le 21 Février 1738, a été un des plus grands fçavans de l'Allemagne. Voyez le *Nouveau Supplém.* de Moréri.

BAYERNE : *écartelé, aux* 1 *& 4 d'azur, à un Z d'argent, pofé en bande ; aux* 2 *& 3 coupé d'argent & de gueules, à l'étoile de même de l'un en l'autre.*

BAYGNAN, en Touraine : *d'argent, au chevron de fable, accompagné de trois râles de même, deux en chef & un en pointe, membrés & becqués de gueules.*

BAYLENS - DE - POYANNE, ancienne Maifon de Béarn, qui a donné quatre Chevaliers des Ordres du Roi : le premier en 1599, le fecond en 1633, le troifième en 1661, & le quatrième de nos jours, le 2 Février 1767, dans le Marquis *de Poyanne*, Commandant des Carabiniers, dont nous parlerons ci-après.

N'ayant reçu aucun mémoire fur cette Maifon, nous ne pouvons en parler que très-fuccintement, d'après l'*Hiftoire des Grands Officiers de la Couronne.* Elle commence à ETIENNE DE BAYLENS, Seigneur de Poyanne, marié à *Jeanne d'Antin*, dont il eut entr'autres enfans :

BERTRAND DE BAYLENS, Baron de Poyanne, Capitaine de 50 hommes d'armes, Gouverneur de la Ville & Château d'Acqs, & Sénéchal des Landes de Bordeaux, nommé Chevalier des Ordres, le 2 Janvier 1599. Il époufa *Louife de Caffagnet-Tilladet,* dont entr'autres enfans :

BERNARD DE BAYLENS, Seigneur de Poyanne, Confeiller d'Etat, Lieutenant-Général au Pays de Béarn, Gouverneur de Navarreins &

d'Acqs ; il fut créé Chevalier du Saint-Efprit le 14 Mai 1633, & époufa *Anne de Baffabat-de-Bordeac,* dont entr'autres enfans :

HENRI DE BAYLENS, Marquis de Poyanne, Sénéchal des Landes de Bordeaux, Gouverneur de Navarreins & d'Acqs, & Lieutenant-Général en la Principauté de Béarn, nommé Chevalier des Ordres le 31 Décembre 1661. Il mourut en Mars 1667, laiffant, de *Jeanne-Marie*, Marquife de *Caftelnau*, fille d'*Antoine de Caftille*, Marquis de *Caftelnau*, & de *Jeanne Valliers.*

1. ANTOINE, qui fuit ;
2. Et JEANNE-MARIE-JOSÈPHE, mariée, en 1683, à *Louis de Pardaillan*, Comte de Gondrin.

ANTOINE DE BAYLENS, Marquis de Poyanne, Gouverneur de Navarreins & d'Acqs, Sénéchal des Landes de Bordeaux, époufa, en 1684, *Marie-Bérénice Avice*, fille d'*Aubin Avice,* Seigneur de Mongon, & d'*Artémife de Nemond*; petite-fille de *Marie d'Aubigné-Surinau.* De ce mariage eft forti :

PHILIPPE DE BAYLENS, Marquis de Poyanne, marié, 1° en 1710, à *Marie-Anne-Martin*, morte le 4 Mai 1716, fille de *Jean-Louis-Martin*, Seigneur d'Auzielles, Fermier-Général, dont il ne paroît pas qu'il ait eu d'enfans ; & 2° en Mai 1717, à *Marie de Gaffion*, feconde fille de *Pierre*, Marquis de *Gaffion*, Préfident au Parlement de Pau, & de *Madeleine du Terron*, dont il eut entr'autres enfans :

BERNARD DE BAYLENS, Marquis de Poyanne, fucceffivement Moufquetaire du Roi dans fa feconde Compagnie, le 5 Septembre 1732, Capitaine de Cavalerie en 1735, Guidon des Gendarmes de la Garde ; Colonel du Régiment de Bretagne, Cavalerie, en 1741, après la mort du Marquis *de Gaffion*, fon coufin germain ; Brigadier le 2 Mai 1744, Maréchal-de-Camp le 1er Janvier 1748, Infpecteur-Général de Cavalerie en 1754, Meftre-de-Camp Lieutenant des Carabiniers de Monfeigneur le Comte de Provence en 1758, Lieutenant-Général des Armées du Roi, le 1er Mai 1758, & créé Chevalier des Ordres le 2 Février 1767. Il a époufé, 1° le 8 Mars 1745, *Antoinette-Madeleine Olivier*, Marquife de Leuville, née le 2 Octobre 1730, morte à Paris le 10 Juillet 1761. Elle étoit fille de *Louis-Thomas Dubois-de-Fienne*, dit *Olivier*, Marquis de Leuville, Lieutenant-Général des Armées du Roi, mort le 3 Avril 1742, devant Egra, en Bohême, & de *Marie Voisin*, morte le 28 Février 1746, & 2° *Marie-Augustine Erard-de-Ray*, veuve, dès 1750, de *N... Dupleix-de-Bacquencourt*, & fille de *Gabrielle de Château-Thierry*, Baronne de Ray, seconde femme du troisième Marquis de *l'Aigle*. Il a eu de son premier mariage :

HENRIETTE - ROSALIE DE BAYLENS-DE-POYANNE, morte le 14 Octobre 1772. Elle avoit épousé, par contrat du 17 Février 1767, *Maximilien-Alexis de Béthune*, Duc de Sully. Voyez BÉTHUNE.

Les armes : *écartelé, aux 1 & 4 d'or, au lévrier rampant de gueules colleté d'argent*, qui est de BAYLENS; *aux 2 & 3 d'azur, à trois canettes d'argent, posées 2 & 1*, qui est de POYANNE.

BAYLES : *d'azur, à la roue de Sainte-Catherine d'or.*

BAYMERES : *écartelé d'or & d'azur.*

BAYNE, en Languedoc : *d'argent, à un lion de sinople, armé & lampassé d'argent, surmonté d'un lambel aussi d'argent à trois pendans, chargés chacun de trois tourteaux de gueules.*

BAYNES : *de sable, à deux os de mort d'argent, posés en croix.*

BAYOL, famille originaire du Royaume d'Ecosse, qui se transplanta en Provence dans le XII° siècle, lors des anciennes guerres Civiles qui désoloient ce pays. Ceux de ce nom y occupoient le premier rang, ainsi que l'ont remarqué l'auteur du *Nobiliaire d'Ecosse*, & M. de Voltaire, dans son *Abrégé de l'Histoire Universelle*.

RAIMONDUS DE BAYOL, le premier de ce nom connu en Provence, naquit à Glascow, en Ecosse, & épousa à Marseille, en 1208, *Blanche de Berre*, dont :

GODEFROY DE BAYOL, qui étoit Bailli de Briolles & de Saint-Maximin. Il possédoit des biens considérables dans le territoire de cette Ville, ainsi qu'il est prouvé par les anciens Livres Terriers de ladite Ville de Saint-Maximin, en foi de quoi les Juges, Maires & Consuls, ont certifié que cette noble & ancienne famille les y a possédés jusqu'à nos jours. Ce GODEFROY DE BAYOL se qualifioit dans les actes d'*Eques* & de *Miles*. Il étoit Commandant de toute la Gendarmerie enrôlée pour le service du Roi.

il avoit épousé, en 1262, *Julie de Clary*.

RAIMONDUS DE BAYOL, II° du nom, son fils, épousa, en 1305, *Anne d'Avalde*, dont :

1. LOUIS, qui suit ;
2. Et CHARLES, qui s'établit à Varayes, où ses descendans ont vécu noblement, l'espace de 300 ans.

LOUIS DE BAYOL épousa, en 1351, *Jeanne Bertrande*, dont :

1. JACQUES, qui suit ;
2. Et ETIENNE, marié à Cuers, en 1390, qui eut pour enfans :

JACQUES & ETIENNE DE BAYOL, qui furent successivement Gouverneurs de Bregançon.

JACQUES DE BAYOL, I° du nom, se maria, en 1388, avec *Lucrèce de Quantelme*, dont plusieurs enfans, entr'autres :

1. ANTOINE, qui suit ;
2. Et PIERRE, qui s'établit à Marseille, & dont la postérité a fini dans une fille, mariée dans la Maison d'*Avenne*.

ANTOINE DE BAYOL épousa, en 1431, *Eléonore d'Errequyrma*, dont :

ELZÉAR DE BAYOL, marié, en 1460, avec *Marguerite de Blanque*. Il en eut :

ANTOINE DE BAYOL, II° du nom, qui fut tué pendant les guerres Civiles, étant du parti du Roi. Il épousa, en 1492, *Catherine de Veteris*, & laissa, entr'autres enfans, JEAN & PIERRE.

PIERRE DE BAYOL se maria, à Avignon, en 1530, avec *Louise de Séron*, dont est issue la branche de BAYOL, établie à Avignon, qui a donné de père en fils 14 assesseurs à ladite Ville, & JOSEPH DE BAYOL, mort depuis peu, Doyen de la Rothe.

PAUL-CÉSAR DE BAYOL, Sieur de Saint-Ferréol, est le chef de cette branche; il a deux sœurs, N..., mariée à N... *de Ferres*; & ELISABETH BAYOL, mariée à N.... *d'Ayard*, ancien Officier dans Royal Italien.

De cette branche s'est formée celle des Comtes d'*Urne*, en Hollande, lorsque LOUIS XIV réunit la Principauté d'Orange à la Couronne.

LOUIS DE BAYOL, Officier dans les Troupes Hollandoises qui composoient la Garnison du Château d'Orange, passa en Hollande, & y épousa *Catherine d'Olberge*, Comtesse d'Urne, dont :

1. RICHARD, Ecuyer du Prince d'Orange, Stathouder de la République de Hollande ;
2. GUILLAUME, Capitaine des Cuirassiers de la

République de Hollande, mort de nos jours;
3. Et JEAN, qui fuit.

JEAN DE BAYOL a continué la poftérité en Provence, par fon mariage, en 1530, avec *Honorade Cabro*, dont :

JACQUES DE BAYOL, IIe du nom, marié, en 1570, avec *Marie Coculde*.

CLAUDE DE BAYOL, fon fils, époufa, en 1621, *Catherine de Simiane-la-Cofte*, dont il eut :

JACQUES DE BAYOL, IIIe du nom, qui après avoir été Lieutenant dans le Régiment de Mazarin, & s'être trouvé aux fameux fiège de Crémone, acquit la Seigneurie de Peirefc, la Charge de Confeiller-Secrétaire du Roi, & celle de Greffier-Criminel en Chef au Parlement de Provence. Il avoit époufé, en 1674, *Sibylle de Solery*, dont il eut entr'autres enfans :
1. MATHIEU, qui fuit;
2. BONIFACE, qui fervit dans les Gardes-du-Corps du Roi, & fe trouva à la bataille de Malplaquet;
3. Et HILAIRE, qui fut Provincial des Chanoines Réguliers de la Trinité.

MATHIEU DE BAYOL, Seigneur de Peirefc, après avoir fervi 12 ans dans les Gardes-du-Corps du Roi, & s'être trouvé à plufieurs fièges & batailles, fut pourvu de la Charge de fon père. Il a eu de fon mariage, contracté en 1706, avec *Thérèfe de Miolles* :
1. CÉSAR, Seigneur de Peirefc, qui a fervi, comme fon père, dans les Gardes-du-Corps du Roi, & eft aujourd'hui Capitaine d'Infanterie;
2. BALTHASARD, qui fuit;
3. Et MARGUERITE, mariée avec *Jofeph de Mine*, dont plufieurs enfans, l'aîné eft Lieutenant des Vaiffeaux du Roi, au département de Toulon.

BALTHASARD DE BAYOL, Seigneur de Peirefc, a fervi pendant 21 ans dans les Gardes-du-Corps du Roi, Compagnie de Luxembourg, où il eft entré en 1743, & en eft forti en 1764, pour exercer la Charge de Major-Commandant pour le Roi dans la Ville, Tour & Citadelle de Saint-Tropez, où il fait fa réfidence. Sa Majefté, en confidération de fes fervices, & de ceux de fes ancêtres, lui a accordé une penfion fur fa caffette, en 1754, & la Commiffion de Capitaine de Cavalerie en 1759. La feue Reine a figné fon contrat de mariage, en 1755, avec *Marie-Louife-Françoife de Flotte*, dont le frère eft Enfeigne de Vaiffeaux du Roi, au département de Toulon. De ce mariage font nés :

1. JOSEPH-LOUIS-LAURENT DE BAYOL-DE-PEIRESC, admis à l'Ecole Royale Militaire, le 15 Mai 1767;
Et quatre filles, MARIE-ANNE-PAULINE, FÉLICITÉ, PHILIPPINE, & JULIE DE BAYOL.

Les armes : *d'azur, au croiffant d'argent, abaiffé fous deux colombes de même, qui fe becquètent, & en chef un lambel de gueules.* Ces armes fe voyent dans une Chapelle de l'Eglife des Auguftins de la Ville d'Aix, où cette famille a depuis long-tems fa fépulture. (*Mémoire envoyé.*)

* BAYON, Château & Bourg fur la Mofelle, à cinq lieues de Nancy, en Lorraine, érigés en Marquifat, par Lettres du 7 Octobre 1720, en faveur de *Marie-Elifabeth de Ludres*, Chanoineffe de Pouffay, depuis fille d'Honneur de l'Impératrice Reine MARIE-THÉRÈSE D'AUTRICHE. Voyez LUDRES.

BAYONNE : *d'argent, à la bande de gueules chargée de trois alérions d'or, au lambel de cinq pendans d'azur.*

BAYS, en Bretagne : *de gueules, à trois boiffeaux ou quarts d'argent, chargés chacun de cinq moucheture d'hermines de fable.*

BAYS (DE), en Bretagne : *de gueules, à trois cuviers d'argent, cerclés de fable, pofés 2 & 1.*

BAZAN, en Franche-Comté : *de gueules, au chevron d'argent, accompagné de trois befans d'or, pofés deux en chef & un en pointe.*

BAZAN-DE-FLAMENVILLE, en Normandie, Généralité de Caen. C'eft une des plus anciennes nobleffes de la Province, qui vient de s'éteindre.

La Roque, dans fon *Hiftoire d'Harcourt*, pag. 446, parle de ROBERT BAZAN, de *Jean le Fort*, & de *Jean le Demeslé*, qui avoient différend avec *Roger des Mares*, lequel défendoit les intérêts de *Louis d'Harcourt*, Patriarche de Jérufalem, le 25 Avril 1465.

Le même auteur fait mention de RICHARD BAZAN-DE-FLAMENVILLE, Bachelier à la revue faite au Mont-Saint-Michel, en Juin 1424.

THOMAS BAZAN, Seigneur de Flamenville, époufa *Jeanne Jallot*, dont il eut :

GUILLAUME BAZAN, marié à *Gabrielle de Renty*, fœur de la Dame *Patrix*, bifayeule du Maréchal Duc *de Coigny*, fille de *Jacques*, Bailli d'Alençon, & de *Françoife Nantier*, Dame de Landelles, remariée à *Gabriel de Rabodanges*, Seigneur de Fontaineriant.

HERVIEU BAZAN, leur fils, Marquis de Flamenville, Baron de Trianville, de Sionville
de Defpieux, de Gronville, de Benoifeville,
de Saint-Paul, de Baubigny, & Bailli du
Cotentin, fe maria, 1° vers 1603, à *Jeanne
d'Argouges*, morte fans poftérité; & 2° à
Agnès Molé, fœur de *Marie*, femme de *Georges de Monchy*, Marquis d'Hocquincourt,
fille de *Jean Molé*, Seigneur de Jufanvigny,
Préfident des Enquêtes, & de *Jeanne-Ga-
brielle Molé*, fille du premier Préfident.

De ce fecond mariage font fortis:

1. JEAN-RENÉ, qui fuit;
2. CHARLES-MATHIEU, Comte de Flaménville,
Capitaine-Enfeigne des Gendarmes d'Anjou, tué au combat de la Marfaille, le 4 Octobre 1693. Il époufa *Bonne des Noyers*, ou *du
Noyer*, fœur de Madame de *Lattaignant*;
3. JEAN, mort en Janvier 1721, Evêque de
Perpignan;
4. Et NICOLAS-EDOUARD, Chevalier de Malte,
Commandeur de Troyes.

JEAN-RENÉ BAZAN, Marquis de Flamenville, Seigneur de Baubigny, de Saint-Paul,
de Creffenville, Capitaine-Lieutenant des
Gendarmes Bourguignons, mort le 14 Avril
1715, époufa, en 1690, *Marie-Anne le Camus*, fille de *Nicolas*, premier Préfident de la
Cour des Aides, dont:

1. JEAN-JACQUES, qui fuit;
2. Et N... Comte de Flamenville, Capitaine
en pied au Régiment de Dragons du Roi,
mort fans alliance.

JEAN-JACQUES BAZAN, mort le 27 Novembre
1752, avoit époufé *Françoife-Bonaventure
de Mauconvenant*, appelée *Mademoifelle de
Sainte-Sufanne*, dont les armes font: *de
gueules, à neuf quinte-feuilles d'argent*, 3,
3, & 3. De ce mariage font iffues:

1. MARIE-FRANÇOISE-ELISABETH, feule héritière, qui fuit;
2. Et MARIE-BONAVENTURE, morte à l'âge de
17 ans, le 4 Avril 1750.

MARIE-FRANÇOISE-ELISABETH DE BAZAN,
morte le 12 Avril 1761, dans fa trentième
année, avoit époufé, le 14 Mars 1747, *Jean-
Jofeph le Conte-de-Nonant*, Marquis de Ra-
ray, Enfeigne des Gendarmes de la Reine,
fils de *François-Louis*, Marquis de Néry,
mort le 22 Mars 1736, & de *Louife-Jofé-
phine Chevalier*, morte le 24 Janvier 1744,
fille de *N... Chevalier*,, & de *Louife-Françoife d'Ailly*, morte le 25 Mars 1749.

Une FRANÇOISE BAZAN-DE-FLAMENVILLE

époufa *Jacques du Moncel*, tige des Seigneurs
de *Martinvaft*, & feptième ayeul [d'*Henri-
Jacques du Moncel*, marié, le 13 Août 1755,
à *Françoife-Elifabeth de Bailleul*.

Les armes de BAZAN-FLAMENVILLE: *d'azur,
à deux jumelles d'argent, furmontées d'un
lion de même paffant, armé, lampaffé & couronné d'or*.

BAZIN-DE-BEZONS, famille noble,
qui a donné un Maréchal de France & un
Archevêque de Rouen, dans les deux frères,
JACQUES, qui fuit; & ARMAND BAZIN DE BE-
ZONS, qui obtint, en 1671, l'Abbaye de Notre-
Dame de Reffons, Ordre de Prémontré, Diocèfe de Rouen; fut fait Agent général du
Clergé de France en 1680, reçut le Bonnet
de Docteur en Théologie de la Faculté de Paris, de la Maifon & Société de Sorbonne, le
17 Décembre 1682; fut nommé à l'Evêché
d'Aire au mois d'Août 1685, transféré le 29
Mars 1698 à l'Archevêché de Bordeaux; Député de cette Province aux Affemblées Générales du Clergé de France, le 25 Mai 1705,
1710, 1711 & 1715; fut un des huit Préfi-
dents à cette dernière; Abbé de Notre-Dame
de la Grâce-Dieu, Diocèfe de Carcaffonne, le
14 Août 1715; du Confeil de Confcience en
1715; & du Confeil de la Régence, Abbé d'E-
vron, Diocèfe du Mans, en 1718; & nommé
à l'Archevêché de Rouen en 1719. Il mourut
le 8 Octobre 1721, dans fon Château de Gaillon, âgé de 66 ans. Ils avoient une fœur, MA-
RIE BAZIN-de-BEZONS, Prieure perpétuelle des
Religieufes de Bon-Secours, Ordre de Saint-
Benoît, rue de Charonne, Faubourg Saint-
Antoine, à Paris, morte le 6 Août 1729, âgée
de 71 ans.

JACQUES BAZIN, Comte de Bezons, Maréchal de France, fut un des deux Maréchaux
de France qui furent invités au Sacre du Roi,
le 25 Octobre 1722, Il fut nommé, le 2 Février 1724, Chevalier des Ordres du Roi, &
mourut à Paris le 22 Mai 1733, âgé de 80
ans. Il eut de *Marie-Marguerite le Menef-
trel-de-Hauguel*, fille d'*Antoine*, Grand-Audiencier de France, & de *Marguerite Berbier-du-Metz*:

1. LOUIS-GABRIEL, qui fuit;
2. Et ARMAND, né le 30 Mars 1701, Abbé Commendataire de l'Abbaye Royale de Saint-
Jouin-les-Marnes, Diocèfe de Poitiers, le 6
Novembre 1717, de celle de Notre-Dame
de Grâce, Diocèfe de Carcaffonne, au mois

d'Octobre 1721, Prieur Commendataire des Prieurés de Saint-Dié & de Saint-Gautier, titulaire de la Chapelle de Saint-Louis, dans l'Eglise Cathédrale d'Avranches, a été Député de la Province de Rouen à l'Affemblée générale du Clergé en 1725, & nommé à l'Evêché de Carcaffonne au mois de Mars 1730;

3. JACQUES-ETIENNE, dit *le Chevalier de Bezons*, né le 13 Décembre 1709, d'abord Capitaine du Régiment Dauphin, étranger, Cavalerie, depuis Colonel du Régiment de Beaujôlois, Infanterie, par Commiffion du 20 Février 1734, mort à Paris le 3 Février 1742;

4. SUSANNE, née le 23 Octobre 1695, morte le 19 Juin 1726. Elle avoit époufé, au mois de Janvier 1716, *Jean-Hector de Fay*, Marquis de la Tour-Maubourg;

5. MARIE-MARGUERITE, née le 2 Novembre 1696, morte le 22 Mai 1722. Elle avoit époufé *Jean-Claude de Laftic*, Marquis de Saint-Jal, Vicomte de Beaumont, &c., Meftre-de-Camp de Cavalerie;

6. JEANNE-LOUISE, née le 3 Octobre 1698, morte Religieufe au Monaftère de Bon-Secours, au mois de Décembre 1723;

7. Et CATHERINE-SCHOLASTIQUE, née le 10 Février 1706, mariée le 28 Avril 1727, avec *Hubert-François*, Vicomte d'*Aubuffon*, Comte de la Feuillade.

LOUIS-GABRIEL BAZIN, Marquis de Bezons, Baron de Frefne, en Soiffonnois, né le 1er Janvier 1700, fut fait Meftre-de-Camp d'un Régiment de Cavalerie au mois de Mars 1718; du Régiment Dauphin, étranger, auffi Cavalerie le 29 Mai 1719; pourvu, en furvivance du Maréchal fon père, du Gouvernement de la Ville & Citadelle de Cambray au mois de Janvier 1721, Brigadier des Armées du Roi le 20 Février 1734, Maréchal-de-Camp le 24 Février 1738, & mort à Paris le 22 Juillet 1740. Il avoit époufé, le 28 Novembre 1723, *Marie-Anne Bernard des Maifons*, fille de *Jacques Bernard*, Seigneur des Maifons, & de *Marie-Madeleine-Sabine de la Quieze*, morte le 5 Mai 1740, âgée de 34 ans, au Château des Maifons, près Bayeux, en Normandie. Leurs enfans font:

1. JACQUES-GABRIEL, qui fuit;
2. ALEXANDRE-LOUIS, Chevalier de Bezons;
3. MARIE-MARGUERITE-FRANÇOISE, née le 28 Novembre 1726, mariée, par contrat du 16 Mars 1743, à *Henri de Poudenx*, IIIe du nom, Vicomte de *Poudenx*;
4. FRANÇOISE-GABRIELLE-JACQUELINE, née le 7 Septembre 1728;

5. Et LOUISE-JOSÈPHE, née le 25 Janvier 1731, mariée, le 7 Mai 1753, à *Philippe-Jacques de Herici*, Marquis de Vauffieux.

JACQUES-GABRIEL BAZIN, Marquis de Bezons, né le 21 Octobre 1725, Colonel d'un Régiment de Cavalerie de fon nom en 1749, ayant eu avant un Régiment d'Infanterie; Brigadier le 5 Juin 1747, Maréchal-de-Camp le 1er Mai 1758, Lieutenant-Général le 25 Juillet 1762, a époufé, le 18 Septembre 1752, *Anne-Marie de Briqueville*, morte le 4 Septembre 1770, âgée de 35 ans, fille d'*Henri*, Marquis de la Luzerne, & de *Marie-Anne-Catherine Boutet-de-Guignonville*. (Voyez BRIQUEVILLE). De ce mariage font iffus:

ARMANDE-MARIE-GABRIELLE, née le 26 Juillet 1753;

Et GABRIEL-JACQUES, né le 21 Février 1755.

L'Abbé *de Champigny*, Prêtre, Docteur en Droit-Canon, de la Faculté de Paris, Chanoine de la Sainte-Chapelle Royale du Palais, à Paris, & Prieur de Saint-Pierre-du-Mont-de-Marfan, Diocèfe d'Aire, mort le 31 Août 1736, âgé de 78 ans, étoit de la même Famille que les Seigneurs de BEZONS, & coufin iffu de germain du feu Maréchal de BEZONS.

Les armes: *d'azur, à trois couronnes Ducales fleuronnées de cinq pièces d'or, 2 & 1.*

Voyez fur cette Maifon, le P. Anfelme & Moréri.

BAZOCHES: *de fable, à la croix engrêlée d'or.*

BAZOCHES: *d'azur, au lion bureté d'argent & de gueules.*

BAZOGES, en Berry. ROBERT DE BAZOGES, Ecuyer, Seigneur de Bois-Maître, fut maintenu dans fa nobleffe par Sentence du 8 Novembre 1588, de Meffieurs les Commiffaires départis dans la Généralité d'Orléans. Il avoit époufé, le 9 Novembre 1576, *Marguerite de Caftelnau*, fille de *Jean*, Seigneur de la Mauviffière, & de *Jeanne du Menil*, dont poftérité.

Les armes: *d'azur, au lion d'argent, armé & lampaffé de gueules.*

BAZON: *échiqueté d'argent & de fable, de quinze pièces.*

BAZONNIÈRE (DE LA), en Normandie, Généralité de Caen: *d'hermines, au lion de gueules.*

BÉARN. Les anciens Vicomtes de Béarn defcendoient d'EUDES, Duc d'Aquitaine, & par conféquent de la race des MÉROVINGIENS. L'Empereur LOUIS-*le-Débonnaire* en confirma la donation, en 820, à CENTULLE Ier, un des fils de LOUP-CENTULLE, Comte de Gafcogne. Elle avoit été faite par fes coufins, fils du Duc *de Garfimire*; & parce qu'il n'eut point de part à la révolte de fon père, cet Empereur l'inveftit de toute la Terre de Béarn, fous le titre feulement de *Vicomté*.

CENTULLE II, fon fils, vivoit en 845. A CENTULLE II fuccéda un autre, dont on ignore le nom.

CENTULLE II étoit Vicomte de Béarn. Il eut pour fucceffeur fon petit-fils:

GASTON Ier, qui fut père de :

CENTULLE III, furnommé *le Vieux*, qualifié Vicomte de Béarn & d'Oléron. Il eut GASTON, qui fuit, & N..., & un fils naturel, nommé ANERLOUP, à qui il donna une partie de la Vicomté d'Oléron.

GASTON II fuccéda en 1004. Il fut père de :

CENTULLE IV, dit *le Jeune*, affaffiné en 1068 par les habitans de la Vicomté de Soule.

GASTON III, fon fils, marié à *Adélaïde d'Armagnac*, mourut avant fon père.

CENTULLE V, qui fuccéda à fon ayeul, réunit au Béarn la Vicomté de Montaner, très-confidérable. Il fit bâtir & dota le Prieuré & l'Eglife de Sainte-Foi de Morlas, qu'il mit fous l'obéiffance de *Hugues*, Abbé de Cluny. Il eft qualifié, dans un acte du Monaftère de la Penna, Comte de Bigorre, de Béarn & d'Oléron. Cependant fes fucceffeurs préférèrent l'ancien titre de Vicomte à celui de Comte. Allant, en 1088, en Aragon mener du fecours au Roi *Sanche Ramir*, il fut affaffiné une nuit, avec fes gens, dans la Maifon de *Garcias*, fils d'*Aznar-Athon*, fon homme-lige. Il fe fépara de fa femme, *Gilles*, qui étoit fa parente, y étant engagé par le Pape. Il la fit conduire à Cluny[1], pour prendre le voile. Elle fut Religieufe dans le Monaftère de Marciniac, bâti par *Hugues*, Abbé de Cluny, pour des veuves & des femmes féparées de leurs maris. Il fe remaria à *Béatrix*, héritière en 1080 du Comté de Bigorre, par la mort de fon frère. Il laiffa trois fils, dont les deux derniers, nés de la feconde femme, furent fucceffivement Comtes de Bigorre.

GASTON IV, né du premier lit, lui fuccéda

dans les Vicomtés de Béarn & d'Oléron, qu'il augmenta des Vicomtés de Soule & d'Acqs. Il fonda des Chanoines Réguliers. Il périt dans une embufcade en 1130, fut enterré dans l'Eglife de Sainte-Marie-Majeure de Saragoffe. Il en avoit fondé le Chapitre Collégial, dont quatre Chanoines devoient être Béarnois, & avec fa femme *Taléfie*, il fonda l'Abbaye de Saubalade & l'Hôpital de Faget. Il eut CENTULLE & GUISCARDE, qui fuivent;

CENTULLE VI fut le dernier des Vicomtes de Béarn, de la race mafculine d'EUDES, Duc d'Aquitaine.

GUISCARDE hérita de la Vicomté de Béarn, à laquelle fuccéda PIERRE DE GAVARET, fon fils. Il mourut en 1150.

GASTON V mourut fans enfans. MARIE, fa fœur, fon héritière, fit hommage à ALPHONSE, Roi d'Aragon, pour elle & pour fes fucceffeurs, tant des fiefs qu'elle poffédoit en Aragon que de ceux qui lui appartenoient en Gafcogne, & du Béarn même, & promit de ne fe marier que de fon confentement. Ce Prince lui fit époufer *Guillaume de Moncade*, Sénéchal de Catalogne.

Les armes de la Maifon de MONCADE font : *de gueules, à fix befans d'or, pofés en pal.*

Les Béarnois, indignés du traité fait par MARIE avec le Roi d'Aragon, fe révoltèrent, & élurent pour leur Seigneur un Chevalier de Bigorre, dont ils fe défirent un an après, pour avoir violé leurs privilèges, & élurent CENTULLE D'AUVERGNE, tué deux ans après pour le même fujet. Ils élurent en fa place GASTON, furnommé *le Bon*, fils de MARIE & de GUILLAUME DE MONCADE. Il mourut fans enfans en 1214.

GUILLAUME-RAYMOND, fon frère jumeau, lui fuccéda, & laiffa le Béarn en 1223 à

GUILLAUME, fon fils, qui eut:

GASTON VII, lequel fut fon héritier. Il mourut en 1290, fans enfans mâles, & eut pour héritière fa feconde fille,

MARGUERITE, femme de ROGER-BERNARD, IIIe du nom, Comte de Foix, qui porte pour armes: *d'or, à trois pals de gueules.* Ils eurent pour fils & héritier GASTON Ier, Comte de Foix, & Vicomte de Béarn, dont la poftérité écartela *les vaches de Béarn.* Les *Foix-Rabats* n'en defcendent pas. GASTON Ier mourut en 1315, & laiffa entr'autres enfans :

GASTON II, mort à Séville en 1343, père de:

GASTON-PHŒBUS, qui perdit fon fils unique

en 1382, & eut le chagrin de voir éteindre en lui fa poftérité.

Les armes du Comte de Foix font: *écartelé, aux* 1 *&* 4 *de* Foix, *qui eft d'or, à trois pals de gueules, aux* 2 *&* 3 *de* Béarn.

MATHIEU DE FOIX, arrière-petit-fils de GASTON Ier, fuccéda à GASTON-PHŒBUS. Il mourut fans enfans, & eut pour héritière fa sœur:

ISABELLE DE FOIX, femme d'*Archambaud de Grailly*, Captal de Buch.

JEAN, leur fils aîné, Comte de Foix & de Bigorre, & Vicomte de Béarn, fut père, entr'autres enfans, par fa troifième femme, *Jeanne d'Aragon*, de:

GASTON V, Vicomte de Béarn, quatrième Comte de Foix, mort en 1472.

FRANÇOIS-PHŒBUS, fon petit-fils, lui fuccéda, joignit aux Etats paternels le Royaume de Navarre, du chef de fon ayeule *Eléonore de Navarre*. Il mourut à Paris, le 29 Janvier 1482, fans alliance, empoifonné avec une flûte.

Les armes de la Maifon de GRAILLY font: *d'argent, à une croix de fable, chargée de cinq coquilles d'argent*.

Sa sœur, CATHERINE DE FOIX, qui lui fuccéda, époufa, en 1484, JEAN D'ALBRET, Comte de Penthièvre & de Périgord, Vicomte de Limoges, fils d'ALAIN, Sire d'Albret. Ils eurent entr'autres enfans:

HENRI D'ALBRET, Roi de Navarre, Prince de Béarn, Comte de Foix, de Bigorre & de Périgord. Il époufa, en 1527, MARGUERITE DE VALOIS, sœur unique de FRANÇOIS Ier. Il en eut une fille unique:

JEANNE D'ALBRET, héritière du Royaume de Navarre, des Comtés de Foix, de Bigorre & de Périgord, & des Vicomtés de Béarn & de Limoges, qu'elle porta dans la Maifon de Bourbon, par fon mariage avec ANTOINE DE BOURBON, Duc de Véndôme.

Les armes de la Reine JEANNE D'ALBRET font: *coupé d'un parti en chef de* 3, *en pointe de* 4, *qui fait fept quartiers; au* 1 *du chef*, de Navarre; *au* 2 *écartelé*, d'Albret; *au* 3 d'Aragon; *au* 4 *& au* 1 *de la pointe, écartelé* de Foix & de Béarn; *au* 5 d'Armagnac & de Rhodès, *au* 6 d'Evreux, *au* 7 de Caftille & de Léon; *fur le tout* de Bigorre.

HENRI IV, furnommé *le Grand*, fils du Duc de Vendôme, lui fuccéda. Etant parvenu au Trône de France, il réunit à la Couronne tous ces Etats, qui revinrent de cette maniè-

re à leur fource primitive. Voyez l'*Abrégé chronologique des Rois de France*.

BÉARN: GALARD DE BÉARN. Voyez ce mot.

BÉARN-DE-DOUMY. JACQUES DE BÉARN, Seigneur de Savignac, Baron de Doumy, fils d'ANTOINE DE BÉARN, Baron de Doumy, époufa *Catherine de Falciche*, qui lui apporta en mariage la Baronie de Viella; elle fut mère d'ANTOINE DE BÉARN, Baron de Viella & de Doumy, marié, le 24 Février 1625, à *Marie de Laure*, dont naquit:

CATHERINE DE BÉARN, qui porta la Baronie de Viella à fon mari *Jacob Labay*, fils de *Jean Labay*, Baron de Doumy, par l'acquifition qu'il en avoit faite d'ANTOINE DE BÉARN, laquelle terre de Doumy fut depuis vendue, vers 1680, à *Dominique-Defclaux-Mefplez*, Evêque de Lefcar. Celle de Viella fut érigée en Comté, en faveur de *Louis de Labay*, par Lettres du mois de Mars 1725. Il avoit époufé *N... de Hyton*, dont il a eu:

JACOB, dit *le Marquis de Viella*, marié, en 1744, à *N... de Noé*, dont trois garçons & trois filles.

Les armes de *Labay-de-Viella*, en Armagnac, font: *écartelé, au* 1 *d'or, à deux vaches de gueules, accornées, accolées & clarinées d'azur; au* 2 *d'or, au lion de gueules; au* 3 *d'azur, à* 2 *balances d'or l'une fur l'autre; au* 4 *de gueules, à une tour ajourée & baftillée d'or, fur le tout d'argent à deux fangliers de fable*.

BÉARN-DE-GERDEREST. BERNARD DE BÉARN, Sénéchal de Foix, fils naturel de JEAN, Comte de Foix, époufa la fille unique d'*Arnaud*, Vicomte de Lavédan, qui lui porta en dot *Gerdereft*, une des 12 premières Baronies de Béarn. Il fut trifayeul de GABRIEL DE BÉARN, Baron de Gerdereft, qui fut décapité en 1569, & fur lequel la Reine JEANNE DE NAVARRE confifqua la Baronie de Gerdereft, avec fes autres biens, qu'elle donna au Seigneur de Montgommery. HENRI IV les rendit à HENRI D'ALBRET, Baron de Mioffens, qui avoit pour bifayeule CATHERINE DE BÉARN-GERDEREST. LOUIS DE LORRAINE, Prince de Pons, vendit le 12 Octobre la Baronie de Gerdereft à *Jean de Noguès*.

JEAN DE BÉARN, fils naturel de JEAN, Comte de Foix, Souverain de Béarn, affifta pour lui, & comme Procureur de fa femme, au ferment de fidélité de *Gafton*, Comte de Foix,

Vicomte de Béarn, fait aux habitans de fa Terre, le 12 Juillet 1436. Il époufa *Angline*, héritière de la première race des Barons de *Mioffens*, qui lui porta en mariage la terre de Mioffens. Il eut:

1. PIERRE, ou PÉEZ, qui fuit;
2. Et JEAN, Seigneur de Saint-Maurice, qui vivoit en 1465, & époufa *Brunette de Lion*, dont naquit JEAN DE BÉARN, IIᵉ du nom, Seigneur de Saint-Maurice, qui époufa *Jeanne d'Antin*, remariée, en 1508, à *Hugues de Galard*, Baron de Braffac. Elle eut de fon premier mariage JEANNE, Dame de Saint-Maurice, mariée à *François de Galard*, Baron de Braffac.

PÉEZ DE BÉARN, Baron de Mioffens, Sénéchal de Marfan, fut Grand-Ecuyer de MADELEINE DE FRANCE, Princeffe de Viane. Il époufa *Chrétienne de Condeuil*, dont il eut:

1. FRANÇOIS, qui fuit;
2. Et ROGER. C'eft de ce dernier que l'on fait fortir une branche qui fubfifte encore aujourd'hui.

FRANÇOIS DE BÉARN, Baron de Mioffens, Sénéchal de Marfan, fut allié à CATHERINE DE BÉARN-DE-GERDEREST. Elle fut mère de:

FRANÇOISE DE BÉARN, héritière de Mioffens, qui porta cette Baronie à *Etienne-Arnault d'Albret*, fils de *Gilles d'Albret*, Seigneur de Caftelmoron, & d'*Anne d'Aguillon*. Il céda la jouiffance de la Baronie de Mioffens à fon frère naturel, *Etienne*, bâtard d'*Albret*, qui, ayant été fon tuteur, avoit procuré fon mariage & fait des avances pour lui.

ROGER DE BÉARN, que l'on croit le deuxième fils de PÉEZ DE BÉARN, Baron de Mioffens, & de *Catherine de Condeuil*, époufa *Gratiane de Saint-Martin*, de laquelle naquit:

JEAN DE BÉARN, allié, en 1532, à *Bertrane de Pouey*. De ce mariage fortit:

JACQUES DE BÉARN, père, par fa femme *Claude de Larmandie*, en Périgord, de:

TIMOTHÉE DE BÉARN, qui fe maria avec *Jeanne de Nays*. Ils eurent entr'autres enfans:

JACQUES DE BÉARN, allié, en 1642, à *Jeanne de Marque*, Dame d'Uffeau, qui eut cinq fils, dont quatre allèrent fervir l'Electeur de Brandebourg.

CYRUS DE BÉARN, l'aîné, mourut fort âgé, laiffant de *N... de Séchen*:

1. JACOB;

Tome II.

---

2. & 3. JEAN & GABRIEL.

BÉATRIX, Seigneur des Pierelles, de Bellecroix & de Maranville, en Normandie, Généralité de Caen: *d'argent, au lion de fable, lampaffé de gueules & couronné d'or à l'antique, ayant le col & l'épaule chargés de cinq croifette du champ,* 3 & 2.

BEAU. Louis XV a accordé en 1747 des Lettres de Nobleffe à JOSEPH BEAU, Avocat à la Cour du Parlement d'Aix, & Maire de la ville d'Antibes. Elles ont été enregiftrées au même Parlement le 12 Octobre 1750.

Les armes: *d'or, à la bombe de fable, enflammée de gueules au chef d'azur, befanté d'or.*

BEAUBIGNÉ, au Maine: *d'azur, à cinq chaudrons d'or, pofés en fautoir.*

BEAUBOIS: *écartelé, aux 1 & 4 de gueules, au croiffant d'argent, chargé de quatre fafces d'azur; & aux 2 & 3 d'argent, à la bande d'azur.*

BEAUBOURG: *écartelé, aux 1 & 4 d'azur, à trois tours d'argent, à la bordure engrêlée de gueules; aux 2 & 3 d'argent, à la bande de fable, chargée de trois molettes du champ.*

BEAUBOYS, Seigneur & Baron de Nevet, en Bretagne, portoit anciennement pour armes: *de gueules, à neuf quarte-feuilles d'or, pofées* 3, 3 & 3; *enfuite de gueules, au croiffant d'argent, chargé de trois fafces d'azur;* & actuellement, *d'or, au léopard de gueules.*

* BEAUCAIRE, ancienne Baronie, en Périgord, Diocèfe & Election de Périgueux, Parlement & Intendance de Bordeaux, acquife, le 11 Mai 1461, d'*Armarieu de Lévi*, Chambellan du Roi, par *Jean*, Seigneur de *Pechpeyrou*, de la Motte & de Montbarla. Voyez PECHPEYROU.

BEAUCAIRE-PUYGUILHEM: *d'azur, au léopard lionné d'or.*

BEAUCAMP: *d'argent, à la bande de fable frettée d'or.*

BEAUCAMPS, Seigneur de Saint-Germain: *d'argent, à l'arbre de finople abaiffé fous une fafce en divife de gueules, furmonté d'un croiffant d'azur, & le fuft de l'arbre accofté de deux étoiles de même.*

M m

BEAUCÉ, en Meleffe, Evêché de Rennes: *d'argent, à une aigle de fable, becquée & membrée de gueules, au bâton ou cotice d'or, brochant fur le tout en bande.*

*BEAUCHAMP, Terre & Seigneurie, en Provence, Diocèfe d'Avignon, Parlement & Intendance d'Aix, Viguerie & Recette de Tarafcon, qui fut érigée en Marquifat par Lettres du mois de Janvier 1658, regiftrées le 16 Janvier 1669, en faveur de *Jean-Baptifte de Doni.* Voyez DONI.

BEAUCHAMP: *d'azur, à deux jumelles d'or, au lion paffant de même en chef.*

BEAUCHAMP, au Maine: *d'or, à un dard de gueules, à l'orle de huit merlettes de même.*

BEAUCHAMP: *d'hermines, à deux faces de finople.*

BEAUCHAMP - RAULIN: *de gueules, à trois clefs d'or, pofées en pal, 2 & 1.*

BEAUCHAMPS (DE), Seigneur de Merle: *d'azur, à la bande d'argent, chargée de trois merlettes de gueules.*

BEAUCHAMPS (DE): *d'azur, au chevron d'or, accompagné en chef de deux étoiles, & en pointe d'un foleil, le tout de même ; le chevron furmonté de deux burelles auffi d'or, & le foleil abaiffé fous une nuée d'argent.*

BEAUCHE: *d'or, à la croix ancrée de gueules.*

BEAUCLERC (DE), Seigneur d'Achères, de Rougemont, d'Eftiau, &c.: *de gueules, au chevron d'or, accompagné en chef de deux têtes de loup de même, & en pointe d'un loup entier paffant auffi d'or ; au chef d'azur, chargé d'un croiffant d'argent.*

BEAUCOURT, Seigneur de Bellière, en Normandie, Généralité de Rouen, famille maintenue dans fa Nobleffe le 11 Mars 1669, dont les armes font : *d'argent, à l'aigle de gueules.*

BEAUDENIS: *d'argent au fautoir de gueules engrêlé, accompagné de quatre têtes de lions de fable.*

BEAUDINAR, en Provence: *de gueules, au lion d'or.* Voyez SABRAN.

* BEAUFFORT, Terre, Seigneurie & Baronie, fituée près d'Avefnes, qui a donné fon nom à une ancienne & illuftre Maifon de la Province d'Artois, dont nous donnerons ci-après la Généalogie.

Par Lettres-Patentes du mois de Juillet 1733, regiftrées à l'Election, au Confeil Provincial & Souverain d'Artois, & au Bureau des Finances de Lille, les Terres de Moulle & de Buiffeheure, &c., furent érigées en Comté, fous la dénomination du Comté de *Beauffort,* en faveur de CHRISTOPHE-LOUIS DE BEAUFFORT, Comte de Croix, &c.

Par autres Lettres-Patentes du mois de Mars 1735, regiftrées à l'Election & au Confeil Provincial & Souverain d'Artois, & au Bureau des Finances de Lille, le Roi LOUIS XV a permis à CHARLES-ANTOINE DE BEAUFFORT, Marquis de Mondicourt, de prendre le titre de *Marquis de Beauffort,* & d'appliquer ce titre fur telles de fes Terres que bon lui fembleroit.

La Maifon de BEAUFFORT, en Artois, eft connue dès le XIIe fiècle, & tire fon nom de cette Terre de *Beauffort,* près d'Avefnes-le-Comte, en ladite Province, où elle s'eft divifée en plufieurs branches.

I. ALLÉAUME, Seigneur de Beauffort & de Noyelles-Wion, Chevalier, paroît dans une Charte de l'Abbaye de Saint-Jean-au-Mont de l'an 1198 avec COLARD, dit *Baudouin de Beauffort,* Seigneur d'Oiran, & GOISSEVIN DE BEAUFFORT, élu Evêque de Tournay en 1204, fes deux frères; & dans une Charte de ladite Abbaye, de l'an 1203. Il mourut en 1219, & eut d'*Athalie,* aliàs *Marguerite de Brimeu,* Dame de Saire & de Ceffoye:

1. WAUTIER, qui fuit;
2. Et GUY, rapporté après fon frère.

II. WAUTIER DE BEAUFFORT, mort avant fon père en 1212, n'eût que les Terres de Saire & de Ceffoye, & fit l'acquifition de celle de Brie. Il eft qualifié *Miles generofus,* dans une Charte de 1211, & par fon mariage accordé avec *Marie,* Dame d'*Angres,* il fut auteur d'une branche qui s'éteignit en la perfonne de PHILIPPE DE BEAUFFORT, Chevalier de l'Ordre du Roi d'Aragon, & Capitaine d'Arras, lorfque cette Ville fut affiégée, en 1414, par le Roi CHARLES VII. Il fut tué en duel, avec fon frère unique, le 24 Octobre 1437.

SECONDE BRANCHE.

II. Guy de Beauffort, qualifié du titre de *Monseigneur*, hérita en 1219 des terres de Beauffort & de Noyelles-Wion, à l'exclusion des enfans de *Wautier*, son frère aîné (la représentation n'ayant point lieu en Artois.) Il épousa *Alix*, aliàs *Marie d'Arras*, veuve de lui en 1250, fille de *Gilles*, Châtelain d'Arras, & nièce de *Névelon d'Arras*, Maréchal de France, dont il eut:

1. Jean, qui suit;
2. Et Jacques, Chevalier, Seigneur de *Noyelles-Wion*, dont sa postérité prit le nom. De son mariage avec *Adèle d'Antoing*, est issue toute la Maison de *Noyelles-Wion*, qui s'est rendue illustre dans les Pays-Bas par ses alliances & par ses services, & qui a produit, entr'autres grands Hommes, Beaudot de Beauffort, dit de *Noyelles-Wion*, Seigneur de Casteau, fait Chevalier de la Toison d'Or en 1433.

III. Jean de Beauffort, Ier du nom, Chevalier, Seigneur de Beauffort & de Metz, fut à la Croisade de l'an 1248, & est qualifié *Monseigneur & Chevalier* en 1259. Il mourut en 1282, & eut de *Julienne de Saveuse*, Dame de Markais:

1. Gilles, Chevalier de l'Ordre des Templiers;
2. Jean, ou Jeannet, qui suit;
3. Raoul, auteur de la branche des Seigneurs de *Metz* & de *Markais*, rapportée ci-après;
4. Et Béatrix, femme de *Guy de Cayeu*.

IV. Jean ou Jeannet de Beauffort, IIe du nom, dit *Payen*, fit partage avec ses frères & sœurs en 1287; se trouva en 1299 à la journée de Cambray avec trois Ecuyers, & mourut en 1306 au service de son Roi, ayant fait la même année son testament. Il fut père, par *Sainte d'Hamélaincourt*, de:

V. Froissard de Beauffort, Chevalier, Seigneur de Beauffort, qui fut tué aux pieds d'Eudes, Duc de Bourgogne, à la journée de Saint-Omer en 1340, laissant de *Jeanne*, aliàs *Alix de Mailly*, fille de *Jean*, dit *Maillet*, Seigneur de Lorsignol, & de *Jeanne de Pecquigny*;

VI. Mathelin de Beauffort, dit *Froissard*, Chevalier, Seigneur de Beauffort, qui servit à la guerre de Gueldres, dès l'an 1366. Il eut de *Marie*, Dame de Ransart:

1. Regnaud, dit *Froissard*, Gouverneur de Béthune, mort sans alliance;

2. Et Colard, qui suit.

VII. Colard de Beauffort, dit *Payen*, Chevalier, Seigneur de Ransart, puis de Beauffort, après la mort de son frère, fut Conseiller & Chambellan du Duc de Bourgogne; & est qualifié dans plusieurs actes *Noble & Puissant Seigneur*, *Monseigneur*; vivoit encore en 1460, & fut lors accusé faussement d'être *Vaudois*. Il avoit épousé *Isabelle d'Ollehain*, fille d'*Hugues*, Seigneur d'Estaimbourg, & d'*Isabeau de Sainte-Aldegonde*, dont il eut:

1. Philippe, qui suit;
2. Et Antoine, Auteur des branches de *Corvin*, & de *Boisleux*, toutes deux éteintes dans le XVIIe siècle, après avoir donné des Gouverneurs aux Villes de Renty, du Quesnoy, de Bapaume, &c., & plusieurs Chanoinesses au Chapitre de Maubeuge, dont la dernière, nommée Anne-Chrétienne de Beauffort, mourut Abbesse en 1698.

VIII. Philippe de Beauffort, Ier du nom, dit *le Barbu*, Chevalier, Seigneur de Beauffort, Capitaine de la Ville d'Arras, pour le Duc de Bourgogne, en 1473 & 1476, en laquelle année il fut fait Chevalier des mains même de ce Prince, & mourut en 1478. Il avoit épousé *Jeanne le Josne*, veuve d'*Antoine*, Seigneur de Habarcq, & fille de *Guillaume*, Seigneur de Contay, Maître-d'Hôtel du Duc de Bourgogne, dont il eut:

IX. Jean de Beauffort, IIIe du nom, Chevalier, Seigneur & Baron de Beauffort, mort Gouverneur d'Arras en 1503, ayant eu de *Marie de Lannoy*, fille de *Jean*, Chevalier de l'Ordre de la Toison d'Or, & de *Jeanne de Ligne*:

1. Philippe, qui suit;
2. Et Jeanne, mariée, en 1525, à *Anne de Montmorency*, Seigneur de Croisilles, fils de *Marc*, & de *Marie de Hallain*.

X. Philippe de Beauffort, IIe du nom, Chevalier, Seigneur & Baron de Beauffort, Seigneur de Ransart, Montenancourt, Reusines, Grincourt, &c., Chambellan de l'Empereur Charles-Quint, & Grand-Bailli de Tournay, mort en 1530, épousa *Jeanne*, fille de *Georges*, Seigneur de *Halwin*, & d'*Antoinette de Sainte-Aldegonde*, dont vinrent:

1. Georges, Seigneur & Baron de Beauffort, qui fut Gentilhomme de l'Empereur Charles-Quint, & Gouverneur de l'Ecluse, & mourut en 1556 sans enfans, de *Marie*, fille de *Charles*, Comte de *Berlaimont*,

Chevalier de l'Ordre de la Toifon d'Or, & d'*Adrienne de Ligne ;*

2. PHILIPPE, qui fuit ;
3. BONNE, Chanoineffe à Andenne ;
4. Et MARGUERITE, Chanoineffe à Nivelle, toutes deux mortes jeunes, avant leur père.

XI. PHILIPPE DE BEAUFFORT, IIIe du nom, Chevalier, Seigneur & Baron de Beauffort, &c., Député général & ordinaire du Corps de la Nobleffe des Etats d'Artois, mourut en 1582, ne laiffant de *Madeleine de la Marck,* fille de *Jean,* Seigneur de Waffenaër, Chevalier de la Toifon d'Or, & de *Joffine d'Egmont,* qu'une fille unique :

ANNE DE BEAUFFORT, mariée, en 1582, à *Philippe de Croy,* Comte de Solre, Chevalier de la Toifon d'Or. De ce mariage defcendent les Princes de *Croy-Solre,* encore poffeffeurs de la Baronie de Beauffort.

TROISIÈME BRANCHE.

IV. RAOUL DE BEAUFFORT, Chevalier, Seigneur de Metz & de Markais, fils puîné de JEAN, Ier du nom, Seigneur de BEAUFFORT, & de *Julienne de Saveufe,* fut en 1306 exécuteur du teftament de JEAN, IIe du nom, dit *Payen,* fon frère aîné, & mourut en 1317. Il avoit époufé *Ifabellote de Moreul,* fille de *Bernard,* Chevalier, Seigneur de Moreul, & d'*Iolente de Soiffons,* dont il eut :

V. JACQUES DE BEAUFFORT, Ier du nom de cette branche, dit *Beaudouin,* Chevalier, Seigneur de Metz & de Markais, qui fe trouva, en 1328, à la bataille de Caffel ; en 1339 à l'Oft de Tournay ; & en 1340 à celui de Bouvines. Il eft qualifié *Capitaine de Thérouanne,* en 1345, dans une Charte de l'Abbaye de Cantimpré. Il eut de fon mariage, contraCté en 1310 avec *Madeleine de Géronvilliers,* Dame du Saulchoy & de Tencquette, fille unique de *Huy,* Seigneur defdits lieux, & de *Jeanne de Prouvy,* fille de *Gérard,* Sire de Prouvy, & d'*Ides de Guines,* entr'autres enfans :

1. GUYON, qui fuit ;
2. Et ROBERT, Seigneur de Rollecourt & de Saint-Valery, Confeiller & Chambellan du Roi, qui vivoit encore en 1374, & fut père de ROBINET DE BEAUFFORT, Chevalier, Seigneur de Rollecourt & Gournay, allié à *Jeanne de Corbeille,* veuve de lui en 1417.

VI. GUYON DE BEAUFFORT, Seigneur de Metz, de Markais, de Tencquette & du Saul-

choy, fut attaché à la Cour des Rois PHILIPPE DE VALOIS, & JEAN, qu'il fervit en plufieurs grandes occafions. Il eft qualifié *Nobilis & potens Dominus,* dans une Chartre de l'Abbaye de Cantimpré, de l'an 1353, & dans d'autres titres. Il avoit époufé *Marie de Souaftre,* fille de *Beaudouin,* IIe du nom, Seigneur de Souaftre, & de *Marguerite de Rely,* dont il eut :

VII. TASSART DE BEAUFFORT, Seigneur du Saulchoy & de Markais, qui fuivit le Duc de Bourgogne, en qualité d'*Ecuyer-Banneret,* dans toutes fes guerres, & fut fait prifonnier à la bataille de Rosbecque en 1383 ; il vivoit encore en 1407 avec *Marie de la Perfonne,* Dame d'Herfin, fa femme, fille d'*Antoine,* Seigneur de Verloing, & de *Marie d'Ailly,* dont il eut :

VIII. JACQUES DE BEAUFFORT, IIe du nom, Seigneur du Saulchoy, de Markais, d'Herfin, &c., lequel, à l'exemple de fes ancêtres, paffa la meilleure partie de fa vie au fervice du Duc de Bourgogne, fon Souverain. Il eft qualifié de *Noble & Puiffant Seigneur,* dans le contrat de mariage de fon fils aîné, en 1424, & mourut en 1441. Il étoit en 1423 du nombre des Seigneurs & Gentilshommes qui efcortèrent PHILIPPE, dit *le Bon,* Duc de Bourgogne, au Tournoi qui fe donna lors à Arras, que ce Prince honora de fa préfence, combattit au mois de Mai 1428 à celui qui fe donna dans la même Ville, auquel ce même Prince affifta. Il avoit époufé *Jeanne de Bruce,* fille de *Richard de Bruce,* Echanfon & Chambellan de *Louis de Masle,* Comte de Flandres, & de *Marguerite de Nevelle,* dont il eut :

IX. JEAN DE BEAUFFORT, Ier du nom de fa branche, Chevalier, Seigneur du Saulchoy, de Markais, d'Herfin, &c., lequel tefta en 1453, & avoit époufé, en 1424, *Marie de Paris,* Dame de Bullecourt, Laffus, Beaurains, Saulchoy en Heudecourt, &c., fille unique de *Jean,* Seigneur des mêmes lieux, & d'*Hélène de Bernémicourt,* dont il eut :

1. JACQUES, qui fut Chevalier de Rhode ;
2. Et JEAN, qui fuit.

X. JEAN DE BEAUFFORT, IIe du nom, Chevalier, Seigneur de Bullecourt, de Markais, d'Herfin, du Saulchoy, &c., fut Capitaine de 50 hommes d'armes, & époufa *Jeanne le Borgne,* fille de *Jacques le Borgne,* Chevalier, Seigneur d'Oriaumont, Capitaine d'une Compagnie de 100 lances, & de *Françoife d'Auft,*

Dame de Ligny. Elle étoit veuve de lui en 1505, & en eut, outre plusieurs enfans, qui tous se distinguèrent au service de leur Prince, auprès duquel ils eurent des emplois considérables :

1. Jean, qui suit ;
2. Jeannet, Chevalier, Seigneur de Markais, &c., qui épousa *Jeanne de Beauffremez*, dont il eut Jeanne de Beauffort, Chanoinesse de Mons, morte sans alliance, avant lui ;
3. Et Marie, mariée, en 1494, à *Robert*, Chevalier, Seigneur *du Bos-Bernard* & d'Oppy, fils *de Jean*, Seigneur des mêmes lieux, Gouverneur de Thérouanne, & de *Jeanne de Lens*, dite de *Lower*, & de *Hourdes*, dont elle eut *Jeanne & Marie du Bos-Bernard*, Chanoinesses de Mons & de Nivelle en 1512.

XI. Jean de Beauffort, IIIᵉ du nom, Chevalier, Seigneur de Bullecourt, Markais, Saulchoy, Lassus, Beaurains, &c., épousa, 1° en 1513, *Madeleine de Sac-Epée*, fille de *Robert*, Seigneur d'Escout & de Jumelle, & d'*Agnès de Carnin* ; & 2° en 1533, *Cornille de Kils*, fille de *Jean*, Chevalier, Seigneur d'Haansbergue, Gouverneur de Bapaume, & de *Marie de Sumenburg*.

Il eut du premier lit :

1. Romain, qui suit ;
2. Et Barbe, reçue en 1532 Chanoinesse à Andenne, & morte Doyenne de ce Chapitre en 1588.

Du second lit il n'eut que :

3. Hugues, auteur de la branche des Seigneurs de *Lassus*, du *Saulchoy* & du *Cauroy*, rapportée ci-après.

XII. Romain de Beauffort, Chevalier, Seigneur de Bullecourt, de Markais, de Beaurains, &c., Guidon des Ordonnances du Roi de la Compagnie du Gouverneur-Général du Pays & Comté d'Artois, & Capitaine de Chevaux, donna des preuves de sa valeur dans toutes les occasions où il se trouva, & mourut à Arras en 1562, des blessures qu'il avoit reçues au service de son Prince, auquel service il aliéna la plus grande partie de ses biens, & des anciennes Terres de sa Maison. Il épousa, 1° en 1549, *Antoinette*, fille de *François*, Seigneur *de Warluselle*, Gouverneur de Bapaume, & d'*Antoinette de Bonnières-de-Souastre* ; & 2° en 1555, *Madeleine de Scoonveliet*, Dame de Ghinderon.

Du premier lit il eut :

1. 2. & 3. Jean-Romain, Philippe-Antoine, & Jacques, tous trois morts au service de France & d'Espagne, sans alliances ;
4. Et Antoinette, Chanoinesse de Munster-Bilsen.

Du second lit il eut :

5. Gilles, qui suit.

XIII. Gilles de Beauffort, Chevalier, Seigneur de Mondicourt, de Montdiès, de Grincourt, de Beaulieu, &c., Capitaine de Chevaux, servit avec distinction aux sièges de Bouchain, de Cambray, de Doullens, & au secours d'Amiens, & mourut en 1631, ne laissant des enfans que de son second mariage avec *Susanne de Fournel*, fille d'*Antoine*, Seigneur de la Rachie, & de *Marguerite de Roussel-Witendaël*, sçavoir :

1. Robert, qui suit ;
2. Et Renom, auteur de la branche des Seigneurs de *Beaulieu*, rapportée ci-après.

XIV. Robert de Beauffort, Chevalier, Seigneur de Mondicourt, Montdiès, Malmaison, &c., Capitaine d'une Compagnie de 300 hommes, servit le Roi d'Espagne, son souverain, avec distinction, & fut du Conseil de Guerre en 1638, pendant le siège de Saint-Omer, où il fit des actions considérables. Il fut aussi député à la Cour pour le Corps de la Noblesse des Etats d'Artois, en 1652 & 1653. Il avoit épousé, en 1632, *Isabelle de France*, sœur de *Jérôme-Gaspard de France*, Baron de Boucault, & de *Christophe de France*, Evêque de Saint-Omer, dont il eut :

XV. Philippe-Louis de Beauffort, Chevalier, Seigneur de Mondicourt, Montdiès, Acquembronne, &c., Capitaine des Cuirassiers au service d'Espagne, qui mourut en 1698, ne laissant des enfans que de son second mariage avec *Marie-Charlotte de Quaëtionek*, fille & unique héritière de *François*, Comte de *Quaëtionek*, Seigneur de Wierlincove, &c., Colonel de Cavalerie au service de l'Empereur, & de *Marie-Marguerite de Saint-Omer*, dite *de Zuytpéesse*, sçavoir entr'autres :

XVI. Charles-Antoine, Marquis de Beauffort & de Mondicourt, qui fut Capitaine de Dragons. Il avoit épousé, 1° en 1703, *Clotilde-Radegonde de Cupère-de-Drinckam*, fille de *François-Marie*, Baron de *Drinckam* ; & 2° *Agnès de Croisilles*. Il eut du premier lit :

1. Charles-Louis-Alexandre, qui suit ;

2. ANTOINE - FRANÇOIS, dit *le Chevalier de Beauffort*, qui fut Capitaine au Régiment de Vermandois, Infanterie, & mourut en Bavière au mois de Mai 1743, fans alliance;

3. Et MARIE-CLOTILDE-JOSÈPHE, mariée, le 20 Juin 1751, à *Philippe - François - Joseph d'Audenfort*, Seigneur de la Potterie.

XVII. CHARLES-LOUIS-ALEXANDRE, Marquis DE BEAUFFORT & de Mondicourt, Vicomte de la Wifche, &c., né le 19 Août 1704, Député général & ordinaire du Corps de la Nobleffe des Etats d'Artois, a époufé, le 25 Septembre 1746, *Florence-Louife-Josèphe de Beauffort*, fa coufine au IV° degré, née le 29 Juin 1725, dont il a:

1. CHARLES-LOUIS-JOSEPH, Chevalier, Marquis de Mondicourt, né le 12 Décembre 1753;

2. ANGE-LOUIS-JOSEPH, né le 14 Octobre 1759;

3. CHARLES - LOUIS - FERDINAND - BALTHASAR, Chevalier, Vicomte de Beauffort, né le 8 Janvier 1761;

4. PHILIPPE - LOUIS - CHARLES - HENRI, Chevalier, dit *le Chevalier de Beauffort*, né en 1766;

5. MARIE-LOUISE-HENRIETTE, dite *Mademoifelle de Beauffort*, née le 4 Janvier 1752;

6. VICTOIRE - LOUISE - MARIE - CAROLINE, dite *Mademoifelle de Mondicourt*, née le 27 Août 1756, reçues toutes deux Chanoineffes à Denain en 1766;

7. Et FÉLICITÉ-LOUISE-MARIE-ELÉONORE-DOROTHÉE, dit *Mademoifelle de la Wifch*.

BRANCHE
des Seigneurs DE BEAULIEU, GRINCOURT, MOULLE, &c., *iffue de celle des Seigneurs* DE MONDICOURT.

XIV. RENOM DE BEAUFFORT, Chevalier, Seigneur de Beaulieu, Grincourt, Moulle, &c., fils puîné de GILLES, Seigneur de Mondicourt, &c., & de *Sufanne de Fournel*, fut Meftre-de-Camp d'un Régiment de vingt Compagnies de Gens de Pied, & Capitaine d'une Compagnie de Chevaux-Légers, le tout entretenu au fervice d'Efpagne, & mourut en 1647. Il avoit époufé, en 1635, *Alexandrine de Maffiet*, Dame de Moulle, fille de *Denis de Maffiet*, Baron de Ravesbergue, & de *Marie d'Affignies-d'Alloifne*, dont il eut:

XV. RENOM-FRANÇOIS DE BEAUFFORT, Chevalier, Comte & Seigneur de Moulle, &c., qui fut Capitaine d'Infanterie au Régiment du Comte de Solre, fon parent, & mourut en 1702, laiffant d'*Antoinette de Croix*, fœur germaine de *Pierre*, Comte de Croix, de

Wafquehal, Colonel du Régiment Royal de Cavalerie Wallonne, & Brigadier des Armées du Roi:

1. LOUIS-FRANÇOIS, Comte de Moulle, mort fans alliance en 1718, Capitaine de Cavalerie;

2. CHRISTOPHE-LOUIS, qui fuit;

3. Et CHRÉTIENNE-FRANÇOISE, née en 1675, admife Chanoineffe de Mouftier-fur-Sambre, & morte fans avoir encore pris poffeffion de fa prébende, le 26 Août 1686.

XVI. CHRISTOPHE-LOUIS, Comte DE BEAUFFORT, de Croix, de Moulle, &c., mourut en 1748. Il avoit époufé, 1° le 3 Juillet 1716, *Claire-Angélique de Croix*, fa nièce à la mode de Bretagne, riche héritière, & fille aînée de *Charles-Adrien*, Comte de Croix, Seigneur de Prefcau & d'Oyembourg, &c., & 2° en 1723, *Marie-Anne-Françoife de Croix*, fa coufine, héritière de la branche des Seigneurs de *Malannoy*.

Du premier lit il n'eut point d'enfans, & du fecond il eut:

1. LOUIS-EUGÈNE-MARIE, qui fuit;

2. MARIE-LOUIS-BALTHASAR, Vicomte de Beaufort, Comte de Croix, &c., Lieutenant au Régiment du Roi, Infanterie, mort fans poftérité le 18 Novembre 1763. Il avoit époufé, le 15 Septembre 1763, *Marie-Ferdinande-Pélagie*, Baronne de *Stéenhuys*, remariée, le 2 Juin 1765, à *Jean-Charles de Joigny*;

3. Et FLORENCE-LOUISE-JOSÈPHE, mariée le 25 Septembre 1746, à CHARLES-LOUIS-ALEXANDRE, Marquis de *Beauffort* & de Mondicourt, fon coufin au IV° degré. (Voyez les *Tabl. Généal.*, part. VII & VIII, & le *Mercure de France*, du mois de Novembre 1746, page 196.)

XVII. LOUIS - EUGÈNE - MARIE, Comte DE BEAUFFORT, de Moulle, &c., Député à la Cour, pour le Corps de la Nobleffe des Etats d'Artois en 1756 & en 1761, a époufé, par contrat du 1ᵉʳ Octobre 1748, *Catherine-Elifabeth-Henriette de Lens-de-Recourt-de-Boulogne-de-Licques*, fille aînée de *Ferdinand-Gillon*, Marquis & Baron de Licques, & d'*Elifabeth de l'Efpinay-de-Marteville*. De ce mariage font nées:

1. LOUISE-FERDINANDE-HENRIETTE DE BEAUFFORT, née le 5 Décembre 1752, reçue Chanoineffe du Chapitre de Nivelle, en Brabant, en 1759, puis mariée, le 26 Septembre 1769, à *Balthafar-Philippe*, Comte de

Mérode, de Montfort & du Saint-Empire.
Elle a été préfentée le 18 Février 1770 ;

2. Et EUGÉNIE-FRANÇOISE, née le 10 Avril 1761, morte jeune.

BRANCHE
des Seigneurs DE LASSUS, DU SAULCHOY & DU CAUROY, *iffue des Seigneurs* DE BULLECOURT, &c.

XII. HUGUES DE BEAUFFORT, Chevalier, Seigneur de Laffus, du Saulchoy, époufa, par contrat du 7 Août 1561, *Marguerite de Leval*, Dame du Ponchet & de Warnecamp, fille & héritière de *Jean*, Seigneur defdits lieux, & de *Marguerite de Mailly-Couronnel*, dont entr'autres enfans :

XIII. JEAN-BAPTISTE DE BEAUFFORT, Chevalier, Seigneur de Laffus, &c., qui époufa, en 1613, *Jeanne de Belvalet*, fille d'*Antoine*, Seigneur de Pommerat & de Famechon. De ce mariage vint entr'autres enfans :

XIV. ANTOINE-JOSEPH DE BEAUFFORT, Chevalier, Seigneur de Laffus, du Saulchoy, du Cauroy, &c., qui s'allia, par contrat du 26 Février 1675, avec *Antoinette-Adrienne du Mont-Saint-Eloy*, Dame des Boucharderies, fille de *Nicolas*, Baron de Nédonchel, & d'*Antoinette de Maillé*, dont :

1. FRANÇOIS-JOSEPH, qui fuit ;
2. MARIE-MADELEINE, mariée, en 1696, à *Gafton-François de Saint-Vaaft*, Baron & Marquis d'Honnecourt, dont vint *Alix-Barbe-Guye de Saint-Vaaft*, héritière d'Honnecourt, mariée, en 1720, à *Charles-Ignace-François*, Comte de *Lannoy*, de Beaurepaire & du Saint-Empire, avec poftérité ;
3. Et JEANNE-ISABELLE, mariée, 1° en 1699, à *Guy de Moncheaux*, Chevalier, Seigneur de Moncheaux & d'Anecamps, fans enfans ; & 2° en 1702, à *François-Jofeph de Partz-de-Preffy*, Marquis d'Efquières.

XV. FRANÇOIS-JOSEPH DE BEAUFFORT, Chevalier, Seigneur de Laffus, du Cauroy & du Saulchoy, Baron de Nédonchel, &c., époufa, par contrat du 13 Avril 1722, *Marie-Florence de Coupigny*, fille aînée de *Philippe-Conftant de Coupigny*, dit *Malet*, Chevalier, Seigneur de Foucquières & de Salau, & de *Marie-Jofèphe du Pont-de-Tayneville*, dont :

1. JEAN-BAPTISTE-CHARLES-ADRIEN, dit *le Baron de Beauffort* ;
2. EMMANUEL-CONSTANT-JOSEPH, dit *le Chevalier de Beauffort*, Capitaine au Régi-

ment du Roi, Infanterie, marié, en 1777, à *Victoire-Louife-Caroline de Beauffort* ;

3. MARIE-ALBERTINE-JOSÈPHE, mariée, en 1761, à *Charles-Philippe-Bernard de Hybert*, Chevalier, Baron de la Motte, Capitaine au Régiment de Montmorin ;
4. MARIE-JOSÈPHE-ANTOINETTE, dite *Mademoifelle de Beauffort*, morte fans alliance ;
5. MARIE-HENRIETTE-CONSTANCE, Chanoinefse-Régulière de la noble Abbaye d'Etrunles-Arras ;
6. Et MARIE-JEANNE-BARBE-FLORENCE, appelée *Mademoifelle de Plouych*.

Les armes : *d'azur, à trois jumelles d'or.*

BEAUFFOU. La Maifon de BEAUFFOU eft fi ancienne, & il y a fi long-tems quelle eft finie, qu'on n'en peut parler que confufément. Elle tire fon origine du Bailliage de Caen, où la Terre de *Beauffou* eft fituée, vers le Pays d'Auge.

Guillaume, Moine de Jumièges, qui décrit l'origine de cette Maifon, commence par RAOUL, Seigneur DE BEAUFFOU, qui accompagna le Duc GUILLAUME-*le-Conquérant* à la conquête du Royaume d'Angleterre, l'an 1066, & vivoit l'an 1069. Il eut pour fils & fucceffeur :

RICHARD, Seigneur de BEAUFFOU, vivant en 1081. Il figna en ce tems à une Charte pour l'Abbaye de Saint-Evroult, & époufa *Emme de Bayeux*, fille de *Raoul d'Amy*, Comte de Bayeux, & d'*Alberede*. De ce mariage fortirent :

1. ROBERT, qui fuit ;
2. GUILLAUME, Chevalier, attaché à GUILLAUME *le Roux*, Roi d'Angleterre, en 1130 ;
3. RICHARD, Evêque d'Avranches en 1140 ;
4. EMME ;
5. JEANNE ;
6. Et ALIX, femme de *Hugues de Montfort*.

ROBERT, Seigneur de BEAUFFOU, après avoir été marié à une femme dont le nom eft inconnu, fe fit, avec fes deux fils, Religieux dans l'Abbaye du Bec. Ses enfans furent :

1. RICHARD, Moine dans l'Abbaye du Bec ;
2. GUILLAUME, Moine auffi dans l'Abbaye du Bec ;
3. Et EMME, héritière de cette Maifon, qui fuit.

EMME, Dame de BEAUFFOU, après que fon père & fes frères fe furent mis dans la Religion, fut mariée avec un Chevalier nommé *Robert Baniel* ou *Baynel*, qui prit le nom

& les armes de BEAUFFOU. Ils laissèrent pour fils :

HENRI, Seigneur de BEAUFFOU en 1210, qui présida à l'Echiquier de Normandie, tenu à Rouen l'an 1213, & est nommé entre les Chevalier portant Bannières sous le Roi PHILIPPE-AUGUSTE. Il laissa un fils :

RICHARD, Seigneur de BEAUFFOU, Chevalier, vivant l'an 1250, & c'est à lui que les *Mémoires* de cette Maison manquent.

Il y a eu depuis de cette Maison trois sœurs héritières :

1. LUCE, Dame DE BEAUFFOU & de Beuvron, qui épousa 1º *Jean*, Sire *de Tilly*, & 2º *Raould'Harcourt*, Seigneur de Charentonne;

2. ISABEAU DE BEAUFFOU, qui épousa *Robert*, Sire *de Percy;*

3. Et JEANNE DE BEAUFFOU, qui fut femme de *Guillaume*, Sire *de Folligny.*

Dans le compte de *Jean le Mire*, Trésorier des Guerres, de l'an 1339, est nommé JEAN DE BEAUFFOU, Chevalier; & dans celui de *Guillaume d'Anfernet*, aussi Trésorier des Guerres, de l'an 1382, est nommé JEAN DE BEAUFFOU, Chevalier; celui-ci peut avoir été père de ces trois héritières ci-devant, dont l'aînée porta la Terre de *Beauffou* dans la Maison de *Tilly*, qui, par succession de tems tomba dans celle *d'Harcourt*, de la branche de *Beuvron*, où elle est encore à présent.

RAOUL, Iᵉʳ du nom, Seigneur *d'Argouges*, épousa, vers 1308, EMME DE BEAUFFOU.

RICHARD DE BEAUFFOU, du consentement de GUILLAUME, Duc de Normandie, donna à l'Abbaye de Saint-Amand de Rouen le Patronage d'Almerville, & un Fief contenant 100 acres de terres.

Il y a une Chartre de *Jean*, Seigneur d'*Hibernie*, & Comte de Mortain, pour l'Abbaye de Jéripont, donnée à *Licestre*, en laquelle est témoin AMAURY DE BEAUFFOU.

Une autre Charte de *Thibaut Vautier*, Echanson d'*Hibernie*, pour le Monastère d'Arkeld, nomme pour témoins, AIMERY DE BEAUFFOU, *Geoffroy de Stanton*, & autres.

Cette ancienne Maison portoit pour armes : *d'argent, au lion de gueules, l'écu semé de billettes d'or;* quelques-uns les ont blasonnées : *d'argent, au lion de gueules, l'écu semé de billettes de même;* mais c'est de la première façon dans tous les Armoriaux.

* BEAUFORT. C'est une petite Ville en Champagne, qui fut donnée, avec la Terre de Soligny, à *Louis d'Evreux*, Comte d'Etampes, par CHARLES, Dauphin de Viennois, Régent du Royaume, en 1357, Louis XI, par Lettres du mois de Septembre 1477, donna à *Thierry, de Lenoncourt*, IIIᵉ du nom, les Comté, Terres & Seigneurie de Beaufort. Louis XII donna le Comté de Beaufort, en 1507, à GASTON DE FOIX. Ce même Prince, après la mort de GASTON, en donna la jouissance à GERMAINE DE FOIX, Reine d'Aragon, sa sœur. HENRI IV, en 1597, érigea le Comté de Beaufort & la Baronie de Jaucourt en Duché & Pairie, en faveur de *Gabrielle d'Estrées*. Le Duché-Pairie de Beaufort fut le partage de *François de Vendôme*, qui périt au siège de Candie, sans laisser de postérité, le 25 Juin 1669, & cette Pairie fut éteinte.

Charles-Frédéric de Montmorency-Luxembourg, Duc de Luxembourg, acquit la Terre de Beaufort, & obtint, en 1688, l'érection de la Terre de Beaufort en Duché, seulement en faveur de lui & de ses enfans & descendans, tant mâles que femelles, à perpétuité. Louis XIV, par d'autres Lettres du mois d'Octobre 1689, ordonna que le Duché de Beaufort seroit dorénavant appelé *le Duché de Montmorency*. Voyez MONTMORENCY-LUXEMBOURG.

* BEAUFORT. L'ancien nom de ceux de cette Maison étoit ROGER. Leur Seigneurie étoit la Terre de Rosiers, dans le Bas-Limousin, puis celle de Beaufort, en Anjou.

I. PIERRE ROGER, Seigneur de Rosiers, est le premier de cette Maison, dont nous ayons connoissance. Il vivoit en l'an 1300, & laissa :

1. GUILLAUME, qui suit;
2. NICOLAS, Archevêque de Rouen en 1342;
3. Et PEYRONNE, femme de *Pierre*, Seigneur de *la Vigerie*

II. GUILLAUME, Iᵉʳ du nom, épousa *Guillemette de la Monstre*, & en eut :

1. GUILLAUME, qui suit;
2. PIERRE, Moine de la Chaise-Dieu, & puis Pape, sous le nom de CLÉMENT VI, en 1342. Il fut le premier des Papes qui fit apposer sur les Bulles le sceau des armes de sa famille : *Contra morem antecessorum*, dit Albert de Strasbourg. Il mourut en 1352;
3. HUGUES, Moine de Tulle, en Limousin, & ensuite Cardinal;
4. GUILLEMETTE, femme de *Jacques de la Jugie*, père & mère des Cardinaux de ce nom;

5. ALMODIE, mariée à *Jacques de Beffe*, dont *Nicolas de Beffe*, Cardinal;

6. Et BERTRANDE, mariée à *Nicolas de Beffe*.

III. GUILLAUME, II° du nom, Seigneur de Rofiers, de Beaufort, par la donation que lui en fit le Roi PHILIPPE DE VALOIS, à la confidé-ration du Pape CLÉMENT VI, fut marié 1° à *Marie du Chambon*; 2° à *Guérine de Canillac*, fille unique de *Marquis*, Seigneur de Ca-nillac, & d'*Alix de Poitiers*; & 3° en 1366, à *Catherine de la Garde*, de la Maifon d'*Ad-hémar de Monteil*. Du premier lit font iffus:

1. GUILLAUME, qui fuit;
2. PIERRE, qui fut Pape fous le nom de GRÉ-GOIRE XI;
3. NICOLAS, Seigneur d'Hermne & de *Li-meuil*, rapporté ci-après;
4. JEAN, Archevêque de Rouen, puis de Nar-bonne;
5. RAYMOND, fait prifonnier de guerre, près de Lille en Flandres, l'an 1339, *lequel, de-puis qu'il fe fut rendu prifonnier, fut occis par la convoitife de fes belles armes*, dit Froiffard;
6. HÉLIS, mariée 1° à *Guillaume de la Tour*; & 2° à *Aymar de Poitiers*;
7. DAUPHINE, mariée à *Hugues de la Roche*, Maréchal de la Cour de Rome, & Gouver-neur du Comté Venaiffin;
8. MATHE, femme de *Guy de la Tour*;
9. MARGUERITE, femme de *Géraud de Venta-dour*, Seigneur de Donzenac;
10. Et MARIE, mariée 1° à *Guérin*, II° du nom, Seigneur d'Apchier, & 2° à *Raymond de Nogaret*, Seigneur de Cauviffon.

Du fecond lit font nés:

11. MARQUIS, Seigneur de Canillac, auteur de la branche de *Canillac*, rapportée ci-après;
12. Et JEANNE, filleule du Roi JEAN.

Du troifième lit vint:

13. RAYMOND, Vicomte de Valerne, mort fans ligée.

IV. GUILLAUME, III° du nom, Comte de BEAUFORT, Seigneur de Canillac, acheta la Vicomté de Turenne de *Cécile de Comminge*, fœur aînée de fa femme, laquelle étoit mariée à *Jacques d'Aragon*, Comte d'Urgel, fils d'AL-PHONSE IV, Roi d'Aragon. Il époufa *Aliénor de Comminge*, fille de *Bernard*, VI° du nom, Comte de Comminge, & Vicomte de Tu-renne, par la donation que lui en fit *Mar-guerite de Turenne*, fa feconde femme, & de *Mathe de l'Isle-Jourdain*, fa troifième fem-me. Leurs enfans furent:

1. RAYMOND, qui fuit;

Tome II.

2. ALIÉNOR, Comteffe de Beaufort & Vicom-teffe de Turenne, après la mort d'*Antoi-nette de Beaufort*, fa nièce. Elle époufa *Edouard de Beaujeu*, II° du nom, Seigneur de Beaujeu & de Dombes;
3. CÉCILE, mariée à *Louis de Poitiers*, II° du nom, Comte de Valentinois & Diois;
4. MARGUERITE, mariée 1° à *Armand*, V° du nom, Vicomte de *Polignac*; & 2° à *Jean le Vayer*, Seigneur de Coefme;
5. Et JEANNE, morte en 1404, qui avoit époufé, 1° *Raymond de Baux*, en Provence; & 2° *Guy de Chauvigny*, Seigneur de Château-roux, en Berry, & Vicomte de Broffe.

V. RAYMOND DE BEAUFORT fut un perfon-nage fameux. Il époufa, en 1375, *Marie de Boulogne*, fille de *Jean*, I° du nom, Comte d'Auvergne & de Boulogne, & de *Jeanne de Clermont*, Princeffe du Sang Royal de France. Ils n'eurent qu'une fille unique:

ANTOINETTE, qui fut mariée, du vivant de fon père, en 1393, à *Jean le Meingre*, dit *Bou-cicaut*, Maréchal de France, fils de *Jean le Meingre*, I° du nom, dit *Boucicaut*, Ma-réchal de France, & de *Florie de Lignières*. ANTOINETTE DE BEAUFORT mourut fans en-fans en 1416, pendant que le Maréchal de Boucicaut, fon mari, étoit prifonnier en An-gleterre, & fes biens pafférent à *Aliénor de Beaufort*, Dame de Beaujeu, fa tante.

BRANCHE
des Seigneurs DE LIMEUIL.

IV. NICOLAS DE BEAUFORT, fils de GUIL-LAUME II, fut marié 1° avec *Marguerite de Galard*, morte en 1370, fille unique & hé-ritière de *Jean de Galard*, Seigneur de Li-meuil, en Périgord, & de *Philippine de Lau-trec*; 2° en 1396, à *Mathe de Montault*, ap-pelée *Mathe d'Hautefort* ou *de Muffidan*, fille de *Raymond de Montault*, Seigneur de Muffidan & de Blaye, & de *Marguerite d'Al-bret*. Du premier lit vinrent:

1. JEAN, qui fuit;
2. PIERRE, mort jeune;
3. Et MARGUERITE, morte auffi en bas âge.

Du fecond lit font nés:

4. AMANIEU, mort fans avoir été marié;
5. PIERRE, Vicomte de Turenne, rapporté ci-après;
6. Et MARGUERITE, femme de *Bertrand de la Tour*, II° du nom, Seigneur d'Oliergues.

V. JEAN DE BEAUFORT fut déshérité par fon père, pour avoir fuivi le parti des Anglois, & mourut à Avignon, en 1420, fans laiffer d'enfans. Il avoit épousé, du consentement de son père, *Marguerite de Montault*, fille de *Raymond*, Seigneur de Mussidan. Il semble qu'en faveur de ce mariage, Nicolas de Beaufort rendit son affection paternelle à Jean, son fils. Ces faits sont constants; mais de sçavoir ce qu'étoit la femme du père à la femme du fils, c'est ce qu'aucun Généalogiste n'a encore débrouillé, ou du moins nous n'en avons pas de connoissance.

V. Pierre de Beaufort, après la mort de Jean & d'Amanieu, ses frères, qui n'avoient pas laissé d'enfans, se mit en possession de la Vicomté de Turenne, & des autres biens d'*Aliénor*, en vertu de la substitution ouverte à son profit. Ce Pierre devint si éperdument amoureux de *Blanche de Gimel*, fille de *Jean de Gimel*, qu'il l'épousa *sans délibération de ses parens & sans le sçû de son conseil.* Le contrat de mariage est du 8 Juillet 1432. Cette *Blanche de Gimel* étoit parente de Pierre de Beaufort, & ils eurent besoin d'obtenir dispense, quelque tems après leur mariage. Elle étoit sœur de *Jeanne de Gimel*, femme de *Jean de Noailles*; d'une autre, l'aînée de toutes, mariée dans la Maison de *Budes*, & de deux qui furent Religieuses dans l'Abbaye de la Règle, à Limoges. De ce mariage il eut:

1. Anne, Comtesse de Beaufort, & Vicomtesse de Turenne, mariée à *Agnès de la Tour*, IVe du nom, auquel elle porta les biens de sa succession;
2. Et Catherine, femme de *Louis de Ventadour*, fils de *Charles*, Comte de Ventadour.

BRANCHE
des Seigneurs DE CANILLAC.

IV. Marquis de Beaufort, Seigneur de Canillac, Vicomte de la Motte, fils de Guillaume de Beaufort, IIe du nom, & de *Guérine de Canillac*, épousa, l'an 1366, *Catherine*, fille de *Beraud* Ier, Comte de *Clermont*, Dauphin d'Auvergne, & de *Marie de Villemur*. Le Dauphin, son frère, lui constitua en dot 7000 florins d'or, & les rentes qu'il avoit en Auvergne dans les Chatellenies & Mandemens de Langeac, de la Motte & d'Aubusson, qu'il promit lui faire valoir 40 livres par an. De ce mariage naquirent:

1. Marquis de Beaufort, Seigneur de Canillac, qui, d'*Elis de la Voute*, eut:
   Louis, Marquis & Jean, morts jeunes;

2. Louis, qui suit;
3. Beraud, Vicomte de Valerne, en Provence, qui mourut sans laisser de postérité de *Louise de Polignac*, fille de *Louis*, dit *Armand*, & d'*Isabelle de la Tour d'Auvergne;*
4. Marquise, dite DE Canillac, femme de *Germain Guérin*, Seigneur de la Tournoelle;
5. Guérine, femme de *Guillaume*, Vicomte de *Narbonne;*
6. Et Antoinette, femme de *Sébastien*, Seigneur de *Marillac*, fils de *Bertrand de Marillac*, & de *Susanne de Lastic.*

V. Louis de Beaufort, Marquis de Canillac, Comte d'Alest, Vicomte de la Motte & de Valerne, prit pour femme, *Jeanne de Norri*, dont il eut:

1. Marquis de Beaufort, mort avant son père, sans laisser d'enfans de *Jeanne de Chabanois;*
2. & 3. Robert & Charles, morts jeunes;
4. Jean, qui fut d'Eglise;
5. Jacques, qui suit;
6. Isabeau, femme de *Jean*, IIIe du nom, Seigneur de *Montboissier;*
7. Anne, femme de *Godefroy de la Tour*, Seigneur de Montgascon;
8. 9. & 10. Marguerite, Agnès & Jeanne, Religieuses.

Jacques de Beaufort, Marquis de Canillac, Comte d'Alest, Vicomte de la Motte & de Valerne, n'ayant point eu de postérité, & étant resté le seul mâle de la Maison de Beaufort, donna tous ses biens à *Jacques de Montboissier*, son neveu, fils de *Jean*, Seigneur de *Montboissier*, & d'Isabeau de Beaufort, sa sœur, à la charge de porter le nom & les armes de Beaufort. Voyez MONTBOISSIER. Il avoit épousé, en 1425, *Jacqueline de Créquy*.

Les armes: *d'argent, à la bande d'azur, accompagnée de six roses de gueules, mises en orle.*

BEAUFORT, en Dauphiné: *d'azur, à une bande d'or, accompagnée en chef de trois molettes d'éperon de même, 2 & 1, & en pointe d'une tour d'argent maçonnée de sable.*

BEAUFORT: *d'argent, au lion de gueules, semé de billettes de même.*

BEAUFORT: *écartelé, aux 1 & 4 de gueules, semé de fleurs-de-lys d'or; aux 2*

& 3 *d'argent, à une aigle éployée & à deux têtes, de sable, membrée & becquée d'or.*

BEAUFORT, en Savoie: *de gueules, au lion d'argent.*

BEAUFORT: *d'azur, à trois écuffons d'argent, 2 & 1.*

BEAUFORT: *d'or, à trois fafces de gueules.*

BEAUFORT, en Bourgogne: *de gueules, à trois écuffons d'hermines, pofés 2 & 1.*

BEAUFORT, en Languedoc: *écartelé, aux 1 & 4 d'azur, au lion d'argent; aux 2 & 3 de gueules, au lévrier auffi d'argent.*

BEAUFORT: *d'or, à la bande de gueules, chargée de deux filets d'or.*

BEAUFORT (DE), Seigneur de Saint-André: *de finople, à deux lévriers courans d'argent, l'un fur l'autre, accolés d'or.*

BEAUFORT, en Bretagne: *de gueules, à trois écus d'hermines, pofés 2 & 1.*

BEAUFORT, en Champagne: *d'argent, à trois bandes de gueules.*

BEAUFORT, en Champagne: *d'azur, au Fort d'argent, bâti dans des ondes de même.*

BEAUFORT DE POTHEMONT, en Champagne. GUILLAUME DE BEAUFORT, dit *Moulon*, Ecuyer de *Jean de Série de Châteauvilain*, étoit marié, en 1402, à *Engothe de Chamelitte*, & ledit *Jean de Série de Châteauvilain* leur donna un bichet de froment par chaque femaine, à prendre fur la mouture du moulin de Pont-la-Ville, & tout le bois pour leur chauffage, à prendre dans tel endroit qu'il leur plaira dans fes forêts, en récompenfe des bons & agréables fervices qu'ils lui avoient rendus. De ce mariage naquit:

ALEXANDRE DE BEAUFORT, Ecuyer & premier Gentilhomme de la Vénerie du Roi, Gouverneur de Pommerol, qui eut de *Catherine de Beleftat*:

LOUIS DE BEAUFORT, Ecuyer, Seigneur de Buffier & de Pont-la-Ville en partie, Gentilhomme de la Vénerie du Roi, marié, par contrat du 18 Mars 1486, à *Marguerite de Serry*, fille de *Charles*, Ecuyer, Sieur de Sou, & de *Jeanne d'Arfouck*, dont eft forti:

NICOLAS DE BEAUFORT, Ecuyer, Seigneur de la Marche, d'Orge, & de Pont-la-Ville en par-

tie, homme d'armes fous la charge du Sieur, Comte d'Aumale. Il s'allia, par contrat du 2 Septembre 1537 à *Catherine de Vaudremont*, Dame de Crefpy en partie, veuve de *Jean Dupont*, Ecuyer. De ce mariage naquit:

HECTOR DE BEAUFORT, Ecuyer, Seigneur de la Marche, d'Orge, & de Pont-la-Ville en partie, marié, par contrat du 2 Mai 1585, à *Jeanne de Robins*, dont il eut:

CHRISTOPHE DE BEAUFORT, Ecuyer, Seigneur de Blegnicourt, Capitaine au Régiment d'Aumont, qui s'allia, par contrat de mariage, paffé le 1er Juin 1649, à *Pérette Berbier-du-Metz*, qui eft de la même famille que celle de M. le Préfident *du Metz*, dont:

CHRISTOPHE DE BEAUFORT, IIe du nom, Seigneur de Pothemont, qui fe maria, par contrat du 12 Juillet 1684, avec *Bonne de Tance*, fille de *Guy de Tance*, Ecuyer, Seigneur de Frampas & d'Argentolle en partie, & de *Claude de Cahier*, dont:

JEAN DE BEAUFORT, Ecuyer, Seigneur de Pothemont & de Frampas en partie, Lieutenant au Régiment de Tavannes, qui époufa, par contrat du 22 Septembre 1709, *Edmée-Madeleine de Montangon*, fille *d'Honoré de Montangon*, Ecuyer, & *d'Edmée de la Rue*, dont:

JEAN-BAPTISTE-JACQUES DE BEAUFORT, Ecuyer, Seigneur de Pothemont, de Frampas en partie & de Crefpy, Petit-Mefgny, Chaumefgny, &c., qui a époufé, par contrat paffé le 4 Octobre 1750, *Louife-Charlotte-Edmée de Serpe Defcordal*, fille de *Louis-François de Serpe*, Ecuyer, Seigneur Defcordal, de Matignicourt, de Blumeré & Humbercin, & de *Charlotte de Brifeux-de-Montbeillard*, dont:

FRANÇOISE-CLAUDINETTE DE BEAUFORT, née le 13 Juin 1755;

Et JEAN-BAPTISTE-CHARLES-PHILIPPE DE BEAUFORT, né le 8 Décembre 1756.

Les armes: *de fable à la bande d'argent chargée d'un lion de gueules, accompagnée de deux étoiles d'argent.*

Cette famille a été maintenue dans fa nobleffe par Arrêt du Confeil d'Etat du Roi, en date du 13 Juin 1672.

BEAUFORT, à Provins en Brie. N... DE BEAUFORT, Chevalier, Seigneur de la Grandcourt, ancien Moufquetaire dans la feconde compagnie, marié, le 25 Octobre 1746, à *Ca-*

therine-Antoinette Gouault, de la Province de Champagne, morte au mois d'Octobre 1762. De ce mariage font nés :

1. FRANÇOIS-ETIENNE, né le 9 Octobre 1750, Moufquetaire du Roi le 11 Octobre 1765 ;
2. Et MARIE-ANTOINETTE, née le 31 Mai 1748, mariée, le 9 Décembre 1767, à *Charles-Louis Barentin,* Marquis de Montchal, Seigneur de Noyant-fur-Seine, Capitaine de Cavalerie dans le Régiment Royal.

Les armes : *d'azur, à deux levrettes d'or, lancées, accompagnées d'une étoile d'or & d'un croiffant d'argent.*

BEAUFRANCHET. JEAN DE BEAUFRANCHET, Ecuyer, Seigneur dudit lieu, époufa, le 23 Janvier 1553, *Louife de Gilbertés,* fille de *Guillaume,* Chevalier, l'un des 100 Gentilshommes de la Maifon du Roi, & Ecuyer de la Reine CATHERINE DE MÉDICIS.

GILBERT-ANTOINE DE BEAUFRANCHET, Ecuyer, fon arrière-petit-fils, Seigneur d'Ayat, dans le Diocèfe de Clermont en Auvergne, a eu de *Marie de Servière :*

AMABLE DE BEAUFRANCHET, Ecuyer, Seigneur de Gramont & d'Ayat, né le 13 Août 1687, qui fit hommage de fa Terre & Seigneurie d'Ayat, mouvante du Roi à caufe de fon Duché d'Auvergne, au Bureau des Finances & du Domaine à Riom, le 28 Mars 1724. Il époufa, le 1er Juin 1718, *Françoise-Antoinette de Sirmont,* de laquelle il eut entr'autres enfans :

AMABLE-FRANÇOISE-CATHERINE DE BEAUFRANCHET-D'AYAT, née le 18 Juillet 1723, & reçue à Saint-Cyr le 11 Septembre 1734, fur fes preuves de nobleffe. Voyez l'*Armorial de France,* reg. I, part. I, pag. 54.

Les armes : *de fable, à un chevron d'or, accompagné de trois étoiles d'argent, pofées deux en chef & une à la pointe de l'écu.*

BEAUGAY, en Anjou : *de gueules, à la croix ancrée d'or.*

BEAUGENDRE, Seigneur des Effarts, de Cricqueville & d'Eftaville, en Normandie, Généralité de Caen : *de gueules, au chevron d'argent, accompagné de trois coquilles d'or, deux en chef & une en pointe.*

BEAUGIE : *de gueules, au lion d'hermines, couronné d'or.*

ϙ BEAUHARNAIS (& quelquefois *Beau-*

harnoys, & de *Beauharnoys,* fuivant les titres), dans l'Orléanois & à Paris , famille diftinguée dans l'ordre de la Nobleffe par fes anciens fervices, foit dans le Militaire, foit dans la Magiftrature. Elle remonte fa filiation à :

I. GUILLAUME BEAUHARNAIS, Ier du nom, Seigneur de Miramion & de la Chauffée, qui époufa, le 20 Janvier 1390, *Marguerite de Bourges,* dont :

1. JEAN, l'un des témoins au procès fait pour la juftification de la Pucelle d'Orléans, qui époufa, en 1423, *Anne de Loynes,* dont il eut :

     N... BEAUHARNAIS, Confeiller du Roi, Maître des Requêtes ordinaire de fon Hôtel, qui fut commis à l'adminiftration du Duché d'Orléans, pendant que le Duc, depuis Roi, fous le nom de LOUIS XII, étoit détenu prifonnier à Bourges. Il mourut fans enfans.

2. GUILLAUME, qui fuit ;
3. Et JEANNE DE BEAUHARNAIS, mariée avec *Jean-Hilaire,* iffu d'une famille ancienne & diftinguée de la ville d'Orléans.

II. GUILLAUME BEAUHARNAIS, IIe du nom, Seigneur de Miramion & de la Chauffée, époufa, le 15 Novembre 1425, *Jacquette le Maire,* dont il eut :

1. & 2. JACQUES ET PIERRE, morts fans alliance ;
3. JEAN, qui fuit ;
4. Et MARION BEAUHARNAIS, veuve, en 1493, de *Pierre de Payeres,* dit *Moireau.*

III. JEAN BEAUHARNAIS, Seigneur de Miramion & de la Chauffée, époufa, par contrat du 7 février 1472, *Jeanne de Boyleve,* dont il eut :

IV. GUILLAUME BEAUHARNAIS, IIIe du nom, Seigneur de Miramion & de la Chauffée, de la Grillière & de Villechauve, lequel donna fon aveu à la Chambre des Comptes de Paris en 1504, des Terres de Miramion & de la Chauffée. Il avoit époufé, le 20 Septembre 1499, *Marie le Vaffor,* fille d'*Aignan,* & de *Jeanne Compain.* Leurs enfans furent :

1. PIERRE, Chanoine de l'Eglife de Saint-Aignan d'Orléans, & Prieur de Saint-Barthélemy de Sémoy ;
2. GUILLAUME, qui fuit ;
3. AIGNAN, auffi Chanoine de l'Eglife de Saint-Aignan d'Orléans ;
4. JEANNE, mariée, le 13 Novembre 1517, à *François de Contes,* dont poftérité ;

5. MARIE, mariée, le 19 Juillet 1521, à *Nicolas Buaftier;*
6. CLAUDINE, mariée le 29 Juin, *aliàs* le 19 Août 1531, à *Jacques de Contes,* Seigneur de Briou & de Villechauve;
7. Et ANNE BEAUHARNAIS, Religieufe de l'Ordre de Fontevrault au Couvent de la Madeleine-lès-Orléans.

V. GUILLAUME BEAUHARNAIS, IV⁰ du nom, Seigneur de Miramion, de la Chauffée, d'Outreville, de la Grillière, de Longuefve, de Villechauve, de Beaumont, de Sédenay, &c., vivoit encore le 5 Avril 1564. Il avoit époufé, le 11 Février 1531, *Jeanne de Saint-Mefmin,* Dame de Sédenay, fille de *François,* & de *Marie le Clerc.* De ce mariage eft iffu:

VI. FRANÇOIS BEAUHARNAIS, Iᵉʳ du nom, Ecuyer, Seigneur de Miramion, de la Chauffée, de Sédenay, d'Outreville, de la Grillière, de Longuefve & de Beaumont, compris en l'état de la nobleffe du Châtelet de la ville d'Orléans, dans le procès-verbal fait le 13 Avril 1583, pour la rédaction de la coutume; il mourut avant le 8 Mars 1588. Il avoit époufé, le 27 Avril 1561, *Madeleine Bourdineau,* qui vivoit encore le 9 Juin 1593, & mourut avant le 15 Mars 1599. Elle étoit fille de *Jacques,* Seigneur de Villemblin ou Villembly & de Buffy, & d'*Anne de Troyes.* Leurs enfans furent:

1. CHARLES, Seigneur de Villechauve, mort au fervice du Roi avant le 25 Mai 1589, fans laiffer de poftérité;
2. GUILLAUME, Ecuyer, Seigneur d'Outreville, de la Chauffée, de la Boiffière & de Sédenay, né vers 1567, qui partagea avec fa mère & fes frères & fœurs, le 25 Mai 1589, la fucceffion de leur père. Il embraffa d'abord la profeffion des armes, & fe fit pourvoir depuis d'une charge de Préfident, Tréforier-Général de France au Bureau des Finances d'Orléans; fut nommé, le 18 Janvier 1620, Confeiller du Roi en fes Confeils d'Etat & Privé, à caufe des fervices qu'il avoit rendus à Sa Majefté; prêta ferment pour cette charge le 24 Février 1621, entre les mains du Chancelier de Sillery; fut confirmé dans cette dignité le 15 Juin 1635; fit fon teftament le 10 Février 1642, & depuis trois codicilles, le premier du 12 Février 1642, & les autres des 29 Mai 1646 & 10 Novembre 1653, & mourut le 27 Novembre 1653. Il avoit époufé, le 25 Juillet 1699, *Marie Rouffeau,* fille de *Jacques,* Confeiller du Roi, Tréforier-Général de fa Maifon, & de *Jeanne Allego.* Ils n'eu-

rent pas d'enfans, mais GUILLAUME BEAUHARNAIS a eu, de *Françoife Pothier,* fon amie, un fils naturel:

GUILLAUME BEAUHARNAIS, Seigneur de la Bretefche, légitimé au mois de Mai 1641, & qui fut légataire de fon père en 1642.

3. FRANÇOIS, qui fuit;
4. JACQUES, Seigneur de Sédenay, Confeiller du Roi, Contrôleur-Général de l'extraordinaire des Guerres & de la Cavalerie-Légère, mort fans alliance;
5. AIGNAN, Seigneur de Miramion & de la Chouarde, *aliàs* de la Choüarde, Confeiller d'Etat & Contrôleur-Général de l'extraordinaire des Guerres & de la Cavalerie-Légère, le 27 Février 1628, mort à Paris au mois de Mai 1652. Il avoit époufé, le 13 Septembre 1618, *Marguerite de Choify,* fille de *Jean de Choify,* Seigneur de Baleroy, Confeiller d'Etat, & de *Madeleine le Charron.* De ce mariage naquirent:

JEAN-JACQUES DE BEAUHARNAIS, qualifié *Chevalier,* Seigneur de Miramion, Confeiller au Parlement de Paris, reçu en 1644, mort à Paris, au mois de Novembre 1645. Il avoit époufé, le 27 Avril 1645, *Marie Bonneau,* morte le 23 Mars 1696, âgée de 66 ans, fille de *Jacques,* Seigneur de Rubelles, Confeilleur-Secrétaire du Roi, & de *Marie d'Ivry.* De ce mariage vint:

1. MARIE-MARGUERITE DE BEAUHARNAIS, morte à Paris le 6 Novembre 1725, âgée de 80 ans. Elle avoit époufé, le 22 Juin 1660, *Guillaume de Nefmond,* qualifié *Chevalier,* Seigneur de Saint-Dizan, Confeiller du Roi en fes Confeils, Préfident à Mortier au Parlement de Paris, mort fans poftérité le 19 Mars 1693;
2. Et MADELEINE DE BEAUHARNAIS, Religieufe au Couvent de la Vifitation de Saint-Denis en France.

6. MARIE DE BEAUHARNAIS, morte de la pefte, le 20 Juin 1597. Elle avoit époufé, par contrat du 4 Juin 1597, & célébration le 14 Juin fuivant, *André Charreton,* Seigneur de la Douze, Confeiller au Parlement de Paris;
7. MARGUERITE, morte auffi de la pefte le 20 Juin 1597;
8. Et ANNE DE BEAUHARNAIS, morte à Paris au mois de Janvier 1653. Elle avoit époufé, le 11 Juin 1605, *Paul Phélypeaux,* Chevalier, Seigneur de Pontchartrain, mort le 21 Octobre 1621.

VII. François de Beauharnais, II° du nom, Seigneur de la Grillière & de Ville-chauve, fut fucceffivement Confeiller-Magif-trat au Bailliage & Siège Préfidial d'Orléans, & depuis premier Préfident & Lieutenant-Général audit Bailliage en 1598, Maître des Requêtes ordinaire de la Reine le 2 Janvier 1610, & enfin Confeiller du Roi en fes Con-feils d'Etat, Privé & Finances, le 20 Septem-bre 1616. Sa Majefté l'ayant confirmé dans cette dignité le 1ᵉʳ Juillet 1635, en confidé-ration des fervices qu'il lui avoit rendus de-puis 38 ans en ladite qualité de Préfident au Préfidial & Lieutenant-Général au Bailliage d'Orléans, il en prêta le ferment le 9 Juillet 1635, & jouiffoit en cette qualité de 2000 li-vres de gages. Il fut Député à l'affemblée des Etats tenue à Paris au mois d'Octobre 1614, & mourut avant le 20 Octobre 1651. Il avoit époufé, le 17 Février 1599, *Anne Brachet*, Dame de la Boifche, morte avant le 27 Fé-vrier 1628, fille d'*Antoine,* Ecuyer, Seigneur de Marolles & de la Boifche, & de *Jeanne Ja-met*. Leurs enfans furent:

1. François de Beauharnais, III° du nom, Seigneur de la Grillière & de Villechauve, Confeiller d'Etat & du Confeil de Gafton, Duc d'Orléans. Il étoit auffi Confeiller de la Reine mère du Roi, & Maître des Re-quêtes ordinaire de fon Hôtel, fuivant un acte du 27 Février 1628; fut nommé en 1635 Préfident & Lieutenant-Général au Bailliage & Siège Préfidial d'Orléans; par-tagea, le 20 Octobre 1651, les fucceffions de fes père & mère, & de *Jeanne Jamet* fon ayeule maternelle, veuve d'*Antoine Brachet*, avec Jean de Beauharnais, fon frère, Anne & Madeleine de Beauharnais, fes fœurs, & fut confidéré de Gafton, Duc d'Orléans, comme il paroît par une Lettre que ce Prince écrivit le 31 Décem-bre 1651, aux Officiers-Généraux & autres qui paffoient aux environs des métairies & fermes fitués dans l'étendue du Duché d'Orléans appartenant audit Seigneur de Villechauve. Cette lettre fe trouve inférée tout au long dans l'*Armorial de France*, & commence ainfi: Meffieurs, *l'eftime que je fais du Sieur de Villechauve de Beau-harnais*, &c., *figné*, Gafton. Ce Prince lui fit encore, le 8 Avril 1654, don du profit de rachat qui lui étoit dû par la fucceffion du feu Sieur d'Outreville-Beauharnais, de la Maifon, Terre & Jardin de la Chauffée fis au faubourg d'Orléans, & qui étoit mouvant de fon Châtelet d'Orléans, *voulant lui donner*

dit-il, *dans cette occafion des marques de fa bienveillance & de l'eftime qu'il faifoit de fa perfonne.* Il partagea, les 13 Juin & 3 Juillet 1654, la fucceffion de Guillaume de Beauharnais, fon oncle, Seigneur d'Ou-treville, Confeiller d'Etat, &c., avec fes frères & fœurs & autres co-héritiers. Il époufa, 1° le 27 Février 1628, *Anne de Mareau*, morte fans enfans, fille d'*Hector*, Ecuyer, Seigneur de Villerégis & de Chil-ly, Gentilhomme ordinaire de la Maifon du Roi, & de *Geneviève Lamirault; &* 2° le 10 Février 1630, *Charlotte Bugy*, fille unique de *Jean*, Seigneur de Moulinet, & de *Charlotte Colas*. Il eut du fecond lit:

> François de Beauharnais, Seigneur de la Grillière, mort fans alliance;
> Charlotte, morte auffi fans avoir été ma-riée;
> Et Marie-Anne, mariée, le 16 Septem-bre 1683, à *Jean Phélypeaux*, fon cou-fin, Chevalier., Comte de Montlhery, Seigneur d'Outreville, Confeiller d'Etat & Intendant de Paris.

2. Jacques de Beauharnais, qui, fous le nom du *Sieur de la Grillière-Beauharnais*, fut fait Directeur des Fortifications de Lérida en Catalogne, le 22 Septembre 1642, & tué au fiège de Cafal;

3. Guillaume, qui fervit le Roi dans le Corps de la Marine, & fut fait Capitaine d'un na-vire de la flotte commandée par l'Arche-vêque de Bordeaux en 1640;

4. Jean, qui fuit;

5. Michel, Prêtre, Docteur de Sorbonne & Aumônier de Gafton, Duc d'Orléans;

6. Anne, mariée, par contrat du 27 Février 1628, à *Nicolas Thoynard*, depuis Con-feiller du Roi & Préfident au Siège Préfi-dial d'Orléans. Ils vivoient encore enfem-ble le 20 Octobre 1651;

7. Et Madeleine de Beauharnais, qui fonda à perpétuité 30 places de pauvres entrete-nus dans l'Hôpital d'Orléans, à la nomi-nation de l'aîné de la famille de Beauhar-nais, & tefta le 14 Novembre 1682. Elle avoit époufé, le 7 Juillet 1641, *Claude le Gloux*, Ecuyer, Confeiller du Roi, Tréfo-rier de France, & Général de fes Finances en la Généralité de Soiffons, mort en 1651, fans enfans.

VIII. Jean de Beauharnais, Chevalier, Seigneur de la Boifche, de Villechauve, de Beaumont & de la Chauffée, fut d'abord Se-crétaire de la Chambre du Roi Louis XIII, Gentilhomme ordinaire de fa Chambre & Gentilhomme à la fuite de Gafton, Duc d'Or-léans; fervit auffi en Catalogne; fut fait Confeiller, Maître-d'Hôtel ordinaire du Roi, le 4 Septembre 1652; & ayant été nommé Chevalier de l'Ordre de Saint-Michel le 30 Avril 1653, il en reçut le collier le 15 Juin fuivant, des mains du Maréchal d'Eftrées, Chevalier des Ordres, que le Roi avoit commis à cet effet. Il mourut en fa Maifon de la Chauffée, au mois d'Avril 1661, & fut enterré le 18 de ce mois dans le cimetière de l'Eglife de Saint-Laurent des Orgeries - lès - Orléans. Il avoit époufé, par contrat du 12 Avril 1636, *Marie Mallet*, fille de *Claude*, Ecuyer, Sieur de Mérifau, & de *Marie de Varanne*, dont il eut:

1. François, qui fuit;
2. Elisabeth, morte fans enfans. Elle avoit époufé, *Charles de Drouin*, fils d'*Henri*, Marquis de Bouville, Gouverneur de Pithiviers;
3. Et Agnès de Beauharnais, mariée, par contrat du 16 Juillet 1673, à *Charles Egrot*, Seigneur d'Hurdy, &c., Confeiller du Roi, Magiftrat au Bailliage & fiège Préfidial d'Orléans.

IX. François de Beauharnais, qualifié *Chevalier*, Seigneur de la Boifche, de la Chauffée, de Beaumont, de Beauville, &c., fervit avec diftinction lors de la convocation de la nobleffe du Royaume, & reçut quittance le 15 Novembre 1676 de la fomme de 100 livres qu'il avoit payée pour être déchargé du fervice perfonnel qu'il devoit au ban & arrière-ban de la Généralité d'Orléans comme étant du Corps de la Nobleffe. Il époufa, par contrat du 14 Septembre 1664, *Marguerite-Françoife Pyvart de Chaftullé*, qui vivoit encore le 26 Juin 1700, fille de *Jacques Pyvart*, Confeiller du Roi, Maitre ordinaire en fa Chambre des Comptes de Blois, & de *Catherine Thierry*. De ce mariage naquirent 14 enfans, entr'autres:

1. Jacques de Beauharnais de la Boische, nommé Lieutenant dans le Régiment du Maine le 12 Avril 1687, Capitaine d'Infanterie dans le même Régiment par commiffion du 7 Juin 1688, qui fut tué au fiège de Mayence en 1688, fans avoir été marié;
2. François, qualifié *Chevalier*, Baron de Beauville, Seigneur de la Chauffée, de Beaumont, &c., Confeiller du Roi en fes Confeils, Intendant Général de fes Armées navales, & qualifié auffi *Haut & Puiffant Seigneur*, dans les actes qui le concernent. Il fut fucceffivement Commiffaire de la Marine, Commiffaire-Général des Armées navales, Intendant de Juftice, Police & Fi-

nances des pays de la Nouvelle-France Acadie, Isles de Terre - Neuve & autres pays de la France Septentrionale, le 1er Avril 1702; Intendant Général de la Marine en 1704; Intendant de l'Armée navale du Roi, commandée par le Comte de Touloufe le 1er Janvier 1706. Il obtint, le 2 Avril 1707, un Brevet par lequel le Roi voulant favorifer le deffein qu'il avoit de former un établiffement à la côte d'Acadie, au lieu appelé *le Port Maltois*, qui ne feroit pas moins avantageux à ceux de fes fujets qui voudroient aller s'y établir qu'à ceux qui viendroient y faire la pêche, lui fit don dudit lieu de *Port Maltois*, la rivière comprife, de quatre lieues de front fur deux de profondeur, tirant du côté de la Heve, à l'eft - quart - nord - eft, avec les Isles & Islettes adjacentes, pour en jouir par lui, fes héritiers ou ayant caufe, à perpétuité, comme de leur propre, à titre de *Fief & Seigneurie*, haute, moyenne, & baffe Juftice, droit de chaffe, pêche & traite avec les fauvages, & autres droits feigneuriaux, à la charge de porter foi & hommage au Château de Saint-Louis de Québec; & Sa Majefté érigea en fa faveur ladite Terre & Seigneurie de *Port Maltois* en Baronie fous le nom de *Beauville*, par Lettres-Patentes du 25 Juin 1707, duement regiftrées, *en confidération de fes fervices* & de ceux de fa famille. François de Beauharnais fut auffi Intendant de la Marine, ayant infpection générale fur les claffes des Officiers-Mariniers & Matelots du Royaume le 1er..... 1710; Intendant de la Marine à Rochefort le 24 Mars 1710; Intendant de Juftice, Police & Finances de la Généralité de la Rochelle le 30 Mars 1710, & commiffaire départi pour l'exécution des ordres du Roi dans le pays d'Aunis & Isles adjacentes, & dans les provinces de Saintonge & d'Angoumois; Intendant des Armées navales dans la mer Océane, & enfin Intendant Général des Armées navales le 1er Avril 1739. Il mourut le 8 Octobre 1746, après 60 ans de fervices, âgé de 81 ans. Il avoit époufé *Anne des Grés*, morte fans enfans le 24 Septembre 1731, âgée de 63 ans;
3. Jean - François, Chevalier, Seigneur de Moulon, Chevalier de Saint - Louis, qui étoit Lieutenant des Vaiffeaux du Roi au mois de Juillet 1707. Il avoit époufé, par contrat du 26 Juin 1700, *Marie-Madeleine de Penillon*, Dame de *Moulon*, qui lui porta en dot cette Terre. Elle étoit fille de *Nicolas de Penillon*, Ecuyer, Seigneur de Mondreville, de Courbaffon & de Moulon,

Seigneur & Patron d'Ouzouer-des-Champs, & de *Jacqueline des Prés-de-Mondreville-de-Moulon*. De ce mariage font iſſues:

1. MARIE - MADELEINE DE BEAUHARNAIS, mariée, à *Georges-François de Ravault*, qualifié Chevalier, Seigneur de Mouſſeaux;
2. MARGUERITE - FRANÇOISE DE BEAUHARNAIS, Religieuſe au Couvent de Saint-Dominique-lès-Montargis;
3. Et ANNE DE BEAUHARNAIS DE MOULON, mariée, par contrat du 8 Mai 1741, à *Guillaume Bouvier*, Chevalier, Marquis de Cépoy.

4. CHARLES DE BEAUHARNAIS DE LA BOISCHE, appelé d'abord *le Chevalier*, enſuite le *Marquis de Beauharnais*, qualifié *haut & puiſſant Seigneur*, dans les actes qui le concernent. Il fut d'abord admis dans la compagnie des Gentilshommes-Gardes de la Marine, ſucceſſivement Enſeigne le 1er Janvier 1692, puis Lieutenant des Vaiſſeaux le 1er Janvier 1696, Capitaine d'une compagnie franche d'Infanterie de la Marine le 18 Janvier 1699, Capitaine de frégates le 9 Mai 1707, Capitaine de Vaiſſeaux le 23 Avril 1708, Chevalier de Saint-Louis, Gouverneur particulier des ville & château de-Québec, Gouverneur & Lieutenant-Général pour le Roi au pays de la Nouvelle-France & autres pays de la France Septentrionale, dans l'Amérique, le 11 Janvier 1726, Commandeur ſurnuméraire de l'Ordre Militaire de Saint-Louis le 22 Mars 1732, avec permiſſion du Roi, datée du même jour, pour en porter les honneurs, en attendant ſa réception. Le Comte de Maurepas, alors Miniſtre de la Marine, lui écrivit, au ſujet de ce titre de Commandeur qu'il lui obtint du Roi, une lettre qui commence en ces termes: *Vous ne devez pas douter* (dit-il), *du plaiſir que je me ſuis fait de vous procurer une grâce que vous déſiriez & que vous aviez méritée*, &c., & ſe trouve en partie inſérée dans l'*Armorial de France*. CHARLES DE BEAUHARNAIS fut Chef d'Eſcadre des Armées navales le 1er Mai 1741; & enfin Lieutenant-Général deſdites Armées navales le 1er Janvier 1748. Il parvint à tous ces grades par ſes ſervices ſignalés, & donna des marques de la plus grande valeur dans toutes les occaſions qui ſe préſentèrent. Il mourut le 12 Juin 1749, après 63 ans de ſervice. Il avoit épouſé, le 6 Août 1716, *Renée Pays*, morte ſans enfans, le 14 Août 1744, veuve 1º de N.... *Galichon*, 2º de *Pierre Hardouineau*, Ecuyer, Seigneur de Laudianière. Elle étoit ſœur de *Louis Pays*, Sieur de Bourjolly;

5. CLAUDE, qui ſuit;
6. GUILLAUME DE BEAUHARNAIS DE BEAUVILLE, Chevalier, qui ſervit 40 ans dans le Corps de la Marine, fut ſucceſſivement l'un des Gentilshommes-Gardes de la Marine en 1697, Lieutenant d'Infanterie au Canada en 1702, Capitaine d'une Compagnie du détachement de la Marine audit pays le 1er Juin 1704, bleſſé d'un coup de fuſil au bras, dans un combat naval où il ſe trouva en 1705, Enſeigne de Vaiſſeaux le 1er Novembre 1705, Aide-Major des Armées navales & du port de Rochefort, & Capitaine d'une Compagnie-Franche d'Infanterie de la Marine le 20 Avril 1711, Lieutenant de Vaiſſeaux en 1711, Chevalier de Saint-Louis le 23 Décembre 1721, reçu le 20 Janvier 1724, & enfin Capitaine de Vaiſſeaux le 10 Mars 1734. Il ne ceſſa de donner des preuves de ſa valeur dans toutes les occaſions qui ſe préſentèrent, & mourut au Petit-Goave, Isle de Saint-Domingue, en 1741, ſans avoir été marié;
6. JEANNE-ELISABETH DE BEAUHARNAIS, mariée à *Michel Bégon*, Chevalier, Seigneur de la Picardière, &c.;
7. ANNE DE BEAUHARNAIS, mariée, le 26 Juin 1700, à *Pierre-François le Juge*, Chevalier, Seigneur de Loigny, de Gourry, de Bagneaux, de Bazoches, &c.;
8. Et CATHERINE-FRANÇOISE DE BEAUHARNAIS, qui aſſiſta, le 26 Juin 1700, au contrat de mariage de JEAN-FRANÇOIS DE BEAUHARNAIS, ſon frère, Seigneur de Moulon.

X. CLAUDE DE BEAUHARNAIS DE BEAUMONT, Chevalier, Seigneur de Beaumont & de Villechauve, fut ſucceſſivement l'un des Gentilshommes-Gardes de la Marine, Enſeigne, puis Lieutenant des Vaiſſeaux, Capitaine d'une Compagnie Franche d'Infanterie de la Marine le 12 Mai 1707, Capitaine de Frégates le 25 Novembre 1712, nommé Chevalier de Saint-Louis le 28 Juin 1718, & reçu le 10 Juillet ſuivant, par le Roi en perſonne, étant à Paris; & enfin Capitaine des Vaiſſeaux le 17 Mars 1727. Il obtint encore du Roi, le 1er Février 1736, une penſion de 1000 liv., & mourut au mois de Janvier 1738, après avoir ſervi 38 ans dans le Corps de la Marine. Il avoit épouſé, par contrat du 11 Mai 1713, *Renée Hardouineau*, fille de *Pierre*, Ecuyer, Seigneur de Laudianière, de Laoul, de la Pivauterie, &c., Conſeiller du Roi, Receveur-Général des domaines & bois de la Généralité de la Rochelle, & de *Renée Pays*, remariée à *Charles*, Marquis de BEAUHARNAIS. Il a eu:

François, qui fuit;
Et Claude, rapporté après fon frère.

XI. François de Beauharnais, Chevalier, Marquis de la *Ferté-Beauharnais*, ci-devant de la *Ferté-Aurain*, Baron de Beauville, Seigneur de Villechauve, de Montvoy, &c., qualifié *haut & puiſſant Seigneur* dans les actes qui le concernent, naquit à la Rochelle le 8 Février 1714. Il a été fuccceſſivement l'un des Gentilshommes-Gardes de la Marine en 1729, Enſeigne en 1733, puis Lieutenant des Vaiſſeaux du Roi en 1741, Chevalier de Saint-Louis en 1749, Capitaine des Vaiſſeaux en 1751, Major des Armées navales en 1754, Gouverneur & Lieutenant-Général des Isles de la Martinique, la Guadeloupe, Marie-Galande, Saint-Martin, Saint-Barthélemy, la Déſirade, la Dominique, Sainte-Lucie, la Grenade, les Grenadins, Tabago, Saint-Vincent, Cayenne avec ſes dépendances & autres Isles du vent de l'Amérique, par proviſions du 1er Novembre 1756; & nommé enfin Chef d'Eſcadre des Armées navales en 1764. Il a obtenu du Roi, au mois de Juillet 1764, des Lettres-Patentes duement regiſtrées, portant érection de la Châtellenie, Terre & Seigneurie de la *Ferté-Aurain* en Marquiſat, ſous le nom de la *Ferté-Beauharnais*, en conſidération des ſervices de ſa famille & de ceux qu'il avoit rendus à Sa Majeſté depuis plus de 35 ans, tant dans le Corps de la Marine, qu'en qualité de Gouverneur-Général de la Martinique, dont il avoit chaſſé, dans la dernière guerre, & avant ſon retour en France, les Anglois qui avoient débarqué dans cette Isle pour s'en emparer. Il épouſa, par contrat du 6 Septembre 1751 (célébration le 13 du même mois), *Marie-Anne-Henriette Pyvart de Chaſtullé*, ſa couſine germaine, morte le 5 Octobre 1767, fille de *François*, Chevalier, Seigneur de *Chaſtullé*, &c., & de *Jeanne Hardouineau*. Il a eu:

1. François, mort en bas âge;
2. Autre François, né à la Rochelle, le 12 Août 1756;
3. Et Alexandre-François-Marie de Beauharnais, né à la Martinique le 28 Mai 1760.

XI. Claude de Beauharnais, Chevalier, Comte des Roches-Baritaud, Seigneur de la Chauſſée, de la Boufferie, de la Cour, &c., né à Rochefort le 16 Janvier 1717, qualifié *Haut & Puiſſant Seigneur* dans les actes qui le concernent, eſt entré au ſervice vers 1733, en

qualité de l'un des Gentilshommes-Gardes de la Marine, & eſt parvenu ſucceſſivement aux grades d'Enſeigne & de Lieutenant de Vaiſſeaux & de l'Artillerie de la Marine; a auſſi été pendant quatre ans Commandant de l'Artillerie au Canada, fait Capitaine de Galiote d'Artillerie & de Bombardiers du Roi, tant dans ſes ports qu'à la ſuite de ſes Armées navales le 15 Novembre 1754, Chevalier de Saint-Louis & Capitaine des Vaiſſeaux le 15 Mai 1756. Il a obtenu du Roi, au mois de Juin 1759, des Lettres-Patentes duement regiſtrées, portant érection de la Châtellenie, Terre & Seigneurie des *Roches-Baritaud* en Comté, en conſidération des ſervices de ſes ancêtres & de ceux qu'il avoit rendus à Sa Majeſté en qualité de Commandant de ſes Vaiſſeaux, & en dernier lieu de *la Bellone*, avec laquelle il avoit eſſuyé un combat de cinq heures, des plus meurtriers, contre deux Vaiſſeaux Anglois, où il venoit de donner des marques de ſa valeur. Il a épouſé, par contrat du 1er Mars 1753, *Marie-Anne-Françoiſe Mouchard*, née en 1738, fille de *François-Abraham-Marie*, Ecuyer, Seigneur de la Garde-aux-Valets, de Croix-Chapeaux & de Chamboneil, Conſeiller-Secrétaire du Roi, Receveur-Général des Finances de Champagne, & d'*Anne-Louiſe Laʒur*. De ce mariage ſont iſſus trois enfans nés à la Rochelle, ſçavoir:

1. Claude, né le 26 Septembre 1756;
2. Marie-Françoise, née le 7 Septembre 1757;
3. Et Anne-Amédée de Beauharnais, née le 8 Janvier 1760.

Les armes: *d'argent, à une faſce de ſable ſurmontée de 3 merlettes de même*. Deviſe: Autre ne sert.

Voyez, pour un plus long détail, l'*Armorial de France*, reg. V, part. I.

* BEAUJEU, petite Ville de France au Pays de Baujolois, avec un Château conſidérable par ſon antiquité, & par la valeur & la nobleſſe des Seigneurs qui le poſſédoient anciennement, a donné le nom à cette Maiſon.

Le premier connu eſt Beraud, Sire de Beaujeu, mort avant 967, marié à *Wandelmode*. Elle a donné un Connétable de France dans la perſonne d'Humbert, Ve du nom, Sire de Beaujeu, qui ſervit les Rois Philippe-Auguste & Louis VIII, ſon fils, en la guerre des Albigeois. Il força le Comte de Toulouse à ſe renfermer dans la ville de Toulouſe, & fit tant de dégât aux environs, qu'il obligea le Comte à demander la paix. Il accompagna BAUDOUIN DE COURTENAY, IIe du nom, Empereur de Conftantinople, fon coufin, au voyage qu'il y fit avec plufieurs grands Seigneurs de France. Il affifta à fon Couronnement, & après fon retour, il fit fon teftament au mois de Juillet 1248, & ne vivoit plus en 1251.

Cette branche finit par GUICHARD DE BEAUJEU, IVe du nom, qui fut Ambaffadeur en Angleterre, & y mourut fans poftérité.

GUICHARD DE BEAUJEU, fecond fils de GUICHARD, IIIe du nom, Comte de Clermont & de Montferrand, mort avant 1256, portoit pour armes: *d'argent, au lambel de cinq pendans d'azur, au chef de gueules.* Il fit la branche des Seigneurs de *Montpenfier* & de *Montferrand,* par fon mariage avec *Catherine,* Dauphine d'*Auvergne,* fille de *Guillaume,* Dauphin d'*Auvergne.* Il eut:

1. HUMBERT DE BEAUJEU, Chevalier, Seigneur de Montpenfier, d'Aigue-Perfe, de la Roche-d'Agoux, d'Hermene & de Rouane, qui accompagna le ROI Saint-Louis en fon premier voyage d'Outre-mer, & fignala fon courage à la bataille de Maffoure en 1280. Il le fuivit auffi à fon voyage d'Afrique, où il fervit au fiège de Tunis en 1270. Il contribua à la prife de Pampelune, & à la réduction du Royaume de Navarre fous l'obéiffance de PHILIPPE-le-Hardi, & fervit très-dignement ce Prince. Il mourut, en 1285, Connétable de France. Son fceau étoit *un écu femé de fleurs-de-lys, à un lambel de trois pièces; chaque pièce chargée de trois châteaux; l'écu accofté de deux épées.* Au contre-fceau, *une tête de lion.* C'eft le plus ancien fceau que l'on ait trouvé avec les épées de Connétable. Il portoit pour armes: *d'or, au lion de fable, furmonté d'un lambel de cinq pendans de gueules.*
2. Un fils;
3. Et LOUIS DE BEAUJEU, Chevalier & Seigneur de Montferrand, qui accompagna le Roi SAINT-LOUIS en Afrique, & mourut en 1280.

Cette branche a fini en la perfonne de LOUIS DE BEAUJEU, IIe du nom, Seigneur de Montferrand, qui mourut en 1296, père de deux enfans, morts fans alliances.

Cette Maifon des anciens Sires de BEAUJEU a donné un Archevêque de Lyon en 1193, dans RENAUD, mort en 1227; un Evêque de Bayeux dans GUILLAUME DE BEAUJEU, mort le 7 Octobre 1337; & un Maréchal de France dans EDOUARD, Sire de BEAUJEU & de Dombes, né le 11 Avril 1316, qui fe fignala en plufieurs occafions, fe trouva à la bataille de Crécy, fut fait Maréchal de France en 1343, par la démiffion de *Charles,* Sire de *Montmorency,* & fut tué au combat d'Ardres contre les Anglois en 1351. Il portoit pour armes: *d'or, à un lion de fable, armé & lampaffé de gueules.*

La Maifon de BEAUJEU, fortie des Comtes de *Forets,* comme on l'a dit, a pour tige, *Louis de Forets,* Seigneur de Beaujeu & de Dombes, fecond fils de *Renaud,* Ier du nom, Comte de *Forets,* & d'*Ifabeau,* Dame de *Beaujeu.* Il prit le nom & les armes de *Beaujeu,* qu'il laiffa à fa poftérité.

GUICHARD, fon fils, Seigneur de BEAUJEU, de Dombes & de Sémur, furnommé *le Grand,* fervit fous les Rois PHILIPPE-le-Bel, LOUIS-le-Hutin, PHILIPPE-le-Long, CHARLES-le-Bel & PHILIPPE-de-Valois. Il eut plufieurs guerres avec fes voifins; commanda le troifième bataillon François à la journée de Montcaffel en 1328, & tefta en 1331.

EDOUARD, Seigneur de Perreux, fuccéda à ANTOINE DE BEAUJEU, fon coufin, en 1374, aux Seigneuries de Beaujeu & de Dombes, & mourut à Perreux le 11 Août 1400.

Les Seigneurs d'*Amplepuis* font une branche fortie des Seigneurs de BEAUJEU. Voyez AMPLEPUIS.

L'*Armorial de France,* reg. I, part. I, pag. 55, parle de la branche des Seigneurs de *Chazeul* & de *Jaule* en ces termes:

JEAN DE BEAUJEU, Seigneur de Chazeul & de Jauge, Chevalier de l'Ordre du Roi, époufa, le 19 Décembre 1526, *Gilberte de Beaurepaire,* fille de *Jean de Beaurepaire,* Seigneur du Chefne, dont il eut:

FRANÇOIS DE BEAUJEU, Seigneur de Jauge, en faveur duquel CLAUDE DE BEAUJEU, Seigneur de Beaujeu & de Vallon au Comté de Bourgogne, par fon teftament du 30 Septembre 1574, fit une fubftitution de fes biens en confidération de ce qu'il étoit fon coufin, moyennant qu'il porteroit le nom & les armes de cette Maifon.

EDME DE BEAUJEU, fon petit-fils, Ecuyer, Seigneur de Jauge & de la Thuillerie, a eu de fon mariage avec *Geneviève-Françoife de Baugi,* fille de *Nicolas de Baugi,* Seigneur de Villecien, Ambaffadeur pour Sa Majefté en Hollande:

CHARLES-LOUIS DE BEAUJEU, Seigneur de Saint-Hubert & de Jauge, Lieutenant-Colonel du Régiment de Flandres, Brigadier des Armées du Roi, Chevalier de l'Ordre Royal & Militaire de Saint-Louis, & Commandant à Marfal, qui fut marié, le 22 Février 1709, avec *Françoise de Pallas*, décédée le 26 Octobre 1724, laiffant :

1. FRANÇOIS, Ecuyer, Seigneur de Jauge, Capitaine dans le Régiment de Flandres ;
2. EUGÈNE, deftiné à l'Eglife ;
3. CHARLES, Lieutenant dans le Régiment de Flandres ;
4. LOUIS, auffi Lieutenant dans le même Régiment ;
5. ALEXANDRE-NICOLAS-JOSEPH ;
6. 7. 8. & 9. CLAIRE, GENEVIÈVE, CÉCILE & GABRIELLE ;
10. MADELEINE-CHARLOTTE, reçue à Saint-Cyr le 18 Avril 1724 ;
11. MARIE-ANNE-URSULE, auffi reçue à Saint-Cyr le 5 Mai 1727 ;
12. Et ANNE-FRANÇOISE, reçue à Saint-Cyr le 26 Novembre 1731.

Dans l'Églife de *Beaujeu* fur Saône, au Comté de Bourgogne, eft une Chapelle appartenant à Meffieurs de BEAUJEU, où l'on voit l'épitaphe de CLAUDE, mentionné ci-deffus, & qui eft en ces termes :

Cy-gît honoré Seigneur CLAUDE DE BEAUJEU, lui vivant, le miroir de vertu, & maintenant la mémoire d'honneur, Seigneur de Vallon, Prantigny & dudit Beaujeu en partie, &c., lequel trépaffa le 9e jour d'Octobre 1574. Dieu ait fon âme.

A côté de celle-ci eft celle de *Jeanne de Mailly-Clinchamps* fa femme.

Les armes de BEAUJEU, repréfentées fur cette épitaphe, font : *un écu de gueules, à cinq burelles d'argent, timbré d'un heaume d'argent, la vifière d'or, bordée & clouée de même, les lambrequins & le bourrelet d'argent & de gueules.* Supports : *deux griffons d'or.* Cimier : *un griffon auffi naiffant d'or.*

A côté de ces armes font celles de *Jeanne de Mailly-Clinchamps*, & autour de l'infcription font auffi figurées les armes de *Cernay* & de *Marcenai*, de *Meligni*, de *Prie* & de *la Baume-de-Montrevel.*

On ne fçait pas pourquoi ces armes font ainfi figurées fur cette épitaphe avec les cinq burelles, car dans tous les endroits du Château de Beaujeu, où feu M. d'Hozier déclare dans fes Mémoires les avoir vues faines & entiè-

res, elles font repréfentées *de gueules, à quatre fafces d'argent*, & l'on préfume que MARC DE BEAUJEU, Seigneur de Montet, qui fut exécuteur du teftament defdits CLAUDE DE BEAUJEU & *Jeanne de Mailly-Clinchamps*, fit conftruire cette épitaphe avec les mêmes armes qu'il portoit, & que Meffieurs de *Jauge* ont commencé de porter depuis ; fçavoir : *de gueules à cinq burelles d'argent.*

BEAUJEU : *de fable à trois jumelles d'argent.*

*BEAUJEUX, en Franche-Conté, Diocèfe, Parlement & Intendance de Befançon, Terre & Seigneurie qui fut érigée en Comté par Lettres-Patentes du mois de Novembre 1715, enregiftrées à Dôle en faveur de *Jean-Claude de Heuneçey*, Seigneur de cette Terre.

BEAULAC, famille noble du Languedoc, d'où font fortis plufieurs Confeillers & Préfidens de la Chambre des Comptes & Cour des Aides de celle de Montpellier, laquelle s'eft éteinte dans FRANÇOIS DE BEAULAC.

* BEAULIEU, Seigneurie en Auvergne, qui a donné fon nom à une branche cadette de la Maifon de *Monteynard*. Cette branche a fini en 1614. Voyez MONTEYNARD.

BEAULIEU, Seigneur de Béthomas & de Richebourg en Normandie, Généralité de Rouen, famille maintenue dans fa nobleffe le 26 Janvier 1668. M. de Boulainvilliers, dans fon *Etat de la France*, met cette famille au nombre des plus anciennes de la Normandie.

N......... DE BEAULIEU, Baron de Béthomas, fut député pour la Nobleffe aux Etats de Normandie le 23 Novembre 1518.

ELÉONOR DE BEAULIEU-DE-BÉTHOMAS fut reçu Chevalier de Malte le 15 Février 1645, & felon Maffeville, dans fon *Hiftoire de Rouen*, Grand'Croix de cet Ordre, & Chef d'Efcadre des Galères de France. Il mourut en 1702. Voyez BETHOMAS.

Les armes : *d'argent, à fix croix pattées*, ou *de Malte, de fable, 3, 2 & 1.*

BEAULIEU, Seigneur de Rochefort, en Normandie, Généralité d'Alençon, famille maintenue dans fa Nobleffe le 18 Mai 1667, dont les armes font : *d'argent, au croiffant de fable, accompagné de fix croix ancrées de même, rangées en fafces, 3 en chef & 3 en pointe.*

BEAULIEU, en Bretagne: *d'azur, à neuf befans d'or, pofés 3, 3 & 3, au lion d'argent brochant fur le tout.*

BEAULIEU (de), en Champagne: *d'azur, au vol plein d'argent, furmonté de deux étoiles d'or.*

BEAULIEU-DE-BARNEVILLE. Henri de Beaulieu, Ecuyer, Seigneur de Barneville-fur-Seine en 1575, naquit dans la ville de Valenciennes en Hainaut, & fut naturalifé par Lettres-Patentes en forme de charte, données dans la ville de Pont-de-l'Arche au mois de Juin 1571, regiftrées en la Chambre des Comptes de Paris le 13 Juin 1572.

Jérôme-Augustin de Beaulieu, fon petit-fils, Seigneur de Barneville, de Maurox en Bretagne, & de Pavilly en Normandie près de Rouen, Capitaine de Vaiffeaux du Roi & de l'Arfenal de Toulon, Chevalier de Saint-Louis, fit un accord le 4 Octobre 1690, avec Marthe de Beaulieu fa fœur, où elle eft qualifiée de veuve-douairière de *Pons-de-Léon*, Vice-Amiral d'Efpagne; il époufa *Marie-Thérèfe de Cambis*, fille de *François de Cambis*, Marquis de Velleron, & de *Jeanne de Forbin-de-Janfon* fœur du Cardinal de ce nom, Grand-Aumônier de France.

Toussaint-Augustin de Beaulieu-de-Barneville, leur fils, fut Garde de la Marine au département de Toulon en 1705, puis Cornette dans le Régiment de Royal-Etranger en 1709, & Capitaine dans le même Régiment le 24 Mars 1711, Chevalier de Saint-Louis le 26 Janvier 1721. Du mariage qu'il contracta, le 18 Juillet 1722, avec *Thérèfe-Victoire de Gombert*, il eut entr'autres enfans:

1. François-Augustin-Toussaint de Beaulieu, né le 29 Décembre 1726;
2. Jérôme-Victor de Beaulieu, né le 8 Avril 1729;
3. Et Claire de Beaulieu, née le 10 Juillet 1724, reçue à Saint-Cyr le 7 Juillet 1736.

(*Armorial de France*, reg. 1, part. I, pag. 856.)

Les armes: *d'azur, à un chevron d'or, accompagné de trois grelots de même, pofés 2 e chef & 1 en pointe.*

BEAULIEU-RUZÉ, du furnom de *Razac* ou d'*Arzac* en Provence. Gaston de Beaulieu commandoit 500 hommes de pied lorfqu'il fuivit *Jean de Foix*, Comte de Carmin. En 1537 il porta les armes fous fix différens Princes, & fe trouva dans les combats qui fe

donnèrent, & aux fièges qui fe firent de fon temps. Le Roi Charles IX, en récompenfe de fes fervices, le pourvut de la Charge de Concierge de fa Maifon de Marfeille. Il fut Gouverneur des villes de Toulon & de Sifteron. Il mourut à Marfeille, âgé de 103 ans, après en avoir fervi plus de 70. Il eut de *Catherine Raynaud* 32 enfans: parmi les mâles, qui étoient au nombre de 20, douze furent tués au fervice du Roi; des filles il y en eut deux de mariées, l'une à *N... de Flotte-Roquevaire*, & l'autre à *N... de Faudran*.

Gaston de Beaulieu, IIe du nom, a continué la poftérité par fon mariage avec *Catherine de Gantès*, fille de *Pierre*, IIe du nom, Seigneur de Valbonnette, & de *Françoife de Bus*, du Comtat d'Avignon.

Pierre-Paul de Beaulieu-Ruzé, Seigneur de Razat, qui prit le parti des armes, & qui mourut des bleffures qu'il reçut au fiège de Montmélian, avoit époufé, en 1611, *Honorée de Saint-Martin*, dont il eut quatre enfans, parmi lefquels on compte:

Barthélemy de Beaulieu-Ruzé, Chevalier de l'Ordre de Saint-Michel, commandant une Galère pendant le combat de Gênes, où il fut tué.
Et Nicolas, qui fuit.

Nicolas de Beaulieu-Ruzé, Lieutenant des Galères du Roi, marié, en 1637, avec *Anne de Flotte*, laiffa:

Barthélemy de Beaulieu-Ruzé-de-Razat, Capitaine au Régiment de la Marine, qui fit alliance, en 1674, avec *Melchiore de Monté*, en Bourgogne, dont il eut:

Jacques-Madeleine de Beaulieu-Ruzé, Aide-Major des Galères du Roi à Marfeille, Chevalier de Saint-Louis.

François de Beaulieu-Ruzé, Commandant du fecond Bataillon du Régiment de Poitou, Chevalier de Saint-Louis, s'eft marié, en 1708, avec *Marie-Charlotte-Louife de Villougne*, en Champagne. Il en eut:

1. Charles-Antoine de Beaulieu, mort Lieutenant des Galères du Roi, Chevalier de Saint-Louis;
2. Et Charles-Jean de Beaulieu-Ruzé, qui a été Officier dans le Régiment de Poitou, dernier du nom, fans poftérité.

Les armes: *d'or, à trois corneilles de fable, becquées & membrées de gueules.* Le *Promptuaire armorial* de Jean Boiffeau, édition de 1657, in-fol., IIe part., pag. 34, dit:

de gueules, au chevron ondé d'argent & d'a-
zur, accompagné de trois lions d'or, 2 en
chef & 1 en pointe.

BEAUMAIS, Seigneur de Marolles, de
Cifay, en Normandie, Généralité de Rouen,
famille maintenue dans fa Nobleffe le 17 Février 1667, qui porte : *d'azur, au chevron*
d'or, accompagné en chef de deux molettes
d'éperon, & en pointe d'une patte d'oifeau,
le tout de même.

BEAUMANOIR, Maifon des plus anciennes & des plus illuftres du Pays du Maine,
dont parle Auguftin du Paz, & laquelle a
donné un Maréchal de France : on en trouve
la Généalogie dans l'*Hiftoire des Grands*
Officiers de la Couronne, tom. VII, pag. 79
& fuiv.

Le premier de ce nom dont on ait connoiffance eft :

I. Hervé, Seigneur ou Sire de Beaumanoir, Chevalier, vivant en 1202. Il fe trouva
la même année aux Etats tenus à Vannes,
pour avoir la réparation de l'affaffinat d'Artus, Ier du nom, Duc de Bretagne, commis
par Jean Santerre, Roi d'Angleterre, fon
oncle.

II. Geoffroy, Seigneur de Beaumanoir,
Chevalier, étoit marié lorfqu'il fe trouva aux
Etats de Bretagne avec fon père : il approuva
à l'affemblée de la Nobleffe à Nantes la veille
dé la Pentecôte 1225, les Privilèges accordés
par Pierre Mauclerc, Duc de Bretagne, aux
habitans de Saint-Aubin-du-Cormier, & confentit que ces privilèges euffent lieu dans fes
Terres. Il eut de fa femme, dont on ignore
le nom :

   1. Robert, qui fuit ;
   2. Et N..... de Beaumanoir, à laquelle on
   donne pour mari, *N.... de Cliffon,* frère de
   la femme de Robert de Beaumanoir.

III. Robert, Seigneur de Beaumanoir, Chevalier, àuquel on donne pour époufe, *N... de*
Cliffon, eut pour fils :

IV. Jean, Ier du nom, Seigneur de Beaumanoir, Chevalier, vivant en 1281, qui vendit au mois de Septembre 1294, à Jean, Seigneur de Maure, Chevalier, le droit qu'il
avoit en la Paroiffe de Saint-Benoît-des-On-
des, fous la Seigneurie de Châteauneuf. Il fut
préfent le 3 Octobre 1311, à l'apanage donné
par Artus II, Duc de Bretagne, aux enfans
du fecond lit de ce Prince. Voyez Lobineau,

Hift. de Bretagne, liv. IX, pag. 296. Il eut
de *Jeanne,* Dame de *Médrignac* & de la
Hardouinaye :

   '1. Jean, qui fuit ;
   2. Guillaume ;
   3. Et Robert, Maréchal de Bretagne pour
   Charles de Blois. Il affiégea & reprit la
   ville de Vannes en 1342, conduifit l'arrière-
   garde à une bataille donnée le 3 ou 9 Juin
   1346, & fut fait prifonnier à celle de la Ro-
   che-Dérien avec Charles de Blois, le 18
   Juin 1347. L'*Hiftoire de Bretagne,* liv. X,
   pag. 330, 339 & 340, lui donne pour femme *N... de Rochefort.*

V. Jean, IIe du nom, Seigneur de Beaumanoir & de Médrignac, Chevalier, s'allia
avec *Marie de Dinan,* fille de *Robert,* Seigneur de Montafilan, & de *Thomaffe de Châ-*
teaubriand, laquelle eut 200 livres de rente
en mariage. Leurs enfans furent :

   1. Jean, qui fuit ;
   2. Et Robert, auteur de la branche des Seigneurs de *Beffo,* rapportée ci-après.

On trouve dans le même tems Marie de
Beaumanoir, femme de *Briant de Château-*
briand, Seigneur de Beaufort, & de *Thomine*
le Moine.

VI. Jean, IIIe du nom, Seigneur de Beaumanoir, de Médrignac, de la Hardouinaye, &
de Moncontours, Chevalier, Maréchal de
Bretagne après Robert, fon oncle, pour Charles de Blois, Capitaine de Joffelin, & Lieutenant-Général de fon armée contre les Anglois, fut chef des combattans, à la bataille
des 30 Bretons, le quatrième Dimanche de
Carême 1351, contre les 30 Anglois, qu'ils
vainquirent, mais où il fut bleffé en rempor-
tant la victoire. Il fe trouva à la bataille de
Mauron en 1352, & fut un des Ambaffadeurs en Angleterre la même année. Il étoit
Gouverneur de Bretagne, lorfque le Duc de
Lancaftre lui remit, par conventions, les clefs
de la ville de Rennes l'an 1357. Il fut un des
ôtages du traité d'Evran le 12 Juillet 1363,
après la bataille d'Auray, où Charles de
Blois fut tué. Jeanne de Bretagne, fa veuve,
le députa pour la paix de Guérande, & le
qualifie fon *coufin* dans fa procuration de
1365. Il époufa 1° *Thiphaine de Chemillé* en
Anjou ; & 2° *Marguerite de Rohan,* remariée à *Olivier de Cliffon,* Connétable de France. Elle étoit fille d'*Alain,* VIIe du nom, Vicomte de Rohan, & de *Jeanne de Roftrénan.*

Du premier lit vint :

1. JEAN, qui fuit;
2. ROBERT, rapporté après fon frère aîné;
3. 4. & 5. Trois filles, mariées.

Du fecond lit vinrent:

6. JEANNE, femme de *Charles de Dinan*, Seigneur de Châteaubriand & de Montafilan;
7. ISABEAU, femme de *Jean de Tournemines*, Chevalier, Seigneur de la Hunaudaye, fils de *Pierre*, Seigneur de la Hunaudaye, & de *Jeanne de Craon*;
8. Et MARGUERITE, femme de *Galhot*, Seigneur de *Rougé*, de Derval, & de la Rochediré, Vicomte de la Guerche en Touraine, fils de *Bonabes de Rougé*, Seigneur dudit lieu, de Derval, &c., & de *Jeanne de l'Isle*.

VII. JEAN, IVe du nom, Seigneur de BEAUMANOIR, de la Hardouinaye, & de Médrignac, rendit de grands fervices à JEAN, Duc de Bretagne; fuivit le Connétable du Guefclin en 1370, avec 19 Ecuyers, & paffa en Poitou la même année, où il fit plufieurs conquêtes avec les autres Seigneurs Bretons l'an 1372. Il fe trouva avec Olivier de Cliffon, au fiège d'Auray, qui fe rendit le 15 Août 1377, & il quitta le parti du Roi en 1378. Il fut l'un des quatre principaux chefs de la Ligue que la Nobleffe fit en faveur du Duc de Bretagne, au-devant duquel il fut en 1379, lorfqu'il vint à Dinan. La même année il entra avec 200 lances en Normandie, où il fit beaucoup de ravages; & revint en Bretagne chargé de butin. Il fut choifi l'un des Arbitres de la Paix par le Duc de Bretagne, qui l'envoya en Ambaffade en Angleterre l'an 1380, & le traite de fon *Amé Coufin* dans l'acte de cette députation. Il fut avec les autres Seigneurs Bretons, à la guerre de Flandres l'an 1382; & le 14 Février 1385, il fut tué, à coup de hache, par Roland de Noyfan, fon Métayer, ne laiffant point d'enfans de *Thiphaine du Guefclin*, fille de *Pierre*, Seigneur du Pleffis-Bertrand, & de *Julienne*, Dame de Dénonval.

VII. ROBERT, Seigneur de BEAUMANOIR, après la mort de fon frère aîné, étoit en 1383, l'un des 14 Chevaliers de la Compagnie d'Eon de Lefnerac, Capitaine de Cliffon, qui furent au fecours du Duc de Bretagne en Flandres, contre les Anglois. Il affifta aux Etats tenus à Rennes le 14 Mai 1386. Il combattit & vainquit le Seigneur de Tournemines, comme l'auteur de la mort de fon frère; il embraffa le parti du Connétable de Cliffon, avec lequel il fut arrêté prifonnier en 1387. Le Connétable de Cliffon, par fon teftament

du 6 Février 1407, le députa pour porter & rendre au Roi l'épée qu'il avoit reçue quand il avoit été fait Connétable de France. Il mourut auffi fans enfans le 16 Février 1408.

BRANCHE
des Seigneurs & Vicomtes DU BESSO.

VI. ROBERT DE BEAUMANOIR, fecond fils de JEAN, IIe du nom, & de *Marie de Dinan*, fut Chambellan du Duc de Bretagne, & Capitaine de Vannes, & eut de *Thiennette*, Dame du *Beffo*:

1. JEAN, qui fuit;
2. Et GUILLAUME, auteur de la branche des Seigneurs de *Lavardin*, rapportée ci-après.

VII. JEAN DE BEAUMANOIR, Ier du nom de fa branche, Chevalier, Vicomte du Beffo, fut l'un des 42 Capitaines des Compagnies d'hommes d'armes, qui s'engagèrent l'an 1419, à venir fervir le Duc de Bretagne toutes les fois qu'il lui plairoit de les commander, & eut le poing coupé l'année fuivante, en voulant s'oppofer aux Penthièvre, qui firent le Duc de Bretagne Prifonnier au Loroux. Il écartela fes armes de celles de fa mère, qui font: *d'or, à trois chevrons de fable*. Il eut de *Jeanne Boutié*, fille d'*Alain*, Seigneur de la Motte-Boutié, Ecuyer, & d'*Aliette de Montelien*, Dame de la Claye:

1. JEAN, qui fuit;
2. CHARLES, Tuteur & Garde de BRIANT, fon petit-neveu, qui lui fit partage le 12 Octobre 1456;
3. Et ISABEAU, femme de *Pierre Yvette*.

VIII. JEAN DE BEAUMANOIR, IIe du nom, Chevalier, Vicomte du Beffo, Seigneur de la Claye, fut Chambellan du Duc de Bretagne, & Chef de fes Gendarmes. Il mourut au fervice de fon Prince aux Landes & Mares de Tannères avant fon père. Il laiffa d'*Yvette de Boishamont*, Dame de la Touche-Huet, Paroiffe de la Mézière, & de Montgerval, Paroiffe de Genefey, fille de *Pierre*, Seigneur du Boishamont, & de *Jeanne de la Bérue*:

1. JEAN, qui fuit;
2. Et JEANNE, femme de *Charles de Landegen*, Seigneur de Saint-Jouan.

IX. JEAN DE BEAUMANOIR, IIIe du nom, Chevalier, Vicomte du Beffo, Seigneur de la Claye, de la Touche-Huet, & de Montgerval, en 1448, époufa *Jeanne*, Dame de la Bérue, de Ceffon, de Gennes, & de la Barre, fille de

Raoul, Seigneur des mêmes lieux, & de *Jeanne-Edmée Bernard*, dont :

1. Briant, qui suit;
2. Et Bertrand, Chevalier, Seigneur de Cesson.

X. Briant de Beaumanoir, Chevalier, Vicomte du Besso, Seigneur de la Claye, de la Touche-Huet, de Montgerval, de la Bérue, de Gennes & de la Barre, eut pour tuteur Charles de Beaumanoir, son grand-oncle; fut fait Chevalier à la bataille de Castillon, puis Chambellan du Roi Louis XI, Capitaine de Melun, & Seigneur de l'usufruit de cette Ville. Il mourut environ l'an 1485. Il avoit épousé, en 1458, *Marguerite de Creux*, morte en 1495, Dame de la Folie, de Loublarie, & de la Ville-Odiernie, fille d'*Olivier*, & d'*Isabeau de Tréal*. Il laissa :

XI. Gilles de Beaumanoir, Chevalier, Vicomte du Besso, Seigneur de la Claye, &c., Chambellan de François II, Duc de Bretagne, qui servit à la conquête de Naples faite par le Roi Charles VIII, en 1495; fut fait Chevalier à la bataille de Fornoue, & mourut en 1498. Il avoit épousé *Jacquemine du Parc*, Dame de la Motte-du-Parc, & de Trébit, laquelle fut tutrice de ses enfans le 6 Janvier 1699. Elle étoit fille de *Charles*, aussi Chambellan du même Prince, Capitaine de 100 hommes d'armes, & de *Marguerite Painel*. Il laissa :

1. François, Chambellan du Roi Louis XII, fait Chevalier à la bataille d'Aignadel contre les Vénitiens en 1509, & mort à son retour à Angers, le 25 Novembre 1509;
2. Charles, qui suit;
3. Marguerite, qui eut de son frère la Seigneurie de la Bérue, & épousa *Hervé de Malestroit*, Seigneur d'Usel, de la Soraye, & du Marchais;
4. Catherine, morte sans enfans;
5. Et Marguerite, morte en bas âge.

XII. Charles de Beaumanoir, Chevalier, Vicomte du Besso, qui succéda à son frère, retira par échange la Seigneurie de Beaumanoir de Charles de Bourbon, Prince de la Roche-sur-Yon, & de *Philippe de Montespédon*. Il mourut au mois de Décembre 1552, & avoit été marié avec *Isabeau Busson*, Dame de Gazan, du Val, de la Motte, de la Grève & de Villaines, fille de *Guillaume*, & de *Jeanne de Sévigné*, dont :

1. René, mort enfant;
2. Jacques, qui suit;
3. Gilles, lequel après avoir été Protono-

taire du Saint-Siège, embrassa la Religion Protestante, se maria, & mourut le 5 Janvier 1572, laissant de sa femme, nommée *Susanne*, Samuel de Beaumanoir, Chevalier, Seigneur de Gazan, qui épousa N...... *de Cayres*, dont Marguerite de Beaumanoir, Dame de la Claye, de la Motte, &c., mariée à N..... *du Maz*, Vicomte de Terchamp;

4. Fiacre, mort jeune;
5. Mathurin, qui accompagna en Turquie M. d'Aramont, Ambassadeur de France, & mourut peu après son retour, par la trahison d'un faux ami;
6. Et Jean, Chevalier de Malte, tué au siège de Malte en 1565.

XIII. Jacques de Beaumanoir, Chevalier, Vicomte du Besso, & de Médrac, Seigneur de Villaines, &c., Echanson du Roi Henri II, & Gentilhomme ordinaire du Dauphin en 1559 & 1560, fut marié, 1° par contrat du 13 Juin 1538, avec *Adélice de la Feuillée*, veuve de *Charles de Kermaouan*, & seconde fille de *François*, Chevalier, Seigneur de la Feuillée, & de *Cyprienne de Rohan*; & 2° le 12 Février 1550, avec *Jeanne de Quellenec*, fille de *Jean*, Baron du Pont, & de *Jeanne de Maure*.

Du premier lit vinrent :

1. Marguerite, Dame de la Touche-Huet, & de Montgerval, femme de *Tannegui*, Sire de Rosmadec, fils d'*Alain* & de *Jeanne de la Chapelle*;
2. Jeanne, femme de *Noël de Tréal*, Seigneur de Beaubois, de l'Aventure, & de Laurigan.

Et du second lit :

3. Toussaint, qui suit;
4. Et Jacquemine, femme de *François*, Baron de Guemadeuc, dont elle eut plusieurs enfans.

Jacques de Beaumanoir eut un fils naturel :

Fierabras, qui vivoit en 1530.

XIV. Toussaint de Beaumanoir, Chevalier, Vicomte du Besso, Baron du Pont & de Rostrénan, baptisé à Jugon le 1er Novembre 1554, créé Chevalier de l'Ordre du Roi, Capitaine de 50 hommes d'armes de ses Ordonnances, Maréchal de ses Camps & Armées en Bretagne, mort à Rennes le 12 Mars 1590, d'une blessure qu'il avoit reçue devant Ancenis, n'eut d'*Anne de Guemadeuc*, fille de *François*, & d'*Hélène de la Chapelle*, qu'une fille nommée

HÉLÈNE DE BEAUMANOIR, Baronne du Pont, & de Roftrénan, Vicomteffe du Fou, &c., morte fans enfans en 1636. Elle avoit époufé 1° *René de Tournemines*, Baron de la Hunaudaye, mort fans enfans le 28 Février 1609; & 2° *Charles de Coffé*, Marquis d'Acigné, fecond fils de *Charles*, Comte de Briffac, Maréchal de France, & de *Judith*, Dame d'*Acigné*.

BRANCHE
des Seigneurs & Marquis DE LAVARDIN, *iffue de celle des Vicomtes* DU BESSO.

VII. GUILLAUME DE BEAUMANOIR, Chevalier, fecond fils de ROBERT, Vicomte du Beffo, & de *Thiennette du Beffo*, retenu Chambellan du Roi par Lettres du 25 Août 1402, époufa *Jeanne Girard*, Dame de Landemont, fille & héritière de *Philippe Girard*, Seigneur de la Gillière, dont:

VIII. JEAN DE BEAUMANOIR, Ier du nom de fa branche, Chevalier, Seigneur de Landemont, de Boisbiil, &c., Ecuyer d'Ecurie du Roi, en 1425, fit la foi & hommage au Duc d'Anjou, le 4 Août 1454, de fa Terre de Landemont, & tefta le 6 Novembre 1459. Il eut de *Marie Riboulle*, fille puînée de *Fouques*, Seigneur d'Affé-le-Riboulle, de Lavardin, &c., & de *Jeanne de Montejan*, entre autres enfans:

IX. GUY DE BEAUMANOIR, Chevalier, Seigneur & Marquis de Lavardin, de Landemont, &c., à qui le Roi accorda un marché & quatre foires par an, à fa Terre de Lavardin, & rendit hommage au Comte du Maine, le 4 Mars 1473, & mourut le 15 Juin 1486, fuivant fon épitaphe qui eft fur fon tombeau avec fes armes, en l'Abbaye de Champagne, au Maine. Il fut marié, 1° le 19 Août 1451, avec *Jeanne d'Eftouteville*, Dame de Presles, &c., fille de *Blanchet*, Seigneur de Villebéon, & de *Marguerite de Vendôme*, fa première femme; elle eft enterrée, avec fon mari, en l'Abbaye de Champagne, au Maine; & 2° fans enfans, avec *Marguerite de la Foffille*, laquelle étant veuve en 1488, plaidoit pour fon douaire, & fe remaria en 1500, à *Pierre le Maire*, Ecuyer. Elle étoit fille de *Jean*, & de *Marguerite Baraton*. Les enfans du premier lit font:

1. JEAN, qui fuit;
2. CHARLES, vivant en 1485;
3. LANCELOT, Abbé de Champagne, mort en 1531, & enterré dans fon Abbaye;

4. JULIENNE, mariée, 1° le 5 Avril 1477, à *René de Champagne*, Seigneur de Longchamp; 2° à *Robert Lavocat*, Seigneur de Langevinaye. Elle vivoit encore avec lui en 1487;
5. MARIE;
6. Et FRANÇOISE, mariée, avant le 21 Oétobre 1480, à *Pierre de Mauny*, Seigneur de Saint-Aignan.

X. JEAN DE BEAUMANOIR, IIe du nom, Chevalier, Seigneur de Lavardin, &c., étoit mort en 1509. Il avoit époufé 1° *Catherine de la Rochefoucauld*, veuve de *Jacques de Mathéfélon*; elle donna, par fon teftament, à fon fecond mari, la Terre d'Anthoigné, qu'elle avoit eue de fon premier, n'ayant eu d'enfans ni de l'un ni de l'autre. Elle étoit fille de *Guillaume de la Rochefoucauld*, Seigneur de Nouans, & de *Marguerite de Torfais*, Dame de Melleran; & 2° *Hélène de Villeblanche*, fille de *Pierre*, & de *Jeanne du Perrier*, dont:

1. CHRISTOPHE, qui tranfigea de fes droits fucceffifs en 1509;
2. JACQUES, mort en 1501, & enterré dans l'Abbaye de Champagne, au Maine;
3. FRANÇOIS, qui fuit;
4. ANNE, femme de *Bonaventure*, Seigneur de *Mareuil* & de *Moulhard*;
5. MARIE, femme de *François de Billy*, Baron de Courville, fils de *Perceval de Billy*, IIe du nom, & de *Louife de Vieux-Pont*;
6. Et MARQUISE, Dame du Val, mariée 1° à *Jean d'Argenfon*, Seigneur de Vaubuiffon; & 2° à *Raymond*, Seigneur de Saltan.

XI. FRANÇOIS DE BEAUMANOIR, Chevalier, Seigneur de Lavardin, &c., tranfigea, en 1519, avec MARIE, fa fœur, à laquelle il donna la Seigneurie de Beauchefne. Il mourut le 18 Novembre 1544, & fut enterré en l'Abbaye de Champagne, au Maine. Il avoit époufé, par contrat du 9 Juillet 1525, *Jeanne de Tucé*, veuve de *Claude d'Aumont*, Seigneur d'Eftrabonne. Elle mourut le 30 Décembre 1545, & fut enterrée en l'Abbaye de Champagne. Elle étoit fille de *Baudouin de Tucé*, & de *Françoife l'Epervier*. De ce mariage vinrent:

1. N....... DE BEAUMANOIR, vivant en 1534, & mort depuis fans alliance;
2. CHARLES, qui fuit;
3. CHRISTOPHE, mort le 22 Mars 1530, & enterré dans l'Eglife de Saint-Gemmes, près Anthoigné;
4. Et SUSANNE, féparée de biens, en 1552, de *Jacques de la Bécaire*, fon mari.

XII. CHARLES DE BEAUMANOIR, Chevalier, Seigneur de Lavardin, après fon frère aîné, s'étant fait Huguenot, appuya ce parti de tout fon crédit, commanda, au rapport de Dupleix, l'avant-garde à la bataille de Saint-Denis; mena la Nobleffe d'Anjou, du Maine & de Bretagne, qui fuivoit le même parti, à la Rochelle, au Prince de Condé; fournit quatre Cornettes de Cavalerie, & deux Compagnies d'Arquebufiers, au fiège de Poitiers ; & fut tué au maffacre de la Saint-Barthélemy, le 24 Août 1572, après avoir été, comme dit M. de Thou, quelque tems Gouverneur du Roi de Navarre. Il avoit époufé, 1º par contrat du 14 Janvier 1545, *Marguerite de Chourfes*, fille de *Félix*, & de *Marguerite de Bailli;* 2º *Catherine de Bellay*, feconde fille & héritière de *Martin*, fi renommé pour fes Mémoires, & d'*Ifabeau Chenu*, Princeffe d'Yvetot.

Du premier lit vinrent:

1. JEAN, qui fuit;
2. Et MADELEINE, femme, le 7 Juillet 1571, d'*Olivier du Fefchal*, Seigneur de Poligny & de Marboué: étant veuve fans enfans, elle donna la Terre de la Génaudière à un de fes neveux.

Et du fecond lit :

3. MARTHE, morte fans enfans. Elle avoit époufé 1º *René de Bouillé*, Comte de Créance, Chevalier de l'Ordre du Roi; & 2º *N..... de la Guiche*, Seigneur de Saint-Gérand;
4. MARIE, morte fans alliance;
5. Et ELISABETH, qui fut partagée avec fes fœurs, par fon frère confanguin, le 18 Novembre 1572, & mariée, le 10 Août 1597, à *Louis de Cordouan*, Seigneur de Mimbré, au Maine.

XIII. JEAN DE BEAUMANOIR, IIIº du nom, Chevalier, Seigneur & Marquis de Lavardin, Comte de Négrépeliffe, Baron de Tucé, Seigneur de Malicorne, &c., Chevalier des Ordres du Roi, Capitaine de 50 hommes d'armes, Gouverneur du Maine & du Perche, né en 1551, fut élevé auprès du Roi de Navarre, pour lequel il fe trouva au fiège de Poitiers, dans l'armée des Huguenots, en 1569. Il fe fit Catholique après la mort de fon père, & fut bleffé au fiège de Saint-Lô en 1574. Sur le refus que le Roi HENRI III lui fit de la charge de Capitaine des Gardes-du-Corps, qui lui avoit été promife, il excita HENRI, Roi de Navarre, de fe retirer de la Cour, & fut

fait Colonel de l'Infanterie Françoife. Il fe rendit maître de Villefranche en Périgord, de Cahors, en 1580, & d'Eauffe, au Comté d'Armagnac, en 1584. Etant devenu fufpeĉt au parti Huguenot, il fe retira en Poitou, auprès de *Jean de Chourfes*, Seigneur de Malicorne, Gouverneur de la Province, fon oncle maternel. Il eut la furvivance de fon Gouvernement, avec le Commandement de l'Armée du Roi, en l'abfence du Duc de Joyeufe, en 1586. Il commanda la Cavalerie Légère à la bataille de Coutras, en 1587, fervit au fiège de Mauléon, fous le Duc de Nevers, en 1588, & fous le Comte de Soiffons au combat de Château-Giron, en 1589, où il fut battu. Il fe trouva auffi aux fièges de Paris, de Chartres & de Rouen, & au combat d'Aumale, où il fut bleffé: il fe démit du Gouvernement de Saint-Denis, en faveur de Dominique de Vic, & fut pourvu de celui de la Province du Maine. Le Roi l'honora du Collier de fes Ordres, le 7 Janvier 1595, de l'Office de Maréchal de France la même année, & le choifit, en 1602, pour commander fon armée en Bourgogne. Il fit la fonĉtion de Grand-Maître de France au facre de Louis XIII, fut Ambaffadeur Extraordinaire en Angleterre en 1612½, d'où étant de retour, il mourut à Paris en fon Hôtel, au mois de Novembre 1614. Son corps fut porté au Mans, & enterré dans l'Eglife Cathédrale, en la Chapelle Saint-Jean. Il avoit époufé, le 27 Décembre 1578, *Catherine de Carmain*, Comteffe de Négrépeliffe, Baronne de Launac, fille unique & héritière de *Louis*, Comte de Négrépeliffe, & de *Marguerite de Foix-Candale*, dont:

1. HENRI, qui fuit;
2. JEAN, Baron de Tucé, mort en 1615, laiffant, de *Catherine de Longueval*, N..... DE BEAUMANOIR, femme d'*Annibal de Longueval*, Vicomte d'Haraucourt;
3. CHARLES, Evêque du Mans, Abbé de Beaulieu, & de Saint-Lignaire ;
4. CLAUDE, auteur de la branche des Vicomtes de *Saint-Jean*, Baron de *la Trouffière*, rapportée ci-après;
5. Autre CLAUDE, Seigneur de Launac, Meftre-de-Camp du Régiment de Piémont, bleffé à mort au fiège de Saint-Anthonin, en 1622;
6. MARTIN, Baron de Milleffe, tué au fiège de Saint-Jean-d'Angely en 1621;
7. EMMANUEL, Seigneur de Mézangères, Abbé de Saint-Liger en Poitou, mort jeune;

8. JEAN-BAPTISTE-LOUIS, Chevalier de l'Ordre du Roi, Baron de Lavardin & d'Anthoigné, Sénéchal du Maine, qui conduifit l'arrière-ban en 1635. Il avoit époufé *Marguerite de la Chevrière*, fille de *Jean*, Seigneur de la Roche-de-Vaux, & de *N.... de la Foffe*. Elle étoit veuve en 1658. Ils eurent: CHARLES DE BEAUMANOIR, Comte d'Anthoigné, Lieutenant de Roi ès Pays du Maine & du Perche, mort fans enfans, environ l'an 1682, & trois filles;

6. Et CATHERINE, femme, le 31 Janvier 1612, de *François du Pleffis*, Marquis de Jarzé, en Anjou, Seigneur de la Roche-Pichemer, & du Pleffis-Bourré, Chevalier de l'Ordre du Roi, fils de *René*, auffi Chevalier de l'Ordre du Roi, Gentilhomme ordinaire de fa Chambre, & de *Renée de Bourré*, Dame de Jarzé. Elle eut en mariage 120000 livres.

XIV. HENRI DE BEAUMANOIR, Ier du nom, Chevalier, Seigneur & Marquis de Lavardin, Comte de Beaufort-en-Vallée, Seigneur de Malicorne, &c., Gouverneur des Comtés du Maine, du Perche & de Laval, mourut au mois de Mai 1633. Il avoit époufé, par contrat du 7 Avril 1614, *Marguerite de la Baume*, fille de *Roftaing de la Baume*, Comte de Suze, & de *Madeleine de Prez-Montpézat*, laquelle fe remaria à *Efprit Raymond*, connu fous le nom de *Comte de Modène*. Les enfans de fon premier mariage furent:

1. HENRI, qui fuit;
2. PHILIBERT-EMMANUEL, Evêque du Mans, Abbé de Beaulieu, & Commandeur de l'Ordre du Saint-Efprit, en 1661, mort à Paris, le 26 Juillet 1671;
3. Et MADELEINE, morte à Paris, le 25 Décembre 1682, âgée de 64 ans, qui avoit époufé, par contrat du 7 Novembre 1638, *René*, Sire *de Froulay*, Comte de Teffé, fils de *René*, & de *Marie d'Efcoubleau-de-Sourdis*.

XV. HENRI DE BEAUMANOIR, IIe du nom, Marquis de Lavardin, Comte de Beaufort, &c., Maréchal des Camps & Armées du Roi, reçut un coup de moufquet à la hanche, au fiège de Gravelines, la nuit du 28 au 29 Juin 1644, & mourut cinq jours après de fa bleffure, âgé de 26 ans. Il avoit époufé 1° *Catherine de Vaffé*, dite *Grognette*, morte en 1638, fix mois après fon mariage, fille d'*Henri*, Seigneur de *Vaffé*, Baron de la Roche-Mabile, & de *Renée le Cornu*; & 2° par contrat du 8 Mars 1642, *Marguerite-Renée de Roftaing*,

qui vivoit encore le 23 Juillet 1687. Elle étoit fille de *Charles*, Marquis de Roftaing, & d'*Anne-Hurault-Chiverny*, & ne laiffa qu'un fils:

XVI. HENRI-CHARLES DE BEAUMANOIR, Marquis de Lavardin, &c., Chevalier des Ordres du Roi, Lieutenant-Général au Gouvernement de la Haute & Baffe-Bretagne, qui fe trouva au combat de Saint-Gothard, en Hongrie, en 1664, à la prife de Courtray en 1667, fuivit le Roi à la conquête de la Franche-Comté en 1668, & à la guerre de Hollande en 1672; fervit auffi en plufieurs autres occafions l'année fuivante; fut envoyé en ambaffade extraordinaire à Rome en 1687; fait Chevalier des Ordres du Roi en 1688, & mourut à Paris le 29 Août 1701, âgé de 57 ans. Il avoit époufé, 1° le 3 Février 1667, *Françoife-Paule-Charlotte d'Albert*, morte en couches en 1670, fille de *Louis-Charles*, Duc de Luynes, & de *Marie Séguier-d'O*, fa première femme; & 2° *Louife-Anne de Noailles*, fille d'*Anne*, Duc de Noailles, & de *Louife Boyer*.

Les enfans du premier lit font:

1. MARIE-CHARLOTTE, née en 1668, femme, le 13 Mai 1694, de *Louis-Charles-Edme de la Châtre*, Comte de Nançay, Lieutenant-Général des Armées du Roi, fils de *Louis*, & de *Charlotte-Louife d'Hardoncourt*;
2. N... DE BEAUMANOIR, appelée *Mademoifelle de Malicorne*, née en 1670, Religieufe Bénédictine, au Cherche-Midi.

Et du fecond lit:

3. EMMANUEL-HENRI, Marquis de Lavardin, Lieutenant-Général pour le Roi, en Baffe-Bretagne, né au mois de Juillet 1684, tué, étant Colonel de Cavalerie, à la bataille de Spire, le 15 Novembre 1703. Il avoit époufé, fans enfans, le 20 Février 1703, *Marie-Françoife de Noailles*, fille d'*Anne-Jules*, Duc de *Noailles*, & de *Marie-Françoife de Bournonville*;
4. MARIE-ANNE-ROMAINE, née à Rome, le 11 Septembre 1688, femme, le 21 Juillet 1704, de *Louis-Augufte d'Albert d'Ailly*, Duc de Chaulnes. Voyez ALBERT & COLBERT.
5. Et MARIE-LOUISE-HENRIETTE, morte à Paris, le 14 Décembre 1755. Elle avoit époufé, le 9 Février 1708, *Jacques-Louis de Béringhen*, Marquis de Châteauneuf, mort le 1er Novembre 1723, ne laiffant qu'une fille, Religieufe Bénédictine.

BRANCHE

des Vicomtes DE SAINT-JEAN, *Baron de la Trouſſière,&c., iſſue de celle des Seigneurs* DE LAVARDIN.

XIV. CLAUDE DE BEAUMANOIR, Iᵉʳ du nom de ſa branche, Chévalier, quatrième fils de JEAN, IIIᵉ du nom, Maréchal de France, & de *Catherine de Carmain,* Vicomte de Saint-Jean, Maréchal des Camps & Armées du Roi, mort le 6 Février 1654, épouſa, en 1616, *Renée de la Chapelle,* Dame de Varenne, de la Trouſſière, &c., morte le 26 Mars 1672, fille unique de *Philibert,* & de *Charlotte Ferre,* dont:

1. CLAUDE, qui fuit;
2. LOUIS, rapporté après ſon frère aîné;
3. JEAN-BAPTISTE, Abbé de Beaulieu, facré Evêque de Rennes, le 20 Février 1678, Abbé de Monſtier-Ramey, le 12 Avril 1696, mort le 23 Mai 1711;
4. PHILIBERT;
5. CHARLES, Chevalier de Malte, reçu le 4 Décembre 1656, & mort à Malte;
6. MADELEINE, femme 1º de *Jean-Jacques de Birague,* Baron d'Entrâmes, fils de *René* & de *Françoiſe d'Erbré;* 2º d'*Antoine de Boiſſonade,* Seigneur d'Ortie;
7. MARGUERITE, Religieuſe au Prieuré de Gaine, Ordre de Fontevrault, le 4 Mai 1645, Abbeſſe de la Périgne, Diocèſe du Mans, le 17 Juillet 1653, morte le 22 Mars 1691, âgée de 63 ans;
8. RENÉE, Abbeſſe de la Périgne après ſa fœur, le 18 Décembre 1691, morte le 13 Novembre 1713, âgée de 78 ans. *Françoiſe-Eléonore Morel-d'Aubigny,* ſa nièce, lui ſuccéda;
9. HENRIETTE, Religieuſe dans la même Abbaye, le 23 Août 1654, morte le 18 Décembre 1686;
10. MARIE, femme, par contrat du 8 Avril 1663, d'*Antoine Morel,* dit *le Comte d'Aubigny,* près Falaiſe, Vicomte de Neufvillette, mort le 10 Octobre 1689, âgé de 58 ans, dont poſtérité. Voyez MOREL;
11. Et LOUISE, morte en 1690.

XV. CLAUDE DE BEAUMANOIR, IIᵉ du nom, Chevalier, dit *le Comte de Lavardin,* Maréchal des Camps & Armées du Roi, Lieutenant-Général des Pays du Maine, de Laval & du Perche, mort au Mans, le 10 Mai 1676, & enterré dans l'Egliſe Cathédrale de cette Ville. Il avoit épouſé, le 27 Septembre 1643, *Marie de Neuchèze,* Dame de Baudiment, remariée, le 7 Octobre 1678, à *Charles de*

Laurens de Beauregard, avec lequel elle vivoit ſans enfans en 1702. Elle étoit fille aînée & héritière de *Jacques,* & de *Jeanne de Launay-d'Onglée,* & laiſſa du premier lit:

1. MARIE-CLAUDE, femme, au mois d'Octobre 1680, de *Pierre-Emmanuel Thibaud,* Seigneur de la Rochethulon, en Beaujolois, Colonel d'un Régiment de Dragons;
2. Et MARIE-FRANÇOISE, morte ſans alliance en 1690.

XV. LOUIS DE BEAUMANOIR, Baron de la Trouſſière, ſecond fils de CLAUDE, Iᵉʳ du nom, Vicomte de Saint-Jean, & de *Renée de la Chapelle,* mourut à la Guénaudière, chez le Marquis de la Rochethulon, ſon neveu, & fut enterré en l'Egliſe de Graitz, en Bouère. Il épouſa, 1º par contrat paſſé à Laval, le 10 Avril 1644, *Jeanne Garnier,* fille de *Jean,* Seigneur du Pin, & de *Louiſe Jamin;* & 2º *Eſther de Domagné-de-la-Rochehue.*

Du premier lit vinrent:

1. LOUISE, mariée à Laval, le 18 Mai 1681, avec *Jacques de la Dufferie,* Chevalier, Seigneur de Martigné-ſous-Laval, & de la Motte-Huffon;
2. MARGUERITE, femme d'*Alexandre Martinetʒ,* Seigneur de Fromentière;
3. N... DE BEAUMANOIR, Religieuſe à Saumur;

Et du ſecond lit:

4. Et une fille morte jeune.

Il y a une autre branche des Seigneurs du *Bois-de-la-Motte,* dont on n'a point la jonction avec les précédens. Elle a pour auteur, JEAN DE BEAUMANOIR, Chevalier, Seigneur du Bois-de-la-Motte, qui étoit mort en 1381, & dont la poſtérité a fini au VIᵉ degré, à FRANÇOIS DE BEAUMANOIR, mort ſans alliance, avant ſon père JACQUES DE BEAUMANOIR, qui fut Conſeiller & Chambellan du Roi CHARLES VIII, le 29 Mars 1491, & mourut en 1540. Voyez pour cette branche le Père Anſelme, tom. VII, pag. 389.

Les armes: *d'aʒur, à onʒe billettes d'argent, poſées 4, 3 & 4.*

BEAUMANOIR, nom de lieu en Normandie. N..... DE GAILLIARD DE LA BOISSIÈRE DE BEAUMANOIR a épouſé N....... *Preaudeau,* ſœur du Fermier-Général, & nièce des trois Meſſieurs *Bouret,* Fermiers-Généraux.

BEAUMANOIR - EDERS, Seigneur de Quincy: *de gueules, à la faſce d'argent, accompagnée de trois quinte-feuilles de même, 2 en chef & 1 en pointe.*

BEAUMEN, en Provence : *coupé, parti, emmanché d'or & d'azur, de l'un en l'autre.*

* BEAUMENIL, subdélégation de Bellesme. La Baronie de *Beaumenil* est une très-ancienne Terre, qui a appartenu à M. le Marquis de Chamilly, dont est sortie Madame la Comtesse de Graville, qui possède actuellement cette Baronie, comme héritière de la Maison de Chamilly. Elle a eu de son premier mariage *Mademoiselle de Martel,* mariée au *Comte de Martel.* La Justice de la Baronie de Bauménil s'étend sur sept Paroisses, dont le Seigneur du lieu a droit de patronage.

BEAUMERLY : *de gueules, à la bande fuselée d'or.*

BEAUMESNIL : *de gueules, à deux fasces d'hermines.*

BEAUMEZ, en Picardie. Hugues, Châtelain de Beaumez est le premier de cette Maison dont on ait connoissance; il épousa, selon Lambert d'Ardres, *Béatrix de Guines,* veuve de *Guillaume Faramus*, Seigneur de Tingry, & fille d'*Arnould de Gand*, Comte de Guines, & de *Mahaud de Saint-Omer*. Ils vivoient ensemble l'an 1173, & eurent entr'autres enfans :

Gilles, Châtelain de Beaumez & de Bapaume, qui se maria avec *Agnès de Coucy*, fille de *Raoul*, Ier du nom, Seigneur de Coucy, de Marle, de la Fère, Verneins, Pinon & autres lieux, & d'*Alix de Dreux*. Ils sont nommés dans un titre de 1214. Ils laissèrent :

1. Gilles, qui suit;
2. Raoul, qui fut dans son tems un vaillant Chevalier, mais il mourut sans enfans d'*Ide*, Dame de Baudour, veuve de *Baudouin de Walincourt;*
3. Thomas, qui succéda, à l'Archevêché de Reims, à *Henri de Dreux*, son cousin;
4. Et Robert, Auteur d'une branche rapportée ci-après.

Gilles, Châtelain de Beaumez & de Bapaume, IIe du nom, eut pour femme *Jeanne de Bailleul*, sœur de *Jacques*, Seigneur de *Bailleul* en Hainaut, de laquelle il eut :

1. Gilles, IIIe du nom, mort sans hoirs de l'héritière de *Beauvoir;*
2. Robert, qui suit;
3. N...... femme de *Jean de Pecquigny*, Vidame d'Amiens ;
4. N...... femme du Seigneur de *Sombresse* en Brabant;
5. N...... femme du Seigneur de *Waencourt*, dont elle n'eut point de lignée;
6. N...... Abbesse de Premy;
7. Et N....... Abbesse du Verger.

Robert, Châtelain de Beaumez & de Bapaume, prit alliance avec *Isabeau de Cany*, fille de *Raoul le Flamen*, Seigneur de Cany, qui le rendit père, entr'autres enfans, de :

1. Gilles, qui suit;
2. Et Robert, Seigneur de *Bombers*, qui fit une branche, dont nous parlerons ci-après.

Gilles, IVe du nom, Seigneur Châtelain de Beaumez & de Bapaume, épousa *Ide d'Escayencourt*, fille de *N*..... Seigneur d'*Escayencourt*, & d'*Isabeau*, Dame *de Croisilles*, dont il eut une fille unique :

Roberte de Beaumez, Châtelaine de Bapaume, Dame de Beaumez & de Croisilles, mariée 1° à *Louis de Marigny*, fils d'*Enguerrand de Marigny*, Comte de Longueville & d'Aleps, de Mons, dont elle eut *Ide de Marigny*, femme de *Jean de Melun*, Comte de Tancarville, morte sans enfans; & 2° à *Guy Mauvoisin*, Seigneur de Rôny, fils de *Guy Mauvoisin*, Seigneur de Rôny, & de *Laure de Ponthieu*, dont sortirent trois filles.

Robert de Beaumez, Seigneur de Bombers, second fils de Robert, Châtelain de Beaumez, & d'*Isabeau de Cany*, eut pour femme une Dame nommée *Isabeau*, qui lui donna :

1. Marguerite, Dame de Bombers, femme *de Hugues de Lorraine*, Seigneur de Bones & de Rumigny, qui mourut sans lignée;
2. Joye, femme de *Jean*, Comte de *Sancerre;*
3. Et Isabeau, morte sans avoir été mariée.

BRANCHE
des Seigneurs de Beaumez, en Bretagne.

Robert de Beaumez, quatrième fils de Gilles, Châtelain de Beaumez, & d'*Agnès de Coucy*, fut élevé à la Cour de Pierre de Dreux, dit *Mauclerc*, Duc de Bretagne, son cousin, à raison de quoi on le surnomma de *Bretagne*. Il prit une femme dans la même Province, dont il eut: Mabille de Rohan fille d'alain v et d'Eléonore de Porhoët 1251

1. Raoul, dit *de Bretagne*, qui, étant né bossu, fut fait d'Eglise, & tint la dignité de Chanoine & Trésorier en l'Eglise de Reims;
2. Et Thomas, qui suit.

Thomas de Beaumez, dit *de Bretagne*, succéda aux terres paternelles sises en Bretagne, & laissa de son épouse, de laquelle le nom nous est inconnu.

Geoffroy de Beaumez, dit *de Bretagne*,

qui acquit la Terre de Tenailles près Origny. Sainte-Benoîte lui échut par la mort de RAOUL, son oncle. Nous n'avons pas davantage de connoissance de sa postérité.

Les armes: *de gueules, à la croix dentelée d'or.*

* BEAUMONT, en Hainaut, Diocèse de Liège, Terre, Seigneurie & Baronie qui fut érigée en Comté en faveur de *Guillaume de Croy*, Duc de Sorria, qui mourut l'an 1521, sans postérité, & eut pour héritier son neveu, *Philippe de Croy*, Duc d'Arschot, dont la petite-fille, *Anne de Croy*, porta le Duché de Croy & le Comté de Beaumont dans la Maison de *Ligne-Arenberg*.

* BEAUMONT, Terre située en Provence, près de la Durance, entre Aix & Manosque, qui a eu long-tems divers Co-Seigneurs. En 1199, *Gérard de Beaumont* vendit une portion de la Justice à *Guillaume de Forcalquier*. En 1481, *Antoine-René de Bouliers* la vendit à *Etienne de Vesc*. Elle passa ensuite à *Raymond d'Agoult*, & de celui-ci à *François de Bouliers*, qui avoit épousé *Jeanne d'Agoult*, sœur de *Raymond*. *François de Bouliers* la vendit, en 1506, à *Pierre d'Arlatan*, dont le fils, *Antoine*, la vendit à *Jean-Louis-Nicolas de Bouliers*, lequel l'engagea à *Jean de Riquetti*, Seigneur de Mirabeau, en 1584; mais *Gaspard & Alphonse de Bouliers* ayant repris cette Terre, la vendirent irrévocablement en 1635, à *Antoine de Riquetti*, Seigneur de Negreaux, & à son neveu, *Thomas de Riquetti*, Seigneur de Mirabeau. Ce dernier s'en étant accommodé avec son oncle, cette Terre a toujours appartenu depuis à ses descendans. Elle fut érigée en Comté par Lettres-Patentes du mois de Septembre 1713, enregistrées au Parlement d'Aix, en Janvier 1714, en faveur de *Jean-Antoine de Riquetti*, Marquis de Mirabeau, Brigadier des Armées du Roi. *(Tabl. gén.* part. VII, p. 192.) Voyez RIQUETTI.

BEAUMONT, en Provence, dont est chef JOSEPH-MELCHIOR DE BEAUMONT, qui a cinq enfans de *Madeleine Négrel-Bruni-de-Roquevair*. Il y a une branche de cette famille établie à Brignoles. Voyez *Armorial de France*, reg. I, pag. 117.

Les armes: *tranché d'argent sur gueules, à trois voiles d'argent enflées & posées en bande.*

BEAUMONT, en Provence: *d'or, à une bande d'azur, accompagnée de trois molettes de gueules, 2 en chef & 1 en pointe.*

BEAUMONT, en Provence : *de gueules, à six losanges d'or, posés en bande.*

* BEAUMONT, dans le Comté Venaissin, Diocèse de Vaison, Terre & Seigneurie, qui est un Fief avec haute, moyenne & basse Justice. Cette Terre étoit possédée dans le XVe siècle, par la Maison de *Brancas*. Elle l'a été ensuite par celle de *Laurens*, & elle appartient aujourd'hui à la Famille de *Fallot-de-Beaupré*.

* BEAUMONT en Vivarais, Terre & Mandement qui consiste dans les trois Terres de Beaumont, Saint-Melany & Donnac, & qui appartenoit à la Maison de *Beaumont* dans le XIe siècle. *Pons de Beaumont*, nommé *Magnificus & potens vir Dominus Pontius de Bellomonte, eques*, affranchit volontairement ses habitans, qui étoient serfs & taillables, *ad omni-modum domini voluntatem*, & réduit à quatre cas cet ancien droit de Taille-à-Merci, par acte d'affranchissement du 12 Janvier 1209. C'est sur cet acte, & sur plusieurs titres des XIIIe & XIVe siècles, que le Parlement de Toulouse a condamné les habitans dudit Mandement de *Beaumont*, & les a déclarés *taillables* en quatre cas envers le Seigneur de Beauvoir-du-Roure-de-Beaumont, Comte de Brison, par ses deux Arrêts du 29 Juillet 1754, & 3 Juin 1763.

La possession de cette Terre remonte jusqu'à la postérité la plus reculée, & il paroit certain que les Seigneurs de *Beaumont* ont donné leur nom à cette Terre, qui étoit appelée *Chabrilles*, dans les titres les plus anciens. Le Mandement de *Beaumont* fut donné à *Foulques de Beauvoir-du-Roure* par *Smaragde de Beaumont* sa mère, épouse de *Guillaume de Beauvoir-du-Roure*, IVe du nom, par testament du 4 Décembre 1435, & par *Pons de Beaumont* son ayeul maternel, par testament du 6 Février 1435, à la charge, par ledit *Foulques*, de porter le nom & les armes de *Beaumont*, ce que ses descendans ont exécuté jusqu'à ce jour.

Le Mandement de *Beaumont* fut érigé en Baronie par Lettres-Patentes du Roi LOUIS XIII, du 18 Août 1616. Ces Lettres portent que, *Sa Majesté voulant reconnoître les bons & agréables services de* Rostaing, *Seigneur de* Beaumont , *Capitaine de cent hommes d'armes, & de fes prédéceffeurs, a érigé & érige, par Lettres-Patentes, la Terre de* Beaumont *en Baronie.* Voyez BRISON.

BEAUMONT, Maifon originaire de Dauphiné, l'une des plus anciennes & des plus illuftres de cette Province. On voit dans la Vallée de Gréfivaudan, peu éloignée des frontières de Savoie, les reftes du Château de Beaumont, qui a appartenu à cette Maifon dès le XIᵉ fiècle, & qui n'en eft forti qu'en 1617, par la vente qu'en fit un Seigneur de Beaumont établi en Languedoc. Elle eft du nombre de celles que les Auteurs qualifient de *très-noble & très-ancienne Chevalerie.* Depuis le commencement du XIVᵉ fiècle, elle eft divifée en deux branches principales qui en ont formé plufieurs autres.

Guy Allard, dans la *Vie du Baron des Adrets;* Le Laboureur, dans fes *Mafures de l'Isle-Barbe;* Chorrier, dans fon *Etat Politique de Dauphiné,* ont donné des Généalogies de la Maifon de BEAUMONT; mais, dit l'Editeur de Moréri, Edit. de 1759, ces Auteurs ont manqué d'exaétitude en plufieurs points, parce qu'ils n'ont pas eu une connoiffance exaéte des anciens titres de cette Maifon, qui étoient reftés dans les Châteaux de la Freyte, Crolles, Montfort & des Adrets. Les Seigneurs qui les poffèdent aujourd'hui, ont communiqué ces titres à l'Editeur de Moréri; le dépôt de la Chambre des Comptes de Grenoble en a d'ailleurs fourni un grand nombre. C'eft d'après les uns & les autres qu'a été dreffée la Généalogie de cette Maifon, dont le premier Seigneur connu eft:

I. HUMBERT, Iᵉʳ du nom, Seigneur DE BEAUMONT, qui foufcrivit à une Charte d'*Odon Alleman,* Seigneur d'Uriage: cette Charte, confervée au Cartulaire du Prieuré de Domène, eft d'environ 1080. Sa femme fe nommoit *Béatrix,* & étoit de la Maifon des *Aynards,* Seigneurs de Domène, & Fondateurs du Prieuré de ce nom. Leurs enfans furent:

1. PIERRE, dont on ignore la poftérité;
2. GUIGUES, qui fuit;
3. Et GUITFRED ou WITFRED, connu par une Charte, dont on parlera au IIIᵉ degré, qui pour lors avoit deux fils, GUITFRED ou WITFRED, & BERLION.

II. GUIGUES, Iᵉʳ du nom, Seigneur DE BEAUMONT, foufcrivit à une Charte de donation, faite l'an 1106 au Prieuré de Domène par

GUILLAUME, fon oncle, Seigneur de Domène, qui y prit l'habit religieux dans fa dernière maladie. GUIGUES, petit-fils de GUIGUES le *Vieux,* tige de la première race des Dauphins, & fa femme, nommée *Regina,* foufcrivirent la même Charte. Deux aétes de 1108, confervés au Cartulaire de Grenoble, font mention de GUIGUES & de fa poftérité. On apprend par l'un d'eux que fa femme fe nommoit *Mathilde.* Ses enfans furent:

1. GUILLAUME;
2. GUIGUES, qui fuit;
3. Et GUITFRED ou WITFRED.

III. GUIGUES, IIᵉ du nom, Seigneur DE BEAUMONT. Un titre, qui fe trouve à la grande Chartreufe, porte que GUITFRED, fils de GUIGUES, GUIGUES, fon frère, avec fa femme & fes enfans, & WITFRED, leur oncle, avec fes enfans, donnèrent à la grande Chartreufe l'Alpe de Bovinant, voifine du Château de Beaumont. Cet aéte eft fait en préfence de *Saint-Hugues,* Evêque de Grenoble: il eft par conféquent antérieur à 1132, que mourut cet Evêque. Sa femme & fes enfans n'y font pas nommés; mais, felon l'ordre des tems, un de fes fils a été:

IV. SIBUET, Seigneur DE BEAUMONT & de la Freyte. On apprend d'une Charte d'*Eudes* ou *Odon,* Doyen, & depuis Evêque de Valence, de l'an 1152, que cet Evêque étoit fils de *Guy de Chaponay* & d'ANNE, fille de SIBUET DE BEAUMONT, Seigneur de la Freyte. Cette qualification fixe fa defcendance dans ceux du même nom, qui, au fiècle fuivant, poffédoient ces deux Châteaux, voifins l'un de l'autre. On trouve vers ce tems-là un SOFFREI DE BEAUMONT, qui foufcrivit avec *Bernard de Roffillon* & *Humbert de Bocfoxel,* à une Charte par laquelle AMÉDÉE III, Comte de Savoie, confirme les privilèges de l'Abbaye de Saint-Sulpice en Bugey, que ce Prince avoit fondée en 1130; Guichenon rapporte cette Charte, qu'il a tirée du Cartulaire de la même Abbaye. Allard parle d'une Bulle datée des Ides de Mai 1163, par laquelle le Pape ALEXANDRE III inféoda des dixmes à un SOFFREI DE BEAUMONT, en confidération du voyage qu'il avoit fait à la Terre-Sainte avec AMÉ, Comte de Savoie, lorfque ce Prince y paffa en 1147 avec le Roi LOUIS *le Jeune.*

V. GUILLAUME, Iᵉʳ du nom, Seigneur DE BEAUMONT, foufcrivit avec *Guillaume,* Seigneur *de Cruffol,* à une Charte de 1179, par laquelle le même *Eudes*, Evêque de Valence, fait donation de la Terre de Beauchaſtel, à *Eudes de Rétortor*, ſon neveu.

VI. HUMBERT, II° du nom, Seigneur DE BEAUMONT, rendit à l'Egliſe de Saint-Maurice de Vienne les dixmes de Saint-Pierre de Paladru dans le Viennois; la Charte de cette donation, datée de l'an 1200, ſe trouve au Cartulaire de Saint-Maurice. On connoît par cette Charte que la femme d'HUMBERT ſe nommoit *Agnès*, & que ſes enfans étoient:

1. & 2. GUILLAUME & ALBERT;
3. PIERRE, qui ſuit;
4. Et AALIS ou ALISE, qui fut Abbeſſe des Hayes, Monaſtère de l'Ordre de Citeaux, peu éloigné du Château de Beaumont.

VII. PIERRE, Seigneur DE BEAUMONT, eſt nommé préſent avec ſes fils à un acte de la Dauphine *Béatrix*. Cet acte ſe voit à la Chambre des Comptes de Grenoble, & eſt de 1198.

VIII. ARTAUD, Ier du nom, Seigneur DE BEAUMONT & de la Freyte, Chevalier, eſt celui depuis lequel la filiation eſt ſuivie & prouvée par titres. Quoiqu'on n'en ait recouvré aucun qui apprenne expreſſément qu'il deſcende d'HUMBERT II, ou de quelqu'un de ſes fils, nommés dans la Charte de 1200, il eſt vraiſemblable qu'il tiroit ſon origine des anciens Seigneurs du même nom, qui poſſédoient les mêmes Terres, & qu'il eſt un des fils de PIERRE, dont il eſt parlé dans l'acte de 1198. ARTAUD reçut, le jour des Ides de Mai 1245, la reconnoiſſance féodale de noble Dame *Gerſe de la Terraſſe* & de *Guillaume*, ſon fils, pour tout ce qu'ils poſſédoient dans le Mandement de Beaumont & dans la Paroiſſe du Touvet; & cet ARTAUD les en inveſtit. Par acte du 10 des Calendes de Juin 1250, ARTAUD donna à la Chartreuſe de Saint-Hugon tout le droit qu'il pouvoit avoir à la montagne du Sueil, au-deſſus du Château de Beaumont. Sa femme, nommée dans cet acte, s'appeloit *Ambroſie*. Il en eut quatre fils, mentionnés dans les actes ci-deſſus, ſçavoir:

1. ARTAUD, qui ſuit;
2. JEAN;
3. AMÉDÉE, qui, conjointement avec ARTAUD, ſon frère, donna à la Chartreuſe de Saint-Hugon, le 6 des Calendes de Juin 1271, les pâturages des Alpes de Larc, de Lencor & du Sueil. Il eut un fils nommé JEAN, qui, en qualité de ſon ſucceſſeur, fit hommage le 14 Septembre 1310 à *Hugues*, frère du Dauphin, & Seigneur de Faucigny;

4. Et FRANÇOIS.

IX. ARTAUD, II° du nom, Chevalier, Seigneur DE BEAUMONT & de la Freyte, confirma en 1271, avec AMÉDÉE, ſon frère, la donation faite par ſon père en 1250 à la Chartreuſe de Saint-Hugon, & en fit de nouvelles. De *Philippe*, ſa femme, nommée dans un traité daté de la veille de la Madeleine 1273, entre *Aimon*, Comte de Genève, & ſon *cher & fidèle* ARTAUD, Seigneur DE BEAUMONT, Chevalier, par lequel le Comte *Aimon*, rend en fief à ARTAUD tout ce qui lui avoit été donné par elle, il eut trois fils, connus par le partage qu'il fit de ſes biens entr'eux en 1304:

1. ARTAUD, qui ſuit;
2. FRANÇOIS, qui ſervoit en qualité d'Ecuyer dans l'armée du Roi de France, contre les Flamands en 1301. Il mourut avant ſon père, & laiſſa deux filles, PHILIPPE & FRANÇOISE;
3. GUIGUES, dit *Guers*, qualifié de *Chevalier* dans tous ſes actes, qui eut dans ſon lot la Terre des Adrets; & reçut, la même année 1304, les reconnoiſſances de ſes Cenſitaires & des Feudataires de ce Château. Il reçut, le 6 des Ides de Janvier 1316, de *Guillaume*, Comte de Genève, des biens en augmentation de fief. On voit par ſon teſtament, daté du Mardi après la Sainte-Antoine 1317, qu'il avoit eu deux femmes, *Artaude* & *Béatrix*, dont il ne laiſſa pas d'enfans. Il y inſtitue héritier ſon neveu ARTAUD IV, fils aîné d'ARTAUD III, ſon frère, & fait des legs à différentes perſonnes de ſa famille;
4. HUGONE;
5. Et AMBROSIE, femme d'*Aimon d'Arces*, Chevalier.

X. ARTAUD, III° du nom, Seigneur DE BEAUMONT & de la Freyte, Damoiſeau, eut le Château de Beaumont par le partage que ſon père fit avec ſes enfans en 1304. Il fut marié 1° à *Marguerite*, & 2° à *Agnès de Bellecombe*. Il eut du premier lit:

1. ARTAUD, qui ſuit, dont la poſtérité ſe diviſa en pluſieurs branches, deſquelles il reſte celle d'*Autichamp* & celles de *Saint-Quentin*, de *Montaut* & de *Saint-Sauveur*, forties de la branche des *Adrets;*
2. BERARD;
3. AGNÈS, mariée à *Ancelot d'Avalon;*
4. MARGUERITE, mariée, en 1295, à *Albert Bigot*, Seigneur de la Pierre.

Et du ſecond lit:

5. GUIGUES, dit *Guers*, qui, le 9 Janvier 1334, fit hommage à HUMBERT II, Dauphin, pour les biens que ſon père avoit poſſédés à Ava-

lon. Il eut un fils, nommé AMBLARD, qui mourut avant lui;

6. ARTAUD, qui époufa *Jacquemette de Serravalle*, dans le Briançonnois;

7. AMBLARD, Ier du nom, Seigneur DE BEAUMONT & de *Montfort*, qui a formé la feconde branche principale, rapportée ci-après, de laquelle font forties les branches de *Pompignan-Peyrac* & du *Repaire*, auffi rapportées ci-après;

8. HENRI, qui tefta en 1328;

9. FRANÇOISE, mariée à *Joffrei de Galles*, qui fut un des Nobles à qui le Dauphin HUMBERT II & les Commiffaires du Roi PHILIPPE *de Valois* confièrent la garde des Châteaux Delphinaux, après le premier tranfport du Dauphiné à la France en 1343;

Et deux filles, Religieufes.

PREMIÈRE BRANCHE
PRINCIPALE,
qui eft celle des Seigneurs DE LA FREYTE, D'AUTICHAMP, DES ADRETS & DE SAINT-QUENTIN.

XI. ARTAUD DE BEAUMONT, IVe du nom, nommé *Artaudet* du vivant de fon père, rendit hommage à *Amédée*, Comte de Genève, le 3 Décembre 1326; il vivoit encore en 1359. Il eut de *Marguerite de Rochefort:*

1. FRANÇOIS, qui fuit;

2. Et CATHERINE, mariée 1° à *Humbert de Loras*, dont elle eut deux fils, tués à la guerre; & 2° à *Pierre Roffillon*, Chevalier, Seigneur de Bouchage, dont elle étoit veuve le 24 Janvier 1403.

XII. FRANÇOIS DE BEAUMONT, Seigneur de la Freyte, des Adrets en Gréfivaudan, &c., eft qualifié dans tous fes actes *noble & puiffant Homme*. En 1377, il fit hommage à *Pierre*, Comte de Genève, de fon Château des Adrets. Il eut de *Polie de Chabrillan:*

1. ARTAUD, qui fuit, & eut en partage le Château de la Freyte;

2. HUMBERT, qui eut les Terres d'Autichamp, de Pelafol & de Barbières, & fit les branches de *Pelafol* & d'*Autichamp;*

3. Et ARNAUD, qui eut le Château des Adrets, & fit la branche qui en porta le nom, de laquelle font fortis les Seigneurs de *Saint-Quentin, Montaut* & *Saint-Sauveur.*

XIII. ARTAUD DE BEAUMONT, V^e du nom, Chevalier, Seigneur de la Freyte, étoit l'un des 67 Gentilshommes de la Compagnie d'Antoine de la Tour, Seigneur de Vinay, qui, fuivant leur montre faite à Auxerre le 8 Sep-

tembre 1386, alloient fervir le Roi à fon paffage en Angleterre. Sa femme fut *Antoinette de la Baume*, qui tefta en 1413, & inftitua fes quatre fils, les fubftituant les uns aux autres. Elle étoit fille & héritière d'*Aimon*, Chevalier, qui poffédoit de grands biens dans les Mandemens de Tullin, de Moreftel & de Renage. Leurs enfans furent:

1. FRANÇOIS, qui fuit;

2. AYNARD, mort fans poftérité;

3. ARTAUD, Damoifeau, qui mourut fans enfans de *Jeanne de Buffevant*, fille de *Pierre*, & de *Françoife de Nerpol;*

4. AIMON, mort fans poftérité;

5. JEANNE, Religieufe à Montfleuri, près Grenoble;

6. Et MARGUERITE.

XIV. FRANÇOIS DE BEAUMONT, IIe du nom, Seigneur de la Freyte, &c., Grand-Bailli du Gréfivaudan, marcha à l'arrière-ban commandé par Henri de Saffenage en 1424, & combattit à la bataille de Verneuil, où 300 Gentilshomme du Dauphiné furent tués. Il tefta le 27 Mars 1446, & eut d'*Aynarde de Guiffrey*, fille d'*Antoine*, Seigneur de Boutière, qui étoit veuve au mois de Décembre 1446:

1. CLAUDE, qui fuit;

2. JEAN, mort fans poftérité;

3. GEORGES, mort auffi fans poftérité;

4. Et une fille mariée à noble *Jacques Bompar.*

XV. CLAUDE DE BEAUMONT, en confidération de fes fervices, obtint, le 15 Février 1453, du Dauphin LOUIS, fils du Roi CHARLES VII, fous lequel il avoit fervi, une remife des droits de lods pour des acquifitions qu'il avoit faites, comme fon père l'avoit déjà obtenue. Il vivoit encore le 8 Mars 1482. Il avoit époufé, par contrat du 26 Janvier 1450, *Antoinette de Saint-Agnan*, fille de *Béraud*, Seigneur de Gaftine & de Confolens en Auvergne, dont il laiffa:

PHILIPPE DE BEAUMONT, Dame de la Freyte, qui fut mariée à *Humbert de la Tour*, Chevalier, Seigneur du Vinay. Cette Dame vendit le Château de la Freyte au Seigneur de *Luxembourg*, & ce Château revint depuis au Baron *des Adrets.*

BRANCHE
des Seigneurs DE PELAFOL, BARBIÈRES, LA BASTIE-ROLLAND & AUTICHAMP, *fortie des Seigneurs* DE LA FREYTE.

XIII. HUMBERT DE BEAUMONT, IIIe du nom,

fils de François, Ier du nom, & de *Polie de Chabrillan*, nommé dans quelques actes Imbert, fervoit avec Artaud, fon frère, en 1386, fous la bannière d'Antoine de la Tour, Seigneur du Vinay, Chevalier-Banneret. Il fut auffi grand guerrier que puiffant en biens. Il combattit vaillamment à la bataille d'Anton, gagnée en 1429 fur le Prince d'Orange par Raoul de Gaucourt, Gouverneur de Dauphiné. Il tefta le 15 Novembre 1436, & fut marié 1° avec *Pernette de Cordon*, fille de *Rodolphe*, & de *Marie de Duin*, Dame d'Evieu en Bugey; & 2° avec *Bruniffande de Cornillan*, fille de *Pierre*. Du premier lit il eut:

  1. Louis, qui fuit;

Et du fecond:

  2. André, qui fervit à l'arrière-ban du Dauphiné, commandé par Jacques, Baron de Saffenage, & acquit beaucoup de gloire à la bataille de Montlhéry en 1465, où il fut tué avec 50 autres Gentilshommes de la même Province. Il eut en partage les Terres d'Autichamp & d'Antoiles, & fit la branche des anciens Seigneurs d'*Autichamp*, finie en 1556 en la perfonne de Humbert, fon petit-fils, lequel, de fon mariage avec *Gilette de Saffenage*, ne laiffa que des filles;

  3. Marie;

  4. Louise, morte fans enfans en 1490. Elle avoit époufé, en 1442, Noble *Pierre Grange* de Chambéry;

  5. Françoise;

  6. N..., Religieufe aux Chartreufes de Salette, en Dauphiné;

  7. Et Polie, mariée à *Jean Alleman*, Seigneur de Sechilienne.

XIV. Louis de Beaumont, Seigneur de Pelafol, &c., reçut en 1424, en confidération de fes fervices, de Louis de Poitiers, Seigneur de Saint-Vallier, l'inveftiture de plufieurs biens qu'il avoit acquis à Creft. Il tefta le 2 Octobre 1439, & laiffa à *Louife de Grolée*, fa femme, fille d'*Humbert* & de *Jeanne de Gruères*, d'une ancienne Maifon de Savoie, & à François de Beaumont, Seigneur de la Freyte, fon coufin germain, la tutelle de fon fils unique:

XV. Guillaume de Beaumont, IIe du nom, Chevalier, Seigneur de Pelafol, &c., qui tefta au Château de la Baftie-Rolland le 11 Avril 1515. Il avoit époufé, avec difpenfe en 1460, *Antoinette Alleman*, fa parente, fille d'*Aimon*, Seigneur de Champ & de Taulignan, dont:

Tome II.

  1. Claude, qui fuit;

  2. Claire, femme, en 1515, de *Philippe de Bellecombe*, en qui finit la Maifon de *Bellecombe*, dont les biens pafsèrent à *Guigues Guiffrey*, connu fous le nom de *Capitaine Boutières*;

  3. Louise;

  4. Et Jeanne, Religieufe au Monaftère de Saint-Verain d'Avignon.

XVI. Claude de Beaumont, Seigneur de Pelafol, &c., fuivit le Roi Charles VIII en Italie. Il tefta le 8 Octobre 1516, & avoit époufé, le 10 Mars 1498, *Ragonde d'Urre*, fille de *Jourdan*, Co-Seigneur d'Urre au Diocèfe de Valence, dont:

  1. Jean, qui en 1519 étoit un des 100 Gentilshommes de la Maifon du Roi, fous la charge du Seigneur de Saint-Vallier. Il mourut fans alliance en 1559;

  2. Antoine, qui fuit;

  3. Claude, qui laiffa un fils naturel, nommé *Alexandre de Beaumont*;

  4. Olivier;

  5. Françoise, alliée, en 1559, à *Guillaume Athenoul*, dit *Gordon*, d'une ancienne Nobleffe de Diois;

  6. Et Louise, mariée à *Maurice Jaubert*, dont elle étoit veuve en 1559.

XVII. Antoine de Beaumont, Chevalier, Seigneur de Pelafol, Barbières, &c., tefta le 7 Octobre 1569, étant dans l'intention d'aller en France trouver la perfonne du Roi, pour continuer l'exercice des armes à fon fervice. Il ne vivoit plus en 1574. Il avoit époufé, en 1555, *Marguerite de Monteux*, fille de *Jérôme*, Seigneur de Miribel en Dauphiné. Il eut:

  1. Gaspard, qui fuit;

  2. 3. & 4. Madeleine, Françoise & Antoinette.

XVIII. Gaspard de Beaumont, Seigneur d'Autichamp, Pelafol, Barbières, &c., étant encore fort jeune en 1574, tefta, *étant, dit-il, dans la réfolution de faire un voyage, & de fe mettre à la fuite de quelques Princes ou grands Seigneurs, comme la coutume eft aux Gentilshommes de fon âge*. Il tefta une feconde fois en 1585, étant fur le point d'aller fervir le Roi en Guyenne; & une troifième fois le 8 Octobre 1600. Il vécut encore quelques années. Il époufa, par contrat du 26 Novembre 1578, *Antoinette de Villette*, fille de Noble *Charles de Villette*, Seigneur du Mey au Comtat-Venaiffin, & d'*Aymare de Sauvaing*, fille du Seigneur de Cheylar, dont:

1. Louis, mort fans alliance, après avoir tefté en 1648 ;
2. Charles, Seigneur d'Autichamp, Gouverneur d'Exilles en Dauphiné, mort auffi fans alliance ;
3. Antoine, qui fuit ;
4. Claude, qui fut Gouverneur pour le Roi du Château d'Exilles, étant âgé de 70 ans. Il avoit époufé *Louife Alleman*, fille de *Gafpard*, Baron d'Uriage, & de *Marguerite de Bouliers*, dont il n'eut point d'enfans ;
5. Et Louise, mariée, en 1606, avec Noble *François du Faure*, Seigneur du Cherveau en Vivarais.

XIX. Antoine de Beaumont, IIe du nom, Seigneur d'Autichamp & de Roche, époufa, le 1er Septembre 1609, *Françoife de Florence*, fille de Noble *Guichard*, Seigneur de Gerbeis, & d'*Hélène de Vaux*. Ils firent un teftament mutuel dans leur Maifon de Saint-Rambert le 6 Septembre 1640. Leurs enfans furent :

1. François, qui fuit ;
2. Charles, Seigneur de Miribel, &c., Gouverneur des Ville & Château d'Angers, né en 1621. Il commença à fervir en 1639 dans le Régiment d'Infanterie du Comte d'Harcourt. Il fervit 21 ans dans ce Régiment, fe trouva au combat de Liorens en Catalogne en 1645, où il fut bleffé à la tête de fa Compagnie ; au fiège de Lérida, où il eut trois chevaux tués fous lui en 1646 ; fur le canal de Nieuport en 1647, où il foutint avec fa Compagnie le feu de 2000 Cavaliers ; & en 1648 à la bataille de Lens, où il commanda le Régiment, les Capitaines qui étoient avant lui ayant été tués ou bleffés. En 1650 & 1651, il fit la charge de Maréchal-des-Logis à l'Armée de Guyenne. Le Comte d'Armagnac, Gouverneur d'Anjou, le demanda au Roi en 1666, pour être fon Lieutenant au Gouvernement des Ville & Château d'Angers. Il époufa 1° *Louife de Roftaing*, fille de *Jacques*, Seigneur de Geffans, & d'*Efpérance d'Iferan-Geffans* ; & 2° *Françoife de Jony*, fille d'*Antoine*, & d'*Emerentienne de Chabert*. Il eut du premier mariage : -

    Jean-Claude de Beaumont, Chevalier, Seigneur de Miribel, Moufquetaire du Roi en 1675, Capitaine & Major du Régiment de Cavalerie du Comte d'Armagnac, Lieutenant du Roi au Gouvernement d'Anjou, Ville & Château d'Angers, mort fans alliance en 1644 ;
    Joseph, Chevalier d'Autichamp, qui fervit dans le Régiment de Cavalerie de Brionne jufqu'à la Paix de Nimègue ;

Et Louise-Olympe, veuve en 1710 avec trois filles de *Pierre Binet*, Chevalier, Seigneur de Montifray, Capitaine de Carabiniers. La première & la feconde des filles ont été mariées, l'une au Marquis d'*Autichamp*, & l'autre au Comte, fon frère, dont il fera parlé ci-après.
3. Anne, mariée à Noble *François de Pourroy*, de la Ville de Creft ;
4. Et Hélène, mariée, en 1640, à *Jean de Laube*, Baron de Bron, Seigneur de Saint-Trivier.

XX. François de Beaumont, Seigneur d'Autichamp, &c., fit hommage le 31 Mai 1645 pour fa Terre d'Autichamp ; & lors de la recherche générale de la Nobleffe il fit preuve en 1667 de fon ancienne extraction noble, par titres, remontés jufqu'à la féparation des branches de *la Freyte* & de *Pelafol* ou *Autichamp*, & fut maintenu, comme noble d'ancienne race, par Jugement avec Charles, fon frère, Seigneur de Miribel, Gouverneur & Lieutenant pour le Roi en la Ville & Château d'Angers, & avec Claude de Beaumont, leur oncle. François tefta dans fon Château de Beaumont le 6 Janvier 1681, & ne vivoit plus le 14 Novembre fuivant. Il avoit époufé, à l'âge de 48 ans, le 9 Juillet 1644, *Louife-Olympe de Breffac*. Il laiffa :

1. Charles Just, qui fuit ;
2. Laurent-François, Colonel d'un Régiment de Cavalerie de fon nom en 1703, mort fans alliance en 1718 ;
3. Joseph, qui prit le parti de l'Eglife, mort en 1696 ; .
4. Marie, alliée à N..... *Brunier*, Seigneur de Larnage ;
5. & 6. Marie-Marguerite, & Louise-Hélène, Religieufes à la Vifitation de Valence ;
7. Et Marie-Anne, Religieufe à Sainte-Urfule de Montelimart.

XXI. Charles-Just de Beaumont, Seigneur d'Autichamp, &c., Lieutenant de la Meftre-de-Camp du Régiment de Villequier, quitta le fervice après la mort de fon père. Il commanda l'arrière-ban du Dauphiné en 1690, & mourut en 1708. Il avoit époufé, le 14 Novembre 1661, *Gabrielle de la Baume-Pluvinel*, fille d'*Antoine*, Seigneur de la Vallée de Quint, Gouverneur des Ville, Tour & Château de Creft, & d'*Alexandrine de Tertullé-de-la-Roque*. Il laiffa :

1. Antoine, qui fuit ;
2. Joseph, Comte d'Autichamp, Page du Roi en fa Grande-Ecurie en 1702, Capitaine de-

Cavalerie en 1708, Exempt des Gardes-du-Corps en 1713, Chef de Brigade en 1733, Brigadier des Armées du Roi en 1734, mort à Versailles le 19 Janvier 1739, âgé de 53 ans. Il avoit épousé, en 1719, *Marie-Eulalie de Montifray*, sa cousine, sœur de la femme du Marquis d'*Autichamp*, son frère aîné mentionné ci-après, morte en 1750 chez les Dames de Miramione à Paris;

3. François, Grand-Doyen de la Cathédrale d'Angers, Abbé d'Oigny en 1736, Evêque de Tulle en 1740, Abbé de la Victoire de Senlis en 1754, mort en 1764 ou 1765;

4. Louis-Imbert, Chevalier d'Autichamp, Page du Roi en sa Grande-Ecurie en 1711, ensuite Mestre-de-Camp de Cavalerie, Exempt des Gardes-du-Corps, & Brigadier des Armées du Roi en 1740;

5. Marie-Gabrielle, alliée, en 1698, à *Henri Pelletier-de-la-Garde-de-Pariol*, près Carpentras;

6. Anne, Religieuse au Monastère de la Visitation de Crest, lors du testament de son père en 1708;

7. Et Thérèse, Religieuse au même Monastère.

XXII. Antoine de Beaumont, IIIe du nom, appelé *le Marquis d'Autichamp*, Page du Roi en sa Grande-Ecurie en 1699, Lieutenant de Roi de la Province d'Anjou, & Commandant des Ville & Château d'Angers en survivance du Seigneur de Miribel, son cousin, & en exercice après sa mort en 1744, épousa, en 1710, *Jeanne-Olympe Binet de Montifray*, fille de *Pierre*, Capitaine de Carabiniers, & de Louise-Olympe de Beaumont-d'Autichamp-de-Miribel. En faveur de ce mariage, MM. d'Autichamp-de-Miribel, oncles de l'épouse, lui firent donation de leurs biens. Antoine de Beaumont n'en eut que:

XXIII. Louis-Joseph de Beaumont, dit *le Marquis d'Autichamp*, Seigneur de Montmoutier, &c., successivement Page de la Grande-Ecurie, Mousquetaire du Roi, Guidon & Enseigne de Gendarmerie, Lieutenant de Roi des Ville & Château d'Angers, Colonel-Lieutenant du Régiment d'Enghien, Infanterie, fut tué à la bataille de Lawfeld le 2 Juillet 1747. Il avoit épousé, le 26 Juin 1737, une nièce de la Maréchale *de Broglie*, nommée *Marie-Céleste-Perrine Locquet-de-Grandville*, fille de *Charles*, Seigneur de Grandville, Maréchal des Camps & Armées du Roi, & de *Marie-Céleste de Gaubert*, dont:

1. Jean-Thérèse-Louis, qui suit;

2. Charles-Antoine-François, né le 30 Mai 1739, dit l'*Abbé d'Autichamp*, Vicaire-Général de l'Archevêché de Toulouse;

3. Et Antoine-Joseph-Eulalie, né le 10 Décembre 1744, appelé *le Vicomte d'Autichamp*, Capitaine de Dragons au Régiment de son frère. Il est marié, & a deux fils.

XXIV. Jean-Thérèse-Louis de Beaumont, dit *le Marquis d'Autichamp*, né le 17 Mai 1738, d'abord Lieutenant au Régiment du Roi, aujourd'hui Colonel du Régiment de Dragons de son nom, ci-devant Carman, & *Autichamp* depuis 1761; & Lieutenant de Roi d'Angers; a fait la campagne de 1757 en qualité d'Aide-de-Camp du Maréchal Duc de Broglie. Il a épousé, en 1763, *N... Maussion-de-la-Court-Augé*, veuve du Marquis *de Vastan*.

BRANCHE

des Seigneurs des Adrets & de Saint-Quentin, *issus des Seigneurs* de la Freyte.

XIII. Aynard de Beaumont, Seigneur des Adrets & de Saint-Quentin, dernier fils de François de Beaumont, Ier du nom, Chevalier, Seigneur de la Freyte & des Adrets, & *de Polie de Chabrillan*, eut en partage la Terre des Adrets, & par son mariage celle de Saint-Quentin. Il servoit à la guerre sous le titre d'*Ecuyer*, & le premier des dix que commandoit Geoffroy d'Argenton, Chevalier, l'an 1388. Il est compris parmi les Nobles de Dauphiné dans une révision des feux de 1450, & il mourut fort vieux. Sa femme fut *Aymonette Alleman*, fille de *Guigues*, Seigneur d'Uriage, & d'*Anne de Châteauneuf*. Il en eut:

1. Aynard, qui suit;

2. Jacques, Seigneur de Saint-Quentin, mari de *Marguerite de Sassenage*. Il fit la branche des anciens Seigneurs de *Saint-Quentin*, éteinte 100 ans après par le décès, sans enfans, de Melchior & Gaspard de Beaumont, Seigneurs de Saint-Quentin, ses arrières-petits fils, & fils de Laurent de Beaumont, qui suivit le Roi Charles VIII à la conquête du Royaume de Naples, & combattit vaillamment à la bataille de Marignan, & d'*Anne de Sassenage*, fille de *François*, & de *Guicharde d'Albon*;

3. Louis, Sieur de la Tour, mort sans enfans. Il avoit épousé *Gabrielle Terrail*, fille de *Pierre*, Seigneur de Bayard, tué à la ba-

taille de Montlhéry en 1465, & de *Marie de Bocſoʒel*, tante du Chevalier *Bayard;*

4. Louise, Religieuſe à Montfleury, près Grenoble;

5. & 6. Jeanne & Claudine, Religieuſes.

XIV. Aynard de Beaumont, IIe du nom, Seigneur des Adrets, fit hommage de cette Terre au Roi-Dauphin en 1488, & commanda une Brigade dans l'arrière-ban de Dauphiné, qui marcha en 1495. Il teſta le 20 Septembre 1499. De *Françoiſe de Laire* il laiſſa :

1. Georges, qui ſuit;

2. Antoine, Auteur de la branche des Seigneurs de *Tencin*, rapportée ci-après;

3. Claude, Prieur Clauſtral de l'Iſle - Barbe l'an 1509: c'eſt lui qui a donné occaſion à le Laboureur, Auteur des Maſures de cette Abbaye, de faire la Généalogie de cette Maiſon;

4. François, Religieux à Boſcodon, dont Jean de Beaumont étoit Abbé;

5. Et Gabrielle, mariée 1° à Noble *Nourry du Motel*, dont la famille eſt éteinte depuis peu d'années; & 2° à Noble *Guelis de Menʒe*, Seigneur de Beaujeu en Gapençois, Maître-d'Hôtel du Dauphin.

XV. Georges de Beaumont, Seigneur des Adrets, épouſa *Jeanne Guiffrey*, fille de *Sébaſtien*, Seigneur de Boutières, & de *Lionette Arcoud*. Elle étoit ſœur de *Guigues Guiffrey*, connu ſous le nom de *Capitaine Boutières* dans les guerres d'Italie ſous François Ier. De ce mariage naquirent :

1. François, qui ſuit;

2. Claude, Moine de l'Abbaye de l'Iſle-Barbe;

3. Et Gabrielle, femme de *Claude Guiffrey*, Seigneur de Freſné.

XVI. François de Beaumont, IIe du nom, Seigneur des Adrets & de la Freyte, fut un des Gentilshommes de France dont le courage & les actions militaires firent le plus de bruit dans les guerres de religion ſous Charles IX. Guy Allard en a donné la Vie; le P. Daniel, M. de Thou, Davila, Chorrier & beaucoup d'autres, en ont amplement parlé. On peut encore conſulter Moréri, édition de 1759, où l'on trouve un abrégé de ſa vie, ſur laquelle nous paſſons pour ne nous attacher qu'à la partie généalogique de cette Maiſon. Le Baron *des Adrets* fit hommage au Roi-Dauphin le 24 Août 1540, & donna l'aveu de ſes Châteaux des Adrets & de la Freyte. (Le Château de la Freyte avoit appartenu à la branche aînée de ſa Maiſon, & en étoit ſorti

par la vente que l'héritière de cette branche avoit faite au Seigneur *de Luxembourg*). Le Baron *des Adrets* teſta le 2 Janvier 1586, & mourut en 1587. Il avoit épouſé, par contrat du 26 Mars 1544, *Claude de Gumin*, veuve de Noble *Guillaume de Vachon*, qui teſta le 19 Mai 1578. Elle étoit fille de Meſſire *Antoine de Gumin*, Chevalier, Seigneur de Romaneſche, & de *Louiſe de Rochefort*. Ses enfans furent :

1. Laurent, Baron des Adrets, Gentilhomme de la Maiſon du Roi Charles IX en 1572, & du Roi Henri III en 1575;

2. Claude, qui, ſelon Brantôme, ne s'épargna pas au maſſacre de *la Saint-Barthélemy*, & mourut en 1573, étant Lieutenant de M. du Gua, au ſiège de la Rochelle, *en grande contrition*, dit le même Brantôme, *du ſang qu'il avoit répandu;*

3. Laurent, Page du Roi Charles IX. Ce Prince lui ayant ordonné d'aller appeler ſon Chancelier, ce Page le trouva à table. Le Chancelier lui ayant répondu qu'après dîné il iroit recevoir les ordres du Roi: *comment*, dit le Page, *faut-il retarder d'un moment lorſque le Roi commande? vîte qu'on marche ſans excuſe.* Le Chancelier le raconta lui-même au Roi, qui répondit en riant que *le fils ſeroit auſſi violent que le père.* C'eſt lui vraiſemblablement qui portoit le nom de *la Freyte*, & qui, lorſque ſon père fut arrêté à Grenoble en 1570, alla demander & obtint ſa délivrance. Ces trois fils du Baron *des Adrets* dont on vient de parler, ſont morts avant lui;

4. Susanne, Dame des Adrets & de la Freyte après la mort de ſon père. Elle en fit hommage au Roi en 1600, & vendit en 1603 le Château de la Freyte à *Florent de Reynard*, premier Préſident de la Chambre des Comtes de Grenoble. Elle teſta le 18 Octobre 1626 en faveur de ſon dernier mari, dont elle n'avoit point d'enfans ; & par là la Terre des Adrets a paſſé dans la Maiſon de *Vauſſerre*, où elle eſt encore. Elle avoit été mariée, 1° le 26 Février 1574, avec *Jean-Baptiſte Roux*, Comte de Tarvanas en Piémont; & 2° le 24 Avril 1608, étant déjà fort âgée, avec *Céſar de Vauſſerre*, Seigneur de Saint-Dizier.

5. Et Esther, mariée, en 1583, à *Antoine de Saſſenage*, Seigneur d'Izeron & de Monteillez.

BRANCHE
des Seigneurs de la Tour-de-Tencin.

XV. Antoine de Beaumont, ſecond fils d'Aynard, IIe du nom, Seigneur des Adrets,

& de *Françoise de Laire*, eſt auteur de cette branche, qui ſe diviſa encore en deux par ſes deux fils CLAUDE & ENNEMOND, qui devinrent Co-Seigneurs de Saint-Quentin par le décès, ſans enfans, de MELCHIOR & GASPARD, leurs couſins, qui poſſédoient cette Terre. Ils tranſigèrent ſur leurs droits ſucceſſifs avec la fille du Baron *des Adrets*.

CLAUDE fit la branche des Seigneurs du *Beſſet*, de *la Tour-de-Tencin* & de *Rochemure*, qui s'établit en Auvergne, où elle s'eſt éteinte à la fin du dernier ſiècle.

ENNEMOND forma la branche des Seigneurs *de Lisle* & *de la Modrinière*, qui ſubſiſte en Dauphiné dans les trois rameaux de *Saint-Quentin*, de *Montaut* & de *Saint-Sauveur*.

Du premier eſt:

> PIERRE-LOUIS DE BEAUMONT, Seigneur de Saint-Quentin, né en 1731, qui a ſervi dans le Régiment de Normandie, & a épouſé, à Metz en 1757, *N... du Prat*. Il a des frères & des ſœurs.

Du ſecond rameau ſont:

> JOSEPH, FRANÇOIS & PIERRE, fils de défunt PIERRE DE BEAUMONT, Seigneur de Montaut, qui fut bleſſé dangereuſement en 1692 à la bataille de Steinkerke, & eſt mort en 1742. JOSEPH ſe maria, & mourut ſans enfans. Les deux autres ſont au ſervice & ne ſont pas mariés.

Du troiſième rameau ſont:

> 1. MELCHIOR-ANTOINE, ancien Gouverneur pour le Roi de la ville de Saint-Marcelin, marié, 1º en 1727, à *Marie-Marguerite de Nyèvre*; & 2º en 1754, à *N... de Garnier*, fille de *N... de Garnier*, Conſeiller au Parlement de Grenoble, & de *N... d'Armand-de-Brion*;
> 2. CHARLES-JACQUES, dit *le Chevalier de Beaumont*, Capitaine au Régiment de Normandie, où il a ſervi depuis 1720 juſqu'en 1759 au moins;
> 3. HENRI, Chanoine & Infirmier de l'Egliſe Collégiale de Saint-Pierre de Vienne, où il fit ſes preuves de Nobleſſe en 1734 pour y être reçu;
> 4. Et LOUIS-JUSTIN, Chanoine de la même Egliſe, auſſi ſur ſes preuves faites en 1747;

Ils ont encore d'autres frères & deux ſœurs, ſçavoir:

> 5. GABRIELLE, Abbeſſe de Saint-Juſt de Romans, Ordre de Cîteaux;
> 6. Et MARIE-ADÉLAÏDE, veuve d'*Antoine de Brenier-de-Belair*, dont un fils, Lieutenant au Régiment de Normandie.

SECONDE BRANCHE
PRINCIPALE,

qui eſt celle des Seigneurs DE BEAUMONT & DE MONTFORT *en Dauphiné*, DE POMPIGNAN *en Languedoc*, & DE PEYRAC, *en Quercy*, *d'où eſt iſſue la branche* DU REPAIRE.

XI. AMBLARD DE BEAUMONT, Iᵉʳ du nom, Seigneur de Beaumont & de Montfort, Chevalier, fils d'ARTAUD, IIIᵉ du nom, Seigneur de Beaumont & de Bellecombe, eſt qualifié dans ſes actes de *Noble & Puiſſant Seigneur*, & dans pluſieurs *Magnifique & Puiſſant Seigneur*. Il eut toute la confiance du dernier Dauphin HUMBERT II, dont il fut le Miniſtre, & qu'il détermina à donner ſes Etats à la France. (Voyez ſon article dans Moréri, édit. de 1759, p. 259). Il teſta le 19 Décembre 1372, & vivoit encore en 1374. Il épouſa, par contrat du 19 Mai 1336, *Béatrix Alleman-de-Vaubonnois*, qui ſurvécut à ſon mari, & teſta le 21 Octobre 1381. Elle étoit fille de *Guillaume*, Seigneur de Vaubonnois, Chevalier, & d'*Agnès de Thoire-Villars*, parente du Dauphin, du chef de *Béatrix*, ſa biſayeule. Leurs enfans furent:

> 1. AYMARD, qui ſuit;
> 2. AMBLARD, qui continua la poſtérité;
> 3. Et ALIX, Abbeſſe des Hayes en 1410, qui vivoit encore en 1417, & ſe qualifioit alors, *par la grâce de Dieu*, Abbeſſe des Hayes.

XII. AYMARD DE BEAUMONT, Seigneur de Beaumont & de Montfort, Chevalier, eſt qualifié dans tous ſes actes *Noble & Puiſſant Homme*. Il ſe diſtingua en pluſieurs occaſions à la tête de cent hommes d'armes, contre les Anglois, qu'il mena enſuite en Italie au ſecours des Florentins, dans l'armée que commandoit le Duc de Touraine contre Jean Galéas, Duc de Milan, & dont François, Baron de Saffenage, étoit Lieutenant-Général. Il n'eut point d'enfans, & teſta au Château de la Terraſſe le 11 Juillet 1382. Par ſon teſtament il défend de mener à ſon convoi ſes chevaux caparaçonnés; mais veut ſeulement qu'on y porte ſon caſque ou timbre, ſon écu & ſon épée, qui ſeront préſentés par des Nobles. Son père l'avoit accordé, par contrat paſſé le 23 Janvier 1350, avec noble Demoiſelle *Anne de Vaulx*, fille aînée & héritière de *Drodet*, ou *Drodon de Vaulx*, Seigneur de la Terraſſe & du Millieu, & d'*Agnès de Fay*.

XII. AMBLARD DE BEAUMONT, IIᵉ du nom,

Seigneur de Beaumont & de Montfort, fuc-céda à fon frère dans fes Châteaux, auxquels il étoit fubftitué. On le trouve le troifième des fept Ecuyers de la Compagnie de Collandon, dans la montre générale qui en fut faite à Chartres, le 5 Septembre 1380, pour fervir le Roi. Il mourut en 1398, laiffant de *Philippe de Saint-Agnan :*

1. AMBLARD, qui fuit ;
2. LOUIS, marié à noble *Claude Garnier*, dont il n'eut point d'enfans ;
3. HENRI, Doyen du Monaftère de Mauriac, qui fut pourvu du Prieuré du Touvet en 1443 ;
4. Et BÉATRIX, alliée à *Hugues d'Arces*, Seigneur de la Baftie-de-Meylan.

XIII. AMBLARD DE BEAUMONT, III° du nom, Seigneur de Beaumont & de Montfort, Chevalier, fit au Dauphin, le 18 Juin 1399, un hommage femblable à ceux de fes prédécef-feurs qu'il rappelle. Il fonda, le 3 Avril 1417, une Chapelle dans la Paroiffe de Crolles, & l'on apprend, par fon teftament du 10 Mars 1427, qu'il avoit époufé *Euftachie de Mont-maïeur*, Dame d'une illuftre Maifon de Savoie, qui a donné des Chevaliers à l'Ordre de l'Annonciade dès le tems de fon inftitution. Leurs enfans furent :

1. AMBLARD, qui fuit ;
2. AIMON, qui continua la poftérité ;
3. ANTOINE, Religieux de l'Ordre de Saint-Antoine en Viennois ;
4. CLAUDE, deftiné Religieux par le teftament de fon père ;
5. Et ANTOINETTE, Religieufe à l'Abbaye des Hayes, lors de ce teftament.

XIV. AMBLARD DE BEAUMONT, IV° du nom, Seigneur de Beaumont & de Montfort, eft qualifié, comme fes prédéceffeurs, *Noble & Puiffant* dans fes actes. Lui & AIMON, fon frère, font nommés les premiers dans un cé-lèbre concordat de famille du 7 Novembre 1446, où ces deux frères, qui defcendent d'AMBLARD Ier, ratifièrent avec les chefs des autres branches de leur Maifon, qui defcen-doient d'ARTAUD IV, frère d'AMBLARD Ier, les différens pactes faits avec leurs ayeux pour la confervation des Terres de leur Maifon dans leur defcendance mafculine par des fub-ftitutions réciproques & perpétuelles. Mais cet engagement folennel & réciproque n'em-pêcha pas qu'AMBLARD, qui avoit déja aliéné la plus grande partie de fes cens & rentes fei-gneuriales, ne continuât fes diffipations. Il

vendit à la plupart des Nobles, fes Feudatai-res, les hommages qu'ils lui devoient. Il époufa, au mois de Janvier 1438, *Margue-rite de Saffenage*, fille d'*Henri*, III° du nom, Baron de Saffenage, & d'*Antoinette de Saluces*.

XIV. AIMON DE BEAUMONT, Seigneur de Beaumont & de Montfort, qualifié dans plu-fieurs actes *Noble & Puiffant Homme*, fouf-crivit avec fon frère AMBLARD, IV° du nom, au concordat de famille, ci-devant mentionné, pour fe mettre en état de réparer les diffipa-tions de fon frère, & de rentrer dans les biens aliénés qui devoient lui revenir en vertu de la fubftitution. *Michel Caffard*, père de fon époufe, lui conftitua en dot tous les différens cens & droits feigneuriaux dépendans du Châ-teau de Beaumont qu'il avoit acquis, & il fut convenu que le furplus de la dot en argent fe-roit employé à retirer d'autres aliénations faites par AMBLARD, après la mort duquel il en-treprit de rentrer dans les biens de fa Mai-fon. C'eft ce que l'on peut voir dans les Con-feils CXL & CXLIII de Guy-Pape, où la defcen-dance de ces deux frères, depuis AMBLARD, Ier du nom, eft très-détaillée. AIMON DE BEAU-MONT ne vivoit plus en 1481, & eut de *Girar-de Caffard*, qui tefta le Ier Juin 1497 :

1. AMBLARD, qui fuit ;
2. LOUIS, deftiné par le teftament de fon père à être Chevalier de Rhodes ;
3. Et FRANÇOISE, mariée, en 1481, à *Pierre de Montfort*, Seigneur du Châtelard, de Bernin & de Craponod. Ce mariage man-qua de caufer la ruine de la Maifon de BEAU-MONT ; & les procès qui furvinrent ne fu-rent terminés que par Arrêt de 1515.

XV. AMBLARD DE BEAUMONT, V° du nom, Seigneur de Beaumont & de Montfort, qua-lifié, comme fes prédéceffeurs, de *Noble & Puiffant Homme* dans tous fes actes, com-battit vaillamment à la bataille de Marignan. Etant dans le deffein d'entrer en religion & de prendre l'Ordre de Prêtrife, il tefta le 14 Juin 1517. Il fit en effet profeffion le 12 du même mois chez les Chanoines Réguliers de la Cathédrale de Grenoble. Il vivoit encore en 1552, lors du teftament de fon fils, qui pour-vut à l'affurance de fa penfion. Il avoit épou-fé, le 8 Septembre 1504, *Marguerite Alle-man*, fille de *Charles*, & de *Clémence de Laydun*. Il eut pour fils unique :

XVI. LAURENT DE BEAUMONT, Chevalier,

Seigneur de Beaumont & de Montfort, qui testa 1° le 2 Avril 1550, & 2° le 5 Mars 1552, & mourut en 1564 ou 1565. Il étoit devenu Seigneur de Pompignan en Languedoc, & de Peyrac en Quercy, par son mariage que *Laurent Alleman*, son tuteur & oncle maternel lui fit faire le 1er Décembre 1538, avec *Delphine de Verneuil*, fille aînée & héritière de *Gratien de Verneuil*, Seigneur de Pompignan & de Peyrac, & de *Jeanne de Durfort*, alors sa veuve, aux conditions que l'un des enfans mâles qui sortiroit de ce mariage porteroit le nom de *Beaumont-de-Verneuil* pour conserver la mémoire & les armes de *Gratien de Verneuil* & de la Maison *de Peyrac*, conformément au testament du même *Gratien* du 1er Août 1537; & ce mariage fixa l'établissement dans ces Provinces. Ses enfans furent:

1. LAURENT, qui suit;
2. CHARLES, auteur de la branche *du Repaire*, rapportée ci-après;
3. ARTAUD, mentionné aux testamens de son père;
4. Et ISABEAU, déjà morte lors de ces testamens.

XVII. LAURENT DE BEAUMONT-VERNEUIL, IIe du nom, Seigneur de Beaumont & de Montfort en Dauphiné, de Pompignan & de Peyrac, est qualifié *noble & puissant Seigneur* dans l'inventaire qu'il fit faire au mois de Septembre 1565 après la mort de son père, tant de ses biens que des titres & actes de sa Maison, qui étoient alors au Château de Crolles dans la Terre de Montfort, le Château de Beaumont ayant été ruiné par les troubles passés. (C'est par le moyen de cet inventaire judiciaire, trouvé depuis peu au Parlement de Grenoble, & de la recherche faite en conséquence dans les Châteaux de Crolles & du Touvet, où ces titres étoient restés, lors de la vente de ces Terres en 1617, qu'on est parvenu à rectifier les méprises de Jean le Laboureur & d'Allard, dans les Généalogies qu'ils ont données de cette Maison). LAURENT eut des procès considérables au sujet des substitutions des biens de la branche d'*Allemand-Laval* & des *Cassard*, qui le retinrent longtems en Dauphiné. Il fit hommage-noble au Roi-Dauphin à la Chambre des Comptes de Grenoble le 6 Février 1594, pour ses Châteaux & Seigneuries de Beaumont, Crolles & Montfort. Il testa le 30 Octobre 1607, &

avoit épousé, en 1577, *Marguerite de Pelgry-du-Vigan*, fille de *Raymond*, Seigneur du Vigan, & de *Madeleine de Lauzières-Thémines*, dont il eut:

1. LAURENT-PHILIBERT, qui suit;
2. GRATIEN, marié, en 1630, avec *Gabrielle de Bourzolles*, veuve de *Jean de Rochefort*, Seigneur de Saint-Angel, & fille de *François*, Seigneur de Bourzoles, & de *Françoise de Caumont;*
3. FRANÇOISE, femme, en 1607, de *Gabriel d'Abzac*, Seigneur de la Serre;
4. ANTOINETTE, femme, en 1607, de *François de Geniez*, Seigneur de l'Angle;
5. SUSANNE, Religieuse à la Dorade de Cahors;
6. Et CATHERINE, alliée, en 1614, à *Hercule de Bonnot*, Seigneur de la Tuque.

XVIII. LAURENT-PHILIBERT DE BEAUMONT-VERNEUIL, Seigneur de Beaumont, Crolles, Montfort, Peyrac & Pompignan, épousa, le 17 Octobre 1611, *Catherine de Clermont*, fille de *Guion de Clermont*, Seigneur & Baron de Clermont-Vertillac, Chevalier de l'Ordre du Roi, Capitaine de 50 hommes d'armes, & de *Françoise de Clermont-de-Piles*. Ses enfans furent:

1. LAURENT, qui suit;
2. ANGÉLIQUE, mariée, en 1642, avec *Antoine de Verbais*, Seigneur de Masseclas & de Laval;
3. ANNE, femme du Baron *de la Jant;*
4. ANTOINETTE, alliée à *Pierre du Bois*, Seigneur de Reynac;
Et deux filles, Religieuses.

XIX. LAURENT DE BEAUMONT-VERNEUIL, IIIe du nom, Seigneur de Peyrac & de Pompignan, né le 7 Juillet 1626, épousa, le 25 Janvier 1654, *Hélène de Cheverry*, fille de *François*, Baron de la Réolle en Biscaye, &c., & de *Catherine de la Rochefoucauld-Montendre*. Il laissa pour enfans:

1. LAURENT, Seigneur de Pompignan & de Peyrac, né en Décembre 1654, mort le 7 Décembre 1727, sans enfans. Il avoit épousé, le 6 Novembre 1697, *Anne de Joubert*, fille de *François*, Seigneur de Rassiols, & d'*Angélique de Gasquet;*
2. GRATIEN, qui suit;
3. JACQUES, Officier d'Infanterie, mort sans enfans en Octobre 1737, qui avoit épousé à Die en Dauphiné, *Henriette de Roquebeau;*
4. JEAN-LAURENT, auteur d'un rameau rapporté ci-après;
5. CÉSAR, mort sans enfans le 7 Mai 1707;

6. Antoine, allié à *Anne de Gaillardy*, dont il n'a laiffé qu'une fille, nommée Isabeau, mariée à *Jean de Martin-de-Donneʒ*, Seigneur du Perget;

7. François, mort jeune à Charlemont, où il fervoit dans la Compagnie des Cadets; -

8. Laurent, mort en bas âge;

9. Françoise, morte Religieufe au Couvent des Bénédictines de Cahors;

10. Et Marie, morte Religieufe au même Monaftère.

XX. Gratien de Beaumont-Verneuil, Seigneur de Peyrac & de Pompignan, mort le 14 Octobre 1713, avoit époufé, par contrat du 12 Juillet 1710, *Anne de Longuet*, laiffant pour enfans:

1. Jacques, qui fuit;

2. Et Marie, alliée avec *Ebrard de Ventejou*.

XXI. Jacques de Beaumont-Verneuil, Seigneur de Peyrac, né le 12 Novembre 1712, a été marié, par contrat du 3 Juillet 1742, avec *Théréfe de Longuet*, fa coufine germaine maternelle, dont il a:

1. Jacques-Abraham, Marquis de Beaumont, né le 20 Avril 1743, marié le 17 Octobre 1768, à *N... Richier de Beaupré*, morte, laiffant un fils;

2. François, né le 17 Avril 1744;

3. Bertrand, né le 27 Septembre 1745;

4. Joseph, né le 31 Mai 1749;

5. Anne-Théréfe, née le 10 Octobre 1750;

6. Et Marie-Marguerite, née le 20 Juillet 1753.

RAMEAU
de Pompignan & Villeneuve, *forti de la branche de* Beaumont-Verneuil & Peyrac.

XX. Jean-Laurent de Beaumont, Seigneur de Marignac, quatrième fils de Laurent III, & d'*Hélène de Cheverry*, né le 10 Septembre 1662, fervit dans le Régiment du Pleffis-Bellière. Il fuivit avec fes frères le procès fur la fubftitution des Terres de leur Maifon en Dauphiné, dans lequel ils établirent leur defcendance depuis Amblard III & *Euftachie de Montmaïeur*, & mourut le 29 Juin 1743. Il époufa, par contrat du 15 Novembre 1694, *Marguerite du Cos-de-la-Hitte*, fille de *Jofeph*, Seigneur de Gafpard, & d'*Antoinette de la Salvetat*. Il a laiffé:

1. François, qui fuit;

2. Et Gratien, nommé *le Chevalier de Verneuil*, né le 3 Juillet 1703, mort fans alliance le 1er Septembre 1738.

XXI. François de Beaumont, Seigneur de Villeneuve, dit *le Comte de Beaumont-Pompignan*, né le 11 Avril 1697, époufa, par contrat du 28 Septembre 1733, *Marie-Anne-Louife de Plaibault-de-Villars-Lugin*, fille de *Louis-Ignace*, Brigadier des Armées du Roi, mort d'un coup de canon à Marchiennes en 1712, venant d'être nommé Maréchal-de-Camp, & d'*Elifabeth du Bois-de-Lauré*. Il en a:

Aimable-Elisabeth-Jeanne, mariée, le 29 Août 1751, avec *Jofeph-François de Caylus*, Marquis de Caylus, Seigneur & Baron de Venes, Réalmont, &c., Chevalier de Saint-Louis, l'un des Barons des Etats de Languedoc, fils de *Pierre-Jofeph-Hyacinthe*, Marquis de *Caylus*, Lieutenant-Général des Armées du Roi, Grand-Croix de l'Ordre de Saint-Louis, Lieutenant-Général de la Province de Rouffillon, Conflans & Cerdagne, Commandant audit Pays, Gouverneur des Ville & Citadelle de Mont-Louis, & d'*Elifabeth de Brunet-de-Pujol-de-Villeneuve-Lautrec*.

BRANCHE
des Seigneurs du Repaire & de la Roque, *iffue de celle de* Pompignan-Peyrac.

XVII. Charles de Beaumont, fecond fils de Laurent, Ier du nom, Seigneur de Baumont, & de *Delphine de Verneuil-Peyrac*, fervit fous le titre d'homme d'armes dans la Compagnie de 50 Lances des Ordonnances du Roi, fous la charge de M. de Clermont-Lodève, & depuis pendant les troubles de l'Etat en 1576 & 1577. Il tranfigea avec fon frère fur tous fes droits paternels & maternels, & fur ceux qui pouvoient lui appartenir dans les biens de la Maifon d'*Alleman-de-Laval* & de Noble *Michel Caffard*, leur trifayeul. Il tefta dans fon Château du Repaire le 24 Septembre 1605, inftitua fa femme, héritière, & fubftitua fon fils. Il étoit devenu Seigneur du Repaire, de Nabirac & de Saint-Aubin en Périgord, par fon mariage, du 3 Mars 1577, avec *Antoinette du Poujet*, fille d'*Imbert*, Seigneur des mêmes Terres, & de *Florette de Bar*. Il eut:

XVIII. Laurent de Beaumont, Chevalier, Seigneur du Repaire, Nabirac & Saint-Aubin, qui tefta le 24 Février 1645. Il avoit époufé, 1º le 30 Juillet 1595, *Marguerite de Salignac*, fille de *Jean*, Seigneur de la Mothe-Fénélon, Capitaine de 50 hommes d'armes, & d'*Anne de Pellegrue*, dont il n'eut point d'enfans; & 2° le 20 Novembre 1605, *Françoise de Chaunac-de-Lanzac*, fille de *Barthélemy*, Seigneur de Lanzac, & de *Catherine de Clermont*. Il laiffa:

1. Barthélemy, qui fuit;
2. & 3. Armand & Raymond;
4. Antoine, Religieux Capucin;
5. Catherine, mariée à *Bernard de Roufteau*, Seigneur du Puy-Lavaife;
6. Antoinette, mariée à *Jofeph de Meynard*, Seigneur de Clarefage, de la Maifon des Seigneurs de *Chaffenejoux*, en Limoufin;
7. Et Françoise, Religieufe de Sainte-Claire lors du teftament de fon père.

XIX. Barthélemy de Beaumont, Chevalier, Seigneur du Repaire, &c., Gentilhomme ordinaire de la Chambre du Roi, fe diftingua en 1753 à la prife de Sarlat, lorfque cette ville fut emportée par le Sieur de Marin, Lieutenant-Général, qui avoit été envoyé par le Duc de Candale. Il fut Commandant pour le Roi des Ville & Château de Domme en Périgord, & ·tefta le 12 Mars 1667. Il avoit époufé, par contrat du 17 Mai 1633, *Louife de Baynac*, qui eut la Terre de la Roque par le décès, fans enfans, de *François de Baynac*, fon frère, & tefta le 18 Janvier 1679. Elle étoit fille de *François*, Chevalier, Seigneur & Comte de la Roque, & de *Diane de Hautefort*. Leurs enfans furent:

1. François, qui fuit;
2. Jean, Chanoine & Chantre de l'Eglife Collégiale de Saint-Avit, lors du teftament de fon père;
3. Gratien, Sieur de la Boiffière, tué au fervice du Roi en Hollande;
4. François, Sieur de Saint-Avit, mort au fervice de Sa Majefté en Allemagne;
5. Armand, Chevalier du Repaire;
6. Un autre Jean, Seigneur de la Baftide;
7. Françoise, Demoifelle de Nabirac;
8. Marie, femme, lors du teftament de fon père, de *François de Toulon*, Seigneur de Guiral;
9. Et Anne, Religieufe au Couvent de Sainte-Claire du Poujet.

XX. François de Beaumont, Chevalier, Comte de la Roque, Seigneur du Repaire, &c., Guidon des Gendarmes de *Monfieur*, frère unique du Roi, après la bataille de Caffel, gagnée par ce Prince en 1677, tefta le 20 Avril 1704 & mourut en 1710. Il avoit époufé, 1° le 15 Juillet 1690, *Jeanne d'Aubuffon*,

Tome II.

fille de *Jean*, Chevalier, Marquis de Miremont, & de *Louife d'Aubuffon-de-Caftel-Nouvel*, dont il a eu des enfans qui moururent jeunes; & 2° le 4 Janvier 1699, *Marie-Anne de Loftanges-de-Saint-Alvaire*, morte le 17 Mars 1747, dans une Communauté de Religieufes à Sarlat, âgée de 80 ans, fille d'*Emmanuel-Galiot*, Marquis de Saint-Alvaire, Sénéchal & Gouverneur de Quercy, & de *Claude-Simonne d'Ebrard-de-Saint-Sulpice*, Dame du Vigan. Leurs enfans font:

1. Armand, qui fuit;
2. Louis, Chevalier du Repaire, Capitaine au Régiment de Richelieu, depuis Rohan, qui ayant été dangereufement*bleffé au combat de Dettingen, n'a pû fervir depuis;
3. Et Christophe, né le 26 Juillet 1703, Evêque de Bayonne en 1741, Archevêque de Vienne en 1745, Archevêque de Paris en 1746, reçu Commandeur des Ordres du Roi le 1er Janvier 1748, Duc & Pair de France le 22 Décembre 1750, & Provifeur ·de Sorbonne.

XXI. Armand de Beaumont, Chevalier, Comte de la Roque, Seigneur du Repaire, Nabirac, Saint-Aubin, Meyrals, Caftel, &c., a époufé, par contrat du 15 Mars 1724, *Marie-Anne de la Faurie*, fille de *Jean-Baptifte*, Seigneur de Guilhome, & Co-Seigneur de Saint-Gery, & de *Jeanne de Calmont*, dont:

1. Louis, qui fuit;
2. Christophe, Chevalier de Beaumont, né le 11 Avril 1731, fucceffivement Sous-Lieutenant aux Gardes-Françoifes, Aide-Major-Général de l'Armée du Bas-Rhin, & Colonel du Régiment de la Fère en 1759. Il a époufé, en 1761, *Marie-Claude de Baynac*;
3. Antoine-François, Vicomte de Beaumont, né le 3 Mars 1733, qui fut fait Garde-de-la-Marine en 1751, & Enfeigne de Vaiffeaux au mois d'Octobre 1755;
4. Et Marie-Anne, morte en 1752.

XXII. Louis, Comte de Beaumont, né le 30 Avril 1728, Sous-Lieutenant au Régiment des Gardes-Françoifes, a époufé, le 27 Janvier 1761, *Marie-Jacquette de Birau*, Comteffe de Goas.

· Les armes: *de gueules, à la fafce d'argent, chargée de trois fleurs-de-lys d'azur;* devife: *impavidum ferent ruinæ.*

· BEAUMONT, en Dauphiné: *échiqueté d'argent & d'azur.*

· BEAUMONT, famille noble, originaire de Vendôme.

GERVAIS DE BEAUMONT, Ecuyer, vint s'établir à Aix, où il avoit été pourvu de l'Office de premier Préſident en la Cour du Parlement, par Lettres données le 24 Septembre 1508.

LOUIS DE BEAUMONT, un de ſes deſcendans, Capitaine au Régiment de Meuſe, s'eſt marié à Ferrat, en Artois, & il a un fils Capitaine au Régiment de Milice de Normandie.

NICOLAS DE BEAUMONT, frère de LOUIS, eſt auſſi dans le ſervice. Voyez ſur cette famille Artefeuil, tom. Ier, pag. 116.

Les armes : *d'or, à la bande d'azur, accompagnée de trois étoiles en chef, de gueules, 2 à ſéneſtre, & 1 à dextre en pointe.*

BEAUMONT, en Champagne : *d'azur, à l'écuſſon d'argent en abîme, & une bande de gueules, brochante ſur le tout.*

BEAUMONT, en Anjou : *de gueules, à la bande d'or.*

BEAUMONT (DE), en Saintonge : *d'argent, au lion de gueules, armé, lampaſſé & couronné d'or.*

BEAUMONT, en Bretagne : *palé d'or & de gueules de ſix pièces.*

BEAUMONT (DE), Seigneur du Breil, Varenne : *d'azur, à trois pieds de biche d'or, 2 & 1.*

BEAUMONT : *d'argent, à la quintefeuille de gueules.*

BEAUMONT (DE), *d'or à la bande de ſable, accoſtée de deux roſes de gueules.*

BEAUMONT : *d'or, à la fleur de ſept feuilles, de ſinople, percée du champ.*

BEAUMONT, en Languedoc : *parti au 1 d'argent, au lion de gueules, armé & lampaſſé d'argent, au chef échiqueté de ſable & d'argent ; au 2 d'or, à une bande d'azur chargée de deux étoiles d'argent.*

* BEAUMONT-LE-BOIS, en Gâtinois, Châtellenie de Château-Landon. *Jacques Cœur*, Argentier de CHARLES VII, en fit l'acquiſition : elle fut confiſquée, lors de ſa diſgrâce, en 1453. Etant mort en 1456, cette Terre, ainſi que ſes autres biens, fut rendue à ſon fils *Geoffroy Cœur*, Echanſon de LOUIS XI, qui d'*Iſabeau Bureau-de-Monglay*, ſa femme, eut pour fille, *Germaine de Cœur*, Dame de *Beaumont*, qu'elle porta en mariage à ſon mari, *Louis de Harlay*, Seigneur de

Cely, la Ferté-Loupière, & Champvalon ; elle fut érigée en Comté au mois de Septembre 1612, par Lettres regiſtrées au Parlement de Paris le 18 Mars 1649, & en la Chambre des Comptes le 21 Juin 1650, en faveur de *Chriſtophe de Harlay*, petit-fils de *Louis*, & ayeul d'*Achille* III, Comte de *Beaumont*, premier Préſident du Parlement, le 18 Novembre 1689. Il eſt ayeul de *Marie-Louiſe de Harlay*, Comteſſe de *Beaumont*, morte le 7 Septembre 1749, femme de *Chrétien-Louis*, Maréchal de Montmorency. Voyez MONTMORENCY.

BEAUMONT-BRESSUIRE. La famille de BEAUMONT-BRESSUIRE, en Poitou, remonte à :

THIBAUT DE BEAUMONT, Chevalier, Seigneur de Breſſuire & de Glenay, qui vivoit l'an 1313. Il eut :

1. THIBAUT, qui ſuit ;
2. Et MILET, Seigneur de *Glenay*, Auteur d'une branche rapportée ci-après.

THIBAUT DE BEAUMONT, Seigneur de Breſſuire, épouſa l'an 1363, *Yolande d'Argenton*, fille de *Geoffroy*, IVe du nom, Seigneur d'Argenton, & de *Surgères*, dont :

1. GEOFFROY, qui ſuit ;
2. GUYART, Chevalier, mort ſans hoirs ;
3. Et GUILLAUME, Seigneur des Dorides, qui fit une branche, dont nous parlerons ci-après.

GEOFFROY DE BEAUMONT, Seigneur de Breſſuire, épouſa *Catherine de Fougeray*, dite de la *Haye*, dont il eut :

1. LOUIS, Seigneur de Breſſuire, mort ſans hoirs ;
2. ANDRÉ, qui ſuit ;
3. Et MARIE, femme de *Guy de Chourſes*, Seigneur de Malicorne, fils de *Geoffroy de Chourſes*, Seigneur de Malicorne, & de *Philippe de Châteaubriand*.

ANDRÉ DE BEAUMONT, Seigneur de Lozay, mort avant ſon père, épouſa *Jeanne de Torſay*, fille de *Jean de Torſay*, Grand-Maître des Arbalêtriers de France, de laquelle il laiſſa :

1. JACQUES, qui ſuit ;
2. Et JEAN, mort jeune.

JACQUES DE BEAUMONT, Seigneur de Breſſuire, Chevalier, Conſeiller & Chambellan du Roi LOUIS XI, Sénéchal de Poitou & d'Angoumois, prit pour femme *Jeanne de Rochechouart*, fille de *Jean de Rochechouart*, Seigneur de Mortemart, & de *Jeanne Turpin*, ſa première femme, de laquelle il laiſſa :

1. JEANNE, Dame de Breſſuire, femme de THI-
BAUT DE BEAUMONT, Seigneur de la Foreſt
& de Commequiers, morte ſans enfans ;
2. PHILIPPE, Dame de Breſſuire, femme de
Pierre de Laval, Seigneur de Loué, fils de
Guy de Laval, Seigneur de Loué, & de
Charlotte de Sainte-Maure ;
3. Et LOUISE, femme d'*André de Vivonne*,
Seigneur de la Chaſteigneraye, fils de *Ger-
main de Vivonne*, Seigneur d'Anville, & de
Marguerite de Broſſe.

BRANCHE
des Seigneurs DE LA JARRIE.

GUILLAUME DE BEAUMONT, Seigneur des Dorides, troiſième fils de THIBAUT DE BEAUMONT,
Seigneur de Breſſuire, & d'*Yolande d'Argenton*, fut père de :

PHILIPPE DE BEAUMONT, Seigneur des Dorides, Chevalier, lequel, entr'autres enfans,
eut pour fils :

FRANÇOIS DE BEAUMONT, Seigneur des Dorides & de la Macairière, qui épouſa *Nicole
Chaſteigner*, Dame de la Jarrie & du Breuil
de Chalans, fille & héritière de *René Chaſteigner*, Seigneur du Breuil & de la Jarrie, &
de *Françoiſe Fagnelin*, dont ſortirent :

1. JACQUES, Seigneur de la Jarrie, mort ſans
lignée. Il avoit épouſé *Françoiſe d'Appelvoiſin*, fille de *Charles-Tiercelin d'Appelvoiſin*, Baron de la Roche du Maine, & de
Claude de Châtillon ;
2. Et SUSANNE, héritière de ſon frère, qui
épouſa *Louis de la Rochefoucauld*, Seigneur de Bayers, fils de *Louis de la Rochefoucauld*, & d'*Angélique Gilliers.*

BRANCHE
des Seigneurs DE GLENAY.

MILET DE BEAUMONT, Seigneur de Glenay,
deuxième fils de THIBAUT DE BEAUMONT, Seigneur de Breſſuire en 1380, eut pour femme
Philippe Beau, de laquelle ſortit :

GUYARD DE BEAUMONT, Seigneur de Glenay,
qui épouſa, l'an 1416, *Marguerite d'Appelvoiſin*, fille de *Louis d'Appelvoiſin*, Seigneur
de Chaligné, & de *Jeanne de Chaſteigner*,
dont il eut :

1. JEAN, qui ſuit ;
2. LOUIS, Seigneur de la Broſſardière & des
Molières ;
3. Et JEANNE, femme de *Jean de Faye*, Seigneur de Marſay.

JEAN DE BEAUMONT, Chevalier, Seigneur de
Glenay en 1446, épouſa *Louiſe de Rouhaut*,

fille de *Jean de Rouhaut*, Seigneur de Boiſ-
menard & de *Jeanne du Bellay*, dont il eut :

1. JEAN, qui ſuit ;
2. ANTOINE, Seigneur de la Broſſardière &
des Molières ;
3. JOACHINE, femme de *Jean Chaudrier*, Seigneur de Norterre ;
4. LOUISE, Religieuſe à Saint-Jean de Thouars ;
5. JACQUETTE, morte fille ;
6. Et MARGUERITE, morte fille.

JEAN DE BEAUMONT, Seigneur de Glenay, ſe
maria avec *Catherine Ratant*, fille de *Jacques Ratant*, Seigneur de Curçay ; de ce mariage ſortirent :

1. MADELEINE, Dame de Glenay, femme de
Merlin de Saint-Gelais, Seigneur de Saint-
Severin ;
2. LOUISE, femme de *Louis de Montberon*,
Seigneur de Fontaines-Chalandray ;
3. Et JEANNE, femme de *Philippe*, Seigneur
de *la Roche-Landry.*

Les armes : *de gueules, à l'aigle d'or, à
l'orle de fers de lances,* que quelques-uns
diſent *de chauſſetrapes d'argent.*

BEAUMONT-DE-GUITÉ, en Bretagne :
*d'argent, à trois pieds de biche de gueules,
onglés d'or, & poſés 2 & 1.*

BEAUMONT-DE-JUNIES, en Touraine.
Les Seigneurs de *Junies* ſont iſſus d'une
branche de la Maiſon de *Touchebœuf*, qui a
pris le nom de BEAUMONT vers 1390, par le
mariage de

Bertrand de Touchebœuf avec GALLIENNE
DE BEAUMONT, que PIERRE DE BEAUMONT, Chanoine de Saint-Martin de Tours, ſon oncle,
avoit inſtituée ſon héritière univerſelle, à la
charge de faire porter le nom de BEAUMONT à
ſon mari & à ſes deſcendans. De ce mariage
vint :

JEAN DE TOUCHEBŒUF, *dit* DE BEAUMONT,
Seigneur de Pierre-Taillade, qui laiſſa de
Pernette de Ferrières, fille de *Guy de Ferrières*, Seigneur de Sauvebœuf, & de *Perrette d'Hélias* :

JACQUES DE BEAUMONT, Seigneur de Pierre-
Taillade, qui épouſa *Jeanne de Plamont*, dont
il eut :

JEAN DE BEAUMONT, Seigneur de Pierre-
Taillade, père de :

ANTOINE DE BEAUMONT, Seigneur de Ferrières & de Pierre-Taillade, triſayeul de
FRANÇOIS DE BEAUMONT, Baron de Junies, Seigneur de Ferrières, de Flaugeat & autres
lieux, mort le 4 Février 1751, âgé d'environ

77 ans, inhumé dans l'Eglife des Religieufes Jacobines de Junies, dont les Seigneurs de Junies font fondateurs, & où ils ont leur fépulture. François eut de fon mariage avec *Charlotte de Montalembert* :

1. Jean-François, Comte de Junies, marié;
2. François, Capitaine au Régiment de Normandie, tué à la bataille de Fontenoy le 11 Mai 1745;
3. Charles-Gabriel, Capitaine au Régiment de Normandie ;
4. Jean-Antoine, Docteur en Théologie de la Faculté de Paris, Vicaire-Général de l'Archevêché de Tours, nommé Evêque de Rennes en Février 1759 ;
5. Et Henriette-Louise, mariée à *Charles de Veylats*, Seigneur de Laftours. (*Mercure de France*, du mois d'Avril 1751).

' BEAUMONT-AU-MAINE ou BEAUMONT-LE-VICOMTE, comme on le trouve en latin, *Bellomontium-Vice-Comitis*, eft une Ville fituée fur la rivière de Chartres, entre le Mans & Alençon. Le plus ancien Seigneur de *Beaumont-le-Vicomte* eft:

Raoul, Ier du nom, Vicomte du Mans, Seigneur de Beaumont en 994. Il vivoit encore en 1061.

La Vicomté de *Beaumont* entra dans la Maifon de *Brienne*, avant le 12 Février 1253, par le mariage d'Agnès, Vicomteffe de Beaumont, fœur & héritière de Richard, IIIe du nom, Vicomte de Beaumont, mort fans enfans, avec *Louis de Brienne*, dit d'*Acre*.

Marie de Brienne, Vicomteffe de *Beaumont*, fille & unique héritière de *Jean de Brienne*, IIe du nom, Vicomte de *Beaumont*, époufa *Guillaume Chamaillard*, dont la fille & héritière:

Marie Chamaillard porta en mariage la Vicomté de *Beaumont*, à *Pierre* II, Comte d'Alençon, Pair de France.

Françoife d'Alençon, fœur & héritière de *Charles*, Duc d'Alençon, Pair de France, obtint au mois de Septembre 1543, du Roi François Ier, l'érection des Vicomté de *Beaumont*, Terre, Baronies & Seigneuries de *Sonnois*, de *la Flèche* & de *Château-Gontier*, en Duché fous le nom de *Beaumont*.

Antoine de Bourbon, Roi de Navarre, Duc de Vendôme, Pair de France, fut Duc de *Beaumont*.

Henri IV réunit, en 1589, ce Duché au Domaine de la Couronne.

Les armes: *de gueules, à cinq chevrons brifés d'argent.*

BEAUMONT-MEULANG : *de fable, au lion d'or.*

BEAUMONT-SUR-OISE, ancienne Maifon qui tiroit fon origine d'Yves, Ier du nom, Comte de Beaumont, vivant en 1028, & qui s'eft éteinte en la perfonne de Thibaut de Beaumont, Seigneur de Luzarches, qui fut auffi Comte de Beaumont-fur-Oife ; & tranfporta ce Comté au Roi Saint Louis, qui lui céda d'autres Terres en récompenfe.

Voyez Duchefne, *Hiftoire de Montmorency*. Elle portoit pour armes: *d'azur, au lion d'or.*

BEAUMONT-PIED-DE-BŒUF : *d'argent, à trois pieds de bœuf de gueules, onglés d'or, pofés 2 & 1.*

' BEAUMONT-LE-ROGER, Bourg ou petite Ville avec Titre de Comté, en Normandie, fituée fur la rivière de Rille entre Evreux & Lifieux, que Saint *Houes* acquit de fes premiers Seigneurs en 1253. Cet ancien Comté étoit poffédé, en 1255, par les Comtes de Meulan.

Raoul de Meulan, Ier du nom, tranfporta le Comté de *Beaumont-le-Roger* au Roi Saint Louis, qui en acquit tous les droits: il fut érigé en Pairie au mois de Février 1328, en faveur de *Robert* d'Artois, IIIe du nom, Comte de *Beaumont-le-Roger*. Il fut confifqué fur lui en 1331, & donné par Philippe de Valois, à Philippe de France, un de fes fils pour le tenir en Pairie.

Le Roi Jean le reprit de fon frère au mois de Mars 1353, & après l'avoir érigé de nouveau en Pairie, avec Breteuil, les Seigneuries de Conche & de Pont-Audemer, il les donna à Charles II, Roi de Navarre, au mois de Janvier 1354.

Son fils Charles III, Roi de Navarre, renonça au droit qu'il avoit fur ce Comté & fur d'autres Terres, pour Nemours qui fut érigé en fa faveur en 1404.

C'eft de ce *Beaumont-le-Roger* que furent furnommés les bâtards d'*Evreux de Navarre*, Comtes de Lerins en Navarre, dont l'héritière époufa N..... *de Tolède*, duquel font defcendus les Ducs d'Albe, fondus dans la Maifon de Sylva: ces Ducs d'Albe ajoutoient à leur nom de *Tolède* celui de *Beaumont*,

& en écarteloient les armes, qui étoient : *losangé d'or & d'azur.*

On ne connoît ni le tems de l'érection, ni en faveur de qui le Comté de *Beaumont-le-Roger* a été érigé. Il fut réuni à la Couronne par le Roi CHARLES VII. Il en a été démembré en faveur de la Maison de *Bouillon,* qui en jouit présentement avec titre de Comté. Voyez TOUR-D'AUVERGNE.

Mais l'on sçait que l'ancienne Maison de *Beaumont-sur-Rille,* qui possédoit *Beaumont-le-Roger,* étoit sans contredit l'une des plus illustres de la Province. On n'a connoissance que d'*Yves,* Seigneur de Beaumont qui vivoit en 1029, dont la postérité a fini, à ce que nous présumons, à *Thomas de Beaumont,* qui plaidoit en 1454, contre le Seigneur de Pirou, son oncle.

Les armes de cette ancienne Maison de *Beaumont* étoient : *gironné de dix pièces d'argent & de gueules.* Le *Promptuaire Armorial* de Jean Boisseau, édition de 1657, in-fol., IIᵉ part., pag. 35, donne pour armes à BEAUMONT-LE-ROGER : *de gueules, au griffon d'or.*

BEAUMONT - SUR - VIGENNE , en Bourgogne.

Cette Maison est tombée dans celle de *Vergy,* & une branche de ses puînés en a pris le nom & les armes. Elle tire son origine des Comtes de Dijon.

GUEBIN , Seigneur de BEAUMONT-SUR-VIGENNE, eut :

1. HUGUES, qui suit ;
2. Et GUEBIN, dit *le Viel,* Évêque de Châlons-sur-Marne.

HUGUES, Iᵉʳ du nom, Seigneur de BEAUMONT sur Vigenne, fut Comte de Dijon après *Rodolphe* ou *Raoul,* Seigneur de Vergy, sous le Roi LOTHAIRE, fils de Louis-d'*Outremer* ; de lui & d'*Adalburge,* son épouse, naquirent :

1. RICHARD, qui suit ;
2. GEBRIEN, ou GUEBIN, dit *le Jeune,* Evêque de Châlons après son oncle ;
3. HUGUES, rapporté ci-après ;
4. Et EUDES, mentionné avec ses frères dans la Chronique de l'Abbaye de Saint-Bénigne de Dijon.

RICHARD DE BEAUMONT, Comte de Dijon, épousa une Dame nommée *Adela,* dont il eut LETALDUS, Comte de Dijon, mort sans lignée, & laissant pour héritier son oncle qui suit :

HUGUES, IIᵉ du nom, Comte de BEAUMONT, puis de Dijon, après la mort de son neveu, sans enfans, en 1015 ; il fut aussi Seigneur d'Autrey, & il eut pour femme *Ermengarde,* énoncée avec lui dans une Charte de l'Abbaye de Saint-Etienne de Dijon, dont il eut :

1. HUGUES, qui suit ;
2. NORDUIN, Chevalier, mentionné dans une Charte de 1027, avec *Eçelme,* sa femme, dont il eut EUDES, Chevalier, marié à une Dame, dite *Gertrude,* dont il n'eut point de lignée, & HUGUES ;
3. GEDUIN, Ecclésiastique ;
4. Et GUY, décédé sans enfans.

HUGUES, IIIᵉ du nom, Comte de BEAUMONT, Seigneur d'Autrey, vivoit ès années 1032 & 1044 ; il épousa *Letgarde,* de laquelle sortirent :

1. ULRIC, ou ODOLRIC, mort jeune ;
2. Et ERMENGARDE, qui suit.

ERMENGARDE , héritière de Beaumont & d'Autrey, épousa un Seigneur de Bourgogne, appelé *Fouques,* qui s'intitula *Comte de* BEAUMONT, à cause d'elle, comme on l'apprend d'une Charte de l'Abbaye Saint-Germain-des-Prez, de l'an 1055. De leur mariage naquit entr' autres enfans :

GEOFFROY, lequel quittant le titre de *Comte,* se qualifia seulement *Seigneur de Beaumont & d'Autrey.* Il épousa une Dame nommée *Gertrude,* dont il eut :

1. HUGUES, qui suit ;
2. FOUQUES, mort jeune, pour lequel GEOFFROY, Seigneur de BEAUMONT, son père donna à *Etienne,* Abbé, & aux Religieux de Bèze, tout ce qu'il possédoit à Lentilly, l'an 1114.

HUGUES, IVᵉ du nom, Seigneur de BEAUMONT & d'Autrey, eut de N... :

1. HUGUES, qui suit ;
2. Et GEOFFROY, surnommé *Martel,* mort en guerre, & inhumé dans l'Abbaye de Bèze, par Geoffroy, Evêque de Langres.

HUGUES, Vᵉ du nom, Seigneur de BEAUMONT & d'Autrey, est nommé, avec son père & son frère, dans une Charte de 1134. Il fit le Voyage de la Terre-Sainte l'an 1147, & laissa *de Mahaut :*

ADELAIS DE BEAUMONT, Dame de Beaumont & d'Autrey, mariée à *Guy,* Seigneur *de Vergy,* fils de *Simon,* & d'*Élisabeth.* Il amortit, avec cette ADELAIS, Dame de Beaumont, à l'Eglise de Cîteaux, tout ce que *Henri de*

Vergy, son oncle, tenoit de fief à Deston, par Lettres de 1169, & laissa :

1. HUGUES DE VERGY, Seigneur de Vergy & d'Autrey, auteur de la Maison de *Vergy*. Voyez ce mot ;
2. SIMON DE VERGY, Seigneur de Beaumont, qui suit ;
3. Et RENAUD DE VERGY, Evêque de Mâcon l'an 1192.

SIMON DE VERGY, Seigneur de Beaumont sur Vigenne, quitta le nom & les armes de VERGY pour prendre celles de BEAUMONT, & vivoit du tems de PIERRE, Evêque de Châlons, l'an 1194. Il épousa *Ermengarde*, veuve de *Fouques*, Seigneur *de Mailly*, dont il eut :

1. HUGUES, qui suit ;
2. GUILLAUME DE VERGY, dit *de Beaumont*, qui épousa, en 1218, *Ode de Neuilly*, fille de *Villain*, Seigneur *de Neuilly*, & d'*Ode* ;
3. Et GUY DE VERGY, dit *de Beaumont*, Seigneur de la Roquette en 1216.

HUGUES, VIe du nom, Seigneur de BEAUMONT sur Vigenne, rendit hommage à THIBAUT, Comte de Champagne, par Lettres de 1216, & mourut vers 1243. Il épousa *Alix de Saint-Seigne*, fille de *Hugues*, Seigneur de Saint-Seigne sur Vigenne, & laissa :

1. JEAN, Seigneur de Beaumont sur Vigenne, qui transporta, avec sa mère, tout le droit qu'ils avoient au fief de Saint-Seigne, en 1252, du consentement de HUGUES, Duc de Bourgogne. Nous ignorons sa postérité ;
2. YVES DE VERGY, dit *de Beaumont*, Abbé de Cluny en 1257. Il fonda à Paris le Collège de Cluny, & mourut l'an 1275 ;
3. MILES DE VERGY, d'abord Prieur de Saint-Martin-des-Champs à Paris, puis de la Charité-sur-Loire ;
4. HUGUES DE VERGY, Prieur de Saint-Martin-des-Champs, après son frère, l'an 1262 ;
5. Et ALIX DE VERGY, dite *de Beaumont*, mariée au Seigneur de *Chasaut*. D'eux naquit, entr'autres enfans, *Inès de Chasaut*, qui succéda à son oncle dans l'Abbaye de Cluny.

Les armes : *d'argent, à trois tours de sinople, crénelées & maçonnées de gueules, posées 2 & 1*.

BEAUNAY, Seigneur de Villenville, d'Imanville, en Normandie, Généralité de Rouen, famille maintenue dans sa Noblesse le 17 Février 1667. La Roque, dans son *Histoire d'Harcourt*, pag. 116, dit que JEAN DE BEAUNAY est nommé dans un Rôle de la Chambre des Comptes, entre les 300 Ecuyers, Chevaliers & autres, auxquels le Roi JEAN pardon-

na tout ce qui s'étoit passé jusqu'au 12 Décembre 1360, pour avoir suivi le parti de CHARLES II, Roi de Navarre.

Le même auteur dit que CLAUDE BEAUNAY, Sieur du Tot, épousa, le 28 Août 1559, *Madeleine d'Espinay-Saint-Luc*, fille de *Louis des Hayes*, l'un des 100 Gentilshommes de la Chambre du Roi ; & que CHARLES-FRANÇOIS BEAUNAY-DU-TOT, fut reçu Chevalier de Malte le 3 Juin 1693.

Voici l'état actuel de cette famille.

PREMIÈRE BRANCHE.

NICOLAS DE BEAUNAY, Marquis du Tot, a épousé, en 1745, N... *du Castillon*, dont est né :

N... DE BEAUNAY, appelé le *Comte d'Auzeville*.

SECONDE BRANCHE.

LOUIS-FRANÇOIS, Marquis DE BEAUNAY & du Boyhimont, marié, en 1743, à MADELEINE DE BEAUNAY, sa cousine germaine, dont :

1. ALEXANDRE-LOUIS, appelé *Marquis de Boyhimont*, né en 1746, Cornette au Régiment de Condé, Cavalerie ;
2. N... né en 1760, Chevalier de Malte de minorité ;
3. MADELEINE, *Mademoiselle de Beaunay*, née en 1745 ;
4. BARBE, *Mademoiselle de Boyhimont*, née en 1747 ;
5. Et N.... *Mademoiselle de la Peynierre*, née en 1749.

TROISIÈME BRANCHE.

CHARLES-ABRAHAM-LAURENT, appelé *Comte de* BEAUNAY, né en 1736, marié, le 6 Septembre 1762, à *Louise-Antoinette Desmiers d'Archiac de Saint-Simon*, fille aînée de *Louis-Antoine*, Comte d'Archiac, Brigadier & Mestre-de-Camp de Cavalerie, Commandeur de l'Ordre de Saint-Louis.

Frère : FRANÇOIS-ALEXANDRE DE BEAUNAY, appelé *Chevalier de Beaunay*.

Les armes : *fascé d'or & d'azur de 6 pièces*.

BEAUNE, famille originaire de Tours, du nom de *Fournier*, à cause que LOUISE DE SAVOIE, mère du Roi FRANÇOIS Ier, donna à *Jacques Fournier*, dit *de Beaune*, la Baronie de Samblançay, & la Vicomté des Ponts de Tours. On trouve JEAN DE BEAUNE, Bourgeois de Tours, vivant en 1455. Il exerça la Charge d'Argentier des Rois LOUIS XI & CHARLES

VIII. Il étoit mort en 1480. Cette famille, qui a fini à JEAN DE BEAUNE, premier Maître-d'Hôtel de la Reine CATHERINE DE MÉDICIS, Chevalier de l'Ordre du Roi, a donné dans REGNAULT DE BEAUNE, un Grand-Aumônier de France, sous HENRI IV, qui en cette qualité fut Commandeur de l'Ordre du Saint-Esprit. Il travailla si puissamment à la conversion de ce Prince, qu'il le reçut à sa profession de Foi dans l'Eglise de l'Abbaye de Saint-Denis, & assista à son Sacre à Chartres en 1594. Il passa de l'Eglise de Bourges, dont il étoit Archevêque, à celle de Sens; & après avoir rendu de fidèles services au Roi & à la Patrie, il mourut à Paris le 27 Septembre 1606, âgé de 79 ans. Voyez Moréri.

Les armes : *de gueules, au chevron d'argent, accompagné de 3 besans d'or, 2 en chef & 1 en pointe.*

BEAUNE. Les Vicomtes de ce nom, en Auvergne, qui portoient pour armes : *flanqué d'argent & de gueules,* sont fondus dans la Maison de *Montagu-Bouzols,* à la charge que celle-ci en porteroit le nom & les armes.

BEAUPOIL, BAUPEL, ou BAUPEIL; on trouve indifféremment ces noms dans les anciens titres. Maison très-ancienne, originaire de Bretagne. Le premier du nom de Beaupoil que l'on trouve est JEAN de Beaupoil qui vivoit en 1369. Le P. Anselme commence la généalogie de cette Maison à GUILLAUME DE BEAUPOIL-SAINT-AULAIRE, Seigneur de Neumalet, qui vivoit en 1410.

La branche aînée a fini à LOUIS DE BEAUPOIL, Marquis de SAINT-AULAIRE, Maréchal-de-Camp des Armées du Roi, Colonel du Régiment d'Enghien, Infanterie, tué au combat de Rumersheim, dans la haute Alsace, le 26 Août 1709. Il ne laissa que :

THÉRÈSE-EULALIE DE BEAUPOIL-SAINT-AULAIRE, morte le 3 Novembre 1739. Elle avoit épousé, le 7 Février 1725, *Pierre d'Harcourt,* Marquis de Beuvron, puis Duc d'Harcourt.

L'Abbé DE BEAUPOIL-SAINT-AULAIRE, Vicaire-Général de l'Archevêché de Rouen, a été nommé par le Roi, en Avril 1753, à l'Abbaye de Saint-Taurin d'Evreux, Ordre de Saint-Benoît.

CHARLES-DENIS-JACQUES DE BEAUPOIL-SAINT-AULAIRE, Archidiacre & Vicaire-Général de Poitiers, Abbé de la Réole, Ordre de Saint-Benoît, Diocèse de Tarbes, un des Aumôniers du Roi, est mort à Lucienne, le 12 Juillet 1761, âgé de 39 ans.

BRANCHE
des Seigneurs & Marquis de LANMARY.

Elle a pour auteur PIERRE DE BEAUPOIL, mort en 1564.

LOUIS DE BEAUPOIL, Marquis de Lanmary, Seigneur de Coutures, &c., d'abord Capitaine de Cavalerie au Régiment de Sourches, ensuite Capitaine-Lieutenant des Gendarmes de la Reine, pourvû de la charge de Grand-Echanson de France, sur la démission du Marquis de Crénan, mourut à Cazal-Major, en Italie, au service du Roi, le 22 Juillet 1702. Il avoit épousé, par contrat du 30 Mai 1681, *Jeanne-Marie Perrault,* morte le 28 Janvier 1719, après s'être remariée, le 31 Janvier 1704, à *Gilbert-François de Rivoire,* Marquis du Palais. Elle étoit fille unique de *Jean Perrault,* Président en la Chambre des Comptes de Paris, & de *Marie-Anne Lemoine.* Ils eurent entr'autres enfans :

1. MARC-ANTOINE-FRONT DE BEAUPOIL-SAINT-AULAIRE, Marquis de Lanmary, né le 25 Octobre 1689, Baron de Milly, Seigneur de Coutures, de Celles, de Bertry, de Chabannes, de Sorges, de Peudry, d'Augerville, &c., d'abord Mestre-de-Camp de Cavalerie, depuis Sous-Lieutenant des Gendarmes de Bourgogne, ensuite Sous-Lieutenant des Gendarmes de Bretagne. Il prêta, le 17 Janvier 1703, entre les mains du feu Prince de Condé, le serment qu'il devoit au Roi, pour sa Charge de Grand-Echanson : il s'en est démis au mois de Mai 1731, en faveur d'André, Comte de Benon. Il a été Ambassadeur en Suède, nommé Chevalier des Ordres du Roi en 1749, & mourut le 24 Avril 1759, à Stockholm, sans avoir été reçu. Il avoit épousé, en 1711, *Elisabeth de Neyret de la Ravoye,* fille de *Jean de Neyret,* Grand-Audiencier de France, dont :

ANNE-ELISABETH DE BEAUPOIL-SAINT-AULAIRE, mariée à HENRI-FRANÇOIS DE BEAUPOIL-SAINT-AULAIRE, Comte de Lanmary.

2. Et HENRI-FRANÇOIS, qui suit.

HENRI-FRANÇOIS DE BEAUPOIL, Comte de Lanmary, né le 17 Janvier 1694, Enseigne des Gendarmes de Flandres, mort en 1748, avoit épousé ANNE-ELISABETH DE BEAUPOIL-SAINT-AULAIRE, fille de MARC-ANTOINE-FRONT DE BEAUPOIL, Marquis de Lanmary, dont :

MARC-ANTOINE-FRONT DE BEAUPOIL-SAINT-AULAIRE, Marquis de Lanmary, Baron de Milly, &c., Guidon de Gendarmerie, mort à Wefel de la petite-vérole, en fa 22e année, le 16 Juin 1761. Il avoit époufé, le 18 Février 1760, *Charlotte-Bénigne le Ragois-de-Bretonvilliers*, remariée, le 20 Juin 1763, à *Charles-François - Céfar le Tellier*, Marquis de Montmirail. Elle étoit fille de *Bénigne le Ragois*, Marquis de Bretonvilliers, & de *Félicité de Milani de Cornillon*.

De cette branche cadette font fortis les Seigneurs de *Fontenilles*, par ANNET DE BEAUPOIL, fecond fils de PIERRE DE BEAUPOIL, Seigneur de Coutures, & de *Catherine de Laurière*, Dame de Lanmary. Le dernier de cette branche, ANDRÉ-DAVID DE BEAUPOIL, Seigneur de Fontenilles, étoit Enfeigne de Vaiffeau en 1678.

Les Seigneurs de *Caftel-Nouvel* ont eu pour auteur JEAN DE BEAUPOIL, Seigneur de Caftel-Nouvel, mort en 1478, & ont fini à FRANÇOIS DE BEAUPOIL, qui ne laiffa qu'une fille, en 1576, fous la tutelle de *Philippe d'Aubuffon*, mariée 1° à *François de Vivonne*, & 2° à *François de Caumont*, dont font defcendus les Seigneurs & Ducs *de la Force*. Voyez le Père Anfelme.

Cette famille eft encore nombreufe; il en exifte entr'autres une branche connue fous le nom des Seigneurs de *Gorre*, dont il y a plufieurs enfans, parmi lefquels une fille, N... DE BEAUPOIL DE SAINT-AULAIRE-DE-GORRE, mariée avec N... *de Morfanges*, Chevalier, Seigneur de Volry (qui fe prononce Vaury), y demeurant Diocèfe & Généralité de Limoges.

Les Barons de *la Luminade*, en Périgord, Seigneur de Montplaifir, du Mas-en-Limoufin, &c., diftingués par les fervices Militaires & leurs alliances, fe font féparés de la branche aînée au commencement du XVe fiècle, par FRANÇOIS, l'un des fils de JEAN DE BEAUPOIL, Seigneur de Saint-Aulaire, & de *Marguerite de Bourdeilles*. Il étoit Capitaine dans la Légion de Guyenne, & fut bleffé au fiège de Perpignan, à une fortie que firent les Efpagnols. Il fit fon teftament le 22 Juillet 1542 & mourut de fes bleffures. Il avoit époufé, par contrat du 7 Mai 1621, *Ifabeau de Boyral*.

Son fils, PIERRE DE BEAUPOIL, fut Aide-de-Camp de FRANÇOIS, Prince de Bourbon, à la bataille de Cerifole, Capitaine dans la Légion de Guyenne, où il donna des preuves de valeur à la bataille de Moncontour. HENRI, Duc d'Anjou, depuis Roi de France, lui donna fon épée, marquée d'une *H & trois fleurs-de-lys*, comme une marque de fatisfaction. Il fit une fondation, & tefta l'an 1578.

ALAIN DE BEAUPOIL, fon fils, fervit, & fut Commandant des Garnifons de Savillan & de Peroufe, qui furent rendues à l'avènement au trône de HENRI III, au Duc de Savoie, en 1574. Il avoit emporté l'Etendart de l'Amiral de Coligny, à Moncontour, & tefta le 19 Juin 1611. Il eut:

1. JEAN, qui fuit;
2. Et HÉLIE, qui eut pour fils FRANÇOIS, Capitaine de Chevaux-Légers, par Brevet du 20 Janvier 1656, qui fut bleffé à la bataille de Lens & de Charenton, & mourut de fes bleffures.

JEAN DE BEAUPOIL, Capitaine fous M. Caftel-Bayard, au fervice de HENRI IV, il fut enfuite Maréchal de bataille, fous le Maréchal de la Châtre, fervit fous LOUIS XIII, contre les factieux, & tefta le 26 Mai 1640. Il eut:

1. RAYMOND, qui fuit;
2. & 3. ANTOINE & HÉLIE, qui furent tués Capitaines dans le Régiment de Gramont;
4. FRANÇOIS, Seigneur de Planège, tué Capitaine dans celui de Lambertye;
5. Et un autre FRANÇOIS, qui fut tué dans le même Régiment.

RAYMOND DE BEAUPOIL, dont les Terres furent érigées en Baronie par Lettres-Patentes de 1655, fut Maréchal des Camps & Armées le 15 Mai 1653. Il avoit fervi très-jeune, fous LOUIS XIII & LOUIS XIV, fe diftingua au fiège de Saverne le 26 Août 1650, fut Maréchal de Bataille le 2 Décembre 1651, Capitaine d'une Compagnie franche; fit lever le fiège aux factieux en plufieurs Villes & Châteaux en Périgord, celui de Dagonot, de Riberac & de Saint-Aftier. Les factieux brulèrent & pillèrent en fon abfence les Châteaux de la Luminade & de la Garde. Le Roi le nomma Capitaine des Chaffes du Périgord en 1654. Il tefta en 1674, & mourut en 1679. Il avoit époufé 1° *Jeanne de Leftrade-de-la-Caufte*, & 2° *Jeanne de la Baylie*, veuve du Marquis de Bouillen.

Il eut de fon premier mariage:

1. ANTOINE, qui fuit;
2. JEAN-CHARLES, Capitaine de Grenadiers, tué

à la bataille de Saint-Denis, près Mons;
3. Et CHARLES, Capitaine dans le Régiment de Louvigny, tué à la guerre de Hollande.

ANTOINE DE BEAUPOIL fut d'abord Page, puis Lieutenant au Régiment de Berry, où il se diftingua, comme il eft rapporté par les certificats des Maréchaux de Catinat & de Vauban. Il emporta une demi-lune au fiège de Cambray, qui occafionna la prife de cette place, où il fut bleffé grièvement, ce qui l'obligea de quitter le fervice. Il y rentra le 8 Février 1708, & obtint une Compagnie de Cavalerie dans les Cravates, qui fut détruite à la bataille d'Oudenarde. Il fit confirmer l'érection de la Baronie des terres de la Luminade en 1655, par Lettres regiftrées à Bordeaux. Il tefta le 28 Février 1723, & laiffa de fon mariage avec *Françoife de Garoux:*

1. YRIEUX ou YRIER, qui fuit;
2. Un autre YRIEUX ou YRIER, Abbé de Beaupoil, & de Saint-Georges-fur-Loire, Vicaire-Général de Nantes, Directeur Général du Séminaire de Saint-Sulpice, à Paris, où il eft mort le 19 Janvier 1766 dans fa 80e année;
3. Et JEAN-BAPTISTE, Capitaine dans le Régiment de Berry, qui fut Ingénieur en Chef de l'Isle d'Oléron, & a laiffé:
   ANTOINE, Lieutenant de Vaiffeau, Seigneur du Mas, en Limoufin;
   JEAN, Garde de la Marine, tué fur mer en 1757;
   Et N..., mariée en Agénois avec M. *Vignet-de-la-Segrirue*, dont elle a des enfans.

YRIEUX DE BEAUPOIL, Ier du nom, Baron de la Luminade, &c., fut Capitaine dans Montforeau, le 4 Janvier 1706. Il avoit époufé, avec difpenfe de Rome, *Joféphine de Bardicault*, fille du Baron d'*Auriac*, & de *Julie d'Aubuffon-de-la-Feuillade*, dont:
1. YRIEUX, qui fuit;
2. JEAN-BAPTISTE, rapporté après fon frère aîné;
Et deux filles.

YRIEUX DE BAUPOIL, IIe du nom, fe maria, en 1732, avec *Marie d'Abʒac-de-Mayac*, fille de *Henri d'Abʒac-de-la-Douʒe*, Marquis de Mayac, Seigneur de Pomier, Migre, Monplaifir, &c., dont il a un fils unique:
PHILIPPE ○○○ÇOIS DE BEAUPOIL, né en 1732, Baron de la Luminade, Seigneur de Monplaifir, &c., qui a fervi dès l'âge de 13 ans, Cornette au Meftre-de-Camp-Général, Cavalerie, fut réformé à la paix de 1749, entra Moufque-

taire, d'où il paffa Lieutenant au Régiment de la Sarre en 1751, fut fait Capitaine-Aide-Major en 1756, paffa à une Compagnie en 1759, réformé la même année; en 1763 remplacé au Régiment de Recrue de la Ville de Paris, réformé le 1er Mai 1767. Il a époufé, le 10 Août 1760, *Marie-Catherine de Bréard*, fille de *Jacques-Michel de Bréard*, Seigneur des Portes, Commiffaire de la Marine, de la Maifon des *Bréard*, de Normandie, près Valogne, noble de très-ancienne extraction, prouvée par tous leurs titres des XIIIe, XIVe & XVe fiècles. Il a de fon mariage:

1. JEAN-BAPTISTE-FRONT-YRIEUX DE BEAUPOIL, Baron, né à Paris le 1er Mai 1763;
2. ALEXANDRE-LOUIS, né aux Portes, en Poitou, en 1765;
3. MARIE-CATHERINE-EUSTACHE-VICTOIRE, née en 1761, tenue fur les fonts de baptême par Anne d'Harcourt, Marquis de Beuvron, & par Marie-Catherine Rouillé, fon époufe. Elle eft élevée à l'Abbaye de Beaumontlez-Tours, fous la protection de fon Alteffe Séréniffime Madame de Vermandois, Abbeffe, & de Mademoifelle de Bourbon-Condé, fille de M. le Prince de Condé;
4. Et MARIE-CATHERINE, née en 1764.

JEAN-BAPTISTE DE BEAUPOIL, fecond fils d'YRIEUX, IIe du nom, & de *Joféphine de Bardicault*, né le 14 Septembre 1712, Capitaine du Corps-Royal d'Artillerie, Ingénieur en chef de l'Isle d'Oléron, a époufé, le 28 Mai 1742, *Marguerite Grénot*, dont il a eu:
1. JEAN-YRIEUX, Lieutenant au Régiment de la Fère en 1761;
2. Et PIERRE-PORPHIRE, Garde de la Marine, à Rochefort, fortant de l'Ecole Royale-Militaire.

Les armes: *de gueules, à trois couples de chiens d'argent, mis en pal, & pofés deux & un.*

BEAUNON: *coupé de gueules & d'or, au lion d'argent fur le tout.*

BEAUPRÉ, ancienne Baronie qui eft entrée, au commencement du XVIe fiècle, dans la Maifon de Choifeul, par le mariage d'*Anne de Saint-Amadour*, avec *Pierre de Choifeul*, IIIe du nom, Chevalier, Seigneur d'Aigremont & de Meufe, mort en 1527. Voyez CHOISEUL.

BEAUPRÉ, autre Seigneurie qui appartient à une branche de la famille de Pelletier. Voyez PELLETIER.

* BEAUPRÉAU, Seigneurie qui fut érigée en Marquisat, au mois de Février 1554, en faveur de *Charles de Bourbon*, Prince de la Roche-sur-Yon, à qui cette Terre étoit venue par *Philippe de Montespedon*, sa femme. Ce même Prince obtint du Roi CHARLES IX, au mois de Juin 1552, l'érection du Marquisat de Beaupréau en Duché. Voyez les *Grands-Officiers de la Couronne*.

Le Marquisat de Beaupréau appartient aujourd'hui à la Maison de *Scepeaux*. Voyez ce mot.

BEAUQUERRE : *écartelé, aux 1 & 4 d'azur, au léopard d'or, aux 2 & 3 de gueules, à la croix ancrée d'argent.*

BEAURAINS, Seigneur de Montmort, famille originaire de Picardie, & établie dans le Valois, Élection de Compiègne.

Louis DE BEAURAINS, Chevalier, Seigneur de la Douie, avoit été maintenu dans sa noblesse par Arrêt du Conseil d'Etat, du 18 Août 1667, & inscrit dans le Catalogue des Gentilshommes de l'Election de Compiègne. Il avoit épousé *Françoise de Leirit*, Dame de Montmort, & de Dauven en partie, & laissa :

1. Louis DE BEAURAINS, Enseigne au Régiment des Gardes-Françoises, mort sans postérité ;
2. ANTOINE, qui suit ;
3. ANNE DE BEAURAINS, fille aînée, mariée, le 21 Mars 1679, à *Michel Sublet*, Chevalier, Marquis de Noyers ;
4. GENEVIÈVE DE BEAURAINS, mariée à *François Joli*, Chevalier, Seigneur d'Harville ;
5. HENRIETTE DE BEAURAINS, morte Abbesse de Moncelles, près de Pont-Saint-Maxence ;
6. CATHERINE DE BEAURAINS, Religieuse à la même Abbaye ;
7. Et ELISABETH DE BEAURAINS, morte sans avoir été mariée, au Couvent de Bon-Secours, Faubourg Saint-Antoine, à Paris.

ANTOINE DE BEAURAINS, Chevalier, Seigneur du Plessis-Châtelain, de la Douie & de Montmort, Grand-Hôtel, Petit-Puizieux, &c., Mousquetaire du Roi, en 1691, Aide-de-Camp de Sa Majesté, par Brevet du 6 Mai 1694, fut confirmé dans sa noblesse par Arrêt du 12 Avril 1698, après avoir prouvé qu'il étoit fils de Louis DE BEAURAINS, Chevalier, Seigneur de la Douie. Il épousa 1° *Marie-Jeanne Lamer*, morte sans enfans, fille

de *François Lamer*, Ecuyer, Seigneur de la Beuvine ; & 2° par contrat du 10 Août 1707, *Louise-Madeleine Messageot*, fille de *Laurent Messageot*, Ecuyer, Secrétaire du Roi, Maison & Couronne de France, & de *Catherine Dupuis*. Il a eu de ce second mariage :

1. ANTOINE, qui suit ;
2. JOSEPH DE BEAURAINS-DU-PLESSIS, Mousquetaire de la seconde Compagnie, mort à Lille de ses blessures, le 12 Juillet 1744 ;
3. Et ALEXANDRINE DE BEAURAINS, morte Religieuse à l'Abbaye de Moncelles.

ANTOINE DE BEAURAINS, Chevalier, Seigneur de Montmort, du Plessis-Châtelain, de la Douie, &c., Capitaine au Régiment de Penthièvre, a commencé de servir dans la Compagnie des Cadets-Gentilshommes de la Citadelle de Metz, le 10 Octobre 1730, est entré dans le Régiment de Penthièvre en 1732, a été fait Chevalier de Saint-Louis, le 18 Juillet 1748, a obtenu du Roi une pension de retraite, à cause de ses blessures, le 1er Avril 1755. ANTOINE DE BEAURAINS a obtenu que la Terre de Glaigne fut réunie à la Seigneurie du Plessis-Châtelain & à celle de la Douie, & autres fiefs adjacens, & érigée en Comté pour lui & ses hoirs mâles, portant ses nom & armes, en considération de ses services. Les Lettres-Patentes de cette érection sont données à Compiègne au mois de Juillet 1764, enregistrées au Parlement de Paris le 13 Janvier 1765, & à la Chambre Domaniale de Soissons le 27 Juin 1765. Elles portent que le Comté de Glaigne-Montmort relèvera en plein fief & en une seule foi & hommage du Duché de Valois. Voyez l'*Histoire de Valois*, supplém. au tom. II, pag. 424. Il a épousé, le 4 Mai 1753, *Marie Anjorrant*, fille de *Basile-Claude-Henri Anjorrant*, Chevalier, Seigneur du Haut & Bas-Traci, Conseiller au Parlement, & de *Jeanne-Catherine Coutard*, dont :

1. ANTOINE-CLAUDE DE BEAURAINS, né le 22 Septembre 1758 ;
2. Et ANGÉLIQUE-JEANNE DE BEAURAINS, née le 29 Juin 1757.

Les armes : *d'azur, à la fasce d'or, chargée de trois merlettes de ▉ surmontée d'un soleil d'or.* Supports : *deux lions.*

BEAURAINS (DE), Seigneur du Plessis : *d'azur, au chevron d'or, accompagné en chef de deux étoiles d'argent, & en pointe d'une colombe paſſante de même, tenant en ſon bec un rameau d'olivier.*

BEAURÁINS: *d'aʒur, à l'écu d'argent en chef, à l'orle de huit coquilles de même.*

BEAUREGARD, dans le Comté de Lauraguais. Voyez DAVID.

BEAUREGARD en Anjou. MATHURIN DE BEAUREGARD, Chevalier, vivoit avec *Louiſe de Beʒe*, ſa femme, avant 1507; RENÉ DE BEAUREGARD, ſon petit-fils, Seigneur du Verger, épouſa *Jacqueline du Bouchet-de-Sourches*, mère de GABRIEL DE BEAUREGARD, Seigneur du Verger, Chevalier de l'Ordre du Roi, & d'HONORAT-BENJAMIN DE BEAUREGARD, Ecuyer, Seigneur de Freſne, Cornette de la Compagnie des Chevaux-Légers de M. de Vendôme, & Maître-d'Hôtel du Roi, marié avec *Jeanne le Clair-de-Lourmaie*, dont il a eu:

CHARLES-FRANÇOIS DE BEAUREGARD, Ecuyer, Seigneur de la Lande, marié, le 2 Janvier 1707, avec *Marie Sourdille*. De ce mariage naquirent:

LOUIS-CHARLES & RENÉ-CHARLES-MAGLOIRE DE BEAUREGARD, tous deux Pages du Roi dans ſa Petite-Ecurie, l'un le 10 Décembre 1730, & l'autre le 26 Mars 1734, ſur les preuves de leur Nobleſſe. Voyez l'*Armorial de France*, reg. I, part. I, pag. 57.

Les armes: *d'argent, à un chevron de ſable, bordé d'aʒur, & accompagné en chef de deux lions de gueules affrontés.*

* BEAUREGARD, Terre, Seigneurie & Château, dans le Blaiſois, qui eſt ſituée à l'une des extrémités de la Forêt de Ruſſy. Par Lettres du mois de Juillet 1654, regiſtrées le 7 Septembre ſuivant, la Terre & Seigneurie de Beauregard fut érigée en Vicomté, en faveur de *Paul Ardier*, Préſident en la Chambre des Comptes de Paris. Le Château de Beauregard, dont il eſt queſtion, eſt ſi magnifique, qu'on le nomme dans le pays *Beauregard-le-Royal*.

BEAUREGARD: *de gueules, à la bande d'or, accoſtée d'une étoile en chef, & en pointe d'un croiſſant; le tout de même.*

BEAUREGARD-BLONDEAU: *d'argent, à trois pommes de pin de gueules, 2 & 1.*

BEAUREPAIR, en Sologne. CHARLES DE BEAUREPAIR, Ecuyer, Seigneur du Cheſne, fils de N... & de *Marie de la Creſte*, épouſa, le 16 Janvier 1630, *Renée de Perovin*, fille de *Jacques*, Seigneur de la Noiſellière, & de *Renée de Marville*, dont PIERRE, Ecuyer, Seigneur du Cheſne.

Les armes: *d'argent, au lion de ſable, armé & lampaſſé de gueules.*

BEAUREPAIRE, Seigneur de Cauvigny & de Jor, en Normandie, Généralité d'Alençon. FRANÇOIS DE BEAUREPAIRE, Seigneur de Cauvigny, fut reçu Chevalier de Malte, le 6 Avril 1645; & RENÉE DE BEAUREPAIRE fut mariée, vers 1700, à *Jacques Duhamel*, Seigneur de Saint-Sauveur.

On lit dans l'*Hiſtoire de la Maiſon d'Harcourt*, par la Roque, pag. 614, que noble homme SAMSON DE BEAUREPAIRE, Ecuyer, fut nommé, en 1511, Procureur de Jean d'Harcourt, pour accorder & appointer tous les procès, tant civils que criminels, mus & à mouvoir, entre lui & noble homme *Jean de Feſchal*, Chevalier, Seigneur de Grippon.

Les armes: *de ſable, à trois gerbes de bled d'or, 2 & 1.*

BEAUREPAIRE, en Champagne. De cette Famille étoit MORETTE DE BEAUREPAIRE, veuve, en 1456, de *Pierre de Souvré*. Elle ſe remaria, en 1468, à *Charles de Magny*, Seigneur de Fleurs, qui portoit pour armes: *d'aʒur, à l'anneau châtonné d'or, à la bordure denchée de même.*

BEAUREPAIRE: *d'argent, au chevron d'aʒur.*

BEAUREPAIRE, Seigneur du Trévégant & du Bourblanc, près Tréguier en Bretagne, portoit anciennement: *de gueules, à une faſce d'argent, chargée de deux têtes de Maures tortillées d'argent*; & actuellement: *de gueules, à une tour crénelée d'or, ſommée d'un tourillon de même.*

BEAUSANG: *de Montmorency, au franc-canton d'or, chargé d'une merlette de ſable.*

BEAUSÉJOUR, branche de la famille de Chauvelin, ſortie d'un quatrième fils de *Jacques de Chauvelin*, Tréſorier de France. Voyez CHAUVELIN.

BEAUSEMBLANT: *de gueules, à la croix engrêlée d'argent.*

BEAUSIRE, Seigneur de Bréguigny en Normandie, Généralité de Rouen, famille maintenue dans fa Nobleffe le 9 Mars 1667, qui porte : *d'azur, à la fafce d'argent chargée d'une étoile d'or, & accompagnée de cinq autres étoiles de même, 3 en chef & 2 en pointe.*

BEAUSOBRE (DE), ancienne nobleffe qui fubfifte en plufieurs branches établies, l'une en France, l'autre en Pruffe, la troifième en Suiffe, & la quatrième en Ruffie. Deux Mémoires Généalogiques, l'un fait en 1617, par le Curial Domo, le Curial Durus, le Miniftre Perréau de Mont-la-Ville & de Cuarmens, le Miniftre Romey de Gollion, & trois Gentilshommes : noble Seigneur de Villerming, Seigneur de Montrichier & de Monnaz, de noble de la Ville-de-Berolles, & de noble de Murizet-de-Cully, fignés au bas, & le tout confirmé par l'atteftation y jointe des Seigneurs Bannerets & Confeillers de la Ville de Morges en Suiffe, avec la fignature de leur Secrétaire, *Bernard Marquix*, à côté de leur grand fceau ; le fecond Mémoire conprenant depuis l'an 1617 jufqu'en 1703, avec l'atteftation & le fceau de ladite Ville & la fignature de leur Secrétaire *Pappan* ; & inventoriés, le 14 Mai 1771, par *Louis Moifant*, Notaire de la ville de Laigle, légalifés & certifiés véritables par M. *Loizel de Précourt*, Confeiller du Roi & Vicomte de Laigle, nous apprennent que cette Maifon, originaire de Provence, dont le nom primitif eft DE BEAUX, remonte à

I. JONAS-BALTHA, qui portoit pour armes, ou plutôt pour devife *(car les armes n'étoient pas encore en ufage) une grande étoile à 16 rayons,* au bas de laquelle étoit écrit en lettres gothiques BALTHA. Il fe maria, en 890, (dit le premier de ces Mémoires), avec *Sibylle de Lavemberg,* dont il eut entr'autres enfans :

II. CASIMIR DE BEAUX, qui époufa, en 926, *Mathilde de Maffa,* dont PONS, qui fuit, & quelques autres enfans.

III. PONS DE BEAUX, marié, en 971, avec *Propheta de la Tour,* fut père de :

IV. HUGUES DE BEAUX, qui fit alliance, en 1006, avec *Léonore de Caftro,* de laquelle vint :

V. GUILLAUME DE BEAUX, qui fe maria, l'an 1039, avec *Tiburge de Vienne,* laquelle fut mère de :

VI. HUGUES DE BEAUX, IIᵉ du nom, marié, en 1088, avec *Vierme de Suze,* dont :

VII. RAYMOND DE BEAUX, marié, en 1130,

à *Etiennette de Provence.* Ces fept degrés portoient : *de gueules, chargé d'une étoile de 16 rayons d'argent, & furmonté de 3 heaumes.* Il laiffa :

VIII. BERTRAND DE BEAUX, qui fe maria, en 1160, avec *Tiburge d'Orange,* & eut :

IX. GUILLAUME DE BEAUX, IIᵉ du nom, lequel, en 1210, fit alliance avec *Ermengarde de Sabran,* dont :

X. RAYMOND DE BEAUX, IIᵉ du nom, marié, l'an 1240, avec *Malberoue d'Aix,* de laquelle vint :

XI. BERTRAND DE BEAUX, IIᵉ du nom, qui époufa, l'an 1268, *Léonore de Genêve.* Il en eut :

   1. GUILLAUME, qui fuit ;
   2. Et RAYMOND, qui s'empara des biens de fon frère après fa mort.

XII. GUILLAUME DE BEAUX, IIIᵉ du nom, époufa, en 1308, *Tiburge d'Anduze.* De ce mariage fortirent BERTRAND, qui fuit, & GUILLAUME, lefquels par fon décès, il laiffa en bas âge entre les mains de RAYMOND, fon frère cadet, qui vécut très-longtems, s'empara de la Seigneurie de *Beaux,* donna quelqu'argent à fes deux neveux, & les chaffa de chez lui.

XIII. BERTRAND DE BEAUX, IIIᵉ du nom, fe retira vers fes parens, en Italie ; mais ayant embraffé l'héréfie des Albigeois, il fut contraint d'en fortir, & vint retrouver à *Beaux,* fon oncle, qui ne voulut pas le recèvoir. Il alla enfuite à Alby, & à caufe du Tribunal de l'inquifition établi à Touloufe, contre les Albigeois, il paffa dans la Province de Guyenne, & fe retira en Armagnac en 1373, où il eut une Compagnie d'Ordonnance. Ses armes étoient les mêmes que celles de fes prédéceffeurs, mais au-deffus des *heaumes* étoit écrit *intaminatâ virtute fulget.* Il mourut le 3 Septembre 1389. On voit fon épitaphe en latin dans l'Eglife de Baffoves, & à côté de la fienne eft celle de BERTRAND, fon fils. Il avoit époufé *Bernardine,* fille d'*Augufte,* Sire *de Pouforb-Combres* & de Baffoves. Il laiffa :

XIV. BERTRAND DE BEAUX, IVᵉ du nom, qui plaida en Provence pour l'héritage de fa grand-tante ALIX DE BEAUX ; mais RAYMOND fon grand-oncle l'emporta fur lui, & les biens d'ALIX lui furent adjugés. Ce BERTRAND, IVᵉ du nom, accufé d'héréfie & fils d'hérétique, fut enfermé dans la grande tour, d'où il fe fauva en fautant du haut en bas, ce qui lui fit donner le furnom de *Beauffare.* Il fe trouva à la bataille d'Azincourt en 1415. La moitié de l'écu de fes armes étoit celles de fes prédéceffeurs, & il avoit chargé l'autre moitié de *deux chevrons d'or fur un fond d'azur, croifés à contre-fens, l'un ayant la pointe en haut, & l'autre la pointe en bas, appuyée fur le bord de l'écu*. Il mourut, & fut enterré à côté de fon père, le 8 Novembre 1457. Il avoit époufé, le 12 Août 1439, *Marguerite*, fille de *Jofeph*, Seigneur *de Macaut*-fur-Gironde, d'Aubre ou de Saubre. De ce mariage vint :

XV. LÉONARD DE BEAUX, né le 5 Mai 1442. Il étoit en 1489 le troifième des 100 Gentilshommes de la grande Garde du Roi, fous le commandement de M. de Miolans. On le furnommoit *de Beauffare*, comme fon père, & M. de Miolans l'appeloit dans fes mandemens *Mons de Beaux-du-Saubre*. Il fut en 1500 Porte-Cornette blanche, mourut à Paris en 1520, & fut enterré à la Madeleine le 23 Décembre. Il avoit époufé, le 20 Décembre 1502, *Étienne* ou *Étiennette*, fille de *Charles*, Seigneur *de Ferrières*, de Sabrin & en Langoiron, dont :

XVI. LÉONARD DE BEAUX, IIᵉ du nom, né en Décembre 1505, Seigneur de Saubre-lez-Albin, dit auffi Sobre, de Ferrières, Soubreboft, Sabrin & en Langoiron, furnommé *de Beaufare*, qui étoit en 1534 dans la première Compagnie des 100 Gentilshommes de la grande Garde du Roi, fous les Ordres de M. de Nevers. Il alla en Novembre 1527 faire vifite à BERNARDIN DE BEAUX, Chevalier de Saint-Jean de Jérufalem, fon parent, tourmenté alors de la pierre. Il n'en put rien obtenir ayant nommé le Roi fon héritier. A caufe des troubles de la Religion, il fe retira à Alançon, mais dans le temps du maffacre de la Saint-Barthélemy, en 1572, il y fut bleffé & mourut la même année à Soubreboft, comme le marque fon épitaphe du 30 Octobre 1573. Il avoit époufé, en 1530, *Henriette*, fille de *Henri de Basbel*, Seigneur dudit lieu fur la Gironde, & de Soubreboft en Limoufin, dont :

1. JEAN, qui entra en 1546 dans la première Compagnie des 100 Gentilshommes de la Garde du Roi, fous M. de Boiffy, qui l'appelle dans une miffive, *Mons de Beaux, mon Compagnon*. Depuis le mois d'Août 1572, il n'eft plus queftion de lui ;

2. PIERRE, qui fit la guerre en Picardie en 1545, fut Capitaine-Particulier de l'arrière-ban, fous le nom de *Beaux-Langoiron*. On

n'en fçait plus rien depuis le maffacre de la Saint-Barthélemy ;

3. GUILLAUME, Sergent de bataille en 1558 de l'armée du Roi HENRI II, delà les monts, Il eft appelé dans deux mandemens *de Beaux-de-Ferrières* , & mourut en ces guerres ;

4. ODET, qui entra dans la première Compagnie des 100 Gentilshommes de la Garde du Roi. M. de Boiffy l'appelle dans un mandement *Mons de Beaux-de-Sabrin*, *mon Compagnon*. Il fut affaffiné en paffant par Orléans, pour fe retirer en Guyenne, fuyant le maffacre de la Saint-Barthélemy. Il avoit époufé, en 1560, *Helène*, fille de *N...* *de Charri*, Meftre-de-Camp du Régiment des Gardes, dont un fils appelé *Mons de Sabrin*, dans une lettre pour aller prendre le commandement d'une Compagnie au même Régiment des Gardes. Sa Compagnie fut réformée, & il mourut en 1600 ;

5. ARNAULT, qui fuit ;

6. GAILLARDINE, mariée à *N...*, *de Cypière*, ou *Sipierre*, Seigneur de Thoefi-Sipierre, près Saulieu ;

7. & 8. JEANNE & HÉLÈNE.

XVII. ARNAULT DE BEAUX, né à Soubreboft en Limoufin, le 30 Avril 1541, fervoit en 1556 dans la première Compagnie des 100 Gentilshommes de la Garde du Roi, fous M. de Boiffy, qui l'appelle dans un mandement *Mons de Beaux-de-Soubreboft*. Il fe trouva en 1562 au fiège de Rouen, fut nommé en 1568 Major du Régiment des Gardes, paffa la même année au fervice du Prince de Condé, & en 1572 pour fe fauver du maffacre de la Saint-Barthélemy, il fe retira près de Saulieu à Thoefi-Sipierre, chez M. *de Sipierre*, fon beau-frère. En 1576 il paffa à Genève, où les Seigneurs de cette République lui firent un grand accueil. Il logea chez le premier Syndic nommé Baudichon, obtint le droit de Bourgeoifie, & fut membre du Confeil des 200. Il mourut à Morges en Suiffe, pays de Vaud (où il s'étoit retiré), en 1610, de chagrin d'avoir été maltraité & volé par des brigands mafqués, comme il alloit à Aubonne, payer la fomme convenue pour l'achat de cette Baronie. Les Seigneurs Bannerets & Confeillers de la noble Bourgeoifie de la ville de Morges, donnèrent à fes enfans le droit de Bourgeoifie. Cet ARNAULT ne fignoit point dans ce pays *de Beaux-de-Saubre* ni *de Soubre*, mais toujours *de Beauffobre*, & on l'appeloit *le Sire* ou *le Seigneur de Beauffobre*, ou feu-

lement *Noble* Arnault de Beaussobre. Dans
fon fecond contrat de mariage, fait à fon arrivée de France à Genève, fcellé du fcel de la
République, il eft dit feulement *Noble* Arnault de Beau-Soubre, fils de *Noble* Léonard de Beau-Soubre, & de ces deux mots
s'eft formé par abréviation le nom de *Beau-
fobre*, que fa poftérité a confervé. Il portoit
pour armes : *coupé de gueules & d'azur, le
gueules chargé d'une étoile à 16 rayons
d'argent; & l'azur de deux chevrons d'or
croifés à contre-fens, la pointe de l'un en
haut & la* ⬤ *te de l'autre en bas, appuyée
fur le bord de l'écu.* Arnault de Beausobre
avoit époufé 1° *Clémence*, fille de feu Sire
Abraham deDijon, & de Dame *de Saumaife*,
& 2° le 27 Juin 1583, *Marthe du Feu.* Il eut
du premier lit:

1. Adolf, dit de Beausobre, qui, fe voyant
tant de frères & fœurs, & peu de biens,
paffa en France. Il eut en 1599 une Lieutenance au Régiment des Gardes, dans la
Compagnie de Sabrin, fon oncle. Celui-ci
étant mort, il en eut une dans le Régiment
de Navarre, & M. de Boeffe, qui en étoit
Meftre-de-Camp, l'appeloit dans fes lettres
Adolf de Beaux. Depuis 1606, il n'eft plus
fait mention de lui.

Du fecond fit vinrent:

2. Jean, qui fuit;
3. Elysée, né le 16 Mars 1595. Il étoit en 1635
en Allemagne, Commandant du Régiment
du Prince de Crodorf. On ignore fa deftinée;
4. Etienne, né le 30 Janvier 1598, Lieutenant dans le Régiment de Navarre en 1620,
fous M. de Palluau, Meftre-de-Camp. En
1622, il fe trouva au fiège de Saint-Antonin & on n'en fçait rien de plus;
5. Isaac, auteur de la troifième branche rapportée ci-après;
6. Marie, née le 22 Octobre 1584;
7. Marthe, née le 18 Novembre 1589;
8. Et Clémence, née le 5 Mai 1592.

XVIII. Jean de Beausobre, Iᵉʳ du nom,
époufa, en 1617, *N... du Ris*, fille de *Guillaume*, Seigneur du Ris en Bourgogne, & de
N... de Boulaire de la Montagne, dont:

1. François, qui fuit;
2. Jean-Gabriel, né le 20 Janvier 1627, marié, en 1678, à *Catherine*, fille de *Charles*,
Seigneur *de Jouet-fur-la-Loire*. Il en eut
Pierre-Daniel, né le 24 Août 1679, Lieutenant dans le Régiment de Courten. Sa
poftérité s'eft éteinte dans fon fils Samuel

de Beausobre, Capitaine au même Régiment, tué à la bataille de Fontenoy le 11
Mai 1745;
3. Jacques, auteur de la feconde branche rapportée ci-après;
4. Pierre, né le 21 Juin 1631, Lieutenant au
Régiment de Bourgogne, marié, en 1666,
à *Sufanne-Marie*, fille du Colonel *Man-
drot*, dont:

     Jean-Jacques, né le 5 Mai 1676, mort
     fans poftérité;
     Et Hélène, Rose & Gabrielle;

5. Marthe, née le 30 Décembre 1618;
6. Et Anne, née le 23 Décembre 1621.

XIX. François de Beausobre, né le 27 Octobre 1624, entra au mois de Mars 1641 dans
la première Compagnie des 100 Gentilshommes de la Garde du Roi, fous M. de Lauzun,
& époufa, en 1656, *Jeanne*, fille de *Charles
de Jouet*-fur-la-Loire, & de *Pernette Jayn*,
petite-fille du Seigneur de Jayn-fur-l'Allier,
dont:

1. Jean-Gabriel, né le 16 Février 1658, Lieutenant dans le Régiment de Bourgogne en
Mai 1674, Capitaine en 1690 & mort en
Décembre 1690 fans poftérité;
2. Jean-Paul, qui fuit;
3. Jean, rapporté ci-après;
4. Marie-Françoise, née le 26 Novembre
1659;
5. Pernette, née le 1ᵉʳ Décembre 1663;
6. Et Jeanne-Françoise, née le 15 Janvier
1668.

XX. Jean-Paul de Beausobre, Lieutenant
en 1660 dans le Régiment de Bourgogne, &
enfuite Capitaine dans les troupes du pays,
eut de fon mariage, contracté en 1687, avec
Judith, fille de *N...de Regis-de-Launay*, Seigneur Banneret, Benjamin, qui fuit, & une
fille.

XXI. Benjamin de Beausobre, né le 7 Novembre 1697, fit la campagne de Majorque
fous fon oncle Jean II, Commandant d'un
bataillon du Régiment de Courten, & mourut
en 1762. Il avoit époufé, en 1731, *Marie*,
fille de *N... de Gumoens*, Seigneur de Gu-
moens-la-Ville, Gumoens-le-Château, Orfou,
Général en Hollande, Colonel d'un Régiment
Suiffe, & de *N... Cartier*. Il laiffa:

1. Louis, né en 1733, Capitaine au Régiment
de Chamborant, Huffards, avec Brevet de
Major, puis de Colonel de Cavalerie en
Janvier 1772, Chevalier de l'Aigle-Rouge
de Brandebourg, avec permiffion du Roi,

Seigneur de Bouchsbach, &c., non encore marié;

2. SAMUEL, né en 1736, ancien Capitaine du Régiment Royal de Deux-Ponts;

3. BENJAMIN, né en 1737, qui a été Capitaine dans le Régiment de Lowendal;

4. FRANÇOIS-VINCENT, né en 1738, mort de fes bleffures en 1762, Lieutenant dans le Régiment de la Marck;

5. Et MARIE-JUDITH, née en 1732, mariée à *Emmanuel de Gumoens*, Major au Régiment du May, Suiffe, au fervice de Hollande.

XX. JEAN DE BEAUSOBRE, IIᵉ du nom, né le 5 Mars 1666, fut Enfeigne en 1687 dans le Régiment de Stoppa. Il fit une action d'éclat & avantageufe près Maubeuge, & eut en 1689 le brevet de Capitaine-Lieutenant avec 4000 livres de gratification. Il follicita à la Cour la reftitution des Terres confifquées fur fes ayeux, comme on le voit par les Lettres de M. Stoppa, l'aîné, Général des Suiffes, qui lui écrivit par ordre du Miniftre (M. de Louvois). Le Comte de Trauttmanfdorff, Ambaffadeur de l'Empereur en Suiffe, voulant l'attirer au fervice de fon Maître, lui envoya fon Secrétaire, qui, pour l'y déterminer, lui dit qu'en reftant au fervice de France, il nuiroit à fa famille, laquelle ne fe releveroit jamais étant dans une efpèce d'obfcurité : *point d'obfcurité*, répliqua-t-il, *où eft l'honneur*. Il fit la guerre en Flandres, en Efpagne, à Majorque, fur la Mofelle & fur le Rhin. Il eft parlé de lui dans les Nouvelles de ce tems. Renouvelant fes prétentions fous la Régence de M. le Duc d'Orléans, ce Prince nomma M. le Comte du Luc & M. de Reinold, Colonel des Gardes-Suiffes, pour lui en rendre compte, & finit en difant : *qu'il faudroit être un Mathufalem pour juger cette affaire*. Il lui fit donner une penfion avec Brevet de Colonel. Il mourut en Décembre 1722. Il avoit époufé, en 1703, JEANNE DE BEAUSOBRE, fa coufine, & laiffa :

1. JEAN-JACQUES, qui fuit;

2. FRANÇOIS, Capitaine au Régiment de Bourqui, mort à Paris en 1751;

3. Et JEAN, mort en 1735, en repaffant les Alpes après la fin de la campagne.

XXI. JEAN-JACQUES, Comte DE BEAUSOBRE, né le 15 Mars 1704, Enfeigne en 1716, Aide-Major en 1728, Capitaine de Grenadiers dans le Régiment de Courten en 1734, Commandant à Traerbach en 1734, puis fur le Rhin

en 1735, eut un bon du Roi en 1738 pour le Régiment de Hainaut; mais n'étant pas riche, il préféra la commiffion de Colonel dans celui d'Appelgrin. Il fut envoyé par le Roi faire la guerre de Hongrie en l'armée Autrichienne, & affifta à la paix conclue le 17 Septembre 1739 dans les lignes de Belgrade. En Janvier 1740, Sa Majefté lui donna par Brevet la permiffion de porter le titre de Comte & de Marquis, ainfi qu'aux parens de fon nom, & en conféquence le nomma ainfi dans le Brevet d'Aide-Maréchal-Gé████ des Logis de l'Armée qui paffa en Boh████ █n 1743, la Cour le força de prendre u██ ██giment de Huffards. Il a été fait Brigadier en 1744, Maréchal-de-Camp en 1748, Lieutenant-Général en 1759, & a fervi avec diftinction dans toutes les guerres que le Roi a eues depuis 1716 jufqu'à préfent. Il a été fait Chevalier de l'Ordre de l'Aigle-Rouge de Brandebourg en 1738 avec la permiffion du Roi, & nommé Grand-Croix de cet Ordre en 1765. Il s'eft retiré au Château de Biffeuil en Normandie, où il poffède la Seigneurie de ce nom, celle de Grébert, la Folie, les Baffes-Londes, Croifilles, &c.

SECONDE BRANCHE.

XIX. JACQUES DE BEAUSOBRE, troifième fils de Jean, Iᵉʳ du nom, & de N... du Ris, né le 10 Février 1629, époufa, en 1668, *Marie*, fille de N... *de Collet*, & de N... *Damont*, petite-fille de *Pierre*, Seigneur de Collet en Périgord, & de *Sufanne de Montrevel*, & nièce de *Philibert de Collet*, Procureur-Général du Parlement de Dombes. De ce mariage vinrent :

1. JEAN-FRANÇOIS, né le 24 Avril 1674, qui fervit dans le Régiment de Piémont, Infanterie, où il fut long-tems Capitaine. Sa poftérité mafculine s'eft éteinte en Bohême dans la perfonne de fon fils FRÉDÉRIC, qui y fut tué, étant Capitaine de Dragons. Il refte une fille mariée à N... *de Martine*;

2. IMBERT-FRANÇOIS, qui fuit;

3. Et JEAN-CLAUDE, rapporté après la poftérité de fon frère.

XX. IMBERT-FRANÇOIS DE BEAUSOBRE, né le 4 Décembre 1676, fervit quelques années, fe maria, & eut pour fils :

XXI. ANTOINE DE BEAUSOBRE, né en 1704, lequel a auffi fervi quelques années en France. Il eft Châtelain de Morges, & a de fon mariage :

César de Beausobre, Officier au Régiment d'Erlach, Suiffe (en 1772) ; Salomée & Suséte.

XX. Jean-Claude de Beausobre, né le 6 Juin 1681, laiffa de *N... le Clerc :*

XXI. Isaac de Beausobre, qui s'eft marié à *N... de la Flefchère*, & a un fils Officier au fervice de Hollande dans le Régiment du May, Suiffe.

TROISIÈME BRANCHE.

XVIII. Isaac de Beausobre, né le 13 Décembre ⬤ dernier fils d'Arnault, & de *Marthe* ⬤ *u*, dernier rejeton de l'ancienne Maifon *du Feu*, fa feconde femme, fut Lieutenant en 1624 dans le Régiment de Piémont, dont étoit Meftre-de-Camp M. de Fontenay. En 1627, allant à l'Isle de Ré où il étoit envoyé avec un renfort, il fut pris par les Anglois & conduit en Angleterre, d'où s'étant fauvé, il fit naufrage près des Sables d'Olonne. Paffant par le Poitou, il tomba malade & fut accueilli par M. & Madame de *Lefcalle*, qui le reçurent dans leur Maifon & lui firent époufer leur fille le 21 Décembre 1632. Il en eut Isaac, qui fuit, & trois filles.

XIX. Isaac de Beausobre, IIe du nom, s'établit en Allemagne, & s'y maria deux fois. Il eut du premier lit :

1. Charles, mort en 1752 ;
2. Albert, tué au fiège de Belgrade en 1717, à l'âge de 22 ans, étant Capitaine d'Infanterie ;
3. Léopold, auteur d'un rameau établi en Ruffie, qui fuit ;

Et du fecond :

4. Frédéric, auteur de celui établi à Berlin, rapporté après fon frère ;
5. Et Léopold, tué à l'âge de 15 ans le 1er Juin 1757 au fiège d'Olmutz, étant Lieutenant.

XX. Léopold de Beausobre, mort en Ruffie en 1754, où il étoit l'un des plus anciens Généraux, & Colonel d'un Régiment de Dragons, avoit époufé *N... de Hoech*, dont il a laiffé :

1. Alexandre, âgé de 25 ans en 1772, Major au Régiment de Mofcou, Cuiraffiers ;
2. Et Jean, Major du Régiment d'Oranburg, Dragons.

XX. Frédéric de Beausobre, né en 1730, fils d'Isaac, IIe du nom, & de fa feconde femme, eft Confeiller Privé du Roi de Pruffe & Membre de l'Académie de Berlin, a voyagé quelques années aux frais de Sa Majefté Pruffienne, & a époufé, 1º en 1769, *N... de Bavas-de-la-Baume*, morte en 1769; & 2º en Janvier 1771, *N... de Reck*, fille de *N.... de Reck*, Seigneur de Callies, de Ramin, &c. Les armes de ces différentes branches font les mêmes que portoit Arnault de Beausobre, fçavoir : *coupé de gueules & d'azur, le gueules chargé d'une comète ou étoile à feize rayons d'argent ; & l'azur chargé de deux chevrons d'or croifés à contre-fens, la pointe de l'un en haut, & celle de l'autre en bas appuyée fur le bord de l'écu.*

BEAUSOBRE (de) : *d'azur, à deux chevrons d'or, dont l'un renverfé & entrelaffé ; au chef coufu de gueules, chargé d'une ombre de foleil d'or.*

BEAUSOLE : *de gueules, au chevron d'or, accompagné de trois têtes de léopard de même, 2 en chef & 1 en pointe.*

BEAUSSAN, Seigneur de Sefert en Normandie, Généralité de Caen : *d'azur, à l'Agnus Dei d'or, à la croix d'argent & à la banderole de même, chargée d'une croix de gueules.*

BEAUSSAN. N... Marquis de Beaussan, Exempt des Gardes du Corps, Compagnie de Luxembourg, marié, par contrat du 9 Février 1766, à N... de Vaucel, fille du Tréforier des Aumônes.

BEAUSSART, en Flandres, Terre & Seigneurie érigée en Comté. Un de *Melun* étoit Comte de *Beauffart* en 1725.

Il y a eu d'autres Seigneurs du nom de *Beauffart*, qui avoient pour tige *Jean de Dreux*, Ier du nom, Seigneur de Châteauneuf & de Beauffart, fils puîné de *Robert de Dreux*, IIe du nom, Seigneur de Beu, qui vivoit en 1347.

Nicolas de Dreux, Vidame & Baron d'Edefval, le dernier mâle de cette branche, mourut fans enfans le 2 Août 1540. Ces Seigneurs de *Beauffart* portoient pour armes : *échiqueté d'or & de gueules.*

BEAUSSE (de) : *d'azur, au cœur de gueules enflammé d'or, accompagné en chef d'un foleil de même, aux flancs dextre & feneftre d'une gerbe de bled auffi de même liée de gueules, & en pointe d'un croiffant d'argent.*

BEAUSSEY : *de gueules, à la croix en-grêlée d'or.*

BEAUSSIER, en Provence, famille ancienne, diftinguée, par un nombre confidérable de Militaires qu'elle a donnés. Elle jouiffoit déjà de quelque réputation, lorfque le Pays étoit gouverné par les Comtes. On en voit la preuve dans une donation qu'un de ces Princes lui fit des Salins, du Mourrillon, en récompenfe de fes fervices.

JEAN DE BEAUSSIER, Ecuyer, qui vivoit en 1375, eft le plus ancien de ce nom dont on ait connoiffance. Ses defcendans ont pris la qualification de *Nobles* ou d'*Ecuyers* dans leurs contrats de mariage, teftamens & autres actes publics.

Cela n'empêcha pas que FÉLIX DE BEAUSSIER, Capitaine d'un des Vaiffeaux du Roi, & Chevalier de l'Ordre Militaire de Saint-Louis, ne fut attaqué, en 1707, par les Commiffaires députés par le Roi pour la recherche des Ufurpateurs de la Nobleffe ; mais ayant préfenté fes titres, il fut déchargé par ordonnance de M. le Bret, Intendant de Provence, qui le déclare iffu de *noble race & lignée*, &c.

Cette famille fort riche autrefois, & divifée en plufieurs branches, ne fubfifte plus qu'en deux.

La branche aînée eft continuée par FRANÇOIS DE BEAUSSIER, Seigneur de Terre de Chaulane, Capitaine d'un des Vaiffeaux du Roi, Chevalier de Saint-Louis, qui commandoit cinq Frégates avant l'affaire de Mahon, & un Vaiffeau de ligne, pendant le combat de l'Efcadre de M. de la Galiffonnière contre les Anglois, en 1756.

N...... DE BEAUSSIER, Juge Royal à Toulon, eft chef de la branche cadette.

Les armes : *d'azur, à trois coquilles d'or, fans oreilles.*(Voy. Artefeuil, tom. I. pag. 118.)

* BEAUTEVILLE. Les Barons de ce nom font une branche de la Maifon de *Buiffon*, qui poffède, en Lauraguais, cette Seigneurie, depuis près de trois fiècles. Voyez BUISSON.

BEAUTOT, BAUTOT, ou BEAUTHOT, Seigneurs de la Rivière, de Vibeuf, de Fontelay, en Normandie, Généralités de Rouen & d'Alençon, famille maintenue dans fa nobleffe le 5 Septembre 1669.

Le Père Anfelme parle de ROBERT DE BEAUTOT, qui rendit hommage, le 16 Janvier 1485, de la Seigneurie de Mézières près Falaife,

que lui avoit apportée en dot *Marguerite d'Aumont*, fa femme.

JEAN DE BEAUTOT, Sieur de Mézières & d'Aubeville, époufa, le 5 Septembre 1514, *Madeleine du Merle-Blanc-Buiffon.*

Et la Roque, dans fon *Hiftoire de la Maifon d'Harcourt*, parle de GABRIEL DE BEAUTOT, Sieur de Mézières, qui poffédoit une partie de la Baronie de Grimbofc. Il étoit marié, avant 1578, avec N..... *du Quefnoy*.

Les armes : *d'argent à trois coqs de fable, crêtés & barbés de gueules*, 2 & 1.

* BEAUVAIS. C'eft une des plus anciennes Villes de l'Isle-de-France, dont JULES-CÉSAR fait mention dans fes Commentaires. Elle eft la Capitale du Beauvoifis, dans le Gouvernement de l'Isle-de-France. L'Evêque de Beauvais fe qualifie *Comte & Pair de France, Vidame de Gerbroy* ; au facre du Roi, l'Evêque de Laon & lui accompagnent l'Archevêque de Reims, lorfqu'il va recevoir Sa Majefté à la porte de l'Eglife, la veille de la cérémonie ; & le lendemain ces deux Evêques font députés, l'un comme Duc, l'autre comme premier Comte, Pair Eccléfiaftique, pour aller lever le Roi de deffus fon lit, & l'emmener entr'eux deux à l'Eglife. C'eft l'Evêque de Beauvais qui, dans la cérémonie, préfente le Manteau Royal.

Les armes du Comté-Pairie de Beauvais font : *d'or, à la croix de gueules, cantonnée de quatre clefs de même pofées en pal.*

BEAUVAIS, Seigneur dudit lieu, & de Taillis, en Normandie, Généralité d'Alençon, famille maintenue dans fa nobleffe le 30 Juin 1666. Les Regiftres de la Chambre des Comptes font mention de JACQUES DE BEAUVAIS, Ecuyer en 1312. JEAN DE BEAUVAIS, Ecuyer, fut Châtelain & Garde de la Tour de Quetinhaft, au Mont Cabaret, pour le récompenfer des fervices qu'il avoit rendus au Roi, fuivant les Lettres du 7 Février 1417. ANTOINE DE BEAUVAIS époufa *Perrette de Vauquignier*, dont JEAN DE BEAUVAIS, mentionné dans trois contrats des années 1475, 1497 & 1504. Il avoit époufé *Marguerite d'Efchelles*, dont JOACHIM DE BEAUVAIS, qui époufa *Charlotte le Clerc*, père & mère de MICHEL DE BEAUVAIS, qui époufa, en 1590, *Jeanne de Mezenges*, dont MICHEL DE BEAUVAIS, IIe du nom, qui fe maria, en 1613, avec *Charlotte de Bailleul.*

La Roque, dans fon *Hiftoire de la Maifon d'Harcourt*, parle de François DE BEAUVAIS, Seigneur de Putanges, qui fe maria, le 1er Juillet 1551, avec *Marie d'Harcourt*, veuve, le 13 Décembre 1571.

Cette famille a fait fes preuves de nobleffe en 1598 & 1599.

Les armes : *d'azur, à trois fafces d'or.*

BEAUVAIS, Sieur de Vouty, de Nullemont & de Bonnelles, en Normandie, Généralité de Rouen. On lit dans l'*Armorial de France*, qu'ALEXIS DE BEAUVAIS, Sieur de Vouty, avoit époufé *Madeleine - Louife Roger*, Dame de Bonnelles, dont il eut CHARLES-FRANÇOIS DE BEAUVAIS, Sieur de Vouty, de Nullemont, de Bonnelles, qui époufa, le 19 Juin 1724, *Marie-Anne le Ver*, dont il eut, entr'autres enfans, MARIE-MARTHE DE BEAUVAIS-DE-VOUTY, reçue à Saint-Cyr, en 1736, fur les preuves juftifiées, depuis PIERRE DE BEAUVAIS, Seigneur de Vouty, fon cinquième ayeul, vivant avant 1568.

Les armes : *d'argent, à une croix de gueules, chargée de cinq coquilles d'or, écartelées de cinq points d'azur, équipolés à quatre points d'argent & un chef de gueules.*

✠ BEAUVAIS, très-ancienne Nobleffe, d'où font fortis les Seigneurs des *Angles*, des *Ifles* & du *Bufe-Huet*, en la Paroiffe de Sainte-Croix, près Buchy, en Normandie.

HILLON, Châtelain DE BEAUVAIS, fonda l'Eglife collégiale de Saint-Barthélemy de Beauvais, en 1037.

LANCELIN, fils de FOULQUE DE BEAUVAIS, Châtelain dudit lieu, fonda l'Abbaye de Villers-Saint-Sépulcre en 1060.

FOULQUE DE BEAUVAIS, Evêque, Comte de Beauvais, vivoit en 1090. Le premier, depuis lequel on a une filiation fuivie, eft :

I. ODON, Chevalier, Châtelain DE BEAUVAIS, Seigneur de Vafcœuil, vivant en 1200, qui époufa *Pétronille de Vafcœuil*, dont vint :

II. ADAM, Chevalier, Châtelain DE BEAUVAIS, Seigneur de Vafcœuil & de Saint-Denis-le-Thiboult, qui vivoit en 1214, & époufa *Marguerite de Braquemont*, de laquelle il eut :

III. GUILLAUME, Ier du nom, Chevalier, Châtelain DE BEAUVAIS, vivant en 1242, qui époufa *Aliénor de Crefpin*, Dame de Ferrière & de Ry, dont :

IV. RENAULT, Ier du nom, Châtelain DE BEAUVAIS, vivant en 1299, marié à N..... *de Saucourt*. Leurs enfans furent :

1. GUILLAUME, qui fuit;
2. RENAULT, tige de la troifième branche, mentionnée en fon rang;
3. Et MARGUERITE DE BEAUVAIS, première femme de *Jean*, Seigneur de *Crequy*, dit l'*Etendart*.

V. GUILLAUME, IIe du nom, dit *le Vélu*, Châtelain DE BEAUVAIS, Seigneur de Vafcœuil, Saint-Denis-le-Thiboult, de Ry & de Ferrière, fut un des Barons mandés, le 12 Novembre 1318, pour fe trouver à Paris à la Chandeleur, & aller contre les Flamands, affifta, pendant 23 jours, au tournoi que fit le Comte du Mans en 1322, & eft nommé préfent à la conceffion que le Roi Charles IV fit, en 1325, à Hervé de Léon, Seigneur de Noyon-fur-Andelle, pour fa terre de Bourgbalde. Il mourut en 1329. Il avoit époufé *Jeanne d'Eftouteville*, fille de *Robert*, IVe du nom, Seigneur d'Eftouteville, & d'*Alix Bertrand de Briquebec*, dont :

1. COLLART, qui fuit;
2. ELIPES, mariée 1º à *Robert de Marigny*, & 2º à *Robert d'Evreux*, qui fut Châtelain de Beauvais, après la mort de JACQUELINE DE BEAUVAIS, fa coufine, dont il fera parlé ci-après;
3. Et JEANNE DE BEAUVAIS, alliée à *Jean*, Seigneur de *Crevecœur*, dit *le Flamand*.

COLLART, Châtelain DE BEAUVAIS, Seigneur de Vafcœuil, &c., fervit, en 1346, en Normandie, fous le Connétable d'Eu. Il époufa *Marguerite de Roye*, Dame de Germigny, fille de *Dreux de Roye*, Seigneur de Germigny, & d'*Alix de Garlande-Poffeffe*. De ce mariage naquirent :

1. GUILLAUME, qui fuit;
2. RICARD, ou RICHARD, tige de la branche des Seigneurs des *Minières*, des *Angles*, &c., rapportée ci-après;
3. JEANNE, Dame de Fayel, vivante en 1402, morte fans alliance;
4. Et MARGUERITE DE BEAUVAIS, Dame de Remaugîs, première femme de *Pierre*, dit *Hutin*, Seigneur d'*Aumont*, Porte-Oriflamme de France.

Nota. Les fix Châtelains, dont on vient de parler, & ladite *Jeanne d'Eftouteville*, font inhumés en l'Abbaye de Notre-Dame de l'Isle-Dieu-fur-Andelle, dont ils ont été bienfaiteurs, comme il appert par chartes des années

1209, 1310, 22 Septembre 1315, 1322 & 1349; lesquelles fondations furent amorties, par Lettres-Patentes du Roi CHARLES V, données à Paris au mois de Juin 1365.

VII. GUILLAUME, IIIe du nom, Châtelain DE BEAUVAIS, Seigneur de Vafcœuil, Confeiller & Chambellan du Roi, Grand-Queue de France, étoit Gouverneur de Beauvais en 1359, fervit le Roi dans fes Armées pendant plufieurs années, & fut pourvu, l'an 1367, de la charge de Grand-Queue de France, qu'il exerça jufqu'à fa mort, arrivée l'an 1390. GUILLAUME & fon époufe font inhumés dans l'Eglife des Jacobins de Beauvais, fuivant l'épitaphe qui eft au-deffus de leur tombeau. Il avoit auffi fait une fondation à l'Abbaye de l'Isle-Dieu, comme il paroît par une charte, datée du jeudi d'après la Notre-Dame d'Août 1375. Il avoit époufé *Jeanne de Raineval,* Dame de Luillier, morte en 1389, fille de *Raoul,* Seigneur de *Raineval,* Grand-Pannetier de France, & de *Philippe de Luxembourg,* fa première femme. De fon mariage il eut :

VIII. JACQUELINE, Châtelaine DE BEAUVAIS, héritière des grands biens de fon père, qui époufa *Jean de Bordes,* & mourut fans enfans. Après fon décès, *Aubert d'Evreux,* Seigneur de Waliquerville, fon coufin iffu de germain, recueillit fa fucceffion, & fut Châtelain de Beauvais.

TROISIÈME BRANCHE, éteinte.

V. RENAULT DE BEAUVAIS, fecond fils de RENAULT, Ier du nom, Châtelain DE BEAUVAIS, & de *N... de Saucourt,* fit auffi une fondation à l'Abbaye de l'Isle-Dieu en 1299, fervit fous Raoul, Comte d'Eu, Connétable de France en 1346, & fe trouva à la bataille de Poitiers, où il demeura prifonnier. De *Marguerite de Trie* il eut :

VI. PHILIPPE DE BEAUVAIS, qui fut fait prifonnier à la bataille de Poitiers avec fon père, fervit fous Hue de Châtillon, Grand-Maître des Arbalêtriers en 1368, & vivoit encore en 1388. Il avoit époufé *Alix,* dite *la Blonde,* Dame de *la Forêt-le-Roi,* dont :

1. PIERRE, Seigneur du fief de Noyers, mort fans alliance;
2. COLLARD, dit COLINET, mort auffi fans alliance;
3. JEANNE, Dame de la Forêt-le-Roi, mariée 1° à *Bureau de Dicy,* premier Ecuyer du corps, & Maître de l'Ecurie du Roi; & 2° le 3 Novembre 1421, à *Jean le Clerc,* Chancelier de France, dont elle fut la troifième femme; & à caufe d'elle, Seigneur de la Forêt-le-Roi, & maintenu, par Arrêt du 5 Mai 1428, en la poffeffion de la Châtellenie de Beauvais, & de toutes les terres qui avoient appartenu à Guillaume, IIe du nom, Châtelain DE BEAUVAIS „ & à *Aliénor de Crefpin.* Voy. CLERC DE FLEURIGNY. Après la mort fans enfans d'*Aubert d'Evreux* ils vendirent enfemble cette Châtellenie à Eftout d'Eftouteville, Seigneur de Beaumont, qui prit depuis la qualité de Châtelain de Beauvais.

4. CATHERINE, morte fille;
5. Et ALIX DE BEAUVAIS, mariée à *Robert de Marigny,* Seigneur de Mainneville & de Boifroger, lequel fe fignala dans les guerres de Gafcogne contre les Anglois. Il eft qualifié Sire de Tourny, Maréchal du Roi de France ès parties du Languedoc & de Saintonge, & mourut fans poftérité.

BRANCHE.
des Seigneurs des MINIÈRES *& des* ANGLES, &c., *fubfiftante.*

VII. RICARD, ou RICHARD DE BEAUVAIS, fecond fils de COLLART, Châtelain DE BEAUVAIS, & de *Marguerite de Roye,* époufa *Marie Bufquet,* & fut, à caufe d'elle, Seigneur du Mont-Lambert & d'Amecourt, comme il paroît par actes paffés devant les Tabellions de Longchamp & de la Ferté, les 3 Août 1378, & 29 Mai 1424. Il eut pour fils :

VIII. GUILLAUME DE BEAUVAIS, Seigneur d'Incarville, de la Villette-en-Bray, & de Martigny, marié à *Catherine du Bofc,* iffue de la Maifon du *Bois-d'Ennebourg,* de laquelle vinrent :

1. JEAN, qui fuit;
2. GUILLAUME, lequel, par acte paffé devant les Tabellions de Pont-de-l'Arche le 9 Août 1478, eut en partage de fon père le manoir d'Incarville, le fief de la Motte, fis au Vaudreuil, à Lery & Tournedos-fur-Seine, & le fief d'Amecourt, fis au village de Gifors; il mourut fans alliance;
3. Et CRESPIN DE BEAUVAIS, auquel fon père donna pour fa part les fief & Seigneuries de Pierreval & de Maudetour, le fief du Puis-fur-Ry, fis à Elbœuf-fur-Andelle, la Vavafforie de Sainte-Croix-fur-Buchy, &c., à la charge du douaire de fa mère, ne fe réfervant que les fiefs d'Alix, d'Aubry & de Martigny. Ledit CRESPIN céda à Jacques le Pelletier, Ecuyer, par contrat paffé devant les Tabellions de Saint-Saens le 28 Janvier

1483, ledit fief de Maudetour, contre celui des Angles, fis à Sainte-Croix, & un autre fief, fitué au Bois-Guilbert. Il décéda auffi fans alliance.

IX. JEAN DE BEAUVAIS, Ier du nom, Seigneur des Minières, & du Mont-Lambert, partagé par fon père le 9 Août 1478, des fiefs des Minières, fis à Romilly, Pitres, & le Pont-Saint-Pierre, du Mont-Lambert, fitué à Catenay, & de la Prévôté d'Ally avec fes dépendances, époufa, par contrat paffé devant les Tabellions de Neufmarché le 28 Mars 1480, *Catherine de Guiffancourt*, fille de *Pierre de Guiffancourt*, Ecuyer, & de *Jeanne de Bouchevilliers*. Leurs enfans furent:

1. PHILIPPE, qui fuit;
2. ETIENNE, mort fans alliance;
3. GUILLAUME, vivant encore en 1547, mort auffi fans alliance;
4. Et MATHURIN DE BEAUVAIS, marié à *Jeanne le Foreftier*, dont MICHEL DE BEAUVAIS, qui époufa *Catherine le Parmentier*, & en eut:

ODOUART DE BEAUVAIS, Sieur de Bofcavin, demeurant à Ally, marié 1° à *Catherine le Monnier*, dont il n'eut point d'enfans; & 2° à *Catherine du Buiffon*, de laquelle fortit:

LOUISE DE BEAUVAIS, femme de *Charles de Bocquemare*, Sieur de Verclives; ce qui eft juftifié par une Sentence du 17 Novembre 1580, donnée par les Commiffaires députés du Roi à Rouen, fur le fait des francs-fiefs, & nouveaux acquêts, & par une autre Sentence du 20 Octobre 1617, rendue entre Madame la Comteffe de Chaligny, lors Châtelaine de Beauvais, & ledit ODOUART DE BEAUVAIS, par laquelle il eft prouvé qu'il defcendoit des anciens Châtelains de Beauvais.

X. PHILIPPE DE BEAUVAIS, Seigneur des Minières, du Mont-Lambert & de Beauficelle, tranfigea avec GUILLAUME, fon oncle, fur la fucceffion de CRESPIN DE BEAUVAIS, auffi fon oncle, & devint, par ce moyen, propriétaire du fief des Angles, par un acte paffé devant les Tabellions de Pont-de-l'Arche, le 3 Octobre 1502, &c., fut fait homme d'armes de la Compagnie de Villebon, par Brevet du 12 Mai 1512, & étoit mort le 4 Novembre 1526. Il avoit époufé *Jeanne le Sénéchal*, fille de *Jacques le Sénéchal*, Ecuyer, dont:

1. JEAN, qui fuit;
2. CATHERINE, mariée, par contrat du 27 Mai

1527, à *Richard Regnard*, Ecuyer;
3. Et JEANNE DE BEAUVAIS, mariée, par contrat reconnu au fiège de la Ferté le 6 Juillet 1539, à *Nicolas Morel*, Ecuyer, Sieur de Bultot, dont il eut pour fils *Antoine Morel*, Ecuyer.

XI. JEAN DE BEAUVAIS, IIe du nom, Seigneur des Minières, des Angles & de Saint-Aubin en partie, fervit en qualité d'homme d'armes en la Compagnie de M. le Marquis d'Aligre. Il époufa, par contrat du 23 Avril 1537, *Marie du Quefne*, remariée à *Adrien Pelletot*, Ecuyer, Sieur de Saint-Martin. Elle étoit fille de *Louis*, Ecuyer, & de *Catherine Houdetot*. De fon premier lit elle eut:

XII. JEAN DE BEAUVAIS, IIIe du nom, Seigneur des Angles, des Minières, & de la Huanière, qui fut exempté de l'arrière-ban, à caufe de fes fervices, & de ceux d'*Alexandre de Camp*, fon gendre, par acte du 31 Juillet 1597. Il mit fes enfans hors de fa garde, par une fentence de la Ferté du 30 Avril 1599, & avoit époufé, par contrat du 17 Septembre 1563, *Louife de Lannion*, fille d'*Antoine*, Ecuyer, Sieur d'Amecourt & de Boutavent, & de *Françoife de Courcelles*. A cet acte fut préfent JEAN DE BEAUVAIS, Ecuyer, Sieur d'Amecourt, fon coufin. De ce mariage naquirent:

1. MATHIEU, qui fuit;
2. JACQUES, mort fans alliance;
3. ANTOINE, marié, par contrat du 2 Avril 1607, à *Madeleine de Baudouin*, fille aînée de *Jean*, Ecuyer, Sieur de la Quaifne & d'Ecalles, & de *Barbe de Saint-Simon*, dont vint:

LAMORAL DE BEAUVAIS, mort fans poftérité;

4. CLAUDE, mort auffi fans poftérité;
5. CATHERINE, femme d'*Alexandre de Camp*, Ecuyer, vivant en 1611;
6. Et CHARLOTTE DE BEAUVAIS, morte fans alliance.

XIII. MATHIEU DE BEAUVAIS, Seigneur des Angles & des Minières, époufa, par contrat du 30 Septembre 1602, *Marguerite du Mefniel*, fille de *Jean*, Seigneur de Hemye, Sommery, la Pommeraye & de Rocfort, & de *Marguerite de Quefnel*, dont:

1. LOUIS, qui fuit;
2. ANTOINETTE, Religieufe de St.-Amand de Rouen;
3. Et MARIE DE BEAUVAIS, Religieufe du tiers ordre de St.-François à Neufchatel.

XIV. Louis de Beauvais, Seigneur des Angles & de Saint-Aubin en partie, maintenu dans fa Nobleſſe, le 31 Décembre 1667, mort au mois d'Août 1678, avoit épouſé, par contrat paſſé devant les Tabellions d'Abbeville, le 4 Octobre 1634, *Madeleine Piquet*, fille de *Gédéon Piquet*, Ecuyer, Seigneur d'Aveleſges, & de *Marie le Roi*, de laquelle il eut :

1. Jean, qui ſuit;
2. René, Sieur de Sionval, Lieutenant-Colonel au Régiment de Talendre, par Brevet du 17 Février 1704, mort ſans poſtérité;
3. Et Louise de Beauvais, morte fille.

XV. Jean de Beauvais, IVᵉ du nom, Chevalier, Seigneur des Angles, épouſa, par contrat paſſé devant les Notaires d'Eſneval, le 1ᵉʳ Mai 1680, *Juſtine de la Houſſaye*, fille de *Pierfē*, Ecuyer, Sieur de la Bourdonnière & de Francourt, & d'*Angélique du Bourdonné*, dont :

1. Guillaume de Beauvais-des-Angles, Lieutenant d'Infanterie, tué en Flandres par un parti de Huſſards;
2. Hubert, qui ſuit;
3. Jean-Baptiste, Sieur de Croville, Capitaine au Régiment d'Arſy, par Brevet du 25 Octobre 1710, mort ſans alliance;
4. Etienne, Sieur des Buhots, Lieutenant d'Infanterie audit Régiment d'Arſy, qui a épouſé *Marie de la Foſſe*, dont :
   Etienne de Beauvais, Officier de Vaiſſeau en l'Isle de Pondichéry, duquel on ignore l'exiſtence;
   Et Marie-Justine vivante, non mariée en 1777;
5. Et autre Etienne de Beauvais, mort Curé de Maulevrier.

XVI. Hubert de Beauvais, Chevalier, Seigneur des Angles, Capitaine d'Infanterie au Régiment de Talendre, par Brevet du 25 Juillet 1702, épouſa, en 1725, *Catherine de Cheveſtre*, fille de *Pierre*, Chevalier, Seigneur de Beaucheſne, & de *Marguerite du Peiroy*, dont :

1. Pierre-Hubert-Louis, qui ſuit;
2. & 3. Jean-Gabriel & Hubert;
4. & 5. Jacqueline & Catherine-Marguerite de Beauvais, tous quatre morts en bas âge.

XVII. Pierre-Hubert-Louis de Beauvais, Chevalier, Seigneur des Angles, des Isles & du Buſe-Huet, ancien Officier d'Infanterie, a épouſé 1º *Françoiſe Aubert d'Armanville*,

Dame des Isles, morte ſans enfans; & 2º en 1762, *Marguerite-Félicité Houxé de Saint-Paul*, fille de *Jean-Baptiſte*, Ecuyer, Sieur de Saint-Paul, Commiſſaire-Provincial d'Artillerie, Chevalier de Saint-Louis, & de *Marguerite l'Hériter de Chêſel*. De ce ſecond mariage ſont iſſus :

1. François-Hubert, né le 28 Octobre 1763, mort en 1777;
2. Louis-Hubert, né le 12 Août 1768, élève de l'Ecole Militaire à Paris;
3. Et Alexandre-Louis-Pompée, Chevalier de Beauvais, né le 4 Avril 1772, élève du collège Royal de Saint-Louis de Metz.

Les armes : *d'argent, à la croix de ſable, chargée de cinq coquilles d'or.* Supports : *deux lions.* (Généalogie dreſſée ſur titres originaux communiqués).

BEAUVAIS, Seigneur des Angles, de Soret en Normandie, Généralité de Rouen, famille maintenue dans ſon ancienne Nobleſſe le 31 Décembre 1667, qui porte : *de gueules, à cinq coquilles d'or,* aliàs *d'argent, poſées 3 & 2.*

BEAUVAIS (de) : *d'argent à la faſce de gueules, chargée de trois roſes mal ordonnées du champ, 1 & 2, accoſtées de deux coquilles d'or, l'une à dextre des roſes & l'autre à ſéneſtre.*

BEAUVAIS (de), Seigneur de Faverolles en Picardie : *d'azur, à une croix d'or, chargée de cinq roſes de gueules.*

BEAUVAIS (de), Seigneur de Gentilly, de la Boiſſière : *d'azur, à un cœur d'or, ſoutenu d'un croiſſant d'argent, & ſurmonté d'une nuée de même.*

BEAUVAIS, Seigneur de l'Ecu en Bretagne : *d'azur, à ſix billettes d'argent, au chef couſu d'azur, chargé de trois targes d'argent.*

BEAUVAIS, Seigneur d'Herbelay : *d'or, au chef de ſable, chargé d'une faſce vivrée d'argent.*

BEAUVAIS, en Picardie : *échiqueté d'argent & d'azur,* aliàs *d'argent, à trois pals de gueules.*

BEAUVAIS, en Normandie, Généralité de Caen : *écartelé, aux 1 & 4 de gueules, à la roſe d'argent; aux 2 & 3 de gueules, au lion d'argent.*

BEAUVAIS, Seigneur de la Gaillardière ou Guillaudière, en Normandie, Généralité d'Alençon, famille maintenue dans fa Nobleffe le 26 Juillet 1667, dont les armes font: *d'argent, au chevron de fable; au chef de gueules.*

BEAUVAIS, Ecuyer, Sieur de la Gaillardière, ancienne Nobleffe employée dans la recherche de 1666, Election de Mortagne, Généralité d'Alençon en Normandie, porte: *coupé d'argent & de gueules, le premier chargé d'un chevron abaiffé de fable.*

BEAUVAIS, Seigneur de Maury en Normandie, Généralité de Rouen, famille maintenue dans fa Nobleffe le 14 Octobre 1666, qui porte: *de gueules, à deux piques d'argent, emmanchées d'or, & pofées en chevron, accompagnées de trois hauffe-cols d'or, deux en chef & un en pointe.*

BEAUVAIS, en Bretagne: *de gueules, à une croix vuidée & cléchée d'or, pommetée d'argent, au franc-canton de même, chargé d'un lion de gueules.*

BEAUVAIX: *d'argent, au pal de gueules.*

BEAUVAU, Maifon illuftre & ancienne originaire d'Anjou, qui tire fon nom de la Terre de Beauvau, qui fait partie du Marquifat de Jarzé. Des Auteurs la font defcendre des anciens Comtes d'Anjou, & croient que, quand même les titres ne juftifieroient pas cette origine, elle eft affez prouvée par les dictions fingulières qui s'obfervèrent dans les cérémonies de l'hommage que RAOUL, Seigneur de Beauvau & de Jarzé, rendit en 1025, conjointement avec GIRAULT, fon frère, au Comte d'Anjou; car RAOUL DE BEAUVAU fit hommage *l'épée au côté & le chapeau fur la tête,* à caufe de leur parenté, *cum gladio & birettâ propter Parentagium,* ainfi que porte un titre de l'Abbaye de Saint-Serge d'Angers, au lieu que les autres Seigneurs s'acquittoient de ce devoir *à genoux, tête nue & fans épée.* La Chronique d'Anjou remarque que la Nobleffe de cette Province marchoit toujours fous la bannière de Beauvau, ce qui fait préfumer que les Comtes d'Anjou reconnoiffoient les Comtes de Beauvau pour leurs parens, puifqu'il n'euffent pas fouffert que la Nobleffe de leurs Etats marchât fous une ban-

nière étrangère. Le premier de cette Maifon qui foit connu eft:

I. FOULQUES DE BEAUVAU, Ier du nom, Chevalier, Seigneur de Beauvau & de Jarzé, qui mourut à Angers l'an 1090, trois jours après Pâques, comme il a été prouvé, lors de la vérification de la nobleffe de JACQUES DE BEAUVAU, Chevalier, Marquis du Rivau, pour être confervé au nombre des 100 Chevaliers de l'Ordre de Saint-Michel, faite en 1665, devant le Marquis de Sourdis, Commiffaire député en cette partie. Il fut père de:

1. RAOUL, qui fuit;
2. Et GIRAULT, dont il a été ci-deffus parlé.

II. RAOUL DE BEAUVAU, Ier du nom, Chevalier, Seigneur dudit lieu & de Jarzé, rendit hommage, comme nous venons de le rapporter ci-deffus, conjointement avec fon frère, au Comte d'Anjou, en 1025, pour les Châteaux de Beauvau & de Jarzé, & le droit de chaffe à toutes bêtes dans la forêt de Chambrières, *l'épée au côté & le chapeau fur la tête,* à caufe de leurs alliances avec les Comtes d'Anjou, fuivant ce qu'en rapporte Trinquant, dans fon *Extrait des Archives de Saint-Aubin d'Angers.* Il fut père de:

III. GEOFFROY DE BEAUVAU, Ier du nom, Chevalier, Seigneur dudit lieu & de Jarzé, qui fit une donation à la Chapelle très-ancienne de Beauvau, fous le titre de Saint-Martin, pour y établir les Religieux de fon Ordre, fuivant le CLXVII Article du premier Cartulaire de l'Abbaye de Saint-Serge d'Angers, dont il étoit Bienfaiteur. Il vivoit en 1060, & fut père de:

IV. JEAN, Ier du nom, Chevalier, Seigneur de Beauvau & de Jarzé, qui foufcrivit à la donation de fon père, & époufa *Berthe de Mayenne,* fille de *Geoffroy,* Seigneur de Mayenne, & de *Gervaife de Châteaugontier,* dont il eut:

V. GEOFFROY, IIe du nom, Chevalier, Seigneur de Beauvau & de Jarzé, qui époufa *Euphrofine de Lude,* dont il eut:

VI. FOULQUES, IIe du nom, Chevalier, Seigneur de Beauvau & de Jarzé, qui fit fon teftament en 1137, par lequel il ordonna à fon fils, de le faire inhumer au pied de fon père dans la Chapelle *encommencée par lui* en l'Eglife de Saint-Martin de Beauvau, *qui ja par mauvaifeté normande avoit été détruite.* Il avoit époufé *Jeanne de Boiffei-le-Châtel.* Il laiffa:

VII. RAOUL DE BEAUVAU, IIe du nom, Chevalier, Seigneur de Beauvau, dénommé dans le teftament de fon père de 1137, qui eut de fa femme, dont ont ignore le nom :

VIII. FOULQUES DE BEAUVAU, IIIᵉ du nom, Chevalier, Seigneur dudit lieu & de Jarzé, qui fut tué à la guerre contre les Infidèles. Il avoit époufé *Claudine de Landry*, laquelle vivoit veuve en 1200, fuivant un acte du jour de la Nativité-Notre-Dame de cette année, par lequel elle fait don, préfence & du confentement de ROBERT DE BEAUVAU, fon fils, qui fuit, aux Religieux de la Pénitence de J.-C. habitués à Angers, d'une maifon fife en cette Ville, provenante de fa dot, à la charge de prier Dieu pour le repos de fon âme & de celle du feu Sieur fon mari.

IX. ROBERT DE BEAUVAU, Chevalier, Seigneur dudit lieu & de Jarzé, qui vivoit en 1200, mourut en 1227, après avoir, par fon teftament, recommandé fes enfans à noble Seigneur *Amauri de Craon*, fon compagnon d'armes. Il avoit époufé *Judith d'Acigné*, dont il eut :

BAUDOUIN DE BEAUVAU, qui fuit ;
Et AGATHE, mariée à *N...... de Voyer*, Seigneur de Paulmy en Touraine.

X. BAUDOUIN DE BEAUVAU, Chevalier, Seigneur dudit lieu & de Jarzé. Ses biens furent faifis par Arrêt du Parlement tenu à Paris le jour de la Nativité-Notre-Dame de l'an 1259, faute d'hommage dû au Roi, pour 100 liv. de fonds, qu'il avoit aliénées pour le mariage de RENÉ, fon fils, qui fuit. (Voyez l'Extrait du Regift. *Olim.* par le Laboureur). Il époufa *Jeanne de la Jaille*.

XI. RENÉ DE BEAUVAU, Chevalier, Seigneur & Baron de Beauvau (MM. de Sainte-Marthe n'ont commencé la Généalogie de cette Maifon qu'à ce RENÉ), accompagna en 1265 CHARLES, Comte d'Anjou, frère du Roi St. Louis, dans fon Expédition de Naples. Après la réduction de ce Royaume, il en fut nommé Connétable ; y mourut en 1266, des bleffures qu'il avoit reçues, & y fut inhumé dans la Chapelle qu'il avoit fait bâtir en l'Eglife de Saint-Pierre. Il avoit époufé, du vivant & du confentement de fon père, *Jeanne de Preuilli*, dont il eut :

1. MATHIEU, qui fuit ;
2. Et N...... qui s'établit en Calabre, d'où fa poftérité fe répandit en Efpagne, & y a fubfifté quelque tems.

XII. MATHIEU, *aliàs* MACÉ DE BEAUVAU,

Chevalier, Seigneur & Baron de Beauvau, Sénéchal d'Anjou, fit rebâtir les Cordeliers d'Angers en 1281, où il fut inhumé avec *Jeanne de Rohan*, fa femme, de laquelle il eut :

1. JEAN, qui fuit ;
2. JAMET, Chevalier, mort fans poftérité ;
3. Et MATHIEU, auteur de la branche des Seigneurs de *la Beffière* & *du Rivau*, rapportée ci-après.

XIII. JEAN DE BEAUVAU, IIᵉ du nom, Chevalier, Seigneur & Baron de Beauvau, époufa *Jeanne de Coulaine*, fille du Seigneur de Poiffonnière en Anjou, dont il eut :

1. JEAN, qui fuit ;
2. JAMET, Chevalier, qui fut Lieutenant de Roi au Gouvernement de Tarente ;
3. Et MARIE, femme de *Louis Gilbert*, Chevalier, Seigneur de Fontaines en Loudunois, dont font iffus les Seigneurs de *Châteauneuf* en Poitou.

XIV. JEAN DE BEAUVAU, IIIᵉ du nom, Chevalier, Seigneur & Baron de Beauvau, Gouverneur & Châtelain de la ville & château de Tarente, au Royaume de Naples, rendit de grands fervices aux Rois Louis Iᵉʳ & Louis II. Il avoit époufé *Jeanne de Tigny*, fille de *Jean*, Seigneur de Tigny en Anjou, & d'*Agnès du Pleffis*, & en eut :

1. PIERRE, qui fuit ;
2. Et BERTRAND, auteur de la branche de *Précigni*, rapportée ci-après.

XV. PIERRE, Seigneur de BEAUVAU, Iᵉʳ du nom, fut auffi Seigneur de la Roche-fur-Yon & de Champigny, Gouverneur d'Anjou & du Maine, Sénéchal d'Anjou & de Provence, Exécuteur teftamentaire de LOUIS II, Roi de Sicile, en 1429, dont il étoit Chambellan, & Ambaffadeur de LOUIS III, fon fils, pour traiter fon mariage avec *Marguerite de Savoie*, fille du Duc *Amédée*. De fon mariage avec *Jeanne de Craon*, morte en 1421, veuve d'*Ingelger d'Amboife*, IIᵉ du nom, Seigneur de la Rochecorbon, de Montils, de la Ferrière, de Marans, &c., & fille de *Pierre de Craon*, Seigneur de la Sufe, de Chantocé & d'Ingrande, & de *Catherine de Machecou*, vinrent :

1. LOUIS, qui fuit ;
2. Et JEAN, dont la poftérité fera rapportée après celle de fon frère.

XVI. LOUIS, Seigneur de BEAUVAU, de Champigny, de la Roche-fur-Yon, &c., Grand-Sénéchal de Provence, Gouverneur & Capitaine de la Tour de Marseille, premier Chambellan de René Iᵉʳ, Roi de Sicile, & son Ambassadeur à Rome vers le Pape Pie II, en 1472, mourut la même année. Il épousa 1° *Marguerite de Chamblet* morte en 1456, fille de *Ferri*, Seigneur de Chambley en Lorraine, & de *Jeanne de Launai* ; 2° *Jeanne de Baudricourt*, dont il n'eut point d'enfans; & 3° *Jeanne de Beaujeu*, fille d'*Edouard*, Seigneur d'Amplepuis, & de *Jacqueline de Linières*.

Du premier lit sortit :

1. Isabeau, qui suit.

Et du troisième vint :

2. Et Alix, mariée à René de Beauvau, Seigneur de la Bessière & du Rivau.

XVII. Isabeau de Beauvau, Dame de Champigny & de la Roche-sur-Yon, morte en 1474, fut enterrée en l'Eglise de Saint-Georges de Vendôme, auprès de son mari. Elle avoit épousé, en 1454, Jean de Bourbon, IIᵉ du nom, Comte de Vendôme. De leur mariage sortit François de Bourbon, Comte de Vendôme, Bisayeul du Roi Henri IV; & par cette alliance, toutes les têtes couronnées de l'Europe descendent de la Maison de Beauvau.

XVI. Jean, Seigneur de Beauvau, IVᵉ du nom, fils puîné de Pierre, & de *Jeanne de Craon*, fut aussi Seigneur de Sarmaises, des Rochettes & des Essarts en Anjou, Baron de Manonville, de Rorté & de Lorraine, Sénéchal d'Anjou, Gouverneur du Château d'Angers, Conseiller & Chambellan du Roi Louis XI & de René, Roi de Sicile, Duc d'Anjou & de Lorraine. Il écartela ses armes avec celles de *Craon*, qui porte *losangé d'or & de gueules*, que sa postérité porte encore à présent. Il mourut en 1468, laissant de *Jeanne*, Dame de Manonville, fille unique & héritière de *Jean de Manonville* en Lorraine, & d'*Alarde de Chamblet*, sœur de *Marguerite*, femme de Louis, Seigneur de Beauvau, son frère aîné, sçavoir :

1. Pierre, qui suit;
2. Jacques, mort jeune;
3. Louise, mariée à *Jean*, Seigneur de *Florainville* en Lorraine;
4. Claude, mariée à *Antoine de Ville*, Seigneur de Dom-Julien, Duc du Mont Saint-Ange, au Royaume de Naples;
5. Hélène, femme de *Charles d'Estouteville*, Seigneur de Villebéon près Chartres;

6. Et Françoise, morte sans alliance.

Jean de Beauvau eut encore d'une Maîtresse :

Achille, qui, par sa bravoure, sous le règne de René II, mérita le Gouvernement de Neufchâteau, & la Charge de Grand-Maître de l'Hôtel de Lorraine. Il laissa de *Jeanne d'Abancourt*, Louise de Beauvau, mariée à *René de Florainville*.

XVII. Pierre, IIᵉ du nom, Seigneur de Beauvau, Baron de Manonville & de Rorté, Sénéchal de Lorraine, Chambellan de René II, Roi de Sicile, mourut en 1521. Sa succession fut partagée entre ses enfans par acte passé devant *Gérard Henaudet* & *François Goffroy*, Notaires à Toul, le 6 Juillet 1521. Il avoit épousé 1° *Marguerite de Montbéron*, fille de *Guichard*, Seigneur de Mortagne, & de *Catherine Martel* ; & 2° *Agnès de Bichoël*.

Du premier lit naquirent :

1. Alof, Conseiller & Chambellan d'Antoine, Duc de Lorraine, Bailli de Bar, mort en 1547, sans postérité de *Marguerite d'Averton;*
2. René, qui suit;
3. Pierre, Ecclésiastique;
4. Antoinette, femme de *Pierre d'Urfé*, Marquis dudit lieu, Bailli de Forez, Grand-Ecuyer de France;
5. Françoise, mariée à *Jacques du Châtelet*, Baron du Châtelet & de Forez & Bailli de Saint-Mihel;
6. Cécile, Abbesse de Remiremont.

Et du second lit :

7. Et Claude, Seigneur de Sandaucourt, Baron de Rorté, &c., qui fut, en 1541, Ambassadeur vers l'Empereur Charles V, pour négocier le mariage du Duc François de Lorraine avec Christine de Danemark, & laissa de *Claude du Fay*, fille de *Jean*, & d'*Antoinette de Bettencourt*:

1. Marie, Dame de Sandaucourt, alliée à *Claude de Reinack*, Seigneur de Saint-Barlemont;
2. Nicole, mariée à *Jean de Damas;*
3. Et Claude, femme de *Claude de Marcossei*.

XVIII. René, Seigneur de Beauvau, IIᵉ du nom, Baron de Manonville & de Rorté, Seigneur de Novian, de Tremblecourt, d'Hamonville, &c., Gouverneur de Darnei, Sénéchal du Barrois, & Chambellan d'Antoine, Duc de Lorraine, mourut vers 1549. Il avoit épousé *Claude de Baudoche*, Dame de Panges, fille de *Claude*, Seigneur de Panges & de Moulins, & de *Jeanne de Serrieres*, dont:

1. CLAUDE, qui suit;
2. ALOF, Auteur de la Branche de *Rorté*, rapportée ci-après;
3. PIERRE, Seigneur de Panges, &c., premier Gentilhomme de la Chambre de FRANÇOIS de Lorraine, Grand-Prieur de France, mort sans postérité d'*Agnès d'Esche;*
4. JEAN, Seigneur de Panges, après son frère, qui a fait la branche de *Panges*, rapportée ci-après;
5. LOUIS, mort au voyage de Naples;
6. MARGUERITE, alliée, en 1549, à *Jean de la Guiche*, Seigneur de Nanton, Bailli de Châlons;
7. FRANÇOISE, Chanoinesse de Remiremont;
8. Et ISABELLE, Abbesse de Saint-Hoïld.

XIX. CLAUDE, Baron de BEAUVAU, Seigneur de Manonville, Novian, &c., Bailli & Gouverneur d'Hatton-Châtel, Gouverneur de la personne de HENRI, Duc de Bar, puis de Lorraine, Grand-Maître de la Garde-robe d'ANTOINE DE BOURBON, Roi de Navarre, mourut en 1597. Il avoit épousé 1º *Nicole de Lutzelbourg* fille de *Nicolas*, Seigneur de Fléville & de Germini, & de *Marguerite de Lucy*; & 2º en 1556, *Jeanne de Saint-Bauffant.*

Les enfans du premier lit furent:

1. CHARLES, qui suit;
2. CLAUDE, mariée à *Jean Frénau*, Seigneur de Pierrefort, &c.

Et du second lit vinrent:

3. JEAN, Marquis de Novian, Seigneur de St.-Bauffant, &c., Bailli de Bassigny, Sénéchal du Barrois, qui, d'*Antoinette d'Urre-de-Tessière*, fille de *Charles*, Seigneur de Commercy, & de *Marie de Marcossei*, eut ANNE-FRANÇOIS DE BEAUVAU, Marquis de Novian, à qui on donna le nom de *François*, parce qu'on crut l'avoir obtenu par l'intercession de *Saint-François de Paule*, dont il porta l'habit jusqu'à l'âge de sept ans. Il se fit Jésuite sur la fin de ses jours, fut fait Prêtre le 3 Mai 1661, & mourut le 23 Mai 1669. Il avoit épousé, en 1637, *Marguerite de Raigecourt*, laquelle, pour entrer dans les pieux sentimens de son mari, fit publiquement, l'an 1660, vœu de continence perpétuelle entre les mains d'*André du Saussai*, Evêque de Toul. Elle étoit fille de *Bernard*, Seigneur de Raigecourt, Sénéchal de l'Evêché de Metz, Général de l'Artillerie de Lorraine, Bailli & Gouverneur de Ste-

Tome II.

nay, & de *Barbe d'Haraucourt*. De ce mariage sortirent:

1. JOSEPH, qui se fit Jésuite avant son père, & mourut le 20 Août 1694;
2. JOSEPH-GABRIEL - BERNARD, mort sans alliance;
3. MARIE-JOSÈPHE, Religieuse à la Visitation de Sainte-Marie de Pont-à-Mousson, morte le 24 Septembre 1660;
4. Et JEANNE-ANTOINETTE, mariée à *Jean Claude de Cussigny*, Comte de Vianges, Seigneur de Coing & de Passavant, Conseiller d'Etat & Maréchal de Lorraine;

4. LOUIS, Colonel dans les Armées d'ALEXANDRE FARNÈSE, puis commandant 6000 hommes de pied & 800 chevaux Lorrains pour le service de France, Capitaine fameux par les sièges & les batailles où il s'est toujours signalé, mort sans alliance en 1596, avec la réputation d'un grand Général;
5. Et FRANÇOISE, mariée à *Henri*, Seigneur de *Montricher*.

XX. CHARLES, Baron de BEAUVAU, Seigneur de Manonville, &c., premier Gentilhomme de la Chambre de HENRI, Duc de Bar, Bailli & Gouverneur de Hatton-Châtel en 1577, sur la démission de son père, épousa, en 1577, *Philiberte de Saulx*, veuve de *Jean de Nicey*, Chevalier de l'Ordre du Roi, & fille de *Théodore de Saulx*, & de *Catherine d'Haraucourt*, dont:

1. HENRI, qui suit;
2. Et ANTOINETTE, femme de *Charles de Marteau*, Baron d'Oison, Gentilhomme de la Chambre de CHARLES, Cardinal de Lorraine.

XXI. HENRI, Baron de BEAUVAU, Iᵉʳ du nom, Seigneur de Manonville, Conseiller d'Etat de HENRI, Duc de Lorraine, premier Gentilhomme de sa Chambre, & Grand Gruyer de Lorraine, fit ses premières campagnes en Hongrie, sous l'Empereur RODOLPHE II, passa ensuite au service de l'Electeur de Bavière, d'où étant retourné en Lorraine, il fut nommé Ambassadeur vers le Pape PAUL V, au sujet du mariage que HENRI DE LORRAINE, Duc de Bar, avoit contracté avec CATHERINE DE BOURBON, sœur du Roi HENRI IV. Il parcourut l'Europe, l'Asie & l'Afrique, & donna à son retour la relation de ses voyages. Il leva depuis un corps de 2000 hommes de pied & de 1000 chevaux, qu'il joignit à l'armée du Comte de Mansfeld. Il avoit épousé, en 1607, *Catherine d'Haraucourt*, fille d'*Elysée*, Mar-

U u

quis de Fauquemont, Gouverneur de Nancy, & de *Chriſtine de Marcoſſei*, dont il eut pour fils unique :

XXII. Henri, Marquis de Beauvau, IIe du nom, Gouverneur de Charles V, Duc de Lorraine, & d'Emmanuel, Electeur de Bavière, Auteur des Mémoires de ſon nom. Il avoit épouſé *Catherine d'Haraucourt*, ſa couſine germaine, fille de *Henri*, Général d'Artillerie, & d'*Anne de Joyeuſe*, dont :

1. Louis, qui ſuit ;
2. Charles, Chevalier de Malte ;
3. François, Grand-Prevôt de Saint-Dié ;
4. Et Anne-Catherine, mariée à *Jean-Nicolas de Rouſſelz*, Seigneur d'Aubigny & de Varneville.

XXIII. Louis, Ier du nom, Marquis de Beauvau, Seigneur de Fléville, de Faims, &c., Conſeiller d'Etat & Capitaine des Gardes-du-Corps du Duc de Lorraine, épouſa 1º *Charlotte de Florainville*, fille de *Henri*, Seigneur de Faims, Maréchal des Camps & Armées du Roi, Gouverneur de Tortone, & d'*Eve-Françoiſe de Lützelbourg* ; & 2º *Anne de Ligny*, fille de *François*, Comte de Charmel, & de *Henriette de Gournai*.

Les enfans du premier lit ſont :

1. Louis, qui ſuit ;
2. Paul, Capitaine des Gardes-du-Corps de la Compagnie des Carabiniers du Duc de Bavière, Gentilhomme de la Clef, tué à la bataille d'Hochſtett, le 13 Août 1704 ;
3. Marie-Louise, mariée à *Charles-Louis*, Marquis de *Baſſompierre* ;

Ceux du ſecond lit ſont :

4. Marc, rapporté après ſon frère Louis ;
5. Et Catherine-Diane, mariée 1º à *Anne-François-Joſeph*, Marquis de *Baſſompierre* ; & 2º à *Charles-François de Stainville*, Comte de Couvonges, Conſeiller d'Etat, & Grand-Maître de l'Hôtel du Duc de Lorraine.

XXIV. Louis, IIe du nom, Marquis de Beauvau, Seigneur de Fléville, de Faims, &c., épouſa *Jeanne-Marie-Madeleine de Ludre*, morte le 8 Avril 1715, fille de *Henri*, Comte d'Afrique, & de *Jeanne-Catherine-Madeleine de Savigni* en Réthelois, dont :

1. Louis-Charles ;
2. Louis-Antoine, né au mois d'Avril 1715, appelé *le Marquis de Beauvau*, Chevalier de Saint-Louis, ſucceſſivement Colonel du Régiment de la Reine, Cavalerie, Brigadier & Maréchal des Camps & Armées du Roi, qui mérita, par ſon application au ſervice

& par les grands talents avec leſquels il étoit né pour la guerre & pour les négociations, d'être employé de bonne-heure auprès du Roi de Pruſſe & de l'Empereur Charles VII. Il donna, dans les Campagnes de Philippsbourg, de Prague & de Menin, des preuves de ſa valeur, & trouva ſous les yeux du Roi Louis XV régnant, une mort glorieuſe en ſe rendant maître du chemin-couvert d'Ypres, le 23 Juillet 1744 ;

3. Marie-Louise, mariée à *Louis-Alexandre*, Marquis de *Salles*, en Lorraine ;
4. Et Anne de Beauvau, mariée, en 1727, à *Antoine-Bernard*, Comte des *Armoiſes*, aujourd'hui Marquis d'Aunoy.

XXV. Marc de Beauvau-Craon, Prince de Craon & du Saint-Empire par Diplôme de l'Empereur Charles VI, daté de Vienne, du 13 Novembre 1722, Grand d'Eſpagne de la première claſſe par Lettres de Philippe V, du 8 Mai 1727, Chevalier de la Toiſon-d'Or, Grand-Ecuyer de Son Alteſſe Royale de Lorraine, Grand Duc de Toſcane, depuis Empereur ſous le nom de François Ier, ſon Miniſtre Plénipotentiaire, Chef & Préſident de ſon Conſeil de Régence à Florence, Marquis d'Harroué, né le 29 Avril 1679, mort le 11 Mars 1754, avoit épouſé, le 16 Septembre 1704, *Anne-Marguerite de Ligniville*, morte le 12 Juillet 1772, Dame-d'honneur de feue Son Alteſſe Royale Madeleine-Charlotte, Ducheſſe de Lorraine. Elle étoit fille de *Melchior*, Maréchal de Lorraine, & d'*Antoinette de Bouſey*. De ce mariage ſont nés :

1. Nicolas-Simon-Jude, Prince de Beauvau, né à Lunéville le 28 Octobre 1710, nommé en ſurvivance à la Charge de Grand-Ecuyer de Lorraine par Lettres du 3 Février 1718 ; mais ayant conſacré à Dieu ſes dignités, ſa fortune & ſes talens à l'âge de 21 ans, pour embraſſer l'état Eccléſiaſtique, on le connut depuis ſous le nom d'*Abbé de Craon*. Il mourut à Rome au mois de Mai 1734, après y avoir reçu les Ordres ſacrés ;
2. François-Vincent-Marc, né le 23 Janvier 1713, Abbé de l'Isle en Barrois, mort à Paris le 9 Juin 1742 ;
3. Léopold-Clément, Chevalier de Malte de minorité, né le 27 Avril 1714, mort à Paris le 27 Février 1723 ;
4. Charles-Just, qui ſuit ;
5. Ferdinand-Jérôme, né le 5 Septembre 1723, reçu Chevalier de Malte de Minorité, Maréchal-de-Camp, Inſpecteur de Cavalerie ;
6. Alexandre, né le 16 Décembre 1725, fait Colonel du Régiment de Hainaut en 1744,

:appelé *le Comte de Beauvau-Craon*, tué à la bataille de Fontenoy, le 11 Mai 1745, ~~fans avoir été marié~~;

7. HILARION, né le 21 Septembre 1728, mort quatre jours après;

8. ANTOINE, né le 18 Janvier 1730, mort à Harroué;

9. ELISABETH-CHARLOTTE, née le 29 Novembre 1705, mariée, le 29 Juillet 1723, à *Charles-François-Ferdinand de la Baume*, Marquis de Saint-Martin, mort le 19 Novembre 1736;

10. ANNE-MARGUERITE-GABRIELLE, née le 28 Avril 1707, mariée, 1º le 19 Août 1721, avec *Jacques-Henri de Lorraine*, Prince de Lixin, mort le 2 Juin 1734; & 2º le 2 Janvier 1739, avec *Pierre-Louis de Levis*, Maréchal héréditaire de la Foi, Marquis de Mirepoix, mort le 25 Septembre 1757;

11. GABRIELLE-FRANÇOISE, née le 31 Juillet 1708, Chanoinesse de Pouffai en Lorraine, morte le 22 Juillet 1758. Elle avoit épousé, le 19 Août 1725, *Alexandre d'Alsace*, Prince de Chimay, mort le 18 Février 1745, âgé de 74 ans;

12. MARIE-PHILIPPE-THECLE, née le 23 Septembre 1709, Chanoinesse de Remiremont;

13. MARIE-FRANÇOISE-CATHERINE, née le 8 Décembre 1711, Chanoinesse de Remiremont, mariée, le 19 Avril 1735, avec *Louis-François*, Marquis de *Boufflers*, mort le 2 Février 1752;

14. LOUISE-EUGÉNIE, née à Craon le 29 Juillet 1715, élue Abbesse d'Espinal le 7 Août 1728, & morte à Nancy en 1736;

15. HENRIETTE-AUGUSTINE, née le 28 Août 1716, Chanoinesse de Pouffai, Religieuse de la Visitation à Paris;

16. CHARLOTTE, née le 8 Novembre 1717, Coadjutrice, & ensuite Abbesse de Pouffai par la démission volontaire de Madame de Gramont, au mois d'Avril 1730, une des Dames de Madame, mariée, le 21 Décembre 1734, avec *Léopold-Clément*, Marquis de *Bassompierre*;

17. ANNE-MARGUERITE, née le 10 Février 1719, Religieuse de la Visitation à Paris;

18. ELISABETH, née le 29 Janvier 1722, Chanoinesse de Pouffai, & aussi Religieuse de la Visitation;

19. GABRIELLE-CHARLOTTE, née le 29 Octobre 1724, Chanoinesse de Remiremont en Lorraine, Religieuse en l'Abbaye Royale de Juvigny en Clermontois, près de Stenay, & nommée Abbesse de Saint-Antoine de Paris le 28 Septembre 1760, dont elle a pris possession le 24 Janvier 1761;

20. Et BÉATRIX-ALEXISE, née le 17 Juillet 1727, morte le 9 Mars 1730.

XXVI. CHARLES-JUST DE BEAUVAU, né à Lunéville le 10 Novembre 1720, quatrième fils de MARC, & d'*Anne-Marguerite de Ligniville*, Prince de Beauvau-Craon & du Saint-Empire, Grand d'Espagne de la première classe, fut d'abord Colonel du Régiment des Gardes-Lorraines. Pendant que ce Régiment se formoit, ce Prince fit la campagne de Prague en qualité de Volontaire auprès de M. le Maréchal de Belle-Isle, & reçut un coup de Mousquet à la cuisse. A son retour de Prague le Roi lui donna la Croix de Saint-Louis. Il a été nommé successivement Lieutenant-Général, Chevalier de ses Ordres, & Capitaine des Gardes-du-Corps & a épousé, 1º le 3 Avril 1745, *Marie-Sophie-Charlotte de la Tour-d'Auvergne*, née le 20 Décembre 1729, morte le 6 Septembre 1763, fille d'*Emmanuel-Théodose*, Duc de Bouillon; & 2º au mois de Mars 1764, *Marie-Sylvie de Rohan-Chabot*, née le 12 Décembre 1729, mariée, 1º le 7 Septembre 1749, à *Jean-Baptiste-Louis de Clermont-d'Amboise*, Marquis de Renel, mort le 18 Septembre 1761. Elle étoit fille de *Guy-Auguste de Rohan*, Comte de Chabot, & d'*Yvonne-Sylvie du Breil de Rais*. Il eut du premier lit:

ANNE-LOUISE-MARIE DE BEAUVAU, née le 1er Avril 1750, mariée, le 9 Septembre 1767, à *Louis-Philippe-Marc-Antoine de Noailles*, Prince de Poix.

BRANCHE des *Seigneurs* DE RORTÉ.

XIX. ALOF DE BEAUVAU, second fils de RENÉ, Seigneur de Beauvau, IIe du nom, & de *Claude de Baudoche*, Dame de Panges, fut Baron de Rorté, &c. Il épousa, 1º par contrat passé devant *Relange*, Tabellion à Neufchâtel, le 3 Février 1551, *Claude de Ludre*, fille de *Jean*, Chevalier, Seigneur dudit lieu, Maître de l'Artillerie, & Chambellan d'ANTOINE, Duc de Lorraine, Bailli & Gouverneur d'Hatton-Châtel, & d'*Eve de Ligniville*, remariée à *Claire de Saulx*; & 2º *Madeleine d'Espenses*, fille & héritière de *François*, Seigneur d'Espenses, & de *Françoise de Sac-Epée*. Du premier lit vinrent:

1. RENÉ, qui suit;
2. MARGUERITE, alliée 1º à *Claude de Fresnels*; & 2º à *Jean-Philippe de Savigni*, Bailli de Vosges;
3. NICOLE, mariée, en 1566, à *François du*

U u ij

Maultoi, Seigneur de Nubecourt, Maréchal des Camps & Armées du Roi.

Les enfans du second lit furent :

4. JEAN, rapporté après son frère aîné ;
5. ALOF, Seigneur de Louvernau ;
6. Et MAXIMILIEN, Seigneur de Begni-Pont & de Merigni.

XX. RENÉ DE BEAUVAU, Baron de Rorté, &c., Page d'honneur de Monseigneur le Marquis de Pont-à-Mousson de Lorraine, puis Sénéchal du Barrois, & Capitaine de Darnei, épousa *Guillemette des Salles,* fille de *Philippe,* Baron de Combervaux, Seigneur de Chardogne, Vernancourt, &c., Capitaine de Neufchâteau, & de *Renée d'Haussonville,* dont :

1. RENÉ, mort sans lignée ;
2. Et MARIE, femme 1° de *Georges,* Seigneur de *Saint-Astier;* & 2° de *François de Riquet,* Seigneur de Barizet, Capitaine de 100 Archers de la Garde du Corps de la Duchesse NICOLE DE LORRAINE.

XXI. JEAN DE BEAUVAU, fils puîné d'ALOF, Baron de Rorté, & de *Madeleine d'Espenses,* sa seconde femme, fut Seigneur d'Espenses, &c., & marié 1° avec *Sara des Salles,* fille de *Claude,* Seigneur de Gorecourt ; & 2° par contrat du 25 Octobre 1600, avec *Anne d'Angennes,* fille de *François,* Seigneur de Montlouet. Du premier lit vint :

1. SAMUEL, Seigneur de Varimont & Poix en Champagne, d'abord Capitaine de Chevaux-Légers par commissions des 8 Avril & 1er Août 1630 ; Colonel d'un Régiment de Cavalerie par autre commission du 24 Janvier 1638, & Colonel d'un Régiment de Cavalerie étrangère par autre du 21 Mai 1645, sous le Roi LOUIS *le Juste.* Il avoit épousé, par contrat passé devant *Lombard,* Notaire Royal à Vitry, résidant à Banteville, le 25 Septembre 1622, *Françoise d'Alaumont,* fille de *Daniel,* Seigneur de Banteville, Cornay & Fléville, & de *Madeleine de Cresay.*

Et du second sortirent :

2. FRANÇOIS, Seigneur de Noirlieu, mort au siège de Bois-le-Duc en 1630, Cornette du Duc de Bouillon, sans enfans de *Marguerite Pasquet ;*
3. JACQUES-CHARLES, tué Mestre-de-Camp d'un Régiment de Chevaux-Légers au siège de Paris en 1649 ;
4. JACQUES, Seigneur de Meri, Colonel de Cavalerie, Lieutenant-Général des Armées du Roi, & Gouverneur du Quesnoy ;
5. CHARLES, Seigneur de Noirlieu, Capitaine de Cavalerie au Régiment de Varimont ;

6. LOUIS, Seigneur de Grandru, Lieutenant-Colonel au Régiment de son frère, puis Maréchal des Camps & Armées du Roi ;
7. MADELEINE, femme de *Charles de Meaux,* Seigneur de Charni en Brie ;
8. LOUISE, alliée à *Maximilien Auberi,* Seigneur de Maurier en Poitou ;
9. Et ANTOINETTE, mariée, par contrat passé devant *Suaire,* Notaire Royal à Vitry, le 29 Mars 1638, à *Henri de la Marche-des-Contes,* Chevalier, Seigneur & Baron de l'Echelle, Seigneur de Fontaines-Denis, Colonel d'un Régiment de Cavalerie étrangère, fils d'*Antoine,* Gouverneur des Ville, Château & Souveraineté de Sédan, & d'*Anne de Maucourt.*

BRANCHE des Seigneurs DE PANGES.

XIX. JEAN DE BEAUVAU, quatrième fils de RENÉ, Seigneur de Beauvau, II° du nom, & de *Claude de Baudoche,* Dame de Panges, fut Seigneur de Panges, Conseiller d'Etat, & Chef des Finances de CHARLES III, Duc de Lorraine. Il avoit épousé *Marie de Salcède,* fille de *Pierre,* Seigneur d'Anvilliers, dont il eut :

1. JEAN, Seigneur de Panges, tué à la bataille d'Yvry en 1590 ;
2. GABRIEL, qui suit ;
3. ANNE, mariée à *Louis de Fremicourt,* Gouverneur de Vitry-le-François ;
4. MADELEINE, morte sans alliance ;
5. BLANCHE, morte à Remiremont ;
6. Et DIANE, alliée 1° à *Antoine Myon,* Seigneur d'Esquinvilliers ; & 2° à *André de Faultreau,* Baron de la Mare.

XX. GABRIEL DE BEAUVAU, Seigneur de Panges, Conseiller d'Etat du Duc de Lorraine, servit en Hongrie, sous le Duc de Mercœur, & en France, sous Henri de Bourbon, Prince de Condé. Il épousa 1° *Anne de Bildstein ;* & 2° *Claude-Françoise de Grandmont,* dont il eut des enfans.

BRANCHE des Seigneurs DE PRECIGNI & DE PIMPEAN.

XV. BERTRAND DE BEAUVAU, Seigneur de Sillé-le-Guillaume & de Briançon, second fils de JEAN, III° du nom, Seigneur de Beauvau, & de *Jeanne de Tigny,* fut Baron de Precigni, Conseiller & Chambellan du Roi, premier Président Laïc de la Chambre des Comptes, & Grand-Conservateur de son Domaine en 1462, ensuite Conseiller & Grand-

Maître-d'Hôtel de RENÉ, Roi de Sicile; Capitaine du Château d'Angers., & Sénéchal d'Anjou. Il mourut, en 1474, ayant été marié 1° à *Jeanne de la Tour-Landry*; 2° à *Françoise de Brezé*; 3° à *Ida du Châtelet*; & 4° à *Blanche d'Anjou*, Dame de *Mirebeau*, dont il n'eut point d'enfans.

Du premier lit vinrent :

1. LOUIS, mort fans poftérité ;
2. ANTOINE, qui fuit ;
3. JEAN, Evêque d'Angers en 1447, Adminiftrateur de l'Archevêché d'Arles, & Chancelier de RENÉ, Roi de Sicile, Comte de Provence, mort le 23 Avril 1479;
4. CATHERINE, mariée à *Philippe de Lenoncourt*, Seigneur de Gondrecourt ;
5. CHARLOTTE, femme d'*Yves de Scepeaux*, Premier Préfident au Parlement de Paris ;
6. Et MARGUERITE, Dame des Effars, en Anjou, alliée à *N..... de Magneville*, Seigneur de la Haye-du-Pui.

Du fecond lit fortirent :

7. JEAN, Seigneur de Tigny, mort fans alliance ;
8. JACQUES, Seigneur de Tigny, après fon frère, mort fans poftérité de *Hardouine de Laval*, fille de *Guy de Laval*, II° du nom, Seigneur de Loué, & de *Charlotte de Sainte-Maure* ;
9. CHARLES, Seigneur de Paffavant, puis de Tigny, après fes frères, auteur de la branche de *Tigny*, rapportée ci-après;
10. BERTRAND, Seigneur de Saint-Laurent-des-Mortiers, qui, de *Louife de Fontaine-Guerin*, eut Jean DE BEAUVAU, Seigneur de Saint-Laurent-des-Mortiers ;
11. PIERRE, Archidiacre d'Angers;
12. ISABELLE, mariée 1° à *Pierre de la Salle*, Grand-Sénéchal de Provence ; & 2° à *Artus de Nelor*, Seigneur de la Chapelle, en Loudunois;
13. MATHURINE, femme de *Charles de Maillé*, Seigneur de Chefelles & de Cravant;
14. Et CHARLOTTE, alliée à *N..... de Saint-Simonian*, Seigneur de Préaux.

Les enfans du troifième lit furent :

15. RENÉ, Baron de Moigneville, qui, de *Marguerite d'Hauffonville*, fille de *Jean*, Sénéchal de Lorraine, & de *Madeleine de Haraucourt*, eut pour fille unique, MADELEINE DE BEAUVAU, Dame de Moigneville, mariée à *Jacques de Clermont-d'Amboife*, Baron de Buffy ;
16. JEAN, mort fans alliance ;
17. Et GUYONNE, qui époufa 1° *Jean Jouvenel-des-Urfins*, Seigneur de la Motte-Jouffe-

rand; & 2° *René de Laval*, Ier du nom, Seigneur de Bois-Dauphin, &c.

XVI. ANTOINE DE BEAUVAU, fecond fils de BERTRAND, & de *Jeanne de la Tour-Landry*, Comte de Policaftre, Baron de Precigni, &c., fuccéda à fon père en 1472, en la charge de Premier Préfident Laïc de la Chambre des Comptes; fut auffi Confeiller & Chambellan du Roi, & Chevalier de fon Ordre. Il mourut en 1489, laiffant entr'autres enfans d'*Anne Hingant*, que l'on croit fille de *Raoul Hingant*, Seigneur du Hac, & de *Françoife de Saint-Amadour*:

1. LOUIS, qui fuit ;
2. Et MARGUERITE, femme de *Gilles de Couvran*, Baron de Sacé.

XVII. LOUIS DE BEAUVAU, Baron de Precigni & de Sillé-le-Guillaume, Seigneur de Vandœuvre & de Pimpean, époufa *Regnaude de Hure* dont il eut pour fils unique :

XVIII. RENÉ DE BEAUVAU, Seigneur de Pimpean, &c., qui laiffa d'*Olive le Maffon*, fille de *René*, Seigneur de Fouletorte :

1. ANDRÉ, qui fuit;
2. GUYONNE, femme de *Jean de Savonnières*, Seigneur de la Bretefche ;
3. Et MARGUERITE, alliée à *Charles de Savonnières*, Seigneur de Linières.

XIX. ANDRÉ DE BEAUVAU, Seigneur de Pimpean, &c., époufa *Philippe de Naillac*, fille de *René*, Seigneur des Roches, premier Ecuyer du Roi CHARLES IX, & de *N..... Pot*, dont :

1. JEAN-BAPTISTE, qui fuit;
2. RENÉE, mariée à *Léonor Barjot*, Seigneur de Mouffy ;
3. Et GABRIELLE, femme de *Louis Arbalefte*, Vicomte de Melun.

XX. JEAN-BAPTISTE DE BEAUVAU, Seigneur de Pimpean, des Roches, &c., marié, en 1597, fans poftérité, à *Françoife du Pleffis*, morte en 1615. Elle s'étoit remariée, en 1603, avec *René de Vignerot*, Seigneur de Pontcourlai, dont elle eut des enfans. Elle étoit fœur du Cardinal de Richelieu, & fille de *François du Pleffis*, Seigneur de Richelieu, Chevalier des Ordres du Roi, Grand-Prevôt de l'Hôtel, & de *Sufanne de la Porte*.

BRANCHE

des Seigneurs DE TIGNY & DE PASSAVANT.

XVI. CHARLES DE BEAUVAU, troifième fils de BERTRAND, Baron de Precigni, & de *Fran-*

çoife de Brezé, fa feconde femme, Baron de Paffavant, puis de Tigny, après la mort de fes frères, époufa 1° Bonne de Chauverfon, dont il n'eut point d'enfans; & 2° Barbe de Talanges, dont:

1. JACQUES, qui fuit;
2. CHARLES, II° du nom, Seigneur de Paffavant, qui, de Barbe de Choifeul, fille de Nicolas, Seigneur de Praslin, & d'Alix de Choifeul, eût pour fille unique, ANNE DE BEAUVAU, Dame de Paffavant, mariée 1° à Théodore de Haraucourt, Seigneur de Paroye; & 2° à Antoine du Châtelet, Seigneur de Châteauneuf, Bailli de Nancy;
3. JEANNE, femme d'Edmond de Prie, Baron de Bufançois;
4. Et ISABEAU, mariée, en 1512, à Jean de Seraucourt, Seigneur de Belmont.

XVII. JACQUES DE BEAUVAU, dit de Tigny, Ier du nom, Seigneur dudit lieu, &c., laiffa de Jeanne d'Epinai, fille de Henri, Sire d'Epinai, en Bretagne, & de Catherine d'Eftouteville:

1. JACQUES, qui fuit;
2. Et MARTHE, femme de Jacques Gabori, Seigneur du Pineau & de la Challiere.

XVIII. JACQUES DE BEAUVAU, II° du nom, Seigneur de Tigny, &c., époufa 1° Anne du Pleffis, fille de Charles, Seigneur de la Bourgonniere, & de Louife de Montfaucon; & 2° Marguerite Bigot, fille de Charles, Seigneur d'Iffai.

Du premier lit il eut:
1. CLAUDE, qui fuit.

Et du fecond:
2. ESTHER, femme de Gilles de Jubilles, Seigneur des Moulins-Carbonel;
3. JACQUELINE, mariée à François Menard, Seigneur de Touche-Près & des Herbières, en Poitou;
4. Et MARGUERITE, mariée à Charles de Brie, Seigneur de Serrant.

XIX. CLAUDE DE BEAUVAU, Seigneur de Tigny, fut marié à Anne de Chezelles, fille de Charles, Seigneur de Neuil-fous-Faye-la-Vineufe, dont:

1. JACQUES, mort en 1611, âgé de 32 ans, fans poftérité;
2. CLAUDE, mort en 1604, âgé de 20 ans;
3. CHARLES, qui fuit;
4. ANGÉLIQUE, morte en 1612, fans alliance;
5. Et RENÉE, mariée à Ancel Chefnel, Seigneur de Gréfillon & de la Roche-Méfangé.

XX. CHARLES DE BEAUVAU, Seigneur de Tigny, a laiffé de Perrine de Guerineau:

1. JACQUES, qui fuit;
2. Et CLAUDE, mort fans alliance.

XXI. JACQUES DE BEAUVAU, III° du nom, Seigneur de Tigny, mort en 1690, avoit époufé, en 1645, Jeanne de Sefmaifons, & laiffa:

1. CLAUDE-CHARLES, qui fuit;
2. CHARLES-RENÉ, tué à la bataille de la Marfaille, le 4 Octobre 1693;
3. FRANÇOISE-ELISABETH, mariée, en 1695, à Guillaume de Laage, Seigneur de la Bretoliere;
4. CHARLOTTE, alliée à Vincent Bohier, Seigneur de la Roche-Guillaume;
Et quatre filles, religieufes.

XXII. CLAUDE-CHARLES DE BEAUVAU, Marquis de Tigny, étant Moufquetaire, entra le premier dans Valenciennes, lorfque cette Ville fut prife, en 1697, fut bleffé à la bataille de Fleurus, & fe retira, après 29 ans de fervices. Il époufa, en 1700, Thérèfe-Eugénie le Sénéchal, fille de Barthélemy-Hyacinthe-Anne, Marquis de Kercado, & de Louife de Lannion, dont:

1. ANNE-LOUIS, qui fuit;
2. & 3. N. & N.... DE BEAUVAU, dont un appelé le Commandeur de Beauvau;
4. GABRIELLE-ELISABETH-EUGÉNIE, mariée, le 28 Octobre 1726, à Nicolas de Fuffey, Seigneur de Melay;
5. Et THÉRÈSE-CHARLOTTE-DOROTHÉE, mariée, par contrat du 8 juillet 1730, à Jofeph de Quengo, Seigneur de Crenolle.

XXIII. ANNE-LOUIS DE BEAUVAU, Marquis de Tigny, mourut le 1er Mars 1770, âgé de 65 ans. Il avoit époufé, le 14 Janvier 1740, Louife-Marguerite le Sénéchal, dont:

XXIV. N... DE BEAUVAU, Capitaine au Régiment de Gardes-Lorraines.

BRANCHE
des Seigneurs DE LA BESSIÈRE, & Marquis DU RIVEAU.

XIII. MATHIEU DE BEAUVAU, troifième fils de MATHIEU, Ier du nom, Seigneur de BEAUVAU, & de Jeanne de Rohan, époufa, N.... le Roux, fille de Hugues, Seigneur d'Expeti, & d'Alix de Mauvoifin, & fut père de:

XIV. GUILLAUME DE BEAUVAU, Sénéchal & Gouverneur d'Anjou, qui eut:

1. MATHIEU, qui fuit;
2. Et JEANNE, mariée à Jean le Boul, Ecuyer.

XV. MATHIEU DE BEAUVAU, II° du nom, Seigneur de la Beffière, Ecuyer d'Ecurie de LOUIS II, Roi de Sicile, Capitaine du Château de Tarente, au Royaume de Naples, Capitaine du Château d'Angers, & Gouverneur du Comté de Roucy, mourut le 28 Décembre 1421. Il avoit épousé *Jeanne Beſſoneau*, morte le 22 Août 1429. De ce mariage naquit, entr'autres enfans :

XVI. Pierre de Beauvau, Seigneur de la Beſſière, du Riveau, &c. Conſeiller & Chambellan du Roi, qui ſervit ſous le règne du Roi Charles VII, en la guerre contre-les Anglois, où il aſſiſta *Jean d'Anjou*, Duc de Calabre, en 1450, & ſous *Jean*, Bâtard d'Orléans, Comte de Dunois, fut bleſſé à la bataille de Caſtillon, en 1453, & mourut trois jours après. Il avoit épouſé, en 1438, *Anne de Fontenais*, fille d'*Ambroiſe*, Seigneur de Saint-Gaſſien, en Loudunois, & de *Marguerite du Pui*, dont :

   1. René, qui ſuit ;

   2. Jean, Chanoine d'Angers ;

   3. Renée, élevée fille d'Honneur de Marie d'Anjou, Reine de France, mariée à *Philippe de la Rochefoucauld*, Seigneur de Mellerau;

   4. Catherine, femme de *Guillaume de-Prunelé*, Seigneur de Herbaut & de Gazeran ;

   5. Et Françoise, mariée à *Jacques de Briſaï*, Seigneur de Douſſan.

XVII. René de Beauvau, Seigneur de la Beſſière & du Riveau, Baron de Saint-Gaſſien Ecuyer de Charles d'Anjou, Comte du Maine, & Capitaine de la ville de Mayenne, mourut le 25 Mars 1510. Il épouſa, 1º en 1481, *Antoinette de Montfaucon*; & 2º Alix de Beauvau, fille de Louis de Beauvau, Seigneur de Champigni & de la Roche-ſur-Yon, & d'*Anne de Beaujeu*, ſa troiſième femme.

  Il eut du premier lit :

   1. François, Seigneur de la Beſſière, du Riveau, &c., Capitaine de 50 hommes d'armes, mort ſans poſtérité dè *Jeanne de Beauvilliers ;*

   2. & 3. Charles, jumeau de François, IIº du nom, Protonotaire Apoſtolique ;

   4. Anne, mariée, en 1516, à *Jacques de Partenai*, Seigneur du Rétail ;

   5. Louise, femme de *Philippe de Vernon*, Seigneur de Gracei ;

   6. Et Marie, qui épouſa, le 7 Février 1518, *Hervé Errault*, Seigneur de Chemans.

  Les enfans du ſecond lit furent :

   7. Antoine, qui ſuit ;

   8. Et Jacques, Seigneur de Courville, mort ſans poſtérité.

XVIII. Antoine de Beauvau, Seigneur de la Beſſière, du Riveau, &c., porta d'abord la qualité de *Seigneur de Saint-Clair*, & laiſſa de *Jacqueline de la Mothe*, fille de *Mathurin*, Seigneur des Aulnais, & de *Françoiſe Freſneau*, un fils unique :

XIX. Gabriel de Beauvau, Seigneur de la Beſſière, du Riveau, &c., qui ſe trouva à la bataille de Saint-Denis en 1567. Il fut marié 1º à *Marguerite Foucaut*, Dame de la Salle, fille de *Pierre*, Seigneur de la Salle, & d'*Antoinette Gourjault*; 2º à *Françoiſe du Frêne*, fille de *René*, Baron de Vaux, & de *Marguerite de la Mothe*; & 3º à *Françoiſe de la Jaille*.

  Du premier lit ſortirent :

   1. François, Seigneur du Riveau, tué en 1569, à la bataille de Jarnac, ſans alliance ;

   2. Jacques, qui ſuit ;

   3. Louis, auteur de la branche des Seigneurs de *Rivarennes*, rapportée ci-après ;

   4. Et Gabrielle, mariée à *Charles d'Allemagne*, Seigneur de Nallières.

  Du ſecond lit il eut:

   5. Marguerite, femme de *René Vaſſelot*, Seigneur de Dannemarie ;

  Et du troiſième lit vint:

   6. Gabriel, Chevalier, nommé dans le partage des biens de la ſucceſſion de ſon père, fait en 1583.

XX. Jacques de Beauvau, Seigneur du Riveau, de la Beſſière, &c., ſervit ſous les Rois Henri III & Henri IV; ſe trouva au combat d'Arques, où il fut fait priſonnier & bleſſé par un parti de la Ligue, près de Poitiers, dont il mourut en 1592. Le Roi l'avoit honoré du Brevet de Chevalier des Ordres; mais ſa mort en empêcha l'effet. Il eut de *Françoiſe le Picard*, fille & héritière de *Joachim*, Seigneur du Boilet:

   1. Jacques, qui ſuit;

   2. Louis, Seigneur de la Beſſière, marié, le 10 Mai 1621, à *Louiſe Dallé*, dont il eut Louis de Beauvau, Prêtre;

   3. François, Baron de la Beſſière, Lieutenant au Régiment de Piémont, puis Prêtre;

   4. Renée, alliée, en 1606, à *Charles de l'Hôpital*, Marquis de Choiſi;

   5. Françoise, épouſe de *Jean de la Baumele-Blanc*, Seigneur de la Gaſſerie, de la Vallière, &c.;

   6. Gabrielle, mariée 1º à *Bonaventure Gillier*, Baron de Saint-Gervais; & 2º à *Jacques de Champagné*, Seigneur de la Mothe-Ferchaut;

7. Et Louise, femme de *François d'Aloigny*, Seigneur de la Chenie & de la Groye.

XXI. Jacques de Beauvau, IIe du nom, Seigneur du Riveau, de la Beffière, &c., fervit fous les Rois Henri IV & Louis XIII, & fut Lieutenant-Général en Poitou. Il époufa, 1° *Renée d'Apchon*, fille unique de *Charles*, & de *Louife de Châtillon-d'Argenton*, dont il n'eut point d'enfans ; & 2° *Ifabeau de Clermont*, fille de *Henri*, Comte de Tonnerre, & de *Catherine-Marie d'Efcoubleau-de-Sourdis*, dont :

1. Jacques, qui fuit ;
2. Pierre-François, Evêque de Sarlat, mort en 1701 ;
3. Joseph, Chevalier de Malte, tué au fervice du Roi ;
4. & 5. Louis & Claude, morts jeunes ;
6. Henri, Religieux Bénédictin ;
7. Françoise, mariée à *Jacques de Voyer*, Vicomte de Paulmy ;
8. Madeleine, alliée 1° à *Denis Thevin ;* & 2°. à *Antoine*, Marquis *du Bellai ;*
9. Et Antoinette, Religieufe.

XXII. Jacques de Beauvau, IIIe du nom, Maréchal des Camps & Armées du Roi, & Capitaine des Gardes-Suiffes de Gaston de France, Duc d'Orléans, obtint l'érection de la Terre du Riveau en Marquifat, par Lettres du 14 Juillet 1664, fous le nom de *Beauvau-du-Riveau*, & mourut en 1702. Il eut de *Diane-Marie de Campet*, morte en 1702, fille de *Samuel-Eufèbe*, Baron de Soujon, & de *Marthe de Viau-Chanlivaut :*

1. Jacques-Louis, Enfeigne de Gendarmerie, mort fans alliance ;
2. Gaston-Jean-Baptiste, mort fur mer ;
3. Gabriel, Marquis du Riveau ;
4. Pierre-Madeleine, Marquis de Beauvau, Maréchal des Camps & Armées du Roi, Capitaine-Lieutenant des Chevaux-Légers de Bourgogne, Infpecteur-Général de la Cavalerie-Légère de France, marié, en 1711, à Marie-Thérèse de Beauvau, fa coufine, fille de Gabriel-Henri, Marquis de Montgoger ;
5. René-François, Evêque de Bayonne en 1700, de Tournay en 1707, Archevêque de Touloufe en 1713, de Narbonne en 1719, & mort le 4 Août 1739. Voyez fon article dans Moréri, édition de 1759, pag. 280 ;
6. & 7. Louis-Henri & Joseph, Capitaines de Vaiffeau, morts fur mer ;
8. Marie-Catherine, femme de *Claude de Bullion*, Marquis d'Atilli ;
9. Et Isabelle de Beauvau.

BRANCHE
des Seigneurs DE RIVARENNES *&* DE MONTGOGER.

XX. Louis de Beauvau, Seigneur des Aulnais, de Bugni & de Rivarennes, troifième fils de Gabriel, Seigneur du Riveau, & de *Marguerite Foucaut*, fervit fous Henri IV, à la bataille d'Ivry, aux fièges de Paris, de Laon & d'Amiens. Il eut de *Charlotte Brillouet*, fille unique de *Jacques*, & de *Guyonne Baraton :*

1. Louis, qui fuit ;
2. Gabriel, Evêque de Nantes en 1636, mort en 1667, ou peu après ;
3. Anne, mariée 1° à *Antoine d'Appelvoifin*, Seigneur de la Chataigneraye ; & 2° à *Jean de Boué*, Seigneur de Larmond, Gouverneur d'Ardres ;
4. Antoinette, femme de *Jacques d'Allemagne*, Seigneur de Nallières ;
5. Et Françoise, alliée à *Léonard du Mefnard*, Seigneur de Vintenat, en Limoufin.

XXI. Louis de Beauvau, IIe du nom, Seigneur de Rivarennes, &c., Capitaine de Chevaux-Légers, mourut au fervice du Roi Louis XIII, à Turin, le 6 Janvier 1641. Il avoit époufé *Charlotte de Fergon*, fille unique de *Martin*, Seigneur de la Mothe-d'Uffeau, en Poitou, dont entr'autres enfans :

1. François, qui fuit ;
2. Jean-Louis, Prieur de Notre-Dame du Pré ;
3. Et Louis, Seigneur de Courquoi, qui, de *N... de la Chenaye*, Dame de la Broffe, eut Louis de Beauvau, Seigneur de la Broffe, dont la fille unique a époufé N..., Comte de *Lucé*.

XXII. François, Marquis de Beauvau, Seigneur de Rivarennes, né en 1624, avoit époufé *Louife de la Baume-le-Blanc*, fille de *Jean*, Seigneur de la Vallière, & de *Françoise de Beauvau-du-Riveau*, dont :

1. Martin, tué à la bataille de Senef, le 11 Août 1674 ;
2. Jacques, Capitaine des Gendarmes de Philippe de France, Duc d'Orléans, tué à la bataille de Caffel, en 1677 ;
3. Gilles-Jean-François, Evêque de Nantes, en 1677, mort le 7 Septembre 1717 ;
4. Gabriel-Henri, qui fuit ;
5. Anne-Louise, Religieufe à la Vifitation ;
6. Et Thérèse-Agathe, Religieufe Carmélite.

XXIII. Gabriel-Henri de Beauvau, Marquis de Beauvau & de Montgoger, Capitaine des Gardes-du-Corps de PHILIPPE DE FRANCE, Duc d'Orléans, mourut à Paris, le 12 Juillet 1738, âgé de 83 ans. Il avoit épousé, 1º en 1682, *Marie-Angélique de Saint-André*, fille de *Pierre de Saint-André*, Tréforier-Général de la Marine & des Galères de France, & de *Marie Aimé-Dieu*; & 2º en 1694, *Marie-Madeleine de Brancas*, fille de *Louis-François*, Duc de Villars, & de *Marie-Madeleine Girard*, fa feconde femme.

Du premier lit font iffues:

1. MARIE-THÉRÈCE, mariée, en 1711, avec PIERRE-MADELEINE, Marquis de BEAUVAU, fon coufin;

2. HENRIETTE-LOUISE, morte le 28 Mars 1737. Elle avoit épousé, le 28 Avril 1711, *Hubert*, dit le *Marquis de Choifeul*.

Et du fecond lit il a eu:

3. GABRIEL-FRANÇOIS;
4. HENRI-LOUIS, mort jeune;
5. ANNE-MARIE-THÉRÈSE;
6. ANNE-AGNÈS, morte le 3 Mars 1742. Elle avoit épousé, le 3 Juin 1717, *Agéfilan-Gafton de Groffolles*, Marquis de Flamarens, mort au mois de Décembre 1762;
7. MADELEINE-LOUISE, Religieufe;
8. MARIE-HÉLÈNE, mariée le 11 Avril 1731, à *Euftache-Louis-Antoine de Bernart*, Comte d'Avernes;
9. MARIE-LOUISE-MADELEINE, morte le 11 Juillet 1763. Elle avoit épousé, le 4 Août 1733, *Pierre-Louis*, Comte d'*Ailly*;
10. GABRIELLE-ELISABETH, mariée le 17 Février 1738, à *François-Louis-Jofeph de Pardieu*, Comte d'Avremenil;
11. Et MARIE-CANDIDE DE BEAUVAU, encore fille en 1738.

On peut confulter fur cette Maifon MM. de Sainte-Marthe, *Généalogie de Beauvau*; Ménage, *Hiftoire de Sablé*, &c., & Moréri, édition de 1759, tom. II, pag. 274.

Les armes: *d'argent, à 4 lionceaux de gueules, cantonnés, couronnés, armés & lampaffés d'or.*

BEAUVAU: *d'azur, au léopard d'or.*

BEAUVERGER-MONGON: *écartelé en fautoir, le chef & la pointe d'azur, les flancs d'hermines, à la bande d'or, brochante fur le tout.*

BEAUVILAIN: *palé d'or & d'argent de fix pièces.*

BEAUVILAY: *fafcé d'or & d'azur de fix pièces.*

BEAUVILLIERS, ancienne Maifon qui a pris fon nom de la Terre & Seigneurie de *Beauvilliers*, fituée au Pays Chartrain, entre les Villes de Chartres & d'Orléans. Les Seigneurs de cette terre ont donné ce nom à plufieurs autres qu'ils ont poffédées en Beauce, en Berry & ailleurs.

I. HERBERT, Iᵉʳ du nom, Seigneur de BEAUVILLIERS, du Lude, de Martinville, de Maleloup & du vieux Alonne, eft qualifié, dans un Nécrologe de l'Eglife de Chartres, écrit avant 1200, fils d'une Dame nommée *Engelfende*. Il devoit être mort dans le XIᵉ fiècle, auffi bien que *Mathieu Ruffin*, mentionné après lui dans le même titre.

II. GEDOIN, Iᵉʳ du nom, Seigneur de BEAUVILLIERS, &c., eft qualifié fils d'HERBERT-EMUSSENT, & foufcrivit en cette qualité à une donation qui fe trouve dans un Cartulaire de Notre-Dame de Chartres, concernant la Prévôté de Voue, près Beauvilliers, dès 1138. Il étoit mort avant 1179, que fes enfans tranfigèrent avec le Chapitre de Chartres au fujet des Terres de Beauvilliers, Lude & Martinville. Il eut de fa femme, dont le nom eft inconnu:

1. HERBERT, qui fuit;
2. & 3. HUGUES & GEDOIN, rapportés l'un & l'autre dans la tranfaction de 1179.

III. HERBERT, IIᵉ du nom, Seigneur de BEAUVILLIERS, du Lude & de Martinville, qui tranfigea en 1179 avec le Doyen & le Chapitre de Notre-Dame de Chartres, eft encore mentionné dans un titre du Cartulaire couvert d'argent de l'Abbaye de Saint-Père de Chartres. Ses enfans furent:

1. GEDOIN, qui fuit;
2. 3. & 4. HUGUES, HENRI & EUDES, mentionnés dans la tranfaction qu'ils firent en 1208 avec le Supérieur de l'Abbaye de Bonneval, en Beauce, pour quelques dépendances du Prieuré de Touret. EUDES eft qualifié de *Clerc* dans ce titre.

IV. GEDOIN, IIIᵉ du nom, Seigneur de BEAUVILLIERS, &c., eft mentionné dans un titre de *Pétronille*, femme de *Raoul* le jeune, Seigneur de la Ferté-Nabert, pour l'Abbaye de Saint-Memin, près d'Orléans, & y eft qualifié *Dominus* JODOINUS DE BEAUVILLIERS. Il eut d'*Urtiffa* ou *Orbiffa*:

1. HERBERT, qui fuit;
2. Et N... DE BEAUVILLIERS. Ils confentirent l'un & l'autre, avec leur mère, à la dona-

tion faite par leur père à Notre-Dame de Baugency en 1212.

V. Herbert, IIIe du nom, Seigneur de Beauvilliers, &c., eut différend avec les Chanoines de Saint-Aignan d'Orléans, pour avoir abattu les fourches patibulaires qu'ils avoient dans la Mairie de Villaines, & auxquelles étoit pendu un Larron. Il fut excommunié à ce sujet, & Manassès, Evêque d'Orléans, l'obligea de les rétablir. Il ne s'est point trouvé de titres qui déterminent positivement l'ordre & la naissance des enfans d'Herbert III, mais il y a beaucoup d'apparence qu'il fut père d'Eudes, Chevalier, & le père ou l'ayeul de Gedoin, IVe du nom, qui suit, auteur de la branche des Ducs de Saint-Aignan.

VI. Gedoin de Beauvilliers, IVe du nom, Chevalier, Seigneur du Lude, en Beauce, de Bretigny, près Chartres, &c., fils ou petit-fils d'Herbert, IIIe du nom, épousa, 1o suivant les titres de l'Abbaye de Bonneval, des années 1248 & 1250, Adelice de Membrolles, fille de N... de Membrolles, & d'Adelice, Dame de Villebon. Elle fut enterrée à l'Abbaye de Voisines, près Mun, à laquelle elle avoit fait une donation; & 2o Jeanne, qui pouvoit être femme du Seigneur de Bretigny. Il eut de son premier mariage:

VII. Robert de Beauvilliers, Ier du nom, Chevalier, Seigneur du Lude, de Binas, &c., qui approuva, en 1260, avec Jacqueline, sa femme, les donations & aumônes d'Adelice sa mère, & de Jeanne, sa belle-mère, en faveur de l'Abbaye de Voisines. Ses enfans furent:
1. Geoffroy, qui suit;
2. Et Jean, Chevalier, qui servit le Roi en Flandres avec huit Écuyers, & reçut en payement 67 liv. 10 sols, à Arras, le 10 Septembre 1302, suivant sa quittance en cire verte.

VIII. Geoffroy de Beauvilliers, dit Pichot, Chevalier, Seigneur de Binas, du Lude en Beauce, & du Lude en Sologne, est qualifié seulement, Ecuyer, dans le partage qu'il fit, l'an 1292, avec le Doyen & le Chapitre de Saint-Sauveur de Blois, & Chevalier dans l'aveu qu'il donna de Binas, & de ce qu'il tenoiten Fief, le Dimanche 1er Septembre 1302. Ses biens passèrent à Gedoin de Beauvilliers, Ve du nom, qui suit, que l'on peut regarder comme son fils, par la convenance des tems & la conformité des armes, qu'il portoit comme Geoffroy, qui sont: fascé avec des merlettes, sans aucune marque de brisure.

IX. Gedoin de Beauvilliers, Ve du nom, Chevalier, Seigneur de Binas, &c., est qualifié, dans les actes qu'on a de lui de 1336, Noble Homme, Haut & Puissant, & il est employé dans la Pancarte du Duché d'Orléans, sous le nom de Monseigneur Gedoin de Beauvilliers. Il épousa Marie d'Orléans, de la même Maison que Payen d'Orléans, Grand-Bouteiller de France en 1093 & 1106, & que Jean d'Orléans, surnommé le Vaillant, lequel fut noyé au voyage d'Outre-Mer. Il en eut:
1. Robert, qui suit;
2. Et Jeanne, mariée à Guillaume Bouffart, Seigneur de Masières, Ecuyer.

X. Robert de Beauvilliers, IIe du nom, Chevalier, dit le Normand, Seigneur de Binas, &c., servoit Charles de Blois, Duc de Bretagne en 1341, étoit de l'Armée du Roi en Flandres en 1347. Il est qualifié Monseigneur Robert de Beauvilliers, Chevalier, Seigneur du Lude, avec Jeanne de Saint-Briçon, sa femme dans l'acquisition qu'ils firent de la Terre & Seigneurie de Dizier, de Philippe Basset, Ecuyer, en 1349. Ses enfans furent:
1. Jean, qui suit;
2. Humbert de Beauvilliers, Ecuyer, Seigneur de Dizier, qui servoit sous Louis de Sancerre, en 1370, 1379, 1380 & 1383. Il épousa, en 1361, Jeanne le Bugle, Dame de Bastardes, veuve de Jean de la Ferté-Hubert, remariée, en 1375, fille de Geoffroy & de Jeanne le Redde. Il en eut Marguerite de Beauvilliers, Dame de Dizier, &c., mariée, le 3 Août 1396, à Jean de Tillières, Seigneur de Chesnebrun & de Brusoles, en Normandie;
3. Et Hervé, rapporté après son frère aîné.

XI. Jean de Beauvilliers, Ier du nom, Chevalier, Seigneur du Lude, en Sologne, &c., servit en qualité d'Ecuyer, sous Randon du Puy, le 10 Juin 1375; sous Guy le Baveux, Chevalier en 1379; sous Pierre de Mornay, le 6 Août 1383; & sous Guillaume de Manchecourt, Chevalier, le 1er Septembre 1386. Il étoit mort avant 1392. Il épousa Pernelle de Manchecourt, remariée avant le 8 Juillet 1390. Elle étoit fille de Guillaume de Manchecourt, Chevalier. Il eut:
1. Jean, IIe du nom, dit le Camus, Ecuyer, Seigneur du Lude, en Sologne. Il fit montre avec 15 Ecuyers de sa Chambre à Baugency, le 1er Avril 1418. Il servoit le Roi

en la Compagnie du Comte de Vertus le 15 Juin 1419; au fiège de Partenay avec 19 autres Ecuyers. Il étoit mort fans enfans l'an 1429;

2. Et ISABEAU DE BEAUVILLIERS, Dame du Lude, &c., qui, après la mort de fon frère, fe maria, le 20 Février 1431, avec *Jean l'Arabe*, Ecuyer, dont elle eut une fille, qu'elle maria à *Guichard Raffin*, auquel elle céda un quart de la Seigneurie du Lude, & elle avoit déjà beaucoup démembré de cette Seigneurie, qui étoit une des plus anciennes de la Maifon de Beauvilliers.

XI. HERVÉ DE BEAUVILLIERS, Seigneur de Binas, du Lude, &c., fervoit dans la Compagnie de Galiot de Saint-Simon, Chevalier, le 30 Avril 1479; fous Pierre de Mornay, Chevalier, le 6 Août 1483; & dans l'Armée deftinée pour le paffage d'Angleterre, le 12 Septembre 1488. Il époufa 1° *Jeanne de la Ferté*, Dame de Montgouaut, fille de *Jean*, & de *Jeanne le Bugle*, Dame de Baftardes; & 2° *Philippe*, Dame de *Ruau* & de *Peray*, pour lefquelles Terres fon mari donna aveu à caufe d'elle, le 4 Juillet 1405. Les enfans de fon premier mariage furent :

1. JEAN, qui fuit;
2. GUYOT, Chevalier de Saint-Jean de Jérufalem en 1408;
3. GUILLOT, qui fe trouve au nombre des 29 Gentilshommes qui accompagnèrent le Duc d'Orléans au voyage qu'il fit à Gien en 1410. Il fervit le Roi CHARLES VII contre les Anglois, fous Jean, bâtard d'Orléans;
4. ROBERT;
5. Et SIMONNE, qui étoient mineurs & fous la garde ou le bail de leur père, le 13 Mars 1498.

XII. JEAN DE BEAUVILLIERS, III° du nom, dit *Bourles*, Seigneur du Lude, de Binas, &c., Gouverneur des Villes & Comtés de Blois & de Dunois, fut tué l'an 1428 d'un coup de flèche ou de Vireton, en défendant fon Château, affiégé par les Anglois. Il laiffa d'*Alix d'Eftouteville*, Dame de Thoury, &c., veuve de *Raoul*, Seigneur de Saint-Remy, tué à la bataille d'Azincourt en 1415, & fille & héritière de *Robert d'Eftouteville*, & de *Robine de Saint-Briçon*, Dame de la Ferté-Hubert :

1. MICHEL, qui fuit;
2. MARGUERITE, mariée, par contrat du 13 Juillet 1438, à *Robinet d'Eftampes*, le jeune, Chevalier, Confeiller & Chambellan du Roi, Maréchal & Sénéchal du Bourbonnois;
3. ROBINETTE, qui vivoit encore le 10 Mai

1469. Elle époufa, par contrat du 28 Septembre 1444, *Jeannequin Kent*, Ecuyer, Seigneur de Saint-Ulface, mort en Janvier 1464;

4. Et ANNETTE, mariée, 1° le 28 Septembre 1444, à *Pierre Garreau*, Ecuyer, Seigneur de Châteauvieux, mort en 1461, laiffant une fille unique, *Alizon Garreau*; & 2° à *Guichard de Loiches*; ils vivoient enfemble le 28 Février 1483.

XIII. MICHEL DE BEAUVILLIERS, Seigneur de la Ferté-Hubert, &c., Chevalier de l'Ordre du Camail, Echanfon du Roi, Bailli de Mantes & de Meullent, Capitaine & Gouverneur de Montereau & de Chartres, né en 1418, fut Capitaine de 24 Archers de la Garde du Roi, conjointement avec Claude de Châteauneuf, en 1456. Il mourut âgé de 45 ans, après avoir fait fon teftament, fuivant un acte du 15 Décembre 1462. Il avoit époufé *Anette de Tillay*, Dame de Brano, Dame d'Honneur de MARIE D'ANJOU, femme du Roi CHARLES VII, morte vers la fin de l'hiver 1472, après s'être remariée fur la fin du mois de Janvier 1466, à *Pierre*, dit *Pierroquin de Prunelé*, Seigneur d'Ouarville en Beauce. Elle étoit fille de *Jamet*, Bailli de Vermandois, & de *Jeanne d'Anneville*, & laiffa de fon premier lit :

1. JEAN, Seigneur de la Ferté-Hubert, &c., né le 26 Juin 1455, qui fut fait Lieutenant de la Compagnie d'Ordonnances d'Engelbert, Comte de Nevers, par Lettres du 14 Avril 1491. Il accompagna le Roi CHARLES VIII, en Italie, avec la Compagnie d'Ordonnance du Comte de Nevers en 1494, & mourut au mois de Juillet 1496, fans enfans d'*Antoinette d'Illiers*, fille de *Jean*, Sire d'Illiers, & de *Marguerite de Chourfes*;
2. MERY, qui fuit;
3. TANNEGUY, né le 12 Février 1457, il ne voit plus lorfque fon père mourut en 1462;
4. ANTOINE, mort jeune;
5. MARGUERITE, née le 24 Avril 1456, mariée avec *Yvon d'Illiers*, Chevalier, Seigneur de Raderets;
6. Et JEANNE, femme de *Gilles d'Efcheles*, Seigneur de Raoullet & de Saint-Flomer. Elle eut 2000 écus en mariage.

XIV. MERY DE BEAUVILLIERS, Chevalier, Seigneur de Thoury, &c., Confeiller & Chambellan du Roi, nommé Gouverneur & Bailli de Blois par LOUIS XII, tefta dans fon Château de la Ferté-Hubert, le 23 Septembre 1511. Il époufa, par contrat du 12 Mai 1489,

1º *Jacquette d'Eftampes*, fille de *Jean*, & de *Marie de Rochechouart*; & 2º par contrat du 25 Décembre 1496, *Louife de Huffon*, morte au mois d'Août 1540, fille de *Charles*, Comte de Tonnerre, Seigneur de Huffon, de Saint-Aignan, &c., & d'*Antoinette de la Trémoïlle*. Leurs enfans furent :

1. CLAUDE DE BEAUVILLIERS, Iᵉʳ du nom, Chevalier, premier Comte de Saint-Aignan, Seigneur de la Ferté-Hubert, qui fut Gentilhomme ordinaire de la Chambre du Roi, Capitaine de 50 Lances des Ordonnances, Gouverneur & Bailli de Blois. Il obtint au mois d'Avril 1537 l'érection de la Baronie de Saint-Aignan en Comté. Il mourut fans enfans, à Saint-Aignan, le 14 Août 1539, & fut enterré en l'Eglife Collégiale de ce lieu, dans le tombeau des anciens Seigneurs & Barons de Saint-Aignan. Il époufa, 1º par contrat de l'an 1524, *Charlotte de Tranchelion*, Dame de Paluau, fille unique de *Charles*, & de *Françoife de Silly*; & 2º, en 1537, *Claude de Rohan*, remariée avec *Julien de Clermont*, Seigneur de Thoury à caufe d'elle. Elle étoit fille aînée de *Charles*, Seigneur de Gié, & de *Jeanne de Saint-Severin*, fa feconde femme ;
2. RENÉ, qui fuit ;
3. GABRIELLE, Religieufe, & enfuite Abbeffe de Notre-Dame d'Angers en 1514;
4. JEANNE, qui tefta le 24 Janvier 1550, & fit fes héritiers *Charles* & *Antoine de Beauvau*, fes beaux-frères. Elle avoit époufé, 1º le 15 Février 1514, *François de Beauvau*, Seigneur de la Beffière, près Mayenne, mort au voyage de Pavie, en 1524, fils de *René*, & d'*Antoinette de Montfaucon*; & 2º le 13 Février 1529, *Charles de Gaillon*, Chevalier, Baron du Puifet. Il ne paroît pas qu'elle ait eu des enfans de fes deux maris;
5. MARGUERITE, mariée, le 28 Décembre 1517, avec *René Taveau*, Baron de Mortemer, Seigneur de Lufflac & du Bouchet, en Brenne. Elle étoit veuve, & avoit la Gardenoble de fes enfans les 10 Février 1530, 31 Janvier 1532, 4 Juillet 1536, & 17 Juillet 1542;
6. MARIE, qui fit profeffion en l'Abbaye de Bellomer en 1525, & qu'on croit avoir été Abbeffe de la Virginité du Mans ;
7. MADELEINE, mariée, par contrat du mois de Juillet 1517, à *Charles du Bec*, Seigneur de Bouris & de Vardès, Chevalier de l'Ordre du Roi, Vice-Amiral de France, fils aîné de *Jean*, & de *Marguerite de Roncherolles*, Dame du Marais-Vardier;
8. ANNE, Religieufe à l'Abbaye de la Trinité de Poitiers;

9. Et FRANÇOISE, Religieufe non profeffe au Couvent de la Madeleine d'Orléans.

XV. RENÉ DE BEAUVILLIERS, Chevalier, Comte de Saint-Aignan, Baron de la Ferté-Hubert, &c., Gentilhomme Ordinaire de la Chambre du Roi & de Monfeigneur le Dauphin, Abbé des Abbayes de Celles, en Berry, en 1531, & de Saint-Satur, fous Sancerre, en 1535, Prevôt de Vierzon en 1537, & Doyen de Saint-Aignan, garda fes bénéfices jufqu'après la mort de fon frère, par laquelle, étant devenu héritier de fa Maifon, il prit le titre *de Comte de Saint-Aignan*. Il fe trouve pourvu, le 2 Mai 1540, d'une Charge de Pannetier du Roi, qu'il garda jufqu'en 1545. Il eft employé dans les Etats de la Maifon du Roi en 1547, en qualité de Gentilhomme ordinaire de fa Chambre, & mourut après une longue maladie & incommodité à une jambe, en fon Château de Chemeré, à trois lieues de Saint-Aignan, le 8 Août 1557, & fut porté à Saint-Aignan, & mis dans la fépulture de fes ancêtres. Il avoit époufé, par contrat du 12 Mars 1540, *Anne de Clermont*, Dame d'Honneur de la Reine en 1548. Elle affifta à la Cérémonie de fon Couronnement, & à fon entrée à Paris en 1549. Elle étoit fille d'*Antoine*, Vicomte *de Clermont* & de Tallard, en Dauphiné, & d'*Anne de Poitiers*. Il en eut :

CLAUDE, qui fuit.

On lui donne auffi une fille naturelle :

JEANNE DE BEAUVILLIERS, mariée à *Pierre de Vaux*, Seigneur de la Chevrolière, qui eut par fon contrat de mariage la Mairie de Crouy, que CLAUDE DE BEAUVILLIERS, Comte de Saint-Aignan, racheta en 1574.

XVI. CLAUDE DE BEAUVILLIERS, IIº du nom, troifième Comte de Saint-Aignan, Seigneur & Baron de la Ferté-Hubert, &c., Chevalier de l'Ordre du Roi, Gentilhomme Ordinaire de fa Chambre, Confeiller & Chambellan Ordinaire du Duc d'Alençon, Lieutenant & commandant fa Compagnie de 90 hommes d'armes, Chef & Surintendant de fes Confeils, Gouverneur & Lieutenant-Général pour le Roi des Provinces de Berry, d'Anjou & de la Ville de Bourges, Confeiller du Confeil d'Etat & Privé, né le 18 Octobre 1542, eut de grands différends avec fa mère, qui furent portés au Parlement en 1564. Il fe trouva à la malheureufe entreprife d'Anvers, où il fut tué en 1583. Il avoit époufé, par contrat du

18 Février 1559, *Marie Babou*, morte en 1582, fille de *Jean*, Seigneur de *la Bourdai-fière*, Gouverneur du Duc d'Alençon, frère du Roi, Grand-Maître de l'Artillerie de France, & de *Françoise Robertet*, dont il eut :

1. HERCULE, Comte de Saint-Aignan, né au Château de la Bourdaifière, le 3 Mai 1563, tenu fur les Fonts par le Duc d'Alençon, fait Gentilhomme de la Maifon de ce Prince en 1575, Chambellan Ordinaire en 1576, & d'Affaires en la place de fon père en 1578, fut bleffé à l'entreprife d'Anvers, où fon père fut tué, & mourut le 23 Février 1583;

2. LÉONOR, Comte de Saint-Aignan, Baron de la Ferté-Hubert, &c., né le 1er Janvier 1565, fut fait, à 13 ans, Chambellan Ordinaire du Duc d'Alençon en 1578. Il rendit hommage pour lui, fes frères & fœurs, pour le lieu du petit Panel, le 23 Décembre 1583, voyagea en Italie l'année fuivante, d'où il ne revint qu'en 1586, fit hommage du Comté de Saint-Aignan en 1588, & en remit en 1589 la Ville & le Château au Roi, pour empêcher que les Ligueurs ne s'en empa-raffent. Il y fut tué au mois de Mars 1589, par un accident du feu qui prit à des poudres;

3. HONORAT, qui fuit;

4. ANNE, née le 4 Octobre 1564, morte en 1636. Elle avoit époufé 1º *Claude du Châtelet*, Gentilhomme ordinaire de la Chambre du Roi, tué au fiège de Dieppe en 1589; & 2º *Pierre Forget*, Seigneur de Frêne, mort en 1610, & enterré dans l'Eglife de Montmartre, près Paris, où fe voit fon épitaphe, ainfi que celle de fa femme;

5. FRANÇOISE, née le 30 Janvier 1572, morte au Château de Saint-Aignan le 2 Septembre 1580;

6. CLAUDE, née le 4 Avril 1573, reçue Religieufe à Montmartre par *Catherine de Clermont*, fa grand-tante, qui en étoit Abbeffe le 1er Février 1587. Elle fut depuis Abbeffe du Pont-aux-Dames, près Meaux;

7. MARIE, née le 26 Avril 1574, qui fut d'abord Religieufe à Beaumont-les-Tours, nommée coadjutrice d'*Anne Babou*, fa tante maternelle, qui en étoit Abbeffe, puis nommée Abbeffe de Montmartre par le Roi HENRI IV; morte dans fon Monaftère le 21 Avril 1656, ayant gouverné cette Abbaye 59 ans;

8. JEANNE, dont il eft parlé dans un acte du 13 Janvier 1589;

9. Et FRANÇOISE, née le 7 Juin 1580, Abbeffe d'Avenay en 1620.

XVII. HONORAT DE BEAUVILLIERS, Chevalier, Comte de Saint-Aignan, Baron de la Ferté-Hubert, &c., Gentilhomme ordinaire de la Chambre du Roi, Meftre-de-Camp-Général de la Cavalerie-Légère de France, Capitaine de 50 hommes d'armes des Ordonnances du Roi, Confeiller en fes Confeils d'Etat & Privé, Lieutenant-Général au Gouvernement des Pays & Duché de Berry, né à la Ferté-Hubert, le 26 Mai 1579, fut pourvu le 30 Décembre 1599, fur la démiffion de fon beau-père, de la charge de Meftre-de-Camp de la Cavalerie-Légère, & d'une Compagnie de 40 Maîtres, pour y être incorporés. Il commanda en 1615 la Cavalerie de l'Armée qui conduifit de Bordeaux à Bayonne la Reine d'Efpagne, & qui ramena de Bayonne à Bordeaux la Reine, nouvelle époufe du Roi LOUIS XIII, fut créé Lieutenant-Général au Gouvernement du Pays & Duché de Berry en 1617, & mourut au mois de Février 1622. Il avoit époufé, le 4 Mai 1604, *Jacqueline de la Grange*. Elle fut du voyage de Bayonne, affifta à la Cérémonie du mariage du Roi LOUIS XIII en 1615, & mourut, le 8 Juin 1632 à Saint-Aignan. Elle étoit fille de *François*, Seigneur de Montigny, de Sery, &c., Chevalier des Ordres du Roi, Meftre-de-Camp de la Cavalerie-Légère de France, Gouverneur de Paris, & Maréchal de France, & de *Gabrielle de Crévant*. De ce mariage vinrent :

1. PIERRE, né à Paris le 31 Décembre 1607, mort jeune;

2. FRANÇOIS, qui fuit;

3. MARIE, qui vivoit encore le 17 Août 1630;

4. ANNE-MARIE, Dame d'Atours de la Reine MARIE-THÉRÈSE d'Autriche, & morte le 12 Novembre 1688, âgée de 78 ans. Elle avoit époufé, par contrat du 29 Novembre 1629, *Hippolyte de Bethune*, dit *le Comte de Bethune*, Marquis de Chabris;

5. CATHERINE-HENRIETTE, née en Mars 1615, qui fut Coadjutrice de fa tante, Abbeffe de Montmartre, & mourut avant elle;

6. & 7. LOUISE-CLAIRE & FRANÇOISE, mortes jeunes;

8. ANNE-BERTHE, qui vivoit encore en 1632;

9. GABRIELLE, morte jeune;

Et deux ou trois enfans morts jeunes, & dont on ignore les noms.

XVIII. FRANÇOIS DE BEAUVILLIERS, feptième Comte & premier Duc de Saint-Aignan, Pair de France, Baron de la Ferté-Hubert, de Chemery, Seigneur de Luffay, en Beauce, Vicomte de Valogne, &c., Capitaine des Gardes de GASTON, Duc d'Orléans, premier Gentilhomme de la Chambre du Roi, Chevalier de fes Ordres, Confeiller en fes Confeils, Lieutenant-Général de fes Armées, Gouverneur & Lieutenant-Général de la Province de Touraine, des Ville & Citadelle du Hâvre de Grace & dépendances, l'un des 40 de l'Académie-Françoife, de celle de Padoue, & Protecteur de l'Académie Royale d'Arles, né en 1610, fervit en 1634 & 1635, en qualité de Capitaine d'une Compagnie de Chevaux-Légers dans l'Armée commandée par le Cardinal de la Valette, en Allemagne; fe trouva aux combats de Steimbrug & de Vaudrevanges; fe fignala à la retraite de Mayenne, où il foutint par fa valeur & fa prudence, avec 400 chevaux, les efforts de plus de 4000 chevaux ennemis, étant refté feul de tous les Commandans, à la tête de fon Efcadron; en 1636, au fiège de Dôle, en Franche-Comté, où il fut bleffé à la cuiffe, & à la reprife de Corbie, en Picardie, à celui de Landrecies, & d'autres Places en Flandres. Il mourut à Paris, le 16 Juin 1687, avec autant de réputation pour fon amour des Belles-Lettres, que pour fa valeur. Voyez fon éloge dans Moréri, édition de 1759. Il avoit époufé, 1º par contrat du 1er Janvier 1633, *Antoinette Servien*, morte à Paris le 19 Janvier 1679, fille de *Nicolas*, Seigneur de Montigny, Confeiller du Roi en fes Confeils d'Etat & privé, & de *Marie Groulart*; & 2º par contrat du 7 Juin 1680, *Françoife Geré-de-Rancé*, dite *Mademoifelle de Lucé*, morte le 3 Avril 1728, dans fa 86e année, fille de *Jacques*, & de *Claude de Nevers*.

Du premier mariage vinrent:

1. FRANÇOIS, Comte de Sery, né à Paris le 4 Octobre 1637, qui fut fait Meftre-de-Camp d'un Régiment d'Infanterie, le 18 Mai 1650, Capitaine d'une Compagnie de Chevaux-Légers de 90 Maîtres, le 31 Mai 1650; pourvu, fur la démiffion de fon père, de la Charge de premier Gentilhomme de la Chambre du Roi, le 21 Février 1657. Il fervit au fiège de Montmedy la même année, fît la campagne de 1663, comme Volontaire dans l'Armée de l'Empereur; paffa en Hongrie contre les Turcs en 1664, eut un cheval tué fous lui au combat de Quermen, & reçut un coup de flèche au bras à celui de Saint-Gothard. Il fut fait Colonel du Régiment d'Auvergne, Infanterie, après la mort du Marquis de Mouchy, le 26 Septembre 1665, & mourut à Paris le 1er Octobre 1666;

2. PIERRE, dit *le Chevalier de Saint-Aignan*, né le 14 Août 1641, Abbé Commendataire de l'Abbaye de Ferrières en 1659, fortit de France au fujet d'une querelle entre les Seigneurs de *la Frète*, fes coufins germains, & le Prince de Chalais, dans laquelle il s'étoit engagé. Il fît le voyage de Hongrie, contre les Turcs, & fut tué le 25 Juillet 1664, au combat de Saint-Gothard, au paffage de la rivière de Raab, après avoir donné des preuves de fa valeur, & s'être enveloppé dans fon drapeau, pour le défendre jufqu'à la mort;

3. & 4. N... & N..., morts jeunes;

5. PAUL, qui fuit;

6. ANNE, née à Paris en 1634, Religieufe Profeffe de Cîteaux, enfuite Abbeffe de Beauvoir, du même Ordre, Diocèfe de Bourges, le 27 Août 1653, & nommée à l'Abbaye de Notre-Dame de Romorantin, Diocèfe d'Orléans, le 2 Juin 1662, eft morte en 1668;

7. GABRIELLE, née à Paris en 1635, morte jeune;

8. ELISABETH, née en 1636, nommée, en 1653, Coadjutrice de l'Abbaye de la Joie, près Nemours, puis Abbeffe de Notre-Dame de Romorantin, le 14 Mai 1668, après la mort d'ANNE, fa fœur aînée. Elle mourut en 1704;

9. GABRIELLE, née le 1er Février 1643, Abbeffe de Beauvoir, fur la démiffion de fa fœur aînée, le 30 Octobre 1664. Elle fe démit volontairement, en 1676, & mourut le 24 Mai 1694;

10. ANNE-CATHERINE, nommée Abbeffe de Nidoifeau, Ordre de Saint-Auguftin, Diocèfe d'Angers, au mois d'Avril 1684, morte en 1700;

11. ANNE, née en 1652, Coadjutrice de l'Abbaye de la Joie en 1669, puis Abbeffe, fur la démiffion de fa fœur, s'eft retirée d'abord aux Bernardines d'Argenteuil, & enfuite aux Bénédictines de Notre-Dame-des-Prés, à Paris, où elle eft morte le 15 Février 1734;

12. Et MARIE-ANTOINETTE, morte à Paris le 13 Octobre 1729 âgée de 76 ans. Elle avoit époufé, par contrat du 10 Janvier 1678, *Louis Sanguin*, Marquis de Livry, premier Maître-d'Hôtel du Roi, mort le 6 Novembre 1723.

Les enfans du fecond lit font:

13. FRANÇOIS-HONORAT-ANTOINE DE BEAUVILLIERS, né à Paris, le 6 Octobre 1682, Abbé de Saint-Germer de Fleix, Ordre de Saint-Auguftin, Diocèfe de Beauvais, en 1701, Evêque & Comte de Beauvais, le 1er Avril 1713, prêta ferment & prit féance au

Parlement en qualité de Pair de France, le 22 Février 1714, fut député de la Province de Reims à l'Assemblée Générale du Clergé, tenue à Paris en 1715, & fit ses fonctions de Pair au sacre du Roi Louis XV, le 25 Octobre 1722. Il se démit de son Evêché, & l'Abbaye de Saint-Victor de Marseille lui fut donnée le 18 Février 1728. Il mourut le 19 Août 1751, dans l'Abbaye de Prémontré, où il s'étoit retiré depuis plusieurs années;

14. PAUL - HIPPOLYTE, Duc de Saint-Aignan, Pair de France, rapporté après son frère aîné;

15. Et MARIE-FRANÇOISE, née à Paris, le 6 Avril 1681, morte le 18 Novembre 1748. Elle avoit épousé, 1º le 10 Janvier 1703, *Jean-François de Marillac*, dit le *Marquis de Marillac*, Colonel du Régiment de Languedoc, Brigadier des Armées du Roi, & Gouverneur de Béthune, tué à la bataille d'Hochstett, le 13 Août 1704; & 2º le 12 Mai 1710, *Louis-François*, dit le *Marquis de l'Aubespine*.

XIX. PAUL DE BEAUVILLIERS, Duc de Saint-Aignan, sous le nom de *Beauvilliers*, Pair de France, Grand d'Espagne de la première classe, Comte de Montrésor, Chaumont, &c., né en 1648, d'abord destiné à l'Etat Ecclésiastique, fut pourvu de l'Abbaye de Saint-Pierre de Châlons. Il s'en démit après la mort de FRANÇOIS, Comte de Sery, son frère aîné, & prit alors le titre de *Comte de Saint-Aignan*. Sur la démission de son père, il fut pourvu de la charge de premier Gentilhomme de la Chambre du Roi, le 10 Décembre 1666. Il alla en 1671, à Londres en qualité d'Envoyé Extraordinaire du Roi, pour complimenter de sa part, le Roi d'Angleterre, sur la mort de la Duchesse d'Orléans. Son père se démit en sa faveur, en 1679, de son Duché Pairie, & il prit le titre de *Duc de Beauvilliers*, pour laisser à son père celui de *Duc de Saint-Aignan*. Le Roi le nomma chef de son Conseil des Finances, en 1685; le pourvut, après la mort de son père, du Gouvernement du Havre-de-Grâce, & de celui de Loches & de Beaulieu, en 1687, & en même tems de la charge de Grand Arpenteur de France. Il accompagna, en 1688, M. le Dauphin dans sa première campagne, fut reçu, le 31 Décembre de la même année, Chevalier des Ordres. Le Roi le nomma Gouverneur de la personne du Duc de Bourgogne, premier Gentilhomme de sa Chambre, & Grand-Maître de sa

Garde-Robe, le 6 Août 1689, & Ministre d'Etat au mois de Juillet 1691. Il accompagna au mois de Décembre 1700, le Roi d'Espagne & les Princes ses frères, jusque sur les frontières d'Espagne. Le 2 Décembre 1706, il se démit de son Duché-Pairie en faveur de PAUL-HIPPOLYTE, son frère, & mourut en sa maison de Vaucresson, près Versailles, après une longue maladie, le 31 Août 1714. Il avoit épousé, le 21 Janvier 1671, *Henriette-Louise Colbert*, nommée Dame du Palais de la Reine, MARIE-THÉRÈSE D'AUTRICHE, le 16 Avril 1680, & morte le 19 Septembre 1733, âgée de 76 ans & 9 mois. Son corps fut porté à Montargis au Couvent des Religieuses Bénédictines, où elle est enterrée auprès de son mari; elle a fait sa légataire universel *Charles-Auguste*, Duc de *Rochechouart*, premier Gentilhomme de la Chambre du Roi, fils de sa fille, la Duchesse de *Mortemart*. Elle étoit fille de *Jean-Baptiste*, Marquis de Seignelay, & de *Marie Charron de Menars*. De ce mariage vinrent:

1. LOUIS DE BEAUVILLIERS, né à Versailles, le 10 Février 1690, mort le 2 Décembre 1705; de la petite vérole;

2. N..., né au mois d'Avril 1691, destiné à l'Ordre de Malte;

3. PAUL-JEAN-BAPTISTE, Comte de Sery, né le 10 Août 1692, mort le 5 Novembre 1705;

4. JEAN-BAPTISTE-JOSEPH, Marquis de BEAUVILLIERS, né le 9 Août 1693, mort en 1694;

5. MARIE-FRANÇOISE, née en 1672, morte en Octobre 1674;

6. MARIE-ANTOINETTE, née le 29 Janvier 1679, Religieuse aux Bénédictines de Montargis, au mois d'Octobre 1696, & Prieure perpétuelle de ce Monastère;

7. MARIE-GENEVIÈVE, née le 6 Mars 1680, dite *Mademoiselle de Sery*, puis Religieuse aux Bénédictines de Montargis, sous le nom de *Sœur Marie-Anne de Jésus*;

8. MARIE-LOUISE, née le 9 Août 1681, dite *Mademoiselle de Montigny*, puis Religieuse avec ses sœurs, sous le nom de *Sainte-Scholastique*, morte; le P. Anselme dit le 9 Avril 1710, & Moréri, le 9 Avril 1717;

9. MARIE-THÉRÈSE, née le 22 Octobre 1683, dite *Mademoiselle de la Ferté*, Religieuse avec ses sœurs, sous le nom de *Sainte-Gertrude*, puis Prieure perpétuelle des Bénédictines de Champ-Benoît, transférées à Provins;

10. MARIE-HENRIETTE, née le 14 Avril 1685, morte à Paris, le 4 Septembre 1718. Elle avoit épousé, par dispense, le 19 Décembre

1703, *Louis de Rochechouart*, Duc de Mortemart, fon coufin germain ;

11. Marie-Paule, dite *Mademoifelle de Bufançois*, née le 9 Avril 1686, Religieufe avec fes fœurs, fous le nom de *Madame de l'Enfant Jéfus;*

12. Marie, dite *Mademoifelle de Montréfor*, née le 19 Septembre 1687, Religieufe avec fes fœurs, fous le nom de *Madame de Séraphin*, morte ;

13. Et Marie - Françoise, dite *Mademoifelle d'Argy*, née le 24 Septembre 1688, Religieufe avec fes fœurs, fous le nom de *Sainte-Cécile*, morte en Janvier 1716.

XIX. Paul- Hippolyte, Duc de Saint-Aignan, en Berry, né à Paris, le 25 Novembre 1684, Pair de France, Comte de Montréfor, en Touraine, Baron de la Ferté-Hubert, dite à préfent de *Saint-Aignan*, en Blaifois, de la Salle-lès-Clery & de Chemery, dans l'Orléanois, Chevalier des Ordres du Roi, Gouverneur & Lieutenant-Général du Havre-de-Grâce & Pays en dépendans, de Loches, en Touraine, Grand Bailli de Caux, l'un des quarante de l'Académie-Françoife, & Honoraire de celle des Infcriptions & Belles-Lettres, en 1732, & de l'Académie des *Infecondi*, à Rome, le 10 Août 1738, fut d'abord deftiné pour être Chevalier de l'Ordre de Saint-Jean-de Jérufalem, dans lequel il fut admis de minorité, en 1686. Il étoit à Malte fur le point de faire fes vœux, lorfque le Duc de Beauvilliers, fon frère, qui venoit de perdre fes deux fils, le rappela à Paris. Il lui acheta un Régiment de Cavalerie, dont il fut fait Meftre-de-Camp par Commiffion du 15 Novembre 1706, & lui fit donation de fon Duché-Pairie, le 2 Décembre de la même année. Il prit alors le titre de *Duc de Saint-Aignan*, refta prifonnier au combat d'Oudenarde, le 11 Juillet 1708, & fût bleffé à la bataille de Malplaquet, le 11 Septembre 1709. Il fut fait premier Gentilhomme de la Chambre du Duc de Berry, au mois de Mars 1711. Le Roi le nomma, au mois de Novembre 1714, pour aller complimenter la nouvelle Reine d'Efpagne, à fon paffage en France; & il fut déclaré, au mois de Mai 1715, Ambaffadeur en Efpagne. En cette qualité, il tint fur les fonts de baptême l'Infant *Don Philippe*, le 25 Août 1716, & fut nommé au mois de Juillet 1718, Plénipotentiaire pour les négociations, au fujet de la tranquillité de l'Europe. Comme fa perfonne devint fufpecte aux Miniftres d'Efpa-

gne, il eut ordre de fortir de Madrid; & de retour à Paris, le 6 Janvier 1719, il fut déclaré Confeiller au Confeil de Régence, & au mois d'Octobre 1730, à l'Ambaffade de Rome, où il arriva le 13 Mars 1732, & mourut le 22 Janvier 1776. Il avoit époufé, 1° le 22 Janvier 1707, *Marie-Geneviève de Montlezun*, Dame de Paumeufe, &c., morte à Rome le 15 Octobre 1734 & inhumée dans l'Eglife de Saint-Louis des François. Elle étoit fille & unique héritière de *Jean-Baptifte-François de Montlezun*, Marquis de Befmaux, Meftre-de-Camp de Cavalerie, premier Cornette des Chevaux-Légers de la Garde du Roi, mort le 10 Octobre 1696, & de *Marguerite - Geneviève Colbert de Villacerf*, morte le 28 Décembre 1696, & petite-fille & feule héritière de *François de Montlezun*, Seigneur de Befmaux, Maréchal des Camps & Armées du Roi, Gouverneur du Château de la Baftille à Paris, & du Fort de Notre-Dame de la Garde à Marfeille, mort le 17 Décembre 1697, âgé de 86 ans ; & 2° par contrat du 9 Novembre 1757, *Françoife - Hélène - Etiennette Turgot*, née le 20 Septembre 1729, fille de *Michel-Etienne*, Marquis de Saufmont, Confeiller d'Etat, Prevôt des Marchands de Paris, & de *Madeleine-Françoife Martineau*, & fœur de *Michel - Jacques*, Préfident du Parlement de Paris. Les enfans qui vinrent du premier lit font :

1. Paul - François de Beauvilliers, Comte de Saint-Aignan, né le 16 Août 1710. Le Duc de Beauvilliers, fon oncle, lui fit donation de 160000 livres, dues par fes père & mère, & fubftitua cette fomme à fes enfans mâles, à leur défaut, à fes frères, puis aux filles, & enfuite à la Ducheffe de Mortemart, & à fes defcendans, par acte du 15 Mars 1711. Il accompagna fon père dans fon Ambaffade à Rome, & fit la campagne de 1733, dans laquelle le Milanois entier fut conquis par les armes de France & de Sardaigne. Il fervit en qualité de volontaire, & fut fait Meftre-de-Camp d'un Régiment de Cavalerie de fon nom, ci-devant Cayeux, le 20 Février 1734. Sur la démiffion du *Duc de Saint - Aignan*, fon père, il prit le titre de *Duc de Beauvilliers*. Il mourut fans enfans, le 7 Janvier 1742. Il avoit époufé, le 30 Décembre 1738, *Marie-Sufanne - Françoife de Creil*, née le 28 Août 1716, Dame d'Honneur de Madame, première bru du Duc de Saint-Aignan, & titrée *Ducheffe-Douairière de Beauvilliers*,

fille unique de *Jean-François*, Intendant de la Généralité de Metz ;

2. Paul-Louis, qui fuit ;

3. Paul-Hippolyte, né le 26 Décembre 1712, appelé *Marquis de Saint-Aignan*, Chef d'Efcadre, le 1ᵉʳ Octobre 1764 ;

4. Paul-Louis-Victor, Abbé, Comte de Lagny, en Brie, Diocèfe de Paris, né le 24 Octobre 1714 ;

5. Paul-François-Honorat, Chevalier de Malte, né le 7 Janvier 1724, appelé *Comte de Saint-Aignan*, Brigadier de Cavalerie en 1762, & Meftre-de-Camp d'un Régiment de Cavalerie de fon nom, le 17 Décembre 1757 jufqu'en 1762, que ce Régiment fut incorporé dans le Commiffaire-Général ;

6. & 7. Marie-Geneviève, née le 27 Janvier 1709, & Marie-Paule-Françoise, née le 5 Juillet 1720, Religieufes à Montargis ;

8. Marie-Anne-Paule-Antoinette, dite *Mademoifelle de Chemery*, née le 26 Juillet 1721, morte le 21 Janvier 1743, au Château de Saint-Aignan, fans laiffer d'enfans. Elle avoit époufé, le 28 Août 1736, *Louis-Armand de Seglières-de-Soyecourt*, né le 29 Janvier 1722, fils de *Joachim-Adolphe*, Marquis de Soyecourt, Brigadier des Armées du Roi, & Chevalier de Saint-Louis, & de *Pauline-Corifante de Pas-de-Feuquières ;*

9. Et Marie-Paule-Thérèse, née le 10 Décembre 1729, appelée *Mademoifelle de Montréfor*, morte le 10 Novembre 1758. Elle avoit époufé, le 22 Août 1753, *Jean-François-Charles de Molette*, Comte de Morangiès, Colonel du Régiment de Languedoc, Infanterie.

XX. Paul-Louis de Beauvilliers, né à Verfailles le 8 Novembre 1711, titré *Duc de Beauvilliers*, après la mort de fon frère aîné, a été tué à la bataille de Rosbach, le 9 Novembre 1757, étant Colonel d'un Régiment de Cavalerie. Il avoit époufé, 1° le 8 Avril 1745, *Augufte-Léonore-Olympe-Nicole de Bullion*, troifième fille d'*Anne-Jacques*, Marquis de Fervaques, Lieutenant-Général des Armées du Roi, & Commandeur de fes Ordres, mort le 23 Avril 1745, & de *Marie-Madeleine-Hortenfe Gigaut-de-Belfonds ;* & 2° le 22 Novembre 1753, *Charlotte-Sufanne des Nos*, auffi titrée *Duchesse-Douairière de Beauvilliers*, une des Dames nommée pour accompagner Madame, fille de *Jean-Baptifte des Nos*, Comte de la Feuillée, & de *Marie-Marguerite de Cardouan*. Les enfans du premier lit font :

1. Paul-Etienne-Auguste, qui fuit ;

2. Charles-Paul-François, auffi rapporté après fon aîné ;

3. Anne-Paul-François, Comte de Montréfor, né le 29 Décembre 1747, mort au mois de Mai 1752 ;

4. Et Colette-Marie-Paule-Hortense-Bernardine, fille unique, née le 20 Août 1749, mariée, le 3 Janvier 1771, à *Antoine-Charles-Guillaume*, Marquis de *la Roche-Aymon*.

XXI. Paul-Etienne-Auguste, titré *Duc de Beauvilliers*, né le 26 Décembre 1745, nommé, en 1765, Capitaine-Commandant de la Lieutenance-Colonelle de la Meftre-de-Camp-Général de Cavalerie, a époufé, par contrat du 17 Avril 1763, & célébré le 16 Novembre 1763, *Marie-Madeleine de Roffet*, fille d'*André-Hercule*, Duc de *Fleury*, née le 27 Janvier 1744, dont une fille, née fur la fin de 1764.

XXI. Charles-Paul-François de Beauvilliers, né le 17 Décembre 1746, Comte de Bufançois. Sa Majefté Catholique lui a confervé le titre de Grand d'Efpagne, de la première claffe, dont étoit revêtu le Duc de Beauvilliers, Gouverneur de Philippe V ; & le 28 Juin 1765, S. M. T. C. l'a mis en poffeffion des honneurs. Il a époufé, par contrat figné du 21 du même mois, *Marie-Louife de Mailly*, feule fille d'*Alexandre-Louis*, Comte de *Mailly*, & d'*Anne-Louife de Saint-Chamans*.

Les armes : *fafcé d'argent & de finople, les fafces d'argent chargées de 6 merlettes de gueules, 3, 2 & 1.*

Il y a plufieurs autres branches de la Maifon de Beauvilliers, qui font éteintes, mais dont la jonction n'eft pas affez prouvée, & fur lefquelles on peut confulter le tom. IV, pag. 724 & fuiv. des *Grands Officiers de la Couronne.*

BEAUVIS : *d'or, au chevron de fable, accompagné de trois chouettes de même, becquées & membrées de gueules, 2 en chef & 1 en pointe.*

BEAUVOIR, en Bourgogne, ancienne Maifon qui a donné un Maréchal de France. Jean, Seigneur de Bordeaux & d'Auxerre, Chevalier, vivoit en 1340, & étoit mort en 1350. *Jacquette*, fon époufe, fille de *Guy d'Oftun*, Chevalier, Seigneur d'Aarcoucay, de Villiers-Lienas & de Beauvoir, lui apporta en dot la

Terre de Beauvoir, en Bourgogne, dont ſes deſcendans ont pris le nom.

CLAUDE DE BEAUVOIR, ſon petit-fils, Seigneur de Chaſtellux, de Bordeaux, & Vicomte d'Avalon, ſuivit toute ſa vie le parti des Ducs de Bourgogne, dont il étoit né ſujet, & deſquels il reçut beaucoup de faveurs. Le Duc JEAN le reçut Conſeiller & Chambellan, par Lettres du 15 Juin 1409. Il fut envoyé, en 1414, pour faire lever le ſiège de la Motte, de Bar-ſur-Aube, aſſiégée par le Bailli de Chaumont. Il eſt mort en Mars 1453. Sa branche a fourni VIII degrés, & a fini à *Léon de Chaſtellux*, Seigneur de Baſerne, qui vivoit en 1610. Il eut d'*Anne de Moroge* un fils, mort à 17 ou 18 ans, & trois filles mariées. De cette branche ſont ſorties celle des Seigneurs de *Chaſtellux*, & celle des Seigneurs de *Coulanges*.

La branche des Seigneurs de Chaſtellux a commencé à *Louis de Chaſtellux*, troiſième fils de *Philippe*, Seigneur de Chaſtellux, & de *Barbe de Hochberg*. Cette branche ſubſiſte. Voyez CHASTELLUX.

La branche des Seigneurs de Coulanges, qui a commencé à *Olivier de Chaſtellux*, vivant en 1588, quatrième fils de *Philippe*, Seigneur de Chaſtellux, & de *Barbe de Hochberg*, ſa ſeconde femme, n'a formé que trois degrés, & a fini à *Alexandre de Chaſtellux*, qui, d'*Anne de Gauville*, eut trois fils, morts ſans poſtérité, & une fille mariée.

BEAUVOIR, en Franche-Comté : *d'aʒur, à trois loſanges d'argent, poſées 2 & 1, ſurmontées en chef d'un lambel d'or à trois pointes.*

BEAUVOIR : *d'or, à deux bandes de gueules.*

BEAUVOIR : *d'aʒur, à deux loups paſſans d'or, l'un ſur l'autre.*

BEAUVOIR DU ROURE-GRIMOARD.

GUILLAUME DE BEAUVOIR, Ier du nom, qui teſta le 11 des Calendes de Juillet 1297, eſt le premier de cette famille qu'on a fait connoître, lors de la maintenue de ſa nobleſſe, qui eſt du 8 Juillet 1669. Il fut père de :

GUY, Ier du nom, lequel fut père de :

GUILLAUME, IIe du nom, celui-ci fut père de :

GUY, IIe du nom, dont le fils :

MAURICE, fut père de :

ARMAND, qui eut :

GUILLAUME DE BEAUVOIR, IIIe du nom, Chevalier, Baron du Roure, qui épouſa, en 1392, *Smaragde de Beaumont*, de laquelle deſcendent les Barons de Beaumont, Seigneurs de Briſon. Il eut :

1. GUY, qui ſuit ;
2. Et FOULQUES, auteur de la branche de *Beaumont-Briſon*.

GUY DE BEAUVOIR, IIIe du nom, Seigneur du Roure, inſtitué héritier des biens de ſon père par teſtament de 1415, eut :

GUILLAUME DE BEAUVOIR, Seigneur du Roure, de Saint-Florent & de Caſtillon, qui teſta le 19 Septembre 1499. Il avoit épouſé *Urbaine de Grimoard*, Dame de Griſac, de Bellegarde & de Verfeuille, qui teſta le 4 Octobre 1530, ordonnant que ſes enfans porteroient le nom & les armes de la Maiſon de *Griſac*, dont elle étoit iſſue. De ce mariage vint :

CLAUDE DE GRIMOARD-DE-BEAUVOIR, Baron du Roure, de Griſac, de Verfeuille, Capitaine de 100 hommes d'armes, marié, en 1520, à *Fleurie des Porcellets*, fille de *Pierre*, Seigneur de Maillane, dont :

1. LOUIS, Baron de *Saint-Florens*, qui a formé la branche de ce nom ;
2. JACQUES, Seigneur d'*Elʒe*, auteur des Seigneurs de ce nom ;
3. Et ANTOINE, qui ſuit.

ANTOINE DE GRIMOARD-DE-BEAUVOIR, Comte du Roure, Marquis de Griſac, par Brevet de CHARLES IX, Capitaine de 100 hommes d'armes, épouſa, en 1556, *Claudine de la Fare-Montclar*, dont il eut :

1. JACQUES, qui ſuit ;
2. ANTOINE, Comte de Saint-Remere, qui n'eut qu'une courte poſtérité ;
3. CLAUDE, Seigneur de Combalet, marié à *Marie d'Albert de Luynes*, dont :
   ANTOINE, Seigneur de Combalet, marié à *Marie-Madeleine de Vignerot de Pontcourlay*, depuis Ducheſſe d'Aiguillon, morte le 1er Avril 1675 ;
4. Et ANNE DE BEAUVOIR, morte le 18 Février 1686. Elle avoit épouſé, au mois de mai 1620, *Charles*, Duc de *Créquy*.

JACQUES DE GRIMOARD-DE-BEAUVOIR, Maréchal-de-Camp, en faveur duquel Griſac fut érigé en Marquiſat, & la Baronie du Roure en Comté, par Lettres du mois de Janvier 1608, mourut en 1637. Il avoit épouſé, en 1599, *Jacqueline de Montlaur*, dont entr'autres enfans :

SCIPION DE GRIMOARD-DE-BEAUVOIR, Comte

du Roure, Lieutenant-Général des Armées du Roi en 1650 & de la Province de Languedoc, créé le 31 Décembre 1661, Chevalier du Saint-Esprit, qui mourut en 1669. Il avoit épousé, 1° en 1639, *Grefinde de Baudan*, fille unique de *Pierre*, Président en la Cour des Comptes de Montpellier ; & 2° en 1664, *Jacqueline de Borne-de-Laugère*, morte sans enfans, au mois de Janvier 1712, âgée de 86 ans. Elle avoit épousé, 1° par dispense du Pape, ALEXANDRE VII, *Charles-Auguste*, Marquis de *la Fare*, son oncle. Du premier lit vinrent entr'autres :

1. Louis, marquis de Grifac, mort en 1728 sans postérité. Il avoit épousé *Madeleine-Françoise d'Apchier*, morte le 3 Juin 1763, en sa 74° année ;
2. LOUIS-PIERRE-SCIPION, qui suit ;
3. Et JACQUELINE DE GRIMOARD-DE-BEAUVOIR, morte le 7 Novembre 1721. Elle avoit épousé *Louis-Armand*, Vicomte de *Polignac*.

LOUIS - PIERRE - SCIPION DE GRIMOARD - DE-BEAUVOIR, Comte du Roure, Gouverneur du Pont-Saint-Esprit, épousa, par contrat du 9 Janvier 1666, *Marie*, fille d'*Achille du Guast*, Seigneur d'Artigny, & de *Marie le Coutellier*, dont entr'autres enfans :

LOUIS-SCIPION DE GRIMOARD-DE-BEAUVOIR, Comte du Roure, Capitaine des Chevaux-Légers, Lieutenant-Général pour le Roi en sa Province du Languedoc, Gouverneur de la ville & citadelle du Pont-Saint-Esprit, tué à la bataille de Fleurus le 1er Juillet 1690. Il avoit épousé, le 8 Mars 1688, *Louise-Victoire de Caumont la Force*, fille de *Jacques-Nompar de Caumont*, Duc de la Force dont :

1. LOUIS-CLAUDE-SCIPION, qui suit ;
2. Et ADÉLAÏDE DE GRIMOARD-DE-BEAUVOIR, morte le 3 Janvier 1760. Elle avoit épousé, au mois d'Août 1714, *Gabriel de Montmorency*, Comte de Laval.

LOUIS - CLAUDE - SCIPION DE GRIMOARD-DE-BEAUVOIR DE MONTLAUR, Comte du Roure, né posthume en 1690, Lieutenant-Général le 1er Janvier 1748, & premier Sous-Lieutenant des Mousquetaires, mourut le 15 Juillet 1752. Il avoit épousé, le 16 juillet 1721, *Marie-Antoinette-Victoire de Gontaut*, morte le 26 mars 1770, fille de *Charles-Armand*, Maréchal-Duc de Biron, & de *Marie-Antoinette de Bautru*, dont entr'autres enfans :

1. DENIS-AUGUSTE, qui suit ;
2. N..... mariée, en 1741, à *Scipion-Louis-Jo-*

seph de la Garde, Marquis de Chambonas ;
3. N...mariée, au mois de Janvier 1750, à N.... *de la Rivoire*, Marquis de la Tourette ;
4. Et MARIE-MADELEINE, morte le 18 Avril 1748. Elle avoit épousé, le 26 Avril 1746, *Anne-Gabriel-Henri Bernard*, Président de Boulainvilliers.

DENIS-AUGUSTE DE GRIMOARD-DE-BEAUVOIR, Marquis du Roure, né le 25 Novembre 1735, Colonel des Grenadiers de France en 1753, de Saintonge en 1761, de Dauphin, & Brigadier le 25 Juillet 1762, a épousé, le 24 Janvier 1759, *Françoise-Sophie-Scholastique de Baglion*, fille de *Pierre-François-Marie de Baglion*, Comte de la Salle, & d'*Angélique-Louise-Sophie de Louville d'Allonville*,

C'est ce que nous savons sur l'état actuel de cette maison, faute de Mémoire.

Les armes sont de six pièces : *coupé parti de 2 ; au* 1 *du Roure, d'azur, au chêne d'or, les branches entrelacées ; au* 2 *de Montlaur, d'or, au lion vairé couronné ; au* 3 *de Grimoard, de gueules, au chef emmanché d'or de trois pièces ; au* 4, *qui est le premier de la pointe, de Maubec, d'or, à deux léopards, d'azur ; au* 5 *d'or, à la tour de gueules ; alias d'azur, à la tour d'argent ; au* 6 *de sable au lion d'argent, à la bordure engrêlée de même.*

BRANCHE
de BEAUMONT-BRISON.

FOULQUES DE BEAUVOIR-DU-ROURE (a), auteur de la Branche de *Beaumont de Brison*, fut nommé par *Pons de Beaumont*, son ayeul maternel, dans son testament du 4 Février 1435, héritier de toutes ses Terres & Seigneuries, à la charge de porter le nom & les armes de Beaumont ; ce qu'il exécuta, & ce qu'ont fait ses successeurs jusqu'à ce jour, en joignant les armes de Beaumont à celles du Roure. Sa mère *Smaragde* le nomma aussi son héritier dans son testament du 24 Décembre 1435, dans lequel elle se dit fille de noble & puissant Seigneur *Pons de Beaumont*, & veuve de noble & puissant Seigneur GUILLAUME DE BEAUVOIR-DU-ROURE. FOULQUES testa le 25 Avril 1481. Il avoit épousé, en 1442, *Ca-*

(a) Aucun des sept ayeux de FOULQUES ne s'est surnommé *Grimoard*, malgré ce qu'en disent les Continuateurs du *Dictionnaire* de Moréri, dans l'édition de 1725. Ce seroit faire tort aux Barons de Beaumont de Brison, d'appeler leur auteur FOULQUES DE GRIMOARD, comme le fait ce *Dictionnaire*, première colonne, p. 431.

therine de Montbrun, Dame de |Maurillac, qui tefta le 12 Avril 1490. Il eut:

1. ANTOINE, mort fans enfans;
2. JEAN, qui fuit;
3. JEANNE, mariée, par contrat du 15 Septembre 1472, avec *Louis de Beaune,* Vicomte dudit lieu;
4. Et BLANCHE, mariée, par aĉte du 12 Juin 1479, avec le Seigneur de *Jonchières.*

JEAN DE BEAUVOIR-DU-ROURE-DE-BEAUMONT, Ier du nom, Chevalier, &c., héritier des Terres de fes père & mère, Porte-Enfeigne en la Compagnie des 100 Gentilshommes de l'Hôtel du Roi, fous la charge & conduite du Duc de Longueville, par commiffion du 27 Juillet 1514, époufa, le 2 Juin 1510, *Hélène de Châteauneuf-de-Rochebonne,* de laquelle font fortis:

1. JEAN, qui fuit; •
2. Et LOUIS DE BEAUVOIR-DU-ROURE, Protonotaire du Saint-Siège Apoftolique.

JEAN DE BEAUVOIR-DU-ROURE-DE-BEAUMONT, IIe du nom, Chevalier, &c., Capitaine d'une Compagnie de 100 hommes d'armes, inftitué héritier de fon père, par teftament du 24 Mai 1520, fe maria 1° à *Anne Adhemar de Grignan,* dont il n'eut point d'enfans; & 2° le 9 Mars 1537, à *Anne de Comtes,* Dame de Sivagues, dont il a eu:

1. ROSTAING, qui fuit;
2. LOUIS DE BEAUMONT, Protonotaire du Saint-Siège Apoftolique;
3. ANTOINE DE BEAUMONT, marié, le 28 Avril 1585, à *Françoife d'Aujole;*
4. ROBERTE, mariée, en 1572, avec le Seigneur de *Sarjat;*
5. SUSANNE, mariée, le 6 Décembre 1579, au Seigneur d'*U\chi ès;*
6. Et LUCRÈCE, mariée, en 1588, avec *François de Chebeuil,* Seigneur dudit lieu.

ROSTAING DE BEAUVOIR-DU-ROURE, Ier du nom, Baron de Beaumont, Chevalier, &c., Capitaine d'une Compagnie de 100 hommes d'armes, inftitué héritier par le teftament de fon père du 4 Septembre 1570, obtint, par Lettres du 18 Août 1616, l'éreĉtion de fa Terre de Beaumont en Baronie. Il époufa, le 4 Mars 1576, *Jeanne de Caires de la Baftide-d'Antraygues,* à laquelle *Louife de Gavarel-de-Saint-Didier,* fa coufine, veuve de noble *Gabriel de Brifon,* fit, le 12 Décembre 1583, une donation entre vifs de tous fes biens, tant provenant de fon patrimoine, qu'à elle avenus de la légitime fucceffion de fes en-

fans, & du feu Seigneur de Brifon, fon mari, confiftant en Château, Rentes & Domaine de Brifon, & autres biens, Terres, &c., & dèslors ROSTAING DE BEAUMONT prit la qualité de Seigneur de *Brifon,* que fes fucceffeurs ont toujours depuis conférvée. Ses enfans furent:

1. JOACHIM DE BEAUMONT, Baron de Brifon, qui fuit;
2. ANNE, mariée, le 12 Février 1607, avec *Jacques de Montjou,* Seigneur de Chaffaignes;
3. Et LOUISE, mariée, le 10 Oĉtobre 1611, avec *Jean Dagrain,* Seigneur des Hubas.

JOACHIM DE BEAUVOIR-DU-ROURE-DE-BEAUMONT, Chevalier, Baron de Brifon, &c., inftitué héritier par teftament de fon père, le 30 Août 1622, Gentilhomme de la Chambre du Roi, Meftre-de-Camp d'un Régiment de pied François, Maréchal des Camps & Armées de Sa Majefté, par Brevet du 27 Août 1626, Gouverneur de la ville de Nîmes, connu dans l'Hiftoire fous le nom de *Brave Brifon,* eut le malheur de férvir à la tête du parti Proteftant contre l'Armée du Roi : il défendit, contre le Connétable de Lefdiguières, les villes de Privas & du Pontin, en Vivarais, dont la capitulation fut fignée à des conditions avantageufes, entre le Connétable & lui, le 27 Juillet 1626. Il reçut un mois après fon Brevet de Maréchal-de-Camp, & obtint le 10 Novembre 1626, des Lettres-Patentes portant abolition de tout crime de rébellion. Il fervit enfuite dans les Armées du Roi; & au mois de Janvier 1628, il fut affaffiné par un Proteftant, nommé *Trémolée,* dans la même ville de Privas, qu'il avoit fi vaillamment défendue. Il avoit époufé, le 30 Mars 1624, *Ifabeau de Fortia-d'Urban.* Il eut :

ROSTAING DE BEAUVOIR-DU-ROURE-DE-BEAUMONT, IIe du nom, Chevalier, Baron de Brifon, Capitaine par commiffion, en date du 14 Novembre 1647, d'une Compagnie de Chevaux-Légers dans le Régiment de Cavalerie du Comte d'Alais, Colonel-Général de la Cavalerie-Légère de France, qui fe maria, le 7 Novembre 1654, à *Françoife d'Urre-Dupuy-Saint-Martin,* dont il eut :

1. FRANÇOIS, qui fuit;
2. JOSEPH, Abbé de Saint-Félix;
3. ANTOINE, Capitaine dans un Régiment de Cavalerie;
4. N..., mariée avec *N... le Julien,* Seigneur de Vinezac;
5. Et N...., mariée avec *N.... Dagrain-des-Hubas.*

FRANÇOIS DE BEAUVOIR-DU-ROURE-DE-BEAU-MONT, Chevalier, Marquis de Brifon, Baron de tous les Etats de Languedoc, Baron de la ville de Largentière, de Beaumont, Brifon, Saint-Melani, Donnat, Rocles, Sanilhac, Chaffies, Saint-Sernin & Fonds, Comte du lieu de Bocz-le-Creftel, Bouffieu-le-Roi, Saint-Barthélemy, le Pin, Colombier-le-Vieux, Seigneur de Roynac, &c., né le 13 Décembre 1658, Capitaine de Cavalerie dans le Régiment Royal-Cravate, par commiffion du 20 Octobre 1683, eft mort le 11 Octobre 1734, & avoit époufé, le 8 Janvier 1688, *Françoife des Bocz de Solignac*, fille de *Henri des Bocz*, Gentilhomme ordinaire de la Chambre du Roi, & de *Laurence de Clermont-Montoifon*, dont il a eu :

1. JOSEPH, qui fuit ;
2. JOSEPH - LAURENT, Bailli-Grand-Croix de l'Ordre de Saint-Jean de Jérufalem, Commandeur de Saint-Paul de Romans & de Blandaix ;
3. ANNE-JOSEPH, Commandeur de Tortebeffe, mort en 1751 ;

Et trois filles, mortes Religieufes.

JOSEPH DE BEAUVOIR-DU-ROURE-DE-BEAU-MONT, Chevalier, Comte de Brifon, &c., né le 17 Mai 1694, Capitaine dans le Régiment du Roi, Cavalerie, par commiffion du 24 Décembre 1712, qui tefta le 2 Mai 1735, & mourut le 21 Novembre 1738. Il fuccéda à toutes les Terres de fes père & mère, & époufa, le 28 Septembre 1721, *Marie - Fleurie de la Fare*, qui tefta le 9 Juin 1736. Elle étoit fille de *Denis-Augufte*, Comte de la Fare-Tournac, Maréchal des Camps & Armées du Roi, Commandeur de l'Ordre Royal & Militaire de Saint-Louis, Lieutenant de Roi des Ville d'Agde, Port & Fort de Brefcou, Baron des Etats-Généraux du Languedoc, Baron de Tornac, &c., & de *Fleurie-Thérèfe du Roure*. Leurs enfans font :

1. FRANÇOIS-DENIS-AUGUSTE, qui fuit ;
2. MARIE-VICTOIRE, morte à Montelimart, le 4 Avril 1747 ;
3. & 4. MARIE-ANNE & MARIE-LOUISE, toutes deux Religieufes de la Vifitation de Montelimart ;
5. Et ANNE, Penfionnaire dans l'Abbaye de Saint-Benoît, à Aubenas.

FRANÇOIS-DENIS-AUGUSTE DE BEAUVOIR-DU-ROURE-DE-BEAUMONT, Chevalier, Comte de Brifon, né le 29 Août 1723, Baron des Etats Généraux du Languedoc, & des Etats Parti-culiers du Vivarais, Seigneur de Beaumont, Brifon, Sanilhac, Rocles, Saint-Melani-Donnac, l'Argentière, Chaffies, Saint-Sernin & Fonds, Baron de Tornac, Comte de Bocz, Seigneur de Roynac, &c., fut Lieutenant dans le Régiment du Roi, Infanterie, depuis 1741 jufqu'à la campagne de 1746 inclufivement, Capitaine de Cavalerie dans le Régiment de Saint-Simon, par commiffion du 10 Mars 1747. Il époufa, le 2 Mai 1752, *Anne-Fran-çoife de Chaponay*, fille de *Nicolas de Cha-ponay-Feyfins*, fecond Préfident à Mortier du Parlement de Dauphiné, & de *Françoife de Virieu-Pupetières*, dont il a eu :

1. NICOLAS-LOUIS-AUGUSTE, né le 25 Août 1753 ;
2. FRANÇOIS-LOUIS-JOSEPH, né le 25 Août 1756, Chevalier de Malte de Minorité, le 26 Mai 1757 ;
3. DENISE-ALEXANDRINE, née le 11 Octobre 1758 ;
4. Et DENIS-SCIPION, né le 31 Décembre 1759.

Les armes de la branche de Beaumont-Brifon font : *parti au 1 de gueules, au chêne arraché & glandé d'or*, qui eft Grimoard de Beauvoir-du-Roure ; *au 2 d'azur au lion d'or, au chef échiqueté d'argent & de fable*, qui eft de Beaumont.

BEAUVOIR-LA-PALU : *écartelé d'or & de gueules.*

BEAUVOISIEN (LE), Seigneur de la Beauvoifinière, en Normandie, Généralité d'Alençon, famille maintenue dans fa nobleffe le 7 Juillet 1666. La Roque parle de JEANNE DE BEAUVOISIEN, Dame de Livarot, morte en 1332.

JEAN LE BEAUVOISIEN, Baron de Courtomer, fervit le Roi CHARLES VII, & eft repréfenté dans un Arrêt de l'Echiquier de 1463. Il eut :

1. FRANÇOIS, Ier du nom, Seigneur de Courtomer, marié, vers 1467, à *Jeanne de Vierville* ;
2. Et GUILLAUME, qui fuit.

GUILLAUME LE BEAUVOISIEN, Baron de Courtomer, époufa *Catherine de Montberon*, Dame du Coudray, dont fortit :

FRANÇOIS LE BEAUVOISIEN, IIe du nom, Baron de Courtomer, marié à *Marguerite du Bois*. De ce mariage eft iffue :

ELÉONORE LE BEAUVOISIEN, Baronne de Courtomer, qui époufa, en 1563, *Arthus de Saint-Simon*, Seigneur de Sainte-Mère-Eglife. C'eft par cette alliance que la Baronie de

Courtomer eft entrée dans la Maifon de *Saint-Simon.*

D'une autre branche étoit JEAN LE BEAUVOISIEN, qui époufa *Girarde Pelet*, dont fortit :

OLIVIER LE BEAUVOISIEN, Chevalier, Bailli d'Alençon, qui eut pour femme *Marine le Gris.* Leur fils fut :

JEAN LE BEAUVOISIEN, IIe du nom, Seigneur de Sainte-Colombe, Gafprée & Fontaine-Rian, qui époufa *Jeanne d'Achey*, fille de *Jean*, VIIe du nom, Seigneur d'Achey, & de *Marie Auvé*, dont :

RENÉE LE BEAUVOISIEN, mariée 1º l'an 1505 avec *Charles*, bâtard *d'Alençon ;* & 2º avec *René de Silly*, Seigneur de Vaux.

D'une autre branche étoit encore GABRIEL LE BEAUVOISIEN, Seigneur de Combray, qui époufa *Anne de Saint-Germain-de-Rouverou,* dont :

1. JEAN, Seigneur de Combray, qui époufa *Anne Mallet-de-Heffey ;*
2. Et FRANÇOISE, femme de *Thomas Mallet*, Seigneur de Heffey, frère d'*Anne Mallet*, fa belle-fœur.

Les Mémoires de Monfieur Bigot, Confeiller à la Cour des Aides de Normandie, font mention de JEAN LE BEAUVOISIEN, Seigneur, d'Angy-fur-Sarthe.

PIERRE LE BEAUVOISIEN, Seigneur de Quatre-Puis, figna à un contrat l'an 1474.

Les armes : *de fable, fretté d'argent.*

BEAUVOLIER, famille de Poitou, dont étoit MARIE DE BEAUVOLIER-DES-MALARDIÈRES, née en 1671, & reçue à Saint-Cyr au mois de Juin 1687, après avoir prouvé qu'elle defcendoit de GILLES DE BEAUVOLIER, Seigneur des Malardières, qui vivoit en 1505, & étoit fon cinquième ayeul.

Les armes : *de gueules, à deux fers de lance à l'antique, ornés d'argent, & pofés en pal.*

BEAUXONCLES. JACQUES DE BEAUXONCLES, Ier du nom, vivant en 1400, fut père de:

JEAN DE BEAUXONCLE, Écuyer, Seigneur du Fay, qui époufa *Catherine de Saint-Martin*, dont :

1. PIERRE, qui fuit;
2. Et CATHERINE, Dame du Pleffis, Saint-Martin, Ville, Gohiblin, &c., femme, vers 1480, de *Robert de Beauvilliers*, Chevalier, Seigneur de Theclaus, dont des enfans.

PIERRE DE BEAUXONCLES, Ecuyer, Seigneur de Cigogne, dont il fit la foi au Comte de Dunois en 1505, eft ayeul de JEAN DE BEAUXONCLES, Chevalier, Seigneur de Cigogne & de Rocheux, Capitaine des Gardes-du-Corps en 1572, qui époufa, en 1526, *Edmonde Rerciers,* fille d'*Antoine.* Elle fut mère de :

JEANNE DE BEAUXONCLES, Dame de Cigogne, femme, en 1572, de *Claude de Mervilliers*, Ecuyer, Seigneur du Heaulme.

JEAN DE BEAUXONCLES, qui pouvoit être fils du précédent, & arrière-petit-fils de PIERRE, fut Seigneur de Courcelles & d'Aunoy-la-Rivière, à caufe de fa femme *Hélène Lucas*, fille de *Jacques*, Seigneur defdits lieux, & de *Madeleine l'Hôpital-Vitry.* On le croit père de :

CHARLES DE BEAUXONCLES, Ier du nom, Chevalier, Seigneur de Courbouzon, Vieuvy, Oucques, qui époufa, *Marie de Saintré*, dont :

1. JEAN, Seigneur d'Oucques, marié à *Anne de l'Hôpital-de-Saint-Mefme ;*
2. Et CHARLES, qui fuit :

CHARLES DE BEAUXONCLES, IIe du nom, Chevalier, Seigneur de Courbouzon, Vieuvy, Armeville & la Coudrais, époufa, le 2 Décembre 1641, *Geneviève de l'Amiraut,* fille de *Hervé*, Ecuyer, Seigneur de Marché-Lambert, & de *Madeleine de Champgrand,* dont :

1. ALEXIS, Seigneur de Courbouzon, qui époufa, en 1672, *Anne Thoinard*, fille de *Jacques*, aliàs *Nicolas*, Ecuyer, Seigneur de Lautray, & de *Marie Lemarrier*, dont MARIE DE BEAUXONCLES, Dame de Courbouzon, femme, en 1692, d'*Armand-Jacques Gujon*, Ecuyer, Seigneur de Saint-Didier & de Champoulet, dont des enfans;
2. CHARLES-MARCEL, Seigneur d'Armeville, qui eut de *Cécile Salomon*, CÉCILE DE BEAUXONCLES, Dame d'Armeville & de Villeromard;
3. Et ELÉONOR, Chevalier, Seigneur de Vieuvy, marié, en 1693, à *Elifabeth de Serizy*, de laquelle il eut CHARLES-ELÉONOR, Chevalier, Seigneur de Vieuvy, marié, en Août 1752, à N... de *Vizel-de-Paray.*

BEAUXYEUX : *d'argent, au chef de gueules, chargé d'un chevron ondé d'argent.*

BEC, en Provence. PIERRE-PAUL BEC, Seigneur du Bourget & de Bagaris, fils de MATHIEU BEC, Avocat au Parlement de Paris, & de *Marguerite de Bermonde*, fut reçu Vifiteur Général des Gabelles de Provence par Arrêt de la Cour des Chambres le 11 Octobre 1669. Cette famille jouit des mêmes privilèges, dont jouiffent celles des Officiers de la Cour des comptes, fuivant les Edits des mois de Mai 1577 & 1583, & la déclaration du Roi du 28 Janvier 1576. Il laiffa de *Madeleine Grognard* :

ANDRÉ BEC, qui fuccéda à la Charge de fon père par Arrêt du 24 Mars 1703. Il époufa *Chriftine de Bœuf*, fille de *Dominique*, Tréforier-Général de France, dont :

MARIUS-BRUNO BEC, pourvû de la Charge de fon père & de fon ayeul, par Arrêt du 12 Juin 1731. Il eft marié avec *Thérèfe-Félicité-Perpétue Bourgerel-de-Foncienne*, fille de *Louis*, Confeiller à la Cour des Comptes. Il a plufieurs enfans qui forment le IVᵉ dégré depuis PIERRE-PAUL BEC, qui a donné la nobleffe à cette famille.

Les armes : *de gueules, à trois oifeaux d'or, à long bec.*

BEC (DU), Seigneur de Vardes, de la Broffe, de Bouri, en Normandie, Généralité de Rouen, famille maintenue dans fa nobleffe le 16 Septembre 1669. Il paroît par la Généalogie du Bec, rapportée dans Moréri, que les Seigneurs de Vardes, fortent ou pourroient être de la Maifon *du Bec-Crêpin*.

Le P. Anfelme parle de GEOFFROY DU BEC, Seigneur de la Motte-Duffeau, qui avoit époufé *Marie de Poftel*. Il fut père de GUILLAUME DU BEC.

On trouve à la Bibliothèque du Roi deux actes originaux, paffés en préfence d'un GUILLAUME DU BEC, Notaire & Secrétaire du Roi, l'un du 17 Février 1441, & l'autre du 12 Octobre 1450.

Quoi qu'il en foit, les Seigneurs DU BEC-DE-VARDES ont donné un Prélat-Commandeur de l'Ordre du Saint-Efprit en 1599, dans PHILIPPE DU BEC, Archevêque & Duc de Reims en 1594; & deux Chevaliers du même Ordre du Saint-Efprit en 1619 & 1661, dans RENÉ DU BEC, Marquis de Vardes, Gouverneur du Thiérache, marié à *Hélène d'O*, & dans fon fils FRANÇOIS-RENÉ DU BEC, Marquis de Vardes, Capitaine des Cent-Suiffes de la Garde du Roi, dont il eft parlé dans Buffi-Rabutin, pour fes intrigues galantes, qui le firent arrêter prifonnier, & exiler de la Cour.

Les armes : *lofangé d'argent & de gueules.*

BEC-CRÊPIN, ancienne Maifon de Normandie qui a donné un Cardinal, des Archevêques de Reims & de Narbonne, des Evêques de Paris, de Laon, de Nantes, de Saint-Malo & de Vannes; un Maréchal de France, un Chevalier des Ordres du Roi, &c. On prétend que cette Maifon eft fortie des *Grimaldi*, Princes de Monaco, depuis le Xᵉ fiècle, & qu'elle s'établit en Normandie, où elle a fait diverfes branches. C'eft *Gilbert de Brionne*, dit *Crépin*, Baron du Bec-Crêpin, qui aida, en 1034, *Hellouin* ou *Herluin*, premier Abbé du Bec, en Normandie, à fonder cette Abbaye. GUILLAUME du BEC étoit Maréchal de France en 1283. JEAN DU BEC mourut en 1451. Cette Maifon s'eft éteinte dans FRANÇOIS-RENÉ DU BEC, Marquis de Vardes, Gouverneur d'Aigues-Mortes, Capitaine des Cent-Suiffes de la Garde ordinaire du Roi, Chevalier de fes Ordres, mort à Paris en 1688, ne laiffant de *Catherine Nicolaï*, fille d'*Antoine*, premier Préfident à la Chambre des Comptes, & de *Marie Amelot*, que MARIE-ELISABETH DU BEC, née le 4 Avril 1661, mariée, le 8 Juillet 1678, à *Louis de Rohan-Chabot*, Duc de Rohan. Voyez la Généalogie de cette Maifon dans les *Grands Officiers de la Couronne*, tom. VI, pag. 631 ; Moréri, le Laboureur, du Chefne, Sainte-Marthe, la Roque, &c.

Les armes : *fufelé d'argent & de gueules.*

BEC-DE-LIÈVRE, en Bretagne, dont fept branches fubfiftent encore; les trois premières & la cinquième font reftées dans cette Province; la quatrième a paffé dans le Maine; les deux dernières en Normandie. Elles fortent toutes de :

I. PIERRE DE BEC-DE-LIÈVRE, vivant en 1363, qui, de *Raoulette Huguet*, eut :

II. THOMAS DE BEC-DE-LIÈVRE, Iᵉʳ du nom, vivant en 1411, qui fut père de :

III. GUILLAUME DE BEC-DE-LIÈVRE, Seigneur du Bouexic, qui eut de *Jeanne Sorrel*, fille de *Pierre*, Seigneur de la Gelimays, & de *Marie Morio* :

1. THOMAS, qui fuit;
2. LOUIS, Recteur de Saint-James-de-la-Lande, mort avant le 8 Octobre 1486, que fa fucceffion fut partagée avantageufement entre RAOUL, fon neveu, & fes oncles;
3. PIERRE, Doyen de Loheac, Maître des Requêtes du Duc de Bretagne FRANÇOIS II, en Février 1487;
4. Un autre PIERRE, Seigneur *du Boisbaffet*, rapporté ci-après, dont les branches *du*

Boisbaffet & de *Saint-Maur* éteintes, & celles des Seigneurs de *Penhouet*, de *Belair* & *du Broffay* exiſtantes ;

5. CHARLES, Seigneur de Chavaignes, auteur des branches des Marquis de *Cany*, des Seigneurs de *Freſne-Saint-Georges* & de *Bonnemare;*

6. Et FRANÇOISE, mariée, par contrat du 12 Mai 1466, à *Guillaume Robellot*, Seigneur de la Voltays.

Il ſe trouve encore FRANÇOIS DE BEC-DE-LIÈVRE, Prieur de Henc, qui obtint, le 6 Décembre 1486, des Lettres de Sauve-garde du Duc FRANÇOIS II.

IV. THOMAS DE BEC-DE-LIÈVRE, IIᵉ du nom, Seigneur du Bouexic & de la Fauvelays, compris en la montre des Nobles tenue à Châteaubriand ſous le Sire de Laval, en 1472, étoit mort avant le 1ᵉʳ Février 1473, que *Perrine Gillot*, ſa veuve, eut la garde-noble de ſes enfans :

1. RAOUL, qui ſuit ;
2. ETIENNE, Seigneur de Bury, compris au rôle des nobles de l'Evêché de Saint-Malo en 1513, qui, de *Jeanne d'Autye*, eut GILLES, Seigneur de Bury, qui rendit aveu au Roi le 15 Janvier 1550 du fief de la Motte au Chancelier, conjointement avec *Jeanne Juhel*, ſa femme, dont il eut GILLES, IIᵉ du nom, Seigneur de Bury, reçu Conſeiller au Parlement de Brètagne le 26 Mars 1571, mort ſans alliance ;
3. THOMAS, Seigneur de Gouen, qui fut partagé comme *juveigneur* par RAOUL, ſon frère, le 1ᵉʳ Février 1505. Il eut de *Jeanne le Chanoine :*

   N..., mariée au Seigneur *de la Porte;*
   Et N..., mariée au Seigneur *de Launay-Perault.*

4. PIERRE, Doyen de Loheac après ſon oncle, qui teſta le 19 Mars 1510;
5. GUILLAUME, Recteur de Combleſſac, qui fit ſon teſtament le 17 Septembre 1522;
6. Et LAURENCE, qui épouſa, par contrat du 5 Juin 1478, *Jean de la Fouays*, Seigneur de Bois-au-Vayer.

V. RAOUL DE BEC-DE-LIÈVRE, Seigneur du Bouexic, compris au nombre des Nobles-tenans du Comté de Laval pour les fiefs de Maupertuis, de Rendumel & de la Rochière, en l'aveu du 28 Juin 1494, fut Lieutenant de Rennes pour le Roi CHARLES VIII par Lettres du 9 Juin 1496. Il épouſa, par contrat du 27 Novembre 1489, *Guillemette Challot*, fille de *Jean*, Seigneur de la Challouſays, & de *Philippine du Pé*, dont il eut :

1. GILLES, Seigneur du Bouexic, mort ſans enfans. Il avoit épouſé, par contrat du 22 Juin 1520, *Gillette de la Chaffe;*
2. ETIENNE, qui ſuit;
3. PERRINE, femme de *Jean Peſchard*, Seigneur de la Chavagnière ;
4. Et ROSE, qui épouſa, par contrat du 22 Septembre 1511, *Jean du Freſche*, Seigneur du Perret.

VI. ETIENNE DE BEC-DE-LIÈVRE, Seigneur du Bouexic, Lieutenant de Rennes pour le Roi FRANÇOIS Iᵉʳ, par commiſſion du 21 Janvier 1527, rendit aveu pour ſa Terre de la Fauvelays, en la Chambre des Comptes de Bretagne le 4 Novembre 1539. Il épouſa, 1⁰ par contrat du 26 Mai 1535, *Gillette de Vaucouleur*, Dame de la Ville-du-Bout; & 2⁰ par contrat du 9 Mai 1541, *Gillette du Han*, fille de *Jean*, Seigneur de Launay, & de *Jacquette Brullon-de-la-Muce*. Les enfans du premier lit ſont :

1. FRANÇOISE, mariée, par contrat du 9 Janvier 1567, à *René de Boiſadam*, Seigneur dudit lieu & de la Rozaye;
2. GILLETTE, qui épouſa, 1⁰ par contrat du 21 Mai 1568, *Jean Peſcherel*, Seigneur de Rochus; & 2⁰ *François d'Eſpinay*.

Et du ſecond lit il eut :

3. FRANÇOIS, qui ſuit;
4. JEAN, Seigneur de la Maultays, qui a fait la branche des Marquis DE BEC-DE-LIÈVRE, rapportée ci-après;
5. Et CLAUDE, qui épouſa, en 1576, *François du Pleſſis*, Seigneur & Vicomte de Grenedan.

VII. FRANÇOIS DE BEC-DE-LIÈVRE, Seigneur du Bouexic, épouſa, par contrat du 26 Mai 1572, *Françoiſe du Châtellier*, qui eut la Terre du Châtellier par les partages qu'elle fit avec *Julienne*, ſa ſœur, femme de *Bertrand du Gueſclin*, Seigneur de la Roberie. Elle étoit fille de *Jean*, Seigneur du Châtellier & des Flèges, & d'*Orphraiſe de Coueſnon*. Ils eurent :

1. RENÉ, mort Chartreux à Paris;
2. JEAN, qui ſuit;
3. MARGUERITE, mariée, par contrat du 28 Mai 1602, à *Guy de Renouard*, Seigneur de Villayer;
4. FRANÇOISE, mariée, par contrat du 20 Mai 1606, à *Nicolas du Boays*, Seigneur du Boays-Robert;
5. OLIVE, Religieuſe à l'Abbaye de Saint-Georges de Rennes;
6. Et CLAUDE, mariée, par contrat du 25 Juil-

let 1611, à *Julien Bonamy*, Seigneur du Châtellier.

VIII. Jean de Bec-de-Lièvre, Vicomte du Bouexic par érection du mois de Février 1637, épousa, 1º par contrat du 25 Septembre 1617, *Guyonne Cheville*, fille de *Jean*, Seigneur de la Flourie, & de *Bertranne Frotet*; & 2º par contrat du 31 Juillet 1644, *Peronnelle de la Ville-Eon*, fille de *François*, Seigneur de Boisfeuillet, & d'*Isabeau de la Fresnaye*. Il eut du premier lit:

1. Françoise, mariée, par contrat du 9 Août 1640, à *Jean Hingam*, Seigneur de Kerisac;
2. Bertranne, Religieuse à l'Abbaye de Saint-Georges de Rennes;
3. Anne, mariée, par contrat du 8 Septembre 1650, à *René*, Seigneur de *la Saudrays*;
4. Guyonne, mariée, par contrat du 3 Juin 1660, à *Georges du Goullay*, Seigneur du Boisguy.

Et du second lit:

5. François, qui suit;
6. Et Georges-Alexis, Prêtre maintenu dans sa noblesse d'ancienne extraction par Arrêt des Commissaires établis pour la réformation de la noblesse de Bretagne, le 14 Mai 1669.

IX. François de Bec-de-Lièvre, IIº du nom, Vicomte du Bouexic, Seigneur du Châtellier, maintenu dans sa noblesse & dans la qualité de *Chevalier*, par Arrêt du 14 Mai 1669, épousa, par contrat de l'année 1676, *Madeleine d'Espinay*, fille d'*Urbain*, Marquis de Vaucouleur, & de *Susanne de Tremigon*.

X. Pierre de Bec-de-Lièvre, IIº du nom, Vicomte du Bouexic, Seigneur du Châtellier, marié, par contrat du 10 Janvier 1702, à *Louise Gabard*, Dame de Teilhac, fille & héritière de *Claude*, Seigneur de Teilhac, & d'*Antoinette de Chardonnay*, dont il a eu:

1. Jean-Baptiste-Antoine, Vicomte du Bouexic, né le 27 Décembre 1702, mort sans enfans. C'est sur lui que la Vicomté du Bouexic a été décrétée en 1756, & adjugée à M. *de Boissix-de-Pinieux*. Il avoit épousé, par contrat du 14 Décembre 1735, *Charlotte de Cornulier*, Dame de Montreuil, fille & héritière de *Claude*, Seigneur de Montreuil, & de *Charlotte le Tourneux*;
2. Charles-Prudent, né en 1705 à Nantes, sacré Evêque de Nîmes le 12 Janvier 1738;
3. Joseph-Pierre, reçu Chevalier de Malte le 14 Février 1718, Enseigne des Vaisseaux du

Roi, mort à bord du *Mercure* dans l'Escadre du Duc d'Anville, le 13 Septembre 1746;

4. Pierre-Joseph, qui suit;
5. Louis-Toussaint, dit *le Chevalier de Bec-de-Lièvre*, né le 31 Octobre 1719, Officier de Marine & Chevalier de Saint-Louis;
6. François-Pierre, né le 14 Juillet 1725, dit *le Chevalier de la Roche-Hervé*, Officier de Marine;
7. Louise, morte Religieuse à la Visitation de Rennes le 11 Octobre 1725;
8. Pélagie, morte le 19 Juillet 1746. Elle avoit épousé, par contrat du 31 Mai 1732, *Pierre Picaud*, Seigneur de la Pommeraye;
9. Marie-Anne, morte le 18 Décembre 1745. Elle avoit épousé, par contrat du 12 Avril 1742, *Charles-Henri d'Ornac*, Baron de Verteuil, Seigneur de Saint-Marcel, au Diocèse d'Uzès;
10. Et Louise-Françoise-Aimée, mariée, par contrat du 20 Juin 1742, à *Jean-Francois-Joseph de Raynaud-de-Boulogne*, Seigneur de Lascours au Diocèse d'Alais.

XI. Pierre-Joseph de Bec-de-Lièvre, Seigneur de Teilhac, né le 10 Mars 1718, mort en 1766, avoit épousé, par contrat du 1er Octobre 1753, *Thérèse-Marie-Gabrielle Gilard-de-Keranflech*, fille de *Mathieu-Joseph*, Seigneur de Keranflech, & de *Marie-Hyacinthe Louvard*. Il eut:

XII. Laurence-Antoinette de Bec-de-Lièvre, Dame de Teilhac, née le 4 Février 1758.

BRANCHE
des Marquis de Bec-de-Lièvre.

VII. Jean de Bec-de-Lièvre, Ier du nom, Seigneur de la Maultays, fils puîné d'Etienne, Seigneur du Bouexic, & de *Gillette du Han*, reçut partage le 5 Mai 1585 de François, Seigneur du Bouexic, son frère aîné, & fut reçu Conseiller au Parlement de Bretagne le 14 Août 1591; il testa le 5 Mai 1608, & épousa *Françoise le Duc*, qui ne vivoit plus en 1602. Elle étoit fille de *Julien le Duc*, reçu Conseiller au Parlement de Bretagne le 2 Août 1554, lors de l'érection. Il en eut:

VIII. François de Bec-dé-Lièvre, Seigneur de la Bunelaye, reçu Conseiller au Parlement de Bretagne le 14 Août 1620, puis premier Président de la Chambre des Comptes de Bretagne le 9 Janvier 1633, qui épousa, par contrat du 7 Juillet 1621, *Jeanne Blanchard*, fille de *Jean*, Seigneur de Lessongère, Conseiller d'Etat, & premier Président en 1634,

Tome II. X x

après la mort de fon gendre, & de *Madelei-ne Savineau*. Leurs enfans furent :

1. JEAN-BAPTISTE, qui fuit ;
2. Et FRANÇOISE, qui époufa, par contrat du mois d'Août 1640, *Guy du Pont*, Seigneur de Chevilly, reçu Confeiller au Parlement le 23 Mai 1643.

IX. JEAN-BAPTISTE DE BEC-DE-LIÈVRE, Seigneur de la Bunelaye, fut d'abord Avocat-Général en la Chambre des Comptes le 17 Juillet 1646, enfuite Confeiller au Parlement le 12 Janvier 1649; reçu Préfident du Parlement le 30 Décembre 1656. Il avoit époufé, par contrat du 16 Juin 1647, *Loüife d'Harrouys*, fille & héritière de *Louis*, Seigneur de la Seilleraye, premier Préfident de la Chambre des Comptes, & de *Simonne-de-Bautru-Nogent*, dont il eut :

1. JEAN-BAPTISTE, qui fuit ;
2. LOUIS, maintenu avec fon frère par l'Arrêt de 1670, mort Capucin ;
3. Et FRANÇOISE, Religieufe à Fontevrault.

X. JEAN-BAPTISTE DE BEC-DE-LIÈVRE, II° du nom, Seigneur de la Bunelaye, maintenu en la qualité de *Chevalier* par Arrêt de la Chambre établie pour la réformation de la nobleffe de Bretagne du 29 Novembre 1670, fut Confeiller au Parlement le 7 Juillet 1677, premier Préfident de la Chambre des Comptes le 5 Septembre 1678, & mourut en Décembre 1736, âgé de 84 ans. Il avoit époufé, par contrat du 22 Août 1677, *Renée de Sefmaifons*, fille & héritière de *René*, Seigneur de Tréambert, & de *Françoife Juchault*, dont il eut :

1. GUILLAUME-JEAN-BAPTISTE-FRANÇOIS, qui fuit ;
2. Et HILARION-MARIE, reçu Préfident en la Chambre des Comptes le 1er Février 1723, mort fans alliance au mois de Juin 1737.

XI. GUILLAUME-JEAN-BAPTISTE-FRANÇOIS DE BEC-DE-LIÈVRE, Marquis de Bec-de-Lièvre, par éreċtion de Tréambert & autres Seigneuries, par Lettres du mois de Février 1717, fut reçu premier Préfident de la Chambre des Comptes en furvivance de fon père le 31 Décembre 1716, & fur fa démiffion le 27 Novembre 1722. Il mourut le 7 Novembre 1733, âgé de 47 ans. Il avoit époufé, par contrat du 30 Juillet 1705, *Françoife le Nobletẓ*, fille & héritière de *René*, Seigneur de Lefcus, & de *Marie-Agnès du Châtel*, dont il eut :

1. HILARION-FRANÇOIS, qui fuit ;

2. GUY-MARIE-HILARION, né le 14 Août 1713, reçu Chevalier de Malte en Janvier 1715, Lieutenant au Régiment des Gardes-Françoifes, mort en Décembre 1740.
3. Et JEANNE-MARIE, née le 16 Août 1706, morte fans enfans au mois de Décembre 1740. Elle avoit époufé, par contrat du 3 Janvier 1723, *Charles-Jean-François*, Marquis de *la Rivière*, aîné de la Maifon de *la Rivière* en Bretagne.

XII. HILARION-FRANÇOIS DE BEC-DE-LIÈVRE, Marquis de Bec-de-Lièvre, né le 9 Décembre 1707, reçu premier Préfident de la Chambre des Comptes de Bretagne le 31 Décembre 1733, a époufé, par contrat du 25 Septembre 1740, *Marie-Anne Danviray-Machonville*, fille & héritière de *Pierre*, Baron de Beaudemont, Préfident en la Chambre des Comptes & Cour des Aides de Normandie, & de *Catherine-Charlotte le Jongleur*, dont il a :

1. HILARION-ANNE-FRANÇOIS-PHILIPPE, qui fuit.
2. ANNE-HENRIETTE-PERRINE, née le 11 Mai 1744, mariée, par contrat du 2 Mai 1765, avec *François-Julien de Rofily*, Seigneur dudit lieu & de Méros, en Bretagne ;
3. Et ANNE-FRANÇOISE, née le 18 Mai 1753.

XIII. HILARION-ANNE-FRANÇOIS-PHILIPPE DE BEC-DE-LIÈVRE, Marquis de Bec-de-Lièvre né le 6 Février 1743, eſt Confeiller au Parlement de Bretagne, & non encore marié.

BRANCHE des *Seigneurs* DU BOISBASSET.

IV. PIERRE DE BEC-DE-LIÈVRE, IIᵉ du nom, Seigneur du Boisbaffet & du Hautbois, fils puîné de GUILLAUME, Seigneur du Bouexic, & de *Jeanne Sorrel*, eſt compris en la montre des nobles de l'Evêché de Rennes des 3 & 4 Mai 1483. Après la mort du Duc FRANÇOIS II, il fut difgracié pour être entré dans le parti que Madame de BEAUJEU, Régente de France, avoit en Bretagne ; & la Ducheffe ANNE donna ordre, le 20 Avril 1491, à Gilles de Coëtlogon, Seigneur de Mejuffeaume, fon Chambellan, de faifir tous fes biens, dans lefquels il rentra, le mariage de CHARLES VIII s'étant fait. Il rendit la foi & hommage, & l'aveu qu'il devoit à la Ducheffe ANNE pour fa Terre du Boisbaffet les 22 Avril 1502 & 16 Juin 1503. Il mourut le 1er Février 1504, & fut inhumé dans le chœur des Cordeliers de Rennes, fous une tombe en demi-relief où il eſt repréſenté armé. Ses armoiries ſont ſur ſa cotte d'armes, & une épitaphe autour de la tombe. Il avoit épouſé 1° *Robine Tremblaye*, fille de *Pierre* & de *Jeanne du Rochel*; & 2° *Jeanne de Bourgneuf*, fille de *Pierre*, Seigneur de Cuſſé, & d'*Olive Blanchet*. Il eut de ſon premier mariage :

1. JEANNE, mariée, par contrat du 3 Août 1501, à *Bertrand*, Seigneur *de Cacé*;

Et du ſecond vinrent :

2. LOUIS, qui ſuit;
3. ARTHUSE, qui épouſa, 1° *Jean le Saige*, Seigneur de la Gontraye ; & 2° *Pierre de Saint-Pern*, Seigneur de la Hongueraye, avec lequel elle rendit aveu au Roi, le 16 Décembre 1539, de la Terre de Noyal-ſur-Saiche ;
4. FRANÇOISE, mariée à *Guyou Brillet*, Seigneur de Lobinière au Maine ;
5. Et GILLETTE, mariée à *Guillaume Peſcherel*, Seigneur de la Villeneuve.

V. LOUIS DE BEC-DE-LIÈVRE, Seigneur du Boisbaſſet & du Hautbois, filleul du Roi Louis XII, ſe trouve compris au nombre des Nobles de la paroiſſe de Maure, Evêché de Saint-Malo, en la réformation de 1513, où il eſt mentionné Seigneur du Hautbois & de Launay. Il épouſa *Julienne de la Boulaye*, qui vivoit encore en 1530, & dont il eut :

1. GILLES, mort en 1541, ſans poſtérité de *Perrine du Masle*, qui ſe remaria à *François de Sérent*, Seigneur de la Rivière;
2. Et PIERRE, qui ſuit ;

VI. PIERRE DE BEC-DE-LIÈVRE, IIIᵉ du nom, Seigneur du Hautbois & du Boisbaſſet, obtint en cette qualité, & comme fils de LOUIS, & petit-fils de PIERRE DE BEC-DE-LIÈVRE & de *Jeanne de Bourgneuf*, Sentence des Grands-Jours tenus à Ploermel le 2 Août 1541, contre Jean le Prêbtre contre qui il plaidoit pour des droits Seigneuriaux de la Terre du Boisbaſſet; cette Sentence fut ſuivie d'Arrêts des 22 Septembre 1542 & 3 Avril 1545. Le 1ᵉʳ Juillet 1549, *Jeanne de Boiſoreaut*, veuve de noble homme *de Croixelay*, Seigneur de la Violays, lui rendit aveu pour ſa Terre de la Rouxelays, comme mère & tutrice de *Nicolas de Croixelay*, ſon fils aîné. Il épouſa *Jeanne du Masle*, fille de *Pierre*, Seigneur du Masle, & d'*Iſabeau de Montauban*, dont il eut :

1. JEAN, qui ſuit;
2. Autre JEAN, Religieux à l'Abbaye de Saint-Mellaine de Rennes, puis Recteur de Maure ;
3. FRANÇOIS, qui a fait la branche des Seigneurs de *Saint-Maur* & de *Penhouet*, rapportée après celle de ſon frère aîné ;
4. JULIENNE, mariée, par contrat du 15 Mai 1575, à *Jean Faurel*, Seigneur de la vallée Saint-Juſt ;
5. Et CATHERINE, mariée à *Pierre de Goula*, Seigneur de la Verguiette, en Anjou.

VII. JEAN DE BEC-DE-LIÈVRE, Iᵉʳ du nom, Seigneur du Boisbaſſet & du Hautbois, fut Lieutenant-Général des Eaux & Forêts de Bretagne. Il épouſa, par contrat du 15 Août 1569, *Louiſe Pellerin*, Dame de Penhouet, fille d'*Yves*, Seigneur de la Guichardays & du Bohurel, dont il eut :

1. FRANÇOIS, qui ſuit ;
2. MATHURIN, mort ſans alliance ;
3. FRANÇOISE, mariée à *Jacques de Privé*, Seigneur des Bignons & de Pompeau ;
4. GILLETTE, qui épouſa 1° *Jean de Gerrille*, Seigneur de la Barre-Chevry ; & 2° *Nicolas de Kerjan*, Seigneur de Préelo ;
5. Et N..... femme de *N..... de Leʒenet*, Seigneur du Valnéant.

VIII. FRANÇOIS DE BEC-DE-LIÈVRE, Seigneur du Boisbaſſet & du Hautbois, donna partage à FRANÇOISE, ſa ſœur, le 30 Novembre 1596, & mourut le 20 Avril 1639. Il avoit épouſé *Jeanne de Limoges*, Dame de Chuſſeville, dont il eut :

1. JEAN, qui ſuit;
2. Et NICOLE, mariée, en Septembre 1633, à *René Rouault*, Seigneur de Tregniel-Lanvaux.

IX. JEAN DE BEC-DE-LIÈVRE, IIᵉ du nom, Seigneur du Boisbaſſet, du Hautbois & de Chuſſeville, rendit aveu au Roi de la terre du Boisbaſſet le 30 Août 1642, & épouſa, par contrat du 20 Décembre 1630, *Louiſe de la Ruée-Saint-Marcel*, fille de *Guillaume*, Seigneur de Beauregard, & de *Gillonne de Saint-Pern*, dont il eut :

1. GILLONNE, Dame du Boisbaſſet, qui épouſa 1° *Gilles-Henri*, Seigneur de *Bohal*. Etant veuve, elle fut maintenue dans ſa nobleſſe par Arrêt de la Chambre de la Réformation, du 27 Juin 1669, & épouſa 2° *N..... Tafin*, Seigneur de la Rouairie, Brigadier des Armées du Roi.
2. Et JEANNE, mariée à *Chriſtophe de Bedée*, Seigneur de Belleville.

BRANCHE
des Seigneurs DE SAINT-MAUR & DE PENHOUET.

VII. FRANÇOIS DE BEC-DE-LIÈVRE, Seigneur de Gouvello, & de Saint-Maur, fils puîné de PIERRE, IIIe du nom, Seigneur du Boisbaſſet, & de *Jeanne du Masle*, reçut partage de JEAN, ſon frère aîné, le 6 Novembre 1569. Il fut reçu le 27 Oêtobre précédent Conſeiller au Parlement de Bretagne, qui avoit été érigé en 1554, & étoit mort le 17 Avril 1603, que ſe fit, en la Juridiêtion de Peillac, la tutelle de ſes enfans. Il épouſa *Grégorine de la Corbinière*, dont il laiſſa :

1. FRANÇOIS, qui ſuit ;
2. FRANÇOISE-JULIENNE, morte ſans alliance ;
3. Et ANNE, qui reçut partage de ſon frère, le 21 Février 1614, & épouſa *Pierre de Perchays*.

VIII. FRANÇOIS DE BEC-DE-LIÈVRE, IIe du nom, Seigneur de Saint-Maur, mort le 4 Mars 1632, épouſa, par contrat du 28 Avril 1613, *Françoiſe le Marchand*, Dame de la Geurivays, fille de *Pierre*, Seigneur de la Gitays, & de la Geurivays, dont il eut :

1. RENÉ, Seigneur de Saint-Maur, qui épouſa, 1° le 25 Septembre 1639, *Marthe de Kerveno ;* & 2° par contrat du 12 Mars 1644, *Antoinette le Pennec*, fille de *René*, Seigneur de Trégron, & de *Jeanne de Guerrier*, dont il eut JULIENNE-MARIE DE BEC-DE-LIÈVRE, Dame de Saint-Maur, qui épouſa, par contrat du 2 Mai 1662, *Jean-Georges de la Motte*, Seigneur de la Vallée-Pimodam, fils de *François*, Seigneur de la Vallée-Pimodam, & de *Françoiſe de Voyer*, dont deux filles, mariées aux Seigneurs de la *Ferronays* & de *Kervillio ;*
2. GUILLAUME, qui ſuit ;
3. CLAUDE, qui a fait la branche des Seigneurs *du Broſſay*, rapportée ci-après ;
4. Et GILLES, Seigneur du Houx, qui reçut partage proviſionel de RENÉ, ſon frère aîné, le 1er Avril 1639, mort ſans alliance.

IX. GUILLAUME DE BEC-DE-LIÈVRE, Seigneur de Penhouet, reçut partage de RENÉ, Seigneur de Saint-Maur, ſon frère aîné, le 19 Septembre 1642, fut maintenu dans ſa nobleſſe, avec ſes deux fils JULIEN-ANTOINE & JEAN, lors de la réformation, par Arrêt du 27 Juin 1669. Il épouſa, par contrat du 20 Janvier 1645, *Julienne du Mur*, Dame de Pommerel, fille de *Julien*, Seigneur du Mur, & d'*Hélène de Gueriſſ*, dont il eut :

1. JULIEN-ANTOINE, qui ſuit ;
2. Et JEAN, qui a fait la branche des Seigneurs de *Belair*, rapportée ci-après.

X. JULIEN-ANTOINE DE BEC-DE-LIÈVRE, Seigneur de Penhouet, mort en 1703, avoit épouſé, par contrat du 23 Juin 1670, *Madeleine Coſnier*, fille de *René*, Seigneur de la Clergerie, & de *Jeanne Carts*, dont il eut :

1. RENÉ-JEAN-BAPTISTE, qui ſuit ;
2. Et JULIEN-ANTOINE, Seigneur de Saint-Maur, marié à *Renée Deniſot* dont il a eu ANTOINETTE DE BEC-DE-LIÈVRE, Dame de Saint-Maur, mariée, par contrat du 10 Janvier 1729, à *Charles-Louis le Fournier*, Seigneur de Tréello.

XI. RENÉ-JEAN-BAPTISTE DE BEC-DE-LIÈVRE, Seigneur de Penhouet, mort le 24 Décembre 1736, épouſa, 1° par contrat du 4 Janvier 1689, *Jeanne de Gallais*, fille de *Jean*, Seigneur de la Villerault, & de *Jeanne Coſtard*, dont il n'eut point d'enfans ; & 2° par contrat du 25 Février 1725, *Jeanne-Hélène le Noir-de-Carlan*, fille de *Guillaume*, Seigneur de Tournemine, & de *Jeanne-Françoiſe Rado-du-Matz*, dont il a eu :

1. JEAN-MARIE, qui ſuit ;
2. GABRIEL-FRANÇOIS-LOUIS, dit *le Chevalier*, *de Bec-de-Lièvre*, né le 15 Septembre 1734, Lieutenant d'Infanterie au Régiment d'Enghien, bleſſé dangereuſement à la bataille d'Aſtenbeck en 1757 ; puis Capitaine au Régiment des Volontaires de Dauphiné en Janvier 1760 ;
3. Et FLAVIE-SUSANNE, Religieuſe Urſuline à Redon, morte le 2 Juillet 1756.

XII. JEAN-MARIE DE BEC-DE-LIÈVRE, Seigneur de Penhouet, né le 8 Décembre 1727, a épouſé, par contrat du 24 Septembre 1757, *Suſanne de la Tullaye*, fille & héritière de *Pierre-Alexandre*, Seigneur de Kernavellon, & de *Marguerite le Clerc*, dont :

1. ANNE-MARIE-ALEXANDRE, né le 10 Janvier 1760 ;
2. GABRIEL-ANTOINE, né le 18 Février 1761 ;
3. Et JEAN-VINCENT, né le 27 Juin 1762.

BRANCHE
des Seigneurs DE BELAIR, ſortie des Seigneurs DE PENHOUET.

X. JEAN DE BEC-DE-LIÈVRE, Seigneur de Belair & de Peruit, fils puîné de GUILLAUME, Seigneur de Penhouet, & de *Julienne du Mur*, né le 2 Février 1648, fut compris en l'Arrêt de maintenue de nobleſſe, le 27 Juin 1669, & épouſa *Anne Olive*. Elle étoit veuve le 3

Février 1697, qu'elle tranfigea avec JULIEN-ANTOINE DE BEC-DE-LIÈVRE, Seigneur de Penhouet, fon beau-frère, fur la fucceffion des père & mère de fon mari, comme tutrice de fes fils, qui font:

1. JULIEN-JOSEPH, qui fuit;
2. Et FRANÇOIS-JEAN, mort le 17 Juin 1708.

XI. JULIEN-JOSEPH DE BEC-DE-LIÈVRE, Seigneur de Belair, né le 25 Avril 1685, mort le 19 Août 1707, époufa, par contrat du 26 Septembre 1706, *Anne Dagues*, fille de *Simon Dagues*, Confeiller au Préfidial du Mans, & de *Renée des Aulnays*, dont il eut:

XII. ANTOINE DE BEC-DE-LIÈVRE, Seigneur de Belair, né pofthume le 5 Mars 1708, mort le 5 Décembre 1740, qui avoit époufé, par contrat du 7 Mars 1733, *Charlotte de Defniaux-de-la-Garenne*, fille de *Jacques*, Seigneur de la Garenne, & d'*Anne de Phlines*, dont il a eu:

1. ANTOINE-PIERRE, qui fuit;
2. Et CHARLES-JACQUES-DENIS, dit l'*Abbé de Bec-de-Lièvre*, né le 17 Septembre 1735, Chanoine de Saint-Brieuc, & Grand-Vicaire du Diocèfe.

XIII. ANTOINE-PIERRE DE BEC-DE-LIÈVRE, Seigneur de Belair & de Piruit, né le 9 Octobre 1734, Garde de la Marine en 1756; périt avec le Vaiffeau *le Théfée*, commandé par M. de Kerfaint, dans le combat donné le 20 Novembre 1759, entre le Maréchal de Conflans & l'Amiral Haukue.

BRANCHE
des Seigneurs DU BROSSAY, *fortie des Seigneurs* DE SAINT-MAUR.

IX. CLAUDE DE BEC-DE-LIÈVRE, Seigneur de la Motte & du Broffay, troifième fils de FRANÇOIS, IIᵉ du nom, Seigneur de Saint-Maur, & de *Françoife le Marchand*, reçut partage de RENÉ, Seigneur de Saint-Maur, fon frère aîné, le 19 Novembre 1642; il époufa *Gillonne Coftard*, qui étoit veuve, & tutrice de GABRIEL, leur fils, lors de l'Arrêt de maintenue de nobleffe du 27 Juin 1669, dans lequel ils furent compris. Il en eut:

1. GABRIEL, qui fuit;
2. Et MARGUERITE, qui reçut partage de GABRIEL, fon frère, le 24 Septembre 1689, & époufa *Georges Saulnier*, Seigneur de Rohermand.

X. GABRIEL DE BEC-DE-LIÈVRE, Seigneur du Broffay, émancipé par acte de la Juridiction

de Derval, du 25 Juin 1680, rendit aveu en cette Baronie de la Terre du Broffay, & époufa, par contrat du 11 Septembre 1683, *Gillonne Rouault*, fille de *René*, Seigneur de Tregniel-Lanvaux, & de *Marguerite Maudet*, dont il eut:

1. RENÉ-FRANÇOIS, qui fuit;
2. PIERRE, dit *le Chevalier du Broffay*, mort fans alliance;
3. Et ANNE-MARIE, morte en 1754, fans enfans, femme du Seigneur de *Kerhouet*.

XI. RENÉ-FRANÇOIS DE BEC-DE-LIÈVRE, Seigneur du Broffay, donna partage, le 21 Juin 1731, à PIERRE, fon frère; il époufa, par contrat du 15 Février 1713, *Gabrielle Saulnier*, fille & héritière de *Georges*, Seigneur de Rohermand, & de MARGUERITE DE BEC-DE-LIÈVRE, dont il eut:

XII. ALEXANDRE-GABRIEL DE BEC-DE-LIÈVRE, Seigneur du Broffay, qui, affifté de PIERRE, Chevalier du Broffay, fon oncle & fon curateur, rendit aveu au Comté de Maure de la Seigneurie de Pouffehard, le 7 Avril 1739. Il époufa, par contrat du 12 Septembre 1735, *Marie Moraud*, fille de *Louis-Jofeph*, Seigneur du Deron, commandant la Nobleffe de l'Evêché de Rennes, & de *Françoife de Montaudouin*, dont il eut:

1. PIERRE, qui fuit;
2. Et LUCRÈCE-AUGUSTINE, née le 2 Septembre 1741, mariée, en 1764, au Seigneur de *Fourché-de-Quéhillac*, Chevalier de Saint-Louis, & ancien Officier de Dragons.

XIII. PIERRE-LOUIS DE BEC-DE-LIÈVRE, Seigneur du Broffay, né le 11 Novembre 1738, reçu Page du Roi en la Grande-Ecurie en 1754, Cornette dans le Régiment de Cavalerie de Talleyrand en 1756.

BRANCHE
des Marquis DE CANY.

IV. CHARLES DE BEC-DE-LIÈVRE, Seigneur de Chavaignes, cinquième fils de GUILLAUME DE BEC-DE-LIÈVRE, Seigneur du Broffay, & de *Jeanne Sorrel*, fuivit en France la Ducheffe *Anne de Bretagne*, lorfqu'elle époufa le Roi CHARLES VIII. Il tranfigea, le 21 Juillet 1500, avec RAOUL, Seigneur du Bouexic, fon neveu, fur la fucceffion de PIERRE, fon frère, Doyen de Loheac; il époufa 1º *Gillonne de Beaune-Samblançay*, morte avant 1490, fœur de *Jacques*, Seigneur de Samblançay & de la Carte, Vicomte de Tours,

Chambellan du Roi, Bailli & Gouverneur de Touraine; & 2° *Pernelle Dreux.*

Il eut de son premier mariage:

1. Gilles, mentionné dans la ratification de la transaction du 29 Mars 1514, mort sans alliance;
2. René, qui suit;
3. Guy, dit *Guyon,* Chanoine de l'Eglise Métropolitaine de Rouen, Prieur de Saint-Ymer, qui fit donation, le 6 Septembre 1538, de la Terre de Chemaille, en Touraine, à René, son frère, en faveur des enfans qu'il auroit de son second mariage;
4. Jeanne, morte, lors de l'accord du 2 Avril 1548, femme de *Martin Fumée.*

Et du second lit vinrent:

5. Charles, Seigneur de Sautonne, de Sanoye & de la Leurie, en Anjou & Touraine, qui ratifia, tant pour lui que pour Gilles, Guyon, François & Jacques, ses frères, l'accord du 21 Juillet 1500, par acte passé devant les Notaires de Rennes, le 29 Mars avant Pâques 1514 avec Raoul, Seigneur du Bouexic, son cousin germain. Il étoit mort sans postérité avant le 2 Avril 1548;
6. François, Seigneur de Launay & de Vauthibault, qui servit aux guerres de Piémont sous le Prince de Melphes, & transigea le 2 Avril 1548, Férie & lendemain de Pâques, par acte passé à Loudun avec Charles, Seigneur de Sazilly, son neveu, sur les successions de Jacques, Gilles, Guy & Charles de Bec-de-Lièvre, ce dernier, Seigneur de Sautonne, & de Jeanne de Bec-de-Lièvre, ses frères & sœur, oncles & tante de Charles, Seigneur de Sazilly. Il fit cession, par acte passé devant les Notaires de Chinon le 5 Août 1555, de tout ce que les enfans du premier mariage de Charles, Seigneur de Chavaignes, avec *Gillonne de Beaune,* devoient à ceux de son second mariage avec *Pernelle Dreux,* ainsi que de ce qui lui appartenoit dans les Seigneuries de Sanoye & de la Leurie. Il épousa *Bertrande du Pin,* dont il eut:

    Guillaume, homme d'armes de la Compagnie du Seigneur de Montmorency, qui fut présent à la prise de possession que Charles, II° du nom, Seigneur de Sazilly, fit le 27 Décembre 1560, de la Terre de Sanoye; mort sans alliance;

7. Jacques, mort avant le 15 Mars 1574, sans alliance;
8. Louise, Dame Destors, veuve, le 18 Mars 1527, de *Denis Duval,* vivante en 1538, comme il apparoît par un titre de l'Abbaye du Val;

9. Et Renée, femme de *Martin de Peguigneau,* Seigneur de Villaumer & de la Motte.

V. René de Bec-de-Lièvre, Seigneur de Sazilly, suivit Louis XII à la conquête du Milanois, qui le fit, en 1502, Gouverneur & *Podestat* de la Ville d'Alexandrie; après la perte de ce Duché, le Roi lui donna, en 1512, une Charge de Conseiller-Clerc en l'Echiquier de Normandie; il succéda au Cardinal d'Amboise dans la Charge de Garde-des-Sceaux de la Chancellerie, près ce Parlement, & mourut le 14 Avril 1545. Il avoit épousé, 1° par contrat du 17 Janvier 1513, *Marie d'Osmont,* morte le 10 Décembre 1531. Elle étoit veuve de *Robert de Croismare,* Seigneur des Alleurs, & fille de *Nicolas d'Osmont,* Seigneur de Berville; & 2° par contrat du 4 Septembre 1538, *Marguerite de Bonshoms,* fille de *Jean,* Seigneur de Hautonne & de Couronne.

Il eut de son premier mariage:

1. Charles, qui suit;
2. Françoise, née le 31 Décembre 1523, mariée, par contrat du 14 Septembre 1541, à *Jean de Bonshoms,* Seigneur de Couronne & de Hautonne.

Et du second mariage:

3. Marie, morte sans postérité. Elle avoit épousé, par contrat du 21 Mars 1553, *Adrien,* Sire de *Breauté,* Châtelain de Neville, Bailli de Gisors, Gentilhomme ordinaire de la Chambre du Roi, Chevalier de son Ordre, & Capitaine d'une Compagnie de ses Ordonnances.

VI. Charles de Bec-de-Lièvre, II° du nom, Seigneur de Sazilly & de Quevilly, né le 20 Janvier 1520, transigea le 15 Mars 1548, avec François, Seigneur de Vauthibault, son oncle; il fit hommage au Roi, le 30 Mai 1556, pour sa Terre de Quevilly; fut élu par la noblesse de la Province, en 1588, pour répondre aux cahier & articles présentés par l'Archevêque de Lyon, & autres Commissaires députés par le Roi en Normandie, & député le 8 Novembre 1593, du Corps de la noblesse du Bailliage de Rouen, pour assister aux Etats tenus à Caen par M. le Duc de Montpensier. Il épousa, 1° au mois de Mars 1548, *Françoise Surreau,* fille de *Jean,* Seigneur de Farceaux, & de *Marguerite de la Vieille;* 2° sans enfans, par contrat du 5 Mai 1558, *Anne du Hamel,* fille de *Nicolas,* Seigneur de Feuguerolles; & 3° par autre contrat du 22 Septembre 1574, *Geneviève Rufé*, fille de *Louis*, Seigneur de la Herpinière, & de *Geneviève le Tur*.

Il eut de fon premier mariage :

1. PIERRE, qui fuit ;
2. FRANÇOIS, qui a fait la branche des Seigneurs de *Bonnemare*, rapportée après la poſtérité de fon frère aîné ;
3. CHARLOTTE, mariée, par contrat du 20 Septembre 1566, à *Jean de la Place*, Seigneur de Ronfeugère & de Fumechon.

Il eut de fon troiſième mariage :

4. Et GENEVIÈVE, qui époufa, par contrat du 28 Novembre 1594, reconnu devant Notaires le 15 Janvier fuivant, *Jacques de Boſcregnoult*, Seigneur dudit lieu & du Moulin.

VII. PIERRE DE BEC-DE-LIÈVRE, II° du nom, Seigneur de Quevilly & de Brumare, Chevalier de l'Ordre du Roi, Gentilhomme ordinaire de fa Chambre, fervit à la bataille de Saint-Denis en 1587, fous M. le Duc de Longueville, aux guerres de la Baſſe-Normandie, aux fièges de Domfront & de Saint-Lô, fous le Seigneur de Matignon, en 1589; & en 1590 fous M. le Duc de Montpenfier, & au fiège de Rouen, en 1591, en la Compagnie du Seigneur de Sainte-Marie; partagea, le 15 Décembre 1575, avec *Hervé de Longaunay*, Seigneur dudit lieu, Chevalier de l'Ordre du Roi, & Lieutenant-Général pour Sa Majeſté en Baſſe-Normandie, mari de *Catherine Surreau*, fa tante, & fon co-héritier en la fucceſſion de *Thomas Surreau*, Seigneur de Farceaux, Gentilhomme ordinaire de la Chambre du Roi, mort fans enfans de *Sufanne de Monchy-Senarpont*; & fit hommage au Roi, le 19 Juillet 1605, pour fa Terre de Quevilly. Il avoit époufé, le 10 Octobre 1576, *Catherine Martel,* fille & héritière d'*Artus*, Seigneur d'Hocqueville & de Bertheauville, & de *Catherine Boivin de Bonnetot*, dont il eut :

1. CHARLES, qui fuit ;
2. PIERRE, Seigneur de Quevilly, Confeiller au Parlement de Rouen, maintenu dans fa nobleſſe le 6 Février 1641, qui mourut fans poſtérité avant le 8 Mars 1653, que fa fucceſſion fut partagée entre fes neveux. Il avoit époufé, 1° par contrat du 14 Juillet 1616, *Marie de Clainville,* fille de *Jacques*, Seigneur de Beaucourfel, & de *Catherine Boulays;* & 2° par autre contrat du 9 Mars

1619, *Marguerite Marc*, fille de *Louis*, Seigneur de la Ferté, & de *Marguerite de Baudouin;*
3. CHARLES, dit *le Jeune*, Seigneur de Frefnes & de Saint-Georges, Gentilhomme ordinaire de la Chambre du Roi; il partagea, avec fes frères, la fucceſſion de leur père & mère, le 17 Mars 1622, & fut tué en duel le 3 Janvier 1640. Il avoit époufé, par contrat du 22 Octobre 1624, *Anne le Brument*, fille de *Pierre*, & d'*Anne de His*, dont il eut :

1. PIERRE, Seigneur de Frefnes, né le 3 Janvier 1635, maintenu dans fa nobleſſe par Ordonnance de M. de la Galiſſonnière, Intendant de Rouen, le 3 Juin 1668, mort fans alliance ;
2. RENÉ, Seigneur de Saint-Georges, né le 7 Avril 1637, Capitaine au Régiment de Rambure en 1659, enfuite au Régiment de la Marine, puis Colonel-Lieutenant du Régiment du Roi, Infanterie, le 6 Janvier 1676, & Brigadier de fes Armées, par Brevet du 24 Février fuivant, fervit en cette qualité en 1677 dans l'Armée de Flandres, commandée par MONSIEUR, Duc d'Orléans, qui gagna la bataille de Caſſel; & fut tué, la campagne fuivante, à la bataille de Saint-Denis, que M. le Maréchal de Luxembourg gagna contre le Prince d'Orange, en 1678;
3. Et JEANNE, née en Décembre 1627, mariée, par contrat du 10 Novembre 1646, à *François du Four*, Seigneur de Nogent ;
4. CATHERINE, mariée, par contrat du 15 Mai 1598, à *Antoine de Parey*, Seigneur de Combray;
5. MARGUERITE, femme de *Pierre de Vinéfay*, Seigneur de la Bataille ;
6. JEANNE, mariée, par contrat du 25 Novembre 1610, à *Charles de Clercy*, Seigneur de Mouyaux, du Frefnay & de Fulletot;
7. Et GENEVIÈVE, femme de *Pierre Gouel*, Seigneur des Parcs & de Normanville.

VIII. CHARLES DE BEC-DE-LIÈVRE, III° du nom, Seigneur d'Hocqueville & de Brumare, né le 26 Février 1579, fuivit le Duc de Mercœur aux guerres de Hongrie, & fe diſtingua au fiège de Canife, fut pourvu de la Charge de Maître-d'Hôtel du Roi HENRI IV le 4 Mars 1610, de celle de Gentilhomme ordinaire de la Chambre de LOUIS XIII, le 30 Décembre 1614; fut nommé Confeiller d'Etat d'Epée, par Brevet du 4 Juin 1619; Meſtre-de-Camp d'Infanterie appointé, par Brevet du 11 Février 1620, reçut Commiffion le 11 Juillet, pour commander un Régiment de 500 hommes à pied, François, dans l'Armée que le Duc d'Elbeuf affembloit en Normandie, & le Roi lui écrivit de la Sufe le 4 Août 1620. Il mourut le 15 Novembre 1622, & avoit époufé, par contrat du 2 Novembre 1604, *Jeanne de Morant*, Dame du Bois d'Aubigny, fille de *Thomas*, Seigneur d'Efterville, & de *Maffiotte de Morel-Putanges*, dont il eut :

1. PIERRE, qui fuit;
2. THOMAS, Seigneur de Brumare, mort en 1643, fans alliance;
3. CATHERINE, mariée, par contrat du 6 Septembre 1626, à *Thomas de Franquetot*, Seigneur de Carquebuc & de Vaffy, l'un des 24 Gentilshommes ordinaires de la Maifon du Roi;
4. Et MADELEINE, femme de *Marc-Aurèle de Giverville*, Seigneur d'Argence.

IX. PIERRE DE BEC-DE-LIÈVRE, IIIe du nom, Marquis de Quevilly, d'Hocqueville & de Cany-Barville, Châtelain de Grainville, premier Préfident de la Cour des Aides de Normandie, Confeiller d'Etat ordinaire & au Confeil-Privé, par Lettres du 4 Décembre 1656, fut maintenu dans fa nobleffe par Ordonnance de M. de la Galiffonnière, du 30 Juin 1668. En faveur de fes fervices & de ceux de fes pères, le Roi érigea, au mois de Mai 1654, la Seigneurie de Quevilly & Fiefs y joints, en titre de *Marquifat*. Il mourut le 13 Juillet 1685, & fut inhumé dans l'Eglife des Carmes Déchauffés de Rouen, qu'il avoit fait bâtir. Il avoit époufé, par contrat du 7 Février 1637, *Madeleine de Moy*, fille de *Pierre*, Seigneur de Bieurville, & de *Barbe Hebert*, dont il eut :

1. PIERRE, Marquis d'Hocqueville & de Cany, Châtelain de Grainville, où il fonda un Hôpital de Religieux de la Charité, premier Préfident de la Cour des Aides de Normandie, par provifion du 9 Décembre 1678, mort en 1726, fans poftérité. Il avoit époufé, par contrat du 20 Mai 1672, *Françoife le Boultz*, fille & héritière de *Noël*, Seigneur de Chomot, Confeiller en la Grand'-Chambre du Parlement de Paris, & d'*Anne Defprez*;
2. THOMAS-CHARLES, qui fuit;
3. BARBE, mariée, par contrat du 29 Mai 1659, à *Pierre le Guerchois*, Seigneur d'Autretot & de Sainte-Colombe, Procureur-Général du Parlement de Normandie;
4. GENEVIÈVE, mariée, par contrat du 19 Mai

1663, à *Balthafar le Marinier*, Marquis de Cany-Veauville;
5. Et MADELEINE, mariée, par contrat du 19 Mai 1670, à *Jacques Danviray-Machonville*, Baron de Beaudemont, Préfident en la Chambre des Comptes de Normandie.

X. THOMAS-CHARLES DE BEC-DE-LIÈVRE, Marquis de Quevilly, Préfident à Mortier au Parlement de Normandie, par provifion du 15 Janvier 1681, fit hommage au Roi, le 26 Juin 1690, pour fon Marquifat de Quevilly, & mourut le 26 Décembre 1711. Il époufa, par contrat du 31 Janvier 1674, *Marie-Anne Pellot*, fille de *Claude*, Comte de *Tréviers*, premier Préfident du même Parlement, & de *Claude le Camus*, dont il eut :

1. CLAUDE, Marquis de Quevilly, Préfident à Mortier du Parlement de Normandie, qui époufa, 1º par contrat du 4 Décembre 1703, *Marguerite Bouchard*, fille & héritière d'*Alexandre*, Seigneur, Vicomte de Bloffeville, & d'*Elifabeth-Sufanne-Marie Vauquelin*; & 2º par contrat du 8 Janvier 1728, *Marie-Angélique-Charlotte-Henriette du Moucel*, fille de *Jacques-Alexandre-Henri*, Seigneur de Lourailles, Préfident à Mortier du Parlement de Rouen, & de *Marie-Madeleine-Cécile Maignard-de-Bernières*;
2. PIERRE, Capitaine d'Infanterie au Régiment de Bigorre, par Commiffion du 15 Février 1693, fous-Lieutenant de la Compagnie Colonelle des Gardes-Françoifes, par Lettres du 12 Mars 1694; tué à Tournay en 1697, ayant l'agrément d'un Régiment;
3. CHARLES-FRANÇOIS, Religieux Bénédictin de Cluny, Prieur de Bort, de Befu & de Saint-Aubin-des-Frefnes;
4. PAUL-RENÉ, Carme Déchauffé, Vifiteur général, & affiftant du Général de fon Ordre, mort le 9 Décembre 1741;
5. FRANÇOIS-ALEXANDRE, Capitaine d'Infanterie au Régiment de la Marine, par Commiffion du mois de Novembre 1704, tué au combat de Caffano, au mois d'Août 1705;
6. HENRI, Garde de la Marine, tué fur le Vaiffeau de M. le Comte de Touloufe, au Combat de Malaga, en 1704;
7. LOUIS, qui fuit;
8. CLAUDE-LOUIS, mort en bas âge;
9. MARIE-ANNE, morte Religieufe à l'Abbaye de Saint-Louis de Rouen;
10. MADELEINE, Religieufe Urfuline à Rouen, morte le 7 Décembre 1768;
11. JEANNE-THÉRÈSE, morte veuve & Carmélite à Rouen, le 14 Décembre 1755. Elle avoit époufé, par contrat du 15 Mai 1700,

Louis de Carrel, Préſident de la Chambre des Comptes de Normandie;

12. MARIE-BARBE-URSULE, mariée, par contrat du 3 Mars 1709, à *Robert-Vincent d'Eſ-malleville*, Marquis de Panneville, Baron de Fréville, Chevalier de Saint-Louis;

13. GENEVIÈVE, morte le 1ᵉʳ Juin 1767. Elle avoit épouſé, par contrat du 14 Septembre 1711, *Pierre de Varroc*, Seigneur d'Houe-feville;

14. Et ELISABETH, Religieuſe Urſuline à Rouen, morte le 28 Octobre 1763.

XI. LOUIS DE BEC-DE-LIÈVRE, Iᵉʳ du nom, Marquis de Cany & de Quevilly, né le 20 Août 1687, rendit foi & hommage au Roi de ces Seigneuries en 1733, & mourut le 4 Novembre 1740. Il avoit épouſé, 1º par contrat du 9 Mai 1711, *Emerique-Thérèſe-Marc de la Ferté*, fille de *Charles*, Seigneur de Reux, & de *Marie Amyot*; 2º par contrat du 15 Avril 1713, *Marie-Anne Coſté-de-Sai* *Suplix*, fille d'*Alexandre*, Seigneur de S Suplix, & de *Marguerite le Blais*; 3 contrat du 3 Mai 1717, *Anne-Henriette therine Touſtain*, fille & héritière de *Ja ques-Nicolas*, Seigneur d'Herbeville & de *Madeleine-Angélique de Lannoy*; & 4º par autre contrat du 24 Juillet 1723, *Marie-Madeleine de Houdetot*, morte le 4 Septembre 1761, fille & héritière d'*Adrien-Joſeph*, Marquis *de Houdetot*,& de *Madeleine de Chal-lons*.

De ſon ſecond mariage il a eu:

1. MARGUERITE-LYDIE, morte le 3 Avril 1741. Elle avoit épouſé, par contrat du 1ᵉʳ Mars 1734, *Louis-Roger d'Eſtampes*, Marquis d'Eſtampes, Baron de Mauny. Voyez ES-TAMPÉS.

De ſon troiſième mariage, il a eu:

1. PIERRE-JACQUES-LOUIS, qui ſuit;
2. Et MARIE-ANGÉLIQUE-CLAUDINE-HENRIETTE, morte le 10 Août 1760. Elle avoit épouſé, par contrat du 29 Mars 1742, *Charles-Louis d'Argouges*, Marquis de Ranes. Voyez ARGOUGES.

Et de ſon quatrième mariage:
PERONNE, morte le 13 Août 1732.

XII. PIERRE-JACQUES-LOUIS DE BEC-DE-LIÈVRE, Marquis de Cany & de Quevilly, né le 18 Avril 1718, rendit hommage au Roi du Marquiſat de Quevilly, le 7 Août 1743, & mourut le 5 Octobre 1771. Il avoit épouſé, par contrat du 30 Août 1733, *Charlotte de Paulmier-la-Bucaille*, morte le 25 Janvier

Tome II.

1754, fille & héritière de *Pierre*, Seigneur *de Préteval*, & de *Geneviève Marette*, dont il a eu:

1. LOUIS-PIERRE, Comte de Cany, né le 25 Août 1737, Capitaine de Dragons au Régiment de la Reine, en Septembre 1755, Guidon de la Gendarmerie en Août 1759; Sous-Lieutenant du même Corps, & Meſ-tre-de-Camp de Cavalerie par commiſſion du 3 Mars 1762; & mort ſans alliance, le 29 Mai 1767;
2. ANNE-LOUIS-ROGER, qui ſuit;
3. Et HENRIETTE-JEANNE-HÉLIE, née le 14 Novembre 1742, nommée en Décembre 1768, Dame de Compagnie de Madame ADÉLAÏDE DE FRANCE. Elle avoit épouſé, par contrat ſigné le 22 Juillet 1767, *Louis-François*, Vicomte *de Talaru*. Voyez TALARU.

XIII. ANNE-LOUIS-ROGER DE BEC-DE-LIÈ-VRE, dit *le Comte de Cany*, né le 13 Août reçu Chevalier de Malte de minorité , Page du Roi en ſa Petite-Ecurie en on premier Page en 1757, Capitaine agons le 18 Janvier 1760, Guidon de la darmerie en Février 1761, Meſtre-de-Camp de Cavalerie en Février 1770, & Sous-Lieutenant de Gendarmerie en 1771, a épouſé, par contrat ſigné le 18 Juin 1768, *Eliſa-beth-Marie Boutren-d'Hattenville*, Dame de Gros-Menil, fille & héritière de *Jean-François-Marie*, Seigneur d'Hattenville, Conſeiller de Grand'Chambre au Parlement de Rouen, & d'*Eliſabeth-Marie-Françoiſe Boulais*, Dame de Catteville, dont il a:

ARMANDE-LOUISE-MARIE, dite *Mademoiſelle de Cany*, née le 20 Juillet 1769.

BRANCHE
des Seigneurs DE BONNEMARE, *ſortie de celle des Seigneurs* DE QUEVILLY, *Marquis* DE CANY.

VII. FRANÇOIS DE BEC-DE-LIÈVRE, fils puî-né de CHARLES II, Seigneur de Quevilly, & de *Françoiſe Surreau*, ſa première femme, fut Seigneur de Bonnemare, de Farceaux, de Farin & de Villers, par les partages de la ſuc-ceſſion de *Thomas Surreau*, Gentilhomme ordinaire de la Chambre du Roi, ſon oncle maternel, ſuivant les actes du 28 Janvier, & jours ſubſéquens de 1576, & reçut pour par-tage de PIERRE II, Seigneur de Quevilly, ſon frère aîné, en la ſucceſſion de CHARLES leur père, le 19 Décembre 1600, la Seigneurie du Manoir-Segouin; il ſervoit dans la Compagnie du Capitaine Boifdannebourg en 1576; étoit homme d'armes de la Compagnie de François d'Orléans, Marquis de Rothelin, en 1587, & fut Gentilhomme ordinaire de la Chambre du Roi, par lettres de retenue en 1612. Il époufa, en 1580, *Anne Hallé,* fille de *Barthélemy,* Seigneur *de la Haule,* & de *Marie de Clainville,* dont il eut :

1. François, Seigneur de Bonnemare, qui fut d'abord homme d'armes de la Compagnie de M. le Comte de Soiffons en 1611, Gentilhomme ordinaire de la Chambre du Roi, & Capitaine de 100 hommes d'armes de fes Ordonnances en 1622, Capitaine au Régiment de Vardes, & en 1625 en celui de Lefmont. Par Lettres données à Tours le 7 Septembre 1617, le Roi ayant indiqué les Etats à tenir à Rouen, il fut élu Député de la Nobleffe du Bailliage de Gifors, le 6 Novembre 1617, & mourut fans alliance 1625 ;

2. Pierre, Seigneur de Farceaux, q̣̣... du Roi, après la mort de fon frèr̀... çois, la Compagnie d'Infanterie , ... infirmités ne lui permirent pas de ga... & mourut fans alliance;

3. Henri, Prêtre & Curé de Saint-Denis-le-Ferment, devenu Seigneur de Bonnemare , qui céda fesTerres à Jacques, fon frère puîné, en faveur de fon mariage ;

4. Jacques, qui fuit;

5. Anne, morte avant 1626, femme de *Nicolas Boulloche,* Maître des Requêtes de la Reine, mère de Louis XIII ;

6. Et Marie, qui époufa, 1º par contrat du 4 Octobre 1621, *Guillaume de Banaftre,* Seigneur de Routes; & 2º *Jean Coftard,* Seigneur des Ervollus.

VIII. Jacques de Bec-de-Lièvre, Seigneur de Bonnemare, de Farceaux, de Farin & de Villers, Capitaine au Régiment de Lefmont, fur la démiffion de Pierre, fon frère, puis dans celui du Tot en 1637, qu'il fervoit en l'armée commandée par M. le Duc de Longueville, époufa, par contrat du 8 Avril 1643, *Charlotte Allorge,* morte le 17 Septembre 1666, fille de *Georges,* Seigneur de Malicorne, & d'*Elifabeth de Lieuray.* Il en eut :

1. François-Henri, Seigneur de Bonnemare & de Farceaux, Maréchal-des-Logis d'une Compagnie de Chevaux-Légers, mort fans poftérité. Il avoit époufé, par contrat du 2 Décembre 1668, *Florentine Rouault,* fille de *Mathurin,* Seigneur des Rouairies, & de *Florentine de Bonardy;*

2. Georges-François, Seigneur de Villers, Ca-

pitaine de Dragons; mort fans poftérité de *Marguerite de Sainte-Marie d'Agneaux;*

3. Jacques-Philippe, qui fuit;

4. Pierre, Capitaine au Régiment de la Marine, mort fans alliance;

5. Anne-Elisabeth, femme d'*Anne Allorge,* Seigneur de Malicorne ; ils vivoient enfemble en 1669;

6. Et Marie-Catherine, mariée , par contrat du mois de Février 1672, à *Charles du Caron,* Seigneur de Ronfeugère.

IX. Jacques - Philippe, Seigneur de Bonnemare, né le 7 Février 1651, mort le 11 Décembre 1719, époufa, par contrat du 2 Janvier 1675, *Madeleine le Marchand,* fille de *Jacques,* & d'*Anne Tribout,* dont il eut :

X. Jacques - Georges de Bec-de-Lièvre , Seigneur de Bonnemare, né le 3 Novembre 1677, qui fut Lieutenant d'Infanterie au Régiment de Montenay, & mourut le 2 Avril ...7. Il avoit époufé, par contrat du 2 Dé...re 1702, *Françoife de Cacqueray,* fille ...an, Seigneur de Montval, dont il eut :

Jean-Jacques-René, qui fuit ;

2. Pierre - Marie , né le 3 Novembre 1715, Prêtre & Curé d'Ouainville, mort en 1770;

3. Françoise-Hélène, née le 1er Décembre 1704, morte le 14 Décembre 1732. Elle avoit époufé, par contrat du 14 Février 1726, *Louis Martel,* Seigneur de Gravetel, fils de *Louis,* Seigneur de Gravetel, & de *Madeleine de Sainte-Marie;*

4. Et Susanne-Angélique, née le 12 Janvier 1707, mariée, par contrat du 2 Juillet 1729, à *Robert le Mancel,* Seigneur de Secqueville, mort le 16 Août 1730, fils de *Louis Aignean,* Seigneur de Secqueville, & de *Louife de Bellanger.*

XI. Jean-Jacques-René, Seigneur de Bonnemare, né le 15 Mars 1709, Chevalier de Saint-Louis, Capitaine de Cavalerie, par Commiffion du 1er Septembre 1751, Meftre-de-Camp de Cavalerie le 1er Juin 1762, Officier dans la première Compagnie des Moufquetaires de la Garde du Roi.

Les armes : *de fable , à deux croix tréflées au pied fiché d'argent, accompagnées d'une coquille oreillée de même en pointe.* Devife : Hoc tegmine tutus.

(Généalogie dreffée fur titres originaux).

BEC-DE-VILLAINE : *écartelé, aux 1 & 4 d'argent, à trois lions de fable; au franc-quartier de* Caftille *; & aux 2 & 3 de* Léon.

BECARIIS, en Provence : *de gueules, à*

un *taureau furieux d'or; au chef cousu d'a-*
zur, embelli de trois fleurs-de-lys d'or, 2 & 1,
sous un lambel de trois pendans de gueules.

BECART, en Bourgogne : *d'or, à treize*
billettes arrondies par le haut, sommées
d'une aigle éployée de sable.

BECCARIE-DE-PAVIE, en Languedoc.
JEAN DE BECCARIE-DE-PAVIE, Seigneur en 1478
de la Salle-de-Quincieu, au Diocèse de Lyon,
(Terre maintenant possédée depuis long-tems
à titre de Comté par la Maison *de Baglion-*
de-la-Salle), fut fait Conseiller au Parlement
de Toulouse par LOUIS XI en Janvier 1466 ;
& acquit, le 18 Juillet 1497, de *Jean d'Ysal-*
guier, son beau-frère, Seigneur de Sainte-
Livrate, la Baronie de Fourquevaux près
Toulouse. Il s'est toujours qualifié de *Messire*
& de *Chevalier,* & dans les registres du Parlement de Toulouse du 12 Juin 1512, où sa
mort est annoncée; il est qualifié de *Messire*
& de *Chevalier,* titres qui ne se donnoient
jamais alors en Parlement aux simples Conseillers; aussi avoit-il été présenté au Roi en
1495 pour être premier Président, mais sans
succès. Il portoit quelquefois le nom de *Rouer,*
de *Royers* ou de *Roüedis,* qui lui venoit de son
ayeule paternelle, & que son fils & son petit-
fils ont aussi porté quelquefois. Il avoit épousé
Jeanne d'Ysalgier, fille de *Jean,* & de *Cathe-*
rine de Pardaillan. Son fils se nommoit FRAN-
ÇOIS, & son petit-fils RAYMOND. Ce dernier,
connu dans l'Histoire de son tems sous le nom
de Seigneur de Fourquevaux, servit avec
distinction dans de grands Emplois sous cinq
Rois, FRANÇOIS Ier, HENRI II, FRANÇOIS II,
CHARLES IX & HENRI III, au commencement
du règne duquel RAYMOND mourut le 4 Juillet 1574. Il fut Chevalier de l'Ordre du Roi,
son Ambassadeur en Espagne pendant 9 ans,
& Gouverneur de Narbonne. Il épousa *Mar-*
guerite de la Jugie-de-Rieux, fille de *Jac-*
ques de la Jugie, Baron de Rieux en Languedoc, & *d'Antoinette d'Oraison.* Il eut :

    1. CLAUDE, mort jeune;
    2. Et FRANÇOIS, qui suit.

  FRANÇOIS, IIe du nom, mort en 1611, se
maria avec *Marguerite de Chaumeilh,* veuve
d'Antoine du Buisson, Baron de Bournezel,
Sénéchal & Gouverneur de Rouergue. Elle
étoit fille de *François de Chaumeilh,* Seigneur de Caillac, Chevalier de l'Ordre du

Roi, Gouverneur de Boulogne & Boulonnois, & *d'Hélène de Montamat.* Il laissa :

    1. CHARLES, qui n'eut que des filles;
    2. Et FRANÇOIS, qui suit.

  FRANÇOIS, IIIe du nom, qui après la mort
de CHARLES en 1648 recueillit la substitution
que son père lui avoit faite. Il épousa, en
1627, *Foi de Baulac,* fille *d'Arnaud-Guilhem*
de Baulac, Seigneur de la Pomarède & de
la Chapelle en Lomagne, & de *Catherine du*
Gout-du-Bouzet. De ce mariage vint :

  JEAN-BAPTISTE DE BECCARIE-DE-PAVIE, Baron de Fourquevaux, & Seigneur de la Chapelle, en faveur duquel la Baronie de Fourquevaux fut érigée en Marquisat par Lettres-
Patentes du mois de Mars 1687, registrées au
Parlement de Toulouse le 15 Avril 1687, &
en la Cour des Comptes & des Aides de Montpellier le 6 Mars 1688, & dans lesquelles il est
[marqué] que le Roi les accorde, tant en considération de la naissance distinguée de JEAN-
BAPTISTE, qui tire son origine de l'ancienne
famille de BECCARIE en Lombardie, laquelle a
possédé autrefois la souveraine autorité dans
Pavie, qu'en considération des services rendus par ledit JEAN-BAPTISTE & ses ancêtres
depuis leur établissement en France, services
qui sont marqués en détail de degré en degré.
Il fut marié, par contrat du 9 Août 1664, avec
Marie-Gabrielle de Mauléon-de-Foix, fille
de *Paul,* Vicomte de Couserans, & de *Marie*
de Clary, dont il eut :

  PAUL-GABRIEL DE BECCARIE-DE-PAVIE, qui,
après avoir été Page de la Chambre, Mousquetaire, Capitaine de Cavalerie dans Noailles-
Duc, Capitaine de Carabiniers, & enfin Mestre-de-Camp d'un Régiment de Cavalerie de
son nom, & s'être beaucoup distingué au service, mourut à Strasbourg le 31 Octobre 1704,
âgé de 38 ans, des blessures qu'il avoit reçues
à la bataille d'Hochstett, où il étoit à la tête de
son Régiment dans l'Armée de M. le Maréchal
de Marcin. Il épousa, le 1er Novembre 1692
Marie de Prohenques, fille de *Guillaume de*
Prohenques, Conseiller au Parlement de Toulouse, & de *Catherine de Rudelle.* Il laissa :

    1. JEAN-BAPTISTE-RAYMOND, Ecclésiastique;
    2. FRANÇOIS-DENIS-CHARLES-GABRIEL, qui suit;
    3. MARIE-GABRIELLE, veuve de *Clément-Julien*
       de Sede, Baron de Lioux ;
    4. Et LOUISE-HÉLÈNE, mariée, le 20 Mai 1740,
       à *Michel-Jean-André de Saint-Félix,* Ba-
       ron de Mauremont, mort.

FRANÇOIS-DENIS-CHARLES-GABRIEL DE BEC-CARIE-DE-PAVIE, Marquis de Fourquevaux, Seigneur de la Chapelle, &c., fut marié, 1º le 1er Mars 1722, avec *Henriette de Caftellan*, morte le 2 Janvier 1752, fille de *Jean-Bap-tifte de Caftellan*, Confeiller au Parlement de Touloufe, & de *Marie de Bourguine-de-Boiffet*; & 2º le 6 Novembre 1754, avec *Cé-cile-Rofe-Colombe de Guy*, veuve de *Louis-François de Rangueil*, & fille de *Jean-Ga-briel de Guy*, Seigneur de Pompertufat. De fa première femme font iffus :

1. JEAN-LOUIS-GABRIEL-BASILE, Marquis de Fourquevaux, né le 14 Juin 1726, Mouf-quetaire du Roi dans la feconde Compa-gnie ;
2. MARIE-JEANNE-THÉRÈSE, née le 18 Janvier 1722 ;
3. Et MARIE-ANGÉLIQUE-FÉLICITÉ, née le 4 Février 1737.

Les armes : *vairé d'or & de finople, &c.*, telé de gueules à l'aigle d'or éployée, à deux têtes couronnées de même à l'antique, &. ayant fur l'eftomac une aigle de fable auffi éployée, à deux têtes couronnées.*

Cette aigle d'or en champ de gueules, &c., dont font écartelées les armes de BECCARIE-DE-PAVIE, vient d'une conceffion faite à Venife le 5 Mars 1403 par l'Empereur MANUEL PALÉO-LOGUE, à CHASTELAIN DE BECCARIE-DE-PAVIE, dont le Marquis de Fourquevaux a un titre authentique, qui a été communiqué à M. d'Hozier, & dont il a donné un extrait en fon reg. II, au commencement de l'article de BEC-CARIE.

Il y a eu à Pavie, dans le Duché de Milan, une famille du nom de BECCARIE, qui avoit même poffédé la fouveraineté de cette ville, avant qu'elle tombât fous la domination des Ducs de Milan, qui, foit avant cet évènement, foit depuis, joignoit quelquefois à fon nom celui de la ville, comme une marque de fes droits. Sur la fin du XVIe fiècle & au commen-cement du XVIIe, on voyoit encore en diffé-rens lieux des monumens de fa grandeur.

BECEL, en Picardie. JACQUES DE BECEL, Sieur de Pulmont, ci-devant Capitaine dans le Régiment d'Oléron, fut maintenu dans fa nobleffe par Ordonnance de M. *Bignon*, Con-feiller d'Etat, & Commiffaire départi dans la Généralité d'Amiens, du 28 Mai 1701. (Voyez *Armorial de France*, reg. I, part. I, p. 58).

Les armes : *d'azur, au chevron d'or, ac-compagné de trois cygnes d'argent*, 2 en chef & 1 en pointe.*

BECEREL, en Breffe. GUY, Seigneur DE BECEREL, Chevalier, vivant l'an 1270, eut de *Marguerite* :

1. ROBERT, qui fuit ;
2. Et JEANNETTE, femme, en 1317, d'*Etienne*, Seigneur *de la Teffonnière*.

ROBERT, Seigneur DE BECEREL, Chevalier, vivoit en 1300, & laiffa de fon époufe, dont le nom ne nous eft pas connu :

1. GEOFFROY, qui fuit ;
2. JEAN, Damoifeau en 1320 ;
3. Et PIERRE, auffi Damoifeau.

GEOFFROY, Seigneur DE BECEREL, Chevalier, le Vendredi 18 Novembre 1323, fit homma-ge au Comte de Savoie de ce qu'il tenoit en fief de lui à caufe de Bourg. Il époufa *Gui-charde de Beyniers*, fille de *Ponce de Bey-niers*, Damoifeau, de laquelle fortirent :

1. HUGONIN, qui fuit ;
2. JEAN, Prêtre & Curé d'Attigna en 1365 ;
3. PIERRE, Damoifeau, qui laiffa FRANÇOISE DE BECEREL, mariée, 1º l'an 1361, avec *Jean de Chandée*, Damoifeau ; & 2º l'an 1364, avec *Pierre du Saix*, Seigneur de Barbarel, en Dombes ;
4. Et GUILLEMETTE, morte fille.

HUGONIN, Seigneur DE BECEREL, Chevalier, époufa, le Dimanche après la Saint-Vincent 1327, *Guicharde de Rogemont*, fille d'*Etien-ne de Rogemont*, & d'*Ifabelle de Maforna*, dont :

1. JEAN, qui fuit ;
2. Et GUICHARDE, femme d'*Othelix*, Seigneur de Beyniers, dont elle étoit veuve l'an 1387.

JEAN, Seigneur DE BECEREL, de Marlia, &c., époufa, le 5 Août 1353, *Catherine de Chan-dée*, Dame de Vaux, fille de *Hugues de Chandée*, Seigneur de Montfalcon, & de *Jean-nette de Châtillon*. Leurs enfans furent :

1. PIERRE, qui fuit ;
2. GUICHARDE, mariée, le 2 Avril 1386, à *Pier-re de Saint-Sulpis*, Seigneur de la Poype.

PIERRE, Seigneur DE BECEREL, Marlia & Vaux, époufa, le 9 Juillet 1398, *Ifabelle de Marmont*, fille d'*Hugonin*, Seigneur de Marmont, & d'*Eléonore de Vienne*. Il en eut :

1. CLAUDE, qui fuit ;
2. HUGONIN, Co-Seigneur de Marlia, mort fans lignée l'an 1470 ;
3. Et FRANÇOIS, mort jeune.

CLAUDE DE BECEREL, Seigneur de Marlia, de Vaux & de Malatrait, tefta le 18 Mars 1481. Il avoit époufé, le 1ᵉʳ Octobre 1447, *Marguerite de Berchod*, fille de *Jean de Berchod*, Seigneur de Malatrait, & d'*Aimée de Seyturier*. Il eut :

1. GUILLAUME, Damoifeau, mort fans lignée ;
2. PIERRE, qui fuit ;
3. JEAN, Religieux & Grand-Vicaire à Saint-Claude ;
4. JEAN, dit *le jeune;*
5. & 6. JEANNE & FRANÇOISE.

PIERRE DE BECEREL, IIᵉ du nom, Seigneur de Marlia, de Vaux & de Malatrait, époufa, le 22 Mai 1522, *Philiberte d'Oncieux*, veuve d'*Aimé de Berchod*, Co-Seigneur de Malatrait, & fille de *Philippe d'Oncieux*, Seigneur de Montiernos, & de *Jacqueline de Montfonnent*, dont :

1. CLAUDE, qui fuit ;
2. CLAUDINE, morte fille ;
3. Et JEANNE, Religieufe à Neufville.

CLAUDE DE BECEREL, IIᵉ du nom, Seigneur de Marlia, de Vaux & de Malatrait, tefta le 5 Novembre 1577. Il avoit époufé, le 12 Septembre 1560, *Louife de la Gellière*, Dame de la Baftie, en Breffe, morte en 1593, après s'être remariée à *Claude de Chabeu*, Seigneur de Becerel, fils de *Jean de Chabeu*, Seigneur de Becerel, & de *Françoife de Sivria*. Elle étoit fille de *Claude de la Gellière*, Seigneur de Cornaton, & de *Jacqueline de Rogemont*. Les enfans de fon premier mariage furent :

1. RENÉ, qui fuit ;
2. FRANÇOIS, Seigneur de *Marlia*, auteur d'une branche rapportée ci-après;
3. LOUIS, Seigneur de Colonges, mort jeune ;
4. PHILIBERT, mort auffi jeune ;
5. LAURENCE, femme de *Claude*, Seigneur de *Noblens;*
6. ISABEAU, religieufe à Sainte-Claire de Bourg, en Breffe ;
7. MARIE, femme de *Jean-François de Candie*, Seigneur de Loefe ;
8. 9. & 10. JEANNE, CLAUDINE & ANNE, mortes fans alliance;
11. & 12. FRANÇOISE & LOUISE, Religieufes à Neufville.

RENÉ DE BECEREL, Seigneur de Malatrait, époufa 1° *Jacqueline Roffel*, & 2° *Antoinette de la Cons*, remariée au Sieur *de Santereau du Fay*, en Dauphiné. Elle étoit fille de *François de la Cons*, Seigneur de Genoft, & de

Claudine d'Oncieux. Il eut de fa première femme :

1. MATHIEU, qui fuit;
2. CLAUDE, Religieux d'Ambronay ;
3. CLAUDINE, femme d'*Aimé-Aymon de Montefpin*, Seigneur de la Beynière;
4. Et CHARLOTTE, femme d'*Aimé de la Griffonnière*, Co-Seigneur de Pirajoux.

MATHIEU DE BECEREL, Seigneur de Malatrait, époufa *N..... de Pauyot*, fille de *François de Pauyot*, Seigneur de Ferrières, Grand-Prévôt de Breffe, Bugey, Valromey & Gex, & d'*Anne Druays de Franclieu*, dont il eut :

1. & 2. THOMAS & CHARLES;
3. Et CHARLOTTE.

BRANCHE
des Seigneurs DE MARLIA.

FRANÇOIS DE BECEREL, Seigneur de Marlia, deuxième fils de CLAUDE DE BECEREL, IIᵉ du nom, Seigneur de Marlia, & de *Louife de la Gellière*. Il époufa, par difpenfe du Pape, le 26 Janvier 1588, *Huguette d'Oncieux*, fa parente, fille de *Charles d'Oncieux*, Seigneur de Montiernos, & de *Claudine de Lugny*. De ce mariage fortirent :

1. CLAUDE, qui fuit ;
2. CHARLES, Seigneur de la Baftie en Breffe, Chanoine, Prevôt, puis Sacriftain en l'Eglife & Comté de Lyon, & Chanoine de Saint-Pierre de Mâcon ;
3. Et LOUISE, mariée à *Jules-Céfar des Amarots*, Gentilhomme Mantouan, Seigneur des Granges, dont *Claude-François*, Religieux de l'Ordre de Saint-Ruf; *Jacques*, Enfeigne au Régiment d'Enghien ; *Philippe*, Enfeigne au Régiment de Lyonnois; *Humbert-Louis*, Religieux du même Ordre de Saint-Ruf; *Charlotte*, Religieufe à Sainte-Urfule de Châtillon; & *Lucrèce*.

CLAUDE DE BECEREL, IIIᵉ du nom, Seigneur de Marlia, la Baftie, Vaux & Colonges, tefta le 12 Février 1625. Il avoit époufé, le 25 Juin 1618, *Philiberte de Teney*, fille de *Marc de Teney*, Baron de Montaney, & de *Philiberte du Molard*. Il laiffa :

1. CLAUDINE-FRANÇOISE, Religieufe à Sainte-Marie de Bourg ;
2. HUGUETTE, femme de *Claude Damas*, Seigneur du Rouffet ;
3. Et PHILIBERTE, mariée, le 6 Juin 1647, à *Louis d'Hoftun*, dit *de Gadagne*, Comte de Verdun, fils de *Balthafard d'Hoftun*, dit

de Gadagne, Marquis de la Baune, & de *Françoife de Tournon*.

Les armes : *d'argent, à la bande de gueules, chargée de trois quinte-feuilles d'argent.*

* BECHAMEIL. La Seigneurie de Nointel, en Soiffonnois, fut érigée en Marquifat, par Lettres du mois d'Octobre 1691, enregiftrées le 12 Novembre fuivant, en faveur de Louis de Bechameil, Marquis de Nointel, Surintendant des Maifons, Domaine & Finance de feu Philippe, fils de France, Duc d'Orléans, mort le 4 Mars 1703, laiffant de *Marie Colbert*, décédée le 3 Avril 1686 :

Marie-Louise de Bechameil, morte à Paris le 2 Avril 1740, âgée de 79 ans. Elle avoit époufé, au mois d'Avril 1692, *Artus-Timoléon-Louis de Coffé*, Duc de Briffac, mort le 2 Juillet 1701. Voyez COSSÉ-BRISSAC.

Les armes : *d'azur, au chevron d'or, accompagné de trois palmes de même, deux en chef & une en pointe.*

BECHET : *de gueules, au fautoir d'or, accompagné de trois croifettes d'azur de l'un en l'autre en pointe, accoftées de deux étoiles d'or.*

BECHET : *d'argent, au chevron de gueules, accompagné en chef de deux étoiles d'azur, & en pointe d'un arbre de finople ; au chef d'azur, chargé de trois croiffans du champ.*

BECHEVEL, Sieur du Caftel, ancienne Nobleffe, Election de Vire, en Normandie, qui porte : *de gueules, à trois quinte-feuilles d'argent, 2 en chef & 1 en pointe.*

⚜ BECK (de), proche de Tarare, dans le Lyonnois. Adrien de Beck, Seigneur de la Motte Saint-Vincent, de Boiffet, de la Cour, du Crozet, de la Buffière, du Rouget, de Gauthier & d'Olivier, reçut du Roi Charles IX, une lettre de 1570, confervée dans la famille, & qui eft remplie de témoignages d'une affection toute particulière, par laquelle ce Prince lui demandoit une de fes filles, pour être Fille d'honneur de la Reine.

La Cour des Aides de Paris rendit en faveur d'Adrien, le 23 Mars 1565, un Arrêt contre la ville de Tarare, qui avoit voulu l'inquiéter au fujet des biens qu'il poffédoit du chef de fa mère près cette Ville, entre'autres

la Terre & le Château de la Buffière, dont il portoit le nom, & où il réfidoit par préférence au Château de Roâne en Lyonnois, qui étoit de tems immémorial la réfidence de fes ancêtres. On trouve dans cet Arrêt un précis de l'inventaire de la production faite par Adrien, contenant quantité d'actes qui fourniffoient la preuve, que fes auteurs, dès le tems de fon cinquième ayeul, jouiffoient des dénominations, titres, honneurs & prérogatives qui n'étoient accordés qu'aux anciens Nobles, & qui conftatoient la nobleffe de fes ancêtres, & fa filiation jufqu'à Hugues de Beck, fon cinquième ayeul, avec les commiffions, tant pour lui que pour fes auteurs, mandemens, certificats de fervices militaires & ambaffades, Lettres d'Etat & Ordonnances, conceffions & Bulles des Papes, une entr'autres de 1484, qui agrée tel Confeffeur que voudra choifir Jean de Beck, Seigneur de la Motte, grand-père d'Adrien.

C'étoit fous le Roi Philippe de Valois que vivoit Hugues de Beck, qui dès-lors avec Geoffroy de Beck, fon coufin, chef d'une autre branche éteinte peu après, étoit Co-Seigneur de la Terre de la Motte-Saint-Vincent ; & il rendit avec lui la foi & hommage à la manière des nobles pour cette Seigneurie aux anciens Comtes de *Beaujeu*, à caufe de leur Seigneurie de Perreux.

Alphonse, fils de Hugues, en rendit auffi hommage à *Edouard*, dernier de ces anciens Comtes de Beaujeu, le 8 Juillet 1396.

Jean de Beck, Ier du nom, fon fils aîné, rendit le même hommage le 16 Février 1409, à Louis II, Duc de Bourbon, Sire de Beaujeu, & il époufa *Anceline de Saint-Romain-de-Valorge*, dont il eut :

Jean de Beck, IIe du nom, Seigneur de la Motte-Saint-Vincent, qui obtint, en 1484, une Bulle du Pape pour choifir tel Confeffeur qu'il voudroit. Il fut marié à *Marguerite de Saint-Prieft*, de laquelle il eut pour fils aîné :

Gilbert, qui fuit ;
Et N.... de Beck, femme de *Guichard du Vernay* (le dernier d'une ancienne Maifon du Beaujolois, qui portoit : *d'hermines, au chef de gueules,*) dont elle n'eut point d'enfans, ce qui fit paffer à la femme de Gilbert, fon frère, & à fes enfans, tous les biens des *du Vernay*, à qui une héritière venoit d'apporter le château & les biens de l'ancienne Maifon de *la Buffière*, & une au-

tre, peu auparavant ceux de *Dalmas-Bon-tevrault*.

GILBERT DE BECK, Seigneur de la Motte-Saint-Vincent, &c., époufa *N... du Vernay*, fœur de *Guichard du Vernay*, dont vinrent :

ADRIEN, qui fuit ;

Et LOUISE DE BECK, mariée à *Jean de Fornillon*, Seigneur de Butherg & de l'Efpinaffe, Maifon du Beaujolois, encore exiftante.

ADRIEN DE BECK, Seigneur de la Motte-Saint-Vincent, de Boiffet, de la Cour, du Crozet, de la Buffière, du Rouget, de Gauthier & d'Olivier, le même dont nous avons parlé au commencement de cet article, fe diftingua à la Cour & dans les Armées, fe trouva au fiège d'Amiens, lorfque cette ville fut prife en 1597, fur les Efpagnols, par HENRI IV ; & dès l'an 1587, il étoit un des Commandans de l'arrière-ban. Il époufa *Françoife de Vaurion*, dont il eut :

1. PIERRE, mort fans poftérité, de *Blanche Pelot*, fille d'un Tréforier de France ;
2. CLAUDE, qui fuit ;
3. RENAUD, Chevalier de Malte, Commandeur de Montbrifon ;
4. JEAN-BAPTISTE, tige de la branche de *la Valfonnière*, rapportée ci-après ;
5. LOUISE, mariée à *Jean du Says*, Seigneur de Tharvé, Maifon éteinte depuis peu ;
6. « Et MARIE DE BECK, femme de *Jean Gletain*, de laquelle il n'eut point d'enfans. »

CLAUDE DE BECK, fervit fous le Connétable de Lefdiguières. Il eut d'abord une Compagnie dans le Régiment de Saint-Chaumont, enfuite dans celui de Villeroy, dont il fut auffi Commandant, & fut fait Chevalier de l'Ordre du Roi. Il abandonna la Terre & le Château de la Buffière à la famille de la veuve de fon frère PIERRE, pour fes reprifes, & il reprit le nom *de la Motte*, comme fes ayeux. Il époufa *Léonore de Chevriers-Saint-Mauris*, & en eut :

1. CLAUDE-FRANÇOIS, qui fuit ;
2. LÉONARD, mort Chanoine de Saint-Claude ;
3. Et ANTOINETTE DE BECK, morte Chanoineffe à Villeneuve-les-Dames, en Breffe.

CLAUDE-FRANÇOIS DE BECK, *de la Motte-Saint-Vincent*, époufa, *Charlotte*, fille de *Pierre de Gelas-Lautrec*, Chevalier de l'Ordre du Roi, & fon Gentilhomme ordinaire. Elle lui apporta entr'autres la Baronie de Céfan en Savoie, qui fut échangée contre la terre de Sainte-Hilaire, par fon fils unique :

LOUIS DE BECK, *de la Motte-Saint-Vincent*, qui fervit dans le Régiment du Perche, & époufa *Elifabeth de la Mure*, Dame de Champlong, près Roanne, qu'elle lui apporta en dot. Il en eut :

Deux fils, Officiers d'Infanterie, tués, l'un à la bataille de Parme en 1734 ; l'autre à la bataille de Guaftalle le 19 Septembre 1734 ;

Et une fille, élevée à Saint-Cyr, fous le nom de *Mademoifelle de Saint-Vincent*, veuve 1º *d'Anne de Chanzey*, à Renaifon, fur la côte Saint-André, près Roanne ; & 2º de *N... de Rochefort*, Seigneur de Beauvoir en Forez, de la branche d'*Epercienne*, dont elle a deux fils, Officiers d'Infanterie en 1772.

BRANCHE
DE LA VALSONNIÈRE.

JEAN-BAPTISTE DE BECK, Iᵉʳ du nom, quatrième fils d'ADRIEN, & de *Françoife de Vaurion*, époufa *Andrée*, fœur de *Jean-Gletain de Chavane*, Seigneur de la Valfonnière, par fa mère *Marguerite de Valenciennes*, lequel, *Jean Gletain*, époufa en même tems, MARIE, fœur de JEAN-BAPTISTE DE BECK, Iᵉʳ du nom, dont il n'eut point d'enfans, ce qui fit paffer la terre de la Valfonnière à fa fœur, & aux enfans de ce JEAN-BAPTISTE DE BECK, fçavoir :

1. JEAN-BAPTISTE, qui fuit ;
2. Et BALTHASAR DE BECK, Seigneur *du Crozet*, auteur de la branche des Seigneurs de ce nom, éteinte après trois générations.

JEAN-BAPTISTE DE BECK, IIº du nom, époufa *Catherine de Ratton*, fœur de la Marquife d'Apchon-de-Saint-André, mère de la Marquife de Saint-Georges, dont :

1. CAMILLE, qui fuit ;
2. CHRISTOPHE, mort Procureur à la Chartreufe de Sainte-Croix, près le Puy, en Velay, après avoir été Capitaine au Régiment de Lyonnois ;
3. Et MARIE DE BECK, morte fans alliance, dans un âge fort avancé.

CAMILLE DE BECK, Chevalier, Seigneur de la Valfonnière & d'Avergne en Lyonnois, de la Cofte, & de Fontville en Beaujolois, ancien Capitaine, & Major au Régiment de Lyonnois, fut tenu fur les fonts de baptême, par le grand Camille de Villeroy, Archevêque de Lyon. Il époufa *Marie-Anne de Saint-Prieft*. Voyez SAINT-PRIEST. De ce mariage font nés :

1. THOMAS-FRANÇOIS, Seigneur de la Valfonnière, &c., qui époufa 1º *Marie*, fille de

N... Philippon, Tréforier de France; & 2º *N... de Faure,* Dame de Saint-Sylveftre, fœur du Marquis de Satilleu en Vivarais. Il a eu du premier lit plufieurs enfans, dont il ne refte qu'une fille, Religieufe Carmélite à Lyon ; & du fecond lit, il n'a eu qu'une fille unique, morte jeune;

2. ANTOINE, qui fuit ;
3. MARIE-ANNE, fœur jumelle d'ANTOINE, nommée par le Roi, Abbeffe de Saint-Jean-le-Grand d'Autun, ordre de Saint-Benoît, en Août 1749, ci-devant Religieufe de l'Abbaye de Saint-Pierre, à Lyon;
4. Et ANTOINETTE-MARIE DE BECK, alliée à *Antoine-Marie du Creft-de-Montigny,* Seigneur du Moufleaux, près de Saint-Gengoux, ci-devant Lieutenant du Régiment de Saintonge. Voyez CRESTₑ (DU).

ANTOINE DE BECK, devenu Seigneur de la Valfonnière, &c., par la mort de fon frère, a été Garde du Roi dans la Compagnie de Villeroy , & s'eft appelé *le Chevalier de Beck,* jufqu'à fon mariage, contracté en 1743, avec *Marie-Anne Maffe,* fille de *Pierre Maffe,* Maître particulier des Eaux & Forêts du Duché d'Aumale, & de *Marie-Anne Ferrette,* d'une ancienne Maifon d'Alface. Voyez MASSE. Il a eu de ce mariage :

MARIE-ANNE-CAMILLE & PIERRETTE-THOMAS.

Les armes: *d'argent, à une aigle à deux têtes de fable, becquée & armée d'or.* Comme cette aigle eft très-commune en Allemagne, elle paroît appuyer une tradition conftamment foutenue, fuivant laquelle cette Maifon eft originaire d'Allemagne , & une branche Allemande de ce nom, originaire de Danemark. Les preuves de nobleffe de cette famille ont été produites deux fois au Juge d'armes de France, la première vers 1720, pour Madame de *Rochefort,* connue à Saint-Cyr fous le nom de *Mademoifelle de Saint-Vincent;* la feconde en 1766, comme nous l'avons vu par une lettre écrite le 21 Mars de la même année, par le Juge d'armes de France, père de Meffieurs d'Hozier d'aujourd'hui , à M. DE BECK, demeurant à Bonneftable, lequel nous a fait paffer cet extrait généalogique avec ceux du *Crefte,* de *Maffe,* en Provence, & des anciens Marquis de *Saint-Prieft* en Forez.

BECQUEL, Seigneur du Mesle, en Normandie, Généralité de Rouen , famille maintenue dans fa Nobleffe le 2 Janvier 1668.

BECTOZ, en Dauphiné: *d'azur, au chef*

d'argent, chargé de trois têtes d'aigles arrachées de fable & lampaffées de gueules.

* BEDEILLES, petite Souveraineté dans le Béarn, qui appartenoit à la Maifon d'*Albret-Moiffens,* d'où elle a paffé, en 1692, à *Charles de Lorraine,* Comte de Marfan, par la donation que lui en fit fa première femme, *Marie d'Albret,* la dernière de fa Maifon. Voyez MARSAN.

BEDEL (LE), Seigneur des Londes, Election de Caen en Normandie, famille annoblie aux francs-fiefs, dont les armes font: *d'azur, au chevron d'argent, chargé de trois tourteaux de fable, & accompagné de trois glands d'or, 2 en chef & 1 en pointe.*

BEDEY (LE), Sieur d'Arnelles, Election de Bayeux, en Baffe-Normandie, famille annoblie en 1598, dont les armes font: *d'azur, à trois lofanges d'argent, 2 & 1, au chef coufu de gueules, chargé de trois rofes d'argent.*

BEDFORT. Le Duc de BEDFORT, arrivé à Paris le 12 Septembre 1762, a eu fon audience le 17 en qualité de Miniftre Plénipotentiaire d'Angleterre, & a figné le 3 Novembre, les Articles préliminaires de la Paix.

BEDONNIÈRE : *d'azur, à fix billettes d'argent, chargées chacune d'une autre billette du champ.*

* BEDUER, en Quercy, Diocèfe de Cahors, Terre & Seigneurie qui appartenoit à *Jean de Narbonnès,* Baron de Puylaunès, lequel en fit donation à fa veuve *Jeanne de Luzech,* qui fe remaria à *François-Louis de Loftanges de Saint-Alvaire,* Colonel d'un Régiment d'Infanterie, en faveur duquel cette Terre fut érigée en Vicomté l'an 1610.

BÉER, en Flandres. JEAN DE BÉER, IIᵉ du nom, Chevalier, Seigneur de Merchen, de Gramene & de Lendelé, Secrétaire & Audiencier de CHARLES-le-Hardi, Duc de Bourgogne, & Commiffaire au renouvellement des Magiftrats de Gand, en 1488, fils de JEAN DE BÉER & de *Marguerite de Dixmude,* époufa 1º *Marguerite de Baenft;* & 2º *Cornélie de Veyfe,* héritière de la Terre de Meulebecke. Il eut de cette alliance:

PHILIPPE DE BÉER, Seigneur de Meulebecke, mort en 1526, laiffant de *Marie Vanheurne,* décédée en 1520.

CHARLES DE BÉER, mort en 1578, ayant été marié, en 1548, à *Jacqueline de Gros,* Dame de Beaudignies, & de la Chapelle, décédée en 1559, dont:

JEAN DE BÉER, mort en 1608, premier Bourgmeftre de Bruges. Il avoit épousé 1° *Anne Vandert-Gracht;* & 2° *Roberte d'Aubremont,* fille de *Pontus,* Seigneur du Quefnoi, & de *Madeleine de Borchove,* de laquelle vint:

ADRIEN DE BÉER, Seigneur de Meulebecke, Grand-Bailli de Courtrai, mort en 1627. Il avoit été marié, en 1612, à *Agnès d'Aubremont,* fa coufine, décédée en 1644, mère de:

NICOLAS-IGNACE DE BÉER, Colonel au fervice d'Efpagne, Grand-Bailli de Gand, en faveur duquel la Terre de Meulebecke fut érigée en Baronie, par Lettres du Roi Catholique, du.... 1655. Il avoit épousé, en 1649, *Anne-Marie Caluwaer*, Dame de Zeveren, de laquelle il eut:

GASPARD-IGNACE, Baron de Meulebecke, Seigneur de Zeveren, mort en 1728, qui, de *Catherine Morrhe,* décédée en 1701, a laiffé:

1. GASPARD-ROBERT-FRANÇOIS, qui fuit;
2. Et PHILIPPE-JOSEPH, dont la poftérité fera rapportée après celle de fon aîné.

GASPARD-ROBERT-FRANÇOIS DE BÉER, Baron de Meulebecke, Capitaine de Cavalerie, époufa, en 1706, *Françoife-Camille d'Ennetières,* morte en 1745, fille de *Jacques-Hippolyte,* Marquis des Mottes, de laquelle font fortis:

1. GASPARD, mort fans avoir eu d'alliance;
2. JEAN-JOSEPH, Chanoine d'Herlebeke;
3. PHILIPPE-ALEXANDRE, Baron de Béer & de Meulebecke, marié, 1° en 1732, à *Marie-Sivine de Béer,* fa coufine germaine, morte en 1741, fans enfans; 2° à *Charlotte,* fille de *N...,* Baron d'*Overfchie,* & 3° à *N....* de *Venderhem,* fille d'*Hermann,* Baron de Venderhem & de Nederftin. Il n'a point eu d'enfans de ces trois femmes;
4. PIERRE-CHARLES, Capitaine aux Gardes Wallones en Efpagne;
5. LIVINE-HIPPOLYTE, Dame de Morfelle, mariée à *Nicolas de Lens,* Seigneur d'Oyeghem, Maréchal héréditaire de Weft-Flandres;
6. Et MARIE-HYACINTHE DE BÉER, alliée à *Nicolas-Jofeph de Viefteren,* Baron de Laerne.

PHILIPPE-JOSEPH DE BÉER, fecond fils de GASPARD-IGNACE, & de *Catherine Morrhe,* fut Seigneur de Zeveren & de Beveren. Il mourut en 1746. Il avoit épousé 1° *Marie-Anne*

d'Overloop; & 2° en 1722, *Jeanne-Régine Pullaert.* Il a eu du premier lit:

1. MARIE-LIVINE DE BÉER, morte en 1741, femme de *Philippe-Alexandre,* Baron de Béer, fon coufin germain;
2. MARIE-CAMILLE DE BÉER, morte en 1743. Elle avoit époufé, en 1734, *Charles-Jofeph,* Comte de *Lalain* & de *Tildonck,* Chambellan de l'Empereur, qui en a eu *Maximilien,* Comte de *Lalain,* Page de l'Impératrice-Reine.

Du fecond lit il a eu:

3. JEAN-FRANÇOIS DE BÉER;
4. MARIE-RÉGINE, mariée, en 1751, à *François-Antoine,* fils de *Gébard,* Baron de *Plotho,* d'Ingelmunfter & de l'Empire;
5. Et JEANNE-JOSÈPHE DE BÉER, non mariée en 1756. (*Tab. Généal.,* part. VIII, pag. 431.)

BEFFROY, en Champagne: *de fable, au lion d'argent, armé & lampaffé de gueules.*

◊ BÉGACZON, ou BÉGASSON, fuivant les titres, au Diocèfe de Saint-Malo en Bretagne. La généalogie de cette ancienne nobleffe, qui fe trouve dans l'*Armorial de France,* reg. II, part. I, remonte par filiation fuivie à

I. MARQUIS DE BÉGACZON, frère juveigneur & germain de père & de mère de PERROT DE BÉGACZON, qui, comme aîné, lui avoit donné plufieurs héritages, & entr'autres chofes l'hébergement de Bégaczon, fans compter quelques rentes que MARQUIS DE BÉGACZON avoit retirées pour fon droit de *prefmerie* (vieux mot de pratique qui fignifie parenté ou proximité, &, qui, felon Mefnage, vient du latin *proximus,* le plus proche.) Il époufa *Jeanne de Brignac,* d'une nobleffe des plus anciennes de la province, dont vint:

II. JEAN DE BÉGACZON-DE-LA-COMBE, Ier du nom, mentionné dans une tranfaction de 1430, paffée en la Cour de Ploermel, avec THIBAUT DE BÉGACZON, fon parent. Il étoit mort en 1446, & laiffa:

III. JEAN DE BÉGACZON, IIe du nom, qui rendit le 31 Août 1497, à Jean, Sire de Rieux, aveu du moulin à eau de Bégaczon, fis fur la rivière de Cleix, & mouvant en fief de la Terre & jurifdiction de Rieux. Il eut:

IV. JEAN DE BÉGACZON, IIIe du nom, qualifié *Noble & Ecuyer,* Seigneur de Bégaczon, dans un titre du 12 Juin 1509, paffé fous les fceaux de la Cour de Maleftroit. LOUIS XII, Souverain Duc de Bretagne, lui accorda, le

28 Août 1512, des Lettres-Royaux qui le maintinrent dans la possession de sa maison de Bégaczon. Il mourut le 9 Avril 1532. Il avoit épousé *Jeanne de Couldebouc*, dont il eut :

1. JEAN, qui suit ;
2. OLIVIER, tige de la branche des Seigneurs des *Métairies* & de *la Villeguichart*, rapportée ci-après ;
3. Et SUSANNE-SIMONE DE BÉGACZON, aînée de ses frères, mariée au Seigneur de *la Morinaie*, du surnom *du Bochschet*, d'une famille noble & ancienne.

V. JEAN DE BÉGACZON, IVᵉ du nom, Ecuyer, Seigneur de Bégaczon, ayant perdu sa mère & tutrice, fut remis sous la tutelle d'Yvon Bugault, Seigneur de Trebedan, qui, le 24 Septembre 1534, rendit aveu pour son pupille, des manoir & hébergement de Begaczon mouvans à foi & hommage des Terres, juridiction & Seigneurie de Rochefort, à Claude, Sire de Rieux. Il fut encore ensuite sous la tutelle de SUSANNE-SIMONE DE BÉGACZON, sa sœur ; rendit lui-même personnellement aveu, le 18 Avril 1554, à Guy, Comte de Laval, Marquis de Nesle, & étoit mort le 2 Novembre 1565. Il avoit épousé 1º *Péronelle de la Haye*, fille de *Jean*, & de *Françoise Cancouet*, tous deux d'une famille dont l'ancienneté est connue dans la Province ; & 2º le 7 Mai 1555, *Jacquette le Coutellier*, fille de *François*, Seigneur de Brossay, & de *Jeanne de Lieurre*. Il eut du premier lit :

1. PÉRONELLE DE BÉGACZON, accordée du vivant de son père, le 14 Juin 1561, avec *Julien Michel*, Ecuyer, Sieur de la Haye en Reignac.

Du second lit vinrent :

2. JEAN, qui suit ;
3. Et JUDITH DE BÉGACZON, morte sans enfans.

VI. JEAN DE BÉGACZON, Vᵉ du nom, Ecuyer, Seigneur dudit lieu & de la Herbelinaie, étant resté en bas âge, fut, avec JUDITH, sa sœur, mis sous la tutelle de leur mère, le 3 Novembre 1565, par sentence de la Cour & juridiction de Rochefort, & le 9 Février 1566, elle rendit aveu des manoir & hébergement de Bégaczon à Guy, Comte de Laval, puis de Rochefort. Il passa ensuite sous l'administration d'OLIVIER DE BÉGASSON, son oncle, qui, en qualité de curateur, paraît deux fois avec *Jacquette le Coutellier*, le 7 Juillet 1573 & le 22 Avril 1575. Le premier acte qu'on ait

de sa majorité fut un aveu qu'il rendit de sa maison de Bégasson, le 23 Juillet 1583, à François de Coligny, Sire de Rieux, où il déclara que cette maison & les autres héritages lui étoient échus par le décès de JEAN, son père, duquel il étoit héritier principal & noble. Il étoit mort le 7 Avril 1599. Il avoit épousé 1º *Julienne Robitel*, fille de *Guillaume*, Sieur de la Herbelinaie, & de *Françoise le Berruyer* ; & 2º *Julienne-Perrine Bouan*, de la Maison du *Tertre*-en-Pleucadeuc. Il laissa du premier lit :

1. JEAN, qui suit ;

Du second lit vint :

2. MADELEINE DE BÉGASSON, mariée, le 30 Juin 1607, à *Alain Couillé*, Ecuyer, Sieur du Vivier.

VII. JEAN DE BÉGASSON, VIᵉ du nom, Ecuyer, Seigneur de Bégasson, de la Lardaye, &c., fut mis à la mort de son père sous la tutelle de *Jacquette le Coutellier*, son aïeule, qui, le 7 Avril 1599, obtint des Lettres-Royaux pour la cassation d'un accord désavantageux que JEAN DE BÉGASSON, son fils, père du pupille, avoit fait, le 18 Décembre 1586, avec OLIVIER, son oncle. Il servit dans la compagnie des 100 hommes d'armes des Ordonnances du Roi, dont étoit Capitaine le Duc de Vendôme, César de Bourbon, fils naturel de HENRI IV. Ce ne furent pas là ses seuls services, car il avoit mérité d'être fait Chevalier de l'Ordre du Roi, qualité qu'il a dans un titre du 8 Avril 1646, avec celle de Seigneur de la Lardaye, de la Bouexière, du Ronceray, de la Pagoudaye, Terres situées dans la Paroisse de Maure, mouvantes de Peillac, au bailliage du Plessis-Mahé, & qui lui vinrent de son mariage avec *Jeanne de Guillou*, par succession de *Jacques*, son père, Ecuyer, Seigneur de la Lardaye, &c., & de *Jacques de Guillou*, frère de ladite *Jeanne*, lequel fit profession dans la maison des Chartreux de Nantes. Leurs enfans furent :

1. CLÉMENT, qui suit ;
2. FRANÇOISE, Dame de la Lardaye, mariée, le 13 Décembre 1639, à *Jean Collobel*, Seigneur du Bot, &c. ;
3. RENÉE, mariée, le 18 Janvier 1631, à *Olivier de Saint-Martin*, Seigneur de Kerpondarme ;
4. Et MARGUERITE DE BÉGASSON, Dame de la Bouexière, mariée, le 15 Février 1639, à *Jean Gouro*, Sieur de la Boulaye, qui fut

avantagé par *Anne du Lieu*, fa mère, en faveur de cette alliance, des prétentions qu'elle avoit fur la maifon de la Boulaye & fes dépendances, fans en excepter même fon douaire.

VIII. CLÉMENT DE BÉGASSON, Ecuyer, Seigneur de Bégaffon, & de la Lardaye, époufa, le 8 Avril 1646, *Marie Guido*, fœur de *Pierre Guido*, Seigneur de Refto, Tréforier des Finances en Bretagne, & fille de *Jean Guido*, Seigneur de Kerdejaroult, Garde du Scel-Royal au Siège Préfidial de Vannes, & de *Jeanne le Méʒec*, remariée à *François Loénan*, dont :

1. GILLES-JEAN, qui fuit;
2. JULIEN, rapporté après la poftérité de fon aîné;
3. PÉRONELLE, morte après le 10 Juillet 1676;
4. FRANÇOISE, Religieufe au premier couvent de la Vifitation de Rennes en 1681;
5. Et PRUDENCE-MARGUERITE DE BÉGASSON, mariée à *Jean-Renaud de Keraly*, Ecuyer, Seigneur du Fos.

IX. GILLES-JEAN DE BÉGASSON, Ecuyer, Seigneur de Bégaffon, la Lardaye, &c., fut, avec JULIEN, fon frère, fous la tutelle de leur mère, qui fut affignée devant la Chambre établie à Rennes, pour la réformation de la nobleffe de Bretagne, par Lettres-Patentes du Roi, du mois de Janvier 1668. Mais fur la production des titres de fon mari, il fut permis à GILLES-JEAN DE BÉGASSON, fon fils aîné, de prendre la qualité de *Chevalier*, & JULIEN, fon frère, celle d'*Ecuyer*, & ils furent maintenus dans leur ancienne nobleffe. Il laiffa de *Marie Gabart* :

X. JULIEN-RENÉ DE BÉGASSON, Seigneur de Bégaffon & de la Lardaye, Confeiller au Parlement de Bretagne, pourvu en même-tems de l'office de Lieutenant des Maréchaux de France, dans la Juftice de Machecoul, mort depuis plufieurs années. Il avoit époufé, le 11 Février 1703, MARIE-FRANÇOISE DE BÉGASSON, fa coufine germaine. Il a laiffé un garçon, dont nous ignorons l'état actuel.

DEUXIÈME BRANCHE.

IX. JULIEN DE BÉGASSON, Ecuyer, Seigneur de la Lardaye & de Kergars, fecond fils de *Clément*, & de *Marie Guido*, fut maintenu dans la qualité d'Ecuyer, par arrêt du 18 Février 1669, & eft mort en 1727, Lieutenant des Maréchaux de France au bailliage de Quimperlé en Bretagne. Il avoit époufé, par con-

trat du 10 Avril 1683, *Marie du Bochet*, Dame de la Grandririère, dont :

1. FRANÇOIS-RENÉ, qui fuit;
2. FRANÇOIS-EXUPERE;
3. MARIE-FRANÇOISE, mariée à JULIEN-RENÉ DE BÉGASSON, fon coufin germain;
4. Et APOLLINE DE BÉGASSON.

X. FRANÇOIS-RENÉ DE BÉGASSON, Ecuyer, Seigneur de la Lardaye, Page de la Grande-Ecurie du Roi au mois de Mars 1703, Lieutenant des Maréchaux de France le 13 Février 1727, époufa, le 19 Avril 1720, *Anne-Marie-Charlotte Grimaudet*, Dame de la Lande, fille unique de *Charles-Marie*, Seigneur de la Lande, & de *Marie-Elifabeth de la Vallée de Bury*, dont :

XI. JOSEPH-RENÉ DE BÉGASSON, Ecuyer, Seigneur de la Lardaye, né le 20 Juillet 1722, qui a été reçu Page du Roi en fa Grande-Ecurie le 5 Mars 1738. Nous en ignorons l'état actuel.

BRANCHE
des Seigneurs des MÉTAIRIES & de la VILLEGUICHART.

V. OLIVIER DE BÉGASSON, Seigneur des Métairies, fecond fils de JEAN, III° du nom, & de *Jeanne de Couldebouc*, connu par des actes du 7 Mai 1555, 3 Novembre 1565, 16 Juin 1572, 15 Juillet 1573 & 22 Avril 1575, eut en partage, par accord fait antérieurement avec fon frère aîné, dans la fucceffion de fes père & mère, les lieux & la maifon noble des Métairies, fitués dans la Paroiffe de Meffiriac. Il étoit mort le 5 Août 1594, & avoit époufé 1° *N...*, & 2° *Catherine Jouchet*, de la Maifon noble de *la Villeguichart*. Il laiffa du premier lit :

1. JEAN, qui fuit.

Et du fecond :

2. GUILLAUME, mentionné ci-après;
3. Et PIERRE DE BÉGASSON, Seigneur de la Porte Bregan, qui, avec fon frère aîné, fut fous la tutelle de *Jacques Jouchet*, coufin germain de leur mère, par acte judiciaire paffé en la juftice de Maleftroit le 18 Août 1594.

VI. JEAN DE BÉGASSON, Seigneur des Métairies, époufa, le 22 Novembre 1582, *Françoife de Couedro*, fille de noble homme *Jean de Couedro*, dont :

ISABEAU DE BÉGASSON, mariée au Seigneur de *Kerpondarme*.

VI. GUILLAUME DE BÉGASSON, Seigneur de

Z z ij

la Villeguichart, qualifié Ecuyer, fecond fils d'Olivier de Bégasson, & de *Catherine Jouchet*, fa feconde femme, étoit mort le 7 Juillet 1621. Il laiffa de *Jeanne Rion* :

VII. Clément de Bégasson, Seigneur de la Villeguichart, né le 5 Décembre 1601, qui époufa, par contrat du 7 Février 1622, *Marguerite du Bot*, iffue de l'ancienne Maifon de *Kerbot*, remariée à N... *Dubois de la Salle*, dont Susanne, à laquelle Clément de Bégasson, fon frère utérin, donna en partage quelques biens fitués au Petit-Molac. Guillaume de Bégasson laiffa :

1. Clément, qui fuit ;
2. Et Catherine de Bégasson.

VIII. Clément de Bégasson, IIe du nom, Seigneur de la Villeguichart, la Béraudaye, &c., fut affigné en 1668, pour faire fes preuves de nobleffe, & prouva fa defcendance depuis Olivier de Bégasson, Seigneur des Métairies, & la liaifon du même Olivier, avec les auteurs de Clément de Bégasson, père de Gilles-Jean, chef de la famille, & mourut au mois de Juin 1679. Il avoit époufé, par contrat du 30 Octobre 1655, *Françoife de Kerraut*, fille ainée & principale héritière de *François*, Seigneur de Tremarden, Confeiller du Roi. Il laiffa :

1. Hélène-Gilette, mariée à *René de Kermabon*, Seigneur de Kerprugent au Diocèfe de Tréguier ;
2. Et Mathurine -Sébastienne de Bégasson, mariée, le 12 Novembre 1686, à *Guy-Henri Grignart de Chamfavoy*, Seigneur dudit lieu, du Refto & de Jehardière, en la Paroiffe d'Evran, au Diocèfe de Saint-Mâlo.

Les armes : *d'argent, à une bécaffe de gueules.*

BEGAIGNON , Seigneur de Rumen, en Pleftin près Tréguier : *d'argent, au fretté de gueules de fix pièces.*

BEGASSOUX (le), en Bretagne : *d'azur, à trois têtes de bécaffes d'or, pofées 2 & 1.*

BEGAT (le), en Champagne : *de fable, à la croix engrêlée d'argent, cantonnée aux 1 & 4 d'une étoile de même.*

BÉGON, famille noble originaire de Blois, qui a été une des plus confidérables du pays; mais elle doit fon principal luftre à Michel Bégon, IIIe du nom, qui s'eft rendu recommandable par fon amour pour les Belles-Let-

tres, & par fon zèle pour ce qui regarde le bien public. Après avoir rempli les principales charges de la robe dans fon pays, le Marquis de Seignelay le fit entrer dans la Marine en 1677; il fut fucceffivement Intendant du Havre, des Colonies Françoifes en Amérique, des Galères, Confeiller d'honneur au Parlement de Provence, Intendant du Port de Rochefort, avec la Généralité de la Rochelle, en 1694. Il mourut le 14 Mars 1710, & a laiffé de *Madeleine Druilon* :

1. Michel, qui fuit ;
2. Scipion-Jérôme, Abbé de Saint-Germerde-Fleix, puis Confeiller du Roi en fon Confeil d'Etat, Evêque - Comte de Toul, Prince du Saint-Empire, mort le 28 Décembre 1753, âgé de 77 ans ;
3. Claude-Michel, Lieutenant des Vaiffeaux du Roi, Capitaine de Compiègne, Chevalier de Saint-Louis ;
4. & 5. Deux filles, Religieufes Carmélites à Blois.
6. N.... mariée à *Jofeph d'Arcuffia*, d'une ancienne nobleffe de Provence ;
7. N.... mariée à *Roland Barrin-de-la-Galiffonnière*, Lieutenant-Général des Armées du Roi ;
8. Et N... mariée à *N...... Foyal de Denuri*, Gouverneur de Blois.

Michel Bégon, IVe du nom, Chevalier, Seigneur de la Picardière, de Saint-Sulpice, de Pommeraye, de Marbelin, de la Siftière, de Sérigny, de Meunes, &c., Confeiller du Roi en fes Confeils & en fa Cour de Parlement de Metz, premier Préfident au confeil fouverain, Intendant du Canada, & depuis Intendant du Havre & des Armées Navales, a époufé, en 1711, *Jeanne - Elifabeth de Beauharnais*, fille de *François de Beauharnais*, Seigneur de la Boifche, & de *Marguerite-Françoife Pyvart de Chaftullé*, dont font iffus :

Michel, qui fuit ;
Deux filles, mariées ;
Et une fille, Religieufe.

Michel Bégon, Ve du nom, né le 22 Février 1717, Confeiller Honoraire du Parlement de Metz, ancien Intendant de la Marine à Dunkerque, a époufé, le 3 Juin 1743, *Anne-Françoife de Pernot*, morte le 4 Août 1745, dont :

Michel Bégon, né le 28 Juillet 1745, mort au mois d'Avril 1747.

Il y a auffi de cette famille Michel Bégon,

Seigneur de Montfermeil, mort Directeur de la Compagnie des Indes le 5 Avril 1728, âgé de 73 ans, laissant de *Catherine de Guymont*, MARIE-FRANÇOISE BÉGON, morte le 8 Août 1742. Elle avoit épousé, le 9 Mars 1720, *Louis-Michel Berthelot*, Seigneur de Monchesne, mort Conseiller-d'honneur au Parlement en 1741. Voyez BERTHELOT.

Les armes : *d'azur au chevron, accompagné en chef de deux roses, & en pointe d'un lion, le tout d'or.*

◆ BEGUE (LE), ancienne noblesse originaire de Normandie, & établie en Lorraine depuis plus de 200 ans. Elle est distinguée par ses services militaires.

I. THOMAS LE BEGUE, Seigneur d'Hannerville, *Chevalier*, est ainsi qualifié dans une lettre du 25 Janvier 1349, adressée par JEAN, fils aîné du Roi de France, Duc de Normandie, au Bailli de Caen ; il y est dit que ce THOMAS LE BEGUE tenoit en hommage un fief-franc de *Haubert*, baillé à Richard de Gache, Ecuyer. Cette lettre est enregistrée en la Chambre des Comptes de Normandie. Il fut père de :

II. COLIN LE BEGUE, Ecuyer, Seigneur d'Hannerville, qui vendit, de concert avec *Guillemette Maupetit*, son épouse, en 1394, un fief provenant de THOMAS LE BEGUE, son père, & eut :

1. GUILLAUME, qui suit ;
2. Et GEORGES LE BEGUE, auteur de la branche des Seigneurs de *Duranville*, &c., Comtes de *Germiny* & du Saint-Empire.

III. GUILLAUME LE BEGUE, Chevalier, Seigneur d'Hannerville, partagea avec son frère la succession de ses père & mère, le 11 Mars 1448, & épousa *Jeanne de Tilly*, Dame de Sourville. Il eut :

IV. COLIN LE BEGUE, IIe du nom, Seigneur d'Hannerville, marié, en 1463, à *Jacqueline Baron*, Dame d'Arvaut. Il eut :

V. THOMAS LE BEGUE, IIe du nom, marié, en 1491, à *Gilette de Canonville*, dont :

GILETTE LE BEGUE, mariée, en 1520, à GEORGES, Baron de *Saint-Germain*.

BRANCHE
des Seigneurs DE DURANVILLE, *&c.,* *Comtes de* GERMINY *& du Saint-Empire.*

III. GEORGES LE BEGUE, Ecuyer, fils puîné de COLIN, Ier du nom, & de *Guillemette Maupetit*, partagea avec son aîné le 11 Mars 1448,

fut Seigneur de Duranville & de Mallerville, du chef de sa femme *Marie de Cramesnil*, qui, étant veuve & tutrice d'ANTOINE LE BEGUE, son fils, transigea avec *Jeanne de Tilly*, sa belle sœur. Elle étoit fille de *Ferry*, Seigneur de Duranville & de Mallerville, & eut :

IV. ANTOINE LE BEGUE, Ecuyer, Seigneur de Duranville & de Mallerville, qui épousa, en 1484, *Jeannette d'Aschey de Serquigny*, dont :

1. GEORGES, marié à *Jeanne de Mouy*. Il eut :
   MARIE LE BEGUE, mariée à *Jean de Moncel*, Chevalier, Seigneur d'Estoubeville ;
   Et CATHERINE, mariée à *Audier*, Seigneur de *Vassy*.
2. RENÉ, qui suit ;
3. & 4. PIERRE & JACQUES LE BEGUE, Prêtres.

V. RENÉ LE BEGUE, homme d'armes des Ordonnances du Roi, Ecuyer, sous la charge du Comte de Montrevel, testa le 25 novembre 1540, & avoit épousé *Jeanne*, fille de *Jean de Queu*, Seigneur de la Queurière, & de *Jeanne le Veneur*. Leurs enfans furent :

1. FRANÇOIS, qui suit ;
2. Et RENÉ LE BEGUE, Ecuyer, qui fut père de JEAN & de NICOLAS.

VI. FRANÇOIS LE BEGUE, dit PISTOR, Capitaine d'une Compagnie de 100 hommes de pied au service de France, passa en Lorraine & testa le 22 Avril 1603. Il avoit épousé, par contrat du 1er Mars 1545, *Marie*, fille de *Francisque Pistor*, Gentilhomme servant de la Duchesse de LORRAINE, & de *Jeanne de Bourgogne*. Il s'obligea, par ce contrat, de joindre le nom & les armes de sa femme aux siennes, & eut :

VII. JEAN ou VIAN PISTOR LE BEGUE, Seigneur de Vitrey, Gauviller, Germiny, Praye au Comté de Vaudemont, d'un fief à Vellefur-Moselle & des Voueries de Crespey & Viterne, qui, après avoir servi dans les guerres de Flandre, & en France pendant la ligue, & y avoir donné des preuves de valeur, fut chargé de plusieurs commissions importantes par le Duc Charles III vers le Sieur de Rône, Comte d'Etages, Maréchal-de-Camp, Général des Armées Espagnoles aux Pays-Bas. Ce prince le créa, par Lettres-Patentes du 15 Décembre 1607, Conseiller en son Conseil d'Etat & privé. Le Duc Henri le fit aussi Conseiller d'Etat en 1610, & l'envoya en commission vers l'Archiduc aux Pays-Bas. Le Duc François le nomma en 1618 Sous-Gouverneur de la perfonne & Maifon du Prince Charles IV fon fils, pendant fa jeuneffe, duquel il fut enfuite Secrétaire d'Etat & Ambaffadeur vers l'Electeur de Brandebourg. Il acquit en 1611, 1624 & 1627, plufieurs portions en la Seigneurie de Germiny, tefta le 31 Juillet 1641, & mourut à Vezelife le 11 Novembre 1645, âgé de 85 ans. Il avoit époufé, par contrat du 30 Janvier 1599, *Anne de Serre*, morte en 1637. Elle étoit veuve de *Pierfon des Moynes*, Maréchal des Logis du Duc Charles III, & apporta à JEAN LE BEGUE, le château bas de Germiny, & la Seigneurie en dépendante, qu'elle eut, pour partage le 7 Janvier 1610 de la fucceffion de *Jacques de Serre*, & d'*Oudette du Doyer*, fes père & mère. Il laiffa:

1. CHARLES, qui fuit;
2. GASPARD LE BEGUE, né le 25 juin 1610, mort en 1635, qui eut de *Barbe Nicolas*, pour enfans naturels:
   1. ISABEAU, morte jeune;
   2. Et NICOLAS LE BEGUE, né le 30 Août 1635, lequel jouit, en qualité de *fils naturel de Gentilhomme*, des privilèges de nobleffe, conformément à la coutume de Lorraine, & y fut autorifé par arrêt du Parlement de Metz du 25 Août 1662, à la charge de porter le nom & les armes de fon père, *barrées*. Il fut Seigneur d'Igney, de Girmont & du fief Saint-Diez, fis à Hoyecourt, pour lefquelles Terres il fit fes reprifes au Duc Léopold le 13 mars 1700, & époufa *Hélène de Beauvais*, dont:
      1. CHARLES-ANTOINE LE BEGUE, Chanoine de Saint-Pierre-le-Vieux à Strasbourg;
      2. JEAN-FRANÇOIS-AUGUSTIN, Seigneur de Girmont, Igney, Villoncourt & du fief de Bayecourt, pour lefquelles Terres il fit fes reprifes les 17 & 19 Juillet 1712. Il a laiffé poftérité;
      3. Et ANNE-MARIE LE BEGUE, mariée à *Nicolas-François de Manefy*, Ecuyer, Seigneur de Maxe, Capitaine-Prevôt du Pont-Saint-Vincent.
3. Et ANNE LE BEGUE, mariée, en 1621, à *Jean l'Efpée*, Seigneur de Saint-Valier & Labenville, Confeiller d'Etat.

VIII. CHARLES LE BEGUE, Seigneur de Germiny, Olchey, Gauviller, Ognéville, Vitrey, Chantreine, Dompfevrin, des Voieries, de Crefpey & Viterne, fut Miniftre & Secrétaire du Duc Charles IV, auquel il rendit fes foi &

hommage le 20 Juin 1664, pour fes Terres. Il partagea avec fes beaux-frères & belles-fœurs, la fucceffion des père & mère de fa femme le 10 Juin 1643, & mourut à Nancy le 16 Juillet 1667, dans la 68e année de fon âge. Il avoit époufé, par contrat du 30 Janvier 1630, *Marguerite de Rutant*, morte le 20 Octobre 1669, inhumée avec fon mari dans le chœur de l'églife paroiffiale de Notre-Dame de Nancy, où l'on voit leur épitaphe. Elle étoit fille de *Jean*, Seigneur de Maizey, Gerbeuville, Relincourt, Senonville, Savonnières, Maizerey, Troyon, Lisle, la Croix-fur-Meufe, Saint-Bauflan, Varvigney, Effey en Voivre, Amblay, Montfot, Chantreine & Dompfevrin, Confeiller d'Etat, & Lieutenant-Général du Bailliage de Saint-Mihiel, & d'*Anne de Marien*. Leurs enfans furent:

1. FRANÇOIS LE BEGUE, Abbé Commendataire de Bouzonville, Grand-Doyen de l'églife de Saint-Diez, puis de la Primatiale de Nancy, Grand-Vicaire du Primat, Miniftre & Secrétaire d'Etat des Ducs Charles IV, Charles V & Léopold, & Garde des Sceaux de Lorraine. Il fubftitua à perpétuité aux aînés mâles de fon nom, la Terre & Seigneurie de Germiny, en réédifia le château, & mourut à Nancy le 19 Janvier 1699. Il fut inhumé dans l'églife Primatiale;
2. CHARLES-HENRI, Abbé Commendataire de Domevre au Diocèfe de Toul, mort en 1688;
3. CHARLES LE BEGUE, Baron de Vitrey, Seigneur en partie de Germiny, Colonel-Commandant du Régiment des Cuiraffiers de Baffompierre pour le fervice de l'Empereur, puis Grand-Bailli & Gouverneur du Comté de Vaudemont, marié, par contrat du 15 Février 1681, à *Madeleine le Preudhomme*, fille de *Chriftophe*, Chevalier, Seigneur de Vitrimont, Monhairon, Nicey, Confeiller d'Etat, & premier Maître des Requêtes de l'hôtel du Duc Charles IV de Lorraine, & d'*Elifabeth de Caboat*. Il eut:
   1. BARBE-FRANÇOISE LE BEGUE, Baronne de Vitrey, Dame en partie de Germiny, morte en 1746. Elle avoit époufé *Nicolas-Jofeph*, Comte de Bouzey, Confeiller d'Etat du Duc Léopold, & Maréchal de Lorraine & Barrois;
   2. Et MARGUERITE LE BEGUE, morte en 1712. Elle avoit époufé, le 13 Mars 1706, *François-Hermann*, Comte d'Hunolftein.
4. JOSEPH, qui fuit;
5. MARGUERITE, morte fans alliance;

6. Et ELISABETH LE BEGUE, née le 5 Avril 1657, au château de Germiny, morte le 20 Avril 1748. Elle avoit épousé, par contrat du 10 Décembre 1678, *Dieudonné de Bettainviller*, Chevalier, Seigneur de Mensberg Bettainviller, Amnéville, Moyeuvre, Romba, Clouange, Bouffange, Gandrange, Mondelange, & Sainte - Marie - au - Chêne, son cousin germain maternel, mort le 11 Janvier 1743.

IX. JOSEPH LE BEGUE, Comte du Saint-Empire, & de Germiny, Baron de Thelot & de Torcheviller, Seigneur de Chantreine, Dompsevrin, la Neuville, Olchey, Gauviller, premier Miniftre d'Etat & Garde des Sceaux du Duc Léopold de Lorraine, fut créé Comte du *Saint-Empire* par diplôme du 30 Avril 1714, en confidération de son *ancienne nobleffe* & des fervices que lui, ses frères, père & aïeul avoient rendus à la maifon d'Autriche, & de ceux par lui rendus au Duc Léopold, qu'il avoit toujours fuivi, ayant même reçu une bleffure confidérable à la journée de Temefwar en Hongrie, étant près de fa perfonne. Ce prince érigea en fa faveur la Terre de Germiny avec fes dépendances en Comté par Lettres-Patentes du 8 Février 1724. (Voyez GERMINY). Il rendit de grands fervices, en qualité de Plénipotentiaire, au congrès de Ryfwick, pour le rétabliffement de S. A. R. dans fes Etats, & au traité d'Utrecht & de Baden; s'acquitta enfuite de plufieurs commiffions importantes dans les Cours de France, d'Angleterre & de Hollande, mourut à Lunéville le 30 Janvier 1730, âgé de 82 ans, & fut inhumé à Nancy dans l'églife paroiffiale de Notre-Dame, en la fépulture de fes père & mère. Il avoit épousé, par contrat du 16 Février 1688, *Jeanne-Françoife de Rennel*, morte à Nancy le 19 Février 1729, dans fa 64e année. Elle étoit fille de *François*, Comte de *Rennel*, & du Saint-Empire, Confeiller du Duc Charles IV, & d'*Antoinette le Maréchal*, fa feconde femme. Il eut:

1. LÉOPOLD-JOSEPH, qui fuit;
2. CHARLES-ERNEST, né le 28 Mars 1701, reçu Chevalier de Malte de minorité au Grand-Prieuré de Champagne en 1703, élevé Page du Duc Léopold, enfuite Chambellan de ce Prince, puis de l'Empereur fon fils, & de l'Impératrice Reine de Hongrie & de Bohême; pourvu en 1744 des Commanderies de Châlons & de Pontaubert, & mort en celle de Châlons en 1754;

3. MARIE, Religieufe Bénédictine à Saint-Avold;
4. Et ANNE-MARIE-ELISABETH LE BEGUE, née à la Haye en Hollande en 1709, mariée, par contrat du 13 Mai 1727, à *Louis-Hubert le Danois*, Marquis de Joffreville, Colonel aux Grenadiers de France.

X. LÉOPOLD-JOSEPH LE BEGUE, Comte du Saint-Empire & de Germiny, Baron de Torcheviller, Seigneur de Gauviller, Holchey, Chantreine, Dompfevrin & la Neuville, né le 15 Mars 1700, Chambellan du Duc Léopold; obtint de ce Prince la charge de Bailli du Comté de Vaudemont, en furvivance du Comte de Gournay; fut mandé à Vienne pour y affifter au mariage de S. A. R. avec l'Archiducheffe; fit la campagne de Hongrie avec le Duc de Lorraine, en qualité de fon premier Maître-d'Hôtel, & fut envoyé à Lunéville, de la part de ce Prince, pour, en fon nom, complimenter la Princeffe, fa fœur, fur fon mariage avec le Roi de Sardaigne. Il acquit, des enfans de la Maréchale de Bauzey, fa coufine germaine, le 2 Avril 1732, le château bas de Germiny & la part de Seigneurie en dépendante, qu'ils avoient eue de la fucceffion de leur mère; ce qui fut uni à la fubftitution du Comté de Germiny. Il eft mórt à Vienne en Autriche le 14 Septembre 1738, & avoit épousé, par contrat du 29 Mai 1724, fa nièce, à la mode de Bretagne, *Gabrielle - Agnès d'Hunolftein*, morte à Bouxières, le 5 Mars 1760, âgée de 50 ans. Il laiffa:

1. ANTOINE-FRANÇOIS, qui fuit;
2. Autre ANTOINE-FRANÇOIS LE BEGUE, Comte du Saint-Empire, né le 1er Décembre 1727, Lieutenant de Vaiffeaux en la Marine du Roi à Breft, en 1774, marié 1º en Améririque, en 1754, à *N.... le Bray*, morte fur le vaiffeau, en revenant en France, & en couches d'un enfant, mort de même peu après fa naiffance. Elle étoit fœur de la Vicomteffe de *Choifeul*; & 2º à Breft, à N... Nous ignorons s'il en a poftérité;
3. LOUIS, mort en bas âge;
4. CHARLES-ERNEST LE BEGUE, Comte du Saint-Empire, né le 13 Décembre 1730, reçu Page du Duc Charles de Lorraine, frère de l'Empereur, puis Officier dans fon Régiment d'Infanterie en 1774. Il a épousé à Nancy, le 4 Août 1772, N... *de Sonet*, Dame de Belleau, fille de N... *de Sonet*, Seigneur d'Auffon en Franche-Comté, & de N.... *Pifchard*. Nous ignorons s'il en a poftérité;

5. Et REINE-CHARLOTTE LE BEGUE, née le 5 Octobre 1733, Religieuſe à l'Adoration perpétuelle du Saint-Sacrement, à Paris.

XI. ANTOINE-FRANÇOIS, Comte de LE BEGUE, du Saint-Empire & de Germiny, Baron de Torcheviller, né le 1ᵉʳ Juin 1725, Capitaine de Cavalerie au Régiment de Roſe, Allemand, mort à Nancy en 1761, avoit épouſé, le 25 Février 1747, *Françoiſe-de-Sales de Thyrmois de Sacy*, fille unique de *Jacques-Raoul*, Seigneur de Sacy & de Saint-Chriſtophe en Normandie, Conſeiller au Parlement de Rouen, & d'*Angélique-Catherine-Françoiſe Langlois de Motteville*, dont :

XII. GABRIEL-JACQUES-RAOUL, Comte de LE BEGUE, du Saint-Empire & de Germiny, Baron de Torcheviller, Seigneur de Sacy & Saint-Chriſtophe, né à Nancy le 23 Octobre 1752, Cornette au Régiment Meſtre-de-Camp-Général des Dragons, puis Capitaine en 1772, a épouſé à Rouen, en 1772, N..... *de Puiſmartin*. Nous ignorons ſ'il en a poſtérité.

Les armes : *écartelé, aux 1 & 4 d'azur, au poiſſon d'ombre d'argent, mis en faſce, aux 2 & 3 d'azur, à un écuſſon d'argent*; & ſur le tout, *d'argent, à l'aigle éployée de ſable.*

BEGUE DE MAJAINVILLE (LE), en

Lorraine. CHARLES LE BEGUE, Seigneur de Majainville, Tréſorier-Général des Maiſons & Finances du Duc d'Orléans, & auparavant Tréſorier-Général des Bâtimens du Roi, mourut le 4 Juillet 1704. Il avoit épouſé, le 1ᵉʳ Octobre 1662, *Anne Fouges-d'Ecures*, morte le 29 Mai 1729, & laiſſa :

1. CHARLES LE BEGUE, Seigneur de Majainville & de Saunières, Conſeiller en la Grand-Chambre du Parlement de Paris;
2. LOUIS LE BEGUE-DE-MAJAINVILLE, né le 22 Juillet 1664, Prêtre, Docteur en Théologie de la Faculté de Paris le 30 Mai 1692, Abbé commandataire de l'Abbaye du Val-Chrétien, ordre des Prémontrés, Diocèſe de Soiſſons, depuis 1693, Chantre & Chanoine de l'Egliſe Collégiale de Saint-Honoré à Paris, mort le 16 Janvier 1737;
3. Et CLAUDE LE BEGUE, Chanoine de l'Egliſe de Chartres, puis Docteur en Théologie de la même Faculté, Conſeiller-Clerc au Parlement de Paris depuis 1726.

Selon l'*Armorial de France*, reg. Iᵉʳ, part. I, pag. 58. Il eut encore pour fils :

PIERRE LE BEGUE DE MAJAINVILLE, Seigneur de Jonville & de Conteville, premier Ecuyer de S. A. R. Madame la Ducheſſe de Lorraine, marié à Nancy, le 10 Août 1710, à *Marie-Thérèſe de Fiquelmont*, Fille d'Honneur de cette Princeſſe, & fille de *Jean-François de Fiquelmont*, Baron de Paroi, Grand-Bailli de Luneville, & de *Marguerite de Chauvirey*, dont :

THÉRÈSE LE BEGUE, née le 21 Mars 1714.

Les armes : *d'azur, au ſep de vigne d'or, fruité de même, tortillé autour d'un échalas auſſi d'or, & ſurmonté en chef d'une merlette d'argent entre deux croiſſans de même.*

BÉHAGUE ou BÉHAGLE, ainſi qu'il

s'écrit en Flamand. C'eſt une ancienne nobleſſe Militaire des Pays-Bas, dont pluſieurs de ce nom ont eu leur ſépulture à Hulft & à Oudenarde, dans la Chapelle de Saint-Jean, où l'on diſtingue encore les armoiries de cette famille. Un *Béhague* étoit Gouverneur de Hulft en 1592.

Les troubles, dont les Pays-Bas furent agités, firent qu'il y eut des *Béhague* qui s'attachèrent, les uns à Marguerite d'Autriche, d'autres au parti du Prince d'Orange, & que quelques-uns ſuivirent celui du Duc d'Anjou. Voilà l'époque de la perte des biens que poſſédoit la famille de *Béhague*, & de leur diſperſion.

A l'inſpection du tableau de filiation, qui nous a été communiqué, on remarque trois branches de *Béhague*, paſſées & depuis long-tems attachées au ſervice de France.

Les alliances de la première de ces branches ſont avec les Maiſons de *Fitz-James, Brindelet, Caſtella, de Baye, d'Aligre, Puyſégur, Calonne-Courtebonne, Molé, Saint-Quentin, Herfort, Colbert, Broglie*, &c.

I. JACOB DE BÉHAGUE, IIᵉ du nom, fils de JACOB, Iᵉʳ du nom, eut de ſa femme :

1. JACOB, qui ſuit;
2. ROBERT, dont la poſtérité ſera rapportée ci-après;
3. & 4. MARTIN & PHILIPPE, auteurs de deux autres branches qui exiſtoient en 1686. La première à Fleſſingue, & la ſeconde à la Haye.

II. JACOB DE BÉHAGUE, IIIᵉ du nom, eut :
1. JACOB, qui ſuit;
2. Et JUDITH, qui épouſa N..... *de Wonner*, originaire du Canton de Berne, Lieutenant-Colonel d'un Régiment Suiſſe, dont elle eut un fils, qui mourut auſſi Capitaine au même Régiment. Après la mort de ſon mari & de ſon fils, elle rejoignit ſon frère.

III. JACOB DE BÉHAGUE, IVᵉ du nom, entra

dans la conjuration du Prince d'Orange, en 1567, & fut obligé de fe réfugier à Werchot, en Boulonnois, avec fa femme & fa fœur JU-DITH. Il y fut inquiété pour caufe de Religion, & fe retira à la Ville-Baffe de Calais, où il fe dit être Catholique. Pour accréditer cette déclaration, il envoya aux fonts de St.-Pierre, le fils qu'il venait d'avoir de fon époufe. Cet enfant, qu'il recommanda de baptifer fous le nom de *Martin*, le fut par erreur fous celui de *Marin*. Il en conclut que c'étoit en mépris de la Religion Proteftante, dont il étoit fufpecté, & il abandonna la Ville-Baffe de Calais, pour aller s'établir à Guines avec fa famille. Les Huguenots lui reprochèrent le baptême de fon fils; il s'en juftifia & les raffura par le dépôt de fes titres & papiers, refte précieux de fes biens, qu'il configna dans leur Temple, qui, par une fuite des ravages que les Efpagnols commirent en ce pays, devint la proie des flammes. Il profeffa conftamment, jufqu'à fa mort, la Religion Proteftante, & y éleva fon fils. Il avoit époufé, en 1566, N..., dont il laiffa:

IV. MARIN DE BÉHAGUE, mort en 1654, qui eut de *Madeleine Gaignon*:

1. PIERRE, qui fuit;
2. Et MICHEL, qui eut la même éducation que fon frère aîné, & à qui on fit auffi faire abjuration.

V. PIERRE DE BÉHAGUE, Ier du nom, reçut le baptême de fes pères. Devenu orphelin en bas âge, fon éducation fut confiée à des mains étrangères, qui lui firent faire abjuration dans l'Eglife de Notre-Dame de Calais. Il y fut élevé. En 1686, il mena fon fils en Hollande. Il fut retenu à Fleffingue par un de fes parens de la branche de MARTIN, troifième frère de JACOB, fon bifayeul. Il fe rendit enfuite à la Haye, où il trouva un autre de fes coufins, defcendant de PHILIPPE, qui tenoit un dés premiers rangs dans la Compagnie des Indes, & jouiffoit d'une fortune confidérable. Il eft mort fans enfans. Il importe aux defcendans de PIERRE de découvrir l'année du décès de ce parent, & ce que font devenus les biens qu'il a laiffés. PIERRE mourut en 1705, & laiffa de *Marie-Jeanne de Préaux*:

1. PIERRE, qui fuit;
2. Et MARIE-JEANNE, mariée à Meffire *Louis-Armand de Cancer*, Chevalier, Seigneur & Baron de Pignan, Meftre-de-Camp de Cavalerie, Exempt des Gardes-du-Corps du Roi, Chevalier de Saint-Louis, Syndic de la Nobleffe du Pays conquis & reconquis dont il refte un fils, ancien Capitaine de Cavalerie, Chevalier de Saint-Louis, Commandant pour le Roi à Guines, & Syndic de la Nobleffe du Calaifis & Ardrefis.

VI. PIERRE DE BÉHAGUE, IIe du nom, mort en 1761, & enterré à Calais dans l'Eglife de Notre-Dame, avoit époufé *Marie-Anne-Eléonore de Genthon*, d'une famille noble originaire du Dauphiné. Il a eu:

1. JEAN-PIERRE-ANTOINE, qui fuit;
2. JACQUES-FRANÇOIS-MARIE-ELÉONOR-TIMO-LÉON, rapporté après fon frère aîné;
3. MARIE-LOUISE-ELÉONORE, née en 1724, mariée 1° par contrat paffé devant *David*, Notaire à Calais, le 11 Octobre 1752, à *Pierre de Conftant*, IIe du nom, Chevalier, Seigneur de Bohaz; & 2° (ce fecond mariage eft problématique) à N..... *de Maffoul*, Chevalier de Saint-Louis, ci-devant Capitaine au Régiment d'Infanterie de Provence, Lieutenant de Roi de Neuville, dont le fils aîné eft entré à l'Ecole Royale Militaire, en 1766, après avoir fait fes preuves de nobleffe;
4. Et MARIE-CHARLOTTE-ADÉLAÏDE, née en 1734, mariée, le 5 Octobre 1762, à *Luc Alen de Saint-Wolftons*, Chevalier, Lieutenant-Colonel d'Infanterie, Chevalier de Saint-Louis, penfionnaire du Roi, &c.

VII. JEAN-PIERRE-ANTOINE DE BÉHAGUE, né en 1727, entré au fervice en qualité de Cornette au Régiment de Cavalerie d'Egmont, par Brevet du 1er Septembre 1744; a paffé dans la feconde Compagnie des Moufquetaires de la Garde du Roi, immédiatement après la réforme qui fuivit la paix de 1748. Il y a fervi jufqu'au 1er Septembre 1755, qu'il fut nommé à une Compagnie de Dragons au Régiment d'Harcourt. Il a été fait Lieutenant-Colonel le 18 Novembre 1761; Chevalier de Saint-Louis le 5 Mars 1762, a été commis à la défenfe de Cayenne & de la Province de Guyane, par Lettres du Roi du 15 Avril 1762; a été chargé en même tems par Sa Majefté d'une miffion particulière; a fuccédé au Gouvernement de la Guyane, en qualité de Commandant-Général, par Lettres-Patentes du 15 Avril 1763; a eu permiffion de repaffer en France, pour y continuer fes fervices; & après avoir rendu compte de fa miffion, a été nommé une feconde fois, pour retourner dans la Guyane, en qualité de Commandant en chef; a été préfenté au Roi, avant fon départ, par le Miniftre de la Guerre & de la Marine eft revenu continuer fes fervices en France, conformément aux ordres de Sa Majefté ; a obtenu 3000 livres de traitement en appointemens, & a été fait Brigadier des Armées du Roi, le 20 Avril 1768. Il n'eft pas encore marié.

VII. Jacques-François-Marie-Eléonor-Timoléon de Béhague, frère cadet du précédent, né en 1742, eft entré au fervice en 1751, en qualité de furnuméraire dans la feconde Compagnie des Moufquetaires de la Garde du Roi, a paffé au Régiment d'Infanterie de Périgord, en qualité de Lieutenant, par Lettres du 1er Septembre 1755, a été nommé Major d'Artillerie, par Brevet du 1er Août 1764, & s'eft marié, en 1765, à N... Verdelhan des Fourniels, fille de Jacques, Seigneur des Fourniels, & de Marie-Madeleine Morin.

SECONDE BRANCHE.

II. Robert de Béhague, Ier du nom, fecond fils de Jacob, IIe du nom, eut :

1. Robert de Béhague, IIe du nom, qui vécut fans alliance, & mourut Gouverneur de la ville d'Hulft en 1592, âgé de 32 ans. Il eft enterré à Hulft;
2. Et Martin, qui fuit.

III. Martin de Béhague, Ier du nom, mourut en 1615. Il eft enterré à Oudenarde dans la Chapelle de St.-Jean. Sur fa tombe eft une infcription en Flamand, furmontée de fes armes. Il a eu de Jeanne Van-Meldert :

Martin, qui fuit;
Et Philippe, Robert, André, Michel, Laurent, Jeanne, Pétronille, Anne, une autre Jeanne & Cornille.
Des autres garçons de Martin, Ier du nom, font forties diverfes branches, telles que celles de Francfort, & celle d'Artois, de laquelle il exifte trois frères. L'aîné a fervi dans le Régiment de Foix ; le fecond dans Beccary, & le troifième dans le Bataillon d'Artois. Leur grand-père a fervi dans la Maifon du Roi ; leur grand-oncle dans le Régiment des Dragons de Parpaille, où il a été tué. Le père & l'oncle dans le Régiment de Nuaillés.

IV. Martin de Béhague, IIe du nom, mort en 1668, & enterré à Oudenarde, dans la Chapelle de St.-Jean, a laiffé de N... Wachter :

V. Philippe de Béhague, enterré à Beauvais dans l'Eglife de Saint-Thomas, qui a époufé, en 1669, Anne Van-Hoven, dont :

1. Philippe, qui voyagea en Ruffie, où les

bontés du Czar le fixèrent. Il y eft mort comblé de marques de diftinction;
2. Jean-Joseph, mort fans alliance;
3. Jean-Baptiste, qui fuit;
4. Jean-François, mort à Saint-Domingue;
5. Nicolas, enterré à Beauvais dans l'Eglife de St.-Thomas;
6. Marie-Anne-Françoise, mariée à N.... de Vigneron, Chevalier, Seigneur de Bretheuil, ancien Capitaine d'Infanterie;
7. Marie-Adrienne, morte à Paris;
8. Et Claude-Georgette, morte à Compiègne, mariée à N... de Pincemaille.

VI. Jean-Baptiste de Béhague a laiffé de Marie Bricard :

VII. Jean-François de Béhague, aujourd'hui chef de la feconde branche, qui s'eft marié, par contrat du 14 Décembre 1733, avec Marie-Hélène Roettiers, dont :

1. Jean-Baptiste-Emmanuel, qui fuit;
2. Et Marie-Laurent.

VIII. Jean-Baptiste-Emmanuel de Béhague, né en 1735, entré au fervice en 1756, en qualité d'Enfeigne au Régiment d'Infanterie de la Tour-du-Pin, nommé Lieutenant en 1757, eft aujourd'hui Capitaine au même Régiment, par commiffion du 5 Mai 1762.

Le Tableau de cette famille, d'après lequel nous venons de dreffer la Généalogie, eft fuivi d'un certificat de Nobleffe, donné à Calais, le 18 Octobre 1769, par M. le Baron de Pignan, Commiffaire pour la répartition de la capitation des Nobles du Gouvernement de Calais & d'Ardres, qui confirme que Jean-Pierre-Antoine de Béhague, Brigadier des Armées du Roi, & Jacques-François-Marie-Eléonor-Timoléon, Chevalier de Béhague-d'Hartincourt, Major d'Infanterie, font enfans de feu Meffire Pierre de Béhague, Ecuyer, Seigneur de Villeneuve, Létang & autres lieux, & font iffus d'une noble & ancienne famille d'origine étrangère, que les malheurs des guerres & les révolutions des Pays-Bas ont fait fortir de la Flandre-Impériale. A ce certificat font appofés la fignature & les fceaux des Gentilshommes du Gouvernement de Calais & d'Ardres, qui reconnoiffent l'exactitude de fon contenu, lequel eft auffi reconnu véritable par M. de Becquet de Cocove, Confeiller du Roi, Préfident-Juge-Général au fiège de la Juftice-Royale de Calais & Pays reconquis.

Les armes : parti, coupé au 1 parti d'or, à trois épis de bled fur leur terraffe, de

*trois tiges chacune de finople ; au 2 parti,
1 coupé de finople à trois têtes d'aigle arrachées d'argent, au 2 coupé d'azur à la
fleur-de-lys d'or* (donnée pour fervices rendus, par MARIE, Duchefle de Bourgogne, femme de MAXIMILIEN D'AUTRICHE), *au chef d'argent, chargé d'une rofe de gueules ; l'écuffon fupporté par deux aigles éployées, le
tout couronné d'un cafque de fafce à cinq
grilles, bords d'argent, orné d'un bourelet
de chevalerie.* Devife : BON GUET CHASSE MAL
AVENTURE.

BEHUCHET : *de . . . . . à une tige à
trois rofes de. . . . accompagnée de quatre
étoiles de. . . . . . deux en chef & deux en
pointe.*

BEIM : *de gueules, à trois annelets d'argent,* 2 & 1.

BEINAC : *de gueules, au lion d'argent
courant, pofé en bande.*

* BEINE ou BEYNES en Provence, Diocèfe de Riez. La Terre & Seigneurie de *Beine*
fut acquife de *Jean de Caftillon,* par fon coufin germain, *René de Caftillon,* Baron d'Aubagne, mort en 1498, & quatrième ayeul de
Pierre de Caftillon, Grand-Sénéchal d'Arles, en faveur duquel cette Terre fut érigée en
Marquifat par Lettres du mois d'Avril 1673,
regiftrées à Aix le 12 Mars 1674. Ce dernier
fut père de *Marc-Antoine,* Marquis de *Beine,*
marié, le 11 Septembre 1717, à *Marie-Anne,*
fille de *Jean Duché,* Avocat-Général en la
Cour des Aides de Montpellier, dont vint
Jean-Pierre de Caftillon, né le 9 Septembre 1718, Marquis de *Beine,* ci-devant Page
de la Petite-Ecurie du Roi, marié à Arles avec
N.... de Serre, Dame de la Roque.

BEINS (DE), Seigneur de Vifancourt, en
Dauphiné : *d'azur, au chevron d'or, furmonté de trois étoiles d'argent rangées en fafce, & accompagné en pointe d'un foleil d'or.*

BEISSIER, Seigneur de Pizany : *de finople, à une plante de lis d'argent.*

BEIVIÈRE (LA) : *de gueules, à une croix
d'or, fleurdelifée.*

BEL (LE), Seigneur de la Boiffière, de Buffy, en Picardie : *de finople, à la fafce d'argent.*

BEL (LE), Seigneur du Hommet, & de Julie, en Normandie, Election de Valognes, fa-

mille annoblie en 1647, en la perfonne de Ju-
LIEN, dont le fils JACQUES, fut maintenu dans
fa Nobleffe en 1665, qui porte : *d'azur, à
trois befans d'argent, pofés* 2 & 1, *à la bordure d'or.*

BEL (LE), Seigneur de France, près Rhé-
don, en Bretagne : *d'argent, à trois fleurs-
de-lys de gueules, pofées* 2 & 1.

BEL (LE), même Province : *d'azur, au
fretté d'or de fix pièces.*

BEL (LE), en Champagne : *d'argent, à la
fafce d'azur, chargée de trois boucles d'or,
& accompagnée en chef de deux hures de
fanglier de fable, défendues d'argent, & en
pointe d'une étoile auffi de fable.*

* BÉLABRE ou BELLABRE, dans la
Haute-Marche, Diocèfe de Bourges, Terre &
Seigneurie qui relève immédiatement du Roi,
à caufe de fa Tour de *Maubergeon de Poitiers.* La Seigneurie de *Bélabre* étoit poffédée dans le XIVᵉ fiècle, par *Jean Périchon
de Naillac,* fur lequel elle fut confifquée,
parce qu'il avoit fervi le parti des Anglois. Le
Roi CHARLES V la donna, en 1372, à *Jean de
Poquières,* dont la poftérité l'a poffédée jufqu'en 1595. Elle paffa alors à titre de fucceffion à *Armand-Léon de Durfort,* Seigneur
de Born, Surintendant des Fortifications de
France, nommé en 1613, Chevalier des Ordres du Roi, & pourvu de la charge de Lieutenant-Général de l'Artillerie de France, le
18 Février 1616, enfuite à fon fecond fils
Léon de Durfort, fur lequel elle fut vendue
par décret, en 1648, & retirée par retrait li-
gnager, par *Eléonore de Chaumont,* troifième femme de *Jacques le Coigneux,* Préfident du Parlement de Paris, & Chancelier
du Duc d'Orléans, frère de LOUIS XIII, en
faveur duquel la Châtellenie de *Bélabre* fut
unie aux Terres d'Anjou & de la Lurefaife,
& aux Châtellenies du Châtelier-Guillebaud
& de la Salle, & érigée en titre de Marquifat,
en confidération de fes fervices, par Lettres
du mois de Février 1650, regiftrées au Parlement & à la Chambre des Comptes de Paris, les 8 & 29 Juillet fuivant, & au Bureau
des Finances de Poitiers, le 1ᵉʳ Mars 1684.
Il avoit été promu au Cardinalat par un Bref
du Pape URBAIN VIII, du 15 Février 1631,
fur la nomination du Roi LOUIS XIII; mais
fon troifième mariage empêcha que cette grâce

n'eût son effet. Il mourut en 1651. Il avoit épousé 1º N....., 2º N...., & 3º *Eléonore de Chaumont*, fille du Seigneur de Mornay, en Saintonge. Il avoit eu de sa première femme :

JACQUES LE COIGNEUX, Marquis de Montmé-lian, aussi Président du Parlement de Paris.

Et de la seconde :

FRANÇOIS LE COIGNEUX-DE-BACHAUMONT, Baron de la Roche-Turpin, Conseiller d'Etat, morts l'un & l'autre sans postérité.

Il laissa du troisième lit :

GABRIEL LE COIGNEUX, qui suit.

GABRIEL LE COIGNEUX, Marquis de Bélabre, décédé en 1709, laissa de *Madeleine Pollart* :

1. JACQUES LE COIGNEUX, Marquis de Bélabre, Brigadier, Mestre-de-Camp du Régiment de Dragons de son nom, mort en 1728, ayant épousé en 1714, *Marie-Anne de Neyeret-de-la-Ravoye*. Il laissa :

LOUIS-JACQUES LE COIGNEUX, né en 1716, Marquis de Bélabre, retiré du service, & marié, en 1747, à *Françoise-Victoire Thomé*, fille de N..... Thomé, Conseiller au Parlement de Paris ;

2. GABRIEL LE COIGNEUX, Baron de la Roche-Turpin, Mestre-de-Camp d'un Régiment de Dragons, mort en 1741. Il avoit épousé 1º N... *d'Armagnac* ; & 2º *Elisabeth Frottier-de-la-Mosselière*. Il eut du premier lit :

GABRIEL-JOSEPH LE COIGNEUX, Baron de la Roche-Turpin, Cornette des Chevaux-Légers de la Garde du Roi, tué le 27 Juin 1743, à la bataille de Dettingen.

Et de son second mariage :

GABRIELLE-ELISABETH LE COIGNEUX, Baronne de la Roche-Turpin & de la Flotte, née en 1741 ;

3. Et GABRIEL LE COIGNEUX, dit *le Chevalier de Bélabre*, né en 1694.

Les armes : *d'azur, à trois porcs-épics d'or, 2 & 1.*

BELAC : *d'azur, à la tour crénelée d'argent, bâtie au milieu des ondes, surmontées de trois fleurs-de-lys d'or en chef.*

BELAIR, Seigneur de Ploudiry, en Bas-Léon *d'azur, au croissant d'argent.*

BELAIR, Sieur de Kerguz & Troffagan, près Saint-Paul de Léon : *d'argent, à une trompe, ou cors-de-chasse d'azur, enguiché de gueules, en sautoir.*

BELAMPRISE : *de gueules, au chef d'or,*

chargé de trois croix recroisettées, au pied fiché de sable.

BELANGER : *écartelé, aux 1 & 4 losangé d'or & de gueules ; aux 2 & 3 d'azur, à la bande d'argent, chargée de trois coupes de gueules.*

BELANGER (DE), Seigneur de Tarotte, de Blacy, de Fontenay, en Champagne : *d'azur, au chevron d'or.*

BELANGRISE, en Picardie : *de gueules, au chef d'or, chargé de trois molettes d'éperon de sable.*

BELASTRE : *d'argent, à quatre quinte-feuilles de gueules.*

BELAUDIÈRE, Baron de Rouet, & Vicomte de Lescoat, en Léon : *d'azur, à trois roues d'or, posées 2 & 1.*

BELAY : *parti d'argent & d'azur, à deux clefs adossées, passées de l'une en l'autre.*

BELAY, au Maine : *de sable, à trois molettes d'éperon d'argent, posées 2 & 1.*

BELAY : *d'argent, au loup passant de sinople,*

⧫ BELCASTEL D'ESCAYRAC, famille noble, originaire de Rouergue, une des plus illustres & des plus anciennes de cette Province & établie depuis 300 ans dans celle de Quercy, où subsistent les première & troisième branches ; la seconde est établie en Poitou. Elle est connue dans les titres Latins sous la dénomination, de *Bellocastro*, étymologique d'un nom de terre, & de la famille, comme il conste des mêmes noms & armes, insérés dans les Nobiliaires du Rouergue & du Périgord, des alliances distinguées, entr'autres avec les Maisons de *Loslanges-Sainte-Alvère*, de *Durfort*, *Montalembert*, & même de *Monte quiou-d'Artagnan*, & d'autorités convaincantes, notamment des Archives de Narjac, Vignerie en Rouergue, qui constatent sa noblesse, & la possession des Fiefs. Elle a aussi donné plusieurs Officiers de distinction, a fait ses preuves à Malte, aux Chapitres Nobles de l'Eglise de Notre-Dame de Bouxières, & de Sainte-Marie de Metz ; ce dernier réuni à celui de Saint-Pierre, sous le titre de Saint-Louis, à la Maison Royale de St.-Cyr, à l'Ecole Royale Militaire, &c. Le plus ancien dont on ait connoissance est :

FLOTTARD DE BELCASTEL, qualifié Noble & Damoiseau, en latin : *Nobilis Flotardus de Bellocastro, Domicellus*, suivant les Archives de la Vignerie de Nayac en Rouergue, lequel fit foi & hommage en 1285, sous le Roi *Philippe-le-Bel*, pour les terres & fiefs dépendans de celles de *Belcastel* & autres, entre les mains de l'Archevêque de Narbonne, & du Maréchal de Mirepoix ; il portoit pour armes : *d'azur, à une tour d'argent à trois donjons crénelés, ajourés & maçonnés de sable*, les mêmes que portent les branches de BELCASTEL D'ESCAYRAC, ET DE BELCASTEL DE MONTLAUZUN, auquel les armes de *Montvaillant* ont été depuis réunies.

Louis, Comte de BELCASTEL, qualifié *Nobilis de Bellocastro Comes*, possédant les mêmes terres, & portant les mêmes armes que le précédent, & dont la famille étoit distinguée par ses services Militaires, fut fait Châtelain de la ville de Cahors, vers 1400, à cause de ceux qu'il avoit rendus à l'Etat.

On trouve ensuite Noble PIERRE DE BELCASTEL, Seigneur d'Espech en Rouergue, qui fut père de CÉCILE DE BELCASTEL, mariée à Noble *Pierre Delrieu* en latin (de *Rivo*) ; duement autorisée par son père, elle vendit avec son mari, en 1425, à Noble *Guiscard de la Motte*, fils de *Ramon*, Seigneur de Saint-Paul, tous les biens héréditės, cens, rentes, pâturages, prés, bois, jardins, vignes, & dépendances quelconques, qui leur appartenoient, & généralement tout ce qu'ils possédoient, dans la terre & juridiction de Castello, excepté ce qu'ils avoient à la Barthe ; ladite vente faite pour le prix de 40 *écus d'or*, par acte passé devant *Pierre Favery*. Mais la filiation, non interrompue de cette famille, ne commence qu'à

I. JEAN DE BELCASTEL, Chevalier, Seigneur de Belcastel, &c., qui épousa, en 1300, Noble *Christine de Sauniac*, & en eut :

II. RAYMOND DE BELCASTEL, Chevalier, Lieutenant d'une Compagnie d'hommes d'armes, marié, par contrat du 4 Février 1526, avec Noble *Jeanne de Montvaillant*, fille de Noble *Jean-Louis de Montvaillant*, Seigneur de Castanet, Caderlés & autres lieux, en Languedoc, & de *Clotilde de Roquefeuille*. C'est par cette alliance que la terre de Montvaillant passa dans la famille de BELCASTEL, avec les armes qui sont : *de gueules, à trois lames d'or en pal, la pointe vers le chef*, qu'elle a

depuis ce tems *écartelées* des siennes, & que les descendans dudit RAYMOND ont ainsi portées jusqu'à présent. De ce mariage vinrent :

1. JEAN DE BELCASTEL, Seigneur de la Pradelle & du Colombier en Rouergue, qui fit la constitution de dot à son frère ROBERT, le 7 Avril 1571 ;
2. ROBERT, qui suit ;
3. RAYMOND, auteur de la branche des Seigneurs de *Montlauzun*, rapportée ci-après ;
4. Et autre JEAN DE BELCASTEL, Chevalier de Malte en 1580.

III. ROBERT DE BELCASTEL, Chevalier, Seigneur de Montvaillant, épousa, le 7 Avril 1571, noble *Philippe de Boutiers*, Dame de la terre d'Escayrac en Quercy, fille de noble *Jean de Boutiers*, Seigneur de Péchon, de Catus, & autres lieux, & de noble *Anne de Course*, dont :

IV. JEAN DE BELCASTEL de Montvaillant, Chevalier, Seigneur d'Escayrac, qui obtint, en considération des services de son fils aîné, une sauve-garde du Roi, pour son château d'Escayrac. Il fut marié le 27 Janvier 1597, avec noble *Marguerite de Mauléon*, fille de noble *Denis de Mauléon*, Seigneur de Savaillan, Saint-Soby & autres lieux, & de noble *Catherine de Maulezun*. Leurs enfans furent :

1. JACQUES, qui suit ;
2. DENIS, rapporté après son frère aîné ;
3. Et JEAN DE BELCASTEL, auteur de la branche *de Belcastel-Montsabès*, rapportée en son rang.

V. JACQUES DE BELCASTEL d'Escayrac, qualifié haut & puissant Seigneur, Messire & Chevalier, Maréchal des Camps & Armées du Roi, & Gouverneur de la Citadelle de Metz, épousa *Dorothée de Schauvembourg*, & en eut :

1. MARGUERITE, reçue Chanoinesse prébendée au Chapitre noble de l'Eglise collégiale & séculière de Notre-Dame de Bouximes près Nancy en Lorraine, le 30 Juillet 1632, sur ses preuves de huit quartiers, ceux du côté paternel furent de BELCASTEL, de BAUTIERS, de MAULÉON, de MONTLAUZUN ; & du côté maternel, *de Schauvembourg*, *de Mittelhusen*, *de Custine & de Roussez*, chacune de ces lignes prouva 200 ans de filiation de noblesse d'ancienne chevalerie, sans aucune mésalliance ni dérogeance. C'est ce qui appert d'une attestation faite à Bouxières, le 5 Novembre 1762, signée des Abbesse, Doyenne & Chanoinesses du Chapitre ;

2. ANNE, auſſi reçue Chanoineſſe prébendée au Chapitre noble de Sainte-Marie de Metz, réuni à celui de Saint-Pierre, ſous le titre de Saint-Louis, où elle eſt morte le 14 Juin 1753, & y a été inhumée;

3. Et N... DE BELCASTEL, auſſi reçue Chanoineſſe au même Chapitre, ſur leſdites preuves de nobleſſe d'ancienne chevalerie.

VI. DENIS DE BELCASTEL de Montvaillant, Ier du nom, Chevalier, Seigneur d'Eſcayrac, de Saint-André, de Troupenac, & autres lieux, ſecond fils de JEAN II, & de *Marguerite de Mauléon*, fut Capitaine de 100 hommes de pied dans le Régiment de Fimarion, puis Capitaine au Régiment de Chambert, & enfin Capitaine-Commandant de la Compagnie Royale de Chevrières. Il s'acquit tellement l'eſtime du Roi, que Sa Majeſté lui en donna des preuves, par une de ſes lettres du 4 Avril 1623. Il épouſa, le 22 Avril 1626, *Clémence de Boutiers*, fille de noble *Geoffroy de Boutiers*, Seigneur de Catus, de la Cardonnie, & autres lieux, & de noble *Françoiſe d'Hébrard du Rocal*, dont :

VII. JEAN-LOUIS DE BELCASTEL de Montvaillant, Chevalier, Seigneur d'Eſcayrac, &c., qui épouſa, le 8 Février 1660, noble *Clémence de Bonnafous*, fille de noble *Barthélemy*, Seigneur de Bonnafous, & de noble *Marguerite du Breuil d'Eſpanel*. Il eut entr'autres enfans :

DENIS, qui ſuit;

Et N.... DE BELCASTEL, appelé *le Comte de Belcaſtel*, Capitaine au Régiment de Bourgogne, qui, lors de la révocation de l'Edit de Nantes, paſſa en Hollande, où il devint Lieutenant-Général au ſervice des Etats-Généraux, & fut nommé leur Ambaſſadeur en la Cour de Turin. Il mourut Généraliſſime des troupes Hollandoiſes, après la bataille de Saragoſſe, où il commandoit.

VIII. DENIS DE BELCASTEL de Montvaillant, IIe du nom, Chevalier, Seigneur d'Eſcayrac, &c., épouſa, le 5 Octobre 1694, *Marguerite de Durfort*, fille de haut & puiſſant Seigneur Meſſire *François de Durfort*, Chevalier, Seigneur de Roquecave & de Montamel, &c., & de noble *Clémence de Vielcaſtel*, dont :

IX. FRANÇOIS DE BELCASTEL de Montvaillant, Chevalier, Seigneur d'Eſcayrac, &c., marié le 18 Décembre 1724, à noble *Jeanne-Nicole de la Tourrille*, fille de *Gratian de la Tourrille*, Chevalier de Saint-Louis, & de

noble *Jeanne de l'Archer*. De ce mariage ſont iſſus :

1. JEAN, qui ſuit;

2. & 3. ANNE-ANTOINETTE & MARIE-LOUISE DE BELCASTEL, toutes les deux reçues à Saint-Cyr, la première en 1741, & la ſeconde en 1745.

X. JEAN DE BELCASTEL de Montvaillant, IIIe du nom, Chevalier, Seigneur d'Eſcayrac, &c., né en 1737, ancien Cornette au Régiment d'Héricy, Cavalerie, demeurant en la ville de Cauſſade en Quercy, a épouſé, le 19 Décembre 1767, noble *Marguerite-Thérèſe de Guitton de Monrepos*, fille de *Joſeph de Guitton de Monrepos*, Ecuyer, ancien Lieutenant-Général de Juſtice & Police de Montréal en Canada, & de noble *Thérèſe du Duc des Bordes*. Leurs enfans ſont :

1. RAYMOND, Chevalier, né en 1768, agréé par le Roi au Collège Royal de la Flèche, le 3 Août 1777;

2. Et LOUIS DE BELCASTEL, né en 1772, appelé le Chevalier *de Belcaſtel*.

BRANCHE
DE BELCASTEL DE MONTSABÈS, *établie en Poitou.*

V. JEAN DE BELCASTEL, Chevalier, Seigneur de Montſabès, troiſième fils de JEAN DE BELCASTEL de Montvaillant, IIe du nom, Chevalier, Seigneur d'Eſcayrac, & de *Marguerite de Mauléon*, Lieutenant-Colonel au Régiment de Navarre, épouſa, le 1er Août 1635, *Catherine de Montet*, fille de *Philippe de Montet*. Il eut :

Cinq garçons, dont les deux aînés furent tués à la priſe de Mont-Midi, Capitaines au Régiment de la Ferté, le troiſième, nommé SAINT-ETIENNE, fut tué, Lieutenant de Vaiſſeau, le quatrième fut le Sieur de SAINT-ANDRÉ, & le cinquième eſt JEAN-LOUIS DE BELCASTEL, qui ſuit.

VI. JEAN-LOUIS DE BELCASTEL de Montſabès, Chevalier, Seigneur de Ferrière, Lieutenant au Régiment de Louvigny, tué au ſervice, le 11 Septembre 1681, avoit épouſé, le 20 Novembre 1675, en Lorraine, *Anne-Gabrielle de Foes*, fille de noble *Nicolas de Foes*, Seigneur de Fercomoulin, & d'*Anne-Marie Amaldo*, dont :

VII. ANTOINE DE BELCASTEL de Montſabès, Chevalier de Saint-Louis, qui a été Capitaine de Grenadiers au Régiment de Périgord, puis Aide-Major, avec Brevet de Commandant de la ville de Sarrelouis, & eft décédé le 14 Juillet 1768. Il avoit époufé, le 2 Avril 1738, *Marie-Jacobée de Léonardy*, fille de *Jean-Henri de Léonardy*, Capitaine d'Artillerie, à la réfidence de Phalsbourg, & de *Jeanne de Foes*, de laquelle font iffus :

1. Mathieu-Sébastien, Chevalier, né le 16 Mai 1745, qui entra d'abord en 1755 à l'Ecole Royale Militaire, d'où il eft forti Chevalier de l'Ordre Militaire de Saint-Lazare, Capitaine au Régiment de Gâtinois, Infanterie, qui a pris le nom de Royal-Auvergne, par Ordonnance du 11 Juillet 1782, mort à Saint-Domingue le 7 Septembre 1780 ;
2. Jean-Baptiste, qui fuit ;
3. Et Marie-Anne-Charlotte de Belcastel, Demoifelle, reçue en la Maifon Royale de Saint-Cyr en 1741, fur fes preuves de nobleffe. Elle eft première Dame d'honneur, & aujourd'hui Grande-Maîtreffe de la Cour de fon Alteffe Royale Madame la Landgrave régnante de Heffe-Caffel, née Princeffe de Pruffe, & a époufé, le 25 Juin 1781, *Henri*, Baron de *Choenfeld*, Chevalier du Mérite Militaire, Général-Major de la Cavalerie Heffoife, Grand-Echanfon de fon Alteffe Monfeigneur le Landgrave régnant de Heffe-Caffel, & Colonel de fes Gardes-du-Corps.

VIII. Jean-Baptiste, appelé le Chevalier de *Belcaftel*, né le 26 Octobre 1748, Chevalier, Seigneur de Lairé, Lemazey, Laubilière, & autres lieux, auffi Elève de l'Ecole Royale Militaire, Chevalier de l'Ordre de Saint-Lazare, ci-devant premier Lieutenant au Régiment de Gâtinois, Infanterie, & actuellement Capitaine attaché au Régiment de Royal-Marine, Infanterie, a époufé, le 23 Mars 1778, célébration dans la Chapelle du Château de Lairé, *Henriette-Catherine Joufferant de Lairé*, fille unique de noble *François-Frédéric de Joufferant*, Seigneur de Lairé, & de *Jeanne-Catherine de Vaucelle*, tous les deux d'une nobleffe d'ancienne extraction du Poitou. Lefdits *Joufferant de Lairé* font reconnus pour tels, & poffèdent la terre de Lairé depuis l'an 1100, qu'ils en étoient alors Seigneurs. Cette famille eft diftinguée, tant par fes emplois militaires, que par fes alliances avec les Maifons de *Laval*, *Saint-Georges de Vérac*, *la Rochefoucauld*, *Fénélon*, &c. Le premier Prieur qui fonda la grande Chartreufe de Paris, étoit de la famille de *Joufferant de Lairé*. Leurs enfans font :

1. Charles-Auguste de Belcastel, Chevalier, né le 14 Juin 1780 ;
2. Et Marie-Henriette-Charlotte de Belcastel, née le 29 Avril 1782.

BRANCHE
des Seigneurs de Montlauzun, établie en Quercy.

III. Raymond de Belcastel de Montvaillant, Chevalier, troifième fils de Raymond, Chevalier, Lieutenant d'une Compagnie d'homme d'armes, & de *Jeanne de Montvaillant*, fut marié le 6 Octobre 1573, avec noble *Anne de Domergue*, Dame de Montlauzun, qu'elle lui porta en dot, fille de noble *Antoine de Domergue*, Gentilhomme ordinaire de la Maifon de Navarre, & de noble *Françoife de Ferrières de Montlauzun*. Il en eut :

IV. Jean de Belcastel, Ier du nom de fa branche, Chevalier, Seigneur de Montlauzun, marié, 1º le 3 Mai 1601, à noble *Ifabeau d'Efcayrac*, fille de noble *Charles d'Efcayrac*, & de noble *Jeanne de la Boiffière-Gayral* ; & 2º le 2 Août 1609, à noble *Jeanne de la Duguye*, fille de noble *Guyot de la Duguye*, Seigneur de la Capelle & de Mauroux. Du premier lit il eut :

1. Jean, qui fuit.

Et du fecond lit :

2. Louis de Belcastel de Permilhac, Chevalier, Maréchal-des-Logis de la Cavalerie-Légère, a joui, ainfi que Jean-Bernard fon frère, de la plus grande confidération à la Cour de Lorraine ; ce qui eft juftifié par nombre de Brevets, ou commiffions militaires, de charges honorables, & de lettres de la part des Princes & Princeffes. De fon mariage, contracté à Nancy, il a eu :
   1. Nicolas de Belcastel de Permilhac, Chevalier, Chambellan de S. A. R. Léopold Ier, Duc de Lorraine & de Bar, mort fans alliance ;
   2. Louis, reçu Bailli d'Epée à Metz, mort fans avoir été marié ;
   3. Anne-Françoise de Belcastel, morte femme du Baron d'*Eyffen* ;
   4. Et une autre fille, mariée au Marquis d'*Audiffret*.

3. Et Jean-Bernard de Belcastel, Chevalier, Maréchal des Camps & Armées, & Gouverneur de Neufchatel, marié à Metz avec noble *Chriftine de Stainville*, & mort fans poftérité.

V. Jean de Belcastel, IIe du nom, Chevalier, Seigneur de Montlauzun, fils de Jean Ier, & d'*Ifabeau d'Efcyrac*, fa première femme, fut Capitaine au Régiment de Boiffe, Infanterie, & reçut plufieurs lettres du Duc d'Epernon, par lefquelles ce Seigneur le prioit de courir, lui & fes vaffaux, au-devant de fes ennemis, tant dans le Rcuffillon, que dans la Guyenne, & du côté de Bordeaux. Il avoit époufé, le 23 Septembre 1640, noble *Jeanne du Brun*, fille de noble *François du Brun*, Seigneur de la Grézette, &c., & de noble *Françoife de Molegat*, dont :

VI. Jean de Belcastel, IIIe du nom, Chevalier, Seigneur de Montlauzun, qui reçut plufieurs lettres du Préfident d'Auffonne, Lieutenant-Général de la Province, & Chef de la Nobleffe, pour fe trouver à diverfes convocations, & aller contre les ennemis de l'Etat. Il époufa, le 23 Juin 1678, noble *Anne de Jerjan*, fille de noble *Bertrand de Jerjan*, Vice-Sénéchal d'Agenois & Condomois, & de noble *Ifabeau de Germat*, & en a eu :

VII. Pierre-Joseph de Belcastel, Chevalier, Seigneur de Montlauzun, de la Grézette & autres lieux, mort le 1er Octobre 1757, avoit époufé, le 27 Janvier 1716, noble *Jeanne de Lautron de Saint-Hubert*, fille de noble *Gabriel de Lautron de Saint-Hubert*, Seigneur de la Baratie & autres lieux, & de noble *Thérèfe de Molières*, dont :

Jacques, qui fuit ;

Et Joseph, appelé le Chevalier *de Belcaftel*, Capitaine au Régiment Royal-Marine, en 1778.

VIII. Jacques de Belcastel, Chevalier, Seigneur de Montlauzun, de la Grézette, &c., réfidant à Cahors, a recueilli la fucceffion des Belcastel-de-Permilhac de Nancy, & de M. de Belcastel, établi à Metz après la mort d'Anne-Françoise de Belcastel-de-Permilhac, Baronne d'Egeren. Il vit fans alliance.

Les armes : *écartelé, aux 1 & 4 d'azur, à une tour d'argent, furmontée de trois donjons crénelés, ajourés & maçonnés de fable*, qui eft de Belcastel, & *aux 2 & 3 de gueules, à trois lances d'or, pofées en pal, la pointe en haut*, qui eft de Montvaillant. Supports : *deux lions d'or lampaffés de gueules*.

BELCASTEL, en Languedoc : *parti de finople & de gueules ; le premier chargé de deux flambeaux d'or, allumés de gueules, &*

le fecond d'une tour d'argent, maçonnée de fable, furmontée d'une colombe auffi d'argent, tenant un pied fur la tour, & l'autre fur une branche de finople, pofée en pal.

BELCHAMPS. Suivant un Extrait des regiftres du Parlement de Metz, du 22 Janvier 1728, cette famille noble remonte à

I. Baudouin de Belchamps, marié à *Odillette de Sancy*, née en 1372, fille de *Thomas de Sancy*, Prevôt dudit lieu, & d'*Ifabelle de Hugues*, dont :

1. Louis, qui fuit ;
2. Marguerite, mariée, en 1444, à *Genot de Haut-Ecuyer*, fils de *Henri-Thomas*, Seigneur de Valleri, & de *Marie de Mornet*.

II. Louis de Belchamps, qui a rendu fes foi & hommage, le 15 Décembre 1487, à René, Duc de Lorraine, pour le fief de Molanville, mouvant du Duché de Bar, à caufe de la Châtellenie de Dun. On lui donne pour fils :

III. Gérard de Belchamps, qui rendit les mêmes foi & hommages, le 28 Novembre 1509, à Antoine, Duc de Lorraine, pour le fief de Molanville, mouvant dudit Duché de Bar, à caufe de la Châtellenie de Dun.

IV. Jean de Belchamps, Ier du nom, fon fils, Ecuyer, époufa *Jeanne Wamaux*. De leur mariage eft iffu :

V. François de Belchamps, Ier du nom, Ecuyer, Sieur de Tonne-Laloin, qui époufa *Catherine le Jeune*. De ce mariage vinrent :

1. Jean de Belchamps, Ecuyer, Sieur de Toillot, Lieutenant en la Prévôté de Dieppe, qui époufa *Claude de Dieuves*, fille de *Gérard de Dieuves*, & de *Barbe Anchevin*, auteur de la branche aînée qui va s'éteindre ;
2. François, qui fuit ;
3. Et Barbe de Belchamps, mariée à *Nicolas Lornet*, Ecuyer.

VI. François de Belchamps, IIe du nom, Ecuyer, Lieutenant en la Prevôté de Tilly fur Meufe, fe maria avec *Jacqueline de Dieuves*, fille d'*Ardien de Dieuves*, Prevôt de Tilly, dont :

1. Jean de Belchamps, Chanoine & Grand-Chantre de l'Eglife de Metz, Docteur en Droit, Archidiacre de Sarrebourg, Protonotaire Apoftolique, Confeiller, Aumônier du Roi, Prieur Commendataire de Zèle, & Adminiftrateur de l'Evêché ;
2. Pierre, qui fuit ;
3. Et Quentine de Belchamps, mariée à *Di-*

dier de la Hauſſe, Ecuyer, Contrôleur à Charny.

VII. Pierre de Belchamps, Ecuyer, Seigneur de Monthairon, teſta le 4 Octobre 1622. Il avoit épouſé, par contrat du 29 Mai 1599, *Marie d'Ambly*, fille d'*Herbin d'Ambly*, Ecuyer, & de *Barbe des Gableſt*. De leur mariage ſont iſſus :

1. Mathias de Belchamps, Chanoine de l'Egliſe Cathédrale de Metz ;
2. François, qui ſuit ;
3. Jeanne de Belchamps, mariée à *Nicolas de Watronville*, Ecuyer, Magiſtrat de Verdun ;
4. Et Anne de Belchamps, Religieuſe.

VIII. François de Belchamps, IIIᵉ du nom, Ecuyer, Seigneur de Monthairon, Avocat au Parlement, aſſocié à pluſieurs Académies du Royaume, teſta le 18 Janvier 1646. Il avoit épouſé *Nicole de Meſligny*, dont il eut :

1. Jean, qui ſuit ;
2. André de Belchamps, Ecuyer, Seigneur de Talange, & Avocat au Parlement, mort ſans poſtérité. Il avoit épouſé *Marguerite Conrard*, fille de *Nicolas Conrard*, Procureur du Roi au Bailliage & ſiège Préſidial de Metz, & de *Marguerite Fanchon ;*
3. François de Belchamps, Chanoine de l'Egliſe Cathédrale de Metz ;
4. Antoine de Belchamps, mort en bas âge ;
5. Et Bernard de Belchamps, Ecuyer, Lieutenant du Régiment du Roi, & depuis Capucin.

IX. Jean de Belchamps, IIᵉ du nom, Ecuyer, Sieur de Mondelange, Avocat au Parlement, teſta le 16 Décembre 1674. Il avoit épouſé *Marguerite Geoffroy*, fille de *Nicolas Geoffroy*, Ecuyer, Commiſſaire Provincial d'Artillerie, & de *Marguerite Machon*. Il eut :

1. Balthasard, qui ſuit ;
2. Et Charles, mort en bas âge.

X. Balthasard de Belchamps, Ecuyer, ci-devant Aide-Major au Régiment Lyonnois, depuis Conſeiller au Parlement de Metz, né le 18 Octobre 1666, mort le 31 Mars 1721, avoit épouſé, le 16 Décembre 1692, *Béatrix d'Auburten*, fille de *Charles d'Auburten*, Ecuyer, Conſeiller au Bailliage, & de *Nicole Conrard*. De ce mariage ſont iſſus :

1. Laurent, qui ſuit ;
2. Nicolas-François, rapporté ci-après ;
3. Pierre-Nicolas de Belchamps, Chevalier, Seigneur de Vaux, Juſſy & Sainte-Ruffine,

mort ſans poſtérité. Il avoit épouſé *Marie-Suſanne de Buʒelet*, fille de *Jacques de Buʒelet*, Ecuyer, Seigneur de Bagneux, Chevalier de l'Ordre de Saint-Louis, Lieutenant-Colonel du Régiment Dauphin Dragons, & de *Catherine Harquel ;*
4. Laurette-Béatrix de Belchamps, mariée à *Etienne-François le Bourgeois-du-Cheſray*, Ecuyer, Seigneur de Merry, Préſident au Préſidial de Verdun. De ce mariage ſont nés :

   Henri-Jean-Baptiſte, Garde-du-Corps du Roi ;
   Louis-Etienne, Chevalier de Saint-Louis, & ancien Commandant de Bataillon au Régiment de la Marck ;
   Jacques-Dominique-Laurent, ancien Capitaine d'Infanterie, & Garde-du-Corps du Roi ;
   Et une fille.

5. Elisabeth de Belchamps, morte ſans poſtérité. Elle avoit épouſé *Jean Ferry*, Seigneur de Lorry, Vaux, Juſſy & Sainte-Ruffine, Conſeiller Honoraire au Parlement de Metz ;
6. Et Anne de Belchamps, mariée à *Jacques-Dominique la Croix*, Seigneur du Sauly, Avocat du Roi au Bureau des Finances, dont :

   Jean, Capitaine d'Infanterie ;
   Françoiſe, mariée à *N.... d'Henʒelin*, Chevalier, Seigneur d'Hanonville ;
   Et *Marie-Nicole*.

X. Laurent de Belchamps, né le 12 Novembre 1699, Chevalier, Seigneur de Talange & de Montrequienne, Chevalier des Ordres de Saint-Lazare & de Notre-Dame du Mont-Carmel, s'eſt marié, le 13 Avril 1735, avec *Marie Gomé*, fille de *François-Brice Gomé*, Ecuyer, Secrétaire du Roi, Seigneur de la Grange, Manon & autres lieux, & de *Françoiſe Ory*, dont :

1. Jean de Belchamps, mort en bas âge ;
2. Marie-Susanne-Charlotte de Belchamps, mariée, le 15 Décembre 1761, à *Laurent-Adolphe Durand*, Ecuyer, Seigneur de Crepy, Chevalier de Saint-Louis, ancien Capitaine de Cavalerie au Régiment de Chabrillan, fils de *François-Benoît Durand*, Ecuyer, Seigneur de Diſtrof, Conſeiller Honoraire au Parlement de Metz, dont *François-Benoît-Charles-Pantaléon*, Seigneur de Crepy, né le 20 Janvier 1765 ;
3. Et Marie-Elisabeth de Belchamps, morte ſans poſtérité, le 13 Décembre 1758. Elle avoit épouſé, le 21 Février 1758, *N.... Macklon-de-Coligny*, Chevalier, Seigneur

de la Foreſt, Chevalier de Saint-Louis, Capitaine au Régiment de la Couronne.

X. Nicolas-François de Belchamps, Ier du nom, Seigneur de Sainte-Ruffine, Vaux & Juffy, Lieutenant des Maréchaux de France au département de Metz, ancien Officier au Régiment de Tournaiſis, s'eſt marié, le 22 Juillet 1738, avec *Marie-Louiſe du Bant*, fille de *Nicolas du Bant*, Conſeiller du Roi, Élu en l'Election de Sainte-Menehould, & de *Marie-Anne Langlois*, dont:

XI. Nicolas-François de Belchamps, IIe du nom, né le 27 Août 1740, marié, le 27 Février 1767, à *Marie-Adélaïde d'Origny*, fille de *Philippe-Louis d'Origny*, Chevalier, Sieur d'Agny, & de *Marguerite de Cambrai*, dont:

1. Antoine - Laurent - Dieudonné de Belchamps, né le 26 Octobre 1769.
2. Et Marie-Louise-Adélaïde-Rose-Nicole de Belchamps.

(Généalogie dreſſée ſur un Mémoire domeſtique envoyé).

Les armes : *écartelé, d'azur au pal componné de ſix pièces argent & gueules, à la croix d'or, chargée d'une molette de ſable.*

BELER : *d'argent, à deux faſces de ſable.*

* BELESTAT , Terre érigée en Comté, dont eſt titré le fils du Marquis de Gardouch, en Languedoc. Voyez GARDOUCH.

BELET-SAINT-GÉNAULT : *d'azur, à deux cotices engrêlées d'argent, ſeneſtrées en chef d'une belette d'or, accolée de gueules.*

BELGIOJOSO, Maiſon, l'une des plus anciennes & des plus célèbres d'Italie, connue dans les premiers tems ſous le nom de *Cunio*, qui étoit comptée parmi les plus illuſtres de Ravennes en 880. La Généalogie de cette Maiſon, qu'on trouve dans Moréri, commence à *Rainerio*, IIe du nom, dixième Comte de *Cunio*, qui fit en 1139, avec *Evido*, ſon frère, la guerre à la ville de Faenza. Pluſieurs de ce nom ſe ſont diſtingués au ſervice de France. Louis de Belgiojoso fut un grand homme de guerre, s'attacha à la France, & ſervit avec diſtinction en Italie & ſur les frontières d'Eſpagne, depuis 1510, juſqu'en 1516. Le Roi François Ier le fit ſon Conſeiller & ſon Chambellan, & l'envoya à Parme en 1521, pour

défendre cette ville contre les troupes réunies de l'Empereur & du Pape.

Albéric de Belgiojoso, frère cadet du précédent, ſe diſtingua auſſi dans les armées de France en Italie, juſqu'à la bataille de Pavie; & Pierre-François, Comte de Belgiojoſo, frère des précédens, ſervit auſſi le Roi de France depuis 1516 juſqu'en 1526, qu'il paſſa avec ſon frère Albéric au ſervice de l'Empereur Charles-Quint.

Antoine, Comte de Belgiojoſo, fut ſucceſſivement Envoyé de la Cour de Vienne en celles de Turin, de Modène & de Parme. L'Empereur Charles VI le fit ſon Chambellan, & l'Impératrice Reine de Hongrie l'a déclaré ſon Conſeiller Intime actuel d'Etat, par Lettres - Patentes du 23 Avril 1741. Il eſt mort le 26 Octobre 1769, laiſſant de *Barbe d'Adda*, fille de *Conſtance*, Comte d'Adda :

1. Albéric, qui ſuit ;
2. Louis-Charles-Marie, né le 2 Janvier 1728, Chevalier de Malte, Chambellan de Leurs Majeſtés Impériales, & Capitaine d'Infanterie au Régiment de Platz ;
3. Et Antoinette, mariée au Comte *della Somaglia*, Chambellan de Leurs Majeſtés Impériales.

Albéric, Comte de Belgiojoſo, né le 20 Octobre 1725, eſt Lieutenant-Colonel & Capitaine des Gendarmes du Corps de l'Archiduc Léopold d'Autriche, Grand Duc de Toſcane, & Chambellan de Leurs Majeſtés Impériales. Voyez Moréri, édition de 1759.

* BELHEM , Seigneurie en Flandre, qui fut érigée en Baronie par Lettres du Roi Catholique, du 25 Janvier 1655, regiſtrées à Lille, en faveur de *Charles de Rym*, Ecuyer, Seigneur de Belhem, de Schuerwelt & de Leckenbecke, l'un des ayeux d'*Anne-Thérèſe de Rym*, Baronne de Belhem, mariée à *Louis-François*, Prince de *Montmorency*, Comte de Logny, Vicomte de Roulers. (*Tablettes Généalogiques*, part. V, pag. 382.)

BELIARDI.N... Abbé Beliardi chargé en Eſpagne des affaires de la Marine & du Commerce de France, nommé en Juin 1767 Abbé de Saint-Florent-lès-Saumur, Ordre de Saint-Benoît, Diocèſe de Nantes.

BELIERE (la), Sieur de la Lorie, Election d'Avranches, ancienne nobleſſe, qui porte : *d'argent, au chef de fable, chargé de 2 molettes du champ.*

BELIERE : *parti d'argent, emmanché de fable.*

BELIERE : *d'or, au chef enté de fable.*

BELIERE (LA), en Bretagne, portoit anciennement : *de gueules, à une croix ancrée d'argent, chargée de cinq mouchetures d'hermines de fable;* & depuis : *écartelé, aux 1 & 4 d'or, au chef endenché de fable ; aux 2 & 3 contre-écartelé d'argent & de fable.*

BELIN, Sieur de la Rivière, Election de Coutances, famille annoblie en 1610, porte : *d'or, à la flamme de gueules, au chef d'azur, chargé de trois étoiles d'or.*

BELINGANT, Seigneur de Kerbabu, en Lanilis, Evêché de Léon : *de gueules, à trois quinte-feuilles d'argent, pofées 2 & 1.*

BELISAL, en Saint-Martin, Evêché de Léon : *de gueules, à fix befans d'or, pofés 3, 2 & 1.*

BELISLE, en Perdenec : *de gueules, à un croiffant d'argent, en abîme, accompagné de cinq coquilles de même, trois en chef & deux en pointe.*

BELISLE, près Guingamp, Evêché de Tréguier : *d'hermines, à une fafce de gueules, chargée de trois molettes d'éperon d'or.*

BELLANG-DE-TOURNEVILLE : *de gueules, femé de croifettes recroifettées au pied fiché d'argent, à trois befans de même, brochans fur le tout, pofés 2 & 1.*

BELLANGER, Seigneur d'Hôtel-la-Faux, de Nanteuil-la-Foffe : *de gueules, au lion d'argent ; au chef coufu d'azur, chargé de deux molettes d'éperon d'or, & foutenu d'une devife de même.*

BELLANGER (DE), en Normandie, Généralité de Caen : *de gueules, à deux aigles éployées d'argent, pofées l'une fur l'autre.*

BELLANGER, en Champagne : *d'azur, au chevron d'or.*

BELLANGER, à Paris : *de gueules, au lion d'argent ; au chef coufu d'azur, chargé de deux molettes d'éperon d'or, & foutenu d'une trangle, auffi d'or.*

BELLANGER : *d'argent, à la bande d'azur.*

BELLANGÈRE-TOURNEVILLE : *de gueules, femé de croix recroifettées d'argent, à trois tourterelles de même, fur le tout, pofées 2 & 1.*

BELLAY, Maifon éteinte, originaire d'Anjou, qui a été confidérable, non-feulement par les grands hommes qu'elle a produits, par les dignités qu'ils ont poffédées, & par les fervices importans qu'ils ont rendus à l'Etat, mais encore par fon ancienneté.

MATHIEU DU BELLAY eft nommé *Pannetier du Roi,* dans un don de 50 livres parifis de rente, qui lui fut fait à héritage, le 12 Juillet 1372.

GUILLAUME DU BELLAY, connu fous le nom de *Seigneur de Langei,* fignala fon courage en diverfes occafions, & fe fit admirer par fa conduite & par fa valeur, fous le règne de FRANÇOIS Ier. Le Cardinal JEAN DU BELLAY, fon frère, Evêque de Paris, s'appliqua à l'étude des Belles-Lettres avec tant de fuccès, qu'il eut la réputation de très-bien écrire en latin, & de faire de très-beaux vers en cette langue. Le Roi FRANÇOIS Ier lui confia des emplois confidérables, & le nomma à quantité d'Ambaffades. Ce fut lui qui fe fervit de fa faveur pour l'avancement des Lettres, & qui fe joignit au fçavant Budé, pour perfuader au Roi de fonder le Collège Royal ; ce que ce grand Prince fit en 1529.

Cette Maifon a formé plufieurs branches. La première a fini à *Giraud,* IIIe du nom, Seigneur de *Montreuil-Bellay,* qui ne laiffa de *Marguerite Avant* qu'une fille unique, nommée *Agnès,* Dame de Montreuil-Bellay, mariée 1º à *Guillaume,* Vicomte de *Melun ;* 2º à *Valeran d'Ivri* ; 3º à *Etienne de Saumur :* elle a eu des enfans de fes trois maris, & entr'autres du premier, *Adam,* Vicomte de *Melun,* Seigneur de Montreuil-Bellay, qui laiffa cette dernière Terre à fa poftérité, d'où elle paffa dans la Maifon d'Harcourt, qui la porta dans celle de Longueville, & fut vendue au Maréchal de la Meilleraye.

La feconde branche, qui eft celle des Seigneurs du *Bellay* & de *Thouarcé,* a commencé à HUGUES DU BELLAY, fils puîné de BERLAY, IVe du nom, qui vivoit en 1227, & a fini au XXe degré, à CHARLES, Marquis DU BELLAY, Prince d'Yvetot, mort fans laiffer de poftérité. Il avoit époufé, en 1622, *Hélène de Rieux.* Après fa mort, la fubftitution fut déclarée ouverte au profit d'*Antoine-Saladin d'Anglure-*

Savigny, Comte d'Eftoges, fils aîné de *Charles Saladin*, & de *Marie Babou*. Leur defcendant aîné mâle portoit le nom & les armes *du Bellay*, & en poffédoit la Terre. Voyez ANGLURE.

La troifième branche eft celle des Seigneurs de *la Courbe*, & de *la Feuillée*, qui a eu pour chef EUSTACHE DU BELLAY, fecond fils de JACQUES DU BELLAY, Baron de Thouarcé, & d'*Antoinette de la Palu*, qui vient de finir dans GUILLAUME DU BELLAY, Colonel du Régiment de Brie, Brigadier des Armées du Roi, qui paffa, en 1741, au fervice du Roi des Deux-Siciles, qui le fit Maréchal-de-Camp. Il eft mort à Naples en 1752.

La quatrième branche eft celle des Seigneurs de *la Palu* & des *Buarts*, qui a commencé à JACQUES DU BELLAY, fils puîné d'EUSTACHE, & de *Guionne d'Orange*, Dame de la Feuillée & de la Courbe, & a fini à RENÉ DU BELLAY, IIᵉ du nom, Baron de la Flotte, Gouverneur de Metz, & Lieutenant de Roi de la Province de Touraine, qui a laiffé de *Catherine le Vayer* :

    RENÉE, Dame de la Flotte, mariée à *Charles*, Seigneur d'*Hautefort*;
    Et CATHERINE DU BELLAY, alliée à *Philippe de Bigni*, Seigneur d'Ainay.

La cinquième & dernière branche eft celle des Seigneurs de *Langei*, & n'a formé que II degrés. MARTIN DU BELLAY, Seigneur de Langei, après la mort de fon frère aîné, mourut le 9 Mars 1559, & laiffa d'*Ifabelle Chenu*, Princeffe d'Yvetot :

    MARIE, Princeffe d'Yvetot, & Dame de Langei, mariée à RENÉ, Seigneur du BELLAY, fon parent;
    Et CATHERINE DU BELLAY, alliée à *Charles de Beaumanoir*, Seigneur de Lavardin. Voyez pour la filiation de ces différentes branches, Moréri.

Les armes : *d'argent à la bande fufelée de gueules, accompagnée de 6 fleurs-de-lys, 3 en chef, pofées 2 & 1, & 3 en pointe, mifes en bande.*

La branche de THOUARCÉ portoit : *d'or, à la bande fufelée d'azur, accompagnée de fix fleurs-de-lys de même, pofées en orle,*

BELLEAU, famille noble & ancienne, dont étoit JEAN DE BELLEAU, Seigneur de Châlons-le-Meldeux, marié à *Lucie de Gernicourt*, dont entr'autres enfans PERRETTE DE BELLEAU, Dame de Châlons-le-Meldeux, femme de *Jean Gigault*, Seigneur d'Orinville, fils de Jac-

ques, Seigneur de Han, & de *Jeanne Olivier*, Dame d'Orinville, dont poftérité. Les armes : *d'azur à trois coquilles d'or*, 2 & 1.

BELLEAU (DE), Seigneur de Petite-Ville, de Jumelière, en Normandie, Election de Verneuil, noble & ancienne famille, dont étoit GERVAIS DE BELLEAU, Evêque de Séez, mort en 1363, & dont les armes font : *d'argent, à deux fafces d'azur, accompagnées de cinq mouchetures d'hermines de fable, 4 en chef, & 1 en pointe.*

BELLEAU (DE), même Province, Généralité d'Alençon & Election d'Argentan, noble & ancienne, famille qui porte : *d'hermines, à deux fafces d'azur.*

BELLEAU (DE), Seigneur de Courtonne, même Province, Généralité & Election de Lifieux, noble & ancienne famille, dont les armes font : *d'hermines, à trois fafces d'azur.*

BELLECOMBE, en Dauphiné : *d'or à la bande de fable.*

BELLECOMBE : *de gueules, à la fafce d'or, chargée de trois fleurs-de-lys d'azur, au lion d'argent, iffant de la fafce.*

BELLÉE, mêmes Province & Généralité, Election de Domfront, noble & ancienne famille, qui porte : *de fable, à trois quinte-feuilles d'argent 2 & 1.*

BELLEFAYE : *écartelé, aux 1 & 4 d'azur, au chevron d'or, aux 2 & 3 d'or, à la fafce de fable.*

BELLEFONDS. Jeanne de Graffignone, Dame de Bellefonds, fille de *Jean*, Seigneur de Bellefonds, & de *Jacquette de Boue*, porta cette Seigneurie, en 1488, à fon mari *Hélion Gigault*. Voyez GIGAULT DE BELLEFONDS.

BELLEFONS : *d'azur, au chevron d'or, accompagné de trois lofanges d'argent, 2 en chef & 1 en pointe.*

BELLEFORIÈRE, en Artois, anciennement BELLEFOURIÈRE, Maifon qui a donné un Chevalier des Ordres, un Grand-Maître de la Garderobe, & un Grand-Veneur de France dans CHARLES-MAXIMILIEN-ANTOINE DE BELLEFORIÈRE, Marquis de Soyecourt, rapporté ci-après. Le premier connu de ce nom eft :

    I. JEAN, Seigneur DE BELLEFORIÈRE, qui fervoit en Normandie en 1353 fous le Maréchal d'Audenhehan, & en Picardie en 1355 fous le même Maréchal. Il fervit auffi en Flandre fous le Seigneur de Conci, & vivoit encore en 1383. Il fut marié 1° avec *Marie de Vaifières* ; & 2° avec *Agnès de Rimaucourt.* Il eut du premier lit :

1. JEANNE, mariée à *Jean de Chièvres*, Châtelain de Lens.

Et du fecond :

2. ROBERT, qui fuit ;
3. Et PIERRE, Commis à la Garde de la Ville d'Ardembourg, tué auprès de Gand.

II. ROBERT, Seigneur DE BELLEFORIÈRE, &c., rendit aveu en 1385, de la Terre de Belleforière, au Duc de Bourgogne, Comte de Flandre & d'Artois, comme mouvante de fon Château de Lens, & fervoit en Flandre en 1396 avec 100 Lances, dit Froiffard, tom. IV, p. 44. On lui donne pour femme *Marie*, fille de *Jacques de la Vieuville*, Seigneur de Flers, & de *Marie de Ghiftelles*, dont :

III. JEAN, II° du nom, Seigneur DE BELLEFORIÈRE & d'Ittre, qui vivoit en 1397, & fut Confeiller & Chambellan de JEAN & de PHILIPPE, Ducs de Bourgogne. Il mourut le 31 Octobre 1438, laiffant de *Jeanne de Landas*, morte le 1er Mars 1449, fille de *Mathieu de Mortagne*, Baron de Landas & de Bouvignies, & d'*Ifabeau de Bourzies* :

1. PERCEVAL, qui fuit ;
2. Et JACQUES, Seigneur de Romeri, qui d'*Anne de Bouvet*, fille de *Jean le Bout*, dit *Bouvet*, eut PHILIPPE DE BELLEFORIÈRE, Gouverneur du Château de Hall en 1488, mort fans poftérité d'*Ifabelle de Vaülieze.*

IV. PERCEVAL, Seigneur DE BELLEFORIÈRE & d'Ittre, Confeiller & Chambellan du Duc de Bourgogne en 1471, & depuis Confeiller & Chambellan de l'Empereur MAXIMILIEN Ier, tefta en 1475, & mourut âgé de 80 ans. Il avoit époufé, le 24 Novembre 1452, *Jacqueline*, fille de *Renaud de Longueval*, Seigneur de Thenelles, & de *Jeanne de Montmorency*. Il eut :

1. MICHEL, Seigneur de Belleforière, d'Ittre & de Noyelle-le-Godard, Confeiller & Chambellan du Roi CHARLES VIII, Bailli & Gouverneur de Lens & de Hénin-Liétard, qui n'eut pas d'enfans de *Jeanne de Neuville*, remariée à *Gilbert de Lannoy*, Seigneur de Villerval. Elle étoit fille de *Jean*, Seigneur de Bombers, & d'*Ifabeau de Ligne* ;
2. PIERRE, qui fuit ;
3. Et JEANNE, mariée, le 14 Juin 1469, avec

Jean de Sains, dit *l'Aigle*, Seigneur de Caveron & de Guyencourt.

V. PIERRE DE BELLEFORIÈRE, Seigneur de Thun, Saint Martin & de Beaumanoir en Cambréfis, fuccéda à fon frère aîné ès Terres de Belleforière, d'Ittre, de Noyelle-le-Godard, &c. Il fut Gouverneur de Corbie en 1496, & élu le 23 Janvier 1515 tuteur honoraire de LOUIS DE BOURBON, Comte de Marle, fils aîné de CHARLES, Duc de Vendôme, dont il étoit Confeiller & Chambellan. Il mourut en 1530. Il avoit époufé, le 22 Février 1512, *Madeleine de Coucy*, remariée le 7 Septembre 1535, avec *Antoine de Hames*, Seigneur d'Andifer. Elle étoit fille de *Raoul*, & d'*Hélène de la Chapelle*. Leurs enfans furent :

1. CHARLES, qui fuit ;
2. CLAUDE, auteur de la branche des Seigneurs de *Thun* & de *Belleforière*, rapportée ci-après ;
3. FRANÇOISE, *aliàs* LOUISE, alliée à *Jacques de Moreuil*, Seigneur de Frefnoy & de Tanques ;
4. MADELEINE, Abbeffe d'Origni ;
5. Et ANTOINETTE, Religieufe à la Fère.

VI. CHARLES, Seigneur DE BELLEFORIÈRE, d'Ittre, Cagni, le grand & le petit d'Olezy, &c., Confeiller & Chambellan du Roi, Chevalier de fon Ordre, Gentilhomme de fa Chambre, & Gouverneur de Corbie en Juin 1556, mourut en 1567. Il eut de *Catherine de Saintau*, fille de *Philippe*, & de *Charlotte de la Foreft* :

1. PONTUS, qui fuit ;
2. ROBERT, Seigneur d'Olezy, Capitaine de Chevaux-Légers, Gouverneur de Bohain, tué en une fortie devant Cambray en 1594, fans laiffer de poftérité de *Marie d'Etampes*, veuve de *Louis de Hallincourt*, & fille de *Jacques*, Seigneur de Valençay, & de *Jeanne Bernard* ;
3. ADRIENNE, mariée à *Charles du Châtelet*, Seigneur de Moyencourt, fils de *Charles*, Chevalier, & d'*Antoinette de Moyencourt* ;
4. Et ANTOINETTE, femme d'*Antoine de Hallincourt*, Seigneur de Gonteville.

VII. PONTUS, felon le P. Anfelme, & PONTHIS felon Moréri, Seigneur DE BELLEFORIÈRE, d'Ittre, de Noyelle-le-Godard, &c., Chevalier de l'Ordre du Roi, Gentilhomme de fa Chambre, Guidon le 20 Février 1579 de la Compagnie des Gendarmes du Marquis d'Elbeuf, vendit fa Terre de Belleforière à CLAUDE, fon oncle, auteur de la feconde branche, rapportée ci-après. Il fut tué, lors de la prise de Corbie, en 1636, de laquelle il étoit Gouverneur, par le Seigneur d'Humières. Il avoit épousé *Françoise*, Dame *de Soyecourt* & de Tilloloi, veuve de *Jean de Thuis*, Colonel de l'Infanterie Françoise ; remariée à *Thibaut de Mailly*, Seigneur de Remaugis & d'Orvilliers, dont elle eut aussi des enfans. Elle étoit fille aînée & principale héritière de *François*, Seigneur *de Soyecourt*, & de *Charlotte de Mailly*. En vertu de ce mariage, ses descendans se sont qualifiés *Seigneurs de Soyecourt*. Il laissa :

1. ALBERT, mort jeune le 25 Février 1586 ;
2. MAXIMILIEN, qui suit ;
3. Et GEOFFROY, Seigneur d'Ittre & de Cagni, qui eut de *Léonore de Bournonville*, fille de *Louis*, Seigneur du Quesnoi, & d'*Antoinette de Moreuil*, ARTUS, mort sans alliance ; THIBAUT, mort à la bataille de Rocroy, le 19 Mai 1643 ; CHARLES, tué en duel près Amiens ; FRANÇOIS, mort jeune ; & ANTOINETTE, morte âgée de 16 ans.

VIII. MAXIMILIEN DE BELLEFORIÈRE, Seigneur d'Ittre & de Soyecourt, Marquis de Guerbigni, & Comte de Tilloloi, successivement Colonel d'un Régiment d'Infanterie, Maréchal-de-Camp, & Lieutenant-Général au Gouvernement de Picardie & de Boulonnois en 1634, commandoit dans Corbie lorsque cette Place fut assiégée & prise par les Espagnols en 1636. Son procès lui fut fait pour n'avoir pas fait assez de résistance ; il se sauva en Angleterre, d'où il revint en France après s'être justifié, & se retira dans le Couvent des Jacobins de la rue du Bac à Paris, où il mourut le 22 Mars 1649. Il épousa, le 27 Septembre 1618, *Judith de Mesmes*, morte le 5 Mai 1659, fille de *Jean-Jacques*, Conseiller d'Etat, & d'*Antoinette de Grossaines*. Il eut :

1. CHARLES-MAXIMILIEN-ANTOINE, qui suit ;
2. CHARLES - LOUIS, Comte de Tupigny, tué devant Bar-le-Duc en 1649, sans avoir été marié ;
3. Et FRANÇOISE-ANTOINETTE, Religieuse aux Filles de la Visitation-Sainte-Marie, rue Saint-Antoine à Paris.

IX. CHARLES-MAXIMILIEN-ANTONIE DE BELLEFORIÈRE, Marquis de Soyecourt, &c., Chevalier des Ordres du Roi, & Grand-Maître de la Garderobe, dont nous avons parlé au commencement de cette Généalogie, mourut le 12 Juillet 1679. Il avoit épousé, le 23 Fé-

vrier 1656, *Marie-Renée de Longueil*, morte le 1er Octobre 1712, fille de *René*, Marquis de Maisons, Président à Mortier au Parlement de Paris, Ministre d'Etat & Surintendant des Finances, &c., & de *Madeleine*, alias *Anne de Boulenc-de-Crevecœur*, Dame de Grisolles. De ce mariage vinrent :

1. LOUIS, mort en 1674 ;
2. JEAN-MAXIMILIEN, Marquis de Soyecourt, Colonel du Régiment de Vermandois, tué à la bataille de Fleurus le 1er Juillet 1690, sans avoir été marié ;
3. ADOLPHE, dit *le Chevalier de Soyecourt*, Capitaine-Lieutenant des Gendarmes Dauphins, mort le 3 Juillet 1690 des blessures qu'il reçut à la même bataille ;
4. MARIE-RENÉE, qui suit ;
5. Et ELISABETH, morte au mois d'Avril 1725. Elle avoit épousé, 1° le 6 Août 1682, *Louis de Romillé*, Marquis de la Chesnelaye & de Mauçon en Bretagne, Gouverneur de Fougères ; & 2° le 6 Octobre 1713, *Joseph-Joachim du Maz*, Comte de Brossay.

CHARLES-MAXIMILIEN-ANTOINE DE BELLEFORIÈRE eut encore deux fils naturels :

Louis, né de *Marie Hennemer*, le 15 Septembre 1666 ;
Et *Jean*, dit *Tirbous*, dont la mère est inconnue, qui se fit Religieux Augustin déchaussé en 1689, & fut ensuite reçu en 1708 parmi les Ecclésiastiques de l'Ordre de Saint-Jean de Jérusalem.

X. MARIE-RENÉE DE BELLEFORIÈRE prit après la mort de ses frères la qualité de *Marquise de Belleforière*, & mourut le 25 Avril 1739, âgée de 82 ans. Elle avoit épousé, par contrat du 5 Février 1682, *Timoléon-Gilbert de Seiglières*, Seigneur de Boisfranc, Maître des Requêtes ordinaire de l'Hôtel du Roi, & Chancelier de PHILIPPE DE FRANCE, Duc d'Orléans, frère unique du Roi LOUIS XIV, mort le 1er Février 1695, fils de *Joachim de Seiglières*, Seigneur de Boisfranc, Chancelier & Garde-des-Sceaux du même Prince, & de *Geneviève de Gedouin*, dont des enfans. Voyez SEIGLIÈRES.

BRANCHE
des Seigneurs DE THUN *&* DE BELLEFORIÈRE.

VI. CLAUDE DE BELLEFORIÈRE, fils puîné de PIERRE, & de *Madeleine de Coucy*, fut Seigneur de Thun, puis de Belleforière par acquisition. Il épousa 1° *Marie de Saint-Blai-*

fe, d'une ancienne nobleſſe de Champagne, de laquelle il n'eut point d'enfans; & 2º *Marie de Waſtini,* veuve d'*Antoine de Habart,* Vicomte de Harteu, dont il eut :

1. MAXIMILIEN, Seigneur de Thun, Capitaine d'une Compagnie de Cavalerie, qui épouſa *Louiſe de Bernimicourt,* fille unique de *Georges de Bernimicourt,* Seigneur du Meſnil, & de *Marie de Pingret,* dont il eut ROBERT, Chevalier, Seigneur de Thun, mort, laiſſant de *Marguerite de Wigles,* fille de *N.... de Wigles,* Seigneur de Meuves, & de *Marie de Wedeville,* entr'autres enfans, un fils tué en duel en 1647; MARIE, femme de *Charles de Bonmarchez,* Seigneur de la Brielle; & FRANÇOISE, Religieuſe à Bourbourg.
2. JEAN, qui ſuit;
3. & 4. FRANÇOISE & MARIE, toutes deux mortes ſans alliance.

VII. JEAN DE BELLEFORIÈRE, Chevalier, Seigneur de Belleforière, de Rots, Warendin & Courcelles-aux-Bois, épouſa *Anne de Nédonchel,* fille de *François,* Seigneur d'Ibergnes, & d'*Iſabeau du Biez,* dont il eut :

1. ALEXANDRE, qui ſuit;
2. Et MADELEINE, mariée, en 1622, à *Robert de Lens,* Chevalier, Seigneur de Blendecques, fils d'*Oudard de Lens,* Seigneur du même lieu, & de *Marguerite de Nédonchel.*

VIII. ALEXANDRE DE BELLEFORIÈRE, Chevalier, Seigneur de Belleforière, &c., eut de *N.....* entr'autres enfans :

IX. PHILIPPE-MAXIMILIEN-IGNACE DE BELLEFORIÈRE, Chevalier, Seigneur de Thun, qui fut d'abord Page du Roi dans ſa Grande-Ecurie en 1691, & mourut, laiſſant pluſieurs enfans, tous morts ſans poſtérité.

Les armes : *de ſable, ſemé de fleurs-delys d'or.*

* BELLEGARDE, Ville ſur la Saône en Bourgogne, qui étoit autrefois aſſez forte, & portoit le nom de *Seurre;* elle eſt à environ cinq ou ſix lieues de Châlons au-deſſus de Verdun, ſur les frontières de la Franche-Comté. Elle ne porte le nom de *Bellegarde* que depuis qu'elle fut érigée en Duché-Pairie, en faveur de *Roger de Saint-Lary,* Seigneur de Bellegarde, Grand-Ecuyer de France, Chevalier des Ordres du Roi, & de ſes hoirs & héritiers mâles, au mois de Septembre 1619. Les titres de Duché-Pairie furent depuis transférés au mois de Décembre 1645 ſur le Marquiſat de Choiſy-aux-Loges en Gâtinois,

acquis par le Préſident *Gautier de Baſſigny.* Le nom de *Bellegarde* eſt reſté à cette dernière Terre, qui a appartenu à M. le Duc d'*Antin.* Quant à la ville de *Seurre,* premier Duché de Bellegarde, elle appartient au Prince de Condé, qui ſe qualifie *Duc de Bellegarde,* ainſi qu'ont fait ſes ancêtres depuis HENRI DE BOURBON, IIᵉ du nom, Prince de Condé.

BELLEGARDE, Maiſon originaire de Flandre, & depuis long-tems établie en Savoie, où elle eſt fort diſtinguée par ſes alliances & ſon ancienneté.

I. JEAN-NOEL, Seigneur de BELLEGARDE, Maître-d'Hôtel de CHARLES III, Duc de Savoie, eut de *Claudine de Saint-Triviers,* Dame de Monts :

II. FRANÇOIS-NOEL DE BELLEGARDE, Seigneur de Monts & des Marches, Gouverneur de Nice, Ambaſſadeur du Duc de Savoie, auprès de l'Empereur CHARLES-QUINT, marié, le 4 Octobre 1546, à *Gaſparde de Menthon,* dont :

III. JEAN-FRANÇOIS DE BELLEGARDE, Iᵉʳ du nom, Marquis d'Antremont & des Marches, Colonel des Gardes de CHARLES-EMMANUEL, Duc de Savoie. Par ſon teſtament du 3 Août 1537, il inſtitua pour héritier ſon fils. Il avoit épouſé *Florentine de Perrache,* dont :

IV. CLAUDE-ANDRÉ DE BELLEGARDE, Marquis d'Antremont & des Marches, marié à *Gaſparde d'Oncieux,* dont il eut :

1. JEAN-FRANÇOIS, qui ſuit;
2. PIERRE, Abbé de Saint-Sixte;
3. GUILLAUME, Comte d'Antremont, marié à *Anne-Françoiſe de Loche;*
4. Et CLAIRE, mariée le 27 Août 1646, à *Charles de Broſſes,* Baron de Montfalcon, Seigneur de Tournay, Grand-Bailli de Gex, dont elle a poſtérité.

V. JEAN-FRANÇOIS DE BELLEGARDE, Marquis d'Antremont & des Marches, Capitaine de Cavalerie, épouſa, le 13 Avril 1632, *Madeleine Portier-de-Mieudry,* dont il a eu :

VI. JANUS DE BELLEGARDE, Marquis d'Antremont & des Marches, Ambaſſadeur du Roi de Sicile, Duc de Savoie, à la Cour de France, marié, le 23 Avril 1687, à *Catherine-Françoiſe de Regard-de-Varo,* dont :

1. JOSEPH-FRANÇOIS, qui ſuit;
2. Et CLAUDE-MARIE, Comte de Bellegarde & d'Antremont, Envoyé Extraordinaire du Roi de Pologne, Electeur de Saxe, à la Cour

de France, mort à Paris le 26 Février 1755. Il avoit époufé, en 1736, Marie-Anne, créée à fa naiffance, en 1706, Comteffe Rutowska, mariée, 1º au mois d'Octobre 1725, à *Michel*, Comte *Bielinski*. Elle étoit fille naturelle de Frédéric - Auguste Ier, Roi de Pologne, & d'*Aurore-Marie*, Comteffe de *Kœnigfmarck*, & fœur de *Maurice*, Comte de Saxe, Maréchal de France. Il a laiffé :

1. N..., Chambellan du feu Roi de Pologne, marié à Drefde ;
2. Et N.... de Bellegarde, établi & marié à Prague.
3. Et N.... de Bellegarde, Gouverneur des Princes de Saxe.

VII. Joseph-François de Bellegarde, Marquis des Marches & de Courfinge, Comte d'Antremont, Commandeur de l'Ordre de Saint-Maurice, Gentilhomme de la Chambre du Roi de Sardaigne, marié à *Françoife-Charlotte Ogletorpe*, en a :

N... de Bellegarde, Colonel au fervice d'Angleterre ;
N... mariée au Seigneur *de Maffingy*, Marquis de la Pierre ;
Et Charlotte-Eléonore, Chanoineffe en Lorraine. (*Mercure de France* du mois de Mai 1755.)

Les armes : *d'azur, aux rayons droits & ondés alternativement, mouvans d'une portion de cercle du chef vers la pointe de l'écu d'or, chaque intervalle de rayons rempli d'une flamme renverfée de même, au nombre de fix en tout, au chef d'or, chargé d'une aiglette de fable.*

BELLEGARDE : *d'azur, à la cloche d'argent, bataillée de fable.*

BELLEHACHE, Seigneur d'Outreval, Election de Mortagne, Généralité d'Alençon, en Normandie, noble & ancienne famille qui porte : *de gueules, à la croix d'argent, cantonnée de quatre merlettes de même.*

*　BELLE-ISLE, avec un Fort, fituée fur les Côtes de Bretagne, donnée par Charles IX à *Charles de Gondy*, Comte de Retz, tué en 1596, & érigée en fa faveur en Marquifat en 1570. Voyez FOUQUET & GONDY.

BELLEMARE, en Normandie, Diocèfe d'Evreux, ancienne nobleffe, dont parle la Roque, & plufieurs autres Ecrivains de Normandie. Un Bellemare paffa dans la Terre-Sainte en 1214 avec Saint-Louis. Un autre

Guillaume de Bellemare fut appelé à l'arrière-ban en 1442. Un autre Bellemare fut Sergent de bataille & Gouverneur de Sainte-Ménehould. On trouve auffi un Bellemare, Chambellan du Roi Charles VII ; un Bellemare, Exempt des Gardes-du-Corps ; & un autre, Favori du Grand Dauphin, fils de Louis XIV, ce qui fe prouve par plufieurs Lettres de ce Prince, que l'on conferve dans la famille, mort au Camp de Timéon, à deux lieues de Charleroy, & inhumé le 23 Mai 1675 dans l'Eglife dudit Village.

Il y a trois branches dans cette famille, la première eft celle de Bellemare-Duranville, dont nous n'avons nulle connoiffance, non plus que de la feconde, qui eft Bellemare-Neuville, dont fort M. de Bellemare-Thiebert, Seigneur de Valhebert & autres lieux.

La troifième eft celle de Bellemare-de-Saint-Cyr, dont nous allons donner la filiation, fuivant un *Mémoire* qui nous a été envoyé.

BRANCHE
des Seigneurs de Bellemare-Saint-Cyr.

Jean de Bellemare, Ier du nom, Ecuyer, Seigneur & Patron de Beaugra, vivoit en 1300. Il eut pour fils :

Robert de Bellemare, Ecuyer, marié, en 1386, avec *Jeanne de la Queze*, fille de *Guillaume de la Queze*, Ecuyer. Il partagea les biens de *Guillaume de la Queze* avec la fœur cadette de fa femme en 1391 ; & les Terres qu'il eut font encore dans la famille. De fon mariage vint :

Jean de Bellemare, IIe du nom, Ecuyer, qui époufa, par contrat paffé devant *Echallard*, Garde pour le Roi, en la Vicomté d'Orbec le 22 Mai 1454, *Guillemette de la Rivière*, dont vint :

Jean de Bellemare, IIIe du nom, Ecuyer, qui s'allia, par acte paffé devant *Guillaume & Michel de Bailhache*, Tabellions Royaux, au Bourgthéroulde, le 19 Octobre 1491, avec *Jeanne le Muet*, fille d'*Artus le Muet*, Ecuyer. De ce mariage vint :

Louis de Bellemare, Ecuyer, qui fe maria, par contrat paffé devant les Tabellions du Neuf-Bourg, le 4 Octobre 1518, avec une des filles de *Charles du Bofguyon*, Ecuyer, Sieur des Jardins. Leur fils fut :

François de Bellemare, Ier du nom, Ecuyer, qui époufa, le 31 Août 1556, *Fran-*

coiſe Eude, fille de *Guillaume Eude*, Ecuyer, Sieur de Norois. De ce mariage vint :

ANTOINE DE BELLEMARE, Ecuyer, marié, le 21 Octobre 1601, avec *Marguerite de Mongoubert*, fille d'*Antoine de Mongoubert*, Ecuyer. Il fut père de :

PHILÉMON DE BELLEMARE, Ecuyer, qui, par contrat paſſé devant les Tabellions de Pont-de-l'Arche, le 6 Février 1635, ſe maria avec *Anne de Malhortie*, Dame de Neufvillette, fille héritière en partie de *Marguerin de Malhortie*, Ecuyer, Sieur de la Garenne.

FRANÇOIS DE BELLEMARE, IIe du nom, Ecuyer, leur fils, fit alliance, par acte paſſé devant les Tabellions de Saint-Georges-du-Vieuvre le 24 Février 1669, avec *Anne des Perrières*, fille de *Jacques des Perrières*, Ecuyer, dont :

1. PHILÉMON-FRANÇOIS, qui ſuit ;
Et deux autres garçons, l'un tué à Malplaquet le 11 Septembre 1709, & l'autre dans un combat particulier.

PHILÉMON-FRANÇOIS DE BELLEMARE, marié, en 1699, avec *Françoiſe de Hayes-de-Goſſard*, fille de *N... de Hayes*, Ecuyer, a eu pour enfans :

1. CYR-SÉBASTIEN-FRANÇOIS, qui ſuit ;
2. FRANÇOIS, qui a ſervi très-long-tems dans l'Infanterie, & dans les Indes-Orientales. Il a épouſé Demoiſelle *des Perrières-de-Saint-Marc*, dont ſont iſſus deux garçons : l'aîné a huit ans, & le cadet cinq ;
3. NICOLAS, Capitaine au Régiment des Graſ-fins, & Chevalier de Saint-Louis. Il s'eſt trouvé au ſiège de Prague, à l'action de Mesle en Flandre, à la bataille de Fontenoy, & à celle de Lawfeld, où il reçut pluſieurs bleſſures dont il eſt mort en 1747. Sa bonne conduite & ſa valeur l'ont fait regretter de ſes Officiers Généraux ;
4. MARC-ANTOINE, Chevalier de Saint-Louis, appelé *le Chevalier de Saint-Cyr*, Brigadier des Mousquetaires du Roi dans la ſeconde Compagnie, & Gouverneur des Ville & Château de Conche ;
Et quatre filles.

CYR-SÉBASTIEN-FRANÇOIS DE BELLEMARE, Ecuyer, Chevalier, Seigneur & Patron de Saint-Cyr & de Salerne, Chevalier de Saint-Louis, & Lieutenant de MM. les Maréchaux de France, a épouſé, par contrat paſſé le 15 Novembre 1744, & dépoſé devant les Conſeillers du Roi, Notaires au Châtelet de Paris le 4 Avril 1745, *Eliſabeth de Canonville*,

Tome II.

fille de *Georges de Canonville*, laquelle lui a apporté en dot les Terres, Seigneuries & Patronages des Paroiſſes du Meſnil-au-Vicomte, Burey, Louverſey en partie, le Breuil, Poignard, & le Clos-Marin. Il ne reſte de l'illuſtre Maiſon de *Canonville* que le Marquis *de Ravetot*, & une branche qui ſubſiſte en Angleterre, ſous le nom de *Caneville*. De ce mariage ſont nés :

1. NICOLAS, qui a été Page de la Reine, & eſt depuis 1769 Mousquetaire du Roi dans ſa ſeconde Compagnie ;
2. GEORGES-CYR-MARC, élevé à l'Ecole Royale Militaire, Chevalier de l'Ordre de Saint-Lazare, & Officier au Régiment de Cambréſis ;
3. GEORGETTE-ELISABETH-ANNE-FOI ;
4. Et ELISABETH, Elève de la Maiſon Royale de Saint-Cyr.

Les alliances ſont avec les Maiſons de *la Luzerne, Beuzeville, Blancménil, la Fonds; Guitry, Chaumont, Merle, Rupierre, Bonnet-de-la-Tour, Nocey, le Roux-d'Eſneval, Chambray, Nollent, Lieurey, Franqueville*, &c.

Les armes : *de gueules, faſcé d'argent, à trois carpes de même, deux en chef, & une en pointe.*

BELLÊME & CHATEAU-GONTIER.

Voici une des plus grandes & des plus illuſtres Maiſons du Royaume, & qui eſt éteinte depuis ſi long-tems, qu'on n'en peut parler dans toute la régularité qu'on auroit voulu. Comme ce tems qu'elle ſubſiſtoit les armes n'étoient pas encore fixes dans les familles, on ne peut pas aſſurer de celles de cette Maiſon; néanmoins les derniers qui en ont été portoient : *d'argent, à trois chevrons de gueules.*

IVES DE BELLÊME, Comte de Bellême & d'Alençon, un des plus grands & des plus riches Seigneurs de ſon tems, épouſa *Godechilde*, dont il eut :

1. GUILLAUME, qui ſuit ;
2. IVES, qui fit la branche des Seigneurs de *Château-Gontier* ;
3. AVESGAUD, Evêque du Mans ;
4. HILDEBURGE, femme de *Hamon* ou *Hamelin*, Seigneur de *Château-du-Loir* ;
5. Et GODECHILDE, dont on ignore l'alliance.

GUILLAUME DE BELLÊME, Ier du nom, Comte de Bellême & d'Alençon, eut de *Mathilde* :

1. Robert, Comte d'Alençon & de Bellème, mort fans hoirs;
2. Guillaume, qui fuit;
3. Et Ives, Comte de Bellème, Evêque de Séez.

Guillaume de Bellème, IIe du nom, Comte d'Alençon & de Bellème, furnommé *Talvas*, épousa *Hildeburge*, de laquelle il eut:
1. Arnoul, mort jeune;
2. Et Mabille, Comteffe de Bellème, d'Alençon & de Séez, femme de *Roger*, Seigneur *de Montgommery*.

BRANCHE
des Seigneurs de Chateau-Gontier.

Ives de Bellème, fecond fils d'Ives, Comte de Bellème & d'Alençon, & de *Godechilde*, fut père de:

Renaud de Bellème, Ier du nom, Chevalier, qui reçut la Terre de Château-Gontier en don de *Geoffroy Martel*, Comte d'Anjou, qui lui fit époufer *Béatrix*, fa nièce, dont il eut:
1. Alard, qui fuit;
2. Renaud, qui fit branche;
3. Et Geoffroy, mort fans enfans.

Alard, Ier du nom, Seigneur de Chateau-Gontier, prit pour femme une nommée *Elifabeth*, qui lui donna pour fils:

Renaud, IIe du nom, Seigneur de Chateau-Gontier, qui fit le voyage de la Terre-Sainte, & époufa *Burgondie de Chantocé*, fœur de la Dame *de Craon*, dont il eut:
1. Alard, qui fuit;
2. Et Laurence, mère de *Herbert Turpin*.

Alard, IIe du nom, Seigneur de Chateau-Gontier, époufa *Mahaud de Briolay*, furnommée *Exulate*, dont il eut:
1. Renaud, qui fuit;
2. & 3. Alard, dit *le jeune*, & Geoffroy.

Renaud, IIIe du nom, Seigneur de Chateau-Gontier, vivant en 1150 & 1178, laiffa pour fils & fucceffeur:

Alard, IIIe du nom, Seigneur de Chateau-Gontier en 1193, qui époufa *Emme de Vitré*, dont il eut:

Jacques, Seigneur de Chateau-Gontier & de Nogent-le-Rotrou en 1227, lequel époufa *Havoife de Montmorency*, fille de *Mathieu*, IIe du nom, Seigneur *de Montmorency*, Connétable de France, & d'*Emme de Laval*, fa feconde femme. Il eut:
1. Emmette, femme de *Geoffroy*, Seigneur *de Poancé* en 1248;
2. Et Philippe, Dame de Hérouville.

BRANCHE
des Seigneurs de Chateau-Renaud.

Renaud de Chateau-Gontier, fecond fils de Renaud, Ier du nom, Seigneur de Château-Gontier, & de la nièce de *Geoffroy-Martel*, Comte d'Anjou, fit bâtir le Château appelé de fon nom *Château-Renaud*, & laiffa Guicher, qui fuit; & un fils naturel nommé *Lesbert*.

Guicher, Ier du nom, Seigneur de Chateau-Renaud (ce fut fur lui que Renaud, IIe du nom, Seigneur de Chateau-Gontier ufurpa le Château bâti par fon père), laiffa pour fils & fucceffeur:

Guicher, IIe du nom, Seigneur de Chateau-Renaud, qui recouvra fon Château, de Renaud, dit *Seigneur de Château-Gontier*, fon parent. Nous ignorons s'il a eu lignée.

BELLEMONT: *d'azur, à trois fafces d'or.*

BELLENAVE-LELOUP: *écartelé, aux 1 & 4 d'azur, au lion d'or, la queue fourchue, couronné de même; aux 2 & 3 contre-écartelé* d'Anjou-Sicile.

BELLENGER, Généralité d'Alençon, Election de Falaife, en Normandie, Écuyer, Sieur des Brières, famille annoblie en 1595, & qui porte: *d'azur, à deux épées d'argent, la garde & la poignée d'or, pofées en fautoir, & accoftées de deux petits poignards d'argent, la pointe en bas.*

BELLENGER ou **BERRENGER**, famille noble & ancienne, reconnue en 1666, lors de la recherche ordonnée dans la Généralité d'Alençon, Election d'Argentan, en Normandie, qui porte: *d'azur, au chevron d'argent, accompagné de trois glands d'or, 2 & 1.*

BELLENGREVILLE. Melchior de Bellengreville, Chevalier, Seigneur des Alleux, Lieutenant de 1000 hommes de pied fous la charge du Sieur de Saint-Aubin; fon oncle, eut d'*Antoinette le Vaffeur*:
1. Nicolas de Bellengreville, Chevalier, Seigneur des Alleux & de Brehen, Gentilhomme ordinaire de François, Duc d'Alençon, frère de Charles IX;
2. Jean, Chevalier, Seigneur de la Cour-du-Bois;
3. Joachim, qui fuit;
4. Et Isabeau de Bellengreville.

Joachim de Bellengreville, Seigneur de

Neuville, de Gambais, &c., Chevalier des Ordres du Roi, Grand-Prevôt de France, fe fignala fous Henri IV, à la défenfe de Meulan. Il reçut commiffion du Roi en date du 1er Juillet 1586, pour la charge de Meftre-de-Camp des vieilles Bandes de Cambray, depuis appelées le Régiment de Cambray; & une autre commiffion en 1589 pour commander 100 Chevaux-Légers, avec lefquels il s'acquit tant de gloire à Meulan qu'il défendit pendant deux mois contre la Ligue en 1590. Il fut admis au rang de Confeiller d'Etat en 1597, obtint le Gouvernement d'Ardres en 1598, & la Charge de Grand-Prevôt de France en 1604.

Le Grand-Prevôt de Bellengreville fe voyant fans enfans, pour maintenir le luftre de fa Maifon, fubftitua fes biens aux enfans d'Antoine de Bellengreville, fon coufin. Il fut reçu au nombre des Chevaliers des Ordres en 1619 ou 1620.

Jean, Marquis de Bellengreville, defcendant de la branche aînée, réfigna en 1617, après la mort de fon frère aîné, les Abbayes dont il étoit pourvu, à Charles de Fontenay, fon coufin, & recueillit en 1623 la fucceffion, & la fubftitution faite à fon profit par le Grand-Prevôt de Bellengreville. Il mourut en 1678, & laiffa trois enfans.

Jean de Bellengreville, IIe du nom, fon fils aîné, Marquis de Bellengreville, époufa, le 26 Novembre 1672, Catherine Scyver, fa nièce, dont font iffus:

1. Nicolas, qui fuit;
2. & 3. Guillaume-Joachim-Africain & Jean-Charles;
Et Anne, Gabrielle & Catherine.

Nicolas, Marquis de Bellengreville, né le 2 Mai 1679, décédé le 7 Février 1723, avoit époufé, le 16 Février 1722, Marguerite-Charlotte le Boucher, née le 10 Août 1703, morte le 8 Décembre 1728, dont:

1. Nicolas-Pascal, né le 6 Décembre 1728;
2. Marie-Charlotte, née le 8 Décembre 1723;
3. Et Catherine-Victoire, née le 3 Novembre 1724. Voyez Moréri.

Les armes: d'azur, à la croix d'or, cantonnée de quatre molettes de même. Le Promptuaire Armorial de Jean Boiffeau, édition de 1657, in-fol. IIe part. p. 36, dit cantonnée de quatre merlettes d'argent.

BELLEPEUCHE: échiqueté de gueules & d'argent.

BELLET: d'azur, à deux bandes d'argent dentelées, au mouton d'or grimpant au-deffus de la feconde.

BELLETRUCHES, en Bourgogne: écartelé, aux 1 & 4 de gueules; aux 2 & 3 d'argent, à la fafce d'azur.

BELLEVAL, en Picardie: de gueules, à la bande d'or, accompagnée de fept croix potencées de même, quatre en chef & trois en pointe.

BELLEVILLE (de), Election de Valognes, en Normandie, noble & ancienne famille qui porte: d'azur, au fautoir d'argent, cantonné de quatre aigles de même.

BELLEVILLE DE HARPEDANE. Il y a un titre original de cette famille, qui prouve que Jean de Harpedane, Chevalier Anglois, vivoit en 1318 avec Catherine Sénéchal, fa femme, morte en Angleterre, fans enfans, fille de Guy Sénéchal, Seigneur de Dienne & de Mortemer, & de Sibylle de Gourville. Ce Jean eft peut-être l'oncle ou le père de

Jean de Harpedane, Ier du nom, Anglois de nation, qui fut Général de l'Armée Angloife, en Guyenne & Connétable d'Angleterre. Il s'attacha enfuite au fervice du Roi Charles VI, qui le fit fon Chambellan, puis fon Capitaine-Général de la Province de Périgord, & Capitaine des Gendarmes en 1388. Il mourut avant le 14 Juin 1406; il avoit marié avec Jeanne de Cliffon, Dame de Belleville, fille d'Olivier de Cliffon, Sire de Cliffon, & de Jeanne de Belleville, Dame dudit lieu de Belleville, en Poitou, de Montagut, de Palluau, de Châteaumur, & de Beauvoir-fur-Mer.

Jean de Harpedane, dit de Belleville, IIe du nom, fon fils, Seigneur de Belleville & de Saint-Hilaire, acheta le 10 Octobre 1415, 8000 écus d'or, les Terres de Cofnac & de Mirambeau, de François de Montberon, Vicomte d'Aunay, & de Louife de Clermont, fa femme. Il avoit époufé 1° Jeanne de Muffidan, & 2° Jeanne Penthièvre. Il eut du premier lit:

Jean de Harpedane, IIIe du nom, Chevalier, Seigneur de Belleville, de Cofnac, en Saintonge, de Mirambeau & de Montagut,

C c c ij

Conſeiller & Chambellan du Roi, qui épouſa, 1º Marguerite de France, dite *de Valois*, fille naturelle du Roi Charles VI, & d'*Odette de Champdivers*, & légitimée par Lettres du Roi Charles VII, données à Montrichard, au mois de Janvier 1427 ; 2º en 1458, *Jeanne de Blois*, dite *de Bretagne*, fille de *Jean de Châtillon-de-Blois*, dit de *Bretagne*, Comte de Penthièvre & de Goello, Vicomte de Limoges, Seigneur d'Avaugour, &c., & de *Marguerite de Cliſſon*. Il n'eut point d'enfans de cette ſeconde femme. De la première il a eu :

1. Louis, Chevalier, Seigneur de Belleville & de Montagut, marié, le 27 Novembre 1455, avec *Marguerite de Culant*, Dame de Montmorillon, fille de *Charles de Culant*, Chevalier, Seigneur de Culant, de Châteauneuf & de Saint-Déſiré, Chambellan du Roi, Gouverneur de Mantes, de Paris & de Chartres, & Grand-Maître de l'Artillerie de France ;

2. Et Gilles, qui ſuit.

Gilles, dit *de Belleville*, Chevalier, Seigneur de Coſnac-ſur-Gironde, Conſeiller & Chambellan du Roi, épouſa *Guillemette de Luxembourg*, veuve d'*Amé de Saarbruck*, Comte de Roucy, & fille de *Thibaut de Luxembourg*, Seigneur de Fiennes & d'Armentières, & de *Philippe de Melun-Epinoy*. Il eſt le troiſième ayeul de :

Godefroy de Belleville, anciennement *de Harpedane*, Ecuyer, Seigneur de Richemont, qui épouſa *Madeleine Chevalier-de-la-Coindardière*, dont :

Philippe-Jacques de Belleville, Ecuyer, Seigneur de Richemont, marié, le 28 Mai 1714, avec *Suſanne Jaudouin*, mère de :

Jean-Philippe de Belleville, né le 7 Mars 1716, & reçu Page du Roi, dans ſa Petite-Ecurie, le 12 Décembre 1731, ſur les preuves de ſa Nobleſſe.

(*Armorial de France*, reg. I, part. I, pag. 58.)

Les armes : *gironné de vair & de gueules de 10 pièces*, aliàs *de 12*.

BELLEVÊVRE. Cette ancienne nobleſſe éteinte tiroit ſon origine du bourg de ce nom, ſitué au Duché de Bourgogne, ſur les frontières de la Franche-Comté.

Marguerite de Bellevêvre épouſa dans le XIIIᵉ ſiècle *Henri d'Antigny*, Sire de Sainte-Croix, & fut mère de *Huguette de Sainte-*Croix, femme d'*Etienhe de Saint-Diẑier*. Anselme de Bellevêvre fut Evêque d'Autun. Guillaume de Bellevêvre, ſon neveu, étoit Evêque de Châlons en 1297. Béatrix de Bellevêvre fut Abbeſſe de Lons-le-Saulnier en 1336. Jean de Bellevêvre Chevalier, Seigneur de Chay, vivoit en 1362, ſuivant un titre de la Chambre des Comptes de Dôle.

BELLEZAIS, Ecuyer, Sieur de la Chevalerie, ancienne nobleſſe, employée dans la recherche de 1666, Election de Mortagne, Généralité d'Alençon, en Normandie, qui porte : *de ſable, à trois loſanges d'or*, 2 & 1.

BELLIEVRE, famille originaire de Lyon, qui a donné un Chancelier de France. Huguenin de Bellièvre eſt le premier que l'on connoiſſe ; il étoit Echevin de Lyon en 1460, 1469, 1475 & 1478. Claude de Bellièvre, Seigneur de Hautefort, né vers 1487, étoit fils de Barthélemy de Bellièvre, Secrétaire & Intendant de la Maiſon du Cardinal *de Bourbon*, Archevêque de Lyon. Claude entra dans la Magiſtrature, & rendit de grands ſervices à ſa Patrie, en qualité de Conſeiller-Echevin de Lyon. François Iᵉʳ lui donna en 1541 la Charge de premier Préſident du Dauphiné ; il eut un grand goût pour l'antiquité, ce qui lui fit raſſembler quantité d'inſcriptions Romaines. Il mourut en 1557, laiſſant de *Louiſe Faye*, Pomponne, qui ſuit, & Jean.

On trouve un Claude de Bellièvre, de Lyon, vivant dans le XIIIᵉ ſiècle, qui a fait en 1262 un Traité latin ſur les différends qu'eurent enſemble les Chanoines de Saint-Jean de Lyon, & ceux de Saint-Juſt. Ce Traité eſt inſéré dans l'*Hiſtoire de Lyon*, du Père Méneſtrier, in-fol., 1696.

Pomponne de Bellièvre, Seigneur de Grignon, né à Lyon en 1529, fut d'abord Conſeiller au Sénat de Chambéry (Blanchard dit au Parlement de Chambéry), Lieutenant-Général au Bailliage de Vermandois, au ſiège de Laon, le 13 Mars 1562, auſſitôt après la reſtitution de la Savoie ; il fut envoyé en Ambaſſade vers les Suiſſes & Griſons, par le Roi Charles IX, fut gratifié de l'Office de Préſident au Préſidial de Lyon, le 14 Avril 1569 ; & créé Conſeiller d'Etat le 1ᵉʳ Juillet 1570. Après la funeſte journée de la Saint-Barthélemy, arrivée en 1572, il fut une ſeconde fois envoyé en Ambaſſade vers les Suiſſes. En récompenſe de ſes ſervices, le Roi lui donna la

Charge de Surintendant des Finances vers 1575 ; il fut reçu Préfident au Parlement de Paris, le 8 Avril 1576, envoyé quelque tems après en Angleterre vers la Reine ELISABETH, pour la détourner du deffein qu'elle avoit de faire mourir MARIE STUART, Reine d'Ecoffe, qu'elle tenoit prifonnière à Londres ; & n'ayant pu rien obtenir, ils'en revint en France. Le Roi HENRI III étant mort, il rendit un fignalé fervice à l'Etat, en perfuadant aux Colonels Suiffes & à leurs Troupes de ne point abandonner le nouveau Roi, dans un tems où il avoit befoin d'eux. Il affifta à l'Affemblée, tenue à Vervins en 1598, pour traiter de la paix entre les Couronnes de France & d'Efpagne, où il conferva l'avantage & les prééminences de la France fur l'Efpagne ; & enfin fut fait Chancelier de France, par Lettres données à Blois, le 2 Août 1599, vérifiées le 7 Septembre fuivant. Il mourut à Paris, le 9 Septembre 1607, & fut enterré dans la Chapelle de Saint-Germain l'Auxerrois, où fe voit fa fépulture avec fon épitaphe. Il laiffa :

ALBERT DE BELLIÈVRE, nommé Abbé de Jouy, par le Roi HENRI IV, en 1594, & facré Archevêque de Lyon en 1599 ;
Et CLAUDE DE BELLIÈVRE, Confeiller au Parlement, Archevêque de Lyon, fûr la démiffion d'ALBERT, facré en 1640.

Cette famille s'eft éteinte dans la perfonne de POMPONNE DE BELLIÈVRE, Chevalier, Seigneur de Grignon, né en 1606, qui fut reçu Confeiller au Parlement, le 22 Février 1629, Maître des Requêtes, le 16 Août 1631, Préfident à Mortier, fur la démiffion de fon père, au mois de Novembre 1642, & premier Préfident au Parlement de Paris en 1651. Il s'eft rendu recommandable par fes Ambaffades d'Italie, de Hollande & d'Angleterre. Ce fut lui qui entreprit l'établiffement d'un Hôpital-Général à Paris, pour y renfermer les pauvres de cette grande Ville. Il mourut à Paris le 13 Mars 1657, fans laiffer de poftérité.

Les armes : *d'azur, à la fafce d'argent, accompagnée de trois trèfles d'or, 2 en chef & 1 en pointe.*

BELLIN-DAVERTON : *écartelé, aux 1 & 4 de gueules, à trois jumelles d'argent ; aux 2 & 3 d'azur, à la croix d'or, parti d'argent, au lion de gueules.*

BELLINGHEN : *d'azur, à trois fafces d'or ; au chef d'argent, chargé de huit rofes de gueules.*

BELLISSEN, famille noble, originaire d'Allemagne, dont il y a plufieurs branches établies en Languedoc, & autres Provinces voifines.

Les Seigneurs de BELLISSEN ont poffédé la Baronie de Malves, ainfi que les Châtellenies de Sallelles, Limoufis & Trafanel, pendant plus de 500 ans, avec les Terres & Seigneuries de Saint-Gougat, Bourgeolles, Barberac, Hurban, Caillavel, Camps, Airoux, Milgrand, Milpetit, Roftigues, & autres Terres fituées en Languedoc.

Ils font divifés en plufieurs branches, qui poffèdent la plus grande partie de ces Terres, & plufieurs Seigneurs du nom de BELLISSEN fubfiftent encore en Allemagne.

I. FRÉDÉRIC DE BELLISSEN, qualifié de *Chevalier,* fe croifa dans la guerre contre les Albigeois, fit fa réfidence dans fes Terres, fituées aux environs de Carcaffonne, fut enterré dans l'Eglife Cathédrale de cette Ville, & fut père de :

II. OTHON DE BELLISSEN, Chevalier, duquel font iffus toutes les différentes branches de BELLISSEN, tant éteintes que fubfiftantes actuellement, foit en Languedoc, ou dans d'autres Provinces voifines. Il eut pour fils :

III. JEAN-PIERRE DE BELLISSEN, Chevalier, Baron de Malves, Sallelles, Limoufis, Trafanel, Cannes & autres lieux ; il eut :

1. GUILLAUME, qui fuit ;
2. Et PIERRE, dit *le Chevalier,* Seigneur de Sallelles, qui fut Chambellan de LOUIS XII, & l'un des Commiffaires qui préfidèrent aux Etats de Languedoc, en 1499. Il fe trouva à la prife de Milan.

IV. GUILLAUME DE BELLISSEN, Ier du nom, Chevalier, Baron de Malves & de Sallelles, Seigneur de Limoufis, Trafanel, Saint-Gougat, Milhay ou Milhan, Milhareft, Barberac, Roftigues, &c., tefta très-âgé, le 19 Avril 1598. Il avoit époufé *Raymonde N...,* & fut père de :

1. PIERRE, Chevalier, Seigneur de Sallelles, de Limoufis, qui en avoit rendu l'hommage au Roi CHARLES VIII, le 11 Avril 1497, lequel du vivant de fon père GUILLAUME, & en confidération des fervices qu'il lui avoit rendus dans fes guerres au delà des Monts, pourvut & nomma ledit PIERRE, Viguier de fa Ville de Carcaffonne, & Châtelain de

Four d'Epine, par fes provifions du 7 Juin 1498. Il a formé la branche des Barons & Marquis de *Malves*, éteinte par le décès de JEAN-CLAUDE DE BELLISSEN, Marquis de Malves & de Talairan, décédé à Narbonne en 1750;

2. JEAN, Chevalier, Seigneur de Bourgeolles & de Saint-Gougat, Ecuyer du Roi FRANçois Ier, puis Connétable, Prevôt & Gouverneur de la Ville de Carcaffonne, par don du même Roi, fuivant les provifions du 28 Août 1522. Il tefta le 20 Janvier 1536. Il a fait la branche des Seigneurs de *Milgrand*, de *Camps* & d'*Airoux*, qui fubfifte encore en Languedoc;

3. JEAN-PIERRE, marié du vivant de GUILLAUME fon père, & décédé avant lui, dont la branche fubfiftante va être rapportée ci-après;

4. BERTRAND, Chanoine de l'Eglife Cathédrale de Carcaffonne, & auquel GUILLAUME fon père avoit fait un legs confidérable, par fon teftament de l'an 1498;

5. LISETTE, mariée à un Seigneur nommé *Affalit*;

6. Et CLARETTE, mariée au Seigneur *Jean Geoftri*.

V. JEAN-PIERRE DE BELLISSEN, Chevalier, Seigneur de Barberac, mort avant fon père GUILLAUME, tefta le 1er Mars 1496. Il avoit époufé *Anne de Monnier*. Il eut pour fils:

VI. ARNAUD DE BELLISSEN, Chevalier, Seigneur de Barberac, Lieutenant de la Compagnie des Gendarmes du Comte de Naffau, & auquel GUILLAUME DE BELLISSEN, fon ayeul, laiffa, par fon teftament du 19 Avril 1498, la Terre & Seigneurie de Barberac & autres. Il époufa, le 10 Janvier 1520, *Ifabelle Mathieu*, fille de *Jean Mathieu*, Chevalier, Lieutenant des Gendarmes de M. de Fiennes, & fut père de:

VII. GUILLAUME DE BELLISSEN, IIe du nom, Chevalier, Enfeigne de la Compagnie d'Arquebufiers du Comte de Rœux, qui époufa, le 4 Septembre 1548, *Marguerite Georges*, & eut pour fils:

VIII. PIERRE DE BELLISSEN, Chevalier, Guidon de la Compagnie des Gendarmes de M. le Duc de Guife, qui époufa, le 5 Mars 1576, *Angélique Foucher*, & fut père de:

IX. LOUIS DE BELLISSEN, Ier du nom, Chevalier, Major de la Ville de Narbonne, qui tefta le 6 Février 1651. Il avoit époufé, le 8 Octobre 1608, *Marie Defperiers*. Il eut:

1. LOUIS, qui fuit;

2. Et MARIE, mariée à *Henri de Verzeilles*, Chevalier, Seigneur d'Argens.

X. LOUIS DE BELLISSEN, IIe du nom, Chevalier, fervit dans la Compagnie des Gendarmes de M. le Duc de Guife. Il époufa, le 30 Décembre 1630, *Delphine de Portanier*, de laquelle il eut:

1. JEAN, qui fuit;

2. Et CHARLES, premier Théologien du Pape INNOCENT XII, & nommé à l'Evêché de Cavaillon.

XI. JEAN DE BELLISSEN, Chevalier, époufa, le 15 Juin 1670, *Marguerite de Mainier*, & eut:

XII. PIERRE DE BELLISSEN, IIe du nom, Chevalier, Sieur de Melun, qui époufa, le 7 Février 1708, *Françoife de Flatrier*, & eut:

XIII. JEAN-PAUL DE BELLISSEN, Chevalier, Greffier & Secrétaire de l'Ordre Royal, Militaire & Hofpitalier du Saint-Efprit de Montpellier, en deça des Monts, par Brevet du 15 Janvier 1755, & Commandeur de la Commanderie de la Fauvette, du même Ordre, dite *au Chevalier*, lequel a époufé, le 5 Octobre 1731, *Marie-Renée du Moulin*, veuve de *Philippe de Rocher*, Chevalier, Sieur de Mandeville, Capitaine au Régiment de Chartres, oncle à la mode de Bretagne, dudit JEAN-PAUL DE BELLISSEN, lequel a eu:

1. JEAN-PAUL-ELÉAZAR, qui fuit;

2. MARIE-ADÉLAÏDE, mariée à *Jean-Baptifte Fauchard*;

3. Et MARIE-MARGUERITE.

XIV. JEAN-PAUL-ELÉAZAR DE BELLISSEN, Chevalier, eft Greffier & Secrétaire général dudit Ordre Royal & Hofpitalier du Saint-Efprit, en furvivance de fon père.

BRANCHE
des Seigneurs DE BELLISSEN, *dont les Marquis* D'AIROUX.

V. JEAN DE BELLISSEN, fecond fils de GUILLAUME, Chevalier, Seigneur de Bourgeolles, Saint-Gougat & Milhan, Prevôt, Connétable & Gouverneur de la Ville de Carcaffonne, tefta le 20 Janvier 1536. Il avoit époufé, 1° en 1526, *Madeleine le Roux*; & 2° *Guillemette Ameline*.

Il eut de fon premier mariage:

1. PIERRE, qui fuit;

2. ARNAUD, Chevalier, Seigneur de Bourgeolles;

3°. Jacques, Prevôt de Milhan, & Chanoine de l'Eglife Cathédrale de Carcaffonne;

4. Philippe, auffi Chanoine de Carcaffonne;

5. Claire, mariée à *Renaud de Garand*, Seigneur de Montequiere;

6. Raymonde, mariée à *Jean de Saix*, Seigneur de Pontignan;

7. Et Giraude, mariée à *Denis Roubin*, Confeiller au Parlement de Touloufe.

VI. Pierre de Bellissen, Ier du nom, Chevalier, Seigneur de Saint-Gougat & Milhan, fut Capitaine, Prevôt, Connétable & Gouverneur de la Ville de Carcaffonne, & tefta le 21 Décembre 1549. Il eut d'*Ifabeau d'Aftergues-Ayevilles*:

1. Pierre, qui fuit;

2. & 3. Jacques & Philippe;

4. Et Françoise.

VII. Pierre de Bellissen, IIe du nom, Chevalier, Seigneur de Saint-Gougat & Milhan, tefta le 3 Janvier 1575. Il avoit époufé, 1° le 5 Juin 1559, *Béatrix d'Antiquamareta*, fille de Meffire *François d'Antiquamareta*, Seigneur de Louberens, Confeiller au Parlement de Touloufe; & 2° le 11 Septembre 1569, *Ifabeau de Manent de Bellot*, veuve de *Louis de Polaftron*.

Il eut de fon premier mariage:

1. Philippe, qui fuit;

2. Béatrix, non mariée;

3. Marguerite, mariée au Sieur de *Galibert;*

4. Et Judith, mariée à Meffire *Jean de Marfant.*

VIII. Philippe de Bellissen, Chevalier, Seigneur de Saint-Gougat & Milhan, tefta le 18 Mars 1601. Il avoit époufé, le 30 Avril 1557, Françoise de Bellissen, fa coufine, fille d'Antoine de Bellissen, Chevalier, Baron de Malves, Seigneur de Sallelles, Trefant, Germiffant, & Saint-Pierre-d'Elles, Viguier de Carcaffonne, Cabardès & Minerbois, Gouverneur des Châteaux de Cabardès. Il eut:

1. Philippe-Jean, qui fuit;

2. & 3. Germaine & Isabelle.

IX. Philippe-Jean de Bellissen, Chevalier, Seigneur de Saint-Gougat & de Milgrand, tefta le 10 Janvier 1644. Il avoit époufé, le 1er Novembre 1619, *Marie Poitiers de la Palme*. Il eut:

1. Jacques-Henri, qui fuit;

2. Philippe-François, décédé en Suède, fans poftérité, étant Colonel d'un Régiment des Gardes de la Reine, Dragons;

3. Isabeau, mariée à *Jean de Beçard*, Seigneur de Brouffes;

4. Marie-Claire, mariée à Meffire *Guillaume de Molinier*, Confeiller au Parlement de Touloufe;

5. Et Marie-Anne, Religieufe au Couvent de Sainte-Urfule de Carcaffonne.

X. Jacques-Henri de Bellissen, Chevalier, Seigneur de Millaret & de Camps, Major des Cadaquès, & Commandant du Régiment de Mérainville, & du Château de la Trinité en Catalogne, époufa, le 26 Mai 1669, *Dorothée de Sainte-Colombe*. Il eut:

1. Jean, qui fuit;

2. Et Jeanne de Bellissen, décédée majeure, après avoir tefté le 12 Septembre 1700.

XI. Jean de Bellissen, Chevalier, Seigneur de Camps, Colonel d'un Régiment d'Infanterie, époufa, le 3 Juillet 1696, *Françoife de Banne d'Avejan*, de laquelle il eut:

XII. Jacques-Henri de Bellissen, Chevalier, Marquis d'Airoux, qui a époufé, en 1733, *Anne de Grave*, & en eut:

1. Jean-Hyacinthe, qui fuit;

2. N...... de Bellissen, dit *le Chevalier de Belliffen*, Lieutenant dans le Régiment de Normandie, tué en 1760, à l'affaire de Vefel;

Et quatre filles.

XIII. Jean-Hyacinthe de Bellissen, Chevalier, Marquis d'Airoux, Gouverneur des Châteaux de Cabardès, né en 1736, a été d'abord reçu Page du Roi, fur les preuves de fa nobleffe, & eft aujourd'hui Lieutenant au Régiment de la Meftre-de-Camp, Dragons.

(Extrait d'un Mémoire fourni par la Famille).

Voyez *les Antiquités* de Beze; *l'Hiftoire du Languedoc; l'Hiftoire du Cardinal d'Amboife, & le Recueil des Pièces Fugitives, pour fervir à l'Hiftoire de France, avec des notes hiftoriques & géographiques,* tom. II, imprimé à Paris, chez Chaubert & Hériffant, avec Approbation & Privilège du Roi, 1759.

Les armes: *d'azur, à trois bourdons d'argent, pofés en pal, au chef coufu de gueules chargé de trois coquilles d'argent.* Supports: *deux fauvages armés de maffues.*

BELLOCIER, Seigneur de Blerainville: *de gueules, à l'aigle efforante d'or, accompagnée en chef de deux étoiles de même.*

BELLON, en Provence. Le premier connu de ce nom eft:

I. Barthélemy Bellon, qualifié de *Noble*

& d'*Ecuyer* dans fon teftament du 15 Mai 1528, paffé devant *Honoré Balardi*, Notaire. Il eut de *Philippe de Treffemane :*

1. RAYMOND, qui fuit;
2. Et JACQUES, auteur de la branche des Seigneurs de *Sainte-Marguerite*, rapportée ci-après.

II. RAYMOND BELLON, Ecuyer, époufa, par contrat paffé devant *Legier*, Notaire, le 21 Septembre 1555, *Anthorenne Thubieras*, dont il eut :

III. FRANÇOIS BELLON, Ecuyer, marié, par contrat paffé devant *Jean Meinard*, Notaire de Draguignan en 1604, avec *Jeanne de Pafcalis-de-Mercadier*. De ce mariage vint :

IV. SIMON BELLON, Ecuyer, qui fit alliance, le 30 Juin 1647, avec *Madeleine de Court*, dont il eut :

V. JEAN-FRANÇOIS BELLON, Ier du nom, qui époufa, par contrat paffé devant *Pierre Artaud*, Notaire de Correns, le 24 Décembre 1675, *Claire Toucas*, de laquelle vint :

VI. BENOÎT BELLON, qui fut maintenu en fon ancienne nobleffe, par Arrêt de la Cour des Comptes de Provence, du 3 Décembre 1737. Il avoit époufé, par contrat paffé devant *Aubert*, Notaire, le 27 Août 1720, *Madeleine d'Aubert*. De ce mariage vint, entr'autres enfans :

VII. JEAN-FRANÇOIS BELLON, IIe du nom, Ecuyer, ancien Juge-Royal de la ville de Brignolle, qui a des enfans de *Félicité de Court*.

SECONDE BRANCHE.

II. JACQUES BELLON, Ecuyer, fecond fils de BARTHÉLEMY, & de *Philippe de Treffemane*, époufa, par contrat du 30 Octobre 1558, *Marguerite Guerin*, de laquelle il eut, entr'autres enfans :

1. GASPARD, qui fuit;
2. Et JEAN, Ecuyer de M. le Duc de Guife, & Gentilhomme ordinaire de la Chambre de LOUIS XIII, qui obtint de ce Prince les *Isles de Sainte-Marguerite*, dont ceux de cette Famille ont toujours porté le nom depuis.

III. GASPARD BELLON, Ecuyer, Seigneur de Sainte-Marguerite, époufa, par contrat paffé devant *Berenguier*, Notaire à Carnoulles, le 3 Décembre 1598, *Claire de Monier*, des Seigneurs de *Châteauvieux*. Il en eut :

IV. FRANÇOIS BELLON, Ecuyer, Seigneur de Sainte-Marguerite, qui s'allia, par contrat du

24 Novembre 1655, avec *Marguerite Taneron*, de laquelle il eut :

V. JEAN-BAPTISTE BELLON, Ecuyer, Seigneur de Sainte-Marguerite, marié, le 12 Mai 1716, avec *Jeanne de Brignolle*, de laquelle eft iffu :

VI. LOUIS-AUGUSTIN-ANTOINE BELLON, Ecuyer, Seigneur de Sainte-Marguerite, qui a époufé *Marie-Hyacinthe du Pujet*, des Seigneurs de *Bras*, dont il a poftérité.

Les armes : *d'argent, au cerf de gueules grimpant*. (Voyez Artefeuil, tom. I, pag. 119 & fuiv.)

BELLON, Seigneur de Turin en Piémont : *écartelé, aux 1 & 4 d'or, à trois pals de gueules ; aux 2 & 3 lofangé d'argent & de gueules ; & fur le tout : d'azur, au bœuf paffant d'or, accompagné en chef de trois fleurs-de-lys de même.*

BELLONET, en Provence. JEAN DE BELLONET, de la Ville de Forcalquier, Lieutenant-Colonel d'Infanterie, Surintendant des Fortifications de l'Armée, fut envoyé par Sa Majefté à la République de Venife pour des affaires importantes, ainfi qu'on l'apprend par une Lettre du Roi en date du 13 Mai 1634. Il époufa *Elifabeth de Pontevès*, dont il eut :

JEAN-VICTOR DE BELLONET, auquel LOUIS XIV accorda des Lettres de nobleffe au mois de Mai 1702, qui furent enregiftrées aux Archives de Sa Majefté en Provence, le 23 Décembre fuivant, regiftre fæculum, Arm. B, fol. 302, & au Parlement la même année, fol. 698. Il a époufé *Catherine de Caftellane-Adhémar*, de laquelle il eut plufieurs enfans, dont il ne refte plus que FRANÇOIS DE BELLONET, qui a fervi avec diftinction, & qui vit à Paris, en 1770, à l'Hôtel-Royal des Invalides, fans poftérité.

Les armes : *d'azur, à une tour d'or, furmontée d'une étoile d'argent, & accoftée de 2 croiffans de même contournés.*

BELLOT, Sieur de Caillonville, Franqueville, Election de Carentan, en Normandie, famille annoblie pour fervices en 1594, & qui porte : *d'azur, au chevron d'or, accompagné en chef de deux lions affrontés, & en pointe d'un fer de pique, le tout de même.*

BELLOUAN, en Bretagne, nobleffe qui n'eft pas moins recommandable par fes illuftres alliances, que par fon ancienneté.

GRÉGOIRE DE BELLOUAN, Seigneur dudit lieu, épousa en 1401 *Jeanne de Lestrieux*, sœur puînée de *Guillaume Normand-de-Lestrieux*, qui lui donna en partage la Seigneurie de la Villefief. De ce mariage vint, entr'autres enfans :

JEAN DE BELLOUAN, Seigneur dudit lieu, de Vay & de la Villefief, marié à *Blanche d'Avaugour*, petite-fille de *Louis d'Avaugour*, & d'*Anne de Malestroit*, & arrière-petite-fille de *Juhaël d'Avaugour*, Seigneur de Kgrois, comme il fut vérifié par l'Arrêt de Nobleffe du Seigneur d'Avaugour du Bois-de-Cargrois, en date du 27 Septembre 1670. JEAN DE BELLOUAN s'obligea, par fon contrat de mariage, de prendre le nom & les armes d'*Avaugour*. Il eut pour enfans :

1. LOUIS, qui fuit;
2. GUILLAUME, rapporté après fon aîné ;
3. Et ANTOINE.

LOUIS prit le nom d'*Avaugour*, & de lui font defcendus les Seigneurs de *Kgrois*, éteints dans la famille de *la Lande*, dite depuis de *Machecoul-de-Vieille-Vigne* ; les Seigneurs d'*Avaugour de Saint-Laurent*, du *Bois de la Motte*, éteints dans la Maifon des *Grées*, & les Seigneurs du *Bois de Kgrois*, dont le dernier eft le Comte d'*Avaugour*.

GUILLAUME DE BELLOUAN, Seigneur de la Villefief, épousa *Anne Blanchet*, dont il eut :

1. JEAN, qui fuit;
2. ALLIETTE, qui fut mariée à *Maurice*, Seigneur de Quejeau, de Lefnée & autres lieux. *Marie*, Dame de Quejeau, leur petite-fille, & unique héritière des Seigneurs de Quejeau, de Lefnée & du Higno, fut mariée, en 1560, à *Julien*, chef du nom & des armes de la famille des *Grées*, Chevalier, Seigneur dudit lieu, du Gafre, de la Tourville, de Boguode, de Gergny, de Branbes & autres lieux ;
3. JEANNE DE BELLOUAN, qui épousa *Jean Bernard*, Seigneur de Lefnée, dont fut héritière la Marquife de *Pontbriand;*
4. Et CHARLOTTE DE BELLOUAN.

JEAN DE BELLOUAN, Chevalier, Seigneur de la Villefief, épousa 1° Dame *Guillard*, de la famille de *Villeder*; & 2° *Guillemette Paftourelle*. Il eut du premier lit :

GUILLEMETTE DE BELLOUAN, mariée, par contrat du 21 Mars 1558, à *Guillaume de Saint-Perne*, Seigneur dudit lieu.

Tome II.

Et du fecond lit :
JEAN, qui fuit.

JEAN DE BELLOUAN, Chevalier, Seigneur de la Villefief, &c., épousa *Françoife d'Arragon*, fille aînée du Seigneur de Quinipily, dont l'héritière fut mariée dans la maifon de *Lannion*. Il eut :

1. PHILIPPE DE BELLOUAN, Chevalier, Seigneur dudit lieu & de la Villefief, mort garçon à Villefief, en 1594;
2. Et CLAUDE DE BELLOUAN, Dame de la Villefief, mariée à *François de la Frénaye*, Chevalier, Seigneur dudit lieu.

Les armes : *de fable, à une aigle éployée d'argent.*

BELLOŸ, nobleffe qui fubfifte encore aujourd'hui avec une grande diftinction. Les Seigneurs de ce nom, qui ont poffédé la Terre du Belloy en France, fe font toujours diftingués par leurs fervices militaires dans toutes les guerres de nos Rois; ils ont les qualités de *Miles*, ou de *Chevalier-Banneret*, de *Bachelier*, de *Monfeigneur*, de *Sire*, de *Meffire*, de *Noble, Puiffant Seigneur*.

On trouve parmi eux des Chambellans de nos Rois, des Gentilshommes Ordinaires de leur Chambre, des Chevaliers de leur Ordre, c'eft-à-dire de Saint-Mic el, des Pannetiers, Echanfons, Ecuyers-Tranchans & Maîtres-d'Hôtel; des Capitaines, Gouverneurs & Commandeurs de différentes Villes & Places ; des Officiers de Terre & de Mer; deux Généraux & Chefs d'Armées, fous les Rois CHARLES VII & LOUIS XI, l'un tué à la bataille de Verneuil en 1424, l'autre étant à la bataille de Guinegate l'an 1479; des Chevaliers de Malte, des Chevaliers de l'Ordre Militaire de Saint-Louis, &c.

Les alliances de la Maifon du BELLOY font avec celles d'*Araines*, d'*Ardres*, d'*Argicourt*, *Beauvais, Biencourt, Billy, Bouconvilliers, Bourlemont, Brouilly, Calonne, Carmonne, Carvoifin,* d'*Achy, Choifeul-Langues, Clement, Courtenay-Chevillon, la Croix de Caftries, des Effarts, l'Eftendart, Eftrées,* du *Fay-de-Château-Rouge,* le *Fèvre-de-Caumartin,* de *Fontaines, Foffeufe, Francières, Frefnoy, Guiry, Hallencourt, Halwin, Hénin-Liétard, Lille, Marivaut, Lannoy, Laudencourt, Ligny-du-Lys-Livron, Mailly*, plufieurs fois *Margival, Mauvoifin, Meaux, Molincourt, Montmorency* deux

883 •   BEL

fois, *Morancy*, *la Motte-de-Ville*, *Pertuis*, *Picquigny*, *Poix*, *la Rivière*, *Sainte-Gene-viève*, *Rouſſel*,*la Rue*,*la Salle*, *de Senicourt*, *Soiſi*, *Soiſſons-Tanques*, *Soués*, *Suhart*, *Vaudremont*, *la Vieuville*, *d'Arvilliers*, *Villemontée*, *Villers-de-Croy*, *Villiers-l'Is-le-Adam*, *Villiers-Saint-Paul*, &c.

Les BELLOY tenoient un rang très-diſtingué dès le règne de PHILIPPE-AUGUSTE; un d'eux fut du nombre des Seigneurs qui jurèrent & ſi-gnèrent la trève que ce Prince conclut avec le Roi d'Angleterre, après la bataille de Bouvines en 1214. Un autre fut Capitaine & Comman-dant de la ville d'Amiens, & nommé pour l'un des Conſervateurs en Picardie & en Pon-thieu, de la trève conclue à Rouen entre le Roi CHARLES VI & le Roi d'Angleterre, le 24 Décembre 1419.

La Généalogie de cette Maiſon, publiée en 1747, eſt diviſée en trois chapitres.

Le premier contient les Seigneurs du BEL-LOY de MORANGLE, de Villaines, de Moiſelles, &c., comme étant ceux qui ont poſſédé plus anciennement la Terre du Belloy en France, avec pluſieurs autres dans ſes environs. L'Au-teur, dans le premier Chapitre, commence à HUGUES DU BELLOY, qui vivoit avant le commencement du XIIᵉ ſiècle. Il le finit à CLAUDE-FRANÇOIS-MARIE DU BELLOY, Cheva-lier, Seigneur de Champneuville, né le 28 Octobre 1719, marié à *Louiſe-Françoiſe le Meſſier de Menillet*, fille de *Louis le Meſſier*, Chevalier, Seigneur de Veſſe, &c. & de *Ma-rie-Eléonore Paulet*, dont :

1. N.... DU BELLOY, né le 28 Juillet 1747 & ondoyé le 30 ſuivant;
2. ADÉLAÏDE-FRANÇOISE DU BELLOY, née le 29 Septembre 1743;
3. Et ANASTASIE-FRANÇOISE-MARIE DU BELLOY-D'ARVILLIERS, née le 3 Février 1746.

Le ſecond Chapitre comprend les Seigneurs du BELLOY DE CANDAS, d'Amy, de Francières, de Caſtillon; il commence à GARIN ou VA-RIN, Seigneur du Belloy, Chevalier vivant en 1208, & finit à ALEXANDRE DU BELLOY, appelé le *Marquis de Caſtillon*, marié, en 1702, à *Françoiſe-Charlotte le Maréchal*, dont il eut MARIE-LOUISE DU BELLOY, fille unique, mariée à *Agnan de Gouſſancourt*, Chevalier, Seigneur de Gouſſancourt. Le même Chapi-tre contient encore les Seigneurs de *Latin*, de *Ciry*, de *Sermoix*, de *Sulſonne*, leſquels ont fait preuve de leur nobleſſe en 1667, de-

vant l'Intendant de Soiſſons.

Le troiſième & dernier Chapitre con-tient:

1° Les Seigneurs du BELLOY-DE-SAINT-LÉO-NARD, près d'Araines, dans l'Amiénois, d'*Y-vrène* & de *Vieulaines*, puis du *Belloy* en France, de *Morangle*, de *Fontenelles*, &c., par le mariage de l'héritière de la branche aî-née de *Morangle*, environ l'an 1550, leſquels ſont éteints ſur la fin du XVIIᵉ ſiècle.

2° Les Seigneurs de *Landrethun*, auſſi éteints.

3° Les Seigneurs de *Beauvoir*, du *Pont-de-Metz*, de *Buires*, de *Cardonnoy*, de *Villeroy*, &c.

4° Les Seigneurs de *Rogehan de la Mai-ſon-Neuve*, de *la Maiſon-Forte*, & fief de *Sarra*.

5° Les Seigneurs de *Prouremont*, de *Fi-ſancourt*, de *Saint-Martin*, de *Lotingan*, d'*Epaumenil*.

6° Les Seigneurs de *Vercourt* & d'*Halivil-liers*, &c.

Les Seigneurs de *Beauvoir*, du *Pont-de-Metz*, &c., commencent à ALEAUME DU BEL-LOY, Iᵉʳ du nom, Ecuyer, Seigneur de Beau-voir-ſur-Hoquincourt, vivant l'an 1300, & fi-niſſent par FRANÇOIS DU BELLOY, Chevalier, Seigneur de Beauvoir, Cardonnoy, Hoquin-court, Belle-Fontaine, Vicomte de Granſart, Eſtalmeny & Bécourt, marié, le 1ᵉʳ Juin 1721, à *Marguerite-Hélène de Maiſmelle*, fille de *Pierre de Maiſmelle*, & de *Marguerite de Pingré*. Le dernier nommé des Seigneurs de Cardonnoy, eſt JEAN-PHILIPPE-NICOLAS DU BELLOY, né le 8 Mars 1741, fils de JEAN-PHI-LIPPE-NICOLAS DU BELLOY, Chevalier, Seigneur de Villeroi, de Contes & de Guiſchart en par-tie, & de *Marie-Jeanne le Vaſſeur de Neuil-ly*, fille de *Jean-Baptiſte le Vaſſeur*.

Les Seigneurs de *Rogehan*, connus dès le commencement du XVIᵉ ſiècle, finiſſent aux enfans d'ANTOINE-CLAUDE DU BELLOY, Cheva-lier, Seigneur de Rogehan, &c., dont le der-nier eſt né le 9 Juillet 1732.

Les Seigneurs de *la Maiſon-Neuve* com-mencent à LOUIS DU BELLOY, Chevalier, Sei-gneur de la Maiſon-Neuve & de Puiſeux, en partie, vivant en 1645, & finiſſent aux en-fans de NOEL-LOUIS DU BELLOY :

1. JACQUES-LOUIS, né le 20 Novembre 1726, Lieutenant dans le Régiment de Lyon-nois;

2. JACQUES-MARIE, né le 2 Novembre 1735 ;
3. Et GUILLAUME, né le 18 Novembre 1737 ;

Les Seigneurs de *la Maison-Forte* & du fief de *Sarra* ne comprennent que PIERRE DU BELLOY, qui a eu trois filles, dont deux mariées, l'une en 1736, l'autre en 1746, & la troisième Religieuse au Couvent de la Madeleine de Trefnel, à Paris.

Les Seigneurs de *Saint-Martin de Lantignan*, de *Prouremont, Fifancourt*, &c., remontent à THESEUS DU BELLOY, ancien Capitaine dans le Régiment de Bourbon, Infanterie, dont des enfans de fes deux mariages, le fecond contracté en 1745.

Outre toutes ces branches & celles qui font éteintes, dont la filiation eft bien prouvée, on trouve à la fin de la Généalogie de cette Maifon une lifte chronologique de ceux du nom DU BELLOY, dont on n'a point trouvé les places dans la Généalogie.

La Généalogie de cette Maifon a été dreffée fur titres originaux, & approuvée par M. *Clairambault*, imprimée en 1747, chez Thibouft, ouvrage de 155 pag. in-4°, donné au Public par M. CLAUDE-FRANÇOIS-MARIE, Chevalier, Marquis titulaire DU BELLOY.

Les trois branches DU BELLOY portent des armes différentes :

BELLOY-DE-CANDAS, d'Amy, de Francières & de Caftillon, porte: *d'argent, à quatre bandes de gueules.*

BELLOY-DE-SAINT-LÉONARD porte: *d'argent, à trois fafces de gueules.*

BELLOY-MORANGLE porte: *de gueules, au lion d'or;* & du Buiffon dit : *de gueules, à 7 lofanges d'or*, 3, 3 & 1.

* BELLOY, Terre érigée en Baronie, par Lettres du mois de Mai 1646, enregiftrées au Parlement, le 19 Décembre fuivant, & en la Chambre des Comptes, le 15 Avril 1644, en faveur de *Jacques de Roddes.*

BELLY : *d'or, à deux ogoeffes de fable, ou tourteaux de Cardonniere, celui du chef renverfé.*

BELONI : *de gueules, au pal d'argent.*

BELONI : *d'azur, au B capital d'or.*

BELOSSAC, en Bretagne : *de vair, à une fafce de gueules.*

BELOT, en Franche-Comté, famille qui entre dans tous les Chapitres Nobles, & dans la noble Confrérie de Saint-Georges. Elle fubfifte dans HENRI BELOT-VILLETTE, Chevalier de la noble Confrérie de Saint-Georges en Franche-Comté, fils de *Jean-François Daudel,* Seigneur de Villette, Mans, Larians,&c., & de *Françoife-Sufanne de Meffey*, & petit-neveu d'*Eléonor de Belot*, dit l'*Abbé de Larians*, Grand-Prieur de Gigny, en Franche-Comté, & de la Confrérie de Saint-Georges.

Les armes: *d'azur, à trois lofanges d'argent, au chef d'or, baftillé de trois pièces.*

BELOT-DU-PEZAI, dans le Bléfois, famille qui fubfifte en deux branches.

PREMIÈRE BRANCHE.

MICHEL BELOT, Ier du nom, Ecuyer, Seigneur de Guillonnière, vivoit en 1547, avec *Anne Sénéchal*, fa femme.

VALENTIN BELOT, leur petit-fils, Ecuyer, Seigneur de Moulins, du Clos & de la Buffière, reçu Confeiller & Avocat du Roi au Baillage & fiège Préfidial, Chambre des Comptes, Eaux & Forêts, Prévôté & Maréchauffée de France à Blois, en 1599, & Confeiller du Roi, Lieutenant-Criminel au même Baillage, en 1608, avoit époufé, en 1599, *Marguerite Ribier*, dont il eut :

MICHEL, qui fuit ;
Et GUILLAUME, qui a formé la branche des Seigneurs de *Moulins*, rapportée ci-après.

MICHEL BELOT, IIe du nom, Ecuyer, Sieur de Moulins en partie, fut, ainfi que fes prédéceffeurs, Confeiller du Roi au Baillage & fiège Préfidial de Blois. Il avoit époufé, en 1643, *Elifabeth le Roux*, dont il a eu :

JACQUES, qui fuit ;
Et FLORENT, Ecuyer, Sieur de Moulins, Prieur de Champigni, en 1677, Chevalier de Saint-Lazare & de Notre-Dame du Mont-Carmel en 1700.

JACQUES BELOT, Confeiller du Roi en fes Confeils, Lieutenant-Général au Baillage, fiège Préfidial & Gouvernement de Blois, acquit en 1680 la terre de Pezai.

MICHEL BELOT, IIIe du nom, fon petit-fils, né le 7 Septembre 1686, fervit dans la Marine, & s'en retira en 1727, étant alors Sous-Brigadier des Gardes de la Marine, au département de Rochefort.

Les armes de cette branche font : *d'azur, à un lac d'amour d'or, furmonté en chef d'une rofe de même, accoftée de deux étoiles auffi d'or.*

SECONDE BRANCHE.

GUILLAUME BELOT, Ier du nom, Ecuyer, Sieur de Moulins, & en partie du Clos, de Laleu & de la Mothe, Confeiller du Roi, Commiffaire ordinaire des Guerres, troifième fils de VALENTIN, IIe du nom, & de *Marguerite Ribier,* mourut en 1691, laiffant entr'autres enfans :

GUILLAUME BELOT, IIe du nom, Ecuyer, Seigneur de Moulins, de la Mothe & Laleu, né le 24 Février 1671, Enfeigne de Vaiffeau en 1705, marié, en 1717, avec *Marguerite de Beauchefne,* dont il a eu :

1. GUILLAUME-VALENTIN BELOT-DE-MOULINS-DE-PEZAI, Ecuyer, né le 4 Janvier 1724, reçu Page de la Grande-Ecurie du Roi, le 18 Mars 1740, fur les preuves de fa nobleffe ;
2. MARGUERITE-HÉLÈNE BELOT, mariée, par contrat du 22 Juin 1738, à *Claude-Guillaume de Verneffon,* Ecuyer, Seigneur des Forges de la Haute-Cour, &c. ;
3. MADELEINE, Religieufe ;
4. ANNE, vivante en 1759 ;
5. Et ROSALIE-ANNE, morte au berceau. (*Armorial de France,* reg. I, part. I, p. 60, & reg. II, p. 2.)

Les armes de cette branche : *d'azur, au lac d'amour d'or, furmonté en chef de deux étoiles de même.*

BELOUAN. Voyez BELLOUAN.

BELOUZE, en Provence: *d'or, à l'écuffon de fable, en abîme.*

BELRIEU (DE): *d'azur, à un croiffant d'argent; au chef d'or, chargé de trois étoiles de gueules.*

BELSUNCE, ancienne & illuftre Maifon du Royaume de Naples, qui étoit autrefois en poffeffion de deux Châteaux de fon nom, l'un fitué dans la Haute-Navarre, à fix lieues de Pampelune, où il fubfifte encore; & l'autre dans la Baffe-Navarre, au pays d'Arberoue, à trois lieues de Bayonne.

I. ROGER, Seigneur de BELSUNCE, tranfmit à fa poftérité la dignité de *Vicomte,* par l'acquifition qu'il fit de la Vicomté de Macaïe au pays de Labour, & des Château & Seigneurie de Pagandure, demeure ordinaire du Vicomte. Il fut père de :

II. CHICON DE BELSUNCE, Vicomte de Macaïe, qui fut l'un des Seigneurs qui foufcrivirent à la charte des privilèges accordés à la ville de Bayonne par RICHARD, Roi d'Angleterre & Duc d'Aquitaine en 1170. De lui naquit :

III. GUILLAUME DE BELSUNCE, qui tefta en 1209, laiffant :

IV. CHICON DE BELSUNCE, IIe du nom, Vicomte de Macaïe, vivant en 1240, père de :

V. GUILLAUME-CHICON DE BELSUNCE, Vicomte de Macaïe, marié, en 1273, à *Michelotte,* fille d'*Arnauld,* Seigneur d'*Uza,* dont :

ARNAULD, qui fuit ;
Et trois autres fils.

VI. ARNAULD DE BELSUNCE, Vicomte de Macaïe, fut gratifié, avec fes trois frères, de penfions, alors confidérables, par le Roi PHILIPPE le Bel, qui poffédoit le Royaume de Navarre, du chef de fa femme. Son fils fut :

VII. GARCIE-ARNAULD DE BELSUNCE, Vicomte de Macaïe, fait Chevalier par CHARLES le Bel, Roi de France & de Navarre, en 1022. De lui vint :

VIII. GUILLAUME-ARNAULD DE BELSUNCE, Vicomte de Macaïe, Chevalier, qui fut Grand-Chambellan & *Ricombre* de Navarre (c'eft un titre qui répond à celui de *Haut & Puiffant Seigneur,* & qui étoit en Navarre, comme en Efpagne, le plus éminent, auquel la haute nobleffe pouvoit prétendre. Parmi les Maifons de Navarre établies en France, l'on ne connoît que celles de *Gramont,* de *Luxe* & de *Belfunce,* qui foient parvenues à cette dignité; les deux premières en 1350, & la dernière peu de tems après). GUILLAUME-ARNAUD DE BELSUNCE n'avoit encore que le titre d'*Ecuyer,* lorfque le Roi CHARLES II, Comte de Navarre, furnommé depuis *le Mauvais,* lui fit don d'un certain bien pour en jouir pendant fa vie, à condition qu'il feroit obligé de le fervir, accompagné d'un Cavalier bien armé & à fes propres dépens durant 40 jours, dans fes armées en tems de guerre, ou de le fuivre dans fes chevauchées (comme on parloit alors) en tems de paix, quand il lui feroit mandé de fe rendre auprès de fa perfonne. Les diftinctions qu'il reçut de ce Prince l'attachèrent fi fort, qu'il le fuivit dans toutes fes malheureufes entreprifes contre la France, & il fut compris dans les Lettres d'abolition accordées au Roi de Navarre par le Traité de Paix du 14 Mars 1360, ftyle ancien. Il eut d'*Agnès de Luxe* :

IX. ANTOINE DE BELSUNCE, Vicomte de Macaïe, Maire & Capitaine général de la ville de Bayonne en 1362 (titre dont la Maifon *de Gramont* s'eft depuis rendue comme héréditaire). Il époufa *Eléonore d'Aroüe*, fille de N..... *d'Aroüe*, Vicomte de Saint-Martin, dont :

X. GARCIE-ARNAULD DE BELSUNCE, IIe du nom, Vicomte de Macaïe, qui figna avec les Seigneurs *de Gramont* & *de Luxe*, le Traité de Paix fait en 1384 entre la France & l'Efpagne. Il eut de *Blanche*, héritière de la Maifon & Abbaye laïque de Barvix :

1. ARNAULD, qui fuit ;
2. Et GASTON-ARMAND, qui, dit-on, délivra fon pays vers 1407 d'un dragon monftrueux, qui avoit trois têtes, & faifoit de grands ravages aux environs de Bayonne ; mais il fut enfeveli dans fon triomphe, puifqu'on le trouva étouffé fous le cadavre du dragon. C'eft ce qui fait que depuis cet événement les Seigneurs de BELSUNCE ont ajouté un dragon à l'écu de leurs armes par permiffion du Roi de Navarre, CHARLES III, dit *le Noble*.

XI. ARNAULD DE BELSUNCE, IIe du nom, dit *Arnauton*, Vicomte de Macaïe, premier Seigneur de Liffague, écartela le premier d'un *dragon* les armes de fes ancêtres. Il tefta en 1346, & avoit époufé *Marie de Léon*, que l'on tient iffue des anciens Rois de Léon, dont :

XII. JEAN DE BELSUNCE, Ier du nom, Vicomte de Macaïe, Seigneur de Liffague. Il fut fait en 1480 Maître-d'Hôtel de FRANÇOIS-PHŒBUS, Comte de Foix. Il eut de *Madeleine de Gramont*, fille de *Gratien, Ricombre* de Navarre, & de *Marguerite*, furnommée *de Navarre* :

XIII. JEAN DE BELSUNCE, IIe du nom, Vicomte de Macaïe, Seigneur de Liffague, Grand-Ecuyer en 1510 de JEAN D'ALBRET, Roi de Navarre, fe maria à *Jeanne de Chaux*, fille de N.... *de Chaux*, Vicomte de Bayonne en Baffe-Navarre. La Maifon *de Chaux* s'eft éteinte dans la perfonne de *Bertrand de Chaux*, Evêque de Bayonne, puis Archevêque de Tours, premier Aumônier du Roi, Prélat-Commandeur du Saint-Efprit, mort en 1641. Il avoit l'honneur d'être parent du Roi HENRI IV, par la Maifon d'ALBRET. JEAN DE BELSUNCE eut :

XIV. JEAN DE BELSUNCE, IIIe du nom, Vicomte de Macaïe, Seigneur de Liffague, premier Pannetier du Roi de Navarre, puis fon premier Maître-d'Hôtel, & enfin fon Grand-Chambellan. FRANÇOIS Ier le mit au nombre des 100 Gentilshommes de fon Hôtel par Lettres du 18 Septembre 1534. Par d'autres Lettres du 31 Décembre 1544, le même Roi le fit Capitaine de 300 hommes d'Infanterie. ANTOINE DE BOURBON, Roi de Navarre, deftinoit ce Vicomte pour Gouverneur de la perfonne de fon fils HENRI, Roi de Navarre ; mais il mourut avant d'en pouvoir faire les fonctions. C'eft à lui que l'*Alcade* du pays d'Arberoue voulut contefter la première place des Etats de ce canton, fous prétexte de prefcription, & que cette préféance bleffoit l'autorité royale dont il étoit revêtu ; l'affaire fut portée au Tribunal du Roi de Navarre : l'*Alcade* fut débouté de fes prétentions, & le Vicomte maintenu dans fon droit par Arrêt de la Chancellerie du 29 Avril 1555. Ses fucceffeurs depuis en ont joui paifiblement. JEAN DE BELSUNCE avoit époufé *Marie d'Armendarits*, fille de *François*, Seigneur dudit lieu en Baffe-Navarre, & de *Catherine d'Armendarits*, fa coufine, dont :

1. JEAN, qui fuit ;
2. FLORENCE, mariée à *Bertrand de Harambure*, Seigneur de Picafari, Gouverneur de Mauléon & pays de Soulles, mort au commencement de 1561 ;
3. JEANNE, époufe de *Triflan d'Aroüe*, Vicomte de Saint-Martin ;
4. MARIE, alliée à *François d'Alçate*, Vicomte d'Urtubie ;
5. Et FRANÇOISE, femme de *Jean de la Lane*, Colonel de l'Infanterie Béarnoife.

XV. JEAN DE BELSUNCE, IVe du nom, Vicomte de Macaïe, Ecuyer, Confeiller & Chambellan du Roi de Navarre, depuis Roi de France fous le nom de HENRI IV, fut nommé par le Roi HENRI II, Capitaine de 300 hommes de pied pour garder les frontières de Guyenne. Il fut enfuite Gouverneur des Ville & Château d'Acqs. La Reine JEANNE DE NAVARRE eut une grande confiance en lui ; HENRI, fon fils, n'en eut pas moins. Ce Vicomte avoit été marié du vivant de fes père & mère, par contrat du 21 Décembre 1555, à *Catherine de Luxe*, fille de *Jean*, Chevalier, &

d'*Isabeau de Gramont*. La Maison *de Luxe* s'est éteinte par une héritière, nièce de *Catherine*, dans celle de *Montmorency-Bouteville*, d'où sont issus les Ducs *de Montmorency-Luxembourg*; ce qui a donné de grandes alliances au Vicomte de BELSUNCE.

De ce mariage vinrent :

1. JEAN, qui suit ;
2. ANTOINE, Gouverneur de Paymirol en Agénois, Mestre - de - Camp d'Infanterie, qui se signala à la bataille de Coutras en 1587. Il fut tué au siège de Rouen dans une vive sortie des assiégés le 25 Février 1592 ;
3. CHARLES, Seigneur d'Higuières en Béarn, Procureur-Général au Parlement de Navarre ;
4. N...... DE BELSUNCE, qui s'attacha au service des Hollandois, alliés de la France, & eut dans leurs troupes un Régiment de son nom. S'étant trouvé à la défense d'Ostende, il y fit paroître tant de bravoure, que la garnison ayant perdu son Gouverneur, le choisit pour suppléer à sa place. Il fut tué depuis dans une occasion où il commandoit l'avant-garde de l'armée de Maurice de Nassau, Prince d'Orange ;
5. JEANNE, mariée à *Charles d'Aroüe*, Vicomte de Saint-Martin ;
6. Et DIANE, épouse d'*Anchot de Mesples*, Seigneur d'Esguiolles.

XVI. JEAN DE BELSUNCE, V^e du nom, Vicomte de Macaïe, &c., fut Capitaine & Gouverneur du Château de Mauléon & du pays de Soulles, & soutint dignement la réputation que son père s'étoit acquise. Il épousa, par contrat du 19 Mars 1584, *Rachel de Gontaut*, fille d'*Armand de Gontaut*, Seigneur de Saint-Geniès, & de *Jeanne de Foix*. De ce mariage vinrent :

1. ARMAND, auteur de la première branche, qui suit;
2. ELIE DE BELSUNCE, Capitaine dans le Régiment de Montpouillan, de la Maison de la Force. Le Roi lui donna ensuite, par commission du 24 Mars 1653, ce Régiment, qui prit alors le nom de *Belsunce*, qui, en 1659, fut uni à celui du Duc de Modène, mais il en eut toujours le commandement sous ce Prince, & il fut tué à la tête de ce Régiment;
3. Et JACQUES, qui a fait la seconde branche, rapportée ci-après.

PREMIÈRE BRANCHE.

XVII. ARMAND DE BELSUNCE, Vicomte de Macaïe, Capitaine & Gouverneur des Château de Mauléon & Pays de Soulles par Lettres du Roi du 16 Novembre 1610, Bailli pour Sa Majesté du pays de Mixe, contrée de la Basse-Navarre, dépendante des Vicomté & Evêché d'Acqs, vendit, du consentement de sa femme, de celui de son fils aîné & de la femme de celui-ci, au Seigneur *de Castalounès*, son gendre, la Vicomté de Macaïe, qui lui étoit déjà presque tout engagée & la Maison seigneuriale de cette Vicomté, nommée la *Salle de Pagandure*, moyennant la somme de 90937 livres, dont partie servit à acquitter la dot de sa fille, à payer les légitimes de ses deux frères ELIE & JACQUES, & à satisfaire quelques créanciers de la Maison. Il épousa, par contrat du 14 Mai 1600, *Marie*, Vicomtesse *de Meharin*, fille & héritière de *Bertrand*, Vicomte de Meharin, dans le pays d'Arberoue, Chambellan du Roi & Bailli du pays de Mixe. Ses enfans furent :

1. CHARLES, qui suit;
2. 3. & 4. Trois garçons, successivement Colonels du Régiment de *Belsunce*, & tués au service du Roi;
5. ESTHER, morte avant la vente de la Vicomté de Macaïe. Elle avoit épousé N..... *du Pont*, Avocat - Général au Parlement de Navarre ;
6. Et JEANNE, femme de *Jacques de Grenier*, Seigneur de Castalounès, Aide des Camps & Armées du Roi, Capitaine au Régiment de Toneins, puis Lieutenant- Colonel du même Régiment, présente à l'acquisition que fit son mari de la Vicomté de Macaïe, dont une fille, héritière de cette Terre, qui épousa ARMAND DE BELSUNCE, Vicomte de Meharin, son cousin.

XVIII. CHARLES DE BELSUNCE, Vicomte de Meharin, & Titulaire de Macaïe, Bailli d'Epée au pays de Mixe, épousa, par contrat du 14 Août 1639, *Sara de Ferrières*, fille de *Samuel de Ferrières*, Ecuyer, Conseiller du Roi au Présidial de la Rochelle, & de *Marie de Genais*, dont :

1. CHARLES, qui suit ;
2. Et SARA, mariée à *Jacob de Gassion*, neveu du Maréchal de ce nom, Seigneur de Château-d'Abere & d'Aslon, Capitaine de Cavalerie, mort en 1708.

XIX. CHARLES DE BELSUNCE, IIe du nom, Vicomte de Meharin, Bailli de Mixe, reçut en 1700 commission du Roi de régler, de concert avec l'Intendant de la Province, les différends qui étoient entre le haut & le bas Navarrois fur les limites des deux pays. Il eut d'*Angélique de Cazaux*, fille de *Henri-Augufte*, Procureur-Général au Parlement de Navarre :

1. ARMAND, Vicomte de Meharin, Bailli de Mixe, mort en 1718 fans enfans de fa coufine *N... de Grenier-Caftalounès*, héritière de la Vicomté de Macaïe, remariée à *Antoine d'Arneder*.

2. CHARLES, qui fuit ;

3. FRANÇOIS, Capitaine dans le Régiment de Nivernois, mort en 1717;

4. LOUIS, dit *le Chevalier de Belfunce*, qui, étant paffé en Efpagne du confentement de LOUIS XIV, fut Lieutenant dans le Régiment des Gardes-Valonnes de Sa Majefté Catholique, & enfuite Colonel de fon Régiment de Navarre. Après avoir fervi avec ce Régiment en Sardaigne & en Sicile, il revint en France, où il obtint une penfion du Roi & la commiffion de Lieutenant-Colonel réformé, à la fuite de la ville de Bayonne;

5. Et ARMAND, mort en 1723.

XX. CHARLES DE BELSUNCE, IIIe du nom, Vicomte de Meharin, Bailli de Mixe, après la mort de fon frère aîné, a fervi long-tems en qualité de Capitaine dans le Régiment de Nivernois, & a époufé *Marie-Anne d'Ardener*, fœur d'*Antoine*, à qui fa belle-fœur s'eft remariée, dont :

1. ARMAND, qui fuit ;

2. HENRI-FRANÇOIS-XAVIER, rapporté après fon frère aîné ;

3. Et MARIE-ANNE.

XXI. ARMAND, Vicomte de BELSUNCE, Lieutenant-Général des Armées du Roi, Gouverneur des Ifles d'Oléron, enfuite de Belle-Ifle, côte de Bretagne, s'eft rendu célèbre par fes exploits militaires à Gottingen, dans l'Electorat de Hanovre en 1760 & 1761 ; & il eft mort à fon arrivée de Saint-Domingue en 1763, où Sa Majefté l'avoit envoyé en qualité de Gouverneur-Général.

XXI. HENRI-FRANÇOIS-XAVIER, Vicomte de BELSUNCE après la mort de fon frère aîné, Colonel du Régiment de Béarn le 16 Novembre 1764, par la mort de M. de Boifgelin, a époufé, en 1761, *N.... de la Live-d'Epinay*.

SECONDE BRANCHE.

XVII. JACQUES DE BELSUNCE, troifième fils de JEAN, Ve du nom, & de *Rachel de Gontaut*, Seigneur des Château & Paroiffe de Borne en Agénois, &c., Aide-des-Camps &

Armées du Roi par Brevet du 16 Août 1631; Capitaine d'Infanterie dans le Régiment de Piémont, par commiffion du 26 Mars 1634, Commandant pour le fervice des Ville & Château de Soiffons, durant l'abfence du Duc de Montbazon par Lettres du Roi LOUIS XIII du 12 Juillet 1637; tranfigea avec fon frère aîné en 1634 fur fes droits de légitime, & lors de la recherche de la Nobleffe (étant âgé de 70 ans) il prouva la fienne par titres, qu'il produifit en Février 1667 par-devant M. *Pelot*, Intendant de Bordeaux, & il fut reconnu pour noble d'ancienne extraction: il vivoit encore en 1668. Il avoit époufé, par contrat du 1er Décembre 1631, *Jeanne de l'Effe*, fille de *Jacob*, Seigneur du Coudray, & de *Marie de Loube*, Dame de la Gateline. De ce mariage naquirent :

1. N...... DE BELSUNCE, Capitaine dans le Régiment de fon nom, tué au fervice du Roi au combat du Faubourg Saint-Antoine, où il commandoit les Enfans perdus en 1652;

2. ARMAND, qui fuit ;

3. JACOB, Capitaine dans le Régiment de Turenne, tué au combat de Sintzecin en 1674;

4. N...... Lieutenant-Colonel des Cuiraffiers du Roi, tué à la bataille de Senef, le 11 Août 1674;

5. ELIE, dit *le Comte de Belfunce*, Chevalier de Saint-Louis, Colonel du Régiment de Nivernois, créé Brigadier des Armées du Roi en 1694. Ses infirmités l'obligèrent de quitter le fervice, & il vivoit encore en Février 1724;

6. ANNE, mariée, en 1667, à *Jean de Montalembert*, Seigneur de Montbeau, dont des enfans ;

7. CHARLOTTE, alliée, après le 21 Juillet 1668, à *Jean de Caumont-la-Force ;*

8. OLYMPE, femme d'*Antoine*, Seigneur *de la Lane*, Colonel d'un Régiment Hollandois, dont une fille unique, mariée à *Nicolas de Fumel ;*

9. Et LOUISE, feconde femme, le 22 Septembre 1667, d'*Armand Nompar-de-Caumont*, Duc de la Force.

XVIII. ARMAND, Marquis de BELSUNCE & de Caftelmoron, Baron de Gavaudun, Seigneur de Borne en Agénois, &c., Sénéchal & Gouverneur des Sénéchauffées d'Agénois & Condomois le 30 Mars 1699, Capitaine dans le Régiment de Schomberg, fervit en cette qualité en Portugal fous le Comte de Schomberg en 1667, & fut enfuite Capitaine dans le Régiment Royal. Il époufa, par contrat du 21

Juillet 1668, *Anne de Caumont-de-Lauzun*, petite nièce du Maréchal-Duc de la Force, préfent à ce contrat, & qui lui donna en confidération de ce mariage, la terre & feigneurie de Caftelmoron. Elle eft morte le 6 Octobre 1712. Elle étoit troifième fille de *Gabriel-Nompar de Caumont*, Comte de Lauzun, & de fa feconde femme *Charlotte de Caumont-la-Force*. Ils eurent :

1. ARMAND, Marquis de Caftelmoron, Colonel en 1701 du Régiment de Nivernois, puis en 1704, Capitaine-Lieutenant des Gendarmes de Bourgogne, Brigadier des Armées du Roi le 30 Janvier 1709, Chevalier de Saint-Louis, commandant la Gendarmerie en Flandre en 1712, qui eft mort de fes bleffures le 18 Juillet 1712. C'eft le neuvième de fa Maifon qui a perdu la vie dans les Armées. Il avoit époufé, en 1700, *N... du Buiffon-de-Bournazel*, morte en 1712, fans enfans. Elle étoit fille & héritière de *N.... du Buiffon*, Marquis de Bournazel & de Mirabel, Sénéchal de Rouergue ;

2. HENRI-FRANÇOIS-XAVIER DE BELSUNCE-CASTELMORON, nommé à l'Evêché de Marfeille le 3 Avril 1709, facré à Paris le 30 Mars 1710, député de la Province d'Arles, à l'Affemblée du Clergé de cette année, Abbé de Notre-Dame de Chambons, Diocèfe de Viviers, & de Montmorel, Diocèfe d'Avranches, & pourvu étant très-jeune, le 12 Août 1688, de l'Abbaye de la Réole, Diocèfe de Lefcars, dont il fe démit peu après, ainfi que de celle de Notre-Dame de Chambons en 1729 ; il fut nommé à l'Abbaye de Saint-Arnoul de Metz. Le zèle & la charité de ce Prélat éclatèrent durant la pefte qui affligea la ville de Marfeille pendant les années 1720 & 1721. Le Roi le nomma en 1723 à l'Evêché de Laon, fecond Duché-Pairie du Royaume, & il remercia Sa Majefté cinq femaines après, ne croyant pas pouvoir quitter une époufe qui lui étoit fi chère, pour en prendre une autre plus honorable. Le Roi, en confidération de la Duché-Pairie, dont il fe privoit, lui accorda par une grâce fingulière de porter en première inftance à la Grand'Chambre, toutes fes caufes, tant pour le temporel de fes Bénéfices, que pour la Juridiction fpirituelle, fi elle étoit attaquée. Il mourut en 1755 ;

3. ANTONIN, Capitaine de Frégate, mort à Saintes le 28 Octobre 1712 ;

4. CHARLES-GABRIEL, qui fuit ;

5. Et ANNE-MARIE-LOUISE, Grande-Prieure de l'Abbaye de Saintes, & depuis Abbeffe de Roncerai à Angers, après que *Françoife*

de Caumont-Lauzun s'en fut démife en fa faveur le 19 Mars 1709.

XIX. CHARLES-GABRIEL DE BELSUNCE, Marquis de Caftelmoron, Seigneur de Montpont, Colonel du Régiment de *Belfunce*, Capitaine-Lieutenant des Gendarmes Bourguignons en 1713, Chevalier de Saint-Louis, pourvu à titre de furvivance de fon père en 1717 de la charge de Sénéchal & Gouverneur des Sénéchauffées d'Agénois & Condomois, Brigadier de Cavalerie le 1er Février 1719, époufa, par contrat du 30 Avril 1715, *Cécile-Geneviève de Fontanieu*, fille de *Moïfe-Auguste*, Secrétaire du Roi, Intendant & Contrôleur-Général des Meubles de la Couronne, & de *Geneviève d'Odun*, dont :

XX. ANTONIN-ARMAND DE BELSUNCE, Comte de Caftelmoron, Grand-Louvetier de France en 1736, mort le 17 Septembre 1741. Il avoit époufé, en 1737, *Charlotte-Alexandrine Sublet-d'Heudicourt*, dont fon fils unique :

XXI. LOUIS-ANTONIN, Marquis de BELSUNCE, né vers 1740, marié, par contrat du 2 Janvier 1763, à *Adélaïde-Elifabeth d'Hallencourt-de-Drofmenil*, préfentée par la Comteffe de BELSUNCE, Dame pour accompagner MADAME, morte à Bagnères dans fa 24e année le 4 Octobre 1770.

Les armes de cette Maifon font celles de Béarn : *d'or, à deux vaches de gueules accornées, accolées & clarinées d'azur*. Mais depuis 1407 ceux de cette Maifon *écartèlent aux 2 & 3 d'argent, à une hydre de finople à fept têtes, dont l'une eft coupée, & tient encore un peu au col avec quelques gouttes de fang qui coulent de la bleffure*.

S'il étoit permis de s'appuyer en pareil cas fur des conjectures, les armes des anciens Comtes de Béarn, que la Maifon de BELSUNCE porte depuis un tems immémorial, feroient un beau préjugé pour elle. Les Seigneurs de BELSUNCE font en poffeffion du titre de *Vicomte* depuis le milieu du XIIe fiècle, & le Chef de la Maifon eft Colonel-né des Milices du Val d'Arberoue, à la tête defquelles eft la nobleffe du Pays dont il commande la principale partie ; & dans les affemblées des Etats, il y précède l'*Alcade* ou *Juge Royal*, & fe place toujours au-deffus de lui, pendant que le refte de la nobleffe, affife fur le même banc, eft au-deffous de cet Officier. (*Dictionnaire des Gaules*.)

BELVEDER, *d'argent, à trois pals de*

gueules, à la bande d'azur, brochant fur le tout, chargée de trois befans d'or.

BELVESER : porte mêmes armes, fans la bande.

BELY : *de gueules, au rocher alaifé d'argent, accompagné en chef d'une couronne de Marquis d'or.*

BENAC, famille noble & ancienne, originaire de la Sénéchauffée de Bigorre, où elle a poffédé long-tems la Baronie de fon nom.

I. Manaud de Bénac, Iᵉʳ du nom, Chevalier, Seigneur & Baron de Bénac, fuivant un dire par écrit qui eft aux Archives d'Offun, eut :

1. Guilhém-Arnaud ;
2. Et Raymond-Arnaud, qui fuit.

II. Raymond-Arnaud de Bénac, Chevalier, Seigneur de Lane, époufa *Anxiette de Las,* Dame du Caftera, dont il eut :

1. Manaud, qui fuit ;
2. Et Berdot, qui mourut fans poftérité, après avoir inftitué Manaud de Bénac, IIIᵉ du nom, fon neveu, fon héritier.

III. Manaud de Bénac, IIᵉ du nom, Chevalier, Seigneur de Lane, époufa, vers 1389, *Conftance de Caftelbajac,* Dame de Boüilh, Saint-Luc & Locrap, morte avant 1405, fille de noble Chevalier *Arnaud-Raymond de Caftelbajac,* IVᵉ du nom, Seigneur & Baron de Caftelbajac, &c. Il en eut :

1. Manaud, qui fuit ;
2. Anglese, qui fut mariée avec noble *Arnaud de Barège,* & fut mère de *Bourguine de Barége,* laquelle époufa *Arnaud,* Seigneur d'Offun.
3. Et Marguerite, qui fut héritière de fon père, avec fubftitution en faveur de fa fœur, & fut mariée, 1º fans poftérité, avec Noble *Bertrand de Bécans,* Seigneur de Lane ; & 2º également fans enfans, avec Noble *Bertrand de Montefquiou,* Baron dudit lieu, qu'elle inftitua fon héritier par fon teftament du 18 Juillet 1428.

IV. Manaud de Bénac, IIIᵉ du nom, Chevalier, Seigneur de Lane, de Boüilh, Saint-Luc & Locrap, fut héritier de Berdot de Bénac, fon oncle paternel, ainfi que de *Bernard de Caftelbajac,* fon oncle maternel, qui avoit été affaffiné. Le Parlement de Paris ordonna qu'il feroit fourni par l'héritier de ce dernier la fomme de 1200 francs d'or pour agir contre les meurtriers. Il étoit encore mineur en 1405, fuivant qu'il paroît par Sentence rendue par *Jean de la Lane,* Bachelier en Droit, Lieu-

Tome II.

tenant de Guidamor & d'Aula, Chevalier, Sénéchal de Bigorre, & Avocat du Roi en la Sénéchauffée, le 29 Mai 1405, qui lui nomme pour tuteur *Noble & Puiffant Seigneur Bernard de Caftelbajac,* Seigneur dudit lieu, fon coufin germain maternel, & noble Manaud de Bénac, fon père. Ce dernier, pour faire ladite fomme de 1200 francs d'or, vendit en ladite qualité la Terre de Boüilh audit *Jean de la Lane,* moyennant 200 florins d'Aragon, par acte du 15 Mai 1408. Il mourut majeur, fans poftérité, laiffant pour héritière de tous fes biens Madame *d'Offun,* fa fœur.

Il y a la Famille de *Montaut-de-Bénac,* dont nous parlerons en fon lieu.

* BENAON, Terre & Seigneurie en Poitou, Diocèfe de la Rochelle, érigée en Comté, & cédée avec le Château de Fontenay-l'Abbatu, par Lettres du mois de Septembre 1378, à *Triftan Rouault,* & à *Perrenelle,* Vicomteffe de Thouars, fa femme, en échange des droits qu'ils avoient fur le Comté de Dreux. *Ifabeau de Thouars* fuccéda à fa fœur, & devint Comteffe de Benaon, & Vicomteffe de Thouars. De fon fecond mari, *Ingelger d'Amboife,* Iᵉʳ du nom, vint *Ingelger II,* père de *Louis d'Amboife,* Vicomte de Thouars & Comte de Benaon. Celui-ci eut pour fille unique *Marguerite d'Amboife,* qui porta le Comté de Benaon & la Vicomté de Thouars à fon mari *Louis,* Iᵉʳ du nom, Sire *de la Trémouille.* Voyez TRÉMOILLE.

BÉNARD, Sieur de Rotot, Maifons, Vauville, ancienne nobleffe, Election de Caen en Normandie, qui porte : *d'azur, à trois lys de jardin, fleuris & d'argent, pofés 2 & 1.*

BÉNARD, Sieur de Monville, Election de Caen, famille annoblie aux Francs-Fiefs en 1471, dont les armes font : *d'azur, à trois feuilles de chêne d'or, pofées 2 & 1.*

BÉNARD, autre famille annoblie la même année que la précédente, qui porte: *d'argent, à la feuille.... de gueules, accoftée de deux croiffans d'azur.*

BÉNARD, Seigneur de la Fortereffe: *d'azur, au chevron d'or, accompagné en chef de deux fleurs de foucis de même, & en pointe d'une tour d'argent ; au chef coufu de gueules, chargé d'un croiffant d'or, accofté de deux étoiles d'argent.*

BÉNARD, Seigneur de Rezay: *d'argent, à deux fafces ondées d'azur; au chef coufu de fable, chargé de trois échecs d'or.*

BENAUD ou BENAULT-DE-LUBIÈRES, en Provence.

Cette famille tire fon origine d'Auvergne, où elle tenoit un rang diftingué parmi les nobles dans les XIIᵉ & XIIIᵉ fiècles. Elle n'eft connue en Provence que depuis MASSÉ DE BENAUD, qui reçut en 1406, en préfence & du confentement de LOUIS II, Comte de Provence, le bâton de Viguier de Marfeille, des mains de *Guillaume de Lafcaris.* Il n'y avoit alors que les principaux Gentilshommes du pays, qui puffent être revêtus de cette dignité.

Son petit-fils, JEAN DE BENAUD, Seigneur de Villeneuve-lez-Pallerandes en Auvergne, &c., fut Confeiller & Chambellan de CHARLES DU MAINE; ce Prince le fit légataire de la fomme de 1500 écus d'or, dans le même teftament où il inftitua LOUIS XI fon héritier. Ce dernier Prince l'employa en diverfes négociations. Il fut Gentilhomme de la Chambre de CHARLES VIII, & commanda un Corps d'armée, lors de la conquête du Royaume de Naples. Il avoit époufé *Catherine de Villeneuve,* fœur du premier Marquis *de Trans,* furnommé *le Grand.* Il eut:

1. JEAN, qui fuit;
2. Et HONORÉE, mariée avec *Jean de Boniface,* Seigneur de la Mole.

JEAN DE BENAUD, IIᵉ du nom, Chevalier de l'Ordre du Roi HENRI II par Lettres du 17 Décembre 1548, & Lieutenant de Roi en Provence, commanda dans le Pays fous les ordres du Gouverneur Claude, Comte de Tende, & tefta le 20 Mai 1556 en faveur de fes enfans. Il époufa, en Juillet 1521, *Jeanne de Lubières,* héritière univerfelle de la Maifon de ce nom, à la charge d'en prendre le nom & les armes, que fa poftérité porte encore actuellement. Il laiffa:

1. ANTOINE DE BENAUD-DE-LUBIÈRES, qui fut légataire d'un autre ANTOINE;
2. GALEAS, qui commanda les Galères du Roi, dont il étoit le plus ancien Capitaine. Il fe diftingua dans plufieurs occafions où il fe trouva. Il fe battit dans un combat particulier proche Jarnac, & mourut des bleffures qu'il reçut en cette occafion;
3. JEAN-BAPTISTE;
4. Et FRANÇOISE, mariée à *Honoré de Rodulf,* qui fut mère du Connétable *de Luynes.*

ANTOINE DE BENAUD, Chevalier de l'Ordre du Roi en 1573, fut envoyé par CHARLES IX en Provence, pour pacifier les troubles qu'il y avoit en cette Province. Il étoit Gentilhomme ordinaire de la Chambre du Roi HENRI III. Il fut encore Colonel des Légionnaires de Provence en 1576, Gouverneur du Château de Tarafcon & de fa Viguerie. Il avoit époufé *Marie de Corlieu,* dont il eut:

ANNE DE BENAUD-DE-LUBIÈRES, qui époufa 1º *Madeleine de Varadier,* fille de *Gabriel de Varadier-de-Saint-Andiol,* & de *Louife-Aube de Roquemartine;* & 2º *Marie de Leftaud,* fille de *Louis,* & de *Françoife de Durand,* de Tarafcon. De ce dernier mariage naquit:

HENRI DE BENAUD, Seigneur du Breuil, qui eut:

DOMINIQUE DE BENAUD, reçu Confeiller au Parlement de Provence en 1655, marié, le 26 Décembre 1653, avec *Sufanne de Laurence,* fille de *Pierre,* Marquis de Saint-Martin, Confeiller en la même Cour, & de *Jeanne de Séguiran-de-Bouc.* De ce mariage font iffus entr'autres enfans:

1. HENRI, qui fuit;
2. Et PIERRE, mort Capitaine d'un des Vaiffeaux du Roi.

HENRI DE BENAUD-DE-LUBIÈRES, IIᵉ du nom, hérita de la famille *d'Aube,* & fut en conféquence Marquis de Roquemartine. Il fuccéda en l'Office de fon père en 1682, & s'allia avec *Victoire de Gazel,* dont eft forti:

PIERRE-JOSEPH DE BENAUD, Marquis de Roquemartine, reçu Confeiller au Parlement en 1718, & marié avec *Thérèfe-Françoife de Brancas-Laudun,* des Comtes de Forcalquier, fille de *Henri,* Baron de Villeneuve, & de *Louife des Porcellets.* Il a laiffé:

1. N... DE BENAUD, qui fert dans les armées du Roi en qualité de Capitaine de Cavalerie;
2. LOUIS-FRANÇOIS, Marquis de Roquemartine, qui exerça l'Office de fes père, ayeul & bifayeul;
3. N... DE BENAUD, mariée à N.... *de Julien-de-Pegneirolle,* Préfident à Mortier au Parlement de Touloufe;
4. Et N... DE BENAUD.

(Voy. Artefeuil, tom. I, p. 122.)

Les armes: *d'or, à trois têtes de maure de fable, 2 & 1, les deux du chef affrontées, celle de la pointe renverfée, tortillées & col-*

letées d'argent, enchaînées ensemble à leur collier par trois chaînes de même, & liées en cœur à un anneau aussi d'argent.

BENAVIDES: *d'azur, au lion bandé d'or & d'azur.*

BENAVILLE: *palé d'argent & de gueules de six pièces.*

BENCE, Seigneur du Buisson, de Garembourg & de Cracoville, Généralité de Rouen. Jean Bence, Seigneur du Buisson, Garembourg, &c., épousa *Françoise de Mallevove,* dont il eut:

Jacques Bence, Seigneur du Buisson, Garembourg & de Cracoville, qui épousa, le 9 Novembre 1676, *Françoise de Nocei,* dont il eut entr'autres enfans :

Angélique-Madeleine Bence-de-Garembourg, reçue à Saint-Cyr le 4 Janvier 1707 sur les preuves de sa noblesse, remontée par titres jusqu'à Robert Bence, son sixième ayeul, Ecuyer, Seigneur du Buisson, de Garembourg, qualifié *Maréchal de Honfleur* en 1463, & pourvu de l'office de Bailli de Gien le 18 Juin 1443.

Les armes : *de gueules, à la fasce d'argent, accompagnée de trois molettes d'éperon d'or, deux en chef & une en pointe.*

BENCE : *d'azur, au chevron d'or, accompagné en chef de deux molettes d'éperon de même, & en pointe d'une foi d'argent.*

BENEDICTI, en Franche-Comté : *de gueules, à la bande engrêlée d'or.*

BENEVANS: *fretté d'or & de gueules, semé d'écussons d'argent.*

BÉNÉVENT, en Languedoc. I. Jean de Bénévent, fils de noble Pierre, Seigneur de Salles, & d'*Anne d'Hautpoul,* eut des provisions de la Capitainerie de Castelnaudary en Lauraguais, de la Reine-mère, datées du 17 Mars 1591, étoit mort le 8 Février 1608, & il avoit épousé, par contrat passé devant *Radulphe,* Notaire à Narbonne, le 7 Mars 1573, *Louise de Cheneteau,* qui, du consentement de Jean-Antoine, son fils, qui suit, passa bail des héritages de feu son mari en 1608. Elle étoit fille de noble *Geoffroy de Cheneteau,* Maréchal des Logis du Roi Henri II, & de *Jacquette Dedier.*

II. Jean-Antoine de Bénévent, Seigneur de Salles, testa le 18 Février 1648, voulut qu'on l'enterrât dans l'Eglise de Saint-Julien dudit lieu de Salles, & institua son héritier Jean-Pierre qui suit. Il avoit épousé, par contrat passé devant *Cazéer,* Notaire à Mont-Réal, Diocèse de Narbonne, le 8 Mai 1633, *Antoinette de Maireville,* fille de noble *Jean de Maireville,* Seigneur de Montgranier & de Perles, & de *Louise de Plantavit.*

III. Jean-Pierre de Bénévent, Seigneur de Salles, au Diocèse de Narbonne, testa le 25 Avril 1676, ordonna qu'on l'enterrât dans l'Eglise des Cordeliers de la ville de Narbonne, & institua son héritier Jean-Gabriel, qui suit. Il avoit épousé, par contrat passé devant *Ancourel,* Notaire du lieu de Laurens, Diocèse de Béziers, le 21 Février 1662, *Jacquette de Ferroul,* fille de Messire *Jean-Gabriel Ferroul,* Seigneur & Baron de Laurens & de Foussillon, & d'*Anne de Thezan-Saint-Geniez.*

IV. Jean-Gabriel de Bénévent, Seigneur de Salles, né & baptisé le 22 Février 1663 dans l'Eglise de Saint-Just de Narbonne, épousa, par contrat passé devant *Rouaut,* Notaire à Narbonne, le 21 Novembre 1689, *Anne de Sauret,* dont il eut :

V. Hyacinthe-Joseph de Bénévent-de-Salles, né & baptisé le 21 Février 1699 dans l'Eglise de Notre-Dame de Lamajour à Narbonne, qui fut présenté vers 1714 pour être reçu Page du Roi dans sa Petite-Ecurie, après ses preuves faites des degrés ci-dessus mentionnés. Nous en ignorons la postérité.

Les armes: *d'argent, à trois bandes de gueules; au chef d'azur, chargé d'un lambel de trois pendants d'or.* Du Buisson dit : *à trois barres,* &c.

BENEVERT, en Bretagne: *d'argent, au chêne de sinople, fruité d'or, un sanglier de gueules passant au pied.*

BENEVILLE, en Provence : *de gueules, à trois mains sénestres, appaumées d'or, posées 2 & 1.*

BENGY, Seigneur de Cornet : *d'azur, à trois étoiles d'argent, posées 2 & 1.*

BENNERAYE (la), en Plemeleuc: *d'or, à trois glés de gueules, posés 2 & 1. Le glé* est un petit animal que nous appelons aujourd'hui *loir,* qui ressemble au *rat,* & vit de poissons, qu'il va chercher au fond de l'eau.

BENNERVEN, en Bretagne *d'argent, à un chêne de sinople, glanté d'or, & un san-*

glier de gueules paſſant au pied. Cette famille paroît être la même que celle de BENE-VERT ci-deſſus.

BENNEVILLE, Seigneur des Granges & de Précaire, en Normandie, Généralité de Rouen.

PIERRE DE BENNEVILLE, ſuivant la Roque, eut pour fils :

GUILLAUME DE BENNEVILLE, compris dans un Arrêt de la Cour des Aides de Rouen du 24 Décembre 1495. Il fut père de :

JACQUES DE BENNEVILLE, qui épouſa *Gravette d'Aniſy*, fille du Seigneur de Criqueville, dont il eut :

GILLES DE BENNEVILLE, qui épouſa *Catherine Perrot*, dont il eut :

1. NICOLAS, marié à *Françoiſe d'Harcourt*, qui lui apporta en dot la Terre des Granges ;
2. Et HENRI, marié, vers 1530, à *Jacqueline d'Harcourt*, l'une & l'autre filles de *Jean d'Harcourt*, Seigneur de Juvigny.

JACQUES DE BENNEVILLE, Seigneur des Granges, Conſeiller au Parlement de Rouen en 1570, fils de NICOLAS, épouſa *Jacqueline* ou *Françoiſe Mallet-de-Craſménil*, dont :

JACQUES DE BENNEVILLE, Seigneur des Granges & de Précaire, Conſeiller au Parlement de Rouen en 1606.

Et JACQUELINE DE BENNEVILLE, mariée, en 1653, à *Jean d'Harcourt*, Baron de Lougey.

Les armes : *d'azur, au lion léopardé d'or.*

BENNEVILLE, en Normandie : *de ſable, au chef d'or, chargé de trois roſes du champ.*

BENOISE. MICHEL BENOISE étoit quartinier de la ville de Paris en 1555.

CHARLES-AUGUSTE DE BENOISE fut Conſeiller au Parlement de Paris, puis Conſeiller de la Grand'Chambre en la même Cour, & mourut le 17 Mars 1762. Il avoit épouſé, en 1712, *N... Berthelot*, fille d'*Etienne Berthelot*, & de *Marie-Henriette-Françoiſe Galland*, dont :

MARIE-FRANÇOISE-CHARLOTTE-BENOISE DE MAREUIL, morte le 2 Novembre 1742, qui avoit épouſé, le 10 Mars 1734, *Marie-Louis de Caillebot*, Marquis de la Salle.

N... BENOISE, ſœur de CHARLES-AUGUSTE, ne prit pas d'alliance.

Les armes : *d'argent, à la faſce d'azur, chargée d'un cœur & d'une fleur-de-lys d'or,*

& *accompagnée de trois roſes de gueules, 2 en chef & 1 en pointe.*

BENOIST, en Provence, famille noble qui ſubſiſte dans FRANÇOIS BENOIST, Avocat du Roi au Bureau des Finances de la Généralité de Provence.

Les armes : *de gueules, au lion d'or, tenant un globe d'azur, cerclé & croiſé d'argent, à la bordure d'or.*

BENOIST : *d'azur, au lion d'or.*

BENOIST, Seigneur de Vielchaſtel : *écartelé, aux 1 & 4 d'azur, à l'aigle d'or ; aux 2 & 3 de gueules, au ſautoir treſlé & alaiſé d'or.*

BENOIST, Seigneur de Saint-Port : *d'argent, à une faſce de ſable, accompagnée de deux jumelles de gueules, une en chef & l'autre en pointe.*

BENOIST, en Normandie, Généralité de Caen, famille annoblie en 1586, dont les armes ſont : *d'argent, à l'aigle de ſable, onglée & languée de gueules.*

BENOIST-DE-LA-PRUNAREDE. I. ANDRÉ, dit *le Capitaine Benoiſt*, vivoit en 1476 ; il eſt connu par le teſtament de JEAN, ſon fils.

II. JEAN BENOIST, I.er du nom, Seigneur de la Ciſternette, teſta le 24 Décembre 1557. Il avoit épouſé 1.º *Anne Damet* ; & 2.º *Philippine de Régis.*

Il eut de ſon premier mariage :

1. ANDRÉ, qui ſuit ;
2. Et Louis, Capitaine d'une Compagnie de 100 hommes de pied, marié à *Marguerite de Patau.*

III. ANDRÉ BENOIST, Seigneur de la Ciſternette, Capitaine d'une Compagnie de 200 hommes de pied, épouſa, 1.º le 7 Février 1554, *Anne Durand* ; & 2.º *Françoiſe du Caylar*, fille de *N.. du Caylar*, Gouverneur de Béziers.

Il eut du premier mariage :

1. JEAN, qui ſuit.

Et du ſecond :

2. Et Louis, qui teſta le 25 Novembre 1581.

IV. JEAN BENOIST, II.º du nom, Seigneur de la Ciſternette, Capitaine de 100 hommes de pied François, Gouverneur du Port de Saint-Jean-de-Foy, épouſa, le 10 Décembre 1593, *Jacquette de Gineſtous-de-Mondardier.* Il eut :

1. Charles, qui fuit ;
2. & 3. François & Jacques.

V. Charles Benoist, Seigneur de la Cifternette & de la Prunarede, Capitaine d'Infanterie au Régiment de Saint-Aunais qui obtint
un Arrêt contre le Traitant des Francs-Fiefs,
dans lequel font vifés les aѐtes, commiffions
& Brevets mentionnés dans cet Arrêt en date
du 5 Oѐtobre 1658. Il époufa, le 30 Juillet
1623, *Ifabeau de Peiran*, Dame de la Prunarede. Il eut :

    1. Henri, qui fuit ;
    2. François, Seigneur de la Verarié, Briga-
       dier des Gardes-du-Corps du Roi, bleffé au
       combat de Leuze en 1691 ;
    3. Et Balthazard, Prêtre, qui tefta le 24 No-
       vembre 1659.

VI. Henri Benoist, Seigneur de la Prunarede, de la Cifternette, de la Sefguière & Di-
reѐte de Saint-Jean-de-Foy, perdit un œil au
fiège de Paris en 1665. Il époufa, le 19 Juillet 1661, *Gabrielle de la Treilhe*. Il eut :

    1. Philippe, qui fuit ;
    2. François, dit *de la Cifternette*, Capitaine
       de Cuiraffiers, tué au fiège de Landau en
       1702;
    3. Henri, Chanoine, Archidiacre & Vicaire-
       Général du Diocèfe de Lodève ;
    4. Autre Henri, Seigneur de la Sefguière, Ca-
       pitaine de Dragons au Régiment Dauphin,
       Chevalier de Saint-Louis;
    5. Et Gabriel, dit *de la Prunarede*, Major
       du Régiment de Noailles, qui a fait la bran-
       che cadette.

VII. Philippe Benoist, Seigneur de la Prunarede, de la Cifternette, du Caffelet & de Saint-
Maurice, Capitaine de Dragons, enfuite Lieutenant-Colonel d'un Régiment d'Infanterie,
levé en 1701 par la Province de Languedoc,
Colonel des Compagnies du Diocèfe de Lo-
dève par Brevet du Roi, époufa, en 1699, *N...
de Gineftous*, dont il eut :

    Gabrielle Benoist, mariée avec *N... de Bar-
       beyrac*, dont le fils, Marquis de Saint-Mau-
       rice, a obtenu en 1753 l'éreѐtion des fufdites
       terres en Marquifat. Il fut tué à la bataille
       d'Hochftett le 13 Août 1704.

BRANCHE CADETTE.

VII. Gabriel Benoist-de-la-Prunarede,
Major du Régiment de Noailles, a époufé,
en 1716, *Ifabeau de la Treilhe-Fofières*. Il
en a eu :

    1. Jean-Gabriel, Abbé de Saint-Guilhem,

Chanoine, Sacriftain & Vicaire-Général de
Montpellier ;

    2. Jean-François, mort en bas âge ;
    3. Henri, qui fuit ;
    4. Guillaume-Gabriel, Doyen de Saint-Mar-
       tin de Tours ;
    5. Jean, Capitaine de Cavalerie au Régiment
       Royal-Lorraine, Chevalier de Saint-Louis;
    6. Et Henriette, mariée avec *Armand de
       Gineftous*, Seigneur de Maron, morte fans
       enfans.

VIII. Henri Benoist-de-la-Prunarede,
Seigneur de Navacelle & de Serifières, Capitaine de Dragons au Régiment Royal, Chevalier de Saint-Louis, a obtenu le Brevet de
Lieutenant-Colonel pour une aѐtion de bravoure, devant Zieremberg en 1761. Il a époufé *Marie de Navacelle*, dont il a Henriette
Benoist.

 ·Les armes : *d'azur, à trois bandes d'or.*

BENSERADE, famille noble qui a donné
un Grand-Maître, Capitaine général de l'Artillerie dans Paul de Benserade, Chambellan
de Louis XII, & Capitaine-Gouverneur du
Château de Milan, tué d'un coup de canon au
fiège de Ravenne en 1512. Isaac de Benserade, né en 1612 à Lions proche Rouen, en
étoit iffu. Il eft connu parmi les Sçavans par
la fécondité de fon génie, fes fines & délicates
railleries, fa préfence d'efprit, fes bons mots :
il fut reçu à l'Académie Françoife en 1674 ;
il étoit contemporain de Voiture. Il mourut
en 1691.

    La Famille de Benserade étoit alliée à la
Maifon de *la Porte*, à celle de *Wignacourt*,
&, felon quelques-uns, à celle du Cardinal *de
Richelieu*.

    Les armes : *d'or, à quatre pals de gueu-
les.*

BENTHEIM, Bourg & Château d'Allemagne, & Comté dans la Weftphalie, entre l'E-
vêché de Munfter & la Province d'Over-Yffel,
qui a donné fon nom à la Maifon de Bentheim.
Elle a formé trois branches. Le premier que
l'on connoiffe des Comtes de Bentheim, eft
Eberwein de Gutterswick, qui acquit ce
Comté en époufant Hedwige, fille de Henri,
IIᵉ du nom, & fœur de Simon-Bernard, derniers Comtes de Bentheim. Leur fils Arnoul,
chef de toutes les branches, mourut en 1506.

    Les Comtes de Bentheim fe divifent en
deux branches, fçavoir : en Bentheim-Teck-
lenbourg-Rheda, & en Bentheim-Bentheim.

Cette feconde branche fe fubdivife en deux branches : en Bentheim-Bentheim-Steinfurt, & en Bentheim-Bentheim-Bentheim.

BRANCHE AINÉE
des Comtes de Bentheim-Tecklenbourg-Rheda.

Elle a pour tige Adolphe, fils aîné d'Arnoul.

Maurice, né le 31 Mai 1615, mort en 1674, laiffa de *Jeanne-Dorothée*, morte en 1695, fille du Prince *Jean-Georges d'Anhalt-Deffau*, Ier du nom :

Frédéric-Maurice, né le 27 Octobre 1653, Colonel au fervice du Roi de Danemark, mort le 13 Décembre 1710. Il avoit époufé 1º *Sophie-Thérèfe*, morte en 1694, veuve du Comte *Frédéric-Guillaume de Linange-Wefterbourg*, fille du Comte *Jean-Aldert de Ronoir*; & 2º *Chriftiane-Marie*, morte en 1732, fille du Comte *Cafimir de la Lippe-Brake*. Il eut du premier lit :

Comte Maurice-Casimir, Ier du nom, né le 8 Mars 1701, marié, 1º le 3 Juillet 1727, à *Albertine-Henriette*, morte le 26 Septembre 1749, fille du Comte *Georges-Albert d'Ifenbourg-Meerholz*; & 2º le 2 Juillet 1750, à Amélie-Isabelle-Sidonie, fa coufine, fille du Comte Charles-Frédéric de Bentheim-Steinfurt.

Du premier mariage font nés :

1. Maurice-Casimir, IIe du nom, né le 12 Septembre 1735, marié, le 2 Septembre 1761, à *Hélène-Charlotte*, fille du Comte *Louis-François de Sayn-Wittgenftein-Berlebourg*, dont plufieurs enfans;
2. Et Frédérique-Louise-Anne, née en 1729, morte en 1747.

DEUXIÈME BRANCHE.

La tige de la feconde branche des Comtes de Bentheim-Bentheim-Steinfurt, eft Ernest-Guillaume, fils aîné d'Arnoul-Jodoc.

Charles-Paul-Ernest, né le 24 Novembre 1703, mort le 7 Juin 1733, avoit époufé *Françoife-Charlotte*, morte en 1738, fille du Comte *Frédéric-Adolphe de la Lippe-Detmold*. De ce mariage font nés :

1. Charles-Paul-Ernest, qui fuit;
2. Emilie-Isabelle-Sidonie, née le 25 Avril 1725, mariée, le 2 Juillet 1750, à fon coufin le Comte Maurice-Casimir de Bentheim-Tecklenbourg;

3. Caroline-Frédérique-Henriette-Marie, née le 2 Juin 1726, morte le 6 Juin 1754. Elle avoit époufé, le 30 Janvier 1747, le Comte *Frédéric de Gronsfeld*.

Charles-Paul-Ernest, Comte régnant, né le 30 Août 1729, Major-Général au fervice de l'Electeur de Hanovre, Roi de la Grande-Bretagne, Chevalier de l'Ordre de Saint-Hubert, a époufé, en 1748, *Charlotte-Sophie-Louife*, morte le 2 Avril 1759, fille du Prince *Frédéric-Guillaume de Naffau-Siegen*, de la branche Proteftante, dont :

1. Charles, né le 13 Février 1753;
2. Geldric-Guillaume-Louis, né le 1er Octobre 1756;
3. Anne-Polixène-Sidonie-Charlotte, née le 29 Septembre 1749;
4. Sophie-Ernestine, &c., morte en bas âge;
5. Eléonore-Auguste-Amélie-Charlotte, née le 29 Avril 1754;
6. Auguste-Clémentine-Louise, née le 3 Septembre 1755;
7. Et Caroline-Marie-Elisabeth-Madeleine, née le 25 Janvier 1759.

TROISIÈME BRANCHE.
des Comtes de Bentheim-Bentheim-Bentheim.

Le Chef de cette branche eft aujourd'hui le Comte Frédéric-Charles-Philippe. Il eft né le 17 Mars 1725, paffa au fervice de France, & a cédé, en vertu d'un Traité daté de Paris le 9 Mai 1753, fes Etats à l'Electeur de Hanovre pour 30 années. Il a époufé, en 1746, *Marie-Lydie*, fille du Marquis *Wolfgang de Bournonville* en Flandre, dont il a eu un fils né en 1748, & mort en bas âge. Il a une fœur unique, Chanoineffe au Chapitre de Thorn. (*Almanach généalogique de Francfort*, en Allemand.)

Les armes : *tiercé en chef, coupé & parti en pointe, à cinq quartiers, & un* fur le tout; *au 1 de gueules, à 18 befans d'or, pofés 4, 4, 4, 3, 2 & 1, qui eft de* Bentheim; *au 2 d'argent, à trois cœurs de gueules, pofés 2 & 1, qui eft de* Tecklenbourg; *au 3 d'azur, à l'ancre pofée en pal d'or, qui eft de* Lingen; *au 4 d'or, au cygne de gueules, becqué & membré de fable, qui eft de* Steinfurt; *au 5 d'argent, au lion de gueules, couronné d'azur, qui eft de* Linbourg; & *fur le tout, parti de deux, coupé d'un; au 1 de gueules, à deux fafces d'argent, qui eft de* Wevelingshofen; *au 2 d'argent, au lion de fable, qui eſt de* Rhéda; *au* 3 *d'or, à deux pattes d'ours de fable, qui eſt* Hoya; *au* 4 *de gueules, au lion d'argent, qui eſt* d'Alpen; *au* 5 *coupé de gueules & d'argent, au lion d'or* fur le tout, *qui eſt de* Helffenftein; *& au* 6 *burelé de gueules & d'or de dix pièces, qui eſt de* Cologne.

BENTIVOGLIO, Maiſon qui tire ſon origine, à ce qu'elle prétend, d'ENTIUS, Roi de Sardaigne. Elle a été alliée aux Rois d'Aragon, aux Ducs de Milan, & à divers autres Souverains. Elle a poſſédé aſſez long-tems la Seigneurie de la ville de Bologne. ANTOINE DE BENTIVOGLIO y fut extrêmement conſidéré. Sur la fin du XIVᵉ ſiècle, le Pape JULES II chaſſa JEAN DE BENTIVOGLIO & toute ſa famille de Bologne; ſes biens furent pillés, & ſa maiſon démolie par le peuple. Cette Maiſon ſe retira à Ferrare. Elle a donné pluſieurs Cardinaux, entr'autres GUY DE BENTIVOGLIO, mort en 1644, qui a laiſſé des ouvrages qui rendront ſon nom vénérable à la poſtérité; CORNEILLE DE BENTIVOGLIO D'ARAGON, Cardinal-Prêtre de *Sainte-Cécile,* né à Ferrare le 27 Mars 1668, Nonce à la Cour de France en 1711, Archevêque de Carthage en 1712, créé Cardinal le 29 Novembre 1719, eſt mort le 30 Décembre 1732. Son frère LOUIS DE BENTIVOGLIO-D'ARAGON a eu:

HIPPOLYTE DE BENTIVOGLIO-D'ARAGON, Noble Vénitien, Patrice de Ferrare, Grand d'Eſpagne, eſt mort à Mantoue en Novembre 1729, âgé de 35 ans;

GUY DE BENTIVOGLIO, Camérier-d'honneur du Pape, depuis la mort de ſon frère aîné, a quitté la Prélature, & a été inſtitué par le Cardinal de BENTIVOGLIO, ſon oncle, pour ſon héritier;

Et une fille, mariée au Sénateur *Albergati* à Bologne.

BÉON. Faute d'un Mémoire inſtructif pour dreſſer la généalogie de cette Maiſon, nous allons en donner une ſimple notice.

On a en Guyenne une idée ſi avantageuſe de la Maiſon de BÉON, qu'on lui donne pour origine un puîné des Vicomtes *de Béarn.* La tradition s'en eſt conſervée dans les Provinces de Guyenne & de Béarn. L'on trouve dans les titres de cette Maiſon un Mémoire qui dit que *Centulle,* Vᵉ du nom, Vicomte *de Béarn,* donna pour apanage à *Arnaud-Guilhem,* ſon troiſième fils, la Vallée de Béon, dans le Diocèſe d'Oléron, par acte du jour de Pâques

1133, qui fut enregiſtré la même année dans la *Cour-Majour* de Morlas.

Les Vicomtes de Béarn deſcendoient de *Loup-Centulle,* Duc de Gaſcogne, & ce dernier de la première race de nos Rois.

RAYMOND-ROGER, Comte de Foix, prend, dans un titre daté de Mazères le 19 Novembre 1204, la qualité d'oncle d'ARNAULD-GUILHEM DE BÉON, Seigneur de la Vallée de ce nom; & ROGER, IVᵉ du nom, Comte de Foix, petit-fils de RAYMOND-ROGER, établit PHILIPPE DE BÉON, petit-fils d'ARNAUD-GUILHEM, ſon couſin, pour Capitaine & Gouverneur de Foix par Lettres du 3 Novembre 1260.

Un Seigneur de BÉON fut tuteur de GASTON-PHŒBUS, Comte de Foix, & de GERMAINE, ſa ſœur, mariée à FERDINAND *le Catholique,* Roi de Navarre, en qualité de leur oncle.

Beaudouin, dans ſon *Hiſtoire de Navarre,* dit qu'un Seigneur de BÉON tenoit le premier rang parmi ceux qui aſſiſtèrent au Couronnement d'ALPHONSE *le Grand,* Roi de Navarre; & l'Hiſtorien des anciens Comtes de Brabant cite pour exemple la Maiſon de BÉON, comme tirant ſon origine des anciens Souverains du Béarn, dont elle a conſervé les armes, & prit le nom de la Vallée de Béon, qui lui fut donnée en apanage.

Cette Maiſon étoit déjà diviſée en deux branches principales, dès le XIIIᵉ ſiècle, ſçavoir: celle des Seigneurs d'*Armantieu* ou de *la Palu,* & celle des Seigneurs Vicomtes de *Sere.*

BRANCHE
des Seigneurs DE BÉON-ARMANTIEU ou LA PALU.

ARNAUD DE BÉON, Chevalier, Seigneur d'Armantieu, vivoit en 1290 avec BERNARD DE BÉON, Damoiſeau, ſon frère. Ils ſont tous deux compris dans une Enquête de 1300, faite par ordre du Roi PHILIPPE *le Bel,* ſur la valeur des fiefs & arrière-fiefs du Comté de Bigorre.

Cet ARNAUD DE BÉON, affiſté de PHILIPPE, Seigneur de la Vallée de Béon, & de PIERRE DE BÉON, Vicomte de Sere, paſſa contrat de mariage, le 6 Janvier 1269, avec *Jeanne de la Palu,* fille de *Georges,* Seigneur de la Palu, Belloc, Montcaſſin, Noueilhan, Semezies, Armantieu, &c. La Terre d'Armantieu en Rivière-Baſſe, & celles de la Palu, Belloc & Montcaſſin en Aſtarac en Guyenne, ſont encore dans la Maiſon de BÉON. ARNAUD laiſſa:

PIERRE, qui ſuit;

Et Navarine de Béon, qui inftitua Raymond, fils de Pierre, fon neveu, pour fon héritier dans fon teftament de 1335. Ce teftament fe trouve en forme dans les Archives du Chapitre de la ville de Narciac, parce que ladite Navarine y fit une fondation qui fubfifte encore.

Pierre de Béon, Seigneur d'Armàntieu, eut pour fils Raymond.

Sentouret de Béon, Seigneur d'Armantieu, &c., eut pour fils Mathieu, fuivant le teftament de ce dernier. Miramonde, fa fille, époufa, par contrat de 1475, *Amadou de Montefquiou.*

Arnaud de Béon tefta le 16 Mai 1450 en faveur de Jean, fon neveu.

Odet de Béon & *Catherine d'Antin*, fon époufe, teftèrent le 11 Novembre 1488 en faveur de leur fils :

Bertrand de Béon, qui tefta le 10 Février 1537 en faveur de fon fils Gabriel. Il avoit époufé, le 17 Janvier 1501, *Jeanne d'Ornefan,* dont :

Gabriel de Béon qui prit alliance, le 17 Août 1556, avec *Catherine de Saint-Lary-Bellegarde*, & en eut :

Pierre de Béon, qui époufa, le 31 Décembre 1579, *Marguerite de Noé.* Elle tefta le 22 Novembre 1638, & inftitua pour fon héritier fon fils :

Jean-Antoine de Béon, qui tefta le 29 Mai 1646 en faveur de François, fon fils. Il avoit époufé *Marguerite de Montefquiou-Meffencome*, dont :

François de Béon, qui tefta le 23 Mars 1685 en faveur de fon fils aîné. Il avoit époufé, le 17 Octobre 1663, *Françoife de Moura,* fille de *Jacques*, Seigneur de Maferolles, & d'*Hilaire de Saint-Paul,* dont :

1. François, qui fuit;
2. Jean-Antoine, Capitaine au Régiment de Conquin, tué au fiège de Lille, en 1667;

Et cinq filles, mortes fans avoir été mariées.

François de Béon, IIᵉ du nom, Seigneur d'Armantieu, la Palu, &c., Chevalier de l'Ordre Militaire de Saint-Louis, époufa *Marie-Catherine de Rollet,* fille de *Jean-Baptifte,* Doyen du Confeil Souverain d'Alface, & de *Véronique de Hupc,* dont :

1. François, qui fuit;
2. Jean-Antoine, Vicomte de Béon, Brigadier des Armées du Roi, & Colonel du Régiment de Boulonnois;
3. Nicolas, Aumônier de Madame :

4. Jean-Louis-Joseph, Capitaine-Aide-Major au Régiment de Boulonnois, tué à Bayonne au mois de Juillet 1755;
5. Autre Jean-Louis-Joseph, Grand-Vicaire d'Aire;
6. François-Auguste, Commandant pour le Roi au Fort d'Andaye;
7. & 8. Marie-Marguerite & Marie-Anne, Religieufes-Profeffes à l'Abbaye de Fabas en Comminges;
9. Marie-Catherine, mariée à N...la Motte Seigneur de Saint-Crift, Baron de Begolle;

Et plufieurs autres enfans, morts en bas âge.

François, IIIᵉ du nom, Comte de Béon, Seigneur d'Armantieu, la Palu, &c., ci-devant Capitaine au Régiment de Boulonnois, a époufé, le 20 Juin 1735, *Anne de Puyberail,* fille de *N... de Puyberail,* Seigneur de Troncens, & de *Paule de Montlezun-Saint-Lary,* dont font nés :

1. François-Frédéric;
2. N..., mort en bas âge;
3. Marie-Jeanne-Josèphe-Paule;
4. Et une fille, auffi morte en bas âge.

La branche des Seigneurs Vicomtes *de Sere,* s'eft fondue dans la Maifon *de Pardaillan-Gondrin,* par N..... de Béon, mariée à *Jean-Louis de Pardaillan-Gondrin,* Baron de Savignac.

Celle des Seigneurs *du Maffès* s'eft formée de Pierre de Béon, Chevalier, fecond fils d'Arnaud-Guillaume, Chevalier, Vicomte de Sere, & s'eft fondue dans la Maifon de *Timbrune-Valence,* par N... de Béon, fille d'*Alexandre,* dernier Seigneur du Maffès.

Celle de *Bouteville-Luxembourg* s'eft formée de Bernard de Béon, Vᵉ du nom, fils d'Aimeri, Seigneur du Maffès, & de *Marguerite de Caftelbajac,* Chevalier, Confeiller du Roi en fes Confeils d'Etat & Privé, Lieutenant-Général des Armées du Roi, Lieutenant-Général ès Provinces de Saintonge, Pays d'Aunis, Haut & Bas-Limoufin, nommé Chevalier du Saint-Efprit.

Jean de Luxembourg, Comte de Ligny & de Brienne, époufa *Guillemette de la Marck,* dont il eut :

Jean-Louis de Béon-Luxembourg, Marquis de Bouteville, qui époufa *Marie de Cugnac-Dampierre.* Il eut :

Charles, qui fuit;

Antoinette-Louise-Thérèse de Béon-Luxembourg, morte le 27 Novembre 1740, âgée de 78 ans. Elle avoit époufé, 1º le 1ᵉʳ Mai

1684, *Hugues Bétauld*, Seigneur de Chémauld, Montbarrois, &c., Confeiller au Parlement de Paris, puis Maître des Requêtes, mort le 2 Mars 1712, âgé de 60 ans; & 2° *Jean-Hippolyte de Beaumont-Gibaut*, Exempt des Gardes-du-Corps, Brigadier le 15 Mars 1740, Enfeigne en 1742, & Maréchal-de-Camp de Cavalerie le 2 Mai 1744. Elle a eu du premier lit *Louis de Bétauld*, & *Jacques-Augufte de Bétauld*, père de:

1. *Hyacinthe-Louife-Augufte de Bétauld-Chémauld*, encore fille en 1755;
2. Et *Hyacinthe-Ifabelle de Bétauld-Chémauld*, mariée à *Pierre-François de Courcy*, Lieutenant pour le Roi & de Noffeigneurs les Maréchaux de France, à Verneuil au Perche;

Et JEANNE DE BÉON-LUXEMBOURG, Religieufe de la Vifitation au faubourg Saint-Jacques à Paris.

CHARLES DE BÉON-LUXEMBOURG, Marquis de Béon, Colonel d'Infanterie, mort fans poftérité, & le dernier de fon nom, le 8 Août 1725, avoit époufé *Anne-Dorothée du Hautoy*, morte en Lorraine le 17 Juin 1755. La moitié de fa fucceffion eft revenue à deux petites-nièces, filles du feu Marquis *de Chémauld*.

La branche de BÉON-CASEAUX fubfifte en la perfonne du Marquis de BÉON, Chef de Brigade des Gardes du Roi, & s'eft formée de JEAN DE BÉON, fecond fils d'AIMERI, Seigneur du Maffès, & de *Marguerite de Caftelbajac*.

FRANÇOIS-PAUL DE BÉON-CASEAUX, Grand-Prieur de Touloufe en 1675, a formé une Commanderie de fon Ordre de Saint-Jean de Jérufalem, en faveur de FRANÇOIS-PAUL DE BÉON, fon neveu & fon filleul, & de tous autres Chevaliers de fa Maifon, à perpétuité. Elle eft aujourd'hui poffédée par le Tréfor, ladite branche de *Cafeaux* n'ayant d'autre mâle que le Marquis de BÉON-CASEAUX, Chef de Brigade des Gardes du Roi.

Les armes: *écartelé, aux 1 & 4 de gueules, à quatre amandes d'argent; & aux 2 & 3 les armes des premiers Souverains de Béarn*, qui font: *d'or, à deux vaches paffantes de gueules, accornées, accolées, clarinées & onglées d'azur*.

BÉOST, en Breffe. Nous ne pouvons donner qu'une fimple notice, faute de Mémoire, de cette ancienne nobleffe de la Province de Breffe.

HENRI DE BÉOST, Chevalier, vivoit en 1250.

Tome II.

Il fit hommage à AMÉ DE SAVOIE, Seigneur de Baugé & de Breffe, de tout ce qu'il poffédoit à Béoft en 1272. Il laiffa de *Jacquette de Lyonniaires*, fille de *Ponce*, Seigneur de Lyonniaires:

1. ETIENNE, qui fuit;
2. Et JEANNETTE, femme, en 1274, de *Guy de Corfan*, Chevalier.

ETIENNE DE BÉOST, Chevalier, Seigneur de Béoft vivoit ès années 1282 & 1306. Il eut de *Guillemette*, Dame de Chintré:

1. GUY, qui fuit;
2. Et ALIX, femme, en 1336, de *Jean le Loup*, Damoifeau.

GUY DE BÉOST, Chevalier, Seigneur de Béoft, tefta le 17 Août 1355. Il avoit époufé *Béraude de Crangeac*, Dame de Mefpilla, fille de *Pierre*, Seigneur de Crangeac, & laiffa:

1. THIBAUT DE BÉOST, Damoifeau, mort avant fon père, fans poftérité;
2. Et BÉATRIX DE BÉOST, Dame de Béoft, femme d'*Odon*, Seigneur de Marmont, fils d'*Etienne*, Seigneur de Marmont.

Cette ancienne famille éteinte portoit pour armes: *d'or, à trois croix ancrées de gueules, 2 & 1*.

BEQUETS: *d'or, au lion de gueules, armé de fable, à la bordure dentelée du fecond*.

BERANCOURT: *d'argent, au lion de fable*.

BERANGERS, en Dauphiné: *gironné d'or & de gueules de huit pièces*.

BERANGERS: *palé d'or & d'azur de huit pièces, à l'écuffon d'argent fur le tout*.

BÉRARD ou BERAR, en Touraine.

PIERRE BÉRARD, Chevalier, Seigneur de Bleré & Chiffé, Maître-d'Hôtel du Roi LOUIS XI, & Tréforier de France, eut de fa femme, dont nous ignorons le nom:

1. JACQUES, qui fuit;
2. Et JEANNE, femme de *Philippe des Effars*, Seigneur de Thieux & de Glatigny, Maître-d'Hôtel du Roi.

JACQUES BÉRARD, Chevalier, Seigneur de Bleré-fur-Cher, de Chiffé, des Roches, Saint-Georges & Gratteloup, & de la Croix-de-Bleré, époufa *Madeleine Châteigner*, Dame de Saint-Pardoux en Gâtine, fille de *Guy Châteigner*, Seigneur de la Rochepofay, & de *Madeleine du Puy*.

De ce mariage naquirent:

1. François, qui fuit ;
2. Et René, rapporté après fon frère aîné.

François Bérard, Chevalier, Seigneur de Bleré, vendit cette Terre en 1572, à François Châteigner, Seigneur de la Rochepofay, fon coufin germain, qui la revendit de-puis à Gafpard de Schomberg, Comte de Nanteuil, fon beau-frère. Il époufa Anne de Ranfard, dont il eut :

1. Louise Bérard, mariée 1º au Seigneur de Faverolles; & 2º à Jofeph d'Efparbès, Seigneur de Luffan, Gouverneur de Nantes;
2. Et Guyonne Bérard, femme du Seigneur de Montagnac en Auvergne.

René Bérard, Chevalier, fils puîné de Jacques, & de Madeleine Châteigner, fut Seigneur de la Croix-de-Bleré, & époufa Ifabeau Richomme, fille de Jean Richomme, Ecuyer, Seigneur de la Goberie en Anjou, & d'Ifabeau de Sainte-Marthe. De ce mariage eft forti entr'autres enfans :

Claude Bérard, Chevalier, Baron de la Croix-Bleré, Lieutenant-Colonel du Régiment de Normandie, &c., mort en Languedoc en 1622, qui époufa Claude Raguier, fille de François Raguier, Seigneur & Baron de Migennes, Lieutenant de la Vénerie du Roi, & Maître-d'Hôtel de la Reine, & de Marguerite de Sercilly, & laiffa :

1. François Bérard, Baron de Migennes, & de la Croix-Bleré, auffi Lieutenant-Colonel du Régiment de Normandie, dans lequel il avoit fait 46 campagnes en 1660. Il époufa 1º Claudine de la Barde, fille de N... de la Barde, & d'Anne Bouthillier; & 2º Claudine de Rigné, veuve de Jofeph de Faverolles, Baron de Bleré. Elle étoit fille de Jacques de Rigné, Seigneur de la Guérinière. Il eut de la première :
   Claude Bérard, IIe du nom, Baron de la Croix & de la Goberie en Anjou, qui étoit fans alliance en 1760;
2. René-Joseph de Bérard, Prieur de Chartrenay;
3. Claude de Bérard, Baron de. Migennes, Lieutenant de Roi, à Sédan, marié avec Marie de Héré;
4. Peronne ou Perrenelle de Bérard, mariée 1º à Jean du Pré, Seigneur de Guypi; 2º à René d'Efcoubleau, Marquis de Sourdis;
5. Et Isabeau.

Les armes : d'argent, à une fafce d'azur, chargée de trois trèfles d'or, & accompagnée de trois fauterelles de finople, 2 & 1.

BÉRARD DU ROURE, en Provence. Suivant un Mémoire envoyé, cette famille tire fon origine d'Alphonse de Bérard, de Vaudemont en Lorraine, qui eut un frère nommé Brancassio, dont Constant, qui fuit.

Dès ce tems-là, cette famille a été illuftrée par le Cardinal de Bérard, qui fut envoyé en 1296, en qualité de Légat, pour traiter de la Paix entre ce même Roi & le Roi d'Angleterre.

N... de Bérard, Seigneur de Mercœuil, fut auffi envoyé Ambaffadeur par le Roi Philippe-le-Bel, en 1304, au Pape Benoît XI, pour le féliciter fur fon Exaltation au Pontificat.

Constant de Bérard fut emmené, en 1282, par Charles Ier, Comte d'Anjou & du Maine, pour le combat qui devoit fe faire entre le Roi d'Aragon & lui, & où fe devoient trouver 100 Gentilshommes de part & d'autre. Il y en eut 62 de Provence, & 38 étrangers, du nombre defquels fut Constant de Bérard. Voyez au Chap. XXIII du quatrième Liv. de Raymond Solery, intitulé : Nicœa Maffilienfium Colonia. Il s'établit dans la ville d'Aix, où il eut :

Antoine de Bérard, qui eut Pons & Aubertine.

Pons fut Conful de la ville d'Aix en 1368, ainfi qu'il paroît dans les Regiftres de la Maifon de la Ville d'Aix. Il eut :

1. Antoine, qui fuit ;
2. & 3. Patrice & René.

Antoine de Bérard fut auffi Conful de la ville d'Aix en 1409, & eut pour fils :

Pierre de Bérard, qui fut père de Jacques-Etienne & de Pierre.

Jacques de Bérard fut du nombre des 72 Confeillers qu'Aymard de Poitiers, Baron de Saint-Volier, Gouverneur de Marfeille, créa en ladite Ville, en 1492, ce qui fut confirmé par Charles VIII, Comte de Provence. Il eut :

Jean, & Louis, qui fuit.

Louis de Bérard, Seigneur de Coutouras, & Co-Seigneur d'Aiglun, vint s'établir à Cucuron. Il époufa, le 16 Octobre 1497, noble Marguerite Textoris, dont :

Raymond de Bérard, qui époufa, le 17 Août 1527, noble Madeleine Turrenque, dont il eut :

Honoré de Bérard, qui époufa, par contrat paffé devant Fulcon, Notaire, le 7 Mars 1563, Philippe Vianot.

PASCAL DE BÉRARD, leur fils, épousa, le 13 Janvier 1602, contrat de mariage paffé devant *Arnaud*, Notaire, noble *Diane de Bouliers*. De ce mariage vint :

JEAN DE BÉRARD, Iᵉʳ du nom, qui épousa, par contrat paffé le 8 Septembre 1625, devant *Girard*, Notaire, *Jeanne de Vocanus*, dont eft iffu :

JEAN DE BÉRARD, IIᵉ du nom, qui, par contrat paffé devant *Chanuis*, Notaire à Pertuis, le 15 Avril 1653, épousa *Louife Roux*, dont :

1. GASPARD, qui fuit ;
2. Et JEAN, Colonel d'Infanterie, commandant une Compagnie de 100 Cadets Gentilshommes, Infpecteur des Milices.

GASPARD DE BÉRARD, Capitaine au Régiment de Foix, & commandant les Milices de Provence, a eu de *Marie-Françoife de Bofco* :

1. JEAN DE BÉRARD, Seigneur du Roure, ancien Officier au Régiment des Gardes Françoifes, Chevalier de Saint-Louis, Lieutenant de MM. les Maréchaux de France, & Gouverneur pour le Roi de la ville de Cucuron ;
2. JEAN-BAPTISTE, qui fuit ;
3. JEAN-GASPARD DE BÉRARD, Chanoine honoraire de St.-Louis du Louvre de Paris, Vicaire-Général du Diocèfe de Perpignan, & Prieur de St.-Nicolas de Noyer ;
4. Et MARIE-FRANÇOIFE, élevée à St.-Cyr, & Religieufe à l'Abbaye-Royale de Poiffy.

JEAN-BAPTISTE DE BÉRARD, ancien Commandant au Régiment d'Auvergne, Chevalier de Saint-Louis, & Lieutenant pour le Roi de Collioure, en Rouffillon, a époufé *Madeleine de Mery de la Canorgue*, fille de *Jofeph de Mery*, Comte de la Canorgue, Confeiller honoraire à la Chambre des Comptes de Provence, & d'*Angélique de Boyer*, des Marquis d'Argens, dont :

MARIE-MADELEINE DE BÉRARD DU ROURE.

Les preuves de nobleffe de cette famille font à la Chambre des Comptes de Provence, & ont été faites par le Juge-d'Armes de France. Les armes : *de gueules, à la bande d'argent, accompagnée d'une étoile en chef, & d'une rofe d'argent en pointe*.

BÉRARD, Seigneur de Villebreuil, de Montalet, &c., en Languedoc.

BERTRAND BÉRARD, Seigneur de Montalet, vivoit avec *Helix de Vefc*, fa femme, avant 1576. Il étoit trifayeul de :

FRANÇOIS BÉRARD, Ecuyer, marié avec *Marie Perfin*, dont il eut :

1. LOUIS-ARMAND, qui fuit ;
2. Et MARC-ANTOINE BÉRARD, premier Conful de la ville de Nîmes.

LOUIS-ARMAND BÉRARD époufa, le 11 Février 1721, *Marie de Planes*, mère de :

N... BÉRARD, Abbé de Villebreuil ;
N... BÉRARD, Abbé de Montalet ;
CLAIRE-COLETTE-MARIE BÉRARD-DE-MONTALET-DE-VILLEBREUIL, morte à Paris en Juillet 1763, veuve 1° de *Joachim-Jacques Trotti*, Seigneur de la Chétardie, Maréchal-de-Camp, Commandant au Vieux-Brifac, & Gouverneur de Landrecies ; 2° de *Ferdinand-Auguftin de Solars*, Comte de Monafterolle, Lieutenant-Général des Troupes de l'Electeur de Bavière, & fon envoyé à la Cour de France. Elle n'a eu de fon premier mari, que *Jacques Trotti*, Marquis de la Chétardie, Colonel de Tournaifis en 1734 ; Brigadier le 1ᵉʳ Janvier 1740 ; Maréchal-de-Camp le 1ᵉʳ Mai 1745 ; Lieutenant-Général le 10 Mai 1748 & mort fans alliance, le 1ᵉʳ Janvier 1758.

Et MARIE-BERNARDINE BÉRARD, née le 17 Septembre 1724, reçue à Saint-Cyr, le 15 Septembre 1736, fur fes preuves de nobleffe. (Voyez l'*Armor. de France*, reg. I, part. I, p. 61.)

Les armes : *d'azur, à un cor de-chaffe d'or, lié de même, à la bordure crénelée d'argent*. Nous trouvons une autre branche de ce nom, Seigneur de *Montalet*, même Province, don les armes font : *de gueules, au demi-vol d'argent*.

BERARD, en Dauphiné, *de gueules, à l'homme armé de toutes pièces d'argent, la vifière levée ; au chef d'azur, chargé de trois étoiles d'or*.

BERARD, même Province : *parti, au 1 d'azur, au lion d'or ; au 2 dé fable, à la panthère d'argent*.

BERARD : *d'argent à la fafce de gueules, chargée de trois trèfles d'or*.

BERARD, en Bretagne : *d'argent, à la fafce de gueules, accompagnée de fix tourteaux de fable, pofés en orle, 1 & 2, 2 & 1*.

BERARD, en Languedoc : *d'azur, au lion d'or, & à la bande de même, brochant fur le tout, & chargée d'un lion d'azur*.

BÉRARDIERE, en Anjou. GUILLAUME-GILLES DE LA BÉRARDIERE, Capitaine de Cavalerie, fils de Jean-Gilles de la Bérardiere, Seigneur de la Grue, épousa, le 30 Janvier 1685, *Françoise*, fille de *François Eveillard*, Conseiller au Parlement de Bretagne. Il a eu : Martin-Gilles de la Bérardiere, Page du Roi Louis XIV, & enfuite Capitaine de Cavalerie, en faveur duquel la Terre de la Barbée a été érigée en Baronie par Lettres du 20 Avril 1752, regiftrées au Parlement de Paris, le 2 Septembre fuivant, & en la Chambre des Comptes de la même Ville, le 12 Septembre 1754. Il a épousé, le 21 Avril 1725, *Marie-Anne Rouffeau*, fille de *Charles Rouffeau*, dont la famille, établie en Anjou & dans le Maine depuis un fiècle, eft une branche de celle des *Rouffeau-la-Patrière*, en Poitou. Leurs enfans font :

1. Claude-Martin-Gilles de la Bérardiere, Baron de la Barbée, né le 21 Avril 1729 ;
2. Et Marine-Françoise-Gilles de la Bérardiere, née le 19 Janvier 1746.

Il y a une autre branche de même nom qui fubfifte en la personne de François-Gilles de la Bérardiere, Seigneur de Fontenaille, en Touraine, iffu d'un frère de Guillaume-Gilles de la Bérardiere, premier poffeffeur de la Seigneurie de la Barbée.

BÉRAUD, en Agenois. Jean de Béraud, Ecuyer, fit fon teftament dans la ville de Caftilloués, en Agenois, le 11 Mars 1490.

Jean de Béraud, Ecuyer, un de fes defcendans au III° degré, fut Seigneur de Canteranne. Il épousa *Marie-Anne du Vivier-de-Saint-Martin*, dont :

Jean de Béraud, Ecuyer, Seigneur dudit lieu, ci-devant Capitaine de Cavalerie dans le Régiment d'Aubuffon, marié le 30 Janvier 1715, qui a eu :

Charles de Béraud, Seigneur de Canteranne, né le 16 Mai 1716, reçu Page du Roi dans fa Grande-Ecurie, le 22 Décembre 1730. (Voy. l'*Armor. de France*, reg. I, part. I, p. 61).

Les armes : *d'argent, au chevron de gueules, & une bande de même, brochant fur le tout.*

BERAUD, Seigneur de Croiffy : *d'azur, à l'aigle d'or ; au chef de gueules, chargé d'une étoile d'or.*

BERAUD, Seigneur de la Haye, de Rioux, en Bretagne : *de gueules, au loup d'argent, accompagné de trois coquilles de même, 2 en chef & 1 en pointe*

BÉRAUD DE COURVILLE, famille du Languedoc, établie dans l'Isle de France, le Luxembourg-François & l'Alface.

François Béraud, Ecuyer, Seigneur de Puiffart, puis des fiefs de Choify, de Hugo, de Grand-Hôtel de Sanois & des Charités, proche Argenteuil, avoit pour fixième ayeul, Imbert Béraud ou de Béraud (*Béraudi* dans tous les contrats de mariage qui font en latin), Seigneur de Chatard, qui vivoit vers 1400. Il fut homme d'armes, & fervit en qualité de Gendarme depuis 1633 jufqu'en 1645. Il fut maintenu de même que Charles Béraud-de-Bonlieu, fon frère, Exempt des Gardes-du-Corps, dans la qualité de Gentilhomme & d'Ecuyer, par Arrêt du Confeil d'Etat, du 21 Avril 1670. Il épousa, en 1639, *Jeanne de Penelle*, fille de *Michel de Penelle*, Ecuyer, Seigneur de la Juftice & Seigneurie des fiefs de Hugo & du Grand-Hôtel, dont font iffus entr'autres enfans :

1. François Béraud, Sieur de Choify, Lieutenant dans le Régiment-Royal des Vaiffeaux en 1678, Aide-Major d'un Bataillon, puis Capitaine par Commiffion du 28 Novembre 1695, Lieutenant-Colonel d'un nouveau Régiment d'Infanterie, formé d'un Bataillon de celui des Vaiffeaux, & Chevalier de Saint-Louis ;
2. César Béraud, Sieur Duperron, d'abord Lieutenant au Régiment Royal-Vaiffeau, puis Capitaine au même Régiment, mort Aide-Major de la ville de Dunkerque ;
3. Et Michel Béraud, qui fuit.

Michel Béraud-de-Courville, Ecuyer, Seigneur de Sanois, de Thonne-lès-Près, en partie, des fiefs de Grand-Hôtel, Hugo, les Charités, Choify, la Cour & Harauchamps, fervit dans le même Régiment que fes frères ; il y étoit Capitaine en 1681. Il épousa, en 1683, *Jeanne Willemard de Châtillon*, dont font iffus :

1. Jean-François, qui fuit ;
2. François-Michel Béraud-de-Sanois, né le 7 Octobre 1690, Lieutenant de la Compagnie-Colonelle du Régiment de Champagne en 1707, puis Capitaine & Chevalier de Saint-Louis. Il eut auffi une Compagnie de Grenadiers dans le même Régiment, en 1734, qu'il quitta en 1735. Il a eu, d'*Agnès-Renée de Beaufort*, Agnès-Félicité ;
3. Charles Béraud-de-Courville, né le 21 Août 1692, Chevalier de Saint-Louis, & Capitaine de Grenadiers au Régiment de Champagne en 1735 ;

4. Jacques-Joseph Béraud-de-Bonlieu, né le 24 Avril 1697, Chanoine de l'Eglife Collégiale de Notre-Dame de Carignan en 1721, nommé en 1740 à l'Abbaye de Saint-Hilaire de la Celle, Diocèfe de Poitiers;

5. Louis, rapporté après la poftérité de fon frère aîné;

6. François-Joseph Béraud-d'Hôtel, né le 22 Mars 1705, Aide-Major dans le Régiment de Champagne, puis Capitaine en 1734, mort de fes bleffures en Bavière en 1735;

7. Christophe Béraud-de-Courville, né le 18 Décembre 1711, Prêtre & Bénéficier de l'Eglife Collégiale de Carignan;

8. Catherine Béraud-de-Courville, née le 16 Avril 1698, reçue le 5 Juin 1709, à Saint-Cyr, où elle eft morte Religieufe en 1727;

9. Et Barbe-Louise Béraud-de-Sanois, née le 18 Octobre 1713, reçue à Saint-Cyr en 1721.

Jean-François Béraud-de-Courville, Seigneur de Sanois, &c., fut marié, le 10 Août 1730, avec *Louife Compagnot.* Leurs enfans font :

1. Louis-Denis-François Béraud-de-Sanois, né le 21 Mars 1740, Moufquetaire de la Garde du Roi dans la feconde Compagnie ;

2. Pierre-Michel Béraud-d'Hôtel, né le 27 Juin 1746, Lieutenant au Régiment de Champagne.

Louis Béraud d'Arimont, Marquis de la Haye, cinquième fils de Michel Béraud, & de *Jeanne de Willemard-de-Châtillon,* né le 24 Janvier 1701, fucceffivement Lieutenant & Capitaine dans le Régiment de Champagne, Chevalier de Saint-Louis en 1736, Capitaine de Grenadiers en 1738, puis Commandant de Bataillon, nommé à la Lieutenance de Roi d'Huningue en 1743, fut premier Veneur & Chambellan de M. le Duc de Berry, & mourut le 24 Mars 1754. Il avoit époufé, en 1744, *Marie-Jeanne de Salomon.* Il laiffa :

1. Charles Béraud, né le 31 Mai 1746, élevé à l'Ecole Militaire, Chevalier de Saint-Lazare, Lieutenant au Régiment de Bretagne ;

2. Jean-Baptiste Béraud, né en 1748, élevé à l'Ecole Militaire, Chevalier de Saint-Lazare, Lieutenant au Régiment d'Alface;

3. Jean Béraud;

4. Jeanne-Catherine, mariée, en 1766, à *Nicolas de Pafcal-Kerenveier,* Chevalier, Capitaine, Aide-Major au Régiment de Limoufin, & Chevalier de Saint-Louis;

5. & 6. Benoîte-Marguerite & Françoise-Elisabeth;

7. Et Jeanne-Catherine.

Les armes : *d'azur, à une bande d'or.*

BÉRAUDIN, famille du Diocèfe de Poitiers. Louis Béraudin, Ier du nom, Seigneur de Pufai, époufa, en 1484, *Catherine de Marconnai.*

Hercule Béraudin, Seigneur de Pufai, époufa, par contrat du 28 Décembre 1617, *Louife de Boifi,* fille naturelle de *Louis Gouffier,* Duc de Roannois.

Henri Béraudin, Chevalier, Seigneur de Pufai, eut de *Marie Poitevin* :

Henriette Béraudin-de-Pusai, née en 1676, qui fut reçue à Saint-Cyr au mois de Juin 1689, après avoir prouvé fa nobleffe depuis Louis de Béraudin, Ier du nom. C'eft tout ce que nous fçavons fur cette famille.

Les armes: *d'azur, à trois fafces d'or, furmontées de trois befans de même.*

BÉRAULT, Seigneur de Villiers, famille dont étoit Antoine-Jacques Bérault, Seigneur de Villiers, entré dans le Régiment des Gardes-Françoifes dès l'âge de 15 ans, en qualité d'Enfeigne, le 21 Avril 1692, monté à une Sous-Lieutenance en 1693, & à une Lieutenance en 1694, qui acheta en 1696 la Compagnie de N.... des Alleurs. Il fut fait, le 29 Mars 1710, Brigadier d'Infanterie, & Maréchal-de-Camp le 1er Février 1719, vendit fa Compagnie en 1727 à N...de Langei, & mourut en 1745, âgé de 68 ans. Il avoit époufé *Marie-Anne Planfon,* morte le 30 Avril 1754, en fa 73e année. On ignore fa poftérité.

Les armes de cette famille font: *d'azur, femé de chauffetrapes d'or, au léopard lionné de même, brochant fur le tout.*

BERAULT, Election de Verneuil en Normandie, Ecuyer, Sieur du Mefnil, de Boifbaril, ancienne nobleffe, qui porte: *d'azur, au chevron d'or, accompagné en chef de deux rofes d'argent, & en pointe d'un coq de même.*

BERAUVILLE (de), Seigneur de Saint-André, Montigny, ancienne nobleffe, Election de Coutances, Généralité de Caen en Normandie, qui porte : *coupé d'argent & de fable, l'argent chargé de cinq tourteaux de fable, rangés en fautoir; & le fable d'un lion léopardé d'argent, armé & lampaffé de gueules.*

BERAY : *d'or, à trois molettes d'éperon de fable, posées* 2 & 1.

BERBESE : *d'azur, à la brebis d'argent, paiſſante ſur une terraſſe de ſinople.*

BERBIDORF, en Dauphiné : *parti d'or & de fable, à deux bras ſupportant une couronne d'or, ſommée d'une étoile de l'un en l'autre d'azur.*

✠ BERBIER DU METZ, famille de robe & d'épée, d'une très-ancienne nobleſſe, originaire de Bourgogne, connue dans cette province, au XVᵉ ſiècle, ſous le nom & les armes de la Mothe.

I. Viennot de la Mothe, Ecuyer, Sieur de la Mothe de Varenne, avoit épouſé *Guillemette de Siguret.* Il eut :

II. Jacques de la Mothe, Ecuyer, qui étoit ſorti de Bourgogne pour s'établir en Champagne. A l'occaſion de ſon mariage, le Sieur Jacques Berbier, Ecuyer, ſon oncle maternel, n'ayant pas d'enfans, lui fit la donation de tous ſes biens, en s'en réſervant l'uſufruit ſa vie durant, à condition qu'il prendroit le nom & les armes de Berbier & qu'il les feroit prendre & porter par ſes deſcendans en légitime mariage. Depuis cette époque, cette famille n'a plus été connue que ſous le nom & les Armes de Berbier, juſqu'en 1636. Alors par Lettres-Patentes du mois d'Août 1636, enregiſtrées au Parlement de Paris, le 29 Novembre de la même année, Jacques Berbier, Sieur du Metz, Seigneur de Chalette, fut autoriſé à ne plus prendre & ſigner que le nom de du Metz, qui depuis eſt reſté à ſa poſtérité. Tous ces faits ſont prouvés par les pièces juſtificatives, produites au Conſeil en 1672, & par l'Arrêt du Conſeil d'Etat, qui s'enſuivit, en date du 2 Avril 1672. Par cet Arrêt, le Roi (Louis XIV) maintient les Sieurs Gédéon, Claude, & Jacques Berbier du Metz, en poſſeſſion de leur nobleſſe, en conſéquence des titres, qu'ils avoient repréſentés depuis Viennot de la Mothe, leur quatrième ayeul, Ecuyer, Sieur de la Mothe de Varenne; ordonne que leurs noms ſeront inſcrits dans le Catalogue des Gentilshommes du Royaume, &c. Voyez l'*Armorial Général de France,* reg. I, part. I, pag. 63.

Jacques de la Mothe-Berbier avoit épouſé, « le 10 Novembre 1524, *Marguerite Peret,* fille de *Jean Peret,* Ecuyer. » Il laiſſa :

III. Gaon Berbier, Ecuyer, Lieutenant-Général au Comté de Vertus, Rônay & Laferté-ſur-Aube, qui fut pourvu en 1582 de la charge de Maître des Requêtes ordinaire de la Reine *Marguerite de Navarre;* il avoit épouſé, le 22 Mai 1553, *Marguerite de Collignon,* fille de *Chriſtophe de Collignon,* Ecuyer, d'une noble & ancienne famille de Champagne. Il eut :

1. Jacques, qui ſuit;
2. Zacharie, qui épouſa *N..... Comparot,* dont il eut un fils, mort ſans poſtérité;
3. Elisabeth, mariée à *Jacques Raulet,* Ecuyer, Sieur de Souain & d'Hievre;
4. Peronne, mariée à Noble homme, *Pierre Manjot;*
5. Et Marguerite Berbier, mariée à *Samſon Raulet,* Ecuyer, Seigneur de Vitry-la-Ville & de Mutigny.

IV. Jacques Berbier, IIᵉ du nom, Ecuyer, Sieur du Metz, exerça, dans ſa jeuneſſe, la profeſſion des Armes, & ſervit en qualité de Capitaine dans les guerres de Champagne, en 1592; il fut enſuite Lieutenant-Général du Comté de Vertus. Il épouſa, 1º le 27 Novembre 1590, *Jeanne Comparot;* & 2º le 26 Novembre 1600, *Marguerite de Vaſſan,* d'une famille noble & ancienne, qui ſubſiſte encore aujourd'hui. Ce ſecond mariage a donné les alliances de *Forget,* de *Courtarvel-Pezé,* de *Montfort,* de *Murat,* d'*Allemans-du-Lau,* de *Maſcrany,* de *Gevres,* de la *Roche-Aymon,* de *Berulle,* de *Miromeſnil,* de *Chazerat,* de *Bullion,* d'*Auvet-de-Rieux,* de *Narbonne-Lara,* de *Mirabeau,* de *Saillant,* de *Cabris,* &c. Jacques Berbier, Sieur du Metz, eut de ſon premier mariage :

1. Charles-Louis, marié, le 27 Octobre 1620, à *Marguerite de Pampelune,* Dame de Pothemont, dont il n'eut que Pérette Berbier du Metz, mariée à *Chriſtophe de Beaufort,* Ecuyer, Seigneur de Pothemont;
2. Jeanne, mariée à *Claude Martineau,* Ecuyer.

Il eut de ſon ſecond mariage :

3. Jacques, qui ſuit;
4. Marie, mariée, en 1638, à *Claude Petit de la Vaux,* Ecuyer, Seigneur, de Rijancourt, Lieutenant d'une Compagnie de Chevaux-Légers;
5. Et Marguerite Berbier du Metz, morte ſans alliance.

V. Jacques Berbier du Metz, IIIᵉ du nom, Ecuyer, Seigneur de Chalette, après avoir paſſé ſes premières années dans la profeſſion des Armes, fut pourvu en 1636 de la charge de Tréforier-Général des Parties Cafuelles, vacante par le décès du Sieur de *Vaffan*, fon oncle. Par Lettres-Patentes du mois d'Août 1636, enregiftrées au Parlement de Paris, ainfi qu'on l'a dit ci-deffus, il fut autorifé à ne plus prendre & figner que le nom de DU METZ. Il avoit époufé, le 28 Avril 1625, *N... le Grand*. Il eut :

1. GÉDÉON, qui fuit;
2. CLAUDE, Chevalier, Seigneur de Chalette, qui fut Lieutenant-Général des Armées du Roi, & de l'Artillerie de France, Gouverneur de Gravelines, Chevalier de l'Ordre Royal & Militaire de Notre-Dame du Mont-Carmel & de Saint-Lazare de Jérufalem; il fe fignala dans les guerres de LOUIS XIV, depuis 1657 jufqu'à la bataille de Fleurus, où il fut tué, le 1er Juillet 1690. Il avoit commandé l'Artillerie de France à plufieurs fièges & combats éclatans, & il la commandoit encore à cette dernière bataille, gagnée par le Maréchal Duc de Luxembourg. Cet Officier, par fa bravoure, fes talens & fes fuccès, s'étoit acquis une réputation diftinguée. Louis XIV l'honora de fon eftime & de fes regrets. Nos Hiftoriens ont célébré fa mémoire : il eft au nombre des Hommes Illuftres de France, dont Perrault a écrit l'Eloge Hiftorique, tom. II, pag. 41, édition in-fol.;
3. LOUIS, Abbé, qui fut Aumônier du Roi, Abbé Commandataire des Abbayes de Huiron & de Sainte-Croix-de-Guingamp;
4. JACQUES, Seigneur de Saint-Remy & de Saint-Martin, qui époufa *N... de la Veuve de Metiercelin;* de ce mariage il eut un fils, Capitaine au Régiment de Vexin, mort fans poftérité, & une fille, mariée, en 1694, à M. de *Remigny de Joux*, d'une noble & ancienne famille de Champagne;
5. MADELEINE, mariée, 1º le 2 Juillet 1645, à *Achille du Four*, Ecuyer, dont elle n'eut point d'enfans; & 2º le 25 Novembre 1656, à *Louis de Moret*, Ecuyer, Secrétaire du Roi, dont elle eut, entr'autres enfans, une fille nommée *Anne Thérèfe de Moret*, mariée le 14 Février 1684, à *Claude-Elzéar*, Comte de Châtillon, Duc & Pair de France, Chevalier des Ordres du Roi, Gouverneur de feu Monfeigneur le Dauphin, père du Roi. Ce mariage a donné à MM. DU METZ, des alliances avec les maifons de *Châtillon*, de *Bethune*, d'*Uzès*, de la *Trémoïlle;* delà font venues auffi les alliances de *Chamborant*, de la *Ferté-de-Reux*, de *Raizay*, de *Mory*, &c.;

6. MARGUERITE BERBIER DU METZ, mariée, en 1665, à *Antoine le Meneftrel-du-Hauguel*, Seigneur de St.-Germain-Laxis, &c. Parmi les enfans iffus de ce mariage, il n'eft refté que *Marguerite le Meneftrel-du-Hauguel*, mariée, en 1694, à *Jacques Bazin de Bezons*, Maréchal de France, Chevalier des Ordres du Roi, Gouverneur de Cambray, & du Cambrefis; & *Marie-Louife le Meneftrel-du-Hauguel*, mariée, en 1703, à *Léon le Cirier*, Marquis de Neufchelles, dont elle n'eut qu'une fille, *Marie-Gabrielle le Cirier de Neufchelles*, mariée, le 26 Juin 1725, à *Samuel-Jacques le Clerc*, Chevalier, Marquis de Juigné, Baron de plufieurs fièges, &c., Colonel du Régiment d'Orléans Infanterie. Le mariage de MARGUERITE BERBIER DU METZ, avec *Antoine le Meneftrel-du-Hauguel*, a donné des alliances avec les Maifons de *Bézons*, de *la Feuillade*, d'*Harcourt*, de *Mortemart*, de *Juigné*, de *Maubourg*. Delà font venues auffi les alliances de *Saint-Jal*, de la *Queuille*, de *Barbançon*, de *Poudenx*, d'*Hericy*, de *Copenne*, de *Pracomtal*, &c.

VI. GÉDÉON DU METZ, Ecuyer, fut honoré de l'eftime & de la confiance du Roi Louis XIV, qui lui confia fucceffivement plufieurs charges importantes. Il fut nommé Intendant & Contrôleur-Général des meubles de la Couronne en 1663, Confeiller d'Etat en la même année, Tréforier-Général des Revenus Cafuels de Sa Majefté, en 1665, Garde du Tréfor Royal en 1674; enfin il fut pourvu d'une charge de Préfident de la Chambre des Comptes de Paris, en 1692. Il fit entrer dans fa famille le Comté de Rônay, ancienne Pairie de Champagne, dont il fit hommage au Roi en fa Chambre des Comptes de Paris, le 4 Août 1700, & qu'il fubftitua aux aînés de fa poftérité. Il avoit époufé, le 23 Août 1680, *Marie Mallet*, d'une famille noble, qui a donné des Magiftrats au Parlement & à la Chambre des Comptes de Paris. De ce mariage font iffus :

1. JEAN-BAPTISTE, qui fuit;
2. CLAUDE-GÉDÉON, rapporté après fon frère aîné, & qui continue la poftérité;
3. Et JACQUES DU METZ, Chevalier, Vicomte de Pernan, Seigneur de Varâtre, Chalette, &c. Il fut reçu Page du Roi en fa Petite-Ecurie, le 29 Avril 1697, & devint fucceffivement Moufquetaire du Roi, Enfeigne dans le Régiment des Gardes-Françoifes, Colonel du Régiment de Vexin, Infanterie, Brigadier des Armées du Roi, Chevalier

de l'Ordre Royal & Militaire de Saint-Louis, & Lieutenant pour Sa Majefté en la ville de Nérac dans le Condomois. Il eft mort fans poftérité.

VII. Jean-Baptiste du Metz, Chevalier, Comte de Rônay, fuccéda à fon père en 1707, dans la charge d'Intendant & Contrôleur-Général des meubles de la Couronne; il fut nommé, en 1715, Capitaine des Gardes de la Porte de S. A. R. Monfeigneur le Duc d'Orléans, Régent du Royaume. Il fut reçu, en 1721, Chevalier de l'Ordre Royal & Militaire de Notre-Dame du Mont-Carmel & de Saint-Jean de Jérufalem. Il mourut fans poftérité en 1731.

VII. Claude-Gédéon du Metz, Chevalier, Seigneur de Rance, Crepy, Eve, Marchemorel, &c. fecond fils de Gédéon du Metz, & de Marie Mallet, fut reçu Confeiller au Parlement de Paris le 13 Août 1704, & fuccéda à fon père dans la charge de Préfident de la Chambre des Comptes de Paris, le 22 Juin 1708. Il devint, par la mort de fon père, aîné & chef de fa famille, & fit hommage au Roi en fa Chambre des Comptes de Paris, le 14 Décembre 1731, pour le Comté de Rônay, mouvant de Sa Majefté. Il époufa, le 13 Décembre 1705, Geneviève-Claude Raguain, fille de Jean-Baptifte Raguain, Ecuyer, Confeiller-Secrétaire du Roi. De ce mariage il eut pour enfans :

1. Claude-Gédéon-Denis, qui fuit ;
2. Et Anne-Marie-Claude du Metz, mariée, 1º le 22 Janvier 1736, à François-Jofeph, Marquis d'Hautefort-d'Ajac, Meftre-de-Camp du Régiment de Touloufe, Cavalerie ; & 2º à Henri-Gabriel de Berry, Marquis d'Efferteaux, Guidon de Gendarmerie, Meftre-de-Camp de Cavalerie.

VIII. Claude-Gédéon-Denis du Metz, Chevalier, Comte de Rônay, Seigneur d'Eve, Marchemorel, &c., a été reçu Confeiller au Parlement de Paris le 7 Août 1742, Préfident en la Chambre des Comptes de Paris le 2 Septembre 1747, honoraire au Parlement le 16 Mars 1759, honoraire en la Chambre des Comptes le 5 Juin 1764. Il a époufé, le 6 Février 1746, Geneviève Pouyvet de la Blinière, fille de Louis Pouyvet de la Blinière, Ecuyer, Seigneur de Bourgon, Bois-au-Parc, Bourgnouvelle, &c., Confeiller du Roi honoraire en fon Grand-Confeil. Ce mariage a donné les alliances de Chifreville, de Tho-

mond, de Choifeul-Praslin, de Breteuil, du Pleffis-Châtillon, de la Chaux, de Folleville, de Saint-Comteft, de Joly-de-Fleury, d'Etampes, de Vauvineux, de Bartillat, de Guitaud, d'Allonville, de Bofredon, &c. De ce mariage font iffus :

1. Claude-Gédéon-Joseph, fubftitué au Comté de Rônay, mort fans poftérité le 13 Décembre 1762 ;
2. Et Claude-Jean-Michel du Metz, qui fuit.

IX. Claude-Jean-Michel du Metz, Chevalier, Seigneur d'Orcheux, fubftitué au Comté de Rônay, Confeiller du Roi en tous fes Confeils, Maître des Requêtes ordinaire de fon Hôtel, a époufé, le 29 Juillet 1777, Armande-Catherine-Claudine le Tellier, fille de Claude-François le Tellier, Chevalier, Capitaine au Régiment des Gardes-Françoifes, Brigadier des Armées du Roi, Chevalier de l'Ordre Royal & Militaire de St.-Louis, d'une branche collatérale de la Maifon de le Tellier-Louvois. Ce mariage a donné des alliances avec les maifons de Coffé, de Rohan-Chabot, de la Rochefoucauld, de Villequier. Delà font venues auffi les alliances de Saint-Chamans, de Sailly, de la Viefville, d'Offun, de Vernouillet, de la Roche-Dragon, de Montaigu, &c.

Les armes : d'azur, à trois colombes d'argent, pofées 2 & 1.

(Généalogie dreffée fur les pièces juftificatives produites au Confeil en 1672, reconnues & confirmées par l'Arrêt du Confeil d'Etat, qui s'enfuivit, & fur d'autres pièces poftérieures & authentiques qui nous ont été communiquées.)

BERBIRZY, BERBIZY ou BERBIZEY. C'eft une famille de Bourgogne très-ancienne, de laquelle étoit Alix de Berbirzy, dite de Bercy, furnommée la Belle, qui époufa, dans le XVe fiècle, Henri Chambellan, Vicomte de Dijon, & Receveur-Général des Finances de Bourgogne. Jean de Berbirzy, Baron de Ventoux, Premier Préfident du Parlement de Bourgogne, depuis le 13 Janvier 1716, dont il fe démit en 1745, & Mathieu de Berbirzy, Chevalier de Malte, Commandeur de Châlons & de Baune, font les feuls de cette famille, qui vivoient alors, dit le père Anfelme, tom. IV, p. 515.

Les armes : d'azur, à la brebis paiffante d'argent, fur une terraffe de finople. Une branche brifoit fes armes: *d'un lambel de trois pendans d'argent, en chef.*

BERBIS: *d'azur, au chevron d'or, accompagné en pointe d'une brebis de même*, aliàs *d'une brebis d'argent.*

BERCEUR (le), Seigneur de Fontenay: *d'azur, à la fleur-de-lys d'or, foutenue d'un croiffant d'argent.*

BERCHÉNY, dénommé dans les plus anciens titres Latins Berezény, dans des titres Allemands Beresény, & dans ceux Hongrois, Bersény, ces derniers prononçant la lettre *S* comme *ch*, conformément au génie de la langue: ancienne famille de Sieules, originaire de Tranfylvanie, où elle s'eft alliée aux plus illuftres Maifons, & a poffédé des domaines confidérables; elle vint s'établir en Hongrie en 1633, eut beaucoup de part aux troubles qui agitèrent ce Royaume, & vint, en 1712, s'établir en France. Le premier connu de cette Maifon eft:

I. Barnabé de Berchény-de-Scekès, Chevalier du Saint-Sépulcre, Gouverneur de Ziged ou Séguedin, qui époufa, en 1440, *Catherine de Mutnoky*, fille de *Pierre*, de la plus ancienne Maifon de Tranfylvanie, Lieutenant-Général de cette Province, & de *Barbe Arady*, fille du Palatin de ce nom, en Hongrie, & eut:

1. Etienne, qui fuit;
2. N... de Berchény, mariée à *Pierre Beffenay*;
3. N... de Berchény, femme de *Pierre Illyeshazy*, Chevalier de la Clef d'Or, & Chambellan de l'Empereur;
4. Et Cécile de Berchény, mariée à *Louis Amadée*, Confeiller & Chambellan de l'Empereur.

II. Etienne de Berchény-de-Scekès, Grand-Chambellan de Jean Bathory, Souverain de Tranfylvanie, étoit marié, en 1480, avec *Catherine de Banfy*, dont il eut:

1. Ladislas, qui fuit;
2. Catherine, mariée à *Jean de Laxar*, Baron libre, Généraliffime en Hongrie;
3. Barbe, mariée à *Jean*, Comte de *Kur*, Ambaffadeur à la Porte;
4. Marguerite, mariée à *Nicolas de Fitter*, Général en Tranfylvanie;
5. Et Susanne, mariée à *Georges*, Comte de *Zéefy*, Grand-Maître des plaifirs du Prince Nicolas Bathory.

III. Ladislas de Berchény, Chevalier de

la Clef d'Or, Ordre dont le Roi de Hongrie ne décoroit que des Gentilshommes de nom & d'armes à fon couronnement, fut Gouverneur de Damasd, époufa, en 1500, *Barbe de Balaffy*, fille du Grand-Echanfon de Jean Bathory, Roi de Hongrie, & de *Marie Niary*, iffue d'une famille des Palatins de Hongrie. Il eut:

1. Emeric, qui fuit;
2. Jean, Feld-Maréchal de l'Empire, marié à *Sufanne de Kemendy*, tante d'un Vaivode de Tranfylvanie de ce nom;
3. Et Louise, mariée au Comte *François d'Antalfy*, Comte Suprême d'Albe.

IV. Emeric de Berchény, Ier du nom, premier Gentilhomme du Prince Bathory, qui ne vivoit plus en 1588, étoit marié, en 1575, avec *Sophie de Saarroffy*, de la première nobleffe de Tranfylvanie, alliée aux Princes *Gabriel* & *Etienne Bettlem*, à *Jean*, Electeur de Brandebourg, aux Bathory, Rois de Pologne, & Princes de Tranfylvanie, aux *Efterhazy*, & aux *Lowenbourg*. Elle étoit fille d'*Etienne Saarroffy*, Grand-Maître de la Maifon du Prince *Gabriel*, & d'*Anne Tholdy*, tante maternelle des deux *Bettlem*. Il eut:

V. Emeric de Berchény, IIe du nom, Chevalier du Saint-Sépulcre & de la Clef d'Or, Baron de Scekès, qui quitta le parti des Mécontens de Tranfylvanie en 1633, & vint fe fixer en Hongrie, où il s'attacha à l'Empereur Ferdinand II, qui le fit Confeiller de la Chambre de Hongrie, & l'envoya en 1634, en qualité de Plénipotentiaire, vers *Georges Rakoczy*, Ier du nom, fon allié, pour traiter avec ce Prince de la reftitution des biens de la veuve de *Bettlem*, fa parente, & de quelques Seigneurs fortis de Tranfylvanie, & lui donner avis que les Turcs prenoient les armes; en 1636 & 1637, Ambaffadeur à la Porte; à fon retour, Colonel d'un Régiment, & Gouverneur de Novigrade. Il mourut en Bohême, au fervice de ce Prince, en 1639, Lieutenant-Général contre les Rebelles du Royaume. L'Empereur Ferdinand III l'avoit reconnu *Baron & Magnat de Hongrie*, en latin *Magnates*..... par Diplôme du 18 Juillet 1639, en confidération de fes fervices & de ceux de fa Maifon, qu'il reconnut pour ancienne & illuftre. Il avoit époufé, en 1612, *Barbe de Lugaffy*, fille unique & fort riche héritière de *Jean Lugaffy*, Gouverneur de

Lippa, & originaire de Valachie, lequel tenoit un rang diſtingué à la Cour de GABRIEL,
Souverain de Tranſylvanie, qui le qualifia
dans différens Diplômes de *Familiaris*, & de
Gouverneur de Lippa, & d'*Anne Birta*,
d'une des premières Maiſons de la Province.
Il laiſſa entr'autres enfans :

1. EMERIC, IIIᵉ du nom, mort en 1656;
2. LADISLAS, Gouverneur de Damasd, mort la
   même année que ſon frère;
3. NICOLAS, qui ſuit;
4. Et SUSANNE, Abbeſſe de Presbourg.

VI. NICOLAS DE BERCHÉNY, Iᵉʳ du nom, Seigneur de Scekès, *Libre-Baron*, Chevalier de
la Clef d'Or & du Saint-Sépulcre, Conſeiller & Chambellan de l'Empereur LÉOPOLD, &
mis au rang des *Comtes & Magnats de Hongrie*, par ce Prince; fut fait, en 1681, Juge
Militaire & Gouverneur des places ſituées
en-deçà des Monts; & en 1682, Lieutenant-
Général de ſes Troupes contre les Turcs, ſous
les ordres de CHARLES V, Duc de Lorraine,
alors Généraliſſime des Troupes Impériales.
Il eut, malgré lui, beaucoup de part aux troubles qui agitèrent le Royaume de Hongrie,
dans le dernier ſiècle, fomentés par le Comte
EmericTekely, & fut, pendant ces révolutions,
un des chefs & la ſeule reſſource du parti des
Mécontens; mais le ſort des armes s'étant déclaré pour la Maiſon d'Autriche, le Comte de
BERCHÉNY fut obligé d'abandonner la Hongrie. Il ſe retira dans les Etats du Grand-Sei-
gneur, d'où il obtint, le 7 Janvier 1683, des
Lettres de rémiſſion de JEAN III, Roi de Pologne, qui étoit chargé des pouvoirs de l'Empereur. Il avoit épouſé, vers 1664, *Eliſa-
beth-Catherine de Rechberg*, veuve du Comte *Georges Forgach-de-Ghimes*, & fille de
Vit-Conrad, Baron de *Rechberg*, d'une ancienne Maiſon d'Allemagne, qui a eu pluſieurs Chevaliers Jurés & reçus dans l'Ordre
de Saint-Georges, & de *Marie-Madeleine*,
Comteſſe de *Fugger*, auſſi d'une très-grande Maiſon. Il en eut entr'autres enfans :

VII. NICOLAS DE BERCHÉNY, IIᵉ du nom,
Libre-Baron de Scekès, Chevalier de la Clef
d'Or, Comte Suprême & héréditaire du Comté Dungwar, Conſeiller & Chambellan de
l'Empereur, chef des treize Comtés de Hongrie, Général & Commiſſaire-Général de Sa
Majeſté dans la Guerre contre les Turcs, décoré par Diplôme de l'Empereur LÉOPOLD, du
Manteau Ducal ſur ſes armes, & des titres

de *Comte perpétuel*, d'*Illuſtriſſime*, *Honorable* & *Magnifique*, qualités pompeuſes,
mais d'autant plus importantes, que l'Hiſtoire nous apprend que SIGISMOND BATHORY exi-
gea de l'Empereur RODOLPHE II, en 1595, de
le qualifier d'*Illuſtriſſime*, en même tems que
ſa Majeſté le reconnoît *Prince de Tranſylvanie & Prince-Libre*. Il eut beaucoup de
part aux troubles de ce Royaume, fomentés
par le Prince *François Rakoczy*, ſon parent,
en 1700, pour ſoutenir les Privilèges, Immu-
nités & Exemptions de la Nation ; ce qui l'o-
bligea de ſe retirer en Pologne, où, ayant
amaſſé un parti nombreux, il fut déclaré, en
1703, dans une aſſemblée de la Nobleſſe, tenue à Onod, *Grand-Général* du Royaume
de Hongrie, & des Armées de la Confédération. Dans une aſſemblée des Etats de Hongrie, tenue en 1705, il fut déclaré *Premier
Sénateur* du Royaume. L'Empereur JOSEPH
voyant les progrès de l'Armée des Confédérés
s'accroître de plus en plus, chargea le Comte
de Széchény, Archevêque de Colocza, d'une
négociation de pacification, & en conſéquence envoya des inſtructions aux Sieurs Tolway
& Jezensky, pour traiter avec le Comte de BER-
CHÉNY, qu'il qualifioit *Palatin du Royaume*;
& à qui il avoit fait offrir, s'il vouloit entrer dans ſes vues, le titre de *Prince de
l'Empire*, la *Toiſon d'Or*, & la charge de
Palatin de ſon Royaume. Ce Comte refuſa
tous ces avantages ; & les Etats de Hongrie,
pour ſe l'attacher davantage, lui conférent,
en 1707, l'emploi de Lieutenant-Ducal, afin
qu'en l'abſence du Prince, il eut la même autorité ; puis Ambaſſadeur en Pologne & en
Moſcovie, pour négocier une alliance qui eut
un heureux ſuccès. L'Empereur ayant gagné
la bataille de Trenezen en 1708, & remporté
divers avantages ſur l'Armée des Confédérés
les années ſuivantes, le Comte de BERCHÉNY
fut obligé d'abandonner la Hongrie. Il ſe retira d'abord en Pologne pendant l'hiver de
1711, d'où il paſſa en Turquie. Il mourut à
Rodoſto, le 6 Novembre 1725, âgé de 61 ans.
Il avoit épouſé, 1º en 1688, *Chriſtine de Drugeth-d'Homonay*, morte en 1690, alliée aux
Bathory, & à pluſieurs Maiſons Souveraines.
(Le premier connu de ce nom, originaire d'Italie, s'attacha, en 800, à un Archiduc d'Autriche, alors à Rome, comme ſon Gentilhomme.) Elle étoit veuve 1º du Comte *André de
Forgatz*, & 2º du Comte *François de Palf-*

fy : Elle étoit fille de *Georges de Drugeth-d'Homonay*, Généraliffime de la Haute-Hongrie, Comte Suprême & Héréditaire des Comtés Dungwar & de Zempline, iffue de Palatins, & de *Marie d'Efterhazy*, fille du Comte *Nicolas d'Efterhazy*, Palatin de Hongrie, & de *Chriftine de Niary*, d'une des plus anciennes & illuftres nobleffes de Hongrie ; & 2° en 1695, à *Chriftine Czaky-de-Kereftzeg*, morte à Rodofto en 1723. Elle étoit veuve 1° du Comte *Nicolas d'Erdœdy-de-Monyorokerek*, Ban de Croatie & Efclavonie, & 2° du Comte *Draskovich*, Grand-Juge du Royaume de Hongrie, fans poftérité. Du premier lit vinrent :

1. LADISLAS-IGNACE, qui fuit ;
2. Et SUSANNE DE BERCHÉNY, mariée à *Pierre*, Comte de *Zeczy-de-Vafonko*, dont elle eut *Pierre de Zeczy*, II° du nom, marié & mort fans poftérité ; & *Nicolas de Zeczy*, Comte de Vafonko, Chambellan & Confeiller Intime de l'Empereur, Comte Suprême du Comté de Zaboltz, mort fans poftérité d'*Elifabeth de Béreny*, fille du Comte *Georges de Béreny*, Comte Suprême du Comté de Zaboltz, d'une ancienne Maifon attachée aux Rois de Hongrie depuis 1212, par les grandes charges du Royaume, & de *Claire d'Uj-Falufy* Comteffe de Divek-Uj-Falufy.

VII. LADISLAS-IGNACE DE BERCHÉNY, Comte de Berchény, né le 3 Août 1689, dans la ville d'Epéries, capitale du Comté de Saros dans la Haute-Hongrie, eft venu s'établir en France, où fes fervices lui ont acquis, dans les Cours de France & de Lorraine, des emplois dignes de fa naiffance. Il avoit fait les Campagnes de 1708, 1709 & 1710, dans la Compagnie des Gentilshommes Hongrois, qui faifoient partie de la Maifon du Prince *Rakoczy* ; & s'étoit trouvé aux batailles de Trenczen & de Romham. Il eft venu en France en 1712, où il obtint du fervice ; fut nommé en 1743 Infpecteur-Général des Huffards, dont il avoit dès 1719 un Régiment de fon nom ; Lieutenant-Général des Armées du Roi en 1744 ; Grand-Croix de l'Ordre Militaire de Saint-Louis en 1753 ; & Maréchal de France le 15 Mars 1758. Il étoit Grand-Ecuyer de Lorraine, Confeiller-Chevalier d'Honneur de la Cour Souveraine de Lorraine & Barrois, par provifions du 21 Avril 1738, fous le règne du feu Roi STANISLAS-LE-BIENFAISANT, Duc de Lorraine & de Bar ; Gouverneur des Villes & Château de la Principauté de Commercy, par Lettres du 11 Mars 1748 ; Grand-Bailli d'Epée le 26 Août 1751. Il eft Seigneur du Lufancy, Meffy, Courcelles, Clerenval, Florrenval, &c., & a époufé, par contrat du 9 Mai 1726, *Anne-Catherine de Wiet-Girard*, alliée aux familles les plus diftinguées du Royaume, & iffue d'une Maifon qui a donné un grand nombre d'Officiers Militaires, dont deux, entr'autres, fe font rendus recommandables aux fièges de Mons & de Valence, où ils étoient Maréchaux-de-Camp, fous les ordres de M. Vauban. Elle eft morte le 24 Août 1766, & étoit fille de *Jacques-Antoine de Wiet-Girard*, Capitaine dans le Régiment d'Humières, dont il eut fa retraite pour caufe de bleffures à la bataille de Malplaquet, fans cependant quitter le fervice ; PHILIPPE, Duc d'Orléans, qui connoiffoit fa capacité, lui ayant fait expédier un Brevet d'Ingénieur, puis de Directeur-Général de toutes les Fortifications d'Alface, & d'*Anne de Camps*. De ce mariage font nés :

1. NICOLAS-FRANÇOIS, qui fuit ;
2. FRANÇOIS-ANTOINE, rapporté après fon frère ;
3. N... DE BERCHÉNY, Abbeffe de l'Abbaye Royale de Flines en Flandre ;
4. & 5. N..... & N..... DE BERCHÉNY, Demoifelles.

IX. NICOLAS-FRANÇOIS DE BERCHÉNY, né le 26 Novembre 1736, Meftre-de-Camp d'un Régiment de Cavalerie Hongroife de fon nom, Chambellan du Roi de Pologne, Duc de Lorraine & de Bar, premier Gentilhomme de la Chambre de Sa Majefté, Grand-Ecuyer & Confeiller-Chevalier d'Honneur en furvivance, de la Cour Souveraine de Lorraine & Barrois, tué à l'armée le 9 Février 1762. Il avoit époufé, le 1er Mai 1757, *Agnès-Victoire de Berthelot*, Dame de Mefdames de FRANCE, & fille de *François de Berthelot*, Baron de Baye, Lieutenant-Général des Armées du Roi, & Commandeur de l'Ordre-Militaire de Saint-Louis, & de *Cécile-Elifabeth Rioult-Douilly-de-Curfay*. Il eut :

1. N... DE BERCHÉNY, Chevalier ;
2. Et N... DE BERCHÉNY, Demoifelle, tous les deux morts en bas âge.

IX. FRANÇOIS-ANTOINE DE BERCHÉNY, né le 17 Juin 1744, fecond fils du Maréchal, & d'*Anne-Catherine de Wiet-Girard*, fut d'abord reçu Chevalier de Malte, le 23 Février

1752; entra au Service en 1756; fut Capitaine du Régiment de Cavalerie Hongroife, de fon nom, après fon frère, puis Meftre-de-Camp du même Régiment, le 2 Mars 1762; premier Gentilhomme de la Chambre du feu Roi de Pologne, Duc de Lorraine & de Bar, le 17 Février 1762; Grand-Ecuyer de Lorraine, en furvivance, le 20 Avril 1768, par la démiffion du Maréchal, fon père, en fa faveur; Gouverneur des Ville & Château de Commercy, & Capitaine de la Capitainerie des Chaffes; nommé par Sa Majefté, en Janvier 1769, Chevalier des Ordres Royaux-Militaires & Hofpitaliers de Notre-Dame du Mont-Carmel & de Saint-Lazare de Jérufalem; eft marié, par contrat du 24 Janvier 1769, avec *Louife-Adélaïde Thomas-de-Pange*, fille de *Jean-Baptifte Thomas*, Chevalier, Marquis de Pange, Seigneur de Villiers, la Qunezy, Domangeville, &c., Commandeur-Tréforier-Général de l'Ordre Militaire de Saint-Louis, & de l'Extraordinaire des Guerres, & de *Marie-Adélaïde de Chambon-d'Abouville*.

Les armes: *parti, au 1 de gueules à la croix pattée d'argent, cantonnée de 4 croifettes de même; au 2 d'azur, à une licorne d'argent, iffante d'une couronne treflée d'or, pofée fur deux montagnes en figure de cœur, entrelaffées d'argent, & mouvantes de la pointe de l'écu.*

(Généalogie dreffée fur un Mémoire envoyé, & partie fur Moréri, édition de 1759.)

BERCHER, Ecuyer, Sieur de Montchevrel, bonne & ancienne nobleffe, employée dans la recherche de 1666, Election de Mortagne, Généralité d'Alençon, en Normandie, qui porte: *d'azur, au cheval cabré d'or, les pieds pofés fur une longue épée de même en bande.*

* BERCHERE, Terre & Seigneurie qui appartient à *N.... le Goux de la Berchère*, famille originaire de Dijon. Voyez GOUX-DE-LA-BERCHÈRE.

BERCHTOLSGADE (*Religion Catholique*). Le Prince Abbé *Michel Balthafard*, Comte de *Chriftalnig*, né le 10 Septembre 1700, élu Coadjuteur le 7 Octobre 1748, Abbé le 4 Juillet 1752.

BERCI, famille de Champagne, de laquelle étoit NICOLE DE BERCI, née en 1678, & reçue à Saint-Cyr au mois de Septembre 1686, fur les preuves qu'elle donna que JACQUES DE BERCI & *Claire du Monnoir*, qui vivoient en 1530, étoient fes trifayeuls.

Les armes: *d'azur, au chevron d'argent, accompagné de trois molettes de même.*

⸙ BERCKHEIM, famille noble originaire d'Alface, avec titre de Baronie, qui tire fon nom du bourg *Mittel-Berckheim*, fitué dans la Baffe-Alface, près de la ville d'Andlau. C'eft une branche fubfiftante de cette Maifon d'Andlau, & qui s'en eft féparée en changeant le nom d'*Andlau* en celui de *Berckheim*. Les hiftoriographes qui parlent de l'Alface & de fa nobleffe, font d'accord fur ce point, comme Schoepfflin, *Alfatia illuftrata*, tom. II, pag. 207 & 379, & les autres qui en parlent tous dans les mêmes termes. Mais la preuve la plus convaincante eft celle qui fe trouve alléguée dans la differtation de Wemker *de jure torneament. Nobil. Argent.*, qui eft un reverfaille de la famille d'Andlau, du lundi avant Saint-Bartholomé en 1485, dont l'original fe conferve dans les archives de la famille BERCKHEIM, par lequel celle d'*Andlau* déclare que celle de BERCKHEIM eft de la même fouche, race, origine de nom & d'armes; que les *Andlau* reconnoiffent les BERCKHEIM pour être de leur même famille. Les armes de BERCKHEIM & d'*Andlau* font les mêmes, c'eft-à-dire *d'or, à la croix de gueules*. Pour les cimiers, ils font différens: BERCKHEIM porte pour cimier *un couffin de gueules*, fur lequel eft debout un *canard d'or*; & d'*Andlau* a pour cimier *la moitié d'un homme blanc couronné*.

La féparation de ces deux familles, qui anciennement portoient le même nom d'*Andlau*, eft provenue de ce qu'une branche étoit établie à Andlau & fe nommoit *Andlau d'Andlau*; & l'autre établie à Mittel-Berckheim, fe nommoit *Andlau de Berckheim*. Mais comme par la fuite des tems il y a eu de grands différends entre ces deux branches, il eft arrivé que celle d'*Andlau de Berckheim* a quitté fon nom d'*Andlau*, n'a conferve que celui de *Berckheim*, & a en même tems changé de cimier à fes armes.

On ne fait pas en quelle année s'eft faite cette féparation, puifque cela fe perd dans l'ancienneté des tems. Cependant on croit qu'elle s'eft faite au commencement du XIIIᵉ fiècle; c'eft ce que rapporte le P. Laguille, dans ſes *Preuves à l'Hiſtoire d'Alſace;* il fait voir que les familles de BERCKHEIM & d'*Andlau*, avant leur ſéparation, n'ont formé qu'une ſeule famille, ſous le nom commun d'*Andlau;* par conféquent celle de BERCKHEIM peut s'attribuer avec juſtice tous les avantages honorifiques attribués à leurs ancêtres. Schoepfflin, tom. II, pag. 708, § 576, avance que les *Andlau* avoient été anciennement regardés de pair aux dynaſtes; & en parlant des titres que l'on donnoit aux Ducs, Comtes & Dynaſtes, il cite un traité fait dans le XIII° fiècle, entre les Ducs de Lorraine & les *Andlau*, & dit qu'ils ont pris, les uns comme les autres, le titre de *nobiles viri*, que, dans ces fiècles là, on ne donnoit qu'aux Ducs, Comtes ou Dynaſtes.

Ainſi la famille de BERCKHEIM, aujourd'hui ſubſiſtante, peut s'attribuer les mêmes prérogatives qu'elle avoit dans le fiècle où elle a été féparée des *Andlau*, & elle peut auſſi prouver que ceux de BERCKHEIM ont été regardés, dans ces tems-là, de Pairs ou Dynaſtes, en ce que CANO DE BERCKHEIM a rempli, ſous l'Empereur LUDOLPHE D'HABSSBOURG, le poſte de Grand-Bailli d'Alſace, poſte qui n'a jamais été occupé au moins que par des Dynaſtes, mais le plus ſouvent par des Electeurs, Princes & Archiducs d'Autriche, ainſi que le prouve la liſte qu'on lit dans l'*Alſatia illuſtrata*.

CANNEMANE DE BERCKHEIM vivoit en 1232, & eſt, ſelon toute apparence, celui qui s'eſt féparé de la Maiſon d'*Andlau*. Il eut:

CUNO DE BERCKHEIM, qui laiſſa entr'autres enfans:

CUNO DE BERCKHEIM, IIᵉ du nom, Sous-Grand-Bailli d'Alſace, que pluſieurs auteurs appellent *præfidem principis in Alſatiá*. Il poſſéda le Château de Crax près d'Andlau, & la ville & fortereſſe de Sermersheim près de Benfeld en Alſace, comme fief d'Empire. Il eut beaucoup de différends avec Conrad, Evêque de Strasbourg, & beaucoup d'autres Seigneurs contre leſquels il eut guerre. Il ſuccomba; ſon château de Crax & ſa fortereſſe de Sermersheim furent aſſiégés, pris & démolis, & les pierres détachées & tranſportées à Lichtenau, dont on batît la ville de ce nom. De ce CUNO DE BERCKHEIM ſortit une branche particulière qui fit pluſieurs acquiſitions, & s'éteignit dans WERNER DE BERCKHEIM, en 1386. Mais entre les enfans de CUNO il y eut:

LUDOLPHE DE BERCKHEIM, qui ſe maria avec

Eliſabeth Tleckenſtein. Ils furent inhumés à Jebsheim, ſelon leur épitaphe de 1341.

Les deſcendans de ce LUDOLPHE vivent encore aujourd'hui en Alſace, & forment la famille des Barons de BERCKHEIM, qui ſe font ſouvent partagés en pluſieurs branches ſucceſſivement éteintes; de façon qu'au commencement du XVIIᵉ fiècle, il ne ſubſiſtoit qu'EGENOLPHE DE BERCKHEIM, qui eut:

N... qui ſuit;

JEAN-LUDOLPHE, auteur de la deuxième branche, rapportée ci-après;

Et EGENOLPHE DE BERCKHEIM, tige de la troiſième branche, qui viendra en ſon rang.

N... DE BERCKHEIM, né en 1585, eſt auteur de la branche de BERCKHEIM établie à Jebſheim. Il étoit Grand-Bailli de la Séréniſſime Maiſon de Wurtemberg, du Comté de Horburg & de la Seigneurie de Techenvich en Alſace. Il eſt mort en 1665, & a laiſſé de *Barbe Lemchengen:*

JULES-EBERHARD DE BERCKHEIM, né en 1631, attaché à la Cour de la Séréniſſime Maiſon de Bade-Dourlach, comme Gouverneur du Prince Charles-Frédéric, qui mourut en 1688. Il avoit épouſé *Anne-Eléonore de Brinning-Koffen*, dont il eut:

1. GEORGES-FRÉDÉRIC DE BERCKHEIM, né en 1662, & mort en 1718. Il avoit épouſé *Charlotte-Eliſabeth de Brieten-Lendenberg*. Il eut:

LOUIS-FRÉDÉRIC DE BERCKHEIM, né en 1698, mort en 1733. Il avoit épouſé *Jeanne-Hélène Eckbrecht-Durckheim.* Il laiſſa:

PHILIPPE-FRÉDÉRIC DE BERCKHEIM, né en 1731, Capitaine au Régiment d'Alſace, Infanterie Allemande au ſervice de France, qui a épouſé *Marie-Octavie-Louiſe de Glaubitz.* Lorſque le Mémoire nous a été fourni, il n'avoit pas encore d'enfant mâle.

DEUXIÈME BRANCHE.

JEAN-LUDOLPHE DE BERCKHEIM, auteur d'une branche établie à Krautergersheim, né en 1587, Capitaine de Cavalerie au ſervice de l'Empereur, enſuite Conſeiller-Aſſeſſeur au Directoire de la nobleſſe immédiate de la Baſſe-Alſace, mourut en 1664. Il avoit épouſé *Suſanne-Barbe de Nippenburg.* Il eut:

CHRÉTIEN-EBERHARD DE BERCKHEIM, né en 1635, Capitaine au ſervice de Suède, enſuite

Conseiller-Asseffeur au Directoire de la noblesse immédiate de la Basse-Alsace, qui a épousé en troisièmes noces *Elisabeth-Marie de Landsperg*, dont il eut :

1. Egenolphe - Sigismond de Berckheim, né en 1694, Lieutenant-Colonel d'Infanterie au service de France & Chevalier de l'Ordre Royal du Mérite Militaire, qui épousa 1° *Françoise-Elisabeth de Landsperg*; & 2° *Sophie de Torschener*, dont il n'a pas eu d'enfans mâles;

2. Et François - Samuel de Berckheim, Mestre-de-Camp de Cavalerie au service de France, Chevalier de l'Ordre Royal du Mérite Militaire & de l'Aigle Rouge, de Brandebourg, Prêteur au Magistrat de la ville de Strasbourg, & Chancelier de cette Université, marié à *Charlotte Saffalle de Landsperg*, dont il n'a pas eu d'enfans.

TROISIÈME BRANCHE.

Egenolphe de Berckheim, né en 1591, a été auteur de la branche établie à *Tibauvillé*. Il mourut en 1636, & avoit épousé *Anne-Marie Truchs de Theinfelden*, dont vint:

Georges-Ludolphe de Berckheim, né en 1629, mort en 1674, qui avoit épousé Sophie-Marguerite de Berckheim, sa parente, sortie de la branche de *Jebsheim*, dont il a eu:

Jean-Guillaume de Berckheim, né en 1652, Major au service de Saxe, mort en 1723. Il avoit épousé *Jeanne-Elisabeth Wurmser de Vendenheim*, dont:

Philippe- Frédéric de Berckheim, né en 1686, Conseiller privé, & Président de la Régence & de la Chambre des Finances du Comté de Hanau - Lichtenberg à Bouxviller en Alsace, & en même tems Bailli de Lichtenau & Witstett, marié à Léonore-Henriette de Berckheim, de la branche de *Jebsheim*, dont :

Louis-Charles de Berckheim, né en 1726, Conseiller privé de la Régence de la Sérénissime Maison de Bade, & son Grand-Bailli du Landgraviat de Sauffenberg & de la Seigneurie de Toettlen, qui demeure à Loyrach ;

Et Chrétien - Louis de Berckheim, né en 1729, Commandant de bataillon au Régiment d'Infanterie Allemande de Royal Deux-Ponts, au service de France, Chevalier de l'Ordre Royal du Mérite Militaire, qui épousa *Sophie-Jacobée de Talhsauhenuen d'Eheuweyher*, dont il n'y a pas d'enfans.

Nous ignorons si cette branche existe encore. Pour faire voir l'illustration de cette famille de Berckheim, le mémoire qui nous a été envoyé nous apprend que ceux de ce nom avoient des vassaux nobles. C'est ce que rapporte Schoepfflin, dans son *Alsatia illustrata*, tom. II, pag. 44, § 414, & dont on a des titres originaux qui subsistent.

Les archives de Saint-Thomas de Strasbourg prouvent clairement que ceux de la famille de *Turdenheim* étoient vassaux de celle de Berckheim, en ce que *Henri de Turdenheim*, Chevalier, vendit, en 1319, au chapitre de Saint-Thomas de Strasbourg, du consentement des Seigneurs Werner, Ebertin & Jean de Berckheim tous les biens dans le ban de *Trutersheim* qu'il tenoit en fief des Seigneurs de Berckheim.

Cette Maison de Berckheim possède encore aujourd'hui les Seigneuries de Jebsheim, Krautergersheim & Innenheim, situées dans la matricule de la noblesse immédiate de la Basse-Alsace ; & aussi la Seigneurie de Schoppenvihz, près de Colmar dans la Haute-Alsace, ainsi que les Seigneuries d'Allmanwegher & Wethenwegher, situées dans la matricule de la noblesse immédiate d'Ortenan, dans l'Empire ; & la famille de Berckheim est encore membre du corps de cette noblesse immédiate de l'Empire. Ceux du nom de Berckheim sont aujourd'hui vassaux du Roi de France ; ils s'étoient autrefois de l'Evêque de Strasbourg, de celui de Metz, de la Maison Palatine, comme Comtes de Tibeaupierre, de la Maison de Hesse-Darmstadt, comme Comtes de Hanau & de la Maison de Wurtemberg, comme Princes de Montbéliard.

Les armes. Voyez ci-dessus.

BERCLÉ, à Léon en Bretagne : *d'azur, à trois lions léopardés d'or, armés & lampassés de gueules, posés l'un au-dessus de l'autre.*

BERCY : *d'argent, à la fasce de sable, dentelée par le haut.*

BERCY-MALON : *d'argent, à trois canettes de sable, posées 2 & 1.*

BERE, en Normandie : *d'argent, à trois léopards d'azur, couronnés & armés de gueules, posés 2 & 1.*

BERENGER, ancienne Maison du Dauphiné qui prétend descendre des anciens Rois

d'Arles par Ismidon, troifième fils d'*Artaud*
III, Comte de Forez & de Lyon, qui vivoit
en 1060, & fe qualifiait *Prince de Royans*,
pendant le règne des premiers Dauphins.
Voyez les Mémoires de M. Bouchu, Intendant de Dauphiné. Ismidon a été bifaïeul de:

Raymond, qui fuit;
Et Pierre, tige de la branche de *Berenger du
Gua.*

Raymond II deBérengereut pour petit-fils:
Aymard de Berenger, Seigneur de Pont-
de-Royans,qui époufa *Béatrix de Saffenage*,
fille de François Ier, Seigneur de Saffenage, &
d'*Agnès de Joinville*, dont:

Henri, Baron de *Saffenage*, de fon chef,
& Seigneur de Pont, du chef de fon père. Il
quitta le nom & les armes de Berenger, pour
prendre ceux de *Saffenage*, que fa poftérité
a confervés jufqu'à préfent, fuivant la difpofition teftamentaire de *François Ier*,Seigneur
de *Saffenage*, fon ayeul maternel, qui l'avoit
fubftitué aux biens de fa Maifon, en casqu'*Albert* II, fon fils, mourut fans enfans.

Raymond Berenger,Grand-Maître de l'Ordre de Saint-Jean de Jérufalem, mourut en
1373.

N.... de Berenger laiffa d'*Antoinette de
Saffenage*, née de *Guigues* :
Georges de Berenger, qui époufa, le 12
Avril 1456, *Guillemette de Saffenage.*

Le Cardinal Berenger ou Berengari mourut le dernier de cette Maifon en Italie, dans
le XVIe fiècle.

Jacques Berenger, Marquis du Gua, Maréchal des Camps & Armées du Roi, mourut
en Dauphiné en Mars 1727, âgé de plus de
80 ans, laiffant:

Charles, Comte de Berenger, Colonel du
Régiment de Bugey, qui époufa, en 1708,
Madeleine-Anne, fille de *Jean-Jacques de
Surbeck*, Colonel du Régiment Suiffe, Lieu-
tenant-Général des Armées du Roi, tué au
fiège de Saint-Venant, le 24 Septembre 1710.

Pierre, Comte de Berenger, Seigneur de
Chanlay près Joigny, Lieutenant-Général des
Armées du Roi,Chevalier de fes Ordres,mort
le 23 Juillet 1751, âgé de 75 ans, avoit époufé *Antoinette-Françoife Bouchay-d'Orfay*,
& laiffa:

1. Raymond-Pierre, qui fuit;
2. N..., Comte de Berenger,Colonel du Régiment de Saintonge depuis 1762;

3. Marie-Françoise, mariée, au mois de Mai
1746, à N..., Marquis de *Dolomieu;*
4. Et Marie-Sylvie de Berenger, mariée, au
mois de Mars 1749, à N...., Comte de
Soyecourt.

Raymond-Pierre, Marquis de Berenger,
Comte du Gua, Chevalier d'Honneur de feu
Madame la Dauphine, Colonel dans le corps
des Grenadiers de France,a époufé, le 2Juil-
let 1755, *Marie-Françoife de Saffenage*,
fille de *Charles-François*, Marquis de Saf-
fenage, fecond Baron du Dauphiné, & de
Marie-Françoife-Camille de Saffenage,
Marquife de Pont-de-Royans.

Achille Berenger de Sassenage, Abbé de
Saint-Jean des Vignes de Soiffons, eft mort
en Août 1762, âgé de 83 ans.

Les Maifons de *Saffenage*, de *Morgues*,
& du *Pipar*, font iffues de la même famille
que les *Berenger.*

Les armes: *gironné d'or & de gueules, de
8 pièces.* Cimier: *lion* naiffant d'or, tenant
de fa patte droite *une épée d'argent garnie
d'or.* Supports: *2 lions.* Devife: *gare la
queue de Berenger; ne s'y frotter, qu'elle
ne pique.*

BERENGER. Il y a plus de deux fiècles
que la famille de Berenger, des Seigneurs de
Grambois & de la Baume, vint de l'Isle de
Corfe s'établir à Marfeille; elle eft originaire
de Florence.

I. François Berengeri, ou Berenger, étoit
Gonfalonier à Florence en 1477. Il eut:
II. Charles, Ier du nom, qui fut exilé de
fon pays par la faction des Médicis, s'établit
en Corfe, où il époufa *Marguerite Gonfille*,
dont il eut:
III. Antoine-Orso Berenger, Ier du nom,
qui eut:
IV. Charles Berenger, IIe du nom, qui
fut père de:
V. Antoine-Orso Berenger, IIe du nom,
qui quitta l'Isle de Corfe, pour venir fixer fa
demeure à Marfeille. Il eut:
VI. Antoine de Berenger, Ier du nom, qui
époufa à Marfeille, *Claire de Gratian.* Il
eut:

1. Jean-François, qui fuit;
2. Et Venture de Berenger, mariée, l'an
1631, avec noble *Henri de Badier*, Seigneur en partie de Roquebrune.

VII. Jean-Françoisde Berenger,Seigneur
de Grambois & de la Baume, fut élu fecond

Conful de Marfeille, l'an 1643, & rétabli dans la nobleffe de fes ayeux, par Lettres du 3 Juillet 1655, enregiftrées aux Archives du Roi en Provence, le 25 Juin 1667. Regiftre fulgur. Arm. B, n° 51, fol. 138. Il époufa *Véronique d'Albert*, fille de *Jacques d'Albert*, Confeiller au Parlement de Provence, & de *Marguerite de Bourguignon de la Mure*. Ils eurent :

1. Antoine de Berenger, qui fuit;
2. Et Brune de Berenger, mariée avec noble *François de Village*, Seigneur de la Grande-Baftide.

VIII. Antoine de Berenger, II° du nom, s'allia, à Solliers, avec N...*Jenfolen*, & laiffa :

1. N...... de Berenger, dont les defcendans continuent leur nobleffe à Marfeille;
2. Et N..... de Berenger, qui époufa, en 1705, *Henri-Hyacinthe d'Albert*, Préfident en la Cour des Comptes, Aides & Finances de Provence.

Les armes : *d'azur, à la croix d'argent*, qui *eft* de Berenger, & fur le tout *un écuffon de gueules, chargé d'un lion d'or*, qui *eft* de Gonfille.

BERENGER, Seigneur des Fontaines, de Cerqueux, de Montaigu, de Languerville, Election de Coutances, en Normandie, ancienne nobleffe, qui porte : *de gueules, à deux aigles d'or, renverfées l'une fur l'autre, becquées & onglées de même*.

BERENGREVILLE : *d'azur, à la croix d'or, cantonnée de quatre molettes de même*.

BERENGUIER, ancienne famille originaire de Tarafcon.

I. Gabriel de Berenguier, par lequel on commence à avoir les papiers en règle, eft qualifié *Noble & Noble Homme* dans plufieurs actes qu'il paffa au commencement du XVI° fiècle. Il époufa, par contrat du 9 Août 1508, *Madeleine Davine*, dont il eut :

II. Antoine de Berenguier, qui fut père de :

III. Jean de Berenguier, I°r du nom, Capitaine d'Infanterie, qui fe maria, en 1591, avec *Marie de Raouffel*.

IV. Pierre de Berenguier, fils de Jean, fervit auffi en qualité de Capitaine, & époufa, par contrat du 10 Novembre 1620, *Marie d'Anfelme*. Ils eurent :

V. Jean de Berenguier, II° du nom, Capitaine d'Infanterie, maintenu dans fa nobleffe par les Commiffaires du Roi, députés pour la vérification des titres de la Nobleffe, le 15 Décembre 1667. Il époufa, par contrat du 7 Novembre 1645, *Madeleine de Camin*, & laiffa :

VI. Balthazard de Berenguier, Officier d'Infanterie, qui époufa, en 1680, N.... *de Guerin*. Il eut :

VII. Charles de Berenguier, qui fut Officier dans le Régiment Dauphin, Infanterie. Il eut de fon mariage avec la fille de M. *Brunau* :

1. Augustin, qui fuit;
2. Et Jean de Berenguier, Capitaine dans le Régiment Dauphin, Infanterie, décédé à Maubeuge.

VIII. Augustin de Berenguier, Chevalier de l'Ordre Militaire de Saint-Louis, Gentilhomme de la Chambre du Roi, époufa, en 1740, N.... *Vincent*, dont :

Jean-Benoît de Berenguier.

Les armes : *d'azur, à 5 pals d'or*; & fur le tout *un petit écuffon, bandé d'argent & de finople de fix pièces*.

BERERD : *d'argent, à deux fafces d'azur; au chef de gueules, chargé d'un lion iffant d'argent*.

BERETTI, Maifon originaire de Pavie. Ceux de ce nom étoient Seigneurs de Frefcarvelo, & ont poffédé le fief qu'on appelle aujourd'hui *la Tour de Beretti*, dans le Territoire de Lomeline; ils ont été nommés tantôt *Beretti*, tantôt *Veretti*, à caufe de la langue efpagnole qui prononce également le *b* par le *v*.

Une branche de cette famille s'établit à Plaifance, & s'y allia avec les meilleures familles de ce pays, tels que font les *Landi*, les *Pallavicini*, les *Anguiciola*, les *Scotti* & autres. Le Marquis de Beretti-Landi, fils de Mutio Beretti, né à Plaifance dans les Etats du Duc de Parme, de l'Académie de *Crufca* de Florence, célèbre parmi les Scavants, mort à Bruxelles au mois d'Octobre 1725, âgé de 74 ans, paffa en 1720, au fervice de Philippe V, Roi d'Efpagne; fut fon Ambaffadeur vers les Cantons Suiffes & Grifons, à la Haye en 1720, & au Congrès de Cambray en 1724. Voyez Moréri fur cette famille.

BEREZAY, près Tréguier en Bretagne : *d'azur, à la lance d'or, la pointe en haut, accoftée de deux épées d'argent, garnies d'or*.

BERGER, Seigneur de Maliffol : *d'azur, au chevron d'or, accompagné de trois têtes de beliers d'argent, posées 2 en chef & 1 en pointe.*

BERGER, famille éteinte, qui portoit d'abord : *d'azur, à deux houlettes d'argent, emmanchées d'or, posées en sautoir, & liées de gueules;* & depuis : *d'azur, au chevron d'or, accompagné en chef de deux étoiles de même, & en pointe d'un mouton paiffant d'argent, langué de gueules, fur une terraffe de finople.*

BERGER, Seigneur de Reffie : *d'azur, à trois fafces d'or, au franc-canton d'hermines.*

BERGER : *d'argent, à trois rofes de gueules, posées 2 & 1, au mufle de léopard de même, en abîme.*

BERGER : *d'or, à trois fafces engrêlées de gueules.*

BERGERAC : *femé de France, parti de gueules, au ferpent aîlé d'or, en pal.*

BERGERET, Seigneur de Frouville : *d'azur, au chevron d'or, accompagné en chef de deux étoiles, & en pointe, d'un mouton paffant fous des rayons fortant de la pointe du chevron, le tout de même.*

BERGERON, Seigneur de la Goupilliere : *d'azur, au lion d'or.*

BERGERONS : *d'or, à trois têtes de lion de fable, lampaffées & couronnées de gueules, posées 2 & 1.*

BERGH DE BETZDORF, dans le Pays de Luxembourg, originaire du Pays de Juliers, qui defcend des Comtes de BERGH du Bas-Rhin.

CHARLES, Baron de BERGH, Brigadier paffé au fervice de France en 1744, époufa *Thérèfe*, baronne de *Bulingen*, dont :

1. CHARLES-EUGÈNE, Baron de Bergh, Brigadier & ci-devant Chambellan de feu Stanislas Roi de Pologne, Duc de Lorraine & de Bar;

2. LOUIS, Baron de Bergh, Colonel par commiffion & Major du Régiment de la Marck, Allemand ;

3. Et JOSÈPHE DE BERGH, mariée au Baron de *Sechvofsfeld*, Brigadier au fervice de France, Colonel-Commandant du Régiment d'Alface.

Les armes: *d'argent à l'aigle éployée de gueules, le bec & les pattes d'azur.*

Tome II.

BERGHE-DE-LIMMINGHE (VANDEN). C'eft, fuivant deux Mémoires que nous avons reçus, une des fept premières familles nobles qui peuplèrent & gouvernèrent la ville de Louvain en 1060.

I. BASTIEN, Comte de *Limminghe*, Gentilhomme Allemand, vint dans ce tems-là, s'établir à Louvain, & eut de N..., fept filles, dont l'aînée *Cunégarde de Limminghe*, fut mariée à ENGELBERT VANDEN BERGHE, qui étoit un des premiers Gentilshommes de cette ville. C'eft ce qui eft prouvé par les meilleurs ouvrages généalogiques & héraldiques du Pays, les archives de cette Maifon, & un diplôme de *Comte* accordé en 1694 à CHARLES VANDEN BERGHE-DE-LIMMINGHE, par CHARLES II, Roi d'Efpagne.

II. LOUIS-WYTTEN VANDEN BERGHE-DE-LIMMINGHE, Chevalier, leur fils, fut Grand-Mayeur de Louvain en 1111, & père de:

1. WAUTHIER, qui fut auffi Grand-Mayeur de Louvain en 1136;

2. Et GODEFROY, qui fuit.

III. GODEFROY VANDEN BERGHE-DE-LIMMINGHE, Ier du nom, eft qualifié, dans une charte de 1146, du titre de *Chevalier*, ainfi que fes enfans, qui furent :

1. GÉRARD, dont la branche s'eft éteinte dans le dernier fiècle ;

2. Et GODEFROY, qui fuit.

IV. GODEFROY VANDEN BERGHE-DE-LIMMINGHE, IIe du nom, nommé avec fon père dans la fufdite charte de 1146, dans laquelle il eft auffi qualifié *Chevalier*, prit *une brifure dans fes armes*, pour fe diftinguer de fon frère aîné, & fut père de :

V. JEAN VANDEN BERGHE-DE-LIMMINGHE, Ier du nom, qui fut fait *Chevalier* en 1214, la veille de la fameufe bataille de Bouvines, & fut auffi père de :

VI. GODEFROY VANDEN BERGHE-DE-LIMMINGHE, IIIe du nom, Chevalier, qui vivoit ès années 1220 & 1257, dont le fils nommé :

VII. ARNOUD VANDEN BERGHE-DE-LIMMINGHE, Chevalier, fe diftingua à la bataille de Wonronck en 1288, & fut père de :

VIII. GODEFROY VANDEN BERGHE-DE-LIMMINGHE, IVe du nom, Chevalier, qui mourut en 1321, & fut inhumé dans l'Eglife des Dominicains de Louvain, laiffant :

IX. GODEFROY VANDEN BERGHE-DE-LIMMINGHE, V^e du nom, Chevalier, qui fe maria, vers 1331, avec *Hermengarde de Heim*, dont:

H h h

X. Jean Vanden Berghe-de-Limminghe, IIᵉ du nom, Chevalier, qui fut premier Bourgmeſre deLouvain ès années 1366, 1367 & 1368, & qui ſe trouve nommé avec ſon père, parmi les *Nobles Vaſſaux* du Brabant, ſous le règne du Duc Jean III. Il avoit épouſé *Catherine Van Raetshoven*, dont il eut :

XI. Godefroy Vanden Berghe-de-Limminghe, VIᵉ du nom, Chevalier, ſecond Bourgmeſtre de Louvain, qui fut tué dans une émeute populaire en cette Ville, en 1379. Il avoit épouſé *Gertrude Van Everweghe*, dont :

   1. Henri, Chevalier, que l'on trouve nommé parmi les *Nobles Vaſſaux* du Brabant ;
   2. Et Godefroy, qui ſuit.

XII. Godefroy Vanden Berghe-de-Limminghe, VIIᵉ du nom, Chevalier, ſervit le Duc Venceslas contre le Peuple de Louvain révolté en 1382, & fut troiſième Bourgmeſtre de cette Ville en 1389. Il avoit été allié avec *Catherine de Vos*, morte en 1409, mère de :

   1. Gilles, Chevalier, qui fut Grand-Mayeur de Louvain en 1411 ;
   2. Et Godefroy, qui ſuit.

XIII. Godefroy Vanden Berghe-de-Limminghe, VIIIᵉ du nom, Chevalier, ſe maria avec *Eliſabeth Van Boucxhorn*, dont :

XIV. Pierre Vanden Berghe-de-Limminghe, Iᵉʳ du nom, Chevalier, mort en 1453, laiſſant de *Mathilde Davits :*

XV. Pierre Vanden Berghe-de-Limminghe, IIᵉ du nom, Chevalier, qui épouſa 1° *Marie Vanden Brughen*, de laquelle on ignore s'il a laiſſé poſtérité ; & 2° *Hélène de Hondt*, dont il eut :

XVI. Augustin Vanden Berghe-de-Limminghe, Chevalier, qui fut pluſieurs fois Echevin de la ville de Louvain, où il mourut le 26 Janvier 1533. Il fut inhumé dans l'Egliſe du Prieuré de Saint-Martin de la même Ville, & à côté de lui *Gertrude de Savernéel*, dite *Waër-Segger*, ſa veuve, morte le 16 Septembre 1545. De ce mariage vint :

XVII. Daniel Vanden Berghe-de-Limminghe, Chevalier, Conſeiller du Conſeil de Flandre, mort le 22 Février 1554, qui s'étoit allié avec *Marie de la Tour-Taxis*, morte le 26 Avril 1601, fille de *Jean-Baptiſte de la Tour-Taxis*, Chevalier, Grand-Maître des Poſtes de l'Empire, & de *Chriſtine de Wachtendonck*. De ce mariage vinrent :

   1. Jean-Baptiste, qui ſuit ;
   2. & 3. Et deux filles, Chanoineſſes au Chapitre d'Andennes en 1578.

XVIII. Jean-Baptiste Vanden Berghe-de-Limminghe, Chevalier, Préſident en la Chambre dès Comptes de Bruxelles, mourut le 4 Novembre 1623. Il avoit épouſé *Anne Baërt-de-Béérentrode*, morte avant lui le 10 Mars 1618, fille de *Nicolas Baërt-de-Béérentrode*, Conſeiller & Receveur-Général des Domaines & Finances de S. M. aux Pays-Bas, & d'*Anne Vanden Heetveld*, dont il laiſſa :

   1. Lamoral, qui ſuit ;
   2. Marguerite, femme de *Georges*, Baron de *Gourcy*, Chevalier, Seigneur dudit lieu, de la branche de *Longuyon*, dont deſcendent les Barons de *Gourcy*, de *Villette* & *Colmey*, & la Comteſſe de Saint-Felix ;
   3. Et Jeanne, épouſe de *Pierre de la Maëda*, Chevalier, Seigneur de Beſquinar.

XIX. Lamoral Vanden Berghe-de-Limminghe, Chevalier, Seigneur de Piéterbais, qui fut pluſieurs fois Echevin & Tréſorier de la ville d'Anvers. Il laiſſa de *Catherine de la Tour-Taxis*, fille de *Charles de la Tour-Taxis*, Chevalier, & de *Catherine de Siéclers :*

   1. Charles, Iᵉʳ du nom, qui laiſſa de *Marguerite de Fourneau-Bajenrieu*, deux fils, morts ſans alliance ;
   2. Lamoral-François, qui ſuit ;
   3. Et Marie-Florence, qui fut la ſeconde femme de *Claude-Philippe de Namur*, Vicomte d'Elzée.

XX. Lamoral-François Vanden Berghe-de-Limminghe, Chevalier, Seigneur de Grez, Piéterbais, Nieuw, Capelle, &c., fut Préſident de la Chambre dès Comptes de Brabant, & ceſſa de porter *la briſure à ſes armes*, à l'extinction de la branche aînée. Il épouſa *Marie-Barbe de Warick*, fille de *Nicolas de Warick*, Chevalier & Vicomte de Bruxelles, Colonel d'Infanterie au ſervice d'Eſpagne, Membre du Conſeil de Guerre, & Margrave de la ville d'Anvers, & d'*Anne-Marie Micault*, Dame de Huyſingue, Buyſinghe & Tourneppe, dont :

   1. Charles, qui ſuit ;
   2. Corneille-François-Joseph, dont la poſtérité ſera rapportée ci-après ;
   3. Norbert, Chevalier, mort ſans hoirs;
   4. Gertrude-Rogère, Chanoineſſe de Mouſtier-ſur-Sambre, qui fut mariée à ſon couſin iſſu de germain, *Philippe-Adrien de*

Warick, Baron de Liberfart, & Vicomte de Bruxelles ;

5. & 6. JEANNE & MARIE, mortes fans alliance.

XXI. CHARLES VANDEN BERGHE-DE-LIMMIN-GHE, II° du nom, Chevalier, Seigneur de Grez, Piéterbais, Nieuw, Capelle, &c., élevé à la dignité de *Comte de Limminghe*, par Lettres-Patentes de CHARLES II, Roi d'Efpagne, du 7 Juillet 1694, mourut à Bruxelles le 30 Novembre 1756, âgé de 96 ans, 7 mois & 18 jours. Il avoit fervi ce Monarque, d'abord en qualité de Cornette dans un Régiment de Cuiraffiers-Allemand, avec lequel il fe diftingua à la bataille de Caftiau en 1676 ; a été fait Sergent-Major, puis Meftre-de-Camp-Général, enfuite Bourgmeftre de Bruxelles, & depuis élu Membre & Député des Etats Nobles du Duché de Brabant, au fervice de l'Augufte Maifon d'AUTRICHE. Il avoit épousé 1° *Anne-Ifabelle Araȝola-d'Ognate*, fille de *Jean Araȝola-d'Ognate*, Chevalier, & d'*Anne-Ifabelle des Cordes*, dite *de Rénialmé* ; & 2° *Jeanne-Thérèfe-Jofèphe de Maffiet*, fille de *Philippe-François de Maffiet*, Chevalier, Seigneur de Beaufart, Lieutenant-Colonel de Cavalerie, & d'*Agnès-Chriftine Van Pulle*.

Du premier lit vinrent :

1. CHARLES-JOSEPH, Chevalier, mort fans poftérité le 9 Août 1744, marié avec fa coufine germaine *N... Araȝola d'Ognate ;*
2. FRANÇOIS-JOSEPH, appelé le *Comte de Limminghe*, Maréchal des Camps & Armées du Roi d'Efpagne, Capitaine de Grenadiers aux Gardes Wallones, Gouverneur & Corrégidor de la ville de Jacca au Royaume d'Aragon, qui fe maria en Efpagne avec *Eléonore O Brien-Onolorgais*, dont il eut :

    PHILIPPINE-CHARLOTTE VANDEN BERGHE-DE-LIMMINGHE, laquelle eft aujourd'hui veuve fans enfans de *Charles*, Comte d'*Albert-Vallangien*, Seigneur d'Ayen, Baron de Noirmont, Comte de Dijon-le-Mont, Chevalier de l'Ordre de Marie-Thérèfe, Général & Colonel propriétaire d'un Régiment de fon nom, Chambellan de Leurs Majeftés Imp. & Royales, & Membre de l'Etat Noble du Duché de Brabant.
3. GUILLAUME-FRANÇOIS-JOSEPH, Chevalier, Seigneur & Comte de Grez, qui fut Echevin de la ville de Bruxelles ès années 1737 & 1744, & eft mort fans alliance au mois de Juin 1769 ;
4. PHILIPPE-CHARLES-LAMORAL, mort Chanoi-

ne du Chapitre de Saint-Pierre à Andrelecht ;

5. MARIE-BARBE, mortė fans enfans en 1750. Elle avoit été mariée 1° à *Jean-Ferdinand*, Comte de *Noftitȝ* & de l'Empire, Chambellan de l'Empereur CHARLES VI ; 2° à *Ferdinand*, Comte de *Noftitȝ* & de l'Empire, coufin germain du fufdit ; & 3° à *N......* Baron de *Kerpen ;*
6. Et CATHERINE-AUGUSTINE-JOSÈPHE, mariée à *Jean-Guillaume-Anne*, Baron de *Waës* & du Saint-Empire, libre Seigneur de Kefenich, dont : *Anne-Salomée-Jofèphe de Waës*, troifième femme, par contrat du 19 Mai 1756, de *Louis-Gabriel des Acres*, Marquis de l'Aigle, Lieutenant-Général des Armées du Roi de France, &c.

Et du fecond lit font nés :

7. PHILIPPE-JOSEPH, qui fuit ;
8. ANNE-PHILIPPINE, femme de *Pierre-Eugène de Fiufco-de-Mataloni*, Chevalier, Seigneur du Sart, dont plufieurs enfans ;
9. Et JUSTINE-NORBERTINE, d'abord Chanoineffe à Andennes dans le Comté de Namur, & depuis mariée à *Louis-Bonaventure de Marbais*, Ecuyer, Seigneur d'Hoves.

XXII. PHILIPPE-JOSEPH VANDEN BERGHE-DE-LIMMINGHE, Chevalier, Comte de Limminghe, Seigneur de Limmelette, &c., ci-devant Capitaine de Cavalerie au fervice de France, puis Echevin de la ville de Louvain, a épousé *Françoife-Caroline-Jofèphe d'Utekem* (dont les armes : *d'argent, à la bande de gueules, chargée de 3 maillets d'or*), fille & troifième enfant de *Charles-Guislain d'Utekem*, Chevalier, Grand-Foreftier de Brabant, Seigneur d'Orbais, de Limmelette & de *Gentinnes*, en faveur duquel cette dernière Terre fut érigée en *Baronie* par Diplôme de l'Empereur CHARLES VI, du 4 Mai 1716, & d'*Anne-Françoife*, libre Baronne de *Nicolartȝ*, dont il a :

1. EUGÈNE-FRANÇOIS-*de-Paule*, Chevalier ;
2. ELÉONORE-CHARLOTTE, Chanoineffe à Mouftier-fur-Sambre ;
3. Et JUSTINE-CHARLOTTE, auffi Chanoineffe au même Monaftère.

SECONDE BRANCHE.

XXI. CORNEILLE-FRANÇOIS-JOSEPH VANDEN BERGHE-DE-LIMMINGHE, Chevalier, fecond fils de LAMORAL-FRANÇOIS, & de *Marie-Barbe de Warick*, fe maria avec *Anne-Marie Vanden Wervé*, fille unique & héritière de *Henri Vanden Werve*, Chevalier, Seigneur de Weftkercke & de Spirenbrock, & d'*Adrienne* de *Rawenſway*, dont pluſieurs enfans, tous morts ſans alliance, excepté le fils aîné :

XXII. Henri Vanden Berghe-de-Limminghe, Chevalier, qui s'eſt marié 1° ſans enfans avec *Françoiſe-Alexandrine-Marquiſe Paſcal*, fille de *François Paſcal*, Gouverneur de Bruxelles ; & 2° avec *N.....Araʐola d'Ognate* (nièce d'*Anne-Iſabelle*, première femme du Comte de Limminghe, ſon oncle), dont il a un fils.

Les armes : *d'or, à 3 pals d'aʐur, au chef de gueules* ; & par un privilège unique dans les Pays-Bas, *leſdites armes, ſurmontées d'une couronne de Comte*, ſont poſées dans une *draperie en forme de pavillon antique, de couleur rouge.* Supports : 2 *lions léopardés d'or, tenant chacun une bannière, celui à dextre aux armes de la maiſon, & celui à ſeneſtre*, d'argent, à la croix de gueules, *en mémoire des croiſades, ſous* Godefroy de Bouillon, *où pluſieurs de cetteMaiſon ſe ſont diſtingués.* ·

BERGHES, ancienne & illuſtre Maiſon qui tire ſon origine en ligne directe de *Jean*, Sire de Glymes, fils naturel de Jean II, Duc de Lorraine inférieure & de Brabant, légitimé par l'Empereur Louis de Bavière, le 27 Août 1344. Le Prince de Berghes, qui étoit Capitaine Général de la Province de Hainaut, & Gouverneur de la ville de Mons, la défendit contre les François en 1691.

Les Seigneurs de Cohen ſont ſortis de la Maiſon de Berghes.

Jean de Berghes, Seigneur de Cohen, &c., fut Grand-Veneur de France, le 2 Juin 1418, commanda les troupes qui allèrent mettre le ſiège devant Montlhéry, en 1418, & fut depuis Gouverneur de la ville d'Abbeville.

Jean-Joseph, Vicomte de Berghes, Seigneur d'Elgheſſent, chef de cette Maiſon, épouſa, 1° le 24 Avril 1715, *Marie-Joſèphe-Iſabelle de Berghes*, Princeſſe de Rache ; & 2° *N... de Créquy-Canaples.* Il eut du premier lit :

1. Philippe-Charles-Joseph de Berghes, Comte de Rache, né le 31 Mars 1716 ;
2. Maximilien-François-Joseph de Berghes, Baron de Zetrud, puis Prince de Rache, né le 19 Novembre 1719, marié, en 1741, ſans enfans, à *Andrée-Armande de Monchy-Senarpont*, fille de *Nicolas*, Marquis de Senarpont ;
3. Eugène-Louis-Joseph de Berghes, né le 24 Janvier 1724 ;

4. Philippe-Pierre-Joseph de Berghes, né le 29 Août 1725 ;
5. Marie-Andrée-Josèphe, née le 18 Février 1718, Chanoineſſe de Maubeuge, puis mariée, en 1734, à *Louis-Albert-François-Joſeph*, Comte de *Houchin*, Seigneur de Hautbourdin, Longaſtre, &c. ;
6. Marie-Françoise-Eugénie-Josèphe, dite *Mademoiſelle de Rache*, née le 24 Décembre 1720, Chanoineſſe à Maubeuge ;
7. Marie-Albertine-Josèphe, née le 14 Novembre 1726 ;
8. Et Ernestine-Françoise-Josèphe, née le 15 Avril 1729, morte ſans enfans. Elle avoit épouſé, en 1746, *Ignace-François Vander Linden*, Baron d'Hooghevorſt.

SECONDE BRANCHE,
iſſue de la précédente.

N... de Berghes-Saint-Winock a eu pour enfans :

1. N... qui ſuit ;
2. N... marié ;
3. N... de Berghes, ancien Officier d'Infanterie, marié, à Toulon, à N... *de Chabert*, fille de N... *de Chabert*, Lieutenant de Vaiſſeaux du Roi, & de *Charlotte de Pontevès*, de la famille des Marquis de *Gien.* Ils ont deux fils ;
4. Et N.... de Berghes, Chanoineſſe à Maubeuge.

N... de Berghes-Saint-Winock, Vicomte d'Arleux, mourut au mois d'Avril 1757. Il avoit épouſé, au mois d'Octobre 1738, *Marie-Françoiſe de Carnin de Lillers*, dont il eut :

1. Adrien-Joseph-Ghislain, qui ſuit ;
2. François-Désiré-Marc-Ghislain ;
3. Et N... de Berghes, dite *Mademoiſelle de Berghes-Saint-Winock*, Chanoineſſe de Maubeuge.

Adrien-Joseph-Ghislain de Berghes-Saint-Winock, né en 1740, Vicomte & Prince de Berghes-Saint-Winock, Cornette au Régiment d'Eſcouloubre, Cavalerie, mourut en 1773. Il avoit épouſé, par contrat du 13 Juillet 1768, *Marie-Thérèſe-Joſèphe de Caſtellane*, fille de *Gaſpard*, Vicomte de Caſtellane. Il a laiſſé :

Une fille en bas âge.

Les armes : *d'or, au lion de gueules, armé & lampaſſé d'aʐur.*

BERGIS, près Tréguier, en Bretagne : *d'argent, à trois quinte-feuilles de gueules, au franc-canton de même, chargé d'un lion d'argent.*

BERI : *de sinople, à trois macles d'argent, posés 2 & 1.*

BERIEN, en Bretagne : *d'argent, à trois jumelles de gueules, au franc-canton d'or, chargé d'un lion de sable.*

BERINGEL. Les Seigneurs de ce nom, Comtes de Prado, Marquis d'Asmidas, sortis des Seigneurs de Sousa, par bâtardise, ont pour auteur *Pierre-Alphonse de Sousa,* fils aîné d'*Alphonse-Denis,* fils aîné du Roi de Portugal ALPHONSE III. *Antoine de Sousa,* IIIe du nom, septième Comte de Prado, servit en Castille, en Aragon & en Catalogne, dans l'armée Portugaise, sous tous les ordres de son ayeul, & mourut en 1722.

Les armes : *écartelé de* Portugal *& de* Léon.

BERINGHEN. PIERRE DE BERINGHEN, natif du Duché de Gueldre, aux Pays-Bas, Seigneur d'Armainvilliers & de Grez, fut premier Valet-de-Chambre du Roi HENRI IV, & employé par ce Prince en d'importantes négociations auprès des Princes d'Allemagne. Il épousa, en 1646, *Madeleine de Bumo,* dont il eut :

HENRI DE BERINGHEN, Seigneur d'Armainvilliers & de Grez, fait premier Ecuyer de la Petite-Ecurie du Roi, le 10 Août 1645, & depuis Gouverneur des Citadelles de Marseille. Il mourut à Paris en 1692, âgé de 89 ans, & est enterré dans la Chapelle de l'Eglise des Feuillans, rue Saint-Honoré. Il avoit épousé, en 1646, *Anne du Blé,* fille de *Jacques,* Marquis d'Uxelles, & de *Claude Phélypeaux,* & laissa :

1. HENRI DE BERINGHEN, reçu en la survivance de la charge de premier Ecuyer de la Petite-Ecurie du Roi, Colonel d'Infanterie du Régiment Dauphin, tué à Besançon, le 18 Mai 1674;
2. JACQUES-LOUIS, qui suit;
3. JACQUES-BALTHASARD, mort jeune, le 4 Mai 1667;
4. ANNE, Abbesse de Farmoutier, en Brie, en 1685;
5. CLAIRE-MARIE, aussi Religieuse à la même Abbaye;
6. Et FRANÇOISE.

JACQUES-LOUIS DE BERINGHEN, Comte de Châteauneuf & du Plessis-Bertrand, Seigneur d'Armainvilliers, Chevalier des Ordres du Roi, premier Ecuyer de Sa Majesté, & Gouverneur des Citadelles de Marseille, fit ses ca-

ravanes à Malte; & lors de la mort de son frère aîné, tué devant Besançon, à la tête du Régiment Dauphin, il quitta l'Ordre, & le feu Roi lui donna un Régiment de Cavalerie, puis le Guidon des Gendarmes de Bourgogne. Il mourut le 1er Mai 1723. Il avoit épousé, le 14 Octobre 1677, *Marie-Madeleine-Elisabeth-Fare d'Aumont,* morte le 18 Octobre 1728, âgée de 66 ans, fille aînée de *Louis,* Duc d'Aumont, Pair de France, & de *Madeleine-Fare le Tellier.* Il eut :

1. JACQUES-LOUIS DE BERINGHEN, Marquis de Châteauneuf, Comte du Plessis-Bertrand d'Armainvilliers, premier Ecuyer du Roi, Maréchal de ses Camps & Armées, Gouverneur des Citadelle & Fort Saint-Jean de Marseille, mort le 1er Novembre 1723, âgé de 43 ans. Il avoit épousé, le 9 Février 1708, *Marie-Louise-Henriette de Beaumanoir,* née le 1er Février 1690, morte le 15 Décembre 1755, & enterrée aux Feuillans de la rue Saint-Honoré, fille d'*Henri-Charles de Beaumanoir,* Marquis de Lavardin, Chevalier des Ordres du Roi, & de *Louise-Anne de Noailles,* sa seconde femme. Il en eut :

   MARIE-LOUISE-NICOLE, née le 13 Novembre 1708, Religieuse en 1731, à Farmoutier, Diocèse de Meaux;

2. FRANÇOIS-CHARLES DE BERINGHEN, Evêque du Puy, Abbé de Sainte-Croix de Bordeaux, Prevôt de Pignans, en Provence, Abbé de Saint-Gilles dans l'Evêché de Nîmes. Il est mort dans son Diocèse, le 17 Octobre 1742, dans la 51e année de son âge;
3. HENRI-CAMILLE, qui suit;
4. ANNE-MARIE-MADELEINE, Abbesse du Pré;
5. LOUISE-CHARLOTTE-EUGÉNIE, Religieuse, puis Abbesse de Farmoutier, morte;
6. ANNE-BÉNIGNE-FARE-THÉRÈSE, morte à Paris, le 26 Septembre 1749, âgée de 67 ans. Elle avoit épousé, le 11 Juillet 1701, *Emmanuel-Armand,* Marquis de *Vassé,* Brigadier des Armées du Roi, dont elle resta veuve en 1710.
7. OLYMPE-FÉLICITÉ, Religieuse, puis Abbesse de Farmoutier, morte à Paris à l'Hôtel de Beringhen, le 10 Août 1743. Elle avoit été obligée, par Lettres de Cachet, de quitter son Couvent, à cause de son appel de la Constitution;
8. MARIE-LOUISE, morte dans sa Terre, près d'Orléans, le 23 Juillet 1746, âgée de 50 ans, mariée, en 1713, à *Guillaume-Alexandre,* Marquis de *Vieux-Pont* & de *Sencée,* en Bourgogne, Lieutenant-Général des Armées du Roi, Lieutenant pour Sa Ma-

jeſté au pays d'Aunis, & Gouverneur de Charlemont, mort ſans enfans en 1728;

9. Et LYDIE, morte le 6 Septembre 1730, dans ſa 26ᵉ année. Elle avoit épouſé, le 22 Novembre 1722, *Hubert de Courtarvel*, Marquis de Pezé, Gouverneur des Châteaux de la Muette & de Madrid, & des Villes & Châteaux de Rennes; Meſtre-de-Camp, Lieutenant-Inſpecteur du Régiment du Roi, Infanterie, Brigadier de ſes Armées, puis Maréchal-de-Camp, le 24 Avril 1727. Il eut la charge de Maréchal-Général des Logis de l'Armée en Italie, pendant les Campagnes des années 1733 & 1734; ſe diſtingua à la bataille donnée ſous les murs de Parme, le 29 Juin 1734, où il eut deux chevaux tués ſous lui, fut fait Lieutenant-Général le 1ᵉʳ Août 1734. Il reçut un coup de fuſil au travers du corps, & un autre dans le bras droit, à la bataille de Guaſtalla en Italie, le 19 Septembre 1734, & le Roi le nomma, le 27 du même mois, Chevalier de ſes Ordres, pour le premier Chapitre qu'il tiendroit; & il mourut de ſes bleſſures à Guaſtalla, le 23 Novembre 1734, âgé de 52 ans, laiſſant deux filles mineures, dont une morte en 1736.

HENRI-CAMILLE, Marquis de BERINGHEN, d'Uxelles, Comte du Pleſſis-Bertrand, Baron de Tenare & d'Orme, Seigneur d'Ivry, de Buſſy, de Monthelie & d'Armainvilliers, en Brie, premier Ecuyer du Roi, le 7 Février 1724, Lieutenant-Général au Gouvernement de Bourgogne, & Gouverneur des Ville & Citadelle de Châlons-ſur-Saône, Chevalier des Ordres du Roi, de la promotion de 1731, ci-devant Meſtre-de-Camp d'un Régiment de Cavalerie de ſon nom, & auparavant Chevalier non Profès de l'Ordre de Malte, & Commandeur de Piéton, eſt né le 1ᵉʳ Août 1693. Le Roi lui donna, le 20 Décembre 1734, le Gouvernement des Châteaux de la Muette & de Madrid, & la Capitainerie des Chaſſes du Bois de Boulogne, vacante par la mort du Marquis de Pezé, ſon beau-frère. Il mourut en Février 1770, ſans poſtérité. Il avoit épouſé, le 20 Mars 1743, *Angélique-Sophie d'Hautefort*, née le 22 Septembre 1702, mariée, 1° le 12 Novembre 1730, à *Jean-Luc de Lauzières*, Marquis de Themines en Quercy, Meſtre-de-Camp de Cavalerie, & Gentilhomme ordinaire de la Chambre de feu M. le Duc d'Orléans, mort ſans enfans. Elle étoit fille puînée de *Louis-Charles d'Hautefort*, Marquis de Surville, Lieutenant-Général des

Armées du Roi, & *d'Anne-Louiſe de Crévant-Humières*.

Les armes : *d'argent, à trois pals de gueules, au chef d'azur, chargé de deux quintefeuilles d'argent.*

• BERKELEY, petite ville d'Angleterre du Comté de Gloceſter, qui a donné ſon nom à l'ancienne & noble famille *de Fitz-Hording*, ſous le règne de HENRI II, laquelle deſcendoit de *Robert Fitz-Hording*, qui étoit du Sang Royal des Danois.

Ce fut dans le Château de Berkeley que le Roi EDOUARD II fut inhumainement tué après avoir abdiqué la Couronne.

GUILLAUME, Lord BERKELEY, deſcendu de MAWBRAY, fut fait en 1482, par RICHARD III, Vicomte de Berkeley, peu après Comte de Nottingham & Grand-Maréchal d'Angleterre, & enfin Marquis de Berkeley, par HENRI VII. Etant mort ſans enfans, ſes titres finirent avec lui, à la réſerve de celui de *Lord Berkeley*, qui fut conſervé dans la ligne collatérale.

GEORGES DE BERKELEY, petit-fils de HENRI, épouſa *Eliſabeth*, ſeconde fille de *Michel Stanhope*. Il en eut :

JACQUES, noyé en paſſant à Dieppe en 1640;
GEORGES, qui ſuit;
Et une fille.

GEORGES DE BERKELEY fut créé par CHARLES II, en 1649, Vicomte de Durſclei & Comte de Berkeley. Il épouſa *Eliſabeth*, fille aînée de *Jean Maſſenberg*, Marchand de Londres, Membre de la Compagnie des Indes Orientales, de laquelle il a eu pluſieurs fils & filles.

L'aîné de ſes fils, Lord DURSCLEI, fut employé pendant la vie de ſon père, en qualité d'Ambaſſadeur auprès des Provinces-Unies, & a été depuis Lord-Juſticier d'Irlande.

JEAN BERKELEY, Baron du Royaume d'Angleterre, envoyé Ambaſſadeur en France, mourut à Londres en 1668, laiſſant entr'autres enfans :

JEAN, qui fut pendant quelque tems Amiral de la Flotte d'Angleterre dans la Manche. Voyez, ſur cette ancienne & illuſtre Maiſon d'Angleterre, Imhoff & le *Dictionnaire anglois*.

Les armes : *de gueules, avec un chevron & dix pals, traverſés d'argent.*

BERLE, famille originaire de Flandre,

établie en Champagne dès le XVe siècle, où elle poffédoit plufieurs Terres & Fiefs. Quoique ce nom foit ancien dans l'ordre de la Nobleffe, nous ne pouvons remonter, faute de *Mémoire*, qu'à:

ENARD DE BERLE, Seigneur de Guignicourt-fur-Venze, marié, avant 1499, avec *Jacqueline de Savigny*, dont il eut:

1. GARLACHE, qui fuit;
2. Et JEAN, marié avec *Marguerite de Mailly*.

GARLACHE DE BERLE, Seigneur de Guignicourt, rendit, en 1533, foi & hommage de cette Terre à l'Evêque de Conferans. Il eut entr'autres enfans, de fa femme, dont on ignore le nom:

1. ODET ou ODART, qui fuit;
2. Et FERRI, qui, le 20 Juillet 1550, étant homme d'armes dans la Compagnie de M. de la Marck, Seigneur de Jametz, paffa en revue au *Chêne-le-Pouilleux*. Voyez le *Dépôt des titres de la Bibliothèque du Roi*. Vol. de 1548 & de 1551.

ODET ou ODART DE BERLE, Seigneur de Guignicourt, homme d'armes dans la Compagnie du Duc de Bouillon, partagea, le 17 Novembre 1543, la fucceffion de fes père & mère avec fes frères & fœurs, & eut de *Louife d'Adeline*:

RENÉ DE BERLE, Seigneur de Guignicourt, qui fervit d'abord dans les Compagnies d'Ordonnances, & paffa enfuite dans l'Infanterie. Il époufa, le 3 Février 1608, *Louife de Fautrey*, dont:

1. FRANÇOIS, mort jeune;
2. NICOLAS, mort fans poftérité;
3. ANTOINE, qui fuit;
4. Et CLAUDE, marié avec *Gabrielle de Saulx*, dont il eut plufieurs enfans, entr'autres un fils, qui fut tige de la branche de BERLE-TRIEFRAIN.

ANTOINE DE BERLE, Seigneur de Maffrecourt, Gendarme dans la Compagnie du Cardinal Mazarin, fuivant fes certificats de fervices du 8 Juillet 1663, laiffa d'*Elifabeth de Fourault*, entr'autres enfans:

HENRI DE BERLE, Seigneur de Maffrecourt, Capitaine au Régiment de la Marine, qui ne fe maria, que dans un âge avancé, en 1731, avec *Elifabeth de Maillet*, fille de *Claude*, Seigneur des Planches, & de *N..... Hocalt*, dont:

1. LOUIS, Capitaine au Régiment Royal de Vaiffeaux, mort fans alliance en Bretagne

en 1759, après s'être trouvé à l'affaire de Saint-Caft;
2. CLAUDE, qui fuit;
3. Et ELISABETH, Dame des Planches, Moivres & Saint-Hilaire, mariée avec *Adam-Claude d'Origny-d'Agny*, Seigneur de Braux, Saint-Lottin, des Planches, &c., Capitaine au Régiment de Champagne.

CLAUDE DE BERLE, Seigneur de Maffrecourt, après avoir fervi dans le Régiment de Bourbon, a époufé *Etienne-Marie-Toinette Troquet-de-Blémy*, dont des enfans.

Les armes: *d'azur, au fautoir d'or, accompagné de quatre lionceaux de même, armés & lampaffés de gueules*.

BERLEGHEM, Terre & Seigneurie en Flandre, érigée en *Baronie*, par Lettres du Roi d'Efpagne du 27 Juillet 1682, en faveur de *Lopez-Rodrigue Devora & Vega*, Chevalier de l'Ordre Militaire de Saint-Jacques.

BERLETTE, en Normandie: *gironné d'argent & de gueules de fept pièces*.

BERLI, en Normandie: *d'azur, au chef d'or, au bâton de gueules, brochant fur le tout*.

BERLIÈRE (LA). Terres & Seigneurie, érigée en *Baronie* par Lettres du Roi Catholique du... 1664, en faveur de *Jacques d'Ennetière*, Préfident en la Chambre des Comptes, Confeiller d'Etat, & Tréforier-Général des Domaines & Finances des Pays-Bas.

BERLIET: *d'or, à trois pals de gueules; au chef d'azur, chargé d'un croiffant d'argent*.

BERLO: *écartelé, aux 1 & 4 d'or, à cinq burelles de gueules; aux 2 & 3 d'argent, au lion de gueules; & fur le tout, d'or, à deux fafces de gueules*.

BERMAN. HANUS DE BERMAN, IIIe du nom, Seigneur du Zémain & d'Ifché en partie, acquit, fur la fin du XVIe fiècle, la Baronie de Lanques. Il avoit époufé 1º *Jeanne le Galland*, Dame de la Grange, d'Acraigne & de Pulligny; & 2º par contrat du 1er Janvier 1587, *Thècle de Choifeul*, fille de *Nicolas*, Seigneur d'Ifché, Chevalier de l'Ordre du Roi & de *Renée de Lutzelbourg* dite de *Luxembourg*, Dame d'Offroicourt. Il eut du premier lit:

1. FRANÇOISE DE BERMAN, mariée à *Simon de Pouilly*, Marquis d'Efme, Comte de Loupy-aux-deux-Châteaux, Baron de Mononville,

Confeiller d'Etat, Maréchal de Lorraine, & Gouverneur de Stenay.

Du fecond mariage vint :

2. Et LOUIS-CLAUDE, qui fuit.

LOUIS-CLAUDE DE BERMAN, Baron de Lanques, Seigneur du Zémain & d'Offroicourt, marié, en 1621, à *Elifabeth de Serocourt,* fille de *Richard,* Seigneur de Romain, Gouverneur de la Motte, & de *Marguerite de Tavigny,* fa première femme. Il eut :

N... DE BERMAN, Baronne de Planques, Dame d'Offroicourt, mariée à *Claude-Godefroy de Chandon-de-Briaille,* Seigneur de Briaille. (*Tabl. généal.,* part. VIII, p. 359.)

BERMAND, en Champagne: *d'or, à un ours de fable debout, portant fur fes pattes une hache d'armes, le manche arrondi d'argent.*

BERMENT ou BERMEN. Cette famille noble & ancienne, qu'on croit originaire d'Ecoffe, & qui s'eft établie à la Ferté-Vidame en Normandie, vers la fin du XIVe fiècle, a été maintenue dans *la Nobleffe de fes ancêtres,* par Arrêt du Confeil d'Etat du Roi, tenu à Paris le 1er Septembre 1667, & par Meffieurs les Intendans d'Orléans, d'Alençon & du Canada ; & enregiftrée *comme Noble* dans plufieurs Elections.

I. LAURENT DE BERMENT, Ier du nom, le plus ancien dont la filiation foit prouvée par titres, Ecuyer, Seigneur de Grainville, Infreville, & du Chefne-aux-Dames, né en 1494, mourut en 1576. Sa fœur MADELEINE DE BERMENT, mariée à *Georges du Fay,* Ecuyer en 1540, figna à fon contrat de mariage paffé devant *Martin Cambert & Thomas Gillet,* Tabellions de la Vicomté de Caudebec, le 22 Novembre 1548, avec *Jeanne Martin,* fille de noble *Jean Martin,* Ecuyer, dont il eut :

II. LAURENT DE BERMENT, IIe du nom, Ecuyer, Seigneur de Grainville, d'Infreville & du Chefne-aux-Dames, né en 1549, qui mourut en 1615. Il avoit époufé, le 15 Décembre 1585, *Marie de Pivain,* & laiffa :

1. LAURENT, IIIe du nom, Ecuyer, Seigneur du Chefne-aux-Dames, mort fans poftérité en 1647 ;
2. JEAN, qui fuit ;
3. Et LOUIS, auteur de la troifième branche rapportée ci-après.

LAURENT DE BERMENT, IIe du nom, avoit encore pour frères ou coufins, vivant en même tems que lui :

1. HANUS DE BERMENT, Ecuyer, Seigneur du Zémain. Voyez BERMAN ;
2. Et JACQUES DE BERMENT, Ecuyer, Seigneur de Condat, qui s'allia, le 3 Octobre 1587, avec *Jacqueline de Montmorin-Saint-Herem,* dont on ignore la poftérité, & remariée, le 3 Juillet 1594, à *Chriftophe de Bunlieu,* Seigneur de Jernière.

III. JEAN DE BERMENT, Ier du nom, Ecuyer, Seigneur de Grainville, d'Infreville, du Chefne-aux-Dames & de la Vallée, né en 1591, l'un des 200 Chevaux-Légers de la Garde ordinaire du Roi, où. il fut tué, fous LOUIS XIII, après 35 ans de fervice. Il avoit époufé, le 14 Mars 1618, *Anne Larcher,* fille de *Nicolas Larcher,* Ecuyer, Seigneur de Barzanne, & laiffa :

1. LOUIS, Ecuyer, né en 1620, & mort en 1693. Il fut Prêtre Religieux de l'Ordre de Saint-Auguftin, & Prieur de l'Amblore & de la Ferté-Vidame, au Diocèfe de Chartres ;
2. JEAN, qui fuit ;
3. Et CHARLES, Ecuyer, Seigneur d'Infreville, né en 1624, qui fervit le Roi dans fes Armées. Il reçut plufieurs bleffures à la bataille de Senef, le 11 Août 1674; fut premier Maréchal des Logis de la Compagnie des Chevaux-Légers de la Garde ordinaire du Roi, Meftre-de-Camp de Cavalerie le 12 Avril 1692 ; Chevalier de l'Ordre Militaire de Saint-Louis le 20 Février 1700, & mourut le 9 Mars 1704. Il avoit époufé, par contrat paffé devant *Antoine Dufay,* Tabellion du Comté de Senonches, le 12 Mai 1679, *Elifabeth Courtin,* dont :

MARIE-ELISABETH DE BERMENT, née en 1680, & morte en bas âge.

Et LÉON DE BERMENT, Ecuyer, Seigneur d'Infreville, né en 1681, Chevalier de l'Ordre Militaire de Saint-Louis, le 2 Janvier 1718 ; Maréchal des Logis de la Compagnie des Chevaux-Légers de la Garde ordinaire du Roi, & Meftre-de-Camp de Cavalerie, le 18 Avril 1735, qui a fervi dans ce corps depuis 1704 jufqu'en 1736. Il eft mort le 9 Mars 1744, fans poftérité. Il avoit époufé, en vertu d'une difpenfe de la Cour de Rome du 18 Juin 1732, & par contrat paffé devant *Jean Vigneron,* Notaire au Bailliage de Chartres, le 24 Septembre fuivant, *Marguerite Courtin,* fa coufine germaine maternelle.

IV. JEAN DE BERMENT, IIe du nom, Seigneur de la Martinière, né le 16 Février 1621, à la Ferté-Vidame, mourut à Paris le 15 Novem-

bre 1700, & fut inhumé en l'Eglife Paroiffiale de Saint-Euftache. Il avoit fervi d'abord
en qualité de Cadet au Régiment des Gardes-Françoifes, puis en celle de Cornette de
la Meftre-de-Camp de celui de Gefvres-Cavalerie, dont il fut fait Capitaine le 13 Février 1648 ; fut fait Exempt des Gardes-du-
Corps du Roi, le 8 Mars 1649, & honoré le
21 Novembre 1651, d'un Brevet de Maréchal de Bataille en fes Armées, en récompenfe de fes actions de valeur en différentes occafions. Suivant 1° un certificat du Duc de
Saint-Simon, Gouverneur de Blaye, ce Seigneur dit que JEAN DE BERMENT *étoit en garnifon à Blaye en 1642, où il portoit les armes pour le fervice du Roi, & que fes premiers exercices dans les Armées ont toujours été accompagnés de zèle & de courage, &c.* 2° Un autre certificat du Maréchal-
Duc d'*Aumont* : ce Seigneur le reconnoît pour
*un homme de cœur & très-affectionné au
fervice du Roi ; qu'il l'a vu dans une occafion importante, donner des preuves de fon
courage & de fa valeur à la bataille des*
Montagnes-Noires de Fribourg & de Brifach
en 1644, *où la chaleur du combat l'ayant
jeté bien avant entre les ennemis, il prit
un Etendart du Régiment de* Gafpard Mer-
ci, *& fe retira glorieux, chargé des dé-
pouilles des ennemis ; & que l'année fuivante* 1645, étant lors Cornette de la Meftre-de-
Camp du Régiment de Gefvres, *il l'a vu en
Allemagne à la bataille de* Nordlingen, *où
il a pareillement donné des preuves de fa
valeur, & fait tout ce qu'un homme de cœur
& expérimenté au fait de la guerre pouvoit faire en femblable occafion, car s'étant
trouvé engagé dans le combat, environné
des ennemis, & bleffé d'une moufquetade à
la cuiffe* (dont il fut très-dangereufement
malade pendant plus de fix mois), *il fit une
retraite honorable, s'étant ouvert le paffage, & ayant fauvé fa Cornette & rallié fa
Compagnie ;* ce qui lui mérita tous les élo-
ges, & d'être fait Capitaine au même Régiment. 3° Un certificat du Maréchal *de Clé-
rambaut* dépofe en faveur de JEAN DE BER-
MENT, mêmes chofes que les précédents. 4°
Un autre certificat du Marquis *de Gefvres*,
Capitaine des Gardes-du-Corps du Roi, &
Lieutenant-Général de fes Armées, dépofe
mêmes chofes que les trois précédents. 5° Un
autre certificat du Marquis *de Montmoren-*

cy-Foffeux, dépofe mêmes chofes que les quatre précédents, & encore *que fa bleffure fut
connue du Prince de Condé, qui commandoit alors. & le recommanda à un Médecin
nommé* Chrétien. 6° Un autre certificat du
Comte de *Saulx-Tavannes*, Lieutenant-Général des Armées du Roi, dépofe que JEAN
DE BERMENT *s'eft toujours fignalé par quelques actions de vertu & de courage ; qu'ayant
un jour été commandé par le Prince de Condé, avec 18 Maîtres, pour aller obferver la
marche des ennemis, avec ordre de ne pas retourner fans faire des prifonniers, il exécuta
cet ordre avec tant de prudence, qu'il ame-
na cinq prifonniers à ce Prince,* lequel, in-
ftruit par eux de la marche des ennemis qu'ils
lui découvrirent, partit en diligence rejoin-
dre le Duc d'Orléans, qui avoit invefti Courtrai ; *mais que la jonction de l'armée du
Prince de Condé obligea de fe rendre* ; &
encore que ledit Sieur DE BERMENT étant Capitaine d'Infanterie, & ayant été commandé
d'attaquer une demi-lune au fiège d'Ypres,
*il l'attaqua avec tant de chaleur & de cou-
rage, qu'il l'emporta, la conferva, & y fit
un logement ; ce qui obligea les affiégés de
capituler,* &c. 7° Un autre certificat de M. *de
Vandi*, Lieutenant-Général des Armées du
Roi, dépofe comme le précédent, & qu'au
fecours d'Arras, y paffant comme volontaire, *il eut un cheval tué fous lui, dans le paffage des lignes, ce qui l'obligea de combattre à pied, où il fit le devoir de foldat
& de Capitaine,* &c. 8° Et un autre certificat du Comte *de Blin*, dépofe comme les deux
derniers. Telles ont été les actions éclatantes
de JEAN DE BERMENT, II° du nom, qui époufa,
par contrat paffé devant Notaire à Paris, le
19 Juin 1650, *Madeleine de Kervert*, fille
de *Jean de Kervert*, Ecuyer, Seigneur de
la Fontaine, & de *Marguerite d'Aufoin*,
dont :

1. ARMAND-LÉON, Ecuyer, Capitaine au Régiment de Navarre, qui fut tué devant
Bruch aux Pays-Bas, en 1674 ;
2. CHARLES, d'abord Clerc-Tonfuré du Diocèfe de Paris, & Prieur Commandataire du
Prieuré de Chênebrun, Ordre de Saint-
Benoît, Diocèfe de Chartres, qui quitta le
parti de l'Eglife, & fut Capitaine dans le
Régiment de Royal-Vaiffeau, fous le nom
de *Chevalier Berment*. Il fut tué à Tolhvis,
au paffage du Rhin en 1672 ;
3. FRANÇOIS, qui fuit ;

4. CHRÉTIEN-FRANÇOIS, auteur de la feconde branche, rapportée ci-après;

5. JEAN-LOUIS, Ecuyer, né à Paris le 5 Décembre 1671, & mort en bas âge;

6. MARIE-GENEVIÈVE, morte fille;

7. MARGUERITE, morte Religieufe en l'Abbaye Royale de Sézanne en Brie;

8. MARIE-NICOLE, née à Paris en 1676, & morte en la même Abbaye, dont elle étoit Prieure, en 1756;

9. Et MARIE-CLAUDE, mariée à *Gédéon le Prevôt*, Chevalier, Seigneur de Belleperche & d'Iray en Normandie, Officier dans les Cuiraffiers du Roi Cavalerie, morts l'un & l'autre, laiffant quatre enfans.

V. FRANÇOIS DE BERMENT, Ecuyer, Seigneur de Sémilly, né à Paris & baptifé fur la Paroiffe de Saint-Euftache, le 17 Septembre 1657, mourut âgé de 80 ans. Il avoit fervi l'efpace de 30 ans, d'abord dans les Moufquetaires du Roi, puis en qualité de Cornette dans le Régiment de Cavalerie des Cuiraffiers, le 17 Janvier 1678, & enfuite en celle de Lieutenant dans le Régiment du Roi-Dragons. Il s'eft trouvé à différentes batailles, où il fut bleffé dangereufement, & dans lefquelles il perdit fes équipages. Il fut, en cette confidération, gratifié de Sa Majefté, & laiffa de *Gabrielle du Hamel*, de la Maifon *du Parcharon-des-Ruiffintes*:

1. ANDRÉ, qui fuit;

2. FRANÇOIS-GABRIEL, appelé *le Chevalier de la Martinière*, ci-devant Lieutenant au Régiment de Ruffec-Cavalerie, qui fut bleffé en 1733, au fiège du Fort de Kell, & fut fait Capitaine d'Invalides détachés. Il mourut à Paris à l'Hôtel-Royal des Invalides, & avoit époufé *Marie-Charlotte-Elifabeth du Bofc-de-Marchainville*, de laquelle il a eu plufieurs enfans morts jeunes;

3. N...., Chevalier, mort jeune;

4. GABRIELLE-CHARLOTTE, morte le 7 Novembre 1735. Elle avoit époufé, le 30 Avril 1711, *Michel-Renaud-Jacquet d'Herlaumont*, Chevalier, Seigneur de Maleftable. Ils laiffèrent 10 enfans;

5. FRANÇOISE-GABRIELLE, dite *Mademoifelle de Sémilly*, morte fille à la Ferté-Vidame, en 1761;

6. Et JEANNE-CATHERINE, dite *Mademoifelle de la Martinière*, née en 1701, & vivante en 1770, fans alliance.

VI. ANDRÉ DE BERMENT, Ecuyer, Seigneur de Sémilly, après avoir été Lieutenant au Régiment de Ruffec-Cavalerie, l'efpace de 20 ans, y eft mort d'accident. Il a époufé, à Verneuil

en 1733, *Geneviève-Louife de Raveneau*, veuve du Sieur *de la Ronce*, Ecuyer, dont:

1. N...., morte fans alliance, âgée de 16 ans;

2. Et ADRIENNE-GENEVIÈVE, née en 1736, & morte le 14 Février 1766. Elle avoit époufé à Verneuil, Meffire *Hyacinthe-Louis de Rambourg*, Ecuyer, Seigneur des Touches, mort Garde-du-Corps du Roi, Compagnie de Beauvau, laiffant de ce mariage quatre enfans.

SECONDE BRANCHE.

V. CHRÉTIEN-FRANÇOIS DE BERMENT, Chevalier, Seigneur de la Martinière, né à Paris le 28 Février 1670, quatrième fils de JEAN, IIe du nom, & de *Madeleine de Kervert*, d'abord Cadet dans la Compagnie des Gentilshommes à la Citadelle de Befançon le 2 Juin 1688, puis Lieutenant au Régiment de Navarre le 3 Juillet 1689, & Capitaine au même Régiment le 5 Septembre 1693; fut obligé de fe retirer du fervice le 5 Mars 1702, à caufe des fuites d'une bleffure qu'il reçut à la bataille de Steinkerque le 3 Août 1692. Il mourut à Châteaudun le 8 Mars 1759, âgé de 89 ans, & fut inhumé en l'Eglife Paroiffiale de Saint-Pierre. Il avoit époufé, par contrat paffé devant Notaires à Paris, le 16 Décembre 1698, *Catherine-Marguerite Gélain* ou *Geslain*, fille de *Marc*, Seigneur de Bellebat, & de *Marie-Louife Courtin*, dont:

1. JEAN-LÉON, né & baptifé fur la Paroiffe de Saint-Lubin de Châteaudun, le 11 Octobre 1699, mort jeune;

2. FRANÇOIS-CHRÉTIEN, né jumeau de fa fœur, dont nous allons parler, le 11 Octobre 1701, à Châteaudun, & baptifé fur la même Paroiffe, lequel, après avoir fervi pendant trois ans en qualité de Cadet au Régiment de Gefvres-Cavalerie, fut ordonné Prêtre le 24 Septembre 1735, & nommé le 25 Novembre 1736, Chanoine de Saint-André de Châteaudun. Il eft mort le 13 Novembre 1766;

3. JEAN-FRANÇOIS, qui fuit;

4. CATHERINE-LOUISE-JULIE, née à Châteaudun, & baptifée fur la Paroiffe de Saint-Lubin, le 16 Septembre 1700, qui fit profeffion le 11 Février 1733, au Couvent des Dames Religieufes de la Congrégation de Notre-Dame de Châteaudun, dont elle mourut affiftante, le 27 Juillet 1762;

5. Et MARIE-MADELEINE-CATHERINE, née jumelle de FRANÇOIS-CHRÉTIEN, ci-deffus, le 11 Octobre 1701, à Châteaudun, & baptifée en la même Eglife, morte jeune.

VI. Jean-François de Berment, Chevalier, Seigneur de la Martinière, né & baptisé le 17 Février 1703, fur la Paroiffe de Saint-Lubin de Châteaudun, mourut en la même Ville, le 8 Mai 1758, & fut inhumé dans le Chœur de la Paroiffe de Saint-Vallerien dudit lieu. Il avoit fervi 15 ans dans les Régimens de Gefvres-Cavalerie, de Lépinay-Dragons, & dans les Gardes-du-Corps; fait les Campagnes de 1734 & 1735; & a été obligé de fe retirer du fervice, le 30 Juin 1738, pour caufe de maladie. Il avoit époufé, en vertu d'une difpenfe de la Cour de Rome, du 15 Juin 1737, & par contrat paffé devant *Nicolas Tiercelin*, l'un des principaux Notaires du Comté & Bailliage de Dunois, réfidant à Châteaudun, le 2 Septembre fuivant, *Marguerite Michau-d'Harbouville*, née le 6 & baptifée à Saint-Lubin de Châteaudun, le 7 Août 1712, fa coufine au IIIe degré, fille de *Marc Michau-d'Harbouville*, Seigneur de la Potterie en Dunois, & de *Marguerite Pillier.* Il eut :

1. François-Louis, qui fuit;
2. Chrétien-Joseph-Louis, Chevalier, né & baptifé le 19 Mars 1744, mort jeune;
3. René-Ambroise, dit *le Chevalier de Bellebat*, né le 18 & baptifé le 19 Octobre 1746, mort jeune;
4. Jean-Baptiste-Alexandre, dit *le Chevalier de Berment*, né le 26 Février 1749, & reçu le 20 Août 1765, fur les preuves de *fa Nobleffe*, Chevau-Léger de la Garde ordinaire du Roi;
5. Marguerite-Catherine, née à Châteaudun, & baptifée fur la Paroiffe de Saint-Vallerien de ladite Ville, le 16 Août 1739, morte jeune;
6. Et Geneviève-Françoise-Anne-Julie, née & baptifée, mêmes lieu & Paroiffe, le 18 Octobre 1714, & mariée, à Châteaudun, le 17 Mai 1762, à *Jean-Jacques le Prevôt*, Chevalier, Seigneur d'Iray & de Chauvigni-en-Iray, en Normandie, fon coufin, dont deux garçons & deux filles.

VII. François-Louis de Berment, Chevalier, Seigneur de la Martinière, né le 16 & baptifé le 17 Octobre 1740, à Châteaudun fur la Paroiffe de Saint-Valérien, Cornette au Régiment de Dauphin-Dragons, depuis le 1er Février 1757, & Lieutenant pour le Roi de la Ville de Châteaudun, le 27 Mai 1768, a fait les Campagnes de 1761 & 1762, & a été réformé à la Paix, le 1er Avril 1763. Il a époufé, par contrat paffé devant *Claude Pi-*

tou, Notaire Royal, réfidant à Châteaudun, le 25 Juin 1764, Marie-Anne de Berment de la Martinière, fa coufine du IVe au Ve degré, née à Québec le 5 Octobre 1746, fille de Meffire Claude-Antoine de Berment, Chevalier, Seigneur de la Martinière, Chevalier de l'Ordre Militaire de Saint-Louis, ancien Capine d'une Compagnie Franche de la Marine au Canada, & Commandant en chef au Fort de Beauféjour en Acadie, & de *Catherine de Parfons*, originaire d'Angleterre. De ce mariage font nés :

1. Marc-François, Chevalier, né le 12 Avril 1765, mort en bas âge;
2. Jean-Baptiste-Alexandre, Chevalier, né le 1er Décembre 1766;
3. Et Jean-Baptiste, appelé *le Chevalier de Berment*, né le 6 Décembre 1769.

TROISIÈME BRANCHE.

III. Louis de Berment, Ier du nom, Ecuyer, Seigneur de la Martinière, troifième fils de Laurent, IIe du nom, & de *Marie de Pivain*, naquit à la Ferté-Vidame, au Diocèfe de Chartres en 1593, & mourut en 1649. Il avoit époufé, par contrat du 13 Septembre 1627, *Françoife de Juchereau*, ou *Jufchereau*, fille de *Jean de Juchereau*, Ecuyer, Seigneur de Maure, & de *N... Pineau.* De ce mariage vinrent :

1. Louis, IIe du nom, Ecuyer, Seigneur de la Martinière, né & baptifé à la Ferté-Vidame, le 18 Octobre 1628, qui fut Gouverneur du Sénégal, & mourut en 1690. Il avoit époufé une Françoife, dont le nom eft inconnu, & de laquelle il eut :
   Marie de Berment, appelée *Mademoifelle de la Martinière*, morte à Verneuil au Perche en 1712, fans enfans, & veuve de *Nicolas de Boiffel*, Ecuyer, mort en la même ville en 1710;
2. Jean-Frédéric, Ecuyer, Capitaine au Régiment de Picardie, mort garçon;
3. Claude, qui fuit;
4. Et Marie, dite *Mademoifelle de la Martinière*, mariée à Verneuil au Perche, avec Meffire *N... de Limbœuf*, Ecuyer, Garde-du-Corps de Sa Majefté, mort fans poftérité.

IV. Claude de Berment, Ecuyer, Seigneur de la Martinière, né & ondoyé à la Ferté-Vidame le 30 Mai 1636, paffa dans la Nouvelle-France en 1661 en qualité d'Officier; enfuite ayant quitté le fervice, il fut fait, par commiffion du Roi du 3 Juin 1678, Confeiller au Confeil Souverain du Canada. Il y a exercé en 1703 la charge de Lieutenant-Géral au Siège de la Prevôté & Amirauté de Québec, & fut fait depuis premier Confeiller-Préfident du même Confeil Souverain. Il mourut à Québec le 24 Décembre 1719, & fut inhumé le lendemain en l'Eglife Cathédrale de ladite ville. Il avoit époufé, 1° par contrat paffé devant *Michel Fillion*, Notaire, le 5 Juillet 1664, *Anne Defprés*, morte fans enfans en 1689, veuve de Meffire *Jean de Laufon*, Chevalier, Grand-Sénéchal du Canada ; 2° par contrat paffé devant *Génale*, Notaire Royal, réfidant en la ville & Prevôté de Québec, en la Nouvelle-France, le 9 Avril 1697, *Marie-Anne Cailleteau*, morte le 30 Novembre 1708, âgée de 38 ans, qui s'étoit remariée à *Michel le Neuf*, Ecuyer, Seigneur de la Vallière & de Beaubaffin, ci-devant Commandant pour le Roi du Pays d'Acadie, & Capitaine d'une Compagnie du détachement de la Marine au Canada, & de la Compagnie des Gardes de Monfeigneur le Comte de Fontenacque, Gouverneur- Lieutenant-Général pour le Roi en tout ledit pays de la France Septentrionale. Elle étoit fille de noble *Jacques Cailleteau*, Seigneur de Champfleuri, & de *Françoife Denis*; & 3° fans enfans, en 1710, *Marie-Catherine du Frefne*, qui mourut veuve en 1732. Il eut de fon fecond mariage :

1. CLAUDE-ANTOINE, qui fuit;
2. JEAN-BAPTISTE, appelé *le Chevalier de Berment*, Seigneur en partie de la Martinière, né à Québec le 26 Décembre 1701, qui paffa aux Isles du Vent de l'Amérique en 1723, où il fut Capitaine-Commandant des quartiers du Bourg-Norrois, & Gros-Cap de la Paroiffe de Saint-Jean-Baptiste du Moule de l'Isle-Grande-Terre, par commiffion du Roi datée de Fontainebleau de 1730; Chevalier de l'Ordre Militaire de Saint Louis; Lieutenant de Roi honoraire defdites Isles, & Commandant d'une partie confidérable de la Guadeloupe en 1757. Il avoit fait un teftament, devant *Guillon*, Notaire Royal en l'Isle de la Guadeloupe, le 30 Novembre 1760, par lequel il inftitue fes légataires univerfels, Meffire FRANçois-Louis DE BERMENT, Cornette au Régiment Dauphin, Dragons, fon coufin, & MARIE-ANNE DE BERMENT, fa nièce, à la charge d'acquitter plufieurs legs, & nomme pour fes exécuteurs MM. *Jean-Charles Coudroye*, Commandant pour le Roi en

Chef préfentement en ladite Isle, & *Paul-Jacques Martin*, Officier de la Compagnie de Cavalerie-Milice audit lieu. Il y eft mort le 21 Août 1761, fans poftérité. Il avoit époufé, à la Guadeloupe, le 12 Février 1727, *Dorothée-Conftance du Verger-de-Maupertuis;*

3. JEAN-ALEXANDRE, Chevalier, né à Québec le 18 Août 1707, & mort en 1708;
4. JEANNE-FRANçOISE, dite *Mademoifelle de la Martinière*, née à Québec le 20 Mai 1699, Religieufe à l'Hôpital-Général de la même ville le 16 Mai 1716, où elle mourut le 5 Octobre 1746;
5. Et FRANçOISE-CHARLOTTE, née à Québec le 17 Septembre 1703, & morte en la même ville le 28 Juin 1709.

V. CLAUDE-ANTOINE DE BERMENT, Chevalier, Seigneur de la Martinière, né le 12 & baptifé le 13 Juillet 1700, en l'Eglife Paroiffiale de Notre-Dame, à Québec; fut fucceffivement Enfeigne des Troupes de la Marine au Canada, le 5 Mai 1722; en pied le 12 Avril 1727, Aide-Major pendant 10 ans, Lieutenant en fecond le 1er Avril 1733, en pied le 20 Mars 1734, Commandant pour le Roi à la Baye Defpuant en 1737, Capitaine le 1er Mai 1743, Chevalier de l'Ordre Militaire de Saint-Louis 1er Avril 1751, & Commandant pour le Roi de l'Acadie depuis le 24 Mai 1753 jufqu'au 28 Juillet 1754. Il obtint fa retraite le 15 Mars 1755, ayant été forcé par fes infirmités de quitter le fervice, fut gratifié par Sa Majefté d'une penfion de 720 livres, & mourut le 24 Décembre 1761, âgé de 61 ans, fur la Paroiffe de Notre-Dame de Québec, dans laquelle il fut inhumé le lendemain. Il avoit époufé, par contrat paffé devant *Raimbault*, Notaire Royal en la Juridiction de Montréal, réfidant à Villemarie le 18 Mars 1729, *Catherine de Parfons*, née en Novembre 1703 à Wulh, près Baftow en la Nouvelle-Angleterre, fille de *N... de Parfons*, tué au fervice d'Angleterre en qualité de Capitaine en 1704, dans la guerre des Sauvages, & d'*Anne de Wheclurigs*. De ce mariage font nés :

1. CLAUDE-JACQUES, Chevalier, né à Québec le 23 Août 1732, & mort le 27 Avril 1733;
2. CLAUDE-GILLES, appelé *le Chevalier de la Martinière*, né à Québec le 14 Septembre 1734, qui fut Enfeigne des Troupes de la Marine à la Guadeloupe, & mourut au Moule de l'Isle-Grande-Terre-Guadeloupe le 1er Septembre 1754, fans alliance. Il avoit

été accordé avec *Conſtance du Verger-de-Maupertuis ;*

3. Marie-Catherine, née à Montréal le 24 Novembre 1730, & Religieuſe à l'Hôpital-Général de Québec le 23 Novembre 1746;

4. Marie-Louiſe, née à Québec le 18 Septembre 1733, & morte le 4 Novembre 1734;

5. Marie-Charlotte, née à Québec le 30 Décembre 1736, & mariée, le 26 Juillet 1756, à *Antoine de Mellis*, Commiſſaire de la Marine ;

6. Marie-Angélique, née à Québec le 15 Décembre 1737, & morte le 27 Juillet 1755 ;

7. Marie-Anne, née jumelle de la précédente, à Québec le 15 Décembre 1737, & morte le 7 Juin 1743;

8. Marie-Joſèphe, née à Québec le 13 Août 1741, & morte le 29 Août 1741;

9. Geneviève-Esther, née le 3 Janvier 1743, & morte le 17 Mai 1744;

10. Et Marie-Anne, née à Québec le 5 Octobre 1746. Elle a paſſé en France en 1763, & y a épouſé, par contrat du 17 Juin 1764, à Châteaudun, Meſſire François-Louis de Bermont, Chevalier, Seigneur de la Martinière.

Les armes : *d'azur, à un chevron briſé d'or, accompagné de trois étoiles de même, 2 en chef & 1 en pointe.* Supports : *deux lions.* Cimier : *une couronne de Marquis.* (Mémoire envoyé.)

BERMEULE-RABODANGE : *d'or, à la croix ancrée de gueules :*

BERMIEULE : *d'or, au créquier de gueules.*

BERMINICOURT : *d'azur, au lambel de gueules, au chef d'argent.*

BERMOND, en Provence, ancienne famillé qui poſſédoit des fiefs, dans le XIII.e fiècle, tems auquel les ſeuls Gentilshommes pouvoient en avoir. Elle eſt la tige des Seigneurs *de Vachères, du Caſtelar, de Bezaure, de Rouſſet,* &c.

Raymond de Bermond fut Seigneur en partie des lieux de Goult & de Beaumettes, dont il rendit hommage en 1304 à la Reine Jeanne, Comteſſe de Provence. De lui deſcendoit par divers degrés :

I. Louis de Bermond, Ecuyer, Seigneur de Rouſſet & de Goult, qui épouſa, à la fin du XV.e fiècle, *Anne de Juſlas,* d'une ancienne famille de Provence. De ce mariage naquirent :

1. Antoine, qui ſuit;

2. Barthélemy, reçu Chevalier de Malte, mort Commandeur de Chirolles ;

3. Et Marguerite, mariée avec Noble *Pierre du Pont.*

II. Antoine de Bermond, Co-Seigneur de Goult & de Rouſſet, fit hommage le 13 Novembre 1531 d'une partie de cette première terre au Baron de Cazeneuve, Il épouſa *Lucrèce de Vachères,* Dame en partie du lieu qui porte ſon nom. Il eut :

III. Vincent de Bermond, père de :

IV. Poncet-Gabriel de Bermond, Seigneur de Rouſſet & de Vachères, qui épouſa *Anne-Thérèſe de Nicolaï,* dont :

V. Jean-François de Bermond, Seigneur de Vachères, qui épouſa *N... de Sáffálin,* de la ville de Manoſque. Il eut :

1. Joseph, Seigneur de Bezaure & de Vachères, Capitaine dans le Régiment du Roi, Cavalerie, marié, ſans enfans, avec *Anne de Poligny,* de la ville de Gap en Dauphiné ;

2. Elzéar, qui ſuit;

3. & 4. Et deux autres fils, dont l'un fut Prevôt de l'Egliſe d'Apt, & l'autre mourut après avoir été nommé à l'Evêché de Vence.

VI. Elzéar de Bermond, Seigneur de Vachères & du Caſtelar, Capitaine d'un des Vaiſſeaux du Roi, épouſa *Eliſabeth de Voire,* dont vinrent :

1. Louis-Elzéar, qui ſuit ;

2. & 3. Et deux autres garçons, morts, l'un Officier de Galères, & l'autre de Vaiſſeaux.

VII. Louis-Elzéar de Bermond, Seigneur de Caſtelar, Capitaine dans le Régiment de Normandie, a épouſé, en 1722, *Françoiſe de Bermond-de-la-Blache,* de laquelle il reſte un fils, qui n'eſt pas encore établi.

Il y avoit autrefois en Provence une autre famille de ce nom, qui avoit poſſédé la Seigneurie de Menerbe ; elle eſt aujourd'hui éteinte. Il ne reſte plus perſonne auſſi des branches, formées de celle dont nous venons de donner la filiation.

Les armes ſont : *d'or, au cœur de gueules.* Voy. Artefeuil, tom. I, p. 129.

BERMOND-DU-CAYLAR, voyez CAYLAR.

BERMONDES, en Champagne : *écartelé, aux 1 & 4 d'or, à la croix treſlée de ſinople ; aux 2 & 3 d'or, au lion de gueules ; & ſur le tout, de gueules, à deux pals d'or, chargés d'une faſce d'azur, ſurchargée de trois loſanges du ſecond.*

BERMONT, en Provence : *d'azur, au chevron d'or, chargé d'un lion naiffant de gueules.*

BERMONT : *d'azur, au chef d'or, chargé d'un lion naiffant de gueules.*

BERNABÉ, famille noble d'Anjou, qui, fuivant les titres originaux communiqués, & que nous avons vérifiés, remonte fa filiation à

SÉBASTIEN DE BERNABÉ, Ecuyer, Sieur de la Boulaye, la Haye-Fougereufe & de la Calonnière en Anjou (fils de THOMAS DE BERNABÉ), homme d'armes du Roi HENRI IV. Il fervit dans l'armée qui fut conduite par le Prince de Conti aux années 1591 & 592,ès pays d'Anjou, Poitou, Touraine, du Maine, Berry, Haut & Bas-Limoufin ; notamment au fecours du Château de Belac en Limoufin, affiégé par le Vicomte de la Guierche, un des partifans de la Ligue, qui fut obligé d'en lever le fiège ; à la prife de Montmorillon en Poitou, dans laquelle ce Vicomte, en fe retirant à Poitiers, laiffa fon canon avec fon Infanterie, qui fut prife d'affaut & taillée en pièces ; aux fièges de Mirebeau, de Selles en Berry, à la bataille de Craon en Anjou ; & depuis au fiège de la Fère en Picardie, & à d'autres occafions de guerre, fous la charge du Comte de la Rochepot, Gouverneur d'Anjou. Il fe comporta avec tant de zèle & de prudence dans plufieurs voyages & affaires où il fut employé par HENRI IV, pour les traités de trève & paix faits ès-années 1594, 95, 96, 97 & 1598, avec le Duc de Mercœur & le Maréchal de Bois-Dauphin, qu'en confidération de fes grands & fignalés fervices rendus, pendant 26. ans, tant fous HENRI IV, qu'au commencement du règne de LOUIS XIII, étant auprès de la perfonne du Comte de la Rochepot, Gouverneur & Lieutenant-Général d'Anjou, Ambaffadeur d'Efpagne, & enfuite auprès du Duc de Rouannois, que LOUIS XIII lui accorda, fans aucune finance, des Lettres de nobleffe, données à Paris au mois de Décembre 1616, pour lui, fes enfans & poftérité, nés & à naître en légitime mariage, enregiftrées en la Cour des Aides le 1er Mars 1617. Il fut encore employé en différentes négociations, ès-années 1614, 16, 17 & 1618, auprès du Duc de Mercœur & du Maréchal de Bois-Dauphin, pour les réfoudre à fe remettre fous l'obéiffance du Roi, qu'il continua de fervir dans toutes les occafions qui fe préfentèrent, & mou-

rut en 1632, en accompagnant Sa Majefté dans le voyage qu'elle fit à Clermont, Metz & Nancy en Lorraine. Il avoit époufé 1° *Léonore Calouyn*, fœur de *Roland Calouyn*, Avocat au Parlement ; & 2° par contrat paffé devant *Etienne Tolleron* & *Antoine Vigeon*, Notaires au Châtelet de Paris, le 21 Novembre 1622, *Madeleine Malingre*, veuve de noble homme *Thierry de Monanteuil*, Avocat au Parlement ; & fœur d'*Ambroife Malingre*, femme de noble homme *Jehan le Pilleur*, Confeiller du Roi, & Contrôleur-Général des Traites foraines de Champagne, qui affiftèrent à ce contrat de mariage, ainfi que LOUIS BERNABÉ, Avocat au Parlement, & *Marguerite Bureau*, fon époufe, frère & belle-fœur dudit SÉBASTIEN DE BERNABÉ. De fon premier mariage il eut pour fils unique :

CLAUDE DE BERNABÉ, Chevalier, Seigneur de la Boulaye, Baron de la Haye-Fougereufe, Gentilhomme ordinaire du Prince de Condé. Il fervit avec beaucoup de valeur, notamment au fecours de l'Isle de Ré contre les Anglois, aux fièges de la Rochelle, de Sufe, Cafal & Privas ; paffa de-là en Lorraine & en Rouffillon ; & fe fignala dans toutes les occafions qui fe préfentèrent ; obtint des Lettres de relief le 20 Septembre 1634, adreffées à la Chambre des Comptes, & de nouvelles Lettres d'adreffe au Parlement le 20 Décembre 1659, pour l'enregiftrement des Lettres de nobleffe de fon père, qui y furent regiftrées le 19 Avril 1660 ; fut pourvu de la charge de Gentilhomme ordinaire d'HENRI DE BOURBON, Prince de Condé, par Lettres du 3 Mars 1641, & confirmé dans cette charge par Arrêt de la Cour des Aides du 5 defdits mois & an. En confidération des fervices de fon père, des fiens & de ceux de fon fils, LOUIS XIV unit & incorpora les Châtellenies du Merle, Fougereufe, le fief l'Evêque, leurs appartenances & dépendances à ladite Châtellenie de la Haye-Fougereufe, mouvante de Sa Majefté, & l'érigea en *Baronie* fous la dénomination de *Baronie de la Haye-Fougereufe* tant pour lui, que pour fes hoirs, fucceffeurs & ayant caufe, par Lettres-Patentes données à Paris au mois de Septembre 1654, enregiftrées au Parlement le 10 Avril 1656, & en la Chambre des Comptes le 23 Août de la même année. Le Roi, par fa Déclaration du mois de Septembre 1664, ayant revoqué toutes les Lettres

d'annobliſſement, accordées depuis 1610,
CLAUDE DE BERNABÉ fut aſſigné par devant le
Commiſſairedéparti enla Généralitéde Tours,
pour repréſenter les titres, en vertu desquels
il prenoit la qualité d'*Ecuyer* ; mais il préſenta ſa Requête au Conſeil du Roi, ſur ce que
Sa Majeſté s'étoit réſervée, par ſa Déclaration, de pourvoir à ceux qui avoient obtenu
leſdites Lettres en *récompenſe de ſervices* ;
& étant dans ce cas, il fut maintenu, par Arrêt du Conſeil d'Etat, tenu à Paris le 28 Avril
1667, dans ſa qualité de *Noble* & d'*Ecuyer*,
lui, ſes enfans nés & à naître en légitime mariage, nonobſtant la révocation portée par la
Déclaration du mois de Septembre 1664, &
l'Arrêt du Conſeil du 13 Janvier de la même
année. Il fut encore confirmé dans ſa *nobleſſe*,
conformément audit Arrêt du Conſeil d'Etat,
par Lettres-Patentes données à Paris au mois
de Mars 1669, enregiſtrées au Parlement le
31 Janvier 1670, en la Chambre des Comptes
le 20 Mars, & en la Cour des Aides le 24 deſdits mois & an. Il avoit épouſé, par contrat
paſſé devant *Moufle* & ſon Confrère, Notaires au Châtelet de Paris, le 7 Février 1633,
Louiſe Deſcamin, fille de *Louis*, Ecuyer,
Sieur de Launay & de Saint-Michel-ſur-Or-
ge, Conſeiller du Roi, Auditeur en ſa Chambre des Comptes de Paris, & de *Marie Aubert*. Le futur fut aſſiſté de *Madeleine Malingre*, ſa belle-mère, alors veuve de SÉBAS-
TIEN DE BERNABÉ, Ecuyer, ſon père; de LOUIS
BERNABÉ, ſon oncle paternel, & autres parens
& amis; & la future, de noble homme *Chriſtophe de Bordeaux*, Conſeiller du Roi, Receveur-Général des Finances en la Généralie-
té de Touraine, ſon beau-frère, mari de *Françoiſe Deſcamin*, ſa ſœur, &c. De ce mariage
vint pour fils unique :

LOUIS DE BERNABÉ, Chevalier, Seigneur de
la Boulaye, Baron de la Haye - Fougereuſe,
Guidon de la Compagnie des Gendarmes du
Duc de Rouannois, Gouverneur du Poitou.
Il ſervit, en cette qualité de Guidon, aux ſiè-
ges de Cognac, Saintes, Taillebourg & de
Bordeaux, où il donna des preuves de ſon
courage, fut enſuite Ecuyer ordinaire de la
Petite-Ecurie du Roi, par Proviſions du 25
Avril 1656; & épouſa, par contrat paſſé de-
vant *Jean Baranger*, Notaire Royal à Sau-
mur, le 19 Décembre 1663, *Marie-Louiſe
Gillier*, Dame de Saint-Gervais, fille de Meſ-
ſire *Jean Gillier*, Chevalier, Seigneur Baron

de Saint-Gervais, & de *Gabrielle de Beauvau*, dont :

JOSEPH, qui ſuit;

Et MARIE - ELISABETH DE BERNABÉ, mariée à
Guillaume Hameau, Ecuyer, Sieur du Marais, dont eſt iſſue *Marie-Perrine Hameau*,
femme de *François-Marie Hameau*, Ecuyer,
Seigneur du Haut - Pleſſis. De ce mariage
ſont ſorties :

Marie-Perrine Hameau, épouſe de *Char-
les-Auguſte de Ravenelle*, Chevalier,
Seigneur dudit lieu, morte ſans enfans ;

Et *Louiſe-Prudence Hameau*, mariée
Pierre-André-Claude Sevalle-Pocquet,
Ecuyer, Seigneur de Livonnière, petit-
fils du célèbre *Pocquet-de-Livonnière*,
ſi connu par ſon Commentaire ſur la
Coutume d'Anjou, dont :

Jean - Marie - Claude Sevalle, Officier dans les Régimens Provin-
ciaux ;

François-Auguſte, étudiant ;
Et *Prudence-Perrine*.

JOSEPH DE BERNABÉ, Chevalier, Seigneur
de la Boulaye, Baron de la Haye-Fougereuſe,
des Châtellenies du Merle, Fief l'Evêque, la
Calonnière, fut Ecuyer ordinaire du Roi en
ſurvivance, par Lettres du 29 Février 1692,
dont il prêta ſerment le 12 Août 1698. Il eſt
décédé en 1732, & avoit épouſé, par contrat
paſſé devant *Naudet* & *Bouraſſeau*, Notaires
en la Cour & Châtellenie d'Ardelay, le 15
Janvier 1701, *Renée-Angélique de la Haye*,
fille aînée d'*Antoine de la Haye-Montbault*,
Chevalier de Saint-Louis, Capitaine des Vaiſſeaux du Roi, & de *Renée Guyraud*, Il eut :

1. ALEXIS-JOSEPH, qui ſuit ;
2. MARIE-ANGÉLIQUE, morte ſans hoirs, mariée 1º à *N... de la Haye-Montbault*, Chevalier ; & 2º à *Louis de Linnière*, Chevalier, Seigneur de la Guyonnière ;
3. Et LOUISE DE BERNABÉ, mariée à Meſſire
Armand de la Fontenelle, Ecuyer, Seigneur
de Vaudoré, ancien Mouſquetaire de la
Garde du Roi, dont eſt iſſue :

Louiſe de la Fontenelle, mariée à *N...
Piard-de-l'Enereau*, Ecuyer, Seigneur
de Dangeu près Pouancé en Anjou. De
ce mariage ils ont pluſieurs enfans, deux
deſquels ſont Pages, l'un chez MON-
SIEUR, & l'autre chez M. le Comte
d'ARTOIS.

ALEXIS-JOSEPH DE BERNABÉ, Chevalier, Seigneur de la Boulaye, Baron de la Haye-Fougereuſe, Saint-Gervais, Châtelain du Merle,
du Fief-l'Evêque, de la Calonnière, Chaveil-

les-Salines, &c., né au mois de Novembre 1712, a fervi dans les Gardes-Françoifes en qualité de Gentilhomme à Drapeau en 1729, 1730 & 1731, & a époufé, par contrat paffé, le 27 Juin 1746, devant les Notaires Royaux à Angers, *Marie-Françoife-Augufte Luthier-de-la-Richerie*, fille de *Claude-Pierre Luthier*, Chevalier, Seigneur de la Richerie, Chevalier de Saint-Louis, & de *Françoife de Boaffé*, dont:

1. MARIE-ALEXIS, qui fuit;
2. MARIE-JEAN-BAPTISTE DE BERNABÉ, né en 1751, Lieutenant au Régiment de Bourgogne, Cavalerie, où il eft entré, en qualité de Volontaire, en 1768;
3. AUGUSTE-ANTOINE, né en 1753, Sous-Lieutenant audit Régiment de Bourgogne, où il eft entré Volontaire en 1770;
4. FRANÇOIS-CHARLES, né en 1754, entré Volontaire, en 1771, au Régiment de Berry, Cavalerie, dont il eft devenu Sous-Lieutenant, décédé au mois de Juin 1777;
5. Et MARIE-ANNE DE BERNABÉ, née en 1759, mariée, par contrat du 5 Août 1776, paffé devant les Notaires Royaux à Angers, avec *Gafpard-Daniel-François-René Rouxeau-de-la-Mefnardière*, Ecuyer, Confeiller-Secrétaire du Roi, Maifon, Couronne de France & à la Chancellerie de la Chambre des Comptes & Cour des Aides d'Aix en Provence, fils de *Gafpard-Daniel Rouxeau*, Ecuyer, Seigneur de la Mefnardière, & de *Renée le Flo-de-Tremelo*.

MARIE-ALEXIS DE BERNABÉ, Chevalier, Seigneur Baron de la Haye, né en 1748, Volontaire dans les Carabiniers en 1766 & 1767, Sous-Lieutenant au Régiment de Bourgogne en 1768, 69 & 1770, a époufé, par contrat paffé devant les Notaires Royaux à Angers, le 10 Juin 1771, *Anne-Marie-Jofèphe Walsh*, fille de *François-Jacques Walsh*, Chevalier, Comte de Serrant, Baron d'Ingrande, Becon, &c., & de *Marie-Anne-Thérèfe Harpert*. De ce mariage font iffus:

1. ALEXIS-MARIE-JOSEPH DE BERNABÉ-DE-LA-HAYE-DE-LA-BOULAYE, né le 9 Septembre 1773;
2. FRANÇOIS-MARIE, né le 23 Décembre 1774;
3. Et LOUIS-AUGUSTE-MARIE, né le 29 Avril 1777.

Les armes: *d'azur, à la croix d'or, cantonnée de quatre colonnes de même*. Cette famille les portoit ainfi avant les Lettres de nobleffe accordées à SÉBASTIEN DE BERNABÉ, en récompenfe de fes fervices.

BERNAGE (DE), à Paris, famille de Robe.

LOUIS DE BERNAGE, Confeiller d'Etat ordinaire, avoit époufé *Anne-Marie Rouillé*, morte à Paris le 21 Novembre 1755, âgée de près de 91 ans, & laiffa:

1. LOUIS-BASILE, qui fuit;
2. Et LOUIS-ANTOINE DE BERNAGE DE CHAUMONT, Lieutenant-Général, enterré le 11 Mai 1761, âgé de 66 ans. Il eut:

   LOUIS DE BERNAGE DE CHAUMONT, Brigadier de 1762, & Colonel du Régiment de Forez, Infanterie;

   Et LOUISE-ANNE DE BERNAGE DE CHAUMONT, mariée, le 9 Avril 1755, à N... *Bernard*, Seigneur de Balainvilliers.

LOUIS-BASILE DE BERNAGE, Seigneur de St.-Maurice, Vaux, Chaffy, &c., Confeiller d'Etat ordinaire, Grand-Croix de l'Ordre Royal & Militaire de Saint-Louis, ancien Prevôt des Marchands, a laiffé de *Marie-Anne Moreau*:

1. JEAN-LOUIS DE BERNAGE DE VAUX, Intendant de Moulins depuis 1744, marié à N... *le Marié*, de la Ville d'Amiens;
2. Et ELISABETH-JEANNE-THÉRÈSE DE BERNAGE DE VAUX, mariée, le 14 Juin 1735, à *Louis-Guillaume Bon*, Marquis de Saint-Hilaire, premier Préfident & Intendant de Rouffillon le 9 Novembre 1753.

Les armes: *d'or, à trois fafces de gueules, chargées chacune de cinq fautoirs d'argent alaifés*.

BERNAGE: *d'argent, à trois levrettes courantes de fable, pofées 2 & 1*.

BERNARD. Seigneur de Javerfac, d'Aftugace, de Monfanfon: *d'or, à trois huchets de gueules, pofés 2 & 1*.

BERNARD, Seigneur d'Egreffins, en Bretagne: *d'or, à trois têtes de Maures de profil de fable, au bandeau d'argent, pofées 2 & 1*.

BERNARD, même Province: *de gueules, au château d'argent, fommé de trois tours de même*.

BERNARD, Seigneur de Saint-Barthélemy: *de gueules, à la bande d'argent, chargée de trois mouchetures d'hermines de fable, au chef d'or chargé de trois rofes de gueules*.

BERNARD, Seigneur de Chintré: *de gueules, à la bande d'or, chargée de trois étoiles d'azur, accompagnée à feneftre d'un cor de chaffe d'or, lié de gueules*.

BERNARD, Seigneur de Saint-Marcellin : *d'azur, au chevron d'argent, accompagné d'une ancre d'or en pointe; au chef d'argent, chargé d'une croix pattée de gueules.*

BERNARD, en Provence : *de gueules, au lion couronné d'or, à une bande d'azur, brochante sur le tout, & chargée d'un croissant d'argent & de deux étoiles d'or.*

BERNARD, Seigneur de Montaigu, en Comté : *de gueules, au croissant d'argent.*

BERNARD, Seigneur de Saffenay : *d'azur, à la fasce d'or, chargée d'une molette d'azur, surmontée d'une hure d'or, au-dessus de laquelle sont deux coutelas d'argent en sautoir, la pointe chargée d'un chapeau aussi d'argent.* D'autres disent la *fasce chargée de trois molettes de sable.*

BERNARD, Seigneur de Maillard : parti au 1, comme les Seigneurs de Saffenay ; au 2, *d'azur, au chevron d'or, chargé d'un tourteau de sable à la croix d'or, & accompagné en chef de deux quinte-feuilles, aussi d'or, & en pointe d'une étoile de même.*

BERNARD, Sieur de Saint-Martin, Election de Coutances, en Normandie, ancienne noblesse, qui porte : *de gueules, à deux fasces d'azur, accompagnées de trois molettes de même, deux en chef & une en pointe.*

BERNARD, autre famille, également ancienne du côté de la noblesse, Election de Vire, qui porte : *écartelé d'or & d'azur, à trois roses de gueules, 2 en chef & 1 en pointe.*

BERNARD : *d'azur, à la croix pattée & alaisée d'argent, chargée en cœur de six étoiles d'or, à la bordure componée d'argent & d'azur.*

BERNARD, Seigneur de Kerbino, Kermagaro, &c., à Vannes : *d'azur, à deux épées d'argent, posées en sautoir, les pointes en haut.*

BERNARD, même Province : *d'argent, à la tour crénelée d'azur, soutenue de deux ours rampans de sable, & affrontés.*

BERNARD, Seigneur de Balainvilliers. SIMON-CHARLES BERNARD, Ecuyer, Seigneur de la Baronie de Balainvilliers & du Comté de Clery, épousa *Marie-Madeleine Labbé,* enterrée le 30 Mars 1758, dont il eut :

1. N..., qui suit;
2 Un fils, Abbé;
3. MARIE-CHARLOTTE, mariée, par contrat du

Tome II.

3 Janvier 1740, à *Marie-Louis Quentin,* Baron de Champlost, né e 5 Septembre 1709, mort le 30 Août 1776;
4. Et une fille, mariée à N..., Vicomte de *Thianges.*

N..., Seigneur de Balainvilliers & du Comté de Clery, Intendant d'Auvergne, Secrétaire-Greffier de l'Ordre de Saint-Louis, marié, le 9 Avril 1755, à *Louise-Anne Bernage de Chaumont,* fille de *Louis-Antoine,* enterré le 11 Mai 1761, âgé de 66 ans.

Les armes : *d'azur, à la gerbe de bled d'or, soutenue d'un croissant d'argent ; au chef de gueules, chargé de trois étoiles d'argent.*

BERNARD, ancienne famille de Normandie, Généralité d'Alençon, qui possédoit autrefois les Terres de Marigny & de la Motte près Séez, & dont étoit :

CHARLES BERNARD, Chevalier, Seigneur de la Bellière, Francheville, le Moncel, la Rosière, Rounay & Gentilly, lequel, de son mariage contracté avec *Hélène-Scholastique de Pilliers,* eut pour fille unique & héritière :

JACQUELINE-ANNE-MADELEINE BERNARD, Dame desdites Terres, troisième femme, par contrat du 9 Juillet 1747, de *Louis,* Marquis de *Chambray,* né, le 16 Juin 1713. Voyez CHAMBRAY.

Les armes : *d'azur, à trois fasces ondées d'or.*

BERNARD, ou BERNARDI. Cette famille est originaire de Dauphiné, du lieu de Bellaffaire, Diocèse d'Embrun, & différente de la suivante, établie en Provence.

I. RAYMOND DE BERNARDI en est la tige. MARIE, Reine de Sicile & de Jérusalem, Comtesse de Provence, lui fit expédier des Lettres-Patentes, données à Avignon le 18 Novembre 1391, par lesquelles il conste qu'il étoit Conseiller du Roi, Maître-d'Hôtel de cette Princesse, son Maître des Comptes, Juge-Majeur des secondes Appellations de Provence, &c. LOUIS II, Roi de Sicile & de Jérusalem, lui accorda d'autres Lettres-Patentes, données à Jérusalem le 1er Mars 1400, qui commencent ainsi : *Potestas attributa magnifico viro Domino* BERNARDI *Militi,* &c. On les trouve dans la Cour des Comptes de Provence, registre *Lividi,* lettre A, fol. 65 de la nouvelle cotte. Ledit RAYMOND fit son testament le 6 Août 1407 (*Jean Michaelis,* Notaire à Avignon), & fut père de :

J j j

1. Fasi, chef d'une branche établie à Tulette en Dauphiné, dont il ne refte plus qu'une fille, veuve du Sieur *Fabri d'Aubenas;*

2. Et Louis, qui fuit.

II. Louis Bernardi alla s'établir à Mazan, Diocèfe de Carpentras. Il eut :

III. Gaspard Bernardi, qui fit fon teftament le 5 Mars 1517. Il avoit époufé, par contrat paffé à Mazan le 29 Mai 1496, *Marguerite de Leftre,* & laiffa entr'autres enfans :

  1. Claude, qui fuit ;

  2. Et Jean, qui tranfigea avec fon frère fur les biens de leur père, le 16 Juin 1542 ; il fut Capitaine d'Infanterie, ainfi qu'il appert par fon Brevet du 5 Octobre 1573, & mourut fans poftérité.

IV. Claude Bernardi époufa *Marguerite de Loques,* dont il eut :

V. Jean Bernardi, marié à Sault, le 7 Février 1579, avec *Honorée de Donodei,* fille de *Sauveur de Donodei,* & de *Françoife de Gaufridi.* Il laiffa :

  1. Elzéar, qui fuit ;

  2. Et Denis, rapporté ci-après.

VI. Elzéar Bernardi tefta le 3 Avril 1649. Il avoit époufé, par contrat paffé à Sault le 2 Juin 1619, *Ifabeau Laborel,* fille de *Claude Laborel* & de *Catherine Pillat,* & laiffa :

  1. Pierre, qui fuit ;

  2. Etienne, dont on ignore la deftinée ;

  3. Et Denis, chef de la branche établie à Rouffillon, Diocèfe d'Apt.

VII. Pierre Bernardi fit fon teftament le 6 Février 1680. Il avoit époufé, le 29 Avril 1648, *Anne Arnoux,* fille de *Poncet,* & de *Madeleine Girard,* & eut :

  1. Elzéar, qui fuit ;

  2. Et Joachim, mort Chanoine & Curé du Bourg de Valenas en Dauphiné.

VIII. Elzéar Bernardi, IIe du nom, fit fon teftament le 5 Juin 1727. Il avoit époufé, par contrat paffé le 25 Juin 1673, *Thérèfe Martin,* fille de *Charles Martin,* & *d'Anne Laugier,* & laiffa :

  1. Balthafard, qui fuit ;

  2. Et Jean-Etienne, Prêtre, Docteur en Théologie, mort Chanoine de l'Eglife Saint-Sauveur d'Aix, Syndic du Diocèfe, Prieur & Co-Seigneur de Tourton, en Provence.

IX. Balthasard Bernardi, époufa, le 16 Décembre 1720, *Angélique-Rofe Roddes,* fille de *Jofeph,* & d'*Auranne Joun,* dont :

X. Joseph-Elzéar Bernardi, marié, le 7 Avril 1750, avec *Louife-Madeleine Demon-*

gé, fille d'*Elzéar,* Seigneur du Caire en Provence, & en partie de Puimichel & d'Hauteval, & de *Françoife de Rabilliaud,* de la ville d'Aix.

VI. Denis Bernardi, fecond fils de Jean, & d'*Honorade de Donodei,* fit fon teftament le 31 Mars 1666. Il avoit époufé, par contrat paffé le 5 Octobre 1622, *Victoire Laborel,* fille de *Claude,* & de *Catherine Pillat,* dont :

  1. Jean-Etienne, qui fuit ;

  2. Et Pompée, qui fit une branche établie à Pernes dans le Comtat-Venaiffin, qui fubfifte en la perfonne d'Antoine-Xavier Bernardi, marié, par contrat paffé à Carpentras le 10 Novembre 1749, avec *Jeanne de Guillini,* fille d'*Efprit-Jofeph,* du lieu de Velleron, & de *Sufanne Martin.*

VII. Jean-Etienne Bernardi fut marié avec *Sufanne d'Aftuard-de-Cheminades,* de la ville de Sault. De ce mariage naquirent :

  1. Denis, mort fans poftérité ;

  2. Esprit, qui fuit ;

  3. Dominique, qui entra d'abord dans les Cadets Gentilshommes, & qui fut enfuite Capitaine dans le Régiment Dauphin, Infanterie, ainfi qu'il confte par fon Brevet & Commiffion du 28 Mai 1689 ;

  Et quatre filles, mariées dans les Maifons de *Camaret* à Caromb, de *Bouvar* à Mazan, de *Silveftre* à Saint-Savournin, & de *Martin* à Sault. Tous ces enfans étoient nommés dans le teftament que fit leur père le 17 Juillet 1679.

VIII. Esprit Bernardi, Vicomte de Valernes, acheta une charge de Tréforier-Général de France en la Généralité de Provence, qu'il exerça pendant 32 ans, & fut marié, le 6 Avril 1684, avec *Jeanne de l'Enfant,* des Seigneurs de *Peirefc.* Il eut :

  1. Jean-Etienne, qui fuit ;

  2. N..., mariée à *Boniface de Fombeton* à Sifteron ;

  3. N.., mariée à M. *Roux de Beauvezet* à Salon ;

  4. N..., mariée à M. *Julien,* frère du Lieutenant-Général des Armées du Roi de la ville d'Orange ;

  5. N..., mariée à M. *Fabri de Brignolles.*

IX. Jean-Etienne Bernardi, Vicomte de Valernes, auquel le Roi, en récompenfe des fervices de fon père & de ceux de fon oncle, accorda des provifions pour la Charge que celui-là avoit exercée le 31 Mars 1732. Il époufa, par contrat du 29 Avril 1723, *Rofe de Caftellane,* fille d'*Henri,* Marquis de Majaftres, & de *Françoife de Ferrier.* Il eut :

1. Pierre-Joseph ;
2. Henri, Chanoine de l'Eglife de Riez ;
3. César-Ignace, Eccléfiaftique ;
4. Esprit-Dominique, Jéfuite ;
5. Jean-Baptiste-Balthasard, Garde de la Marine ;
6. Et Madeleine, mariée avec N... l'Olivier, Baron de Bonne en Dauphiné.

Il fe trouve dans l'Abrégé Hiftorique de Provence par Pierre Louvel, imprimé à Aix en 1676, un Bernardi, Evêque d'Apt en 1353. Il y en avoit un autre en 1351, Evêque de Glandèves : il les foupçonne tous les deux iffus de la famille dont nous venons de parler.

Les armes : *d'azur, au cor d'argent, enguiché de gueules, furmonté d'une trangle d'argent ; au chef de gueules, chargé de trois grenades d'or.*

BERNARD-BEAULIEU, Sieur de Courville en Anjou, famille établie dans le Blaifois & en Bretagne.

Jean Bernard, Seigneur d'Eftiau en Anjou, fut élu Maire de la ville d'Angers en 1485. Il étoit le quatrième ayeul de Pierre Bernard, Ecuyer, Seigneur de Beaulieu & de la Foflerie, qui fuccéda à fon père dans la charge de Maréchal des Logis du Roi, dont il obtint une confirmation en 1636. Ledit Pierre fut maintenu dans fa nobleffe par Lettres du Roi Louis XIV de 1657, & par autres Lettres de 1668. Il époufa, par contrat paffé en 1650, *Charlotte de Barbançon*, fille de *René de Barbançon*, Seigneur de Champs-le-Roi, & de *Françoife de Villebrefme-de-Fougere*. De cette alliance, également diftinguée tant du côté paternel que du côté maternel, naquit entr'autres enfans :

Jacques - François Bernard, Ier du nom, Ecuyer, Seigneur de Beaulieu, né le 27 Mars 1651, Maréchal des Logis du Roi, en furvivance de fon père, par Brevet du 13 Juin 1653, puis Capitaine de 100 hommes de guerre dans le Régiment d'Auvergne en 1671. Il fe rendit à Orléans en Juin 1690 pour fervir dans la Compagnie du Ban de Blois ; &, fuivant un certificat de M. *de Creil-Bournezeau*, Intendant d'Orléans, il fut choifi pour Maréchal des Logis de l'Efcadron des Bailliages de Chartres & de Blois, où il fit ce fervice en chef & avec honneur. Il eut :

Jacques - François Bernard, IIe du nom, né le 12 Juillet 1705, qui entra dans le Régiment d'Auvergne en 1720, où il a fervi pendant 10 ans en qualité de Lieutenant. Il époufa, le 20 Février 1735, *Marie Douineau*, fille de *Gilles Douineau*, Ecuyer, Préfident & Tréforier-Général des Finances de France, Grand-Voyer de la Généralité de Touraine. Il en a eu :

Jacques-François Bernard-de-Beaulieu, III du nom, né le 2 Février 1736.

Il y a auffi une branche de cette famille établie en Bretagne fous le nom de Bernard-de-Courville, qui fubfifte dans la perfonne de :

Guy-André Bernard-de-Courville, né le 3 Août 1713, admis en 1729 au nombre des 600 Cadets Gentilshommes commandés dans la Citadelle de Metz par le Sieur du Bofchet, Enfeigne dans le Régiment de Berry, puis Lieutenant dans le même Régiment en 1735. Il fut maintenu dans fa nobleffe par Lettres du Roi en 1738. Il étoit fils de Julien Bernard, Ecuyer, Seigneur de Courville & de Pichandet, Lieutenant d'une Compagnie d'Infanterie au Régiment de Thianges, depuis Laval, Capitaine en 1702, Chevalier de Saint-Louis en 1710, & trois ans après il eut une Compagnie de Grenadiers. (*Armorial de France*, reg. II, p. 2.)

Les armes : *d'argent, à deux lions de fable, langués & onglés de gueules, & paffant l'un au-deffus de l'autre, autrement léopardés.*

BERNARD - CALONNE, famille originaire de Flandre, dont la feule branche qui fubfifte, réfide en Artois.

I. Arnould de Bernard, Ecuyer, Seigneur de Quelme, Boudigny, Lompré, Taintignie, Florent, époufa *Marie-Jacqueline de Vacque*. Il eut :

II. Michel de Bernard, Ier du nom, Ecuyer, Seigneur de Quelme & du Mont, qui époufa, 1° le 14 Mars 1510, *Antoinette de Croix*, dite de *Rumez* ; & 2° *Marguerite de Landas*. Il eut de ce dernier mariage :

III. Florent de Bernard, Ecuyer, Seigneur de Quelme, Florent, & du Mont, qui fe maria, le 28 Mai 1576, avec Catherine de Bernard, Dame de Jollain, Luchin & Betignie. Ils eurent :

IV. Maximilien de Bernard, Chevalier, Seigneur de Quelme, Jollain, Betignie, Florent, qui s'allia, le 19 Juin 1602, avec *Marie de Corde*, dont il eut :

V. Maximilien de Bernard, Chevalier, Seigneur de Quelme, Jollain, Betignie, Florent, allié à *Marie-Claire de Berghes*, fille de *Philippe*, Chevalier, Seigneur de Rache-Bourbe, Cumay, Haute-Garde, Auberlieu, Baron de Zetrud, premier Pair de Namur, d'où descend le Prince de Rache, & de *Françoise de Halwin*. Il eut:

VI. Louis-François de Bernard, Chevalier, Comte de Bailleul, de Quelme, Jollain, Betignie, Florent, du Mont, Calonne, Ziguescape, &c., Capitaine d'Infanterie au Régiment du Baron de Zetrud, marié, le 4 Avril 1685, à *Marguerite-Charlotte de Berghes*, Dame de Sept-Fontaines, Auberlieu & Vallers, fille de *Philippe de Berghes*, Baron de Zetrud, frère cadet d'*Eugène de Berghes*, Prince de Rache, Chevalier de la Toison-d'Or, Gouverneur de Mons, & Grand-Bailli de Hainaut, dont:

1. Charles-Alexandre, qui suit;
2. François-Eugène, rapporté après son frère aîné;
3. Marie-Louise-Josèphe;
4. Et Marie-Françoise-Josèphe.

VII. Charles-Alexandre, Comte de Bailleul, Seigneur de Quelme, Betignie, Florent, du Mont, Saint-Phorien, marié, le 5 Juillet 1706, à *Marie-Alexie de Lannoy*, fille de *Charles*, Comte de Lannoy, de Vanne, &c., & de *N... de Tienne*, dont:

Marie-Marguerite de Bernard, Dame de Quelme, Bailleul, Betignie, Florent & du Mont, qui épousa *Antoine-Alexandre de Claïbes*, Comte d'Huft, Seigneur de Coyquem. De ce mariage vint:

Marie-Caroline de Claïbes, Comtesse d'Huft, de Quelme, Bailleul & Florent, qui fut mariée, en 1750, à *Ferdinand*, Marquis de *Bruyas-Royon*.

VII. François-Eugène de Bernard, frère puîné de Charles-Alexandre, Comte de Calonne, Seigneur de Vallers, Auberlieu, Souverain-Moulin, Taronie, Binethun & Vimille, Capitaine d'Infanterie au Régiment de Boufflers en 1706, fut marié 1° à *Marie-Claire-Josèphe de Lannoy-d'Arpinghien*, fille de *Robert de Lannoy-d'Arpinghien*, Seigneur d'Amilville & Royaume, & d'*Anne Way-de-Roosendale*; & 2° à *Jeanne-Josèphe Deleval-de-la-Marche*, Dame d'Atin-Beutin, Saint-Cornil & Rouchefay, fille de *François Deleval*, Seigneur d'Atin, & de *N... Roger-d'Ignicourt*: ce fut en ce Fran-

çois *Deleval* que finit le nom de *Deleval*, qui étoit connu en 1265, avec la qualité de Chevalier en 1194 par un Prevôt de Cambray & un Grand-Bailli de Cambrésis en 1267. Il a de ce mariage:

1. Marie-Louise-Josèphe;
2. Et Marie-Josèphe-Françoise de Bernard, née le 5 Février 1753, mariée, par contrat du 1er Juin 1767, à *Adrien-Joseph-Amélie*, Comte de *Bethune* & de Saint-Venant. Voyez BETHUNE.

Les armes: *de gueules, à une épée dont la poignée est garnie d'or, la lame d'argent, la pointe en bas, accompagnée de deux étoiles d'or*. Supports: *deux griffons*. Cimier: *une couronne de Comte*.

BERNARD-COUBERT, à Paris. Samuel Bernard, Conseiller d'Etat, baptisé le 29 Octobre 1651, a obtenu que la Seigneurie de Coubert en Brie fût érigée en Comté en 1720. Il est mort le 28 Janvier 1739. Il avoit épousé 1° *Madeleine Clergeau*; & 2° le 13 Août 1720, *Pauline-Félicité de Sàint-Chamans*, fille de *François*, Marquis de Méry-fur-Seine, & de *Bonne de Chastellux*. Ses enfans du premier lit font:

1. Samuel-Jacques Bernard, Comte de Coubert, né le 19 Mai 1686, Maître des Requêtes, Intendant de la Maison de la feue Reine, Intendant & Commandeur de l'Ordre Royal & Militaire de Saint-Louis, marié, le 12 Août 1715, à *Elisabeth-Louise Frottier-de-la-Coste-Messelière*. De ce mariage il reste:

1. Jacques-Samuel-Olivier, Comte de Coubert, né le 6 Janvier 1730;
2. Louise-Henriette-Madeleine, née le 7 Juillet 1719, morte en 1757. Elle avoit épousé, le 27 Septembre 1732, *Chrétien-Guillaume de Lamoignon*, Président au Parlement de Paris;
3. Louise-Olive-Félicité, née le 7 Juillet 1722, mariée, le 26 Septembre 1739, avec *Nicolas-Hyacinthe de Montvallat*, Comte d'Entragues;
4. Elisabeth-Olive-Louise, née le 26 Janvier 1725, mariée, le 15 Avril 1741, avec *Antoine-Jean-François de Saint-Simon-Courtomer*, appelé *le Vicomte de Courtomer*;
5. Marie-Olive, née le 14 Août 1727, mariée, le 18 Mai 1743, à *Jean-Baptiste de Chabannes*, Comte de Pionzac & d'Apchon;
6. Et une autre fille.

2. N..., mariée au Comte de *Sagone*;

3. Gabriel-Bernard, dit *le Préfident de Rieux*, mort le 13 Décembre 1745. Il avoit époufé, le 29 Juin 1719, *Sufanne-Marie-Henriette de Boulainvilliers*, & laiffa:

Anne-Gabriel-Henri, dit *le Préfident de Boulainvilliers*, né le 10 Décembre 1724, Seigneur de Saint-Saire, de Paffy-lez-Paris & de Saint-Pol-de-Grefolles, qui a époufé, 1º le 26 Avril 1746, *Marie-Madeleine*, morte le 18 Avril 1748, fille de *Louis-Claude-Scipion Grimoard de Beauvoir*, Marquis du Roure; & 2º en Septembre 1748, *N...* *d'Hallencourt*, Dame de Boulainvilliers. Il eut de fon premier mariage:

Charles-Armand-Henri-Gabriel Bernard de Saint-Saire, né le 31 Mai 1747, mort.

Et du fecond lit:

Plufieurs enfans;

Du fecond lit vint:

4. Et Bonne-Félicité Bernard, née le 20 Septembre 1721, mariée, le 22 Septembre 1733, à *François-Mathieu Molé*, ancien premier Préfident du Parlement de Paris.

Les armes: *d'azur, à l'ancre d'argent fenefirée en chef d'une étoile de même, étincelante ou rayonnée d'or.*

BERNARD-MONTEBISE, en Orléanois.

François Bernard, Ecuyer, Seigneur de Montebife, né le 16 Septembre 1587, avoit époufé *Madeleine Parfait*, fille de *Guillaume*, Ecuyer, Seigneur des Tournelles, Confeiller au Parlement de Paris, & de *Marie le Gros*, d'où defcend:

N... Bernard, dit *le Marquis de Montebife*, Chevalier, Seigneur des Tournelles, qui a des enfans de *N... Houel*, fille de *Charles*, Marquis de Houelbourg à la Guadeloupe en Amérique, Maréchal des Camps & Armées du Roi, mort le 29 Janvier 1736, & d'*Anne-Henriette de Cordouan-Langerais*, mariée, le 14 Mai 1703, morte le 20 Décembre 1719.

Les armes de Bernard-de-Montebise font: *d'azur, à la licorne d'argent.*

BERNARD-MONTESSUS, ancienne nobleffe, originaire de Bourgogne.

Voici ce que nous en apprennent une Généalogie manufcrite, & un Procès-verbal dreffé d'autorité du Parlement de Befançon, contenant l'inventaire des titres qu'Antoine-François de Bernard-de-Montessus, Chevalier de Saint-Louis, & Officier au Régiment des Gardes-Françoifes, a produits pour la vérification des Lettres-Patentes qu'il a obtenues de Sa Majefté au mois de Septembre 1770, portant conceffion du titre perfonnel de *Comte* à lui & à fes enfans, & defcendans mâles, nés & à naître en légitime mariage. Ce Procès-verbal eft du 16 Juillet 1771.

Cette Maifon, qui poffède encore en Bourgogne, fans interruption, depuis plus de trois fiècles la Seigneurie de *Monteffus* (nom qu'elle a joint depuis ce tems à celui de Bernard), a été, par Arrêts rendus à la Chambre des Comptes de Dôle & au Parlement de Befançon, les 18 Mai & 20 Novembre 1736, maintenue dans le droit de prendre la qualité de *Chevalier*. Elle a fait fes preuves de nobleffe au Chapitre de Saint-Claude, aux Chanoineffes de Château-Chalon & de Migette, à l'Ordre de Malte & celui du Roi, & dernièrement, en 1767, au Chapitre des Comtes de Lyon. Plufieurs de ce nom fe font diftingués dans les Armées, ont eu des emplois à la Cour de nos Rois, des Gouvernemens de Ville, ont été Gentilshommes ordinaires de la Chambre, ont eu des Compagnies d'hommes d'armes, & des places de Meftre-de-Camp. Elle poffède plufieurs Seigneuries titrées, & a fait de très-belles alliances, comme on le va voir par le détail où nous allons entrer. Les guerres continuelles, & les révolutions arrivées en Bourgogne, ont fait perdre à beaucoup de familles nobles des titres anciens, & celle-ci, qui fubfifte en deux branches, eft du nombre, & ne peut remonter, par filiation, felon le Procès-verbal cité, qu'à:

I. Henri de Bernard, qui époufa, au commencement du XIVᵉ fiècle, *Henriette de Hénin*, dont il eut:

II. Philibert de Bernard, vivant en 1380, qui reprit de fief pour les Terres qu'il poffédoit en Charolois. Il eft qualifié *Meffire* & *Chevalier*, ce qui fuppofe une ancienne nobleffe. Il époufa *Catherine de Montholon*, dont il eut entr'autres enfans:

Pierre, qui fuit;

Et Philippe, Chevalier, qualifié *vir nobilis Dominus* de Bernard, *Miles*, dans un acte de reprife de fief, entre les mains du Chancelier du Duc de *Bourgogne*, en fon Comte de Charolois, par *Hugon de Monay*, Damoifeau, au nom d'*Ifabelle de Damas*, pour les biens qu'elle poffédoit audit Comté de Charolois, relevant à hommage-lige du Duc de *Bourgogne*, ainfi que pour ce que Philippe de Bernard, Chevalier, poffédoit en arrière-fief & hommage de ladite Dame, en qualité d'héritier de noble homme *Philippe de Leſſertet*, Chevalier. Cette repriſe de fief fut faite par acte reçu de *Philippe de Perche*, Notaire au Comté de Charolles, le 20 Juillet 1413.

III. Pierre de Bernard, Chevalier, rendit foi & hommage-lige au Duc de *Bourgogne*, entre les mains de ſon Chancelier, au Bailliage de Mâcon, le 15 Mars 1395, pour les biens qu'il poſſédoit au Comté de Charolles, ſçavoir un moulin & étang, dit *de Gauronjon*, avec la Juſtice & juridiction, ainſi que pour toutes les Terres, Cens & autres biens tenus par lui au lieu & territoire d'Azen. Dans cet acte, reçu par *Denis de Prus*, Notaire, Pierre de Bernard eſt qualifié *vir nobilis Dominus* Petrus de Bernard, *Miles*. Il eſt dit auſſi, dans la Généalogie manuſcrite, qu'il reprit de fief en 1402, pour les Terres qu'il poſſédoit en Charolois, & a dans cette repriſe les mêmes qualifications que ci-deſſus. Il épouſa, en 1415, *Nicole de Damas*, ce qui eſt prouvé par le traité de mariage de ſon petit-fils, dans lequel *Pierre de Damas & Jean de Montholon*, ſont dénommés ſes couſins. De ſon mariage vint:

IV. Jacques de Bernard, Seigneur de Montcenis en partie, de Monteſſus, des Bois, &c., qui reprit de fief à la réunion de la Bourgogne à la Couronne de France, en 1422, entre les mains de M. *Georges d'Amboiſe*; &, ſuivant le Procès-verbal, il obtint des Lettres-Patentes du Roi, qui portent qu'il lui prêta, en la perſonne de l'Evêque d'Alby (*Georges d'Amboiſe*), à ce commis, la foi & hommage qu'il étoit tenu de faire à Sa Majeſté, pour les Terres & rentes nobles qu'il tenoit ès Bailliages de Dijon & de Montcenis: ces Lettres ſont datées de Dijon le 5 Août 1469. Il fit pluſieurs donations conſidérables à l'Egliſe de Montcenis, entr'autres des dîmes de Chapendis. Il épouſa, en 1455, *Béatrix Bourgois*, fille de Meſſire *Jean Bourgois*, Chevalier, Bailli de Dijon, & ſœur de *René Bourgois*, qui, ſuivant Olivier de la Marche, dans ſes Mémoires, portoit la Cornette du Duc de *Bourgogne*, & *faiſoit moult bon & aſſuré devoir dans les batailles*. On lui donne pour enfans:

Hugues, qui ſuit;
Et Philibert-Jacques de Bernard-de-Montessus, qui fit un abandon de ſes biens à ſon fils aîné, le 25 Novembre 1494, lequel en fut

mis en poſſeſſion par acte du 26 Mai de l'année ſuivante.

V. Hugues ou Huguenin de Bernard, Seigneur de Monteſſus, de Brandon, &c., obtint des Lettres, le 26 Janvier 1487, de *Jean de Châlons*, Prince d'Orange, Lieutenant-Général & Gouverneur pour le Roi du Duché de Bourgogne & Comté de Charolois, adreſſées au Bailli du Charolois, leſquelles lui permettent de ſe mettre en poſſeſſion d'une rente de 10 livres ſur un Village de ce Comté, dépendant de Sa Majeſté (rente que ledit Hugues ou Huguenin avoit acquiſe de noble homme *Jean de la Cour*), à charge & condition par lui de la tenir & poſſéder en fief du Souverain, & de lui en faire le devoir & hommage ſelon la nature du fief, quand il en ſera requis & ordonné. Il ſervit pluſieurs années dans les bans & arrière-bans de la nobleſſe, & dans les Compagnies d'Ordonnances. Il épouſa, en 1497, *Bernarde de Sarraſin*, fille de N... *de Sarraſin*, Ecuyer, Seigneur de Fontaine, & de *Marguerite de Voutefuche*, dont il eut:

VI. Pierre de Bernard, IIᵉ du nom, Seigneur de Monteſſus, Brandon, Balore, Montcenis en partie, Soirans, &c., qui rendit foi & hommage à François d'Orléans, Duc de Longueville, Seigneur & Baron de Montcenis, pour les biens & fiefs que lui donna Hugues, ſon père. Il fut Capitaine de 50 lances au ſervice de Louis XII, comme il ſe voit dans l'état de l'armée, rapporté dans les Mémoires du Sieur de Villars en 1550; & épouſa, par contrat paſſé au Château d'Aubigny, devant d'*Artaux Jouves*, Notaire Royal, le 12 Janvier 1539, aſſiſté de Hugues, ſon père, *Barbe du Meix*, fille de noble *Jean du Meix*, Chevalier, Seigneur d'Aubigny, & de *Philiberte de Rye*: elle fut aſſiſtée de *Bernard du Meix*, ſon frère. De ce mariage vinrent:

1. Philibert, qui ſuit;
2. Melchior, auteur de la branche de *Bellevêvre*, rapportée ci-après;
3. Joachim, reçu au Chapitre noble de Gigny en 1590, après avoir fait preuve de 16 quartiers de nobleſſe de nom & d'armes, jurés par quatre Gentilshommes, ſuivant un certificat de ce Chapitre, en date du 18 Juin 1734;
4. Adrienne, mariée à *François de Montagu*, Chevalier, Seigneur de Morſon, ſuivant une tranſaction paſſée entre ſes deux frères à la Citadelle de Châlons, par *Byot*, No-

taire Royal, le 19 Novembre 1583. Elle fut mère de :

Africain & *Jean-Antide de Montagu*, reçus à la Confrèrie de Saint-Georges en 1650 & 1652;

5. Et Jacqueline, morte Chanoineffe en 1606, & inhumée en l'Abbaye de Château-Chalon, où l'on voit encore fa tombe & fes armes.

VII. Philibert de Bernard-de-Montessus, Chevalier, Seigneur de Soirans, Brandon, &c., Chevalier de l'Ordre du Roi, Gentilhomme ordinaire de fa Chambre, Enfeigne de 50 hommes d'armes, & premier Pannetier de la Maifon du Roi de Navarre, partagea avec Melchior, fon frère, la fucceffion de leurs père & mère, par acte paffé au Château de Hautully, & reçu de *Renard*, Notaire, en date du 20 Décembre 1565; & fit fon teftament le 22 Avril 1591, lequel fut publié au Bailliage de Montcenis le 24 Novembre fuivant. Il avoit époufé 1° *Antoinette de Monconis*, fille de *Philibert*, Baron *de Monconis*, Chevalier de l'Ordre du Roi, & Gouverneur des Ville & Citadelle de Châlons, & fœur de *Guillemette de Monconis*, femme de *Georges de Saint-Belin*, Sieur de Bielle, Chevalier de l'Ordre du Roi, & Enfeigne de 50 hommes d'armes. Philibert de Bernard affifta à la création de tutelle & garde-noble des enfans du Sieur de *Saint-Belin*, fes neveux & nièces, laquelle fut faite au Bailliage de Chaumont en 1583, & il époufa 2° *Marguerite de Clugny*, fille de *Ferri*, Chevalier, petit-neveu du Cardinal *de Clugny*, Fondateur du Collège de ce nom à Paris. Du premier lit naquirent :

1. André, qui fuit;
2. Philibert, Chanoine de Saint-Claude & Prieur de Cainfrain. Il fut légataire d'une penfion par le teftament de fon père, du 22 Avril 1591;

Et du fecond lit :

3. Guy, rapporté après fon frère aîné;
4. Et François, Religieux à Beaume-les-Meffieurs.

VIII. André de Bernard-de-Montessus, Seigneur de Soirans, Vitrey & la Vefvre, Chevalier de l'Ordre du Roi, Gentilhomme ordinaire de fa Chambre, Lieutenant de 50 hommes d'armes de la Compagnie de Caufans, époufa, en Franche-Comté en 1596, *Catherine de Faulquier*, fille unique & héritière de *Girard de Faulquier*, Chevalier, Seigneur de Vitrey, & de *Catherine de Saint-*

Julien. La famille de *Faulquier* étoit très-noble, ayant donné plufieurs Abbés de Saint-Claude, & plufieurs Chanoines-Comtes de Lyon, comme on le voit dans les Mémoires du Comté de Bourgogne par Dunod, & dans le *Gallia Chriftiana*. André de Bernard-de-Montessus fe colloqua au décret de la Seigneurie de Vitrey, pour les deniers dotaux de fon époufe, laquelle lui donna procuration le 25 Juillet 1612, pour la part & portion qui lui compétoit dans la fucceffion de feu *Georgette de Malain*, fa tante, Dame de Chilley. Il eut :

Françoise de Bernard-de-Montessus, mariée, par contrat paffé au Château de Soirans, devant *François Huenot*, Notaire Royal, le 12 Avril 1616, à *Charles Chabot*, Gentilhomme ordinaire de la Chambre du Roi, petit-fils de l'Amiral *Chabot*, & fils de *François Chabot*, Chevalier des Ordres du Roi, Marquis de Mirebeau, Comte de Charny, Baron de Fontaine-Françoife, Capitaine de 50 hommes d'armes des Ordonnances de Sa Majefté, & de *Catherine de Silly*. Plufieurs Seigneurs du nom de *Chabot* affiftèrent à ce mariage. Palliot, dans fon livre de la *Parfaite Science des Armoiries*, imprimé à Paris en 1661, dit, p. 650, qu'il y eut procès entre MM. *de Bauffremont* & François de Bernard-de-Montessus, Comteffe de Charoux, &c., comme tutrice de *Jacques Chabot*, fon fils, au fujet de la fubftitution du Comté de Charny, & qu'en 1632 Arrêt fut rendu au Parlement de Grenoble, qui, fur les Ecritures dudit Palliot, adjugea ce Comté à Dame Françoise de Bernard-de-Montessus. Elle eft enterrée en la Sainte-Chapelle de Dijon, où l'on voit fon épitaphe, auprès de *Jacques Chabot*, fon fils, qui mourut en bas âge. *Marguerite Chabot*, fa fille, époufa *Henri*, Comte de *Bonneval*, dont une fille, nommée :

Jeanne de Bonneval, mariée à Marie-Beaune de Bernard-de-Montessus.

VIII. Guy de Bernard-de-Montessus, Chevalier, Baron de Rully, Seigneur de Brandon de Nuas, Paquier, &c., fecond fils de Philibert, & de *Marguerite de Clugny*, fa feconde femme, époufa *Marguerite de Tintry*, fille de *N.... de Tintry*, & d'*Anne de Saint-Léger*, Baronne de Rully, dont :

IX. Philippe de Bernard-de-Montessus, Chevalier, Baron de Rully, &c., qui fe maria avec *Adrienne-Françoife de la Touvière*, fille unique & héritière de *Claude de la Touvière*, Seigneur de Servignat & de Beaurégard, & de *Barbe de Thomaffin*. On trouve la Généalogie de la Maifon de *la Touvière* dans l'*Hiftoire de Breffe,* par Samuel Guichenon. De ce mariage vinrent :

1. Guy, qui fuit;
2. Alexandre, Chevalier de Malte ;
3. René, tué en Flandre, portant l'Enfeigne du Régiment d'Enghien;
4. Claude, Seigneur de Servignat, Lieutenant-Colonel du Régiment de Peſeux, Chevalier de Saint-Louis, lequel n'eut point d'enfans de *N... de Mendre de Savoyeux ;*
5. Et Jacques, Capitaine de Grenadiers au Régiment de Tournon, Chevalier de Saint-Louis, & Seigneur de Villers-Chapey.

X. Guy de Bernard-de-Montessus, II° du nom, Baron de Rully, Seigneur de Servignat, &c., Capitaine au Régiment d'Enghien, commanda la nobleſſe du ban & arrière-ban des Bailliages de Châlons, de l'Auxois, Semur, &c., & fut maintenu dans ſon ancienne nobleſſe, ſur le vu des titres & papiers qu'il produiſit, par Jugement rendu contradictoirement devant l'Intendant de Bourgogne, en 1698, lors de la recherche de la nobleſſe, ordonnée par le Roi. Il épouſa 1° *Anne de Buade,* fille de *N... de Buade ;* & 2° *Françoiſe de Chauſſin,* fille de *Claude de Chauſſin,* & de *Jeanne de Salins,* dont il n'eut point d'enfans. Du premier lit vinrent :

1. Paul-Henri, qui fuit;
2. Charles, marié, en 1719, à *Nicole Berger de Charny,* dont il a laiſſé :
   N..., Capitaine au Régiment Royal-Barrois;
   N..., Chanoine de Montpellier, dont ſon oncle, *N... Berger,* étoit Evêque :
   Françoise de Bernard-de-Montessus, Chanoineſſe de Neuville, où l'on fait preuve de 8 générations paternelles;
3. & 4. Madeleine & Jeanne, Religieuſe à Saint-Bernard de Dijon.

XI. Paul-Henri de Bernard-de-Montessus, Baron de Rully, Caleſtre, Servignat, &c., Capitaine de Dragons au Régiment de Sommery, épouſa, en 1709, Marie-Charlotte de Bernard-de-Montessus, de la branche de *Bellevêvre,* ſa parente du III° au IV° degré, dont :

1. Charles-François, qui fuit;
2. N... dit *le Chevalier de Rully,* Seigneur de Balore;
Et quatre filles, Religieuſes à Châlons-ſur-Saône.

XII. Charles-François de Bernard-de-Montessus, Baron de Rully, Bellevêvre, Ser-

vignat, Soirans, &c., a été Page de la Petite-Ecurie du Roi, & a épouſé, en 1739, *Ferdinande-Agathange de Vaudrey,* fille d'*Eugène de Vaudrey,* Marquis de Beveuge, Lieutenant-Général des Armées du Roi , & de *Gabrielle de Blifterswich ,* laquelle a une ſœur mariée au Marquis *de Grammont,* vivant, Lieutenant-Général des Armées du Roi. De ce mariage ſont iſſus :

N..., Capitaine de Dragons en 1760 ;
N..., Comte de Lyon en 1766 ;
N..., appelée *Mademoiſelle de Rully*, mariée, en 1763, à N... *de Damas ,* Vicomte de Thianges ;
Marie-Charlotte-Eugénie, mariée, par contrat des 17 & 21 Août 1763, à *Marie-Jean-Louis de Riquet,* Comte de Caraman;
Et d'autres enfans, morts en bas âge.

BRANCHE de Bellevêvre.

VII. Melchior de Bernard-de-Montessus, ſecond fils de Pierre, & de *Barbe du Meix,* Chevalier, Seigneur de Monteſſus, de Montcenis en partie & de Balore, biens qu'il a eus de ſon père, d'Eſcouelle & de Pontdevaux, qu'il eut de ſon épouſe, reprit de Fief le 9 Mars 1565, à la Chambre des Comptes du Duché de Bourgogne (tant en ſon nom que pour ſon frère Philibert), pour les Terres & Seigneuries de Monteſſus, Brandon & autres lieux, mouvans du Roi; & fut Gouverneur de la Citadelle de Châlons-ſur-Saône en 1586, où l'on voit ſes armes à la principale porte de cette Citadelle, au-deſſus de celles du Roi & de Monſieur le Prince. Il remit le Gouvernement de ſa Citadelle au Baron de *Malain de Lux,* ſuivant l'Hiſtorien de la ville de Châlons, & le Roi Henri III, le pourvut alors de la Charge de Gentilhomme ordinaire de ſa Chambre. Il épouſa, par contrat reçu de *Claude Poillechat,* Notaire Royal à Dijon, le 10 Octobre 1575, *Jeanne de Vintimille ,* des Comtes *de Vintimille,* fille unique & héritière de *Jacques de Vintimille,* Conſeiller au Parlement de Bourgogne, Seigneur de Civry, Carpet, Bazan & Saint-Barthélemy, ſur la rive de Gênes, & de Magny en partie, & de *N... Gros,* Dame d'Agé. Elle lui apporta tout ce qui lui appartenoit ſur la Rivière de Gênes, dépendant du Comté de Vintimille, comme on le voit dans l'*Hiſtoire du Parlement de Bourgogne,* par Palliot, où la nobleſſe des *Gors d'Agé* eſt auſſi établie. Le même Auteur rapporte la vie de *Jacques de Vintimille*, & dit qu'il étoit allié aux Maisons de *Paleologue* & de *Lascaris*, & que Madame de *Savoie*, mère de *François* & de *Henri de Montmorency*, le reconnoissoit pour son parent. Il est dit dans leur contrat de mariage, que PHILIBERT DE BERNARD-DE-MONTESSUS, Chevalier, Seigneur de Brandon & Soirans, frère aîné de MELCHIOR, ayant fait accord avec lui par leur partage, fera ratifier ledit traité par son frère, sitôt qu'il sera de retour de la Cour, où il est pour le service du Roi. Ces deux frères, PHILIBERT & MELCHIOR, traitèrent, en 1579, avec *N...de Saulx-Tavannes*, pour les droits de *Barbe du Meix-d'Aubigny*, leur mère, dont la famille s'est éteinte dans celle de *Saulx*. MELCHIOR eut de son mariage :

1. PHILIBERT, qui suit;
2. JACQUES, tué au siège de Privas, sans laisser de postérité ;
3. GUILLEMETTE, Chanoinesse de l'Abbaye de Château-Châlon, vivante encore en 1635, comme il est prouvé par une donation entre-vif qu'elle fit en faveur de MELCHIOR, son père, Baron de Sarrigny, frère de ladite GUILLEMETTE, avant de faire ses vœux de profession en ladite Abbaye. Cet acte est daté du 24 Octobre 1611, & une copie a été expédiée sur la grosse, le 10 Avril 1614, par *Taby*, Notaire à Dijon. Son père la rappelle dans son testament, par lequel il lui lègue une pension de 200 livres, en date, à Dijon, du 31 Décembre 1614, & publié au Bailliage de cette Ville le 14 Octobre 1615. Elle fit, à Château-Châlon, la preuve de *Jeanne de Vintimille*, sa mère ;
4. Et MADELEINE, mariée, en 1602, à *Pierre de la Tournelle*, Seigneur de Beauregard, Capitaine de 50 Chevaux-Légers & Gouverneur de Beaugé, fils de Messire *Lazare de la Tournelle*, Chevalier, Seigneur dudit lieu, Lieutenant d'une Compagnie de 100 hommes d'armes des Ordonnances du Roi, & de *Jeanne de Corcelles*.

VIII. PHILIBERT DE BERNARD-DE-MONTESSUS, Chevalier, Baron de Rully, Sarrigny, Balore & d'Escouelle, Gentilhomme ordinaire de la Chambre du Roi, Mestre-de-Camp d'un Régiment d'Infanterie, & Gouverneur des Ville & Château de Beaune, mourut au siège de Montmélian en Savoie, en 163... Il avoit épousé, par contrat du 16 Juin 1608, passé à Beaune en Bourgogne, devant *P. Vacher*, Notaire Royal, *Françoise de Fussey*, fille de *Bernard de Fussey*, Chevalier, Sei-

Tome II.

gneur & Baron de Sarrigny, & d'*Yolande de Trestondans*. Dans son contrat de mariage, PHILIBERT est dit autorisé de *Prosper*, des Comtes *de Vintimille*, son cousin. Il eut pour fils :

IX. MELCHIOR DE BERNARD-DE-MONTESSUS, II° du nom, Chevalier, Seigneur dudit lieu, Baron de Sarrigny, Bellevêvre, Balore, Seigneur de Bellefond, Travoisy, Grandchamp, Vicomte de Lunes, Gouverneur pour le Roi, après son père, des Ville & Château de Beaune, par Lettres-Patentes de Louis XIII, données au Fort des Barraux en 163.., Gentilhomme ordinaire de sa Chambre, Capitaine d'une Compagnie de 100 hommes au Régiment de son père, & ensuite Lieutenant-Colonel du Régiment d'Armagnac. Il épousa, 1° par contrat passé le 11 Janvier 1633, devant *Claude Humbert*, Notaire Royal, en la Maison Seigneuriale de Sarrigny, *Jacqueline de Pinsonnat*, fille de *Théodore*, Conseiller d'Etat, Président de la Chambre des Comptes de Dijon, Baron de Bellevêvre, &c., & de *N... de Galois de Perroux* ; & 2° *Jacqueline de Thiard de Bissy*, fille de *N... de Thiard de Bissy*, & de *N... Bourot*. Du premier lit vinrent :

1. LOUIS, qui suit;
2. MARIE-BEAUNE, Chevalier, Seigneur de Montessus, Baron de Bellevêvre, Gouverneur de la ville de Beaune, & Lieutenant-Colonel du Régiment de Duras. Il épousa, 1° en 1672, *Jeanne de Bonneval*, fille de *Henri*, Comte *de Bonneval*, Chevalier, & de *Marguerite Chabot*, laquelle étoit fille de FRANÇOISE DE BERNARD-DE-MONTESSUS, mentionnée au degré VIII de la première branche ; & 2° en 1677, *Françoise de Choiseul*, fille de *Clériadus de Choiseul*, Chevalier, Marquis de Lanques, & d'*Anne de Verrières*. MARIE-BEAUNE céda à son frère LOUIS la Baronie de Vitrey, pour celle de Bellevêvre. Les enfans qu'il eut du premier lit moururent en bas âge. Ceux du second furent :

1. N... DE BERNARD-DE-MONTESSUS, Baron de Bellevêvre, Capitaine de Cavalerie au Régiment d'Esclainvilliers, & Chevalier de Saint-Louis, mort en 1748, sans alliance;
2. Et MARIE-CHARLOTTE, alliée, en 1709, à PAUL-HENRI DE BERNARD-DE-MONTESSUS, Baron de Rully, &c., son parent, mentionné au degré XI de la première branche, auquel elle porta tous

K k k

les biens de la branche de *Monteſſus-Bellevêvre*;

3. AIMÉ, Chevalier de Malte, mort jeune.

Du ſecond lit il a eu :

4. JACQUES, dit *de Bellefond*, Capitaine de Cavalerie au Régiment d'Auger, avec Brevet de Colonel, tué au ſervice;

5. CLAUDE, Capitaine de Carabiniers, tué au ſervice en 1704;

6. Et MADELEINE, morte en 1707. Elle avoit épouſé, *Etienne de Ganay*, Seigneur de Génélard & Lauger, d'une nobleſſe qui a donné un Chancelier de France. Elle laiſſa un fils unique :

> N... *de Ganay*, héritier de la Terre de Bellefond, Chevalier de Saint-Louis, ancien Meſtre-de-Camp de Cavalerie du Régiment de Bretagne.

X. LOUIS DE BERNARD-DE-MONTESSUS, Chevalier, Baron de Bellevêvre, enſuite de Vitrey, Chauvirey, Chaſſagne, Seigneur de la Perrey, Dampierre, &c., fit hommage au Roi pour ſa Terre de Chauvirey, entre les mains de M. le Marquis de *Montauban*, Lieutenant-Général du Comté de Bourgogne, ſuivant un dénombrement donné, en conſéquence, à la Chambre des Comptes de Dôle en 1680. Il ſervit en qualité de Capitaine, au Régiment de Duras, & épouſa, par contrat paſſé devant *Gaſpard de Cleſſy*, Notaire Royal à Ozole en Charolois, le 13 Décembre 1659, *Jacqueline de la Cour*, fille de *Hugues de la Cour*, Chevalier, Seigneur de Moulins-la-Cour, Saint-Martin, d'Ozole, Chaſſagne, Sommery, &c., & *de Françoiſe d'Eltouf de Pradines*, dont :

1. JEAN-ETIENNE, qui ſuit;

2. N..., mariée à *François de Pointe*, Seigneur de Bourguignon;

3. & 4. NICOLE & FRANÇOISE.

XI. JEAN-ETIENNE DE BERNARD-DE-MONTESSUS, Chevalier, Seigneur & Baron de Vitrey, Chauvirey, Aigrevaux, &c., reprit de fief à la Chambre des Comptes de Dôle, pour ſa Terre de Chauvirey, le 11 Mai 1722; ſervit en qualité de Cornette, dans la Compagnie de ſon oncle, au Régiment d'Auger, & fut enſuite Capitaine de Cavalerie au Régiment de Villars. Il épouſa, par contrat paſſé devant *Regnaud*, Notaire, le 11 Décembre 1693, *Jeanne-Guillemette de Pointe*, fille de *Claude*, Ecuyer, Seigneur de Piſſeloup, Genevreuille, Pomet, Amblans, &c., & de *Françoiſe Chapuis*. Leurs enfans ſont :

1. CLAUDE;

2. PIERRE-FRANÇOIS, mort jeûne, Lieutenant au Régiment Royal-Etranger;

3. FRANÇOIS-SALOMON, qui ſuit;

4. LOUISE, Religieuſe de la Viſitation à Langres;

5. BÉATRIX, Religieuſe Urſuline à Veſoul;

6. Et CHARLOTTE, mariée à *Gaſpard Tenier*, Ecuyer, Seigneur de Pont, dont un fils unique, *N... Tenier*, ancien Capitaine au Régiment de Belſunce & Chevalier de Saint-Louis, vivant en 1775.

XII. FRANÇOIS-SALOMON DE BERNARD-DE-MONTESSUS, Chevalier, Baron de Vitrey, Chauvirey, Ouge, la Carte, Aigrevaux, Seigneur de Moulins & Piſſeloup, obtint en ſa faveur les deux Arrêts (dont on a parlé au commencement de cette Généalogie), l'un rendu à la Chambre des Comptes du Comté de Bourgogne le 18 Mai 1736, & l'autre au Parlement de Beſançon, le 20 Novembre même année, qui le maintiennent dans la poſſeſſion de ſe dire & qualifier *Chevalier*, ſur la production de ſes titres, par leſquels il fut vérifié que ſes ancêtres prenoient cette qualité dès 1400 & auparavant, & étoient d'une nobleſſe diſtinguée dans le Charolois. Il a auſſi obtenu, par Lettres-Patentes de Sa Majeſté, du mois de Juin 1740, duement enregiſtrées tant au Parlement qu'à la Chambre des Comptes de Franche-Comté, l'érection de ſes Terres en *Baronie*. Ces Lettres portent que c'eſt en faveur de ſon ancienne nobleſſe & des ſervices de ſes ancêtres. Il a épouſé, par contrat paſſé devant *Loyſon*, Notaire à Veſoul, le 6 Octobre 1735, *Gabrielle-Valentine de Mongenet*, fille de *Claude-François de Mongenet*, Ecuyer, Seigneur de Janey, &c., & d'*Anne-Françoiſe le Camus*, dont :

ANTOINE-FRANÇOIS, qui ſuit;

Et PIERRE-IGNACE DE BERNARD-DE MONTESSUS, Seigneur de Piſſeloup & Retoncourt, Chevalier de Malte en 1770.

XIII. ANTOINE-FRANÇOIS DE BERNARD, Comte de Monteſſus, Chevalier, Baron de Vitrey, Chauvirey, Ouge, la Carte, Seigneur de Moulins-la-Cour, &c., né à Veſoul, en Franche-Comté, le 24 Octobre 1738, a fait toute la dernière guerre, a été créé Chevalier de Saint-Louis en 1772, & eſt Officier dans le Régiment des Gardes-Françoiſes. Il a obtenu de Sa Majeſté des Lettres-Patentes, datées de Verſailles au mois de Septembre 1770, portant conceſſion du titre perſonnel de *Comte* pour lui, ſes enfans & deſcendans mâles, nés & à naître en légitime mariage, ſur la production de ſes titres, des ſervices de ſes ancêtres, les ſiens & l'illuſtration de ſes alliances, qui ſont en partie avec les Maiſons de *Damas, Choiſeul*, de *Thiard-de-Biſſy*, de *Chabot*, de *la Tournelle, Clugny, Vintimille* & *Vaudrey*. Il a épouſé, par contrat paſſé devant *Quatre-Maire*, Notaire à Paris, le 19 Novembre 1769, *Marie-Anne-Louiſe de Jodrillac*, fille de *Louis de Jodrillac*, Ecuyer, Seigneur de Touſſac, le Pleſſis-Gateblé & la Louptière, & de *Marie Dubois*.

Les armes de Montessus ſont : *d'azur, au chevron d'or, accompagné de trois étoiles d'argent, deux en chef & une en pointe.*

BERNARDI : *d'azur, à deux haches d'armes d'or, poſées en ſautoir; liées par en bas de même.*

BERNARDON : *d'azur, au ſautoir d'or, accompagné en chef d'un croiſſant, & en flancs & en pointe de trois étoiles, le tout de même.*

www.ingramcontent.com/pod-product-compliance
Lightning Source LLC
Chambersburg PA
CBHW050542270326
41926CB00012B/1883